HOSPITALITY STRATEGIC MANAGEMENT

CONCEPTS AND CASES

JEFFREY S. HARRISON

Cornell University

CATHY A. ENZ

Cornell University

WILEY

John Wiley & Sons, Inc.

This book was set in Minion by Leyh Publishing, LLC and printed and bound by Malloy, Inc. The cover was printed by Brady Palmer Printing.

This book is printed on acid-free paper.∞

Published by John Wiley & Sons, Inc., Hoboken, New Jersey.
Published simultaneously in Canada.

For general information on our other products and services or for technical support, please contact our Customer Care Department within the United States at (800) 762-2974, outside the United States at (317) 572-3993 or fax (317) 572-4002.

Wiley also publishes its books in a variety of electronic formats. Some content that appears in print may not be available in electronic books. For more information about Wiley products, visit our web site at www.wiley.com.

Library of Congress Cataloging-in-Publication Data
Harrison, Jeffrey S.
  Hospitality strategic management / Jeffrey S. Harrison, Cathy A. Enz.
    p. cm.

Includes index.
ISBN 0-471-47853-9 (cloth : alk. paper)
  1. Strategic planning. 2. Hospitality industry—Management. I. Enz, Cathy A., 1956– II. Title

HD30.28 .H3758 2005
647.94'068'4—dc22   2003023859

Printed in the United States of America

10 9 8 7 6 5 4

Dedicated to

Marie for her constant support, love, and encouragement.
Beth, Ben, and Jim for always being there.

Contents

CASES

Preface

This book was created in response to an unmet need among hospitality professors and practitioners for a thorough, rigorous, and up-to-date treatment of strategic management in a hospitality context. It is our goal to provide a book that is comprehensive in its treatment of strategy concepts and ideas, but that also illustrates and links these ideas to the competitive dynamics of the hospitality industry. We know the struggles that hospitality faculty have had in finding a book that focuses on the industry and that adequately treats the subject. We think this is the book they have been searching for.

Not only does this text cover strategic management from the perspective of hospitality professionals, but it is also practical in that it is based on what strategic managers actually do. On one hand, they acquire, develop, and manage internal *resources* such as people, knowledge, financial capital, and physical assets. Of equal importance, they acquire, develop, and manage *relationships* with external stakeholders such as guests, suppliers, owners, franchisors, venture partners, and governmental agencies. *Hospitality Strategic Management: Concepts and Cases* provides a realistic, balanced view of the field. It draws heavily from the resource-based perspective that firms can develop competitive advantages through the acquisition, development, and management of resources. It also uses stakeholder theory to help explain when firms should form partnerships, the form they should take, and how to manage them.

This book also contains the most relevant theory and models from what might be called the traditional approach to strategic management. Consequently, combining the resource-based view and the stakeholder view with traditional theory and models provides a comprehensive and managerially useful perspective of strategic management. The focus of this book is on the translation of strategic ideas into hospitality contexts. Using a diverse set of examples, the book seeks to link useful strategies and strategic issues to actions and activities of hospitality firms. Furthermore, we have introduced or created theories and models in key areas that fit the hospitality context better than ideas found in the general strategy literature.

In addition to the balanced approach found in this book, it also contains several other features that are a direct result of current trends in strategic management:

1. *International flavor.* The hospitality industry is a pioneer in globalization; hence global strategic management theory is woven into many of the chapters and discussed in a separate international chapter.

2. *Section on strategic thinking.* Strategic thinking is different from other aspects of strategic management. In fact, some strategists have argued that strategic planning

processes can stifle strategic thinking. The perspective taken in this book is that strategic thinking is an essential, creative aspect of the strategy process.

3. *Chapter on entrepreneurship and innovation.* Innovation and entrepreneurship are vital to strategic success, particularly in the foodservice and lodging industries. The entrepreneurship chapter contains elements of starting a business (such as what a business plan contains), franchising, and entrepreneurship within existing organizations (organizational entrepreneurship or "intrapraneurship").

4. *Section on competitive dynamics.* Firms do not create strategies in a static environment. They need to account for the dynamic elements of industry competition. This book reflects the reality of a dynamic environment in every chapter.

5. *Innovative and comprehensive treatment of implementation and control.* Consistent with the balanced theme of the book, implementation is treated from the perspective of managing internal processes as well as external relationships. A careful treatment of organizational design and a fully integrated strategic control model pull the implementation process together.

6. *Size is not overwhelming.* In spite of all this coverage, the book is only ten chapters. The essential material was included without all the "fluff." Principles and theories are explained with brief examples that get right to the point. The smaller size of the book allows instructors to use more cases, simulations, exercises, or readings.

The exciting cases selected for *Hospitality Strategic Management: Concepts and Cases* include a variety of firms from various segments of the industry. This section begins with a note that helps students to conduct case analyses, followed by seven cases. The cases are current and illustrate key issues of concern in the industry. In addition, the cases in the book can be supplemented by online cases from the Web site at the Center for Hospitality Research, Cornell University (http://www.hotelschool.cornell.edu/chr/research/). The online cases are available free of charge, as are instructor's notes for adopters of the book. You will find cases on companies in a variety of hospitality industries, including lodging, gaming, cruise lines, airlines, and food service.

Hospitality Strategic Management: Concepts and Cases also has several design elements that should appeal to students and instructors. The examples and quotations are in the text rather than boxed, since boxes are often distracting to the flow of the material. In fact, some readers skip boxes. A glossary defines important terms. End-of-chapter materials include a key-points summary and discussion questions. Finally, the book is supported by an instructor's manual (0-471-65951-7) and a user-friendly Web site that contains special features for students and instructors. Please visit www.wiley.com/college/ for instructor's resources.

ACKNOWLEDGMENTS

Book writing is a team activity, and our team has been a pleasure to work with. First we would like to thank Rick Leyh, CEO of Leyh Publishing, for his expertise, guidance, and professionalism in helping us to write this book. We are also grateful to the rest of the staff at

Leyh Publishing and Wiley for their enthusiastic support of this project. Our colleagues and the administrators of the School of Hotel Administration at Cornell University were also supportive. Finally, we had the benefit of thoughtful and supportive reviewers who provided us with insights and observations that have substantially improved this book. They are:

Chris Roberts, *University of Massachusetts*

Dana Tesone, *University of Central Florida*

Michael Sciarini, *Michigan State University*

Peter Ricci, *University of Central Florida*

Howard Adler, *Purdue University*

Michael Russo, *University of Oregon*

Sanjay Goel, *University of Minnesota*

Joseph Bensen, *New Mexico State University*

Michael Goldsby, *Ball State University*

Michael Coombs, *California State University*

W. Jack Duncan, *University of Alabama at Birmingham*

Vikas Anand, *University of Arkansas*

Rose Mary Cordova-Wentling, *University of Illinois*

Olav Sorenson, *University of California at Los Angeles*

William Schultze, *Case Western Reserve University*

Andrew Inkpen, *Thunderbird*

Grant Miles, *University of North Texas*

Garry Bruton, *Texas Christian University*

Richard Menger, *St. Mary's University*

We are also most profoundly thankful for the support and love of our families, who tolerated our evenings and days spent working on this book. To our spouses and children we owe our gratitude for their constant support and understanding. Finally, we would like to acknowledge two extraordinary leaders: Fred G. Peelan, CEO of International Hospitality Consultants and a former senior executive at InterContinental Hotels, and Lewis G. Schaeneman Jr., former CEO of Stop and Shop Groceries. These leaders have served as models to us and have generously provided for the endowed professorships that we hold.

—Jeffrey S. Harrison and Cathy A. Enz

About the Authors

JEFFREY S. HARRISON

Jeffrey S. Harrison is the Peelen Professorship Chair of Global Hospitality Strategy at the School of Hotel Administration, Cornell University. He received his Ph.D. at the University of Utah in 1985 and served on the faculties at Arizona State University, Clemson University, and University of Central Florida prior to his appointment at Cornell.

Dr. Harrison's research interests include corporate-level strategic management, the hospitality industry, and business ethics. Much of his work has been published in prestigious academic journals such as *Academy of Management Journal, Strategic Management Journal, Journal of Management, Journal of Business Ethics,* and *Cornell Hotel and Restaurant Administration Quarterly.* His articles have been published in North America, Europe, and Japan. He has also published many articles in journals specifically targeted at managers such as *Academy of Management Executive, Long Range Planning* (European), and *Prevision* (Japanese). His other book projects include *Foundations in Strategic Management, Strategic Management of Organizations and Stakeholders, Blackwell Handbook of Strategic Management,* and *Mergers and Acquisitions: A Guide to Creating Value for Stakeholders.* Dr. Harrison's contributions to research have been recognized through many research awards.

Dr. Harrison is also an extraordinary teacher who has received awards for his teaching at both the undergraduate and graduate levels. In addition, Dr. Harrison provides highly visible service to the field of management through his positions on the editorial review boards of both *Academy of Management Journal* and *Academy of Management Executive.* He recently guest co-edited a special research forum of the *Academy of Management Journal* entitled "Stakeholders, Social Responsibility and Performance." Many high-level executives seek Dr. Harrison's advice on a wide range of issues.

CATHY A. ENZ

Cathy A. Enz is the Lewis G. Schaeneman Jr. Professor of Innovation and Dynamic Management at the School of Hotel Administration, Cornell University, where she recently completed a term as the executive director of the Center for Hospitality Research. Dr. Enz received her Ph.D. from the Fisher College of Business at Ohio State University. She has been on the faculty at Cornell since 1990, and previously was on the faculty of the Kelley School of Business at Indiana University.

Dr. Enz has published over seventy journal articles and book chapters, and three books in the areas of strategic management and strategic human resources. Her research interests include competitive dynamics, innovation and change management, and human resource investment strategies. Her book, co-authored with three marketing professors, *American Lodging Excellence: The Key to Best Practices in the U.S. Lodging Industry* was the winner of an excellence award from the American Hotel and Lodging Association. This book represents the findings from a comprehensive study of best practices and features over 140 cases of excellence. Her research has been published in a wide variety of academic and hospitality journals such as *Administrative Science Quarterly, The Academy of Management Review, The Journal of Service Research, The Journal of Travel Research,* and *The Cornell Hotel and Restaurant Administration Quarterly.* A fourth book scheduled for release, *The Cornell Handbook of Applied Hospitality Strategy,* will be available in 2005.

Dr. Enz is the recipient of both outstanding teaching and research awards. She teaches a university-wide course in innovation in addition to teaching courses in strategic management. The Hospitality Change Simulation, a learning tool for the introduction of effective change, was developed by Dr. Enz and is available as an online education program of e-Cornell.

In addition to teaching graduates and undergraduates Dr. Enz presents in numerous executive programs in Europe, Asia, and Central America. Dr. Enz consults extensively in North America and serves on the board of directors of two privately owned hotel companies. Prior to her academic activities Dr. Enz held several industry positions including strategy development analyst in the office of corporate research for a large insurance organization, and operations manager responsible for midwestern United States customer service and logistics in the dietary food service division of a large U.S. health care corporation.

HOSPITALITY STRATEGIC MANAGEMENT

CONCEPTS AND CASES

1

Strategic Management

*A*fter decades of impressive growth in sales and profits, McDonald's is in trouble. U.S. sales have flattened and many consumers are turning to fast food restaurants with a more upscale menu, a segment sometimes referred to as "fast casual." In response, McDonald's has tried a number of new menu items in its flagship stores, including a lettuce and tomato "Big and Tasty" burger to compete directly with Burger King's "Whopper" and a variety of high quality salads in an attempt to lure more adults, especially women. They are also experimenting with nontraditional store looks in France. However, the problems at McDonald's are too deep to fix with an upgraded menu or a new face, at least in the longer term.

Perhaps a part of the solution came in the form of a letter from Steven Ells back in 1997. His Chipotle Mexican Grill restaurant in Denver, Colorado, was doing so well that he opened a branch nearby to handle overflow crowds. Although he had the operational expertise, the business skill to expand on his own was lacking. He also needed capital, and venture capitalists at the time were caught up in the technology frenzy. So Ells sent an unsolicited business plan to McDonald's on a hunch. The timing was excellent, as executives were looking for a way to improve growth. After about a year of getting acquainted with Mr. Ells and his business, McDonald's decided to invest in the business, eventually acquiring control.

Although McDonald's is still having trouble growing its flagship chain, Chipotle is experiencing explosive growth, sometimes doubling sales in a single year. In addition to company-owned stores, the company is stepping up its franchise sales, especially to existing McDonald's franchisees. Although per restaurant sales are not as high as a traditional McDonald's restaurant, the initial investment is lower. The kitchen is compact and efficient, and the menu is simple. Russ Smyth, who manages McDonald's' partner brands, envisions thousands of Chipotle restaurants.

The Chipotle venture was the first time McDonald's had made such an investment; however, the company has since acquired the Donatos Pizzeria and Boston Market chains. It is pursuing these other ventures with caution, slowly developing Donatos in Germany and opening only a few new Boston Markets each year. It sold off an investment in a British sandwich shop called Aroma Café and is expanding another upscale sandwich shop called Pret A Manger very slowly. Given the intensity of competition in these other segments, perhaps caution is warranted; however, shareholders' patience may run out.[1]

INTRODUCTION

The hospitality business is fiercely competitive. When McDonald's began its rapid expansion in the middle of the last century, there were few fast-food alternatives. McDonald's did more than any other company to shape the fast-food market, picking up new rivals at every stage. As domestic growth began to level off, the company increased its investments outside the United States. However, other American companies followed and foreign rivals began to develop and expand in their home markets. Now the company faces some of the most difficult problems in its recent history as the domestic U.S. market nears saturation and consumers' tastes are changing. Will McDonald's reinvent itself? Will its diversification strategy succeed over the long term? Or will McDonald's, like the market leaders in many other industries in the past, settle for stagnant growth while it watches upstarts take its place?

Why are some companies successful, while so many other businesses fail? Some organizations may just be lucky. They may have the right mix of products and/or services at the right time. But even if luck leads to success, it probably won't last. Most companies that are highly successful over the long term effectively acquire, develop, and manage resources and capabilities that provide competitive advantages. For example, McDonald's enjoys outstanding brand recognition and a world-class operating system. Marriott enjoys these same benefits in the lodging industry. Successful companies have also learned how to develop and manage relationships with a wide range of organizations, groups, and people that have a stake in their firms. The emergence of a fiercely competitive global economy means that firms have to expand their networks of relationships and cooperate with each other to remain competitive.[2] McDonald's' investment into Chipotle was a cooperative venture. The company later gained control, but Mr. Ells still owns a sizable portion of the business. McDonald's also has ventures or alliances with a number of companies, including Walt Disney.

This book focuses on how organizations can grow and prosper through successful execution of the strategic management process. Strategic management is a process through which organizations analyze and learn from their internal and external environments, establish strategic direction, create strategies that are intended to move the organization in that direction, and implement those strategies, all in an effort to satisfy key stakeholders. Stakeholders are groups or individuals who can significantly affect or are significantly affected by an organization's activities.[3] An organization defines who its key stakeholders are, but they typically include customers, employees, and shareholders or owners, among others. Although larger companies tend to make use of the strategic management process, this process is also a vital part of decision making in smaller companies.

Firms practicing strategic planning processes tend to outperform their counterparts that do not.[4] In fact, in a recent survey of executives, strategic management provided significantly higher levels of satisfaction than did most other management tools. Furthermore, 81 percent of companies worldwide reported doing strategic planning. In North America, the figure was even higher (89 percent).[5] A recent study of hotels in the United Kingdom found that business performance was positively associated with the thoroughness, sophistication, participation, and formality of strategic planning processes.[6] Jack in the Box provides an excellent example of how strategic analysis can help guide business strategy.[7]

> Jack in the Box recently announced plans to open 100 to 150 convenience stores over the next five years. The stores will feature full-sized restaurants, as well as gasoline and other typical convenience items such as bread and milk. How did Jack in the Box arrive at this decision? According to Bob Nugent, CEO, an analysis of the convenience store market indicated that there was plenty of opportunity there. For example, 7-Eleven, Inc., the largest player in the industry, controls slightly over 4 percent of the market. Compare this to fast foods, where McDonald's controls 43 percent of the market and Jack in the Box a mere 4.6 percent. Mr. Nugent also justifies his decision on the basis of research indicating that "a convenience store customer is twice as likely to eat fast food as a non-convenience-store customer."[8]

This book also recognizes that there is a difference between the strategic planning process and strategic thinking, and that both are a part of effective strategic management. The strategic planning process tends to be a rather rigid and unimaginative process in many organizations. Strategic thinking, on the other hand, leads to creative solutions and new ideas. A firm that combines strategic thinking into the strategic planning process has the best of both worlds.

THE ORIGIN OF STRATEGIC MANAGEMENT

The increasing importance of strategic management may be a result of several trends. Increasing competition in most industries has made it difficult for some companies to compete. Modern transportation and communication have led to increasing global trade and awareness. Technological development has led to accelerated changes in the global economy. Regardless of the reasons, the past two decades have seen a surge in interest in strategic management. Many perspectives on strategic management and the strategic management process have emerged. The approach found in this book is based predominantly on three of these perspectives: the traditional perspective, the resource-based view of the firm, and the stakeholder approach. These three perspectives, outlined in Table 1.1, will now be introduced.

THE TRADITIONAL PERSPECTIVE

As the field of strategic management began to emerge in the latter part of the twentieth century, scholars borrowed heavily from the field of economics. For some time, economists had been actively studying topics associated with the competitiveness of industries. These topics included industry concentration, diversification, product differentiation, and market power. However, much of the economics research focused exclusively on industries, and some of it even assumed that individual firm differences didn't matter. Other fields also influenced early strategic management thought, including marketing, finance, psychology, and management. Academic progress was slow in the beginning, and the large consulting firms began to develop their own models and theories to meet their clients' needs. Scholars readily adopted many of these models into their own articles and books.

TABLE 1.1	THREE PERSPECTIVES ON STRATEGIC MANAGEMENT		
	Traditional Perspective	**Resource-Based View**	**Stakeholder View**
Origin	Economics, other business disciplines, and consulting firms	Economics, distinctive competencies, and general management capability	Business ethics and social responsibility
View of Firm	An economic entity	A collection of resources, skills, and abilities	A network of relationships among the firm and its stakeholders
Approach to Strategy Formulation	Situation analysis of internal and external environments leading to formulation of mission and strategies	Analysis of organizational resources, skills, and abilities. Acquisition of superior resources, skills, and abilities	Analysis of the economic power, political influence, rights, and demands of various stakeholders
Source of Competitive Advantage	Best adapting the organization to its environment by taking advantage of strengths and opportunities and overcoming weaknesses and threats	Possession of resources, skills, and abilities that are valuable, rare, and difficult to imitate by competitors	Superior linkages with stakeholders leading to trust, goodwill, reduced uncertainty, improved business dealings, and ultimately higher firm performance

Eventually, a consensus began to build regarding what is included in the strategic management process. The traditional process for developing strategy consists of analyzing the internal and external environments of the company to arrive at organizational strengths, weaknesses, opportunities, and threats (SWOT). The results from this "situation analysis," as this process is sometimes called, are the basis for developing missions, goals, and strategies.[9] In general, a company should select strategies that (1) take advantage of organizational strengths and environmental opportunities or (2) neutralize or overcome organizational weaknesses and environmental threats.[10] After strategies are formulated, plans for implementing them are established and carried out. Figure 1.1 presents the natural flow of these activities.

The model contained in Figure 1.1 is still valid and will provide a framework for understanding the various activities described in this book. However, the traditional approach to strategy development also brought with it some ideas that strategic management scholars have had to reevaluate. The first of these ideas was that the environment is the primary determinant of the best strategy. This is called environmental determinism. According to the deterministic view, good management is associated with determining which strategy will best fit environmental, technical, and human forces at a particular point in time, and then working to carry it out.[11] The most successful organization will be the one that best adapts to existing forces. There is some evidence that the ability to align the skills and other resources of the organization with the needs and demands of the environment can be a source of competitive advantage.[12] However, after a critical review of environmental determinism, a well-known researcher once argued:

> There is a more fundamental conclusion to be drawn from the foregoing analysis: the strategy of a firm cannot be predicted, nor is it predestined; the strategic decisions made by managers cannot be assumed to be the product of deterministic forces in their environments....On the contrary, the very nature of the concept of strategy assumes a human agent who is able to take actions that attempt to distinguish one's firm from the competitors.[13]

FIGURE 1.1 **THE TRADITIONAL STRATEGIC MANAGEMENT PROCESS**

This is basically an argument that firms may choose their environments. For example, a larger firm may decide not to compete in a given environment. Or, as an alternative, the firm may attempt to influence the environment to make it less hostile and more conducive to organizational success. This process is called enactment, which means that a firm can influence its environment. The principle of enactment assumes that organizations do not have to submit to existing forces in the environment—they can, in part, create their environments through strategic alliances with stakeholders, investments in leading technologies, advertising, political lobbying, and a variety of other activities.[14] Of course, smaller organizations are somewhat limited in their ability to influence some components of their environments on their own. For example, a small firm may have a difficult time influencing national government agencies and administrators. However, smaller organizations often band together into trade groups to influence government. Also, they may form alliances with larger entities. In addition, even a small firm may be able to exert a powerful influence in its local operating environment. The key to enactment is understanding that a firm does not necessarily have to adapt completely to the forces that exist in its operating environment. It can at least partly influence certain aspects of the environment in which it competes.

The traditional school of thought concerning strategy formulation also supported the view that managers respond to the forces discussed thus far by making decisions that are consistent with a preconceived strategy. In other words, strategy is deliberate. Deliberate strategy implies that managers plan to pursue an intended strategic course. On the other hand, in some cases strategy simply emerges from a stream of decisions. Managers learn as they go. An emergent strategy is one that was not planned or intended. According to this perspective, managers learn what will work through a process of trial and error.[15] Supporters of this view argue that organizations that limit themselves to acting on the basis of what is already known or understood will not be sufficiently innovative to create a sustainable competitive advantage.[16] In spite of the strength of this example of emergent strategy, it is not a good idea to reject deliberate strategy either. One of the strongest advocates of learning and emergent strategy recently confessed, "We shall get nowhere without emergent learning alongside deliberate planning.[17] Both processes are necessary if an organization is to succeed.

In summary, scholars have determined that both adaptation and enactment are important to organizations. They should adapt to environmental forces when the costs of enacting (influencing) the environment exceed the benefits. However, they should be proactive in creating their own opportunities. In addition, organizations should engage in deliberate strategic planning processes, but they should also be willing to make mistakes and learn from them as they chart a strategic course. In other words, strategy should be both deliberate and emergent, and firms should both adapt to and enact their environments, with the situation determining which option to choose.

THE ORGANIZATION AS A BUNDLE OF RESOURCES

In recent years, another perspective on strategy development has gained wide acceptance. The resource-based view of the firm has its roots in the work of the earliest strategic management theorists.[18] It grew out of the question, "Why do some firms persistently outperform other firms?" An early answer to that question was that some firms are able to develop distinctive competencies in particular areas.[19] One of the first competencies identified was general management capability. This led to the proposition that firms with "high quality" general managers will outperform their rivals. Much research has examined this issue. Clearly, effective leadership is important to organizational performance. However, it is hard to specify what makes an effective leader. Also, although leaders are an important source of competence for an organization, they are not the only important resource that makes a difference.

Economic thought also influenced development of the resource-based view. Nearly two centuries ago, an economist named David Ricardo investigated the advantages of possessing superior resources, especially land.[20] One of Ricardo's central propositions was that the farmer with the most-fertile land has a sustained performance advantage over other farmers. More recently, another economist, Edith Penrose, expanded on Ricardo's view by noting that various skills and abilities possessed by firms can lead to superior performance. She viewed firms as an administrative framework that coordinates the activities of numerous groups and individuals, and also as a bundle of productive resources.[21] She studied the effects of various skills and abilities possessed by organizations, concluding that a wide range of skills and resources can influence competitive performance.

A common thread of reasoning in the distinctive competency literature and the arguments of Ricardo and Penrose is that organizational success can be explained in terms of the resources and capabilities possessed by an organization. Many modern scholars have contributed to this perspective of the firm.[22] According to this view, an organization is a bundle of resources, which fall into the general categories of (1) financial resources, including all of the monetary resources from which a firm can draw; (2) physical resources, such as plants, equipment, locations, and access to raw materials; (3) human resources, which pertains to the skills, background, and training of managers and employees, as well as the way they are organized; (4) organizational knowledge and learning; and (5) general organizational resources, including the firm's reputation, brand names, patents, contracts, and relationships with external stakeholders.[23] The organization as a bundle of resources is depicted in Figure 1.2.

Envisioning the firm as a bundle of resources has broad implications. For example, the most important role of a manager becomes that of acquiring, developing, managing, and discarding resources. Also, much of the research on the resource-based perspective has demonstrated that firms can gain competitive advantage through possessing superior resources.[24] Superior resources are those that have value in the market, are possessed by only a small number of firms, and are not easy to substitute. If a particular resource is also costly or impossible to imitate, then the competitive advantage may be sustainable. A sustainable competitive advantage may lead to higher-than-average organizational performance over a long period.[25]

> The success of Marriott is largely attributable to advantages created by resources that have been difficult to duplicate by other companies in the hotel industry. The first is financial controls. Marriott can determine and anticipate construction and operating costs with nearly exact precision. Second, Marriott has developed a distinctive competence in customer service, or "becoming the provider of choice." Looking to the future, Marriott is actively engaged in creating a third organizational capability as the "employer of choice." Marriott executives reason that with fewer people entering the labor force in the eighteen- to twenty-five-year-old age group, good workers will become increasingly difficult to attract. Also, good workers are especially important in a service business like hotels because they interact directly with customers.[26]

FIGURE 1.2   THE ORGANIZATION AS A BUNDLE OF RESOURCES

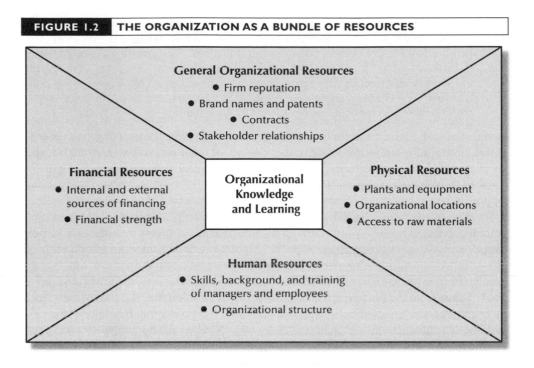

General Organizational Resources
- Firm reputation
- Brand names and patents
- Contracts
- Stakeholder relationships

Financial Resources
- Internal and external sources of financing
- Financial strength

Organizational Knowledge and Learning

Physical Resources
- Plants and equipment
- Organizational locations
- Access to raw materials

Human Resources
- Skills, background, and training of managers and employees
- Organizational structure

Many strategy scholars believe that acquisition and development of superior organizational resources is the most important reason that some companies are more successful than others.[27] Most of the resources that a firm can acquire or develop are directly linked to a company's stakeholders. For example, financial resources are closely linked to establishing good working relationships with financial intermediaries. Also, the development of human resources is associated with effective management of organizational stakeholders. Finally, organizational resources reflect the organization's understanding of the expectations of society and the linkages it has established with stakeholders.

THE ORGANIZATION AS A NETWORK OF RELATIONSHIPS WITH STAKEHOLDERS

A *Fortune* magazine cover story described modern business in these terms: "Business already is moving to organize itself into virtual corporations: fungible modules built around information networks, flexible work forces, outsourcing, and webs of strategic partnerships."[28] Negotiating and contracting have always been important to business. However, the trend in business is toward more strategic alliances, joint ventures, and subcontracting arrangements with stakeholders. The fact is that some of a firm's most valuable resources may extend beyond the boundaries of a firm.[29] Consequently, business organizations are becoming a tangled web of alliances and contracts. For example, Toyota, the automobile giant, chooses to rely on outside suppliers rather than produce supplies in-house. Only two suppliers are owned outright by Toyota, with everything else provided by more than two hundred outside sources.[30] Of course, the hotel business contains many examples of the network approach.

The hotel business is a tangled web of alliances between major competitors. It is not uncommon for a company to own a hotel property that is managed by one of its competitors. Nor is it uncommon to share brand affiliations. For example, Starwood Lodging owns the Princeton Marriott, a 294-room hotel in Plainsboro, New Jersey. A third party to the venture, Princeton University, leases the land upon which the Marriott is built. Similarly, Wyndham's Performance Hospitality Management group manages hotels under nonproprietary brand names such as Hilton, Holiday Inn, and Hyatt.[31]

In the mid-1980s, a stakeholder approach to strategic management began to emerge. It was developed as a direct response to the concerns of managers who were being buffeted by increasing levels of complexity and change in the external environment.[32] The existing strategy models were not particularly helpful to managers who were trying to create new opportunities during a period of such radical change. The word "stakeholder" was a deliberate play on the word "stockholder." Much of the strategy literature at the time was founded, either explicitly or implicitly, on the idea that stockholders were the only important constituencies of the modern for-profit corporation. Stakeholder theory contradicted this idea by expanding a company's responsibility to groups or individuals who significantly affect or are significantly affected by the company's activities, including stockholders.[33] Figure 1.3 contains a typical stakeholder map. A firm has internal stakeholders, such as employees, that are considered a part of the internal organization. In addition, the firm has frequent interactions with stakeholders in what is called the operating (or task) environment. The firm and stakeholders in its operating environment are both influenced by

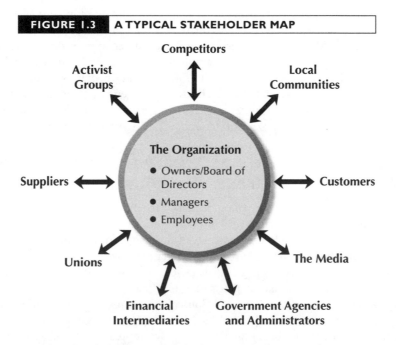

| FIGURE 1.3 | A TYPICAL STAKEHOLDER MAP |

Note: Two-headed arrows signify both two-way influence and a two-way dependent relationship between an organization and its stakeholders.

other factors such as society, technology, the economy, and the legal environment. These other factors form the broad environment, which will be discussed in Chapter 2.

This section has laid a foundation upon which the rest of this book will be built. The three perspectives that will be incorporated are the traditional, the resource-based, and the stakeholder views of strategic management and the firm. Now the strategic management process will be introduced in more detail.

THE STRATEGIC MANAGEMENT PROCESS

To this point, three perspectives on strategic management have been discussed: the traditional model, the resource-based view, and the stakeholder approach. In this book, these three approaches are combined (see Table 1.2). The basic strategic management process is most closely related to the traditional model. However, each one of the stages of this process is heavily influenced by each of the three approaches.

Chapter titles have been added to the simple model of the strategic management process introduced earlier (see Figure 1.4). The typical sequence of activities begins with (1) a situation analysis of the broad and operating environments of the organization, including internal resources, and both internal and external stakeholders; (2) establishment of strategic direction, reflected in mission statements and organizational visions; (3) formulation of specific strategies; (4) strategy implementation, which includes designing an organizational structure, controlling organizational processes, managing relationships with stakeholders, and managing resources so as to develop competitive advantage. While these activities may occur in the order specified, especially if a firm is engaging in a formal strategic planning program, they may also be carried out in some other order or simultaneously.

TABLE 1.2	A COMBINED PERSPECTIVE OF STRATEGIC MANAGEMENT
Process	Firms conduct external and internal analysis (situation analysis), both of which include analysis of stakeholders. On the basis of information obtained, they create strategic direction, strategies, and tactics for implementing strategies and control systems.
Origin	Traditional, resource-based, and stakeholder perspectives.
Adaptation vs. Enactment	Influence the environment when it is economically feasible to do so. Take a proactive stance with regard to managing external stakeholders. Monitor, forecast, and adapt to environmental forces that are difficult or costly to influence.
Deliberate vs. Emergent	Firms should be involved in deliberate strategy-creating processes. However, they should learn from past decisions and be willing to try new things and change strategic course.
Source of Competitive Advantage	Firms can obtain competitive advantage from superior resources, including knowledge-based resources, superior strategies for managing those resources, and/or superior relationships with internal or external stakeholders (which are another type of resource).
Creation of Strategic Alternatives	Firms develop strategies to take advantage of strengths and opportunities or overcome weaknesses or threats. They arise as organizations conduct resource analysis, analysis of organizational processes, and through analyzing and partnering with external stakeholders.

FIGURE 1.4 **THE STRATEGIC MANAGEMENT PROCESS**

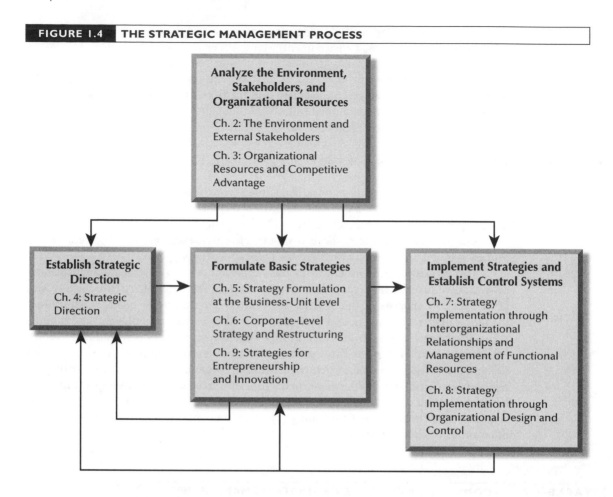

The feedback loops at the bottom of Figure 1.4 indicate that organizations often cycle back to earlier activities during the strategic management process, as new information is gathered and assumptions change. For instance, a company may attempt to develop strategies consistent with its strategic direction and, after a trial period, discover that the direction was not reasonable. Also, an organization may discover rather quickly (or over a longer period of time) that a proposed strategy cannot be implemented feasibly. As a result, the firm may have to cycle back to the formulation stage to fine-tune its strategic approach. In other words, organizations may learn from their own past actions and from environmental forces, and they may modify their behavior in response.

Entrepreneurial start-up firms rarely engage in all of the processes depicted in Figure 1.4. Start-ups often begin with an entrepreneur who has an idea for a product or service that he or she believes will lead to market success. Venture capital is raised through a variety of public or private sources, and a new business is born. The entrepreneur may establish an informal sense of direction and a few goals, but the rest of the formal strategy process may be overlooked. If the organization is successful, it will typically expand in both sales and personnel until it reaches a critical point at which the entrepreneur feels a loss of control. At this point, the entrepreneur may attempt to formalize various aspects of strategic planning, either by hiring outside consultants, by creating planning positions within the firm, or by involving other managers in planning activities. This same process is typical of nonprofit start-ups as well, except that the nature of the cause (i.e., humanitarian, educational) may place tighter constraints on the way the firm is financed and organized.

Consequently, the model in Figure 1.4 is not intended to be a rigid representation of the strategic management process in all organizations as they currently operate. Nevertheless, the progression of activities—from analysis to plan to action and control—provides a logical way to study strategic management. Furthermore, the activities relate equally well to for-profit, nonprofit, manufacturing, and service entities, although some of the differences in the way these organizations approach strategic management will be described throughout the text.

Now that the strategic management process has been introduced, each of its components will be described in more detail—situation analysis, strategic direction, strategy formulation, and strategy implementation.

SITUATION ANALYSIS

Many of the stakeholders and forces that have the potential to be most important to companies were presented in Figure 1.3. All of the stakeholders inside and outside of the firm, as well as the major external forces, should be analyzed at both the domestic and international levels. Chapter 2 will deal with the external environment, which includes groups, individuals, and forces outside of the traditional boundaries of the organization that are significantly influenced by or have a major impact on the organization.[34] External stakeholders, part of a company's operating environment, include competitors, customers, suppliers, financial intermediaries, local communities, unions, activist groups, and government agencies and administrators. The broad environment forms the context in which the company and its operating environment exist, and includes sociocultural influences, economic influences, technological influences, and political/legal influences, domestically and abroad. One organization, acting independently, can have very little influence on the forces in the broad environment; however, the forces in this environment can have a tremendous impact on the organization. The internal organization, discussed in Chapter 3, includes all of the stakeholders, resources, knowledge, and processes that exist within the boundaries of the firm.

Analyzing the environment and the company can assist the company in all of the other tasks of strategic management.[35] For example, a firm's managers should formulate strategic direction and specific strategies based on organizational strengths and weaknesses and in the context of the opportunities and threats found in its environment. Strengths are company resources and capabilities that can lead to a competitive advantage. Weaknesses are resources and capabilities that a company does not possess, to the extent that their absence places the firm at a competitive disadvantage. Opportunities are conditions in the broad and operating environments that allow a firm to take advantage of organizational strengths, overcome organizational weaknesses, and/or neutralize environmental threats. Threats are conditions in the broad and operating environments that may stand in the way of organizational competitiveness or the achievement of stakeholder satisfaction.

STRATEGIC DIRECTION

Strategic direction pertains to the longer-term goals and objectives of the organization. At a more fundamental level, strategic direction defines the purposes for which a company exists and operates. This direction is often contained in mission and vision statements. Unlike shorter-term goals and strategies, mission and vision statements are an enduring part of planning processes within the company. They are often written in terms of what the organization will do for its key stakeholders. For example, the mission and vision of Fairmont Hotels and Resorts Inc. are:

> Mission: We will earn the Loyalty of our Guests by exceeding their expectations and providing warm and personal service in distinctive surroundings.

> Vision: We will inspire an open innovative learning organization that is energetic and exciting for our Colleagues. We will demonstrate a relentless commitment to understand, anticipate and fulfill the needs of our Guests. We will deliver superior operating performance and financial returns for our Owners and Investors to ensure growth for the company and reinvestment in our hotels.[36]

A well-established strategic direction provides guidance to the stakeholders inside the organization who are largely responsible for carrying it out. A well-defined direction also provides external stakeholders with a greater understanding of the company and its activities. Strategic direction is the central topic of Chapter 4. The next logical step in the strategic management process is strategy formulation.

STRATEGY FORMULATION

A strategy can be thought of in either of two ways: (1) as a pattern that emerges in a sequence of decisions over time or (2) as an organizational plan of action that is intended to move a company toward the achievement of its shorter-term goals and, ultimately, toward the achievement of its fundamental purposes. In some organizations, particularly those in rapidly changing environments and in small businesses, strategies are not "planned" in the formal sense of the word. Instead, managers seize opportunities as they come up, but within guidelines or boundaries defined by the firm's strategic direction or mission. In those cases, the strategy reflects the insight and intuition of the strategist or business owner, and it becomes clear over time as a pattern in a stream of decisions.

Strategies as "plans" are common in most organizations. Strategy formulation, the process of planning strategies, is often divided into three levels—corporate, business, and functional. One of the most important roles of corporate-level strategy is to define a company's domain of activity through selection of business areas in which the company will compete. Business-level strategy formulation, on the other hand, pertains to domain direction and navigation, or how businesses should compete in the areas they have selected. Sometimes business-level strategies are also referred to as competitive strategies. Functional-level strategies contain the details of how functional resource areas such as marketing, operations, and finance should be used to implement business-level strategies and achieve competitive advantage. Basically, functional-level strategies are strategies for acquiring, developing, and managing organizational resources. These characterizations are oversimplified, but it is sometimes useful to think of corporate-level strategies as "where to compete," business-level strategies as "how to compete in those areas," and functional-level strategies as "the functional details of how resources will be managed so that business-level strategies will be accomplished."

Perhaps a more accurate way to distinguish among the three levels is to determine the level at which decisions are made. Corporate-level decisions are typically made at the highest levels of the organization by the CEO and/or board of directors, although these individuals may receive input from managers at other levels. If an organization is involved in only one area of business, then business-level decisions tend to be made by these same people. However, in organizations that have diversified into multiple areas, which are represented by different operating divisions or lines of business, business-level decisions are made by division heads or business-unit managers. Functional-level decisions are made by functional managers, who represent organizational areas such as operations, finance, personnel, accounting, research and development, or information systems. Figure 1.5 shows the levels at which particular strategy decisions are made within a multibusiness firm.

Chapter 5 is concerned primarily with business-level strategies. Chapter 6 contains a more detailed discussion of the corporate-level strategies of concentration, vertical integration, and diversification. Chapter 9 focuses on entrepreneurship in both independent companies and in corporations. Functional-level resource-management strategies are used to support all other types of strategies. You will find them discussed throughout the entire book, beginning in Chapter 3, where the various functions are presented as potential sources of competitive advantage. They are revisited in Chapter 5 as tools to carry out business-level strategies; in Chapter 7, where they become tools of strategy implementation; and in Chapter 9 as they relate to entrepreneurial activities. The order in which the strategy formulation activities are discussed is not important. For example, many instructors prefer to discuss corporate-level strategies before business-level strategies.

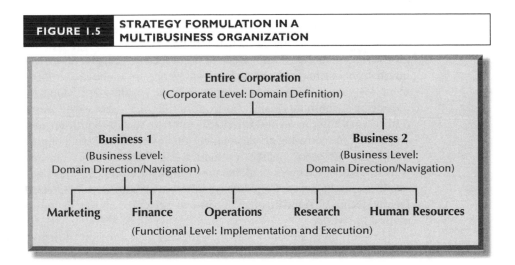

FIGURE 1.5 **STRATEGY FORMULATION IN A MULTIBUSINESS ORGANIZATION**

Entire Corporation
(Corporate Level: Domain Definition)

Business 1
(Business Level: Domain Direction/Navigation)

Business 2
(Business Level: Domain Direction/Navigation)

Marketing   Finance   Operations   Research   Human Resources
(Functional Level: Implementation and Execution)

STRATEGY IMPLEMENTATION

Strategy formulation results in a plan of action for the company and its various levels. On the other hand, strategy implementation represents a pattern of decisions and actions that are intended to carry out the plan. Strategy implementation involves managing stakeholder relationships and organizational resources in a manner that moves the business toward the successful execution of its strategies, consistent with its strategic direction. These topics are discussed in Chapter 7. Implementation activities also involve creating an organizational design and organizational control systems to keep the company on the right course. Organizational control refers to the processes that lead to adjustments in strategic direction, strategies, or the implementation plan, when necessary. Thus, managers may collect information that leads them to believe that the organizational mission is no longer appropriate or that its strategies are not leading to the desired outcomes. On the other hand, a strategic-control system may tell managers that the mission and strategies are appropriate, but that they have not been well executed. In such cases, adjustments should be made to the implementation process. Chapter 8 deals with organizational design and organizational control systems.

In summary, the four basic processes associated with strategic management are situation analysis, establishment of strategic direction, strategy formulation, and strategy implementation. Morrison Restaurants is among many hospitality firms that make full use of these processes. The company, with more than $1 billion in revenues, "has developed and implemented an integrated strategic plan for each of its divisions and concepts."[37] Based on a strategic analysis, the company developed its strategies on the basis of its strengths, weaknesses, opportunities and threats. Its plan and goals, which are widely used and understood by managers and team members, support its mission statement.

GLOBAL COMPETITIVENESS IN THE HOSPITALITY INDUSTRY

Most successful organizations, like McDonald's, eventually find that their domestic markets are becoming saturated or that foreign markets offer opportunities for growth and profitability that often are not available domestically. Many forces are leading firms into the international arena.[38] For example, global trends are leading to a more favorable environment for foreign business involvement. Trade barriers are falling in Europe (i.e., the European Community) and North America (i.e., the North American Free Trade Agreement). Also, newly industrialized countries such as South Korea, Taiwan, and Spain are leading to increasing global competition and new marketing opportunities. There is a worldwide shift toward market economies, as in Germany and China, and financial capital is now readily exchanged in global markets. In addition, communication is easier due to satellites and the Internet, and English is becoming a universally spoken business language. Finally, technical standards have started to become uniform in industrialized countries around the world.

In addition to global trends, organizations have a variety of firm-specific reasons for international involvement. Sometimes firms are so successful that they have saturated their domestic markets, so they look overseas. For example, McDonald's expects more growth in its international markets than in the United States. Also, in some cases, international markets are more profitable than domestic markets. Coke, for instance, makes higher profits in its foreign operations than it does at home.[39] Latin America has substantial business potential. Chile, in particular, has enjoyed rapid development in recent years.[40] Other once-battered nations such as Vietnam are emerging as profitable places for investment. Both Eastern Europe and China, despite political turmoil, offer substantial investment opportunities, due to low labor rates and untapped consumer markets.

> Over the past decade, few developments in international economics have been more important than the sudden emergence of China as a dominant recipient of foreign direct investment (FDI) in the world. From an almost isolated economy in 1979, China has become the largest recipient of FDI in the developing world, and globally the second-largest recipient (after the United States), since 1993.[41]

In order to remain competitive, organizations need to acquire state-of-the-art resources at the lowest prices possible. Sometimes the best product or service is not available in the home country, but in a foreign country. The same is true of lowest-cost goods and services. For example, many lodging companies have expanded into emerging nations such as Indonesia, India, Mexico, or Chile, where the wage rates are relatively low. Finally, foreign investments offer opportunities to acquire technical knowledge and managerial techniques that can then be applied across the entire firm.

The strategic management implications of increasing globalization are profound. Managers cannot afford to ignore opportunities in foreign markets. However, business methods and customs differ from country to country. These differences make stakeholder analysis and management even more important. Analysis of broad environmental forces such as society, technology, and political influences must also be expanded to each of the areas in which an organization conducts business. People also differ greatly from country to country. They cannot be managed in the same way. One example occurs in Vietnam:

> Once war-torn and destitute, Vietnam is emerging as a potential source of profitable business opportunities. Tran Xuan Gia, Planning and Investment Minister, notes that Vietnam has a relatively stable political and social environment, which minimizes the risk for investors. Vietnam's economy has been growing at a fast rate in recent years, sometimes as much as 8 percent per year. The nation is turning from a planned to a market economy. Even during a recent regional economic downturn, Vietnamese firms demonstrated remarkable resilience. For example, Vietnam Airlines increased its passenger loads during the period.
>
> Western business executives need to exercise due care when conducting business in Vietnam. For example, the Vietnamese often communicate through subtle messages in the stories they tell. Also, the concept of "right relationship," with roots in ancient ancestor cults and Confucianism, means that every person has his or her place in the organization, which defines right, duties, and responsibilities. In addition, relationships should be developed over time in a step-by-step fashion. "Relationships in Vietnam move through layers. First-time visitors are graciously welcomed acquaintances, second-time visitors return as friends, third-time visitors as old friends. Foreigners should consider managing layers of intimacy by making multiple visits that move both the relationship and project plans forward step-by-step."[42]

The tools, techniques, and models found in this book apply well to strategic management in a global environment. The methods and theories are used by top strategic planners in business situations around the globe. However, there are differences between strategic management in a domestic setting versus in an international setting. Each of the four basic parts of the strategic management process (e.g., situation analysis, strategic direction, strategy formulation, and implementation) is a little different when applied to an international environment. First, analysis of the environment associated with a situation analysis is complicated by the fact that the organization is involved in multiple environments with varying characteristics. Second, strategic direction must consider stakeholders with a much broader range of needs. Third, the number of alternative strategies is greatly increased as a firm considers options arising from foreign environments. Finally, the specific details associated with implementing strategies will be very different from country to country due to differences in customs, resources, and accepted business practices.

International issues associated with strategic management will be handled in various ways in this text. First, the theory of strategic management will be illustrated with a variety of U.S. and non-U.S. organizational examples. Second, theories and models dealing with global strategy will be included in various chapters of the book and in Chapter 10. Finally, many country-specific illustrations will be used to demonstrate how strategic management is likely to differ in a variety of global contexts.

The challenges of an increasingly competitive global marketplace can be addressed through a well-devised strategic management process. However, strategic planning does not always lead to the kinds of changes that are necessary to remain competitive over the long term. Ineffective strategic planning is often the result of a missing ingredient, strategic thinking, which is the topic of the next section.

STRATEGIC THINKING

What does it take for a company to be on the cutting edge in its industry? Organizational leaders can learn a great deal from studying the strategies of competitors. Clearly, an organization can learn things from competitors that will lead to improvements in performance. However, by the time a firm develops the skills and acquires the resources that are necessary to imitate industry leaders, those leaders probably will have moved on to new ideas and strategies. Consequently, industry leaders break out of traditional mind-sets and defy widely accepted industry practices. Gary Hamel, a well-known strategic management author and consultant, calls these firms "Industry Revolutionaries." He says that revolutionaries don't simply seek incremental improvements to existing business systems to increase efficiency, nor do they focus exclusively on individual products or services. Instead, they invent new business concepts. According to Hamel, "Industry revolutionaries don't tinker at the margins; they blow up old business models and create new ones."[43] For instance, Southwest Airlines decided to reject the hub-and-spoke operating model so prevalent in the industry in favor of a point-to-point system.

Bill Gates, CEO of Microsoft, has said that his company is "always two years away from failure."[44] At any time, a competing firm may develop a software product that is perceived as superior to whatever version of Windows Microsoft is selling, and, within a couple of years, become the market leader. Indeed, Microsoft almost missed a huge opportunity with the Internet and had to play catch-up to Netscape. Strategic thinking does not mean that a firm should randomly try new things until something works. Instead, it allows creative thought to emerge, which should then be accompanied by systematic analysis to determine what should actually be done.

Much will be said in this book about the importance of innovation and how to foster organizational entrepreneurship. An excellent way to start this discussion is with the topic of strategic thinking, since such thinking runs parallel to both innovation and entrepreneurship. It is important to understand from the outset that strategic thinking is not a replacement for the strategic planning process. There are certain aspects of the process, such as analysis of the external environment, that foster strategic thinking. Also, parts of the strategic planning process should be done very systematically, such as the evaluation of alternatives and the development of control systems. However, strategic thinking helps organizations move beyond what is tried and proven. Effective strategic management includes both strategic thinking and the essential elements of the strategic planning process.

STRATEGIC PLANNING CAN DRIVE OUT STRATEGIC THINKING

The term "strategic thinking" is used in so many ways that it is difficult to determine what people mean when they use it. In fact, most people probably don't know exactly what they mean. They may use the word to mean "thinking about strategy" or use it interchangeably with "strategic management" or "strategic planning."[45] According to a well-known strategist, Henry Mintzberg, strategic planning is an analytical process aimed at carrying out strategies that have already been identified. Strategic planning results in the creation of a plan. On the other hand, strategic thinking involves intuition and creativity. It is a way to synthesize stimuli from the internal and external environments to create an "an integrated perspective of the enterprise."[46] According to Mintzberg, strategic planning is so rigid that it tends to drive out creative-thinking processes. The following true story illustrates this point. The actual name of the company is disguised to protect the firm from embarrassment. However, many companies, especially larger ones, have strategic planning processes that mirror the ones described in this example:

> One of the largest companies in the world, with vast operations around the globe, has a very systematic strategic planning process. The organization is divided into many companies. Each year, all of the companies prepare a two-day presentation for corporate administrators to whom they report. They present highly detailed plans of the objectives the company will reach over the next few years, and the specific strategies that will be pursued in order to reach them. Hundreds of PowerPoint–style slides are used. A rigid format is followed, so that the presentations of each company contain the same elements, and corporate executives know what to expect. In preparing for the presentations, company managers are very cautious. They are hesitant to bring up highly innovative ideas that could lead to dramatic changes because the managers know that once they commit to their performance targets, the managers will be held accountable for reaching them. The managers are afraid to fail because the organization penalizes failure. In general, the organization doesn't reward unconventional thinking. Consequently, the company has been limping along for several years now, with many performance problems and low shareholder returns.[47]

This kind of approach to strategic planning can be referred to as "strategy as form filling," whereas strategic thinking is "crafting strategic architecture."[48] The next section provides more detail on the essential elements of strategic thinking.

CHARACTERISTICS OF STRATEGIC THINKING

Strategic thinking is intent focused, comprehensive, opportunistic, long-term oriented, built on the past and the present, and hypothesis driven. A summary of these characteristics is found in Table 1.3.[49]

Intent Focused

Strategic thinking is not a random process of trial and error. Instead, it involves strategic intent, which is a vision with regard to where an organization is or should be going. Strategic intent "implies a particular point of view about the long-term market or competitive position that a firm hopes to build over the coming decade or so. Hence, it conveys a sense of direction. A strategic intent is differentiated; it implies a competitively unique point of view about the future. It holds out to employees the promise of exploring new competitive territory. Hence, it conveys a sense of discovery. Strategic intent has an emotional edge to it; it is a goal that employees perceive as inherently worthwhile. Hence, it implies a sense of destiny. Direction, discovery, and destiny. These are the attributes of strategic intent."[50]

Comprehensive

Strategic thinking is based on a "systems perspective" that envisions the firm as a part of a complete end-to-end system of value creation. Furthermore, strategic thinking means that decision makers are very aware of the interdependencies in the system.[51] This type of thinking fits very well within the stakeholder view of the organization, which is one of the

TABLE 1.3	ELEMENTS OF STRATEGIC THINKING
Intent Focused	Built on a managerial vision of where the firm is going and what it is trying to become. This is called strategic intent.
Comprehensive	A "systems" perspective. Envisions the firm as a part of a larger system of value creation. Understands the linkages between the firm and the other parts of the system.
Opportunistic	Seizes unanticipated opportunities presented to the firm.
Long-term Oriented	Goes beyond the here and now. Looks several years into the future at what the firm will become, based on its strategic intent.
Built on Past and Present	Does not ignore the past or present. Instead, learns from the past and builds on a foundation of the realities of the present.
Hypothesis Driven	A sequential process in which creative ideas are then critically evaluated. Is willing to take a risk. Learns from mistakes.

Source: This table was strongly influenced by J. M. Liedtka, "Strategy Formulation: The Roles of Conversation and Design," in *The Blackwell Handbook of Strategic Management*, ed. M. A. Hitt, R. E. Freeman, and J. S. Harrison (Oxford: Blackwell Publishers, 2001), 70–93.

important perspectives upon which our model of strategic management is based. Organizational managers each possess a "mental model," which is a view of "how the world works."[52] Mental models should include an understanding of both the internal and external organization. An industry-based model of the external environment has dominated for many years.[53] However, a more promising model views the company not as a member of a single industry, but as a part of a larger business system that crosses a variety of industries. Companies co-evolve around innovations, and they work both in competition and cooperatively to satisfy the demands of a wide variety of stakeholders, including customers, suppliers, and broader society and its governments, as well as to create or absorb the next round of innovation.[54] Organizations are a part of one or more value chains, to which they can contribute in a number of ways.

Managers who want to think strategically must also understand and appreciate the internal pieces that make up the whole of their companies. The role of each person within the larger system must be identified, as well as the effect of that role on other people and groups within the organization and on the outcomes of the organization. It is impossible to optimize an organizational system in, for example, satisfying customer needs, without understanding how individuals fit into the system.[55] So the strategic thinker observes and understands the connections between and among the various levels of a business, as well as the linkages between the business and stakeholders in the external environment.

Opportunistic

Although strategic thinking is based on strategic intent, there has to be room for what might be called "intelligent opportunism."[56] Intelligent opportunism can be defined as the ability of managers at various levels of the organization to take advantage of unanticipated opportunities to further intended strategy or even redirect a strategy. For example, Marriott saw an opportunity for growth in the lower-priced segment of the lodging industry when Courtyard was introduced. Of course, the company has a long history of bold entrepreneurship, beginning with a root beer stand started in 1927 by John and Alice Marriott. They added hot food, incorporated, and expanded their Hot Shoppes into a regional chain. The next major move was Marriot's first hotel, the Twin Bridges Marriott Motor Hotel, which opened in Arlington, Virginia, in 1957. With the increase in airline travel, Marriott built several hotels at airports during the 1970s. Each of these ventures was in response to an opportunity and each was a vital part of building the Marriott that exists today. Intelligent opportunism is consistent with the traditional strategic planning model. According to that model, strategies often come from taking advantage of opportunities that arise in the external environment.

Long-term Oriented

Managers, especially in America, are often accused of making shortsighted decisions.[57] Perhaps a research project is canceled because the payoff looks too far away, or employees are laid off only to be rehired within a few months. In contrast, strategic thinking is long-term oriented. Actions that a firm must make now should be linked to a vision of what the firm should become, based on the strategic intent of its top managers. This type of thinking is driving many hoteliers into international markets on a much larger scale.

Built on Past and Present

Although strategic thinking is long-term oriented, it does not ignore the present or the past. In fact, it might be referred to as "thinking in time":

> Thinking in time (has) three components. One is recognition that the future has no place to come from but the past, hence the past has predictive value. Another element is recognition that what matters for the future in the present is departures from the past, alterations, changes, which prospectively or actually divert familiar flows from accustomed channels....A third component is continuous comparison, an almost constant oscillation from the present to future to past and back, heedful of prospective change, concerned to expedite, limit, guide, counter, or accept it as the fruits of such comparison suggest.[58]

Strategic thinkers need to consider the past. The past forms a historical context in which strategic intent is created. Learning from past mistakes helps the firm avoid making them again. Also, analysis of the past behaviors of important stakeholders such as customers, competitors, unions, or suppliers can help a firm anticipate how the stakeholders will react to new ideas and strategies.

The present is also important to strategic thinking, because it places constraints on what the organization is able to accomplish. While strategic thinking is a creative process, it is also a well-reasoned process. Although it may lead firms to consider unconventional ideas, the ideas that are actually pursued are selected based on rational analysis, including consideration of the organization's current resources, knowledge, skills, and abilities.

Hypothesis Driven

Organizations should test their decisions to see if they are appropriate or likely to be successful. This process is similar to the scientific method, in which hypotheses are developed and tested. Hypothesis development is a creative process, whereas hypothesis testing is an analytical process. A typical process begins as managers suggest ideas regarding what the firm might want to do. Those that are considered reasonable are then subjected to rigorous analysis of potential using a well-developed methodology. After analysis, managers determine which of the ideas are worthy of implementation. However, the company may decide not to make a full commitment to each of them at first. Instead, they may allocate enough resources to implementing the ideas so that the company will be able to tell whether they are going to work out. The ideas that are successful are given additional resources. In this description, hypothesis testing occurred twice. The first test was the rigorous analysis conducted by managers in the organization. The second test occurs as the company tries the ideas in the marketplace.

If you combine all six of the elements of strategic thinking, what you have is a long-term thinker who builds a vision for the future on the foundation of the present and the past. It is someone who understands how the organization fits within its external environment, and who has a firm grasp of relationships with external stakeholders. Furthermore, it is someone who is willing to break out of traditional mind-sets and to seize opportunities, but who uses a rational approach to test ideas to prevent the organization from moving indefinitely in an inappropriate direction.

MOTIVATING MANAGERS AND EMPLOYEES TO THINK STRATEGICALLY

We live in a fast-paced world. To keep up, organizations should encourage strategic thinking. Organizations can encourage strategic thinking in a number of ways. First, managers and employees can receive training that describes strategic thinking and how to do it. Second, an organization can encourage and reward employees that generate new ideas (hypotheses). For example, Disney allows some of its employees an opportunity each year to present new ideas to top managers. With a similar philosophy Virgin, well known for its unconventional airline, created a one-stop bridal-services company because one of its flight attendants was having a hard time lining up those services for a friend's wedding.[59] Virgin Bride, the name of the venture, is now Britain's largest bridal emporium. Third, a company can actually implement a strategic planning process that incorporates the elements of strategic thinking. Such a process would include a thorough evaluation of the external environment, with a special emphasis on relationships with stakeholders. It would also include the generation of new ideas and facilitate their testing. Finally, to encourage strategic thinking, an organization has to be willing to take risks. It was risky for Sam Walton to build large discount department stores in rural areas; however, the strategy worked so well that Wal-Mart is now the largest department-store retailer in the United States.

STRATEGIC MANAGEMENT IN THE HOSPITALITY INDUSTRY

Hotels and restaurants are among the most competitive businesses in the world. The hospitality industry primarily consists of businesses that provide accommodation, food, and beverage or some combination of these activities. Hospitality businesses provide services, which differ from tangible products because they are immediately consumed and require a people-intensive creation process. They differ from other service establishments by providing for those who are in the process of traveling away from home in contrast to local residence, although restaurants often serve both travelers and local guests. The offering of an experience is also an important component of hospitality. In addition, a wide range of business formats exist in hospitality such as direct ownership by chains, franchising, asset management, and consortia. Today, the hospitality industry has become more complex and sophisticated with a movement away from the "mine host" and cost control framework of the past to a more strategic view of the business, in both investment and operations domains.

"Travel and tourism" is a broad term used to capture a variety of interrelated businesses that provide services to travelers. Tourism is the largest industry worldwide, and the third largest in the United States.[60] Besides the traditional hospitality businesses of hotels and restaurants; the tourism industry includes a broad range of businesses like airlines, cruise lines, car rental firms, entertainment firms, travel agents, tour operators, and recreational enterprises. The focus of this textbook will be on those hospitality businesses primarily engaged in providing food and lodging to traveling guests. However, we will include discussions of other travel-related businesses such as casinos, airlines, cruise lines, time-shares, travel agents, tour operators, and governmental tourism institutions.

THE FOODSERVICE INDUSTRY—THE PLAYERS

The foodservice industry consists of a wide variety of different businesses including institutional providers and food contractors such as Aramark Corp., Sodexho Alliance, Autogrill SpA's, HMS Host, and Compass Group. Institutional and military foodservice are small segments of the industry and consist of non-commercial institutions that operate their own foodservice. Contractors operate for-profit services to commercial, industrial, university, school, airline, hospital, nursing home, recreation, and sports centers. Management is provided by the contractor of restaurant services, but the institution may provide the facilities and personnel for these operations.

Contract companies are highly consolidated after aggressive merger and acquisition behavior to give them strong positions in the various on-site segments (e.g., school, corporate, and healthcare). Compass Group North America, for example, purchased Bon Appetit Management Company, a $300 million provider of upscale foodservice for corporations and universities to expand its coverage in various key segments.[61] In the latest rankings, Aramark is the leading contract chain in U.S. systemwide sales ($5.3 billion) and market share (29.4 percent share of aggregate sales of contract chains in top 100).[62] Sodexho has divisions in school services, healthcare services, corporate services, and campus services all of which top the list of chains ranked by sales growth, with Sodexho school services reporting a 82.58 percent growth in 2003.[63]

The restaurant industry is the largest private-sector employer in the United States, and consists of commercial dining and drinking establishments, like restaurants, bars, cafeterias, ice cream parlors, and cafes. It dominates the foodservice industry. Within foodservice, the restaurant industry is by far the largest segment with 870,000 restaurants in the U.S., sales projected to reach $426.1 billion in 2003 and an annual growth rate of around 7.5 percent.[64]

Common convention is to split the restaurant industry into two main segments, quick-service and full-service. Quick-service, commonly called fast-food or fast-service restaurants are defined as eat in or take out operations with limited menus, low prices and fast service. This segment of the industry is further broken down into sandwiches (e.g., hamburgers and tacos), pizza, and/or chicken. Leaders in market share in the sandwich segment are McDonald's, Burger King, Wendy's, Subway, and Taco Bell, while the chicken segment is lead by KFC, Chick-fil-A, and Popeyes Chicken and Biscuits.[65] The pizza segment is led by two strong players: Pizza Hut with 43 percent of the market and Domino's Pizza with a 25 percent market share.[66]

Full-service restaurants offer eat in service, with more expansive menus, and prices that range from low to high. In providing annual comparisons, *Nation's Restaurant News* divides full-service restaurants into family, grill-buffet, and dinner house segments. Family chains include players like Denny's and IHOP/ International House of Pancakes, and grill-buffet segment leaders include Golden Corral, Ryan's Family Steak House, and Ponderosa Steakhouse.[67] Finally, the large dinner house segment, is aggressively focusing on new product development, with several major players including Applebee's Neighborhood Grill and Bar, Red Lobster, Outback Steakhouse, Chili's Grill and Bar, Olive Garden, and T.G.I. Friday's.[68] Key players in this segment are the multi-concept operators and franchisors like Darden and Brinker. Large companies in the restaurant industry, such as Yum! Brands are aggressively developing portfolios of restaurants, and international expansion continues to serve as a viable growth strategy for firms like Starbucks. Small operators and independent restaurants compete with the large chains in an industry known for its low barriers to entry and entrepreneurial opportunities.

THE LODGING INDUSTRY—THE PLAYERS

Lodging in the United States is a $102.6 billion industry, with over 42,000 hotels and around 4.4 million guestrooms.[69] Like the foodservice industry, consolidation has been a theme for the last decade with most of the largest companies being publicly owned. Hyatt Hotels, owned by the Pritzker family, and Carlson Companies are exceptions to this rule, with Carlson being one of the largest privately held companies in the U.S.

Providing a bed, bathroom, television, and phone are hotel basics, but additional amenities and services are common. Segmentation is a strategy that distinguishes properties on the basis of price, service, function, style, offerings, and type of guest served. Hotel chains have been utilizing segmentation, particularly since the 1980s to enable growth, expand their customer base, and leverage corporate resources and expertise. A widely-used approach to classifying segments of the lodging industry was devised by Smith Travel Research and Bear Stearns', and includes five segments: luxury (upper upscale), upscale, midscale with food and beverage services, midscale without food and beverage services, and economy. Extended stay hotels are also included in many classifications as either upper or lower tier depending on the range of services they offer. Many of the largest hotel chains have developed brands in a variety of segments, from luxury to economy. Accor hotels for example has the Sofitel brand in the upscale segment, Novotel in the midscale with food and beverage, Etap, Ibis, Motel 6, and Formula 1 in the budget segment, and Red Roof Inn in the economy segment.[70] This chain also offers Studio in the lower-tier, economy extended stay category.

A hotel may be owned by one company, franchised by another, and operated by a third, or any combination of these choices. It is the complex web of business relationships that can often make the question of business identity confusing for those who do not understand the structure of the industry. Companies who chose to own hotels can select from a variety of different forms including corporations, partnerships, and real estate investment trusts (REITs). A company that owns hotels may also be part of a franchise.

Management companies run the operation of a hotel, and may also be franchisors. These companies may actually own the hotels they manage, or operate hotels that others own. Companies managing the most hotels worldwide in a recent *Hotels* 2003 survey were Marriott International (838 managed and a total of 2,557 hotels), Accor SA (484 managed and a total of 3,829 hotels), Extended Stay America (455 managed and a total of 455 hotels), Interstate Hotels and Resorts (390 managed and a total of 390 hotels), and Tharaldson Enterprises (350 managed and a total of 350 hotels).[71] As these rankings suggest, Marriott and Accor are also franchisors and owners of hotels. The top five franchise hotels worldwide are Cendant Corporation (6,513 franchised and a total of 6,513 hotels), Choice Hotels International (4,664 franchised and a total of 4,664 hotels), InterContinental Hotels Group (2,834 franchised and a total of 3,333 hotels), Hilton Hotels Corporation (1,721 franchised and a total of 2,084 hotels), and Marriott International (1,612 franchised and a total of 2,557 hotels).[72] Overall, the top players based on the number of rooms they hold around the world are in order: Cendant Corporation, InterContinental Hotels Group, Marriott International, Accor, Choice Hotels International, Hilton Hotels Corporation, Best Western International, Starwood Hotels and Resorts Worldwide, and Hilton Group plc. As this list suggests, 70 percent of the largest chains are North American headquartered, although this percentage drops to half when the list includes the top fifty corporations.

As firms in the industry have evolved and transitioned into more consolidated international operations, so too has the mind-set of managers moved to a more strategic way of thinking about the business. Many of the assumed differences between hospitality firms and other businesses have disappeared, being replaced with a clear understanding of business practice. While there are differences between hospitality firms and firms of other types, in most ways hospitality firms are not that different. From one perspective, hotels and restaurants are a big assembly operation, much like a manufacturing operation. However, they are seldom studied in this manner. Also, all hospitality firms can be studied in terms of their cash flows, just like other types of firms. And like other firms, they all rely on markets for capital, human resources, customers, and supplies. They are subject to economic, technological, and governmental and societal influences and trends. They have competitors. In summary, there are more similarities than differences between hospitality firms and firms of other types.

Consequently, the general strategic management process does not require substantial modifications to be applicable to hospitality firms. The process begins with analysis of the firm and its environment, which forms the foundation for development of strategic direction, strategies, and implementation plans. Of course, the outcomes from this process will be different for each hospitality firm because results depend on the specifics of the situation. In addition, certain ideas require modification to understand their use and application in services. The most unique aspect of this book compared to general strategic management texts is the translation of ideas into service contexts through the use of hospitality industry examples. These examples should be helpful to you as you learn the strategic management process. Also, they will help you to become more aware of strategies and strategic issues in the industry. However, the most up-to-date theories and ideas of strategic management are also contained herein. We will use nonhospitality examples occasionally when they better illustrate the point we are trying to make.

One of the most important strategic issues facing the hospitality industry today is the ability to leverage human capital.[73] In particular, managers are concerned about human resource activities such as attracting, retaining, and developing the workforce. Although human resources are an area of concern in every business, the hospitality business faces particularly great challenges because of relatively low wage rates and a large percentage of routine jobs. Managers are also very interested in effective use of capital, aligning the interests of stakeholders such as employees, customers, and owners, understanding their customers better, and applying information technology. Of course, many hospitality businesses are still trying to survive or prosper in the post–September 11 environment. Because of their importance to the industry, these issues will receive special attention in this book.

KEY-POINTS SUMMARY

This chapter emphasized the important role of the strategic management process in modern organizations. The strategic management process includes (1) analysis of the external environment and the organization, (2) the establishment of a strategic direction, (3) strategy formulation, and (4) strategy implementation and development of a system of controls. Each of these processes was described in detail. Organizations seldom begin with a thorough strategic management process. Instead, they usually begin with basic financial planning or forecasting. Over time, they develop methods that are more closely associated with what we refer to as strategic management.

The traditional approach to strategy development was that firms should adapt to their environments. According to this deterministic view, good management is associated with determining which strategy will best fit environmental, technical, and human forces at a particular point in time, and then working to carry out that strategy. However, strategists determined that organizations may, in part, create their own environments. The principle of enactment assumes that organizations do not have to submit to existing forces in the environment—they can, in part, create their environments through strategic alliances with stakeholders, investments in leading technologies, advertising, political lobbying, and a variety of other activities. The traditional strategy formulation model also supported the view that managers create strategies in a very deliberate fashion; however, a more reasonable approach also suggests that, through trial and error, managers can also learn as they go.

The resource-based view of the firm explains that an organization is a bundle of resources, which means that the most important role of a manager is that of acquiring, developing, managing, and discarding resources. According to this view, firms can gain competitive advantage through possessing superior resources. Most of the resources that a firm can acquire or develop are directly linked to an organization's stakeholders, which are groups and individuals who can significantly affect or are significantly affected by an organization's activities. A stakeholder approach depicts the complicated nature of the management task. This book combines the best of the traditional, resource-based, and stakeholder perspectives of strategic management.

Many trends and forces are leading firms into global markets at increasing rates, which has led to a high level of global economic interconnectedness. While the tools, techniques, and models of strategic management apply well to a global environment, there are differences between managing in a domestic or an international arena. Consequently, global examples and well-accepted international theories will be woven into each of the chapters. In addition, a separate chapter will be devoted to international topics.

Often industry leadership is associated with breaking out of traditional mind-sets and defying widely accepted industry practices. Strategic planning results in the creation of a plan. On the other hand, strategic thinking involves intuition and creativity. It is intent-focused, comprehensive, opportunistic, long-term oriented, built on the past and the present, and hypothesis driven. Organizations can encourage strategic thinking through training, rewards systems, integrating elements of strategic thinking into the strategy-making process, and by encouraging risk taking.

DISCUSSION QUESTIONS

1. Explain each of the activities in the definition of strategic management. Which of these activities do you think is most important to the success of an organization? Why?
2. Explain the major perspectives of strategic management.
3. Explain the traditional, resource-based, and stakeholder perspectives of strategic management.
4. What are some of the considerations that are motivating U.S. companies to go global?
5. What is the difference between the strategic planning process and strategic thinking? Which of these is essential to effective strategic management?
6. What are the important characteristics associated with strategic thinking? How can an organization encourage this sort of thinking?

NOTES

1. A. Zuber, "Chipotle," *Nation's Restaurant News,* 28 January 2002, 58–59; J. Dunn, "Free Range Burritos: Is This McDonalds?" *New York Times,* 29 September 2002, 6; J. Forster, "Thinking Outside the Burger Box," *Business Week,* 16 September 2002, 66–67.
2. J. S. Harrison and C. H. St. John, "Managing and Partnering with External Stakeholders," *Academy of Management Executive* (May 1996): 46–59.
3. This is essentially the definition used by Edward Freeman in his landmark book on stakeholder management: R. E. Freeman, *Strategic Management: A Stakeholder Approach* (Marshfield, Mass: Pitman Publishing, 1984).
4. C. C. Miller and L. B. Cardinal, "Strategic Planning and Firm Performance," *Academy of Management Journal* 37 (December 1994): 1649–1665.
5. D. Rigby, "Management Tools and Techniques: A Survey," *California Management Review* 43 (Winter 2001): 139–160.
6. P. A. Phillips, "Strategic Planning and Business Performance in the Quoted UK Hotel Sector: Results of an Exploratory Study," *International Journal of Hospitality Management* 14 (1996): 347–362.
7. Some of this material is also found in J. S. Harrison, "Strategic Analysis for the Hospitality Industry," *Cornell Hotel and Restaurant Administration Quarterly* 44(2)(2003): 139–149.
8. S. Leung and A. Barrionuevo, "Fast-food Chain Makes a Move Out of the 'Box,'" *Wall Street Journal,* 29 October 2002, B1.
9. C. W. Hofer and D. E. Schendel, *Strategy Formulation: Analytical Concepts* (St. Paul: West Publishing, 1978).
10. M. D. Olsen and A. Roper, "Research in Strategic Management in the Hospitality Industry," *Hospitality Management* 17 (1998): 111–124.

11. L. J. Bourgeois III, "Strategic Management and Determinism," *Academy of Management Review* 9 (1984): 586–596; L. G. Hrebiniak and W. F. Joyce, "Organizational Adaptation: Strategic Choice and Environmental Determinism," *Administrative Science Quarterly* 30 (1985): 336–349; M. D. Olsen and A. Roper, "Research in Strategic Management in the Hospitality Industry," *Hospitality Management* 17 (1998): 111–124.

12. T. C. Powell, "Organizational Alignment as Competitive Advantage," *Strategic Management Journal* 13 (1992): 119–134; N. Venkatraman, "Environment-Strategy Coalignment: An Empirical Test of Its Performance Implications," *Strategic Management Journal* 11 (1990): 1–23.

13. Bourgeois, "Strategic Management," 589.

14. L. Smirchich and C. Stubbart, "Strategic Management in an Enacted World," *Academy of Management Review* 10 (1985): 724–736.

15. H. Mintzberg and A. McHugh, "Strategy Formation in an Adhocracy," *Administrative Science Quarterly* 30 (1985): 160–197.

16. H. Mintzberg, "The Design School: Reconsidering the Basic Premises of Strategic Management," *Strategic Management Journal* 11 (1990): 171–196.

17. Mintzberg, "Learning 1, Planning 0," 465.

18. J. B. Barney and Asli M. Arikan, "The Resource-based View: Origins and Implications," in *The Blackwell Handbook of Strategic Management,* ed. M. A. Hitt, R. E. Freeman, and J. S. Harrison (Oxford: Blackwell Publishers, 2001), 124–188.

19. L. G. Hrebiniak and C. C. Snow, "Top Management Agreement and Organizational Performance," *Human Relations* 35, no. 12 (1982): 1139–1157; M. A. Hitt and R. D. Ireland, "Corporate Distinctive Competence, Strategy, Industry, and Performance," *Strategic Management Journal* 6 (1985): 273–293.

20. D. Ricardo, *Principles of Political Economy and Taxation* (London: J. Murray, 1817).

21. E. T. Penrose, *Theory of the Growth of the Firm* (New York: Wiley, 1959).

22. Perhaps the first publication to clearly delineate what is now known as the resource-based view of the firm was B. Wernerfelt, "A Resource-based View of the Firm," *Strategic Management Journal* 5 (1984): 171–180. However, no other scholar has contributed more on this view than Jay Barney. See, for example, J. B. Barney, "Firm Resources and Sustained Competitive Advantage," *Journal of Management* 17 (1991): 99–120.

23. Barney and Arikan, "Resource-based View," 124–188; Barney, "Firm Resources," 99–120; J. B. Barney, *Gaining and Sustaining Competitive Advantage* (Reading, Mass: Addison-Wesley, 1997); J. S. Harrison et al., "Synergies and Post-Acquisition Performance: Differences versus Similarities in Resource Allocations," *Journal of Management* 17 (1991): 173–190; J. T. Mahoney and J. R. Pandian, "The Resource-based View within the Conversation of Strategic Management," *Strategic Management Journal* 13 (1992): 363–380; B. Wernerfelt, "A Resource-based View of the Firm," *Strategic Management Journal* 5 (1984): 171–180.

24. Barney and Arikan, "Resource-based View," 124–188.

25. Barney, "Firm Resources"; Mahoney and Pandian, "Resource-based View."

26. D. Ulrich and D. Lake, "Organizational Capability: Creating Competitive Advantage," *Academy of Management Executive* (February 1991): 79.

27. Barney and Arikan, "Resource-based View," 124–188.

28. J. Huey, "The New Post-Heroic Leadership," *Fortune,* 21 February 1994, 44.

29. J. H. Dyer and H. Singh, "The Relational View: Cooperative Strategy and Sources of Interorganizational Competitive Advantage," *Academy of Management Review* 23 (1998): 660–679.

30. G. G. Dess et al., "The New Corporate Architecture," *Academy of Management Executive* (August 1995): 7–20.

31. M. Pandya, "Starwood Lodging Moves In," *Business News New Jersey,* 18 September 1996, 17.

32. R. E. Freeman and J. McVea, "A Stakeholder Approach to Strategic Management," in *Blackwell Handbook,* 189–207.

33. This is essentially the definition used in Freeman, *Strategic Management.*

34. Freeman, *Strategic Management;* M. Pastin, *The Hard Problems of Management: Gaining the Ethics Edge* (San Francisco: Jossey-Bass, 1986).

35. Harrison, "Strategic Analysis for the Hospitality Industry."

36. Fairmont Hotels and Resorts Inc., from an open letter to faculty and students at the Cornell School of Hotel Administration, dated January 20, 2003, from Jennifer Chase.

37. R. H. Woods, "Strategic Planning: A Look at Ruby Tuesday," *Cornell Hotel and Restaurant Administration Quarterly* 35(3)(1994): 41–57.

38. H. Henzler and W. Rall, "Facing Up to the Globalization Challenge," *McKinsey Quarterly* (Winter 1986): 52–68; T. Peters, "Prometheus Barely Unbound," *Academy of Management Executive* (November 1990): 70–84; M. E. Porter, *Competition in Global Industries* (Boston: Harvard Business School Press, 1986), 2–3.

39. "As a Global Marketer, Coke Excels by Being Tough and Consistent," *The Wall Street Journal,* 19 December 1989, 1.

40. C. Larroulet, "Look to Chile for an Answer to the Latin Malaise," *The Wall Street Journal,* 24 August 2001, A9.

41. K. H. Zhang, "What Attracts Foreign Multinational Corporations to China?" *Contemporary Economic Policy* 19 (2001): 336.

42. J. R. Schermerhorn, Jr. "Planning and Investment Minister Tran Xuan Gia on Foreign Investment and the Vietnamese Business Environment," *Academy of Management Executive* (November 2000): 9–10; L. Borton, "Working In a Vietnamese Voice," *Academy of Management Executive* (November 2000): 23; J. R. Schermerhorn, Jr. "Vietnam Airlines' CEO Dao Manh Nhuong on Strategic Leadership," *Academy of Management Executive* (November 2000): 19.

43. G. Hamel, *Leading the Revolution* (Boston: Harvard Business School Press, 2000).

44. G. Hamel, "The Challenge Today: Changing the Rules of the Game," *Business Strategy Review* 9, no. 2 (1998): 19–26.

45. J. M. Liedtka, "Strategy Formulation: The Roles of Conversation and Design," in *Blackwell Handbook,* 70–93.

46. H. Mintzberg, *The Rise and Fall of Strategic Planning* (New York: Prentice Hall, 1994).

47. This story comes from actual consulting experience.

48. G. Hamel and C. Prahalad, *Competing for the Future* (Boston: Harvard Business School Press, 1994).

49. Many of these points come from Liedtka, "Strategy Formulation."

50. Hamel and Prahalad, *Competing for the Future,* 129–130.

51. Liedtka, "Strategy Formulation."

52. P. Senge, "Mental Models" *Planning Review* (March/April 1992): 4–10.

53. M. E. Porter, *Competitive Strategy* (New York: The Free Press, 1980).

54. J. Moore, *The Death of Competition* (New York: Harper Business, 1996).

55. Liedtka, "Strategy Formulation."

56. Liedtka, "Strategy Formulation."

57. J. S. Harrison and J. O. Fiet, "New CEOs Pursue Their Own Self Interests by Sacrificing Stakeholder Value," *Journal of Business Ethics* 19 (1999): 301–308.

58. R. Neustadt and E. May, *Thinking in Time: The Uses of History for Decision Makers* (New York: The Free Press, 1986), 251.

59. Hamel, *Leading the Revolution.*

60. The American Hotel and Lodging Association website *2003 Lodging Industry Profile,* (September 30, 2003, http://www.ahla.com/products_info_center_lip.asp).

61. P. King, "Major contractors experience boom in business by inking school, healthcare, multisite deals," *Nation's Restaurant News* (June 30, 2003, vol. 37, no. 26: 130).

62. Ibid. pg. 128.

63. Ibid. pg. 128, 130.

64. The National Restaurant Association website 2003 Restaurant Industry Forecast: Executive Summary, (September 29, 2003; http://www.restaurant.org/research/forecast_overview.cfm). The National Restaurant Association website frequently asked questions (September 29, 2003; http://www.restaurant.org/faq.cfm).

65. A. Garber, "Sandwich chains get in shape to meet consumer preference for upscale settings, healthful fare," *Nation's Restaurant News* (June 30, 2003, vol. 37, no. 26: 88) P. Frumkin, "Chicken chains searching for new strategies to differentiate brands, move up in pecking order," *Nation's Restaurant News* (June 30, 2003, vol. 37, no. 26: 100).

66. G. Cebrzynski, "Pizza chains keep new products rolling, but marketing experts see 'commodity' image downside," *Nation's Restaurant News* (June 30, 2003, vol. 37, no. 26: 94).

67. C. Walkup, "Family chains nurture familiar, down-home image while welcoming new customers into dining room," *Nation's Restaurant News* (June 30, 2003, vol. 37, no. 26: 110). J. Hayes, "Grill-buffet chains use sizzling new marketing tactics to boost sales, stake claim in fast-casual," *Nation's Restaurant News* (June 30, 2003, vol. 37, no. 26: 116).

68. M. Prewitt, "Casual dinnerhouse operators serve up diversity on the menu to tempt new diners, boost sales," *Nation's Restaurant News* (June 30, 2003, vol. 37, no. 26: 122).

69. The American Hotel and Lodging Association website *2003 Lodging Industry Profile,* (September 30, 2003, http://www.ahla.com/products_info_center_lip.asp).

70. Accor Company Website (September 30, 2003; http://accor.com/gb/groupe/activites/hotellerie /activites_hotellerie.asp).

71. S. Wolchuk and M. Scoviak, "Hotels' 325, *Hotels* (July 2003, 35-54).

72. Ibid. pg. 38.

73. C. A. Enz, "What Keeps You Up at Night?" *Cornell Hotel and Restaurant Administration Quarterly* (April 2001): 2–9.

CHAPTER 2

The Environment and External Stakeholders

*T*he terrorist attacks of September 11, 2001 had a terrible worldwide effect on virtually every type of business. However, few industries have suffered as much as the hospitality industry. Airline travel was immediately curtailed as a result of government-mandated cancellations followed by a general loss of consumer confidence. The economy, which was weak at the time, took another major blow. Consumers responded by reducing travel even more. Occupancy rates plummeted.

How bad did things get? Monthly hotel sales-tax revenue for Washington, D.C., dropped from nearly $5 million in November 2000 to less than $3 million in November 2001. Revenue per available room (RevPAR) across all U.S. hotels was down over 7 percent for the year 2001, in spite of the fact that the attacks came toward the end of the year. The New England, Middle Atlantic, and Pacific regions endured the largest drops in RevPAR. Hotels in those areas also had further to fall (that is, higher RevPARs) than hotels in the nation's central regions, which fell off more gradually from a less-lofty peak than did the coastal properties. Even within the regions, large cities experienced a greater fall-off in RevPAR than did smaller markets. Particularly hard hit were luxury hotels in major cities, which experienced huge drops in foreign visitors and many event cancellations. Pain spread beyond U.S. boundaries. For example, the Dublin-based Jurys Doyle Hotel Group saw its profits drop 12 percent.

Hotel operators responded to the crisis in a number of ways. In Las Vegas, Strip operators cut back on staffing at their hotels, scaled back larger building projects, and cut room rates to stimulate demand. For example, Bellagio's weekday quoted room rate fell as low as $109, compared to its normal range from $160 to $230. Cost-cutting measures across the industry helped to preserve profits to some degree. In Washington, D.C., hotels launched a campaign featuring Washington as a "City of Inspiration." Nevertheless, by the beginning of 2003, analysts were starting to wonder if demand would ever return to pre–September 11 levels, prompting Standard & Poor's to cut its ratings for a number of hotel holding companies.[1]

INTRODUCTION

The terrible events of September 11, 2001 sent shock waves through the entire business community in the United States and abroad. Organizations and governments increased security, especially in the transportation and entertainment industries. As the example illustrates, reduced travel had a large negative effect on tourism and the airlines. The decline in tourism also had a ripple effect on state tax revenues and an assortment of businesses in U.S. states and foreign countries that rely on tourism for a large part of their revenue. This provided another shock to an already slumping U.S. economy, impacting most businesses either directly or indirectly. Then, in the midst of this crisis came the announcements that the SARS virus was killing people in many popular tourist destinations around the globe.

Successful organizations stay abreast of changes in their external environments to predict trends, anticipate concerns, and generate ideas. These activities lead to the identification of external opportunities and threats, which are then considered by managers as they develop strategic direction and formulate and implement organizational strategies.[2] The external environment can be divided into the broad and operating environments. The operating environment is different for each firm, although similarities may exist among firms in the same industries. On the other hand, the broad environment is not firm specific or industry specific. In other words, the major trends and influences that occur in the broad environment impact many firms and industries, although the type and level of influence may be different from one industry to the next. For example, an event such as September 11 has been felt most strongly in the travel and lodging sectors; however, virtually every industry has been influenced in some way.

The major components of the broad and operating environments are displayed in Figure 2.1. An organization can have a much more significant influence

FIGURE 2.1 THE ORGANIZATION, ITS PRIMARY STAKEHOLDERS, AND THE BROAD ENVIRONMENT

on events that transpire in its operating environment than it can in its broad environment. In fact, this is one way to distinguish between the two environments. For example, it would be difficult for a firm, working independently, to dramatically influence societal views on abortion, drug abuse, free trade with China, or migration to the Sun Belt states in the United States. However, an organization can have a profound impact on the attitude of its customers or suppliers, competitive rivalry, or even government regulations (assuming proactive political activities). Since organizations typically can have only a minimal influence on forces in the broad environment, the emphasis in the first section will be on analyzing and adapting to those forces.

ASSESSMENT OF THE BROAD ENVIRONMENT

This section describes many of the most important forces in the broad environment and how some organizations respond to them. The emphasis in this section will be on monitoring, forecasting, and adapting to broad environmental influences. The broad environment forms the context in which the firm and its operating environment exist. The most important elements in the broad environment, as it relates to a business organization and its operating environment, are sociocultural influences, global economic influences, political influences, and technological influences. These four areas will now be described, as well as examples of successful and unsuccessful organizational responses.

THE SOCIOCULTURAL CONTEXT

Society is composed of the individuals who make up a particular geographic region. Some sociocultural trends are applicable to the citizens of an entire country. For example, a few of the major social issues currently facing the United States are:

- Role of government in health care and child care
- Terrorism and levels of violent crime
- Security of travel and public places
- Importance and role of the military
- Declining quality of education
- Legality of abortion and stem-cell research
- Level of foreign investment/ownership in the United States
- Social costs of restructuring, especially layoffs
- Pollution and disposal of toxic and nontoxic waste

On the other hand, attitudes and beliefs can relate to geographic areas that are larger or smaller than individual countries. For example, people refer to the South, which alludes to the southern states of the United States; to Western culture (globally speaking); or to Latin American countries. These sociocultural groups have meaning to most well-educated people, because of the widely held beliefs and values that are a part of the culture in these areas.

Analysis of societal trends is important from at least four perspectives. First, broader societal influences can create opportunities for organizations. For example, societal interest in fitness has led to the development of state-of-the-art fitness centers as a differentiating feature in upscale hotels. Also, many baby-boomer couples had babies later in life than did past generations, causing a demographic trend toward older couples with children. The higher levels of income of these more established parents means that they are more likely to travel, which has led to the opportunity to develop programs that cater to their special interests. One outgrowth of this trend is the creation of family-friendly cruises such as the Disney Cruise Lines. Although baby-boomer parents and their children have provided growth and profit opportunities for child-friendly hospitality businesses, the countercycle of the baby-boomer trend, the baby-bust generation, will likely reverse the trend.

Second, awareness of and compliance with the attitudes of society can help an organization avoid problems associated with being perceived as a "bad corporate citizen." For example, Denny's was known for many years as one of America's most racist companies. However, Ron Petty, Denny's CEO, introduced initiatives that turned the company into a model of multicultural sensitivity.[3] In general, the public is becoming increasingly distrusting of larger corporation, a part of the aftermath of the Enron scandal.

> December 2, 2001, Enron, once the seventh-largest Fortune 500 company, filed for bankruptcy. Less than a year earlier, Enron's CEO, Jeff Skilling, said in an interview: "Our business is not a black box. It's very simple to model. People who raise questions are people who have not gone through it in detail. We have explicit answers, but people want to throw rocks." In retrospect, a black box was a very good description of Enron in 2001. Debt was hidden behind partnerships. Financial disclosures were kept to a minimum. Earnings were intentionally inflated. Executives made exaggerated statements about how well the company was doing. They have been accused of arrogance, greed, deceit, and financial chicanery.
>
> The Enron collapse tarnished the reputation of what was previously one of America's most trusted organizations, Arthur Andersen LLP. Andersen, the huge accounting firm that audited Enron's financial statements, not only failed to provide realistic assessments of Enron's financial condition, but also sought to cover up its own mistakes through destroying documents. An October 12, 2001 memo directed workers to destroy all audit materials except for some basic working documents.[4]

The fallout from the Enron implosion has had a sweeping impact on firms and industries in America and throughout the world. The whole accounting profession is now under a high level of scrutiny, and a wave of new government regulation is expected. Investors and financial analysts have lost more of their already eroding confidence in the accuracy of financial statements. The financial community is now looking more closely at the statements of a wide range of companies, including hospitality firms, wondering whether they have hidden debt or manipulated numbers. The Enron case is an excellent example of how the external environment can influence firms and industries.

Third, a positive organizational reputation among stakeholders such as customers and suppliers may increase demand for products or lead to increased business opportunities. Companies such as Four Seasons, Marriott, and McDonald's go to great lengths to present themselves in a positive light. Each year, *Fortune* magazine rates corporations on the basis of their reputations. One of these issues began, "Each year we hear of more companies that have made an explicit corporate goal of improving their performance in *Fortune's* annual survey of corporate reputations."[5] Four Seasons, for example, is a hospitality favorite on the Fortune 100 best companies to work for list. A corporate reputation can be a very important organizational resource, since it cannot be imitated completely. The value of this resource will be discussed further in Chapter 3.

Fourth, correct assessment of social trends can help businesses avoid restrictive legislation, which can be a threat to organizational success. Industries and organizations that police themselves are less likely to be the target of legislative activity. Legislative activity is often in response to a public outcry against the actions of firms or industries, as has been the case with some intrusive and unethical telemarketing activity. Business practices of U.S. firms in foreign countries continue to be an issue of social debate. This debate is complicated by a strict government regulation called the Foreign Corrupt Practices Act, as explained below.

The Foreign Corrupt Practices Act (FCPA) was passed by Congress and signed into law by President Carter in 1977. The act was a response to social concern about bribes paid by U.S. companies to foreign government officials. The public and Congress seemed to believe that foreign governments work similarly to the government of the United States. Unfortunately, the "rules of the game" are different in many foreign countries, where payments are demanded as a regular part of business. In the United States, while these types of payments may occur, they are illegal.

Some business writers believe that the FCPA reduced the competitiveness of U.S. firms in foreign markets for two reasons. First, U.S. firms can't compete fairly with firms from countries that do permit bribery. Second, the FCPA requires detailed record keeping and reporting, which adds another administrative expense to international operations and makes them less efficient. The lesson for businesses is fairly clear: "Once legislation that is supposedly ethically motivated is passed, it is almost impossible to rescind. The time to participate forcefully in discussion of ethically motivated legislation is before it is passed, no matter how difficult this appears to be at the time."[6] Another example of avoidable legislation is the U.S. Sentencing Guidelines (USSG), compulsory guidelines courts must use to determine fines and penalties when corporate illegalities are proven. These guidelines, which substantially increase corporate punishments, are a direct response to social distress over the increasing incidence of white-collar crime.[7]

Correct evaluation of societal forces can help direct organizational planning. For instance, understanding demographic forces can help an organization forecast industry demand. Currently, the aging U.S. population is providing opportunities for companies in recreation and nursing homes. Companies in many industries are taking advantage of this trend by offering special services and discounts to senior citizens. Evolving consumer food preferences and dining habits are also of interest to many in the hospitality industry. According to the National Restaurant Association, 38–40 percent of our food dollars are spent away from home.[8]

Predictions abound on what people will be eating, whether it is more herbs such as garlic or more fresh vegetables. A senior manager of a cookware chain makes the following prediction about cooking in the future.

> It's headed toward easier and more convenient cooking. I don't think people will let their favorite dishes disappear, but the kind of cooking done by our grandmothers will. People just don't have the time and there are too many alternatives. People used to cook three meals a day because they had to, even if they did not like to cook. Now there are other options. People today cook on weekends and to entertain.[9]

THE ECONOMIC CONTEXT

Economic forces can have a profound influence on organizational behavior and performance. Economic forces that create growth and profit opportunities allow organizations to take actions that satisfy many stakeholders simultaneously, particularly owners, employees, and suppliers. On the other hand, when economic trends are negative, managers face tremendous pressures as they balance potentially conflicting stakeholder interests, often between employees and owners.

Economic growth, interest rates, the availability of credit, inflation rates, foreign-exchange rates, and foreign-trade balances are among the most critical economic factors (see Table 2.1). Of course, many of these forces are interdependent. Organizations should constantly scan the economic environment to monitor critical but uncertain assumptions

TABLE 2.1	A FEW OF MANY GLOBAL ECONOMIC FORCES TO MONITOR AND PREDICT
Force	**Potential Influences**
Economic Growth	Consumer demand, cost of factors of production, availability of factors of production (especially labor and scarce resources)
Interest Rates	Cost of capital for new projects, cost of refinancing existing debt, consumer demand (due to customer ability to finance purchases)
Inflation	Interest rates, cost of factors of production, optimism or pessimism of stakeholders
Exchange Rates	Ability to profitably remove profits from foreign ventures, government policies toward business
Trade Deficits	Government policies, incentives, trade barriers

concerning the economic future, and then link those assumptions to the demand pattern and profit potential for their products and services. These assumptions often form the base upon which strategies and implementation plans are built.

Economic growth can have a large impact on consumer demand for hospitality services. Consequently, hospitality organizations should consider forecasts of economic growth in determining when to make critical resource-allocation decisions such as additions. Inflation and the availability of credit, among other factors, influence interest rates that organizations have to pay. High interest payments can constrain the strategic flexibility of firms by making new ventures and capacity expansions prohibitively expensive. On the other hand, low interest rates can increase strategic flexibility for organizations and also influence demand by encouraging customers to purchase goods and services on credit. Volatile inflation and interest rates, such as those experienced in the United States in the 1970s and in South American and Eastern European countries, increase the uncertainty associated with making strategic decisions. Therefore, they are worthy of forecasting efforts in most organizations, but especially in those that are highly dependent on debt or have customers who finance their purchases.

Foreign-exchange rates are another major source of uncertainty for global organizations. Companies sometimes earn a profit in a foreign country, only to see the profit turn into a loss due to unfavorable currency translations. Furthermore, the organization may have billings in one currency and payables in another. Foreign-trade balances are relevant to both domestic and global organizations because they are an indication of the nature of trade legislation that might be expected in the future. For example, the United States tends to run a trade surplus with the European Union. As a result, American firms that conduct business with the EU are concerned about new protectionist legislation such as high tariffs that may be enacted to reduce the trade imbalance.[10] These high tariffs could reduce business and potentially business travel between the United States and the EU. Finally, there are a number of economic variables that may be interesting to specific types of firms. For example, gasoline price fluctuations have been found to influence U.S. lodging demand.[11] Executives involved in strategic planning should develop their own sets of economic variables to track and forecast. The variables discussed here are just examples.

Unexpected shocks to the world economy, such as wars or an epidemic such as SARS, can have serious implications for hospitality organizations; however, they are hard to predict. In general, the increasing frequency of such jolts will probably make hospitality firms a little more conservative with regard to financial and workforce planning.

THE POLITICAL CONTEXT

Political forces, both at home and abroad, are among the most significant determinants of organizational success. Governments provide and enforce the rules by which organizations operate. These rules include laws, regulations and policies. In the United States, two of the most widely known regulatory agencies are the Occupational Safety and Health Administration (OSHA) and the Environmental Protection Agency (EPA).

Governments can encourage new-business formation through tax incentives and subsidies, or direct intervention. For example, Mexico is developing a chain of twenty-two government-franchised ports and marinas in the Baja Peninsula in its most ambitious bid to increase tourism since its highly successful Cancun project.[12] Governments can also restructure companies, as in the case of the AT&T breakup. or totally close firms that do not comply with laws, ordinances, or regulations. Alliances among governments provide an additional level of complexity for businesses with significant foreign operations. Also, some countries have established independent entities to counsel them on government policy. For example, the Australian government uses task forces to help devise policy.[13] They are independent of both business and government. Recently, these task forces have examined technological progress and the needs of various industries to evolve in order to become more competitive.

Some organizations find themselves in a situation in which they are almost entirely dependent on government regulators for their health and survival. In many countries, tight regulatory controls are found in a wide variety of industries. In communist countries, such as China or Cuba, the government has significant control over the actions of firms. In the United States, utilities are a good example of a highly regulated environment; however, hospitality firms tend to be less regulated than firms in other businesses.

Although all organizations face some form of regulation, there is a trend toward deregulation and privatization (transfer of government productive assets to private citizens) of industries worldwide. In Portugal, for example, the previously regulated government-owned banking industry is moving toward privatization. In Eastern Europe, many industries are struggling to survive and prosper in an emerging free-market economy. In the United Kingdom, water utilities have been privatized. In the United States, the past twenty years have brought the deregulation of the airline, banking, long-distance telephone, and trucking industries. With deregulation, existing industry competitors face turbulence and unpredictability. The highly volatile airline industry is an excellent example. However, deregulation can provide new opportunities for firms to enter the market. Jet Blue, a relative newcomer, is thriving amid the struggles of other air carriers.

Monitoring and complying with laws and regulations is a good idea from a financial perspective. Involvement in illegal activities can result in a significant loss of firm value.[14] Fines and penalties imposed by government units can run in the millions of dollars. The following example demonstrates what can happen when an organization mishandles or ignores government regulation.

> Buying California's most famous, most beautiful, most historic golf course—the one where Crosby kidded Hope and knocked out ashes from his pipe against the cypress trees—must have seemed the coup of coups to Minoru Isutani, owner of Cosmo World, a Japanese golfing conglomerate. True, the price he paid in September 1990— said to be somewhere between $800 million and $1 billion—seemed high. But Isutani had a plan. He would transform Pebble Beach into a private club, with memberships (at $740,000 each) sold primarily to wealthy Japanese. Golfers of lesser means protested. Under existing rules, anybody willing to endure a waiting list and pay a $200-per-person greens fee could play the course. But if Pebble Beach went private, the best hours would be reserved for members. Enter the California Coastal Commission, all powerful in matters of coastal access: Did the new owners have a commission permit for this conversion? Er . . . no, they didn't. They didn't think they needed one. The commission ruled they did, and withheld it.[15]

A simplified model of some of the major groups in the United States that influence the political environment of business is found in Figure 2.2. Government influences come from (1) lawmakers, (2) regulatory agencies, (3) revenue-collection agencies, and (4) the

FIGURE 2.2	GOVERNMENT INFLUENCES ON ORGANIZATIONS IN THE UNITED STATES

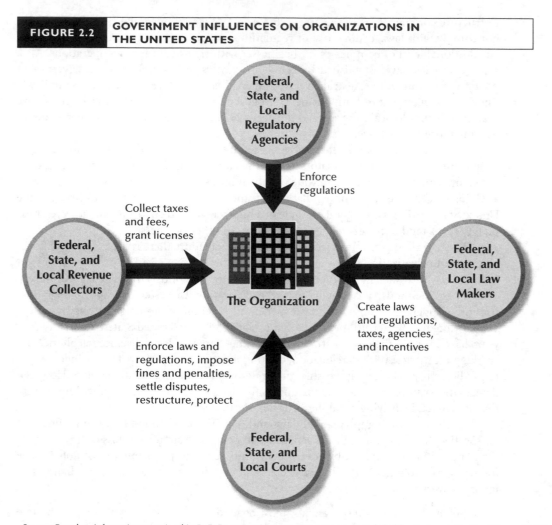

Source: Based on information contained in R. E. Freeman, *Strategic Management: A Stakeholder Approach* (Boston: Pitman, 1984).

courts. Notice that each of these influences can occur at the federal, state, or local levels, which results in twelve major forces instead of four. Involvement in more than one country further increases the number of relevant government forces. All industrialized countries have counterparts for each of the four government influences found in Figure 2.2. For example, the Health and Safety Commission in the United Kingdom functions similarly to many state and federal U.S. regulatory agencies:

> The mission of the United Kingdom's Health and Safety Commission is to ensure that risks to people's health and safety from work activities are properly controlled. The commission aims to modernize, simplify, and support the regulatory framework; to secure compliance with the law; to improve knowledge and understanding of health and safety; and to promote risk assessment and technological knowledge as the basis for setting standards and guiding enforcement activities.[16]

Lawmakers often pursue legislation in response to requests and pressures from constituents. Regulatory agencies and revenue-collection agencies develop the specifics of the regulations needed to carry out new laws, and they serve an enforcement role as well. The courts handle disputes, interpret laws as needed, and levy fines and penalties. Although one organization may not be able to dramatically alter major political forces as a whole, it may have considerable impact within its own specific industries and operating domain. Consequently, major political forces are considered a part of the broad environment, while government agencies and administrators are considered a part of the operating environment. Political strategies for dealing with government within industries will be described later in this chapter.

THE TECHNOLOGICAL CONTEXT

Technological change creates new products, processes, and services, and, in some cases, entire new industries. It also can change the way society behaves and what society expects. Notebook computers, compact discs and players, direct satellite systems, and cellular telephones are technological innovations that have experienced extraordinary growth in recent years, leaving formerly well established industries stunned, creating whole industries, and influencing the way many people approach work and leisure. Computers and telecommunications technologies, for example, have played an essential role in creating the increasingly global marketplace. The Internet, in particular, added a new communications and marketing tool that has led to many new global business threats and opportunities. Organizations that don't embrace technological change may live to regret it.

> Use of online Internet sites for hotel bookings has exploded recently. Originally envisioned as an online alternative to "brick and mortar" travel agencies, these sites have now evolved into online merchants, while putting pressure on room prices. In response, Hilton Hotels Corp, Hyatt Hotels Corp., Marriott International Inc., Six Continents PLC [now Intercontinental Hotels Group] and Starwood Hotels and Resorts Worldwide Inc. have formed a venture to be called Hotel Distribution System LLC that will sell discounted hotel rooms over the Internet. Pegasus Solutions Inc. of Dallas will provide the needed technology. The venture has already inked an agreement with Orbitz LLC to sell rooms that are considered excess inventory.[17]

Technology refers to human knowledge about products and services and the way they are made and delivered. This is a fairly broad definition of technology. Typically, technology is defined in terms of such things as machinery, computers, and information systems. However, technologies don't have to be technically sophisticated. For example, there is a technology associated with cooking or with cleaning a room. Just because these technologies are simple does not mean that technological opportunities do not exist. There is still room for innovation and improvement.

Technological innovations can take the form of new products or processes, such as fax machines and cellular phones. When an innovation has an impact on more than one industry or market, it is referred to as a basic innovation. Examples include the microprocessor, the lightbulb, superconductors, and fiber optics. Basic innovations reverberate through society, transforming existing industries and creating new ones. The hospitality industry has the challenge of selecting appropriate technologies for consumers, whether they be in-room Internet connections or teleconferencing. A recent study reported that although in-room fax machines and cell phone rentals were not popular technologies, Internet reservation systems, management e-mail systems, in-room modems, and voice mail were.[18] The challenge for many hospitality managers is determining which technology innovations are appropriate. In the case of cell phones, consumers' personal phones make the provision of this amenity less profitable.

Technological change is difficult, but not impossible, to predict. An understanding of the three characteristics of innovation can help an organization develop a plan for monitoring technological change. They are: (1) innovations often emerge from existing technologies, (2) a dominant design will eventually be widely adopted, and (3) radical innovations often come from outside of the industry group. These three characteristics will now be discussed.

Innovations from Existing Technologies

As James Utterback pointed out in his book *Mastering the Dynamics of Innovation,* most innovations draw from the existing technologies of the time, but, through a new configuration of some type, they fulfill a new need or fulfill an existing need better.[19] For example, the first personal computers were sold as do-it-yourself kits for electronics enthusiasts and used existing electronics technology. It was only after Apple Computer provided a user-friendly interface and appearance, and software designers provided applications, that the personal computer began to gain legitimacy as a home and office machine. With the entry of IBM into the market, which further signaled the importance of the innovation, the market for personal computers exploded. Since then, innovations in semiconductor and microprocessor manufacturing have lead to smaller, less-expensive components, which has improved affordability and design flexibility. Now business travelers and even tourists often travel with a laptop computer, providing opportunities to hoteliers to provide services such as in-room Internet connections.

Adoption of a Dominant Design

Innovations in the personal-computer industry illustrate a second characteristic of technological innovation. Just like the invention process, commercial innovations tend to evolve through predictable stages—from chaotic efforts to develop variations on the innovation to the emergence of a dominant design as customer needs become clear.[20] The emergence of a dominant design has strategic implications for firms in the industry and for firms considering entering the industry. A dominant design suggests that the industry may evolve as a commodity—with customers comparing prices and businesses finding fewer ways to create differences that customers will pay for. For example, when the personal computer was first emerging, many companies entered the market. They each had different target applications, different keyboard configurations, different operating systems, different microprocessor capabilities, and different overall appearances. Each manufacturer was struggling to create a computer that would appeal to a largely unknown target market. Over time, however, the personal computers began to converge toward a dominant design: operating systems with pulldown menus and user-friendly icons, a standard keyboard, standard word-processing/spreadsheet/graphics applications, and a standard microprocessor. Although computers made by different companies are not identical, they are so similar that few people have trouble moving from model to model. This standardization has made it possible for hotels to provide computer-related services efficiently.

Radical Innovations from Outside the Industry

A third characteristic of the innovation process is that radical innovations usually originate outside the industry boundaries, which makes monitoring of trends outside the immediate competitive group so important. For example, it was not the existing office-machine companies that developed the personal computer, although office machines were ultimately displaced by personal computers. Many innovations in electronics, telecommunications, and specialty materials originated with space and military projects and were adopted by other industries for use in commercial applications. In general, when the rate of improvements with an existing technology begins to slow down, the likelihood of a substitute innovation increases. Hospitality firms should monitor the technological developments in industries other than their own, conducting brainstorming sessions about the possible consequences for their own services and markets. A typical upscale hotel now enjoys a very high level of technology related to its information and communications systems. Early innovators with new technologies enjoy first-mover advantages with regard to winning over and keeping customers.

Dealing with Technological Change

To help identify trends and anticipate their timing, companies may participate in several kinds of technological-forecasting efforts. In general, organizations may monitor trends by studying research journals, government reports, and patent filings. Since the U.S. government is a major sponsor of basic research, government reports and federal technology assessments are often a rich source of information on emerging technologies. Another, more formal method of technological forecasting is to solicit the opinion of experts outside of the organization. These experts may be interviewed directly or contacted as part of a formal survey, such as a Delphi study. A third method is to develop scenarios of alternative technological futures, which capture different rates of innovation and different emerging technologies. Scenarios allow an organization to conduct "what if" analyses and to develop alternative plans for responding to new innovations. In addition to forecasting, some organizations establish strategic alliances with universities to engage in joint research projects, which allows them to keep abreast of trends. For example, the Center for Hospitality Research at Cornell University has research collaborations with numerous hospitality firms. Other hospitality programs have similar programs.

CHANGE AND INTERDEPENDENCE AMONG THE BROAD ENVIRONMENTAL FORCES

Although each of the broad environmental forces has been discussed separately, in reality they are interdependent. For example, social forces are sometimes intertwined with economic forces. In the United States, birthrates (a social force) are low, and, because of improved health care and lifestyles (another social force), people are living longer. This demographic shift toward an older population is influencing economic forces in society.

For instance, the older population means that there are shortages of young workers to fill the service jobs in hospitality while demand for premium services by older consumers is increasing.

To assess the effect of broad environmental forces, including those that are interdependent, organizations often create models of their business environments using different scenarios. The scenarios are composed of optimistic, pessimistic, and best-case assumptions and interpretations of various economic, social, political, and technological data gleaned from an organization's business-intelligence system. Continuing the example of the aging population, a firm providing services for the elderly might develop different demand and wage-rate scenarios as a way of considering several possible future business environments.

Information about broad environmental forces and trends is often available through public and private, published and unpublished sources, but organizations must take deliberate steps to find and use the information. For example, information about U.S. demographic patterns, investment patterns, economic trends, technological advances, and even societal views is widely available through published sources and government reports in libraries. For local economic and sociocultural trends, census data and chamber of commerce reports are just a few of the sources available.

As a review of this section thus far, Table 2.2 contains a chart that can help organizational managers track trends in their broad environments. It is also helpful to students in identifying opportunities and threats as a basis for developing alternatives during case analysis.

Collecting information on the broad environment in an international setting can be a significant challenge. Although most industrialized nations have similar sources of trend data, developing nations will not. Consequently, organizations often rely on a local firm to provide the kinds of broad environmental insights necessary for good strategic decision making, or turn to organizations such as the World Tourism Organization (WTO), which provides statistics and market reports for a wide variety of countries and regions of the world. The next section briefly discusses some of the challenges firms face in the global environment.

INTERNATIONAL ENVIRONMENTS

As an organization becomes involved in or even interested in international business opportunities, the amount of data that must be collected and analyzed increases dramatically. The economic, social, and political environments of various countries and continents can be very different. Africa, for example, must work with serious issues of hunger and poverty. As Dawid DeVilliers, WTO deputy secretary-general, noted, "Passion for Africa and a belief in the power of tourism as a change agent can be major factors in responding to the challenges of poverty and inequity."[21] A few quotations from international business scholars will demonstrate country difference further, beginning with an economic example:

> The Spanish capital market has recently undergone considerable change. Up to a few years ago it was a narrow market worked only by a very few people, as the public in general preferred to put their savings into lower risk, more traditional investments such as fixed term deposits, etc. However the way in which society and the economy in Spain have developed, together with a strong privatization policy, the increasingly global nature of the economy and the internationalization of markets have led to a considerable increase in shareholdings, so that many more Spaniards are now involved in the world of business and in the capital market.[22]

| TABLE 2.2 | ASSESSMENT OF THE BROAD ENVIRONMENT |

Trends, Changes, or Forces	Implication for Organization			Organizational Response, If Any
	Opportunity	Threat	Neutral	
Sociocultural Influences				
• Attitude changes				
• Demographic shifts				
• Sensitive issues				
• New fads				
• Public opinions				
• Emerging public-opinion leaders				
Global Economic Forces				
• Economic growth				
• Interest rates				
• Inflation				
• Foreign-exchange rates				
• Trade deficits				
• Other (depending on business)				
Technological Forces				
• New production processes				
• New products/product ideas				
• Current process-research efforts				
• Current product-research efforts				
• Scientific discoveries that may have an impact				
Political/Legal Forces				
• New laws				
• New regulations				
• Current administrative policies				
• Government stability wars				
• International pacts and treaties				

This chart is a useful tool for organizations that desire to track trends in their broad environments. It can also be used to generate strategic alternatives. On the left, a manager should describe the nature of each trend. The column in the middle can be used to identify each trend as an opportunity, a threat, or as neutral to the organization. The third column should list possible actions the firm could take to respond to the opportunities and threats, if appropriate.

With regard to the political environment, differences also can be significant:

Hours after Prime Minister Lionel Jospin (of France) named Laurent Fabius his new minister of the economy, finance and industry, Socialist Senator Henri Weber hailed the new cabinet member as "the right man in the right place, who will set off fireworks." Fabius's appointment was the cornerstone of Jospin's cabinet reshuffle.… Jospin needed another powerful Socialist leader to become the second ranking person in the government.… Currently, as a part of a strategy being closely coordinated with Jospin—not unrelated to the emerging presidential race—he is working on further cuts in personal and corporate taxes, among the highest in Western, industrialized countries. The total tax burden in France represents 45.6 percent of gross national product and has been climbing.[23]

Of all the elements in the broad environment, perhaps societal differences are the most difficult to analyze, monitor, predict, and integrate into the strategic plan. For example, American firms often have difficulty in China due to differences in the sociocultural environment:

> China is known for rampant corruption that is tolerated by its citizens. Furthermore, Chinese/American relations are often strained due to China's poor attitude towards human rights and its unwillingness to conform to American policies on issues such as copyright protection and arms sales to politically unstable countries. Anti-U.S. sentiment can also be strong at times among some Chinese people. In a recent survey, 90 percent of Chinese youths feel that the U.S. behaves "hegemonistically." When some American movies are played in China, film authorities are swamped with phone calls complaining about the "unhealthy capitalist lifestyles" of some characters. Even the American icon, McDonald's, was attacked with complaints that they were undermining the health of children.[24]

Differences also exist within the technological environment; however, they tend to be a little less severe because of global information sharing and standardized technologies in many industries. The primary differences stem from the fact that some countries are more advanced in certain technologies than are others. Consequently, the global technological environment also deserves attention. In particular, organizations should try to identify where the most-advanced technologies exist so that they can be learned and applied to internal firm processes. As will be discussed later, one of the best ways to do this is through joint ventures with firms that possess the best technologies.

This section has been a discussion of the broad environment and the importance of collecting information on broad environmental trends. The emphasis in this section has been on monitoring, predicting, and adapting to trends in the sociocultural, economic, political, and technological environments. Attention will now turn to an analysis of the operating environment.

ANALYSIS OF EXTERNAL STAKEHOLDERS AND THE OPERATING ENVIRONMENT

The operating environment consists of stakeholders with whom organizations interact on a fairly regular basis, including customers, suppliers, competitors, government agencies and administrators, local communities, activist groups, unions, the media, and financial intermediaries. Not all stakeholders are equally important to firm success, nor do any of them play the same roles. Furthermore, stakeholders have varying levels and types of power to influence an organization.

This section will briefly explore the characteristics that determine the nature of an industry, as well as relationships that exist between an organization and its external stakeholders. It will discuss the power particular stakeholder groups have to influence firm behavior and success. To begin, three of these stakeholder groups will be discussed with regard to economic power in an industry. They are customers, suppliers, and competitors.

Other factors determining the dynamics of industry competition will also be presented. The section will then be expanded to include other important stakeholders such as government agencies and administrators, the media, activists, and local communities. Methods for managing external stakeholders and the operating environment will be presented. In particular, joint ventures and other cooperative relationships will be discussed, as well as political and economic strategies firms might pursue. Relationships with stakeholders and involvement in interorganizational relationships can be sustainable sources of competitive advantage.

PORTER'S FIVE FORCES, ECONOMIC POWER, AND INDUSTRY CHARACTERISTICS

The first step in any type of industry analysis is to determine the boundaries of the industry to be analyzed. Hospitality can be divided into several major industries: lodging, restaurants, other food services, airlines, gaming, cruise lines, theme parks, time share, and tourism. Of course, there is a lot of overlap. A big hotel in Reno, Nevada, may compete in the lodging, gaming, and restaurant industries. Many restaurant and lodging companies are involved in other types of food services. Time-shares are combined with regular lodging in the same resorts. In addition, although resorts are typically included in lodging, they may be better classified as a separate segment. Finally, the tourism industry is not well defined at all; it includes travel agencies, Web-based travel services, vacation planning, and outdoor services and activities. Industries are often difficult to define, but in general they refer to a group of organizations that compete directly with one another to win orders or sales in the marketplace. Consequently, before an analysis is conducted, managers need to define precisely who they consider to be a part of the relevant industry group. Levels are important also. For example, a national hotel chain may consider all hotels in the U.S. market its competitors. However, a single private hotel may only consider other hotels in the same city when conducting an analysis. The right definition of industry is the one that best fits the needs of the firm conducting the analysis.

Michael Porter, one of the most significant scholars in strategic management, developed a model that helps managers evaluate industry competition.[25] Porter described how the economic power of customers and suppliers influences the ability of a firm to achieve economic success. He reviewed factors that lead to high levels of competition among direct competitors. He also noted how entry barriers and the strength of substitute products increase or decrease the level of competition. These five areas of competitive analysis, referred to as the five forces of competition, are presented in Figure 2.3. According to Porter, the five forces largely determine the type and level of competition in an industry and, ultimately, the industry's profit potential.[26] Porter developed the five forces in the manufacturing sector, but they apply well to services also.

An analysis of the five forces is useful from several perspectives. First, by understanding how the five forces influence competition and profitability in an industry, a firm can better understand how to position itself relative to the forces, determine any sources of competitive advantage now and in the future, and estimate the profits that can be expected. For small and start-up businesses, a five forces analysis can reveal opportunities for market entry that will not attract the attention of the larger competitors. An organization can also conduct a five forces analysis of an industry prior to entry to determine the sector's attractiveness. If the firm is already involved in the industry, a five forces analysis can serve as a

FIGURE 2.3	PORTER'S FIVE FORCES MODEL OF INDUSTRY COMPETITION

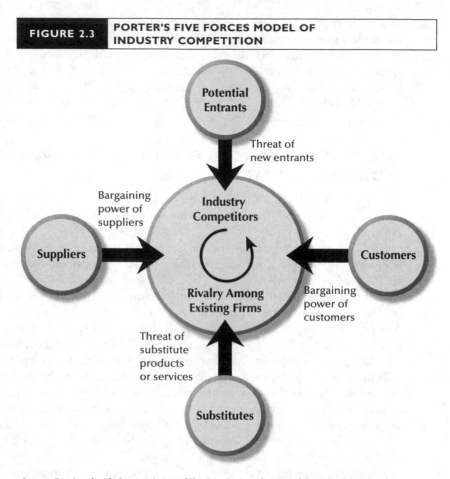

basis for deciding to leave it. Finally, company managers may decide to alter the five forces through specific actions. Examples of such actions will be presented later in the chapter.

Economic Power of Customers

Customers provide demand for products and services, without which an organization would cease to exist. Because customers can withhold demand, they have bargaining power, a form of economic power. They can influence a firm's behavior. However, not all customers have the same amount of bargaining power. For example, Toys "R" Us has substantial influence over the products produced by toy manufacturers. If Toys "R" Us decides not to stock a toy, there is a high likelihood that the manufacturer will stop producing it. According to Porter, customers tend to exhibit greater bargaining power under the following conditions:[27]

- They are few in number. This creates a situation in which an industry competitor can't afford to lose a customer. The number of customers to hospitality firms tends to be large, so this typically is not much of a factor.

- They make high-volume (regular) purchases. High-volume purchasers in the hospitality industry can often dictate contract terms, force price concessions, or demand special services.

- The products they are buying are undifferentiated (also known as standard or generic) and plentiful. This means that customers can find alternative suppliers. Higher-end hotels tend to exhibit much more differentiation than budget or economy hotels.

- They are highly motivated to get good deals. This happens when they earn low profits or when a lot of what they buy comes from the same industry. Terms of a deal may greatly influence whether they will be successful in the next year. It is interesting to note that airlines are asking for concessions from the airports they use because they are making such low profits.[28]

- They can easily integrate backward and thus become their own suppliers. Vertical integration means that a firm moves forward to become its own customer or, in this case, backward to become its own supplier. In general, hospitality firms would have great difficulty becoming their own suppliers. Consequently, this factor typically does not apply. However, we cannot completely discount it either. Note that some cruise lines own jets for transporting guests to their starting ports.

- They are not concerned about the quality of what they are buying. This happens when the products or services don't influence the quality of their own products or services. Since quality is not affected, customers will be interested primarily in obtaining the lowest possible price. For example, office supplies don't influence the quality of services provided by a high-quality hotel or restaurant.

- They have an information advantage relative to the firms they are buying from. Information creates bargaining power. If customers know a lot about the cost and profit structure of firms from whom they are buying, they can use this information to their advantage. For instance, Web-based discount hotel retailers have substantial information about the lodging companies from whom they buy inventory. This puts them at a relative advantage at the bargaining table.

- They are well organized. Sometimes weaker customers come together to increase their bargaining power. For example, tourists may join a clubs or associations to increase their ability to get relevant information or to obtain discounts.

In combination, these forces determine the bargaining power of customers—that is, the degree to which customers exercise active influence over pricing and the direction of product-development efforts. Powerful customers must be given high priority in strategic management activities.

Economic Power of Suppliers

Powerful suppliers can raise their prices and therefore reduce profitability levels in the buying industry. They can also exert influence and increase environmental uncertainty by threatening to raise prices, reducing the quality of goods or services provided, or not delivering supplies when needed. Many of the factors that give suppliers power are similar to the factors that give customers power, only in the opposite direction. In general, supplier power is greater under the following conditions:[29]

- Suppliers are few in number, or, in the extreme case, there is only one supplier for a good or service. This limits the ability of buying organizations to negotiate better prices, delivery arrangements, or quality. In the hospitality industry, this often applies to landowners at popular destinations.

- They sell products and services that cannot be substituted with other products and services. If there are no substitutes, the buying industry is compelled to pay a higher price or accept less-favorable terms. Exotic, but popular, foods are often sold at very high prices, even to restaurants, because they are not substitutable.

- They do not sell a large percentage of their products or services to the buying industry. Since the buying industry is not an important customer, suppliers can reduce shipments during capacity shortages, ship partial orders or late orders, or refuse to accept orders at all, all of which can create turbulence for the buying industry, reduce profits, and increase competition.

- They have a dependent customer. In other words, the buying industry must have what the suppliers provide in order to provide its own services. In a literal way, restaurants must have the foods they prepare in order to remain in business; however, in most markets the abundance of potential suppliers offsets this factor.

- They have differentiated their products or in other ways made it costly to switch suppliers. For example, smaller hotel companies sometimes contract with a reservation service to handle their bookings. If the company later chooses to purchase these services from a different supplier, it must remove the reservation system, purchase or contract for a new system, and retrain employees to use it.

- They can easily integrate forward and thus compete directly with their former buyers. This would happen when a food supplier opens a restaurant.

- They have an information advantage relative to the firms they are supplying. If a supplier knows a lot about the cost and profit structure of firms to which it is selling, the supplier can use this information to its advantage. For instance, if a supplier knows that a buyer is making high profits, a more attractive sales price can probably be negotiated.

- They are well organized. Sometimes suppliers form associations to enhance their bargaining power. In a sense, employees who organize into a union are an example of increasing supplier power.

These forces combine to determine the strength of suppliers and the degree to which they can exert influence over the profits earned by firms in the industry.[30]

Competition, Concentration, and Monopoly Power

Competitive moves by one firm affect other firms in the industry, which may incite retaliation or countermoves. In other words, competing firms have an economic stake in one another. Examples of competitive moves and countermoves include advertising programs, sales force expansions, new-service introductions, capacity expansion, and long-term contracts with customers. In most segments of the hospitality industry, competition is so intense that profitability suffers, as has been the case recently in the airlines and fast-food industries. Some of the major forces that lead to high levels of competition include the following:[31]

- There are many competitors in the industry, and none of them possess a dominant position. Economists sometimes call this pure competition. In a situation of pure competition, organizations must work hard to maintain their positions, since customers have so many options. Consider how many lodging options a tourist has in one of the larger cities of the world.

- The industry is growing slowly. Slow industry growth leads to high levels of competition since the only way to grow is through taking sales or market share from competitors.

- Products in the industry are not easily differentiated (i.e., they are standard or "generic"). Lack of product differentiation puts a lot of pressure on prices and often leads to price-cutting strategies that appeal to customers but reduce the profitability of industry participants. High-end hotels tend to be differentiated; however, at the lower end of the lodging industry the primary competitive factor is typically price (after a certain level of cleanliness and functionality is obtained).

- High fixed costs exist, such as those associated with large hotel properties or a major theme park. High fixed costs mean that firms are under pressure to increase sales to cover their costs and eventually earn profits. It is not easy to cut back on the inventory of rooms in the short term, so hoteliers will cut prices or increase marketing expenses to increase demand.

- High exit barriers exist. When exit barriers are high, firms may lose all or most of their investments in the industry when they withdraw from it. Therefore, they are more likely to remain in the sector even if profits are low or nonexistent.

The relative size of firms in an industry has a great deal to do with competitive dynamics. The first item in the list above describes pure competition as a situation in which sales are spread out over many companies without a dominant firm or firms in the industry. This type of situation fosters competitive rivalry, which in theory is good for consumers because it keeps prices at relatively low levels. At the other extreme are monopoly situations in which one company dominates all others in a sector. Monopolists may misuse their dominant positions through activities such as engaging in unfair practices that limit the ability of competitors to compete, erecting entry barriers to keep new competitors out of the industry, or charging too much for products or services. Consequently, some governments intervene to break up monopolies or penalize them for unfair practices. This is why AT&T was broken up.

Most segments of the hospitality industry are composed of a multitude of competitors. In the lodging industry, even the giants like Starwood, Cendant, and Marriott, in spite of their market power, could not be classified as monopoly players. However, some industries are often characterized by the existence of a few very large firms. These industries are called oligopolies. The theme park industry is a good example of an oligopoly. Some analysts might classify the airline industry as an oligopoly. This is probably an accurate classification if major geographic regions are considered separately. For example, the airline industries in the United States, the European Union, and Asia are dominated by a few large carriers.

Firms in oligopolies may informally cooperate with each other by not pursuing radical departures from existing pricing. They do this because they have learned that price wars hurt the profitability of the entire industry. Formal price-fixing, which is illegal in the United States, is called collusion. On the other hand, some oligopolies are known for severe price-cutting and high levels of competition. The U.S. airline industry has struggled for many years as a result of price wars. If firms in an oligopoly sell products that are hard to differentiate, they are especially prone to a high level of competitive rivalry.

One of the global factors resulting in the creation of increasingly dominant companies and oligopolies is industry consolidation. Competitors in most industrialized countries are merging together to form larger companies with more market power. The major lodging, airline, and restaurant companies have engaged in many consolidating acquisitions. Examples include McDonald's acquisition of Boston Market and Canadian Pacific's acquisitions of Delta Hotels, Princess Hotels, and Fairmont Hotels to form Fairmont Hotels and Resorts.

Richard D'Aveni has identified industries that experience what he calls hypercompetition, a condition of rapidly escalating competition based on price, quality, first-mover actions, defensive moves to protect markets, formation of strategic alliances, and reliance on wealthy parent companies.[32] Short product life cycles, international competitors, global market opportunities, and deep pockets are causing some industries to stay in turmoil. The results of efforts to differentiate are not sustainable because competitors match each other move for move. Competitive practices are forcing profits to lower and lower levels. Airlines are clearly hypercompetitive. Some managers might argue that the lodging industry also has characteristics of hypercompetition.

As a summary of what has been discussed so far, Figure 2.4 contains an abbreviated example of a five forces analysis for the airline industry. In addition to the three forces just described, the figure also includes the similarity of substitute products, as well as barriers that keep new competitors from entering an industry. These forces will now be discussed.

Entry Barriers and Substitutes

Several forces determine how easy it is to enter an industry, and therefore how many new entrants can be expected. New entrants increase competition in a sector, which may drive down prices and profits. The new entrants may add capacity, introduce new products or processes, and bring a fresh perspective and new ideas—all of which can drive down prices, increase costs, or both. Forces that keep new competitors out, providing a level of protection for existing competitors, are called entry barriers. Examples of entry barriers found in many industries include:

- Economies of scale. Economies of scale occur when it is more efficient to provide a service at higher volume. For example, the larger hotels enjoy economies of scale because standard features such as the front desk and communications systems can service multiple rooms simultaneously. If a new entrant will be at a substantial cost disadvantage because of size, few firms will enter.

| **FIGURE 2.4** | **PORTER'S FIVE FORCES FOR THE U.S. AIRLINE INDUSTRY** |

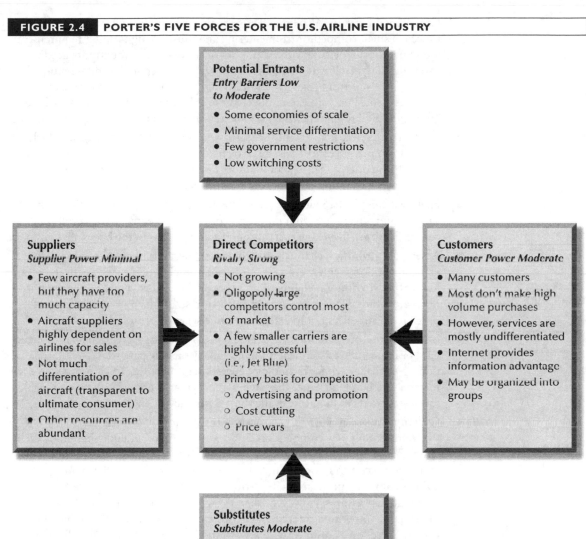

Potential Entrants
Entry Barriers Low to Moderate

- Some economies of scale
- Minimal service differentiation
- Few government restrictions
- Low switching costs

Suppliers
Supplier Power Minimal

- Few aircraft providers, but they have too much capacity
- Aircraft suppliers highly dependent on airlines for sales
- Not much differentiation of aircraft (transparent to ultimate consumer)
- Other resources are abundant

Direct Competitors
Rivalry Strong

- Not growing
- Oligopoly—large competitors control most of market
- A few smaller carriers are highly successful (i.e., Jet Blue)
- Primary basis for competition
  - Advertising and promotion
  - Cost cutting
  - Price wars

Customers
Customer Power Moderate

- Many customers
- Most don't make high volume purchases
- However, services are mostly undifferentiated
- Internet provides information advantage
- May be organized into groups

Substitutes
Substitutes Moderate

- Current fear of flying is turning more consumers to:
  - Automobile transportation
  - Buses and trains
  - Shorter distance vacations
- Business consumers using teleconferences, etc.

- Capital requirements. Also known as start-up costs, high capital requirements can prevent a small competitor from entering an industry. High capital requirements are sometimes associated with economies of scale, since new entrants need to invest in a large facility to be cost competitive. However, high capital requirements also result from research-and-development costs, start-up losses, or expenses associated with extending credit to customers. In the hospitality industry, high capital requirements tend to be closely linked to economies of scale.

- Product differentiation. Established firms enjoy a loyal customer base, which comes from many years of past advertising, customer service, word of mouth, or simply being one of the first competitors in a particular market. These factors make it very hard for a new entrant to compete.

- High switching costs. Switching costs were mentioned earlier in our discussion of supplier and buyer power, but they can also serve as an entry barrier protecting competing firms. Switching costs are almost nonexistent in the hospitality business.

- Access to distribution channels. In industries where supply networks are strong and competition is intense, access to distribution channels may effectively thwart new entry. Distribution channels in the hospitality industry tend to be open to new competitors. However, existing hotels or restaurants in a market can put pressure on suppliers not to extend the same services or prices to newcomers.

- Inimitable resources. Resources that are possessed by industry participants but are hard or impossible to completely duplicate may include patents, favorable locations, proprietary service technology, government subsidies, or access to scarce raw materials such as land. Since these types of advantages are difficult or impossible for new entrants to duplicate in the short term, they often discourage entry.

- Government policy. Sometimes governments limit entry into an industry, effectively preventing new competition. For instance, many Indian tribes enjoy exclusive rights to open casinos on their reservations, while developers in the surrounding communities do not enjoy the same privilege.[33] For many years airlines enjoyed a protected status, with their routes and prices protected from competitive pressures. However, when the airline industry became deregulated, many new competitors entered and existing competitors greatly expanded their routes. These forces resulted in fare wars and lower profitability for all of the firms in the industry. Currently, airline companies are consolidating to build competitive strength.[34]

Taken together, these forces can result in high, medium, or low barriers. Examples of industries that traditionally are associated with high barriers to entry are aircraft manufacturing (technology, capital costs, reputation) and automobile manufacturing (capital costs, distribution, brand names). Medium barriers are associated with industries such as household appliances, cosmetics, and books. Low entry barriers are found in most service industries such as lodging, hotels, and even airlines.[35]

Substitute products are another force outside of the industry that can influence the level of industry competition. If organizations provide goods or services that are readily substitutable for the goods and services provided by an industry, these organizations become indirect competitors. Close substitutes serve the same function for customers and can place a ceiling on the price that can be charged for a good or service.[36] In the service sector, credit unions are substitutes for banks, and bus travel is a substitute for airline travel. Close substitutes also set new performance standards.

Whether a product or service qualifies as a substitute depends on how the boundaries of the industry are drawn. For example, there are few substitutes for the lodging industry in general. Perhaps staying with friends or relatives or camping would qualify. However, it may be more helpful to analyze a particular segment of the lodging industry, such as the luxury segment. It the industry is defined as the luxury segment, then the other segments would become substitutes. This is relevant because the lower segment may improve its services to the extent that consumers would be unwilling to pay the price differential to stay in a luxury hotel. Consequently, luxury hotels need to be aware of and stay ahead of what is happening in lower segments. Regardless of how industries are defined, organizations should pay close attention to the actions of the producers of close substitutes when formulating and implementing strategies.

EXTERNAL STAKEHOLDERS, FORMAL POWER, AND POLITICAL INFLUENCE

The emphasis throughout this section so far has been on economics and bargaining power. Economic analysis is important to strategic management. However, economic power is not the only type of power available to stakeholders, nor do economic factors completely determine the competitiveness of organizations. Figure 2.5 demonstrates that stakeholders can be classified based on their stakes in the organization and the type of influence they have. Such an analysis can help managers understand both the needs and the potential power of their key stakeholders. Internal stakeholders are included in Figure 2.5 for completeness, although our attention in this section will be on external stakeholders.

In Figure 2.5, groups and individuals can have an ownership stake, an economic stake, or a social stake. An ownership stake means that a stakeholder's own wealth depends on the value of the company and its activities. For example, a hotel holding company depends on the operating units for income. Stakeholders also can be economically dependent without ownership. For example, employees receive a salary, debt holders receive interest payments, governments collect tax revenues, customers may depend on what they purchase to produce their own products, and suppliers receive payments for goods and services provided to the company. Finally, a social stake describes groups that are not directly linked to the organization but are interested in ensuring that the organization behaves in a manner that they believe is socially responsible. These are the "watchdogs" of our modern social order, such as Greenpeace.

On the influence side, groups and individuals may enjoy formal power, economic power, or political power. Formal power means stakeholders have a legal or contractual right to make decisions for some part of the company. Regulatory agencies and the Internal Revenue Service have formal power. Economic power, on the other hand, is derived from the ability to withhold services, products, capital, revenues, or business transactions that the firm values. The discussion of Porter's five forces was largely a discussion of economics power. Finally, political power comes from the ability to persuade lawmakers, society, or regulatory agencies to influence the behavior of organizations. Notice that some stakeholders have more than one source of power. For example, creditors sometimes have both economic and formal influence because they have formal contracts and may also have a seat on the company's board of directors.

FIGURE 2.5	TYPICAL ROLES OF VARIOUS STAKEHOLDERS

		Formal (Contractual or Regulatory)	Economic	Political
Stake	Ownership	Managers who own stock in organization Directors who own stock in organization Stockholders in general Sole proprietors	Other companies that own stock in the organization	
	Economic Dependence	All paid managers and directors of for-profit and nonprofit firms Joint venture partners Creditors Internal revenue service	Employees Customers Suppliers Creditors Competitors	Competitors Foreign governments Local communities
	Social	Regulatory agencies (e.g., EPA, OSHA, and SEC) Unpaid trustees or managers of nonprofit organizations	Financial community at large (e.g., large brokerage houses, fund managers, and analysts)	Activist groups (e.g., Nader's Raiders) Government leaders The media

Influence on Behavior

Source: Adapted from R. E. Freeman, *Strategic Management: A Stakeholder Approach* (Boston: Pittman, 1984), p. 63. Copyright 1984 by R. Edward Freeman. All rights reserved.

In general, powerful stakeholders should be given more attention during strategy formulation and implementation. The most important external stakeholders are those with the greatest impact on the firm's ability to survive and prosper. In for-profit organizations, the most important external stakeholders are typically customers.[37] For example, Four Seasons envisions everything it does as a means to "satisfy the needs and tastes of our discriminating customers."[38] At Four Seasons, satisfaction of customers is the key to satisfying other stakeholders. However, the key to effective stakeholder management is that while some stakeholders are given more attention, none of the important stakeholders is ignored. In fact, consideration of a wide range of stakeholders can sometimes lead to creative strategies through partnerships and alliances.

MANAGING THE OPERATING ENVIRONMENT

The operating environment may seem overwhelming to many managers. Powerful customers or suppliers can limit organizational success and profitability. Powerful competitors can make it difficult to remain competitive. Substitute products put pressure on prices and other product features. When entry barriers are low, new competitors enter the industry on a regular basis. Finally, external stakeholders can be powerful and difficult to deal with, based not only on economic power, but on formal or political power as well. However, responding to challenges such as these defines the success of a manager. Fortunately, organizations can pursue a variety of actions to make their operating environments less hostile and thus increase the likelihood of organizational success. These actions tend to fall into three broad categories: economic actions, political actions, and partnering actions.

ECONOMIC ACTIONS

Firms may take a variety of economic actions to offset forces in the operating environment. For example, if entry barriers are low, companies may work to erect new entry barriers that prevent other firms from entering, thus preserving or stabilizing industry profitability. Although a difficult task, the erection of entry barriers can be accomplished through actions such as increasing advertising to create product differentiation or by constructing larger facilities to achieve economies of scale. For example, large lodging companies set up centralized reservation centers or purchasing departments that process large amounts of transactions somewhat more efficiently than do small-volume companies. Similarly, restaurant chains can afford more elaborate advertising campaigns. As another entry barrier, some firms make it unattractive for customers to switch. For example, hotels and airlines set up consumer loyalty programs that encourage repeated consumption. Six Continents (now InterContinental Hotels) in 2002 relaunched its Priority Club Rewards program with several new features that make it easier to enjoy enhanced benefits.[39] Starwood spent $15 million to build consumer awareness for its plan.[40]

Industry rivals apply a variety of competitive tactics in order to win market share, increase revenues, and increase profits at the expense of rivals. Competitive tactics include advertising, new-product launches, cost-reduction efforts, new service methods, and quality improvements, to name a few. Typically, a particular industry can be characterized by the dominance of one or more of these tools. For example, the chain restaurant industry is characterized by high levels of advertising as a competitive weapon. In addition, the entrance of international competitors into the hospitality industry has placed an increasing emphasis on product differentiation through high levels of quality. Other common competitive tactics include providing high levels of customer service and achieving economies of scale (which can lead to lower costs, thus allowing lower prices to customers). Notice that some of these competitive tactics can also lead to the erection of entry barriers, as previously discussed.

Competitive benchmarking is a popular technique for keeping up with competitors. Benchmarking is a tool for assessing the best practices of direct competitors and firms in similar industries, then using the resulting "stretch" objectives as design criteria for attempting to change organizational performance.[41] For example, Disney is often cited as a model for human resource management and Four Seasons provides very high levels of guest satisfaction.[42] Xerox pioneered competitive benchmarking in the United States upon discovering that competitors were selling products at prices that were equal to Xerox's costs of producing them. The company responded by establishing benchmarks as a fundamental part of its business planning.[43]

While benchmarking may help a company improve elements of its operations, it will not help a firm gain competitive advantage. Benchmarking is a little like shooting at a moving target. While a firm is shooting, the target is moving. If an organization benchmarks against an industry leader, that leader will probably have moved on by the time the benchmark is achieved. Coincidentally, Xerox is no longer considered competitive in most of its markets (with the exception of the large copiers). Strategic thinking, described in Chapter 1, can help an organization move beyond what competitors are doing to set new standards and pursue new strategies.

POLITICAL STRATEGIES

Political strategies include all organizational activities that have as one of their objectives the creation of a friendlier political climate for the organization. For example, Enron CEO, Kenneth Lay spent half an hour with U.S. Vice President Dick Cheney to outline what Lay saw as an effective energy policy. Many of his suggestions were incorporated into President George W. Bush's energy plan. How did this happen? Enron had donated $888,000 to the Republican Party, $300,000 to the inaugural committee, and $114,000 to the Bush campaign during the 2000 presidential campaign.[44] After the Enron collapse, this political influence was cast in a highly unfavorable light, but it is still an excellent example of how companies can influence their political environments.

Most organizations don't get half an hour with the vice president to talk about how they would like to be treated by government; however, many hire lobbyists to represent their views to political leaders. While lobbying can be part of a political strategy, it is only a small part of the bigger political picture. Companies may donate to political causes or parties, special-interest groups, or charities. They may pursue community-relations efforts or become involved in community service. Most large organizations have public-relations officers, and many do public-relations advertising.

Some scholars have suggested that individual firm lobbying efforts are often ineffective. Fragmented involvement, in which each company represents its own interests, have resulted in a free-for-all, and the collective interests of business have been the real loser.[45] One suggestion for fixing this problem is increased efforts to strengthen collective institutions such as the Business Roundtable and the Committee for Economic Development.

Collective activity may include membership in trade associations, chambers of commerce, and industry and labor panels. Firms join associations to have access to information and to obtain legitimacy, acceptance, and influence.[46] Trade associations, although not as powerful in the United States as in Japan and Europe, often serve an information-management and monitoring purpose for member firms. They provide information and interpretation of legislative and regulatory trends, may collect market research, and sometimes provide an informal mechanism for exchanging information about competitors. Companies may also join industry and labor panels to manage negotiations with activist groups and unions. In addition, competitors may form alliances of many types in an effort to influence stakeholders such as activist groups, unions, the media, or local communities.

PARTNERING WITH EXTERNAL STAKEHOLDERS

The foregoing discussion of collective political action is a good introduction to the concept of partnering. Organizations may partner for political reasons; however, many other types of partnerships exist. As mentioned previously, a firm's most valuable resources may extend beyond the boundaries of the company.[47] Table 2.3 lists and describes common forms of interorganizational relationships, which is a term that includes many types of organizational cooperation.[48]

A joint venture is created when two or more firms pool their resources to create a separate, jointly owned organization.[49] Joint ventures are often formed to gain access to international markets or to pursue projects that were not mainstream to the organizations involved.[50] For example, Britain's Hilton Group PLC and India's Blue Coast Hotels formed a joint venture to develop first class and luxury hotels and resorts in India.[51] They are also used to pursue a wide variety of strategic objectives, including combining operations to gain scale economies or development of new services.[52]

Networks are constellations of businesses that organize through the establishment of social, rather than legally binding, contracts.[53] Typically, a focal organization sits at the hub of the network and facilitates the coordination of business activities for a wide array of other organizations. Each firm focuses on what it does best, allowing for the development of distinctive competencies. In the automobile industry, for example, Toyota is at the center of a tightly linked network of 180 firms that supply component parts and do joint research. Since network partners concentrate on the components part of the business, Toyota is able to focus specifically on design and manufacture of automobiles.[54] A special type of network form, called a keiretsu, is common in Japan. Keiretsu are organized around an industry and work in much the same way as other networks; however, firms in a keiretsu often hold ownership interests in one another. Lodging firms in other countries are often linked in elaborate networks in which property ownership, branding, and management of operations are shared among competitors. They are not as large as the Japanese keiretsu, but they accomplish many of the same purposes.

TABLE 2.3	COMMON FORMS OF INTERORGANIZATIONAL RELATIONSHIPS
Interorganizational Form	**Description**
Joint Venture	An entity that is created when two or more firms pool a portion of their resources to create a separate, jointly owned entity.
Network	A hub-and-wheel configuration with a local firm at the hub organizing the interdependencies of a complex array of firms.
Consortia	Specialized joint ventures encompassing many different arrangements. Consortia are often a group of firms oriented toward problem solving and technology development, such as R&D consortia.
Alliance	An arrangement between two-or-more-firms that establishes an exchange relationship but has no joint ownership involved.
Trade Association	Organizations (typically nonprofit) that are formed by firms in the same industry to collect and disseminate trade information, offer legal and technical advice, furnish industry-related training, and provide a platform for collective lobbying.
Interlocking Directorate	Occurs when a director or executive of one firm sits on the board of a second firm or when two firms have directors who also serve on the board of a third firm. Interlocking directorates serve as a mechanism for interfirm information sharing and cooperation.

Source: Adapted from *Journal of Management,* Vol. 26, B.B. Barringer and J.S. Harrison, "Walking a Tightrope: Creating Value Through Interorganizational Relationships," p. 383, Copyright 2000, with permission from Elsevier.

Consortia consist of a group of firms that have similar needs and band together to create an entity to satisfy those needs. For example, most U.S. lodging companies participate in data collection and reporting conducted by Smith Travel Research. Research findings are then reported to the members. By banding together, these firms are able to accomplish much more research more affordably than any one or a small group of firms could accomplish on its own. Similar in many ways to consortia, trade associations typically are nonprofit organizations formed within industries to collect and disseminate information, offer legal or accounting services, furnish training, and provide joint lobbying efforts.[55] The primary advantages to belonging to a trade association are collective lobbying, learning, and cost savings through combining efforts in certain areas.

Alliances are agreements among two or more firms that establish some sort of exchange arrangement but involve no joint ownership.[56] They are sometimes informal and do not involve the creation of a new entity. A typical *Fortune* 500 company has sixty strategic alliances.[57] Walt Disney Company and Kellogg Company, the world's leading producer of cereals, formed an alliance in which Mickey Mouse and other Disney characters will show up on everything from cereal boxes to toothbrushes.[58] In the lodging industry, Fairmont Hotels and Resorts has teamed up with the luggage forwarder Virtual Bellhop to create a program in which its guests have their luggage picked up for them at their homes and delivered to their destinations.[59] Fairmont also teamed up with Porsche in a cross-marketing program that provides high-end consumers with a Porsche driving experience.[60]

Finally, interlocking directorates occur when an executive or director of one firm sits on the board of directors of another firm, or when executives or directors of two different companies sit on the board of a third company.[61] In the United States, the Clayton Antitrust Act of 1914 prohibits competitors from sitting on each other's boards. However, they are allowed to sit on the board of a third company. The primary advantage of interlocking directorates is the potential for what is referred to as "co-optation," defined as drawing resources from other firms to achieve stability and continued existence.[62] For example, if a firm develops a new technology, the interlocking director would have access to this information. Also, an organization may add to its board a director from a financial institution in an effort to facilitate financing.

The common characteristic behind all of these forms of interorganizational relationships is that they are an effort to combine resources, knowledge, or power to benefit each participant. They involve partnering and resource sharing. While the emphasis in much of this chapter has been on analysis of the environment in order to formulate strategy, the notion of partnering will be a common theme throughout the rest of this book. Successful interorganizational relationships can be an important source of sustainable competitive advantage.

This concludes our discussion of the broad and operating environments. Information collected during environmental analysis is used in every aspect of strategic planning, including the creation of strategic direction, formulation of strategies, and creation of implementation plans and control systems. Organizations can pursue a variety of economic, political, and partnering actions to make their operating environments more hospitable. The next chapter will explore internal aspects of organizations and the ability of firm resources to provide other sources of sustainable competitive advantage.

KEY-POINTS SUMMARY

The most important elements in the broad environment, as it relates to a business organization and its operating environment, are sociocultural influences, economic influences, technological influences, and political influences. The broad environment can have a tremendous impact on a firm and its operating environment; however, individual firms typically have only a marginal impact on this environment.

Analysis of society is important because broad societal changes and trends can provide opportunities for organizations. It is also important because awareness of and compliance with the attitudes of society can help a company avoid problems associated with being a "bad corporate citizen." A positive organizational reputation among stakeholders such as customers and suppliers may increase demand for products or lead to increased business opportunities. Finally, correct assessment of social trends can help businesses avoid restrictive legislation.

Economic forces such as economic growth, interest rates, availability of credit, inflation rates, foreign-exchange rates, and foreign-trade balances are among the most critical economic factors. Economic forces play a key role in determining demand patterns and cost characteristics within industries.

Technological forces in the broad environment have the power to create and destroy entire industries. In general, (1) innovations usually arise from existing technologies, (2) most products and processes evolve toward a dominant design, and (3) radical innovations tend to come from outside the established group of competitors. An understanding of these characteristics can help a manager develop a system for monitoring technology trends.

Organizations should also track political forces, particularly as they relate to increases and decreases in degree of regulation. Government influences come from (1) lawmakers, (2) regulatory agencies, (3) revenue-collection agencies, and (4) the courts. Each of these influences can occur at the federal, state, or local levels, which results in twelve major forces instead of four. Most industrialized nations have comparable government entities. Involvement in more than one country further increases the number of relevant government forces. Although one organization may not be able to dramatically alter major political forces, it may have considerable impact within its own specific industries and operating domain. Consequently, major political forces are considered a part of the broad environment, while government agencies and administrators are considered a part of the operating environment.

The operating environment includes stakeholders such as customers, suppliers, competitors, government agencies and administrators, local communities, activist groups, the media, unions, and financial intermediaries. One important distinction between the operating and broad environments is that the operating environment is subject to a high level of organizational influence, while the broad environment is not. A firm's industry is composed of companies that compete for the same sales dollars. The nature and level of competition in an industry is dependent on competitive forces that determine rivalry, such as the number of competitors and the growth rate of the industry, as well as the strength of customers and suppliers, the height of entry barriers, and the availability of substitute products or services. These competitive forces are known collectively as the five forces of competition.

Tactics for influencing stakeholders and the operating environment often involve interorganizational relationships, including joint ventures, networks, consortia, alliances, trade associations, and interlocking directorates. Other important tactics include contracting, various forms of stakeholder involvement in organizational processes and decisions, and exercising political influence to promote favorable regulations. Analysis of external stakeholders and the broad environment can result in the identification of opportunities and threats, which are then considered by managers as they establish a strategic direction and develop and implement strategies.

At this point, you should begin to appreciate that stakeholder analysis and management is a difficult and comprehensive management task. The themes, tools, and ideas contained in this chapter will be applied throughout the remaining chapters. The next chapter will focus on the internal organization and resource management.

DISCUSSION QUESTIONS

1. Why is analysis of the broad environment important for effective strategic management?
2. What are the major components of the broad environment? Give an example of a trend in each area that could affect the welfare of a business organization.
3. Why should sociocultural influences be monitored? What are some of the current sociocultural forces in the United States?
4. What are some of the most important factors to track in the global economy? Why are these factors important to organizations?
5. Describe the roles of lawmakers, regulatory agencies, revenue-collection agencies, and the courts as they relate to doing business in the United States. Are these roles likely to be different in other countries?
6. Explain the three characteristics of technological innovation and how an understanding of those characteristics can be used to develop a technological forecasting process.
7. What are the major differences between the operating and broad environments? Can an organization effectively influence its broad environment? Its operating environment?
8. What are the five forces of competition? Describe their potential influence on competition in an industry with which you are familiar (except airlines).
9. What are the primary factors that make some stakeholders more important than others? How should high-priority stakeholders be managed? How do management techniques for high-priority stakeholders differ from those of low-priority stakeholders? Give examples.
10. Describe the major forms of interorganizational relationships, and provide one possible advantage of each form.
11. What role can political strategy play in influencing favorable regulations? How can firms use political influence to balance power with strong competitors, suppliers, or customers?

NOTES

1. C. A. Enz and L. Canina, "The Best of Times, the Worst of Times: Differences in Hotel Performance Following 9/11," *Cornell Hotel and Restaurant Administration Quarterly* 42 (5)(October 2002): 41–52; G. Stafford, L. Yu, and A. K. Armoo, "Crisis Management and Recovery: How Washington, D.C. Hotels Responded to Terrorism," *Cornell Hotel and Restaurant Administration Quarterly* 42 (5)(October 2002): 41–52; M. J. Falcone, E. L. Hausler, and J. H. Simkins, "Las Vegas Back on Track; Will It Derail?" *Gaming Industry Initiation* (August 21, 2002): 18–41; C. Binkley, "Hotel Rebound Is a No-Show," *The Wall Street Journal*, 24 February 2003, B6; "Jurys Doyle Rolls Out More Inns as Profits Take a Dip," *Hotel Report* (January 2002): 3.
2. J. S. Harrison, "Strategic Analysis for the Hospitality Industry," *Cornell Hotel and Restaurant Administration Quarterly* 44(2)(2003): 139–149.
3. F. Rice, "Denny's Changes Its Spots," *Fortune*, 13 May 1996, 133–134.
4. A. Bernstein and B. Grow, "Bracing for a Backlash," *Business Week*, 4 February 2002; J. R. Emshwiller and R. Smith, "Behind Enron's Fall, a Culture of Operating Outside Public's View," *The Wall Street Journal*, 5 December 2001, A1, A10; T. Hamburger and J. Weil, "Second Executive Tells of Andersen E-Mail," *The Wall Street Journal*, 21 January 2002, A3; B. McLean, "Why Enron Went Bust," *Business Week*, 24 December 2001, 59; M. Maremont, J. Hechinger, and K. Damato, "Amid Enron's Fallout, and a Sinking Stock, Tyco Plans a Breakup," *The Wall Street Journal*, 23 January 2002, A1, A4; R. Smith and J. R. Emshwiller, "Internal Probe of Enron Finds Wide-ranging Abuses," *The Wall Street Journal*, 4 February 2002, A3.
5. A. B. Fisher, "Corporate Reputations," *Fortune*, 6 March 1996, 90.
6. M. Pastin, *The Hard Problems of Management: Gaining the Ethics Edge* (San Francisco: Jossey-Bass, 1986), 123.
7. D. R. Dalton, M. B. Metzger, and J. W. Hill, "The 'New' U.S. Sentencing Commission Guidelines: A Wake-up Call for Corporate America," *Academy of Management Executive* (February 1994): 7–16.
8. National Restaurant Association Research Report, 2002.
9. Chuck Williams, founder of the Williams-Sonoma cookware chain as quoted in globalgourmet.com, http://www.globalgourmet.com/food/egg/egg0198/changecook.html.
10. R. A. Melcher, "Europe, Too, Is Edgy about Imports—from America," *Business Week*, 27 January 1992, 48–49.
11. L. Canina, K. Walsh, and C. A. Enz, "The Influence of Gasoline-price Fluctuations on U.S. Lodging Demand: A Study of Branded Hotels from 1988 through 2000," The Center for Hospitality Research, Cornell University, 2002.
12. J. Millman, "Big Dreams for Baja," *The Wall Street Journal*, 15 January 2003, B1.
13. V. Chaudhri and D. Samson, "Business-Government Relations in Australia: Cooperating Through Task Forces," *Academy of Management Executive* (August 2000): 19–29.
14. W. N. Davidson III and D. L. Worrell, "The Impact of Announcement of Corporate Illegalities on Shareholder Returns," *Academy of Management Journal* 31 (1988): 195–200.
15. Adapted from A. Farnham, "Biggest Business Goofs of 1991," *Fortune*, 13 January 1992: 83.
16. W. Altman, "Health and Safety Commission Chair Bill Callaghan on 'Good Health Is Good Business,'" *Academy of Management Executive* 14, no. 2 (May 2000): 8.
17. R. Abramson, "Pegasus Gets a Lift From Online Hotel-Reservation Deal," *The Wall Street Journal*, 12 February 2002, B4; J. N. Ader and T. McCoy, "Web Storm Rising," *Lodging Industry* (August 2002): 1.
18. Judy A. Siguaw, Cathy A. Enz, and Karthik Namasivayam, "Adoption of Information Technology in U.S. Hotels: Strategically Driven Objectives," *Journal of Travel Research* 39 (November 2000): 192–201.
19. J. M. Utterback, *Mastering the Dynamics of Innovation* (Boston: The Harvard Business School Press, 1994).
20. Utterback, *Mastering the Dynamics*.
21. This quote is drawn from a WTO press release on tourism as an instrument of prosperity for Africa, http://www.world-tourism.org/newsroom/Releases/2003/june/angola.htm, June 2003.
22. M. Espinosa-Pike, "Business Ethics and Accounting Information: An Analysis of the Spanish Code of Best Practice," *Journal of Business Ethics* 22 (1999): 249.

23. A. Krause, "Laurent Fabius, France's Minister of the Economy, Finance, and Industry," *Europe* (July/August 2000): 16.

24. Adapted from J. Barnathan, "A Pirate under Every Rock," *Business Week*, 17 June 1996, 50–51; K. Chen, "Anti-U.S. Sentiment Surges in China, Putting a Further Strain on Relations," *The Wall Street Journal*, 15 March 1996, A11; L. Kraar, "The Risks Are Rising in China," *Fortune*, 6 March 1995, 179–180; K. Schoenberger, "Motorola Bets Big On China," *Fortune*, 27 May 1996, 116–124; K. Schoenberger, "Arco's Surprisingly Good Fortune in China," *Fortune*, 5 February 1996, 32.

25. This section is strongly influenced by M. E. Porter, *Competitive Strategy: Techniques for Analyzing Industries and Competitors* (New York: The Free Press, 1980).

26. This section on competitive forces draws heavily on the pioneering work of Michael Porter. See Porter, *Competitive Strategy*, 1–33.

27. Most of these factors came from Porter, *Competitive Strategy*.

28. W. Zellner, "Airports Feel the Carriers' Pain," *Business Week*, 9 June 2003, 46.

29. Most of these factors came from Porter, Competitive Strategy.

30. R. W. Coff, "When Competitive Advantage Doesn't Lead to Performance: The Resource-based View and Stakeholder Bargaining Power," *Organization Science* 10 (1999): 119–133.

31. Most of these factors came from Porter, *Competitive Strategy*.

32. R. D'Aveni, "Coping with Hypercompetition: Utilizing the 7S's Framework," *Academy of Management Executive* (August 1995): 45–57.

33. J. Millman, "House Advantage," *The Wall Street Journal*, 7 May 2002, A1.

34. Barriers to entry form a major portion of the literature in industrial-organization economics. See J. S. Bain, *Barriers to New Competition* (Cambridge, Mass.: Harvard University Press, 1956); J. S. Bain, *Industrial Organization*, rev. ed. (New York: John Wiley, 1967); B. Gold, "Changing Perspectives on Size, Scale, and Returns: An Integrative Survey," *Journal of Economic Literature* 19 (1981): 5–33; Porter, *Competitive Strategy*, 7–17; W. G. Shepherd, *The Economics of Industrial Organization* (Englewood Cliffs, N.J.: Prentice Hall, 1979). For applications of barriers to entry to competitive strategy, see K. R. Harrigan, "Barriers to Entry and Competitive Strategies," *Strategic Management Journal* 2 (1981): 395–412.

35. Bain, *Barriers to New Competition;* H. M. Mann, "Seller Concentration, Barriers to Entry, and Rates of Return in Thirty Industries, 1950–1960," *Review of Economics and Statistics* 48 (1966): 296–307.

36. Porter, *Competitive Strategy*, 23.

37. B. Z. Posner and W. H. Schmidt, "Values and the American Manager: An Update," *California Management Review* 3 (1984): 206.

38. "Our Values," 2001 Annual Report, Four Seasons Hotels and Resorts, 1.

39. G. Wagner, "Six Continents Reinvents Priority Club," *Lodging Hospitality* 58(6)(2002): 9.

40. M. Beirne, "Starwood Ups Loyalty Plan with $15M," *Brandweek*, 27 August 2001, 6.

41. K. Jennings and F. Westfall, "Benchmarking for Strategic Action," *Journal of Business Strategy* (May/June 1992): 22.

42. O. Port, "Beg, Borrow, and Benchmark," *Business Week*, 30 November 1992, 74–75.

43. R. C. Camp, "Learning from the Best Leads to Superior Performance," *Journal of Business Strategy* (May/June 1992): 3.

44. B. Davis and R. Smith, "In Era of Deregulation, Enron Woos Regulators More Avidly Than Ever," *The Wall Street Journal*, 18 May 2001, A1, A6.

45. Empirical support of this phenomenon is found in K. B. Grier, M. C. Munger, and B. E. Roberts, "The Determinants of Industry Political Activity, 1978–1986," *American Political Science Review* 88 (1994): 911–925; a descriptive review of this problem is found in I. Maitland, "Self-defeating Lobbying: How More Is Buying Less in Washington," *Journal of Business Strategy* 7, 2 (1986): 67–78.

46. W. R. Scott, *Organizations: Rational, Natural, and Open Systems*, 3d ed. (Englewood Cliffs, N.J.: Prentice Hall, 1992).

47. J. H. Dyer and H. Singh, "The Relational View: Cooperative Strategy and Sources of Interorganizational Competitive Advantage," *Academy of Management Review* 23 (1998): 660–679.

48. B. R. Barringer and J. S. Harrison, "Walking a Tightrope: Creating Value through Interorganizational Relationships," *Journal of Management* 26 (2000): 367–403.

49. A. Inkpen and M. M. Crossan, "Believing Is Seeing: Joint Ventures and Organizational Learning," *Journal of Management Studies* 32 (1995): 595–618.

50. Y. L. Doz and G. Hamel, *Alliance Advantage* (Boston: Harvard Business School Press, 1998).

51. "Blue Coast Hotels, Hilton in Indian JV," *Reuters,* 16 December 2002, http://global.factiva.com/en/arch.

52. Xerox, *Annual Report* (2000), 9.

53. C. Jones, W. S. Hesterly, and S. P. Borgatti, "A General Theory of Network Governance: Exchange Conditions and Social Mechanisms," *Academy of Management Review* 22 (1997): 911–945.

54. C. T. Edwards and R. Samimi, "Japanese Interfirm Networks: Exploring the Seminal Sources of Their Success," *Journal of Management Studies* 34 (1997): 489–510.

55. Barringer and Harrison, "Walking a Tightrope," 367–403.

56. P. H. Dickson and K. M. Weaver, "Environmental Determinants and Individual-Level Moderators of Alliance Use," *Academy of Management Journal* 40 (1997): 404–425.

57. J. H. Dyer, P. Kale, and H. Singh, "How to Make Strategic Alliances Work," *MIT Sloan Management Review* 42(4)(2001): 37–43.

58. R. Verrier, "Disney, Kellogg Seal Honey of a Deal," *Orlando Sentinel,* 6 September 2001, A1.

59. B. Estabrook, "Taking the 'Lug' Out of Luggage," *The New York Times,* 29 September 2002, 7.

60. C. Binkley, "Fairmont Teams Up with Porsche," *The Wall Street Journal,* 8 October 2002, B9.

61. Barringer and Harrison, "Walking a Tightrope," 367–403.

62. J. Pfeffer and G. R. Salancik, *The External Control of Organizations* (New York: Harper & Row, 1978).

3 Organizational Resources and Competitive Advantage

*C*endant Hotel Group is the largest hotel franchisor in the world. The company has well-known brands such as Days Inn, Ramada, Super 8, and Travelodge. With over half a million rooms in its franchise system, ownership of Avis and Budget rental car companies, and several user-friendly Internet sites, Cendant is also one of the largest Web-based travel service providers. However, Cendant faces a problem with regard to how some of its brands are viewed by consumers. Many of its brands are in lower-priced segments, and since the company does not have absolute control over its franchisees, there is a lot of variability in what a guest might experience. Furthermore, when Cendant cancels a contract due to violations of contract terms, sometimes franchisees delay removal of signs.

In an effort to reduce these problems, Cendant launched a strategic plan called Project Restore. One of the major purposes of the plan is to purge the system of substandard quality hotels. The company will eliminate up to 40,000 rooms, or 7 percent of its domestic U.S. hotel system, in addition to the rooms that are normally terminated each year. According to Steven A. Rudnitsky, recently appointed CEO of the hotel group, "We will work hard to support our good operators, who reinvest their hard-earned profits to maintain their properties and strive to deliver outstanding service, every day." Project Restore will be accompanied by a "new, strategic approach to franchise sales that will enhance the value proposition of our brands." The group also announced plans to cut staff by 15 percent and use the savings to launch a major advertising campaign across all its brands, improve brand Internet sites, and replace outdated property-management systems with state-of-the-art hardware and software. In addition, Cendant forged an agreement with Newtek Small Business Finance Inc. to offer loans to its franchisees for property purchases, construction, renovation, and improvements.[1]

INTRODUCTION

Resources and capabilities are the bread and butter of organizational success. Better resources and capabilities lead to higher levels of success. Poor resources and capabilities lead to failure. However, not all resources and capabilities are equal in their ability to help an organization achieve sustainable performance. Because of its size, Cendant has an advantage with regard to its hotel room booking systems. Furthermore, its brand diversity allows the company to offer a wide variety of options to potential franchisees. However, the reputation of a brand greatly influences the choices of potential franchisees and consumers. Consequently, Rudnitsky is making great efforts to solidify and strengthen the image of Cendant's brands. This chapter will provide tools to evaluate internal firm resources. It will help you understand how managers may identify and/or develop those resources and capabilities that are most likely to lead the firm to obtain a sustainable competitive advantage.

INTERNAL ANALYSIS AND COMPETITIVE ADVANTAGE

Chapter 1 described internal resources and capabilities as falling into five general categories: financial, physical, human, knowledge-based, and general organizational. Figure 3.1 provides examples of the types of resources and capabilities that fall into each of these five areas.

The ability of a resource or capability to lead to a sustainable competitive advantage depends on the answers to six questions:

1. *Does the resource or capability have value in the market?* These types of resources allow a firm to exploit opportunities and/or neutralize threats. For example, Cendant has developed highly sophisticated and user-friendly Internet sites that can provide value across all of its brands.

FIGURE 3.1 | **EXAMPLES OF FIRM RESOURCES AND CAPABILITIES**

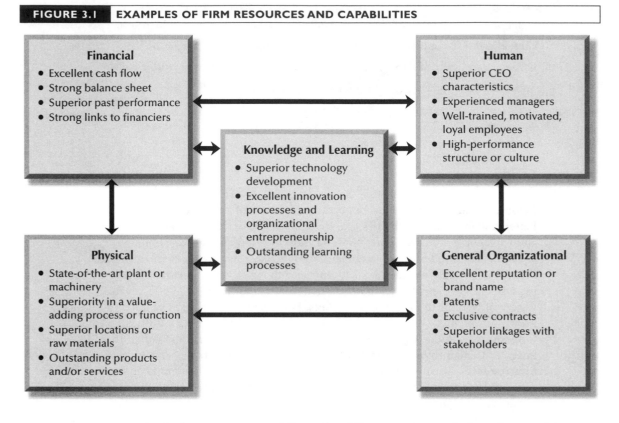

2. *Is the resource or capability unique?* If an organization is the only one with a particular resource or capability, then it may be a source of competitive advantage. If numerous organizations possess a particular resource or capability, then the situation is described as competitive parity—no company has the advantage. Note that uniqueness does not mean that only one organization possesses a capability or resource—only that few firms do. The uniqueness dimension also implies that a resource or capability is not easily transferable. That is, it is not readily available in the market for purchase.

3. *Is there a readily available substitute for the resource or capability?* Sometimes competing organizations may not have the exact resource or capability, but they have easy access to another resource or capability that will help them accomplish the same results. For example, some car rental companies have arrangements with airports that allow them to lease space on the airport premises. This provides a location benefit. However, the benefit is not as large as it could be because competitors offer frequent and convenient shuttle service to car rental lots just outside these airports.

Positive answers to the first two questions and a negative answer to the third question mean that a resource or capability has the potential to lead to a competitive advantage for the firm. However, that potential is not realized unless two other questions are also answered in the affirmative:

4. *Do organizational systems exist that allow realization of potential?* For potential to be realized, the firm must also be organized to take advantage of it. Disney is a master of exploiting profit potential from its animated features. Even before a movie is released, toys featuring the major characters and a soundtrack are available for purchase. Characters quickly become part of parades and shows at its theme parks, and sometimes a major attraction or ride is developed.

5. *Is the organization aware of and realizing the advantages?* One of the great differentiators between successful and unsuccessful companies is the ability of managers to recognize and tap into resource advantages. An organization may have employees who have great potential in an area, but the organization does not know it. The company may have the ability to produce a product that is highly unique and valuable to a particular market segment, but the firm does not realize it. In fact, an organization may even have systems in place that would allow realization of potential. Nevertheless, managers have to be able to identify sources of competitive advantage and take positive actions for potential to be realized.

At this point, an organization is using its systems and knowledge to take advantage of a unique and valuable resource or capability. However, resource advantages may not be sustainable. A final question determines the long-term value of a resource or capability:

6. *Is the resource or capability difficult or costly to imitate?* Competing firms face a cost disadvantage in imitating a resource or capability. The more difficult or costly a resource or capability is, the more valuable it is in producing a sustainable competitive advantage.[2] Investing in people is one powerful way of building capability that is hard to imitate. Cendant Corporation, for example, launched a comprehensive diversity initiative in 1997 composed of franchisee, supplier, and employee development for minorities. The franchise development program, called "Keys to Success," was a financial incentive program in the form of a loan that is forgiven if the franchisee remains in the system for a minimum of fifteen years. This program is difficult to imitate because it involves a variety of stakeholders and involves a long time commitment.[3]

Figure 3.2 demonstrates how resources and capabilities become sustainable competitive advantages. If a resource or capability is valuable, unique, nonsubstitutable, or hard to imitate, and if it also can be applied to more than one business area, it is called a core competency or capability. For example, Marriott has supplied its skill in managing financial assets across a broad range of business segments. Successful companies pay critical attention to developing and applying their core competencies.

Tangible resources can be seen, touched, and/or quantified.[4] Examples include manufacturing processes and product variations. These resources tend to be easy to imitate. Although some products can be patented, a patent provides a measure of protection only until it runs out. On the other hand, some of the most important resources and capabilities are intangible; that is, they are hard to quantify. Intangible resources and capabilities are the hardest to imitate. For example, knowledge about how to innovate is much harder

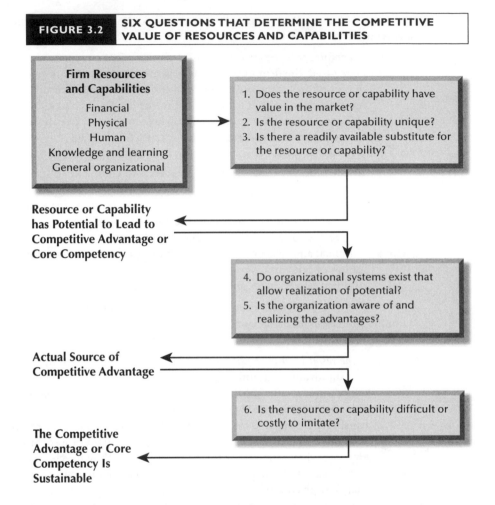

FIGURE 3.2 **SIX QUESTIONS THAT DETERMINE THE COMPETITIVE VALUE OF RESOURCES AND CAPABILITIES**

Firm Resources and Capabilities

Financial
Physical
Human
Knowledge and learning
General organizational

1. Does the resource or capability have value in the market?
2. Is the resource or capability unique?
3. Is there a readily available substitute for the resource or capability?

Resource or Capability has Potential to Lead to Competitive Advantage or Core Competency

4. Do organizational systems exist that allow realization of potential?
5. Is the organization aware of and realizing the advantages?

Actual Source of Competitive Advantage

6. Is the resource or capability difficult or costly to imitate?

The Competitive Advantage or Core Competency Is Sustainable

to imitate than any particular product innovation. Organizational reputations cannot be fully imitated, even in the long term. Other intangibles include good relationships with external stakeholders, a high-performing culture, and a well-known corporate brand. One of the reasons that intangible capabilities are difficult for competitors to imitate is that it is difficult to determine exactly how the source of capability was created (sometimes called causal ambiguity). Whereas a new product can be imitated, the processes used over time to hire, develop, retain, and build loyalty and shared values within the workforce are difficult to observe, and even more difficult to imitate. Consequently, intangible resources and capabilities are often the ones most likely to lead to competitive advantage.

The resources and capabilities that lead to competitive advantage are different in each industry and can change over time. For example, high-performing film studios during the period from 1936 to 1950 possessed superior property-based resources such as exclusive long-term contracts with stars and theaters. However, during the period from 1951 to 1965, knowledge-based resources in the form of production and coordinative talent and budgets were associated with high performance. These findings can be traced to the capabilities needed to deal with increasing uncertainty in the film industry.

The rest of this chapter will discuss resources and capabilities in five sections. For the sake of simplicity, the term resources will sometimes be used to mean both resources and capabilities, unless a specific capability is being described. The five sections are financial resources, physical resources, human-based resources, knowledge-based resources, and general organizational resources. Although these resources will be discussed separately, it is important to note that in reality, they are all tied together. This point is demonstrated in Figure 3.3.

An organization can enter Figure 3.3 at any point, but we will start at financial resources. An organization with very strong financial resources can hire better managers and employees and train them better. A strong financial position can also lead to investments in superior physical assets such as a hotel with distinctive architectural features or a restaurant in an excellent location. In addition, if an organization uses strong financial resources to hire the most-talented people and train them well, those employees are more likely to learn better and innovate. This innovation and learning will result in better operational processes, which reinforces investments in superior physical assets. The result should be better products and services, which lead to a strong brand, an excellent organizational reputation, and excellent relationships with stakeholders. Strong brands and superior products and services are likely to lead to financial success. Thus, the cycle continues.

To be successful over the longer term, companies need to pay attention to all five resource areas. Lack of attention to any of the five areas can remove a firm from the loop.

FIGURE 3.3   COMPETITIVENESS AND RESOURCE INTERCONNECTEDNESS

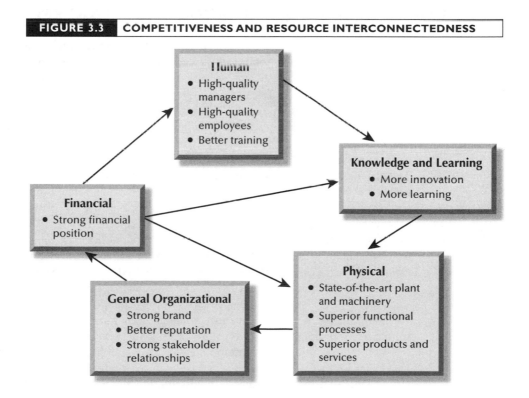

A solid investment strategy should focus on human-resource development and superior physical assets and processes. If financial resources are misused, they will not result in better human resources or superior physical assets and processes. Eventually, the organization will no longer be competitive. Human resources need to be managed effectively so that learning and innovation are the result. If human-resource development is neglected or misguided, learning and innovation will cease and the organization will eventually wear down, thus breaking out of the loop. Knowledge creation and innovative activities should be channeled so as to produce better processes and more innovative services. If this does not happen, the value of a company's brand will be eroded, and its reputation may suffer. Finally, brand names, organizational reputation, and stakeholder relationships should be carefully guarded and developed in order to produce strong financial results. The point here is that all of the resource areas are interdependent, and an organization can't afford to neglect any of them.

Entrepreneurs enter the cycle at any of a number of stages; however, most often an entrepreneur will begin with an idea. He or she will then seek to build an organization around the idea. Financing will need to be arranged. Human resources will need to be acquired. Once a venture is formed, the innovation may lead to superior processes or services. If not, then it is unlikely to be successful. However, if superior processes or services result, financial success may be obtained. The entrepreneur then uses financial success as a platform for building the human resources of the organization. The cycle has begun.

FINANCIAL RESOURCES AND FINANCIAL ANALYSIS

Financial resources can be a source of advantage, although they rarely qualify as "unique" or "difficult to imitate." Nevertheless, strong cash flow, low levels of debt, a strong credit rating, access to low-interest capital, and a reputation for creditworthiness are powerful strengths that can serve as a source of strategic flexibility, which means that firms can be more responsive to new opportunities and new threats. Essex Partners, an independent management company that specializes in operating budget hotels, realized that in order to compete in a very crowded and competitive market, it would have to prove that its operations were more efficient and produced a higher gross operating profit (GOP) than comparable properties. The firm has established a system of budgeting and cost controls that allow it to perform at a level that attracts the attention of both property owners and financial lenders. Part of this success comes because Essex is able to obtain better financing for its owners and to reduce other expenses usually not deemed the management company's responsibility, such as interest rates, insurance, legal, and audit costs.[5] These types of firms are also under less pressure from stakeholders than are their competitors who suffer financial constraints. Financial ratios, such as the ones found in Table 3.1, may be used to determine the financial strength of an organization and its ability to finance new growth strategies. Often companies will track trends of key ratios over several years, assessing changes over time. Also, because ratios are useful for comparisons, firms may compare their numbers against industry averages from a major competitor to assess comparative financial strength.

Profitability ratios are a common measure of overall financial success. They provide a barometer for management with regard to how well strategies are working, and they may also provide warning of downward trends and thus the need for more-dramatic changes.

TABLE 3.1	COMMONLY USED FINANCIAL RATIOS

Ratio	Calculation	What It Measures
Profitability Ratios		
Gross profit margin	$\dfrac{\text{Sales} - \text{COGS}}{\text{Sales}} \times 100$	Efficiency of operations and product pricing
Net profit margin	$\dfrac{\text{Net profit after tax}}{\text{Sales}} \times 100$	Efficiency after all expenses are considered
Return on assets (ROA)	$\dfrac{\text{Net profit after tax}}{\text{Total assets}} \times 100$	Productivity of assets
Return on equity (ROE)	$\dfrac{\text{Net profit after tax}}{\text{Stockholders' equity}} \times 100$	Earnings power of equity
Liquidity Ratios		
Current ratio	$\dfrac{\text{Current assets}}{\text{Current liabilities}}$	Short-run debt paying ability
Quick ratio	$\dfrac{\text{Current assets} - \text{inventories}}{\text{Current liabilities}}$	Short-term liquidity
Leverage Ratios		
Debt to equity	$\dfrac{\text{Total liabilities}}{\text{Stockholders' equity}}$	Extent to which stockholders' investments are leveraged (common measure of financial risk)
Total debt to total assets (debt ratio)	$\dfrac{\text{Total liabilities}}{\text{Total assets}}$	Percent of assets financed through borrowing (also financial risk measure)
Activity Ratios		
Asset turnover	$\dfrac{\text{Sales}}{\text{Total assets}}$	Efficiency of asset utilization
Inventory turnover	$\dfrac{\text{COGS}}{\text{Average inventory}}$	Management's ability to control investment in inventory
Average collection period	$\dfrac{\text{Receivables} \times 365 \text{ days}}{\text{Annual credit sales}}$	Effectiveness of collection and credit policies
Accounts receivable turnover	$\dfrac{\text{Annual credit sales}}{\text{Receivables}}$	Effectiveness of collection and credit policies

External stakeholders pay critical attention to profitability ratios, as they are a primary determinant of share prices, the ability to repay loans, and future dividends. Also, other types of performance measures are highly relevant, depending on the industry. For example, load factors, which are basically a measure of how full planes are on average, are a key metric in the airline industry. In the hotel industry, revenue per available room (RevPAR) is a widely used measure of performance.

Liquidity ratios help an organization determine its ability to pay short-term obligations. Financiers are especially interested in these ratios because lack of liquidity can lead to immediate insolvency during downturns. Insufficient liquidity may be a sign that the company is performing poorly. However, it might also be an indication of the need for more long-term financing. For example, an organization may have relatively low levels of liquidity, but also low levels of long-term debt such as bonds. By selling bonds, the organization can increase its cash flow, thus relieving tight liquidity. This often happens when firms are growing. Consequently, liquidity needs to be measured against other ratios and trends to achieve an accurate picture of financial strength.

Leverage is a common measure of financial risk, which in simple terms may be thought of as the risk of bankruptcy. When a publicly held organization goes bankrupt, its shareholders, financiers, employees, managers, customers, local communities, and suppliers are all adversely affected. For example, the U.S. airlines had so much leverage and such low liquidity before the disaster on September 11, 2001 that the government had to give them billions of dollars within weeks just to help them continue to operate. Finally, Table 3.1 contains a few ratios that measure the efficiency of organizational activities. These ratios may be hard for outside observers to measure. For example, annual credit sales, a factor in two of these ratios, may not be reported. Consequently, you should not be frustrated if you can't get information to calculate all of these ratios. Instead, focus on information that is available. For example, information on sales and total assets, used to calculate asset turnover, is almost always available.

In addition to general financial health, special arrangements such as real estate investment trusts (REIT) can provide financial benefits. A REIT is a financial arrangement in which investors own shares of a holding company that invests in real estate such as hotels and resorts. As long as the REIT pays out at least 95 percent of its income as dividends it does not have to pay income taxes.[6] Many hotels are owned by REITs but managed by other companies. REITs allow hotel management companies such as Marriott to greatly expand their operations by reducing the capital needed for land and buildings. Franchising offers many of the same benefits because the franchisor typically does not have an ownership interest in the real property associated with a particular franchise.

Strong financial resources are increasingly important in the highly competitive environments that make up the hospitality industry. Deep financial resources are needed to wage battles in markets where other forms of advantage are not sustainable for long. In the hotel industry innovations are quickly imitated. Also, the ability to invest in unique, valuable, difficult-to-imitate capabilities is often tied completely to the available financial resources. For example, the ability to build a brand name, to create an innovative process, or to compensate fairly and retain a highly creative workforce depends on financial resources. While financial resources may not be unique, they provide the lever for developing those types of resources elsewhere in the organization.

PHYSICAL RESOURCES AND VALUE-ADDING ACTIVITIES

This section is about physical assets and processes. These are the resources people see when they observe the organization. Superior physical resources such as prime locations and outstanding facilities are obvious sources of competitive advantage. Organizations should develop plans to acquire and develop such assets. However, equally important to a service setting are the ways a firm uses its physical resources to generate customer value. McDonald's was able to turn a filthy restaurant in a terrible location into a model of efficiency and quality through its standard operating procedures:

> McDonald's has a restaurant on the eastbound side of the Connecticut Turnpike Interstate 95 in Darien. For years, the place had been an almost unimaginably filthy highway eatery before being converted into a McDonald's. Three years later, it was one of the busiest McDonald's locations in America.[7]

A hotel or a restaurant can be envisioned as a complicated assembly operation. It may be easy to envision a meal in this way, but it is probably harder to see how this applies to a bed for the night. However, at the core of a hotel are a set of sequential activities that satisfy a guest's needs for rest, comfort, and pleasure. Consequently, one way to think about organizational resources and capabilities is to visualize the activities and processes of an organization and determine how they add value to the services that the organization provides in the marketplace.[8] The value chain divides organizational processes into distinct activities that create value for the customer. Value-adding activities are a source of strength or competitive advantage if they meet the requirements identified earlier, such as value, uniqueness, nonsubstitutability, and inimitability.

Sometimes manufacturing firms divide their activities based on whether they are a primary part of the production chain or an activity that supports those production activities.[9] A similar thought process takes place when a service firm such as a hotel or restaurant divides its activities into what we will call core and support activities. Core activities lead to direct interface with the guest. In a hotel, these core activities include processes such as check-in and check-out, in-room services, and advertising (because the guest experiences the advertisement directly). Support activities allow the hotel to function and to provide the core activities. Examples include management, maintenance, and purchasing. One of the reasons the breakdown between core and support activities is useful is that it can help focus attention on areas in which the experience of a guest is most strongly influenced. Of course, the distinction between these two types of activities is not critical enough to argue. If you feel better about putting advertising as a support activity or reclassifying any of the other activities, it is perfectly acceptable, and may even be better, as long as it works for the firm. The key is to list all the major activities of the firm that add value to the overall process and thus influence performance.

Figure 3.4 provides a starting point for analysis of value-adding activities for a budget hotel chain. The list is not comprehensive nor is the breakdown into boxes reflective of all budget hotel chains, but the example provides an illustration of how a value analysis of firm activities can be conducted. It also demonstrates that value analysis can be conducted at the chain or property levels in a multi-unit firm. In this example, many of the activities that lend themselves to economies of scale are centralized at the chain level. For example, the chain provides legal, marketing research, and purchasing support. The chain also created a standardized information system that all the properties use. If an individual property manager has a problem with the system, assistance is provided by the central office. In the example, the central office does not get involved much in direct contact with the guest. Its core activities

FIGURE 3.4 **EXAMPLE OF ANALYSIS OF VALUE-ADDING ACTIVITIES FOR A BUDGET HOTEL CHAIN**

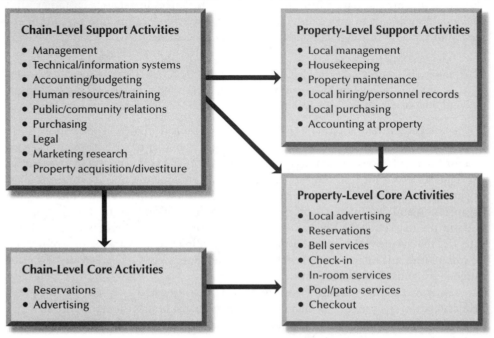

are limited to reservations and advertising. Human-resources services such as training are provided mostly at the chain level; however, a local manager is responsible for local hiring and maintenance of personnel records. Most of the accounting is provided centrally; however, a certain amount of bookkeeping is required at the property.

Once the core and support activities are described, the firm should compare how well it conducts those activities relative to close competitors. A close competitor competes directly for the same sales dollars. For a chain, close competitors include other chains in the same approximate pricing segments and geographic markets. For an individual property, close competitors are typically defined as those in the same general proximity and price range. However, a hotel that aspires to be better may find it useful to expand comparisons to hotels in higher price ranges. Also, a large resort may consider its competitors to include large resorts in other cities that could potentially lure away its business or leisure travelers. The key is to be flexible enough to conduct an analysis at the level at which it is most relevant to the organization.

The cumulative effect of value-chain activities and the way they are linked inside the firm and with the external environment determine organizational performance relative to competitors. An organization can develop a competitive advantage in any of the primary or support activities. For each area, the relevant question is, "How much value is produced by this area vs. our cost of producing that value?" This analysis of value and costs is then compared with competing firms. For example, one firm may have superior human-resources training, accompanied by higher training costs, while another firm may have a superior reservations systems, accompanied by higher reservation costs. These two firms may actually provide an overall service quality that is similar in the market (as indicated by price and demand).

Competitive advantages can also be created through superior linkages with stakeholders in the external environment. For example, a restaurant may develop an exclusive relationship with one of its suppliers, which can lead to a quality advantage. Or an airline can link its reservation systems with those of its competitors (code sharing), creating an advantage for all of the cooperating airlines. As another example, some hotel companies have long-term relationships with particular universities, allowing them greater access to high quality graduates.

HUMAN-BASED RESOURCES

The humans that make up an organization are its lifeblood—its unique and most valuable asset. Most of the other factors of production—such as properties and even special knowledge—may be duplicated over the long term, but every human being is totally unique. This section deals with the internal stakeholders of the firm, which include managers, employees, and owners, including the boards of directors that usually represent them. It begins by highlighting the importance of the chief executive officer in creating organizational success, followed by a general discussion of effective strategic leadership. Organizational governance issues will then be presented, followed by a discussion of employees, structure, and culture. Analysis of the human-based resources of a firm can provide an indication of future competitiveness, as well as highlighting areas that need attention.

STRATEGIC LEADERSHIP

The highest-ranking officer in a large organization can be called by a number of titles, but the most common is chief executive officer, or CEO. Most of the research evidence indicates that CEOs have a significant impact on the strategies and performance of their organizations.[10] In fact, in some cases a CEO can be a source of sustainable competitive advantage. A CEO such as Michael Eisner at Disney, Isadore Sharp of Four Seasons Hotels and Resorts, Bill Gates at Microsoft, or Joseph Neubauer of Aramark can leave little doubt that much of the success or failure of an organization depends on the person at the top. Neubauer, who presides over one of the most successful managed services firms in the world, was recently featured in a front-page *Business Week* story. Corporate raiders once tried to take over his company, while trying to get Neubauer to go along with the deal:

> Instead, he mortgaged his house, took out a personal loan, and helped lead a management buyout with seventy other execs to fend off the raiders. "I felt an obligation to the people who worked with me," he says. "We wanted to control our destiny." It was a winning bet. Last year, he took a larger, more successful Aramark public again to finance overseas growth. "We made 250 people millionaires from hot dogs and dirty laundry. Only in America," he quips.[11]

Neubauer, who emigrated from Israel at age fourteen and worked his way to the top of a highly successful company, epitomizes effective leadership. However, just as excellent leadership can have an enormous positive influence on a firm, poor leadership can have a powerful negative influence. Coca-Cola enjoyed many years of double-digit growth under the leadership of Roberto Goizueta. However, some analysts have argued that since his death in 1997, the company has felt a leadership void and has been struggling as a result.[12]

In the traditional model of leadership, the CEO decides where to go, and then, through a combination of persuasion and edict, directs others in the process of implementation.[13] However, the traditional view of CEOs as brilliant, charismatic leaders with employees who are "good soldiers" is no longer valid in many organizational settings. Turbulent global competitive environments and multibusiness organizations are far too complex for one person to stay on top of all the important issues. Shared leadership is needed because a leader cannot be everywhere at once. It would be naive to assume that a leader can, at any given time, control all the actions of members of an entire business. Also, companies are influenced by multiple stakeholders with competing demands. Consequently, while the CEO is the most important leader in a firm, other leaders are also vital to organizational success. While the smallest organizations may have a single owner/manager who makes all important strategic and operating decisions, in large organizations strategic leadership is distributed among a wide variety of individuals.[14]

The CEO has primary responsibility for setting the strategic direction of the firm, but other executives and managers are expected to show leadership qualities and participate in strategic management activities. Many effective CEOs assemble a heterogeneous group of three to ten top executives that make up the top management team (TMT).[15] Each member of the TMT brings a unique set of skills and a unique perspective of how the organization should respond to demands from a diverse set of stakeholders. CEOs work with TMT members to tap their skills, knowledge, and insights. Consequently, while this section will focus primarily on CEOs as the primary source of leadership in organizations, it is assumed that strategic leadership is distributed among the TMT and other influential managers and organizational members.

The literature on strategic leadership is vast, and there is no consensus on the characteristics that distinguish excellent leaders. However, most scholars would agree on five important responsibilities of strategic leadership that seem to be evident in most successful organizations. They are: (1) creating organizational vision, (2) establishing core values for the organization, (3) developing strategies and a management structure, (4) fostering an environment conducive to organizational learning and development, and (5) serving as a steward for the organization.

Creating Organizational Vision

The traditional view of leaders in organizations is that they set direction, make the important decisions, and rally the followers (usually employees).[16] Many CEOs have been described as visionaries. They have a vision of what the organization should become, and they communicate that vision to other managers and employees. They *make* their vision a reality. The French entrepreneurs Paul Dubrule and Gerard Pelisson have presided over one of the great success stories in the hotel industry. Beginning with a roadside hotel in Lille, France, Accor is now the third-largest hotel group in the world, with nearly half a million rooms in almost 100 countries. Unlike many hotel groups that focus on higher-quality segments, Accor's vision is to appeal to the masses, with around 90 percent of its revenues in the economy and midpriced segments. Brands include Novotel, Etap Formule 1, Ibis Red Roof Inns and Motel 6, among many others. While Dubrule and Pelisson, as founding co-chairmen, continue to fuel their vision of a rapid growth and broad appeal, they have selected as CEO Jean-Marc Espalioux, a graduate of France's elite ENA business school and a veteran of Compagnie Generale des Eaux (now Vivendi).

> Has a hostile global marketplace dampened the expansive vision of Accor's founders and CEO? No. Espalioux continues to add properties around the world. In Europe, which currently accounts for about half the company's revenues, the emphasis continues to be on budget and mid-priced hotels. However, outside North America, Accor is seeking opportunities across a broader market. Espalioux is using a wide range of tools for expansion, including ownership, leasing, franchising and management. The focus is on lodging, as Espalioux has sold off businesses that don't fit the vision such as rental car companies and catering businesses. Acquisitions are another important part of the plan. In 1999, Accor bought Red Roof Inns. Because of efforts to increase room yields and enhance efficiency, Accor's revenues and earnings remained fairly stable through the troubled years following 9/11. The company plans to continue adding hundreds of new properties each year, with fifteen new countries under study for potential expansion.[17]

Visionary leadership can be divided into three stages: (1) envisioning what the organization should be like in the future, (2) communicating this vision to followers, and (3) empowering these followers to enact the vision.[18] Paul Dubrule and Gerard Pelisson developed a vision of making their companies one of the largest hoteliers in the world. Then they tirelessly communicated this vision in word and deed to managers and associates. When they selected a new CEO, they made sure that he shared their vision.

Establishing Core Values

It would be naive to assume that a leader can, at any given time, control all the actions of members of an entire business. Effective leadership is much more subtle. Leaders basically establish a social system that establishes and reinforces desired behaviors. Consequently, when members of a company face an unexpected situation, they are guided by the social system.[19]

One important way that leaders influence the social system in their organizations is through the values they bring to the organization. These values can be conveyed in a number of ways. For instance, they can be communicated directly through public statements, memoranda, and e-mails. Highly visible decisions are also an effective way to communicate a value. For example, a CEO could overturn the decision of a subordinate in favor of a customer in an effort to communicate the importance of customer satisfaction: "The customer is always right." Choice Hotel's CEO Charles Ledsinger Jr. made a very public decision by appointing a highly respected executive, Paul Sterbini, to a position dedicated to the company's fair franchising principles. Ledsinger was quoted as saying:

> Our Fair Franchising Policy, established more than three years ago, dictates a corporate philosophy of fairness, integrity and trust in all issues relating to our franchisee customers. Paul's intimate knowledge of our business, his long-standing relationships with many of our franchisees and his own personal integrity combine to make him the ideal executive for this critical position.[20]

"Small talk" is also vital to effectively establishing organizational values. Small talk refers to private discussions in offices or in lunchrooms. Conversations of this kind are a forum for discussing issues, problems, situations, incidents, processes, and individuals.[21] Leaders can also influence value systems through the way they administer rewards. The organization's individuals that demonstrate the desired attitudes and behavior can be rewarded with salary increases, promotions, attention (i.e., awards), or special privileges.

> Frederick Cerrone, president of Day Hospitality Group, believes there is more to life than just work. After a trip to India he recognized that he was finally taking the time to do something that he had always wanted to do. This realization inspired him to develop a sabbatical program for his relatively young general managers. He instituted a mandatory ninety-day paid sabbatical leave program for every general manager with five years' tenure in his company. The sabbatical concept ties into one of the company's seventeen value statements: "Believe in balanced living in all areas of life—career, family, spiritual, physical, financial, social, and educational."[22]

In addition, core values can provide a basis for determining which alternative strategies to select, how they are to be selected, how strategic decisions will be communicated, and to whom. If leaders are responsive to the values of key stakeholders when making and communicating decisions, the decisions are more likely to be perceived as ethical by those stakeholders.

One example of communicating values is set in Arizona's desert. "Sara Bird-in-Ground sees her mission as telling the world about the rich culture of her community—the Pima and Maricopa tribes of Arizona who for centuries farmed the area, sharing their bounty with travelers."[23] Sheraton Wild Horse Pass resort, a 500-room luxury inn in the desert, has crafted its strategy around providing employees and guests with the Indian tribes' history and culture. Culturally themed programs and events such as the Kid Club, which includes nature walks, pottery making, and basket weaving, are designed to persuade vacation decision-makers to select Arizona hotels over other destinations with sun and great golf.

Developing Strategies and Structure

Strategic leaders are directly responsible for overseeing the development of strategies the organization should follow. For example, Chris Sullivan, CEO of Outback Steakhouse, Inc., is leading his firm in a rapid growth strategy in spite of turbulence after September 11.[24] Eiko Kono, president of Recruit in Japan, has turned around her company by putting its classified-advertising magazines on virtually every newsstand.[25] Effective strategy development implies a strong awareness of the resources and capabilities that an organization has or can develop or acquire that will lead to a sustainable competitive advantage.[26]

In small organizations, the entrepreneur typically serves as the sole strategist. As organizations grow, the top-management team is assembled for the same purpose. Furthermore, as companies grow, they tend to have more managers and more levels of management. The variety and number of these other managers are as varied as the businesses themselves. Strategic leaders have the opportunity to "influence patterns of interaction and to assign responsibility to particular individuals."[27] They do this by creating a management-reporting structure. As organizations continue to grow, they often become involved in more than one business area. As this happens, typically the CEO will delegate responsibility for developing competitive strategies to the managers who are responsible for each business. The reporting structure is then altered accordingly. Specific strategies will be discussed in Chapters 5, 6, and 9, and organization structures will be treated at length in Chapter 8.

Fostering Organizational Learning

Many organizational scholars believe that the true role of a leader is to harness the creative energy of the individual, so that the organization as a whole learns over time.[28] Leaders should create an environment for organizational learning by serving as a coach, teacher, and facilitator.[29] A learning environment is created by helping organizational members question their assumptions about the business and its environment: what customers want, what competitors are likely to do, which technology choices work best, and how to solve a problem. For learning to take place, members must understand that the organization is an interdependent network of people and activities. Furthermore, learning requires that members keep their work focused on creating patterns of behavior that are consistent with strategy rather than reacting haphazardly to problems. Leaders play the essential role in creating an environment where employees question assumptions, understand interdependency, see the strategic significance of their actions, and are empowered to lead themselves.[30] Organizational learning will be treated further later in this chapter.

Serving as a Steward

Finally, effective leaders are stewards for their firms: they care about the company and the society in which it operates, both voluntary and involuntary stakeholders.[31] Leaders must feel and convey a passion for the organization, its contribution to society, and its purpose. They should feel that "they are part of changing the way businesses operate, not from a vague philanthropic urge, but from a conviction that their efforts will produce more productive organizations, capable of achieving higher levels of organization success and personal satisfaction than more traditional organizations."[32]

So far, this section has emphasized some of the most important characteristics of effective strategic leadership, including (1) creating organizational vision, (2) establishing core values for the organization, (3) developing strategies and a management structure, (4) fostering an environment conducive to organizational learning and development, and (5) serving as a steward for the organization. Before leaving this section, a few common approaches to leadership will be presented. Also, the concept of fitting leadership characteristics to organizational circumstances will be discussed.

Leadership Approaches and Organizational Fit

There are many ways to lead, depending on the circumstances and the personality of the individual. Bourgeois and Brodwin identified five distinct leadership approaches or styles.[33] The styles differ in the degree to which CEOs involve other managers and lower-level employees in the strategy formulation and implementation process. The first two styles correspond to the traditional model of leader as director and decision maker; the latter three styles represent more participative styles of leadership that are probably more relevant in today's global economy.

- *Commander.* The CEO formulates strategy and then directs top managers to implement it.
- *Change.* The CEO formulates strategy, then plans the changes in structure, personnel, information systems, and administration required to implement it.
- *Collaborative.* The CEO initiates a planning session with executive and division managers. After each participant presents ideas, the group discusses and agrees to a strategy. Participants are then responsible for implementing strategy in their areas.
- *Cultural.* After formulating a vision and strategy for the company, the CEO and other top-level managers mold the organization's culture so that all organizational members make decisions that are consistent with the vision. In this approach, the culture inculcates organizational members into unity of purpose and action.
- *Crescive.* Under this leadership model, lower-level managers are encouraged to formulate and implement their own strategic plans. The CEO's role is to encourage innovation while filtering out inappropriate programs. Unlike the other models, the Crescive model of leadership uses the creative energies of all members of the organization, which is consistent with the philosophy of Total Quality Management (TQM) influencing American industry.

Not only do different executives have different leadership styles, but they also have varying capabilities and experiences that prepare them for different strategic environments. While managers are capable of adapting to changing environments and strategies, it is not likely that they are equally effective in all situations. A manager who was part of the turbulent growth years of a start-up company may have serious difficulty adjusting to the inevitable slowdown in growth. Look, for example, at the computer industry:

> Steven Jobs, one of the highly successful founders of Apple Computer, had difficulty adjusting to the increasingly large and complex Apple Computer that success had created. He hired John Sculley, a former PepsiCo executive, to bring professional management techniques to Apple. Jobs' management style was incompatible with that of Sculley, and eventually Jobs was forced out of the organization he had created. Then, when Apple desperately needed Jobs' vision again, he was invited to return to the company. On the other hand, the founder of Microsoft, Bill Gates, has successfully managed Microsoft through its early start-up years to its current position as the largest computer-software company in the world.

The debate continues regarding whether it is appropriate to try to fit a manager to a particular organization's strategy.[34] Some research suggests that low-cost strategies are best implemented by managers with production/operations backgrounds because of the internal focus on efficiency and engineering. The research also suggests that differentiation strategies need to be managed by executives trained in marketing and research and development because of the innovation and market awareness that are needed.[35] There is also some tentative evidence that strategic change or innovation in companies is more likely to occur with managers who are younger (both in age and in time in the company) but well educated.[36] Growth strategies may be best implemented by managers with greater sales and marketing experience, willingness to take risks, and tolerance for ambiguity. However, those same characteristics may be undesirable in an executive managing the activities of a retrenchment or some other strategy.[37] For example, Stephen Bollenbach, currently of Hilton, spent time at Trump, Marriott and Disney/ABC/Capitol Records prior to Hilton. During those years, the companies he was working for were pursuing aggressive growth via mergers and acquisitions; however, Bollenbach did not remain once those phases changed.

When radical restructuring is required, an outsider may be needed. The person who helped create problems in the organization is likely to resist selling cherished assets, closing plants, or firing thousands of people. "In many cases, the emotional ties of the career CEO are just too strong," says Ferdinand Nadherny, vice chairman of Russell Reynolds Associates, the nation's largest executive-recruiting firm. "The guy would be firing close friends."[38]

ORGANIZATIONAL GOVERNANCE

Effective leadership can be an important source of sustainable competitive advantage. As the previous section demonstrated, the definition of an effective leader varies somewhat depending on the nature of the environment in which a firm competes. Organizational governance is another aspect of leadership that can be associated with the creation of a sustainable competitive advantage. Although organizational governance is a fairly broad topic, this chapter will focus on the board of directors, especially the role of the board in governing managers and ensuring that shareholder interests are protected and enhanced.

Establishment of Organizational Governance

Many larger companies, as well as smaller companies that need large amounts of capital to support growth, have issued stock. Therefore, their owners are the shareholders. Shareholders are interested primarily in receiving a steady and increasing stream of financial returns. Shares of stock have value because shareholders expect that, at some future point, they will receive dividends. However, many fast-growing or highly profitable organizations decide to reinvest most of their cash flow instead of paying out dividends. Consequently, the value of many stocks depends more on expectations of future dividends than on current payments. If a company does not pay high dividends but the stock increases in value, shareholders can receive the increase in value by selling their stock. Managers have a fiduciary duty to direct the organization in such a way that shareholders' financial returns are as high as they can be, given other constraints such as laws, regulations, formal and informal contracts, and ethics.

The typical ownership structure found in many public corporations is illustrated in Figure 3.5. The interests of shareholders are protected by a board of directors, who are elected by the voting shareholders. In most corporations, each share of common stock has one vote in these elections. However, mutual funds and pension funds often make very large investments in companies. Therefore, they have significant voting power, which often equates to the ability to influence the board of directors and, through the board, even the decisions of top managers.

Boards of directors serve three primary functions.[39] First, the board monitors top managers to make sure they are acting responsibly with regard to shareholder and other stakeholder interests. Specific actions associated with this role include hiring, firing,

FIGURE 3.5 TYPICAL OWNERSHIP STRUCTURE IN A PUBLIC CORPORATION

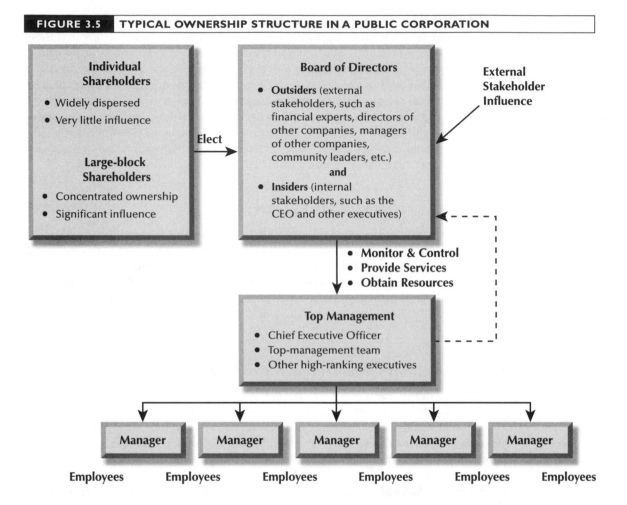

supervising, advising, and compensating top managers within the firm. This function, sometimes called the "control" role, is a legal duty. The courts evaluate whether directors are fulfilling this fiduciary responsibility based on the business-judgment rule, which presumes that directors make informed decisions, in good faith, with the best interests of the corporation in mind, and independently of personal interests or relationships.

Second, directors provide services to top managers. Since they tend to come from diverse backgrounds and have varied skills, directors serve as excellent advisers on a wide range of issues from financing to operations to human-resource management. They can also provide information on what is happening in the external environment that could potentially influence the firm. Boards typically also reserve the right to reject major strategic decisions such as the development of a new line of business, mergers, acquisitions, or entrance into foreign markets. Finally, directors can help establish important linkages with the external environment so that the organization can acquire needed resources. For example, a director may also sit on the board of a supplier company, thus allowing for easy contracting with that supplier. Also, many companies add bankers to their boards to facilitate financial arrangements. Each of the three functions is even more important when a company is in a crisis or experiencing stress.[40]

There are two major and interrelated issues of strategic importance concerning ownership in a publicly held corporation. The first deals with the conflicts of interest that sometimes emerge between owners and managers of the firm. The second major issue deals with the relationship between the composition and behavior of the board of directors and organizational performance. While this section will focus on governance structures in the United States, similar structures for publicly held organizations exist in most other industrialized countries.[41]

Conflicts of Interest and Agency Problems

In sole proprietorships, the owner and top manager is the same individual. Therefore, no owner/manager conflicts of interest exist. This is also the case in privately held or closely held companies in which all of the stock is owned by a few individuals, often within the same family. In these cases, the owners have direct control over their firms. However, as soon as ownership and management are separated, the potential for conflicts of interest exists. In this case, top managers become agents for the owners of the firm—they have a fiduciary duty to act in the owners' best interests.

Theoretically, in a publicly held corporation, both shareholders and managers have an interest in maximizing organizational profits. Shareholders want maximum organizational profits so that they can receive high returns from dividends and stock appreciation. Managers should also be interested in high profits to the extent that their own rewards, such as salary and bonuses, depend on profitability. However, top managers, as human beings, may attempt to maximize their own self-interests at the expense of shareholders. This is called an agency problem. Entrenchment occurs when "managers gain so much power that they are able to use the firm to further their own interests rather than the interests of shareholders."[42] Chief executives can become entrenched by recommending their friends and internal stakeholders such as other managers for board membership. Often the recommendations of the CEO are taken without much resistance.

Agency problems are manifest in a number of ways. Some power-hungry or status-conscious top managers may expand the size of their empires at the expense of organizational shareholders. For example, two decades ago, Harding Lawrence led Braniff Airways to financial ruin through overzealous growth.[43] The highly unsuccessful unrelated acquisitions of the 1960s may have resulted, in part, from managers who were more interested in short-term growth than in long-term performance. This agency problem can be precipitated by compensation systems that link organizational size to pay.

Agency problems often arise because of the way executives are compensated. For example, an executive who is compensated according to year-end profitability may use his or her power to maximize year-end profits at the expense of long-range investments such as research and development.[44] Some business writers argue that the extremely high salaries of some CEOs, which often reach millions of dollars, are evidence that agency problems exist.[45] Sandy Weill's pay package of $151 million at Citigroup or Steve Jobs' $872 million options grant at Apple seem to defy reason. Charles Elson, who runs the University of Delaware's Center for Corporate Governance, refers to such salaries as "outrageous in many cases and unrelated to services rendered."[46] Since shareholders are numerous and often not very well organized, their influence on decisions such as CEO compensation is nominal. Consequently, self-serving forces within the organization can sometimes prevail. For example, Roberto Goizueta of Coke once received an $81 million restricted stock award. The award was initiated by an old associate whose firm had received $24 million in fees from Coke over the previous six years.[47] Unfortunately, conflicts of interest of this type are common.[48]

The real issue concerning salary is whether CEOs are worth what they receive. For example, in *Business Week*'s annual report on executive pay, compensation is compared to the performance of the organizations for which these executives work. This analysis is revealing, and it often demonstrates that some CEOs are a real bargain. CEOs who have more-demanding jobs, as indicated by the amount of information they have to process and the firm's strategy, tend to be more highly paid.[49] Because of all of the ramifications associated with executive pay, it is a decision that is as much ethical as it is financial.

To help overcome problems with excessive compensation of some CEOs, top management compensation should probably be linked to corporate performance.[50] One risk in relating compensation to performance is that a lot of these schemes tie annual compensation to annual, as opposed to long-term, performance. Whenever possible, compensation packages should be developed that encourage, instead of discourage, actions that will lead to high long-term performance. For example, if CEO bonuses depend on profit, board members in charge of compensation should add back research and development expenditures before calculating profits for the year. This helps ensure that CEOs will not hesitate to allocate resources to potentially profitable long-term research and development projects. Another trend in CEO compensation is rewarding with stock instead of cash. When managers receive stock and stock options, they become owners, and their interests should converge with those of other shareholders.[51] Here is an example of how stock options can figure into pay:

> Stock options are a creative way to align CEO interests with the long-term interests of the organization. If a stock is currently selling at $50, a CEO might receive options to buy 100,000 shares of stock at $50, which is called the *strike price*. However, the options may not be exercisable for some specified time, such as three years. If, over the next three years, the stock price rises to $100, the options are now worth $5 million, since the CEO can buy 100,000 shares at $50 and sell them at $100. In this situation, if the stock price declines or remains the same, the options are worthless. Thus, it is in the best interests of the CEO to maximize the share price of the company, which is also in the best interests of the shareholders.

Perhaps the greatest agency problems occur when top managers serve on the board of directors, which is often the case in U.S. corporations. In fact, it is not uncommon to find the CEO in the position of chairman of the board. This condition is known as CEO duality. As chairman of the board of directors, the CEO is in a strong position to ensure that personal interests are served even if the other stakeholders' interests are not. For example, a CEO/chairman may influence other board members to provide a generous compensation package. Also, a CEO/chairman is instrumental in nominating future board members and therefore has the opportunity to nominate friends and colleagues who are likely to rubber-stamp future actions and decisions.

In spite of these theoretical arguments against CEO duality, research findings are inconclusive.[52] However, when a relationship between CEO duality and performance is found, it typically supports the view that duality hurts performance. For example, one study examining the financial performance of 141 corporations over a six-year period discovered that firms opting for independent leadership consistently outperformed those relying upon CEO duality.[53] Of course, CEO duality is not a problem in privately held companies or in companies in which the CEO or the CEO's family owns a very large share of the stock.

Boards of Directors and Organizational Performance

The fiduciary responsibility for preventing agency problems lies with boards of directors. Some business experts believe that many boards of directors have not lived up to their fiduciary duties. These experts argue that for the most part, boards have not reprimanded or replaced top managers who acted against the best interests of shareholders. However, the incidence of shareholder suits against boards of directors has increased.[54] In addition, large-block shareholders such as mutual-fund and pension-fund managers put lots of pressure on board members and directly on CEOs to initiate sweeping organizational changes that will lead to more accountability and higher performance.[55]

The inclusion of several outsiders (nonmanagers) on the board may help ensure that shareholder interests are well served. In fact, the percentage of outsiders on the board of directors is increasing.[56] Boards with a large percentage of outside directors are referred to as independent. In theory, independent boards should lead to higher levels of organizational performance because they are more likely to look out for the interests of shareholders. However, inclusion of outsiders may not be a potent force in reducing agency problems if external board members are personal friends of the CEO or other top managers. These types of relationships limit the objectivity of outsiders. Consequently, a consistent relationship between board independence and firm performance has not been established, at least during normal circumstances.[57] During crises, board independence becomes more important.[58]

Boards play other important strategic roles besides monitoring executive action. As mentioned previously, they provide services to top managers in the form of counseling and information. Boards can also provide guidance to top managers and participate in decisions. Higher performance is found in companies with boards that participate more actively in organizational decisions, compared to companies with "caretaker" boards.[59] Boards need sufficient power to both monitor and discipline CEOs. Vigilant boards are the best defense against executive entrenchment.[60]

In order to gain maximum benefits from the services directors provide to top managers, it is important to include both internal and external stakeholders on the board.[61] Internal stakeholders provide stability and enhanced understanding of internal operations. External stakeholders bring a breadth of knowledge and a fresh point of view to the challenges that face an organization. For example, inclusion of labor union representatives on boards can help firms avoid decisions that are likely to be blocked by the union. By including environmentalists, firms can enhance their social image and decrease the likelihood that a proposal will be resisted due to potential damage to the environment. Some corporations appoint retired government officials, such as generals or presidential cabinet members, to their boards. The knowledge and contacts of these retirees can facilitate government contracting or the acquisition of public lands for development.

Inclusion of outside board members is also important with regard to establishing linkages to facilitate acquisition of needed resources. For example, interlocking directorates can lead to important strategic alliances. Interlocking directorates occur when executives from two companies sit on each other's boards or on a third company's board. As was mentioned in the previous chapter, this is a common practice in many countries, especially Japan (e.g., *keiretsu*). While it is illegal in America to have interlocking directors of direct competitors (e.g., Marriott and Hilton), firms often include representatives from suppliers or customers. Linkages such as these may reduce the monitoring ability of directors. However, interlocks can facilitate contract negotiations and the transfer of information and technology. In some cases, strategic alliances can even create barriers that make it hard for new firms to compete.

Cendant Corporation has assembled a board of directors that follows many of the conventional ideas with regard to effective governance. Like many hospitality companies, the CEO, Henry R. Silverman, is also the chairman of the board. However, Cendant's board is largely independent and very diverse. In fact, the company has established a policy that "At least two-thirds of the Board will be comprised of directors who meet the criteria for independence required by the New York Stock Exchange."[62] These criteria include a lack of any type of business affiliation or employment with the company over at least the previous five years for the candidate and family members. The board has three standing committees with responsibility for auditing, compensation of high-level executives and corporate governance. Detailed duties of board members are also specified. Another policy states, "The Board seeks members from diverse professional and personal backgrounds who combine a broad spectrum of experience and expertise with a reputation for integrity." So what does the board look like? Besides Henry Silverman, the board includes:

Myra J. Biblowit, president, Breast Cancer Research Foundation

James E. Buckman, vice chairman and general counsel, Cendant Corp.

William S. Cohen, chairman and CEO, Cohen Group

Leonard S. Coleman, senior adviser, Major League Baseball

Martin L. Edelman of Counsel, Paul Hastings Janofsky and Walker

Stephen P. Holmes, chairman and CEO, Hospitality Services Group, Cendant Corp.

Cheryl D. Mills, senior vice president, New York University

The Right Honourable Brian Mulroney, senior partner, Ogilvy Renault

Robert E. Nederlander, president, Nederlander Organization, Inc.

Ronald L. Nelson, chief financial officer, Cendant Corporation

Robert W. Pittman, former CEO, AOL Time Warner, Inc.

Pauline D. E. Richards, former CFO, Lombard Odier Darier Hentsch Ltd.

Sheli Z. Rosenberg, vice chairwoman, Equity Group Investments, Inc.

Robert F. Smith, CEO, Car Component Technologies, Inc.[63]

Cendant's board is, perhaps, a little large, but it is diverse, includes mostly outside directors, and includes key insiders who can provide valuable information and stability. In summary, boards of directors play a critical role in supervising managerial actions to ensure shareholder interests are served, providing services such as counseling and information to top executives, and establishing linkages that facilitate resource acquisition. The governance structure of an organization can be a source of competitive advantage that is hard for competitors to imitate. This completes a fairly thorough introduction to the leadership and ownership structure of modern corporations. This section will now turn to two other human-based sources of competitive advantage: employees and culture.

EMPLOYEES

Employees and the way they are managed can be important sources of competitive advantage.

> It was 1988 and CP Hotels had just invested $750 million in the bricks-and-mortar side of the business, updating its hotels nationwide. Management was confident that the newly renovated hotels would attract guests for a first stay, but bringing them back again would be the real ROI challenge. To meet that challenge, CP management looked to its human capital and Carolyn Clark, the newly appointed vice-president, human resources. Human resources had become a strategic player at the boardroom level and now it was time to help the company achieve its overall goals. Clark knew that in the service-intensive hotel industry, people can provide a critical competitive advantage, so her strategic HR plan focused on the development of human capital.[64]

CP Hotels is now known as Fairmont Hotels and Resorts, North America's largest luxury hotel chain. Because of their importance to competitiveness, employees are being given increasing amounts of managerial attention in the organizational planning of a lot of large organizations. In fact, human capital considerations such as the ability to attract qualified workers top the list of factors that concern managers in the hospitality industry.[65]

Unfortunately, many hospitality firms fail to realize the strategic importance of the human resource area. Research has shown that more-sophisticated human-resource planning, recruitment, and selection strategies are associated with higher labor productivity, especially in capital-intensive organizations.[66] Also, a large-sample study of nearly one thousand firms indicated that "high performance work practices" are associated with lower turnover, higher productivity, and higher long- and short-term financial performance.[67] Chapter 7 will describe human-resources strategies hospitality firms can use to maximize competitiveness. For now, the objective is to highlight the importance of this area and to provide guidelines regarding what should be evaluated during an internal analysis of the firm.

Labor productivity and employee turnover are important outcomes that are worthy of assessment. Labor productivity is a good indication of how well managed employees are and their levels of experience and training. For example, hotels often track how many rooms a housekeeper can clean in an hour. Restaurants look at how many meals can be served at various times and with various personnel configurations. Turnover is at least partially an indication of how employees feel about their jobs and the organization, including their satisfaction with compensation and the way they are managed. These are only examples of possible indicators. Human-resources systems and processes should also be examined. These include reporting systems, hiring programs, compensation systems, training programs, and supervisory systems. Finally, the overall quality of the laborers in a hotel or restaurant can be assessed by their motivation levels, attitudes, experience, and the amount of training they have received. If a union is present, relationships with union officials should also be assessed.

Structure and Culture

Leaders, managers, directors, and employees can all be sources of competitive advantage. However, the way they are organized can also lead to competitiveness. Organization structure has a lot to do with how successful a firm will be. For example, in a world where innovations are widely understood by competitors within a year, a flexible structure is a key to success in many companies.[68] Big companies are trying to increase speed and flexibility by altering their organization structures and management systems so that they focus on one core business and allow other firms to fill in the gaps.[69] Accor, highlighted earlier in this chapter, is one such company. Another way large organizations can improve flexibility is by decentralizing responsibility and rewarding employees for innovations and flexibility.[70] Chapter 8 will explore in great detail various organizational structures that are used to support strategic objectives. It is sufficient to say at this point that structure is another potential source of sustainable competitive advantage.

Closely related to structure is an organization's culture, the system of shared values of its members. Organization culture often reflects the values and leadership styles of executives and managers, and is greatly a result of past practices in human resource management, such as recruitment, training, and rewards. Many companies realize the benefits of a shared set of values as a potential source of competitive advantage. There is an intangible quality that stakeholders look for when making decisions about the products and services that they purchase or in selecting alliance partners. They want to be able to rely on the company. They want promises and commitments to be fulfilled. There are many pragmatic benefits to a high-profile organizational culture that can help an organization in its recruiting, employee development, and relationships with customers.[71]

An organization's culture can be its greatest strength or its greatest weakness. Some firms have created cultures that are completely consistent with what the company is trying to accomplish. These are called high-performance cultures. For example, Jet Blue airlines has a culture that stresses a warm and friendly atmosphere, high-quality service, and efficiency. Table 3.2 provides guidelines for identifying the culture of an organization based on factors such as attitude toward customer and competitors, risk tolerance, and moral integrity. For each of these factors, an organization should ask: (1) Which characteristics support the vision and strategies of the organization and should be sustained in the future? (2) Which characteristics do not support the vision and strategies and should be modified? (3) What efforts will be necessary to make the required changes happen?

A strong culture can be a two-edged sword. Sometimes very successful corporations so firmly attach themselves to their successful business practices that they exaggerate the features of the successful culture and strategy, and fail to adapt them to changing industry conditions. Four very common organization orientations associated with excellent performance can lead to four extreme orientations that can lead to poor performance:

- *Craftsmen.* In craftsmen organizations, employees are passionate about quality. Quality is the primary driver of the corporate culture and a source of organizational pride. However, a culture that is focused on quality and detail can evolve to an extreme where craftsmen become *tinkerers.* Obscure technical

TABLE 3.2	DEFINING AN ORGANIZATION'S CULTURE

Dimensions	Description
Attitude toward customers	Respect vs. indifference
Attitude toward competitors	Compliance, cooperation, or competitiveness
Achievement orientation	Industry leader or follower
Risk tolerance	Degree to which individuals are encouraged to take risks
Conflict tolerance	Degree to which individuals are encouraged to express differences
Individual autonomy	The amount of independence and responsibility given to individuals in decision making
Employee relations	Cooperative vs. adversarial relationships among employees
Management relations	Cooperative vs. adversarial relationships between managers and employees
Goal ownership	Identification with goals and concerns of organization as a whole vs. identification with goals and concerns of a work group or department
Management support	Cooperative vs. adversarial relationships between managers and employees
Perceived compensation equity	Perceived relationship between performance and rewards
Decision-making style	Rational and structured vs. creative and intuitive
Work standards	Diligent, high-performing vs. mediocre
Moral integrity	Degree to which employees are expected to exhibit truthfulness
Ethical integrity	Degree to which decisions are expected to be balanced with regard to stakeholder interests vs. focused exclusively on a key objective such as profitability

Source: Adapted from P. McDonald and J. Gandz, "Getting Value from Shared Values," *Organization Dynamics* (Winter 1992), 68; E.H. Schein, *Organization Culture and Leadership* (San Francisco: Jossey-Bass, 1985).

details and obsessive engineering perfection result in products that are overengineered and overpriced. Another version of the obsessive concern for quality is a passion for low costs, which paralyzes an organization's ability to make timely, necessary investments.

■ *Builders.* In builder organizations, growth is the primary goal. Managers are rewarded for taking risks that result in growth, new acquisitions, and new market niches. When efforts to grow and expand become careless, builders become *imperialists,* with high debt, too many unrelated businesses, and neglected core businesses.

■ *Pioneers.* Pioneers build their businesses through leadership positions in new-product and new-technology development. The strengths of these organizations lie in their design teams and flexible structures, which promote idea sharing. Pioneers begin to decline when they evolve into *escapists,* who invent impractical products and pursue technologies with limited customer value.

■ *Salesmen.* Salesmen are excellent marketers who create successful brand names and distribution channels, and pursue aggressive advertising and innovative packaging. They become so confident in their marketing abilities that they ignore product capability and quality, and begin to market imitative, low-quality products that customers do not value. They evolve into *drifters.*[72]

In all of the orientations described above, the organization becomes too focused on its own capabilities, and loses sight of its customers and evolving industry conditions. One stakeholder group becomes too dominant at the expense of others and resists change. Several contributing factors can drive a successful organization to an unsuccessful extreme. First, leadership may get overconfident from its past successes, thinking that what has worked in the past will continue to work in the future. Second, one department may become overly dominant, attracting the best managerial talent and exercising unbalanced influence over the decisions made within other departments. Third, the dominant managers and departments may keep the organization focused on strategies and policies that may no longer be relevant. An acknowledgment that change is needed would erode their base of power and influence. Finally, the successful strategies of the past may have become embedded in the routine policies and procedures of the organization. Those policies and procedures create an air of continuity that is very resistant to change.[73]

In summary, structure and culture can be added to an already impressive list of human-based sources of competitive advantage. Just as these factors can be sources of advantage, they can also be sources of weakness when they are neglected or poorly managed. Attention will now be drawn to knowledge-based and general organizational resources.

KNOWLEDGE-BASED RESOURCES

We live in what is sometimes called a "knowledge economy." More than 50 percent of the gross domestic product in developed economies is knowledge-based, which means that the GDP is based on intangible people skills and intellectual assets.[74] Consequently, wealth is increasingly being created through the management of knowledge workers instead of physical assets. According to David Teece:

> Fundamental changes have been wrought in the global economy which are changing the basis of firm level competitive advantage, and with it the functions of management. The decreased cost of information flow, increases in the number of markets…, the liberalization of product and labour markets in many parts of the world, and the deregulation of international financial flows is stripping away many traditional sources of competitive differentiation and exposing a new fundamental core as the basis for wealth creation. The fundamental core is the development and astute deployment and utilization of intangible assets, of which knowledge, competence, and intellectual property are the most significant.[75]

Knowledge is an intangible asset. Intangible assets differ from physical assets in fundamental ways. First, physical assets can be used only by one party at a time, whereas knowledge can be used by several parties simultaneously. Second, physical assets wear out over time and are depreciated accordingly. While knowledge does not wear out, its value depreciates rapidly as new knowledge is created. Third, it is relatively easy to set a price based on how much of a physical asset is sold or transferred, but it is difficult to measure the amount of knowledge transferred or its value. Finally, rights to tangible property are fairly clear and easy to enforce, whereas it is difficult to protect and enforce protection of intellectual property.[76]

Knowledge can be divided into two general types: core knowledge and integrative knowledge.[77] Core knowledge is scientific or technological knowledge that is associated with actual creation of a product or service. For example, knowledge about integrated circuitry formed the foundation for creation of semiconductors. Integrative knowledge is knowledge that helps integrate various activities, capabilities, and products. For example, an organization that wants to be involved in selling personal computers has to understand how they are assembled and manufactured (core knowledge), but also has to understand how computer manufacturing fits into an entire system, which includes suppliers of component parts, marketing, financing, and even linkages between personal computers and other types of products (integrative knowledge).

Core knowledge is comparatively easier to acquire than integrative knowledge because integrative knowledge deals with a complex system. Consequently, integrative knowledge is probably more likely to lead to a sustainable competitive advantage. Wal-Mart, for instance, developed a complete and unique retailing system that involves complex coordination of codified information across suppliers, distribution centers, and stores; feedback from customers in the form of daily sales information; information about the products themselves; and forecasts of needs. Innovations have included cross docking, which occurs when merchandise is unloaded from suppliers' trucks directly onto Wal-Mart's trucks for distribution to stores.[78]

Another way to differentiate knowledge is based on whether it is codified or tacit. Codified knowledge can be communicated completely through written means. For example, blueprints, formulas, and computer code are codified. On the other hand, "tacit knowledge is that which is difficult to articulate in a way that is meaningful and complete."[79] Creation of an artwork such as a sculpture or a modern dance, for instance, would be very hard to describe in words that would have real meaning. You have to experience it. In general, the easier it is to codify knowledge, the less difficult it is to transfer. Tacit knowledge can be very valuable to organizations in creating a sustainable competitive advantage.

INTERNAL KNOWLEDGE CREATION AND ORGANIZATIONAL LEARNING

Some organizations are clearly more innovative than others. They consistently create greater numbers of successful products or services. Other organizations may not develop a lot of products or services, but they are adept at creating more-efficient ways of creating or delivering them. The distinction here is between product or service development and process development. Still other organizations seem better at both types of innovation. Knowledge creation is at the center of both product or service development and process development. One of the most important managerial tasks is facilitating knowledge (1) creation, (2) retention, (3) sharing, and (4) utilization. Outstanding execution of these tasks can lead to superior performance.[80]

Here is an example of innovation:

"If the day is twenty-four hours long, guests should be able to check in and check out at any time they like," reasoned Ali Kasikci, the charismatic and innovative general manager of the Peninsula Beverly Hills Hotel.[81] The implementation of twenty-four-hour check-in and checkout with no surcharge to guests began as an idea obtained during an executive education program at Cornell's Hotel School. The practice was tested in the summer and fully implemented by the staff of the Peninsula hotel a year later. Kasikci began by discussing the idea with his marketing director, sales managers, and front-office manager. Each of these managers informally collected feedback from customers about the concept and "talked it up" to other managers in the hotel. Customers were very responsive to the idea—especially those from Australia and New Zealand whose fourteen- to seventeen-hour flights generally arrived in the early morning hours and departed late in the evening.

Armed with the support of guests and various managers, the next step was to determine whether it was operationally feasible. With the help of his executive housekeeper, data on departures was gathered and once the idea appeared feasible to implement special equipment was purchased to clean rooms quietly in the dark. Before the practice was put in place Kasikci also discussed the idea with competitor hotels in his market. These competitors were the biggest critics; they said the idea would never work and that the Peninsula would be quickly forced to give up the practice. The housekeeping staff was also hesitant, but their attitudes changed after extensive discussions and efforts to focus on the positive implications for the hotel. The practice, conceived in 1996, is still in use. A lot of ideas are never put into practice because, as Kasikci notes, "we always make excuses that operationally it is not possible." This practice was easy and it astonished the guest, ultimately leading to both customer loyalty and repeat business according to the hotel's managers. As this innovation illustrates, facilitating knowledge can lead to high performance.

Each of the four knowledge facilitation tasks requires different management skills and organizational arrangements. Knowledge creation requires systems that encourage innovative thinking throughout the firm. Most organizations tap only a fraction of the creative potential of employees and managers. An organization that wants to create knowledge will select employees and managers who contribute innovative ideas and will reward those employees and managers through salary increases, recognition, bonuses, and promotions. Some organizations even allow managers or employees the opportunities to lead in the execution of their ideas. Organizations also need to establish forums through which ideas can be conveyed to managers. A suggestion box is a rudimentary system to encourage ideas. Work meetings and interviews are other means of sharing knowledge. To create knowledge, organizations should also allocate human and financial capital to research and development.

Knowledge retention is a second critical activity. A lot of knowledge exists in an organization. Only part of that knowledge is shared, but very little of that sharing gets recorded unless it is associated with an actual research or development project. Low-cost information systems have made it possible to record and store vast amounts of information very affordably. An important part of documentation is recording not only the new knowledge, but how a manager or the organization responded to it. Also, an organization should record information on whether such actions were a success or a failure.

Sharing of knowledge is as important as creating it. For example, Marriott has used knowledge gained in the lodging industry in its time-share business. Disney applied its knowledge in staging dramatic presentations (developed in its theme parks and moviemaking) to Broadway musicals. Many companies have newsletters in which new ideas are shared. Creating an information system for the sharing of ideas is, by itself, a possible source of competitive advantage.

Finally, an organization has to clear the way for knowledge to be translated into new processes and programs. This sometimes means eliminating barriers to innovation. For example, some companies require many signatures and approvals on even the smallest projects before they will be funded. An organization should also encourage taking risks by not harshly penalizing managers whose projects or ideas fail and richly rewarding managers whose projects or ideas succeed. Table 3.3 reviews the four tasks associated with knowledge creation and utilization. Attention will now be drawn to generating knowledge through partnerships with external stakeholders.

KNOWLEDGE CREATION AND INTERORGANIZATIONAL RELATIONSHIPS

If firms perform the tasks associated with internal knowledge creation, they will still be limited in how much knowledge they acquire unless they also have a productive program for acquiring knowledge from outside their organizations. As discussed in Chapter 2, a part of obtaining knowledge from the outside is studying the innovations of others in the industry, other industries, and the technological environment in general. In fact, most of the knowledge that will revolutionize an industry actually comes from outside the industry. For example, semiconductors were developed in the computer industry, but had far-reaching implications for most other industries, including the hospitality industry. Knowledge about

TABLE 3.3	TASKS ASSOCIATED WITH INTERNAL KNOWLEDGE CREATION AND UTILIZATION
Task	**Description**
Knowledge creation	Develop reward systems that encourage innovative thinking.
	Create a forum whereby creative ideas are shared.
	Invest in research-and-development programs.
Knowledge retention	Document findings from research and development programs.
	Create information systems that record and organize innovative ideas.
	Document both the ideas and managerial responses or organizational responses to them.
	Document successes and failures.
Knowledge sharing	Create an information system that shares results from research and development projects with other parts of the organization.
	Routinely pass new ideas on to managers who can act on them.
	Create a database management system to organize ideas generated from employees and managers so that they can be retrieved systematically at a later date.
Knowledge utilization	Reduce bureaucratic barriers that prevent knowledge from resulting in new programs and projects.
	Encourage risk taking.
	Reward success.

innovations in other industries comes into an organization through hiring people with varied backgrounds, through hiring consultants and trainers, through providing educational programs and opportunities to employees, and through assigning researchers to specifically follow various scientific streams through journals, newsletters, books, and seminars.

Another important source of external knowledge comes from interorganizational relationships.[82] Organizations can learn from each other. In fact, knowledge is not always created within a single firm, but rather in a network of firms working together. An example of this phenomenon is found in the biotechnology industry, where there is a large-scale reliance on collaborations to produce innovation.[83]

Several factors can lead an organization to enhance organizational learning from interorganizational relationships. First, relational ability, defined as the ability to interact with other companies, can increase a firm's ability to obtain and transfer knowledge.[84] Firms can enhance their relational ability through practice (e.g., increasing the use of interorganizational relationships) or through hiring managers that have already developed relational skills.[85] Often CEOs develop excellent relational skills. Second, the more embedded into a network of interorganizational relationships an organization becomes, the more it is able to acquire competitive capabilities.[86] Consequently, increasing the use of joint ventures, alliances, and other interorganizational relationships can position a firm in a more central location to what is happening in its industry and across relevant industries. Third, proximity can lead to enhanced learning.[87] The lodging industry is a good example of this, since hotels often cluster in one geographic area. Finally, an organization needs to be deliberate about taking steps to increase its absorptive capacity, which refers to the ability of a firm to absorb knowledge. Just like internally generated knowledge, if knowledge gained through interorganizational relationships is not retained, shared, and used, it is of no worth to the organization.

Andrew Inkpen, an expert on interorganizational relationships, studied forty American-Japanese joint ventures with the intention of finding out what organizational conditions facilitate effective transfer of knowledge. His conclusions, contained in Table 3.4, are a fitting summary to this section on the important role of knowledge in creating a sustainable competitive advantage.

GENERAL ORGANIZATIONAL RESOURCES

The final category of organizational resources is a varied collection of organizational possessions that can have a tremendous impact on financial success and survival. In this section, only a few of many such resources will be discussed. However, the ones that are discussed have been found to be powerful sources of competitive advantage in some instances. They are patents and brand names, organizational reputation, and superior relationships with external stakeholders.

PATENTS AND BRANDS

Patents are the tangible result of knowledge creation. Organizations file for patent protection to prevent other companies from making use of their innovations. Patents can

TABLE 3.4	FACILITATING KNOWLEDGE TRANSFER IN JOINT VENTURES
Facilitation Mechanism	**Description**
Flexible learning objectives	Organizations should enter into a venture with objectives regarding what the organization would like to learn from the venture. However, conditions often change, and managers should be willing to adjust those objectives if needed.
Leadership commitment	At least one strong, higher-level manager must champion the learning objective. This person acts as a catalyst for knowledge transfer. For example, in one case, an American president had a long-standing relationship with the chairman of the Japanese partner. They worked together to facilitate transfer of both technical and management ideas.
A climate of trust	Trust is critical to the free exchange of knowledge. One of the greatest disadvantages of a joint venture is the risk of opportunistic behavior. This is the risk that one of the partners will use information gained in the venture to the disadvantage of the other partner. Consequently, trust must be carefully guarded or information transfer will be stifled.
Tolerance for redundancy	This means that there is deliberate overlapping of company information, processes, and management activities. Redundancy leads to more interaction among participants, and interaction leads to more sharing of information.
Creative chaos	Disruptive or high-stress events can enhance transfer of knowledge by focusing partners on solving problems and resolving difficulties.
Focus on learning in spite of performance	Some ventures perform poorly, at least on financial measures, but organizations can still learn from them. The American firms tended to let poor performance reduce or eliminate learning, whereas the Japanese firms took a longer-term view and were less distracted by short-term performance.

Source: Based on A.C. Inkpen, "Creating Knowledge through Collaboration," *California Management Review* 39, no. 1 (Fall 1996): 123–140

sometimes be a source of competitive advantage for a period of time. However, they do not really offer much protection and eventually they run out. Furthermore, they apply more to manufacturing firms than to hospitality firms.

Brands and their associated trademarks offer a higher level of protection. Consequently, if managed well, brands can be a powerful source of sustainable competitive advantage.[88] Disney takes full advantage of its brand, which is one of its core competencies. According to Michael Eisner, CEO:

> We are fundamentally an operating company, operating the Disney Brand all over the world, maintaining it, improving it, promoting and advertising it with taste. Our time must be spent insuring that the Brand never slides, that we innovate the Brand, nurture the Brand, experiment and play with it, but never diminish it. Others will try to change it, from outside and from within. We must resist. We are not a fad! The Disney name and products survive fads![89]

Club Med also has a widely known brand. In fact, it is one of the top sixty global brands and one of only two from France, with an average recognition rating of 86 percent worldwide.[90] Hotel companies have used their brand names to expand into different segments of the market so as to retain customers, a strategy that has met with some success.[91] For example, someone might be familiar with upscale Marriott properties because of business travel, but may be looking for something less expensive for leisure travel. As a result,

Marriott takes advantage of its highly recognized brand by marketing one of its lower priced chains as "Fairfield Inn by Marriott."

ORGANIZATIONAL REPUTATION

A reputation can be thought of as an economic asset that signals observers about the attractiveness of a company's offerings. A reputation is also an assessment of past performance by various evaluators. It is a part of a social system and is based more on interpretation than fact.[92] Like a brand, an organization's reputation is difficult to imitate. A good reputation may be associated with excellent quality or highly innovative products or services, excellent human-resource management, or other factors. Reputation, which can transcend international borders, is thus a potential source of global competitive advantage.[93] Of course, an organization's reputation is often linked to a well-known brand name.

Much has been said in this book about how to develop a good reputation through socially responsible actions and stakeholder satisfaction. Some of the potential benefits of a good reputation include the ability to attract talented workers, charge premium prices, keep loyal customers, raise capital with less difficulty by attracting investors, avoid constant scrutiny by regulators and activists, or enter international markets with less difficulty.[94] Some business writers have argued that a corporate reputation may be the only source of truly sustainable competitive advantage.[95] They argue that it is the only component of competitive advantage that can't ever be duplicated in its entirety. Therefore, organizations should devote considerable time and effort to safeguarding a good reputation. Organizations with the best reputations in the *Fortune* survey had strong financial performance, but it was combined with strong performance in nonfinancial areas as well.[96]

SUPERIOR RELATIONSHIPS WITH STAKEHOLDERS

Stakeholder relationships were described in detail in the previous chapter. Furthermore, the chapter demonstrated how strong relationships with stakeholders can lead to sustainable competitive advantage. This section will not be redundant with Chapter 2, but it is included to demonstrate an important point. Stakeholder theory and the resource-based view are closely linked.

Relationships with external stakeholders can also be described as an organizational resource. The fact is that all five areas of resources and capabilities described in this chapter are closely linked to external stakeholders. For example, financial resources are based, in part, on relationships with financial intermediaries. The strength of human resources may depend on linkages with unions, trainers, human resources associations, communities, or educational institutions from which an organization recruits. Valuable knowledge comes from interorganizational relationships with competitors, customers, suppliers, or other stakeholders. Inputs necessary to develop physical resources are provided by suppliers. Finally, contracts with many types of stakeholders are a general organizational resource.

Internal resource analysis may be combined with stakeholder analysis to identify strengths and weaknesses, and for uncovering opportunities for cost savings or ways to add value for customers. For instance, the intersection between activist groups and technology development could result in low-cost solutions to problems with pollution and other externalities. Also, customers may be able to help a firm increase the effectiveness of its marketing, sales, or service activities. The combination of stakeholder analysis with resource analysis holds great potential for developing strategies that are both efficient and effective.

The conceptual link between stakeholder theory and the resource-based view has important implications. Basically, an organization that is incapable of successful stakeholder management will have a difficult time developing resources and capabilities that will lead to a sustainable competitive advantage. Also, an organization with weak resources and few capabilities will find it difficult to develop strong stakeholder relationships because stakeholders will find them unattractive for partnerships and contracts.

KEY-POINTS SUMMARY

This chapter evaluated organizational resources and capabilities and their ability to lead to competitive advantage. The value of a resource or capability in leading to a competitive advantage depends on the answers to six questions: (1) Does the resource or capability have value in the market? (2) Is the resource or capability unique? (3) Is there a readily available substitute for the resource or capability? (4) Do organizational systems exist that allow realization of potential? (5) Is the organization aware of and realizing the advantages? (6) Is the resource or capability difficult or costly to imitate? If a capability or resource is valuable, unique, and not easily substitutable, it has potential to lead to a competitive advantage. If the firm has systems to support the resource or capability and is using them, a competitive advantage is created. If the resource or capability is hard to imitate, then the competitive advantage will be sustainable.

Five resource areas were then discussed in detail. The areas are: financial, physical, human-based, knowledge-based, and organizational resources. Although these resources were discussed separately, in reality they are all tied together. An organization must pay close attention to each of the five areas to remain competitive over the longer term.

Financial resources can be a source of advantage, although they rarely qualify as "unique" or "difficult to imitate." Nevertheless, strong cash flow, low levels of debt, a strong credit rating, access to low-interest capital, and a reputation for creditworthiness are powerful strengths that can serve as a source of strategic flexibility. Firms that are in a strong financial position can be more responsive to new opportunities and new threats and are under less pressure from stakeholders than are their competitors who suffer financial constraints. In the lodging industry, special financial arrangements such as real estate investment trusts (REIT) and franchising can provide competitive advantages.

Physical resources were discussed through the concept of value-adding activities. Core activities lead to direct contact with guests, whereas support activities help the firm in its administrative processes as the core activities are supported. After these activities are described, they are then compared with the same activities for close competitors. An organization can develop a competitive advantage by excelling at any of the core or support activities, relative to competitors or by linking internal activities to external stakeholders in unique and productive ways. The cumulative effect of value-adding activities and the way they are linked inside the firm and with the external environment determine firm performance relative to competitors.

Human-based resources and capabilities were discussed next. The humans that make up an organization are its unique and most valuable asset. Several types of internal stakeholders were discussed, including managers, employees, and owners, as well as the boards of directors that usually represent them. The section began with a discussion of the importance of the chief executive officer in creating organizational success. This discussion then led into a more general treatment of the characteristics of effective strategic leadership. Organizational governance issues were then presented, followed by a discussion of employees, structure, and culture.

Owners in a for-profit, publicly held corporation, the shareholders, are typically represented by a board of directors, who act as their agents. Directors have the responsibility to oversee the activities of organizational managers and ensure that shareholder interests are protected. They are obligated to hold CEOs and other organizational officials accountable for their actions. They also provide services to top managers and create linkages with the external environment that can lead to acquisition of essential resources. Agency problems can exist when boards of directors are weak in carrying out these responsibilities, when CEOs also serve as chairmen of their own boards (e.g., CEO duality), or any time CEOs or other managers act in their own personal interests at the expense of shareholders.

Organizations need highly qualified employees if they are going to succeed in the global economy. These trends make training and other human-resource management activities crucial to long-term competitiveness. Innovative human-resource management techniques are increasing employee effectiveness for some successful companies. An organization's structure and culture are also potential sources of competitive advantage. Organization culture is defined as the shared values of its members. Culture often reflects the values of management, the human-resource management practices that create the working conditions, and the experiences of employees. Culture can be a tremendous source of advantage for a firm, or a millstone.

Since we live in a knowledge-based economy, knowledge management is very important to organizational success. The section on internal knowledge management focused on knowledge (1) creation, (2) retention, (3) sharing, and (4) utilization. Also important is acquiring knowledge through interorganizational relationships. Several guidelines for facilitating knowledge transfer through interorganizational relationships were presented.

General organizational resources include superior brands, patents, and reputations. Also included in this category are relationships with external stakeholders, which create a conceptual overlap with Chapter 2 and stakeholder theory. The overlap is useful, since an organization that is incapable of successful stakeholder management will have a difficult time developing outstanding resources and capabilities, and an organization with weak resources and few capabilities will find it difficult to develop strong stakeholder relationships.

DISCUSSION QUESTIONS

1. What are the six questions that must be asked to determine whether a resource or capability will lead to a sustainable competitive advantage?

2. What are the five resource areas that an organization should analyze to determine internal sources of competitive advantage? Why must a firm pay attention to all five areas?

3. Describe the value-adding activities of a typical restaurant (not a chain). Determine which of these activities are core and support. How can the restaurant use this information to help determine ways to create competitive advantage?

4. Describe the five distinct leadership approaches or styles CEOs use. Which of these styles is more authoritarian? Which is more participative? Is any one style the best? Why?

5. Describe the relationships that exist among shareholders, boards of directors, and CEOs. What is an agency problem? How can agency problems be avoided?

6. Why is human resource management becoming an even more important part of strategic management in many organizations?

7. Name four common cultural orientations that are often associated with excellent performance. How can these orientations lead to extremes that ultimately lead to poor performance?

8. What is the difference between core knowledge and integrative knowledge? Which type of knowledge is more likely to be associated with a sustainable competitive advantage? Why? What is the difference between tacit knowledge and codified knowledge? Which type of knowledge is more likely to be associated with a sustainable competitive advantage? Why?

9. Name several factors and organizational conditions that can lead an organization to enhance organizational learning from interorganizational relationships.

10. Which source of competitive advantage is usually more sustainable: a patent or a brand? Why?

11. What is an organizational reputation? What are the benefits of having an excellent organizational reputation? Are those benefits typically sustainable?

NOTES

1. "Cendant's Hotel Group Launches Strategic Plan," www.cendant.com/media/press-release.cgi, November 22, 2002; Cendant Corporation 2002 Annual Report, 3; "SBA Lender Offers Financing to Cendant Hotel Franchisees," *Hotel Executive*, www.hotelexecutive.com/newswire/pub/_364.asp, July 5, 2003.

2. Most of these questions are based on Barney, "Looking Inside for Competitive Advantage" *Academy of Management Executive* 9 (4) (1995) 49-61.; R. L. Priem and J. E. Butler, "Is the Resource-Based 'View' a Useful Perspective for Strategic Management Research?" *Academy of Management Review* 26 (2001): 22–40.

3. L. Dube, C. Enz, L. Reneghan, and J. Siguaw, *American Lodging Excellence: The Keys to Best Practices in the U.S. Lodging Industry* (1999), 62–63.

4. M. A. Hitt, R. D. Ireland, and R. E. Hoskisson, *Strategic Management: Competitiveness and Globalization* (Minneapolis: West Publishing, 1995), 73.

5. Dube, Enz, Reneghan, and Siguaw, *American Lodging Experience*, 95.

6. "Land Grab Real Estate Investment Trusts," http:hedge-hog.com/sub/reits.html, July 7, 2003.

7. J. Hogan, "What Are Your Priorities as a Hotel Owner and/or Manager?" *Hotel Online,* March 2002, http://www.hotel-online.com/Neo/News/PR2002_1st/Mar02_CommonSense.html.

8. We gratefully acknowledge the intellectual contributions of Michael Porter with regard to the creation and use of value chains. His work deals primarily with a manufacturing setting. In this chapter we applied many of the same principles to a service environment. For more information, see M. E. Porter, *Competitive Advantage: Creating and Sustaining Superior Performance* (New York: The Free Press, 1985), chap. 2.

9. M. E. Porter, *Competitive Advantage: Creating and Sustaining Superior Performance* (New York: The Free Press, 1985).

10. S. Finkelstein and D. C. Hambrick, *Strategic Leadership: Top Executives and Their Effects on Organizations* (Minneapolis: West Publishing, 1996), chap. 2.

11. N. Byrnes, "The Straight Shooter," *Business Week,* 23 September 2002, 82.

12. D. Fisher, "Gone Flat," *Forbes Global,* www.forbes.com/global, 15 October 2001.

13. P. Nutt, "Selecting Tactics to Implement Strategic Plans," *Strategic Management Journal* 10 (1989): 145–161.

14. C. Handy, *The Age of Unreason* (Boston: Harvard Business School Press, 1989).

15. R. D. Ireland and M. A. Hitt, "Achieving and Maintaining Strategic Competitiveness in the 21st Century: The Role of Strategic Leadership," *Academy of Management Executive* 13, no. 1 (February 1999): 43–57.

16. P. M. Senge, "The Leader's New Work: Building Learning Organizations," *Sloan Management Review* 32, no. 1 (Fall 1990): 7–24.

17. "The Accor Model," http://www.accor.com/gb/finance/strategie, July 8, 2003; R Evans, "Le Motel 6, C'est Moi," *Barrons,* 30 April 2001, 20–22.

18. F. Westley and H. Mintzberg, "Visionary Leadership and Strategic Management," *Strategic Management Journal* 10 (1989): 17–18.

19. S. Sjostrand, J. Sandberg, and M. Thyrstrup, *Invisible Management: The Social Construction of Leadership* (London: Thomson Learning, 2001).

20. "Choice Realigns Sales Force," *HotelMotel,* http://www.hotelmotel.com/hotelmotel/content, November 5, 2002.

21. Sjostrand, Sandberg, and Thyrstrup, *Invisible Management.*

22. Dube, Enz, Reneghan, and Siguaw, *American Lodging Excellence,* 86.

23. D. Hogan "Cultural Tourism . . . on the Rise: Its Popularity Grows as Hoteliers Pursue Those Shrinking Tourist Dollars," *The Daily Courier,* (Prescott, June 15, 2003), 1D.

24. "Dear Shareholder," *2001 Annual Report,* Outback Steakhouse, Inc.

25. A. Harrington, "The Power 50," *Fortune,* 15 October 2001, 194–201.

26. Ireland and Hitt, "Achieving and Maintaining."

27. Sjostrand, Sandberg, and Thyrstrup, *Invisible Management,* 8.

28. Senge, "Leader's New Work"; C. C. Manz and H. P. Sims, "SuperLeadership," *Organization Dynamics* 17, no. 4 (1991): 8–36.

29. Senge, "Leader's New Work."

30. Senge, "Leader's New Work"; Manz and Sims, "SuperLeadership."

31. Clarkson Centre for Business Ethics, *Principles of Stakeholder Management* (Toronto: Rotman School of Management, 1999), 3

32. Senge, "Leader's New Work," 13.

33. L. J. Bourgeois and D. R. Brodwin, "Strategic Implementation: Five Approaches to an Elusive Phenomenon," *Strategic Management Journal* 5 (1984): 241–264.

34. J. G. Michel and D. C. Hambrick, "Diversification Posture and Top Management Team Characteristics," *Academy of Management Journal* 35 (1992): 9–37; S. F. Slater, "The Influence of Style on Business Unit Performance," *Journal of Management* 15 (1989): 441–455; A. S. Thomas, R. J. Litschert, and K. Ramaswamy, "The Performance Impact of Strategy-Manager Coalignment: An Empirical Examination," *Strategic Management Journal* 12 (1991): 509–522.

35. V. Govindarajan, "Implementing Competitive Strategies at the Business Unit Level: Implications of Matching Managers to Strategies," *Strategic Management Journal* 10 (1989): 251–269.

36. K. A. Bantel and S. E. Jackson, "Top Management and Innovations in Banking: Does the Composition of the Top Team Make a Difference?" *Strategic Management Journal* 10 (1989): 107–124; C. M. Grimm and K. G. Smith, "Management and Organizational Change: A Note on the Railroad Industry," *Strategic Management Journal* 12 (1991): 557–562; M. F. Wiersema and K. A. Bantel, "Top Management Team Demography and Corporate Strategic Change," *Academy of Management Journal* 35 (1992): 91–121.

37. A. K. Gupta and V. Govindarajan, "Business Unit Strategy, Managerial Characteristics, and Business Unit Effectiveness at Strategy Implementation," *Academy of Management Journal* 27 (1984): 25–41.

38. B. Brenner, "Tough Times, Tough Bosses: Corporate America Calls in a New, Cold-eyed Breed of CEO," *Business Week*, 25 November 1991, 174–180.

39. S. Chatterjee and J. S. Harrison, "Corporate Governance," in M. A. Hitt, R. E. Freeman, and J. S. Harrison, *The Blackwell Handbook of Strategic Management* (Oxford: Blackwell Publishers, 2001), 543–563; J. L. Johnson, C. M. Daily, and A. E. Ellstrand, "Boards of Directors: A Review and Critique," *Journal of Management* 22 (1996): 409–438.

40. Chatterjee and Harrison, "Corporate Governance."

41. Sjostrand, Sandberg, and Thyrstrup, *Invisible Management.*

42. S. Weisbach, "Outside Directors and CEO Turnover," *Journal of Financial Economics* 20 (1988): 431–460.

43. J. A. Pearce II and S. J. Teel, "Braniff International Corporation (A) and (B)," in *Strategic Management: Strategy Formulation and Implementation*, 2d ed. (Homewood, Ill.: Richard D. Irwin, 1985), 820–838.

44. J. S. Harrison and J. O. Fiet, "New CEOs Pursue Their Own Interests by Sacrificing Stakeholder Value," *Journal of Business Ethics* 19 (1999): 301–308.

45. J. A. Byrne, "How High Can CEO Pay Go?" *Fortune*, 22 April 1996, 100–122.

46. G. Colvin, "The Great CEO Pay Heist," *Fortune*, 25 June 2001, 64.

47. J. A. Byrne, "What, Me Overpaid? CEOs Fight Back," *Business Week*, 4 May 1992, 142–148.

48. Byrne, "Overpaid?" 147.

49. A. D. Henderson and J. W. Fredrickson, "Information Processing Demands as a Determinant of CEO Compensation," *Academy of Management Journal* 39 (1996): 575–606.

50. E. J. Zajac, "CEO Selection, Succession, Compensation, and Firm Performance: A Theoretical Integration and Empirical Analysis," *Strategic Management Journal* 11 (1990): 217–230.

51. C. W. L. Hill, "Effects of Ownership Structure and Control on Corporate Productivity," *Academy of Management Journal* 32 (1989): 25–46.

52. P. L. Rechner and D. R. Dalton, "The Impact of CEO as Board Chairperson on Corporate Performance: Evidence vs. Rhetoric," *Academy of Management Executive* (May 1989): 141–143; and "CEO Duality and Organizational Performance: A Longitudinal Analysis," *Strategic Management Journal* 12 (1991): 155–160.

53. Rechner and Dalton, "CEO Duality."

54. I. F. Kesner and R. B. Johnson, "Crisis in the Boardroom: Fact and Fiction," *Academy of Management Executive* (February 1990): 23–35.

55. M. Magnet, "Directors, Wake Up!" *Fortune*, 15 June 1992, 86–92.

56. I. F. Kesner, B. Victor, and B. T. Lamont, "Board Composition and the Commission of Illegal Acts: An Investigation of Fortune 500 Companies," *Academy of Management Journal* 29 (1986): 789–799; I. B. Kesner and R. B. Johnson, "An Investigation of the Relationship between Board Composition and Shareholder Suits," *Strategic Management Journal* 11 (1990): 327–336.

57. D. R. Dalton, C. M. Johnson, and A. E. Ellstrand, "Meta-analytic Reviews of Board Composition, Leadership Structure, and Financial Performance," *Strategic Management Journal* 19 (1998): 269–290.

58. Chatterjee and Harrison, "Corporate Governance."

59. W. Q. Judge Jr. and C. P. Zeithaml, "Institutional and Strategic Choice Perspectives on Board Involvement in the Strategic Decision Process," *Academy of Management Journal* 35 (1992): 766–794; J. A. Pearce II and Shaker A. Zahra, "The Relative Power of CEOs and Boards of Directors: Associations with Corporate Performance," *Strategic Management Journal* 12 (1991): 135–153.

60. E. F. Fama and M. C. Jensen, "Separation of Ownership and Control," *Journal of Law and Economics* 26 (1983): 301–325.

61. M. J. Stahl and D. W. Grigsby, *Strategic Management for Decision Making* (Boston: PWS-Kent, 1992), 12–13.

62. All of the quotations in this paragraph came from Cendant Corporation *2002 Corporate Report*, http://www.cendant.com/investors, July 7, 2003.

63. All of the quotations in this paragraph came from Cendant Corporation, *2002 Corporate Report*, http://www.cendant.com/investors, July 7, 2003.

64. R. Langlois, "Fairmont Hotels: Business Strategy Starts with People," *Canadian HR Reporter*, 5 November 2001, 19–25.

65. C.A. Enz, "What Keeps You Up at Night? Key Issues of Concern for Lodging Managers," *Cornell Hotel and Restaurant Administration Quarterly* 42(2)(April 2001): 38–45.

66. M. J. Koch and R. G. McGrath, "Improving Labor Productivity: Human Resource Management Policies Do Matter," *Strategic Management Journal* 17 (1996): 335–354.

67. M. A. Huselid, "The Impact of Human Resource Management Practices on Turnover, Productivity, and Corporate Financial Performance," *Academy of Management Journal* 38 (1995): 635–672.

68. W. M. Bulkeley, "The Latest Thing at Many Companies Is Speed, Speed, Speed," *The Wall Street Journal,* 23 December 1994; J. T. Vesey, "The New Competitors: They Think in Terms of 'Speed-to-Market,'" *Academy of Management Executive* (May 1991): 23–33.

69. S. Tully, "The Modular Corporation," *Fortune,* 8 February 1993, 106.

70. J. B. Tracey, "The Strategic and Operational Roles of Human Resources: An Emerging Model," *Cornell Hotel and Restaurant Administration Quarterly* 43(4)(August 2002): 17–26.

71. J. B. Quinn, *Intelligent Enterprise: A Knowledge and Service Based Paradigm for Industry* (New York: The Free Press, 1992).

72. Based on information from D. Miller, *The Icarus Paradox* (New York: Harper Business, 1990).

73. Based on information from Miller, *Icarus Paradox.*

74. G. G. Dess and G. T. Lumkin, "Emerging Issues in Strategy Process Research," in *Blackwell Handbook,* ed. Hitt, Freeman, and Harrison, 3–34.

75. D. J. Teece, *Managing Intellectual Capital* (New York: Oxford University Press, 2000), 3; see also R. M. Grant, "Toward a Knowledge-based View of the Firm," *Strategic Management Journal* 17 (Special Issue) (1996): 109–122.

76. Teece, *Intellectual Capital.*

77. C. E. Helfat and R. S. Raubitschek, "Product Sequencing: Co-Evolution of Knowledge, Capabilities, and Products," *Strategic Management Journal* 21 (2000): 961–979.

78. Helfat and Raubitschek, "Product Sequencing."

79. Teece, *Intellectual Capital,* 13.

80. D. M. DeCarolis and D. L. Deeds, "The Impact of Stocks and Flows of Organizational Knowledge on Firm Performance," *Strategic Management Journal* 20 (1999): 953–968.

81. Dube, Enz, Reneghan, and Siguaw, *American Lodging Excellence,* 181–182.

82. J. B. Goes and S. H. Park, "Interorganizational Links and Innovation: The Case of Hospital Services," *Academy of Management Journal* 40 (1997): 673–696.

83. W. W. Powell, K. W. Koput, and L. Smith-Doerr, "Interorganizational Collaboration and the Locus of Innovation: Networks of Learning in Biotechnology," *Administrative Science Quarterly* 41 (1996): 116–145.

84. G. Lorenzoni and A. Liparini, "The Leveraging of Interfirm Relationships as a Distinctive Organizational Capability: A Longitudinal Study," *Strategic Management Journal* 20 (1999): 317–338.

85. B. L. Simonin, "The Importance of Collaborative Know-How: An Empirical Test of the Learning Organization," *Academy of Management Journal* 40 (1997): 1150–1174.

86. B. McEvily and A. Zaheer, "Bridging Ties: A Source of Firm Heterogeneity in Competitive Capabilities," *Strategic Management Journal* 20 (1999): 1133–1156.

87. P. Maskell and A. Malmberg, "Localised Learning and Industrial Competitiveness," *Cambridge Journal of Economics* 23 (1999): 167–185.

88. G. Khermouch, "The Best Global Brands," *Business Week,* 6 August 2001, 50–57.

89. Walt Disney Company, *Annual Report* (1995), 6–7.

90. I. Griffiths, "The Accidental Tourist," *The Independent,* 15 September 1999, 1–2.

91. W. Jiang, C. S. Dev and V. R. Rao, "Brand Extension and Customer Loyalty: Evidence from the Lodging Industry," *Cornell Hotel and Restaurant Administration Quarterly* 42(4)(August 2002): 5–16.

92. C. J. Fombrun, "Corporate Reputations As Economic Assets," in *Blackwell Handbook,* ed. Hitt, Freeman, and Harrison, 289–312.

93. J. A. Petrick et al., "Global Leadership Skills and Reputational Capital: Intangible Resources for Sustainable Competitive Advantage," *Academy of Management Executive* (February 1999): 58–69.

94. R. P. Beatty and J. R. Ritter, "Investment Banking, Reputation, and Underpricing of Initial Public Offerings," *Journal of Financial Economics* 15 (1986): 213–232; C. Fombrun and M. Shanley, "What's in a Name? Reputation Building and Corporate Strategy," *Academy of Management Journal* 33 (1990): 233–258; B. Klein and K. Leffler, "The Role of Market Forces in Assuring Contractual Performance," *Journal of Political Economy* 89 (1981): 615–641; P. Milgrom and J. Roberts, "Price and Advertising Signals of Product Quality," *Journal of Political Economy* 94 (1986): 796–821; P. Milgrom and J. Roberts, "Relying of the Information of Interested Parties," *Rand Journal of Economics* 17 (1986): 18–32; G. J. Stigler, "Information in the Labor Market," *Journal of Political Economy* 70 (1962): 49–73.

95. S. Caminiti, "The Payoff from a Good Reputation," *Fortune,* 10 February 1992, 74–77.

96. Reese, "Most Admired."

CHAPTER 4

Strategic Direction

*T*he primary goal of Fairmont Hotels and Resorts is to become "The luxury hotel brand of choice recognized worldwide for distinctive style." This goal is reflected in the mission, vision, and values of the company:

Mission: We will earn the Loyalty of our Guests by exceeding their expectations and providing warm and personal service in distinctive surroundings.

Vision: We will inspire an open innovative learning organization that is energetic and exciting for our Colleagues. We will demonstrate a relentless commitment to understand, anticipate and fulfill the needs of our Guests. We will deliver superior operating performance and financial returns for our Owners and Investors to ensure growth for the company and reinvestment in our hotels.

Values:

Respect—We value the needs, ideas and individuality of others. We treat all Colleagues and Guests with fairness and dignity.

Integrity—We act with honesty and professionalism, guided by the highest standards of ethical conduct. We take accountability for all of our decisions and actions.

Teamwork—We work together to achieve our common goals. We recognize the impact of each individual contribution and the importance of maintaining a co-operative and supportive work environment.

Empowerment—We have the necessary tools, training and authority to exceed expectations. We trust and support each other in making informed decisions and taking appropriate actions.[1]

INTRODUCTION

These statements are excellent examples of the major components of strategic direction. We see that Fairmont has a mission that is centered on satisfying its customers, a vision that encompasses learning and high performance, and values that include the way the company and its colleagues will act. Fairmont's business definition, another element of strategic direction, is made clear in its major goal to be the premier luxury hotel brand.

The central components of strategic direction—mission, vision, business definition, and values—are the primary topics of this chapter. The chapter begins with a general discussion of the importance of strategic direction and the factors that influence it.

INFLUENCES ON STRATEGIC DIRECTION

Top managers are charged with the responsibility of providing long-term direction for their organizations, while at the same time balancing the competing interests of key stakeholders. One of the critical errors that some organizations make is that they do not know who they are, how they got to where they are, or where they are going. They suffer an "identity crisis." For example, Josten's, the Minnesota-based manufacturer of class rings, yearbooks, and other products to schools, had a 34-year record of sales and earnings increases. Then it diversified into computer systems and started losing money. A New York stock analyst who followed the company for years concluded, "Nobody was taking a hard look at what was going on—nobody seemed to be asking the right questions."[2]

Strategic direction is established and communicated through tools such as visions, missions, business definitions, and values, all of which will be discussed in this chapter. There are no widely accepted guidelines managers use to provide strategic direction. In some companies, little is written down. Other companies have adopted formal statements for each of these areas. However, regardless of the medium of communication, high-performing companies tend to create an organizational identity that is understood by both internal and external stakeholders. On the inside, a well-established organizational identity can provide guidance to managers at all levels as they make strategic decisions.[3] In addition, communicating strategic direction to external stakeholders can increase their understanding of the motives of the organization, and it may also facilitate the creation of interorganizational relationships, since potential partners have a greater ability to judge the existence of common goals. One corporate president stated that "his company's mission statement has helped create a 'partnering attitude' instead of an adversarial relationship" between his company and its customers.[4]

As Figure 4.1 illustrates, both internal and external stakeholders influence strategic direction. The amount of influence stakeholders have is proportional to their economic, political, and formal (legal or contractual) power. The broad environment is also influential. For example, an organization usually tries to establish a value system that is consistent with what society expects, or at least appears to be consistent. Also, economic, technical, and political/legal realities influence the selection of business areas in which to compete. Strategic direction forms the foundation from which plans of action are developed. Actions include the firm's competitive strategies, implementation strategies, control systems, and the way internal and external stakeholders and stakeholder relationships are managed.

Organizational actions lead to particular outcomes, such as market successes or failures, and to financial performance, which includes sales growth. Also, stakeholders will respond to the actions of organizations in a variety of ways. For instance, customers could be pleased with the services of an organization, or they could be angry and file a lawsuit

FIGURE 4.1 **INFLUENCES ON STRATEGIC DIRECTION**

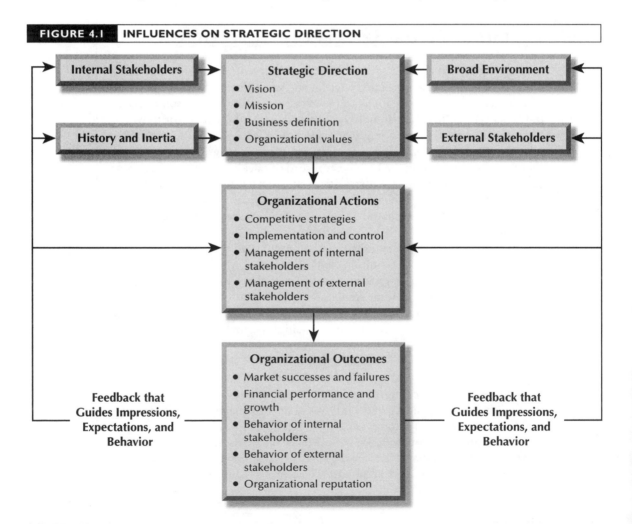

against the company. Employees could be happy, or they could strike. Government regulators could be cooperative, or they could interfere with operations through fines and penalties. These outcomes translate into feedback that the organization can use to adjust strategic direction, actions, or both direction and actions.

Feedback becomes a part of the organization's history. History can potentially assist strategic planning processes, since organizations can learn from past successes and failures. Unfortunately, history can also be a weakness that stands in the way of forward progress. Past successes sometimes create strong structural inertia, the term for forces at work to maintain the status quo.[5] These forces can include systems, structures, processes, culture, sunk costs, internal politics, and barriers to entry and exit. Anything that favors the "status quo" has the potential to cause inertia. Inertia is stronger when an organization has been successful in the past because managers believe that past success will translate into future success, regardless of early warning signals to the contrary. Inertia, then, is another potential threat to the survival and prosperity of an organization.

Structural inertia is related to human nature. Most humans desire a certain amount of predictability in their work. In other words, they have learned to cope with their organizational environment—they are comfortable. They may also fear that changes will reduce their own power or position in the organization or that they will no longer be considered competent. If the forces favoring inertia are strong and if the organization has been successful in the past, people will be highly resistant to any major shift in missions or strategies. Inertia based on past successes was one of the main reasons for the decline of the railroads as a form of passenger transportation. They continued to pursue the same strategies until it was simply too late.[6] According to Leslie Wexner, CEO of The Limited, Inc.:

> Success doesn't beget success. Success begets failure because the more that you know a thing works, the less likely you are to think that it won't work. When you've had a long string of victories, it's harder to foresee your own vulnerabilities.[7]

One of the most common means of communicating strategic direction is in a written mission statement. The next section is a general discussion of organizational mission statements and how they develop over time.

MISSION STATEMENTS

An organization's mission statement provides an important vehicle for communicating ideals and a sense of direction and purpose to internal and external stakeholders. It can inspire employees and managers. It can also help guide organizational managers in resource-allocation decisions. Clearly, not all "opportunities" that organizations face will be compatible with their missions. If used properly, an organization's mission should provide a screen for evaluating opportunities and proposals. Table 4.1 outlines the various uses of mission statements and considerations for writing them.

Sometimes students of strategic management confuse the terms mission and vision. In general, a mission is what the organization is and its reason for existing, whereas a vision is a forward-looking view of what the organization wants to become. However, when mission statements are written, they often include a vision statement, a business definition, or

TABLE 4.1	MULTIPLE USES OF MISSION STATEMENTS	
Use	**Primary Stakeholders Targeted**	**Considerations**
Direct decision making and resource allocations	Managers and employees	Mission statements should use terms that are understandable to internal stakeholders. For example, a clear business definition provides guidance with regard to where an organization should pursue business opportunities. Also, a statement like, "We use state-of-the-art technology" has clear implications for how resources should be allocated. To be effective, missions should be communicated to internal stakeholders on a regular basis.
Inspire higher levels of performance and pride in association	Managers and employees	Mission statements should be worded in such a way that they inspire the human spirit. A person should read the statement and feel good about working for the company. On the other hand, this can be a two-edged sword if the organization does not act accordingly. This can cause a sense of betrayal and hypocrisy.
Communicate organizational purpose and values	Managers, employees, shareholders and potential investors	Organizational purpose and values help managers and employees resolve dilemmas when faced with tradeoffs. They also help external stakeholders know what to expect from the organization in particular situations.
Enhance organizational reputation	Society and most external stakeholder groups, especially customers and potential venture partners	Mission statements should be carefully articulated so that they enhance reputation. Catchy slogans (but not cliché) are helpful so that stakeholders will remember them. They should be short enough so that external stakeholders will attempt to read them and remember them. They should be widely dispersed to media sources and apparent in public settings such as the foyers of office buildings and factories.

statements about the values of an organization. As long as an organization understands what it is, what it values, and where it is going, then it has a well-defined strategic direction. The particular labels are not as important as making sure that all aspects of strategic direction are included. Following is one example of how a company chose its path:

> One hotel general manager's direction-setting experience shows that sometimes the vision emerges in discussions with the senior management staff but is not written down initially. According to the general manager of a Hilton-branded property who crafted a vision for his hotel, it was a change in thinking first and foremost. "We were going to become the best corporate hotel positioned at the top end, but I approached this vision by doing three things, living my values, constantly talking about our vision, and modeling the vision every day. The plan was shockingly devoid of systems or procedures. I felt it and was deeply into it. The hotel needed an identity in the minds of the employees, and my job was to bring a deep belief in what this hotel could become to these people. My agenda? Focus and model, focus and model. I just did what seemed right at the time." It was not until almost six years later when the general manager was executive vice president of the hotel group, a company that owned and managed hotels branded with a variety of different midpriced and upper-priced hotel franchisers, that he created a formal vision of what the hotel aspired to become. After considerable thought he arrived at the simple statement, "the friendliest place to visit."[8]

As organizations are first established, their mission may be as simple as "Provide low-cost lodging to highway travelers while generating a profit for the owner." The mission is often informal and is seldom written down. But notice that even in its simplest form, this mission encompasses a purpose, a brief definition of the business, and two important stakeholders, the owner and the customer. Most businesses begin with a mission that is just as simple as the example given. The mission is an extension of the entrepreneur or entrepreneurs who form the organization.

As companies succeed in their business environments, opportunities arise that allow the firm to grow in revenues and number of employees, and encourage it to expand into new product and market areas. The original mission may seem too restrictive. At this point, the organization will probably begin to pay more attention to previously overlooked or neglected stakeholders. For example, the company may increase employee benefits (employees), hire additional tax specialists (government), designate a public-relations officer (society), attempt to negotiate better discounts with suppliers (suppliers), or increase borrowing to help sustain growth (financial intermediaries). In addition, the firm will certainly pay more attention to the actions and reactions of competitors. These stakeholders and forces in the broad environment then become forces that are considered as the organization adjusts or enlarges its mission.

At some point in the growth of an organization, planning processes are formalized. This may be the first time that a mission statement is put into words. Articulating a mission forces top managers to come to terms with some key issues regarding the current direction of the firm and its future. A well-written mission statement can be an excellent tool for conveying the meaning and intent of an organization to its internal and external stakeholders. A mission statement can also be an effective way to communicate to important stakeholders such as shareholders, customers, and employees that the company is aware there is a problem and is trying to fix it. This is important during a turnaround. The huge North American retailer Sears experienced major setbacks in recent years, including market-share erosion in retailing and loss of the market leadership position to Wal-Mart. Sears' mission statement reflects awareness of difficulties and the outline of a plan for fixing them:

> Sears is a company on the move. Our destination is clear. We're pursuing ways to generate profitable growth. We're striving to become more relevant to our customers. We're learning to celebrate our diversity, work together and perform with urgency. And we're establishing new benchmarks for productivity and continuous improvement. By turning individual success stories into models we can replicate across the organization, we can become the destination of choice for customers, employees and investors.[9]

Unfortunately, in many organizations the process of developing a written mission statement has deteriorated into an exercise in slogan writing. Managers often worry more about writing a catchy, short phrase that can be printed on a business card than about managing with purpose. For an organization's mission to be a management tool, it must be grounded in the realities of the business. One of the first steps in creating a clear sense of mission is to fully understand the nature of the business in which the organization participates. This first step, business definition, will be discussed in the next section.

BUSINESS DEFINITION

One of the most vital questions management can ask is "Who are we?"[10] A clear business definition is the starting point of all strategic planning and management.[11] It provides a framework for evaluating the effects of planned change and for planning the steps needed to move the organization forward.

When defining the business, the question "What is our business?" should be answered from three perspectives: (1) Who is being satisfied? (2) What is being satisfied? (3) How are customer needs satisfied?[12] The first question refers to the markets that an organization serves, the second question deals with the specific functions provided to the customers identified in question 1, and the third question refers to the capabilities and technologies the firm uses to provide the functions identified in question 2. This approach is, admittedly, marketing oriented. Its greatest strength is that it focuses on the customer, an important external stakeholder for most firms. Candlewood Hotel Company defines its business as follows:

> Candlewood Hotel Company, Inc. owns, operates, franchises and manages business-travel hotels. The Company's hotel properties cater to mid-market and upscale business and personal travelers seeking multiple night stays.[13]

While defining a business is helpful in communicating to internal and external stakeholders what the organization is all about, the business definition should not constrain strategic choice. In other words, it is an excellent tool for identifying where a company is, but it should not be used to determine where the company should go in the future.[14] Peter Drucker suggested that the business-definition question should be stated not only as "What is our business?" but also as "What will it be?" and "What should it be?"[15] The second question refers to the direction that the firm is heading at the current time. In other words, where will the business end up if it continues in its current course? The third question, "What should it be?" allows for modifications to the existing strategy to move the company in an appropriate direction. Organizations that struggle to come to grips with those two questions are forced to look forward in time and to think about a vision for the future.

Gary Hamel suggests that rather than determine the future direction of an organization based on what it does, the organization should think in terms of what it knows and the resources it owns.[16] In other words, a company should determine future direction based on its resources and capabilities. This suggestion is consistent with the discussion of resource analysis contained in Chapter 3. As organizations become involved in businesses outside of their current operations, they are increasing what is referred to as their scope. In other words, the scope of an organization is the breadth of its activities both within a market and across markets. Marriott has stated its intent to broaden its business definition to include related markets. Marriott's mission statement, in part, reads:

> Marriott International expects to create significant shareholder value by aggressively growing its existing businesses, and identifying related opportunities which leverage our core skills and can be developed into major new businesses.[17]

Delta Air Lines, like many airlines, has adhered to a narrow business definition. Instead of venturing into new areas, in 1986 Delta acquired Western Airlines. This move allowed Delta to greatly increase its western U.S. route coverage and establish an international presence, thus expanding the geographic size of its markets.[18] However, the type of customer served, function, service, and technologies remained the same. Delta and many other airlines are almost entirely dependent on one business. When the industry experiences downturns and shocks, they have no other businesses to offset losses. This became evident in 2001 when the terrorist attacks in the United States and the associated downturn in demand for air travel led to losses that the airlines could not sustain. When it looked as if many U.S. airlines would go out of business, the federal government provided a multibillion-dollar bailout. On the other hand, Virgin Atlantic Airways is a part of a highly diversified group:

> Led by adventurous founder, chairman, and owner Sir Richard Branson, Virgin Group gets around. The group's travel operations, led by 51 percent-owned Virgin Atlantic Airways, are among its biggest breadwinners. Virgin Atlantic is complemented by its pan-European and Australian low-fare cousins, Virgin Express and Virgin Blue. Virgin Group also operates two UK rail franchises and sells tour packages. The group's Virgin Megastores sell music, videos, and computer games. Other Virgin Group operations include balloon flights, beverages, bridal stores, cosmetics, financial services, health clubs, Internet services, mobile phone services, publishing, and a record label.[19]

Virgin's business definition is at the opposite extreme from many lodging, restaurant, and airline companies that tend to focus on only one type of business. While such high levels of diversity typically are hard to manage, they do provide a cushion against shocks in particular businesses. Choices regarding appropriate levels of diversification will be discussed in depth in Chapter 6. For now, it is sufficient to say that the execution of a corporate-level strategy results in a particular business definition. For example, if a corporate-level strategy includes increased involvement in particular businesses or business segments, the business definition will be changed to reflect these changes.

ORGANIZATIONAL VISION

An organization with a vision has a definite sense of what it wants to be in the future. The CEO has primary responsibility for creating the organizational vision. The vision of Marriott is "to be the world's leading provider of hospitality services."[20] Marriott, with nearly 2,600 properties and 144,000 associates in sixty-seven countries and territories, is arguably fulfilling that vision. Once it is stated, a vision may be used to focus the efforts of the entire organization.[21] For example, plans, policies, or programs that are inconsistent with the corporate vision may need to be altered or replaced. A well-understood vision can help managers and employees believe that their actions have meaning. Unfortunately, sometimes firms have a vision but it produces no positive results because it is not well understood by members of the organization.

> A study was conducted at Cornell's School of Hotel Administration in which students were to make contact with an employee of eighty different lodging companies. Many of these contacts were with reservation agents, the point of first contact with the company for many guests. For the majority of the companies multiple contacts were made as a better indication of actual knowledge possessed by employees. Students asked their contact if they knew the vision of the company. Without embarrassing any one lodging company, we will just say that the overall results were not impressive. Of those contacted, 28 percent knew the vision, 3 percent looked it up, 68 percent did not know the vision, and 1 percent provided a rude response.[22]

While this study was not rigorous from a scientific perspective, it is still possible to draw a few simple, though tentative, conclusions. First, it is possible that many of these firms did not have a vision. Second, those firms that had one were not communicating it very well. Either of these situations results in the same problem. The people who are making contact with guests and other stakeholders don't really understand what their companies are trying to become.

Sometimes a vision is more of a concept than a specific goal. In other words, it is a vision of what the organization should be like. Such a vision can still be very motivating and can help establish a culture that guides the actions of individuals.

> When Michael Snyder saw his son's horse run free without bit or saddle against the picturesque Colorado backdrop of the snow-capped Rocky Mountains, the idea came to him: "What if a guy could run a company that way? What if you had an organization, powerful, all going the same direction with beauty and grace, effortlessly, unbridled, without restraint?"
>
> That was ten years ago when Snyder, now president and CEO of Red Robin International, was just a Red Robin franchisee at the head of The Snyder Group Co. He began applying his unbridled philosophy to his franchise restaurants and, now, after two years in charge of the Englewood, Colorado-based casual-dining, family restaurant/burger joint, he applies his theory to corporate units as well.
>
> A philosopher at heart, Snyder runs Red Robin with a fatherly goodwill towards employees and is modest about his role in the success of the $300-plus million restaurant chain. "I try to surround myself with people who share my values, which are honor, integrity, continually seeking knowledge and having fun, and who are smarter than me," Snyder says. "What I try to do is provide a healthy, productive, profitable, valuing environment for people to continue through life's journey."[23]

ORGANIZATIONAL VALUES

A final but equally important aspect of strategic direction is the establishment of organizational values. Values guide organizational decisions and behavior. Wendy's International Inc., one of the world's largest restaurant-operating and -franchising companies, has a specific statement of values that should drive organizational decisions and operations:

> Integrity—We keep our promises. All actions are guided by absolute honesty, fairness and respect for every individual.
>
> Leadership—We lead by example and encourage leadership qualities at all levels. Everyone has a role to play.
>
> People Focus—We believe our people are key to our success. We value all members of our diverse family for their individual contributions and their team achievements.
>
> Customer Satisfaction—Satisfying internal and external customers is the focus of everything we do.
>
> Continuous Improvement—Continuous improvement is how we think; innovative change provides competitive opportunities.

Community Involvement—Giving back is our heritage. We actively participate and invest in the communities where we do business.

Commitment to Stakeholders—We serve all stakeholders and, through balancing our responsibilities to all, we maximize value to each of them.[24]

Values statements are common throughout the hospitality industry. The value statement of Starwood Hotels and Resorts Worldwide Inc. is found below. Notice that there are some similarities between these value statements, but there are important differences also. These differences are a reflection of the culture and ethics of the company:

Our values serve as the guide for how we treat our customers, our owners, our shareholders and our associates. We aspire to these values to make Starwood a great place to work and do business. We succeed only when we meet and *exceed the expectations* of our customers, owners and shareholders. We have a *passion for excellence* and will deliver the highest standards of *integrity* and *fairness*. We celebrate the *diversity* of people, ideas and cultures. We honor the *dignity* and *value of individuals* working as a team. We improve the *communities* in which we work. We encourage *innovation*, accept *accountability* and embrace *change*. We seek knowledge and growth through *learning*. We share a *sense of urgency, nimbleness* and endeavor to have *fun* too.[25]

High-level managers, especially the CEO, have a great deal of influence on the values of the company. The values of Darden Restaurants were articulated by CEO Joe Lee in a letter to shareholders (see Table 4.2). When a new top manager takes charge, his or her personal values help shape the entire company. Managers who work with the CEO quickly identify his or her value system and communicate it to lower-level managers and employees. The CEO may also discuss organizational values in speeches, news releases, and memos. To the extent that the CEO controls the rewards systems subjectively, managers who make decisions that are consistent with the values of the CEO are likely to be rewarded, thus reinforcing what is expected. Many of the people who strongly disagree with the new values will voluntarily leave the firm. Or, if their own behavior pattern is inconsistent with the new rules of the game, they will be "forced out" through poor performance evaluations, missed promotions, or low salary increases. Thus, over a period of time, the example and actions of the CEO are reflected in most of the major decisions that are made by the organization.[26]

In spite of the power of the CEO, he or she is not the only determinant of organizational values. The values of an organization are also a reflection of the social groups from which managers and other employees are drawn (which makes global management even more challenging). These individuals bring a personal value system with them when they are hired.

In the hospitality industry, often times the values of a social group are part of the service experience. Disney's Polynesian resort, for example, offers an entire training program, "Magic of Polynesia," which is designed to facilitate employee understanding and commitment to the authentic vision of Polynesia.

The case members and management identified four theme values as part of their discussion of "what makes us Polynesian." The values identified as reflecting Polynesian hospitality

TABLE 4.2	**THE VALUES OF DARDEN RESTAURANTS, INC.**

The following is an excerpt from a letter to shareholders authored by Joe R. Lee, chairman and CEO of Darden Restaurants:

While we benefit from competing in an industry that has strong long-term prospects and we have a terrific group of restaurant companies, a great strategy and excellent financial strength, we know we cannot be successful without a clear sense of who we are. We understand and appreciate Darden's core values, values that have been forged over the 64-year heritage started by our founder, Bill Darden. As we continue the journey toward becoming the best casual dining company, we will look to these values for guidance and know they will be especially critical when we're faced with unexpected opportunities or challenges.

As an organization, we value:

- **Integrity and fairness.** It all starts with integrity. We trust in the integrity and fairness of each other to always do the right thing, to be open, honest and forthright with ourselves and others, to demonstrate courage, to solve without blame and to follow through on all our commitments.
- **Respect and caring.** We reach out with respect and caring. We have a genuine interest in the well being of others. We know the importance of listening, the power of understanding and the immeasurable value of support.
- **Diversity.** Even though we have a common vision, we embrace and celebrate our individual differences. We are strengthened by a diversity of cultures, perspectives, attitudes and ideas. We honor each other's heritage and uniqueness. Our power of diversity makes a world of difference.
- **Always learning—always teaching.** We learn from others as they learn from us. We learn. We teach. We grow.
- **Being "of service."** Being of service is our pleasure. We treat people as special and appreciated by giving of ourselves, doing more than expected, anticipating needs and making a difference.
- **Teamwork.** Teamwork works. By trusting one another, we bring together the best in all of us and go beyond the boundaries of ordinary success.
- **Excellence.** We have a passion to set and pursue, with innovation, courage and humility, ever-higher standards.

These values communicate the behaviors and attitudes we cherish as we strive to deliver on Darden's Core Purpose, which is: **"To nourish and delight everyone we serve."** That is what motivates us to be the best.

Source: Darden Restaurants, Inc., 2002 Annual Report, http://www.dardenrestaurants.com/numbers/annual_report.asp, July 8, 2003.

included (1) a sense of *Ohano,* or sense of family, which describes the way they would like their working relationships to be; (2) a sprit of *Aloha,* which means that the basis of their interactions is their desire to be caring and mindful of others; (3) a sense of *ina olea,* the desire to perform all interactions and services in a high-quality way; and (4) a sense of *Mea Ho okipa,* the desire to be the perfect host by "welcoming and entertaining guests and strangers with unconditional warmth and generosity."[27]

If value changes in society are not voluntarily incorporated into a firm, an employee or manager may "blow a whistle," which is an attempt to force the organization to cease a behavior that society finds unacceptable or to incorporate a practice that is in keeping with the new social value. For example, antidiscrimination lawsuits have prompted many organizations to adopt more stringent equal employment opportunity policies and even affirmative action programs. The values of various social groups are constantly changing. Therefore, strategic managers need to keep abreast of these changes in order to successfully position their firms. This task is especially difficult in global organizations.

Stakeholder theory is closely aligned with discussions of values and social responsibility, since one of the principles underlying the theory is that organizations should behave appropriately with regard to a wide range of stakeholder concerns and interests.[28] The increasing incidence of lawsuits against top managers and their companies in recent years provides evidence that many organizations are not satisfying all of their stakeholders' expectations very well.[29]

SOCIAL RESPONSIBILITY

Embedded within the concept of organizational values is the notion of social responsibility. Social responsibility contains four major components: (1) economic responsibilities, such as the obligation to be productive and profitable and meet the consumer needs of society; (2) a legal responsibility to achieve economic goals within the confines of written law; (3) moral obligations to abide by unwritten codes, norms, and values implicitly derived from society; and (4) discretionary responsibilities that are volitional or philanthropic in nature.[30]

McDonald's, the largest global quick-service restaurant company, takes its social responsibility seriously:

> McDonald's in the community means local development, support for local schools, youth sports, and other community programs, help in times of need. Through our support for Ronald McDonald House Charities, we help improve the health and well-being of children and families around the world.
>
> McDonald's has a long-standing commitment to environmental protection. Our restaurants around the world have innovative programs for recycling, resource conservation, and waste reduction. We are working with expert advisors and our suppliers to make further changes so that resources used to meet today's needs will remain available for the needs of future generations.
>
> McDonald's works with our suppliers and expert advisors to improve animal handling practices, help preserve the effectiveness of life-saving antibiotics, ensure the quality and safety of our products and restaurant environments, and promote the protection of workers' health, safety, and human rights.
>
> McDonald's has a People Vision—to be the best employer in each community around the world. Our People Promise and People Principles express our commitment to respect, recognition, openness, and employee development. Diversity is integrated into our business operations and planning around the world.
>
> To guide our social responsibility efforts, McDonald's seeks the advice of independent experts. We have been recognized for our leadership in corporate social responsibility by numerous organizations and publications.[31]

McDonald's is serious about its commitments. It now issues social responsibility reports that highlight what the company is doing in the international communities it serves. For example, the company conducts approximately 500 animal welfare audits throughout the world each year and publishes an animal welfare report. It established the Ronald McDonald House Charities, which are dedicated to improving the health and welfare of children. Over 200 Ronald McDonald houses in twenty-one countries provide families with a home-like atmosphere while their child receives care at a nearby hospital. Ronald McDonald Care Mobiles take medical and dental care directly to underprivileged children. A large grant will provide immunizations to one million children and mothers in Africa. McDonald's has also provided disaster relief in many countries, including Greece, Turkey, India, Chile, and the United States. In addition, the corporation has purchased more than $4 billion of recycled materials. These are just a few examples of the many things McDonald's is doing to be a good citizen.[32]

Research evidence does not unequivocally support the idea that firms that rank high on social responsibility, based on the four components described above, are necessarily any more or less profitable than firms that rank low.[33] However, an organization that maintains an untarnished reputation should enjoy greater opportunities to enhance economic performance over the longer term. Furthermore, firms that have an overall high rank in the four areas listed above (one of which is productivity and profitability) have achieved an end in itself. The old belief, espoused primarily by economists such as Milton Friedman, is that the only valid objective of a corporation is to maximize profits, within the rules of the game (legal restrictions). While it is true that profits are desirable, they are only one outcome of successful corporations.

A corporation that becomes too focused on profits is likely to lose the support and cooperation of key stakeholders such as suppliers, activist groups, competitors, society, and the government. In the long run, this sort of strategy may result in problems such as lawsuits, loss of goodwill, and, ultimately, a loss of profits. One business-ethics expert argued that

> There is a long-term cost to unethical behavior that tends to be neglected. That cost is to the trust of the people involved. Companies today—due to increasing global competition and advancing technological complexity—are much more dependent than ever upon the trust of workers, specialists, managers, suppliers, distributors, customers, creditors, owners, local institutions, national governments, venture partners, and international agencies. People in any of those groups who believe that they have been misgoverned by bribes, sickened by emissions, or cheated by products tend, over time, to lose trust in the firm responsible for those actions.[34]

The case of Manville illustrates these points.

> Nearly fifty years ago, employees and managers of Manville (then Johns-Manville) started to receive information that asbestos inhalation was associated with various forms of lung disease. Manville chose to ignore this information and to suppress research findings. The company even went so far as to conceal chest X-rays from employees in their asbestos operations. When confronted about this tactic, a Manville lawyer was quoted as saying that they would let their employees work until they dropped dead, all in the interest of saving money. Eventually, this neglect of research findings and their own employees led to financial ruin for Manville.[35]

Concerning ethical decision making, the approach of many business organizations seems to be to wait until someone complains before actions are taken. This is the type of attitude that resulted in the savings-and-loan crisis, the Bhopal explosion tragedy in India, and the explosion of the space shuttle *Challenger*. In each of these situations, the organizations involved could have avoided problems by being more responsive to warning signals from key stakeholders. History has taught us that many human-induced disasters and crises could be avoided if organizations were sensitive to what one or another of their stakeholders is saying.

ENTERPRISE STRATEGY

One fundamental question an organization should ask in determining its purpose is "What do we stand for?" This question is the critical link between ethics and strategy. Enterprise strategy is the term used to denote the joining of ethical and strategic thinking about the organization.[36] It is the organization's best possible reason for the actions it takes. Consequently, an enterprise strategy is almost always focused on serving particular stakeholder needs. For example, an enterprise strategy can contain statements concerning a desire to maximize stockholder value, satisfy the interests of all or a subset of other stakeholders, or increase social harmony or the common good of society.[37] Some organizations get very specific about how they will deal with stakeholder interests. For example, the specific stakeholder goals of Hilton Hotels can be found in Table 4.3.

Organizational mission statements containing the elements of an enterprise strategy are more likely to be found in high-performing than in low-performing corporations.[38] Enterprise strategy is a natural extension of the ethics of the organization, which are an extension of the values of key managers within the organization (as was discussed in Chapter 3). The ethics of a firm are not just a matter of public statements. Ethical decision making is a way of doing business. A company that specifically works to build ethics into its business practice, to develop and implement an enterprise strategy, will have a frame of

TABLE 4.3	HILTON HOTELS' STAKEHOLDER GOALS

At Hilton, "minding our business" is about tending to the specific needs of our four primary constituencies: our customers, shareholders, hotel owners, and team members.

For our customers: By providing the best service, value and amenities, along with a wide variety of hotel products and price points, we are focused on our mission of being the first choice of the world's travelers.

For our shareholders: By taking care of our customers, maximizing our growth opportunities in each of our business segments, and effectively managing our costs, we remain dedicated to enhancing shareholder value.

For our owners: By offering the industry's most powerful collection of brands and the tools necessary to continue showing strong market share performance, we are committed to seeing our hotel owners maximize their investments with us.

For our team members: By providing growth opportunities, positive and productive places in which to work, and a commitment to diversity and community services, we strive to build on our reputation as an employer-of-choice in the hotel industry.

Source: Annual Report 2002, Hilton Hotels Corporation, 1, 2, 4, 7, 8.

reference for handling potential ethical problems. For this reason it is not surprising that a recent study of hospitality executives revealed that ethics and integrity were considered the most important competencies for the success of future leaders in the industry.[39]

ETHICAL FRAMES OF REFERENCE

The pattern of decisions made by organizational managers establishes strategy and creates expectations among other organizational members and external stakeholders. For example, a firm that has specialized in the highest-quality services creates an expectation among customers that all services will be high quality. If the firm chooses to change its strategy to include lower-quality services, it runs the risk that customers will perceive the change as a breach of faith. Similarly, if a company has an established relationship with a customer as its sole source of supply of a particular product, then the customer comes to depend on that company. If the supplier then chooses to drop that product from its product line, what might seem to be a clear-cut business decision takes on an ethical dimension: Can the customer's business survive if the product is dropped? Should other alternatives be considered? What obligation does the supplier have to that customer?

These types of decisions carry an ethical dimension because they go against what some important stakeholders think is right. An ethical dilemma exists when the values of different stakeholders of the organization are in conflict. Although there is no real legal dimension, an issue of trust or good faith is apparent. In addition to decisions that violate stakeholder expectations, there are also ethical dilemmas related to the gray area surrounding legal behavior: the definitions of what society views as right and wrong. The values that organizational members bring to their work—the shared values that make up the organizational culture—determine whether the issues of trust, good faith, and obligation are raised when decisions are being deliberated, as well as the degree to which these issues influence the final outcome.

In making decisions that deal with ethical issues, it is important to have a frame of reference. Few ethical dilemmas have simple right-or-wrong answers. Instead, they are complex and require balancing the economic and social interests of the organization.[40] The following are five theoretical models that often influence organizational decisions.[41]

- *Economic Theory.* Under economic theory, the purpose of a business organization is to maximize profits. Profit maximization will lead to the greatest benefit for the most people. Other than profit maximization, there are no ethical issues in business. *Limitations of Economic Theory:* Assumptions of profits being evenly distributed is naive. Not all business decisions relate to profit making, and some ways of increasing profits hurt society.

- *Legal Theory.* Laws are a reflection of what society has determined is right and wrong. Compliance with the law ensures ethical behavior. *Limitations of Legal Theory:* The social and political processes used to formulate laws are complex and time consuming. Since the processes are subject to manipulation, the laws may not truly reflect the interests of society.

- *Religion.* Everyone should act in accordance with religious teachings. *Limitations of Religion:* As a model for business decision making, religious values are difficult to apply. There are many different religious beliefs, and there is no consensus on the behaviors that are consistent with the beliefs.

- *Utilitarian Theory.* Utilitarian theory says to focus on the outcome of a decision. Everyone should act in a way that generates the greatest benefits for the largest number of people. *Limitations of Utilitarian Theory:* Under this model, immoral acts that hurt society or a minority group can be justified if they benefit the majority.

- *Universalist Theory.* Universalist theory says to focus on the intent of the decision. Every person is subject to the same standards. Weigh each decision against the screen: Would I be willing for everyone else in the world to make the same decision? *Limitations of Universalist Theory:* This model provides no absolutes. What one person believes is acceptable for all in society may be offensive to others.

It is obvious that the five models do not provide absolute guidance on how to handle an ethical dilemma. Instead, they provide a departure point for discussing the implications of decisions. In addition, conflicts sometimes are easier to resolve if the two parties to the conflict understand each other's perspectives. An awareness of different frames of reference is especially important for hospitality firms that participate in foreign environments. For example, Eastern countries tend to be much more utilitarian in their approach to decisions, whereas larger industrialized Western countries tend to give economics a lot of weight. The influence of religion is strong in some Latin countries. These are obviously overgeneralizations that do not always hold true, but the key is not so much to pin down exactly what perspective a decision maker favors, but rather to look at decisions and conflicts from a variety of perspectives and to be aware that the other party to a transaction may not share your frame of reference.

CODES OF ETHICS

Many organizations create a code of ethics in a further effort to communicate the values of the corporation to employees and other stakeholders. Another benefit of a code of ethics is that it allows the firm to clarify to employees what behavior is considered appropriate. Some codes of ethics set a minimum standard of behavior by stating that employees are expected to obey all laws. Other organizations make specific statements about values, duties, and obligations to customers, employees, and societies. Clearly, in those cases, the organization expects members to maintain standards of ethical behavior that transcend minimum legal standards. The code of ethics of the Resort Hotel Association, a provider of insurance services to the hospitality industry, states:

> RHA is member driven and managed. As intermediaries between our member resorts and the companies that provide insurance coverage, we recognize that we must be bound by high standards of ethical conduct. Accordingly, it is our responsibility to RHA members:
>
> - To ensure that insurance coverage will be provided by financially stable organizations.
> - To ensure that coverages will be specifically designed to meet the needs of resort hotels.

- To provide adequate limits of coverage.
- To ensure that members' insurance claims are resolved in an equitable, timely and effective manner.
- To provide effective loss-control and risk-management services.
- To strive to make the association a superior insurance risk in the commercial marketplace.
- To adhere to the highest professional standards of conduct.
- To present to our members, accurately and honestly, all facts essential to their buying decisions.
- To maintain strict confidentiality of member information.
- To exemplify the best professional standards of this industry.[42]

To ensure that employees abide by the corporate code of ethics, some companies establish an ethics system, including an audit process to monitor compliance. Employees should be encouraged to report violations to their supervisors or a designated corporate ethics officer. Some companies allow these reports to be anonymous through use of toll-free numbers to reduce the possibility of retribution against employees for making reports of violations.

Sometimes formal systems are not enough to ensure ethical behavior.[43] In an award-winning article, "The Parable of the Sadhu," Bowen McCoy, an investment banker with Morgan Stanley, discussed what he thought was the core, underlying problem when an organization handles ethical dilemmas poorly.[44] In his view, people who are part of an organization often do not personalize ethical issues. It is as if the "organization" is responsible, and the individuals are not. Even individuals who see themselves as very ethical will tend to pass through an ethical dilemma without recognizing it as one, or they will view the dilemma as ultimately someone else's problem. For many ethical dilemmas, one person is not physically capable of correcting the problem alone.

When faced with a major crisis, such as finding that a service is dangerous to the customers who purchase it, many organizations do not know what to do. There is no guiding precept, no system of shared values, to unite the company behind a clear understanding of correct behavior. Although some company members may feel discomfort with the course of action being pursued by the firm, a change in action requires a structured, systematic effort by the entire organization. According to McCoy: "Some organizations have a value system that transcends the personal values of the managers. Such values, which go beyond profitability, are usually revealed when the organization is under stress…. Members need to share a preconceived notion of what is correct behavior, a 'business ethic,' and think of it as a positive force, not a constraint."[45]

The individual has a critical role in the development of the shared values. McCoy writes: "What is the nature of our responsibility if we consider ourselves to be ethical persons? Perhaps it is to change the values of the group so that it can, with all its resources, take the other road."[46]

ETHICS IN GLOBAL ENVIRONMENTS

Dealing with the ethics of employees, customers, and other stakeholders and the society from which they are drawn is a difficult task even in organizations that compete within a single domestic economy. However, the difficulty level increases for global organizations because value systems are highly divergent across international boundaries. For example, a survey of 3,783 female seniors attending 561 universities and colleges in Tokyo revealed that they not only expected sexism in the workplace, but didn't seem to mind it. "More than 91 percent said they would not mind being treated as 'office flowers.' Nearly 25 percent considered that to be a woman's role. Over 66 percent said acting like an office flower would make the atmosphere more pleasant."[47] This attitude concerning the role of women, which is widely held in Japan, would be considered unacceptable in many other countries, including the United States.

This clash of values is illustrative of the types of problems that exist across many international relationships. U.S. companies often experience cultural clashes when doing business with companies in China, Latin America, Russia, and many other countries. And, of course, firms from other countries often have difficulty understanding the values of Americans, Europeans, Australians, and so forth. The problem is a common one. The key to overcoming cultural clashes is working to understand the host country culture and developing strategies that are consistent with that culture instead of fighting it. The discussion of ethical frames of reference found earlier in this chapter is helpful in doing this, since people in many countries tend to favor one or another of the ethical frames.

Although there are dissimilarities among international cultures, it would be an overstatement to say that everything is different. In fact, as organizations grow, develop, and internationalize, they tend to adopt values that are friendlier to a wider group of international constituents. This is certainly true of hospitality companies. The chapter will close with a statement from Luiz Alberto Garcia, chairman of the board of directors of Algar, a large and successful Brazilian company with investments in a wide variety of service, agricultural, and manufacturing businesses. The statement was found at the beginning of Algar's recent annual report. Many of the elements of values, social responsibility, and enterprise strategy are included in the chairman's message. In fact, it could just as well have been the opening statement in the annual report of a U.S., European, or Asian company.

> Algar is known today as being one of the most active companies in Brazil in terms of corporate citizenship as well as one of the best companies in which to work. We take great pride in such recognition. But above all, these are things that are part of our core values and beliefs. We have conducted training programs for our associates for many years now and our companies believe in—and invest in—actions of social responsibility. We know that these projects go hand in hand with the respect we give our human talents, our partners and, of course, our customers. All of these relationships merge into an overall chain of action involving ethics, quality, commitment, and attitude. And believing in a better Brazil is also a business investment.[48]

KEY-POINTS SUMMARY

Strategic managers are charged with the responsibility of providing long-term direction for their organizations, while at the same time balancing the competing interests of key stakeholders. Strategic direction should be established based, in part, on an analysis of the internal and external environments and the history of success or failure of the business. However, managers need to be careful that past success does not lead to failure due to resistance to change. Inertia is the term used to describe the forces that cause a company to resist change.

One of the most commons means to communicate strategic direction is in a written mission statement. An organization's mission statement provides an important vehicle for communicating ideals and a sense of direction and purpose to internal and external stakeholders. It can inspire employees and managers. It can also help guide organizational managers in resource-allocation decisions. Sometimes the terms mission and vision are confused. In general, a mission is what the company is and its reason for existing, whereas a vision is a forward-looking view of what the company wants to become. However, when mission statements are written, they often include a vision statement. Many times, mission statements also include a business definition and statements about the values of an organization.

A clear business definition is the starting point of all strategic planning and management. It provides a framework for evaluating the effects of planned change and for planning the steps needed to move the organization forward. Businesses are defined with answers to three questions: (1) Who is being satisfied? (2) What is being satisfied? (3) How are customer needs satisfied? While defining a business is helpful in communicating to internal and external stakeholders what the organization is all about, the business definition should not be used to limit where the company should go in the future. The business-definition question should be stated not only as "What is our business?" but also as "What will it be?" and "What should it be?" In answering these questions, the organization should think in terms of what it knows and the assets it owns, its resources and capabilities.

The final aspect of strategic direction discussed in this chapter was the establishment of organizational values. Values guide organizational decisions and behavior. Values help determine a firm's attitude toward social responsibility and treatment of various stakeholder groups. Enterprise strategies define how a company will serve particular stakeholder needs. Many organizations create a code of ethics to communicate the values of the corporation to employees and other stakeholders. Viewing problems from multiple frames of reference is an important tool for understanding the values of other cultures, since very few ethical dilemmas have simple right-or-wrong answers. Common frames of reference include economic, legal, religious, utilitarian, and universalist.

Dealing with the ethics of employees, customers, and other stakeholders and the society from which they are drawn is considerably more difficult as organizations become global. Value conflicts are common across international boundaries. The key to overcoming cultural clashes is working to understand the host-country culture and developing strategies that are consistent with that culture instead of fighting it.

DISCUSSION QUESTIONS

1. What, really, is an organizational mission? What is the difference between a mission and a vision? What can a mission include? Does a mission have to be formally written down to be effective?

2. What are some of the key forces influencing strategic direction in an organization? What is inertia, and how can inertia lead a successful firm to failure?

3. Describe the three elements that are critical in defining the business or businesses of an organization. Define the business of a large, diversified organization with which you are familiar. Do not use a company that was described in this chapter.

4. What is corporate-level strategy, and how does it relate to a firm's business definition?

5. What are five common ethical frames of reference? What are their limitations?

6. Due to a decrease in demand for its products, an organization is about to lose money. Managers are considering laying off 10 percent of their workforce. This would be the first layoff in company history. Employees are not organized into a union. The decrease in demand for products is expected to last into the foreseeable future; however, there may be other options for cutting costs. Determine the major issues to consider with regard to this problem from the perspective of each of the five ethical frames of reference.

7. What is an enterprise strategy? Why is an enterprise strategy important to an organization? Write an enterprise strategy for a firm with which you are familiar.

8. Create a mission statement for the university or college you are attending. Make any logical assumptions that are necessary to complete the task. Include all the elements of strategic direction, including vision, business definition, enterprise strategy (what the organization does for its stakeholders), and a statement of what the organization values. (Of course enterprise strategy and values overlap.)

NOTES

1. From an open letter to students and faculty of the School of Hotel Administration, Cornell University, by Jennifer L. Chase, Executive Director Business Development, Fairmont Hotels and Resorts, January 20, 2003.

2. K. Labich, "Why Companies Fail," *Fortune*, 14 November 1994, 53.

3. L. J. Bourgeois, "Performance and Consensus," *Strategic Management Journal* 1 (1980): 227–248; G. G. Dess, "Consensus on Strategy Formulation and Organizational Performance: Competitors in a Fragmented Industry," *Strategic Management Journal* 8 (1987): 259–277; L. G. Hrebiniak and C. C. Snow, "Top Management Agreement and Organizational Performance," *Human Relations* 35 (1982): 1139–1158; Labich, "Why Companies Fail."

4. S. Nelton, "Put Your Purpose in Writing," *Nation's Business* (February 1994): 63.

5. J. Betton and G. G. Dess, "The Application of Population Ecology Models to the Study of Organizations," *Academy of Management Review* 10 (1985): 750–757.

6. T. Levitt, "Marketing Myopia," *Harvard Business Review* 53, no. 5 (September/October 1975): 45–60.

7. G. G. Dess and J. C. Picken, "Creating Competitive (Dis)advantage: Learning from Food Lion's Freefall," *Academy of Management Executive* 13, no. 3 (1999): 97–111.

8. Adapted from C. Enz and D. Corsun "Living a Vision at Hillerman Hotels," *Case Research Journal*. In press.

9. Sears, *Annual Report* (2000), 7.

10. G. Hamel, *Leading the Revolution* (Boston: Harvard Business School Press, 2000), 246.

11. D. F. Abell, *Defining the Business: The Starting Point of Strategic Planning* (Englewood Cliffs, N.J.: Prentice Hall (1980), 169.

12. Abell, *Defining the Business,* 169.

13. "Candlewood Hotel Company," *Hoover's Online,* http://www.hoovers.com, July 8, 2003.

14. Hamel, *Leading the Revolution.*

15. P. F. Drucker, *Management—Tasks, Responsibilities, Practices* (New York: Harper & Row, 1974), 74–94.

16. Hamel, *Leading the Revolution.*

17. This is a part of a mission statement for Marriott from the files of Cathy Enz of the School of Hotel Administration, Cornell University.

18. J. S. Bracker, "Delta Airlines," in *Strategic Management: A Choice Approach,* ed. J. R. Montanari, C. P. Morgan, and J. S. Bracker (Chicago: The Dryden Press, 1990), 657–670.

19. "Virgin Group LTD," *Hoover's Online,* http://www.hoovers.com, July 8, 2003.

20. "Vision," Marriott International, Inc., 2002 *Annual Report,* 2.

21. D. J. Isenberg, "The Tactics of Strategic Opportunism," *Harvard Business Review* 65, no. 2 (March/April, 1987): 92–97.

22. This informal study was based on strategic management students' phone calls to corporate reservation systems as part of a classroom assignment.

23. E. Sturm, "Run, Red Robin, Run." *Market Watch* (March/April 1999): 55.

24. Wendy's International Inc., *2000 Summary Annual Report to Shareholders* (2000), 1.

25. "Company Values," http://www.starwood.com/corporate/company_values.html, July 8, 2003.

26. E. H. Schein, *Organizational Culture and Leadership* (San Francisco: Jossey-Bass, 1985); E. H. Schein, "The Role of the Founder in Creating Organizational Culture," *Organizational Dynamics* (Summer 1983), 14; P. Selznik, *Leadership in Administration* (Evanston, Ill.: Row, Peterson, 1957).

27. L. Dube, C. Enz, L. Reneghan, and J. Siguaw, "Disney's Polynesian Resort: A Value-Based Process of Training and Selection," *American Lodging Excellence: The Keys to Best Practices in the U.S. Lodging Industry,* American Hotel Foundation (1999), 90–91.

28. Clarkson Centre for Business Ethics, *Principles of Stakeholder Management* (Toronto: Rotman School of Management, 1999).

29. I. F. Kesner, "Crisis in the Boardroom: Fact and Fiction," *Academy of Management Executive* (February 1990): 23–35.

30. A. B. Carroll, "A three dimensional model of corporate social performance," *Academy of Management Review* 4 (1979): 497–505.

31. "McDonald's Social Corporate Responsibility," http://www.mcdonalds.com/corporate/social/index.html, July 8, 2003.

32. "McDonald's Social Corporate Responsibility," http://www.mcdonalds.com/corporate/social/index.html, July 8, 2003.

33. K. E. Aupperle, A. B. Carroll, and J. D. Hatfield, "An Empirical Examination of the Relationship between Corporate Social Responsibility and Profitability," *Academy of Management Journal* 28 (1985): 446–463.

34. L. T. Hosmer, "Response to 'Do Good Ethics Always Make for Good Business,' " *Strategic Management Journal* 17 (1996): 501. See also L. T. Hosmer, "Strategic Planning as if Ethics Mattered," *Strategic Management Journal* 15 (Summer Special Issue) (1994): 17–34.

35. S. W. Gellerman, "Why 'Good' Managers Make Bad Ethical Choices," *Harvard Business Review* 64, no. 4 (July/August 1986): 85–90.

36. Hosmer, "Strategic Planning"; D. Schendel and C. Hofer, *Strategic Management: A New View of Business Policy and Planning* (Boston: Little, Brown, 1979).

37. Freeman and Gilbert, *Corporate Strategy.*

38. J. A. Pearce II and F. David, "Corporate Mission Statements: The Bottom Line," *Academy of Management Executive* 1, no. 2 (May 1987): 109–115.

39. B. Chung-Herrera, C. Enz, and M. Lankau, "Grooming Future Hospitality Leaders: A Competencies Model, *Cornell Hotel and Restaurant Administration Quarterly* (June 2003): 1–9.

40. Hosmer, *Ethics of Management.*

41. Based on information in Hosmer, *Ethics of Management.*

42. Resort Hotel Association, "Code of Ethics," http://www.resorthotelinsurance.com/about/code.html, July 9, 2003.

43. J. A. Byrne, "The Best-laid Ethics Programs," *Business Week,* 9 March 1992, 67–69; D. Driscoll, "The Dow Corning Case," *Business and Society Review* 100, no. 1 (September 1998): 57–64; M. B. W. Tabor, "Ex-Dow Corning Executive Faults Company's Ethics on Implants," *The New York Times,* 23 September 1995, 10.

44. B. McCoy, "The Parable of the Sadhu," *Harvard Business Review* 61, no. 5 (September/October 1983).

45. Ibid.

46. Ibid.

47. E. Thornton, "Japan: Sexism OK with Most Coeds," *Business Week,* 24 August 1992, 13.

48. Algar, *Annual Report* (2000), 5.

5
Strategy Formulation at the Business-Unit Level

"*A* crew member stops to help a woman at the head of the queue with her luggage and they chat about her recovery from chemotherapy. A check-in agent extols the merits of Walt Disney World's Space Mountain to two young children and their mother. This is not a typical airport line. There is no moaning, no impatience. Everyone seems, well, happy." Welcome to JetBlue, the airline with the best profit margin in the U.S. In fact, JetBlue enjoys load factors approximately 10 percent above the industry average.

How has JetBlue defied the trends in a highly volatile and troubled industry? JetBlue is a discount airline, and the most frequent reason a traveler will book with JetBlue is price. However, the most common reason a person will recommend JetBlue to friends is service. Friendly employees, leather seats and 24-channel satellite seatback TV systems make the airline truly unique among domestic carriers. These features bring customers back.

On the cost side, JetBlue keeps labor costs low—around 25 percent of revenues compared to 33 percent at Southwest and 44 percent at Delta. The company makes up for low wages with profit sharing and stock options. Reservation-takers work at home, which saves them commute time and helps the company reduce office space. Maintenance costs are about a quarter of what the competition pays because JetBlue has a new fleet of Airbus A320s. The A320s spend an average of twelve hours a day in the air, compared to eleven hours at Southwest and 9 hours at many other airlines. One of the reasons for the extra use is that unlike major competitors that operate large hub-and-spoke networks, JetBlue flies point to point. The large hub-and-spoke systems are a logistical nightmare, making it difficult to keep the planes in the air and on time.

The heart of JetBlue is its charismatic CEO David Neelman. He has been known to pass out refreshments on flights while soliciting feedback from travelers. Having been diagnosed with attention deficit disorder, Neelman refuses to take medication because he is afraid it might rob him of creativity and energy. He works late, sometimes searching the Internet for airline developments after his family has gone to sleep. Some of JetBlue's employees compare him to nuclear fusion. Everyone agrees he and his airline stand out from the competition.[1]

INTRODUCTION

Business-level strategy defines an organization's approach to competing in its chosen markets. Sometimes this type of strategy is referred to as competitive strategy. However, all strategies are competitive strategies so, to avoid confusion, this book uses the term "business level" to describe strategies within particular businesses. The strategy of JetBlue can be described as a combination of low-cost leadership and service differentiation, a combination called best value, which is increasing in popularity in both service and manufacturing businesses. JetBlue achieves low cost through reduced labor and maintenance expenses and by using its fleet efficiently. However, the company is also differentiating its services, thus making them more attractive to customers.

Some of the major strategic management responsibilities of business-level managers are listed in Table 5.1. They include establishing the overall direction of the business unit, ongoing analysis of the changing business situation, selecting a generic strategy and the specific strategies needed to carry it out (strategic posture), and managing resources to produce a sustainable competitive advantage. These responsibilities and the methods for carrying them out are similar in for-profit and nonprofit organizations.[2] They are also similar in both manufacturing and service settings. This chapter will begin with a discussion of the basis for competing in particular markets through specific business-level strategies. Attention will then turn to competitive dynamics—the moves and countermoves of firms and their competitors.

TABLE 5.1	MAJOR BUSINESS-LEVEL STRATEGIC MANAGEMENT RESPONSIBILITIES
Major Responsibilities	**Key Issues**
Direction Setting	Establishment and communication of mission, vision, ethics, and long-term goals of a single business unit
	Creation and communication of shorter-term goals and objectives
Analysis of Business Situation	Compilation and assessment of information from stakeholders, broad environmental analysis, and other sources
	Internal resource analysis
	Identification of strengths, weaknesses, opportunities, threats, sources of sustainable competitive advantage
Selection of Strategy	Selection of a generic approach to competition—cost leadership, differentiation, focus, or best value
	Selection of a strategic posture—specific strategies needed to carry out the generic strategy
Management of Resources	Acquisition of resources and/or development of competencies leading to a sustainable competitive advantage
	Ensuring development of functional strategies and an appropriate organizational design (management structure) to support business strategy
	Development of control systems to ensure that strategies remain relevant and that the business unit continues to progress toward its goals

GENERIC BUSINESS STRATEGIES

Business strategies are as different as the organizations that create them. That is, no two business strategies are exactly alike. However, classifying strategies into generic types helps firms identify common strategic characteristics. For example, a firm that is trying to achieve a competitive advantage by producing at lowest cost should seek some combination of efficiency, low levels of overhead, and high volume. Also, since generic strategies are widely understood, they provide a means of meaningful communication. Instead of having to explain the strategy each time, managers can simply use the generic label.

The generic strategy types proposed by Michael Porter are perhaps the most widely used and understood. Porter advanced the idea that a sustainable competitive advantage is related to the amount of value a firm creates for its most important stakeholder, the customer.[3] According to Porter, firms create superior value for customers either by offering them a basic product or service that is produced at the lowest possible cost or by offering them a preferred product or service at a somewhat higher price, where the additional value received exceeds the additional cost of obtaining it. The first option, called low-cost leadership, is based on efficient cost production. In this book, as in practice, the terms "low-cost leadership" and "cost leadership" are used interchangeably. The second option, referred to as differentiation, requires the company to distinguish its products or services on the basis of an attribute such as higher quality, more-innovative features, greater selection, better service after sale, or more advertising. Both of these strategies assume that an organization is marketing its products or services to a very broad segment of the market.

Porter identified a third strategic option, called focus, in which companies target a narrow segment of the market. According to Porter, a firm can focus on a particular segment of the market through either low-cost leadership or differentiation. Consequently, Porter's original generic strategies were low-cost leadership, differentiation, and focus through either low cost or differentiation (for a total of four strategic approaches).

Porter referred to companies that were not pursuing a distinct generic strategy as "stuck-in-the-middle."[4] According to Porter, these uncommitted firms should have lower performance than committed firms because they lack a consistent basis for creating superior value. He argued that companies that exclusively pursue one of the generic strategies center all of their resources on becoming good at that strategy. However, since that time, many firms have succeeded at pursuing elements associated with cost leadership and differentiation simultaneously. In this book, we refer to this hybrid as best value. Increasing global competition has made a best-value strategy increasingly popular. Combining low-cost, differentiation, and best value approaches with a broad-vs.-narrow market focus results in six generic-strategy types, outlined in Table 5.2. Notice that for each strategy, the term "firms attempt" is used. These describe strategies that businesses are pursuing and do not depend on whether a company is successful in pursuing their strategy. For example, five firms can pursue a cost-leadership strategy, while only one of them will be the cost leader.

It is important to understand that one corporation can be pursuing several business-level strategies simultaneously through its different business units. For example, Marriott owns many brands with a wide variety of strategies. The strategy of Fairfield Inn is probably best described as low-cost leadership because of its broad appeal to the mass market and emphasis on economy. This is not to say that Fairfield is a low-quality lodging brand. In the hotel industry, there are certain quality standards that almost all brands have to meet or consumers will not stay there. In contrast, Ritz-Carlton is clearly focused on elite consumers. Execustay also pursues a focus strategy, but the target market is on business people who need longer-term, temporary housing. Because a single corporation can pursue multiple strategies, this chapter will discuss specific brands instead of their corporate parents. Each of the strategy types will now be discussed in detail.

COST LEADERSHIP

Firms pursuing cost leadership set out to become the lowest-cost providers of a good or service. The broad scope of cost leaders means that they attempt to serve a large percentage of the total market. For instance, Etap and Motel 6 are both pursuing cost leadership.

> Accor is the undisputed worldwide leader in economy lodging. In Europe it has the Etap Brand. The closest U.S. counterpart is Motel 6. Both of these brands cater to a large segment of the population interested in economical lodging. They are both large enough to enjoy economies of scale and provide travelers with the opportunity to stay within the chain on longer trips. They both have huge information and reservation networks. And they both strive to keep costs at absolute minimums while providing clean, functional, and modestly comfortable rooms.[5]

Many hoteliers would bristle at the thought that they are pursuing a low-cost leadership strategy. Rather, they envision their firms as pursuing some sort of balance between low costs and differentiation. However, we must realize that a clean room and linens and

| TABLE 5.2 | GENERIC BUSINESS-LEVEL STRATEGIES |

Business-Level Strategy	Broad or Narrow Market	Desired Source of Advantage	Description
Low-cost leadership	Broad	Lowest-cost production	Firms attempt to manufacture a product or provide a service at the lowest cost to the customer. The product or service is targeted at a very broad segment of the market.
Differentiation	Broad	Preferred product or service	Firms attempt to manufacture a product or provide a service that is preferred above the products or services of competing firms. The product or service is targeted at a very broad segment of the market.
Best value	Broad	Low cost & highly desirable product or service	Firms attempt to manufacture a product or provide a service that is very attractive to customers, but also produced at a reasonably low cost, thus providing the best value for the cost. The product or service is targeted at a very broad segment of the market.
Focus through low-cost leadership	Narrow	Lowest-cost production	Firms attempt to manufacture a product or provide a service at the lowest cost to the customer within a specific segment (niche) of the market.
Focus through differentiation	Narrow	Preferred product or service	Firms attempt to manufacture a product or provide a service that is preferred above the products or services of competing firms within a specific segment (niche) of the market.
Focus through best value	Narrow	Low cost & highly desirable	Firms attempt to manufacture a product or provide a service that is very attractive to customers, but also produced at a reasonably low cost, thus providing the best value for the cost in a particular segment (niche) of the market.

some level of comfort (i.e., telephone and television) is expected at every lodging property. The only exceptions would be independent units in out-of-the-way places that have relatively little serious competition or motels that specialize in providing short-term services for adults. Once the basic quality standards have been met, differentiation occurs as companies offer significantly more than just a clean, comfortable room. Brands like Fairfield Inns, Etap, and Motel 6 do not offer significantly more than the basics. Management in these companies is very good at keeping costs at a minimum. Consequently, they can keep prices low and attract a wide segment of the market interested in an inexpensive room.

To fully appreciate the significance of the cost-leadership strategy, it is important to understand the factors that underlie cost structures in firms. Companies pursuing a low-cost strategy will typically employ one or more of the following factors to create their low-cost positions: (1) accurate demand forecasting combined with high capacity utilization, (2) economies of scale, (3) technological advances, (4) outsourcing, or (5) learning/ experience effects.[6] These factors will now be explained.

High Capacity Utilization

When demand is high and capacity is fully used, a firm's fixed costs are spread over more units, which lowers unit costs. However, when demand falls off, the fixed costs are spread over fewer units, so unit costs increase. This basic concept suggests that a firm that is able to maintain higher levels of capacity utilization, through better demand forecasting, conservative capacity-expansion policies, or aggressive pricing, will be able to maintain a lower cost structure than a competitor of equal size and capability. Consequently, the lodging industry puts high importance on occupancy rates and restaurants pay close attention to meals served per hour.

High capacity utilization is particularly important in industries, like hotels and airlines, in which fixed costs represent a large percentage of total costs. In these situations, entry barriers make industry participants extremely sensitive to even small fluctuations in customer demand. For example, small variations in demand can cause wide fluctuations in profitability. In these types of businesses, where capacity utilization is so important, companies that are faced with falling demand typically attempt to stimulate sales by employing massive price-cutting.

Economies of Scale

The second major factor with the potential to lead to cost advantages is economies of scale. Economies of scale are often confused with increases in the "throughput." As described above, increases in capacity utilization that spread fixed expenses can lead to lower unit costs. However, true economies of scale are associated with size rather than capacity utilization. The central principle of economies of scale is that costs per unit are less in a large facility than in a small facility. For example, the cost of constructing a 200-room hotel will not necessarily be twice the cost of building a 100-room hotel, so the initial fixed cost per unit of capacity will be lower. Also, the manager of the larger facility will not generally receive double the salary of the manager of the smaller facility. In addition, activities such as quality control, purchasing, and reservations typically do not require twice as much time or twice as many laborers. In summary, the larger firm may be able to achieve per-unit savings in fixed costs and indirect labor costs. Diseconomies of scale occur when a firm builds facilities that are so large that the sheer administrative costs and confusion associated with the added bureaucracy overwhelm any potential cost savings.

Technological Advances

Companies that make investments in cost-saving technologies are often trading an increase in fixed costs for a reduction in variable costs. If technological improvements result in lower total-unit costs, then firms have achieved a cost advantage from their investments referred to as economies of technology.[7] For example, the reservation systems maintained by the major airlines and lodging companies represent investments in technology that reduce overall costs and provide a degree of information control that was previously impossible.

Outsourcing

Traditional thinking in management was that organizations should perform as many value-adding functions as possible in-house in order to retain control of the production process and gain technological efficiencies through creating synergies among processes. However, competitive reality has set in, and corporations realize that sometimes another company can perform a process better or more efficiently than they can. This has led to outsourcing, which means contracting with another firm to provide services that were previously supplied from within the company. For example, a hospitality firm could subcontract its accounting, reservations, information systems, or even hotel management. A real estate investment trust is, in essence, subcontracting management of the properties it owns to other firms. Although firms can sometimes gain efficiency through outsourcing, it is important that they continue to control production of the unique features that provide competitive advantage to the company. In other words, they should "nurture a few core competencies in the race to stay ahead of rivals."[8] Outsourcing allows a firm to concentrate resources on the core business activities.

Learning Effects

A final factor that influences cost structures is learning effects.[9] If you are a student, you probably spent a long time the first time you registered for classes. Now, as a veteran of several registrations, you know how to get through the process much faster. When an employee learns to do a job more efficiently with repetition, then learning is taking place. The learning-curve effect says that the time required to complete a task will decrease as a predictable function of the number of times the task is repeated. Dramatic time savings are achieved early in the life of a company. However, as the company matures, tangible cost savings from labor learning are harder to achieve because it takes longer to see a true doubling of cumulative volume, and because most of the opportunities for learning have already been exploited. Also, learning effects do not just happen. They occur only when management creates an environment that is favorable to both learning and change and then rewards employees for their productivity improvements.

Learning effects can be described by a curve such as the one found in Figure 5.1.[10] Following from the logic of this curve, a market-share leader should enjoy a cost advantage relative to competitors because of the extra learning and experience that has occurred by producing the additional output. This concept has led many firms to fight aggressively on price in order to obtain the highest market share and thus move to the right on the curve as far as possible. As the curve flattens, it becomes increasingly difficult to gain cost advantages from learning effects. The same sort of phenomenon exists with respect to economies of scale.

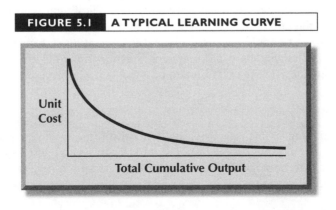

FIGURE 5.1 | **A TYPICAL LEARNING CURVE**

Companies that are able to achieve the lowest cost do not have to charge the lowest price. In other words, a cost leader does not have to be a price leader. If an organization is able to achieve the lowest cost but charge a price that is the same as competitors charge, then it will enjoy higher profits. However, if the low-cost leader's price is the same as or higher than the price others charge, then customers may switch to a competitor, undermining the low-cost producer's efforts to benefit from capacity utilization, learning effects, or other sources of low cost. Consequently, many low-cost leaders try to underprice competitors slightly in order to give customers an incentive to buy from them and to keep their volumes high enough to support their low-cost strategy.

Risks Associated with a Cost-Leadership Strategy

There are some risks associated with a cost-leadership strategy. Firms pursuing cost leadership may not detect changes in services that are becoming expected because of a preoccupation with cost. They run the risk of making large investments in new properties only to see them become obsolete because of changing trends. Their large investments make them reluctant to keep up with changes that are not compatible with their existing facilities. Another risk is that competitors will quickly imitate the technologies that are resulting in lower costs. As Michael Porter observed, "A company can outperform rivals only if it can establish a difference it can preserve."[11]

Another risk associated with a cost-leadership strategy is that the company will go too far and perhaps even endanger customers or employees in the process. ValuJet's "penny-pinching" allowed it to achieve a very low cost position in the airline industry. ValuJet passed the savings on to consumers and experienced unprecedented growth. However, their stinginess came under close scrutiny after the crash of ValuJet flight 592 into the Florida Everglades. Federal investigators found some of ValuJet's procedures, especially maintenance procedures, unsafe, and they ultimately shut down the airline until safety concerns could be worked out.[12]

DIFFERENTIATION

In differentiation strategies, the emphasis is on creating value through uniqueness, as opposed to lowest cost. Uniqueness can be achieved through service innovations, superior service, creative advertising, better supplier relationships leading to better services, or in an almost unlimited number of other ways. The key to success is that customers must be willing to pay more for the uniqueness of a service than the firm paid to create it. As in the cost-leadership strategy, an organization pursuing a differentiation strategy is targeting a broad market; consequently, the differentiated product or service should be designed so that it has wide appeal to many market sectors. Examples of firms that are pursuing differentiation strategies include both Marriott and Hilton (in their brand name hotel groups) by providing very high-quality guest experiences that appeal to both business and personal travelers. Currently many firms in the hospitality industry are using Wi-Fi as a tool for differentiation.

> Wireless Networking or "Wi-Fi" is taking the hospitality industry by storm. Boeing is so excited about it that it hopes to outfit nearly 4,000 planes with the service over the next decade. For a fee, laptop computer users will be able to log on to the Net. Marriott is also equipping hotel rooms with Wi-Fi technology. "Customers are making decisions

about where they stay based on where this technology is available," according to Lou Paladeau, a Marriott vice president in charge of technology development. "If you don't have it, you're not getting them in the door."[13]

Companies pursuing differentiation strategies cannot ignore their cost positions. When its costs are too high relative to competitors' costs, a firm may not be able to recover enough of the additional costs through higher prices. Therefore, differentiators have to keep costs low in the areas that are not directly related to the sources of differentiation. The only way a differentiation strategy will work is if the attributes that makes a service unique are sufficiently valued by buyers so that the buyers are willing to pay a higher price for the service or choose to buy from that firm preferentially. Basically, the extra revenues from differentiation must exceed the additional costs of producing it.

Resource-based Differentiation

Chapter 3 contained a detailed discussion of resource-based sources of competitive advantage. No attempt will be made to repeat that discussion here. However, it is worth mentioning that some resources are more likely to lead to a source of sustainable differentiation. For example, reputations and brands are difficult to imitate, whereas particular service features may be easy to imitate. In general, intangible resources such as a high-performance organizational culture are hard to imitate, whereas a tangible resource such as a particular customer-service policy is easy to imitate. Resources that are hard to imitate are more likely to lead to a sustainable advantage. Intangible resources are associated with what internal stakeholders know or how they are organized, as well as with how external stakeholders feel about a particular organization or its services or how they are linked to the organization.

Risks Associated with a Differentiation Strategy

It is important to recognize that the difference in value may be a result of buyer perceptions rather than actual service attributes. For example, effective advertising may result in a strong brand preference even though the services in a particular segment in the industry are essentially the same. Consequently, the major risks associated with a differentiation strategy center on the difference between added costs and incremental price. One risk is that customers will sacrifice some of the features, services, or image possessed by a unique service because it costs too much. Another risk is that customers will no longer perceive an attribute as differentiating. They may come to a point at which they are so familiar with a service that brand image is no longer important. If a source of differentiation is easy to imitate, then imitation by competitors can also eliminate perceived differentiation among products or services. Returning to the example, as Wi-Fi becomes a standard feature on planes or in hotel rooms it will no longer be a source of differentiation. Consequently, staying ahead of the competition in service development requires constant innovation.[14] As one business writer put it: "For outstanding performance, a company has to beat the competition. The trouble is the competition has heard the same message."[15]

BEST VALUE

Some strategy scholars argue that a combination of strategic elements from both differentiation and low cost may be necessary to create a sustainable competitive advantage: "The immediate effect of differentiation will be to increase unit costs. However, if costs fall with increasing volume, the long-run effect may be to reduce unit costs."[16] Volume is expected to increase because differentiation makes the product or service more attractive to the market. Then, as volume increases, costs will decrease. For example, Anheuser-Busch has created brewing products that have a good image and high quality, yet the company is a cost leader due to efficiencies created by high-volume production and sales.

The key to a best-value strategy is simple supply-and-demand economics. For example, assume that three vendors sell hot dogs on the street corners of a major city. The first vendor pursues a low-cost strategy. She is able to buy hot dogs at 20 cents each and buns at 8 cents each. Her hot dogs are known by locals to be of low quality, but some of them buy from her anyway and she gets almost all of the drive-by business at a price of $1. Her average daily sales are 100, for a gross profit of $72. Her cart costs are $30 per day, so she nets $42. Another vendor specializes in the highest-quality imported sausages. They cost him $2 each and he buys a little better bun at 10 cents. He sells an average of forty sausages for $4 each. His nicer cart costs him $40 per day. After making the calculations, you will see that his gross is $76 and his net is $36.

However, assume that a third vendor can buy a domestic sausage that is almost as good as the imported sausage and sell eighty per day at $3. She buys the sausages locally for $1 each, which is five times as much as the first vendor pays for cheap hot dogs but half the cost of the imported sausages. The better buns are 10 cents each and the nicer cart is $40 per day. Gross profit is $152 and net is $112. Obviously, this third vendor has found a better strategy. Hospitality is often a lot like the hot dog vendors. A little extra service in a room, better technology, or a chocolate on the pillow are not very expensive. Taken together, however, they can enhance the guest experience and thus make the service more valuable in the eyes of consumers.

> Value is the focus for Martyn Levitt, finance director at the privately owned townhouse chain Firmdale Hotels. Levitt has a remarkably unaccountant-like approach to his job and, rather than focusing entirely on costs, as is the accountant reputation, he signs the praises of looking beyond the short-term numbers. It may be alien to some of his fellow members of the British Association of Hotel Accountants, a body Levitt is vice-chairman of. But Levitt is convinced that his current outlook, learnt during his time at Firmdale, a company he joined in May 1993, is the right one.
>
> A key learning for Levitt was that boutiques need something to sell the property. This means that idiosyncratic features such as cinema screening rooms are important to add cachet to a property.[17]

Best value is about making sure that the things that provide the most perceived value to a customer are done very well, while looking for ways to keep costs low through technology, economies of scale, learning, or reducing waste. The JetBlue example at the beginning of the chapter is an excellent illustration of how a best-value strategy can work. Friendliness, leather seats, and personal televisions are very noticeable, yet the company saves money by keeping labor and maintenance costs low and using a different technology in routing its flights.

Quality and Best Value

An emphasis on quality may help hospitality firms that want to pursue a best value strategy. Much has been said and written on the topic of quality. According to the American

Assembly, which consists of sixty-five leaders of business, labor, government, and academia: "This does not mean quality merely to specifications but that improves constantly, quality that is characterized by constant innovations that create a loyal customer. It means achieving this attitude from top to bottom, from the board room to the factory floor."[18] W. Edwards Deming, an expert on quality, argued that producing higher-quality products though superior designs also reduces manufacturing costs.[19] Also, high-quality production eliminates waste through reducing the amount of rework and minimizing the amount of discarded final products. It is less expensive to produce ten products right the first time than to build eleven products and have to throw one away because of quality defects. Although these concepts were developed in a manufacturing setting, there is not reason to believe that they cannot apply equally well in services.

Many organizations have implemented in the past, and some are still pursuing, Total Quality Management (TQM) programs in an effort to improve quality. The principles of TQM are presented in Table 5.3. TQM is so comprehensive in its scope that virtually all parts of an organization are affected.

Six Sigma has also had a pervasive effect on organizations in the United States and elsewhere. It is a philosophy based on minimizing the number of defects found in a manufacturing operation or service function. The term comes from Sigma, the Greek letter that statisticians use to define one standard deviation from the center of the normal bell-shaped curve. At one Sigma, about one-third of whatever is being observed falls outside the range. Two Sigmas means that about 5 percent falls outside the range. Six Sigmas is so far out that virtually nothing is out there. This is the goal with regard to the number of defects that are considered acceptable. "In consultant-speak, it denotes the path to a corporate nirvana where everything—from product design to manufacturing to billing—proceeds without a hitch. In engineer-speak, it means no more than 3.4 defects per million widgets or procedures. In practice, Six Sigma is a statistical quality-control method that combines the art of the efficiency expert with the science of the computer geek."[20] Starwood was one of the first hospitality companies to implement a Six Sigma program.[21]

Although quality is extremely important, it does not guarantee success. The ability of quality to lead to sustainable differentiation depends on how long it takes for rivals to imitate the quality difference.

Risks Associated with a Best-Value Strategy

To review, cost leadership is associated with risks (1) that a firm will become preoccupied with cost and lose sight of the market, (2) that technological breakthroughs will make process-cost savings obsolete, (3) that competitors will quickly imitate any sources of cost advantage, and (4) that the company will take the cost-reduction emphasis too far, thus endangering stakeholders. The risks associated with differentiation are (1) that the company will spend more to differentiate its service than it can recover in the selling price, (2) that competitors will quickly imitate the source of differentiation, and (3) that the source of differentiation will no longer be considered valid by customers.

A best-value strategy represents somewhat of a trade-off between the risks of a cost-leadership strategy and the risks of a differentiation strategy. The risk that technological breakthroughs will make the strategy obsolete is as much a problem with best value as it is with cost leadership. Also, the risk of imitation, found in both of the other two strategies,

TABLE 5.3	**PRINCIPLES OF TOTAL QUALITY MANAGEMENT**

General

1. Get to know the next and final customer.
2. Get to know the direct competition, and the world-class leaders (whether competitors or not).
3. Dedicate to continual, rapid improvement in quality, response time, flexibility, and cost.
4. Achieve unified purpose via extensive sharing of information and involvement in planning and implementation of change.

Design and Organization

5. Cut the number of components or operations and number of suppliers to a few good ones.
6. Organize resources into chains of customers, each chain mostly self-contained and focused on a product or customer "family."

Operations

7. Cut flow time, distance, inventory, and space along the chain of customers.
8. Cut setup, changeover, get-ready, and start-up time.
9. Operate at the customer's rate of use (or a smoothed representation of it).

Human Resource Development

10. Continually invest in human resources through cross-training (for mastery), education, job switching, and multi-year cross-career reassignments; and improved health, safety, and security.
11. Develop operator-owners of products, processes, and outcomes via broadened owner-like reward and recognition.

Quality and Process Improvement

12. Make it easier to produce or provide the product without mishap or process variation.
13. Record and own quality, process, and mishap data at the workplace.
14. Ensure that front-line associates get first chance at process improvement—before staff experts.

Accounting and Control

15. Cut transactions and reporting; control causes and measure performance at the source, not via periodic cost reports.

Capacity

16. Maintain/improve present resources and human work before thinking about new equipment and automation.
17. Automate incrementally when process variability cannot otherwise be reduced.
18. Seek to have multiple work stations, machines, flow lines, cells for each product or customer family.

Marketing and Sales

19. Market and sell your firm's increasing customer-oriented capabilities and competencies.

Source: R.J. Schonberger, "Is Strategy Strategic? Impact of Total Quality Management on Strategy," *Academy of Management Executive* (August 1992): 83. Reproduced with permission of Academy of Management in the format Textbook via Copyright Clearance Center.

is evident in a best-value strategy as well. On the other hand, a firm pursuing best value is unlikely to become preoccupied with either cost or differentiation; instead, it should try to balance these two factors. Also, the company probably would not be prone to take the cost-saving strategy too far, thus endangering employees or customers. Finally, because of the balance between cost and differentiation, a hospitality firm pursing a best-value strategy is less likely than a pure differentiator to put so much into differentiating a service that the company will be unable to recover the additional costs through the selling price.

FOCUS

Focus strategies can be based on differentiation, lowest cost, or best value; however, a focus strategy emphasizing lowest cost would be rare in the hospitality industry because it is hard to please a particular guest segment without some form of differentiation. The key to a focus strategy is providing a product or service that caters to a particular segment in the market. Firms pursuing focus strategies have to be able to identify their target market segment and both assess and meet the needs and desires of buyers in that segment better than any other competitor. Four Seasons focuses on elite consumers with discriminating tastes:

> We have chosen to specialize within the hospitality industry, by offering only experiences of exceptional quality. Our objective is to be recognized as the company that manages the finest hotels, resorts, residence clubs and other residential projects wherever we locate. We create properties of enduring value using superior design and finishes, and support them with a deeply instilled ethic of personal service. Doing so allows Four Seasons to satisfy the needs and tastes of our discriminating customers, and to maintain our position as the world's premier luxury hospitality company.[22]

An even more extreme example of catering to the elite is the Burj Al Arab hotel, a sail-shaped hotel built on a man-made island.

> It stands 321 meters above sea level in the gulf waters of Dubai in the United Arab Emirates. The hotel has 202 suites ranging from about (U.S.) $1,000 to $6,000. The hotel is targeted at members of royal families who visit from Europe, Asia, and the Middle East, as well as celebrities and wealthy industrialists and visitors. The mission of the hotel is "to be the world's most luxurious hotel with a team dedicated to outstanding personalized service, surpassing guest expectations, by providing the ultimate Arabian hospitality experience."[23] Jumeirah International, which owns the hotel, has recently expanded from two hotels in Dubai in 1999 to five, five-star hotels (plus one under construction), two hotels in London and a hotel school for undergraduates in an alliance with Ecole Hoteliere De Lausanne (Switzerland), among other ventures.

Another group of lodging companies is focusing on the "young and affluent" that have different ideas than their parents about what makes a good hotel. These trendy boutique, or designer, hotels "typically emphasize provocative modern design, encourage 'lobby socializing' and are often anchored by bars or restaurants favored by locals, not just standard travelers. They are also celebrity magnets, if one is to believe gossip columnists."[24] W Hotels, owned by Starwood, were born of the frustration of its CEO, Barry Sternlict, over hotel monotony. They have striking interiors and run wild promotions.[25]

The risks of pursuing a focus strategy depend on whether the strategy is pursued through differentiation, cost leadership, or best value. The risks of each of these strategies are similar to the risks faced by adopters of the pure strategies themselves. However, the focus strategy has two risks that are not associated with any of the three pure strategies. First, the desires of the narrow target market may become similar to the desires of the market as a whole, thus eliminating the advantage associated with focusing. Second, a competitor may be able to focus on an even more narrowly defined target and essentially "outfocus the focuser."

This completes our discussion of generic strategies. We have also devoted considerable attention to how to implement those strategies. Low-cost leadership may be achieved through high capacity utilization, scale economies, technological advances, outsourcing, and learning effects. Differentiation is pursued on the basis of providing a preferred product or service. Meaningful differentiation can be achieved through a variety of firm resources and capabilities; however, the intangible resources tend to provide a more sustainable advantage. Best-value strategies combine elements from both differentiation and cost leadership. Many firms are pursuing a best-value strategy through an emphasis on quality or speed. Focus strategies apply one of the generic orientations to a specific market niche.

Business-level strategies should be formulated on the basis of the existing or potential resources and abilities of the organization. However, they should also be selected on the basis of how well the resulting products and services are expected to be received in the market. Otherwise, an organization might develop a wonderful product or service that is largely unsuccessful. "It would be a little like having a concert pianist in a street gang who has a skill that is unique in that environment, but that hardly helps to attain the gang's goals."[26]

COMPETITIVE DYNAMICS

Even well-designed strategies may not be as successful as anticipated due to the reactions of competitors. For instance, suppose a large independent hotel decides to pursue a low-cost-leadership strategy through cutting the price of rooms to increase sales volume. To meet anticipated demand, the company builds a new addition. However, when the firm cuts prices, competitors do likewise. So the organization launches a major advertising campaign. Competitors also increase advertising. These actions may increase demand in the area as a whole, but the increased demand probably is not enough to cover the increased expenses and loss of profit margins. The result is that the organization still has approximately the same market share as before, with an expensive new addition that is not being fully used.

Competitive dynamics are particularly important because of what a well-known economist, Joseph Schumpeter, called "creative destruction."[27] Creative destruction describes the inevitable decline of leading firms due to competitive moves and counter-moves. Competitors pursue creative opportunities in an attempt to eliminate the competitive advantages of market leaders. As long as the playing field is level, which means that the government enforces rules of fair competition, eventually competitors will succeed. Bill Gates, CEO of Microsoft, once said that his company is always only two years away from potential failure because at any time a competitor could produce a product that is better than Windows.

In the past few decades, increasing globalization of markets has made competitive dynamics even more important, as firms now have to contend with a larger group of competitors. Most recently, the Internet has dramatically increased the amount of information available to consumers and hotel competitors around the world. For example, if you want to book a room in Spain from Japan, it is easy to do on the Internet. Also, innovations are adopted at a much higher rate. Consequently, the actions of a hospitality company anywhere in the world now have a ripple effect on all other industry participants. For example, if

Marriott develops a more efficient process for maintaining its customer databases, the technology is likely to be communicated and adopted at other lodging companies in a relatively short amount of time.

Markets are always in a state of flux, in the United States as well as in other countries. The actions of one competitor result in countermoves from other industry participants.[28] Countermoves set off another series of actions, and then reactions to those actions. Across all industries, the number of competitive moves and countermoves has been increasing.[29] In addition, the number of new products introduced and the number of patents issued have both increased. Along with these trends, brand loyalty has been dropping, and the popularity of foreign brands has been steadily increasing. Consequently, increasingly disloyal consumers now have more to choose from, and it comes from a lot more places. It is not surprising, then, that the number of new-business failures is also increasing.[30]

STRATEGIES THAT REFLECT COMPETITIVE DYNAMICS

Given these trends, it is clear that competitive dynamics plays an important role in strategy formulation. An organization can respond in a number of ways to the dynamics in its industry. Offensive strategies such as aggressive competition or seeking first-mover advantages are intended to increase market share and diminish the ability of competitors to compete. Defensive strategies such as threatening retaliation, seeking government intervention, or erecting barriers to imitation are intended to deter or slow down rivals from taking actions that would reduce the effectiveness of a firm's own strategies. Collaboration with stakeholders can be used offensively or defensively. Finally, a firm may avoid direct competition (avoidance) or be so flexible that it can easily leave an industry segment if the battle becomes too intense.

Aggressive Competition

Aggressive competitors use every available resource in an effort to overwhelm rivals, thus reducing the chance that any countermove will be effective. The opening of the Borgata Casino in Atlantic City is an example of overwhelming the competition:

> The opening of the first new casino here in thirteen years would be a big event if the owner of the $1.1 billion Borgata Hotel, Casino and Spa wasn't heralding its debut this July by trashing the opposition. "There is, to a large degree, a generation gap between Borgata and existing properties in Atlantic City," said Robert L. Boughner, chief executive of the casino that rises like a 40-story gold ingot at the north end of this island city. "Many of the other places are just reincarnated old hotels, and they just don't have the technology and the amenities to keep up with us."
>
> Dressed in gunfighter black, Mr. Boughner took a few more shots at his competitors. The other casinos are "slots warehouses," he said in an interview this month, and because they have inadequate ventilation, they smell. "They do—they can't help it," he said. The new Borgata, a joint venture between MGM Mirage Inc. and the Boyd Gaming Corporation, has all the latest casino technology. Instead of opening new restaurants, it features well-known establishments such as the Old Homestead Steakhouse in New York. In addition, the casino features a 35,000 square foot spa and Borgata Babes, reminiscent of the extinct Playboy Bunnys.[31]

Walt Disney Company is another example. Disney uses the most-advanced technologies and the most-talented workers in producing its animated feature films. Then the company floods the market with advertising and promotion. A similar offensive strategy is pursued in its theme parks. High-tech, innovative rides and world-class entertainment based on Disney characters and feature films create a "magical" place that is especially appealing to young people and families.

To be successful, aggressive competition requires significant resources that have high value and are at least somewhat rare. In addition, if those resources are difficult or costly to imitate, the attack may be effective over a longer time frame. Disney has been effective for many years at overwhelming competitors in theme parks and animated feature films due largely to its incredible brand name and its ability to attract the most-talented people for feature films and to attract and train low-cost laborers for its theme parks. Other resources that tend to provide a strong base for aggressive competition include a superior market position; a strong financial position; possession of patents or trade secrets; exclusive contracts; and involvement in a well-organized network of external stakeholders that includes major suppliers, financial institutions, government leaders, and other competitors.

One of the greatest risks of aggressive competition is that a rival will try to match the attack or even top it. Another risk is that the basis for competition may lose power over time. Disney, for instance, enjoyed many decades of almost unchallenged domination in the theme-park industry. The company built its dominant position through a strategy that focuses on children and the families that bring them to the parks, with little that appealed directly to teenagers and young adults with no children. Now Americans are having fewer children and having them later in life. Furthermore, several major competitors have entered the scene with products that have specific appeal to teenagers and young adults. For example, in Orlando, Universal Studios was expanded to become Universal Escape, a complete vacation destination featuring themed resorts and Islands of Adventure, a state-of-the-art, high-tech adventure park that appeals to almost everyone under forty. Vivendi Universal, the French conglomerate that owns Universal, also owns Universal Studios Japan through a joint venture with Osaka Municipal Group. The venture competes directly with Disneyland Tokyo. Disney is still "top dog" in the theme-park market, but its position is weakening and its original strategy in this segment is losing some of its power. In response, Disney has opened its own "adventure park" in California.

In spite of these hazards, aggressive firms tend to have higher performance than do laggards. For example, software firms that engage rivals with a greater number of competitive moves have the highest performance.[32] Also, these sorts of companies tend to elicit slower responses to their moves by competitors, an indication that intimidation is working.[33]

First-Mover Advantage

First-movers also tend to enjoy a competitive advantage. These are firms that stay at the forefront of advances in their industries. Domino's Pizza is an example of a company that has benefited by being a first-mover.

Domino's Pizza built an initial advantage over rivals by being the first to offer home delivery in a half hour or less with a free product guarantee. Rivals at first scorned that tactic, but eventually imitated it. Once most pizza retailers offered home delivery,

Domino's initial advantage was gone. Domino's second action was to offer a giant pizza, the "Big Foot," its third was to distribute direct mail coupons, and fourth was to give its customers handy magnets for easy access to Domino's phone number. Only through a string of actions could Domino's maintain its advantage and keep rivals off guard.[34]

Consistent with the principle of creative destruction, industry leaders are often "dethroned" by aggressive moves by number-two competitors.[35] Consequently, to remain the first-mover in an industry, significant investments in research and development typically are required. Organizational learning ability is also important to this strategy. Not only first-movers, but early imitators as well, or "second-movers" may enjoy higher performance.[36] Some firms have a deliberate strategy of rapidly imitating the innovations of competitors. They enjoy many of the same benefits without all of the research-and-development costs.

Collaboration

Organizations often combine resources in an effort to gain a stronger resource position. In some cases, a leading firm will collaborate with a handpicked group of firms and deliberately exclude others in an effort to weaken them or put them out of business. Or weaker rivals may join forces to gain position relative to a market leader. Collaborative relationships can be hard to duplicate, thus increasing their value as a competitive tool. The joint venture described in Chapter 2 between major competitors Hilton, Hyatt, Marriott, Six Continents, and Starwood to sell discounted hotel rooms over the Internet is an excellent example of this type of collaboration.[37] Rivals will have a hard time duplicating the collective clout of these industry giants. In the airline industry, code-sharing agreements allow airlines sell one another's seats. These types of agreements put airlines without such arrangements at a competitive disadvantage.

Threat of Retaliation

Sometimes organizations will threaten severe retaliation in an effort to discourage competitors from taking actions. For a threat to be believable, an organization should be perceived as having enough resources to carry on an effective battle if one ensues. High liquidity, excess manufacturing capacity, and new-product designs that are being held back for a "rainy day" can be significant in convincing competitors that they would lose more than gain from the conflict.[38]

Multimarket competition means that firms compete in multiple markets simultaneously. When this is the case, a company may fear that its actions in one market could lead to retaliation in another market.

> Historically, Europe's charter carriers did not compete directly with regular airlines. In addition, low-cost carriers were not particularly interested in holiday destination served by the charter airlines. However, the UK's low-cost carriers are now encroaching on holiday business in areas such as Malaga, Alicante and Palma de Mallorca. Also, a sluggish packaged holiday business has led the major charter travel groups to compete more directly with low-cost carriers. For example, the UK company MyTravel (formerly Airtours) has started the budget airline MyTravelLite and in Germany TUI has formed a venture with Germania to launch Hapag-Lloyd Express.[39]

These developments mean that two previously separate transportation segments will be competing against each other in multipoint competition, which is likely to change the dynamics of competition in both industry segments over time. Industries consisting of competitors with a lot of multimarket competition are expected to demonstrate a lot of mutual forbearance, which limits rivalry.[40] Since rivalry is limited, profit margins are expected to be higher in these situations.[41] On the other hand, lack of multimarket contact can lead to more-intense rivalry and lower profit margins.[42]

Government Intervention

Chapter 2 discussed political strategies as a tool to create a more favorable operating environment in which to compete. There will be no attempt here to repeat that discussion. However, it is worth noting that political strategies can be used to attempt to change the rules of the game.

> In a ruling that could reshape the nation's $1.3 trillion credit-card industry, a U.S. district court judge ruled that Visa and MasterCard will no longer be able to bar member banks from issuing cards from rivals. The decision . . . is a major victory for rival card brands American Express and Discover, which effectively have been banned from pursuing relationships with banks that issue Visa or MasterCard.[43]

Barriers to Imitation

One of the most common competitive countermoves is imitation. A "follower" organization can simply imitate the leader's strategy point by point. In fact, most innovations in hospitality are very easy to imitate. Consequently, some leading companies attempt to thwart imitation through erecting a variety of barriers. Some barriers to imitation are similar to barriers to entry discussed in Chapter 2. The primary difference is that barriers to imitation are intended to prevent existing competitors from imitating sources of cost savings or differentiation, whereas barriers to entry are created to discourage other companies from entering the industry. Also, many barriers to entry are possessed by most existing firms; therefore, they affect new entrants rather than incumbent firms. Most automobiles, for example, are built in large factories that enjoy economies of scale. Nevertheless, as a practical matter, many of the entry barriers are the same as imitation barriers.

Organizations may discourage imitation in a number of ways. A company may build a significantly larger and more expensive hotel, thus achieving economies of scale that are hard to duplicate. A firm may develop a highly valuable and hard-to-imitate brand name or trademark. In addition, special relationships with external stakeholders can be difficult to copy. For example, an organization may have special arrangements with a financial institution, an excellent relationship with its union, or an exclusive-supply agreement with one of its suppliers. In addition, an organization may deter entry through new service proliferation, significant investments in advertising, cutting prices, or withholding information about the profitability of a service so that potential competitors will not be eager to duplicate it.[44]

As discussed in Chapter 3, intangible assets are among the most difficult to imitate. For example, a particular service is fairly easy to imitate, but the research-and-development processes that went into creating the service are more difficult to reproduce. Consequently, an organization with an excellent ability to innovate may be able to create a barrier to imitation. By the time competitors have imitated a service, the company has moved on to other new services. Organizational-learning ability is similarly difficult to imitate. Organizational learning can lead to private information (secrets) that results in higher performance. Consequently, an organization can build a barrier to imitation by fostering learning processes (Chapter 9 will cover this topic in detail). Finally, a high-performance organizational culture is difficult to copy.

Strategic Flexibility

Strategic flexibility allows a firm to earn high returns while managing the amount of risk it faces.[45] Flexibility means that a company can move its resources out of declining markets and into more-prosperous ones in a minimum amount of time. Exit barriers influence a firm to remain in a market or industry after it is no longer attractive for investment. For example, an organization may have a significant investment in a large resort. Selling the resort would result in a major loss, and closing it is not a reasonable option. Strategic exit barriers can also reduce flexibility. These barriers are a result of reluctance to sacrifice the benefits of intangible assets that have accumulated through previous investments. Some of these may include loss of synergies created through linkages with other businesses, loss of customers, or loss of a market position.

Organizations can retain strategic flexibility by reducing investments in assets that are likely to create large exit barriers. For example, lodging companies greatly enhance their strategic flexibility when they manage properties that are owned by others. Similarly, restaurants often lease space and many airlines lease their planes. Keeping large capital assets off the balance sheet frees up capital for expansion and reduces potential losses if the assets become unproductive. On the other hand, companies forego the additional revenue potential from owning the assets. The important thing to remember at this point is that the level of strategic flexibility is a decision.

Avoidance

Each of the strategies above can require a great deal of managerial attention and, in some cases, significant other resources. However, some firms simply avoid confrontation completely by focusing on a particular niche in the market in which other firms have little interest (Porter's focus strategy). In hospitality, a niche can be a small segment of the market or a small geographic area. A restaurant company, for instance, might specialize in a particular nationality of food that does not draw a lot of customers. Or a company could locate its hotels in out-of-the-way areas. Or, as in the case of Steve Rushmore, a company can offer services that nobody else is offering.

> Rushmore, founder and president of hotel consulting company HVS International, got his start by performing hotel feasibility studies and appraisals. "Back then [the early 1980s], you had companies such as Laventhol and PKF, both of which could do feasibility studies, but not appraisals," Rushmore recalls. "Then there were the appraisers, and they were regionally oriented generalists. All of the appraisers were economic majors and some were engineers, but none were from hotels schools."[46]

The French retailer Carrefour, the second-largest retailer in the world, has prospered in international markets where Wal-Mart does not have a foothold:

> Carrefour's most significant edge on Wal-Mart, though, is the French group's commanding presence in markets where the Americans—late arrivals on the international retail scene—are either at the startup stage or have yet to plant their flag. "Carrefour is the world's most successful international retailer," says Jaime Vasquez, an industry analyst at Salomon Smith Barney in London, adding, "Wal-Mart has no track record outside North America."[47]

Actually, Wal-Mart is ahead of Carrefour in Mexico and has made recent acquisitions in Germany and Britain. However, in all other international markets, Carrefour is way ahead. It can't last forever. As the two titans continue to grow, they will eventually clash.

RESOURCES, INDUSTRY STRUCTURE, AND FIRM ACTIONS

Many of the strategies contained in this section require a strong resource position or excellent stakeholder relationships.[48] For example, for aggressive competition to succeed, a firm must have better or more resources than competitors do. First-movers need significant resources associated with innovation and learning. Collaboration requires a network of excellent relationships with external stakeholders. Successful government intervention comes from excellent relationships with government leaders or parties. Firms with strong or unused (slack) resources are in a strong position to pursue most of the strategic options. On the other hand, firms with poor resources are limited in their abilities to pursue aggressive strategies. They may need to avoid direct competition or to develop strategic flexibility until their resource positions are stronger.

The characteristics of an industry determine, in part, the tactics an organization will pursue. Rapid industry growth typically is associated with lower levels of rivalry because firms do not have to steal market share to increase sales.[49] Also, a high level of concentration (a few firms hold most of the market share) should reduce the motivation of rivals to compete aggressively. If entry or imitation barriers are high, there is less competitive pressure from potential entrants.[50] Figure 5.2 illustrates the effect firm resources and industry structure have on firm actions and competitor reactions over time. After an organization acts, competitors will respond in turn, thus changing the resource positions of each company, as well as industry structure. The cycle then continues with moves, countermoves, and resulting changes.

Thus far, this discussion has centered on specific strategies firms might pursue to deal with competitive dynamics. Another important aspect of competitive dynamics is anticipating the countermoves of rivals. The question is, "How are competitors likely to respond to a strategic move?" Anticipation of competitor reactions is vital to understanding how effective a strategy may be. The two factors already identified in this section, resource position and industry characteristics, are very important to predicting countermoves. For example, a rival with a strong resource position is much more likely to respond with a countermove. Also, a slow-growing industry is more likely to elicit a response from competitors than is an industry that is growing rapidly. However, several other factors can play a role in determining whether a firm will countermove and what form the response will take.

| FIGURE 5.2 | THE RELATIONSHIP AMONG RESOURCES, INDUSTRY STRUCTURE, AND ACTIONS OVER TIME |

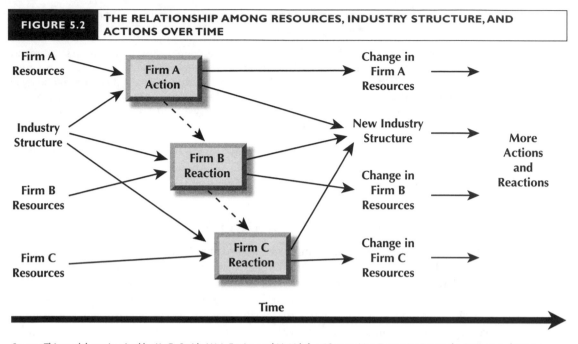

Source: This model was inspired by K. G. Smith, W. J. Ferrier, and H. Ndofor, "Competitive Dynamics Research: Critique and Future Directions," in *The Blackwell Handbook of Strategic Management,* ed. M. A. Hitt, R. E. Freeman, and J. S. Harrison (Oxford: Blackwell Publishers, 2001), 315–368.

Predicting the potential response of a competitor also has a lot to do with the goals of its managers.[51] If a planned strategy is likely to interfere with the goals found in a competitor organization, that organization is likely to respond with a countermove. For example, a company may launch a strategy to grow in a particular market. If another company's goals depend on that market, a strong reaction can be expected.

> Boeing has historically dominated the Japanese market for commercial aircraft. In fact, Boeing's planes account for 84 percent of the nation's commercial fleets. Recently, the European rival Airbus Industrie began an attack on Boeing's dominance through expanding its Japanese office and making allies of Japanese businesses. Airbus recently targeted Japan with its new A380 superjumbo jet, which holds up to eight hundred people. Large jets are important in Japan because its airports are so congested. Airbus should have expected a strong reaction. It came in the form of a newly designed Boeing 747X, a stretch model that will accommodate up to 520 passengers and will cost $20 million less than the Airbus A380.[52]

On the other hand, sometimes companies pursue different segments of the market (avoidance strategy), allowing a less aggressive atmosphere to develop. An organization should also try to understand the assumptions of competing firm managers about their organization and the industry. For example, managers may assume that a countermove will be detrimental because such moves have been harmful in the past. Or firm managers may see their organization as a follower.

Of course, a competitor is not likely to respond if it is unaware that a firm has pursued a strategic action. Consequently, the strength of a firm's environmental-scanning and -analysis abilities and the awareness of its top managers to significant events in the industry also play a role in whether a countermove will be pursued.[53] Newer or smaller organizations are less likely to be aware of precisely what larger, older competitors are doing.

In summary, some of the characteristics that help an organization anticipate the response of a competitor to a particular strategic move include strength of its resource position, characteristics of the industry, goals and assumptions of competing-firm managers, and awareness of competitive actions. When a strategy is formulated, managers should try to anticipate the reactions of competitors in order to more accurately assess the potential outcomes.

TRACKING COMPETITOR MOVEMENT

One way to keep track of the strategies of competing firms is with a strategic-group map such as the one in Figure 5.3. A strategic-group map categorizes existing industry competitors into groups that follow similar strategies. To construct a strategic-group map, first identify strategic dimensions that are important in the industry, such as breadth of services, quality level, or national-vs.-regional participation. The axes of a strategic-group map should describe strategy and not performance. Therefore, variables such as pricing strategy, customer-service approach, level of advertising, and service mix are appropriate, whereas return on assets and earnings per share are not. Furthermore, to reveal more about the industry, the dimensions should not be highly correlated with one another. Once the variables are selected, a grid may be constructed by plotting industry rivals on the relevant dimensions.

Organizations that end up in the same general location on a map are called strategic groups. Consequently, they have similar strategies based on the dimensions found in the map. Strategic-group maps can help an organization understand the strategies of competitors. For example, competitors within the same strategic group, such as Marriott and Hilton, are in direct competition for customers, whereas competitors in different strategic groups, such as Days Inn and the Ritz Carlton, do not compete directly. Strategic-group maps sometimes highlight an area in the industry in which no firms are currently competing (a strategic opportunity). For instance, short-haul, no-frills airlines occupy a competitive arena that was almost empty before airline deregulation.

Strategic-group maps may also be used to track the evolution of an industry over time. In the past few years, traditional low-end fast food restaurants have lost sales dollars to "fast casual" restaurants such as Chipotle and Sbarro. In addition, lower-end family restaurants like Denny's have given up market share to more upscale family restaurants such as Applebee's and Cracker Barrel.

On the other hand, one of the weaknesses associated with strategic-group maps is that organizations can belong to several strategic groups, depending on the dimensions that are used to form the groups. For example, Hilton and Marriott compete in both the high-end and the affordable (through Hampton Inn and Courtyard) hotel categories. Since the choice of dimensions is somewhat subjective and dependent entirely on the industry under study, strategic-group maps do not provide answers, but they help raise relevant questions

---

FIGURE 5.3 | **STRATEGIC-GROUP MAP OF RESTAURANT CHAINS IN THE U.S.**

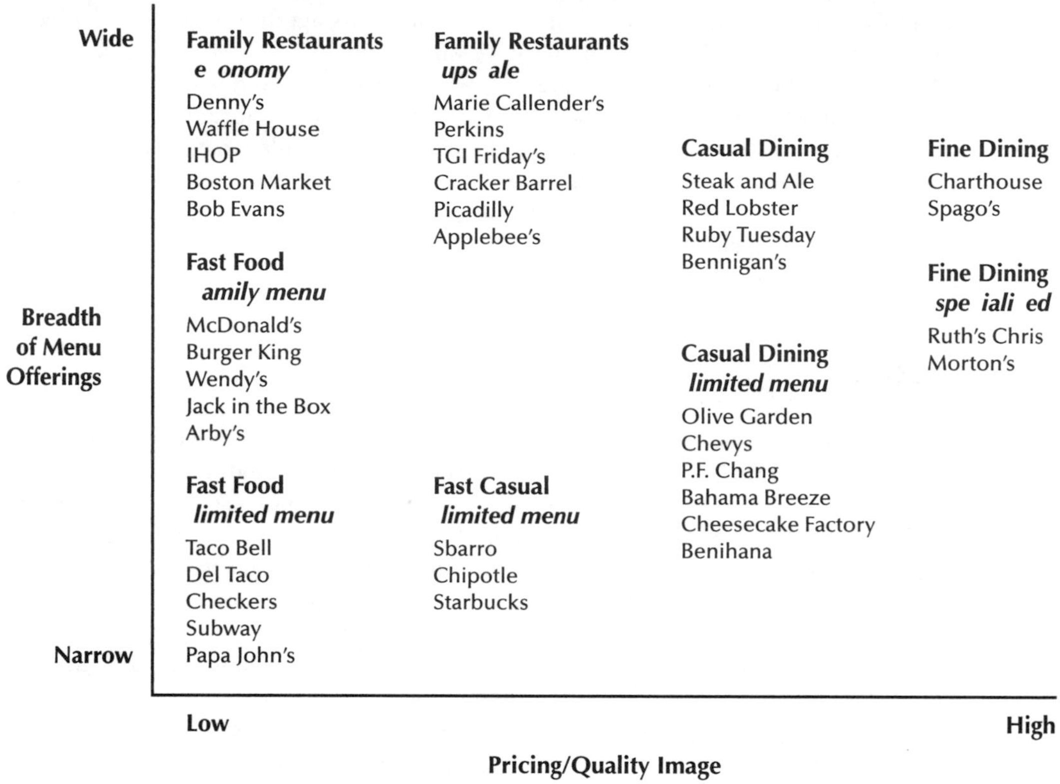

Wide	**Family Restaurants** *e onomy*	**Family Restaurants** *ups ale*		
	Denny's	Marie Callender's		
	Waffle House	Perkins	**Casual Dining**	**Fine Dining**
	IHOP	TGI Friday's	Steak and Ale	Charthouse
	Boston Market	Cracker Barrel	Red Lobster	Spago's
	Bob Evans	Picadilly	Ruby Tuesday	
		Applebee's	Bennigan's	**Fine Dining**
	Fast Food *amily menu*			*spe iali ed*
Breadth of Menu Offerings	McDonald's		**Casual Dining**	Ruth's Chris
	Burger King		*limited menu*	Morton's
	Wendy's			
	Jack in the Box		Olive Garden	
	Arby's		Chevys	
			P.F. Chang	
	Fast Food *limited menu*	**Fast Casual** *limited menu*	Bahama Breeze	
			Cheesecake Factory	
	Taco Bell	Sbarro	Benihana	
	Del Taco	Chipotle		
	Checkers	Starbucks		
	Subway			
Narrow	Papa John's			

Low   **High**

Pricing/Quality Image

about the current state and direction of competitive rivalry. As noted, they may also help firms discover untapped market opportunities.

KEY-POINTS SUMMARY

The responsibilities of business-level managers include establishing the overall direction of a business unit, ongoing analysis of the changing business situation, selecting a generic strategy and a strategic posture through which to implement it, and acquiring and managing resources. The generic business-level strategies described in this chapter are cost leadership, differentiation, best value, and focus. Firms may focus through cost leadership, differentiation, or best value. The distinguishing feature of a focus strategy is that energy is focused on a narrow, as opposed to a broad, segment of the market.

Companies that pursue cost leadership actively seek resources that will allow them to produce services at the lowest possible cost. Hospitality firms that pursue differentiation attempt to distinguish services in such a way that they have greater value to their consumers. Best-value strategies combine elements of both differentiation and low cost. Many organizations have implemented programs that enhance speed or quality in an effort to produce a service that is the best value.

Organizational dynamics is defined as the moves and countermoves of industry competitors. Markets are in a constant state of flux, with a competitive move setting off a series of reactions and countermoves. Organizations can pursue a variety of strategies in response to competitive dynamics. They include aggressive competition, seeking a first-mover advantage, collaborative agreements with stakeholders, threats of retaliation, seeking government intervention, erecting barriers to imitation, remaining flexible enough to move in and out of markets with relative ease, and avoiding direct competition completely. Sometimes organizations combine these approaches.

DISCUSSION QUESTIONS

1. What are the strategic management responsibilities of a business-unit manager? Explain what each of these responsibilities entails.

2. Describe the generic business-level strategies found in this chapter. Provide an example of hospitality brands that you think are pursuing each of these strategies.

3. How can an organization pursue the business-level strategy of low-cost leadership?

4. How can an organization pursue a differentiation strategy?

5. What are some of the risks associated with a cost leadership, differentiation, best value, and focus strategy?

6. How can an emphasis on quality help a firm pursing a best-value strategy?

7. What are competitive dynamics? Why has competition become more dynamic in the past few decades?

8. Describe the eight strategies that reflect competitive dynamics.

9. Of the strategies that reflect competitive dynamics, which one seems to be the highest risk? Why? Which one seems to be the lowest risk? Why?

10. If you were a market leader in a segment of the hotel industry, which of the strategies that reflect competitive dynamics would probably be the most attractive to you? If you were a weak competitor with few resources, which strategy would you likely find attractive?

NOTES

1. Opening quotation and other material come from J. Bloom, "AdAge Special Report: Marketer of the Year: Upstart JetBlue Marketer of the Year," *Advertising Age,* 9 December 2002, 49; C. Woodyard, "JetBlue Soars on CEO's Creativity," *USA Today,* 8 October 2002, B1; M. Wells, "Lord of the Skies," *Forbes,* 14 October 2002, 130–135.

2. H. J. Bryce, *Financial and Strategic Management for Nonprofit Organizations* (Englewood Cliffs, N.J.: Prentice Hall, 1987).

3. This discussion of generic strategies draws heavily from concepts found in M. E. Porter, *Competitive Strategy: Techniques for Analyzing Industries and Competitors* (New York: The Free Press, 1980), chap. 2.

4. Porter, *Competitive Strategy.*

5. R. Evans, "Le Motel 6, C'est Moi," *Barron's,* 30 April 2001, 20–22.

6. This discussion of factors leading to cost savings is based, in part, on Porter, *Competitive Strategy;* M. E. Porter, *Competitive Advantage: Creating and Sustaining Superior Performance* (New York: The Free Press, 1985); and R. W. Schmenner, "Before You Build a Big Factory," *Harvard Business Review* 54 (July/August 1976): 100–104.

7. As defined by Schmenner, "Before You Build."

8. M. E. Porter, "What Is Strategy?" *Harvard Business Review* 74, no. 6 (November/December 1996): 61.

9. The same principles apply to "experience effects." In this book, the two terms will be used synonymously.

10. W. J. Abernathy and K. Wayne, "Limits of the Learning Curve," *Harvard Business Review* 52, no. 5 (September/October 1974): 109–119; Boston Consulting Group, *Perspectives on Experience* (Boston: Boston Consulting Group, 1972); W. B. Hirschman, "Profit from the Learning Curve," *Harvard Business Review* 43, no. 3 (January/February 1964): 125–139.

11. Porter, "What Is Strategy?" 62.

12. A. Paszton, M. Branningan, and S. McCartney, "ValuJet's Penny-pinching Comes under Scrutiny," *The Wall Street Journal,* 14 May 1996, A2, A4.

13. Quotes from C. Binkley and D. Clark, "Wi-Fi Is Now a Must for Big Hotels," *The Wall Street Journal,* 27 February 2003, D3; H. Green, "Wi-Fi Means Business," *Business Week,* 28 April 2003, 86–92.

14. E. Mansfield, "How Rapidly Does New Industrial Technology Leak Out?" *Journal of Industrial Economics* (December 1985): 217.

15. P. Ghemawat, "Sustainable Advantage," *Harvard Business Review* 64, no. 5 (September/October 1986: 53.

16. C. W. L. Hill, "Differentiation versus Low Cost or Differentiation and Low Cost: A Contingency Framework," *Academy of Management Review* 13 (1988): 403. See also A. I. Murray, "A Contingency View of Porter's 'Generic Strategies,'" *Academy of Management Review* 13 (1988): 390–400.

17. "Firmdale's Idiosyncrasies Are Its Key to Success," *Hotel Report* (April 2002).

18. M. K. Starr, ed., *Global Competitiveness: Getting the U.S. Back on Track* (New York: W. W. Norton, 1988), 307.

19. W. E. Demming, *Out of the Crisis* (Cambridge, Mass.: MIT Press, 1982); L. W. Phillips, D. Chang, and R. D. Buzzell, "Product Quality, Cost Position, and Business Performance," *Journal of Marketing* 47 (1983): 26–43; M. Walton, *Deming Management at Work* (New York: Putnam, 1990).

20. C. H. Deutsch, "Six Sigma Enlightenment," *The New York Times,* 7 December 1998; reprinted in E. H. Bernstein, *Strategic Management* (Guilford, Conn: McGrawhill/Dushkin, 2001), 151.

21. "We Encourage Innovation, Accept Accountability and Embrace Change," *Annual Report 2001,* Starwood Hotels and Resorts Worldwide, Inc., 3.

22. "Who We Are," *2001 Annual Report,* Four Seasons Hotels, Inc., 1.

23. "Mission," http://www.jumeirahinternational.com/ji_site/aboutus/aboutus.asp; October 2002; also personal experience of Jatin Bagga, who worked for the hotel for three years.

24. A. Martinez, "The City Life: Hotels with an Attitude," *The New York Times,* 13 August, 2001, A16.

25. M. Beirne, "Let It All Hang Out: When Joe Boxer and W Hotels Team Up, It's 'Let's Hear it for the Boys!' " *Brandweek,* 9 December 2002, 32; D. Goetzl, "Starwood's W Hotel Ads Display Interior Motives," *Advertising Age,* 18 September 2000, 13.

26. G. G. Dess and J. C. Picken, "Creating Competitive (Dis)advantage: Learning from Food Lion's Freefall," *Academy of Management Executive* 13, no. 3 (1999): 100.

27. J. Schumpeter, *The Theory of Economic Development* (Cambridge, Mass.: Harvard University Press, 1934).

28. K. G. Smith, W. J. Ferrier, and H. Ndofor, "Competitive Dynamics Research: Critique and Future Directions," in *The Blackwell Handbook of Strategic Management,* ed. M. A. Hitt, R. E. Freeman, and J. S. Harrison (Oxford: Blackwell Publishers, 2001), 315–361.

29. Predicasts, *Predicasts' Funk and Scott Index, United States Annual Edition* (Cleveland, Ohio: Predicasts, 1993).

30. All of these trends are well documented in C. M. Grimm and K. G. Smith, *Strategy as Action: Industry Rivalry and Coordination* (Cincinnati, Ohio: South-Western College Publishing, 1997).

31. I. Peterson, "A New Casino Is Coming," *The New York Times,* 27 April 2003, 41, 46; http://www.atlanticcityhotelsdirect.com/casinos/borgata_casino_spa.html, July 10, 2003.

32. G. Young, K. G. Smith, and C. Grimm, "Austrian and Industrial Organization Perspectives on Firm-Level Competitive Activity and Performance," *Organization Science* 73 (1996): 243–254.

33. K. G. Smith, C. Grimm, and M. Gannon, *Dynamics of Competitive Strategy* (London: Sage Publications, 1992).

34. Grimm and Smith, *Strategy as Action,* 99.

35. W. Ferrier, K. Smith, and C. Grimm, "The Role of Competition in Market Share Erosion and Dethronement: A Study of Industry Leaders and Challengers," *Academy of Management Journal* 43 (1999): 372–388.

36. H. Lee et al., "Timing, Order, and Durability of New Product Advantages with Imitation," *Strategic Management Journal* 21 (2000): 23–30.

37. R. Abramson, "Pegasus Gets a Lift From Online Hotel-Reservation Deal," *The Wall Street Journal,* 12 February 2002: B4; J. N. Ader and T. McCoy, "Web Storm Rising," *Lodging Industry* (August 2002): 1.

38. P. Ghemawat, *Strategy and the Business Landscape* (Upper Saddle River, N.J.: Prentice Hall, 2001).

39. C. Baker, "Vertical Shift," *Airline Business,* October 2002, 64–65.

40. G. Young, K. G. Smith, C. Grimm, and D. Simon, "Multimarket Contact, Resource Heterogeneity, and Rivalrous Firm Behavior," *Journal of Management* (2003): in press.

41. J. Gimeno and C. Woo, "Multimarket Contact, Economies of Scope, and Firm Performance," *Academy of Management Journal* 42 (1999): 323–341.

42. Smith, Ferrier, and Ndofor, "Competitive Dynamics."

43. J. Sapsford and P. Beckett, "Visa and MasterCard Must Allow Banks to Issue Rivals' Credit Cards, Judge Rules," *The Wall Street Journal*, 10 October 2001, A3.

44. Grimm and Smith, *Strategy as Action.*

45. K. R. Harrigan, "Strategic Flexibility in the Old and New Economies," in *Blackwell Handbook*, ed. Hitt, Freeman, and Harrison, 98–123.

46. R.A. Nozar, "The House That Steve Built," *Lodging Magazine* (October 2002), 44.

47. R. Tomlinson, "Who's Afraid of Wal-Mart," *Fortune*, 26 June 2000, 186–196.

48. Smith, Ferrier, and Ndofor, "Competitive Dynamics."

49. K. G. Smith et al,, "Predictors of Response Time to Competitive Strategic Actions: Preliminary Theory and Evidence," *Journal of Business Research* 183 (1989): 245–259.

50. Smith, Ferrier, and Ndofor, "Competitive Dynamics."

51. Porter, *Competitive Strategy.*

52. S. Holmes, C. Dawson, and C. Matlack, "Rumble over Tokyo," *Business Week*, 2 April 2001, 80–81.

53. Smith, Ferrier, and Ndofor, "Competitive Dynamics."

CHAPTER

6

Corporate-Level Strategy and Restructuring

$\mathcal{M}$arriott International, Inc. is a diversified hospitality company that operates in six business segments:

Full-Service Lodging—Marriott Hotels, Resorts, and Suites; and Renaissance Hotels, Resorts, and Suites

Luxury Lodging—Ritz-Carlton; Bvlgari Hotels and Resorts; and J. W. Marriott Hotels and Resorts

Select-Service Lodging—Courtyard by Marriott, Fairfield Inn by Marriott, SpringHill Suites, and Ramada International Hotels and Resorts

Extended-Stay Lodging—Residence Inn, TownePlace Suites, Marriott ExecuStay, and Marriott Executive Apartments

Vacation Ownership—development, marketing, ownership, and operation of a variety of time-share properties under the names Marriott Vacation Club International, The Ritz-Carlton Club, Horizons by Marriott, and Marriott Grand Residence Club

Synthetic Fuel—operation of coal-based synthetic fuel production facilities

Until recently, Marriott was also involved in senior-living services through ownership and operation of residences for senior citizens, as well as wholesale food distribution. However, management decided to exit these businesses. Marriott has used a variety of growth techniques, including acquisitions, internal development and joint ventures with other companies. For example, Ritz-Carlton was acquired, Courtyard was developed internally, and Bvlgari Hotels and Resorts is a joint venture with luxury goods designer Bvlgari S.p.A. (of Italy).

Marriott also has a special relationship with Host Marriott Corporation, which has been a separate real estate investment trust since 1993. Host Marriott is the largest hotel REIT, with over a hundred hotels. Many, but not all, of Host Marriott's hotels are operated by Marriott International. J. W. Marriott Jr. is the chairman and CEO of Marriott International. Richard E. Marriott is chairman of the board and Christopher J. Nassetta is president and chief executive officer of Host Marriott.[1]

INTRODUCTION

Like many large hospitality companies, Marriott is pursuing a strategy called related diversification. The primary operations of the company focus on lodging, through nightly room rentals, longer-term stays, or time-share. Synthetic fuel operations represent an immaterial portion of the company's operations and are retained solely for tax reasons. As noted, Marriott's related diversification strategy is carried out through developing businesses from within the company, acquisitions, and/or joint ventures.

This chapter begins with a discussion of concentration, vertical integration, and diversification, the three basic corporate-level strategies. A comparison of these three strategies is followed by a detailed analysis of acquisition strategies, an important tactic firms use to diversify. We would like to point out that vertical integration, diversification, and mergers are corporate-level strategies and tactics, but they can also be applied within the business units of larger companies. For example, the president of a single division could decide to diversify the business through an acquisition of a firm in a related industry. The acquisition might have to be approved at the corporate level, but it could still be executed at the business level. Nevertheless, the focus of this chapter will be on the corporate level, while recognizing that much of this discussion can sometimes apply to individual business units as well.

Corporate-level strategy is formulated by the CEO and other top managers. An organization may have several business units or divisions that are run by individual managers. Those managers establish strategy for their own units, but not for the corporation as a whole. At the corporate level, primary strategy-formulation responsibilities include setting the direction of the entire organization, formulation of a corporate strategy, selection of businesses in which to compete, selection of tactics for diversification and growth, and management of corporate resources and capabilities. These responsibilities and the key issues associated with each responsibility are listed in Table 6.1.

TABLE 6.1	MAJOR CORPORATE-LEVEL STRATEGIC MANAGEMENT RESPONSIBILITIES
Major Responsibilities	**Key Issues**
Direction setting	Establishment and communication of organizational mission, vision, enterprise strategy, and long-term goals
Development of corporate-level strategy	Selection of a broad approach to corporate-level strategy—concentration, vertical integration, diversification, international expansion
	Selection of resources and capabilities in which to build corporate-wide distinctive competencies
Selection of businesses and portfolio management	Management of the corporate portfolio of businesses—buying businesses, selling businesses
	Allocation of resources to business units for capital equipment, R&D, etc.
Selection of tactics for diversification and growth	Choosing among methods of diversification—internal venturing, acquisitions, joint ventures
Management of resources	Acquisition of resources and/or development of competencies leading to a sustainable competitive advantage for the entire corporation
	Hiring, firing and rewarding business-unit managers
	Ensure that the business units (divisions) within the corporation are well managed, including strategic management; provide training where appropriate
	Develop a high-performance corporate management structure
	Developing control systems to ensure that strategies remain relevant and that the corporation continues to progress toward its goals

Hospitality organizations typically begin as entrepreneurial ventures providing a single hotel, restaurant, casino, or service, or, in the case of an airline, one or a few flights in a limited market. This type of corporate-level strategy, called *concentration*, is associated with a narrow business definition. As long as an organization has virtually all of its resource investments in one business area, it is still concentrating. With this strategy, a firm may pursue growth through internal business ventures, mergers and acquisitions, or joint ventures. Some organizations never stop concentrating, in spite of their size. For instance, Delta Air Lines is still pursuing a concentration strategy.

As they grow, successful organizations often abandon their concentration strategies due to market saturation, excess resources that they need to find a use for, or some other reason. Through internal ventures, mergers and acquisitions, or joint ventures, they pursue businesses outside their core business areas. Corporate strategy typically evolves from concentration to some form of vertical integration or diversification of products, functions served, markets, or technologies (see Figure 6.1).[2] Diversification that stems from common markets, functions served, technologies, or services is referred to as related diversification. Unrelated diversification is not based on commonality among the activities of the corporation. Organizations may continue to pursue vertical integration and/or diversification successfully for many years, each time expanding their business definitions.

Many organizations eventually come to a point at which slow growth, declining profits, or some other situation forces corporate-level managers to "rethink" their entire organizations. Disgruntled stakeholders—including stockholders, employees, and managers—often drive this process. The result is usually some form of restructuring. Restructuring often involves reducing the business definition combined with refocusing

---

FIGURE 6.1   **CORPORATE-LEVEL STRATEGIES**

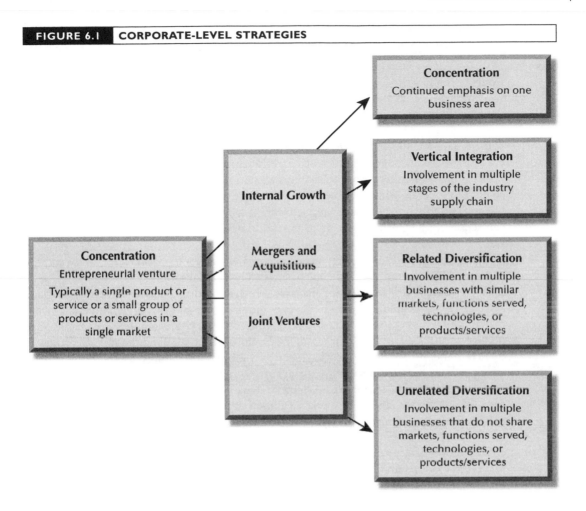

efforts on the things the organization does well. It is interesting to note that prior to recent restructuring, Marriott was significantly more diversified, with significant investment into senior-living facilities and food distribution. However, the company has now reduced the scope of its activities. This type of restructuring strategy is called downscoping. Most successful restructuring efforts result in a leaner (i.e., fewer employees, less capital equipment), less-diversified organization. The organization may then cycle back and begin a cautious, better educated, and more focused program of diversification or vertical integration. Restructuring will be discussed at the end of this chapter.

CONCENTRATION STRATEGIES

Loews Hotels is a 55-year-old company that focuses on owning and operating upscale and unique hotels. The company is currently in the midst of the largest expansion in the chain's history, with many new projects under way. Nevertheless, it continues to be a single business enterprise. The company is based in New York City, and has eighteen hotels in the locations of New York City, Tucson, Washington D.C., Annapolis, Orlando, Nashville, San Diego, Santa Monica, Denver, Miami, Chicago, Philadelphia, Montreal, and Quebec City.[3]

Concentration is the least complicated of the corporate-level strategies, but it is still pursued by many large and successful companies. Domino's Pizza, for example, started out small, with just one store in 1960. By 1983, there were 1,000 Domino's stores, and 5,000 in 1989. Today, there are more than 7,000 stores—including more than 2,000 outside the United States. As the second largest pizza delivery company in the United States, it has an operating network of company-owned and franchise-owned stores, but it continues to be a single-business enterprise.[4] Many regional casinos, airlines, and hotel and restaurant chains also operate with a concentration strategy. Diversification is sometimes a necessity because too much dependence on one business area provides a substantial business risk. Consequently, a concentration strategy is associated with both strengths and weaknesses (see Table 6.2).

The strengths of a concentration strategy are readily apparent. First, concentration allows an organization to master one business. This specialization allows top executives to obtain in-depth knowledge of the business, which should reduce strategic mistakes. Also, since all resources are directed at doing one thing well, the organization may be in a better position to develop the resources and capabilities necessary to establish a sustainable competitive advantage. Domino's, for example, was the innovator behind the sturdy, corrugated pizza box and the "spoodle," a saucing tool that combines the features of a spoon and a ladle, which cuts the time spent saucing a pizza. Furthermore, organizational resources are under less strain. Lack of ambiguity concerning strategic direction may also allow consensus to form among top managers. High levels of consensus are sometimes associated with superior organizational performance. In fact, a concentration strategy has sometimes been found to be more profitable than other corporate-level strategies.[5] Of course, the profitability of a concentration strategy depends largely on the industry in which a firm is involved.

On the other hand, concentration strategies entail several risks, especially when environments are unstable. Since the organization depends on one product or business area to sustain itself, change can dramatically reduce organizational performance. The airline industry is a good example of the effects of uncertainty on organizational performance. Prior to deregulation, most of the major carriers were profitable. They had protected routes

TABLE 6.2	ADVANTAGES AND DISADVANTAGES OF A CONCENTRATION STRATEGY
Advantages	**Disadvantages**
• Allows an organization to master one business	• Dependence on one area is problematic if the industry is unstable
• Less strain on resources, allowing more of an opportunity to develop a sustainable competitive advantage	• Primary service or product may become obsolete
• Lack of ambiguity concerning strategic direction	• Difficult to grow when the industry matures
• Often found to be a profitable strategy, depending on the industry	• Significant changes in the industry can be very hard to deal with
	• Cash flow can be a serious problem

and fixed prices. However, deregulation and the ensuing increase in competition hurt the profitability of all domestic carriers. Since most of the major carriers were pursuing concentration strategies, they did not have other business areas to offset their losses. Consequently, several airlines were acquired or went bankrupt. However, the industry did not seem to learn its lesson. In the aftermath of the September 11, 2001 disasters, most airlines would have gone bankrupt without help from the U.S. government. Once again, inadequate diversification reduced their ability to deal with the shock.

> Airlines have not always followed concentration strategies; in fact, they have often sometimes in the hotel business. Early on Pan Am created the Inter-Continental chain with locations at "every way stop where the company might touch down."[6] Air France started its hotel operations in 1948 with the subsidiary Relais Aeriens FrancaisBack, to provide hotel facilities in African destinations served by the airline. Whether we look at Japan Airlines' (JAL's) Nikko hotels or KLM's partial ownership of Golden Tulip Hotels, the two businesses have often been linked. American Airlines entered the hotel business in the early 1970s, with American Hotels Chain, but exited later in that decade. United Airlines owned the Westin chain. In 1967 Trans World Airlines (TWA) purchased Hilton International as part of its diversification strategy, but was later sold to the corporate raider, Carl Icahn. Today, U.S. airlines have gotten out of the hotel business admitting that it required too much time and effort following deregulation. In addition, the hotel/airline relationships did not provide the necessary offsets in bad times; when one industry was doing poorly typically the other one was also taking losses.[7]

Product obsolescence and industry maturity create additional risks for organizations pursuing a concentration strategy. If the principal product or service of an organization becomes obsolete or matures, organizational performance can suffer until the company develops another product that appeals to the market. Consumer demand for healthy food, for example, spurred McDonald's Corporation to offer new menu items such as a McVeggie burger and to sell burgers free of antibiotics.[8] Some firms are never able to duplicate earlier successes. Furthermore, since they have experience in only one line of business, they have limited ability to switch to other areas when times get tough; consequently, many are eventually acquired by another company or go bankrupt. Fortunately, obsolescence is not a particularly strong influence in the hospitality industry. Services such as lodging, gaming, restaurants, and vacations are not likely to disappear. However, a particular format can become obsolete. For example, many "low-tech" basic casino hotels in Las Vegas have been torn down to make room for trendy casino hotels. Concentration strategies are also susceptible to problems when the chosen industry is undergoing significant evolution and is converging with other industries. For example, as the telecommunications industry evolves, entire segments are converging. Some local telephone operating companies are now offering cable-television services through a modified version of the telephone long-distance lines, which represents a substantial diversification away from local telephone services. In hospitality, technological advancements are also causing a lot of convergence, especially in reservations and the level of technology-based services offered to guests. As the quick-service segment of the restaurant industry matures and evolves, even McDonald's, an organization that has been extremely successful with a concentration strategy, has moved toward diversification. Companies that fail to diversify in ways that are consistent with industry evolution and convergence can often find themselves short of the next generation of products and services.

Concentration strategies can also lead to cash flow problems. While a business is growing, the organization may find itself in a "cash poor" situation, since growth often entails additional investments in capital equipment and marketing. On the other hand, once growth levels off, the organization is likely to find itself in a "cash rich" situation, with limited opportunities for profitable investment in the business itself. In fact, this may be one of the most popular reasons that organizations in mature markets begin to diversify.[9] Having exhausted all reasonable opportunities to reinvest cash in innovation, renewal, or revitalization, organizational managers may look to other areas for growth. Of course, the company might also consider increasing dividends, but at some point managers feel a responsibility to profitably invest cash rather than simply returning it to shareholders. Finally, a concentration strategy may not provide enough challenge or stimulation to managers. In other words, they may begin to get tired of doing the same things year after year. This is less true in organizations that are growing rapidly, since growth typically provides excitement and promotion opportunities.

VERTICAL INTEGRATION STRATEGIES

Some of the most common examples of vertical integration in the hospitality industry are between hotels and restaurants. Ritz-Carlton and Marriott both emerged from restaurants, and Forte, before it merged with Trust House, owned luxury hotels and fast-food restaurants. As noted earlier, numerous attempts have been made to integrate hotels and airlines, although most of these efforts have proved to be unsuccessful. Some industries, such as steel and wood products, contain firms that are predominantly vertically integrated. In hospitality, vertical integration strategies have been frequently tried but have failed to provide the anticipated synergies. Often hotel companies like Hyatt exit from the airline sector, as it did five years after buying Braniff Airlines. However, since research has not generally found vertical integration to be a highly profitable strategy relative to other corporate-level strategies, this may not be a serious issue.[10]

Vertical growth can be accomplished by either backward integration, when a company produces its own inputs, or forward integration, when it provides its own distribution. Importing and roasting coffee beans, acquiring a bakery, or growing its own vegetables are examples of backward integration because the restaurant company assumes functions previously provided by a supplier. Site selection, design, and construction of hotel projects through the late 1980s made Marriott Corporation a backward-integrated hotel developer with skill in constructing large numbers of hotels. Cendant Corporation characterizes itself as "One of the most geographically diverse and vertically integrated travel distribution companies in the global travel industry."[11] Its use of forward integration is reflected in its travel distribution services such as Galileo International, Travelport, Travelwire, Cheap Tickets, and Lodging.com.

As one vertical integration expert explained, vertical integration can "lock firms in" to unprofitable adjacent businesses.[12] Also, just because a firm excels in one part of the vertical supply chain, there is no reason to believe that it will excel in others. Consider the case of a small restaurant chain:

> Like smaller restaurant chains, almost all supplies are acquired from other firms. However, this chain decides that it is not satisfied with the price or quality of the meats it is able to obtain, so it purchases a meat processing facility. After a short time, the

chain realizes that it does not have the expertise to manage the processing of meats in an efficient manner, so it sells the facility.

Examples such as these are common in all industries. However, this does not mean that all vertical integration is unsuccessful. In fact, one study suggested that vertical integration may be associated with reduced administrative, selling, and R&D costs, but higher production costs. The researchers believe that the higher production costs may be a result of a lack of incentive on the part of internal suppliers to keep their costs down. Since internal suppliers have a guaranteed customer, they do not have to be as competitive.[13] An important point to remember with regard to all of the strategies is that some companies are pursuing them successfully.

From a strategic perspective, vertical integration contains an element of risk that is similar to concentration. If a firm is vertically integrated and the principal product becomes obsolete, the whole organization can suffer unless its value-chain activities are sufficiently flexible to be used for other products and services. Researchers have found that both high levels of technical change and high levels of competition reduce the expected profits from vertical integration.[14] Among the most significant advantages are internal benefits such as the potential for efficiency through synergy from coordinating and integrating vertical activities. Vertical integration can also help an organization improve its access to essential components or materials, differentiate its products, or gain greater control over its market. On the other hand, activities associated with vertical integration can increase overhead, link firms to unprofitable adjacent firms, or cause firms to lose access to important information from suppliers or customers.

VERTICAL INTEGRATION AND TRANSACTION COSTS

Transaction-cost economics, which is the study of economic transactions and their costs, helps explain when vertical integration may be appropriate.[15] From this perspective, firms can either negotiate with organizations or individuals on the open market for the products and services they need, or they can produce these products and services themselves. According to Oliver Williamson, an influential transaction-cost economist, "Whether a set of transactions ought to be executed across markets or within a firm depends on the relative efficiency of each mode."[16] If required resources can be obtained from a competitive open market without allocating an undue amount of time or other resources to the contracting process or contract enforcement, it is probably in the best interests of an organization to buy from the market instead of vertically integrating. However, when transactions costs are high enough to encourage an organization to produce a good or service in-house instead of buying it from the open market, a market failure is said to exist. The market is likely to fail, which means that transactions costs are prohibitively high, under a variety of conditions.[17] The following four situations provide examples of conditions when it is better to use vertical integration than to obtain suppliers or distributors in the open market.

- If the future is highly uncertain, it may be too costly or impossible to identify all of the possible situations that may occur, and to incorporate these possibilities into the contract. As a result, the supplier or distributor of the good or service will increase the price during negotiations in order to offset the risks (or demand other unusual contract terms). At some point, the price is going to get so high that it will actually be in the buyer's best interest to produce or distribute the good or service rather than contract it out.

- If there is only one or a small number of suppliers or distributors of a good or service and these companies are opportunistic, which means that they take advantage of the situation, a market failure may occur. In this case, the market failure could take place in the form of a lack of candor or honesty and/or in a high price. Limited supplies of a needed good or service or few distributors are primary reasons a firm might consider producing it in-house or handling its own distribution.

- When one party to a transaction has more knowledge about the transaction or a series of transactions than does another party, once again opportunism can result. This may happen when, for example, a private company is selling to a publicly held corporation, since a lot of information is readily available on the public corporation but not on the privately held corporation. The supplier can use this additional information to its advantage during the bargaining process.

- If a supplier has to invest in an asset that can be used only for the purpose of producing a specific good or service for the other party to the transaction (called asset specificity), the other party can take advantage of the producer after the asset is in place. To offset this risk, the supplier will establish a higher price or difficult contract terms. At some point, it is no longer worth it for the buyer to deal with the supplier. Instead, the buyer produces the product or service in-house.

Where transactions costs are low, an organization would usually be better off contracting for the required goods and services instead of vertically integrating. Remember that transactions costs are assumed to be low only if there are a large number of potential suppliers. Under these circumstances, there is probably no profit incentive to vertically integrate, since competition would eliminate abnormally high profits. For example, a hotel company with resorts in remote locations might rely on tour wholesalers to fill rooms. However, if the company had only one tour wholesaler that sold 95 percent of its inventory, the transaction costs would likely be high, and the wholesaler would have more power in the transaction. If no other wholesalers were available, this company might be better off trying to do its own sales and marketing. Furthermore, vertical integration often requires substantially different skills than those possessed by the firm. In this regard, vertical integration is similar to unrelated diversification.[18] As mentioned previously, a firm that can master one stage of the industry supply chain will not necessarily excel at other stages. Tour wholesalers who book hotels at an agreed-upon rate must sell the rooms or incur the costs, so they prepare and distribute marketing materials to a worldwide distribution network including a wide array of travel agencies. Unlike the hotel company, the wholesaler has invested in building this sales and marketing infrastructure. The hotels located on Caribbean islands or in the jungles of Africa may simply not have the resources to reach their European or American guests.

SUBSTITUTES FOR FULL VERTICAL INTEGRATION

Much of this discussion assumes that when a firm vertically integrates, it will do so at full scale. In other words, the firm will become fully involved in becoming its own supplier or distributor. However, in most cases it is impractical for a hospitality firm to become its own supplier because the skills and other assets needed to produce something like a gaming machine, ground beef, or towels are so different from the skills and assets needed to provide hospitality services. Similarly, being the sole distributor of its services can limit the hospitality firm's ability to access important customers. Few hotel chains can afford to rely on just their own reservation systems and ignore Expedia or Travelocity. However, sometimes the forces that might lead to vertical integration are strong. For example, there may only be one supplier of a good in a given market or the quality or quantity of what is supplied may not be adequate. Resort operators in some remote locations, for example, have sought to reduce their dependence on one or a few large tour operators who control the flow of guests to their destinations. In these situations, a hospitality firm may pursue partial vertical integration to overcome some of the disadvantages of full integration.[19]

> To allow Domino's stores to concentrate on making and delivering pizzas, Domino's developed a central commissary system. This relieves stores from long hours making dough, grating cheese and preparing toppings. The distribution system provides high quality dough and ingredients nationwide, keeping the company's pizza consistently delicious. In fact, through its network of eighteen domestic distribution centers, Dominos regularly supplies more than 4,800 pizza stores with more than 240 products. Other pizza and fast food companies in the U.S have adopted this same system.[20]

Partial vertical integration strategies include taper integration, quasi integration, and long-term contracting. Taper integration means that an organization produces part of its requirements in-house and buys the rest of what it needs on the open market. A restaurant chain may grow some of its own herbs and vegetables but rely on vendors for the rest. Quasi-integration involves purchasing most of what is needed of a particular product or service from a firm in which the purchasing organization holds an ownership stake. For example, by purchasing a 12 percent stake in Grill Concepts, Starwood helps guarantee its access to the full-service Daily Grill and The Grill on the Alley concepts in Sheraton and Westin properties.[21] An example of forward quasi-integration is when a large manufacturer of ice cream acquires part interest in a chain of ice cream stores to guarantee access to the distribution channel. Also, some hospitality firms use long-term contracts to achieve many of the benefits of vertical integration. Long-term agreements are considered to be vertical integration only when the two firms that provide the agreed-upon goods and services to each other do not have contracts with competitor firms. In the hotel business, many firms have long-term contracts that would not be considered a vertical integration strategy because the supplier or distributor is not a "captive company" that although independent does most of its business with the contracting firm. Each of the alternatives to complete integration contains trade-offs. That is, while they each reduce the level of exposure to the ill effects of vertical integration, they also reduce the potential for benefits arising from vertical integration. For example, taper integration, quasi-integration, and long-term contracting all yield less control over resources than does full integration.

Because of the potential disadvantages of vertical integration and the limited potential for profitability that may exist at other stages in the industry supply chain, many organizations don't ever pursue vertical integration. As they feel the need to expand beyond the scope of the existing business, they pursue diversification directly. Other organizations may vertically integrate for a while but eventually pursue diversification. Diversification is the topic of the next section.

DIVERSIFICATION STRATEGIES

Diversification, which is one of the most studied topics in all of strategic management, can be divided into two broad categories.[22] Related diversification implies organizational involvement in activities that are somehow related to the dominant or "core" business of the organization, often through common or complementary markets or technologies. Unrelated diversification does not depend on any pattern of relatedness. Some of the most common reasons for diversification are listed in Table 6.3.[23] They are divided into strategic reasons, which are frequently cited by executives in the popular business press, and personal motives that CEOs may have for pursuing diversification. In addition to these strategic and personal reasons, some diversification may be simply a result of less familiarity with the diversified business areas than with the core business areas of the organization. In other words, diversification opportunities may look good because organizational managers do not possess enough information about problems and weaknesses associated with the diversified areas—they "leap before they look."[24]

RELATED DIVERSIFICATION AND SYNERGY

Related diversification is based on similarities that exist among the products, services, markets, or resource-conversion processes of different parts of the organization. These similarities are supposed to lead to synergy, which means that the whole is supposed to be greater than the sum of its parts. In other words, one organization should be able to produce two related products or services more efficiently than can two organizations each producing one of the products or services on its own. The same reasoning applies to similar markets and similar resource-conversion processes. Most of the research on diversification strategies

TABLE 6.3	COMMONLY STATED REASONS FOR DIVERSIFICATION
Strategic Reasons	**Motives of the CEO**
• Risk reduction through investments in dissimilar businesses or less dynamic environments	• Desire to increase the value of the firm
• Stabilization or improvement in earnings	• Desire to increase personal power and status
• Improvement in growth	• Desire to increase personal rewards such as salary and bonuses
• Use of excess cash from slower-growing traditional areas (a form of organizational slack)	• Craving for a more interesting and challenging management environment
• Application of resources, capabilities, or core competencies to related areas	
• Generation of synergy through economies of scope	
• Use of excess debt capacity (also a form of organizational slack)	
• Ability to learn new technologies	
• Increase in market power	

indicates that some form or other of relatedness among diversified businesses leads to higher financial performance.[25] Related diversification can also reduce risk.[26]

> Hotel companies are branching out into a variety of related businesses, including rental cars, time share, real estate, and e-commerce. Carlson Hospitality Worldwide owns TGI Fridays, Radisson Hotels and Resorts Worldwide, Wagonlit Travel Agency, a lifestyle living complex complete with a club atmosphere and hotel amenities, and Seven Seas cruise lines. According to Curtis Nelson, CEO, "It seemed natural for us, beginning four or five years ago, to develop a brand-management strategy where we had a portfolio to serve customers different needs. Now we can offer more to hotel guests."[27]

Relatedness comes in two forms: tangible and intangible.[28] Tangible relatedness means that the organization has the opportunity to use the same physical resources for multiple purposes. Tangible relatedness can lead to synergy through resource sharing. For example, if two services are provided in the same facility, operating synergy is said to exist. This phenomenon is referred to as economies of scope. Economies of scope occur anytime slack resources that would not have been otherwise used are being put to good use.[29] Sharing facilities can also lead to economies of scale through producing services in an optimally sized (typically larger) facility.[30]

> "The biggest thing that multi-branding offers is the chance to leverage our existing assets that have lower volumes than, say a McDonald's, for instance," notes David Deno, Yum! Brands CFO.[31] Yum! Brands Inc., with such well-known quick-service restaurant brands as Pizza Hut, Taco Bell, KFC, A&W All-American Food, and Long John Silver, is the worldwide leader in multibranding, offering consumers a combination of two of the company's brands in one restaurant location. Starting with combinations of KFC–Taco Bell, and Taco Bell–Pizza Hut, it has added $100,000 to $400,000 per unit in average sales, dramatically improving unit economics. The company and its franchisees operate 1,975 multibrand restaurants.[32]

Other examples of synergy resulting from tangible relatedness include: (1) using the same marketing or distribution channels for multiple related services, (2) buying similar supplies for related services through a centralized purchasing office to gain purchasing economies, (3) providing corporate training programs to employees from different divisions that are all engaged in the same type of work, and (4) advertising multiple services simultaneously.

Intangible relatedness occurs anytime capabilities developed in one area can be applied to another area. It results in managerial synergy.[33] For example, Four Seasons used capabilities from its lodging businesses to help develop Four Seasons Residence Clubs, its vacation ownership business.[34] This example demonstrates effective use of another intangible resource, image or goodwill. Goodwill means that a company that has an established trade name can draw on this name to market new products. Synergy based on intangible resources such as brand name or management skills and knowledge may be more conducive to the creation of a sustainable competitive advantage, since intangible resources are hard to imitate and are never used up.[35]

The potential for synergy based on relatedness in diversified firms is limited only by the imagination. In the case of multibranding, Allied Domecq Quick Service Restaurants, a unit of Britain's Allied Domecq PLC, combined its Dunkin Donuts and Baskin Robbins brands under one roof, sometimes with the Togo's sandwich shop added in to provide a lunch option. The use of a common facility to gain operations synergies is the major benefit of multibranding, although this firm's motivation is different than that of Yum! Allied Domecq keeps customers moving through the store at all hours by offering choices tailored for breakfast, lunch, and snacks.[36]

However, even if relatedness is evident, synergy has to be created.[37] McDonald's, the number one fast-food chain, is a strong brand and would most likely overshadow any other brands added to its stores. Besides, these units operate at volume capacity in most stores, diminishing the capacity-enhancing benefits. The synergies might exist in the future once McDonald's partner brands, like Chipotle Mexican Grill, Donatos Pizza, and Boston Market, have more time to develop and create a market.[38] These concepts could benefit from cobranding by shared advertising and promotion, cross-selling, and capacity improvement. The potential management synergies from multibranding might be limited because this strategy requires a high level of cooperation—for instance, sharing marketing, labor or engineering costs—and some brands guard their autonomy too closely to allow for such cross-fertilization. Finally, companies need to preserve the intangible asset of brand equity even as they compress multiple restaurants into a single outlet.[39] The requirements for synergy creation are outlined in Figure 6.2. Some examples of potential sources of synergy from related diversification are shown in Table 6.4.

Some managers seem to believe that if business units are somehow related to each other, synergy will occur automatically. Unfortunately, this is not the case. One factor that can block the ability of organizational managers to create synergistic gains from relatedness is a lack of strategic fit. "Strategic fit" refers to the effective matching of strategic organizational capabilities. For example, if two organizations in two related businesses combine their resources, but they are both strong in the same areas and weak in the same areas, then the potential for synergy is diminished. Once combined, they will continue to exhibit the same capabilities. However, if one of the organizations is strong in operations but lacks marketing power, while the other organization is weak in operations but strong in marketing, then there is real potential for both organizations to be better off—if managed properly.

Another factor that can block managers from achieving synergistic gains is a lack of organizational fit. Organizational fit occurs when two organizations or business units have similar management processes, cultures, systems, and structures.[40] This makes them compatible, which facilitates resource sharing, communication, and transference of knowledge and skills. Unfortunately, relatedness on a dimension such as common markets or similar resource-conversion processes does not guarantee that business units within a firm will enjoy an organizational fit. Lack of fit is especially evident in mergers and acquisitions. For instance, two related companies may merge in an effort to create synergy but find that they are organizationally incompatible.

> A little more than a year after acquiring Le Meridien Hotels and Resort, Forte PLC found itself the object of a hostile takeover bid from leisure and media titan Granada PLC. A tumultuous two months later, the CEO of Forte left behind a splintered culture comprised of not-nearly-assimilated Meridien executives and Forte's old guard, many of whom were destined to be replaced by new appointees from Granada.[41]

Synergy creation requires a great deal of work on the part of managers at the corporate and business levels. The activities that create synergy include combining similar

| FIGURE 6.2 | **REQUIREMENTS FOR THE CREATION OF SYNERGY** |

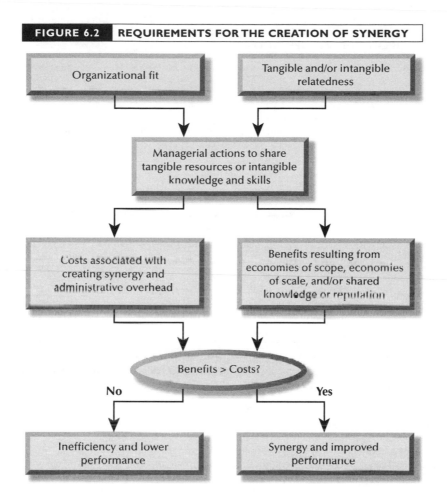

processes, coordinating business units that share common resources, centralizing support activities that apply to multiple units, and resolving conflicts among business units. Many organizations do not engage in these activities to any degree. Synergy, which is supposed to result in 2 + 2 = 5, often ends up 2 + 2 = 3. Not only are the coordinating and integrating activities expensive themselves, but corporate-level management creates an administrative-overhead burden that must be shared by all of the operating units.[42]

Consequently, organizational performance is increased only if the benefits associated with synergy are greater than the costs related to corporate-level administration, combining activities, or sharing knowledge and resources. When the economic benefits associated with synergy are highest, the administrative costs are highest also, because a lot more information and coordination are required to create the synergy.[42] For example, if two business units are unrelated to each other, they do not ever have to communicate or coordinate. On the other hand, if they are related and want to share knowledge or skills, they will have to engage in meetings, joint-training programs, and other coordination efforts. If two related businesses are using the same facility or store, they will have to work out operations (e.g., kitchen design

TABLE 6.4	**POTENTIAL SOURCES OF SYNERGY FROM RELATED DIVERSIFICATION**

Synergies are created by linking value activities between two separate businesses. Here are some examples:

Potential Marketing-Based Synergies

- Shared brand names: Build market influence faster and at lower cost through a common name
- Shared advertising and promotion: Lower unit costs and tie-in purchases
- Shared distribution channels: Bargaining power to improve access and lower costs
- Cross-selling and bundling: Lower costs and more integrated view of the marketplace

Potential Operations Synergies

- Common new facilities: Larger facilities may allow economies of scale
- Shared facilities and capacity: Improved capacity utilization allows lower per-unit overhead costs
- Combined purchasing activities: Increased influence, leading to lower costs and lower-cost shipping arrangements
- Shared computer systems: Lower per unit overhead costs and ability to spread the risk of investing in higher priced systems
- Combined training programs: Lower training costs per employee

Potential R&D/Technology Synergies

- Technology transfer: Faster, lower cost adoption of technology at the second business
- Development of new core businesses: Access to capabilities and innovation not available in the market
- Multiple use of creative researchers: Opportunities for innovation across business via individual experience and business analogy

Potential Management Synergies

- Similar industry experience: Faster response to industry trends
- Transferable core skills: Experience with previously tested, innovative strategies and skills in strategy and program development

and purchasing). Coordination is also required when using the same sales force for related products, combining promotional efforts, and transferring products between divisions. Coordination processes can be costly in time and other resources. Consequently, the benefits of synergy may be offset, in part, by higher administrative costs. The various costs and forces that can undermine the creation of synergies are listed in Table 6.5.

In summary, organizations may pursue related diversification by acquiring or developing businesses in areas that are related on some basic variable, such as a similar production technology, a common customer, a complimentary brand, or any number of other dimensions. However, synergy is not instantaneously created if businesses are related. The creation of synergy requires related businesses to fit together common processes. This can be a difficult managerial challenge. The level of difficulty depends on the amount of strategic and organizational fit that exists among related businesses. In addition to the synergy that can be created through related diversification, corporate-level managers sometimes try to add value to their organizations through the development of corporate-level distinctive competencies that may or may not be associated with a relatedness strategy.

TABLE 6.5	FORCES THAT UNDERMINE SYNERGIES

Management Ineffectiveness

- Too little effort to coordinate between businesses means synergies will not be created
- Too much effort to coordinate between businesses can stifle creativity

Administrative Costs of Coordination

- Additional layers of management and staff add costs
- Executives in larger organizations are often paid higher salaries
- Delays from and expense of meetings and planning sessions necessary for coordination
- Extra travel and communications costs to achieve coordination

Poor Strategic Fit

- Relatedness without strategic fit decreases the opportunity for synergy
- Overstated (or imaginary) opportunities for synergies
- Industry evolution that undermines strategic fit
- Overvaluing potential synergies often results in paying too much for a target firm or in promising too much improvement to stakeholders

Poor Organizational Fit

- Incompatible cultures and management styles
- Incompatible strategies, priorities, and reward systems
- Incompatible production processes and technologies
- Incompatible computer and budgeting systems

UNRELATED DIVERSIFICATION

Large, unrelated diversified firms are often called conglomerates, since they are involved in a conglomeration of unrelated businesses.[44] Cendant Corporation has significant holdings in hospitality in addition to a diverse set of businesses that include tax preparation and retail mortgage origination. Cash-flow management and risk reduction are two reasons corporate strategists adopt strategies of unrelated diversification. For example, if a gaming company has excess cash and wants to spread its risk, it might consider a company with stable and constant cash flows in an industry unrelated to hospitality.

Richard Rumelt documented the rise of unrelated diversification in the United States from the 1950s to the early 1970s.[45] In spite of the popularity of this strategy during the period, he concluded that unrelated firms experience lower profitability than firms pursuing other corporate-level strategies. His findings have been generally, although not unequivocally, supported by other researchers.[46] Perhaps of greater concern, there is some evidence that unrelated diversification is associated with higher levels of risk than other strategies.[47] This is particularly distressing since one of the most frequently cited arguments for unrelated diversification is that it leads to reduced risk.

Unrelated diversification places significant demands on corporate-level executives due to increased complexity and technological changes across industries. In fact, it is very difficult for a manager to understand each of the core technologies and appreciate the special requirements of each of the individual units in an unrelated diversified firm. Consequently, the effectiveness of management may be reduced. By the late 1960s, conglomerates began suffering performance problems. In early 1969, the stock prices of many conglomerates fell by as much as 50 percent from their highs of the previous year, while the Dow Jones Industrial Average fell less than 10 percent during the same period.[48]

Over the years, many conglomerates have acquired hotel chains, often to sell them after a short period. For instance, Granada PLC, the media conglomerate that bought Forte, merged with Compass Group PLC, one of the world's leading food-service and hotel groups, and a year later demerged. The Compass Group then began to sell Meridien Hotels, Posthouse Hotels, London Signature, and Heritage Hotels, all previously part of Forte Hotels.[49] These mergers, acquisitions, and demergers all occurred in a five-year period. Omni Hotels is not unlike others, having been owned by four large corporations:

> The company was founded in 1958 by the Dunfey family of New England. The business, know as Dunfey Hotels grew to more than 8,000 rooms in the 1960s and 1970s, changing owners twice—first to Aetna Insurance and then to Aer Lingus, the Irish national airline. In 1983, the company acquired Omni International Hotels, soon after which it changed its name to Omni Hotels. World International Holdings Ltd. and Wharf Holdings Ltd. of Hong Kong, a diversified trading company representing some 10 percent of the Hong Kong stock market, purchased Omni Hotels in 1988. In February of 1996, TRT Holdings, Inc., a private firm that specialized in oil, gas, and pipelines and expanded into banking, purchased the Omni Hotel chain. TRT Holdings sold its Teco Pipeline subsidiary company in 1997 and brought $400 million dedicated to improving and expanding Omni Hotel properties.[50]

Now managers and researchers alike believe that unrelated diversification typically is not a high-performing strategy. However, some firms have had great success with it. Cendant Corp. is enjoying profitable growth. General Electric, one of the biggest conglomerates in the world, has enjoyed many years of strong financial performance. Jack Welch, recently retired CEO of GE, explained his philosophy this way:

> All our industries don't grow at the same rate. Our plastics business might be more like [a fast-growing company] in terms of top line growth. But in our other businesses, it allows us enormous staying power. For example, next year we'll go from A to B. I think I know exactly how I'm going to go from A to B, and I know the company in total will go from A to B. I'm not sure the 30 or so businesses are going to get from A to B exactly as they planned it, but I've got enough muscle that I can get from A to B.
>
> If one of the businesses is going to be weak, and it's a great business but it's in a difficult moment, I can support it. If I'm a single-product guy in a weak business like that, in a business that cycles dramatically, I get whacked. So the staying power that our businesses have allows us to stay for the long haul.[51]

The 1980s were marked with a dramatic decrease in unrelated diversification, accompanied by an increase in related diversification.[52] Related diversification, accompanied by sell-offs of unrelated businesses, is a continuing trend among U.S. firms.[53]

MERGERS AND ACQUISITIONS

Some companies rely on internal venturing for most of their growth and diversification. However, managers sometimes feel that their own firm's resources are inadequate to achieve a high level of growth and diversification. Consequently, they seek to acquire skills and resources through purchase of or merger with another firm. Many firms in the hotel and restaurant industries focus on acquisitions and mergers as their primary method for growth. Compared to internal venturing, mergers and acquisitions are a relatively rapid way to pursue growth or diversification, which may partially account for the dramatic increase in their popularity over the past few decades.[54]

> Over the last several years, we have seen numerous mergers of hotel organizations in what was widely touted as a period of significant consolidation in the U.S. hotel industry. Driven by inexpensive acquisition capital frequently the result of the frothy pricing of hotel stocks on Wall Street—the "urge to merge" was close to a fever pitch in late 1997 and early 1998.[55]

Mergers occur when two organizations combine into one. Acquisitions, in which one organization buys a controlling interest in the stock of another organization or buys it outright from its owners, are the most common type of merger. Acquisitions are a relatively quick way to (1) enter new markets, (2) acquire new products or services, (3) learn new resource-conversion processes, (4) acquire knowledge and skills, (5) vertically integrate, (6) broaden markets geographically, or (7) fill needs in the corporate portfolio.[56] As a portfolio-management tool, managers often seek acquisition targets that are faster growing, more profitable, less cyclical, or less dependent on a particular set of environmental variables. In the case of restaurants and hotels, underperforming multi-unit operators are also targeted for acquisition.

> A few recent examples of hotel acquisitions include Hilton's $3.7 billion purchase of Promus Hotel Corp., Carnival's acquisition of P&O Princess Cruises, Gaming Corporation's acquisition of CMS, LLC, a leading supplier of casino management systems software, and nH Hotels' (Spain) acquisitions of hotel companies Krasnapolsky (Dutch), Krystal Hotels (Mexican) and Astron (German). nH is now targeting the U.S. for expansion. These examples involve whole companies. Of course, buying and selling individual hotel properties is a normal part of business for many lodging companies.[57]

Industry consolidation, which occurs as competitors merge, is a major trend. For example, significant consolidation has occurred in the hotel, airline, restaurant, health-care, and many other industries. In China, nine airlines were merged into three companies as part of a state-ordered consolidation that gives these firms together 80 percent of the Chinese market.[58] Mergers and acquisitions are on the rise in restaurants as well. Much of the consolidation is due to conversion, such as when Lone Star Steakhouse Inc. acquired Ground Round units or Wendy's purchased Rax Restaurants. Many other acquisitions can be attributed to financial problems being experienced by the sellers, as the following shows:

With so many seats in the marketplace, a trend toward a shakeout-based consolidation is inevitable, according to many foodservice observers and participants. "It's going to happen," said Lone Star chairman and chief executive Jamie Coulter, speaking about the move toward consolidation. "The efficient operators are going to recycle the inefficient ones," he notes. After the churning of the merger and acquisition waters calms down again, the experts expect the restaurant industry to emerge stronger than ever before as the best operators rise to the top, able to take advantage of sites and operations that could no longer be profitably maintained by previous owners.[59]

Corporate raiding is another interesting phenomenon associated with mergers and acquisitions. Corporate raiders are organizations and individuals who engage in acquisitions, often against the wishes of the managers of the target companies. This type of acquisition is called hostile, and it tends to be more expensive than a friendly acquisition because the premium paid to acquire the firm is higher.[60] From a social perspective, some corporate raiders have argued that they are doing society a favor, because the threat of takeover motivates managers to act in the best interests of the organization's stockholders.[61] They believe that they are keeping managers from becoming "entrenched." However, this argument remains to be proved. Hostile takeovers have recently come to the shopping-center industry, as two of the most powerful families in this industry are locked in a bitter takeover battle.

> On one side is David Simon, CEO of the country's largest mall empire, who has launched a hostile bid for the 30 upscale regional centers controlled by Robert Taubman and his family. On the other is the Michigan-based Taubman, who accuses Simon of opportunism and "belligerent badgering." "He said that it was a wonderful opportunity for his company to take over our company and that he really didn't care what we thought," Taubman recounted.[62]

MERGER PERFORMANCE

The shareholders of an acquired firm typically enjoy a huge payoff because they receive an enormous premium over market value for the shares of stock they hold prior to the acquisition announcement.[63] However, most of the research evidence seems to indicate that mergers and acquisitions are not, on average, financially beneficial to the shareholders of the acquiring firm.[64] In one study of 191 acquisitions in twenty-nine industries, researchers found that acquisitions were associated with declining profitability, reduced research-and-development expenditures, fewer patents produced, and increases in financial leverage.[65] John Chambers, CEO of Cisco Systems, made seventy-one acquisitions between 1993 and 2000. Reflecting on that activity, he said, "I don't know how to make large mergers work."[66]

Table 6.6 provides several explanations for why acquisitions, on average, tend to depress profitability (at least in the short term). High premiums, increased interest costs, high advisory fees and other transaction costs, and poison pills (actions that make a target company less attractive) can cause acquisitions to be prohibitively expensive and thus reduce any potential gains from synergy. In addition, strategic problems such as high turnover among target-firm managers, managerial distraction, lower innovation, lack of organizational fit, and increased leverage and risk can reduce any strategic benefits the organization was hoping to achieve. The president and COO of Radisson Hotels and Resorts Worldwide has observed, "Most big-company acquisitions have not been lucrative. Deals are easy on paper, but hard to execute day to day. With that in analysts' minds,

TABLE 6.6	A FEW OF MANY POTENTIAL PROBLEMS WITH MERGERS AND ACQUISITIONS

High Costs

- High premiums typically paid by acquiring firms: If a company was worth $50/share in a relatively efficient financial market prior to an acquisition, why should an acquiring firm pay $75 (a typical premium) or more to buy it?

- Increased interest costs: Many acquisitions are financed by borrowing money at high interest rates. Leverage typically increases during an acquisition.

- High advisory fees and other transaction costs: The fees charged by the brokers, lawyers, financiers, consultants, and advisers who orchestrate the deal often range in the millions of dollars. In addition, filing fees, document preparation, and legal fees in the event of contestation can be very high.

- Poison pills: These anti-takeover devices make companies very unattractive to a potential buyer. Top managers of target companies have been very creative in designing a variety of poison pills. One example of a poison pill is the "golden parachute," in which target-firm executives receive large amounts of severance pay (often millions of dollars) if they lose their jobs due to a hostile takeover.

Strategic Problems

- High turnover among the managers of the acquired firm: The most valuable asset in most organizations is its people, their knowledge, and their skills. If most managers leave, what has the acquiring firm purchased?

- Short-term managerial distraction: "Doing a deal" typically takes managers away from the critical tasks of the core businesses for long durations. During this time period, who is steering the ship?

- Long-term managerial distraction: Because they are too distracted running diversified businesses, organizations sometimes lose sight of the factors that led to success in their core businesses.

- Less innovation: Acquisitions have been shown to lead to reduced innovative activity, which can hurt long-term performance.

- No organizational fit: If the cultures, dominant logics, systems, structures, and processes of the acquiring and target firms do not "fit," synergy is unlikely.

- Increased risk: Increased leverage often associated with mergers and acquisitions leads to greater financial risk. Acquiring firms also take the risk that they will unable to successfully manage the newly acquired organization.

Source: M.A. Hitt, J.S. Harrison and R.D. Ireland, *Mergers and Acquisitions: A Guide to Creating Value for Stakeholders* (New York: Oxford University Press, 2001); S. Chatterjee, et al., "Cultural Differences and Shareholder Value in Related Mergers: Linking Equity and Human Capital," *Strategic Management Journal* 13 (1992); 319–334; J.S. Harrison, "Alternatives to Merger—Joint Ventures and Other Strategies," *Long Range Planning* (December 1987); 78–83; J.P. Walsh and J.W. Ellwood, "Mergers, Acquisitions, and the Pruning of Managerial Deadwood," *Strategic Management Journal* 12 (1991); 201–207.

public companies will be under incredible scrutiny when it comes to acquisitions."[67] Also, if there are several suitors for a company, bids can get so high that that additional premium is hard to offset through any efficiencies created. For example, ITT, owner of Sheraton hotels and Caesars World, was the target of a fierce bidding war between Hilton and Starwood Hotels and Resorts.

Perhaps the most condemning evidence concerning mergers and acquisitions was presented by Michael Porter. He studied the diversification records of thirty-three large, prestigious U.S. companies over a period of thirty-seven years. He discovered that most of these companies divested many more of their acquisitions than they kept. For example, CBS, in an effort to create an "entertainment company," bought organizations involved in toys, crafts, sports teams, and musical instruments. All of these businesses were sold due to lack of fit with the traditional broadcasting business of CBS. CBS also bought the Ziff-Davis publishers, which they unloaded a few years later for much less than they paid after having run all its magazines into the ground. Porter's general conclusion was that the corporate-level strategies of most of the companies he studied had reduced, rather than enhanced, shareholder value.[68]

SUCCESSFUL AND UNSUCCESSFUL MERGERS AND ACQUISITIONS

Does the discouraging evidence about merger performance mean that all mergers are doomed to failure? An examination of the market's reaction to merger and tender-offer announcements in the lodging industry found that the equity markets view lodging mergers and acquisitions favorably.[69] In contrast to the results for the overall market, a study of forty-one lodging acquisitions from 1982 to 1999 revealed a positive stock-price reaction for both the acquiring firms and their targets. While mergers in lodging may be viewed more favorably, their postmerger success is still a challenge for corporate managers. Researchers have identified factors associated with successful and unsuccessful mergers. Unsuccessful mergers are associated with a large amount of debt, overconfident or incompetent managers, poor ethics, changes in top management or organization structure, or diversification away from the core area of the acquiring firm.[70]

Some factors seem to lead to success in mergers. For example, some researchers have found that successful mergers are made by acquiring firms with relatively small amounts of debt. Merger negotiations are friendly (no resistance), which helps keep acquisition premiums to a minimum and helps make postmerger integration of the companies a lot easier.[71] Successful mergers also tend to involve companies that share a high level of complementarity among their resources, thus creating the potential for synergy. Complementarity occurs when two companies have strengths in different areas that complement each other.[72] Furthermore, researchers have discovered that the largest shareholder gains from merger occur when the cultures and the top-management styles of the two companies are similar (organizational fit).[73] In addition, sharing resources and activities has been found to be important to postmerger success.[74] However, it is fair to say that "there are no rules that will invariably lead to a successful acquisition."[75]

One of the most important factors leading to a successful merger is the due-diligence process. Warren Hellman, former CEO of Lehman Brothers, suggests that because so many acquisitions fail, organizations should assume that all of them will fail. The burden is then on the shoulders of the managers who want the merger to take place to prove why their particular deal will be an exception to the general rule.[76] The due-diligence process is an excellent way to obtain the necessary evidence. Due diligence involves a complete examination of the merger, including such areas as management, equity, debt, sale of assets, transfer of shares, environmental issues, financial performance, tax issues, human resources, customers, and markets. Typically, the process is conducted by accountants, investment bankers, lawyers, consultants, and internal specialists.[77] The due-diligence team should be empowered by top managers of both companies with responsibility and authority to obtain all of the necessary data. For those acquisitions that finally occur, information gained during due diligence is invaluable for integration planning.

Many of the major problems with mergers and acquisitions can be avoided through effective due diligence, even if it means avoiding the deal altogether. For example, the president of a billion-dollar division of one of the largest corporations in the United States recently walked away from an acquisition because of accounting irregularities discovered during due diligence.[78] Joseph Neubauer, CEO of Aramark, provides another example:

> It was a crucial moment for Aramark Worldwide Corp. After months of negotiating and millions spent on due diligence, the $7.8 billion outsourcing service company was close to wrapping up deals for a pair of overseas acquisitions. The target companies fit perfectly wit Aramark's goal of expanding internationally, and the price—more than $100 million—was right, too. But when Chief Executive Joseph Neubauer finally got a close look at the operations and books, he didn't like what he saw. Despite the huge investment in time and money, he didn't think twice. Neubauer walked away. "It takes a lifetime to build a reputation and only a short time to lose it all," he says matter-of-factly. "We chose to eat the loss on the time and the money because we couldn't live with their business practices."[79]

Chapter 3 discussed organizational learning through interorganizational relationships. Organizations can also learn through acquisitions. In fact, some experts have argued that "acquisitions may broaden a firm's knowledge base and decrease inertia, enhancing the viability of its later ventures."[80] However, mergers and acquisitions represent a paradox with regard to innovative activities. While organizations can learn from the companies they acquire, acquisitions can lead to reduction in innovative activities. This negative effect may come from a loss of focus on the core business or absorption of new debt that directs cash flow toward interest payments and away from research and development. Regardless of the reasons, acquisitions seem to be a way to "buy" innovation from external sources while damaging internal innovation. Consequently, some experts call acquisitions "a substitute for innovation."[81]

In summary, mergers and acquisitions have a high incidence of failure but, if carefully executed, may enhance firm performance. Once a firm has created a portfolio of businesses—either through acquisitions, joint ventures, or internal growth—the emphasis becomes managing those businesses in such a manner that high organizational performance is achieved. One of the keys to doing so is creating competencies that span multiple businesses. The next section will discuss this important topic.

STRATEGIC RESTRUCTURING

> Less than six months after going public, Cosi—the upscale sandwich chain—is undergoing its second major management shakeup, planning to close up to 13 of its fast-casual restaurants and seeking financing to fund its greatly diminished growth plans. Cosi, whose rapid expansion over the past several years reflected the aggressive grab for market share among many fast-casual players, now doesn't plan to launch any more restaurants beyond the six that have opened in 2003. Cosi's explanation that the change was the result of insufficient financing prompted a flurry of lawsuits by shareholders, who alleged that they were deceived by the firm's growth projections in its IPO prospectus.[82]

Disgruntled stakeholders are often the force that causes corporate-level managers to consider restructuring. For example, stockholders may be dissatisfied with their financial returns, or debt-rating agencies such as Standard & Poor's may devalue firm securities due to high risk. If an organization has spent many years diversifying in various directions, top managers may feel as though the organization is "out of control." This feeling of loss of control is also related to organizational size. In the largest organizations, top managers may even be unfamiliar with some of the businesses in their portfolios. Also, many organizations have acquired high levels of debt, often associated with acquisitions. For these companies, even small economic downturns can be a rude awakening to the risks associated with high leverage.[83] For all of these reasons, restructuring has become commonplace in recent years.[84]

Researchers have observed that as organizations evolve, they tend to move through what is called a period of convergence, followed by a period of reorientation or radical adjustment, and then another period of convergence.[85] During convergence stages, the organization makes minor changes to strategies in an effort to adapt, but for the most part follows a consistent approach. During this time, the structure and systems are more or less stable, performance is acceptable, and managers develop mental models, or assumptions, about how the industry and the organization work.[86] A period of convergence can continue indefinitely, as long as the industry conditions and organization characteristics are not significantly out of alignment.[87] However, when gradual drift results in a substantial misalignment or an environmental discontinuity does occur, the organization is forced to reorient itself. At this time, the mental models that were developed during the convergence period may prevent executives, managers, and employees from recognizing the need for change. The information that doesn't fit the preconceived mental model is just not seen at all. As one researcher described it, "The writing on the wall cannot be read."[88]

A reorientation is a significant realignment of organization strategies, structure, and processes with the new environmental realities.[89] Transformation, renewal, reorientation, and restructuring are all words that describe the same general phenomenon: a radical change in how business is conducted. Some of the most common restructuring approaches will now be described. They include retrenchment or downsizing, refocusing corporate assets on distinctive competencies, Chapter 11 reorganization, leveraged buyouts, and changes to organizational design. Organizations may use any one or a combination of these strategies in restructuring efforts.

TURNAROUND STRATEGIES AND DOWNSIZING

Turnaround strategies (sometimes called retrenchment) can involve workforce reductions, selling assets to reduce debt, outsourcing unprofitable activities, implementation of tighter cost or quality controls, or new policies that emphasize quality or efficiency. Turnaround can occur at the corporate level of a company or on a property-by-property basis.

> Some management companies crave properties that need improvement. Turning around underperforming properties is how management companies develop a reputation and how they acquire more business sources. "I love going into an asset where the previous management company has missed the low-hanging fruit," said Robert Dann, executive v.p. of Boykin Management Co. "To take a hotel and turn it around, people remember that," said David McCaslin, president of MeriStar Hotels and Resorts. "About half our business is with turnaround properties," said William Hoffman, president of Trigild Corp.[90]

Workforce reductions, or "downsizing," have become a common part of turnaround strategies in the United States as a response to the burgeoning bureaucracies in the post–World

War II era. Even the U.S. military has a new focus on a "lighter fighter" division that can respond faster to combat situations. Staff reductions and office closings were key elements of InterContinental Hotels Group's effort to remove $100 million in costs from its balance sheet. The company closed its London headquarters office, consolidated operations, and reduced its global corporate staff by 800.[91] The great mystery is that some companies lay off employees in spite of strong profits. For example, Mobil once posted "soaring" first-quarter earnings—and then announced plans to cut 4,700 jobs.[92]

The evidence is mounting that "downsizing does not reduce expenses as much as desired, and that sometimes expenses may actually increase."[93] Companies may experience problems such as reductions in quality, a loss in productivity, decreased effectiveness, lost trust, increased conflict, and low morale.[94] According to one CEO involved in a major lay-off, "The human impact of our decisions is very real and very painful."[95] Many organizations cut muscle, as well as fat, through layoffs. One reason the muscle is cut is that some of the best employees leave, either because of attractive severance packages or fear of future job loss. Because the best employees can usually get new jobs fairly easily, they may decide to leave while all of their options are open to them. Also, studies have shown that the "surviving" employees experience feelings of guilt and fear that may hurt productivity or organizational loyalty.[96] It is not surprising, then, that the stock market often reacts unfavorably to announcements of major layoffs.[97]

Sometimes layoffs are critical to survival, as was the case following the events of September 11, 2001. According to the Bureau of Labor Statistics, during the five weeks following the terrorist attacks, more than 88,500 workers were discharged. This job loss was across industries and viewed as either a direct or indirect result of the attacks.[98] Indeed, among the workers that were reported laid off, 43 percent belonged to the airline industry and 36 percent to the hotel industry.[99] A Cornell University study in the weeks after the events revealed that seven out of ten hotel general managers surveyed employed some form of staff reduction.[100] "On September 15, Continental announced that it would cut 12,000 jobs. One by one, the other airlines followed suit: United and American announced 20,000 layoffs each; Northwest, 10,000; US Airways 11,000; Delta forecast eliminating 13,000."[101] Obviously, the airlines could not have been prepared for such events, although occupancies in the hotel industry were beginning to erode in the first quarter of the year. Barry Sternlicht, CEO of Starwood Hotels and Resorts, stated: "Our focus in this crisis has been to react flexibly and entrepreneurially and to run a lean, mean machine."[102]

A survey by the American Management Association of 1,142 companies that had been involved in workforce reductions indicated that about half of these companies were poorly prepared for these activities.[103] One of the keys to successful downsizing, then, may be sufficient preparation with regard to outplacement, new reporting relationships, and training, when possible. Of course, another important element in all successful restructuring activities, especially workforce reductions, is effective communication with and examination of the needs of key stakeholders.[104] Managers anticipating layoffs should combine caring with cost consciousness and should "humanize" their approaches to workforce reductions.[105] Many organizations avoid layoffs through hiring freezes, restricting overtime, retraining and redeploying workers, switching workers to part-time, starting job-sharing programs, giving unpaid vacations, shortening the workweek, or reducing pay.[106]

REFOCUSING CORPORATE ASSETS

Most restructuring companies are moving in the direction of reducing their diversification, as opposed to increasing it.[107] For example, Carlson Restaurants sold off its emerging brands division to focus on T.G.I. Fridays and Pick Up Stix.[108] Refocusing activities are generally viewed favorably by external stakeholders such as the financial community.[109] Refocusing entails trimming businesses that are not consistent with the strategic direction of the organization.

> Wyndham International's continued quest to become what chairman and CEO Fred Kleisner called a healthy company will include more management and franchise business and the sale of 55 nonstrategic assets. Kleisner said in New York in early June that the Dallas-based company hopes to increase the management and franchising portions of its business to 20 percent of its earnings before interest, taxes, depreciation and amortization from the 5 percent of EBITDA it now represents. "Growing our management and franchising business is a core strategy," Kleisner said. Wyndham has signed 16 management contracts and 14 franchise agreements in the last three years, according to Kleisner. Since the company's recapitalization in June 1999, it has sold 83 assets for $900 million. "We'll dispose of the final 55 nonstrategic assets by the end of next year. … We will clean up this company and make it simpler."[110]

This type of refocusing is often called "downscoping." Downscoping involves selling off nonessential businesses that are not related to the organization's core competencies and capabilities.[111] Furthermore, innovative activities tend to increase in companies involved in this type of restructuring. You may recall that this is opposite of the impact of acquisitions.[112]

On the other hand, sell-offs that do not improve the strategic focus of the organization may signal failure or market retreat, which can cause concern among stakeholders such as owners, debt holders, and the financial community. For instance, the stock market tends to react positively to divestitures linked to corporate-level or business-level strategies, and negatively to divestitures that are portrayed as simply getting rid of unwanted assets.[113]

A divestiture is a reverse acquisition. In the lodging industry, this type of activity is sometimes referred to as a "demerger." One type of divestiture is a sell-off, in which a business unit is sold to another firm or, in the case of a leveraged buyout, to the business unit's managers. Another form of divestiture is the spin-off, which means that current shareholders are issued a proportional number of shares in the spun-off business. For example, if a shareholder owns one hundred shares of XYZ Company and the company spins off business unit J, the shareholder would then own one hundred shares of XYZ Company and one hundred shares of an independently operated company called J. The key advantage of a spin-off relative to other divestiture options is that shareholders still have the option of retaining ownership in the spun-off business. Six Continents Hotels (previously Bass Hotels and Resorts), renamed for the second time in less than two years as InterContinental Hotels Group, spun off its pub operations from its hotel business. The demerger resulted in two separate, publicly traded companies.[114]

Refocusing may also involve new acquisitions or new ventures to round out a corporate portfolio or add more strength in an area that is essential to corporate distinctive competencies.[115] For instance, Grand Metropolitan bought Pillsbury and simultaneously sold Bennigan's and Steak & Ale restaurants in an effort to redefine its domain in the food-processing industry.[116]

CHAPTER 11 REORGANIZATION

An organization that is in serious financial trouble can voluntarily file for Chapter 11 protection under the Federal Bankruptcy Code: "Chapter XI provides a proceeding for an organization to work out a plan or arrangement for solving its financial problems under the supervision of a federal court. It is intended primarily for debtors who feel they can solve their financial problems on their own if given sufficient time, and if relieved of some pressure."[117] For example, Kmart became the largest retailer in history to file for Chapter 11, "hoping to buy itself time to repay creditors while it restructures its businesses."[118] Chapter 11 became very common in the hospitality industry in the aftermath of September 11, including companies such as Renaissance Cruises, US Airways, Boston Chicken, United Airlines, and Lodgian. Another example is Planet Hollywood:

> At its peak, Planet Hollywood International Inc. and its franchisees had 95 restaurants in 31 countries. The company was backed by celebrity investors such as Bruce Willis and Sylvester Stallone. Many of its movie-themed restaurants are in top destinations such as Disney World, the Las Vegas Strip or Times Square in New York. Citing financial difficulties, the company first filed for Chapter 11 bankruptcy protection in 1999, a day after 32 U.S. restaurants were closed. As the company began to show promise again, the drop in tourism after 9/11 sent it into a tailspin. In October of 2001 Planet Hollywood filed for Chapter 11 protection the second time in two years. By December 2002 the company emerged from bankruptcy proceedings again, this time a much smaller, privately-held company. It now owns 10 stores in top tourist destinations.[119]

While Chapter 11, if executed properly, can provide firms with time and protection as they attempt to reorganize, it is not a panacea for firms with financial problems. Chapter 11 can be expensive. Fees from lawyers, investment bankers, and accountants can total millions of dollars.[120] Another disadvantage is that, after filing, all major restructuring decisions are subject to court approval. Thus, managerial discretion and flexibility are reduced. Researchers do not agree on the potential for successful reorganization. Some researchers have argued that it is in the best interests of organizations that are facing high amounts of adversity to quickly select Chapter 11 (instead of having it imposed on them), unless they have high levels of organizational slack.[121] On the other hand, in a study of firms that had voluntarily filed for Chapter 11 protection, only a little more than half of the companies were "nominally successful in reorganizing," and "two-thirds of those retained less than 50 percent of their assets on completion of the reorganization process."[122]

Facing sales declines and an aging customer base in 2003, the 175-unit Piccadilly Cafeterias considered Chapter 11. As this firm contemplated a range of strategic options including the sale of the company, the chain's chairman, J. H. Campbell Jr., noted, "Bankruptcy protection also is a possibility. Should no workable solutions come from outside sources in the form of a sale or equity injection, the board may avail itself of the reorganization opportunity afforded by the bankruptcy code."[123] While larger firms have a better chance of successfully reorganizing, Chapter 11 should probably still be used as a strategy of last resort.

LEVERAGED BUYOUTS

Leveraged buyouts (LBOs) involve the private purchase of a business unit by managers, employees, unions, or private investors. They are called "leveraged" because much of the money that is used to purchase the business unit is often borrowed from financial intermediaries (often at higher than normal interest rates). An LBO made possible the sale by Compass of its Little Chef and Travelodge units following a strategic review that concluded the two businesses did not fit within its core focus of contract food service.[124] Permira, a leading European-based private equity firm, was granted exclusivity in handling the deal, which involved a debt package from five banks and an additional investor. Because of high leverage, LBOs are often accompanied by selling off the company's assets to repay debt. Consequently, organizations typically become smaller and more focused after an LBO. For example, Planet Hollywood is now a much smaller company and is privately owned, having been a publicly traded company prior to its LBO.

During the late 1970s and early 1980s, LBOs gained a reputation as a means of turning around failing divisions.[125] However, some researchers have discovered that LBOs stifle innovation, similar to what can happen with mergers and acquisitions.[126] Others have found that LBO firms have comparatively slower growth in sales and employees, and that they tend to divest a larger proportion of both noncore and core businesses, compared to firms that remained public.[127] Also, some executives who initiate LBOs seem to receive an excessive return, regardless of the consequences to others. For example, John Kluge made a $3 billion profit in two years through dismantling Metromedia following an LBO.[128] Plant closings, relocations, and workforce reductions are all common outcomes. Consequently, some businesspeople are starting to wonder if LBOs are really in the best interests of all stakeholders. LBOs can certainly do seemingly irreparable damage to organizational resources.

> In 1996, Robert Hass led a LBO of Levi Strauss & Co., putting its future in the hands of four people: himself, an uncle, and two cousins. Other family shareholders had a choice of staying in or cashing out. While most of them stayed, they probably should have cashed out. Under Robert's leadership during the 90s, "Levi's market share among males ages 14 to 19 has since dropped in half, it hasn't had a successful new product in years, its advertising campaigns have been failures, its in-store presentations are embarrassing, and it manufacturing costs are bloated." He launched an $850 million reengineering that was a huge failure. From 1997 to 1999, the company announced plans to shutter twenty-nine factories in the United States and Europe and eliminate 16,310 jobs. Fortune estimated that during the first four or five years of the LBO, Levi Strauss's market value shrank from $14 billion to about $8 billion. In the same time period, Gap, a rival company, grew from $7 billion to over $40 billion.[129]

It is the responsibility of the board of directors to ensure that stakeholder interests are considered prior to approving an LBO:

> When considering a leveraged buyout, board members must treat fairly not only shareholders but other stakeholders as well. Corporate groups—employees, creditors, customers, suppliers, and local communities—claim the right to object to leveraged buyouts on the grounds that they have made a larger investment in—and have a more enduring relationship with—the corporation than do persons who trade share certificates daily on the stock exchanges. ... Similarly, if short-run profit is at the expense of and violates the expectations of employees, customers, communities, or suppliers, companies will find themselves unable to do business. The better employees will leave. Customers will stop buying. Communities will refuse to extend services. Suppliers will minimize their exposure.[130]

Not surprisingly, reports of failed LBOs are not uncommon. Successful LBOs require buying a company at the right price with the right financing, combined with outstanding management and fair treatment of stakeholders.[131]

CHANGES TO ORGANIZATIONAL DESIGN

Organizational design can be a potent force in restructuring efforts. For example, as organizations diversify, top managers have a more difficult time processing the vast amounts of diverse information that are needed to appropriately control each business. Their span of control is too large. Consequently, one type of change to organization design may be a move to a more decentralized product/market or divisional structure. The result is more managers with smaller spans of control and a greater capacity to understand each of their respective business areas. On the other hand, a company may desire more consistency and control over operations, thus moving toward centralization rather than decentralization.

> Choice Hotels International wanted to operate more efficiently and wanted to provide more consistent service to franchisees. To accomplish that, the company underwent a reorganization. The restructuring reduced the regional sales offices from five to three, centralized franchise sales in Silver Spring, Maryland, and realigned marketing operations to increase business.[132]

Because organization structure will be thoroughly covered in Chapter 8, we will not say more about it at this point. However, closely linked to changes in organizational structure are adjustments to the culture of the firm, the unseen glue that holds the structure together. A successful turnaround is often accompanied by a dramatic change in culture. If restructuring activities are precipitated by unusually poor economic or competitive conditions, a strong strategy-supportive culture can be undermined by the actions taken during the restructuring.[133] In other retrenchment situations, the existing culture may be part of the problem: too little focus on quality, too little learning and sharing, a poor attitude toward customers, or a lack of innovation.

If the culture is part of the problem, then the restructuring effort has to address the necessary changes in culture. It is difficult for an organization to throw off its old way of doing business. For instance, many vacation ownership companies have historically been excellent at real estate development, with a depth of knowledge about feasibility, development, and construction design. Once a resort is developed, the sales and marketing know-how then kicks in. Unfortunately, many of these firms are deficient in the financial components of the business and need to undergo significant restructuring in systems. Once acquired these companies need to transition from an entrepreneurial structure to one with much stronger corporate disciplines.[134] Following a hostile takeover, Linda Wachner, CEO of Warnaco, says she had to instill a hardworking, "do it now" culture to improve the organization's performance.[135] In 1999, Sony, the Japanese conglomerate with worldwide sales of more than $56 billion and 170,000 employees, combined a new structure with cultural change in order to create more of an entrepreneurial spirit. When Nobuyuki Idei became president of the company in 1995, he gave managers two slogans: "Regeneration" and "Digital Dream Kids."

Reengineering can also lead to significant changes in the way an organization is designed. "Business Process Reengineering involves the radical redesign of core business processes to achieve dramatic improvements in productivity cycle times and quality. Companies start with a blank sheet of paper and rethink existing processes, typically placing increased emphasis on customer needs. They reduce organizational layers and unproductive activities in two ways: they redesign functional organizations into cross-functional teams, and they use technology to improve data dissemination and decision making."[136] Based on a survey of executives of American firms, more than three-quarters of large firms in the United States were involved in reengineering. However, satisfaction rates were low for reengineering, and use of it has dropped significantly. Some business experts think that reengineering may have been just a fad.

Some authors suggest that restructuring should be a continuous process.[137] Changes in global markets and technology have created a permanent need for firms to focus on what they do best and to divest any parts of their organizations that no longer contribute to their missions or long-term goals. However, most organizations have a hard time achieving significant changes, and managers' mental models cause them to resist change. Consequently, continuous restructuring is a good idea, and perhaps even essential to remaining competitive, but it is certainly difficult to accomplish.

PORTFOLIO MANAGEMENT

Thus far in this chapter we have discussed the basic corporate-level strategies and the techniques organizations use to carry them out. For example, we discussed formulation of a related-diversification strategy and also described how acquisitions can be used to implement it. As a firm begins to diversify, it will start to develop a portfolio of businesses. Consequently, the final corporate-level tool we will discuss in this chapter is portfolio management. Portfolio management refers to managing the mix of businesses in the corporate portfolio. CEOs of large diversified organizations continually face decisions concerning how to divide organizational resources among diversified units and where to invest new capital, as well as which businesses to divest. Portfolio models are designed to help managers make these types of decisions.

Portfolio planning gained wide acceptance during the 1970s, and, by 1979, approximately 45 percent of *Fortune* 500 companies were using some type of portfolio planning.[138] In spite of their adoption in many organizations, portfolio-management techniques are the subject of a considerable amount of criticism from strategic management scholars.[139] However, since these techniques are still in wide use, this book would be incomplete without them. Keep in mind that they are not a panacea and should not replace other types of sound strategic analysis.

The simplest and first widely used portfolio model was the Boston Consulting Group (BCG) Matrix, displayed in Figure 6.3. The model is simple, but most of the other portfolio techniques are adaptations of it. Consequently, if you understand how to use it you can develop a variation of it that fits the company you are studying much better. The BCG Matrix is based on two factors, business growth rate and relative market share. Business growth rate is the growth rate of the industry in which a particular business unit is involved. Relative market share is calculated as the ratio of the business unit's size to the size of its largest competitor. The two factors are used to plot all of the businesses in which the organization is involved, represented as Stars, Question Marks (also called Problem Children), Cash Cows, and Dogs.

The BCG Matrix can be useful in planning cash flows. Cash Cows tend to generate more cash than they can effectively reinvest, while Question Marks require additional cash to sustain rapid growth, and Stars generate about as much cash as they use, on average. According to BCG, Stars and Cash Cows, with their superior market-share positions, tend to be the most profitable businesses. Consequently, the optimal BCG portfolio contains a balance of Stars, Cash Cows, and Question Marks. Stars have the greatest potential for growth and tend to be highly profitable. However, as the industries in which Stars are involved mature and their growth slows, they naturally become Cash Cows. Therefore, Question Marks are important because of their potential role as future Stars in the organization. Dogs are the least attractive types of business. The original prescription was to divest them. However, even Dogs can be maintained in the portfolio as long as they do not

FIGURE 6.3	THE BOSTON CONSULTING GROUP (BCG) PORTFOLIO MATRIX

Source: Boston Consulting Group, copyright © 1970, used with permission.

become a drain on corporate resources. Also, some organizations are successful at positioning their Dogs in an attractive niche in their industries.

One of the central ideas of the BCG Matrix is that high market share leads to high profitability due to learning effects, experience effects, entry barriers, market power, and other influences. In fact, there is evidence, both in the strategic management literature and in the economics literature, that higher market share is associated with higher profitability in some instances. However, some low-share businesses enjoy high profitability.[140] The real relationship between market share and profitability depends on many factors, including the nature of the industry and the strategy of the firm. For example, one researcher found that the market share–profitability relationship is stronger in some industries than in others. He also discovered that beyond a certain market share, profitability tended to trail off.[141]

A lot of the criticism related to the BCG matrix is due to its simplicity. Only two factors are considered, and only two divisions, high and low, are used for each factor. Also, growth rate is an oversimplification of industry attractiveness, and market share is an inadequate barometer of competitive position. A common criticism that applies to many portfolio models, and especially the BCG Matrix, is that they are based on the past instead of the future. Given the rate of change in the current economic and political environments, and the dynamic nature of hospitality firms this criticism is probably valid. Finally, another problem that is inherent in all matrix approaches is that industries are hard to define.

Numerous organizational managers and business writers have developed portfolio matrices that overcome some of the limitations of the BCG Matrix.[142] Virtually any variables or combination of variables of strategic importance can be plotted along the axes of a portfolio matrix. The selection of variables depends on what the organization considers important. By applying resource analysis and environmental analysis to a portfolio model, it may be possible to tap the potential of a business unit as well as its current competitive standing. For example, based on a thorough resource analysis, a firm's competitive position could be determined based on the strength of its human, physical, financial, knowledge-based, and general organizational resources, especially as they relate to competitive advantage. Industry attractiveness may be assessed by evaluating the power of suppliers and customers, the level of competitive rivalry, the threat of substitutes, the height of entry barriers, the amount and type of regulation, the power of unions, rate of growth, current profitability, and resiliency during downturns. From a portfolio-management perspective, businesses that are in a strong competitive position in attractive industries should be given the highest priority with regard to resource allocations.

Portfolio analysis can also be adapted to tourism, in which the focus is not on a specific company but the destination itself, such as a country, region, or a city. Managing destination tourism is often the responsibility of national and regional non-profit tourism organizations, which use a series of factors/variables relating to potential tourism markets, the destination, and the competition to create portfolio matrices. While these organizations typically do not have a direct economic interest in tourism products, they do need to diagnose and strategically assess the attractiveness of each current and potential market segment and their competitive position. Portfolio analysis is a useful tool for tourist destination management and can help focus marketing and promotion activities. In a study of Portugal as a tourist destination, examples of the factors used on the attractiveness axis included market size, market growth rate, disposable income per capita, average daily spending, seasonality, distance from destination, benefits sought by tourists when they travel abroad, and accessibility by air. To measure competitiveness, factors such as levels of prices, travel costs to destination, and quality of services, products, and benefits of tourism were included in the matrices. The study indicated that Portugal is most competitive in Spain, followed by France and the United Kingdom, suggesting that it has different levels of competitiveness for various tourism generating markets.[143]

In conclusion, while portfolio-management models have weaknesses and limitations, they provide an additional tool to assist managers in anticipating cash flows and making resource-allocation decisions. Hotel and restaurant-chain executives may find them especially useful in determining how to allocate resources among a variety of hotel or restaurant brands. Airline and cruise line executives might conduct similar analyses of particular market segments. Finally, not-for-profit tourism organizations can use the analysis for destination management. The key is to apply portfolio techniques in the way that is most useful to the organization in combination with other strategic tools.

KEY-POINTS SUMMARY

Corporate-level strategy focuses on the selection of businesses in which the firm will compete, and on the tactics used to enter and manage those businesses and other corporate-level resources. At the corporate level, primary strategy-formulation responsibilities include setting the direction of the entire organization, formulation of a corporate strategy, selection of businesses in which to compete, selection of tactics for diversification and growth, and management of corporate resources and capabilities. The three broad approaches to corporate-level strategy are concentration, vertical integration, and diversification, which is divided into two broad categories, related and unrelated. These strategies, and their strengths and weaknesses, were discussed in depth.

Concentration is associated with a narrow business definition. As long as a company has virtually all of its resource investments in one business area, it is concentrating. Concentration strategies allow a company to focus on doing one business very well; however, a key disadvantage is that the company depends on that one business for survival. Consequently, most successful organizations abandon their concentration strategies at some point due to market saturation, excess resources for which they need to find a use, or some other reason. Through internal ventures, mergers and acquisitions, or joint ventures, they pursue businesses outside their core business areas.

Vertical integration is a strategy that involves an organization becoming its own supplier (backward integration) or distributor (forward integration). Compared to other corporate-level strategies, vertical integration has not been found to be highly profitable because it reduces strategic flexibility. Vertical integration allows a firm to become its own supplier or customer. According to the theory of transaction cost economics, if required resources can be obtained from a competitive open market without allocating an undue amount of time or other resources to the contracting process or contract enforcement, it is probably in the best interests of an organization to buy from the market instead of vertically integrating.

Diversification that stems from common markets, functions served, technologies, or products and services is referred to as related diversification. Unrelated diversification is not based on commonality among the activities of the corporation. It was a very popular strategy during the 1950s, 1960s, and the early 1970s. However, research results seem to indicate that it did not lead to the high performance that many executives had expected. Many organizations are now restructuring to reduce unrelated diversification. Related diversification, on the other hand, is still a popular strategy. Businesses are related if they share a common market, technology, raw material, or any one of many other factors. However, for a related-diversification strategy to have its full positive impact, synergy must be created. In addition to some form of relatedness, organizational fit is required, as are actions on the part of managers to actually make synergy a reality.

Mergers and acquisitions are the quickest way to diversify; however, they are fraught with difficulties, and most of them fail to meet the expectations of the firms involved. Nevertheless, friendly acquisitions between companies that have complementary skills or resources, executed after a thorough due-diligence process, are more likely to succeed.

Many firms eventually come to a point at which slow growth, declining profits, or some other crisis forces corporate-level managers to "rethink" their entire organizations. The result of this process is usually some form of restructuring. Some of the most common restructuring approaches include turnaround strategies and downsizing, refocusing corporate assets on distinctive competencies, Chapter 11 reorganization, leveraged buyouts, and changes to organizational design. Continuous restructuring may help keep an organization healthy, but it is hard to accomplish and may be too costly.

Portfolio management tools help top executives manage a portfolio of businesses. They are flexible enough to incorporate a variety of strategic variables, but they should be used with caution and only in combination with other tools of strategic management. These techniques for strategic decision making can be applied to tourism destinations as well as company portfolios.

Discussion Questions

1. Describe the three basic corporate-level strategies.
2. What are the strengths and weaknesses of a concentration strategy? What are the strengths and weaknesses of a vertical integration strategy?
3. How is a vertical integration strategy like a concentration strategy? How is it like an unrelated diversification strategy?
4. What is the difference between forward and backward integration? Which is likely to be more profitable for hospitality firms? Why?
5. Why isn't an unrelated diversification strategy generally a good idea?

6. What is required for a related diversification strategy to produce synergy? Please explain.

7. What are ten common reasons for mergers and acquisitions? What are some of the major reasons that mergers and acquisitions often produce unsatisfactory results?

8. Which of the major restructuring techniques is most likely to provide rapid results? Defend your answer.

9. Is downsizing or downscoping typically a more appropriate restructuring technique? Why? Also, what are some of the ill effects from layoffs? How can an organization avoid layoffs and still reduce labor costs?

10. Why do you think Chapter 11 doesn't work out for most firms?

11. What are some of the key factors that lead to success in restructuring, regardless of the technique used to restructure?

12. Create a BCG Matrix for a diversified hospitality firm. Now do a portfolio analysis for a destination. What does this portfolio management tool tell you about organizations and destinations?

NOTES

1. Marriott International, Inc., *Annual Report 2002*; Host Marriott Corporation, *Annual Report 2001*.

2. A. D. Chandler Jr., *Strategy and Structure: Chapters in the History of the Industrial Enterprise* (Cambridge, Mass.: MIT Press, 1962).

3. Loews Hotels, http://www.loewshotels.com. August 16, 2003.

4. Domino's Pizza, http://www.dominos.com. August 16, 2003.

5. R. P. Rumelt, *Strategy, Structure, and Economic Performance* (Boston: Harvard Business School, 1974); R. P. Rumelt, "Diversification Strategy and Profitability," *Strategic Management Journal* 3 (1982): 359–369.

6. D. Nelms, "Strange Bedfellow," *Air Transport World*, September 1993, 60–65.

7. G. Lafferty and A. van Fossen, "Integrating the Tourism Industry: Problems and Strategies," *Tourism Management* 22 (2001): 11–19; D. Nelms, "Strange Bedfellow."

8. A. Garber, "Berger Giants Weigh In with More Healthful Menu Ideas," *Nation's Restaurant News*, 26 May 2003, 1, 6; A. Garber, "It's Not Easy Not Being Green," *Nation's Restaurant News*, 11 August 2003, 66.

9. H. I. Ansoff, *Corporate Strategy: An Analytical Approach to Business Policy for Growth and Expansion* (New York: McGraw-Hill, 1965), 129–130.

10. Rumelt, *Strategy, Structure*; Rumelt, "Diversification Strategy."

11. Cendant Corporation, http://www.cendant.com. August 16, 2003.

12. K. R. Harrigan, "Formulating Vertical Integration Strategies," *Academy of Management Review* 9 (1984): 639.

13. R. A. D'Aveni and D. J. Ravenscraft, "Economies of Integration versus Bureaucracy Costs: Does Vertical Integration Improve Performance?" *Academy of Management Journal* 37 (1994): 1167–1206.

14. S. Balakrishnan and B. Wernerfelt, "Technical Change, Competition, and Vertical Integration," *Strategic Management Journal* 7 (1986): 347–359.

15. O. E. Williamson, *Markets and Hierarchies: Analysis and Antitrust Implications* (New York: The Free Press, 1975); O. E. Williamson, *The Economic Institutions of Capitalism* (New York: The Free Press, 1985).

16. Williamson, *Markets and Hierarchies*, 8.

17. B. Klein, R. Crawford, and A. A. Alchian, "Vertical Integration, Appropriable Rents, and the Competitive Contracting Process," *Journal of Law and Economics* 21 (1978): 297–326; Williamson, *Markets and Hierarchies*, 9–10.

18. R. E. Hoskisson, J. S. Harrison, and D. A. Dubofsky, "Capital Market Implementation of M-Form Implementation and Diversification Strategy," *Strategic Management Journal* 12 (1991): 271–279.

19. K. R. Harrigan, "Exit Barriers and Vertical Integration," *Academy of Management Journal* (September 1985): 686–697.

20. Domino's Pizza, http://www.dominos.com/C1256B4200, August 16, 2003.

21. A. Spector, "Starwood Cooks Up Joint Venture, Buys 12% Stake in Grill Concepts," *Nation's Restaurant News*, 4 June 2001, 4.

22. D. D. Bergh, "Diversification Strategy Research at a Crossroads: Established, Emerging, and Anticipated Paths," in *The Blackwell Handbook of Strategic Management*, ed. M. A. Hitt, R. E. Freeman, and J. S. Harrison (Oxford: Blackwell Publishers, 2001), 362–383.

23. Information on the strategic arguments can be found in Ansoff, *Corporate Strategy*, 130–132; C. W. L. Hill and G. S. Hansen, "A Longitudinal Study of the Cause and Consequence of Changes in Diversification in the U.S. Pharmaceutical Industry," *Strategic Management Journal* 12 (1991): 187–199; W. G. Lewellen, "A Pure Financial Rationale for the Conglomerate Merger," *Journal of Finance* 26 (1971): 521–537; F. M. McDougall and D. K. Round, "A Comparison of Diversifying and Nondiversifying Australian Industrial Firms," *Academy of Management Journal* 27 (1984): 384–398; and R. Reed and G. A. Luffman, "Diversification: The Growing Confusion," *Strategic Management Journal* 7 (1986): 29–35. The personal arguments are outlined in W. Baumol, *Business Behavior, Value, and Growth* (New York: Harcourt, 1967); D. C. Mueller, "A Theory of Conglomerate Mergers," *Quarterly Review of Economics* 83 (1969): 644–660; N. Rajagopalan and J. E. Prescott, "Determinants of Top Management Compensation: Explaining the Impact of Economic, Behavioral, and Strategic Constructs and the Moderating Effects of Industry," *Journal of Management* 16 (1990): 515–538.

24. Ansoff, *Corporate Strategy*, 130–131.

25. A detailed review of this literature is found in R. E. Hoskisson and M. A. Hitt, "Antecedents and Performance Outcomes of Diversification: A Review and Critique of Theoretical Perspectives," *Journal of Management* 16 (1990): 468. More recent evidence is found in P. S. Davis et al., "Business Unit Relatedness and Performance: A Look at the Pulp and Paper Industry," *Strategic Management Journal* 13 (1992): 349–361; J. S. Harrison, E. H. Hall Jr., and R. Nagundkar, "Resource Allocation As an Outcropping of Strategic Consistency: Performance Implications," *Academy of Management Journal* 36 (1993): 1026–1051; J. Robins and M. Wiersema, "A Resource-Based Approach to the Multi-Business Firm: Empirical Analysis of Portfolio Interrelationships and Corporate Financial Performance," *Strategic Management Journal* 16 (1995): 277–299.

26. M. Lubatkin and S. Chatterjee, "Extending Modern Portfolio Theory into the Domain of Corporate Diversification: Does It Apply?" *Academy of Management Journal* 37 (1994): 109–136.

27. A. Salomon, "Hoteliers Diversify to Thrive," *Hotel and Motel Management*, 17 September 2001, 74–75.

28. M. E. Porter, *Competitive Advantage: Creating and Sustaining Superior Performance* (New York: The Free Press, 1985), 317–363.

29. D. J. Teece, "Economies of Scope and the Scope of the Enterprise," *Journal of Economic Behavior and Organization* 1 (1980): 223–247.

30. B. Gold, "Changing Perspectives on Size, Scale, and Returns: An Integrative Survey," *Journal of Economic Literature* 19 (1981): 5–33.

31. A. Zuber, "Accelerated Multibrand Growth Plan Puts Tricon in Driver's Seat," *Nation's Restaurant News*, 15 February 2002, 64.

32. *Annual Report YUM! Brands Inc. 2002.* 33. Ansoff, *Corporate Strategy.*

34. M. Beirne, "Four Seasons Puts Luxury into Leisure," *Brandweek*, 15 April, 2002, 4.

35. H. Itami, *Mobilizing Invisible Assets* (Cambridge, Mass.: Harvard University Press, 1987).

36. L. Weber, "Multibranding Offers All-in-one Fast-food Eats," *Fastfoodsource.com, Reuters News Service*, http://www.qsrweb.com/news_multibranding_20303.htm (2003).

37. P. R. Nayyar, "On the Measurement of Corporate Diversification Strategy: Evidence from Large U.S. Service Firms," *Strategic Management Journal* 13 (1992): 219–235; Reed and Luffman, "Diversification," 29–36.

38. A. Zuber, "To Market, to Market: Chains Find Strength in Numbers, Use Co-branding as Growth Vehicle," *Nation's Restaurant News*, 5 February 2001, 35.

39. Ibid.

40. D. B. Jemison and S. B. Sitkin, "Corporate Acquisitions: A Process Perspective," *Academy of Management Review* 11 (1986): 145–163.

41. T. Cruz, "Full Speed Ahead," *Hotels* (May 1999; 63-64). 42. M. C. Lauenstein, "Diversification—The Hidden Explanation of Success," *Sloan Management Review* (Fall 1985): 49–55.

43. G. R. Jones and C. W. Hill, "Transaction Cost Analysis of Strategy-Structure Choice," *Strategic Management Journal* 9 (1988): 159–172.

44. This section and portions of other sections in this chapter were strongly influenced by M. Goold and K. Luchs, "Why Diversify? Four Decades of Management Thinking," *Academy of Management Executive* (August 1993): 7–25.

45. Rumelt, "Diversification Strategy and Profitability," 361. See also Bergh, "Diversification Strategy Research."

46. A few examples of the many studies that demonstrate low performance associated with unrelated diversification are R. Amit and J. Livnat, "Diversification Strategies, Business Cycles, and Economic Performance," *Strategic Management Journal* 9 (1988): 99–110.; R. A. Bettis and V. Mahajan, "Risk/Return Performance of Diversified Firms," *Management Science* 31 (1985): 785–799; D. Ravenscraft and F. M. Scherer, *Mergers, Selloffs, and Economic Efficiency* (Washington, D.C.: Brookings Institution, 1987); P. G. Simmonds, "The Combined Diversification Breadth and Mode Dimensions and the Performance of Large Diversified Firms," *Strategic Management Journal* 11 (1990): 399–410; P. Varadarajan and V. Ramanujam, "Diversification and Performance: A Reexamination Using a New Two-Dimensional Conceptualization of Diversity in Firms," *Academy of Management Journal* 30 (1982): 380–393. On the other hand, the following studies are among those that support the superiority of unrelated diversification: R. M. Grant and A. P. Jammine, "Performance Differences between the Wrigley/Rumelt Strategic Categories," *Strategic Management Journal* 9 (1988): 333–346; A. Michel and I. Shaked, "Does Business Diversification Affect Performance?" *Financial Management* (Winter 1984): 18–25.

47. Lauenstein, "Diversification"; M. Lubatkin and R. C. Rogers, "Diversification, Systematic Risk, and Shareholder Return: A Capital Market Extension of Rumelt's 1974 Study," *Academy of Management Journal* 32 (1989): 454–465; M. Lubatkin and H. G. O'Neill, "Merger Strategies and Capital Market Risk," *Academy of Management Journal* 30 (1987): 665–684; M. Lubatkin, "Value-Creating Mergers: Fact or Folklore," *Academy of Management Executive* (November 1988): 295–302; C. A. Montgomery and H. Singh, "Diversification Strategy and Systematic Risk," *Strategic Management Journal* 5 (1984): 181–191.

48. R. S. Attiyeh, "Where Next for Conglomerates?" *Business Horizons* (December 1969): 39–44.

49. "History—About Us," http://www.compass-group.com, 20 August 2003.

50. "History," http://www.omnihotels.com, 20 August 2003; "Company Facts, Background Information for TRT Holdings," http://www.hotelreports.com, 20 August 2003.

51. "A Conversation with Roberto Goizueta and Jack Welch," *Fortune,* 11 December 1995, 98–99.

52. Hoskisson and Hitt, "Antecedents and Performance Outcomes," 461–509; Shleifer and Vishny, "Takeovers in the '60s."

53. Hoskisson and Hitt, "Antecedents and Performance Outcomes," 461.

54. M. A. Hitt, J. S. Harrison, and R. D. Ireland, *Mergers and Acquisitions: A Guide to Creating Value for Stakeholders* (New York: Oxford University Press, 2001).

55. R. Kline, "Post–Merger Integration in Hospitality," http://hotel-online.com, Spring 1999.

56. Lubatkin, "Value-Creating Mergers"; J. Pfeffer, "Merger As a Response to Organizational Interdependence," *Administrative Science Quarterly* 17 (1972): 382–394.; J. H. Song, "Diversifying Acquisitions and Financial Relationships: Testing 1974–1976 Behaviour," *Strategic Management Journal* 4 (1983): 97–108; F. Trautwein, "Merger Motives and Merger Prescriptions," *Strategic Management Journal* 11 (1990): 283–295.

57. E. Perez, "Carnival, Winning Princess Bid, Is Poised to Expand Dominance," *The Wall Street Journal,* 28 October 2002, A3, A14; R. Selwitz, "Spain-based Hotel Company Considers U.S. Expansion," *Hotel and Motel Management,* August 2002, 7; "Gaming Announces Acquisition of Casino Management System Software Company," PR Newswire, 13 November 2002.

58. "China Merges Nine Airlines into Three," *Weekly Corporate Growth Report,* http://global.factiva.com, 21 October 21, 2002.

59. "Only the Strong Can Survive the Times: Consolidation Is the Wave of the Future," *Nation's Restaurant News,* 9 June 1997, 31.

60. L. L. Fowler and D. R. Schmidt, "Determinants of Tender Offer Post-Acquisition Financial Performance," *Journal of Management* 10 (1989): 339–350.

61. T. B. Pickens, "Professions of a Short-Termer," *Harvard Business Review* (May/June 1986): 75–79.

62. M. McDonald, "Brawl at the Mall," *U.S. News & World Report,* 17 March 2003, 37,63. Lubatkin, "Value-Creating Mergers."

64. One of the most active proponents of the view that mergers and acquisitions create value for acquiring-firm shareholders is Michael Lubatkin (see Lubatkin, "Value-Creating Mergers"). However, he recently reported strong evidence that contradicts his earlier conclusions in S. Chatterjee et al., "Cultural Differences and Shareholder Value in Related Mergers: Linking Equity and Human Capital," *Strategic Management Journal* 13 (1992): 319–334. Other strong summary evidence that mergers and acquisitions do not create value is found in W. B. Carper, "Corporate Acquisitions and Shareholder Wealth," *Journal of Management* 16 (1990): 807–823; D. K. Datta, G. E. Pinches, and V. K. Narayanan, "Factors Influencing Wealth Creation from Mergers and Acquisitions: A Meta-Analysis," *Strategic Management Journal* 13 (1992): 67–84; K. M. Davidson, "Do Megamergers Make Sense?" *Journal of Business Strategies* (Winter 1987): 40–48; T. F. Hogarty, "Profits from Merger: The Evidence of Fifty Years," *St. John's Law Review* 44 (Special Edition 1970): 378–391; S. R. Reid, *Mergers, Managers, and the Economy* (New York: McGraw-Hill, 1968).

65. M. A. Hitt et al., "Are Acquisitions a Poison Pill for Innovation?" *Academy of Management Executive* (November 1991): 20–35.

66. S. Thurm, "Cisco Says It Expects to Meet Profit Estimate," *The Wall Street Journal,* 4 October 2001, A12.

67. S. Wolchuk, S. Lerner, and M. Scoviak, "325 Hotels," *Hotels,* July 2002: pp. 41-4268. M. E. Porter, "From Competitive Advantage to Corporate Strategy," *Harvard Business Review* (May/June 1987): 59.

69. L. Canina, "Acquisitions in the Lodging Industry: Good News for Buyers and Sellers," *Cornell Hotel and Restaurant Administration Quarterly* 42(6) (December 2001): 47–54.

70. M. Hitt et al., "Attributes of Successful and Unsuccessful Acquisitions of U.S. Firms," *British Journal of Management* 9 (1998): 91–114.

71. Hitt, Harrison, and Ireland, *Mergers and Acquisitions.* See also J. B. Kusewitt Jr., "An Exploratory Study of Strategic Acquisition Factors Relating to Success," *Strategic Management Journal* 6 (1985): 151–169; L. M. Shelton, "Strategic Business Fits and Corporate Acquisition: Empirical Evidence," *Strategic Management Journal* 9 (1988): 279–287.

72. J. S. Harrison, M. A. Hitt, R. E. Hoskisson and R. D. Ireland, "Resource Complementarity in Business Combinations: Extending the Logic to Organizational Alliances," *Journal of Management* 27 (2001): 679–690; J. S. Harrison et al., "Synergies and Post-Acquisition Performance: Differences versus Similarities in Resource Allocations," *Journal of Management* 17 (1991): 173–190; M. A. Hitt, R. D. Ireland, and J. S. Harrison, "Mergers and Acquisitions: A Value Creating or Value Destroying Strategy?" in *Blackwell Handbook of Strategic Management,* ed. Hitt, Freeman, and Harrison, 384–408.

73. S. Chatterjee et al., "Cultural Differences and Shareholder Value in Related Mergers: Linking Equity and Human Capital," *Strategic Management Journal* 13 (1992): 319–334; D. K. Datta, "Organizational Fit and Acquisition Performance: Effects of Post-Acquisition Integration," *Strategic Management Journal* 12 (1991): 281–297; Jemison and Sitkin, "Corporate Acquisitions."

74. T. H. Brush, "Predicted Change in Operational Synergy and Post-Acquisition Performance of Acquired Businesses," *Strategic Management Journal* 17 (1996): 1–24.

75. F. T. Paine and D. J. Power, "Merger Strategy: An Examination of Drucker's Five Rules for Successful Acquisition," *Strategic Management Journal* 5 (1984): 99–110.

76. M. L. Sirower and S. F. O'Byrne, "The Measurement of Post-Acquisition Performance: Toward a Value-Based Benchmarking Methodology," *Applied Corporate Finance* 11 (1998): 107–121.

77. Hitt, Harrison, and Ireland, *Mergers and Acquisitions.*

78. This is one of my private consulting clients. I am not at liberty to disclose the name.

79. N. Byrnes, "The Good CEO," *Business Week,* 23 September 2002, 80.

80. F. Vermeulen and H. Barkema, "Learning through Acquisitions," *Academy of Management Journal* 44 (2001): 457.

81. Hitt, Harrison, and Ireland, *Mergers and Acquisitions*, chap. 7.

82. J. Peters "Cosi Chain Seeks Bread, New CEO, Plans Closings," *Nation's Restaurant News*, 14 April 2003, 4.

83. These arguments are outlined in M. A. Hitt, R. E. Hoskisson, and J. S. Harrison, "Strategic Competitiveness in the 1990s: Challenges and Opportunities for U.S. Executives," *Academy of Management Executive* (May 1991): 7–22.

84. R. E. Hoskisson and R. A. Johnson, "Corporate Restructuring and Strategic Change: The Effect on Diversification Strategy and R&D Intensity," *Strategic Management Journal* 13 (1992): 625–634.

85. C. J. Gersick, "Revolutionary Change Theories: A Multi-Level Exploration of the Punctuated Equilibrium Paradigm," *Academy of Management Review* 16 (1991): 10–37; M. I. Tushman and E. Romanelli, "Organizational Evolution: A Metamorphosis Model of Convergence and Reorientation," in *Research in Organization Behavior*, ed. E. E. Cummings and B. M. Staw (Greenwich, Conn: JAI Press, 1985), 171–222.

86. N. A. Wishart, J. J. Elam, and D. Robey, "Redrawing the Portrait of a Learning Organization: Inside Knight-Ridder, Inc.," *Academy of Management Executive* 10 (February 1996): 7–20; J. P. Walsh, "Managerial and Organizational Cognition," *Organization Science* 6 (1995): 280–321.

87. Gersick, "Revolutionary Change Theories"; Tushman and Romanelli, "Organizational Evolution."

88. Gersick, "Revolutionary Change Theories," 22.

89. Gersick, "Revolutionary Change Theories"; Tushman and Romanelli, "Organizational Evolution."

90. J. P. Walsh, "Operators Turn Underperformers into Gems," *Hotel and Motel Management* 19 March 2001, 1.

91. B. Adams, "IHG Cuts Costs, Maps Brands' Growth Plans," *Hotel and Motel Management*, 16 June 2003, 1.

92. M. Murray, "Amid Record Profits, Companies Continue to Lay Off Employees," *The Wall Street Journal*, 4 May 1995, A1, A6.

93. W. McKinley, C. M. Sanchez, and A. G. Schick, "Organizational Downsizing: Constraining, Cloning, Learning," *Academy of Management Executive* (August 1995): 32.

94. K. S. Cameron, S. J. Freeman, and Aneil K. Mishra, "Best Practices in White-Collar Downsizing: Managing Contradictions," *Academy of Management Executive* (August 1991): 57–73.

95. Adapted from C. Solomon, "Amoco to Cut 8,500 Workers, or 16% of Force," *The Wall Street Journal*, 9 July 1992, A3.

96. J. Brockner et al., "Survivors' Reactions to Layoffs: We Get By with a Little Help from Our Friends," *Administrative Science Quarterly* 32 (1987): 526–541.

97. D. L. Worrell, W. N. Davidson III, and V. M. Sharma, "Layoff Announcements and Stockholder Wealth," *Academy of Management Journal* 34 (1991): 662–678.

98. Bureau of Labor Statistics, "Impact of the Events of September 11, 2001, on the Mass Layoff Statistics Data Series," 30 November 2001.

99. Bureau of Labor Statistics, "Impact of the Events of September 11, 2001, on the Mass Layoff Statistics Data Series."

100. M. Taylor, M and C. Enz, "Voices from the Field: GM's Responses to the Events of September 11, 2001," *Cornell Hotel and Administration Quarterly* 43, no. 1: 7-20 (February 2002).

101. R. Ward, "September 11 and the Restructuring of the Airline Industry," *Dollars and Sense* (May/June 2002), 16.

102. B. Sternlicht, Chairman/CEO, Starwood Hotels & Resorts. *Hotel Business*, 21 October–6 November 2001, 9.

103. D. A. Heenan, "The Downside of Downsizing," *Journal of Business Strategy* (November/December 1989): 18.

104. If you would like to read some of this literature, you can start with Brockner et al., "Survivors' Reactions," and C. Hardy, "Investing in Retrenchment: Avoiding the Hidden Costs," *California Management Review* 29 (1987): 111–125.

105. M. Settles, "Humane Downsizing: Can It Be Done?" *Journal of Business Ethics* 7 (1988): 961–963; Worrell, Davidson, and Sharma, "Layoff Announcements."

106. E. Faltermeyer, "Is This Layoff Necessary?" *Fortune*, 1 June 1992, 71–86.

107. R. E. Hoskisson et al., "Restructuring Strategies of Diversified Business Groups: Differences Associated with Country Institutional Environments," in *Blackwell Handbook of Strategic Management*, ed. Hitt, Freeman, and Harrison, 433–463.

108. R. Ruggless, "Carlson to Divest E-Brands, Focus on Core Concepts," *Nation's Restaurant News,* 4 February 2002, 1.

109. C. Markides, "Consequences of Corporate Refocusing: Ex Ante Evidence," *Academy of Management Journal* 35 (1992): 398–412.

110. J. Higley, "Wyndham Maintains Improvement Course," *Hotel and Motel Management,* 15 July 2002, 4.

111. Hitt, Hoskisson, and Harrison, "Strategic Competitiveness"; R. E. Hoskisson and M. A. Hitt, *Downscoping: How to Tame the Diversified Firm* (New York: Oxford University Press, 1994), 3.

112. Hoskisson and Johnson, "Corporate Restructuring"; Hoskisson and Hitt, *Downscoping.*

113. C. A. Montgomery, A. R. Thomas, and R. Kammath, "Divestiture, Market Valuation, and Strategy," *Academy of Management Journal* 27 (1984): 830–840.

114. C. Goldsmith and A. Raghavan, "Six Continents to Split Businesses," *Wall Street Journal* 13 March 2003, A5.

115. Hitt, Hoskisson, and Harrison, "Strategic Competitiveness," 7–21.

116. R. L. Daft, *Organization Theory and Design,* 4th ed. (St. Paul, Minn.: West Publishing, 1992), 94.

117. D. M. Flynn and M. Farid, "The Intentional Use of Chapter XI: Lingering versus Immediate Filing," *Strategic Management Journal* 12 (1991): 63–64.

118. A. Merrick, "Kmart Lays Out Plans to Trim Its Size, Increase Efficiency in Bankruptcy Filing," *The Wall Street Journal,* 23 January 2002, A3.

119. "Planet Hollywood Wins Court Approval of Reorganization," *Wall Street Journal,* 17 December 2002, A12.

120. E. Thornton and C. Palmeri, "Who Can Afford to Go Broke?" *Business Week,* 10 September 2001, 116.

121. Flynn and Farid, "Intentional Use."

122. W. N. Moulton, "Bankruptcy As a Deliberate Strategy: Theoretical Considerations and Empirical Evidence," *Strategic Management Journal* 14 (1993): 130.

123. R. Ruggless, "Facing Buffet of Problems, Piccadilly Eyes Iffy Future," *Nation's Restaurant News,* 14 July 2003, 8, 54.

124. L. Bushrod, "Little Chef/Travelodge," *European Venture Capital Journal,* 1 April 2003, 1.

125. K. M. Davidson, "Another Look at LBOs," *Journal of Business Strategies* (January/February 1988): 44–47.

126. A good review of these studies, of which there are seven, is found in S. A. Zahra and M. Fescina, "Will Leveraged Buyouts Kill U.S. Corporate Research and Development?" *Academy of Management Executive* (November 1991): 7–21.

127. M. F. Wiersema and J. P. Liebeskind, "The Effects of Leveraged Buyouts on Corporate Growth and Diversification in Large Firms," *Strategic Management Journal* 16 (1995): 447–460.

128. Davidson, "Another Look at LBOs."

129. N. Munk, "How Levi's Trashed a Great American Brand," in *Strategic Management,* ed. E. H. Bernstein (Guildford, Conn.: McGraw-Hill/Dushkin, 2001), 163–168, first published in *Fortune,* 12 April, 1999.

130. Davidson, "Another Look at LBOs," 44–45.

131. M. Schwarz and E. A. Weinstein, "So You Want to Do a Leveraged Buyout," *Journal of Business Strategies* (January/February 1989): 10–15.

132. J. P. Walsh, "Choice Restructures to Offer Better Service to Franchisees," *Hotel and Motel Management,* 5 February 2001, 1.

133. B. O'Brian, "Delta Air Makes Painful Cuts in Effort to Stem Red Ink," *The Wall Street Journal,* 10 September 1992, B4.

134. J. Simoon and T. Fisher, "Vacation Ownership—Rengineering the Financial Platform," *Lodging Hospitality,* May 1998, 14–15.

135. J. M. Graves, "Leaders of Corporate Change," *Fortune,* 14 December 1992, 113.

136. D. Rigby, "Management Tools and Techniques: A Survey," *California Management Review* 43, no. 2 (Winter 2001): 156.

137. J. F. Bandnowski, "Restructuring Is a Continuous Process," *Long Range Planning* (January 1991): 10–14.

138. P. Hapeslagh, "Portfolio Planning: Uses and Limitations," *Harvard Business Review* (January/February 1982): 58–73.

139. J. P. Shay, "Food-Service Strategy: An Integrated, Business-life-cycle Approach," *Cornell Hotel and Restaurant Administration Quarterly* 38(3) (June 1997), 36–49; R. A. Kerin, V. Mahajan, and P. R. Varadarajan, *Strategic*

Market Planning (Needham Heights, Mass.: Allyn & Bacon, 1990), 94; J. A. Seeger, "Reversing the Images of BCG's Growth Share Matrix," *Strategic Management Journal* 5 (1984): 93–97.

140. R. G. Hammermesh, M. J. Anderson, and J. E. Harris, "Strategies for Low Market Share Businesses," *Harvard Business Review* (May/June 1978): 95–102; C. Y. Woo and A. C. Cooper, "Market Share Leadership—Not Always So Good," *Harvard Business Review* (January/February 1984): 50–54.

141. J. Schwalbach, "Profitability and Market Share: A Reflection on the Functional Relationship," *Strategic Management Journal* 12 (1991): 299–306.

142. C. W. Hofer and D. Schendel, *Strategy Formulation: Analytical Concepts* (St. Paul: South-Western College Publishing, 1978).

143. P. Aguas, J. Costa, and P. Rita, "A tourist market portfolio for Portugal," *International Journal of Contemporary Hospitality Management* (7 December 2000): 394–400.

7

Strategy Implementation Through Interorganizational Relationships and Management of Functional Resources

*T*oday more than 50 percent of the airline network traffic is in the hands of five alliances. Global alliances have become the backbone of international aviation since the first such alliance, Star, was formed in 1997. These alliances allow carriers to leverage existing routes and increase marketing power by promoting "code sharing." Code sharing permits one airline to tack its flight number onto a flight operated by a partner carrier. Passengers might buy a ticket on one airline, not even knowing that the plane they take will be operated by another carrier. This allows carriers to expand around the world with what appears to be their own network. Global alliances are not tied by ownership, but the expanding carrier partnerships have made their fates increasingly intertwined.

The Star alliance includes heavyweight carriers such as Lufthansa, Singapore Airlines, United Airlines, and Air Canada, along with smaller carriers Austrian Airlines and Air New Zealand. In 1999, American Airlines and British Airways joined forces by forming Oneworld; they were followed in 2001 by SkyTeam, an alliance among Delta Airlines, Air France, CSA Czech Airlines, AeroMexico, and Korean Air.

Airline alliances are busy strategizing to add more alliance partners. SkyTeam wants to add more European partners, one each in Argentina and Brazil and another in Southeast Asia. The members of this alliance plan to focus on cost-saving initiatives. They launched combined fuel tenders at select airports and slashed ground handling costs by 20–40 percent at five

South American airports by joining forces. SkyTeam also plans joint sales offices and could, in the long term, coordinate aircraft acquisitions. In the airline industry, only three global alliances—Oneworld, SkyTeam, and Star—are expected to survive, expand, and prosper, according to Air France Chairman/CEO Jean-Cyril Spinetta.[1]

INTRODUCTION

As the global airline industry demonstrates, formation of partnerships is one way to take advantage of opportunities that arise in the external environment. Productive interorganizational relationships can be sources of competitive advantage. The interdependent nature of tourism, composed of complementary sectors such as lodging, transportation, food and beverage, attractions, recreation, leisure, travel organizers, government tourist organizations, and wholesale travel agencies makes the management of alliances and cooperative relationships a critical skill. Since 1841, when Thomas Cook packaged the first tour, hospitality and tourism enterprises have relied on long-term cooperative alliances with one another.[2] Cooperative interfirm relationships, common in the industry, involve two firms working together for mutual strategic value. On the other hand, companies may also develop competitive advantages through superior acquisition, development, and management of internal resources and capabilities. Of course, internal and external approaches to strategy implementation are not mutually exclusive. That is, firms use both approaches simultaneously. Hospitality firms compete energetically but are quick to forge cooperative alliances when necessary.

The focus of this chapter is on strategy implementation. It presupposes that the firm has established an appropriate strategic direction and strategies at the corporate and business levels, as well as a growth strategy. The organization then needs to develop specific tactics for executing those strategies. The first section in this chapter emphasizes the collaborative nature of the tourism industry, the role of interorganizational relationships in the successful execution of strategies, and methods of effectively managing relationships with external stakeholders. The second section deals with how companies can manage resources in the functional areas so as to develop competitive advantage. Taken together, these sections provide a wealth of ideas that can help firms achieve competitive success as they implement their strategies.

Chapter 2 introduced common forms of interorganizational relationships, including joint ventures, networks, consortia, alliances, trade groups, and interlocking directorates (see Table 2.4 for a review of these terms). All of these arrangements represent various types of partnerships; therefore, the term partnership will be used interchangeably with interorganizational relationship in the remainder of this text. This section will focus specifically on how such partnerships can be used to implement strategies. Partnerships can help organizations achieve many of the same objectives that are sought through mergers and acquisitions. Some of the most commonly cited reasons for acquisitions are that they can lead to sales growth, to increased earnings, or to a balance in a portfolio of businesses.[3] Working in partnership with other firms can also help establish a destination as a desirable travel site.

INTERORGANIZATIONAL RELATIONSHIPS AND STAKEHOLDER MANAGEMENT IN THE TOURISM INDUSTRY

The travel industry is the world's largest because it is composed of a complex and diverse variety of types of organizations. These firms must work together to provide the overall experience in what is called a tourism cluster or overall system, and thus the motivation to partner is particularly great. Tourism clusters are geographic concentrations of competing, complementary, and interdependent firms. The industry can be divided into three types of organizational sectors that work cooperatively: (1) the direct providers of travel services, (2) support services or suppliers to the industry, and (3) tourism development organizations, agencies, and institutions that affect provider firms, support services organizations, and the traveler.[4] These organizational sectors can represent an important competitive advantage for a city, region, or country. Figure 7.1 illustrates the cooperative system of a tourism cluster in Costa Rica.

At the center of the Costa Rican tourism cluster are the motivations to visit the country. In a circle around motivations are industry sectors with a direct interface with tourists. These are the lodging, transportation, food and beverage, attractions, and promotion sectors. In the peripheral circle are support services, training, support organizations and transportation infrastructure. These are sectors important to the service ultimately received by tourists, although they do not have a direct interaction with visitors. Development and enhancement of the tourism clusters provide benefits to all businesses as they share information and help establish a destination as desirable for travelers. A detailed illustration of this can be seen in the Barra Honda National Park of Costa Rica:

> Visitors to the Barra Honda National Park find services that are typically non-existent in these locations: a local-food restaurant, lodging, camping facilities within a natural dry forest, a deer nursery, a handicraft shop, a parking area, and local guides. All these services are the responsibility of a Pro-Development Association, made up of community members, and are offered on the park periphery to leave the natural reserve untouched. Additionally, this cluster of tourism organizations is voluntarily involved in controlling fires within the park and reforesting with pochote (Bombacopsis quinatum) trees. Finally, training is provided in such diverse topics as food handling, English, fire control, and soil conservation.[5]

FIGURE 7.1 TOURISM CLUSTER IN COSTA RICA

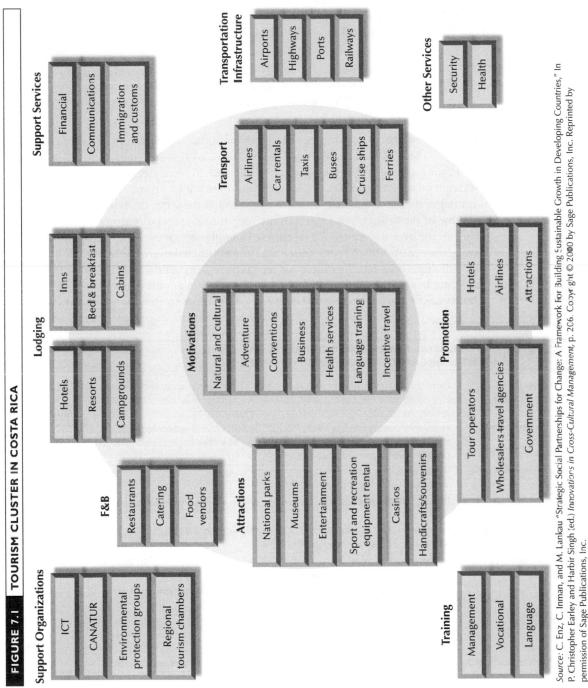

Support Services
- Financial
- Communications
- Immigration and customs

Transportation Infrastructure
- Airports
- Highways
- Ports
- Railways

Other Services
- Security
- Health

Transport
- Airlines
- Car rentals
- Taxis
- Buses
- Cruise ships
- Ferries

Lodging
- Inns
- Bed & breakfast
- Cabins
- Hotels
- Resorts
- Campgrounds

Motivations
- Natural and cultural
- Adventure
- Conventions
- Business
- Health services
- Language training
- Incentive travel

F&B
- Restaurants
- Catering
- Food vendors

Attractions
- National parks
- Museums
- Entertainment
- Sport and recreation equipment rental
- Casinos
- Handicrafts/souvenirs

Promotion
- Hotels
- Airlines
- Attractions
- Tour operators
- Wholesalers travel agencies
- Government

Support Organizations
- ICT
- CANATUR
- Environmental protection groups
- Regional tourism chambers

Training
- Management
- Vocational
- Language

Source: C. Enz, C. Inman, and M. Lankau "Strategic Social Partnerships for Change: A Framework for Building Sustainable Growth in Developing Countries," In P. Christopher Earley and Harbir Singh (ed.) *Innovations in Cross-Cultural Management*, p. 206. Copyright © 2000 by Sage Publications, Inc. Reprinted by permission of Sage Publications, Inc.

ADVANTAGES AND DISADVANTAGES OF INTERORGANIZATIONAL RELATIONSHIPS

Becoming world class means joining the world class. Success in the global economy derives not just from meeting high standards for competition in world contests, but also from strong relationships—networks that link to global markets and networks that build collective local strength.[6]

Many of the potential advantages of interorganizational relationships are summarized in Table 7.1. These advantages are most easily illustrated through joint ventures, a form of interorganizational relationship that results in a separate, jointly owned entity. Consequently, many of the examples that follow are joint ventures. However, most of the advantages are also available to some degree through the other types of partnerships.

One of the primary advantages of interorganizational relationships is that they allow firms to gain access to particular resources. Examples of resource sharing are easy to find. Disney teamed up with the American Automobile Association (AAA) to provide a "Disney-style" multipurpose rest area for travelers.[7] Galileo International partnered with ITN for corporate travel solutions, while WorldRes and Wizcom announced an Internet alliance,[8] CBS formed joint ventures with Twentieth Century Fox to develop videotapes and with

TABLE 7.1	**POTENTIAL ADVANTAGES OF PARTICIPATION IN INTERORGANIZATIONAL RELATIONSHIPS**
Gain access to a particular resource	Firms form relationships to gain access to a particular resource, such as capital, employees with specialized skills, intimate knowledge of a market, or an excellent location or facility.
Speed to market	Firms with complementary skills, such as one firm that is operationally strong and another that has strong market access, partner to increase speed to market in hopes of capturing first-mover advantages.
Enter a foreign market	Partnering with a local company is often the only practical way to gain new access to a foreign market (as in China).
Economies of scale	In many industries, high fixed costs require firms to find partners to expand production volume.
Risk and cost sharing	Many types of partnerships allow two or more firms to share the risk and cost of a particular business endeavor.
Service development	Partnering can provide firms the opportunity to pool skills to develop new services.
Learning	Interorganizational relationships often provide participants with the opportunity to "learn" from their partners (e.g., human resource management in an unfamiliar country).
Strategic flexibility	Creation of partnerships can provide a valuable alternative to acquisitions, because they do not have to be as permanent. They also require less of an internal resource commitment, which frees up resources for other uses.
Collective political clout	Interorganizational relationships can increase collective clout and influence governments into adopting policies favorable to their industries or circumstances.
Neutralizing or blocking competitors	Through a partnership, firms can gain the competencies and market power that is needed to neutralize or block the moves of a competitor.

Source: Adapted from B. B. Barringer and J. S. Harrison, "Walking a Tightrope: Creating Value through Interorganizational Relationships," *Journal of Management* 26 (2000): 385, with permission from Elsevier.

Home Box Office (owned by Time Inc.) and Columbia Pictures (owned by Coca-Cola) to develop motion pictures.[9] All of these joint ventures by CBS were similar in that they resulted in related diversification and drew on the combined strengths of all joint-venture partners. Another example of resource sharing is found in a joint venture between the government of Botswana and Debswana, a diamond mining company:

> Debswana's $31.75m, 100-room, five star hotel project, the most ambitious undertaking of its kind in Botswana is a 50–50 partnership between the government and the South African based mining conglomerate. The government has awarded Debswana a casino and hotel license. It has also allocated the diamond company a prime site at the edge of the Chobe Game Park. Debswana has already lined up four candidates as possible technical partners. These include the flamboyant South African entrepreneur, Sol Kerzner, most famous for creating the Sun City complex in South Africa. Debswana believes a luxury hotel at the site will improve quality access to game viewing. An immediate 950 jobs will be created, with more to come as the result of subsequent downstream economic activity. In addition, more Botswana will be financially involved in the project through pension funds and will be able to invest [10]

Resource complementarity is helpful in partnerships just as it is in mergers and acquisitions.[11] Complementary skills, in particular, can help increase speed to market. If two companies have strengths in different areas, by combining those strengths, they can save a lot of time in creating or expanding services. For example, a joint venture involving The Rank Group, owners of Hard Rock Hotels, and Sol Melia, a leading hotel company in Spain, Latin America, and the Caribbean, will help expand Hard Rock hotels in Europe and Latin America. London-based Rank will control hotel design and brand development, while Sol Melia will manage and market the hotels. The partnership gives both companies entrees into new geographic areas, in addition to blending Hard Rock's distinctive brand with Sol Melia's hotel-management expertise.[12]

In addition to the advantages associated with resource sharing, partnerships can lead to economies of scale through sharing physical facilities, where one firm may not be able to achieve those economies on its own. Peet's Coffee & Tea, Inc., a specialty coffee roaster with seventy-one company-owned stores, opened its first on-campus branded coffee unit in 1966 at the University of California at Berkeley. A partnership with Stanford University followed one year later. The chain's executive vice president, Bill Lilla, says brand association with colleges and universities raised the concept's image because campus dining programs are traditionally creative, intelligent, and aggressive.[13] He calls the early partnerships with universities a key factor in advancing the brand's growth.

Risk and costs are shared among the partners, which minimizes the impact on any one organization if the venture should prove to be unsuccessful. Consequently, compared to mergers or internal venturing, joint ventures are sometimes considered a less risky diversification option. Partnerships also allow firms to pool their resources for development of entirely new services, which can lead to a higher level of competitiveness. In addition, they provide participants with ample opportunity to learn from each other. Learning is considered to be one of the most important reasons to pursue interorganizational relationships.[14]

> The Ohio State University is striking their own deals to bring in brands and profits. But learning curves for chains can be steep. "You have to teach some companies how college foodservice runs, how to get involved in events and the school's calendar," explains Dave Wiseley of Ohio State. He applauds Wendy's, which pitches in with

housekeeping, maintenance, and events. The Ohio Union includes brands such as Freshens, Wall Street Deli, and The Steak Escape, in addition to Wendy's.[15]

Since partnerships often have an ending date or can be canceled with a minimum of difficulty, firms may be able to retain their strategic flexibility by deciding whether to continue a particular venture or allocate venture-related resources elsewhere. Partnerships also have political advantages, since companies can combine their clout with respect to influencing government leaders and agencies. Trade groups are an excellent example of combined political clout, as the alliance between the Travel Business Roundtable (TBR) and the World Travel and Tourism Council (WTTC) illustrates. These two groups joined forces to work with domestic and international governments on the importance of the travel industry. "This alliance reflects the growth of our industry, and will only strengthen our ability to get our message across," says Jonathan Tisch, chairman of TBR and chairman and CEO of Loews Hotels.[16] The Pennsylvania Restaurant Association is another example of a trade group formed to achieve many of the advantages we have just discussed, including combined political clout, learning, and pooling resources:

> The mission of the Pennsylvania Restaurant Association is to represent, promote and educate our members for the improvement of the restaurant and foodservice industry in the Commonwealth of Pennsylvania. Members of the PRA are professional restaurateurs and foodservice operators who provide and serve safe food in a quality manner while also providing outstanding customer service.
>
> Our members will—*Regard* our foodservice industry as an honorable profession. *Serve* food in accordance with the highest standards of sanitation and in the best interests of their customers. *Conduct* themselves and their businesses in a professional manner, guided by the highest level of integrity. *Strive* to improve themselves and their employees in the latest food preparation and service techniques. *Recognize* their responsibility to participate in activities that contribute to improving their communities. *Encourage* new generations to pursue food preparation as a professional career thorough education and training. *Represent* our foodservice industry, individual restaurants and businesses, their local chapters, and the Pennsylvania Restaurant Association by personally adhering to the above Code of Ethics.[17]

Finally, partnerships may be formed as firms try to improve their competitive positions against rivals by locking in exclusive distribution arrangements or by depriving competitors of essential supplies. Bell Atlantic, for instance, signed an exclusive distribution agreement with On Command Corp. to distribute InfoTravel, Bell Atlantic's interactive television-based city guide.[18] These actions can also deter the entry of new competitors.[19]

In spite of their strategic strengths, partnerships may be limiting, in that one organization has only partial control over the activity and enjoys only a percentage of the growth and profitability that are sometimes created. In addition, partnerships sometimes create high administrative costs associated with developing the multiparty equity arrangement and managing the venture once it is undertaken.[20] Company culture clashes can erode cooperation between firms and prevent true partnering from taking place. For instance, partnerships between university foodservice and brand restaurants, while potentially profitable, as is the case with Peet's, can be challenging. Teaching corporate restaurant food-service managers about university culture can frustrate both sides, says Frank Gladu, director of dining at Vanderbilt University in Nashville, Tennessee. "They're used to cookie-cutter systems.[21] While learning a different culture can be challenging, chain restaurants bring needed marketing and training to these noncommercial markets.

Another limiting factor is that joint decision making can be slow and result in too many compromises. Also, there is some evidence that some types of partnerships may not be desirable in particular environments. Harvard University, the third largest self-operated college food-service organization, for example, downplays commercial branding in its partnerships with restaurants, preferring to develop its own brands. They offer Starbucks Coffee, for example, but do not permit the chain to provide logo items like cups and napkins.[22] In fact, partnerships may be no more successful than non-joint ventures, as one researcher discovered when examining joint ventures in the petroleum industry.[23]

Partnerships also entail a risk of opportunism by venture partners. Unfortunately, a stronger venture partner may take advantage of a smaller or less experienced partner, structuring the deal so that the benefits accrue unfairly to the stronger partner. Well written contracts alleviate the risk but cannot eliminate it. Sue Hawkins, director of dining services at the University of California at Santa Barbara, has had her share of unpleasant partnerships. She experienced one chain that neglected to pay rent or compensate the building contractors, and another partner that failed to comply when asked to change a menu item.[24]

As in mergers and acquisitions, organizational fit is important to interorganizational relationships. Lack of organizational fit can reduce cooperation and lead to venture failure. Potential differences among partners range from dissimilar ethics to different languages to disparate managerial techniques to incompatible operating methods.[25] Trust among partners is also critical. If trust breaks down, the venture can fall apart. Also, companies are more likely to form partnerships with firms they trust. Consequently, it is essential that partners manage their interorganizational relationships carefully so as not to violate trust.[26]

In summary, while interorganizational relationships have both benefits and drawbacks relative to other strategic options, many firms have found that they are essential to competitive success.[27] Of course, partnerships are an essential form of business in the hospitality industry. Consequently, partnerships of all types are popular, and many types of partnerships, such as joint ventures, are increasing in use.

SELECTION OF STAKEHOLDERS FOR PARTNERSHIPS

Managers have limited resources, and one of the most important of these is time. Clearly, managers do not have time to pursue interorganizational relationships with all stakeholders. Consequently, deciding when and with whom to partner are significant managerial decisions. In general, organizations should consider partnering with stakeholders that are strategically important. This means that they significantly affect the firm and its future success. Several factors, outlined in Figure 7.2, can increase the strategic significance of a stakeholder, thus making partnering more attractive. One of the most common reasons to partner is to acquire resources, and many of the interorganizational forms that have been described in this section can facilitate resource transfer. One of the most important resources a company may need is, of course, knowledge.

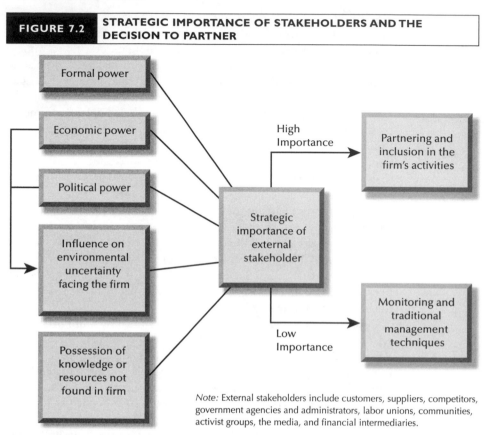

FIGURE 7.2 **STRATEGIC IMPORTANCE OF STAKEHOLDERS AND THE DECISION TO PARTNER**

Note: External stakeholders include customers, suppliers, competitors, government agencies and administrators, labor unions, communities, activist groups, the media, and financial intermediaries.

Partnerships can facilitate organizational learning. However, stakeholders also become important when they hold formal power, which means that they have a legal or contractual right to make decisions that affect some part of the organization (i.e., regulatory agencies or governments). Hotel developers may need to partner with the government to get business done, as is the case in China. However some industry experts caution that in general partnering with a government is not attractive because there is a distortion of the true asset value for the developer. As Art Buser, executive vice president of West Coast operations for Jones Lang LaSalle Hotels, notes, "The government gets you into a deal, but usually the developer doesn't get a good return when it exits."[28]

Another factor that can dramatically affect the strategic importance of a particular stakeholder is its influence on the organizational uncertainty facing the firm.[29] For example, organizations are uncertain of the level of future demand; the price elasticity of demand; the strategic moves of competitors, suppliers, activists, unions, and other key stakeholders; the nature of future government regulations; and the ability to secure adequate resources, whether physical, financial, or human. Stakeholders that have high economic or political power have more influence on the environmental uncertainty facing a firm. Consequently, arrows are drawn from the economic-power and political-power boxes to the environmental-uncertainty box in Figure 7.2. For example, a customer can quit buying from an organization, or a bank can sever a financial agreement. These are examples of exerting economic power. On the other hand, stakeholders with political power have the ability to influence events and outcomes that have an impact on the organization. In one example, some of Wal-Mart's angry competitors have convinced communities and governments in several locations in the northeastern United States that Wal-Mart, by causing small businesses to suffer, harms the community more than it helps it. The result has been adverse legislation, causing Wal-Mart to lose several new locations for its stores.[30]

One way to understand the role of environmental uncertainty is to imagine a situation in which managers knew everything that would happen with regard to customers, suppliers, unions, competitors, regulators, financial intermediaries, and every other relevant external force for the next year. In such a hypothetical situation, management of the company would be a straightforward task of generating maximum revenues at minimum costs so that profits are maximized. Management is difficult because our hypothetical world does not exist. Managers have to make decisions without knowing how customers, suppliers, and competitors will react. Customers are particularly important because their actions have so much impact on how the firm will perform. In other words, they have a large influence on the uncertainty that the firm is facing.

While environmental uncertainty often originates in the broad environment (e.g., economic cycles, social trends), organizations feel most of its influence through external stakeholders. For example, gasoline price increases affect consumers' purchasing power. Automobile travel is not the only casualty of rising fuel prices; so are automobile sales and car purchase preferences. These fuel costs also produce a shock in the broad environment of the lodging industry. According to a recent study, hotels experience a decline in rooms demand when gasoline prices rise.[31] Nevertheless not all lodging operators need to worry that jumps in gasoline prices will affect their demand levels. The study showed that the effects of gas price changes are magnified in hotels located along highways and outside of major metropolitan locations—in short, those that depend on automobile access.

Establishment of the strategic priority of stakeholders provides direction as to the amount of attention they should be given during the development of strategy. However, prioritizing stakeholders also provides clues concerning the types of strategies that may be appropriate in managing them. Strategically important stakeholders should be seriously considered for partnerships. According to Pfeffer and Salancik, two well-known organizational researchers, "The typical solution to problems of interdependence and uncertainty involves increasing the mutual control over each other's activities."[32] Companies may also want to consider including them in organizational processes, such as including a supplier on a research-and-development team to create a new product. Less-important stakeholders should not be ignored. They should be monitored and managed in more traditional ways.

EFFECTIVE STAKEHOLDER MANAGEMENT

Chapter 2 provided a detailed description of the operating environment and the major stakeholders found therein, including customers, suppliers, competitors, government agencies, labor unions, local communities, activists, the media, and special-interest groups. The emphasis in that chapter was on analyzing stakeholders (as well as industry factors) as a foundation upon which to build effective strategies, although a few tactics for managing stakeholders were provided at the end. Thus far, this chapter has thoroughly examined interorganizational relationships, which are one of the most important tools for managing stakeholder relationships. It also provided guidelines for deciding which stakeholders are most attractive for the formation of partnerships. We are now in a position to discuss stakeholder management in more depth.

Organizations use two basic postures when managing relationships with external stakeholders.[33] One posture involves buffering the organization from environmental uncertainty through techniques designed to stabilize and predict environmental influences and, in essence, raise the boundaries. They soften the jolts that might otherwise be felt as the organization interacts with members of its external environment. These are traditional stakeholder management techniques such as marketing research, creation of special departments to handle specific areas of the external environment (e.g., legal, recruiting, purchasing), advertising, efforts to ensure regulatory compliance, and public-relations efforts. For instance, the establishment of a director of diversity is often a buffering technique to respond to concerns about opportunity for minorities in the industry. Buffering techniques focus on planning for and adapting to the environment so that the needs and demands of critical stakeholders are met.

On the other hand, the previous section argued that likely candidates for partnerships of one form or other are stakeholders with attractive resources; with high levels of formal, economic, or political power; and/or with a large influence on environmental uncertainty facing the firm. Partnering activities allow companies to build bridges with their stakeholders in the pursuit of common goals, whereas traditional stakeholder management techniques (buffering) simply reduce shocks and facilitate the satisfaction of stakeholder needs and/or demands. Cendant's approach to diversity illustrates a partnering and inclusion strategy, as shown below:

> Cendant Corporation developed a comprehensive diversity initiative based on a series of meetings with key opinion leaders in the African-American community. First meeting with the National Urban League, the company developed franchise opportunities for African Americans, hired an African American–owned marketing agency, built a mentorship program, and provided charitable donations to the National Association for the Advancement of Colored People (NAACP), The National Urban League, the Jackie Robinson Foundation, and the Inner City Game Foundation.[34]

Table 7.2 lists examples of traditional stakeholder management techniques as well as partnering techniques, grouped by type of external stakeholder. It is nearly impossible to be competitive in the lodging industry on a large scale without effective use of interorganizational relationships. The rest of this section will elaborate on effective management of the external stakeholders listed in Table 7.2, with an emphasis on the creation of partnerships.

Customers

Since customers are so vital to organizational success, many firms place their highest priority on satisfying customer needs. Organizations pursue a number of what might be called traditional management tactics to satisfy customers. Among the most important are customer-service departments, marketing research, on-site visits, and service development. Listening to customers is one of the most important strategies a firm can pursue. Sears, for

TABLE 7.2	**EXAMPLES OF TACTICS FOR MANAGING AND PARTNERING WITH EXTERNAL STAKEHOLDERS**	

Stakeholder	Traditional Management	Partnering and Inclusion Strategies
Customers	Customer service departments Marketing and marketing research On-site visits 800 numbers Long-term contracts	Involvement on teams to create or refine services Joint planning sessions Joint training/service programs Financial investments Appointments to board (interlocking directorate)
Suppliers	Purchasing departments Encourage competition among suppliers Sponsor new suppliers Threat of vertical integration Long-term contracts	Involvement on design teams for new services Integration of ordering system Shared information systems Coordinated quality control Appointments to board (interlocking directorate)
Competitors	Direct competition based on differentiation Intelligence systems Corporate spying and espionage (ethical problems)	Joint ventures or consortia for research and development, manufacturing, marketing, etc. Alliances to pursue a variety of objectives Trade associations for sharing information and collective lobbying Informal price leadership or collusion (may be illegal)
Government agencies and administrators	Legal, tax or government relations offices Lobbying and political action committees Campaign contributions Personal gifts to politicians (ethical problems)	Jointly or government sponsored research Joint foreign development projects Problem-solving task forces on sensitive issues Appointment of retired government officials to board
Local communities	Community relations offices Public relations advertising Involvement in community service Donations to local causes	Task forces to work on special community needs Cooperative training and educational programs Development committees/boards Joint employment programs
Activist groups	Organizational decisions to satisfy demands Public/political relations efforts Financial donations	Consultation with representatives on sensitive issues Joint development programs Appointments to the board
The media	Public/political relations efforts Media experts/press releases	Exclusive interviews or early release of information Inclusion in social events and other special treatment
Unions	Union avoidance through excellent treatment of employees Hiring professional negotiators Mutually satisfactory labor contracts Chapter XI protection to renegotiate contract	Contract clauses that link pay to performance Joint committees on safety and other issues Joint industry/labor panels Inclusion on management committees Appointments to the board
Financial intermediaries	Financial reports Close correspondence Finance and accounting departments High-level financial officer Audits	Inclusion in management decisions requiring financing Contracts and linkages with other clients of financier Shared ownership of projects Appointments to the board

Source: Adapted from J. S. Harrison and C. H. St. John, "Managing and Partnering with External Stakeholders," *Academy of Management Executive* (May 1996): 53. Used with permission of Academy of Management in the format Textbook via Copyright Clearance Center.

many years, ignored the changing needs of its predominantly middle-class customers, who were tightening up their finances due to a significant decline in their spending power. They switched their loyalties to lower-priced stores such as Wal-Mart.[35] Of course, Wal-Mart, as a competitor, is also a stakeholder of Sears. Therefore, Sears could have adjusted its strategy on the basis of information received from either of two stakeholders, customers or a competitor. Instead, Sears, after more than a decade of restructuring, is just now beginning to recover its footing as a retail chain.

Firms are increasingly trying to include customers more in internal processes or form partnerships with them. Even with the growing recognition that forty-one million kids between the ages of five and fourteen have direct buying power, estimated at over $40 billion, many restaurants have not yet learned to value this important stakeholder group by using them in formal product testing.[36] However, chains like Applebee's, Red Lobster, KFC, Friendly's, and Dairy Queen are involving young people in their design teams.

> Dairy Queen, eager to improve its status as a snack destination among young people, relied on a special panel of "'tweens" (8 to 12 year olds) to determine the 2003 Blizzard flavors for the chain, which encompasses more than 5,900 fast-food and frozen-treats outlets. At Red Lobster, after getting initial feedback from children on popular trends and flavors, they develop a variety of items. The dishes are refined based on results from formal product testing with youngsters.[37]

Popular partnering approaches include joint planning sessions to identify driving forces for industry change, joint service- and market-development efforts, enhanced communication linkages, sharing of facilities, and joint training and service programs (other examples are found in Table 2.5). Efforts to strengthen linkages with customers often provide significant benefits. For example, ClubCorp USA, the owner or operator of nearly two hundred golf courses and dozens of sport clubs and resorts has been effective at attracting customers to its operations. This creates a longer-term cooperative relationship that provides steady income for ClubCorp and a steady social group and consistently high-quality recreational facilities for customers.

> Founded in 1957, Dallas-based ClubCorp employs 19,000 workers to serve the nearly 210,000 member households and 200,000 guests who visit ClubCorp properties each year. The company did not plan to invent an industry, or to become the world leader. The goal has been to ensure an unparalleled private club experience for every member and every guest, every time. Along the way, well, a certain magic happened.[38]

Suppliers

Building strong partnerships with key suppliers facilitates competitive advantage and is essential to successful supply chain management. In fact, recent research has revealed that inefficient management of the supply chain can reduce overall corporate performance.[39] More and more hospitality firms are discovering that their suppliers can provide knowledge, technical assistance, and joint problem solving.[40]

> Hilton Hotels Corp. has teamed up with LodgeNet Entertainment to create a broadband, interactive media company. Dubbed InnMedia LLC, the company will promote an interactive digital technology product to Hilton properties and other hospitality companies in the United States and Canada that will give guests video- and music-on-demand services

in the guestroom. Hilton and Sioux Falls, SD-based LodgeNet will each own 50% of InnMedia, which will be marketed via LodgeNet's national distribution system.[41]

Considering the establishment of strong supplier relationships comes at a time when many firms are downsizing their own corporate purchasing activities and outsourcing key activities to others. Outsourcing allows a firm to leverage its own capabilities by focusing resources on high value-added activities. Scarce management talent and time are not wasted on activities that do not add unique value. In addition, outsourcing provides the potential to reap economies of scale through specialized suppliers. However, outsourcing is often approached as a "quick fix" rather than a long-term relationship. Take the owner and general manager of the year-old Charlesmark Hotel in Boston, who has used outsourcing to help him keep costs down in a tough market. He farms out sales and marketing, public relations, information technology, maintenance, and some food preparation to outside companies, but he considers this outsourcing to be a short-term solution while his business gets off the ground.[42] In contrast, Cendant Corporation developed a preferred alliances program with major vendors. With more than 110 preferred alliances, Cendant has used this program as a major selling point for franchisees.[43] What distinguishes the more traditional and contractual supplier relationships noted in the Boston hotel example from strong alliances like those developed by Cendant is that partnering involves technology transfer and training, increased interfirm communication, coordinated quality control, involvement on design teams, and risk sharing.

Because of the commitments required to be a true business partner companies are consolidating by limiting the number of suppliers they do business with.[44] The partnerships that are likely to last are those where a closer relationship is forged. Strong relationships offer both firms several advantages. Suppliers gain preferential treatment and more market security, while buyers benefit from technological development and better response times.[45]

> Talking about partnerships with vendors to hotels, Robert Barnard, managing consultant at PKF notes, "Getting the relationship right depends on very careful preparation for the contract and knowing that you've got a good cultural fit. And it's got to be beneficial for both parties." Hoteliers remain wary of outsourced staff who will not necessarily provide the level of loyalty or commitment that a high-quality establishment relies on.[46]

In partnerships between food-service operators and their suppliers, a recent study found, trustworthiness and problem-solving ability were the most critical traits in the relationship. The research, sponsored by the Center for Hospitality Research at Cornell University, also reported that the major barrier to maintaining strong partnerships was the turnover of the vendor representative.[47] Trust becomes particularly critical when a firm builds dependence on a supplier. This is the situation that often surfaces in hotels that rely on vendors to handle their information technology needs. Information systems will be discussed later in this chapter, but the rapid changes and complexity of this area of hotel operations make the importance of trust-based supplier relationships all the more important.

Competitors

Competitors pose a difficult stakeholder management problem because it is often in the best interests of one competitor to cause another competitor to falter. However, to combat increasing levels of global competition and to get a jump on new emerging technologies, competitors are joining forces in increasing numbers. In fact, about half of all major alliance deals are among rival firms.[48] They are coming together to form alliances for technological advancement, new-product and new-service development, to enter new or foreign markets, and to pursue a wide variety of other opportunities.[49]

As the introductory case revealed, international airlines for some time have been joining forces with competitors to enhance customer service. The underlying motive of some partnerships seems to be to put the remaining firms that are not included in an alliance at a competitive disadvantage. According to one industry analyst, "Regulatory barriers created by firm conduct may be used by groups in the industry as a competitive weapon against other groups."[50] While global alliances are not new, after the September 11 slump, U.S. carriers like Delta, Northwest, and Continental have joined to code share, allow the others to earn and redeem frequent flier miles on flights, and admit the others' airport-lounge members to its own facilities.[51] These carriers must still compete on fares and schedules to comply with antitrust laws, and both the U.S. Transportation Department and the Justice Department's antitrust officials have carefully reviewed the alliance.

In oligopolies, where a few major rivals dominate an industry, the major firms may cooperate with one another in setting prices. Formal price-setting cooperation is called collusion. In the United States and many other countries, collusion is illegal. However, companies may still cooperate informally by being careful not to drop prices enough to start a price war. Price wars can damage the profits of all firms in the sector, as demonstrated several times in the airline industry since it was deregulated. Alternatively, some sectors have an established price leader, usually one of the largest companies in the industry, who establishes a pricing pattern that other firms follow.

In some countries and regions, collusion is not illegal, or it is widely practiced in spite of its illegality. For example, for many years, the Organization of Petroleum Exporting Countries (OPEC) cartel established the price charged for crude oil produced by Middle Eastern countries. Ultimately, the cartel lost some of its power when countries participating in OPEC discovered that great financial rewards were available for individual firms that were willing to violate OPEC agreements.

Working cooperatively with competitors is easier in the hotel industry because of the geographic dispersion of individual properties. Shared resources and cooperative arrangements can be devoted to a particular market, with competition occurring in other areas. The absence of local conflict makes competitor cooperation more effective and eases joint planning, marketing, and development.[52]

Government Agencies and Administrators

Business organizations and governments share a number of common goals, among them creating a favorable environment for international trade, stable market conditions, a healthy economy, and production of desirable goods and services. Consequently, many organizations form alliances with government agencies and officials to pursue a wide variety of objectives, including finding answers to social problems, developing particular parts of cities, or establishing trade policies. Various hospitality organizations work cooperatively with governmental institutions in the development of heritage sights that represent a nation's past and identity, as the following American example shows:

Mount Rushmore National Memorial in the Black Hills of South Dakota is the single largest attraction in that state. This monumental sculpture of four American presidents was initiated by state officials in the 1920s to create a spectacular attraction and take advantage of the increasing popularity of automobile travel in the U.S. The State Cement Plant in Rapid City provided materials for the roads to the monument and President Calvin Coolidge promised federal financing after a visit in 1927. Railway and oil companies also had a vested interest in fostering tourism in the state and provided additional funding. Mount Rushmore could have been carved anywhere and it did not particularly reflect the history or heritage of the West, but it did attract tourist, and still does.[53]

Government/business partnerships are even more widely used outside of the United States, where governments often play a more active role in economic development. One such effort resulted in the formation of the major aerospace company Airbus Industries, jointly owned by aerospace firms from Britain, France, Germany, and Spain. The Japanese Ministry of International Trade and Industry (MITI) targets particular segments of the Japanese industry and provides support for those that are determined to be most closely linked to the growth of the Japanese economy. The relationship between the Australian Gold Coast City Council and the Gold Coast International Tourism Committee, an association of eighteen major destination operators, illustrates the importance of the public and private sectors cooperatively working to market a destination. Promotion of the Gold Coast has relied on formal marketing and informal promotion, by chambers of commerce and tourism promotion associations combined with media reports of events and activities, and advertising by real estate developers.[54]

Governmental actions can profoundly shape the competitive environment in developing countries. In many instances, the government not only regulates businesses but may also have power through state-owned enterprises. These businesses are quite different from their private-enterprise counterparts, often operating at a substantial loss or with unfair advantages. If we return to the government of Botswana's luxury hotel project mentioned earlier in this chapter, we see that existing hoteliers are critical of the proposed project, which is located on the edge of the Chobe Game Park:

Existing hoteliers, perhaps worried about the impact of the new complex on their own tourism receipts, are hostile to the Debswana project. The manager of Kasane's The Garden Lodge notes, "This hotel has the potential to destroy the aesthetic value of the boat cruise completely as well as negatively modify the game viewing." Reacting to the criticism, the managing director of the project states, "We are not going to compete with anybody. Why are they so worried? Some of the people who criticize the government for granting us a site within the Chobe National Park are themselves in the park! What exclusive right do they think they have?" he asked.[55]

Local Communities

The Holiday Inn Miri has always been known to be a committed and caring corporate citizen, These efforts have not gone unnoticed by the chain who awarded the hotel with the Asia-Pacific Bass Hotels & Resorts' Outstanding Performance in Community

Involvement award. Senadin State Assemblyman Lee Kim Shin said Holiday Inn Miri deserves to receive such a prestigious award as it has consistently organized community service activities and events. "They (the hotel) are unlike others because they put extra effort into making a difference in the life of Miri residents by contributing towards the local community," he said.[56]

Organizations take a proactive role in their communities for a variety of reasons. Good relationships with communities and governments can result in favorable local regulation or in tax breaks. For example, the Walt Disney Company received tax breaks and special treatment from the city of New York when the company invested millions of dollars in the development of one of the most crime-filled areas in the city—42nd Street between Times Square and Eighth Avenue in Manhattan. The company constructed a live-production theater, a Disney Store, cinemas, hotels, game parlors, and restaurants.[57] Other organizations find opportunities to achieve financial or operating objectives while satisfying a need in the local community.

Quasi-public alliances between local governments and business leaders are flourishing across many sections of the United States. For example, the Economic Development Commission of Mid-Florida Inc. represents four central Florida counties. The commission works with government and business leaders to create economic plans and initiatives. Recent activities include developing an economic-action plan for Osceola County, promoting an industrial park, matching local companies that sell goods with foreign buyers, and finding ways to use the Orlando Naval Training Center, one of several military facilities the navy has decided to abandon. The commission has a lot of cash, including $425,000 in state and local government grants.[58]

Because the hospitality industry can profoundly affect communities and their citizens, not just as an employer but also in altering the physical surrounds and the economics of a location, it is important to involve communities before development begins. Many firms work closely with local organizations not only to support the long-term success of their enterprises, but also to care for the welfare of the local people. For example, the rapid growth of tourism in some communities can result in a shortage of qualified hospitality employees. To address this problem in Scottsdale, Arizona, a partnership was formed between the Hyatt Regency Scottsdale and a community college, city government, school district, and university. The hotel developed an educational program that was instituted at the high school level and leads directly into a two-year associate degree program at the local community college, which transfers to the hotel program at the university.[59] To implement this program, the hotel had to work closely with the school district, and meetings are held regularly for all the partners to discuss changes and improvements in the program. The program accomplished its goal of providing qualified and skilled workers to the industry while giving young students an opportunity to explore a career in hospitality.

Activist Groups

Activist groups such as the Sierra Club, Greenpeace International, the National Association for the Advancement of Colored People (NAACP), the National Organization for Women (NOW), and Mothers Against Drunk Driving (MADD) represent a variety of social and environmental perspectives. Public-interest groups (e.g., MADD) represent the position of a broad cross-section of society, while special-interest groups (e.g., the NAACP) focus on the needs of smaller subgroups. While these groups are most often seen in an adversarial role relative to the desires of other organizational stakeholders, this does not have to be the case. However, it is difficult for executives to break out of the old mind-set and adopt an attitude of common goal achievement. For example, the recent efforts of public health activists and lawyers to attack the restaurant industry over obesity have led to lawsuits and aggressive name-calling. McDonald's was the target of a lawsuit claiming that the chain was responsible for obesity-related health problems and that fast food, like tobacco, is addictive. McDonald's called the lawsuit frivolous.[60] A spokesperson for the National Council of Chain Restaurants, commenting on the growing movement around healthful menu items and court action, contends:

> They've sucked all the money they can out of the tobacco industry, and now they are moving on to other industries. And let's be clear about this: These lawsuits are not about improving public health. It's about making money.[61]

To adopt a win-win attitude with activist groups, executives should consider potential benefits from partnering activities, especially in situations in which an activist is strategically important. In the case of health, all agree that Americans are getting fatter and that the public-health implications are serious with regard to diabetes, heart disease, and other illnesses that are more likely to occur in overweight people.[62] The Public Health Advocacy Institute and restaurant operators both want to do something about this problem. Building a cooperative approach will be a challenge.

One of the best ways to reduce unfavorable regulation in an industry is to operate in a manner that is consistent with the values of society. Organizations that respond to the widely held positions of public-interest groups on issues such as pollution, fair-hiring practices, safety, and waste management do not need to be regulated. They find themselves in the enviable position of solving their own problems, instead of having a regulatory body of individuals with less experience in the industry dictating how problems will be solved. Aspen Skiing Company (ASC), which operates four mountains, three hotels, and fifteen restaurants in Aspen, is one of many ski resort companies that know protecting the environment assures that the ski industry survives.

> In 1999, more than 150 ski resorts joined Aspen Skiing Company in signing the National Ski Areas Association (NSAA) environmental charter. The agreement is non-binding, so all environmental improvements are voluntary, but small steps are being made. Vail Resorts installed an "earth tub" from Green Mountain Technologies that composts kitchen scraps into fertilizer. Wachusett Mountain Ski Area in Princeton, Massachusetts uses waste heat from snowmaking machines to heat their new Base Lodge, and they've been recognized by the NSAA for their "Science on the Slopes" environmental education program. Though sprawling development and diminishing water and wildlife resources continue to place ski resorts on many environmentalists' blacklists, the charter's signatures are a hopeful step toward more sustainable slopes.[63]

Public-interest groups are particularly important in helping organizations avoid conflicts with social values, which can result in unfavorable media and a damaged reputation. Such groups are experts in the causes they represent. As a result, many companies invite members of public-interest groups to participate in strategic-planning processes, either as advisers or as board members.

Organizations should also consider the needs of special-interest groups, which represent the views of smaller social groups. However, buffering techniques may be more applicable because these groups, by virtue of their smaller social scope, are likely to be less strategically important than are public-interest groups. Both types of activists can also provide an alternative perspective on issues that affect the environment, consumers, minorities, or other interests. This alternative perspective can lead to new ways to solve organizational problems. Another benefit to allowing participation by important public-interest or special-interest groups during planning processes is that there may be fewer obstacles during strategy implementation. The groups involved would be less likely to protest or seek government intervention. This may also result in good public relations and publicity.

Alliances with activist groups can also help companies develop new products or services. The increasing social emphasis on environmental protection has left companies rushing to introduce products that are environmentally acceptable.[64] Examples include McDonald's return to paper packaging and Rubbermaid's environmentally friendly "Sidekick" lunch box. Also, organizations in the mature personal computer industry may find growth opportunities in developing products for the physically and mentally challenged by partnering with the Institute on Applied Technology, a Boston-based nonprofit organization that does research and training on computer applications for these individuals.[65]

The Media

Not only must an organization assess the potential effects of social forces on its business, but it must also manage its relationship and reputation with society at large. The media act as a "watchdog" for society. They are a commanding force in managing the attitudes of the general public toward organizations. Executives have nightmares about their company's being the subject of the next *20/20* program or some other news show. On the other hand, a well-managed media effort can significantly help the image of a firm. Burger King combined local social responsibility with astute media management by announcing that after fourteen years of sponsoring a float in the Orange Bowl Parade, money ordinarily used for the float would be used to support education (primarily scholarships) in Burger King's headquarters city of Miami.[66]

It is rather difficult to pursue an inclusion or partnering strategy in the case of the media. In general, companies will rely on traditional management techniques to deal with this stakeholder. To manage relations with the media, large firms typically employ public-relations (PR) experts. The public-relations staff is usually active in releasing information that will place the company in a favorable light, while being careful not to create the impression that the organization is withholding information from the public. It is not uncommon in the hospitality industry for an owner/operator to build PR around his own name. Wolfgang Puck, the chef known for "California cuisine," has put his name on four operations: Puck's casual-dining, Puck special events, Puck catering, and the Puck fine dining group.[67] Driving the entire engine is Puck, whom some describe as an "icon." This high-profile chef spends 50 percent of his time with some form of media, using his television show to establish the Puck brand.

While it is difficult to include the media directly in the organization, and formal partnerships are out of the question in most countries, managers can make individual reporters feel as though they have a special relationship with the company, thus prompting the reporters to portray the company in a more favorable light. Granting individual interviews to specific reporters, early release of information to a limited set of reporters, or treating a few media people to social activities such as luncheons or golf are some of the many efforts that firms make to cultivate the goodwill of the press. Hotel operators who trade room nights for electronic media placement are engaged in a form of cooperative activity called barter. For more than a decade The Breakers Palm Beach has been using barter as a way to advertise.

> "It is timely to barter in today's economy," says Jody Merl, President of Innovative Travel Marketing, a company that arranges the barter exchange between hotels and media outlets such as television and radio stations. "The opportunity cost for barter is at its lowest because there is so much inventory out there and [hotel operators] should make that inventory work for them. You can never make up the revenue of a lost room night." According to Merl, barter is a $20-billion industry utilized by 80% of Fortune 500 companies."[68]

Images and features found in motion pictures, television, newspapers, and magazines have an important impact on popular culture and consumer interest in tourism destinations. An old television program, *Love Boat,* gave consumers an opportunity to think about a cruise every week they turned in to watch the show. Movies and television familiarize audiences with places and attractions, which is important since familiarity has been found to be an important factor in shaping consumer decision-making. The movie *Braveheart* attracted tourists to Scotland to visit places depicted in the film (although much of the movie was actually filmed in Ireland), according to one study.[69]

Unfortunately, marketers are not likely to have control over how a destination or even a company is portrayed. A 2003 reality television show called "The Restaurant" features a New York chef, Rocco DiSpirito, as he operates his recently opened Manhattan restaurant, Rocco's. While industry opinion generally holds the show to be a ridiculous and sensationalized view of the industry and the owner's handling of staff to be by the "seat of the pants," the restaurant's three-week wait for reservations grew to three months.[70] Clearly, the media can be powerful allies in the hospitality industry.

In some parts of the world such as Africa and the Middle East, state ownership of media is the rule, while North and South American media outlets are often owned by families.[71] In parts of the world where states provide support, biased reporting and favorable coverage of the incumbent government is more likely. Hence the level of cooperation the hospitality industry can obtain with the media will vary widely around the world.

Labor Unions

Unions are formed to protect and advance the welfare of their members. The strength of unions varies from state to state and from country to country. In the United States, union strength has declined to only 13.2 percent of the workforce, down from 35 percent in the 1950s. In the private sector, less than 10 percent of employees are unionized.[72] However, unions are far from dead, particularly for the Hotel Employees and Restaurant Employees International Union (HERE) that reports a rise in membership of 15 percent since 1996. While the potential for cooperation is great, the traditional adversarial relationship has not changed much. For example, the Service Employees International Union (SEIU) employs shock tactics and harassment to influence janitorial contractors to pressure their employees to unionize.[73] As a result, the SEIU is growing steadily. A quick look at news headlines and the first paragraph of each story confirms that the contentious nature of union/management relationships still persist for hotels, casinos, and food-service operators.

- "Ark Las Vegas Loses Court Case," *Las Vegas Review Journal*. A federal appeals court in Washington, D.C., has ruled a Las Vegas company unlawfully fired eight employees who were trying to organize a union.

- "Hotel Union Leaders Prepare for Strike," *Monterey County Herald* (California). Workers at the Hyatt Regency Monterey and Carmel Highlands Inn could strike at any time, now that they have rejected a management contract offer. Members of the HERE Local 483, who work at those two hotels, voted Friday night 278–7 to reject a contract offer by Chicago-based Hyatt Corporation, union officials announced Saturday. Members authorized action that could include a strike.

- "Union Fight with Indians Gets Personal," *Gambling Magazine*. A wage and benefits dispute between a hotel workers union and the Agua Caliente Band of Cahuilla Indians of Palm Springs has escalated into a personal feud between the tribal chairman and a group of activist clergy.

- "Local 5 Members Rally at Waikiki Beach Marriott," *Star Bulletin* (Honolulu). Hundreds of Waikiki Beach Marriott Hotel workers marched in front of the hotel on Kalakaua Avenue yesterday afternoon.

- "Sodexho Cafeteria Workers in Plattsburgh Rally for Unionization." Cardinal Points Sodexho cafeteria workers on campus held a rally Thursday afternoon to support the possibility of a union. The workers at the rally wanted representation by the Local 471 chapter of the Hotel, Motel & Restaurant Employees and Bartenders Union, AFL-CIO.[74]

Because of the variety of tasks performed by hospitality industry employees, they may be organized under the leadership of a number of different unions, including the Teamsters, the Culinary and Bartenders Union, or the AFL-CIO affiliated HERE. The HERE takes an active roll in promoting the welfare of its members and the industries it represents.

> The Hotel Employees and Restaurant Employees International Union (HERE) launched the Web site www.whosesmithsonian.org earlier this month to take the nonprofit Smithsonian to task for what the union calls "a lack of public accountability" in some of its business dealings with companies such as McDonald's Corp. The Web site is the latest in a portfolio of sites intended to turn public opinion against companies and organizations that HERE believes are unfair to union workers. In the past year, HERE also has built three other sites intended to inform Web surfers about alleged unfair employment practices at on-site giant Sodexho and airline caterers LSG Sky Chefs and Flying Food Group. The sites are filled with unflattering information concerning the companies, such as poor food safety reports, labor disputes, pending lawsuits and lists of lost accounts.[75]

Unions are being treated as partners instead of adversaries in some companies with great success. Eleven hotels in the San Francisco area formed a multiemployer bargaining group with the goal of promoting labor/management cooperation and creating a partnership with their workers and the union. They brought this new idea to the union leaders, who agreed that it was time to try a different approach. This partnership began with a joint study to analyze the problems facing hotels in the San Francisco market and resulted in the creation of a "living contract." Unlike more traditional contracts, the living contract permitted changes after the parties finished negotiations to address unforeseen problems and modify the contact. The contract's primary accomplishment was to foster cooperation between the hotels and the union. It allowed a number of interest-based study teams to develop solutions to problems facing the industry. In addition the partnership permitted the hotels and union to revise work rules, create joint training programs, and implement a grievance-mediation program that reduced the traditional formal and costly approach to dispute resolution. This program has dramatically changed the hotel and union relationship from a grievance and arbitration driven one to a partnership based on finding mutually satisfactory solutions to important problems.

> The living contract has allowed study teams made up of line workers and managers at individual hotels to resolve a multitude of departmental and hotel-wide problems. The study team approach permits customization of programs among hotels to account for their differences, but still allows them to operate under the citywide contract's mandatory provisions. At the Holiday Inn Fisherman's Wharf the study team reduced contractual cook classifications in the kitchen from approximately 21 to 7 thereby achieving efficiencies that the hotel had long sought unsuccessfully through bargaining. This partnership helped Hyatt Regency adjust their room inspection process, and the Hilton to manage a complex luggage handling task.[76]

Unions consider the hotel construction stage as one of the best times to organize.[77] This may seem rather early since the hotel may not yet have employees. In fact the union often approaches the hotel to discuss the establishment of a neutrality agreement. A hotel signing one of these agreements promises to stay neutral if the union decides to organize the property. The neutrality agreement means that the hotel does not have the right to contest union organization and the employees do not have the right to vote in a secret ballot to determine whether they wish to be represented. Instead union recognition is based on a card-check procedure where the union is recognized once 50 percent of the bargaining-unit employees sign a union-authorization card.[78] Not all industry experts consider signing neutrality agreements to be a viable approach, arguing that hotels virtually guarantee that the union will be the bargaining agent for their employees. However, in highly unionized cities, this approach may make strategic sense. Four Seasons, for instance, made a strategic decision to form a friendly union partnership at a new hotel:

> As Four Seasons was planning to open a new property in San Francisco, it became evident that unionization of its employees would certainly happen in this strong union town. In fact, the new building was to be located on city property and a neutrality agreement would be a requirement. Consequently, managers at Four Seasons approached the union voluntarily before the hotel even opened and were able to work out a neutrality agreement that would work for the company and the union. It contained terminology consistent with a 5-star hotel. Furthermore, because the company took the initiative, it was able to choose HERE as the contracting body instead of the Teamsters.[79]

Organizations that succeed in labor/management relationships are starting to include representatives from labor unions in strategic-planning decisions. For example, Scott Paper Company formed a committee combining ten of its top executives with ten top officials from the union. They pledged to "work together to meet the needs of employees, customers, shareholders, the union and the community."[80] The results were so successful in terms of cutting costs and boosting quality that now other paper companies are doing the same thing. Of course, one of the most effective ways to deal with a union is to avoid unionization, when possible. For example, a unionization effort at a New Orleans hotel was thwarted because its employees are so well treated. In fact, union organizers were offered coffee in an effort to extend goodwill and hospitality.

Unions are making great strides in pursuing common goals with managers. The AFL-CIO once urged the eighty-six unions it represents to "become partners with management in boosting efficiency."[81] This was an unprecedented move for the AFL-CIO. Unions also finance hotel projects through their equity-based pension funds and their real-estate investment debt funds. The building investment trust of the AFL-CIO has invested millions in hotels through union pension funds, allocating 10–15 percent of its assets to hotel financing.[82] While the trust prefers to participate in public-private partnerships that strengthen local communities, such as loans for affordable housing, it is also involved in projects to create convention centers and build downtown convention hotels. Another player in the pension-fund hotel-investment arena is Union Labor Life Insurance, a debt fund. The Loews New Orleans Hotel is an interesting example: the project is being built with labor union pension fund money and the construction job is 100 percent union.[83] In addition, Loews has agreed not to oppose unionization of the hotel once construction is complete. In these stakeholder roles, unions become financial intermediaries and business partners, a topic we turn to next.

Financial Intermediaries

Financial intermediaries consist of a wide variety of institutions, including banks, stock exchanges, brokerage houses, investment advisers, mutual-fund companies, pension-fund companies, and other organizations or individuals that may have an interest in investing in the firm. This list is not exhaustive, and many financial-service firms play more than one role.

Trust is especially important in dealing with creditors. Disclosure of financial records helps establish trust, as do timely payments. Many organizations, in an effort to manage their relationships with creditors and develop trust, have invited creditor representatives onto the board of directors. For instance, at Mandalay Resorts Group, an entertainment company with a focus on casino gaming, three members of the nine-member board of directors have financial interests in the company, including a venture capital company and a real-estate development firm.[84] In some cases, board membership is a loan requirement. This type of involvement allows creditors to know firsthand the financial condition of the company and to have a say in major financial decisions such as acquisitions, restructuring, and new offerings of stock and debt. Another type of linkage occurs when an organization does business with a company that is represented by the same financial institution. This type of cooperation, which can facilitate contracting and financial transactions, is common among the *keiretsu* in Japan. Banks and other lenders may also participate as part owners of business ventures of client firms.

> In Indonesia, the Bank Restructuring Agency (IBRA) is planning to establish a holding company to manage the unsold property assets surrendered by former bank owners. These property assets include hotels, shops, land, and rice fields. The IBRA was founded to restore the country's banking sector and retrieve state funds that had been extended

to ailing banks. The agency seized massive amounts of assets from banks, including property and collateral for loans, following their failure to repay funds that had been injected into the banking sector at the height of the 1990s financial crisis.[85]

Financial intermediaries are the last of the external stakeholders that will be discussed in this chapter; however, it should be noted that other external stakeholders, of varying importance, exist on a firm-by-firm basis. For example, donors are a key stakeholder in nonprofit organizations. Donors should probably be treated more like customers than anything else. In fact, individuals who donate to charities or religious organizations are forgoing other purchases. Nonprofit organizations should communicate with donors, involve them in the processes of the organization, and create a high-quality service that donors will want to support. In the case of charities, the recipients of goods and services should also be treated as customers.

MANAGING PARTNERSHIPS

Much of this chapter so far has dealt with creating successful partnerships with external stakeholders. It is clear that interorganizational relationships are desirable and are becoming increasingly important activities for strategic advantage. Those that promise the most benefit are also likely to present the greatest implementation challenges. Critical attention to the integration of divergent operational and strategic goals of partners is essential for long-term alliance success. For many large hospitality firms, a variety of partnerships are managed simultaneously, as seen in the business transactions of Accor:

> With 157,000 associates in 140 countries, Accor is the European leader and one of the world's largest groups in travel and tourisms. The company has numerous brands in its portfolio, including Ibis, Etap, Sofitel, Motel 6, and Red Roof Inn. However, the firm is also a part of a global network of business partnerships. A few of these follow:
>
> ■ Transportation: Accor has a long-term partnership contract with Europcar to develop sales synergies and offer customers package deals. Air France has formed a series of alliances with Accor, including a joint customer loyalty program, a project to develop services for Air France customers and joint promotional campaigns. In addition, Accor and SNCF have a "Train + Hotel" partnership. Accor also offers Eurotunnel customers preferred rates and will be opening three new Accor hotels at the French Eurotunnel Calais-Coquelles site through this partnership.
>
> ■ Communications: Accor has a partnership with France Telecom that allows customers to book services directly by dialing Orange 711. Also, customers can book rooms on their cell phones by typing HOTE or 4683. In addition, Accor and Bouygues Telecom deliver Accor's services to customers via a 6th Sense mobile portal through their cell phones or the Internet.
>
> ■ Online Distribution: Accor is a part of the PlacesToStay Internet site, a division of WorldRes Inc. This site features 31,000 hotels around the world.
>
> ■ Finance: Through a partnership with Visa International, Accor will offer benefits such as preferred rates at Sofitel hotels throughout the world to high-end clientele who hold the Infinite, Platinum, or Signature credit cards. American Express, a partner for Compliment and Corporate cards, contributes its expertise in payment methods and loyalty programs.

■ Restaurants and Food: Accor owns a 20 percent stake in the restaurant company Courtepaille and maintains a marketing partnership between the restaurants and its economy hotels. Accor also partners with Danone in coffee and snacks, as well as sponsoring Danone Nation's Cup.[86]

This section will close with a few comments on how to manage partnerships so that they are likely to succeed. Managers should communicate the expected benefits of the venture to important external and internal stakeholders so they will understand the role the alliance will play in the organization.[87] They should also develop a strategic plan for the partnership that consolidates the views of the partners about market potential, competitive trends, and potential threats. There are several additional steps that may be used to improve the likelihood of success:

1. Through careful systematic study, identify an alliance partner that can provide the capabilities that are needed. Avoid the tendency to align with another firm just because forming alliances is a trend in the industry.

2. Clearly define the roles of each partner and ensure that every joint project is of value to both.

3. Develop a strategic plan for the venture that outlines specific objectives for each partner.

4. Keep top managers involved so that middle managers will stay committed.

5. Meet often, informally, at all managerial levels.

6. Appoint someone to monitor all aspects of the partnership, and use an outside mediator when disputes arise.

7. Maintain enough independence to develop your own area of expertise. Avoid becoming a complete "captive" of the alliance partner.

8. Anticipate and plan for cultural differences.[88]

This concludes our discussion of strategy implementation through the creation of partnerships and managing relationships with external stakeholders. The next section focuses on another element of strategy implementation—developing functional-support strategies.

FUNCTIONAL-LEVEL RESOURCE MANAGEMENT

Translating the corporate and business strategies into specific actions is the responsibility of managers in the various functional areas of an organization. Functional-level strategies, by being more specific and short-term, help employees understand what they are to do to accomplish the broader long-term aspirations of the corporation. The Pierre hotel in New York, for example, is a luxury hotel operated by Four Seasons. The marketing function strategy is to maintain rate integrity and focus on individual versus groups sales with an emphasis on foreign markets.[89] To accomplish this strategy the hotel relies on major press tours in Europe to promote the hotel. Similarly the information technology group at Starbuck's is busy working on providing Internet access to guests to fit with the firm's guest loyalty strategy.[90]

Functional-level strategies are about paying attention to details. Some of the most successful companies operate in low-growth, moderately profitable industries and pursue strategies that are not unique. The reason for their extraordinary success is their attention to the details associated with strategy implementation. Organizations are made up of people who interact with one another and with external stakeholders as they perform functions that meet the goals of the organization. Several years ago, researchers found that companies that were most successful in implementing their strategies had created a "pervasive strategic vision" throughout the company, with the full involvement of all employees.[91] In those firms, employees worked as a "coordinated system," with all of their separate but interdependent efforts directed toward the goals of the firm. Consequently, each functional area is one piece of a larger system, and coordination among the pieces is essential to successful strategy execution. For example, coordination of the hotel's various functions was essential for the Newark Gateway Hilton when it implemented its guest check-in on the shuttle bus to the hotel:

> The idea for an express check-in service originated with the president of Hilton Hotels. Acting upon this suggestion, the Newark Gateway Hilton formed a cross-functional team representing front office, security, housekeeping, finance, sales and marketing, and reservations. John Luke, vice president of front-office operations and systems, remarked that it was important to involve these departments in particular, so that each area affected by the decision would have some input into the process. After brainstorming for approximately one month, the team developed the Mobile Zip-in Check-in program. With the implementation of this process, overall guest satisfaction has improved.[92]

From a coordinated-systems perspective, well-developed functional-level resource-management strategies should have the following characteristics:

- *Decisions made within each function will be consistent with other areas.* For example, if a new hotel marketing promotion is developed, it has implications for reservations in explaining the program, human resources in training staff, and rooms division for costs and operational execution.

- *Decisions made within one function will be consistent with those made in other functions.* Interdependencies and linkages exist among the many activities of a firm. It is common for the decisions made by one department to be inconsistent with those of another department. For example, although they are responsible for most of the primary value-adding activities, marketing and operations frequently advocate very different approaches to the many interdependent decisions that exist between them. Left to their own devices over time, it is likely that marketing will make decisions that implement a differentiation strategy, while operations will implement a low-cost leadership strategy. The finance area also tends to conflict with operations, as operations strives for high service satisfaction and finance seeks to reduce costs.

- *Decisions made within functions will be consistent with the strategies of the business.* For example, if a company is pursuing a low-cost competitive strategy, then the bulk of the activities and resources should focus on cost reduction to improve profitability. It is often difficult to adapt to changes in the competitive environment. Suppose a company is pursuing an aggressive-growth strategy in a healthy business environment. Under those conditions, marketing may pursue market-share increases and revenue growth as its top priority. If the business environment changes—demand slows down and profits are squeezed—then the

TABLE 7.3	**CONDUCTING A FUNCTIONAL STRATEGY AUDIT**

Marketing Strategy

- Target customers—few vs. many, what groups, what regions
- Product positioning—premium commodity, multi-use, specialty use
- Product line mix—a mix of complementary products
- Product line breadth—a full-line offering of products
- Pricing strategies—discount, moderate, premium prices
- Promotion practices—direct sales, advertising, direct mail, Internet
- Distribution channels—few or many, sole contract responsibilities
- Customer service policies—flexibility, responsiveness, quality
- Product/service image—premium quality, good price, reliable
- Market research—accuracy, frequency, and methods for obtaining marketing information

Operations Strategy

- Capacity planning—lead demand to ensure availability or lag demand to achieve capacity utilization
- Facility location—near suppliers, customers, labor, natural resources, or transportation
- Facility layout—floor plans, integration of service activities, grounds, and external services
- Technology and equipment choices—degree of automation, use of computers and information technology
- Sourcing arrangements—cooperative arrangements with a few vs. competitive bid
- Planning and scheduling—standard services or custom, flexibility to customer requests
- Quality assurance—process control, standards, feedback gathering processes
- Workforce policies—training levels, cross-training, rewards, use of teams

Information Systems Strategy

- Hardware—local area network (LAN), mainframe, minicomputer, internal systems, links to Internet
- Software—data processing, decision support, Web management, computer automated design (CAD), computer integrated manufacturing (CIM), just-in-time inventory
- Personnel—in-house experts, subcontracting, or alliances
- Information security—hardware, software, physical location and layout
- Disaster recovery—off-site processing, backup procedures, virus protection and treatment
- Business intelligence—management support, marketing, accounting, operations, R&D, human resources, finance
- Internet—communications, marketing, resource acquisition, research, management

(Continues)

focus of marketing may have to change to stability and profit improvement over sales-volume increases. Unless prodded by the organization, marketing may be very reluctant to change from its traditional way of doing business.[93]

The rapid success and subsequent decline of People Express Airlines is a good demonstration of what can happen when there is inconsistency in tactical decisions across departments or between a generic strategy and functional strategies.

Following the deregulation of the airlines, Donald Burr started People Express as a low-cost commuter airline. In the beginning, every management decision supported low costs: aircraft were bought secondhand, pilots kept planes in the air more hours per day

TABLE 7.3	**CONDUCTING A FUNCTIONAL STRATEGY AUDIT (*CONTINUED*)**

Innovation Strategy

- Innovation focus—services, service processes, other applications
- Innovation orientation—leader, early follower, late follower
- Project priorities—budget, quality, creativity, time
- Knowledge creation—training, alliances and ventures, acquisitions, cross-functional teams
- Corporate entrepreneurship—"seed money" grants, time off to develop a venture, management support, rewards for entrepreneurs, ideas come from everyone

Human Resources Strategy

- Recruitment—entry level vs. experienced employees, colleges, technical schools, job services
- Selection—selection criteria and methods
- Nature of work—part-time, full-time, or a combination; on site or off site, domestic or foreign
- Performance appraisal—appraisal methods and frequency, link to rewards
- Salary and wages—hourly, piece rate, commission, fixed, relationship to performance, competitiveness
- Other compensation—stock ownership programs, bonuses
- Management compensation—stock awards, stock options, bonuses linked to performance, perquisites, low-interest loans
- Benefits—medical, dental and life insurance, paid leave, vacations, child care, health club
- Personnel actions—disciplinary plans, outplacement, early retirements
- Training—types of training, availability of training to employees, tuition reimbursement

Financial Strategy

- Sources of capital—debt, equity, or internal financing
- Financial reporting—frequency, type, government, shareholders, other stakeholders
- Capital budgeting—system for distributing capital, minimum ROI for investments, payback
- Overhead costs—allocation of overhead costs based on direct labor, machine use, sales volume, activity
- Financial control—system to ensure accuracy of internal and external financial information, audits
- Returns to shareholders—dividends policy, repurchase of stock, treasury stock, stock splits
- Financial targets—establishment of financial targets for functional areas and business units, method of reporting on progress

than any other airline, terminal leases were inexpensive, and human-resource policies required cross-training, encouraged high productivity, and rewarded employees with profit-sharing plans. In line with its no-frills commuter approach, the company did not book reservations or provide in-flight meals. The airline was extraordinarily successful with its strategy, and achieved the lowest cost position in the industry. However, with success, People Express began to alter its pattern of decisions and, over time, drift from its low-cost strategy. It pursued longer routes, which pulled it into direct competition with the full-service airlines, even though People Express did not have the elaborate reservation systems and customer services. It contracted more-expensive terminal arrangements and purchased new aircraft at market prices. The close-knit, high-performance culture that encouraged an extraordinary work pace in exchange for profit sharing was undermined by rapid growth and too many new faces. Just a few years after its start-up, People Express was in serious financial trouble and was forced to sell out to another airline.

A functional-strategy audit can help determine whether functional strategies are internally consistent, consistent across functions, and supportive of the strategies of the firm. Table 7.3 outlines some of the functional areas to be included in a functional audit. The first step is to determine what an organization is doing in each area. Internal consistency is evaluated, as is consistency across functional areas and consistency with the strategies of the organization. The next step is to develop plans to correct any inconsistencies. A functional-strategy audit is especially helpful as an implementation tool for new strategies. You may personally find it useful if you are doing case analyses in a Strategic Management course. If your instructor requires you to write an implementation section for a strategy you recommend, you can develop your plan, in part, based on the items for each functional area found in Table 7.3.

The collective pattern of day-to-day decisions made and actions taken by managers and employees who are responsible for value-creating activities result in the functional strategies that are used to implement the growth and competitive strategies of the business. Management's challenge is to ensure that the pattern is consistent with what was intended.

Key-Points Summary

This chapter focused on implementing strategy from two perspectives. First, organizations can look outward to external stakeholders, especially through the formation of interorganizational relationships. However, another approach is to look inward to the way organizational resources are managed through the execution of functional-level resource-management strategies. These approaches are not mutually exclusive, but, rather, include a range of options that executives may consider when devising implementation plans.

Interorganizational relationships are an increasingly popular technique for pursuing strategic objectives. One of the most important reasons for forming partnerships is to acquire resources, especially knowledge. High priority for partnerships should be given to stakeholders with a large amount of formal, political, or economic power; stakeholders that have a large impact on the uncertainty facing an organization; and/or stakeholders that possess needed resources. Other stakeholders should not be ignored, but they can be managed with more traditional stakeholder management techniques, with the objective of buffering the organization from their influence.

Strategies are implemented through the day-to-day decisions and actions of employees throughout the organization. Management's challenge is to create a pattern of integrated, coordinated decisions that meets the needs of stakeholders and fulfills the planned strategy of the organization. To this end, strategies are established for functional-level resource areas such as marketing, operations, information systems, innovation, human resources, and finance. In each area, employees interact with different stakeholder groups and manage conflicting expectations. In managing functional strategies, managers must ensure that decisions within each area are consistent over time, with other functions, and with the stated strategies of the firm.

DISCUSSION QUESTIONS

1. Returning to Chapter 2 (Table 2.4), review the definitions of the following interorganizational relationships: joint ventures, networks, consortia, alliances, trade groups, and interlocking directorates.

2. What is a tourism cluster? Provide examples of firms in the three sectors of a cluster for a specific tourism destination.

3. What are the major advantages of interorganizational relationships?

4. Do interorganizational relationships have any disadvantages? If so, what are they?

5. What are the primary factors that make some stakeholders more important than others? How should high-priority stakeholders be managed?

6. How do management techniques for high-priority stakeholders differ from those of low-priority stakeholders? Give examples.

7. What can organizations do to ensure that their partnerships are effective?

8. Why does the hotel industry have so many partnerships among competitors? Is this true for other industries? Which ones?

9. What are some of the methods organizational leaders can use to effectively manage relationships with local communities, activists, the media, unions, and financial intermediaries?

10. What is a functional-level resource-management strategy? Give an example of how a functional-level resource-management strategy can be used to carry out one of the generic business-level strategies, such as low-cost leadership.

11. What characteristics should well-developed functional-level resource-management strategies have?

NOTES

1. P. Sparaco, "Air France Predicts More Consolidation," *Aviation Week & Space Technology*, 2 December 2002, pg. 2; D. Michaels and S. Neuman, "Global Partners may Get Roiled by Turbulence," *The Wall Street Journal*, 6 December 2002, pg. B1; J. Flottau, "SkyTeam Alliance Courts New Members," *Aviation Week & Space Technology*, 7 October 2002, pg. 3.

2. J. Crotts, D. Buhalis, and R. March, "Introduction: Global Alliances in Tourism and Hospitality Management," *International Journal of Hospitality and Tourism Administration* 1, no. 1 (2000): 1–10.

3. J. S. Harrison, "Alternatives to Merger—Joint Ventures and Other Strategies," *Long Range Planning* (December 1987): 78–83.

4. P. Dittmer, *Dimensions of the Hospitality Industry*, 3rd edition (New York: John Wiley and Sons, 2002).

5. C. Enz, C. Inman, and M. Lankau, "Strategic Social Partnerships for Change: A Framework for Building Sustainable Growth in Developing Countries," in P. Christopher Earley and Harbir Singh (ed.), *Innovations in Cross-Cultural Management* (Thousand Oaks, CA: Sage Publishing, 2000).

6. R. Kanter, *World Class: Thriving Locally in the Global Economy*. (New York: Touchstone, 1995), 325.

7. L. Doolittle, "Disney Teams with AAA to Provide Multipurpose Rest Area for Travelers," *Orlando Sentinel*, 25 January 1996, B1.

8. Hotel Online, http://www.hotel-online.com/News. August 17, 2003.

9. R. M. Kanter, "Becoming PALS: Pooling, Allying, and Linking across Companies," *Academy of Management Executive* (August 1989): 183–193.

10. R. Mukumbira, "Botswana: Debswana Hotel Venture to Go Ahead," *African Business,* June 2003: 49.
11. J. S. Harrison et al., "Resource Complementarity in Business Combinations: Extending the Logic to Organizational Alliances," *Journal of Management* 27 (2001): 679–690.
12. M. Krantz, "Hard Rock Hotels Enlists Sol Melia to Help Expand Chain's Reach," *Meeting News,* 14 July 2003, 16.
13. Peet's Coffee & Tea, Inc., Press Release, "Peet's Coffee & Tea, Inc. Reports Second Quarter 2003 Result," http://www.peets.com/abtu/11/4.3.29_newsart.asp; M. Sheridan, "Mutual Attraction," *Restaurants & Institutions,* 15 April 2003.
14. A. C. Inkpen, "Strategic Alliances," in *The Blackwell Handbook of Strategic Management,* ed. M. A. Hitt, R. E. Freeman, and J. S. Harrison (Oxford: Blackwell Publishers, 2001), 409–432.
15. M. Sheridan, "Mutual Attraction."
16. K. Amarante, "TBR/WTTC Partner on Tourism Initiatives," http://www.hotelinteractive.com, 30 January 2002.
17. Pennsylvania Restaurant Association. http://www.parestaurant.org/mission.html, 9 July 2003.
18. "InfoTravel unites with On Command Corp.," *Hotel and Motel Management,* 18 November 1996, 75.
19. B. Kogut, "Joint Ventures: Theoretical and Empirical Perspectives," *Strategic Management Journal* 9 (1988): 319–332.
20. K. R. Harrigan, "Joint Ventures and Competitive Strategy," *Strategic Management Journal* 9 (1988): 141–158; R. N. Osborn and C. C. Baughn, "Forms of Interorganizational Governance for Multinational Alliances," *Academy of Management Journal* 33 (1990): 503–519.
21. M. Sheridan, "Mutual Attraction."
22. P. King, "Harvard Aims to Give Students a Better Read on Food," *Nation's Restaurant News,* 30 June 2003, 20; M. Sheridan, "Mutual Attraction."
23. D. H. Kent, "Joint Ventures vs. Non-Joint Ventures: An Empirical Investigation," *Strategic Management Journal* 12 (1991): 387–393.
24. M. Sheridan, "Mutual Attraction."
25. P. Lorange and J. Roos, "Why Some Strategic Alliances Succeed and Others Fail," *Journal of Business Strategy* (January/February 1991), 25–30.
26. Inkpen, "Strategic Alliances"; E. C. Karper-Fuehrer and N. M. Ashkanasy, "Communicating Trustworthiness and Building Trust in Interorganizational Virtual Organizations," *Journal of Management* 27 (2001): 235–254; R. Gulati, "Does Familiarity Breed Trust? The Implications of Repeated Ties for Contractual Choice in Alliances," *Academy of Management Journal* 38 (1995): 85–112; B. Nooteboom, H. Berger, and N. G. Noorderhaven, "Effects of Trust and Governance on Relational Risk," *Academy of Management Journal* 40 (1997): 308–338.
27. Inkpen, "Strategic Alliances."
28. J. Walsh, "Partnerships Are Key to Developing Abroad," *Hotel & Motel Management,* 4 June 2001, 40.
29. J. S. Harrison and C. H. St. John, "Managing and Partnering with External Stakeholders," *Academy of Management Executive* (May 1996): 46–50; J. D. Thompson, *Organizations in Action* (New York: McGraw-Hill, 1967); J. R. Lang & D. E. Lockhart, "Increased Environmental Uncertainty and Changes in Board Linkage Patterns," *Academy of Management Journal* 33, no. 1 (1990): 106–128; A. D. Meyer and G. R. Brooks, "Environmental Jolts and Industry Revolutions: Organizational Responses to Discontinuous Change," *Strategic Management Journal* 11 (Special Issue 1990): 93–110.
30. J. Perreira and B. Ortega, "Once Easily Turned Away by Local Foes, Wal-Mart Gets Tough in New England," *The Wall Street Journal,* 7 September 1994, B1, B4.
31. L. Canina, K. Walsh, and C. Enz, "Gasoline-price Fluctuations and Demand for Hotel Rooms: A Study of Branded Hotels from 1988 through 2000," *Cornell Hotel and Restaurant Administration Quarterly* 44, no. 4 (2003).

32. J. Pfeffer and G. R. Salancik, *The External Control of Organizations: A Resource Dependence Perspective* (New York: Harper & Row, 1978): 43.

33. This is the view of many organization theorists. For example, see R. L. Daft, *Organization Theory and Design,* 4th ed. (St. Paul, Minn: West Publishing, 1992), chap. 3.

34. L. Dube, C. Enz, L. Renaghan, and J. Siguaw, "Cendant Corporation: Comprehensive Diversity Initiative," *American Lodging Excellence: The Key to Best Practices in the U.S. Lodging Industry* (2000): 62–63.

35. W. Weitzel and E. Jonsson, "Reversing the Downward Spiral: Lessons from W. T. Grant and Sears Roebuck," *Academy of Management Executive* (August 1991): 7–22.

36. L. Lohmeyer, "Chains: Kids' Advice Not Child's Play: Using Youths for Menu Testing Taps Lucrative Niche-market Insights," *Nation's Restaurant News* 23 June 2003, 49.

37. L. Lohmeyer, "Chains: Kids' Advice Not Child's Play."

38. "Welcome to ClubCorp," http://www.clubcorp.com, 20 August 2003.

39. R. Parker, "Supply Chains Put Market Leaders Ahead of the Pack," *Supply Management,* 17 July 2003, 10.

40. J. Brownell and D. Reynolds, "Strengthening the F&B Purchaser-Supplier Partnership: Actions That Make a Difference," *Cornell Hotel and Restaurant Administration Quarterly* 43, no. 6 (December 2002): 49–61.

41. R. Terrero, "Hilton Hotels Corp. Inks Alliance, Forms Company with LodgeNet Entertainment," *Hotel Business,* 3 March 2003, 50.

42. J. Gunn, "Third-party Politics," *Caterer & Hotelkeeper,* 6 February 2003; pg 24.

43. L. Dube, C. Enz, L. Renaghan, and J. Siguaw, "Cendant Corporation: Developing 'Preferred Alliances' with National Vendors."

44. R. Bragg and S. Kumar, "Building Strategic Partnerships," *Industrial Engineer,* June 2003, 39.

45. D. McCutcheon and F. Stuart, "Issues in the Choice of Supplier Alliance Partners," *Journal of Operations Management* 18 (2000): 279–301.

46. J. Gunn, "Third-party Politics."

47. J. Brownell and D. Reynolds, "Strengthening the F&B Purchaser-Supplier Partnership: Actions That Make a Difference," *Cornell Hotel and Restaurant Administration Quarterly* 43, no. 6 (December 2002): 49–61.

48. J. R. Harbison and P. Pekar Jr., *Smart Alliances: A Practical Guide to Repeatable Success* (San Francisco: Jossey-Bass Publishers, 1998).

49. J. Hagedoorn, "Understanding the Rationale of Strategic Technology Partnering: Interorganizational Modes of Cooperation and Sectoral Differences," *Strategic Management Journal* 14 (1993): 371–385; E. R. Auster, "International Corporate Linkages: Dynamic Forms in Changing Environments," *Columbia Journal of World Business* 22 (1987): 3–13; Harrigan, "Joint Ventures and Competitive Strategy."

50. S. Oster, "The Strategic Use of Regulatory Investment by Industry Sub-groups," *Economic Inquiry* 20 (1982): 604.

51. D. Bond, "Recovery, Phase Two: Majors Change Strategy from Super-sized Alliances to Drinks over the Atlantic, Carriers Top Waiting for the Market to Save Them," *Aviation Week & Space Technology,* 2 September 2002; pg 24.

52. J. Lewis, *Partnerships for Profit: Structuring and Managing Strategic Alliances* (New York: The Free Press, 1990).

53. M. Pretes, "Tourism and Nationalism," *Annals of Tourism Research* 30, no. 1 (2003): 125–142.

54. B. Prideaux and C. Cooper, "Marketing and Destination Growth: A Symbiotic Relationship or Simple Coincidence," *Journal of Vacation Marketing* 9, no. 1 (December 2002; pg. 35).

55. R. Mukumbira, "Botswana: Debswana Hotel Venture to Go Ahead," *African Business,* June 2003, 49.

56. "Award for Holiday Inn Miri," *New Straits Times-Management Times,* 11 January 2001.

57. F. Rose, "Can Disney Tame 42nd Street?" *Fortune,* 24 June 1996, 95–104.

58. B. Kuhn, "Business Growth on the Rise: Central Florida Faces Good News, Bad News Scenario," *The Orlando Sentinel,* 10 January 1994, 24; J. DeSimone, "A Boost for Business," *The Orlando Sentinel,* 31 October 1994, 8; A. Millican, "Want New Industry? House It," *The Orlando Sentinel,* 7 October 1994, 1.

59. L. Dube, C. Enz, L. Renaghan and J. Siguaw, "Hyatt Regency Scottsdale: A Community-based Hospitality Training Program for High School Students," *American Lodging Excellence: The Key to Best Practices in the U.S. Lodging Industry* (2000): 62–63.

60. S. Leung, "McDonald's See Glimmers of a Return to Its Salad Days," *The Wall Street Journal*, 1 August 2003, B1.

61. M. Prewitt, "Operators Weigh Options over Fat Suits," *Nation's Restaurant News*, 7 July 2003; 1.

62. B. Thorn, "The Skinny on Foodservice's Fat Fight: Big Problem Requires Large Helping of Ideas," *Nation's Restaurant News*, 21 July 2003; pg. 34.

63. K. Kerlin, "Sustainable slopes," *E: The Environmental Magazine*, November/December 2001; 15.

64. J. J. Davis, "A Blueprint for Green Marketing," *The Journal of Business Strategy* (July/August 1991): 14–17; J. S. Scerbinski, "Consumers and the Environment: A Focus on Five Products," *The Journal of Business Strategy* (September/October 1991): 44–47; Z. Schiller, "At Rubbermaid, Little Things Mean a Lot," *Business Week*, 11 November 1991, 126.

65. T. L. O'Brien, "Aided by Computers, Many of the Disabled Form Own Businesses," *The Wall Street Journal*, 8 October 1993, A1, A9.

66. M. R. Moskowitz, "Company Performance Roundup," *Business and Society Review* (Spring 1995), 74

67. A. Spector, "Puck Express Expands through Franchising," *Nation's Restaurant News*, 11 June 2001; 4.

68. G. Haussman, "Barter Biz Plugging Room Sales Shortfall," http://www.hotelinteractive.com/news/ (25 August 2003).

69. H. Kim and S. Richardson, "Motion Picture Impacts on Destination Images," *Annals of Tourism Research* 30, no. 1 (2003): 216–237.

70. R. Allen, "The Dish on 'The Restaurant': Style over Substance Presents an Unappetizing View of Foodservice," *Nation's Restaurant News*, 25 August 2003; pg. 23.

71. The World Bank, *Building Institutions for Markets: World Development Report 2002* (Oxford University Press, Oxford, England, 2002).

72. D. Whitford, "Labor's Best Hope," *Fortune*, 29 October 2001; pg. 119. C. Wolff, "Hotel Organizing: Down but Not Out," *Lodging Hospitality*, 1 May 2003; pg. 8.

73. M. J. Ybarra, "Janitors' Union Uses Pressure and Theatrics to Expand Its Ranks," *The Wall Street Journal*, 21 March 1994, A1, A8.

74. All of the news items were taken from the union HERE News Web pages, http://www.hereunion.org/here-news/herenews.asp, 28 August 2003.

75. P. King, "Restaurant Union Launches Cyberspace Attacks on Chain Foes," *Nation's Restaurant News*, 19 August 2002, 8.

76. S. Korshak, "A Labor-management Partnership: San Francisco's Hotels and the Employees' Union Try a New Approach," *Cornell Hotel and Restaurant Administration Quarterly* 41, no. 2 (April 2000): 14–29.

77. C. Wolff, "Hotel Organizing."

78. A. Stokes, R. Murphy, P. Wagner, and D. Sherwyn, "Neutrality Agreements: How Unions Organize New Hotels without an Employee Ballot," *Cornell Hotel and Restaurant Administration Quarterly* 42, no. 5 (October–November 2001): 86–96.

79. Based on information obtained directly from in-person meeting with John Young, executive vice president of human resources, Four Seasons Hotels and Resorts, 2003.

80. Ibid.

81. A. Bernstein, "Why America Needs Unions But Not the Kind It Has Now," *Business Week*, 23 May 1994, 70–82.

82. K. Seal, "Union Pension Funds Fill Financing Void for Hotel Projects," *Hotel and Motel Management*, 6 March 2000.

83. R. Mowbray, "Looking for the Union Label Never Easier, Thanks to Hotel; Loews Makes Use of Organized Labor," New Orleans *Times-Picayune*, 9 May 200; pg. C3.

84. Mandalay Resort Group, *2002 Annual Report*, http://www.mandalayresortgroup.com/investor_relations.html, 29 August 2003.

85. M. Taufiqurrahman, "IBRA Moves to Manage Property Assets," *Jakarta Post*, 7 July 2003; pg A6.

86. "Accor Strategic Partnerships," http://www.accor.com/gb/groupe/partenariats/strategiques.asp, visited 21 August 2003.

87. Lorange and Roos, "Strategic Alliances," 25–30.

88. Adapted from various sources, including P. Burrows, "How a Good Partnership Goes Bad," *Electronic Business,* 30 March 1992, 86–90; G. Develin and M. Bleackley, "Strategic Alliances—Guidelines for Success," *Long Range Planning* 21, no. 5 (1988): 18–23.; Lorange and Roos, "Strategic Alliances;" J. B. Treece, K. Miller, R. A. Melcher, "The Partners," *Business Week,* 10 February 1992, 102–107.

89. L. Dube, C. Enz, L. Renaghan, and J. Siguaw, "The Pierre: Maximizing Profitability by Managing the Sales Mix," *American Lodging Excellence: The Key to Best Practices in the U.S. Lodging Industry* (2000): 185–186.

90. A. Liddle, "Operators Chew on Ways to Offer In-store Internet Access," *Nation's Restaurant News,* 11 August 2003; pg. 1.

91. F. W. Gluck, S. D. Kaufman, and A. S. Walleck, "Strategic Management for Competitive Advantage," *Harvard Business Review* (July/August 1980): 154–161.

92. L. Dube, C. Enz, L. Renaghan, and J. Siguaw, "Newark Gateway Hilton: Guest Check-in on the Shuttle Bus," *American Lodging Excellence: The Key to Best Practices in the U.S. Lodging Industry* (2000): 177.

93. R. Hayes and S. Wheelwright, *Restoring Our Competitive Edge: Competing through Manufacturing* (New York: John Wiley and Sons, 1984), 30.

Sea Containers Ltd. is a Bermuda company engaged in three main activities: passenger transport, marine container leasing, and leisure-based (hotel) operations. In addition, Sea Containers' other activities include property development and management, publishing, fruit farming in the Ivory Coast and Brazil, and a United Kingdom–based travel agency.

Sea Containers is a diversified firm with 15,000 employees. In senior management, the firm has begun to search for a new CEO. The founder, president, and CEO, James B. Sherwood, is seventy years old and plans to divide his responsibilities while continuing to occupy the role of chairman of the board. Each of the three segments of this conglomerate has a number of operating businesses.

Passenger and Freight Transportation Division
(Ferry and Rail Companies)

This division is managed by the senior vice president of Passenger and Freight Transport. The passenger transport division of the firm consists of fast ferry and conventional ferry services. The individual companies are Hoverspeed Ltd., Isle of Man Steam Packet Company, SeaStreak, Silja Line, and SNAV-Hoverspeed. Rail operations in the United Kingdom are conducted under the name Great North Eastern Railway (GNER). Ship management and naval architects subsidiaries support the passenger and freight transport division and have outside clients as well.

Marine Container Leasing Division

In this division, the senior manager is the vice president of the Containers Division and also the president of the primary business GE SeaCo. Marine container leasing is conducted primarily through GE SeaCo SRL, a Barbados company owned 50 percent by Sea Containers and 50 percent by General Electric Capital Corporation. GE SeaCo operates one of the largest marine container fleets in the world and partly owns five container service depots, four container manufacturing facilities, and a refrigerated container service business.

Orient-Express Hotels Ltd.

Orient-Express Hotels Ltd. began as a division of the company and is now a subsidiary of Sea Containers Ltd. This publicly traded hotel company (symbol OEH) focuses on the luxury end of the leisure market. The company owns and/or operates twenty-six highly individual deluxe hotels worldwide, six tourist trains, a river cruise ship, and two restaurants. The company's distinctive operations include the Copacabana Palace in Rio de Janeiro, the Venice Simplon-Orient-Express train in Europe and the '21' Club in New York City.[1]

INTRODUCTION

Organizations employ a wide variety of tactics to implement their strategies. In the opening example, Sea Containers Ltd. is using a decentralized divisional management structure to enhance implementation of its unrelated-diversification strategy. In this structure, the Orient Express Hotels operate as an independent company, but it can benefit from having access to capital and other resources of the larger company. In the passenger and freight transport division, the corporation has created five separate businesses operating in various geographic locations: the English Channel, the Irish Sea, the Baltic Sea, the Adriatic Sea, and New York City.

One element of the corporate strategy for Sea Containers is the intention to sell the Isle of Man Steam Packet Company, while a business-level strategy for the SeaStreak fast ferry company in New York includes the introduction of new services and the construction of two new ferries. The corporate and business-level organization structures can have a powerful influence on the execution of these strategies. Success in accomplishing these and other strategic plans rests on the managers and employees' knowing how to get the work done.

An organization that is appropriately organized and has activities, budgets, and programs directed toward the desired objectives will likely succeed in the implementation of strategy.

While there were a few hints at how to do this in earlier chapters, this chapter will add a great deal of understanding. It will begin with a discussion of the key building blocks of organizing (e.g., formalization, specialization, and hierarchy of authority), and then explore the various formal structures and how they can be used to support a particular strategic focus. The section will close with a few comments on some of the newly emerging organizational structures and the importance of lateral relationships.

The final section of this chapter on implementation will review control systems. Beyond the traditional measuring and monitoring functions, managers use control systems to overcome resistance to change, communicate new strategic agendas, ensure continuing attention to new strategic initiatives, formalize beliefs, set boundaries on acceptable strategic behavior, and motivate discussion and debate about strategic uncertainties.[2] Therefore, control systems may also be considered "tools of strategy implementation."[3] A discussion of the increasingly important topic of crisis management will complete this chapter.

ORGANIZATIONAL STRUCTURES

One of the most important activities associated with strategy implementation is designing a strategy-supportive organization. Since so many activities that take place within organizations are performed by people who have not been involved in the strategy formulation process, it is essential that their work be designed to deliver on the strategy. It is systems, not smiles, that make excellent customer service. That is, managers need to carefully design the operating systems to enable effective action and to modify those systems as an organization grows or shifts its strategic focus.

Designing an organization involves defining organizational roles, determining reporting relationships, establishing how to group individuals, and creating ways to coordinate employee efforts. One element of design is the formal structure of how work is organized. The activities and people within corporations are usually subdivided into departments and groups so that employees may specialize in a limited number of activities and focus on a limited set of responsibilities. The formal structure specifies the number and types of departments or groups and provides the formal reporting relationships and lines of communication among internal stakeholders. The purpose of these structures is to coordinate, communicate, and control individual actions to support the strategy, and to facilitate workflow, permit management control, and create doable jobs.

Alfred Chandler was the first researcher to recognize the importance of the structure-strategy relationship.[4] According to Chandler, an organization's structure should be designed to support the intended strategy of the firm.[5] An organization can choose from a variety of structural forms when implementing a chosen strategy. The underlying assumption is that a fit between the strategy and the structure will lead to superior organization performance, which seems logical but has not been proved conclusively. Nevertheless, the connection between organizational structure and performance has been supported by research in the restaurant industry.[6] Higher performing restaurants, defined by growth in unit sales, are less centralized, more formalized, and more specialized. Franchised operations are more formalized, as are companies in the quick-service segment. McDonald's, admired by its supporters and reviled by those who see it as robbing workers of meaningful tasks, is an excellent example of fitting the operating structure to the low-cost provider strategy it uses to sell food.

> To ensure that all McDonald's restaurants serve products of uniform quality, the company uses centralized planning, centrally designed training programs, centrally approved and supervised suppliers, automated machinery and other specially designed equipment, meticulous specifications, and systematic inspections. To provide its customers with a uniformly pleasant "McDonald's experience," the company also tries to mass-produce friendliness, deference, diligence, and good cheer through a variety of socialization and social control techniques. Despite sneers from those who equate uniformity with mediocrity, the success of McDonald's has been spectacular.[7]

Several principles or dimensions may be used to characterize an organization's structure. The dimensions, described in Table 8.1, capture the formal arrangements of people, activities, and decision-making authority. Each of these dimensions represents an organizational-design decision, and these decisions have ramifications with regard to organizational behavior. Conscious decisions are made regarding the degree of specialization, formalization, centralization, and levels of authority necessary to operate an organization. Over time these decisions are revisited and organizations are redesigned to accommodate growth and changes in size, environmental complexity, competition, and entry into new or different businesses. When a new strategy is formulated, administrative problems often emerge and performance declines. This situation requires the establishment of a new structure, which leads to performance improvements. Hence, the careful design and redesign of organizations is essential to ensuring that the execution of a strategy is supported by the right system of coordination, communication, and control.

To illustrate this evolution, let's start with a small business. A chef/owner decides to open an upscale restaurant in Buffalo, New York. This fine-dining establishment has an owner/chef who creates the menu, decides on food preparation methods, purchases the ingredients, cooks the meal, and then moves to the dining room to socialize with the guests.[8] In this small organization, little specialization is evident as the owner does many of the tasks necessary to operate the business. The reporting relationships are very informal, as her family and friends work by her side to deliver the meals. No job descriptions or formal performance reviews exist, and everyone in the restaurant is part of a "family." This type of organization relies on the simplest management structure, the entrepreneurial structure, sometimes called the owner/manager structure. This form is common for smaller hotel and restaurant companies. The owner is the top manager, and the business is run as a sole proprietorship. This means that the owner/manager makes all of the important decisions and directs the efforts of all employees.

As this owner/chef builds her reputation she may need to hire additional kitchen workers to perform specific culinary functions. As the volume of meals served increases, the chef /owner creates departments separating front-of-house service from back-of-house food preparation. She has now doubled the number of departments, increased her staff levels, and increased the level of specialization in the performance of various tasks. She has

TABLE 8.1	DIMENSIONS OF ORGANIZATIONAL STRUCTURE
Dimension	**Description**
Hierarchy of authority	Formal reporting relationships among levels and across functions and departments. A tall, narrow structure means that there are multiple levels between the CEO and the customer. A flat, wide structure means fewer levels and a wider span of control for managers (more people report to them). A flat structure may be associated with more use of cross-functional, self-managed teams.
Degree of centralization	Refers to where in the structure the decision-making authority lies. A highly centralized structure means that high-level managers make most of the critical decisions. A decentralized structure puts more decision-making authority in the hands of lower-level managers and teams.
Complexity	Describes the number of levels in the hierarchy, the number of units such as departments or teams, and the number of markets served.
Specialization	The degree to which the tasks of the organization are divided into separate jobs. Some organizations have a highly specialized structure, with people focusing on one particular task or function. The advantage is that people can get very good at what they do. Other organizations expect people to be skilled in a number of tasks, which improves scheduling flexibility and teamwork.
Formalization	This might also be called bureaucracy. It describes the extent to which formalized rules, policies, and procedures exist within the organization and the extent to which people actually follow them. A high level of formalization can lead to efficiency but may reduce the flexibility that is sometimes required to satisfy customers.
Professionalism	Refers to the amount of formal education and training possessed by employees and managers. High technology firms tend to have more professionalism, while firms engaged in agriculture or basic assembly tend to have less-well educated employees.

Source: R. L. Daft, *Organization Theory and Design* (Cincinnati, OH: South-Western College Publishing, 2001).

created levels of hierarchy, hiring a sous chef to supervise the kitchen and a dining room manager to handle guests. Her restaurant's popularity has lead to an emerging catering business, requiring even more departmentalizing and specialization. The business is becoming more complex, and this entrepreneur must now create a more formalized structure. Our chef decides that now is the time for her to develop an organization chart, a useful tool for showing the various parts of the organization, how they interrelate, and how each position fits into the whole.[9]

Her success leads to careful business analysis and a revised strategy in which she wishes to expand by opening another restaurant in Syracuse, New York, and branching into retail by selling her sauces at a local grocery store called Wegman's. With these moves come increasing levels of hierarchy and complexity, as her organization now serves a number of markets with multiple units and increasing numbers of employees. Many of the critical decisions in the day-to-day operation of each restaurant and the retail business are now delegated to her subordinate managers, making the organization more decentralized. To complete our example: after years of success this small business is now a big business with fifteen units in seven northeastern cities and two separate divisions, one for restaurants and the other for retail sales. Our CEO/owner has expansion in her five-year plan, with a desire to diversify into casual-dining restaurants and to move her fine-dining concept into a franchise operation. Along the way, she has altered the organizational structure several times to reflect the evolution in her strategy.

The key point is that managers need to be deliberate about organizational-design choices because they have ramifications on a firm's ability to execute its chosen strategies. For instance, decentralized decision making is likely to encourage innovation and entrepreneurship, while a high level of formalization (rules and procedures) will have the opposite influence. Generally speaking, restaurant chains have a fairly high degree of formalization, which supports the operating unit strategies, particularly in the quick-service segment. Also, high levels of professionalism (well-educated employees) may be needed to support a strategy of technical leadership. A surprising feature of many multi-unit restaurants is the absence of a specialized research and development function, although this pattern is changing and the function is often considered essential for long-term growth.[10] These are just a few examples of what might happen to the operation of an organization when different decisions are made regarding organizing elements like centralization, formalization, and levels of hierarchy.

As competition increases and the hotel industry matures, hotel strategists have begun to question what should be centralized to corporate headquarters and what belongs more effectively executed at the property level. Choice Hotels, for example, evaluated service delivery and then created a more centralized franchise services function to provide more consistency in delivery and a better focus on customer needs.[11] Centralization has often been found to provide cost savings and efficiency. Examples include the consolidation of food and beverage operations into a single prep kitchen that delivers product to a number of outlets fast and with fewer workers. For some, moving sales and marketing out of the hotel and into regional areas has provided a more effective selling model. Accounting activities such as payroll has also become more efficient when handled at a chain's corporate headquarters, as have central reservation systems (CRS) that serve multiple properties.

> With Wyndham Hotels & Resort's shift from a real estate investment trust (REIT) to a branded hotel operating company, technology purchasing priorities have changed. As a REIT, Wyndham wasn't concerned with having a system-wide CRS, and properties relied on seven different project management systems. But as a branded operating company with a desire for seamless connectivity between properties and a CRS, Wyndham began to have difficulty cost justifying the licensing of seven PMSs and developing seven interfaces to a CRS.
>
> Because Wyndham owns 90% of its hotels, it makes sense to employ a centralized PMS system to which individual properties subscribe on an application service provider (ASP) basis, says Mark Hedley, senior vice president and chief technology officer. Wyndham acts as the central ASP provider of the OPERA PMS by MICROS Systems, loading and configuring software on a single server that is linked to every property in the system. Updates to the server can upgrade all properties overnight, reinvigorating systems in a manner that would take a chain with decentralized, on-property PMSs countless hours of labor."[12]

When making decisions about how to structure an organization, it is important to remember the following:

- Structure is not an end; it is a means to an end. The "end" is successful organizational performance.
- There is no one best structure. A change in organization strategy may require a corresponding change in structure to avoid administrative inefficiencies, but the organization's size, strategies, external environment, stakeholder relationships,

and management style all influence the appropriateness of a given structure. All structures embody trade-offs.[13]

- Once in place, the new structure becomes a characteristic of the organization that will serve as a constraint on future strategic choices.

- Administrative inefficiencies, poor service to customers, communication problems, or employee frustrations may indicate a strategy-structure mismatch.

The various structural forms can be divided into two broad groups, business-level and corporate-level. These groups are consistent in their definitions with the way we have been using the terms business-level and corporate-level in describing strategies. Business-level structures are methods of organizing individual business units, which are often called divisions if they are part of a larger corporation. Another way to think of these units is as separate operating companies. If an organization consists of only one operating company, then its business-level structure is its corporate structure. However, as organizations diversify and form multiple operating companies, they encounter the need to create a corporate-level structure to tie these separate companies together. It is interesting to note that a single corporation, like Sea Containers Ltd., could have two or more business units using different business-level structures. For example, one unit could be organized according to functional activities like marketing, accounting, and human resources, and another unit could be organized according to geographic markets like the East, West, and Midwest. A corporate-level structure ties the business units together. The example below illustrates how a firm designs its operation to run multiple businesses and also develops an overarching corporate structure.

> Morrison Restaurants is divided into three divisions, Morrison's Hospitality Group, Morrison's Family Dining Group, and the Ruby Tuesday Group, that combined generate more than $1.1 billion in annual revenues. Morrison has developed and implemented an integrated strategic plan for the organization as a whole and has developed strategic plans for each of its divisions and concepts.[14]

BUSINESS-LEVEL STRUCTURES

In the hospitality industry, the basic business-level structures include functional, geographic/customer, and project matrix. Some of the essential characteristics, strengths, and weaknesses of these structures are presented in Table 8.2.

Functional Structures

The most common way in which companies organize is called a functional structure and is based on putting people in groupings or departments based on their shared expertise. Functional structures are organized around the common activities or similar tasks performed by individuals.[15] Hotels are most often functionally structured and usually have marketing, human-resources, food and beverage, accounting, and rooms departments, at a minimum. If the hotel is larger in size, it will have other departments, such as engineering, public relations, and convention services. The structure is centralized, highly specialized, and most appropriate when a limited service or product line is offered to a particular

TABLE 8.2	IMPORTANT ATTRIBUTES OF BASIC BUSINESS-LEVEL STRUCTURES		
	Functional	**Geographic or Customer**	**Project Matrix**
Organizing Framework	Functional inputs such as marketing, engineering and manufacturing	Outputs such as types of services or various markets in which they are provided	Inputs and outputs
Degree of Centralization	Centralized	Decentralized	Decentralized with shared authority
Competitive Environment	Tends to work better if the environment is stable and demands internal efficiency or specialization within functions	Works well in a dynamic environment with pressure to satisfy needs of particular customers, markets, or locations	Responds to both internal pressure for efficiency or specialization and external market pressure to satisfy particular needs
Growth Strategy	Supports market penetration well	Useful for market and/or service development	Frequent changes to products and markets
Major Strengths	• Economies of scale within departments may lead to efficiency • Allows development of functional expertise and specialization • Best in organizations with few products or services	• Suited to fast change in an unstable environment • High levels of client satisfaction • High coordination across functions • Best in large organizations with several products or markets	• Achieves coordination • Flexible sharing of human resources • Best in medium-sized firms with multiple products
Major Weaknesses	• Slow response time to environmental changes • Hierarchy overload from decisions collecting at the top • Poor coordination across departments • Restricts view of organizational goals	• Lose economies of scale • Some functions are redundant within the organization • Lose in-depth specialization within functions • May lead to poor coordination and integration across locations, customers or products, depending on the style used	• Dual authority can cause frustration and confusion • Excellent interpersonal skills needed • Additional training required can be expensive • Time consuming due to frequent meetings • Great effort needed to maintain power balance

Sources: R. L. Daft, *Organization Theory and Design* (Cincinnati, OH: South-Western College Publishing, 2001); R. Duncan, "What is the Right Organization Structure? Decision Tree Analysis Provides the Answer," *Organization Dynamics* (Winter 1979): 429–431.

market segment and when the needs of external stakeholders are relatively stable. The functional structure is oriented toward internal efficiency and encourages teamwork and coordination of activities within individual departments or units. It is particularly appropriate in organizations that want to exploit economies of scale, efficiency, and learning effects from focused activities. Small businesses often employ functional structures very effectively (see Figure 8.1). A functional structure can also be effective for a firm pursuing a market-penetration strategy because organizational scope (i.e., number of products and markets) and customer requirements will be relatively stable over time.

FIGURE 8.1 **FUNCTIONAL STRUCTURE FOR A HOTEL**

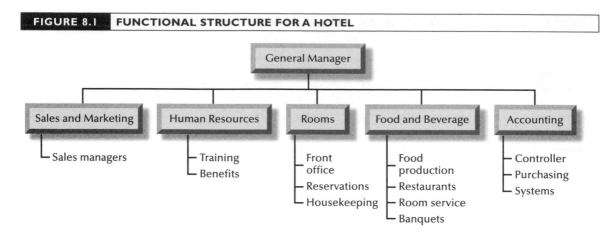

The functional structure is not appropriate in an environment where customer needs are diverse or changing, as when a firm is trying to provide many products or services to many customer groups. The functional structure may result in poor coordination across departments and thus impede the ability of the firm to adapt to changing needs. Over time, the different departments may become insular and focus on departmental goals at the expense of overall organizational goals.[16] Because functional departments concentrate on their own professional or technical activities it is possible for a department to be high performing, but the overall hotel to not be. In addition, interdepartmental conflicts easily emerge when people focus exclusively on their own area of skill. In hotels it is common for departments to be in conflict over service delivery. The sales team books business, but it is the rooms division and banquet staff that must deliver on the promises to customers. Because of the nature of a functional design, it is not easy to handle interdepartmental communication and coordination. It is unlikely that individual departments are capable of resolving across department conflicts and the task of handing these issues falls on the general manager (GM). Hierarchy overload can lead to decisions piling up at the top of the organization, because most interdepartmental issues fall on the general manger. It is not uncommon for a GM to feel overloaded with problems and decisions. Turnover among GMs has been found to be primarily due to management conflict and problems between the property and owners.[17] One way to reduce the problems inherent in this structure is to avoid the tendency to blame other departments and to develop general management skills in the functional managers. Later in this chapter, we will discuss ways in which lateral relationships can help reduce the coordinating challenges faced in functionally designed organizations. The following are examples of problems that can develop across functions in a hotel.

Imagine that the director of sales in under pressure to increase group bookings. Without coordinating with the other hotel departments, here is what might happen:

- Sales might guarantee more rooms for a convention than are actually available, resulting in overbooking, a problem that the front desk and reservations staff will have to handle.

- Sales might book a group that has meeting-room needs the hotel cannot satisfy because of previous commitments. The convention services manager, if consulted, might have avoided this problem.

- Convention services may try to accommodate the meeting needs of the group, but neglect to let food and beverage know of the additional guest needs, causing the coffee service to be missed during a break.

- Finally, the hotel laundry may be unaware of the banquet requirement for clean uniforms with the addition of this new group business and not have the uniforms available.[18]

Geographic and Customer-Based Structures

In the hotel and restaurant industry, organizations often grow by adding hotels or restaurants in new locations. Corporations that organize on the basis of expanding into new locations are using a geographic structure.[19] This form of organizing is common in the hospitality industry because companies operate in diverse geographic markets. Best Western operates 4,000 hotels in eighty-four countries, Darden Restaurants has 1,200 stores in various locations, and MGM Mirage owns or operates eighteen casino properties on three continents. Restructuring of InterContinental Hotels Group PLC into four geographical divisions is an example of a geographic structure and is thought to have streamlined that company.[20] A firm that expands its business from a regional market base to a national market base may form new units around geographic segments. For example, Pegasus Solutions, Inc., a global provider of hotel reservation technologies, has divided its regional offices to cover North America, Latin America, Europe/Middle East/Africa, and Asia Pacific/India.[21] A restaurant chain may be divided into units responsible for eastern and western regions (see Figure 8.2a).

If the organization structures its major units around the characteristics or types of customer, it is a customer-based structure (see Figure 8.2b). Some firms that pursue growth through market development seek out new customer groups. If sales to a particular new type of customer reach sufficient volume, the organization may reorganize around customer groups. For example, a hotel chain may organize around economy and luxury lodging. Similarly, a microcomputer company might organize its business around home-user, business, academic, and mail order customer groups. Or an architectural firm might organize around commercial, military, and residential projects. When a business organizes around geographical regions or type of customer, it may continue to centralize its production or service operations in one area if economies of scale are significant. If not, then each geographic region or market unit may have its own operations facilities. However, in most cases at least some administrative functions, such as legal or research, are still centralized.

Both the geographic and customer organizational structures have as a major strength their focus on unique needs and customer preferences. The goal is to be responsive to local market conditions. A company that uses a geographic structure is better able to serve the unique tastes and needs of customers in various locations. Unfortunately, there may be little sharing of resources across locations or customer groups and obvious duplication of efforts. The following hotel example illustrates how unique a hotel location can be and how difficult it would be to share these resources.

"One day the eyes of the whole world will be on the Amazon," Jacques Cousteau supposedly told a wealthy Brazilian lawyer in 1982. "If you build a hotel up in the trees, people will come." And they have come—to Brazil's Ariau Hotel, a 205-room treetop resort. Tarzan's house is one perch in the world's largest treetop resort. With seven cylindrical towers and two lookout towers rising to 130 feet, and three miles

FIGURE 8.2	GEOGRAPHIC- AND CUSTOMER-BASED STRUCTURES

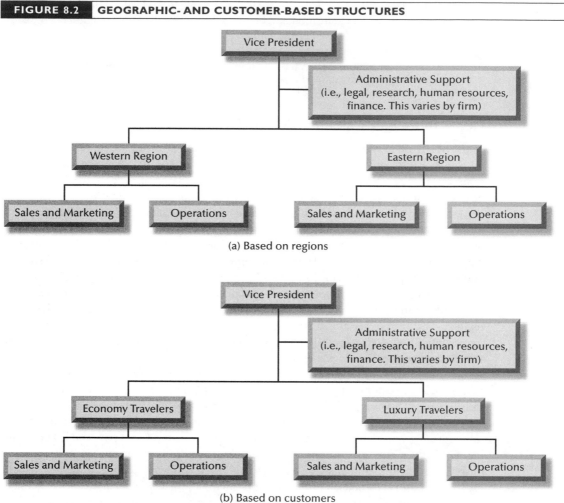

(a) Based on regions

(b) Based on customers

of catwalks connecting them through the multilayered mazeway of the rain forest, Brazil's Ariau Hotel dwarfs the more famous tree lodges of Kenya and California.[22]

Geographic and customer-based structures are suited to a fast-changing environment and high levels of customer satisfaction. They are especially appropriate in larger businesses with multiple types of services, and they are helpful if market or service development is the strategic focus. However, economies of scale are lost if operations are separated, and some functions will be redundant across locations. Also, the company loses some of its in-depth functional specialization and coordination across product lines, which can be a problem.[23] Nevertheless, these structures are popular in larger hospitality companies.

When Jay Witzel took over as president of Carlson Hotels Worldwide, he was determined to inject more of a customer focus. One of the tools he used to do so was to change the organization's structure. "The first thing I wanted to do then was take us out of four or five operating companies and move us into one multi-branded operating company. Then I wanted to split up the globe." In essence, what Witzel did was increase the power of the central administration over the way business would be conducted, while simultaneously increasing the power of each geographic area to satisfy local needs. "We are going to merge all our brand into Rezidor in Europe," said Witzel, "Rezidor will be responsible for Regen, Radisson, Country Inns & Suites and Park Inns." One of the real advantages of centralization is found in marketing. "Up to this point, sales teams for the different brands have been selling on an individual basis. Now we have a centralized team that sells on behalf of all the brands."[24]

Some organizations, particularly large integrated service organizations, use the network, or "spider's web," structure.[25] The network structure is similar to the geographic or customer-based structure; however, it is even more decentralized. It represents a web of independent units, with little or no formal hierarchy to organize and control their relationship. The independent units are loosely organized to capture and share useful information. Other than information sharing, however, there is little formal contact among operating units. A hotel consortium is a good example of a network in which hotels combine resources in order to establish joint purchasing arrangements and marketing services.[26] Best Western is an excellent example of this type of structure. The company is organized as a nonprofit association of member hotels, providing member services such as a reservation system, marketing, brand identity, facilities design, and training.[27] The services are funded by member fees and dues. Tom Higgins, Best Western's president and CEO, characterizes the network as the "ultimate Jeffersonian Democracy."[28] Other examples of a spider web structure include the top five consortia in terms of number of rooms: Utell Ltd., Lexington Services Corp., Unirez, SynXis Corp., and Supranational Hotels.[29] Incorporating the network service provider as a brand is the approach taken by Leading Hotels of the World, Ltd., the eighth largest consortium, providing global distribution, reservations, and luxury marketing support to five-star independent hotels and hotel groups.

Project Matrix Structures

A hybrid structure that combines some elements of functional structures with other forms, discussed earlier, is called a project-matrix structure. For example, a construction company with functional departments could form teams to carry out specific projects. Each team would have individuals from the functional areas reporting to both a project leader and their functional manager. The project-matrix structure is viewed by some as a transition stage between a functional form and other forms, and by others as a complex form necessary for complex environments.[30] Either way, the many stakeholder influences that simultaneously pull an organization toward functional forms and the more diverse geographic, customer, product, or service forms reach an equilibrium in the matrix structure. Project-matrix structures are most common in turbulent or uncertain competitive environments where internal stakeholders are highly interdependent and where external stakeholder demands are diverse and changing.[31] Matrix structures can improve communications between groups, increase the amount of information the organization can handle, and allow people and equipment to be used more flexibly.[32]

In a matrix structure, the organization is simultaneously functional and either product, geographic, customer, or service oriented (see Figure 8.3). Unfortunately, matrix

FIGURE 8.3 THE PROJECT-MATRIX STRUCTURE

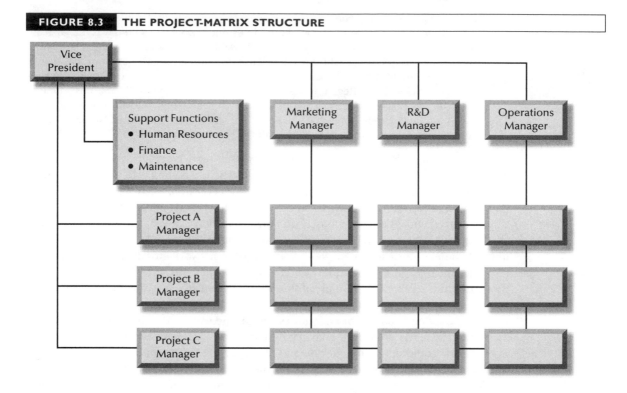

structures can be disconcerting for employees because of the "too many bosses" problem. Power struggles may occur because it is difficult to balance the different lines of authority. Matrix structures require a lot of interpersonal skill because of frequent communications. Meetings can take a lot of time, and it is sometimes difficult to coordinate the many people and schedules. The overall complexity of the structure can create ambiguity and conflict between functional and product managers and between individuals. The sheer number of people that must be involved in decision making can slow the decision processes and add administrative costs.[33]

> "Let's invent," said William Norman on the day he began as president and chief executive officer of the Travel Industry Association (TIA). In a discussion of his experience at TIA, Norman describes a system he calls matrix management. Two prominent features—task teams and an unusually free-spirited quarterly staff meeting—capture the essence of how the matrix functions. Norman looks at an organization as "a cross-functional form," or matrix that should have relatively few barriers between traditional departments. TIA's matrix has broken down many old barriers.[34]

CORPORATE-LEVEL STRUCTURES

Three general types of structures are used by multibusiness organizations: multidivisional, strategic business unit, and corporate matrix. These structures are used when a company begins to diversify its services, enters unrelated market channels, or begins to serve diverse customer groups.[35] These more complex structures are necessary because of the increased coordination and decision making required for handling large and diversified firms. Typically, decision making is decentralized and the corporate headquarters focuses on coordinating all of its divisions or groups of business through reporting systems and corporate planning. Table 8.3 lists the major characteristics of these corporate-level structures.

If we return to Orient-Express Hotels, Ltd., a company we discussed at the beginning of the chapter, we see that its corporate senior management includes three regional vice presidents for hotels in North America, in Europe and Asia, and in Africa, Australia, and South America. Another vice president oversees the operations of trains and cruise ships. The remaining executives include functional areas such as accounting, law, and public relations.

> According to Simon M. C. Sherwood, president of Orient-Express Hotels (OEH), the regional vice presidents play a large role in the company's operational success. Decentralized in its approach, OEH has only 20 to 25 staff at its corporate headquarters who oversee corporate planning and serve as resources for property managers. "Corporate staff is there to help, not to look over anyone's shoulder. I respect the general managers as business people and give them the autonomy to manage their hotels. But that does not prevent me from jumping on a plane if I see a problem," says Sherwood.[36]

Multidivisional Structures

If an organization has relatively few businesses in its portfolio, management may choose a multidivisional (line-of-business) structure, with each business existing as a separate unit.

TABLE 8.3	DISTINGUISHING CHARACTERISTICS OF CORPORATE-LEVEL STRUCTURES		
	Multidivisional	**Strategic Business Unit**	**Corporate Matrix**
Number of Businesses	Few relative to the other corporate-level structures (but at least two independent businesses)	Many businesses grouped into SBUs based on commonalities such as products or markets	Few or many businesses
Degree of Relatedness	No operational or marketing relatedness required; however, sometimes a low level of relatedness exists	Related businesses are grouped into SBUs, but there may be little or no relatedness across SBUs	Typically very high relatedness is required so that people can be transferred throughout the corporation without significant retraining or frustration
Need for Coordination Across Businesses	Typically low coordination across units; coordination required only to the extent that relatedness exists	Coordination required within SBUs; little or no coordination required across SBUs	Significant coordination required to make the structure work
Expected Synergy	Financial synergy can be achieved; limited operational synergies, only to the extent that units are related and coordinated	Financial synergy available across SBUs; operating synergy may be available within SBUs to the extent that strategies and activities are coordinated	High operational synergies are available; may result in high levels of innovation, cost savings, or a greater ability to serve multiple markets

For example, a multidivisional organization may have a time-share division, a corporate services division, a transportation division, and a gaming equipment division. In this type of structure, a general manager—sometimes referred to as a divisional president or vice president—heads up each of the three divisions. Each division has its own support functions, including sales, accounting/finance, personnel, and research and development. Services that are common to all three businesses are housed at the corporate level, such as legal services, public relations, and corporate research. Divisional activities and overall financial control are monitored by the corporate headquarters.

International strategies are often implemented through multidivisional structures. If an organization chooses to produce and sell its products in Europe, management may form an international division to house those activities. If a firm pursues a multidomestic strategy that involves it in several independent national or regional businesses, management may form a separate division for each business. The multidivisional structure is appropriate when management of the different businesses does not require sharing of employees, marketing resources, or operations facilities.

The multidivisional structure, shown in Figure 8.4, has several advantages. By existing as a separate unit, each business is better able to focus its efforts on the needs of its particular stakeholders, without being distracted by the problems of other businesses. Corporate-level management is freed from day-to-day issues and is able to take a long-term, integrative view of the collection of businesses. Corporate executives may monitor the performance of each division separately and allocate corporate resources for specific activities that show promise. This can lead to what is referred to as financial synergy. Financial synergy can be defined as the values added because of the ability to allocate financial resources to the areas that have the highest potential. The result may be increased returns, reduced risk (variability in earnings), or both.

With the multidivisional structure, it is often difficult to decide which activities will be performed at the corporate level and which ones will be held within each division. Competition for corporate resources (research, legal, investment funds) may create coordination difficulties among divisions. Also, organizational efforts may be duplicated, particularly when the different businesses within the corporate portfolio are highly related. It may

| **FIGURE 8.4** | **THE MULTIDIVISIONAL STRUCTURE** |

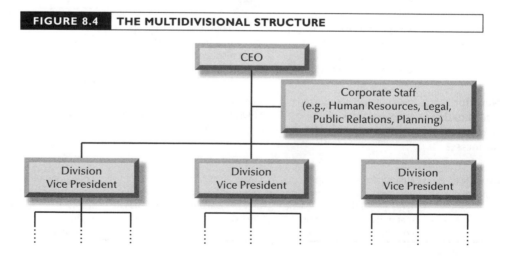

be that shared distribution channels or common-process development could save costs for the two businesses, yet separation in the organization structure discourages cooperation.

A multidivisional structure is well suited to an unrelated-diversification strategy, where there is no attempt to achieve operating synergies through coordinating and combining activities. However, managers sometimes use a multidivisional structure while pursuing a related-diversification strategy. Unfortunately, to exploit operational synergies, managers must structure relationships among businesses and partners in ways that encourage interdependence, and they must manage them over time with shared goals, shared information, shared resources, and cooperative program development.[37] The multidivisional structure makes resource sharing and cooperation difficult, but those two behaviors are necessary for operating synergy to occur.

Strategic-Business-Unit Structures

When an organization is broadly diversified with several businesses in its portfolio, it becomes difficult for top management to keep track of and understand the many industry environments and business conditions. Management may choose to form strategic business units (SBUs), with each SBU incorporating a few closely related businesses and operating as a profit center. Each SBU is composed of related divisions, with divisional vice presidents reporting to the vice president of an SBU or group. If an organization becomes very large, it may combine strategic business units into groups or sectors, thus adding another level of management. Johnson & Johnson uses an SBU structure in the management of its health-care businesses. The corporation has nearly 200 separate operating companies, which are grouped into nineteen SBUs. These SBUs are formed into sectors for pharmaceuticals, consumer products, and professional products.[38] The SBU structure is illustrated in Figure 8.5.

The SBU structure makes it possible for top management to keep track of many businesses at one time. It allows decentralization around dimensions that are meaningful to the business, such as markets or technologies. SBU vice presidents can encourage the members of the SBU to coordinate activities and share information. The intent of the structure is to provide top management with a manageable number of units to keep track of and to force responsibility for decision making lower into the organization, near the important internal and external stakeholders. Financial synergy is possible through allocating resources to the SBUs that have the greatest potential. Operating synergy is also available within SBUs, since they are formed based on relatedness among businesses. Consequently, financial synergy is available across SBUs, while operating synergy is possible only within SBUs.

> The Walt Disney Company is a leading producer and provider of entertainment and information, using a portfolio of brands to differentiate its content, services, and consumer products. With a total market value of $38 billion, the corporation consists of a broadcast group, studios and entertainment, parks and resorts, and consumer products. Within these SBUs are a wide variety of businesses. In broadcasting, for example, rests the ABC television network, ESPN Inc., ABC radio division, ABC cable networks group, and ABC-owned television stations, all overseen by presidents. Disney's ESPN sports channel alone is worth a hefty $20 billion; the other parts would bring in perhaps $50 billion if chopped up and sold. The company may dump ABC's sixty-four radio stations (eighteen are in the top twenty markets), which could sell for about $4 billion. Disney's

FIGURE 8.5 **THE STRATEGIC BUSINESS UNIT (SBU) STRUCTURE**

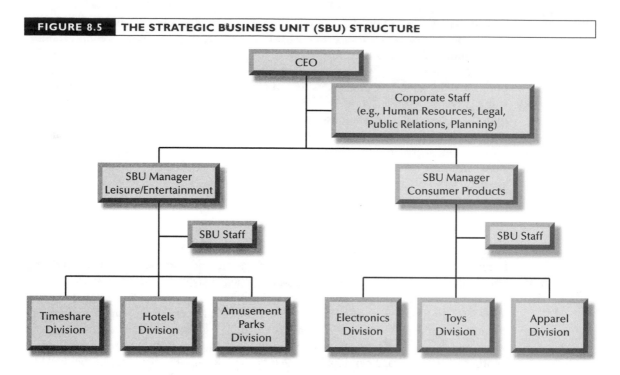

theme parks and resorts are struggling, battered by the weak economy and fears of terrorism. To build new parks and update existing ones, Disney spent about $5 billion in capital expenditures in the past five years. The company is also exploring options for its Disney Store business, including selling the stores in North America and Europe. Overall, Michael Eisner, the CEO, is feeling the pressure to restore Disney's magic.[39]

The difficulty of the SBU structure is that operating units, and therefore the customer, are even further removed from top management than in the multidivisional form. As with the multidivisional form, there is competition for corporate financial and staff resources, which may create conflicts and coordination problems. It is important to assign specific job responsibilities and expectations to business vice presidents, SBU vice presidents, and the corporate president, or conflicts may occur.

Corporate-Level Matrix Structures

The corporate matrix is the corporate-level counterpart to the project-matrix structure described earlier (see Figure 8.6). It is a way to achieve a high degree of coordination among several related businesses. Corporate-matrix structures are used when the individual businesses within a corporation's portfolio need to take advantage of resource, information, or technology sharing in order to succeed in their industries. The corporate-matrix structure tries to reach a balance between the pressures to decentralize units closer to market and technological trends and the pressures to maintain centralized control to bring about economies of scope and shared learning.

| FIGURE 8.6 | **TYPES OF CORPORATE MATRIX STRUCTURES** |

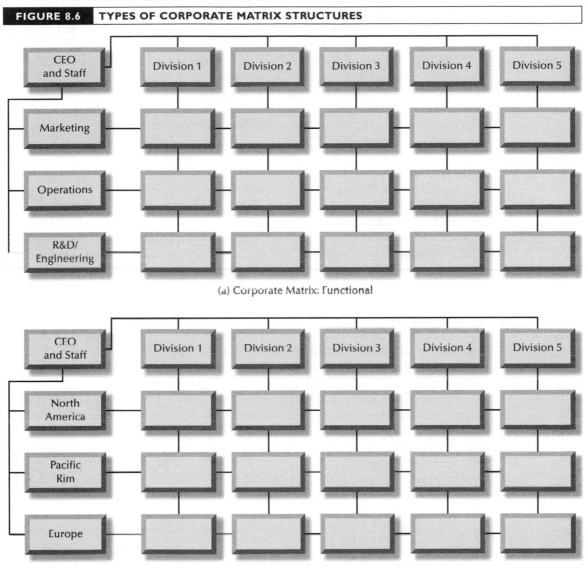

(a) Corporate Matrix: Functional

(b) Corporate Matrix: Regional

The corporate-matrix structure is particularly appropriate for related-diversification strategies and global strategies. For example, a hospitality firm that has businesses in lodging, gaming, and cruise lines may use a matrix structure to capitalize on economies of scale and capture operating synergies in marketing and distribution, as shown in Figure 8.6. Ideally, the corporate-matrix structure improves coordination among internal stakeholders by forcing managers within related businesses to maintain close contact with one another. It can help the organization become more flexible and responsive to changes in the business environment, and it can encourage teamwork and participation.[40] Cendant

Corporation uses a corporate matrix to structure its 60,000-employee conglomerate. For example, the vice president of human resources is responsible for corporate and business-unit human resource functions across the entire organization.[41]

The corporate-matrix form may also be effective in structuring a hospitality company that provides services that are all sold in several nations. A multinational firm may create a matrix structure that groups all products under each national manager and simultaneously groups all nations under each product manager. This type of matrix structure allows the firm to achieve a national focus in its marketing and distribution practices, and it encourages synergies through economies of scale and shared information within each product category. The corporate-matrix structure applied to a multinational organization is shown in the bottom half of Figure 8.6.

A more complex version of the corporate-matrix structure is the transnational form.[42] Whereas the global-matrix structure organizes businesses along two dimensions, the transnational structure organizes businesses along three dimensions: nation or region, product, and function. The transnational form is an attempt to achieve integration within product categories, within nations, and within functions while simultaneously achieving coordination across all of those activities. The transnational form requires three types of managers, who serve integrating roles: (1) country or region managers, who oversee all products and functions performed in their area to maintain a focal point for customers; (2) functional managers, who oversee the activities of a particular function (technology, marketing, or manufacturing) for all products in all nations; and (3) business managers, who oversee all functions and markets supported by a particular service group.[43] When Royal Dutch Shell used a transnational form, its executives often reported to a country, a regional, and a functional head.[44]

The corporate-matrix and transnational structures are plagued by one serious difficulty: sheer complexity may interfere with what they are designed to accomplish. It is difficult to balance the needs of the different functional, national, and product stakeholders. The unusual command structure can create an atmosphere of ambiguity, conflict, and mixed loyalties. The overall complexity and bureaucracy of the structure may stifle creativity and impede decision making because of the sheer number of people who must be involved. Furthermore, the administrative costs associated with decision delays and extra management may overwhelm the benefits of coordination.[45]

This concludes our discussion of the business- and corporate-level structures. Each of the forms contained in this section is a model that provides a general idea of how to structure an organization. With the exception of the simpler forms, it would be unusual to find a firm structured exactly like one of the models in this chapter. Also, it would be unusual to find any two companies structured in exactly the same way. Organizations create their own designs based on their own needs. Also, many companies create hybrid structures that combine elements of two or more of the models discussed in this section. It is not uncommon for a company to have one division based on geography and another based on products, with a functional staff at the corporate level.

Earlier chapters discussed the worldwide trends that are leading firms to increased interorganizational relationships. These trends are causing newer organizational forms to emerge. Modular structures outsource all the noncore functions of the organization. The organization is actually a hub surrounded by networks of suppliers. This type of structure allows the firm to minimize capital investments and to focus internal resources on core activities. A second new form is referred to as the virtual type, a group of units from different firms that have joined into an alliance to exploit complementary skills and resources in the pursuit of a common strategic objective. The term virtual comes from the computer industry, where computers can be programmed to seem as though they have more memory than they actually have. Paramount Communications, through strategic alliances, positioned itself to exploit as many stages of the entertainment industry as possible. Modular and virtual organizational forms present new management challenges for managers.[46]

THE LATERAL ORGANIZATION

To successfully implement strategy, managers must design the lateral (horizontal) organization carefully. The lateral organization consists of the communication and coordination mechanisms that occur across departments or divisions.[47] Building lateral capability enables a company to more flexibly and quickly accomplish organizational objectives by bypassing the movement up through the vertical hierarchy. Recall that the limitation of a functional structure is that it leads to poor coordination among departments, while a product-based structure leads to poor coordination across product lines, and the geographic based structure makes coordination across locations problematic. Lateral linkages allow work to get done at the level in which it occurs, with people communicating directly with those in other departments or divisions, rather than through their managers. Characterized as working in the "white spaces" between the boxes on an organization chart and across divisional boundaries, the lateral organization, while often unseen, is a key part of organizational structure. In fact, the job of organizing is not complete until both the vertical structures, discussed earlier in this chapter, and the lateral linkages are designed. The more highly differentiated a company is the more it will need a high level of integration to make the organizational structure function effectively.

> Coastal Hotel Group developed a buddy system to help newly acquired properties benefit from the experience and skills of department heads in existing properties. The way the system works, corporate management determines the buddy needs of the acquired property and the training timetable. The providing hotel saves payroll costs when the buddy is away, and the new hotel gains knowledge and insights. Before the sharing of skilled workers across hotels, newly acquired hotel staff knew that things could be done better, but they were not seeing it happen. With the buddy system someone is there to help.[48]

There are a variety of lateral coordinating mechanisms a firm can use ranging from the simple and informal to the highly structured (e.g., matrix) and complex. Direct contact among managers from different departments or divisions is the simplest form of coordination, and is it often based on an informal friendship network. Information often gets shared naturally in these networks, making "who you know" an important component of effective implementation. Meetings and committees are also devices used to help coordinate work. When used strategically, these lateral coordinating processes can be extremely effective. One successful CEO, Lewis Schaeneman, was so effective in using meetings and informal ties with his senior management staff at Stop and Shop Companies, Inc., that most of this team went on to senior executive positions in other firms, having learned how to build cooperative teams.

> Lewis G. Schaeneman Jr., the driving CEO of Stop and Shop Companies, Inc., a large New England grocery chain, brought out the best in his senior management staff by encouraging and soliciting open and honest dialogue. If a department head was not willing to be challenged and questioned by his peers, that executive did not survive in this company. Relying on data, Lew would have his senior management team talk and talk and talk about important issues until they had talked them to death and every manager was in agreement about the direction the firm would be taking. By candid, open, and continuous senior management conversations, the group built a commitment to implementation and a clear understanding of every department's or division's role in making the corporate strategy a reality. In Lew's words, "We evolved a system of management that empowered ordinary people to do extraordinary things."[49]

Accenture and other consulting firms were early to develop communities of practice as another way to share information horizontally and network. A "community of practice" is a group of people who share a concern, a set of problems, or a passion about a topic and who deepen their knowledge and expertise in this area by interacting continually.[50] Organizations frequently hold annual meetings and retreats with their general managers to help build commitment and interpersonal relationships as well as to update and inform participants of corporate strategies and new practices.

Teams and task forces bring together individuals from several functions or groups to solve problems or work together to accomplish an overall outcome. Task forces are a common form of coordination in hospitality firms; for instance, Accor North America establishes task forces to help develop practices to improve customer and employee satisfaction.[51] Members of these task forces, from different levels and hotels in the region, perform various designated roles, including the role of conscience, who ends the meeting by giving constructive feedback to each member of the team. It is not uncommon for Accor to also include an outside consultant on their task force teams.

In large firms, boundary-spanning positions are created so that various components of a business fit together and resources are appropriately allocated. These formal integrator positions may be project managers or knowledge managers. Whether these positions are chief knowledge officer (CKO), chief learning officer (CLO), director of intellectual assets, or manager of performance, these roles have been developed because of an awareness of the importance of using the ideas of people at every level of the firm and to ensure that opportunities are not missed and that people and projects are coordinated. Finally, when the need for lateral coordination in a highly differentiated firm is great, the lateral mechanisms we have discussed may fall short, requiring a formal integrating structure like a matrix.

> John Peetz, a partner with Ernst & Young, worked mainly as a consultant, advising clients in fields ranging from the entertainment business to engineering and construction. When he was asked to chair an ad hoc "knowledge committee" in 1992, Peetz had no idea the assignment would result in a career shift. "We obviously needed a better process for managing intellectual capital and a strategy to match it with the company's overall business objectives," recalls Peetz. Two years later, Ernst & Young named him its first chief knowledge officer. "We're decentralized, so at first our tax people couldn't imagine any of their knowledge would be of use to auditors, or that auditor information could help consultants and so on," he notes. Peetz is formally charged with the tasks of organizing, capturing, and cataloging the firm's collective knowledge. He is also busy encouraging the company's 70,000 worldwide employees to share and use emerging information.[52]

ORGANIZATIONAL CONTROL

As mentioned in the introduction to this chapter, top managers use control systems for a variety of important functions, such as overcoming resistance to change, communicating new strategic agendas, ensuring continuing attention to strategic initiatives, formalizing beliefs, setting boundaries on acceptable strategic behavior, or motivating discussion and debate about strategic uncertainties.[53] From the perspective of top executives, a strategic-control system is "a system to support managers in assessing the relevance of the organization's strategy to its progress in the accomplishment of its goals, and when discrepancies exist, to support areas needing attention."[54]

Several types of control will be discussed. Feedback control provides managers with information concerning outcomes from organizational activities. With feedback control, managers establish objectives and then measure performance against those targets at some later time. In addition to feedback controls, organizations use a variety of internal controls to encourage behavior that is consistent with the overall objectives of the firm. In this chapter, we will discuss three types of behavioral controls—bureaucratic, clan, and process controls. Finally, we will conclude with a discussion of crisis prevention and management.

> Scandinavia's SAS Group provides an example of what happens when managers lose control of a company. The SAS Scandinavian Airlines business makes up about 80% of the group's SKr 51 billion in annual revenues, with the remaining 20% in airline-related and hospitality businesses. Certainly, a major jet crash and the crisis that followed 9/11 had a lot to do with the problems SAS is facing. However, Jergen Lindegaard, CEO of SAS Group, acknowledges that the company flooded the market with airline seats at a time when they should have been moving in the opposite direction. "The promise I have made to myself and to everybody else is that never, ever again will we put SAS in the situation where we lose control," says Lindegaard. Referring to huge operating losses, he commented, "If you run a business when you lose that much, you simply lose control of it."[55]

STRATEGIC VS. FINANCIAL CONTROLS

A brief review of the evolution of organizational-control systems will help you to understand how they work and why so many of them fail to live up to expectations. Early in the twentieth century, the increase in diversified and vertically integrated organizations created the demand for systems that could help top managers allocate time, capital, and human resources where they were most needed. E. I. du Pont de Nemours Powder Company, formed from a combination of previously independent companies, was one of the innovators in this area.[56] DuPont created one of the most enduring systems for controlling diversified businesses. The system was based on return on investment (ROI), which was defined as the operating ratio (return on sales) times the stock turn (sales to assets).[57] Sales cancel out, leaving return divided by assets. Using this summary measure of performance for each division, top managers could identify problem areas and allocate capital to the most successful operations and divisions.

> Rooms still offer US hoteliers their best return on investment (ROI) for real estate, although food-and-beverage profits as a percentage of food and beverage revenues has

been climbing since the late 1980s, according to Bjorn Hanson of Pricewaterhouse Coopers. Space dedicated to restaurants in hotels generally still provides just 1/3 the ROI that rooms do.[58]

Since financial-reporting requirements included figures for income, assets, and sales, managers could easily calculate ROI or related measures from existing data. As the multidivisional form of organization proliferated after 1950, the use of financial measures such as ROI gained wide acceptance and application.[59] In many organizations, they became the only important measure of success. In the words of Roger Smith, past CEO of General Motors: "I look at the bottom line. It tells me what to do."[60]

Unfortunately, organizational-control systems that rely primarily on financial controls are likely to have serious problems. The main problem with financial-control systems as a primary basis for control is that high-level managers typically do not have an adequate understanding of what must be done to improve value-adding activities within the organization. According to some control experts, financial-control measures based on accounting data are "too late, too aggregated, and too distorted to be relevant for managers' planning and control decisions."[61] Lateness refers to the long lag times between the organizational transactions themselves and the dates financial reports come out. For example, Pinkerton's didn't know it was in trouble until so much time had passed that the problem became very large.

In an effort to increase revenues, Pinkerton's engaged in a major acquisition program in 1991. It bought a host of small security-guard-contracting firms, with the intention of making the combined businesses more efficient through economies of scale. Executives were telling investors that business was booming. Instead, costs increased dramatically, and the recession hurt profit margins, but no one at Pinkerton's had any idea what was happening. The stock price fell from $36 at the beginning of the year to around $15 by September. A group of shareholders filed a lawsuit charging that executives misled them so that the executives could sell some of their own shares at an inflated price.[62]

The aggregation problem simply means that financial measures based on accounting data do not contain the detail that is necessary to make meaningful improvements to organizational processes. In a study of branded hotels in the United States, the commonly used industry averages of average daily rate (ADR), revenue per available room (RevPAR), and occupancy were found to be distorted by certain markets and price segments.[63] The study showed that reliance on aggregate industry averages can lead to overstating ADR and RevPAR and understating occupancy.

Finally, distortions associated with financial information are well documented (e.g., the Enron scandal). Differences in the way financial-control variables are created make meaningful comparisons difficult across departments, divisions, or companies. Also, changes in the way a department, division, or company calculates a variable from one period to the next can cause distortion. Distortion is especially evident in the way inventories, plant, and equipment are valued and in the way overhead costs are allocated to departments and divisions.

In January 2002, the Securities and Exchange Commission (SEC) pursued its first enforcement action regarding the abuse of pro-forma earnings figures against Trump Hotels & Casino Resorts Inc. The company was charged with making misleading statements in the company's third-quarter earnings release. According to the SEC Trump committed three separate acts that collectively amounted to misleading investors.

1. Trump's earnings release and the accompanying financial data did not use the term "pro forma," even though the net income and earnings per share (EPS) figures contained in the release significantly differed from such figures calculated in conformity with generally accepted accounting procedures (GAAP).

2. Trump's release expressly stated that its net income and EPS excluded an $81.4 million one-time charge. Not until several days later, however, did an analyst's report unveil that Trump's net income and EPS figures included an undisclosed one-time gain of $17.2 million.

3. Trump's release compared its earnings favorably to analysts' earnings estimates without stating that its figures were non-GAAP, pro-forma figures, whereas the analysts' figures were GAAP. Discounting the pro-forma adjustments would have resulted in a decline in revenues and net income, as well as in a failure to meet analysts' expectations.[64]

In addition, accounting-based financial measures sometimes prompt managers to behave in ways that are counterproductive over the long run. For example, financial measures such as ROI discourage investments in long-term research projects because expenses must be paid out immediately, while benefits may not accrue until many financial periods later.[65] Also, managers may cancel services (e.g., turn-down service in the guest room) that appear to be too costly, placing an emphasis on essential services or services that are most efficiently produced. If financial-control information is used as a part of an incentive system to reward managers, then organizations should consider adding back long-term investments such as research and development before calculating ROIs. Another alternative is to create separate accounts for longer-term investment programs that are independent of the rest of the financial-reporting system.

> The overhead cost allocation process is fairly complex, and is not well understood by the lodging industry. The major drawbacks of cost allocation relate primarily to the managers of operating departments and to misunderstandings as to its use. For example, department heads may not understand the process and may resist it. Department heads may defer discretionary costs such as repairs, or otherwise strive to achieve short-run profitability at the expense of the long-run profitability of the company. Finally, fully-allocated department statements are not appropriate for performance evaluation.[66]

Rather than establish a control system based purely on financial controls, top managers should establish a more complete strategic-control system. In the literature on strategic management, some scholars use the term "strategic control" to mean that corporate-level managers become integrally acquainted with the processes and operations of each of their divisions through sharing of "rich" information and face-to-face contact.[67] This kind of knowledge is necessary so that they can evaluate the performance of each division on the basis of factors that are relevant within their own companies and markets. A corporate manager that relies on this type of control puts less weight on financial controls as a source of information for evaluating division performance. Our use of the term "strategic control" is also based on the idea that financial controls should not be relied on exclusively to evaluate performance. They are one of many types of feedback-control systems that should be in place in an organization. The combination of control systems is what we refer to as "strategic control."

FEEDBACK-CONTROL SYSTEMS

Anytime goals or objectives are established and then measured against actual results, a feedback-control system exists. Feedback-control systems perform several important functions in organizations.[68] First, creating specific targets ensures that managers at various levels and areas in the company understand the plans and strategies that guide organizational decisions. Second, feedback-control systems motivate managers to pursue organizational interests as opposed to purely personal interests, because they know they will be held accountable for the results of their actions. This alignment of interests reduces some of the agency problems discussed in Chapter 3. Finally, feedback-control systems help managers decide when and how to intervene in organizational processes by identifying areas requiring further attention. Without good feedback-control systems, managers can fall into the trap of spending too much time dealing with issues and problems that are not particularly important to the future of the firm.

Examples of feedback-control systems are easy to find. Budgets are feedback-control systems because they provide revenue and expense targets against which actual results are measured. For instance, if food costs are set at 31 percent of food sales, and actual food costs are 36 percent, the gap would signal that corrective action might be required. Financial-ratio analysis is another example. Ratios such as ROI or a current ratio are measured against targets that are established on the basis of past performance or in comparison with competing firms. Audits are also a type of feedback-control system because firm conduct and outputs are measured against established guidelines, typically by independent auditors. Financial audits control accuracy within accounting systems, based on generally accepted accounting principles. Social audits control ethical behavior, based on criteria that are established either totally in-house or in conjunction with activist groups, regulatory agencies, or editors of magazines that compile this sort of information (e.g., *Business and Society Review*).

Figure 8.7 contains a flowchart of activities for a feedback-control system as it applies to strategic control. The starting point is the strategic management process, beginning with establishment of strategic direction, followed by identification of basic strategies and implementation plans. Objectives are established as a part of the implementation process. Time passes, and eventually these objectives are measured against actual performance. Performance information is then used as feedback to guide the strategic management process, and the cycle continues. The steps in developing a feedback-control system for strategic control, shown in Table 8.4, will now be explained. They include determining broad goals, establishing links between those goals and resource areas or activities, setting measurable targets for each resource area or activity, and a variety of specific tasks that increase the probability that targets will be achieved.

Determination of Broad Goals

The first step in developing a strategic-control system is determining what needs to be controlled. One way to determine control factors is to ask, "If we achieve our vision, what will be different?" Robert Kaplan and David Norton have developed an approach to designing a strategic-control system that considers organizational performance from four perspectives: (1) financial, (2) customer, (3) internal business, and (4) innovation and learning.[69]

FIGURE 8.7 **FEEDBACK CONTROLS**

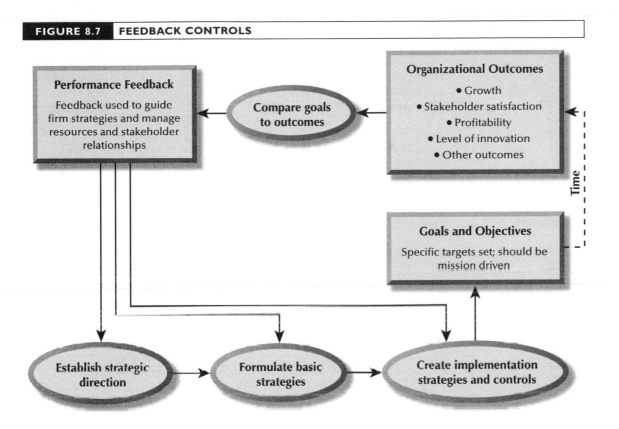

Each of these performance perspectives has its own set of feedback controls and is linked to particular stakeholder groups. For example, stakeholders who evaluate an organization's performance using financial targets will typically look to return on investment, cash flow, stock price, and stability of earnings. Customers, on the other hand, evaluate other types of information: pricing, innovation, quality, value, and customer service. From the perspective of internal stakeholders and processes, other performance indicators become important, such as cost controls, skill levels and capabilities, product-line breadth, safety, on-time delivery, quality, and many others. From an innovation and learning perspective, an organization may consider the foundation it is building for the future, such as workforce morale, innovation, investments in research, and progress in continuous improvement.

While Kaplan and Norton's four areas are important and worthy of control, they do not capture everything that is important to the long-term success of a firm. The stakeholder perspective of organizations provides a fairly comprehensive view of who is important to a firm. Stakeholders that might be worthy of attention include shareholders, customers, employees and managers, suppliers, local communities, government regulators and taxing agencies, creditors, bondholders, unions, or even particular special-interest groups, among others. A company should not establish control systems for every possible stakeholder, but only for the most important.

Examples of the kinds of broad goals an organization could set on the basis of achieving its vision include "We want to have the highest level of customer satisfaction," "We want

TABLE 8.4	STEPS IN DEVELOPING A FEEDBACK-CONTROL SYSTEM	

Step	Description
1. Determine broad goals	If the organization achieves its vision, what will be different? Answer this question from the perspective of the organization and each of its key stakeholders. In other words, what is the organization going to do for each key stakeholder?
2. Establish links between broad goals and resource areas or activities of the organization	Determine which areas are instrumental in achieving each of the broad goals. For instance, if one of the goals is to have the highest level of customer satisfaction, determine which activities, skills, and resources are needed to make this happen. Examples might be customer service, product quality, and pricing. The objective is to identify factors that can be measured.
3. Create measurable operating goals for each resource area or activity	The things that are measured and rewarded are the things that get done. Operating goals are established for each factor that was identified in the last step, including a date by which each goal should be accomplished. Monitoring systems should also be established as a part of this step.
4. Assign responsibility	Each of the goals should be assigned to a specific manager, who is then responsible to make sure it is accomplished.
5. Develop plans for accomplishment	Each manager should develop an action plan for accomplishing each goal, including needed resources (technology, personnel, capital, supplies). Some resources may be available inside the organization, while others will have to be sought through outside contracts, joint ventures, or other forms of interorganizational relationships.
6. Allocate resources	Resources should be allocated to the accomplishment of each goal, as needed.
7. Follow up	At an agreed-upon time, each manager should report on the status of a goal. Following up also means rewarding managers and employees who are responsible for accomplishment of a goal.

to give back to the community through community-service programs," and "We want to maximize shareholder return." The first goal pertains to customers, the second goal relates to the communities in which the organization operates, and the third goal pertains to shareholders. Below is the broad goal of Four Seasons Hotels, an operator of luxury hotel and resorts that also offers vacation ownership properties and private residences:

> Our goal is to create properties of enduring value using superior design and finishes, and support them with a deeply instilled ethic of personal service. Doing so allows Four Seasons to satisfy the needs and tastes of our discriminating customers, and to maintain our position as the world's premier luxury hospitality company.[70]

Identification of Resource Areas or Activities

As shown in Table 8.4, the next step in establishing a feedback-control system is to identify resource areas or organizational activities that are key to accomplishing the broad goals identified in the first step. This identification of resource areas or activities should lead to factors the firm can measure, although the measures do not have to be financial in nature. For example, assume that one of the broad goals is to achieve a very high level of customer satisfaction. Specific factors that lead to customer satisfaction may include a high-quality product, excellent customer service, good value (price relative to features and quality), and excellent hands-on training or instructions. These things can be measured through direct customer surveys or interviews, quality-measurement systems, hiring a research firm, observing repeat business, or conducting competitor-comparison surveys. Notice that the factors identified as important to customers include both resources (a high-quality product) and activities (customer service, training, pricing).

> Hilton's Hotels developed a comprehensive approach to delivering value for all stakeholders. At the heart of the approach were five broad goals: delighted customers, loyal team members, satisfied owners and shareholders, successful strategic partners, and involved community. The four primary resource areas, which they called value drivers, were activity areas that directly contributed to success. The areas that together create value for Hilton's constituencies include: Brand management, Revenue maximization, Operational effectiveness, and Value proposition. Brand management, for example, involves promoting and maintaining consistency in the delivery of services and products expected by customers. In the areas of revenue maximization, Hilton implemented flexible, rational pricing, taking into consideration demand elasticities in different segments and local markets.[71]

Financial measures are appropriate to achieve broad financial goals. Consequently, if a broad goal is a high rate of return for shareholders, as it is in many public corporations, then things such as profitability, debt relative to assets, RevPAR, and short-term cash management should be measured. A study of six major United Kingdom hotel groups indicated widespread adoption of techniques to analyze accounting data and relate it to business strategy. In particular, data on real costs and prices, volumes, market share, cash flow, and resource demands are used.[72] Since the things that get measured are often the things that receive attention in organizations, managers need to be sensitive to the needs of stakeholders and make sure that the critical result areas identified reflect the priorities that have been established concerning satisfaction of various stakeholder needs and interests.

Sometimes a factor will need to be evaluated further so that an appropriate resource area or activity can be identified. For example, profitability is a good thing to measure, but what really causes profitability? Managers should analyze what they think are the key drivers of profitability in their industry and establish measures in those areas as well. They may determine that cost control is the primary driver, or they may decide that occupancy is vital. Whichever factors they decide are most important should then become other factors to control. The same sort of thinking applies to quality. What causes high quality? These factors should be controlled also. A balanced scorecard system of measures based on research has been successfully used by several hotel chains.

> "Hilton Hotels conducted a conjoint study to determine the key attributes on which they were not meeting customer expectations. Overall they discovered that the quality of the guest experience was inconsistent. The study was a catalyst for managers asking whether Hilton was delivering on this standard at all times." Their analysis also showed that a 5 percent increase in customer loyalty at Hilton Hotels (measured as the percentage of customers who indicated they are likely to return to Hilton) in a given year was associated with a 1.1 percent increase in annual revenues the following year at a typical property.[73]

Creation of Measurable Operating Goals

Once identified and linked specifically to financial, customer, internal-process, learning and other stakeholder-driven outcomes, the critical result areas become the objectives that pace strategy implementation. Vision and mission statements include broad organizational goals and lofty ideals that embrace the values of the organization. These ideals can provide motivation to employees and managers; however, they typically provide general, not specific, direction. Specific operating goals or objectives are established in an effort to bring the concepts found in the vision statement to life—to a level that managers and employees can influence and control. As time passes and operating objectives are met, then the broader goals will be met as well, and ultimately the vision will begin to be realized. By specifically linking objectives to the vision, the firm can structure a control system that is strategically relevant.

The terms "objectives" and "goals" capture the same basic concept: they each represent a performance target for an individual, a department, a division, a business, or a corporation. In practice, the term "target" is often used. The important point to remember when using these words is to make sure that people understand how you are using them. In this section, a distinction is made between broad goals and operating goals. Unlike the broad goals contained in vision statements, operating goals in key result areas provide specific guidance concerning desired outcomes. Consequently, they are an important part of strategy implementation. Effective operating goals should be high enough to be motivating yet realistic. They should be specific, measurable, and cover a specific time period. They should be established through a participative process and should be understood by all affected employees.[74]

Goals are established at all levels in the organization. At the corporate level, they encompass the entire organization. At the business level, goals focus on the performance of a particular business unit. Goals are also developed at the functional level, where they provide functional specialists with specific targets. One of the keys to effectively setting goals is that they must be well integrated from level to level. To connect property-level actions with corporate strategy, Hilton Hotels uses an annual business-planning process.

> According to Dieter Huckestein, the president of Hilton Hotels, and Robert Duboff, a management consultant, "Property-specific goals are linked to incentive bonuses, performance reviews, merit-based salary increases and stock-option grants. The result of setting the standard and making sure that everyone understands how those standards are measured is an alignment of actions with goals. People at every level of the organization, from the president to front-line team members, know what is expected of them and how they are doing."[75]

Once the goals and critical results areas are determined, systems for monitoring progress must be put into place. These systems typically involve the accounting, marketing research, and information systems departments, but other departments may be needed. Many larger organizations have an individual or department specifically devoted to strategic planning. If this is the case, then that individual or department typically coordinates the collection of data for monitoring progress.

> Sheraton's customer-service promise, implemented across its 200 North American properties, incorporates technology that tracks any service deficiency the minute it surfaces, identifies patterns and response times across properties, and adjusts training programs quickly. "If a guest calls because he's missing a bar of soap, someone delivers the soap right away, and the incident is recorded electronically," says Norman MacLeod, executive vice president for Sheraton."[76]

Facilitation of Operating Goals

Goals do not get accomplished on their own. Behind each goal should be a manager with responsibility for making it happen. After managers are assigned responsibility for goal achievement, they should develop plans for accomplishment. Often these plans are evaluated and approved by higher-level managers. Plans should include a list of needed resources such as technology, personnel, capital, equipment, and supplies. Some of these resources may be available inside a department or business unit, while other resources might need to be acquired from other units of the organization. The plan might also include resource acquisition from outside the organization through purchases, contracts, joint ventures, or other types of interorganizational relationships.

> In the restaurant business, discipline means setting standards, being a moral leader and sharing ownership shift by shift. "Training, setting goals and then giving [our people] the tools to achieve those goals on the floor is critical to creating a sense of ownership for our hourly team members and managers," said Kirstie Johnson, regional training manager for Dave & Buster's. "Our managers and our shift leaders work together to formulate an operating plan for each shift. They ask, 'What should we focus on today?' By soliciting their input and not relaxing our standards, this allows all of the team members to feel like a bigger piece of the whole and that what they did today at work really matters."[77]

The higher-level managers who assign managers responsibility for achieving a goal should also make sure that required resources are allocated. Then, at the agreed-upon time, the assigned manager should report on progress. Reward systems should be linked to accomplishment of goals. While rewards are usually financial, they do not have to be purely monetary. Besides salary, bonuses, and profit sharing, recognition could include professional advancement, assignment of more responsibility or more personnel, tangible awards, and public recognition.

The purpose of all control systems is to provide information that is critical to decision making. If a control system reveals that something has changed or deviated from expectations, the managers should assess cause and effect in an effort to learn why. This will usually happen at the time goals and outcomes are compared. For example, assume that a passenger airline has established an operating goal that its planes should be 80 percent full for the first quarter of the fiscal year. At the end of the quarter, performance is at 70 percent, which causes enough concern that managers investigate the matter. They look at other goals that were set in support of the 80 percent goal. They look specifically at marketing and other internal functions. They investigate competitor behavior and look at economic variables. They discover that early indicators suggest a slowdown in the economy. The airline uses this information to revise its performance goals. In this case, an adjustment to the goal was warranted because of factors outside the influence of the organization. In other cases, adjustments to operations or marketing might have to be made.

Numerous control systems at multiple levels are necessary to keep an organization and its component parts headed in the right directions. However, they should be integrated in such a way that information can be shared. In other words, information from all parts of the organization should be accessible when and where it is needed to improve organizational processes. To enhance the quantity and quality of organizational learning, comprehensive organizational-control systems should have the following characteristics:

- Information generated by control systems should be an important and recurring item to be addressed by the highest levels of management.

- The control process should also be given frequent and regular attention from operating managers at all levels of the organization.

- Data from the system should be interpreted and discussed in face-to-face meetings among superiors and subordinates.

- The success of the control process relies on the continual challenge and debate of underlying data, assumptions, and strategies.[78]

OTHER TYPES OF CONTROLS

The creation of control systems is a vital part of the implementation process. There are so many types of organizational controls that they are even hard to classify, and there is no consensus with regard to definition of terms or titles. Some controls help guide an organization's progress in the accomplishment of its goals. Other controls ensure that reporting is accurate and that organizational processes are accomplished according to predetermined standards. A special set of controls is used to motivate employees to do things that the organization would like them to do, even in the absence of direct supervision. We will refer to them as behavioral controls, although other names could be used.[79] Behavioral controls work to encourage employees to comply with organizational norms and procedures. They are "real-time" in that they influence the employee as the job is being performed. Among the most important of these systems are bureaucratic controls, clan control, and process controls. We are discussing these particular controls in this chapter because they are particularly relevant to strategy implementation.

Bureaucratic Controls

Bureaucratic control systems consist of rules, procedures, and policies that guide the behavior of organizational members. They are especially appropriate where consistency between employees is important. For example, in an effort to guarantee quality, McDonald's has established standard ways of doing everything from cooking french fries to assembling orders. Rules and procedures outline specific steps for an employee to follow in a particular situation. When a particular problem is routine or arises often, a rule or procedure may be developed so that every employee handles it in the way that is consistent with the organization strategy. Since rules and procedures outline detailed actions, they are usually relevant for specific situations. Unusual situations and quickly changing business conditions can make an existing procedure obsolete or ineffective.

A policy is a more general guide to action. Some policies are stated in broad terms and communicate the organization's commitment to a guiding principle. They guide behavior in a general sense only (e.g., equal-opportunity employer), with specific procedures needed to translate that commitment into action. Other policies are more specific. For example, human-resource policies may specify which employees are eligible for training programs or what employee behaviors deserve disciplinary actions. A marketing policy may specify which customers are to get priority, and an operations policy may describe under what conditions an order of supplies will be rejected. The procedures and policies that most companies employ to govern daily activities such as check approval, price setting, overtime, maintenance, and customer service are all a form of concurrent control and are intended to ensure consistency of action.

Unfortunately, many companies do not see everyday rules, procedures, and policies as "strategic." However, since the rules, procedures, and policies guide the decisions and actions of employees, they are a major determinant of how well strategies are implemented. For example, one of the most successful retailers in the United States, The Gap, uses detailed procedures extensively. The Gap replaces most of its merchandise in stores every two months. At that time, all store managers receive a book of detailed instructions specifying exactly where every item of clothing will be displayed. Company procedures also require that white walls be touched up once a week and wood floors polished every three to four days.[80] Gap management believes this level of procedural detail is necessary to achieve consistency and high levels of performance.

It is also possible for policies and procedures to encourage behavior that works against the strategies of the firm. For example, rules and procedures may stifle employees from improving processes because they feel "rule bound." Merchandise return policies that alienate customers can undermine any attempt at a customer-service advantage. Purchasing policies that require bids to be awarded on the basis of price can erode quality. Frequently, reward policies create tensions among interdependent stakeholder groups.

Clan Control

Clan control is based on socialization processes through which an individual comes to appreciate the values, abilities, and expected behaviors of an organization.[81] Socialization also helps organizational members feel inclined to see things the same way, by espousing common beliefs and assumptions that in turn shape their perceptions. Socialization processes for existing employees take the form of intensive training; mentoring relationships and role models; and formal organizational communications including the vision, mission, and values statements. Clan control is closely linked to the concepts of culture and ethics that were discussed in earlier chapters.

> The general manager of the Simpson House Inn, a bed and breakfast located in Santa Barbara, California, appreciated the power of socialization when she developed training modules that promote understanding, improve staff communication and self-understanding, and enhance self-esteem. She explains the property's philosophy as follows: "Seamless, flawless, gracious service can be given only by people who feel good about themselves and what they are doing, and who are motivated intrinsically by their own competence and sense of personal mission."[82]

Organizations that want to create, preserve, or alter their culture and ethics often use formal and informal orientation programs, mentoring programs, rigorous selection procedures, skills and communications training, and other methods of socialization to instill commitment to organization values. The first step is to define those behaviors that the company finds important, and then stress them in selection, orientation, and training procedures. Some firms select employees on the basis of their existing personal work-related values. Other firms prefer to hire young people and then socialize them toward a required set of values that will support the culture of the organization. Either way, human-resource-management systems play an important role in controlling organizational behavior.

Process Controls

Process controls use immediate feedback to control organizational processes. For example, the warning systems built into navigational equipment on an aircraft tell the pilot immediately if the aircraft falls below an acceptable altitude. The systems don't just feed back an aggregate report at the end of the flight telling the pilot how many times the aircraft fell below acceptable standards. That aggregate feedback information might be important for some uses, such as designing new navigational systems, but it would not be useful for the pilot. Within a business environment, real-time feedback is also useful in some instances but would be a disadvantage in others. Real-time financial feedback, for example, would make managing a business much like operating on the floor of the stock market—a frenzy. On the other hand, real-time controls in service-delivery environments can be very useful. Returning to Hilton's control system, we see how it relies on process controls.

> Hilton developed a continuous-improvement process called Situation–Target–Proposal (STP). The STP takes data and helps determine the actions needed to address a problem. In one hotel, for example, the balanced scorecard revealed low scores on guest-comment cards. Reviewing the report showed that bath and shower facilities fell into the "fix-it now" quadrant of the scorecard. The staff members thought the problem was due to low water pressure and hence an infrastructure issue. However, a process team investigated the problem and after taking apart a showerhead found the problem. When the team removed the unit's centrifugal flow restrictor the water pressure improved and so did customer satisfaction.[83]

To summarize this section, strategic-control systems help companies monitor organizational progress toward the accomplishment of goals and encourage human behavior that supports this progress. In many cases, control systems are used to help managers create and monitor organizational changes. Organizational crises are a type of change that require an immediate response from managers. The final section of this chapter deals with how to prevent and manage crises.

CRISIS PREVENTION AND MANAGEMENT

Organizational crises are critical situations that threaten high-priority organizational goals, impose a severe restriction on the amount of time in which key members of the organization can respond, and contain elements of surprise.[84] Crises such as the outbreak of hoof-and-mouth disease in the United Kingdom in 2001 and the massive power failure in the northeastern United States and in Canada in 2003 are hard to control and cannot be avoided. On the other hand, managers have at least some control over the incidence and resolution of human-induced organizational crises. Examples of these types of crises include the massacre in 1984 at a McDonald's in San Ysidro, California, that left twenty-one people dead and nineteen wounded; the gunman who entered a Brown's chicken unit in a Chicago suburb in 1993 and shot seven workers in the head; the disclosure in 2001 that

McDonald's had been using oil with a beef extract for cooking its fries; and the Norwalk stomach virus outbreaks in the summers of 2002 and 2003 aboard various cruise ships.

> Norwegian Cruise Line, Royal Caribbean, Princess Cruises and Holland America have all been hit by stomach ailment outbreaks. Even with extensive cleaning, the "Farmington Hill" strain of Norwalk is particularly hard to get rid of. The virus contaminates surfaces on cruise ships, prompting cruise lines to pull ships out of service long enough to break the cycle of the virus. Cruise lines have learned from the 2002 outbreaks, increasing training and establishing protocols to contain the virus when it appears. Princess Cruises formed six-member Norwalk crews on each ship, who disinfect the cabins of passengers who fall ill. These ships also carry special Norwalk test kits, allowing health workers to identify the virus within hours of someone becoming sick. Previously, tests for Norwalk took days or weeks.[85]

The five phases of crisis management include signal detection, preparation/prevention, containment/damage limitation, recovery, and learning.[86] Firms that ignore crises until they are involved in one will spend most of their time in the containment and recovery stages, essentially mopping up the damage. Back in 1984, the vice president of McDonald's advised his people to do the right thing and not worry about legal implications and media attention.[87] He focused on helping the survivors and families of the victims. Management experts advise clients to seize the early hours of a crisis to proactively manage local media, employees, the public, and, in the case of a violent incident, the victims' families.

> When Chevys franchisee Stan Knoles left his suburban Salt Lake City unit on a busy Thursday evening, it seemed like a business-as-usual day. "Surreal" is how he described the scene 30 minutes later. Surrounded by police, cameras, and distraught employees and customers, Knoles was caught in a restaurateur's worst nightmare. He couldn't change the fact that a gunman had run off the street into his restaurant, shot and killed the front-of-the-house manager and a customer, and injured another employee and a customer, before fleeing the scene. But he had to act fast to keep a bad situation from getting even worse. Knoles called Chevys headquarters in San Francisco and the public relations manager. With the go-ahead from corporate offices Knoles and the PR manager sat down for a strategy session. The two agreed that their first priority would be the victims—they'd worry about the news cameras later. But even as mangers and employees get on with it, in many cases of restaurant violence the media can often be counted on to dwell on it—only further fixing tragic images in the public's mind. In the wake of the San Ysidro McDonald's killings headlines like "McMurder," "McMassacre," and "Big Mac Attack" filled the papers.[88]

On the other hand, crisis-prepared companies establish early detection systems and prepare for crises, or even prevent them from occurring (left side of the model). For Keaton Woods, the general manager of the Le Meridien Kuwait, extra food was ordered and hidden in the hotel two weeks before the invasion by Iraqi forces during the Gulf War. Later he protected and provided for his guests and avoided being taken hostage by Iraqi soldiers for four months.[89]

> "Vegetarian French Fries in McDonald's India" read the posters made by Amit Jatia and his staff. Amit Jatia's company, Hardcastle Restaurants, owns and manages McDonald's restaurants in India, a country in which half of those eating at a McDonald's are vegetarian. Within hours of the story that McDonald's uses beef extract for cooking fries in

the U.S., the Indian operator jumped into action. PR specialists and a team of corporate and legal experts were assembled to build a strategy for handling the crisis.

On the same day the story broke, Jatia submitted samples of the fries to leading laboratories in Pune and Mumbai. Tests were quickly done by the Bombay Municipal Corporation and FDA and local political parties. Results were posted in the various outlets, and the papers.[90]

Some organizations are crisis prone. Studies conducted at the University of Southern California Center for Crisis Management have identified crisis-prone organizations as those having the following characteristics:

- If these organizations prepare at all, they prepare for only a few of the possible types of crises. Furthermore, their preparations are fragmented and compartmentalized.

- They focus on only one aspect of a crisis, and only after it has already occurred.

- They consider only technical factors (as opposed to human or social) in the cause or prevention of crises.

- They consider few, if any, stakeholders in an explicit fashion.[91]

Safety and security of hotels has become a top-of-the-mind matter for hotel guests and managers since the terrorist attacks in 2001. Hotels themselves have become targets of terrorism, as the 2003 attack on the Marriott in Jakarta illustrates. In response to those concerns, some hotel operators have created new security procedures, such as conducting more detailed background checks on their employees. Hilton Hotels now requires customers to show an ID with a picture on check-in, for instance, while Starwood Hotels and Resorts has raised security standards in its parking garages.[92] The Peninsula New York established a crisis management team to focus on the safety and survival of the guest and employees during a crisis. While many hotels are proactively preparing to handle crises a study conducted at Cornell revealed that U.S. hotels had made few changes to their safety and security arrangements in the aftermath of the September 11 crisis.[93] Overall, general managers were not doing a great deal of reevaluation of their security procedures (only 29 percent indicated they had done much), and even fewer were substantially changing their procedures (only 12 percent reported making a great deal of change). When it came to adding employees, about 70 percent of the GMs responded that they had made no additions to their security staff.

With regard to stakeholders, the key questions organizations should ask are: "Who are the individuals, organizations, groups, and institutions that can affect as well as be affected by crisis management? Can the stakeholders who will be involved in any crisis be analyzed systematically?"[94] As in other types of stakeholder management, open communication with important stakeholders is essential to success.

Organizations can take steps to control organizational crises. These activities fall into the categories of strategic actions, technical and structural actions, evaluation and diagnostic actions, communication actions, and psychological and cultural actions. Examples of these types of actions are found in Table 8.5. Above all, organizations have to plan ahead for things that might happen. Because of its planning, Merrill Lynch was up and running when the stock markets reopened six days after the September 11 terrorist attacks.

In the 1950s and 1960s, the surest way to get a job at Merrill Lynch was to be an ex-marine; the place was full of them. Though that is no longer the case, Merrill employees

| **TABLE 8.5** | **CRISIS MANAGEMENT STRATEGIC CHECKLIST** |

Strategic Actions

1. Integrate crisis management (CM) into strategic planning processes
2. Integrate CM into statements of corporate excellence
3. Include outsiders on the board and on CM teams
4. Provide training and workshops in CM
5. Expose organizational members to crisis simulations
6. Create a diversity or portfolio of CM strategies

Technical and Structural Actions

1. Create a CM team
2. Dedicate budget expenditures for CM
3. Establish accountabilities for updating emergency policies/manuals
4. Computerize inventories of CM resources (e.g., employee skills)
5. Designate an emergency command control room
6. Assure technological redundancy in vital areas (e.g., computer systems)
7. Establish working relationships with outside experts in CM

Evaluation and Diagnostic Actions

1. Conduct legal and financial audit of threats and liabilities
2. Modify insurance coverage to match CM contingencies
3. Conduct environmental impact studies
4. Prioritize activities necessary for daily operations
5. Establish tracking system for early warning signals
6. Establish tracking system to follow up past crises or near crises

Communication Actions

1. Provide training for dealing with the media regarding CM
2. Improve communication lines with local communities
3. Improve communication with intervening stakeholders (e.g., police)

Psychological and Cultural Actions

1. Increase visibility of strong top management commitment to CM
2. Improve relationships with activist groups
3. Improve upward communication (including "whistleblowers")
4. Improve downward communication regarding CM programs/accountabilities
5. Provide training regarding human and emotional impacts of crises
6. Provide psychological support services (e.g., stress/anxiety management)
7. Reinforce symbolic recall/corporate memory of past crises/dangers

Source: I. I. Mitroff and C. Pearson, "From Crisis Prone to Crisis Prepared: A Systematic and Integrative Framework for Crisis Management," *Academy of Management Executive* (February 1993), p. 58. Reproduced with permission of Academy of Management in the format Textbook via Copyright Clearance Center.

still pride themselves on being good marines. Like those graduates of Parris Island, they had planned for worst-case scenarios long ago. In 1999, Merrill installed a global-trading platform that meant all its business was on the same system—and that the system would operate even if part of it went down. And Merrill's chief technology officer, John McKinley, was well versed in disaster planning. The firm had prepared for all kinds of problems: loss of power, loss of water, loss of voice and data communications, loss of an entire building.[95]

In summary, organizational crises have the potential to thwart organizational efforts toward the accomplishment of goals. However, the Japanese symbol for "crisis" is made up of two characters. One elaborate character symbolizes threats, and one simple character symbolizes opportunities. Crisis-prevention and crisis-management programs represent yet another opportunity for organizations to develop distinctive competencies. Distinctive competencies in these areas may be hard to detect, because it is hard to measure, in financial terms, savings from a disaster that does not occur or whose negative effects are reduced. However, as more and more organizations suffer blows from large crises, it is evident that effective crisis prevention and management is critical to steady long-term performance.

KEY-POINTS SUMMARY

This chapter described the organizational structures and control systems that are used in implementing strategies. Centralization, formalization, specialization, and other key dimensions are important to characterizing organizational structures. In configuring the relationships among departments in a single business, organizations usually employ a variation of one of the following structures: functional, geographic/customer group, product/service group, or project matrix. Each of the structures exhibits strengths, weaknesses, and fits with particular strategic choices. The functional form encourages functional specialization and focus, but discourages coordination between functions or departments. Geographic or customer groups are grouped by various locations or customer types. The product/service group structures divide markets into smaller, more-manageable subunits that may improve service or provide different products to customers but result in resource duplication. The project-matrix structure employs a dual-reporting relationship that is intended to balance functional focus and expertise with responsiveness to customer needs. However, it is expensive and may create ambiguity and hinder decision making if managed improperly.

In structuring relationships among multiple business units, managers attempt to create either independence, so that organizations are unencumbered, or interdependence, to exploit operating synergies. Multidivisional and strategic-business-unit (SBU) structures divide businesses into divisions. The multidivisional structure creates the potential for financial synergy as managers allocate financial resources to the most promising divisions; however, the business units are typically so independent and share so few resource similarities that coordination and resource sharing among businesses is difficult. Consequently, operating synergy across divisions is hard to achieve. The SBU structure combines divisions into groups based on commonalities, thus allowing for the creation of operating synergy within an SBU. Corporate-matrix structures are intended to exploit economies, learning, and resource sharing across businesses; however, they require extra measures of coordination to avoid divided loyalties, sluggish decision making, and management conflicts.

Lateral relationships range from simple direct contact, networks, and communities of practice to teams, task forces, and even formal integrators such as knowledge officers. These horizontal coordinating mechanisms are essential for effectively addressing the deficiencies of the vertical structures and for getting work done across departments and divisions.

Strategic controls consist of systems to support managers in tracking progress toward organizational vision and goals and in ensuring that organizational processes and the behavior of organizational members are consistent with those goals. Feedback control provides managers with information concerning outcomes from organizational activities; the information is then used as a basis for comparison with the targets that have been established. The learning processes associated with strategic control form the basis for changes to strategic direction, strategies, implementation plans, or even the goals themselves, if they are deemed to be unreasonable given current conditions. Control systems are developed at the corporate, business, functional, and operating levels in a company. These systems should be integrated in such a way that information can be shared. In other words, information from all parts of the firm should be accessible when and where it is needed to improve organizational processes. Goals should also be integrated from one level to the next and across the firm.

Development of a feedback-control system entails determining broad goals based on strategic direction, establishing links between broad goals and resource areas or organizational activities, setting measurable goals for each resource area or activity, assigning responsibility for completion of each goal to individual managers, allowing those managers to develop plans for accomplishment and allocating resources to them, and following up to ensure completion and provide rewards. The factors that are to be controlled should reflect the interests of various stakeholder groups inside and outside of the organization.

Crisis-prevention and crisis-management systems are a special type of controls, specifically designed to prevent major disasters. Organizational crises are critical situations that threaten high-priority organizational goals, impose a severe restriction on the amount of time in which key members of the firm can respond, and contain elements of surprise. Companies can take steps to control organizational crises. Crisis-prevention and crisis-management activities fall into the general categories of strategic actions, technical and structural actions, evaluation and diagnostic actions, communication actions, and psychological and cultural actions. While the potential for crisis is a threat to an organization, effective crisis prevention and management may also represent an opportunity to develop a distinctive competence

DISCUSSION QUESTIONS

1. Describe each of the dimensions of organizational structure. How are they important?

2. Explain how these dimensions change as an organization grows.

3. Use the resources of your college library and interviews in your community to describe each of the dimensions of organizational structure for a local quick-service and fine-dining restaurant. How and why do the structures differ? Compare the structural dimensions of a Wendy's and a McDonald's. How do the structures differ?

4. For each of the business level structures presented in this chapter, discuss its strengths and weaknesses and when each structure might be most appropriate.

5. What are the primary differences between the functional structure and the geographic/customer structure? How is a project-matrix structure a combination of the two?

6. Discuss the distinguishing characteristics of each of the corporate-level structures presented in this chapter.

7. How are the multidivisional and SBU structures the same? How are they different? When would one structure be more appropriate than the other?

8. What is the primary purpose of the lateral mechanisms of an organization? When would the different types of lateral mechanisms (e.g., direct contact, teams, task forces, full-time integrator) be more appropriate?

9. What is a strategic-control system? Give examples.

10. Describe the problems associated with traditional accounting-based financial controls. Are they ever appropriate? In what circumstances?

11. What is feedback control? Describe the steps associated with developing a feedback-control system.

12. What are the characteristics of accident-prone organizations? Name ten things companies can do to control organizational crises.

NOTES

1. Sea Containers Ltd., *Annual Report 2001,* and Orient-Express Ltd. Investors Site, http://www.orient-express-investorinfo.com, 2 September 2003.
2. R. Simons, "How New Top Managers Use Control Systems As Levers of Strategic Renewal," *Strategic Management Journal* 15 (1994): 169–189.
3. R. Simons, "Strategic Orientation and Management Attention to Control Systems," *Strategic Management Journal* 12 (1991): 49–62.
4. B. Keats and H. M. O'Neill, "Organizational Structure: Looking through a Strategy Lens," in *The Blackwell Handbook of Strategic Management,* ed. M.A. Hitt, R. E. Freeman, and J. S. Harrison (Oxford: Blackwell Publishers, 2001), 520–542.
5. A. D. Chandler, *Strategy and Structure: Chapters in the History of the American Industrial Enterprise* (Cambridge, Mass.: The MIT Press, 1962).
6. E. Tse, "An Empirical Analysis of Organizational Structure and Financial Performance in the Restaurant Industry," *International Journal of Hospitality Management* 10, no. 1 (1991): 59–72.
7. R. Leidner, *Fast Food, Fast Talk: Service Work and the Routinization of Everyday Life* (Berkeley: University of California Press, 1993).
8. This example is drawn from the ideas of E. Nebel, *Managing Hotels Effectively: Lessons from Outstanding General Managers* (New York: Van Nostrand Reinhold, 1991).
9. R. Daft, *Organization Theory and Design,* 8th ed. (Mason, Ohio: South-western, 2004).
10. Ibid.
11. Choice Hotels, Letter to Shareholders, http://media.corporate-ir.net/media_files/nys/chh/reports/2001/ch2001ar02.html, 3 September 2003.
12. J. Marsan, "One for the Money," *Hotels,* January 2001, 67.
13. P. R. Lawrence and J. W. Lorsch, *Organization and Environment* (Homewood, Ill.: Irwin, 1969), 23–39.
14. R. H. Woods, "Strategic Planning: A Look at Ruby Tuesday," *Cornell Hotel and Restaurant Administration Quarterly* 35 (June 1994): 41.
15. A. C. Hax and N. S. Majluf, *The Strategy Concept and Process: A Pragmatic Approach* (Englewood Cliffs, N.J.: Prentice Hall, 1991).
16. R. Duncan, "What Is the Right Organization Structure? Decision Tree Analysis Provides the Answer," *Organization Dynamics* (Winter 1979): 429–431.
17. K. Birdir. "General Manager Turnover and Root Causes," *International Journal of Contemporary Hospitality Management* 14, no. 1 (20 February 2002): 43–47.
18. This example is drawn from the ideas of E. Nebel, *Managing Hotels Effectively: Lessons from Outstanding General Managers* (New York: Van Nostrand Reinhold, 1991).
19. M. Davis and D. Weckler, *A Practical Guide to Organizational Design* (Menlo Park, Calif.: Crisp Publications, 1996).
20. "EMEA Restructure for InterContinental," *Travel Weekly: The Choice of Travel Professionals,* 23 June 2003, 27.
21. Pegasus Solutions, Inc., http://www.rez.com/products_services/services.htm, 3 September 2003.
22. P. Tierney, "The Jungle Booking," *Forbes,* 10 March 1997, 92.
23. Duncan, "What Is the Right Organization Structure?"
24. First two quotations are from S. C. O'Connor, "Witzel Tapped As Group President at Carlson Hotels," *Hotel Business,* 21 October 2002, 6. The third quotation is from B. Serlen, "Carlson Bundles Hotels," *Business Travel News,* 3 June 2002, 3.
25. J. B. Quinn, *Intelligent Enterprise* (New York: The Free Press, 1992).
26. A. Roper, "The Emergence of Hotel Consortia as Transorganizational Forms, *International Journal of Contemporary Hospitality Management* 7, no. 1 (1995): 4–9.

27. Best Western, *Annual Report for 2002,* http://www.bestwestern.com/aboutus/2002.pdf, 3 September 3, 2003.

28. G. Haussman, "Higgins Out to Be 'Premier' Best Western Pres/CEO," *Hotel Interactive,* 29 August 2003. http://www.hotelinteractive.com/news/.

29. "25 Consortia," *Hotels,* July 2002, 62, 64, 67.

30. J. R. Galbraith and R. K. Kazanjian, *Strategy Implementation: Structure, Systems, and Processes,* 2nd ed. (St. Paul, Minn: West Publishing Company, 1986).

31. R. L. Daft, *Organization Theory and Design,* 3rd ed. (St. Paul, Minn.: West Publishing, 1989), 240.

32. R. C. Ford and W. A. Randolph, "Cross-functional Structures: A Review and Integration of Matrix Organization and Project Management," *Journal of Management* 18, no. 2 (1992): 267–294.

33. Ibid.

34. K. Staroba, "Managing the Matrix," *Association Management* 48, no. 8 (August 1996): 64.

35. J. Pearce and R. Robinson, *Formulation, Implementation, and Control of Competitive Strategy,* 7th ed. (Boston: McGraw-Hill, 2000).

36. "Orient-Express Hotels Maximizes Niche Strategy," *Hotels,* May 2002).

37. C. W. L. Hill, M. A. Hitt, and R. E. Hoskisson, "Cooperative versus Competitive Structures in Related and Unrelated Diversified Firms," *Organization Science* 3, no. 4 (November 1992): 501–521.

38. J. Weber, "A Big Company that Works," *Business Week,* 4 May 1992, 124–132; Johnson & Johnson, *Annual Reports* (1990–1991).

39. "Walt Disney . . . and Other Items of M&A News," *Weekly Corporate Growth Report,* 2 June 2003, 11; B. Pulley, "Disney the Sequel," *Forbes,* 9 December 2002, 106; Walt Disney Company, *Annual Report 2002.*

40. Ford and Randolph, "Cross-functional Structures."

41. Based on information provided by Jo Anne Kruse, who served as vice president of human resources at Cendant Corporation.

42. C. A. Bartlett and S. Ghoshal, *Managing across Borders: The Transnational Solution* (Boston: Harvard Business School Press, 1989).

43. C. A. Bartlett and S. Ghoshal, "The New Global Manager," *Harvard Business Review* (September/October 1992): 124–132.

44. Davis and Weckler, *A Practical Guide to Organizational Design.*

45. Ford and Randolph, "Cross-functional Structures."

46. G. G. Dess et al., "The New Corporate Architecture," *Academy of Management Executive* 9, no. 3 (1995): 7–20.

47. J. Galbraith, D. Downey, and A. Kates, *Designing Dynamic Organizations* (New York: American Management Association, 2002).

48. L. Dube, C. Enz, L. Renaghan, and J. Siguaw, "Coastal Hotel Group: Employees on Loan for Training with the Buddy System," *The Key to Best Practices in the U.S. Lodging Industry* (Washington: American Hotel and Motel Association, 2001), 76–77.

49. Personal interviews with Lewis G. Schaeneman (past CEO of the Stop and Shop Supermarket Company) and his senior staff, including Bill Grize, now president and CEO.

50. G. Gregory, "A New Knowledge Management Model," *Information Today,* December 2002.

51. L. Dube, C. Enz, L. Renaghan, and J. Siguaw, "Accor North America: Internal Customer Satisfaction," *The Key to Best Practices in the U.S. Lodging Industry* (Washington: American Hotel and Motel Association, 2001), 36–37.

52. J. Stuller, "Chief of Corporate Smarts," *Training,* April 1998, 28.

53. Simons, R., "How New Top Managers Use Control Systems As Levers of Strategic Renewal" (1994).

54. P. Lorange, M. F. Scott Morton, and S. Ghoshal, *Strategic Control* (St. Paul, Minn.: West Publishing, 1986), 10.

55. M. Pilling, "Getting a Grip," *Airline Business* (October 2002), 34.

56. H. T. Johnson and R. S. Kaplan, *Relevance Lost: The Rise and Fall of Management Accounting* (Boston: Harvard Business School Press, 1987), 10–18.

57. J. F. Weston and E. F. Brigham, *Essentials of Managerial Finance,* 7th ed. (Hinsdale, Ill.: The Dryden Press, 1985), 154.

58. M. Whitford, "Limited-service Trend Crimps Food-and-beverage Profits," *Hotel and Motel Management,* 1 February 1999, 19.

59. O. E. Williamson, *Markets and Hierarchies: Analysis and Antitrust Applications* (New York: The Free Press, 1975).

60. A. Lee, *Call Me Roger* (Chicago: Contemporary Books, 1988), 110.

61. Johnson and Kaplan, *Relevance Lost,* 1.

62. A. Barrett, "Feeling a Bit Insecure: Overexpansion and Too Rosy Forecast Plague Pinkerton," *Business Week,* 28 September 1992, 69–72; "Bogie's Men: Pinkerton," *The Economist,* 5 October 1991, 73; "Pinkerton's Reports Earnings Pressures, Revises 1992 Earnings Expectations," *Newswire,* 19 June 1992, 0618A1456; "Two Investors Charge Pinkerton's Misled Them to Inflate Stock," *The Wall Street Journal,* 26 June 1992, A7.

63. C. Enz, L. Canina, and K. Walsh, "Hotel-industry Averages: An Inaccurate Tool for Measuring Performance," *Cornell Hotel and Restaurant Administration Quarterly* 42 (December 2001): 22–32.

64. D. Heitger, B. Ballou, and R. Colson, "Pro-Forma Earnings," *CPA Journal* 73, no. 3 (March 2003): 44.

65. R. E. Hoskisson and M. A. Hitt, "Strategic Control and Relative R&D Investment in Large Multiproduct Firm," *Strategic Management Journal* 6 (1988): 605–622.

66. N. Geller and R. Schmidgall, "Should Overhead Costs Be Allocated?" In R. Schmidgall, *Hospitality Industry Managerial Accounting,* 4th ed. (Lansing, Mich.: Educational Institute, American Hotel and Motel Association, 1997).

67. M. A. Hitt et al., "The Market for Corporate Control and Firm Innovation," *Academy of Management Journal* 39 (1996): 1084–1119.

68. M. Goold and J. J. Quinn, "The Paradox of Strategic Controls," *Strategic Management Journal* 11 (1990): 43–57.

69. R. S. Kaplan and D. P. Norton, "Putting the Balanced Scorecard to Work," *Harvard Business Review* (September/October 1993): 134–147.

70. Four Seasons, *Annual Report for 2002,* www.fourseasons.com, (7/2003) http://www.fourseasons.com /about_us/investor_information/annual_reports.html.

71. D. Huckestein and R. Duboff, "Hilton Hotels: A Comprehensive Approach to Delivering Value for All Stakeholders," *Cornell Hotel and Restaurant Administration Quarterly* 40 (August 1999): 28–38.

72. P. Collier and A. Gregory, "Strategic Management Accounting: A UK Hotel Sector Case Study," *International Journal of Contemporary Hospitality Management* 7, no. 1 (1995): 16.

73. M. L. Frigo, "Strategy and the Balanced Scorecard," *Strategic Finance* (November 2002), 7; D. Huckestein and R. Duboff, "Hilton Hotels: A Comprehensive Approach to Delivering Value for All Stakeholders," *Cornell Hotel and Restaurant Administration Quarterly* 40 (August 1999): 28–38.

74. G. P. Latham and E. A. Locke, "Goal Setting—A Motivational Technique That Works," *Organizational Dynamics* (Autumn 1979): 68–80; M. D. Richards, *Setting Strategic Goals and Objectives,* 2d ed. (St. Paul, Minn.: West Publishing 1986); M. E. Tubbs, "Goal Setting: A Meta-Analytic Examination of Empirical Evidence," *Journal of Applied Psychology* 3 (1986): 474–475.

75. D. Huckestein and R. Duboff, "Hilton Hotels: A Comprehensive Approach to Delivering Value for All Stakeholders," *Cornell Hotel and Restaurant Administration Quarterly* 40 (August 1999): 31.

76. R. Carey, "Walking the Talk," *Successful Meetings,*(November 2002).

77. J. Sullivan, "Planning Best Way to Grow amid Inevitable Change," *Nation's Restaurant News,* 7 January 2002, 16.

78. Simons, "Strategic Orientation," 50.

79. V. Govindarajan and J. Fisher, "Strategy, Control Systems, and Resource Sharing: Effects on Business Unit Performance," *Academy of Management Journal* 33 (1990): 259–285.

80. R. Mitchell, "Inside the Gap," *Business Week,* 9 March 1992, 58–64.

81. P. McDonald and J. Gandz, "Getting Value from Shared Values," *Organization Dynamics* (Winter 1992): 60–71.

82. C. Enz and J. Siguaw, "Best Practices in Human Resource Management," *Cornell Hotel and Restaurant Administration Quarterly 41* (February 2000): 48–61.

83. D. Huckestein and R. Duboff, "Hilton Hotels: A Comprehensive Approach to Delivering Value for All Stakeholders," *Cornell Hotel and Restaurant Administration Quarterly* 40 (August 1999): 33.

84. C. F. Hermann, ed., *International Crises: Insights from Behavioral Research* (New York: The Free Press, 1972).

85. E. Perez, "Carnival Unit's Ship Has Norwalk Virus Cases," *The Wall Street Journal,* 3 September 2003, D7.

86. I. I. Mitroff, "Crisis Management: Cutting through the Confusion," *Sloan Management Review* (Winter 1988): 19.

87. M. Steintrager, "Lights, Camera, Reaction," *Restaurant Business,* 15 November 2000.

88. Ibid.

89. K. Woods, "When the Tanks Rolled into Town: A GM's Experience in Kuwait," *Cornell Hotel and Restaurant Administration Quarterly* 32 (May 1991): 16–25.

90. S. Gupte, "McDonald's Averts a Crisis," *Ad Age Global*, July 2001; pg. 134.

91. I. I. Mitroff and C. Pearson, "From Crisis Prone to Crisis Prepared: A Systematic and Integrative Framework for Crisis Management," *Academy of Management Executive* 7, no. 1 (February 1993): 48–59.

92. R. Terrero, "Hotels Step Up Security: Prepare for Future Events by Training Employees," *Hotel Business,* 21 October–6 November 2001, 15.

93. C. Enz and M. Taylor, "The Safety and Security of U.S. Hotels: A Post–September 11 Report," *Cornell Hotel and Restaurant Administration Quarterly,* 43 (October, 2002; 119–136); Changes in U.S. Hotel Safety and Security Staffing and Procedures during 2001 and 2002," http://www.chr.cornell.edu, 15 June 2003.

94. C. Enz and M. Taylor, "The Safety and Security of U.S. Hotels: A Post–September 11 Report," *Cornell Hotel and Restaurant Administration Quarterly*, 43 (October, 2002; 119–136).

95. D. Rynecki, "The Bull Fights Back," *Fortune,* 15 October 2001, 132.

CHAPTER 9

Strategies for Entrepreneurship and Innovation

*K*undan and Chanbrakanp Patel bought their first motel in 1980 because Kundan could not find suitable employment as a medical technician. The business was seen as a sound investment that could grow through hard work. According to Kundan, "Indians are hardworking and you can build up clientele with a friendly air." Now the Patels own several lodging properties. Another Indian American, R. C. Patel, bought his first hotel in Pell City, Alabama over twenty years ago when he was just twenty years old. Now the CEO and chairman of the board of the Atlanta-based Diplomat Hotels, this entrepreneur owns fourteen hotels in the southern United States.

These hotel owners are part of a sizable number of Indian American motel and hotel owners. Indian Americans have quietly carved out an unparalleled niche within the industry that is growing in size and influence. According to the Asian American Hotel Owners Association (AAHOA), its members own more than half of all economy hotels and 35 percent of all hotels in the United States.

The Indian influx started in the 1940s when a few immigrants bought cheap single-room occupancy hotels in the San Francisco area, according to Mike Amin, president of AAHOA. But the community's presence as hoteliers really took off in the late 1970s, when many successful Indians living in Uganda were forced out of the country by political turmoil, said Rajiv Bajatia, an India native and vice president of the Cendant Hotel Group. "From the early 1990s to

2000, the Asian ownership in some of our brands tripled. It continues to grow," said Bob Weller, president of Cendant Hotel Group. Of Cendant's 5,000 franchisees, 44 percent are Indian American, while Hospitality Franchise System (HFS), with names such as Howard Johnson and Days Inn, notes that 45 percent of its franchisees are from India. Prime Hospitality Corp. estimates that one-third of its franchisees are Indian American.

The Indian community's participation in the lodging industry is a result of immigration, cultural, and business reasons. Motels and hotels provide jobs for all members of a family, as well as a place to live. Families often provide a lot of support, especially in financing. "When you are an immigrant, it takes a lot of money to buy a business," according to Paresh Patel, owner of the Howard Johnson Inn and Suites on Route 17 in Paramus, New Jersey. "So what they do is pool their resources." His family's holdings include the Hampton Inn in Ridgefield and the Hilton Garden Inn in Secaucus, also in New Jersey. AAHOA Chairman Bakulesh "Buggsi" Patel observes that many younger Indian Americans have grown up in the hotel business, and it is now their challenge to transform their parents' assets into better assets.[1]

INTRODUCTION

In the broadest sense of the term, entrepreneurship is the creation of new business. It involves opportunity recognition or creation, assembling resources to pursue the opportunity, and managing activities that bring a venture into existence. Some ventures are complete start-ups, while other ventures are pursued within an existing organization. According to Arnold Cooper, widely acknowledged as a pioneer in the study of entrepreneurship: "Entrepreneurial ventures, whether independent or within established corporations, might be viewed as experiments. They test to determine the size of particular markets or whether particular technologies or ways of competing are promising. They have good internal communication and enormous commitment from their key people."[2]

This chapter discusses entrepreneurship, innovation, and growth. The first section discusses independent new-venture creation, including franchising, followed by a section on entrepreneurship within established firms.

ENTREPRENEURIAL START-UPS

The U.S. economy relies heavily on entrepreneurship as a source of growth and strength. Hundreds of thousands of small firms are created each year. Annually, more than a million jobs are created by these firms, while *Fortune* 500 companies are cutting their workforces. Eating and drinking places in America are mostly small businesses, with more than half being sole proprietorships or partnerships.[3] More than half of the private workforce is employed in firms with fewer than five hundred employees. These businesses account for about half of the private-sector gross domestic product. Two-thirds of new inventions come out of smaller firms.[4] Nevertheless, entrepreneurship is a high-risk activity. Entrepreneurs in nations with highly developed economies often complain about how difficult it is to keep a new business going, and they are right. However, entrepreneurial efforts in less-developed economies such as Russia are even more difficult: "An unstable government, an undeveloped legal system, overregulation, a virtually unfathomable taxation system, a pervasive mafia, and an inadequate business structure characterize the maze that Russian entrepreneurs must navigate in their attempts to create successful ventures."[5]

Much of what is found in this book is valuable to entrepreneurs. However, this section looks specifically at aspects of entrepreneurship that are different from other types of strategic planning. The topics include characteristics of entrepreneurs, the entrepreneurial tasks of opportunity recognition or creation, creation of a business plan, securing financing and managing a venture through its first year, and common causes of new-venture failures.

THE ENTREPRENEUR

Entrepreneurs have been studied for many years, and lists of their characteristics are numerous. However, some common traits exist among the lists. In general, entrepreneurs today are opportunists, in that they recognize and take advantage of opportunities. They are also resourceful, creative, visionary, hardworking, and optimistic. They are independent thinkers who are willing to take risks and innovate. They also tend to be excellent leaders.[6] Above all, they are dreamers:

> Would-be entrepreneurs live in a sea of dreams. Their destinations are private islands— places to build, create, and transform their particular dreams into reality. Being an entrepreneur entails envisioning your island, and, even more important, it means getting in the boat and rowing to your island. Some leave the shore and drift aimlessly in the shallow waters close to shore, while others paddle furiously and get nowhere, because they don't know how to paddle or steer. Worst of all are those who remain on the shore of the mainland, afraid to get in the boat. Yet, all those dreamers may one day be entrepreneurs, if they can marshal the resources—external and internal—needed to transform their dreams into reality.[7]

Conrad Hilton got his start in the lodging industry by renting out rooms in his home in New Mexico. Everyone around her thought Debbi Fields would fail when she decided to start selling her delicious cookies. She founded Mrs. Fields' Original Cookies, a company with over $100 million in sales and more than 4,000 employees. Not everyone has the internal stamina and drive to be an entrepreneur. Entrepreneurship causes a lot of stress. Disappointments are common. Uncertainty is a constant. However, successful entrepreneurs can also acquire great wealth and personal satisfaction.

ENTREPRENEURIAL TASKS

> In the spring of 1988, Patrick Clark opened an upscale restaurant called Metro in New York City's Upper East Side. He had apprenticed with renowned French chef Michel Guerard and had been chef at Manhattan's Odeon for seven years. He was ready to move from the trendy downtown dining scene to the city's bastion of wealth for his own venture. He had financing, a fine, chic dining room and a sterling reputation. "Like most chefs, I wanted my own place. I had made my reputation, and I felt the time was right," noted Clark. He found a location on East 74th Street, signed a 15-year lease, and set a budget of $1.1 million. His major investors were three Odeon customers. In addition he used his own savings and that of his working partners, Clark's assistant and the maitre d' from Odeon. Metro's was off and running with an average check of $60. Clark ended his first year of operation with gross income of almost $4 million.[8]

The primary tasks associated with a new venture are recognition or creation of an opportunity, creation of a business plan, securing start-up capital, and actual management of the start-up through its early stages. These tasks will now be described.

Opportunity Recognition or Creation

Entrepreneurship is often envisioned as a discovery process. Entrepreneurial discovery entails channeling resources toward the fulfillment of a market need.[9] For a start-up to be successful, this often means meeting a need better than other companies. In the case of Metro, the reviews were mixed about his concept. While *Gourmet* magazine lauded Clark, and both *Esquire* and the *New York Times* wrote mostly positively about the new concept, the press did think that the concept was somehow askew. In other cases, success involves creating a new market.

> Sipping the inordinately expensive but shockingly mediocre French wine jarred the otherwise pleasant dining experience in the opulent settings of the Taj or the Grand Hotel in Mumbai, thought Kapil Grover and his father, Kanwal, in the early 1980s. More than two decades later, those French associates rave about the Indian wine that the Grovers painstakingly developed specially to complement traditionally spicy Indian cuisine. Grover Vineyards was established in 1988 on 40 acres of land at the foot of the Nandi Hills near Bangalore, and the family spent several years experimenting with different types of French grapes and their response to Indian conditions. In 1996, the vintner became a joint venture with Veuve Clicquot, a brand of Paris-based luxury goods giant LVMH Moet Hennessy Louis Vuitton SA. The younger Grover is the director of the company, which now boasts more than 100 acres of world-class varietals under production. Kanwal is the company's chairman. With their winery, the Grovers undertook one of marketing's most exciting and exhausting challenges: creating a market where one did not previously exist.[10]

As this example illustrates, entrepreneurial discovery may be viewed as the intersection of a need and a solution. There are a lot of unmet needs in the world. For example, we need a cure for AIDS, and we need a more efficient way to enforce laws, and we need to be able to communicate more easily in a wide variety of languages. There are also a lot of solutions for which there may be no need at the present time. Scientists and even common people discover things every day. Human creativity is unbounded. Entrepreneurial activity occurs anytime an entrepreneur is able to link a need to a solution in such a manner that a new business emerges. Opportunities to do this are context specific:

What might be an opportunity today in Ukraine may not be an opportunity at all in the United States today or even in Ukraine tomorrow. This means that entrepreneurial opportunities do not necessarily lie around waiting to be discovered by the serendipitous entrepreneur who stumbles upon them, or even be "divined" by entrepreneurial geniuses, if any such geniuses exist. Instead, entrepreneurial opportunities are often residuals of human activities in non-economic spheres and emerge contingent upon conscious actions by entrepreneurs who continually strive to transform the outputs of those non-economic activities into new products and firms and in the process fulfill and transform human aspirations into new markets. In other words, before there are products and firms, there is human imagination; and before there are markets, there are human aspirations.[11]

Creation of a Business Plan

Everything associated with a new venture revolves around a business plan. Creation of the plan forces the entrepreneur to think through the details of the venture and determine whether it really seems reasonable. Table 9.1 contains a description of the various sections. The executive summary has the primary objective of catching the interest of the reader. This is followed by a description of the proposed business venture; an analysis of the environment; a resource analysis; and functional plans such as a marketing plan, operations plan, and a management plan. Financial projections are among the most important elements of a business plan, especially for potential investors. Projections determine when financing will be needed and in what quantity, as well as when investors can expect to begin receiving returns. Projections often take the form of pro-forma financial statements, including financial statements, balance sheets, and cash-flow statements. Pro-forma statements are hard to develop because entrepreneurs seldom have good data upon which to base them. But the process of developing pro-forma statements requires research on how much resources will cost and potential margins that might be expected. Pro-forma statements are an excellent way for an entrepreneur to communicate expected financial needs and performance.

A fully developed implementation schedule may or may not be included in the initial business plan. However, even when a full schedule is not included, a business plan typically outlines a timeline for major events. Investors are also interested in what might be called an "endgame" strategy. This is a plan for concluding the venture, transferring control to others, or allowing potential investors to exit the venture with a high return on their investments. It may also include contingency plans in the event the venture does not succeed (i.e., alternative uses or sales potential for acquired resources), and an executive-succession plan in case the primary entrepreneur leaves the venture. Finally, potential investors will be very interested in the amount of risk found in a venture. Rather than sidestepping this issue, it is probably better to include a section that honestly evaluates financial and operating risks.

In most ways, a business plan closely resembles a strategic plan for an existing business. It contains the basic elements of situation analysis (external and internal), strategy formulation, and strategy implementation. However, in a business plan, there is more emphasis on financing. Also, the perspective from which the two types of plans are written is very different. For instance, strategic plans assume an ongoing business, whereas a new

TABLE 9.1	WHAT'S IN A BUSINESS PLAN?
Section	**Description**
Executive summary	The executive summary contains a brief description of the venture and why it is likely to be successful. It must immediately catch the attention of potential investors and encourage them to read the entire business plan.
Business description	The introduction provides a thorough description of the venture. It should include elements such as where it will be launched, who will be involved, the customers it will serve, and when everything is likely to happen.
Environmental analysis	This section covers the most-relevant characteristics of the external environment in which the new venture will compete. These characteristics often include: • Market analysis (including customer analysis and evaluation of past and expected growth in demand) • Existing-competitor analysis • Supplier analysis • Evaluation of potential substitutes • Discussion of entry and exit barriers and their influence on entering and exiting competitors • Relevant government regulations and regulators • Financial condition of the industry • Availability of funding • Overall economic factors for the host country • Availability of technology • Availability of personnel with appropriate qualifications
Resource analysis	Resource analysis focuses on the special resources the venture already possesses and the resources that will be needed in order to make the venture a success. Such things as personnel, financial capital, equipment, patents and intellectual capital, and physical property are described. The most important resource and the one that should receive the most attention is the entrepreneur(s).
Functional plans	The nature of the venture will determine which functional plans should be included. A marketing plan (how the market will be reached, advertising ideas, distribution strategy, etc.), a management plan (who will be responsible for which activities), and an operating plan are essential. Beyond these, other plans may include research and development, information management strategy, or personnel (training).
Financial projections	Good data for projections typically is not available, but potential investors want to have some sense of the potential market size and growth and the projected margins that will be available. Financial projections (pro-forma statements) also help investors understand timing issues, such as when money will be needed, how much will be needed, and when their investment will begin to provide tangible returns.
Implementation schedule	This is a plan outlining the steps that will be taken as the venture unfolds. It provides a time frame for the accomplishment of various activities.
End-game strategy	Potential investors will be interested in knowing at what point they can exit the venture. Other important elements of an end-game strategy from the perspective of the entrepreneur include an executive succession plan and an exit strategy if the venture is not successful or when the venture has concluded.
Risk analysis	All ventures entail risk. Potential investors appreciate a good analysis of risk. This section is also very helpful to the entrepreneur in determining whether to pursue the venture.

business venture may not be pursued if it is determined to be infeasible. Also, the target audiences of a business plan and a strategic plan are different. Since a business plan will go to potential investors, it must be written in a concise format (no more than thirty to forty pages), and it must answer the types of questions that potential investors would like to have answered. A strategic plan usually includes a lot more detail in the implementation sections, since it serves as a guide for an existing organization. Potential investors are not interested in as much operating detail as are managers in an existing organization.

Securing Start-up Capital

Obtaining start-up capital is probably the most difficult problem facing a potential entrepreneur, and, as will be demonstrated later in this chapter, not obtaining sufficient capital is one of the biggest causes of failure. Some of the most common sources of start-up capital include commercial banks, personal contacts, venture capitalists, corporate partnerships, investment groups and business angels (see Table 9.2). Bank loans result in debt. Personal contacts, such as family financial support in the Indian community or the customers and coworkers of Patrick Clark in his Metro restaurant venture, may be among the most flexible sources of financing because the financiers have a personal interest in the entrepreneur. In the early years of the gaming business in Las Vegas, for example, most of the funding came from the Teamsters Central States Pension Fund because financial institutions steered clear of casino investments.[12] Venture capitalists, corporate partners, investment groups, and business angels may provide loans, receive equity, or own part or all of the property in exchange for the capital they provide. After start-up, if the venture has enough of a track record so that potential investors believe that it will be highly profitable in time, an initial public offering may be pursued.

Some entrepreneurs are able to start with their own financial resources. For example, the first of Colonel Sanders' fried-chicken restaurants was financed with his Social Security check.[13] Anne Beiler (of Auntie Anne's, Inc.) began her first pretzel stand with a $6,000 loan from her in-laws. For larger ventures or once these resources are exhausted, they often turn to a bank. Because of the risks involved, commercial banks don't get very excited about financing entrepreneurial ventures unless substantial secured assets are involved. For example, entrepreneurs often mortgage their homes or offer their automobiles, jewelry, or financial investments as loan security. Banks also consider loans more attractive if a wealthy third party is willing to cosign, thus taking on the financial obligation if the entrepreneur is unable to pay. Occasionally, a bank will make an unsecured loan based on the reputation or credentials of the entrepreneur or on a personal relationship. Restaurants are often considered a bad investment by bankers, who will refuse to finance these ventures because of the low barriers to entry, little collateral value in used restaurant equipment, and the long hours required on-site by owners.[14]

Venture capitalists are another potential source of start-up capital. They are individuals or groups of investors who seek out and provide capital to entrepreneurs with ideas that seem to have the potential for very high returns. Retail and service businesses began to receive more attention from the venture community in the 1990s, although they typically do not get involved in restaurant investments unless they are larger and more established multi-unit operations. They may seek an annual return as high as 60 percent or more on "seed money" for a new venture.[15]

TABLE 9.2	POTENTIAL SOURCES OF CAPITAL FOR ENTREPRENEURS IN HOSPITALITY
Source	**Description**
Commercial banks	Includes asset-backed borrowing, small loans, third-party loan guarantees, leasing, credit cards, and credit lines. Once in a while, a bank will select a venture for funding with very little security, usually based on the track record and credentials of the entrepreneur.
Personal contacts	Family and friends, asset sales
Venture capitalists	Organizations or individuals who evaluate business plans and invest "seed money" in some of them for an ownership interest and other compensation. They expect very high returns on their investments because of the risk they are taking.
Corporate partnerships	Many corporations seek opportunities to invest in new ventures with a high potential payoff. The corporation usually trades money or other resources for an ownership interest.
Investment groups	Wealthy investors or corporations often form investment groups that own most or all of the capital assets associated with a hospitality venture. The operator then pays the investment group for use of the facilities, and the investment group also enjoys the benefits from property appreciation. Real estate investment trusts (REIT) are an example.
Business angels	High net worth individuals who invest in entrepreneurial ventures as an opportunity to grow their wealth at a rate higher than a secure investment would provide. Many angels are also interested in providing opportunities to entrepreneurs.
Initial public offerings	These are usually used during a more advanced stage of the venture, rather than at start-up. The venture has existed long enough to provide adequate information that would lead potential investors to believe that it will be highly successful. The IPO basically provides the capital to pursue the venture at a larger scale.

Sources: J. A. Fraser, "How to Finance Anything," *Inc* (March 1999), 32–48; P. DeCeglie, "The Truth about Venture Capital," *Business Startups* (February 2000), 40–47; K. Schilit, "How to Obtain Venture Capital," *Business Horizons* (May–June, 1987), 76–81; J. Freear, J. E. Sohl, and W. E. Wetzel Jr., "Angels and Non-angels: Are There Differences?" *Journal of Business Venturing* (March 1994), 109–123.

In evaluating business plans, venture capitalists consider the entrepreneur's personality and experience, the product or service characteristics, market characteristics, financial potential, and the strength of the venture team.[16] Financing from a venture capitalist is often combined with capital from other sources such as banks or private investors. In the restaurant industry, venture capitalists often wait till later stages in the company's life cycle to provide capital. The most common first disbursement is usually provided to companies that are about to expand (called third-stage or mezzanine financing) rather than to provide start-up financing to develop an initial unit.[17] The House of Blues, a restaurant and nightclub concept, used three venture capital firms—Aeneas Group, US Venture Partners, and the Platinum Group—to help finance the building of new units and a merchandising operation.

The restaurant industry has many advantages as an investment target, including its fragmented nature with good growth potential, low risk of obsolescence in products, and the potential for mass distribution. Considering the use of venture capital can also benefit the entrepreneur because of access to large amounts of capital and the ability to obtain management expertise and advice to refine and sustain the start-up.[18] Entrepreneurs who seek financing from venture capitalists should prepare a thorough business plan and should answer questions as completely and accurately as possible. They should not expect an immediate decision, embellish facts, dodge questions, hide significant problems, or fixate on pricing.[19]

Entrepreneurs may also turn to corporations to obtain financing. From the entrepreneur's perspective, the chief disadvantage of this form of financing is a partial loss of control and ownership. Large corporations often seek investments in new ventures as a way to obtain new technology, products, or markets. A special type of corporate partnership is the investment group. These are groups of wealthy individuals, business owners, or corporations that take an ownership interest in the capital assets of the venture. For example, an investment group may own a hotel and the property on which it stands. The hotel operator pays the group for use of the property. The investment group also receives the benefits from property appreciation. A common example of an investment group is the real estate investment trust (REIT).

Another potential source of capital is business angels, wealthy individuals who provide start-up capital to entrepreneurs with promise. Many of them were once entrepreneurs themselves. They sometimes seek high returns, but many of them enjoy investing simply for the sake of helping an entrepreneur or advancing the state of technology in an area such as medicine, the arts, or computer technology. Unlike venture capitalists, business angels do not pursue investing full time.

After a venture has established a record of performance, entrepreneurs or venture capitalists may pursue an initial public offering (IPO). An IPO entails selling stock to the public and investors (see Figure 9.1). Assuming a board of directors has been created, the first step is to receive approval from the board to proceed with the IPO. Then an underwriter (investment banker) is selected, and a "letter of intent" is drafted. The letter of intent outlines the financial relationship between the company and the underwriter (e.g., fees), and other conditions of the offering. Attorneys then begin work on a prospectus, being careful to follow guidelines set by the Securities and Exchange Commission. The investment banker will oversee an elaborate "due diligence" process, which is a thorough examination of the company, its financial situation, markets, customers, creditors, and any other important

FIGURE 9.1   **THE INITIAL PUBLIC OFFERING (IPO) PROCESS**

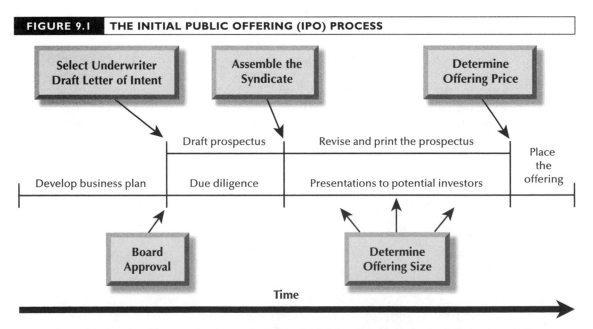

Source: This model is based on information found in Nasdaq, "Going Public" (New York: The Nasdaq Stock Market, Inc., 2000).

stakeholders. After a printer is selected for the prospectus and a preliminary prospectus is filed, the underwriter assembles a syndicate of companies that will help sell the IPO to targeted investors. Venture managers and the investment banker then make a series of formal presentations to potential investors. If everything looks positive after these presentations, the final prospectus is printed, the offering is priced, the size of the offering is determined, and the IPO takes place.[20] In the three years after its IPO, Krispy Kreme (KKD)—a relatively small donut operator, with just 292 stores compared to Dunkin Donuts' 3,600 in the United States alone—experienced notable success. The stock ended the first day of trading at $9.25, split adjusted, and in mid-2003 sold for four times that amount.[21]

Managing the Venture

The early stages of an entrepreneurial start-up are the most difficult.[22] Some of the major tasks of entrepreneurs for the first year of a venture are outlined in Table 9.3. In the early stages, financing and financial management are difficult problems. Even after the difficult process of securing initial financing, the entrepreneur must still set up a system to manage financial flows and keep records necessary to satisfy venture capitalists, creditors, and the

TABLE 9.3	FIRST YEAR AGENDA FOR ENTREPRENEURIAL STARTUPS
Activity	**Description**
Financial management	Once external funding is obtained, the emphasis becomes establishing systems to track revenues and expenses and control costs. A record-keeping system must be established that will satisfy the demands of investors, creditors, and the internal revenue service.
Marketing	Early marketing efforts may include providing a service to a few customers at a nominal price to establish a track record and gain references. Targeted advertising is also appropriate.
Services development	This includes establishment of a system for collecting feedback from early customers so that services can be improved. Continual improvement is essential.
Resource acquisition	This process begins with site selection and construction of a building, if necessary. The site must also be equipped with necessary machinery, furnishings, information systems, utilities, and supplies. Contracts need to be established with suppliers of raw materials, components, and services.
Process development	The focus is on production and operations management to ensure efficiency and quality. Once again, continual improvement is essential.
Management and staffing	One of the most essential activities is recruitment of motivated, well-trained employees and selection of managers, as needed. This area also includes assignment of responsibilities, establishment of personnel policies, overcoming administrative problems, training, and establishing a compensation system, which may include benefits. The entrepreneur is establishing an organizational culture in this first year. It should support the objectives of the venture.
Legal requirements	The venture will need a legal form (sole proprietorship, partnership, corporation). If employees are hired, the venture will need an Employer Identification Number and will need to collect and pay payroll taxes. Patents and trademarks are sometimes necessary to protect the proprietary technology or brand image of the venture. Other legal requirements vary depending on the nature of the venture, the country and industry in which it is formed.

Internal Revenue Service. For those who wish to operate a restaurant or hotel, the uniform systems of accounts provide standardized accounting systems that contain many supplementary operating statements covering budgeting and forecasting. The *Uniform System of Accounts for the Lodging Industry* (USALI) and the *Uniform System of Accounts for Restaurants (USAR)* are designed with the special needs of those industries in mind and permit entrepreneurs to compare their operating results directly with industry standards.[23] Fortunately, there are a lot of inexpensive software packages that can help an entrepreneur track revenues and expenses and prepare to file tax reports. However, sometimes entrepreneurs are not familiar enough with personal computers to fully understand how to implement even a simple system. In this case, it is helpful if one of the first employees hired has the skills to handle a basic financial program. Also, many entrepreneurs secure the services of a tax adviser during the first few years of the venture.

Entrepreneurs often experience cash-flow problems because occupancy rates and other cash flows typically take a while to materialize. Low sales can plague a new venture, especially in the first few months after introduction. Many consumers and businesses wait to see if the new restaurant or hotel receives good reviews. They look for a "track record." In the case of the Metro restaurant, as a general downturn in business hit New York City, customer counts were down to about 175 on the weekend and considerably lower during the week. Clark, the chef, concedes that he may not have been in tune with what his Upper East Side clientele wanted, and by the start of his second year in operation he began trimming his staff and cutting his prices.[24] One strategy for overcoming resistance is to provide services to the first few customers at a nominal price. Those first customers then become references. Targeted advertising is also helpful, and it requires that the entrepreneur carefully define the target markets. In the case of a restaurant, the menu, hours of operation, location, and service must be aligned with what the customer believes is worth buying. Building a strong and stable customer base is important to early operational success.

Another important first-year activity is service development. Entrepreneurs seldom get a service exactly right from the outset. Early consumers will very quickly discover flaws. Entrepreneurs should set up a system that collects feedback from early customers so that services can be improved. Theme restaurants, like the previously bankrupt Planet Hollywood, suffered from low profitability because of the high wages of their entertainers, inflated prices, stagnant menus, and the lack of repeat customers.[25] Continuous improvement is essential because if the product or service is a success, other firms will quickly imitate it. They may be larger firms with more resources. Therefore, it is important to stay one step ahead of the competition in order to enjoy first-mover advantages.

Many resources need to be acquired at start-up. One of the most important decisions in this regard is site selection. The entrepreneur has to determine a size that is small enough to be cost-efficient, yet large enough to take advantage of current and future demand. The site-selection decision is usually made during the development of the business plan, since potential investors will be interested in making sure that a suitable site is available. The site also has to be attractive to personnel who have the skills required for the venture to be a success. It should also be as close as possible to suppliers and customers. If the site does not yet include a suitable building, then construction must be coordinated. Other physical resources that need to be acquired include furnishings, utilities, information systems, and supplies. Contracts need to be established with suppliers of essential materials and services.

"The kitchen was atrocious," noted Clark when he first began the lengthy renovation necessary to convert the long-standing restaurant called Adam's Rib to the Metro. The kitchen walls and floor needed to be retiled, the dining room required massive work on the ceiling arches to bring it into conformance with city codes, and the costs rose. Furnishings like the Tihany designed chairs were $240 each, bringing cost even higher.[26]

In addition to product/service development, process development cannot be neglected. Once a site has been selected, it has to be prepared for service production. The first units of a service are the most expensive to produce. For example, the first meals prepared will take the most time and the first week of a hotel will be very expensive, as all the bugs are worked out and systems are put in place. Entrepreneurs should pay close attention to process issues, should establish a quality-control system, and should focus on obtaining supplies at a minimum of cost. Costs of production should drop rapidly in the early stages of the service life cycle, consistent with the experience curve presented earlier. Other production- and operations-management issues will present themselves and will require immediate attention.

Many entrepreneurial ventures begin with a small group of people; however, successful ventures need more personnel soon. The entrepreneur simply has too much to do. As the venture grows, recruitment and training of personnel and managers become important activities. The entrepreneur has to delegate responsibilities and establish a compensation system, which might even include benefits such as insurance. As the organization grows, it is important to have a culture in place that supports the objectives of the venture. The culture is established very early through the examples of the entrepreneur and other early employees. For example, if the entrepreneur works hard, a cultural norm that values hard work will be established. If customers are given highest priority, then a customer-oriented culture will emerge.

Legal requirements are also a major issue during the first year. First, the entrepreneur should decide which legal form the venture will take. In a sole proprietorship, the entrepreneur is the owner and is financially and legally liable for the venture in its entirety. In a partnership, the partners each contribute resources such as money, physical goods, services, knowledge, and external relationships to the venture. They also share in the rewards. Typically, articles of partnership are drawn up by the partners to define such things as the duration of the venture, contributions by partners, division of profits and losses, rights of partners, procedures for settlement of disputes, and employee management.[27] A limited partnership can be established in which the management responsibility and legal liability of partners are limited, except that at least one partner must be a general partner with unlimited liability. Several forms of limited partnerships exist.[28] A key advantage of a partnership over a corporation is that profits are passed through to partners instead of being taxed at higher corporate rates. Also, the problem of double taxation, in which profits are taxed at the corporate level and then dividends are taxed at the personal level, is avoided.

Corporations and the agency issues surrounding them were discussed in Chapter 3. At this point, the only thing that needs to be added is that one of the advantages of forming a corporation is that the financial risk of a shareholder is limited to the amount invested in the corporation. However, shareholder control over the actions of the company is extremely limited. Also, the tax advantages found in partnerships are lost when a corporation is formed. The only exception is the S corporation, formerly called the Subchapter S corporation (from

Subchapter S of the Internal Revenue Code), which allows tax advantages similar to what are found in a partnership. However, to qualify as an S corporation, organizations must have relatively few shareholders and must adhere to other strict guidelines.[29]

As employees are hired, the entrepreneur will need to file for an Employer Identification Number (EIN) and begin to pay (and collect) payroll taxes. Trademarks or unique processes may need to be protected from competitor infringement. Other legal requirements depend on the nature of the venture and the regulations surrounding it.

This discussion is not intended to be complete, but it does provide an idea with regard to what an entrepreneur faces in the first year or so. For any would-be entrepreneurs, it adds a dimension of realism with regard to what it will take to make it through the first year. Entrepreneurs experience a lot of problems. Figure 9.2 demonstrates that from an external perspective, customer contact is an issue facing more than a quarter of entrepreneurs. Other major concerns are a lack of market knowledge, and problems with market planning. It is interesting to note that most entrepreneurs do not feel that competitors are much of a problem. This point attests to the advantages of being small and introducing a new product or service to the market. From an internal perspective, the most common issues are obtaining adequate capital and managing cash flow. Management problems are also experienced with inventory control, facilities and equipment, human resources, leadership, organization structure, and accounting systems. For some entrepreneurs the benefit of brand recognition, economies of scale, training, access to a reservation system, and marketing support make franchising a viable approach to business ownership. In addition, chain affiliation often gives hotel developers an edge with lending institutions.[30]

FRANCHISING

In the United States, lodging industry franchising is a viable way to start a new venture, with around 70 percent of hotels affiliated with a chain, although this percentage is substantially lower in other parts of the world. Franchising is also popular in the restaurant industry, with the greatest number of franchised concepts being in the fast-food industry.[31] Franchising is when two independent companies form a contractual agreement giving one (the franchisee) the right to operate a business in a given location for a specified period under the brand of the other firm (franchisor). Franchisees agree to give the franchisor a combination of fees and royalties, usually in the form of a percentage of unit sales in restaurants or a percentage of room sales in hotels. Also included in these agreements are an advertising contribution paid to the franchisor as a percentage of unit revenues. Hospitality firms engage in what is called business-format franchising, which is when the franchisor sells a way of doing business to its franchisees. This form of franchising is in contrast to traditional franchising, in which the franchisor is mostly a manufacturer selling its product through a franchise network such as car dealerships.[32]

Is franchising less risky than going into business on one's own? While conventional wisdom might say yes, current research suggests that joining a new and small franchise may be more risky than starting one's own business because success depends on the capacity of the franchisor and the other few franchisees to make the entire chain work. The likelihood of failure is lower when one joins an established chain with many units such as Subway, Pizza Hut, Applebee's Neighborhood Grill and Bar, Panera Bread Company, or Red Lobster.

FIGURE 9.2	INTERNAL AND EXTERNAL PROBLEMS FACED BY ENTREPRENEURS

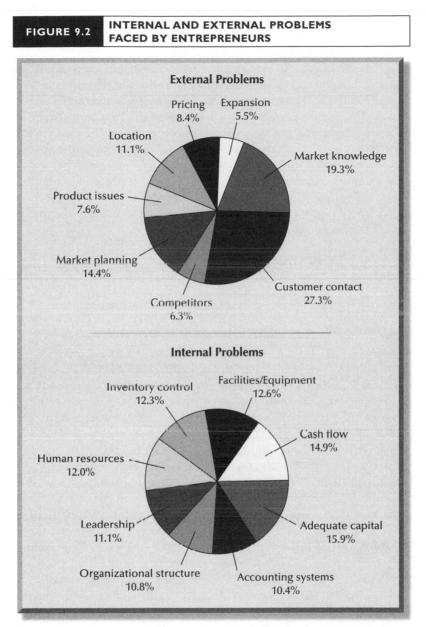

External Problems

- Pricing 8.4%
- Expansion 5.5%
- Location 11.1%
- Market knowledge 19.3%
- Product issues 7.6%
- Market planning 14.4%
- Competitors 6.3%
- Customer contact 27.3%

Internal Problems

- Inventory control 12.3%
- Facilities/Equipment 12.6%
- Cash flow 14.9%
- Human resources 12.0%
- Leadership 11.1%
- Adequate capital 15.9%
- Organizational structure 10.8%
- Accounting systems 10.4%

Source: H. Robert Dodge, Sam Fullerton, and John E. Robbins, "Stage of Organizational Life Cycle and Competition as Mediators of Problem Perception for Small Business," *Strategic Management Journal* 15 (1994): 129. © John Wiley & Sons Limited. Reproduced with permission.

It is important to understand that franchising is not without risks, with one study showing fewer than 25 percent of companies that offered franchises in the United States in 1983 still franchising ten years later.[33]

Finally, an entrepreneur considering franchising as a method of doing business needs to keep in mind that multi-unit franchisee ownership is common in the hospitality industry; for example, the average McDonald's franchisee in the United States owns three restaurants. The multi-unit franchisee will have far more bargaining power in transactions with the franchisor, and hence the new entrepreneur needs to consider their own long-term ownership strategy. Franchising can be very promising, although there will always be opportunities for entrepreneurs who operate independent hotels or restaurant, in which they can reap substantial store-level profits and leverage prime locations and distinctive service features. Whether franchising or non-chain ownership is the method of operation, a variety of factors can cause failure. Some of these causes of failure will be discussed further in the next section.

CAUSES OF FAILURE

> Two years after its promising opening, Metro went out of business.[34] "We did all we could to stay open, but the concept was very expensive to maintain. And the overhead killed us," noted one of Clark's partners. "We were never able to accrue a cash reserve to see us through the slow times."[35]

According to both entrepreneurs and venture capitalists, the most common reasons new ventures fail are internal.[36] Specifically, the number-one reason cited by both groups is lack of management skill. Entrepreneurs often have enthusiasm, optimism, and drive but do not possess the business skills they need to make a venture successful. In addition, many times entrepreneurs lack the ability to manage finances effectively. One of the reasons failure rates are high in the restaurant sector is the ease of entry to the industry. The low barriers make it possible for inefficient operators lacking skill, experience, and capital to enter the industry.[37] A poor management strategy and inappropriate vision are also common problems in failed ventures. These management errors in restaurants can often be seen in the choice of a poor location, poor food or service quality, and mispriced menu items.

According to Dun and Bradstreet's *Business Failure Record,* the retail sector, which includes the restaurant industry, and the service sector, which captures the lodging industry, experienced the highest business failure rate. In addition, within the retail sector, that includes food stores, and general merchandise stores along with other types of businesses, eating and drinking places have more business failures than any other industry.[38] Although no exact figures are available on restaurant failure rates, experts, executives, and the investment community estimate that they are as high as 90 percent in the United States and West European cities.[39] Failure rates are not tracked by the National Restaurant Association, and statistics appear to vary by the source. Of particular concern to many entrepreneurs in recent years are the highly variable reports on the failure rate of franchise operations. The U.S. Federal Trade Commission's consumer protection director notes, "The most widespread myth is that franchises are a safe investment because they have a much lower failure rate than independent business. In fact, there may be much less of a difference than is commonly thought."[40]

Many new ventures fail because of a lack of capitalization. Often businesses need a lot of capital at the beginning if they are going to succeed. Without sufficient capital, the venture may fail even if the idea was good and the management skills were present. For example, a business may need to be a particular size to generate enough efficiency to make a profit. Or a venture may fail because not enough people know about a product or service due to insufficient advertising. A firm that does not initially have enough financial backing may also assume too much debt too early. Interest payments can divert funds away from more important uses, and the risk of insolvency from not being able to make timely payments is a constant threat. When entrepreneurs feel high levels of financial risk, their behavior may change. They may be less willing to take other risks that are necessary for the venture to continue to progress.

Another common problem is that the service delivery system is inefficient or ineffective, thus making the venture uncompetitive. Even if a venture has excellent management, sufficient capitalization, and a good service delivery system, it can still fail if market conditions are not favorable. This is another timing issue. An entrepreneur may launch of a new hotel or restaurant right before a downturn in the domestic economy, as Metro was, or in a foreign economy upon which the new venture is dependent. Tourism is an industry that is extremely vulnerable to localized recessions and seasonal demand. For example, some expatriate-owned bars and cafes may even depend on particular nationalities within the already niche tourism market for their success.[41] In these instances sudden and unpredictable changes in consumer demand can be fatal. The language barrier and ignorance of local customs and regulations can also be sources of failure for expatriates running small businesses.

From an owners' perspective, a variety of factors appear critical to successful hospitality ventures in mass tourist destinations including: access to sufficient capital, sound planning, effective financial management, management experience, industry experience, business training, use of external advisers, and overseas experience.[42] There are many other reasons a venture can fail; however, these are some of the most common. Table 9.4 contains a summary of common problems leading to failure of entrepreneurial ventures.

TABLE 9.4	MOST COMMON SOURCES OF ENTREPRENEURIAL FAILURE
Problem	**Description**
Management skills	This is perhaps the most common problem. It can be manifest in poor planning, a poor management strategy or ineffective organization, or inadequate financial management. Or an entrepreneur may lack "people skills." Inflated owner egos, poor human resource management, and control issues can stifle a venture.
Lack of adequate capitalization	Many entrepreneurial ventures begin "on a shoestring." They lack the financial backing necessary to be large enough to be efficient or effective in reaching the desired customer. Some organizations may also acquire too much debt too early, which can stifle a new venture.
Service delivery problems	Poor service delivery design can hinder success. Or the venture may depend too much on a single customer group. Timing is also an issue. A hotel, restaurant, airline, or casino may be too early or too late into the market to be successful.
External market conditions	An otherwise outstanding venture may still fail if economic conditions turn sour in a domestic or international economy upon which the new venture depends.

Sources: D. E. Terpstra and P. D. Olson, "Entrepreneurial Startup and Growth: A Classification of Problems," *Entrepreneurship Theory and Practice* (Spring 1993), 19; A. V. Bruno, J. K. Leidecker, and J. W. Harder, "Why Firms Fail," *Business Horizons* (March–April 1987): 50–58.

So far, this discussion has focused primarily on entrepreneurial start-ups. However, existing organizations also need entrepreneurship. The next section deals with entrepreneurship and innovation in established firms.

CORPORATE ENTREPRENEURSHIP AND INNOVATION

Most hotel companies are in the business of "selling sleep" to their customers. I teach our staff that we're in the business of "creating dreams."

—Chip Conley, *CEO Joie de Vivre Hotels*

Entrepreneurial success comes from more effectively accumulating, combining, and directing resources to satisfy a need than other firms can. However, the advantage is not likely to last for long due to competitor imitation.[43] Consequently, continued growth requires continual innovation and entrepreneurship. Some argue that small companies tend to be better than large companies at innovation. One reason for the difference is that smaller companies are more flexible. They are not as subject to the constraints of a rigid bureaucracy that can stifle creative activity. They also tend to foster more of an entrepreneurial spirit.[44] As Seth Godin notes, "Why didn't Maxwell House create Starbucks?"[45] Others note that large firms have the complementary resources necessary to commercialize an innovation. If the firm has some degree of monopoly power, it can deploy the economies of scale and leverage its better access to capital to invest more heavily in innovations.[46] The Ford Mustang, 3M's Post-it notes, and Intel's bubble memory are all examples of commercially successful innovations created within large corporate settings.

"If you have a great idea and it takes two years to develop and test it, it may not be so interesting anymore," notes Ron Savelli, the vice president of product research and development at Einstein Bros. Bagels. At Einstein, taste panels are created quickly, items are tried at three to five stores, and new items reach the marketplace within six months of development.[47]

Corporate entrepreneurship, sometimes called intrapreneurship, involves the creation of new products, processes, and services within existing corporations that enable them to grow.[48] The offering of new menu items in restaurants has been accelerating at a dramatic rate (up 31.6 percent since the mid-1990s), although competition and the ease of imitation make these product innovations short lived.[49] Intrapreneurship is more common in organizations that foster innovation. Consequently this section will begin with a discussion of factors that encourage corporate innovation, followed by a description of the various structures firms use when they form internal business ventures. Because so much entrepreneurial activity has been directed recently toward communications technology, this section will close with a discussion of the Internet and e-commerce.

FOSTERING INNOVATION IN ESTABLISHED FIRMS

Innovation cannot be separated from a firm's strategy or its competitive environment, which means that what we consider to be innovative is defined by the context. Innovations may be a recombination of old ideas or a unique approach that is perceived as new by the individuals involved.[50] The development of electronic newspapers from around the world delivered to hotel guests on demand is an example of a recombination of the old idea of providing a copy of a local paper to each guest room. Innovation is the combination of both invention and commercialization. Developing a new product or process is not enough; the innovative firm must know how to convert an idea into a service or product that customers want.

Onity, previously called TESA Entry Systems, is an example of a highly innovative, established firm:

> TESA Entry Systems established itself as a leader in electronic locks for the hospitality industry. However, in the past few years, Onity has repositioned itself in the marketplace as a provider of other innovative technological solutions and services that include cutting-edge smartcard systems, in-room safes, Phillips closed-circuit television surveillance solutions, and Senercomm guestroom energy management systems, in addition to locking systems. Feeling that the TESA Entry Systems name was no longer reflective of what the company had become, Pascal Metvier, vice president of global sales and marketing, explained that the company was searching for a name that was not product focused, but rather service and technology centered. "The company's rebranding as Onity underlies the company's continued migration toward developing and delivering a host of innovative and intelligent facility management solutions." Onity's motto is "Innovative thinking."[51]

Firms innovate in a number of ways, including business models, products, services, processes, and marketing channels with either the goal of maintaining or capturing markets or the desire to reduce costs or prices through greater efficiencies. Researchers have been able to identify several factors that seem to encourage innovation. In addition, they have discovered many impediments to innovative activity. Some of the major factors that encourage or prevent innovation in established firms are listed in Table 9.5.

Large corporations that are successful innovators tend to have a clear-cut, well-supported vision that includes an emphasis on innovation.[52] Their cultures support this vision by encouraging people to discuss new ideas and take risks. The organization should not only tolerate failures, but also encourage employees and managers to learn from them.[53] The cultures of service firms like Disney, Southwest Airlines, Starbucks, and Ben and Jerry's illustrate the

TABLE 9.5	**FACTORS ENCOURAGING OR DISCOURAGING INNOVATION IN ESTABLISHED FIRMS**
Factors Encouraging Innovation	**Factors Discouraging Innovation**
• Vision and culture that support innovation, personal growth and risk taking	• Rigid bureaucracy and conservatism in decision making
• Top management support and organizational champions	• Absence of management support or champions
• Teamwork and collaboration; a flat management hierarchy	• Authoritarian leadership and traditional hierarchy
• Decentralized approval process	• Difficult approval process
• Valuing the ideas of every employee	• Attention given to the ideas of only certain people (researchers or managers)
• Excellent communications	• Closed-door offices
• Innovation grants and time off to pursue projects	• Inadequate resources devoted to entrepreneurial activities
• Large rewards for successful entrepreneurs	• Harsh penalties for failure
• Focus on learning	• Exclusive emphasis on measurable outcomes

importance of having line-level service workers engaged in creating the experience. Innovative cultures also promote personal growth in an effort to attract and retain the best people. Joie de Vivre uses a month-long sabbatical program for its salaried employees to reflect and nourish themselves, often at one of the company's Balinese resorts. The CEO, Chip Coley, expresses the value in promoting growth this way: "Our base line of business is hospitality, so why not give deserving employees an opportunity to experience the legendary graciousness of the island of Bali?"[54]

The best people also seek ownership, and innovative companies often provide it to them through stock incentives and stock options.[55] This is one way to align the interests of the organization with the interests of talented individuals. Finally, a culture that supports innovation encourages employees and managers to challenge old ideas by instilling a commitment to continuous learning and strategic change. "Past wisdom must not be a constraint but something to be challenged. Yesterday's success formula is often today's obsolete dogma. My challenge is to have the organization continually questioning the past so we can renew ourselves every day," notes Yoshio Maruta of Japan's second-largest diversified cosmetics and computer firm.[56]

As J. W. Marriott Jr. describes it: "Success is never final." He continually stresses three things. The first is the constant need to improve, to always try to get better. The second is the sharing of best practices across brands. Practices that are invented in one part of the company should be shared with everyone in the company. Finally, employees should always be looking for new ideas. Customer needs change and competitors improve.[57]

Rigid bureaucracies can stifle innovation. They are characterized by rules, policies, and procedures that make it difficult for an individual to vary from normal activities. People who feel as though they cannot or should not vary from established rules are unlikely to be sources of creativity and innovative thought.

> For years McDonald's has had a very efficient burger-making bureaucracy with extensive policies and procedures covering every detail of it operations. With the slowdown in the low-end fast-food burger market, the company now has to re-invent itself to continue its growth pattern. In addition to acquisitions such as Chipotle Mexican Grill and Boston Market, McDonald's is experimenting with a number of "home-grown" innovations. For example, the company is trying a diner-like Sandwich and Platter Shop and a bakery–ice cream outlet.[58]

Top-management support of innovation is essential, including efforts to develop and train employees with regard to innovation and corporate entrepreneurship.[59] Choice Hotels conducts an annual organization-wide talent review, which includes a mapping of upcoming business initiatives against any possible competency shortfalls by senior executive staff. They use this readiness assessment to determine current leadership capability to pursue new business initiatives.[60] Managers should be persistent in getting projects to market.[61] Because they shape the vision and purpose of the organization, top managers must also serve a disruptive role, making sure that managers and employees don't get too comfortable with the way things are.[62] Richard Branson, CEO of the Virgin Group (including Virgin Airlines), is an excellent example of a CEO who supports innovation. The overall philosophy of the group is to find areas in which Virgin can provide a better service or product to people than they are currently getting. This philosophy has led the group into a wide variety of hospitality, entertainment, and service businesses. Philippe Bourguignon, who was hired to transform Club Med, has also created an innovation-friendly culture:

> Club Med is the most widely recognized holiday company in the world. However, the company became "arrogant with success. It started losing sight of reality," according to Bourguignon. "The company had never made big profits. But when it started making losses it decided to raise prices. But when you raise prices you lose clients, so you cut costs. The quality and level of service fails so more clients are lost. So you raise prices even more. The guests are dissatisfied, the staff is dissatisfied so you lose more clients and you lose market share." In an effort to update the company, many new activities are being introduced. The Flying Trapeze, BMX bikes and climbing walls, in-line skating and half-pipe appeal to a new generation. In addition, the company has created an Internet department and is licensing the Club Med brand for a variety of products. Club Med is also using acquisitions to expand its market base, including an acquisition of the French tour operator Jet Tours.[63]

In addition to top managers, organizational champions are important.[64] A champion is someone who is very committed to a project and is willing to expend energy to make sure it succeeds. Two champions are needed. The first is a managerial champion, a person with enough authority in the company to gather the resources and push the project through the administrative bureaucracy. The second is a technical champion. This is an expert with the knowledge needed to guide the technical aspects of the project from beginning to end.

As top managers support innovation, they also have to be careful not to be too dictatorial in their decision making. Authoritarian management can stifle innovation. This type of management is being replaced by networking, teams, and a "people friendly" style of management.[65] At Chowking Food Corporation, an Asian fast-food restaurant, new product development involves almost all key departments, not just the head cooks and the research and development department, "We are one big team with the president himself heading the product board. All aspects of operations are involved," notes Jojo Ajero, the marketing manager.[66]

To maintain an adaptive, learning atmosphere at all organizational levels, many firms have created self-managed work teams and cross-functional product-development teams, so that multiple perspectives will be brought to problem solving. Teams cut across traditional functional boundaries; a single team might include representatives from engineering, research and development, finance, marketing, information systems, and human resources. These teams are kept small so that they are highly flexible, adaptable, and easy to manage.[67] The management hierarchy in these types of organizations tends to be flat, meaning that there are not a lot of levels of management between the customer and the top manager.[68]

The level at which projects are approved is also a key factor in determining support for innovative activities. Some large corporations require that an idea receive approval from five or more managers before any resources are committed to pursuing it. Innovative organizations allow project teams that do not report through the traditional lines of authority. Consequently, their work does not have to pass through multiple levels for approval.[69]

> The Ritz-Carlton Tysons Corner established an innovative program to shift decision making from management to the hourly staff and to eliminate by attrition certain management positions. The initiative began with the executive committee of the hotel changing

its name to the "guidance team," to help set the tone for what it hoped to achieve. A mission statement was created and signed by all employees, and special attention was given to keeping everyone, especially the hourly workers, fully informed and consulted every step of the way. After considerable discussion the hotel staff identified a number of management tasks for possible transfer to the hourly staff, including forecasting budgets and work scheduling. The results of this initiative were reductions in management costs, lowered employee turnover, increased guest satisfaction, and a more motivated and committed staff.[70]

Innovation is also more likely to emerge from a company with a culture that values the ideas of every person. Gary Hamel, an expert on innovation, talks about his work with companies in which secretaries come up with ideas for multimillion-dollar businesses. He says: "Many companies have succeeded in making everyone responsible for quality. We're going to have to do the same for innovation."[71] Unfortunately, many large companies don't give equal attention to everyone's ideas. They expect researchers or managers to come up with all of the innovations. Along with an egalitarian culture, excellent communications are found in innovative organizations. They encourage communication by having informal meetings whenever possible, forming teams across functions, and planning the physical layout of the facility so as to encourage frequent interaction (they don't let people hide in their offices).[72]

For corporate entrepreneurship to take place, organizations also have to commit resources such as people, money, information, equipment, and a physical location.[73] Some companies, such as 3M, even provide seed money in the form of innovation grants. Giving people time to pursue their ideas is also critical. At 3M, a corporate policy that supports internal venturing allows scientists to spend up to 15 percent of their time on personal research projects. The company's Post-it notepads were invented through this program.[74]

Effective rewards systems are also important. Corporate entrepreneurship allows creative people to realize the rewards from their innovative talents without having to leave the company.[75] Innovation should be rewarded through raises, promotions, awards, perquisites, and public and private recognition. While the upside rewards for innovation should be high, the downside penalties for failed innovation efforts should be minimal.[76]

Corporate entrepreneurship can be viewed as an organizational-learning process directed at developing the skills and knowledge necessary to compete in new domains.[77] Organizational learning is at the center of innovative activities. Chapter 3 discussed activities associated with knowledge (1) creation, (2) retention, (3) sharing, and (4) utilization. As was demonstrated in that chapter, outstanding execution of these activities can be a source of competitive advantage leading to superior performance.[78]

Many of the characteristics of innovative companies are found in General Electric, one of the largest and most successful conglomerates. Jack Welch, Jeff Immelt, and other board members of General Electric discussed the organization's transition to becoming a "learning company."

> Our true "core competency" today is not manufacturing or services, but the global recruiting and nurturing of the world's best people and the cultivation in them of an insatiable desire to learn, to stretch and to do things better every day. By finding, challenging and rewarding these people, by freeing them from bureaucracy, by giving them all of the resources they need—and by simply getting out of their way—we have seen them make us better and better every year. We have a Company more agile than others a fraction of our size, a high-spirited company where people are free to dream and

encouraged to act and to take risks. In a culture where people act this way, every day, "big" will never mean slow. This is all about people—"soft stuff." But values and behaviors are what produce those performance numbers, and they are the bedrock upon which we will build our future.[79]

This is a fitting summary of this section because it mentions so many of the elements of innovative companies. The next section will discuss the Internet and e-commerce, which have profoundly influenced the hospitality industry.

THE INTERNET AND E-COMMERCE

We live in an age of expanding worldwide communication. The Internet is a major part of the Information Revolution. According to Peter Drucker, "The explosive emergence of the Internet as a major, perhaps eventually the major, worldwide distribution channel for goods, services, and, surprisingly, for managerial and professional jobs is profoundly changing economies, markets, and industry structures; products and services and their flow; consumer segmentation, consumer values, and consumer behavior; jobs and labor markets."[80] Firms use the Internet for e-tailing, exchanging data with other businesses, business-to-business buying and selling, and e-mail communications with a variety of stakeholders.

> Webitying a business is not even half of it. Too often today's CEOs view the Web as yet another productivity tool—one that offers the promise of wholesale efficiencies. Yet, despite the fevered claims of Internet boosters and IT vendors, the Web's most profound impact on business will come not in the form of hyperefficient business processes, but in a riotous explosion of new products, new services, new content, new companies, and new organizational forms.[81]

In the 1990s, thousands of entrepreneurs started businesses that came to be known as "dot-coms." These were companies that would register a domain name on the World Wide Web, typically with a ".com" extension, and begin providing some sort of service over the Internet. Companies spent millions of advertising dollars through many forms of media trying to attract users to their Web sites.

> Just suppose you blew a cool $3.5 million in a mere 90 seconds on three television ads starring yourself and hyping your little known dot-com. . . . Having started with just $5.8 million in seed financing, you squandered more than half of your capital in less time than it takes to soft-boil an egg. ... Computer.com, a hand-holding help site for novice computer users, did actually run through 60 percent of its funding in ninety Super Bowl seconds.[82]

Early in the Internet craze, the race was not to achieve profits or even revenues, but to attract "eyeballs." The notion was that if a Web site could become a favorite for users throughout the world, eventually the business owners would figure out a way to make money from it. The founders of these types of Web sites had an inadequate business model for turning eyeballs into profits and cash flow.[83] Eventually, their initial investment capital ran out, and they were left with inadequate cash flow to continue operations. Some of these dot-coms were bought out. Others went out of business. A few of the most successful have continued to hold on. For example, priceline.com Inc., a travel retailer, announced its first-ever profit late in 2001. Other profitable ventures include online broker Ameritrade Holding and Homestore.com, a real-estate listings site.[84] Yahoo! boasts 145 million registered users, more than any other in the world, and is profitable.[85]

A variety of approaches to the Internet have been used. Some dot-coms provide retailing. Many of these dot-com retailers carry no inventory themselves. Rather, they connect buyers and sellers. Other dot-coms provide a service to consumers and sell advertising on their Web sites. For instance, Lycos.com has extensive road-map information, and Google.com is a Web search engine. Monster.com is a job-placement service. Some companies use a combined approach. Amazon.com is a retailer that provides extensive services to its users and sells advertising.

Electronic Tourism Markets

Travel is the most successful commercial sector on the Internet, bringing fundamental changes to both airlines and travel agencies. Airlines in particular were aggressive leaders in using the Internet to bypass their product and service intermediaries. With the advent of electronic ticketing in 1995, airlines reduced distribution costs by combining their established national networks and brand awareness with direct Internet sales. Traditional travel agencies began losing sales not only to airline sites but also to online agencies. According to SABRE, 15 percent of all airline tickets are sold through the Internet, with more than half of those being sold directly by airline Web sites and the rest by online agencies.[86] Travelers have discovered that they can obtain direct access to information, lower rates, and other benefits, as the following airline incentives show.

> To encourage people to book online, airlines offered numerous incentives. They attracted customers to their sites with exclusive Web fares, undercutting the prices offered via Central Reservation Systems (CRSs) and travel agents. They offered mileage bonuses to already-existing frequent fliers, and signing bonuses for travelers joining their loyalty programs. They sent their frequent fliers weekly e-mails, offering special fares not available through travel agencies. They broadened the range of online services and information, and made their sites more user-friendly by reducing the number of keystrokes necessary to search and book.[87]

While airlines were early to take advantage of the Internet, lodging firms have followed their lead, making extensive use of the Internet as a marketing and sales tool. Electronic tourism products and services have evolved with the advances in Internet technologies, beginning with simple systems that only provided travel information like sightseeing or destination guides or the promotion of hotel products. From these simple systems the industry evolved by integrating internal databases with the Web, producing more efficient and convenient information management systems. Many hotels and airlines have adopted these integrated Web/database business models, which link the Web to legacy systems such as customer relationship management (CRM) and back-office enterprise resource planning (ERP) systems.[88]

The one-stop travel services that permit a customer to complete all travel-related activities by visiting one site, such as Travelocity, require yet another level of cooperative relationships among various players, necessitating the development of strategic alliances. The development of electronic tourism, in which levels of integration and cooperation are both very high, continues to be a challenge because customer databases and revenue management systems of many suppliers (e.g., hotels, rental cars, and airlines) are not yet integrated with the Web reservation systems of cyber travel agencies.

Travel Web sites first targeted the airline industry and introduced consumers to heavily discounted e-fares. The hotel industry is next and year-over-year growth in online lodging revenue has already begun outpacing growth in the overall online travel sector. What started simply as an online alternative to bricks-and-mortar travel agencies, travel Web sites have evolved into online merchants, cannibalizing hotel profits in the process. Web sites such as Expedia, Travelocity, Orbitz, and Hotels.com now dominate the online space.[89]

Web bookings have put incredible pressure on prices in the lodging industry. Research at Cornell University has shown that heavy price discounting in hotels did not yield the desired boost in market share or occupancies.[90] Internet intermediaries such as Hotels.com may be to blame for the reported losses in revenue, as consumers have learned that they can get a better price for a hotel room by going to the Internet. To regain some control over their product pricing, several hotel companies have begun to rethink their long-term strategic relationships with third-party Internet distributors. Another approach to retaining control over pricing and inventory has resulted in alliances among major competitors to create their own Web sites. One example is the TravelWeb consortium, led by Marriott, Hilton, and Hyatt.[91] Another circumstance from the proliferation of Web sites is that independent hotels are now as easy to book as the chains, creating further competition and challenging the role of tour operators, particularly in resort locations in developing parts of the world. In fact, Orbitz is expanding its sales of rooms in the independent discount-hotel market.[92]

Learning to use the Web to help differentiate a hospitality product is essential to leveraging the Internet as a channel for distribution, and operators should move from focusing on price to the unique features and services of a product, as research on Web design suggests.

> A recent study by Jupiter Research revealed 87% of consumers have already chosen a destination before searching for a lodging product, however, only 23% of those booking rooms online have decided on a specific hotel. That means it is wise to develop a site that highlights points of differentiation to consumers regarding amenities, activities and services at individual hotels. Hoteliers should create a well-branded site that reflects the flavor and style of the resort. A Las Vegas hotel, for example, should not be afraid to create a site that's "garish," if it's appropriate.[93]

Hotel companies have also joined forces in e-commerce ventures to purchase supplies. For example, Marriott partnered with Hyatt to form Avendra. Intercontinental Hotels Group and Fairmont have also joined the venture.[94]

So how do you make money on the Internet? According to Gary Hamel:

> Electricity created dramatic productivity gains—and shrank margins. The Net is doing the same. The way for companies to avoid the crunch: Be unique. The collective delusion of the dot-com mob was that clicks could readily translate into customers and revenues. The collective delusion of the *Fortune* 500 is that productivity gains translate into plumper profits. Any company that plans to make money from "e" must have a Web strategy that creates unique value for customers, confers unique advantages in delivering that value, and is tough to copy.[95]

It is hard to predict the future of the Internet. However, several trends seem apparent. First, the Internet is an increasingly important tool for the exchange of information, goods, and services. Sales via the Internet are increasing at an astronomical rate. Businesses are using the Internet as a tool for a wide variety of applications. Second, managers and investors are being much more careful as they design business models around the Internet, making sure that there is some way to use invested resources to generate positive returns. Finally, information technologies are changing at such an amazing rate that the Internet is likely to be a source of entrepreneurial ventures for many years to come.

Key-Points Summary

Modern economies rely on entrepreneurship as a source of growth and job creation. Entrepreneurship involves the creation of new business. Some ventures are complete start-ups, while other ventures are pursued within an existing organization. Entrepreneurs are opportunists and dreamers. They are resourceful, creative, visionary, hardworking, and optimistic. They are independent thinkers who are willing to take risks and innovate. They also tend to be excellent leaders.

Entrepreneurial tasks include opportunity recognition or creation, assembling resources to pursue the opportunity, and managing activities that bring a new venture into existence. Entrepreneurial discovery may be viewed as the intersection of a need and a solution. Entrepreneurial activity occurs anytime an entrepreneur is able to link a need to a solution in such a manner that a new business emerges. Opportunities to do this tend to be context specific, and they can emerge from anywhere.

Everything associated with a new venture revolves around a business plan. Creation of the plan forces the entrepreneur to think through the details of the venture and determine whether it is feasible. A business plan includes an executive summary; a description of the proposed business venture; an analysis of the environment; a resource analysis; and functional plans such as a marketing plan, operations plan, and a management plan. It also includes financial projections, which are especially important to potential investors. Some sort of implementation schedule or timeline for major events is also included. Investors are also interested in what might be called an "endgame" strategy, a plan for concluding the venture, transferring control to others, allowing potential investors to exit the venture with a high return on their investments, contingency plans in the event the venture does not succeed, and an executive-succession plan in case the primary entrepreneur leaves the venture. Finally, a business plan should include an honest assessment of potential risks.

Obtaining start-up capital is probably the most difficult problem facing a potential entrepreneur. Some of the most common sources of start-up capital are commercial banks, personal contacts, venture capitalists, corporate partnerships, investment groups, and business angels. After a venture has established a record of performance, entrepreneurs or venture capitalists may pursue an initial public offering (IPO). An IPO entails selling stock to the public and investors.

Some of the major tasks of entrepreneurs for the first year of a venture include financing and financial management, marketing, service development, resource acquisition, process development, management and staffing, and satisfying legal requirements.

Entrepreneurs also need to decide whether to form their new ventures as sole proprietorships, partnerships, or corporations.

Business-format franchising is a popular and viable approach to new venturing in hospitality firms. While affiliation with a large and established franchisor can be relatively low risk, new entrepreneurs need to keep in mind a long-term ownership strategy and realize that going with smaller new franchisors may be more risky than going into business on one's own.

The most common reason for the failure of entrepreneurial ventures is lack of management skill. This is sometimes demonstrated by a poor management strategy, inappropriate vision, or an inability to manage finances effectively. Many new ventures fail because of a lack of capitalization. Other factors that can lead to failure are associated with the service itself, such as poor timing. Even if a venture has excellent management, sufficient capitalization, and a good service, it can still fail if market conditions are not favorable.

Corporate entrepreneurship, or intrapreneurship, involves the creation of new products, processes, and services within existing corporations. This sort of entrepreneurship is more common in organizations that foster innovation. Some of the factors associated with these types of firms include a well-supported vision that includes an emphasis on innovation and a culture that supports this vision, top-management support, organizational champions, teamwork and collaboration, a flat management hierarchy, a decentralized approval process, respect for the ideas of everyone, excellent communications, adequate resources devoted to entrepreneurial activities, a reward system that encourages innovation, and a focus on learning.

Firms are using the Internet for e-tailing, exchanging data with other businesses, business-to-business buying and selling, and e-mail communications with a variety of stakeholders. The hospitality industry extensively uses the Internet as a marketing and sales tool. Web bookings have put incredible pressure on prices in the lodging industry, resulting in alliances among major competitors to create their own Web sites. Another influence from the proliferation of Web sites is that independent hotels are now as easy to book as the chains, creating further competition. Hotel companies have also joined forces in e-commerce ventures to purchase supplies. While it is hard to predict the future of the Internet, it is clearly an increasingly important tool for the exchange of information, goods, and services.

DISCUSSION QUESTIONS

1. What is entrepreneurship, and why is it important?
2. What are some of the characteristics of entrepreneurs? Are you that sort of person? Do you know anyone who would be a good entrepreneur?
3. Describe the entrepreneurial tasks.
4. What does a business plan contain? Is a business plan the same as a strategic plan for an existing business? If not, how are they different?
5. What is the difference between business-format franchising and traditional franchising?
6. Is franchising more or less risky than starting one's own business?
7. What are the primary reasons new business ventures fail?

8. What are some of the typical activities of an entrepreneur during the first year of a venture?

9. Describe the sources to which an entrepreneur can turn for venture capital.

10. How can established firms foster innovation?

11. What are the different business models available to tourism organizations for leveraging the Web? How well do you think the industry is doing at balancing the integration and coordination of databases and Web interface?

NOTES

1. Hugh R. Morley, "Like a Rhyme—Motel, Hotel, Patel, Indian-Americans Own Approximately 35% of All Hotels in U.S.," *The Record,* Hackensack, N.J., Knight Ridder/Tribune Business News, March 6, 2003; Nancy E. Bistritz, "The Evolution of AAHOA." *National Real Estate Investor,* www.nreionline.com (August 7, 2003); Glenn Haussman, "AAHOA Hails 2002 Triumphs, Sets 2003 Goals," *Hotel Interactive,* 30 April 2003 (August 7, 2003); Kathy Hoke, "Downtown Hotel Opening Just As Owner Had Dreamed," *Business First of Columbus,* 4 September 2000; Melwani Lavina, "Diplomat of Hotels: Indian Hoteliers Step Up," *Welcome to India,* http://206.20.14.67/achal/archive/Jul97/hotel.htm. (August 7, 2003).

2. A. M. McCarthy and C. L. Nicholls-Nixon, "Fresh Starts: Arnold Cooper on Entrepreneurship and Wealth Creation," *Academy of Management Executive* 15, no. 1 (February 2001): 29.

3. D. Milton, "Industry Surveys Restaurants," *Standard and Poor's,* 8 May 2003.

4. P. D. Reynolds, M. Hay, and S. Michael Camp, *Global Entrepreneurship Monitor* (Kansas City, Missouri: Kauffman Center for Entrepreneurial Leadership, 1999).

5. S. M. Puffer and D. J. McCarthy, "Navigating the Hostile Maze: A Framework for Russian Entrepreneurship," *Academy of Management Executive* (November 2001): 24.

6. S. J. Min, "Made Not Born," *Entrepreneur of the Year Magazine,* Fall 1999, 80.

7. L. E. Shefsky, *Entrepreneurs Are Made Not Born* (New York: McGraw-Hill, 1994), 10.

8. D. Kochilas, "Manhattan Blues: A Combination of Troubled Times and Wrong Concept Eventually Did Metro In, Despite Rave Reviews," *Restaurant Business,* 20 January 1991.

9. R. Jacobson, "The 'Austrian' School of Strategy," *Academy of Management Review* 17 (1992): 782–807; J. Schumpeter, *The Theory of Economic Development* (Cambridge, Mass.: Harvard University Press, 1934).

10. A. Parmar, "Exposure Wins Indian Vintner Favor" *Marketing News,* 28 October 2002, 6.

11. S. Venkataraman and S. D. Sarasvathy, "Strategy and Entrepreneurship: Outlines of an Untold Story," in *The Blackwell Handbook of Strategic Management,* ed. M. A. Hitt, R. E. Freeman, and J. S. Harrison (Oxford: Blackwell Publishers, 2001), 652.

12. S. Lalli, "A Peculiar Institution," in J. Sheehan, ed., *The Players: The Men Who Made Las Vegas* (Reno/Las Vegas: University of Nevada Press, 1997), 1–22.

13. Shefsky, *Entrepreneurs Are Made Not Born,* 20.

14. P. Rainsford and D. Bangs, *The Restaurant Planning Guide: Starting and Managing a Successful Restaurant* (Dover, N.H.: Upstart Publishing Company, 1992).

15. W. K. Schilit, "How to Obtain Venture Capital," *Business Horizons,* May/June 1987, 78.

16. I. MacMillan, R. Siegel, and P. N. Subba Narasimha, "Criteria Used by Venture Capitalists to Evaluate New Venture Proposals," *Journal of Business Venturing* (Winter 1985): 119–128.

17. B. Hudson, "Venture Capital in the Restaurant Industry," *Cornell Hotel and Restaurant Administration Quarterly* 36, no. 3 (June 1995): 50–61.

18. Ibid.

19. P. DeCeglie, "The Truth about Venture Capital," *Business Startups,* February 2000, 40–47.

20. NASDAQ, "Going Public" (New York: The NASDAQ Stock Market, 2000).

21. A. Serwer, "The Hole Story," *Fortune,* 7 July 2003, 53.

22. D. E. Terpestra and P. D. Olson, "Entrepreneurial Start-up and Growth: A Classification of Problems," *Entrepreneurship Theory and Practice* (Spring 1993): 19.

23. To obtain uniform systems of accounts you can go to the following sources: *Uniform System of Accounts for the Lodging Industry,* 9th rev. ed. (East Lansing, Mich.: Educational Institute of the American Hotel and Lodging

Association, 1996); *Uniform System of Accounts for Restaurants,* 69th rev. ed. (Washington, D.C.: National Restaurant Association, 1990).

24. D. Kochilas, "Manhattan Blues," 92.

25. S. Campbell, "Prosperity Bodes Well for the Hospitality Industry in the New Millennium," *The Black Collegian,* 1 February 2000, 68–75. 26. D. Kochilas, "Manhattan Blues," 86–87.

27. D. F. Kuratko and R. M. Hodgetts, *Entrepreneurship: A Contemporary Approach,* 5th ed. (Fort Worth, Tex.: Harcourt College Publishers, 2001).

28. Interested readers will find a wealth of information on this subject in K. W. Clarkson et al., *West's Business Law,* 7th ed. (St. Paul, Minn.: West Publishing).

29. R. L. Miller and G. A. Jentz, *Business Law Today,* 4th ed. (St. Paul, Minn.: West Publishing).

30. T. Graves, "Industry Surveys—Lodging and Gaming," *Standard and Poor's,* 6 February 2003, 16.

31. D. Milton, "Industry Surveys Restaurants," *Standard and Poor's,* 8 May 2003.

32. F. Lafontaine, "Survey—Mastering Strategy 9 Myths and Strengths of Franchising," *Financial Times,* 22 November 1999, 10.

33. Ibid.

34. D. Kochilas, "Manhattan Blues," 86–87.

35. It is sad to note that Patrick Clark died in February 1998 at the age of 42 while awaiting a heart transplant. Clark, deemed "a terrific chef" by former *New York Times* critic Ruth Reichl, was the winner of the James Beard Award for best Mid-Atlantic Chef in 1995. He was a chef trained in the French tradition who achieved celebrity status and served as a role model for other African Americans interested in the culinary arts. After his venture at Metro he worked as several restaurants, including the nation's most profitable independent restaurant, Tavern on the Green, where he was the first African American executive chef. A cookbook in his honor, *Cooking with Patrick Clark,* was published by Charlie Trotter in 1999; www.booksite.com/texis/scripts/oop/click ord/showdetail.html?sid=4166&isbn=1580080731.

36. L. Zacharakis, G. D. Meyer, and J. DeCastro, "Differing Perceptions of New Venture Failure: A Matched Exploratory Study of Venture Capitalists and Entrepreneurs," *Journal of Small Business Management* (July 1999): 1–14.

37. W. English, B. Josiam, R. Upchurch, and J. Willems, "Restaurant Attrition: A Longitudinal Analysis of Restaurant Failures," *International Journal of Contemporary Hospitality Management* 8, no. 2 (1996): 17–20.

38. Dun and Bradstreet Corporation, *Business Failure Record;* Z. Gu and L. Gao, "A Multivariate Model for Predicting Business Failures of Hospitality Firms," *Tourism and Hospitality Research* 2, no. 1 (2000): 37–49.

39. H. Hubbard, "Putting Your Money Where Your Mouth Is - Restaurants: How to Spot a Hot Investment," *International Herald Tribune,* 11 January 2003, 13.

40. J. Oleck, "The Numbers Game: Failure-rate Statistics Run the Gamut, But Whose Are Right? *Restaurant Business,* 10 June 1993, 86, 91.

41. T. Blackwood and G. Mowl, "Expatriate-owned Small Businesses: Measuring and Accounting for Success," *International Small Business Journal* 18, no. 3 (2000): 60–73.

42. Ibid.

43. K. G. Smith, W. J. Ferrier, and H. Ndofor, "Competitive Dynamics Research: Critique and Future Directions," in *The Blackwell Handbook of Strategic Management,* ed. M. A. Hitt, R. E. Freeman, and J. S. Harrison (Oxford: Blackwell Publishers, 2001), 315–361.

44. J. Naisbitt and P. Aburdene, *Re-inventing the Corporation* (New York: Warner Books, 1985).

45. C. Conley, *The Rebel Rules: Daring to Be Yourself in Business* (New York: Fireside Book, 2001).

46. A. Afuah, *Innovation Management: Strategies, Implementation, and Profits* (New York: Oxford University Press, 1998).

47. L. Yee, "Bold New Day: Top 400 Chains Keep Innovation on the Menu," *Restaurants and Institutions,* 15 July 2001, pg. 24-28, 32.

48. G. Pinchot, *Intrapreneuring* (New York: Harper & Row, 1985); R. A. Burgelman, "Designs for Corporate Entrepreneurship in Established Firms," *California Management Review* (Spring 1984): 154–166.

49. L. Yee, "Bold New Day: Top 400 Chains Keep Innovation on the Menu," *Restaurants and Institutions,* 15 July 2001.

50. A. Van de Ven, D. Polley, R. Garud, and S. Venkataraman, *The Innovation Journey* (New York: Oxford University Press, 1999).

51. "Turn On to Onity," *Hotel and Motel Management,* 21 October 2002, 1.

52. J. B. Quinn, "Managing Innovation: Controlled Chaos," *Harvard Business Review* 63 (May/June 1985): 73–84.

53. Kuratko and Hodgetts, *Entrepreneurship.*

54. C. Conley, *The Rebel Rules.*

55. Naisbitt and Aburdene, *Re-inventing the Corporation.*

56. S. Ghoshal and C. A. Bartlett, "Changing the Role of Top Management: Beyond Structure to Process," *Harvard Business Review* 73 (January/February 1995): 94.

57. L. Dube, C. Enz, L. Renaghan, and J. Siguaw, "J. W. Marriott, Jr. Marriott International, Inc.: Overall Best-Practice Individual Champion in Corporate Management," *American Lodging Excellence: The Keys to Best Practices in the U.S. Lodging Industry* (Washington, D.C.: American Hotel Foundation, 2001).

58. "McDonalds Set to Unveil New Format," *Restaurant Business,* 1 June 2002, 11.

59. J. A. Pearce II, T. R. Kramer, and D. K. Robbins, "Effects of Managers' Entrepreneurial Behavior on Subordinates," *Journal of Business Venturing* 12 (1997): 147–160.

60. L. Dube, C. Enz, L. Renaghan, and J. Siguaw, "Choice Hotels International: In-House Executive Training and Development," *American Lodging Excellence: The Keys to Best Practices in the U.S. Lodging Industry* (Washington, D.C.: American Hotel Foundation, 2001): 68–69.

61. Kuratko and Hodgetts, *Entrepreneurship.*

62. Ghoshal and Bartlett, "Changing the Role," 86–96.

63. I. Griffiths, "The Accidental Tourist," *The Independent,* 15 September 1999, 1–2.

64. P. G. Green, C. G. Brush, and M. M. Hart, "The Corporate Venture Champion: A Resource-Based Approach to Role and Process," *Entrepreneurship Theory and Practice* (March 1999): 103–122.

65. Naisbitt and Aburdene, *Re-inventing the Corporation.*

66. "Innovation Key to Success," *BusinessWorld,* 31 October 2002.

67. Quinn, "Managing Innovation."

68. Ibid.

69. Ibid.

70. L. Dube, C. Enz, L. Renaghan, and J. Siguaw, "The Ritz-Carlton Tysons Corner: Self Directed Work Teams, Job Redesign, and Employee Empowerment," *American Lodging Excellence: The Keys to Best Practices in the U.S. Lodging Industry* (Washington, D.C.: American Hotel Foundation, 2001).

71. G. Hamel, "Avoiding the Guillotine," *Fortune,* 2 April 2001, 140.

72. Kuratko and Hodgetts, *Entrepreneurship.*

73. Burgelman, "Designs."

74. "Lessons from a Successful Entrepreneur," *Journal of Business Strategy* (March/April 1988): 20–24.

75. Naisbitt and Aburdene, *Re-inventing the Corporation.*

76. Kuratko and Hodgetts, *Entrepreneurship.*

77. R. Normann, "Organizational Innovativeness: Product Variation and Reorientation," *Administrative Science Quarterly* 16 (1971): 203–215.

78. D. M. DeCarolis and D. L. Deeds, "The Impact of Stocks and Flows of Organizational Knowledge on Firm Performance," *Strategic Management Journal* 20 (1999): 953–968.

79. J. F. Welch, J. Immelt, and Other Board Members, *GE Annual Report* (2000), 2.

80. P. F. Drucker, "Beyond the Information Revolution," *Atlantic Monthly,* October 1999, 47–57.

81. G. Hamel, "Take It Higher," *Fortune,* 5 February 2001, 169.

82. Salon, "Business As Usual," www.salon.com, 8 May 2000.

83. G. Hamel, "Is This All You Can Build with the Net? Think Bigger," *Fortune,* 30 April 2001, 134–138.

84. J. Angwin, "Latest Dot-Com Fad Is a Bit Old-Fashioned: It's Called Profitability," *The Wall Street Journal,* 14 August 2001, A1, A6.

85. S. Rosenbush, "Empire Builders," *Business Week E. Biz,* 15 May 2000, EB27.

86. National Commission to Ensure Consumer Information and Choice in the Airline Industry, *Upheaval in Travel Distribution: Impact on Consumers and Travel Agents,* 12 November 2002.

87. Ibid., 25.

88. J. Joo, "A Business Model and Its Development Strategies for Electronic Tourism Markets," *Information Systems Management* (Summer 2002): 58–69.

89. J. N. Ader and T. McCoy, "Web Storm Rising: Hotels Face Increasing Pressure on Rate as Web Bookings Increase," http://www.bearstearns.com, August 2002.

90. C. Enz, "Hotel Pricing in a Networked World," *Cornell Hotel and Administration Quarterly* 44 (February 2003): 4–5.

91. M. Rich, "Orbitz to Expand Sales of Rooms in Online Discount-Hotel Market," *The Wall Street Journal*, 13 March 2003, D3.

92. Ibid.

93. G. Haussman, "Consumer Study Identifies Top Web Design Techniques," *Hotel Interactive*, 13 August 2003.

94. C. Binkley, "Checked Out: The Hotel-supply Business Seemed the Perfect Place to Launch an Online Venture: It Wasn't," *The Wall Street Journal*, 21 May 2001: R22; "E Procurement Alliances," *Hotels* (October 2000), 92.

95. G. Hamel, "Edison's Curse," *Fortune*, 5 March 2001, 175.

CHAPTER 10

Global Strategic Management and the Future

$\mathcal{S}$uccessful American companies sometimes have difficulty taking their winning formulas overseas. In an effort to continue rapid growth despite a U.S. market that is quickly becoming saturated, Starbucks has expanded to thirty countries beyond the United States. Japan is Starbuck's most important overseas market. Its first location, in the Ginza district, was an instant success. Since then, the company has opened as many as 117 locations each year in Japan, with revenues of nearly half a billion dollars. Rivals are luring away customers, however, and Starbucks is losing money in Japan. The company is also experiencing competitive problems in many other international markets. In Britain, the company continues to lose money in spite of many efforts to fix problems. In the Mideast, Starbucks closed six stores. The company also ended a joint venture in Switzerland and Austria because sales were not meeting expectations.

Another American giant, Pizza Hut, seems to be losing the competitive battle in Thailand. After a falling out with Pizza Hut, William Heinecke, an American-born citizen of Thailand, opened his first Pizza Company restaurant in March 2001. With spicy toppings and tangy cheese, the Pizza Company catapulted to the number one position in the market within six months and now holds a 60 percent market share in pizza. Heinecke now plans to expand the Pizza Company into China and the Middle East.[1]

Introduction

As these examples show, developing internationally isn't for the faint of heart, but it is for all who are farsighted, notes Jay Witzel, president of Radisson Hotels and Resorts.[2] Many hospitality companies were pioneers in global expansion, with international hotel development starting in the late 1940s and early 1950s and McDonald's opening its first overseas restaurants in the Caribbean and South America in the 1960s.[3] InterContinental, Hilton, and Sheraton were early entrants to international development, followed by Holiday Inns (the largest international company in the late 1970s) and Hyatt.[4] North American companies tended to dominate the international hotel scene, but Club Mediterranee and Novotel from France and Trusthouse Forte and Travelodge from the United Kingdom were also large operations in the 1970s. Three restaurant chains have led the way in international expansion, McDonald's, Pizza Hut, and KFC. KFC was the first fast-food company to enter China, back in 1987, and had grown to two hundred restaurants a decade later. Now this chain has over seven hundred restaurants in China, and the parent company (Yum! Brands) expects to continue opening around one thousand international restaurants annually.[5] Rapid growth and expansion in domestic and international markets dominated the 1980s, while consolidation of large firms through acquisitions and mergers was a theme in hotels of the 1990s. In the early years, most international strategies focused on a single hotel product; today large firms are working with a portfolio of brands and sophisticated worldwide consumers, adding levels of complexity to the challenges of internationalization.

> According to Georges Le Mener, president and CEO of Accor Lodging North America, there are two primary areas to consider when developing a brand internationally: the size of each market and the type of products. "With an upscale brand, you can get critical mass without many properties. If it's upscale you want to be in major cities. When developing a budget brand, you need a large number of hotels in a market." Adding to this analysis, David Martinez, vice president of acquisitions and development for Starwood, distinguishes between critical mass in operations and critical mass in brand awareness. He notes that if you are after a boutique market you can get the job done with a small number of operations. Finally, Marriott believes it is easier to take a brand and build under it, than to push up a brand by entering with a product like Courtyard. According to Susan Thronson, senior vice president of international marketing, "We don't want a Courtyard to be the first Marriott hotel in a country." As these executives' ideas show, there are a variety of factors to consider when devising a global strategy.[6]

In a wide variety of industries, corporations are now making huge investments in foreign markets. One of the outcomes of increasing internationalization is that countries are economically interconnected at an unprecedented level. In the hospitality industry, the connection between local business demand and the prosperity of foreign economies is extremely strong. For example, in the wake of the September 11, 2001 terrorist attacks in the United States, many American businesses announced layoffs and cutbacks. Across the Atlantic, British Airways cut 7,000 jobs. This announcement occurred within one week of the tragedy, and analysts predicted that Europe would follow the United States into economic recession, with Germany the hardest hit.[7] Speculation at the time was that the disasters would result in a decline in Asian exports, which would lead to economic woes across the region.[8] The United Nations predicted that the region's gross domestic product could decrease by 2.4 percentage points as a result of the attacks. In fact, one analyst mentioned that China's relative isolation from the United States might actually reduce the impact of the disasters in that country.[9] The activities of business travelers both domestically and overseas are key elements of building strategy for hotels and restaurants.

To understand the development of hotels it is useful to observe the structure of an economy. Why are new hotels developing in China and Russia? One explanation lies in the fact that as economies grow and develop, different types of businesses are needed.[10] Hotel demand reflects the structure of an economy. As an economy grows and companies begin to serve multiple locations in a region and international markets, the demand for hotel services increases and new opportunities emerge. In an early economic phase, a country or region relies mostly on manufacturing and extractive industries dominated by single-location companies. In these economies demand comes from international business travelers who primarily visit major cities, while domestic business demand is relatively low. Large franchised hotel brands like InterContinental, Hyatt, or Hilton, oriented to overseas visitors, would frequently serve these locations in capital cities.[11] As a country's economy grows and business development leads to nationwide expansion and beyond, more jobs require travel to secondary and tertiary markets. Local and regional hotel companies emerge to service these needs. As an economy makes additional improvements in transportation, such as faster trains, improved roads, and more airline routes, more business travel can be undertaken on day trips. In addition, there is a limit to growth, and in mature markets like the United States, there may be only marginal growth in hotel demand, and in some locations saturation. As various parts of the world evolve economically, the level of competition to provide hotel services will also rise.

When domestic markets begin to show slowed growth, as they did for quick-service restaurants, companies start to think about international expansion. "New Starbucks Opens in Restroom of Existing Starbucks," a joke headline from the pages of *The Onion*, a satirical online publication, highlights the challenges of growth in saturated markets. "We probably self-cannibalize our stores at a rate of 30% a year," notes Howard Schultz, Starbucks founder.[12] Brinker, a casual-dining chain operator, had twenty-three Chili's units in six U.S. states with sales of $30 million twenty years ago, and now has 1,387 restaurants in forty-nine states and twenty-two nations with annual sales in excess of $3 billion.[13] Clearly international expansion can be profitable. Among the most popular reasons companies make foreign investments are to search for new markets or better resources, increase efficiency, reduce risk, or counter the competition (see Table 10.1).[14] Although many countries are significant in the world economy, they tend to fall into three dominant regions,

TABLE 10.1	PRIMARY REASONS FIRMS MAKE FOREIGN INVESTMENTS
Reason	**Description**
New markets	As domestic markets become saturated, companies seek to expand their market reach into other countries.
Better resources	Some countries have more-abundant resources than do others. Firms may seek resources such as raw materials, excellent suppliers, trained workers, advanced technologies, well-developed infrastructures, and good financial markets.
Efficiency	Organizations can create economies of scale through increasing production. Also, they can increase efficiency through cutting costs in countries with inexpensive labor. In addition, fixed investments in certain resources can be applied to multiple markets (economies of scope).
Risk reduction	Although global markets are interconnected, their business cycles do not match up perfectly. Consequently, a recession in Europe may not coincide exactly with a recession in Japan or in the United States. By investing in multiple global regions, a company can theoretically reduce volatility in overall corporate earnings.
Competitive countermove	If a major competitor invests in a particular global region, other competitors may feel obliged to do so to protect their own interests. For example, they may fear that one company will develop better resources or achieve more efficiency.

which are sometimes called the "Triad" regions: North America, Europe, and the Pacific Rim. Some researchers have suggested that in order to remain competitive, larger organizations should be involved in all three of these regions.[15] For example, organizations may find that the best suppliers of a particular good or service are not in their own countries. If they are going to be "world class," they have very little choice but to develop business relationships where the best suppliers operate. Of course, much of the growth in the hospitality industry over the next several decades will take place outside the Triad, in developing nations such as China and India.

Some scholars have argued that global strategic management is "simply the application of strategic management in a larger arena." Others "point to the historical legacy of international economics and trade theory, to the powerful effects of cultural differences, to the role of exchange rate risk, and to the very different institutional conditions in different countries and see the strategic concerns of multinational firms to be intrinsically different from their domestic cousins."[16] Both views are correct. Many of the tools you have learned—such as environmental, stakeholder, and resource analysis; creation of strategic direction; and development of control systems—can be directly applied to global firms. In this book, you have seen numerous applications of the theory and tools of strategic management to firms based or operating outside the United States. Nevertheless, significant differences exist among countries and markets. These differences are worthy of discussion.

This chapter begins with a discussion of the general orientation a firm takes toward international involvement. Consistent with the underlying themes of this book, the next section will describe global stakeholder management and global resource development as they relate to competitive advantage. Various global strategies will then be described, and guidelines will be provided for selecting among countries for investment. The final section will briefly discuss some of the global trends that are likely to be a part of the competitive environment in the future.

GLOBAL ORIENTATION

Multinational strategies tend to fall into two broad categories: international expansion and global integration.[17] International expansion is the process of building an expanding operational presence. This approach was taken by Holiday Inn Worldwide during the early 1990s. Its expansion strategy involved a "core brand" that provided standardized product design and service.[18] As organizations expand their reach, they can enjoy benefits such as increased market size, economies of scale, increased opportunities for learning, a larger pool of resources from which to draw, more opportunities to create partnerships, and more advancement opportunities for their managers. Global integration is the process through which a multinational organization integrates its worldwide activities into a single world strategy through its network of affiliates and alliances. It is a process of coordinating decentralized activities so as to exploit the firm's capabilities across markets. This multinational strategy is illustrated by Hyatt International, which relies on local and regional managers' evaluations of local conditions and property-level business plans. Managers throughout the global network are encouraged to identify and respond to opportunities, while the corporate office provides coordination and support. Global integration can result in cost efficiency, global flexibility, and an ability to apply the firm's resources and skills across multiple markets. In the case of Hyatt, it also enables development opportunities:

> As planning responsibility is shared throughout the global organization, changes in local market conditions can be identified rapidly. When for example, the complex process of change began to gain momentum in Eastern Europe, details of development opportunities began to emerge instinctively from all parts of Hyatt's global organization. The information came from managers at all levels in the organization who were either witnessing change, or gathering market information from talking to business travelers and others with experiential knowledge of what was actually happening.[19]

Not long ago, many U.S. companies, particularly those outside of the hotel and restaurant industry, were not ready for global expansion. According to Sheth and Eshghi, experts on international strategy:

> Many companies become multinational reluctantly. They start off as export houses, and as international business grows and becomes a significant part of corporate revenues, they become more involved in foreign operations. However, the corporate culture still remains domestic, and the international division is treated as a stepchild. The situation becomes one of them vs. us. ... What is lacking is a true worldwide orientation."[20]

Structural inertia within U.S. companies has been a major impediment to their transformation into true global competitors. You may recall from Chapter 4 that inertia describes forces at work to maintain the status quo, including systems, structures, processes, culture, sunk costs, internal politics, and barriers to entry and exit.[21] Inertia is stronger in successful organizations because managers believe that past success will translate into future success. Historically, North American companies were able to prosper by selling their products and services to the largest and richest market in the world. In the past, some managers considered overseas operations nuisances or simply organizational appendages that generated a few extra dollars in sales revenue.[22] However, the United States had a wake-up call, and now American companies are rushing to foreign markets in an effort to catch up. And, of course, American companies are not the only companies that have been guilty of a narrow global vision.[23]

International activities should be accompanied by a new mind-set for all members of an organization, from top managers to the lowest-level employees. Where will this new global mind-set come from? It has to start at the top of the organization. CEOs who want to create global companies can start by expanding their organizational visions to include overseas operations. However, they should also assign specific individuals to monitor global stakeholder groups, economic trends, and markets, and integrate this information into ongoing strategic management processes through the business-intelligence system. To increase its desire to go international with the W brand, Starwood hired a vice president of operations with international experience and a vision of getting into as many international markets as it can by 2006.[24]

CEOs can create a sense of urgency in the organization by constantly discussing global customers, operations, strategies, and successes and failures with subordinates, the board of directors, employees, and the media. They will also want to make visits to global operations as a part of their regular routines. Finally, CEOs can communicate the value of employees from countries that are outside of the home country by making sure that they are both hired and promoted as often as employees from the homeland. For some CEOs, the transition can be painful. There are plenty of minefields when going international, as Starbuck's chairman and chief global strategist, Howard Schultz, learned:

> As Starbucks spreads out, Howard Schultz will have to be increasingly sensitive to those cultural challenges. In December, for instance, he flew to Israel to meet with Foreign Secretary Shimon Peres and other Israeli officials to discuss the Middle East crisis. He won't divulge the nature of his discussions. But subsequently, at a Seattle synagogue, Schultz let the Palestinians have it. With Starbucks outlets already in Kuwait, Lebanon, Oman, Qatar, and Saudi Arabia, he created a mild uproar among Palestinian supporters. Schultz quickly backpedaled, saying that his words were taken out of context and asserting that he is "pro-peace" for both sides.[25]

GLOBAL STAKEHOLDERS AND RESOURCES

Global strategic management provides challenges and opportunities that are not found in domestic markets. Stakeholder management is more complicated because of the diversity of people, organizations, and governments involved. However, a more diverse environment offers more opportunities to develop stakeholder-based competencies through effective management and interorganizational relationships. Also, global diversity provides a much larger pool of resources from which to draw.

STAKEHOLDER MANAGEMENT IN FOREIGN ENVIRONMENTS

Global expansion requires an adjustment in the business definition of the organization. The answer to "Who is being satisfied?" typically is enlarged to include worldwide customers. According to a senior manager at InterContinental, "You have to look to see where there are consumers who have the same needs your brand meets."[26] Answering "How are customer needs satisfied?" may involve relationships with a much broader range of suppliers and partners. When McDonald's entered Europe it could not find local food processors who could handle the high-volume automated production and cryogenic meat freezing that were essential elements of the company's operations.[27] To solve this problem, McDonald's used its established suppliers who build facilities in new countries, sometimes with the restaurant chain serving as a partner in these supplier ventures. Depending on the nature of the venture, any of the stakeholder groups may be enlarged. At a minimum, all global ventures rely on cooperation from a foreign government; however, most foreign ventures involve many other stakeholder groups as well. These new stakeholders add a new dimension to stakeholder analysis and management. They also increase the need for a state-of-the-art business-intelligence system.

Stakeholder analysis, a complicated process in domestic environments, becomes even more demanding when companies are significantly involved in countries other than their home countries. Organizations may respond to this complexity by evaluating stakeholders in all countries simultaneously. This process, which requires a high level of information-system sophistication, results in a comprehensive view that provides the firm with a global picture and helps high-level managers craft missions, goals, strategies, and implementation plans that are applicable in a global setting. On the other hand, many hospitality companies use a decentralized approach to stakeholder analysis, allowing local managers to manage their own information and custom-tailor or modify strategic direction, goals, strategies, and implementation plans. Development directors play a key role in stakeholder analysis and implementation of an international strategy. While average daily rate is the primary factor in hotel market analysis, owners and franchisors also look at the demand generators, supply in the market, and the price of real estate.[28] What makes development more complex in international settings is the unique cultural differences in various markets. A study on the role of development directors in hotel expansion revealed that these individuals serve as critical intermediaries between opportunities in the market and the hotel group. The primary responsibilities of development directors include:

- Development of a strategic plan for the designated geographic area.
- Establishment of a network of productive contacts such as real estate developers, individual and institutional investors, hotel owners, hotel management companies, municipalities, and governmental development organizations.
- Selling the value proposition of the brand, particularly to potential franchisees.
- Assist franchisees with applications and fee payments, and develop relationships with existing local franchisees and owners.[29]

Of course, global stakeholder management is even more taxing than analysis. Going global offers many new management challenges. The fact is that Europeans and the Japanese have different views of business and manage differently from American managers, although management techniques are slowly converging.[30] The following quotations are based on a recent study of differences in management perspectives and styles across the United States, Europe, and Japan, from a European managerial perspective. They illustrate the types of challenges American managers face when doing business abroad:

Jacopo Vittorelli, former deputy chairman of Pirelli: "If you have to close a plant in Italy, in France, in Spain or in Germany, you have to discuss the possibility with the State, the local communities, with the trade unions, everybody feels entitled to intervene. … Even the Church."

Andre Leysen, chairman of the supervisory board of Agfa Gevaert: "We work for profit, but also for people. On the other hand, in the U.S., profit dominates everything, and people are considered as a resource that you can take or leave. This is a major difference. Now you could say that the European philosophy is close to the Japanese. I do not think so. There is a fundamental difference between the two. Europe is an individualistic society whereas the Japanese society is based on the collective."

Justus Mische, member of the board in charge of personnel of Hoechst: "Europe, at least the big international firms in Europe, have a philosophy between the Japanese, long term, and the United States, short term."[31]

Although there are similarities among countries in specific regions of the world, there are also significant differences. It is a mistake to lump all European countries together, all Asian countries in another bloc, and all African or Middle Eastern countries in their respective groups. In fact, the difference between Indonesia and South Korea is probably greater than that between Japan and the United States.

The Danish culture is closer to the Indonesian culture than to the Swedish culture in terms of the mindscape characteristics. Let us take one aspect of the Danish culture as an example. In the Danish culture, the main purpose of interpersonal communication is to maintain a familiar atmosphere and convey affection. … It is impolite to explain things, because such an act assumes that someone is ignorant. It is also impolite to ask questions on anything beyond immediate personal concern, because the respondent may not know the answer. It is often considered aggressive to introduce new ideas. A foreign businessperson eager to discuss what is outside the immediate business needs is likely to be met with a strong, silent resistance. In contrast, in Sweden, the purpose of daily interpersonal communication is transmission of new information or frank feelings. One prefers to be silent unless he or she can convey an important message, while in Denmark one must keep talking. While Danes are affect-oriented, Swedes are performance-oriented.[32]

Management of internal stakeholders such as employees becomes difficult and complex when an organization operates in more than one country. Figure 10.1 illustrates the wide differences that exist from country to country regarding assumptions about manager/subordinate relationships. In countries such as the United States, Sweden, the Netherlands, and Denmark, managers are typically not expected to have precise answers to subordinates' questions. In France, Italy, Indonesia, and Japan, most employees expect managers to be able to deal with most of their questions in a precise manner. Working in different parts of the world takes tremendous human resources know-how and sensitivity to cultural values. Communication can often be a challenge because of language differences and conflicts are common between expatriates and local managers and staff. The challenges that Four Seasons' managers faced when opening a hotel in Bali, Indonesia, are instructive.

Although there were more than 10,000 applicants eager to fill the 580 jobs at the Four Seasons Resort Bali, virtually none were able to speak English, and many didn't have

| FIGURE 10.1 | **CROSS-CULTURAL HUMAN RESOURCE DIFFERENCES** |

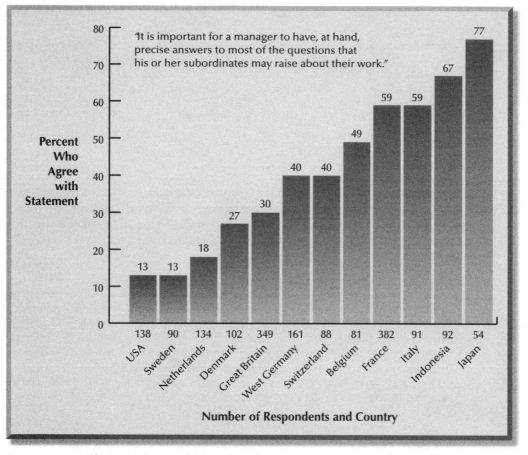

Source: A. Laurent, "The Cross-Cultural Puzzle of International Human Resource Management," *Human Resource Management* 25 (1986), p. 94, Copyright © 1986 by John Wiley & Sons, Inc. This material is used by permission of John Wiley & Sons, Inc.

any concept about world cuisine and western customs. The traditional corporate training methods were fairly useless in educating the indigenous population. The gracious and hospitable Balinese people did not need to be taught the concept of service, they just needed it refined. "It was the specifics of western culture that the native workers needed to learn, like milk goes with cereal, butter goes on toast, and ketchup goes with fries," noted Reny Ratman, director of HR. Middle management and expatriate staff also had several misunderstandings about compensation and allowances packages. Many of the problems were made more difficult because Indonesians avoid conflict. Senior managers five years after the opening still felt they needed to change their focus and proceed slowly so there is time to learn and overcome differences.[33]

Corporate training programs designed to teach operating standards don't always deliver when applied in new cultural setting, but management training can do a lot to help firms cope with global stakeholder management. Companies are sending some of their managers to special training programs to help increase their global awareness and vision. The School of Hotel Administration at Cornell University provides instruction for hundreds of industry professionals from around the world each year through its professional development and general managers programs. The University of Michigan recently provided an intensive, in-depth five-week program for twenty-one executives from Japan, the United States, Brazil, Great Britain, and India to help them become global thinkers. The program first made the participants more aware of the differences that existed between them. Then the trainers helped the participants to work out these differences. The training program was so successful that organizers are planning to make it an annual event.[34] Some South Korean firms have thorough training programs. An example is the use of "culture houses." An employee who will be sent to Germany, for example, is put in a "German house," where the employee is confined until he or she is able to eat, live, and sleep like a German.[35]

Government stakeholders are among the most difficult for a global firm to manage. The level of involvement of government administrators and regulators varies widely from nation to nation. For example, in two Egyptian Red Sea resort cities, Hurghada and Sharm El-Sheikhled, overbuilding and underpricing led the Ministry of Tourism and the Red Sea governate to stop issuing licenses for new hotels. According to the ministry, the decision to end hotel development will put a stop to price wars and a deterioration of service quality.[36]

> Keeping quality high at the Red Sea's resorts is a top priority for the Ministry of Tourism. Hotels that fail to maintain quality standards in keeping with the number of stars they carry are warned and then degraded in ranking. "We are going to take action to maintain our standard worldwide," says Elhamy ElZayat, chairman of the Egyptian Federation of Tourist Chambers.[37]

A communist government such as China has firm control over economic factors, whereas the U.S. government favors more of an open-market system.

> China can be a frustrating place to do business. One of the biggest sources of frustration is the government. China's leaders insist on a high level of control over most aspects of business in their country. Furthermore, the whims of government leaders sometimes take precedence over official rules and laws. For example, Chinese leaders wanted their government's English-language television channel to be broadcast in America in exchange for allowing AOL–Time Warner to connect its services to a few million Chinese homes. Also, Beijing often makes companies officially recognize China's claim on Taiwan before they are allowed to conduct business in the country.
>
> When the Chinese government talks about reforms, they probably are not exactly what most Westerners would expect. According to President Shangquan Gao of the Chinese Economic Reform Foundation, one of the goals of the reforms is that "The state sector is to have more dominance in the national economy in accordance with the fundamental transformation of the economic structure and economic growth mode, and with the needs of opening up further to the outside world." It may seem like a contradiction to proclaim movement toward more state dominance combined with opening up to the outside world; however, this is the mindset of a lot of Chinese leaders. Basically, China wants to retain its monopoly of state ownership in areas such as state security, all industries that supply major products or services to Chinese citizens, and in high or emerging technologies. Leaders also want to control many large and extra-large businesses or groups of businesses in major industrial sectors and highly profitable industries. A final goal is "Withdrawing state ownership from generally competitive

industries in a step-by-step and planned manner." One might draw the conclusion from this reform plan that the Chinese government is only interested in releasing absolute control of areas that it sees as unprofitable or unimportant.

As Chinese government officials retire and are replaced by new leaders, China's economic policies may be revised. However, it is unlikely that China will relinquish its firm grip on the economy. Nevertheless, business opportunities in China will undoubtedly continue to draw foreign investors.[38]

Why do organizations enter such difficult environments? In a word, opportunity. China is a huge market. As David Martinez, who oversees international growth for Starwood Hotels and Resorts put it, "China is a big but growing, awakening giant (for American business)."[39] Hotel companies based in the United States continue to see opportunity in developing hotels throughout Asia. The high barriers to entry that can inhibit construction in the United States and Western Europe are less of an issue in many Asian cities, where desirable sites can be found in existing and emerging heavily trafficked business districts.[40] Other countries in the region, such as South Korea and Vietnam, are seeing some of the same forces driving their growth. In 2003, Starwood Hotels opened its first property in Vietnam and Ramada International Hotels & Resorts, a division of Marriott International, opened its first hotel in South Korea. The section on international market selection at the end of this chapter highlights some of the issues that must be addressed when looking at a specific foreign market.

How should a hospitality firm enter new international markets? A common approach is to enter a new country with a foreign partner that understands the government system. At a minimum, a firm should hire employees and managers who are natives of the host country and have significant business experience specifically to handle government issues such as regulations and taxes. In the Beijing headquarters of McDonald's, only one American, a Chinese speaker, is on the staff. In Japan, decisions in this large quick-service restaurant chain have been in the hands of locals since the company opened its first store in 1971.[41]

> Starwood plans to establish a foothold in China's gateway cities, such as Shanghai and Beijing, through management agreements. "We'll use upscale flags in primary markets as the hub around which we want to build broader distribution," according to David Martinez. Accor continues to expand its mainland China network with plans to operate 9 new hotels by 2004. The Ibis Tianjin will be the first internationally managed economy hotel concept in mainland, funded totally by Accor. "Michael Issenberg, managing director of Accor Asia Pacific, said that the expansion was well timed to take advantage of China's growing domestic travel market while putting Accor hotel brands prominently in the minds of China's potentially huge outbound traveling public.[42]

GLOBAL RESOURCE ADVANTAGES

One of the major advantages of global involvement is that organizations can draw from a much broader and more diversified pool of resources—including human resources; physical resources such as supplies and locations; and technological know-how.[43]

Michael Porter, whose name should now be familiar to you, expanded his analyses of competitive environments to include the global economy. In his book *The Competitive Advantage of Nations,* he developed arguments concerning why some nations produce so many stellar companies in particular industries. For example, Germany is the home base for several top luxury-car manufacturers, and Switzerland has many leading companies in pharmaceuticals and chocolate. The United States is the undisputed world leader in the entertainment industry. Porter explains that four characteristics of countries actually create an environment that is conducive to creating globally competitive firms in certain business areas. The four characteristics are:

- *Factor Conditions.* Some nations enjoy special endowments such as uncommon raw materials or laborers with specific skills or training. Often countries with excellent schools or universities that excel in particular areas produce laborers with superior skills. For example, Japan is well known for producing graduates with outstanding quantitative and technical skills.

- *Demand Conditions.* If a nation's buyers of a particular product or service are the most discriminating and demanding in the world, then firms must achieve product and service excellence just to survive. Since they are so good, these companies can easily outperform foreign companies that compete in the same industry, even in the home countries of those foreign competitors. For example, American consumers are very discriminating in their consumption of movies and theme parks. Consequently, American entertainment companies are very competitive, even in foreign markets and against home-country rivals.

- *Related and Supporting Industries.* If suppliers in a particular country are the very best in the world, then the companies that buy from them are at a relative advantage. Firms in related industries that are also global leaders can also help create a nationally based competitive advantage.

- *Firm Strategy, Structure, and Rivalry.* If the management techniques that are customary in the nation's businesses are conducive to success in a particular industry, then the firms in that nation are at a competitive advantage relative to firms from other countries. Another advantage can come from having an industry that attracts the most talented managers in the nation. Finally, if industry rivalry is strong in a particular industry, then firms are forced to excel. This is similar to the argument with regard to discriminating buyers.[44]

Basically, the reason companies can develop a highly competitive nucleus is that tough market environments create world-class competitors only if the competitors are also endowed with the resources they need to compete. If home markets are uncompetitive, firms will not be sufficiently motivated to produce a quality service or superior product. Greater efficiency and innovation are also found to be benefits of greater competition.[45] On the other hand, if home markets are highly competitive but the factors of production, support industries, and human talent are not available, firms will likewise be incapable of producing globally competitive products.

Some firms buy foreign companies specifically to get a foothold in a world-class industry. For example, Vivendi, a French conglomerate, bought Universal Studios, with operations primarily in the United States. Vivendi Universal can now enjoy the learning benefits from competing head-to-head with other U.S. rivals in an environment with the most discriminating buyers. What Vivendi learns in the United States will help its theme-park joint venture in Japan and any other international theme-park ventures it decides to pursue.

The logical conclusion from Porter's analysis would seem to be to locate subsidiaries in the nations with the strongest home bases in particular industries. However, he argues that this is sometimes hard to do. First, it is difficult in some cases for an "outsider," a foreign firm, to become an "insider." In other words, it may be difficult for a foreign firm to tap into the sources of supply or obtain the highly valued resources that make home-base competitors so successful. Japan, in particular, is a tough nation to penetrate. Second, Porter suggests that it is difficult for the foreign subsidiary in the nation with the natural advantages to influence the parent company "long distance."[46]

Porter suggests that firms should take advantage of their own nation's natural-resource advantages. He also recommends that some of the principles that apply to the competitive advantages of nations can be applied in any company that wants to become more competitive in the world economy. Specifically, organizations can seek out the most discriminating buyers, choose from the best suppliers in the world, seek to excel against the most outstanding global competitors, form alliances with outstanding foreign competitors, and stay abreast of all research findings and innovations that are relevant to their core businesses.

MANAGEMENT OF FOREIGN SUBSIDIARIES

The role of foreign subsidiaries in a multinational company is changing from being treated as simply "branch locations" to a full role in the development of competencies, capabilities, resources, and products.[47] Some early models of multinational companies assumed that foreign subsidiaries would look more or less alike, except perhaps for size.[48] For example, if they were involved in marketing and sales, their structures and functions would be similar. If they were involved in production, their production facilities would be alike. However, multinational firms evolved toward a system that allowed each foreign subsidiary to play a different yet integrated role in the overall organization. Three levels of subsidiary responsibility emerged.

- *Local Implementation.* These subsidiaries have well-defined roles to play and little independence. These local implementers have a single-country scope of operations and, at most, might make minor adjustments to strategy to satisfy local markets.

- *Specialized Contribution.* These subsidiaries belong to an interdependent network of subsidiaries, often in a production role. Each subsidiary makes a unique contribution to the network.

- *Global Mandate.* These subsidiaries have responsibility for an entire global business, not just one part of the value chain. Activities are integrated by the subsidiary itself, instead of by the corporate office.[49]

The role each subsidiary will play depends on its capabilities and resources. If capabilities and resources are limited either by virtue of the country in which a subsidiary operates or by insufficient internal resources, then it might be assigned an implementation role. Subsidiaries that exist in countries with special advantages or that have specific internal-resource advantages are expected to make a specialized contribution. Subsidiaries with a global mandate must have substantial skills and resources from which to draw, both from the country environment and internally. In Shangri-La Hotels, for example, the principal activity of the company is investment holding, while the subsidiaries focus on operations.

The principal activities of the Company's subsidiaries are the ownership and operation of hotels and associated properties and the provision of hotel management and related services. The Company's subsidiaries are also registered proprietors of various trademarks and service marks in various countries, including the brand names "Shangri-La," "Traders," "Rasa," "Summer Palace," and "Shang Palace" and related devices and logos.[50]

Matrix and transnational structures, described in Chapter 8, help integrate activities across subsidiaries, especially where those subsidiaries have highly related activities. As responsibilities for determining strategies become more decentralized, integration across subsidiaries becomes more important.

These decentralized activities, located in highly differentiated subsidiaries, are tied together through intensive and extensive use of electronic communications. Of great importance, though, is the condition that these communications are no longer primarily vertical, from headquarters to subsidiary and back, but horizontal, directly from subsidiary to subsidiary. The global center participates only in headquarters-relevant issues, such as financial reporting, key account management, executive level management, and the like.[51]

The corporate office is responsible primarily for determining the role each subsidiary will play; however, managers of subsidiaries themselves will have a lot of influence on those decisions. Corporate-level managers should envision each subsidiary as a semiautonomous unit that has different skills and resources to contribute to a global network of subsidiaries. In such a situation, strong centralized control is not advisable.

So far, this discussion has assumed that organizations would like to integrate activities and build one integrated global strategy. However, some firms do not pursue such integration. These are companies whose subsidiaries are unrelated to each other. They are pursuing a global unrelated-diversification strategy. For example, corporate-level management could make resource-allocation decisions and reward subsidiary managers based on financial-performance indicators such as ROI. Also, corporate management could make decisions about buying and selling subsidiaries based on performance indicators or needs in the corporate portfolio. The integration activities described in this section are applicable only in situations in which organizations have enough commonality among their subsidiaries to pursue such things as economies of scale or economies of scope.

INTERNATIONAL ALLIANCES AND BUSINESS-FORMAT FRANCHISING

International strategic alliances are an outstanding way to acquire resources, specialized skills, or market knowledge. Resource combinations can lead to increased competitiveness. For example, India's Blue Coast Hotels is involved in a joint venture with Hilton Group PLC (Britain) to develop three hotels in a fast-growing New Delhi market.[52] Virgin Group, owner of Virgin Airlines and many other hospitality-related businesses, uses joint ventures extensively in a variety of areas:

Sprint Corp. and Richard Branson's Virgin Group Ltd. (announced) they have formed a joint venture to offer prepaid wireless telecom services and handsets to the youth market in the United States. Sprint, the No. 3 U.S. long-distance telephone company, beat rivals including AT&T Corp. to supply the U.S. network for a Virgin-branded service modeled after Virgin's wireless ventures in Britain and Australia. The two companies have been in talks since July. The new venture targets fifteen- to thirty-year-old consumers. Virgin will sell digital phones with services such as voice mail, messaging, and games. The company will begin retail sales in Virgin Megastores in New York and Los Angeles, said John Tantum, a senior Virgin executive.[53]

International franchising can be an extremely profitable tool to accomplish branding and growth. In the beginning, the first to export a business-format franchise model to markets outside of the United States were fast-food franchise powerhouses such as McDonald's and KFC (of parent company Yum! Brands).[54] Now these pioneers of international franchising are as common in many other countries as they are in the United States, and they have been joined by other food concepts, hotels and most of the major players in all industries that franchise. For many large franchisors today, the question is not where they have franchises, but rather where they do not.

Yum! Restaurants International (YRI) is the fastest growing and most profitable division of this quick-service restaurant (QSR) chain. In fact, KFC makes more profit outside the U.S.A. than in the U.S.A. In 2002, the YRI system opened a record 1,051 traditional restaurants. With over 6,000 KFCs and over 4,000 Pizza Huts, YRI has the second and third largest QSR brands outside the U.S. The company credits its strong joint venture and franchise partner base for its continued success in key growth markets.[55]

Selection of high-quality franchise partners is one of the most important factors in international markets. Tony Roma's, a Romacorp Inc. brand with the largest number of casual theme restaurants in the world, has found that selection of financially strong, well established, and operationally experienced franchise partners can make a huge difference between success and failure.[56] Operations expertise is key.

Tony Roma's with locations in 22 countries and five continents has franchise partners in every major region of the world. The franchise partners understand the system, understand the guests in their country and have the resources to provide world-class service on a daily basis. If they do not deliver outstanding experiences everyday, the brand is quickly tarnished, growth stops, and future reentry back into the market is almost impossible. Your international franchise partners must know what makes customers in their market tick and be able to deliver what they demand and expect from the brand. A quality franchise partner not only strengthens the concept in their country, but also provides a "worldwide billboard" for your brand.[57]

As mentioned in Chapter 9, business format franchising has been a common strategy for domestic expansion in the hospitality industry. In addition to helping create new businesses in a home country, franchising has historically been an important tool for international expansion. In this form of franchising, an ongoing business relationship between franchisor and franchisee includes the entire business concept itself, not just the product, service, and brand.[58] Marketing strategy, operating manuals and standards, quality control, and continuing assistance and guidance are elements of this type of franchising. "Franchising constitutes an alliance between at least two organizations, where each side benefits from the skill and resources held by (the) other. Independent hotels benefit from the global brand name of the international hotel chain and its reservations system. The franchising firm (foreign) gains quick, often smooth, access to a new market without the risk involved in ownership."[59] However, franchising is a lower-return strategy compared with equity investments in hotels abroad.[60] A franchise strategy may be more difficult outside of North America because of the lack of infrastructure in some countries. Finding franchisees with good sites to build on is also a challenge in light of regulations restricting hotel property development in Europe and other parts of the world.[61] A certain level of learning skill or absorptive capacity is required of a franchisee to adopt the business concept in the overseas location; studies in hotel franchising have shown that franchising is more likely in developed nations because of the greater likelihood that the global partners possess the needed organizational skills.[62] To help deal with the challenges of developing internationally, chains sometimes develop master franchisees as partners.

> TT Resources has the exclusive master franchise rights from Gloria Jean's Gourmet Coffees Franchising Corp for Malaysia, Singapore, Brunei, and Thailand. The five-year agreement allows it to grant sub-franchises for third parties to develop and operate outlets. It may also distribute coffee to hotels, restaurants and retailers. TT Resources has been a Gloria Jean's franchisee since 1999 for Malaysia, Singapore and Brunei. It has been a franchisee for Thailand since 2000. Under the new agreement, TT Resources has to open and operate at least 45 stores, which include existing ones, in Malaysia, Singapore and Brunei. It also has to open at least 25 stores, including existing ones, in Thailand. TT Resources also runs San Francisco Steakhouse, Tai Thong Chinese Restaurants, Shrooms and Stars Oyster & Sushi Bar.[63]

Master franchise agreements involve larger franchisees who have the rights to develop in a specific territory. Cendant, for example, continues to expand through master licenses. In contrast, Marriott doesn't master franchise as much, and not at all with its Ritz-Carlton brand.[64] Markets dictate whether franchising is used; for example, Marriott relies on franchising in Moscow and has a master franchise agreement with Whitbread in the United Kingdom. Often times a master franchise is used in nonstrategic or smaller markets. Curtis Nelson explained the Carlson Hotels' approach to using master franchise arrangements:

> Where you are established, where you have critical mass, it makes sense to do it yourself. Those partnerships are less beneficial the more you are established. It's less important to establish a new [master franchise] after you have distribution of a brand.[65]

Global competition is also causing firms to reevaluate how they acquire knowledge. "New knowledge provides the foundation for new skills, which in turn can lead to competitive success," according to Andrew Inkpen, an expert on international alliances. "In bringing together firms with different skills, knowledge bases, and organizational cultures, alliances create unique learning opportunities for partner firms."[66] For example, Marriott plans to work with a British hotel developer and a bank affiliated with Russia's oil giant Yukos to establish a national chain of forty to fifty midmarket and economy hotels in Russia over the next decade.[67] When it comes to international development the complexity of ownership and franchising rights can make hotel competitors also partners in some settings. These relationships and agreements can also shape decisions on which brands are and are not taken international. To illustrate, Cendant's growth overseas is through Howard Johnson and Days Inn because Marriott owns the franchising right of Ramada internationally, although Cendant has acquired the franchising right in Canada.[68] The Pritzker family of Hyatt Hotels owns the rights to Travelodge in Asia, and Cendant has the rights in North America and the Caribbean.

In summary, global organizations face a much more complicated management task due to diversity of stakeholders and resources. However, this diversity provides opportunities with regard to both stakeholder relationships and acquisition or development of resources that domestic companies do not enjoy. The way global firms manage their foreign subsidiaries has much to do with how they manage their resources. Also, firms can learn new technologies and acquire skills and other resources through international alliances. The next section deals with various strategies that companies apply as they approach global markets.

GLOBAL STRATEGIES

As firms approach international markets, they have several strategic decisions to make. They must select a general approach to their markets, decide on expansion tactics, and formulate global business-level and corporate-level strategies. These strategic decisions are the subject of this section.

GLOBAL PRODUCT/MARKET APPROACH

One of the key issues facing top managers as their organizations pursue international development is selection of a product/market approach. A multidomestic strategy entails handling the approach to the market on a country-by-country basis by tailoring the services provided around individual market needs. Many of the upscale and luxury hotel chains have followed this approach. On the other hand, organizations pursuing a global strategy standardize what they offer so that it is essentially the same in all markets.[69] This approach is more common in the economy and budget hotel brands and in the quick-service restaurant chains. Internationalization patterns in which some hotel companies focus on a global strategy are emerging, but the companies restrict their development to particular countries and locations. Another approach is to deploy a focused geographic strategy relying on a range of different hotel brands in specific countries.[70]

Multidomestic strategies are intuitively appealing from a stakeholder point of view, since they emphasize the satisfaction of segmented customer needs. However, customization may add more costs to the products or services than can be recaptured through higher prices.[71] As a counterargument, some researchers explain that a global product/market strategy is appropriate only if (1) there is a global market segment for a product or service, (2) there are economic efficiencies associated with a global strategy, (3) there are no external constraints, such as government regulations, that will prevent a global strategy from being implemented, and (4) there are no absolute internal constraints.[72]

Some organizations are pursuing a hybrid transnational product/market strategy. An international counterpart to the best-cost strategy discussed previously, a transnational strategy entails seeking both global efficiency and local responsiveness. McDonald's, for instance, has relied on a standardized American concept worldwide, but it has begun to more extensively acknowledge cultural, regional, and national differences, due in part to the criticism of "overarching Americanization" of the world.[73]. The difficult task of pursuing a hybrid strategy is accomplished through establishing an integrated network that fosters shared vision and resources while allowing individual decisions to be made to adapt to local needs.[74] Four Seasons' strategy can best be described as transnational, as the following excerpts demonstrate:

> According to David Richey, president of Richey International, a firm Four Seasons and other hotel chains hired to audit service quality, "Four Seasons has done an exceptional job of adapting to local markets. From a design perspective, they are much more clever than other companies. When you sit in the Four Seasons in Bali, you feel that you are in Bali. It does not scream Four Seasons at you."[75]

On the other hand, there are things about the Four Seasons approach that are the same:

> The seven Four Seasons "service culture standards" expected of all staff all over the world at all times were:
>
> - SMILE. Employees will actively greet guests, smile, and speak clearly in a friendly manner.
> - EYE: Employees will make eye contact, even in passing, with an acknowledgment.
> - RECOGNITION: All staff will create a sense of recognition by using the guest's name, when known, in a natural and discreet manner.
> - VOICE. Staff will speak to guests in an attentive, natural, and courteous manner, avoiding pretension and in a clear voice.
> - INFORMED: All guest contact staff will be well informed about their hotel, their product, will take ownership of simple requests, and will not refer guests elsewhere.
> - CLEAN: Staff will always appear clean, crisp, well-groomed, and well-fitted.
> - EVERYONE: Everyone, everywhere, all the time, will show their care for our guests.
>
> In addition to its service culture standards, Four Seasons had 270 core worldwide operating standards.[76]

INTERNATIONAL EXPANSION TACTICS

Firms can apply a variety of expansion tactics as they pursue global opportunities. In hotels, most chains rely on several tactics including, franchising, joint ventures, management contracts, ownership, and acquisitions, while restaurant chains tend to focus on franchising. Generally speaking, among the most common tactics are:

- *Exporting.* Transferring goods to other countries for sale through wholesalers or a foreign company. Because hospitality firms tend to focus on services rather than goods, this tactic is not particularly relevant.
- *Contractual Arrangements,* such as:
  - *Licensing.* Selling the right to use a brand name in a foreign market. This right typically comes with restrictions that allow the licensing firm to protect its brand image.
  - *Franchising.* Similar to licensing, but franchising typically requires more standardization on the part of the franchisee. A foreign firm buys the legal right to use the name, but it may also be required to apply operating methods or

use supplies from the franchisor company. Marketing arrangements vary, but a lodging franchisee is typically a part of the companywide reservation system. Also, the franchisee typically contributes to a companywide advertising pool. Both hotels and restaurants use this tactic extensively.

- *Long-term Management Contract:* A contract between an owner and a management company. The owner agrees to make a payment from the operation's gross revenues to the management company in exchange for running the business with full management responsibility. This is a common hotel tactic for expansion.

- *Foreign Direct Investment,* such as:

  - *Joint Venture.* Cooperative agreement among two or more companies to pursue common business objectives.

  - *Wholly Owned Subsidiary.* Venture is started from scratch, thus creating a wholly owned foreign subsidiary. These ventures are sometimes called a "greenfield investment."

  - *Acquisition.* Purchase of a foreign firm or the foreign subsidiary of a foreign or domestic firm.[77]

Among the most important criteria when deciding on an option for international growth are cost, financial risk, profit potential, and control. In general, moving down the list of alternatives from first to last entails greater cost and greater financial risk, but also greater profit potential and greater control. Consequently, these alternatives represent a trade-off between cost and financial risk on one hand, and profit and control on the other. Of course, this is a gross generalization. Some of the options, such as joint ventures and acquisitions, are hard to judge on the basis of these four criteria because the exact nature of the agreement can vary so widely from deal to deal. For any international growth decision, these options should be weighed using real data on cost, risk, profit potential, and control, rather than generalizations. Hotel operators tend to rely on more than one of these options, although they may favor a particular approach to others. Accor, for example, has altered its strategy to focus more on growing the company through franchising and management contracts and less on building new hotels.[78] For fast growth acquisition of regional firms and joint ventures are also popular. Choice Hotels International's 55 percent stake in Melbourne-based Flag Hotels is an example of buying local expertise in a market with high barriers to quick growth.[79]

Another factor that seems to influence the decision among international growth options is multinational diversity. Firms that operate in diverse multinational environments have a greater capacity to learn and develop resources and skills. These types of firms are more likely to start a business in a foreign environment, with or without partners, than they are to acquire one.[80] Strategies in service businesses may vary from what produces success in other industries, as Kurt Ritter, Rezidor SAS's president and CEO, observes:

> Big mergers have not shown major economic benefits. Yes, there will be near-term opportunities for takeovers and rebranding, but we believe more in organic growth. Mixing cultures is much harder in the hotel industry than in manufacturing.[81]

Research demonstrates some of the major differences between Western and Japanese firms in the way they enter foreign markets. U.S. firms tend to favor big overseas investments, often through acquisitions. On the other hand, Japanese firms favor sequential investment. They make frequent, smaller investments in foreign operations over a long period. "Typically, Japanese companies make a small initial investment in their core businesses and expand their operations if this investment performs well. The companies might later make big investments."[82] Sequential entry can help an organization reduce the risks associated with foreign investments, regardless of which method of entry is used.

GLOBAL BUSINESS-LEVEL STRATEGY

World markets provide outstanding opportunities with regard to business-level strategy. Organizations that are involved in multiple global markets have advantages available to them in pursuing their business-level strategies. Examples of the many options available for improving competitive position vis-à-vis a global strategy include the following:

- Expanding markets leading to economies of scale. Some companies could not grow large enough to enjoy the lowest possible costs on the basis of domestic demand alone. However, expansion into foreign markets can lead to significant increases in demand.

- Transfer of technological know-how through joint venture (learning from competitors). Joint ventures may provide opportunities to learn new technologies that can lead to significant cost reductions.

- Superior quality through joint venture. Just as U.S. companies can learn cost-saving technologies through joint ventures, they can also learn how to better differentiate their products through higher quality or some other unique feature.

- Licensing of brands or technologies from abroad.

- Forcing an open, learning mind-set. Companies that attempt to differentiate themselves in the international marketplace must develop an innovative mind-set or culture and must be willing to learn from and adapt to a variety of conflicting circumstances. They can then bring what they learn back to the home country and apply it to local businesses.[83]

While world markets provide many opportunities, pursuing these opportunities creates additional costs and risks. Managing businesses in foreign countries can result in additional costs associated with such things as travel, communications (including translation costs), export and import duties and tariffs, transportation of products, advertising, taxes, and fees. In addition, managers may find themselves unable to understand or effectively manage businesses in countries that are unfamiliar to them. This is another reason why hiring a local manager may be desirable.

> The first McDonald's in Japan was a fifty-fifty partnership between McDonald's and Den Fujita. He overruled McDonald's American management for the choice of the first site; instead of choosing a suburban Tokyo drive-in, he chose a high-rent location right in the centre of Tokyo, which he said would give the little known McDonald's brand more prestige. He argued that in order for McDonald's to succeed in Japan it must appear to be a 100% Japanese operation. Den Fujita also asked that the spelling of McDonald's be changed to make it easier for the Japanese to pronounce, so it became "Makudonarudo." While McDonald's would not permit deviation for its operating principles, it did permit Fujita more freedom in the marketing area. At the McDonald's

twenty-fifth anniversary celebration in Tokyo, Fujita (now in his seventies) set a goal for McDonald's Japan to have 10,000 restaurants by 2006.[84]

Many risks are associated with global expansion. Organizations face the risk that citizens in some countries may not be receptive to some foreign services because of prejudices they hold against the home countries of the companies providing the services. Also, the risks associated with managing international joint ventures and currency translations were discussed previously. These are only a few of many potential risks. Wise selection of countries in which to pursue opportunities can reduce costs and risks associated with global expansion.

INTERNATIONAL MARKET SELECTION

Significant changes in the global environment have created great opportunities for organizations that are willing to take a risk and wait patiently for returns. However, these changes have also created significant challenges. Some of the greatest management challenges are experienced by firms entering developing countries—an unstable government, inadequately trained workers, low levels of supporting technology, shortages of supplies, weak transportation systems, and an unstable currency. Furthermore, problems in the financial markets of one emerging nation can have ripple effects on financial markets in other emerging nations.

> Argentina's stock market jumped 8.2 percent, and emerging-market bonds rallied following an $8 billion rescue package from the International Monetary Fund, the IMF's latest effort to head off a potential default in emerging markets. Still, jitters remain. Both investors fear that the aid package won't stave off substantial restructuring of Argentina's $130 billion in public debt. If Argentina is forced to restructure, the process could be far more complicated than previous restructuring efforts by countries like Ecuador and Russia. "A really nasty restructuring would highlight the problems with lending to emerging markets," says Abigail McKenna, an emerging-markets portfolio manager for Morgan Stanley Asset Management. "If the restructuring in Argentina turns out to be a disaster, it could really mar prospects not just for Argentine bonds, but for other emerging-market bonds, too."[85]

Firms also have to struggle with managing stakeholders that are typically very different—in values, beliefs, ethics, and in many other ways—from stakeholders found in the industrialized countries. However, firms that are "first-movers" into developing countries may be able to develop stakeholder-based advantages such as long-term productive contractual and informal relationships with host-country governments and organizations that followers won't have the opportunity to develop. For example, Spanish firms took huge risks by making major investments in Latin America during the first wave of privatizations, and they are now firmly entrenched in one of the world's fastest-growing regions. According to one large Spanish bank executive with significant investments in Latin America: "It's not a new frontier for Spanish companies because we discovered America in 1492. But it's a growth frontier. It's a financial rediscovery of the Americas."[86] Actually, growth in gross domestic product in Latin America averaged 3.2 percent during the 1990s, while poverty decreased dramatically.[87]

In North America, the North American Free Trade Agreement has done much to open up borders and stimulate trade between the United States and its neighbors, Canada and Mexico. In fact, rightly or wrongly, NAFTA is sometimes credited with creating jobs in both Mexico and the United States.[88] After passage of NAFTA more U.S. chain hotels made their presence felt in Mexico and other major hotels throughout Mexico expanded and upgrade their facilities.[89] Mexico has four high-tech convention centers—in Cancun, Monterey, Guadalajara, and Acapulco. The Mexican Tourism Secretariat, SECTUR, plans to develop these areas with support from the private sector. Mexican President Vicente Fox, educated in the United States, has a pro-business attitude.[90] Some U.S. companies are now thriving in Mexico, which is reshaping the Mexican economy.

> Whether the Free Trade Area of the Americas (FTAA)—a proposal to create the world's largest free-trade zone—will actually be implemented by its 2005 deadline remains to be seen, but should it move forward, Cancun is ready to reap the benefits. According to Mexican impresario Francisco de Paula Leon Olea, president of Hemisferia, the $300 million venture will bring trade shows, conventions, and other forums for international exchange to the tip of the Yucatan Peninsula, "with the idea of stimulating free trade. We wanted to create a meeting point of the Americas," he explains. "Cancun is the geographical center and has all the necessary infrastructure—airlift, hotels, plus cultural attractions." The governor of Quintana Roo state, meanwhile, is pushing Hemisferia in the hopes it can attract enough conventions and trade shows to offset the tourism shortfall during the September-December slow season."[91]

Surprisingly, Canada offers economic advantages compared to other industrialized nations, especially with regard to starting new businesses. A 1999 KPMG study of business costs in the United Kingdom, the United States, Japan, Italy, Austria, Canada, France, and Germany found that Canada was the least expensive country in which to build a business. The results are fairly consistent across nine industries studied.[92] Organizations that want to establish centralized call centers are finding that they can operate in Canada for 15 percent to 35 percent less than in the United States. In addition, Canada offers "an available quality labor force that delivers excellent and loyal customer-attracting-and-retaining service, sales and tech support."[93] Fortunately the outbreaks of Severe Acute Respiratory Syndrome (SARS) in Toronto, Ontario, had a relatively modest impact on the economy as a whole, but they severely damaged the hotel, restaurant, and airline sectors of the industry.[94]

> "To the rest of the world (and even to a great many Canadians) Canada is known as the country where everything is cooked in maple sugar." So said the editors in the foreword to Jehane Benoit's 1963 Encyclopedia of Canadian Cuisine, which set out to shatter those stereotypes. The epicurean entrepreneurs have carried on Mme. Benoit's legacy; 40 years later, Canadians can boast of exquisite, first-class hotels and restaurants, and towns like Sooke Harbour that have become world famous. By taking advantage of the bounty of the country's farms and fields, these hospitality stars have made Canada a sweet place to visit for just a meal or an entire vacation.[95]

Another region with a lot of potential is Asia. The "Pacific Century" refers to a forecast that the world's growth center for the twenty-first century will shift across the Pacific Ocean to Asia. Asia is already the world's biggest consumer of steel and the second-fastest-growing market for automobiles. It is General Electric's fastest-growing market.[96] The newly industrialized economies (NIEs) of South Korea, Taiwan, Hong Kong, and Singapore have experienced growth in real gross domestic product at a much higher level than Europe, Japan, or the United States.[97]

While many Western hotel companies have turned their attention to Asia, many Asian hotel companies continue to prosper. International arrivals and domestic travel have been growing in China. Because of the comparative cost advantage of operations in China, manufacturing industries are also relocating to the country. The 2008 Olympic games and the 2010 World Expo, both in China, will provide further economic stimulus. A few examples of Asian-based hotel companies include the following:

> The Hongkong and Shanghai Hotels, Ltd. (Peninsula Group), owns and operates deluxe hotels in international gateway cities, with roots to 1866 and the cities of Hong Kong and Shanghai. This chain has been guided by the Kadoorie family for most of its long history.
>
> New World Development is a large conglomerate strategically focused on Hong Kong and Mainland China. The group's core businesses include property, infrastructure, service, and telecommunications. Their property development portfolio is focused on residential and an investment property portfolio comprising shopping malls, offices, hotels, and service apartments. Their hotel portfolio includes fourteen hotels in Hong Kong, Mainland China, and Southeast Asia.
>
> In India, the Indian Hotels Company is the largest hotel chain in the country, operating the Taj hotels, palaces and resorts. A few of the fourteen subsidiaries are KTC Hotels Ltd. Asia Pacific Hotels Ltd., St. James Court Hotel Ltd., and United Hotels Ltd.
>
> Finally, the Hong Kong-based Shangri-La Hotels and Resorts is the largest Asian-based deluxe hotel group in the region with forty-one deluxe hotels and resorts in key cities of Asia and the Middle East.[98]

China, with more than one billion potential consumers, will provide much of the growth in demand for consumer products over the next several decades.[99] An "open door" policy on the part of the Chinese government has made China the largest recipient of foreign direct investment among developing nations and second among all nations (after the United States).[100] Nevertheless, there are huge risks and difficulties for foreign firms operating in China. Management fraud is a widespread problem.[101] The government dominates the economy through its control over the infrastructure, utilities, pricing, and distribution networks. A subsidiary's board must be chaired by a Chinese citizen, who is nominated by the Communist Party.[102] Successful foreign companies in China form excellent relationships with the government, use joint ventures, make large investments, and "stick it out" over the long term.[103]

> Up to now, China has been the biggest success story in Asian hotel development as U.S.-based hotel companies vie to establish a foothold in what is the region's single largest market. While China remains a development powerhouse, the pace of development is growing in other destinations as well.
>
> Asia-based hotel companies also are expanding their portfolios in the region and are eager to broaden the number of U.S.-based corporations with which they work. Consequently, they may be more willing to negotiate favorable rates as a way of building trial usage with these accounts. Hong Kong-based Shangri-La Hotels and Resorts, for example, in February opened a 120-room hotel in the Putrajaya district of Kuala Lumpur, Malaysia. Putrajaya is the administrative capital of Malaysia's federal government. Reflecting the depth of inventory that local hotel companies have in these markets, Putrajaya is Shangri-La's seventh property in Malaysia.[104]

Japan enjoyed a long period of economic growth and expansion during the 1980s and early 1990s. However, the "economic bubble" burst in 1992. Over the next several years, the yen declined dramatically against U.S. currency, property prices plummeted, and the Nikkei stock market index dropped precipitously. The unemployment rate increased to an unprecedented level, and business investment dropped off. Now an already competitive market has become even more competitive, especially for foreign companies.[105] In what might be called "post-bubble" Japan, much is changing. Table 10.2 describes some of these changes and their implications. Successful foreign companies in Japan are those that understand the Japanese market and play by Japanese rules.[106] High levels of technological capability are also important.[107]

TABLE 10.2	**CHANGES IN JAPAN AFTER THE ECONOMIC BUBBLE BURST**		
Factor	**Pre-Bubble Japan**	**Post-Bubble Change**	**Implications for Foreign-Owned Affiliates**
Japanese business environment	Major obstacles to success in Japan were high operating costs and extreme competitiveness.	Remains a tough, highly competitive environment; price destruction, distribution becoming more concentrated; increasing expectations of fast retailer response.	Power brands; vertical integration to encompass retail sector.
Consumers	Japanese consumers very willing to adopt new products; they work hard and long to support radical spending habits.	Increased balance between work and family; some convergence with "international values."	More and different products consumed in the home.
Heritage	Cramped living conditions in Japanese cities and high concern for aesthetics made Japanese consumers a ready target for luxury products.	Luxury designer products hold strong, but consumers are more price/value conscious; luxury products sold through discount outlets.	Quality and image remain important but are supplemented by functional and value claims.
Consumer interest	Japanese consumers delighted in foreign travel and out-of-home experiences; led to preference for foreign designer brands with premium pricing.	More focus on home; more value-for-money-driven behavior; increased emphasis on functional performance, less brand devotion.	Justify positioning of brands and price levels, value-driven positioning; stress on dependability and function.
Product churning	Japanese companies were known for churning out new products regardless of justification.	Reduction in product-emulation activity.	Products must have genuine consumer justification.
Insider strategy	Success for foreign-owned companies believed to be associated with becoming a part of Japanese "insider," an integral part of the business community.	May still be true, but foreign-owned companies attempting "insider" strategies are struggling.	Adopt those aspects of "insiderism" that are financially justified.
Marketing skills	The pace of change in Japan required a sharpening of marketing skills.	Marketers in Japan still maintain dedicated dialogue with consumers.	Need to gear up to track consumer.

Source: Reprinted with permission from *Journal of International Marketing,* published by the American Marketing Association, D.M. Reid, "Changes in Japan's Post-Bubble Business Environment: Implications for Foreign-Affiliated Companies," 7 (1999): 38–63.

Changes in Europe have made it increasingly important for U.S. companies to be involved there. Privatization programs in the United Kingdom and elsewhere and a fundamental restructuring of the financial capital markets in countries such as Germany have put a lot more assets into the hands of private citizens.[108] A common currency (the euro) and reduction of trade barriers among many European countries have created a more open market of 340 million consumers.[109] Also, differentiation is easier to achieve because organizations can draw freely from the strengths of each nation. Companies that have businesses in Europe already enjoy the advantages of a typically well-educated workforce, a well-developed infrastructure, a sophisticated level of technology, and high consumer demand—all factors that are associated with First World countries. The recent changes in Europe make it even more attractive for investment.

Restaurant chains are making strides in Europe, attracted by the size of the market and the consumer's growing interest in American food. For example, Foster's Hollywood restaurants franchisee, Madrid-based Grupo Zena, operates twenty-five of these restaurants across Spain and has found that American-themed casual dining is a natural culinary product for young European consumers who view American food as being like Italian, Chinese, and Korean.[110] According to a study conducted at the turn of the century by PricewaterhouseCoopers, the hotel sector in Europe has changed faster in the past ten years than at any time in history. With around five million hotels in Europe, mostly in the countries of Italy, Germany, France, Spain, and the United Kingdom; this regional market also is the world's largest for hotel inventory. With around 80 percent of its hotel inventory unbranded, the industry is still fragmented, although the degree of branding varies by country. The Pricewaterhouse Coopers study made the following observations about the structure of the industry:

> Global brands, European regional brands and the independent sector through marketing consortia are all fighting for market share. The industry is being driven by rising travel volumes, rising living standards, and the incentive provided by a weak Euro to internal travel. Most of these features reflect the increasing globalization that is taking place internationally across all sectors, coupled with the expansion of the tourism industry itself; some are features that are specifically a result of the New Europe.[111]

Foreign investment in Russia and the old Soviet bloc is also increasing. However, businesses that desire to invest in Russia often face huge hurdles stemming from "historical precedent as well as the government's mishandling of the economic transition during the 1990s."[112] In the aftermath of the September 11, 2001 attacks, Russian relations with the United States improved dramatically.

> When retired General Fyodor I. Ladygin, a former head of Russian military intelligence, first heard reports that U.S. military cargo planes had landed in the former Soviet republic of Uzbekistan in Central Asia, he figured the Americans had cut a sly deal with the Uzbeks without consulting the Russians. No way, Ladygin told *Business Week* on September 24 (2001), would Russian President Vladimir V. Putin give a green light to stationing the U.S. military in Russia's own backyard. Wrong prediction, General: In a speech that very evening on national television, Putin voiced support for such deployments to assist the U.S.-led campaign against international terrorism. Of all the surprising developments the world has witnessed since the attack on the World Trade Center, the sudden rapprochement between Russia and the United States is one of the most startling.[113]

Many characteristics must be evaluated when considering a foreign country for investment. Many of them fall within the general areas of the broad environment, including the social environment, the economy, the political/legal environment, and the state of technology. Other characteristics are related to specific industries and markets. Questions concerning each of these factors are listed in Table 10.3. These questions are a useful tool for evaluating a potential country for investment.

The wrong answers to any of the questions in Table 10.3 can make a country less attractive. The following are examples that demonstrate this point: (1) an unstable government can greatly increase the risk of a total loss of investment; (2) an inefficient transportation system can reduce demand because people cannot get to hotels, casinos, or other properties; (3) inadequate school systems can result in poorly skilled workers, who may not have the ability to work at a high level of quality; (4) a slowly growing GNP could mean that consumer demand will be sluggish; (5) high foreign tax rates can virtually eliminate profits; and (6) if the local currency cannot be translated into U.S. dollars, the organization will have a tough time removing profits from the country.

One of the most important factors to consider when deciding whether to enter a country is the state of its capital markets. Some economies support very well developed capital

---

TABLE 10.3	**EXAMPLES OF QUESTIONS TO ASK ABOUT A POTENTIAL FOREIGN MARKET**

Social Forces

What currently are the hot topics of debate? How well organized are special-interest groups with regard to the environment, labor, and management issues? Are current policies or behaviors of the organization likely to be offensive in the new host country? What is the attitude of potential consumers toward foreign products/services? Will there be significant cultural barriers to overcome? How difficult is the language? How old is the population? What other differences could cause difficulty for the organization?

The Economy

What is the inflation rate? How large is the gross national product (GNP)? How fast is it growing? What is income per capita? How much impact does the global economy have on the domestic economy? How high is the unemployment rate? What actions does the government take to fuel economic growth? What is the trade balance with the United States? Can the currency be exchanged for the home currency? How high are interest rates? Is the financial sector well organized? How expensive are the factors of production?

Political/Legal Environment

What is the form of government? How much influence does the government have over business? Is the government stable? What is the attitude of the government toward private enterprise and U.S. firms? What is the attitude of the home government toward the foreign government? How high are tax rates compared with the home country? How are taxes assessed and collected? How high are import and export taxes? What is the nature of the court system? Is legal protection available through incorporation or a similar form?

Technology

Is the country technologically advanced? Do schools and universities supply qualified workers? Are the required skills available in sufficient quantity? Are suitable information systems available? Is the infrastructure sound (i.e., roads, transportation systems)? Is an appropriate site available?

Industry Specific

How large is the industry? How fast is it growing? Can it be segmented? How many competitors are there? How strong are they? What is the relative position of industry participants in relation to suppliers and customers? Are substitute products available? What is the primary basis for competition? Is there a possibility of reaching the market through a joint venture?

markets with very efficient financial transactions, while other economies are less well developed (see Figure 10.2). Market-centered economies have well-developed infrastructures, business environments, and external capital markets. Laws and regulations regarding capital markets are well developed and enforced. The capital market is not dominated by either equity or debt as a source of funding. Examples are the United States and the United Kingdom. Bank-centered economies also have well-developed infrastructures and business environments. However, capital markets are not as strong as in the United States or the United Kingdom. Banks and other financial institutions play the most significant role in the external capital markets. One of the advantages of this system is that banks are willing to let companies take on higher debt levels, and then are willing to help the borrowers through tough times. Examples of bank-centered economies are Japan and Germany.

In family-centered economies, families hold a lot of the stock in large corporations, allowing them control. A pyramidal structure is often used to maintain control.[114] At the lower levels, the parent company holds stock in its subsidiaries. At the next level, different parent companies are linked to a large financial institution. At the highest level, these financial institutions are interconnected through "capital networks and interlocking directorates." A good example of a family-centered economy is France, where about a third of the largest companies are still managed by their founders or heirs. Other examples are Sweden and Italy.

Group-centered economies such as South Korea do not have strong financial systems. Groups of companies manage the use of internal capital as a replacement for external capital markets. This system is sometimes created because only the government is able to borrow abroad. The government then channels borrowed money into particular sectors. Firms in those sectors secure funds from the government, diversify their portfolios, and then recycle capital into other ventures. Finally, emerging economies such as Russia and China historically are dominated by government ownership of the economic enterprise, with very little development of financial capital markets. Some of these economies are now pursuing

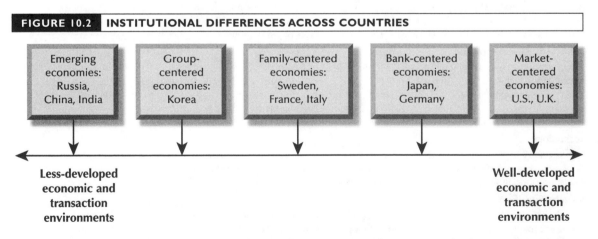

FIGURE 10.2 **INSTITUTIONAL DIFFERENCES ACROSS COUNTRIES**

| Emerging economies: Russia, China, India | Group-centered economies: Korea | Family-centered economies: Sweden, France, Italy | Bank-centered economies: Japan, Germany | Market-centered economies: U.S., U.K. |

Less-developed economic and transaction environments ⟵ ⟶ **Well-developed economic and transaction environments**

Source: R. E. Hoskisson et al., "Restructuring Strategies of Diversified Business Groups: Difference Associated with Country Institutional Environments," in *The Blackwell Handbook of Strategic Management,* ed. M. A. Hitt, R. E. Freeman and J. S. Harrison (Oxford: Blackwell Publishing, 2001), 444. Used with permission.

privatization programs that put economic assets in the hands of private citizens. These programs are experiencing varying levels of success.[115] One notable success story for private enterprise comes from Prince Karim Aga Khan IV, spiritual head of the world's Ismaili Shia Muslims and venture capitalist to the Third World. Through his economic development institutions, he is increasingly taking equity positions in small-scale commercial enterprises including hotels and lodges in Africa.

> Prince Aga Khan was early to push the idea that the dispossessed could find hope in private economic enterprise. He grasped that government handouts and multilaterally funded megaprojects—like those from the United Nations or the World Bank—can often foster dependence in the people they're meant to help. Instead, the Aga Khan's goal is to spur sustainable economic development and individual self-reliance at the grassroots level in South and Central Asia and Africa. Poor countries like Tanzania, Pakistan, and the former Soviet republic of Tajikistan don't otherwise hold much hope of attracting high-profile foreign investors.
>
> The Aga Khan Development Network focuses largely on health care, early childhood and female education, building business opportunities, clean water, farming, and housing. However, tourism is another success story, particularly in Kenya, where the Network's Tourism Promotion Services Ltd. is traded on the local stock exchange. Tourism has been the major generator of foreign exchange—in some cases it has overtaken the traditional foreign exchange earners of tea and coffee. Aga Khan–funded companies have built three lodges in Kenyan game parks and reserves, and hotels in Nairobi and on the Mombasa coast. In 1997–98 the company added three new lodges and a luxury tented camp in Tanzania's fabled Serengeti game reserve and a big hotel on the island of Zanzibar.[116]

STRATEGIC MANAGEMENT IN HOSPITALITY FIRMS IN THE FUTURE

Without question, the greatest managerial challenges lie ahead. It is hard to predict with precision the kind of business environment the next generation of managers will face; however, judging from the recent past, it will probably be associated with increasing global complexity and interconnectedness. Major events like those that transpired on and after September 11, 2001 are hard to predict, yet they result in sweeping global changes in the business environment. Regional and global economic booms and busts, terrorism, and political crises will all shape the performance of the hospitality industry in unpredictable ways. Table 10.4 contains a few of the characteristics that, based on recent trends, might be expected to exist in the business environment of the early twenty-first century.

Globalization and technological innovation are likely to be key factors in the future of hospitality. Large hotel companies will continue to extend their reach and free markets will enable more capital to move across countries and into developing nations. Restaurant chains have learned a great deal from the groundwork of McDonald's and Yum! Brands on how to go global successfully. Technological innovations will enable the development of new distribution channels and ways of managing customer relationship. Some predict that we will see fully mobile reservations and sales, location-aware marketing, the outfitting of all front-line staff with mobile devices, automatic transmission of

TABLE 10.4	STRATEGIC MANAGEMENT FOR THE TWENTY-FIRST CENTURY

- Increasing levels of global trade and global awareness
- Global and domestic social turbulence
- Increased terrorism and a worldwide effort to eliminate it
- Increased sensitivity to ethical issues and environmental concerns
- Rapidly advancing technology, especially in communications
- Continued erosion of buying power in the U.S. and other economies
- Continued development of third world economies
- Increases in U.S. and global strategic alliances
- Revolution in the U.S. health-care industry
- Greater emphasis on security and crisis management

preferences from embedded storage devices, and biometric footprinting of guests.[117] How do you prepare for this future? Advice abounds on how to become ready for what lies ahead, some crucial actions for managers are:

- *Pay global attention* by looking after the global traveler at home and the local traveler abroad and by extending the global reach of your portfolio.
- *Uncover the unexpected* experiences that excite and delight your customers.
- *Invest in your guest* by developing a comprehensive framework for guest interactions.
- *Become agile:* Integrate your businesses across business units, brands, and locations into a common business infrastructure for back-of-house and key front-of-house functions, and consider strategic outsourcing opportunities.
- *Rethink revenues* to focus on "return on investment management."
- *Polish your GEMs* to transform frontline staff into "guest experience managers."
- *Extend the experience* before the trip begins and after it ends.[118]

What kind of leaders will be needed to navigate through the business environment of the future? They will be strategic thinkers—people who are willing to break with conventional norms, but at the same time learn from and respect the past. They will be revolutionaries who don't simply seek incremental improvements to existing business systems to increase efficiency, but invent new business concepts.[119] As Bill Gates said of Microsoft, any company can be "two years away from failure."[120] They will be global thinkers, eager to establish relationships with outstanding companies, to obtain the best resources, and to sell in the most advantageous markets, regardless of where they are found. They will be sensitive to the organizational and external environment, realizing that long-term success requires a broad attitude regarding what and who is important. Finally, they will be able to instill in organizational members an urgent sense of vision.

The tools, theories, and techniques found in this book can help you become an effective leader for the twenty-first century. We encourage you to apply what you have learned to current and future business situations in which you and your organizations are found.

KEY-POINTS SUMMARY

Hospitality firms were pioneers in globalization. From cautious expansion before the 1970s to rapid growth by the early 2000s, international reach continues. One of the outcomes of increasing internationalization is that countries are economically interconnected at an unprecedented level. The evolving economic structures of countries help explain the stages of hotel development. For example, as a country grows and builds commerce, demand for hotels in secondary markets accelerates. Among the most popular reasons companies make foreign investments are to search for new markets or better resources, increase efficiency, reduce risk, or counter the competition.

Multinational strategies tend to fall into two broad categories. International expansion is the process of building an expanding operational presence. Global integration is the process through which a multinational organization integrates its worldwide activities into a single world strategy through its network of affiliates and alliances. Holiday Inn focused on international expansion with a standardized core product in various locations. In contrast, Hyatt International used global integration to build a network of decentralized hotels coordinated by a corporate office.

Structural inertia within some industries and U.S. companies has been a major impediment to their transformation into true global competitors. International activities should be accompanied by a new mind-set for all members of an organization, from top managers to employees at the lowest level. CEOs are instrumental in creating this mind-set.

Global strategic management provides challenges and opportunities that are not found in domestic markets. Stakeholder management is more complicated because of the diversity of people, organizations, and governments involved. However, a more diverse environment offers more opportunities to develop stakeholder-based competencies through effective management and interorganizational relationships. Development directors perform an important role as intermediaries between market opportunities and hospitality firms. Also, global diversity provides a much larger pool of resources from which to draw—including human resources; physical resources such as raw materials, supplies, and locations; and technological know-how. Companies that operate in countries with uncommon factor conditions, demand conditions, related and supporting industries, or exceptional firm strategies, structures, or rivalry may be at a comparative advantage relative to other global competitors.

The role of foreign subsidiaries in a multinational company is changing from being treated as simply "branch locations" to a full role in the development of new competencies, capabilities, resources, and services, depending on the company's capabilities and resources. If capabilities and resources are limited either by virtue of the country in which a subsidiary operates or by insufficient internal resources, then the subsidiary might be assigned an implementation role. Subsidiaries that exist in countries with special advantages or that have specific internal-resource advantages are expected to make a specialized contribution. Subsidiaries with a global mandate must have substantial skills and resources from which to draw, both from the country environment and internally. Matrix and transnational structures are helpful in integrating activities across subsidiaries, especially where those subsidiaries have highly related activities.

International strategic alliances are an outstanding way to acquire both resources and skills. Franchising has been an extremely useful tool for global expansion in hospitality firms. Master franchises involve providing a larger franchisee with the rights to develop a specific territory. This approach to franchising can be particularly useful in developing nations and non-strategic locations. While risk is lower using this model for global expansion, so are the returns.

One of the key issues facing top managers as their organizations pursue international development is selection of a product/market approach. A multidomestic strategy entails handling operations country by country by tailoring services around individual market needs. On the other hand, organizations pursuing a global strategy produce one type of service and market it in the same fashion throughout the world. Quick-service restaurant firms like McDonald's have relied on a strategy that closely approximates a global strategy. Firms must also determine which expansion tactics they will pursue. Common options include exporting, licensing, franchising, management contracts, joint ventures, wholly owned subsidiaries, and acquisitions. Among the most important criteria when deciding on an option for international growth are cost, financial risk, profit potential, and control. Another factor that seems to influence the decision among international growth options is multinational diversity.

Many characteristics should be evaluated before entering a foreign market. They fall into the areas of the broad environment, including the social environment, the economy, the political/legal environment, and the state of technology. Other characteristics are related to specific industries and markets. One of the most important factors to consider when deciding whether to enter a country is the state of its capital markets. Finally, future strategic management in the hospitality industry will be influenced by globalization and technological innovations. The future is in your hands. Good luck!

DISCUSSION QUESTIONS

1. Why were hospitality firms some of the first to internationalize?

2. What are some of the outcomes from increasing global interdependence among companies? Why might a firm want to pursue internationalization?

3. How does the structure of an economy shape international development?

4. How can an organization create more of a global mind-set?

5. What is the role of a development director? Why do so many hotel companies rely on these individuals when expanding into new markets?

6. Why do organizations enter difficult environments? How should a firm enter new markets?

7. Explain the conditions that can lead a nation to produce a disproportionate amount of global leaders in particular industries.

8. Describe the various roles played by foreign-owned subsidiaries. What determines which role they will play?

9. Why is a business-format franchise a popular approach to internationalizing in the hospitality industry?

10. What is the difference between a global and a multidomestic product/market strategy, and what are the advantages and disadvantages of each? Is there a strategy in between these extremes?

11. What are the major expansion tactics, and what are the factors that determine which one is the preferred approach?

12. What should a company consider before entering a foreign market?

13. What do you predict will be key innovations in the hospitality industry of the future? What leadership skills will be necessary to successfully manage global firms in the twenty-first century?

NOTES

1. S. Holmes, "For Starbucks, There's No Place Like Home," *Business Week,* 9 June 2003, 48; "Pizza Hut Loses Battle in Thailand," *The Post Standard,* 29 May 2003, C-6.

2. J. Walsh, "Patience, Adaptability Help Companies Overseas," *Hotel and Motel Management,* 18, pg. 3–4, March 2002.

3. T. Royle, *Working for McDonald's in Europe* (London: Routledge, 2000).

4. D. Litteljohn and A. Roper, "Changes in International Hotel Companies' Strategies," in *Strategic Hospitality Management,* ed. R. Teare and A. Boer (Cassell Educational: London, 1991).

5. Company Source, Press Release, "KFC Opens 700th Restaurant in China: KFC Is China's Largest, Most Popular and Fastest Growing QSR," http://www.kfc.com/about/pr/091302.htm, 14 September 2003.

6. Walsh, "Patience, Adaptability Help Companies Overseas."

7. J. Ewing, "The Fallout in Europe," *Business Week,* 8 October 2001, 52–53.

8. M. L. Clifford, "Trapped in the Tornado," *Business Week,* 8 October 2001, 54.

9. J. Booth, "Terror Attacks to Harm Asian Economies," *The Wall Street Journal,* 16 October 2001, A23.

10. "World Development Report 2002 Building Institutions for Markets" (Washington, D.C.: The World Bank Oxford University Press, 2002).

11. Slattery and Boer, "Strategic Developments for the 1990s."

12. S. Holmes, "Planet Starbucks to Keep Up the Growth: It Must Go Global Quickly," *Business Week,* 9 September 2002, 100.

13. R. Ruggless, "Brooks to Fill McDougall's CEO Post at Brinker International," *Nations Restaurant News,* 16, pg. 1–2, June 2003.

14. H. Henzler and W. Rall, "Facing Up to the Globalization Challenge," *McKinsey Quarterly* (Winter 1986): 52–68; T. Peters, "Prometheus Barely Unbound," *Academy of Management Executive* (November 1990): 70–84; M. E. Porter, *Competition in Global Industries* (Boston: Harvard Business School Press, 1986), 2–3; S. Tallman, "Global Strategic Management," in *The Blackwell Handbook of Strategic Management,* ed. M. A. Hitt, R. E. Freeman, and J. S. Harrison (Oxford: Blackwell Publishers, 2001), 464–490.

15. K. Ohmae, "Becoming a Triad Power: The New Global Corporation," in *Global Strategic Management. The Essentials,* 2d ed., ed. H. Vernon-Wortzel and L. H. Wortzel (New York: John Wiley, 1991), 62–74.

16. Tallman, "Global Strategic Management," 464.

17. M. E. Porter, "Changing Patterns of International Competition," *California Management Review* 28, no. 2 (1986): 9–40; Tallman, "Global Strategic Management."

18. R. Teare, J. Costa, and G. Eccles, "Relating Strategy, Structure and Performance, *Journal of Workplace Learning* 10, no. 2, pg. 58–75, (1998).

19. Ibid.

20. J. Sheth and G. Eshghi, *Global Strategic Management Perspectives* (Cincinnati, Ohio: South-Western Publishing, 1989), 13.

21. J. Betton and G. G. Dess, "The Application of Population Ecology Models to the Study of Organizations," *Academy of Management Review* 10 (1985): 750–757.

22. C. A. Bartlett and S. Ghoshal, "Global Strategic Management: Impact on the New Frontiers of Strategy Research," *Strategic Management Journal* 12 (1991): 5–16.

23. B. Bremner, "The President Has a Will, But No Way," *Business Week,* 15 March 1999, 92–95.

24. J. Walsh, "W Brand Focuses on International Expansion," *Hotel and Motel Management,* 17 June 2002, 217.

25. Holmes, "Planet Starbucks to Keep Up the Growth."

26. Walsh, "Patience, Adaptability Help Companies Overseas."
27. T. Royle, *Working for McDonald's in Europe.*
28. J. Walsh, "Market Analysis Determines Brand Location," *Hotel and Motel Management,* 19 May 2003, 218.
29. L. Altinay and A. Roper, "The Role and Importance of Development Directors in Initiating and Implementing Development Strategy," *International Journal of Contemporary Hospitality Management* 13, no. 7 (2001): 339–346.
30. M. Muller, "Employee Representation and Pay in Austria, Germany, and Sweden," *International Studies of Management and Organization* 29, no. 4 (2000): 67–83; R. Calori and B. Dufour, "Management European Style," *Academy of Management Executive* (August 1995): 61–73.
31. R. Calori and B. Dufour, "Management European Style."
32. Excerpted and adapted from M. Maruyama, "Changing Dimensions in International Business," *Academy of Management Executive* (August 1992): 88–96.
33. C. Solomon, "When Training Doesn't Translate," *Workforce* 76, no. 3 (March 1997).
34. S. Tully, "The Hunt for the Global Manager," *Fortune,* 21 May 1990, 140–144; J. Main, "How 21 Men Got Global in 35 Days," *Fortune,* 6 November 1989, 71.
35. Maruyama, "Changing Dimensions."
36. "Hotels Halted," *Business Today* (Egypt), 13 August 2003.
37. Ibid.
38. D. Roberts and M. L. Clifford, "Power Shift: China Gets Set for New Leaders," *Academy of Management Executive* (February 2002): 54–56; "China Trade(-Offs)," *Christian Science Monitor,* 7 September 2001, 10; quotations of President Gao are from Z. Wang, "Economic Reform Foundation's President Shangquan Gao on Organizational Reform and Sustainable Business Development," *Academy of Management Executive* (February 2000): 9.
39. N. Weilheimer, "Starwood Expands Property in China," *Commercial Property News,* 1 June 2003, 3.
40. B. Serlen, "Starwood, Marriott, Hilton Enter or Expand in Asia," *Business Travel News,* 24, pg. 15, (March 2003).
41. J. Watson, *Golden Arches East: McDonald's in East Asia* (Stanford, Calif.: Stanford University Press, 1997).
42. "Accor Announces Biggest Expansion Plan in China's Mainland Hotel Market," Xinhau, 11 August 2003; N. Weilheimer, "Starwood Expands Property in China."
43. A. McWilliams, D. D. Van Fleet, and P. M. Wright, "Strategic Management of Human Resources for Global Competitive Advantage," *Journal of Business Strategies* 18, no. 1 (Spring 2001): 1–24.
44. M. E. Porter, *The Competitive Advantage of Nations* (New York: The Free Press, 1990).
45. "World Development Report 2002 Building Institutions for Markets."
46. Porter, *The Competitive Advantage of Nations.*
47. N. Nohria and S. Ghoshal, *The Differentiated Network* (San Francisco: Jossey-Bass, 1997).
48. G. S. Yip, *Total Global Strategy: Managing for Worldwide Competitive Advantage* (Englewood Cliffs, N.J.: Prentice Hall, 1992).
49. J. M. Birkinshaw and A. J. Morrison, "Configurations of Strategy and Structure in Subsidiaries of Multinational Corporations," *Journal of International Business Studies* 26 (1995): 729–754.
50. Shangri-La Asia Ltd. *Annual Report 2002,* 40.
51. Tallman, "Global Strategic Management," 485.
52. "Blue Coast Hotels, Hilton in Indian JV," *Reuters News,* http://global.factiva.com/en/arch, 16 December 2002.
53. Reuters, "Virgin, Sprint in Wireless Venture," *Orlando Sentinel,* 6 October 2001, B9.
54. L. Polly, "International Growth Patterns Remain Strong," *Franchising World,* April 2002.
55. Yum company Web site, http://www.yum.com/investors/overview.htm, 11 September 2003; Polly, "International Growth Patterns Remain Strong."
56. F. Steed, "It's a Small, Small World: Growing Your Brand Globally," *Franchising World,* November/December 2001, 14–15.
57. Ibid.
58. U.S. Department of Commerce.
59. J. F. Preble, A. Reichel, and R. C. Hoffman, "Strategic Alliances for Competitive Advantage: Evidence from Israel's Hospitality and Tourism Industry," *Hospitality Management* 19 (2000): 327.
60. F. Contractor and S. Kundu, "Franchising versus Company-run Operations: Modal Choice in the Global Hotel Sector," *Journal of International Marketing* (1998): 28–53.

61. T. Cruz, "Speed to Market," *Hotels* (February 1998).
62. Contractor and Kundu, "Franchising versus Company-run Operations."
63. "TT Resources Bags Deal," *Business Times,* 16 September 2002.
64. J. Walsh, "Franchisors Piece Together Worldwide Master Licenses," *Hotel and Motel Management,* 17 September 2001.
65. Ibid.
66. A. C. Inkpen, "Learning and Knowledge Acquisition through International Strategic Alliances," *Academy of Management Executive* 12, no. 4 (1998): 69.
67. "New Investments Expected in Russia Hotel Sector," *Emerging Markets Economy,* 26, pg N.PAG, February 2003.
68. Walsh, "Franchisors Piece Together Worldwide Master Licenses; 'Corporate 300'," *Hotels,* July 2003, 37.
69. K. Ohmae, "Managing in a Borderless World," *Harvard Business Review* 67 (May/June 1989): 152–161.
70. D. Litteljohn and A. Roper, "Changes in International Hotel Companies' Strategies.""
71. T. Levitt, "The Globalization of Markets," *Harvard Business Review* 61 (May/June 1983): 92.
72. S. P. Douglas and Y. Wind, "The Myth of Globalization," *Columbia Journal of World Business* (Winter 1987): 19–29.
73. R. Smet, "McDonald's: A Strategy of Cross-cultural Approach," *The Journal of Language of International Business* 12, no. 1 (2002).
74. M. A. Hitt, R. D. Ireland, and R. E. Hoskisson, *Strategic Management: Competitiveness and Globalization* (Minneapolis, Minn.: West Publishing, 1995).
75. R. Hallowell, D. Bowen, and C. Knoop, "Four Seasons Goes to Paris," *Academy of Management Executive* 16, no. 4 (2002): 10.
76. Hallowell, Bowen, and Knoop, "Four Seasons Goes to Paris," 10–11.
77. H. G. Barkema and F. Vermeulen, "International Expansion through Start-up or Acquisition. A Learning Perspective," *Academy of Management Journal* 41 (1998): 7–26; C. W. L. Hill, P. Hwang, and W. C. Kim, "An Eclectic Theory of the Choice of International Entry Mode," *Strategic Management Journal* 11 (1990): 117–128; C. W. L. Hill and G. R. Jones, *Strategic Management: An Integrated Approach* (Boston: Houghton Mifflin, 1992), 254–259; R. Schmidgall, *Hospitality Industry Managerial Accounting,* 4th ed., (Educational Institute: American Hotel and Motel Association, Washington, D.C., 1997).
78. J. Walsh, "Accor Shifts Focus to Franchising," *Hotel & Motel Management,* 19; pg. 3,17, May 2003).
79. "Corporate 300," *Hotels,* 38.
80. Barkema and Vermeulen, "International Expansion through Start-up."
81. "Corporate 300," *Hotels,* 38.
82. S. J. Chang, "International Expansion Strategy of Japanese Firms: Capability Building Through Sequential Entry," *Academy of Management Journal* 38 (1995): 383.
83. Some of the options contained in this list were based on information found in Sheth and Eshghi, *Global Strategic Management Perspectives.*
84. T. Royle, *Working for McDonald's in Europe.*
85. C. Karmin and P. Murphy, "IMF Aid Lists Argentina Stocks, But Jitters Remain," *The Wall Street Journal,* 23 August 2001, C1.
86. T. Kamm and J. Friedland, "Spanish Firms Discover Latin America Business As New World of Profit," *The Wall Street Journal,* 23 May 1996, A1, A9.
87. C. Larroulet, "Look to Chile for an Answer to the Latin Malaise," *The Wall Street Journal,* 24 August 2001, A9.
88. C. J. Whalen, P. Magnusson, and G. Smith, "Nafta's Scorecard: So Far, So Good," *Business Week,* 9 July 2001, 54–56.
89. P. Alisau, "NAFTA Fuels Growth in Meeting Facilities," *Incentive* April 1997, pg. 92.
90. J. Cummings and N. King Jr., "Mexico's Fox Gets Commitment from Bush to Reshape Ties, Even if Congress Balks," *The Wall Street Journal,* 7 September 2001, A16.
91. S. Welch, "Cancun & The Riviera Maya," *Successful Meetings,* 30 August 2003.
92. O. Edur, "Setting Up Shop Abroad," *CMA Management* (September 2000): 54.
93. B. B. Read, "Scoring Points Up North," *Call Center Magazine,* September 2001, 36.
94. "Economic Policy," *Country Report: Canada,* August 2003, 6.
95. "Hôtelier De Luxe : Isadore Sharp," *Time Canada* 21, pg. 38–39, July 2003.
96. J. Rohwer, "GE Digs into Asia," *Fortune,* 2 October 2000, 165–178.

97. J. Labate, "The World Economy in Charts," *Fortune,* 27 July 1992, 62.

98. The Hongkong and Shanghai Hotels, Limited company website, member profile page, http://www.chamber.org.hk/info/member_a_week/hksh.asp, 12 September 2003; New World Development company website, http://209.41.56.193/listco/hk/nwd/profile.htm, 12 September 2003; TAJ Indian Hotels Company company website, http://www.tata.com/indian_hotels, 12 September 2003; Sangri-La Hotels and Resorts company website, investors relations page, http://www.shangri-la.com/eng/investor/index.htm, 12 September 2003.

99. L. Kraar, "Asia 2000," *Fortune,* 5 October 1992, 111.

100. K. H. Zhang, "What Attracts Foreign Multinational Corporations to China?" *Contemporary Economic Policy* 19 (2001): 336–346.

101. P. M. Norton and L. Huang, "Management Fraud in China," *The China Business Review* (March/April 2001): 26–35.

102. R. N. Sanyal and T. Guvenli, "American Firms in China: Issues in Managing Operations," *Multinational Business Review* (Fall 2001): 40–46.

103. Ibid.

104. Serlen, "Starwood, Marriott, Hilton Enter or Expand in Asia."

105. D. M. Reid, "Changes in Japan's Post-Bubble Business Environment: Implications for Foreign-affiliated Companies," *Journal of International Marketing* 7 (1999): 38–63.

106. M. G. Allen, "Succeeding in Japan," *Vital Speeches of the Day* 60 (1994): 429–432.

107. H. Yoshihara, "Foreign Companies in Japan—Key Factors for Success and Failure," *Management Japan* 24, no. 1 (1991): 17–24.

108. A. Spicer, G. A. McDermott, and B. Kogut, "Entrepreneurship and Privatization in Central Europe: The Tenuous Balance between Destruction and Creation," *Academy of Management Review* 25 (2000): 630–649; S. Ogden and R. Watson, "Corporate Performance and Stakeholder Management: Balancing Shareholder and Customer Interests in the U.K. Privatized Water Industry," *Academy of Management Journal* 42 (1999): 526–538; M. Johnson, "Germany Gets a Makeover," *Global Finance* 14, no. 11 (November 2000): 31–39.

109. D. Fairlamb and G. Edmondson, "Out from under the Table," *Business Week,* 24 September 2001, 116–120; S. Tully, "Europe 1992: More Unity Than You Think," *Fortune,* 24 August 1992, 136–142.

110. L. Hayes, "Love American Style: European Market Embraces US Restaurant Chains," *Nation's Restaurant News,* 17, pg. 47–49, August 1998.

111. L. Hall (editor), *New Europe and the Hotel Industry* (Price Waterhouse Coopers Hospitality & Leisure Research, London, England, 2000).

112. S. M. Puffer and D. J. McCarthy, "Navigating the Hostile Maze: A Framework for Russian Entrepreneurship," *Academy of Management Executive* (November 2001), 24.

113. P. Starobin, C. Belton, and S. Crock, "Vladimir Putin, Washington's Pal?" *Business Week,* 8 October 2001, 56.

114. P. Windolf, "The Governance Structure of Large French Corporations: A Comparative Perspective," paper presented at the Sloan Project on Corporate Governance at Columbia Law School, May 1998.

115. R. E. Hoskisson et al., "Restructuring Strategies of Diversified Business Groups: Difference Associated with Country Institutional Environments," in *The Blackwell Handbook of Strategic Management,* ed. M. A. Hitt, R. E. Freeman, and J. S. Harrison (Oxford: Blackwell Publishers, 2001), 433–463.

116. P. Gupte, "Venture Capitalist to the Poor," *Forbes,* 31, pg. 58–60, May 1999.

117. M. Erdly and L. Kesterson-Townes, *Experience Rules: PwC Consulting's Vision for the Hospitality and Leisure Industry,* Circa 2010 (PWC Consulting, Transforming Futures Series, New York, NY: 2002).

118. Ibid.

119. G. Hamel, *Leading the Revolution* (Boston: Harvard Business School Press, 2000).

120. G. Hamel, "The Challenge Today: Changing the Rules of the Game," *Business Strategy Review* 9, no. 2 (1998): 19–26.

Cases

Learning Through Case Analysis

Strategic management is an iterative, on-going process designed to position a firm for competitive advantage in its ever-changing environment. To manage an organization strategically, a manager must understand and appreciate the desires of key organizational stakeholders, the industry environment, and the firm's position relative to its stakeholders and industry. This knowledge allows a manager to set goals and direct the organization's resources in a way that corrects weaknesses, overcomes threats, takes advantage of strengths and opportunities, and, ultimately, satisfies stakeholders.

Case analysis typically begins with a brief introduction of the company. The introduction, which sets the stage for the rest of the case, should include a brief description of the defining characteristics of the firm, including some of its outstanding qualities, past successes, failures, and products or services. The industries in which the firm is involved are also identified.

The next section of a case analysis can be either an environmental analysis or an internal resource analysis. Both types of analysis are required before all of the organization's opportunities can be identified.

ENVIRONMENTAL ANALYSIS

An analysis of the external environment includes an industry analysis and an examination of key external stakeholders and the broad environment. Findings are then summarized, with an emphasis on identifying industry growth and profit potential and the keys to survival and success in the industry. Some organizations are involved in more than one industry.

Consequently, a separate industry analysis is done for each of the industries in which a firm is involved.

The Broad Environment

A complete environmental analysis includes an assessment of the broad environment, including social influences, economic influences, political influences, and technological influences. Each of these areas is evaluated only as it relates to the industry in question. Environmental influences should be evaluated at the domestic and global levels, if appropriate. Forces in the broad environment may pose threats or provide opportunities.

Industry Analysis

The first step in industry analysis is to provide a basic description of the industry and the competitive forces that dominate it. Porter's Five Forces are evaluated, along with other relevant issues.

1. What is the product or service? What function does it serve? What are the channels of distribution?

2. What is the industry size in units and dollars? How fast is it growing? Are products differentiated? Are there high exit barriers? Are there high fixed costs? These are some of the forces that determine the strength of competition among existing competitors.

3. Who are the major competitors? What are their market shares? In other words, is the industry consolidated or fragmented?

4. Who are the major customers of the industry? Are they powerful? What gives them power?

5. Who are the major suppliers to the industry? Are they powerful? What gives them power?

6. Do significant entry barriers exist? What are they? Are they effective in protecting existing competitors, thus enhancing profits?

7. Are there any close substitutes for industry products and services? Do they provide pressure on prices charged in this industry?

8. What are the basic strategies of competitors? How successful are they? Are competitors likely to retaliate to competitive moves or countermoves? How rapidly do they respond?

9. Is the industry regulated? What influence do regulations have on industry competitiveness?

10. Are any other external stakeholders important in this industry? Examples might include labor unions, special interest groups, financial institutions, and local communities.

11. To what extent is the industry global? Are there any apparent advantages to being involved in more than one nation?

The findings of this part of the analysis will help you decide whether the industry is "attractive" (growing and profitable) and worthy of further investment (i.e., time, money, and resources). It will also help you identify areas in which the firm may be able to excel in an effort to create a competitive advantage.

Strategic Issues Facing the Industry

A thorough environmental analysis provides the information needed to identify factors and forces that are important to the industry in which your organization is involved and, therefore, your organization. These factors and forces may be categorized as follows:

1. Driving forces in the industry, which are trends that are so significant that they are creating fundamental industry change, such as the opening up of Eastern Europe or networked computer communications. Of course, each industry will have its own unique set of driving forces.

2. Threats, defined as noteworthy trends or changes that threaten growth prospects, profit potential, and traditional ways of doing business.

3. Opportunities, which are important trends, changes, or ideas that provide new opportunities for growth or profits.

4. Requirements for survival, identified as resources and capabilities that all firms must possess to survive in the industry. An example in the pharmaceutical industry is "product purity." These factors do not command a premium price. They are necessary, but not sufficient to guarantee success.

5. Key success factors, which are factors firms typically should possess if they desire to be successful in the industry. An example in the pharmaceutical industry is the ability to create products with new therapeutic qualities. This ability may lead to high performance.

Having completed an analysis of the external environment, you are ready to conduct a more specific analysis of the internal organization.

ORGANIZATIONAL RESOURCE ANALYSIS

Understanding industry trends, growth prospects, profit potential, and key strategic issues can help you critique an organization's strategies and evaluate its strengths and weaknesses. For example, what might qualify as a strength in one industry may be an ordinary characteristic in another industry. A good organizational analysis should begin with a general evaluation of the internal organization.

Evaluation of Strategic Direction and the Internal Environment

The following questions are useful in beginning to assess the internal organization:

1. What is the company's strategic direction, including its vision, business definition, and values? If these factors are contained in a formal mission, share it. If not, you may want to write one. Remember that organizations have a strategic direction even if it is not written down.

2. How has the strategic direction changed over time? Has the evolution been consistent with the organization's capabilities and planned strategies?

3. Who are the principal internal stakeholders? In particular, who are the key managers and what is their background? What are their strengths and weaknesses? Are they authoritarian or participative in their management style? Is this appropriate for the situation? What seems to drive their actions?

4. Who owns the organization? Is it a publicly traded company with a board of directors? If there is a board and you know who is on it, is the composition of the board appropriate? Is there an individual or group with a controlling interest? Is there evidence of agency problems? How active are the owners and what do they value?

5. What are the operating characteristics of the company, including its size in sales, assets, and employees, its age, and its geographical locations (including international operations)? Does the company have any unique physical resources?

6. Are employees highly trained? If a union is present, how are relations with the union?

7. How would you describe the organization's culture? Is it a high performing culture? Is it supportive of the firm's strategies?

Most instructors also require a financial analysis both to identify financial strengths and weaknesses and to evaluate performance. A financial analysis should include a comparison of ratios and financial figures with major competitors or the industry in which the organization competes (cross-sectional), as well as an analysis of trends in these ratios over several years (longitudinal). Financial ratio analysis can provide an indication as to whether the firm is pursuing appropriate strategies. Poor financial trends are sometimes symptoms of greater problems. For example, a firm may discover that administrative costs are increasing at a faster rate than sales. This could be an indication of diseconomies of scale or the need for tighter controls on overhead costs. Financial analysis is also used to indicate the ability of the firm to finance growth. For example, managers of a firm that has very high leverage (long-term debt) may have to be less ambitious in their strategies for taking advantage of opportunities. On the other hand, an organization with a strong balance sheet is well poised to pursue a wide range of opportunities. Strong financial resources are often hard to imitate in the short term.

Analysis of Resources and Capabilities

The foregoing analysis of the internal environment provides an excellent starting point for identifying key resources and capabilities. For example, outstanding resources and capabilities may result from (1) superior management, (2) well-trained employees, (3) an excellent board of directors, (4) a high-performance culture, (5) superior financial resources, (6) effective knowledge-generating processes, or (7) the appropriate level and type of international involvement. However, these potential sources of competitive advantage barely scratch the organizational surface.

You also should evaluate the organization's primary value chain activities to identify resources and capabilities. These activities include its (8) inbound logistics, (9) operations, (10) outbound logistics, (11) marketing and sales, and (12) service, as well as the support activities of (13) procurement, (14) technology development, (15) human resource management, and (16) administration. In addition, an organization may have (17) an excellent reputation, (18) a strong brand name, (19) patents and secrets, (20) excellent locations, (21) outstanding learning capabilities, or (22) strong or valuable ties (i.e., alliances, joint ventures, contracts, or cooperation) with one or more external stakeholders. All of these potential resources and capabilities (and many others) have been discussed in this book. They form a starting point that you can use to help identify the potential sources of competitive advantage. Each company will have its own unique list.

It is useful to screen resources and capabilities based on their long-term strategic value. This process entails asking several questions:

- Does the resource or capability have value in the market?
- Is the resource or capability unique?
- Is there a readily available substitute?

Positive answers to the first two questions and a negative answer to the third mean that the resource or capability has the ability to provide a source of competitive advantage. Two additional questions are then asked:

- Do organizational systems exist that allow realization of potential?
- Is the organization aware of and realizing the advantages?

Opportunities can exist if an organization is not taking advantage of sources of competitive advantage, either because it is unaware of them or because systems are not in place yet to take advantage of them. A final question is then asked:

- Is the resource or capability difficult or costly to imitate?

If it is difficult or costly to imitate a resource or capability, it can be a source of sustainable competitive advantage. A final part of this analysis is to determine whether the resource or capability can be applied to multiple business areas. If this is the case, it can be classified as a core competency or capability.

Performance Evaluation

The next step in internal analysis is to describe and critique the organization's past strategies. In critiquing strategies, you will need to describe them in detail, discuss whether they have been successful, and then *evaluate whether they fit with the industry environment and the resources and capabilities of the organization.*

1. What is the company's pattern of past strategies (corporate-level, business-level, and international)?

2. How successful has the company been in the past with its chosen strategies? How successful is the company now?

3. For each strategy, what explains success or failure? (Use your environmental and organizational resource analyses to support your answer.)

SUMMARY OF SITUATION ANALYSIS

On the basis of your environmental and organizational analyses, you should be in a position to draw some conclusions about the situation your organization is facing, called a situation analysis. Many students will do this by creating lists of strengths and weaknesses, opportunities and threats. Strengths are defined as firm resources and capabilities that can lead to a competitive advantage. Weaknesses, on the other hand, are resources and capabilities that the firm does not possess, resulting in a competitive disadvantage. Consequently, each of the resources and capabilities identified during the organizational analysis should be measured against the factors identified in the environmental analysis.

Opportunities are conditions in the external environment that allow a firm to take advantage of organizational strengths, overcome organizational weaknesses, or neutralize environmental threats. Consequently, now that the organizational analysis is complete, you should re-evaluate your list of opportunities to determine whether they apply to your organization. You should also evaluate threats to make sure they are applicable to your firm. Threats are conditions in the broad and operating environments that may stand in the way of organizational competitiveness or the achievement of stakeholder satisfaction.

DEVELOPING A STRATEGIC PLAN

Your environmental and organizational analyses helped you to evaluate the past strategies and strategic direction of the firm, as well as develop a list of strengths, weaknesses, opportunities, and threats. The next step is to make recommendations concerning the strategies the firm may want to pursue in the future. If the firm is not a stellar performer, this should be an easy task. However, even firms that have been highly successful in the past should consider taking advantage of opportunities and should respond to threats. History has taught us that firms that are unwilling to move forward eventually decline.

Strategic Direction and Major Strategies

You should probably begin your strategic recommendations by focusing on the strategic direction and major strategies of the firm. Based on your earlier analyses, you may want to consider adjustments to the mission of the firm, including its vision or business definition. Determine whether the business definition is still appropriate, given your environmental analysis. Is your dominant industry stagnant? Is it over-regulated? Is competition hurting profitability? Should you consider investing in other industries? If so, what are their defining characteristics? What core competencies and capabilities could be applied elsewhere? What opportunities could be explored that relate to the corporate-level strategies?

The business-level strategy should also be considered. If you determined earlier that the business-level strategy is not as successful as it should be, what adjustments should be made? Could the company have more success by focusing on one segment of the market? Or if the company is pursuing a focus strategy, would broadening the target market be appropriate? If the company is following cost leadership, would a differentiation strategy work better? If differentiation doesn't seem to be working very well, would a cost-leadership strategy be better? Finally, would a best-value strategy be the most appropriate?

It is possible that you may want to leave the strategic direction and major strategies alone, especially if the organization has enjoyed recent success. Regardless of whether you altered the direction and strategies, at this point you have now established what you think they should be. The direction and corporate- and business-level strategies provide guidance for fine-tuning an organization's strategies. Each of the recommendations you make from this point on should be consistent with the strategic direction and major strategies of the organization. At this point, it is time to explore strategic opportunities further.

Evaluation of Opportunities and Recommendations

Using the strategic direction and corporate- and business-level strategies as guides, strategic opportunities should be evaluated further. These alternatives were generated during earlier analyses. They include opportunities that allow a firm to take advantage of organizational strengths, opportunities for the firm to overcome organizational weaknesses, and opportunities for the firm to neutralize environmental threats. Evaluation of opportunities means much more than simply accepting them on the basis of earlier environmental and organizational analyses. They should also be evaluated based on factors such as the following:

1. *Value added to the organization.* Some alternatives may have high potential for growth in revenues while others may be oriented towards improving efficiency, eliminating problems, taking advantage of organizational strengths, or any of a wide range of other factors. Make sure that you look at long-term value as well as short-term value.

2. *Organizational resources required to implement the alternative.* The actual dollar costs to an organization are often difficult for a student to estimate. However, you should always provide a description of all of the resources needed to carry out the alternative.

3. *The extent to which the alternative fits within the organization.* Base this part of your analysis on such things as whether the alternative takes advantage of current distinctive competencies, the ability of the organization to successfully execute the alternative, and whether the existing culture, management, and resources of the organization will support implementation

of the alternative. Make sure to specify whether this alternative is consistent with the current strategic direction of the company or requires new direction.

4. *Risks associated with the alternative.* Consider such things as financial risk, risk to the reputation of the firm or its existing strengths, and risk to particular stakeholder groups such as employees, managers, customers, or suppliers. Part of this analysis should anticipate the reactions of competitors to the strategy and what could happen if they respond in an adverse manner.

5. *Future position.* Will the strategy continue to be viable as the industry and the broad environment undergo their expected changes? Will it provide a foundation for survival or competitive success?

The result of this analysis should be a recommendation or recommendations that the organization should pursue. You may not be required by your instructor to conduct a formal analysis of alternatives based on a standard set of criteria; however, you should still make recommendations concerning changes the organization should make to remain or become competitive and satisfy its stakeholders. Through this entire process, remember that many companies identify areas of strength that are no longer capable of giving the company a competitive edge. What was a key to success yesterday may be a requirement for survival today.

Implementation and Control

Recommendations should always be accompanied by an implementation plan and basic controls. The following are major questions that should be addressed during this section of a case analysis. Items 7 and 8 relate specifically to control.

1. How do the recommendations specifically address concerns that were identified during the analysis?

2. What will be the roles and responsibilities of key internal *and* external stakeholders in carrying out the recommendations and how are they expected to respond? What actions should be taken to smooth out the transition period or avoid stakeholder discontent?

3. Does the organization have the resources (funds, people, skills) to carry out the recommendations? If not, how should the organization proceed in developing or acquiring those resources?

4. Does the organization have the appropriate systems, structures, and processes to carry out the recommendations? If not, how should the organization proceed in creating the appropriate systems, structures, and processes?

5. What is the appropriate time horizon for implementing recommendations? What should the organization and its managers do immediately, in one month, in six months, in a year, and so forth?

6. What are the roadblocks the organization could encounter while implementing the recommendations (i.e., financing, skilled labor shortages)? How can the organization overcome these roadblocks?

7. What are the desired outcomes or changes the organization should expect once the recommendations have been implemented? How will the organization know if the recommendations have been successful? In other words, what are the objectives associated with your recommendations?

8. What were some of the major assumptions you made with regard to the external environment? Which of these factors, if different from expected, would require an adjustment to your recommendations?

In addition, some instructors require separate functional plans for areas such as finance, human resources, or marketing. Chapter 8 contains detailed information that should help you develop these plans.

Following the implementation section, you may want to update your audience (your instructor or other students) concerning actions the firm has taken since the case was written. If a case update is required, it should center on actions that pertain to the focus of your case analysis. If you do an update, remember that what the organization did, even if it appears to have been successful, may not have been the optimal solution.

A NOTE TO STUDENTS

If you are reading this appendix early in the course, you will have the rest of the semester or quarter to practice the case analysis process and study the chapter readings. If you are reading this appendix later in the course, we encourage you to go back to earlier chapters and refresh your memory concerning the concepts that were covered. Just as this course integrates material you learned during your years of business study, the case analysis process integrates material from all sections of the strategic management course.

Since there is not a standard method for analyzing cases, your instructor may teach a method of case analysis that differs from the approach contained herein. Also, cases can be treated in many different formats, including class discussions (complete with discussion questions to be answered before coming to class), written papers, formal presentations, and class debates. Finally, some cases do not lend themselves to comprehensive analysis. After reading this appendix, check with your instructor for specific instructions and requirements.

CASE 1

Six Continents: Demerging for a Better Future?

INTRODUCTION

How would you choose to spend $3 billion? It may sound like an easy question, but it is one that the UK conglomerate Six Continents has been struggling to answer. The inability to make a decision has been a catalyst for change at Six Continents. Today, Six Continents is on the precipice of a major transformation. The failure to spend the $3 billion gained from the sale of their Bass Brewing business has culminated in a decision to return a portion of this capital to their shareholders. Additionally, Six Continents will begin the process of demerging their hotel and soft drink business from their restaurant and pub business.

Chairman Ian Prosser said, "over the past five years we have narrowed our business focus and have paid significant sums to our shareholders. The progression of this strategy is the separation of our hotels and soft drinks businesses from the retail business combined with a return of £700m ($1.1 billion). Our hotel and retail businesses are both very strong businesses with great potential."[1]

Written by Adam Baru, Yinian Hou, Vikas Patel, Bill Spinnenweber, Anjali Talera, and Kem Wilson under the direction of Jeffrey S. Harrison at the School of Hotel Administration, Cornell University.

This case study was written for the purposes of classroom discussion.

In order to best understand Six Continents' corporate strategy, it is essential to first understand the evolution of this conglomerate.

HISTORY

Six Continents PLC, formerly Bass PLC, was founded in 1777 by William Bass when he established a brewery in the English town of Burton-on-Trent. By the early 1800s, the size of the brewery doubled as volume increased to two thousand barrels per year. By the time Michael Thomas Bass, William Bass' grandson, took over in 1827, the brewery was producing ten thousand barrels per year.[2]

In 1837, Bass formed a partnership with John Gretton and Richard Ratcliffe to become known as Bass, Ratcliffe & Gretton. Business growth continued with an enormous boost from the expansion of railroads. Railways allowed Bass to transport its barrels across England and popularized Bass ales amongst the masses. By 1860, Bass had expanded to three breweries as output neared 420,000 barrels.[3]

The year 1876 was a landmark year for Bass as it was recognized as the largest brewery in England. Even more notably, it was also this year that Bass' red triangle trademark became the first trademark to be registered in England. In 1888, the company was incorporated as Bass, Ratcliffe & Gretton Ltd. Output had risen to nearly one million barrels a year, and more than 2,500 men and boys were employed at the breweries.[4]

Beer consumption took a big hit during the World War I era as the radio, cinema, and other forms of entertainment lured customers away from pubs. It was also during this time that the government dealt the brewing industry a blow when it increased taxes. Furthermore, during the early 1900s, it was commonplace for English breweries to run their own pubs as outlets to retail their beer. Therefore, many breweries invested large amounts of capital to improve their pubs. Although Bass owned a number of pubs, the company neglected to improve its pubs and instead relied on the popularity of its brand and the acquisitions of breweries such as Worthington & Company Ltd to spur expansion. Despite this strategy, Bass' failure to modernize proved to be costly. Competitors such as Mitchells & Butler not only improved their pubs, but also coerced their pub managers to sell their firm's beer. Such tactics undercut Bass' market position. By the 1930s, these issues along with a declining economy forced Bass to lay off workers, close factories, and decrease production.[5]

By the late 1940s, recovery was in full stride and Bass continued its expansion through acquisitions. Between the late 1940s and late 1950s, Bass acquired holdings in William Hancock & Company and Wenlock Brewing Company while seeing its net profits increase by over 120 percent. Nevertheless, problems still remained as Bass continued to be obstinate toward change. Notably, Bass refused to update its pricing system, ignored the public's desire for milder beers, and failed to integrate its operations.[6]

Under the leadership of James Grigg, Bass finally recognized the need for modernization. During the 1960s, Bass made two strategic and significant mergers. In 1961 Bass merged with Mitchells & Butler becoming Bass, Mitchells & Butler. Importantly, both companies were able to integrate and modernize their companies' operations. Additionally, both companies recognized the need to diversify, and in 1967 Bass, Mitchells & Butler merged with Charrington United Breweries to become Bass Charrington Ltd. Although Charrington United Breweries controlled a number of regional beer brands, it lacked a premium beer such as Bass. Likewise, Bass, Mitchells & Butler lacked the spirit and soft drinks business Charrington United Breweries excelled in. Therefore, the merger proved extremely beneficial, especially through its improvement of the two companies' national distribution networks.[7]

The year 1970 marked Bass' entrance into the world of hospitality as it purchased about fifty hotels from the oil giant Esso.[8] These hotel holdings became known as Crest Hotels. Renamed Bass PLC in the early 1980s, the company's leisure subsidiaries, including its hotel division, "contributed substantially to Bass' growth and profits."[9] Recently promoted chairman and CEO Ian Prosser saw great growth potential in the hotel industry despite its being minor compared to the brewing business. Therefore, it came as no surprise in 1987 when Bass' hotel division began to make its presence felt. Following a failed attempt to buy the Hilton International hotel chain, Bass won the exclusive rights to the Holiday Inn name outside the United States, Canada, and Mexico for $475 million on September 15, 1987.[10]

The year 1989 saw the advent of legislation upon the brewing industry through Beer Orders. Through Beer Orders legislation, the government sought to limit the vertical integration within the brewing industry by limiting the number of pubs a brewer could own.[11] Bass' response was to continue to focus on and develop its international hotel business. Therefore, on August 25, 1989, Bass made a monumental decision by purchasing Holiday Corporation's flagship Holiday Inn chain for $2.23 billion. Included in this purchase were 1,410 franchised Holiday Inns and 177 company-owned/managed Holiday Inns.[12] The remainder of Holiday Corporation, including Embassy Suites, Hampton Inns, Homewood Suites, and Harrah's Casinos of Nevada and New Jersey, was spun off to shareholders as Promus Companies Inc.[13, 14]

Founded by Kemmons Wilson in 1952, Holiday Inns quickly grew into the largest lodging corporation in the world. A 1951 road trip to Washington, D.C. with his wife and five children had convinced Wilson of a great need for a brand name hotel/motel that families could trust anywhere they traveled. Importantly, Wilson was aware of the soon-to-be construction of a $76 billion federal interstate highway system and planned to take full advantage by building Holiday Inns alongside it. Indeed, his foresight paid off as the interstate highway system popularized travel from coast to coast. Later, in his book *The Fifties*, Pulitzer-prize winning author David Halberstam would call this trip to Washington "the vacation that changed the face of the American road."[15] With the purchase of the Holiday Inn chain, Bass' desire to focus on and develop their hospitality division came full circle. The importance of such a decision is still felt as the hospitality industry defines the company today.

When Bass purchased Holiday Inn, the chain was in the midst of a decline due to aged properties and poor service. Most notably, the all-important business traveler was dissatisfied and unwilling to pay the rates charged at most Holiday Inns. Additionally, the hotel industry was seeing great growth in budget hotel chains such as Hampton Inn. To counter these issues, Bass began a $1 billion renovation project for the Holiday Inn brand, initiated an expansion of its high-end Crowne Plaza hotels, and launched its own budget hotel chain called Holiday Inn Express. Additionally, to improve the reservation capabilities of their hotels, Bass invested $60 million in technology upgrades in 1992.[16]

Despite these investments, Bass' hotel division saw sharp declines in 1991 and 1992, which lowered the overall companies operating results. A lawsuit filed in 1992 against Promus revealed Bass' discontent with its acquisition as many hotels failed to meet zoning laws. The lawsuit was settled in 1995 for $49 million.[17] It was at this time that Bass finally began to see some turnaround in its hotel division. The timing could not have been better as Bass was beginning to experience difficulties in its brewing business.

Between 1994 and 1995, beer sales for Bass declined about 6 percent. Nevertheless, Bass continued to expand this business through a 34 percent acquisition of Prague Breweries in 1993, a strategic alignment with Grolsch to form Grolsch UK in 1994, and the formation of Bass Ginsber Beer Company in China in 1995.[18] However, it was Bass' blocked attempt to acquire 50 percent of Carlsberg-Tetley in 1996 that defined Bass' brewing business in the 1990s. In fact, Bass was poised to become the

number one brewing company in England with a 37 percent market share before the deal was blocked for antitrust reasons.[19]

Meanwhile, significant changes were also taking place within Bass' soft drinks division. In 1995, Bass added Robinsons soft drinks to its Britvic brand by acquiring it from Reckitt & Coleman for 103 million pounds. Under a complicated structure, Robinsons became a subsidiary of Britannia Soft Drinks Ltd., which was 50 percent owned by Bass. Furthermore, Britannia held a 90 percent stake in Britvic, with the other 10 percent held by Pepsico Holdings Ltd. According to chairman and CEO Ian Prosser, "there were substantial synergies between Britvic and Robinson brands."[20]

Bass' retail division also experienced significant changes during the 1990s. Bass' retail division, consisting of bars, pubs, and restaurants, grew with the branding of O'Neills pubs in 1994, the acquisition of the Harvester restaurant chain from Forte in 1995, and the acquisition of Browns Restaurants in 1998.[21] Additionally, from 1997 to 1998 Bass sold off various retail businesses including about three hundred small pubs, the Coral chain of gambling houses, the Gala bingo chain, and the subsidiaries that focused on manufacturing electronic entertainment and gaming machines. In the process, Bass was able to raise 1.3 billion pounds.[22]

Having raised such a significant amount of cash, Bass was now poised to make a much-anticipated major acquisition. In March of 1998, Bass outbid Marriott International, Patriot American Hospitality, and Ladbroke Group to acquire the luxury InterContinental hotel chain from Japan's Saison Group for $2.9 billion. Included in the acquisition were InterContinental's 211 hotels in seventy-seven countries.[23] Thomas Oliver, then chairman and CEO of Bass' hotel division (Holiday Hospitality), summed up the acquisition well when he said that Inter-Continental provides an "excellent geographic complement to Holiday Hospitality's current structure and gives us a broader portfolio of brands spanning the mid-scale and upscale markets around the globe. The purchase … is consistent with our strategy of growing Bass' business in markets which offer long-term growth opportunities."[24] Around the same time, Bass announced its plans to enter the fast-growing extended-stay hotel market with the development of its Staybridge Suites.[25] This development would allow Bass to both enter into a new segment of the hotel market and compete with the likes of Marriott's Residence Inns and Choice Hotels' Mainstay Suites. Even further expansion occurred in early 2000 when Bass acquired fifty-nine hotels from SPHC in Australia for 128 million pounds. This acquisition gave Bass a greater presence in the Asia-Pacific region.[26]

On June 14, 2000, Bass severed its 223-year-old tie to the brewing industry when it entered into an agreement to sell its beer brewing division to Interbrew, a Belgian brewing company, for $3 billion. According to then chairman and CEO Ian Prosser, the beer industry "was consolidating rapidly and only the very biggest players were likely to remain successful."[27] Prosser also stated that Bass would use the proceeds to expand its global hotel business.[28] Analysts praised the sale, stating it was the "right strategic move" at a "phenomenal price." [29] Along with Bass' sale came the cessation of its name and on June 28, 2001, Bass officially became known as Six Continents PLC. The name "Six Continents" alludes to the number of continents in which the company has a hotel. When asked why they did not rename the company "Seven Continents," present-day CEO Tim Clarke replied, "as we have no intention of opening an outlet in Antarctica, we decided on six."[30]

Today Six Continents PLC's operations include three divisions: hotel, retail, and Britvic (soft drinks). Six Continents PLC's strategy is to "create long-term sustainable growth in shareholder value through developing and strengthening the leading brands within its core businesses of high-growth international hotels and high-return restaurants and pubs. Six Continents is deploying its strong management, global infrastructure, and substantial financial resources to drive superior returns from the expansion of its proven brands."[31] Six Continents Hotels owns, operates, or franchises over 3,200 hotels in close to 100 countries under the brands Holiday Inn, Holiday Inn Express, Crowne Plaza, InterContinental, and Staybridge Suites.[32] Six Continents Hotels aspires to both leverage its competitive position as a global hotel brand owner and drive high returns from brand ownership. It plans to accomplish this by:

- using its worldwide experience further to develop strongly differentiated hotel brand offers that appeal to the high value market segments in which hotels can build a sustainable competitive advantage;

- leveraging the synergies of the global system scale in revenue generation and operations to build RevPAR and GOP premiums for its brands in its target markets and to operate a highly efficient support infrastructure;

- using this superior performance to create an unparalleled network of upscale hotels and domestic depth for midscale hotels in major markets; and

- redeploying capital from owned and leased assets once superior performance is achieved, and continuing to develop its people to ensure consistently high service delivery. [33]

Six Continents Retail owns and manages over 2,000 bars, pubs, and restaurants in the United Kingdom and Germany. Its strategy is to strengthen its market leadership, by driving both growth and returns through:

- creating and sustaining consumer brands and formats with high levels of amenity, service, and value;

- developing prime sites into these brands and formats; and

- maximizing the benefits from corporate, brand, and unit scale.[34]

Britvic is a manufacturer of soft drinks and still maintains its complicated structure in which 90 percent is owned by Britannia Soft Drinks of which Six Continents has a 50 percent majority interest in.[35] Britvic's vision is to become the United Kingdom's leading soft drinks company.[36] Notably, Six Continents has been looking to sell its stake in Britvic. In fact, a sale almost took place with Pepsi in 2000 but controlling shareholders of Britvic could not reach an agreement.[37]

With the horde of cash gained from its sale to Interbrew, Six Continents began to aggressively seek a large hotel purchase. In fact, Six Continents has recently been linked to numerous large hotel acquisitions. For instance, in August 2001 Six Continents came very close to sealing a deal to buy Wyndham International for 3 billion pounds.[38] Nevertheless, Six Continents has been unable to make any large hotel acquisitions, but have instead only managed to acquire the seventy-nine-hotel Posthouse chain and the legendary Regent Hong Kong.[39] This unfruitful, aggressive hotel acquisition strategy has angered major shareholders and led to Ian Prosser's announcement that he would not seek reelection as chairman in 2003.[40]

Despite this unease, Six Continents has continued to focus on the future of the company. On October 1, 2002, Six Continents announced that it would be demerging Six Continents Hotels and Britvic from Six Continents Retail. As part of the split, Six Continents plans on returning $1.1 billion in dividends to shareholders. Under this proposal, Tim Clarke, now CEO of Six Continents PLC, will become head of Six Continents Retail and Richard North, now Finance Director and Chairman of Britvic, will head up Six Continents Hotels and Britvic. The process was expected to become final in April 2003.[41] The separation will have the following benefits:

- Two separate UK listed companies offering discrete investment propositions and with clear market valuations

- Greater flexibility for Hotels and Retail to manage their own resources and pursue strategies appropriate to their markets, which have different characteristics and opportunities

- Management rewards more directly aligned with business and stock market performances, helping to attract, retain and motivate the best people

- Sharpened management focus, helping the two businesses maximize their performance and make full use of their available resources

- Improved ability for Hotels and Retail to develop their strong positions through

participation in industry restructuring and consolidation, if appropriate

- Transparent capital structure and an efficient balance sheet for each business[42]

Commenting on this announcement, Tim Clarke said, "I look forward to the benefits that additional management focus and appropriate balance sheets that separating the two businesses will provide. Our Retail business has a strong track record. With proven retail brands and a strong pipeline, I am very confident about our prospects." Additionally, Richard North remarked, "We have a great Hotels business, with the enviable combination of first class people and a strong global brand portfolio. As a separate company we will build on the Hotels business's leading positions to increase market penetration, operational efficiencies and return on capital employed."[43]

ENVIRONMENTAL ANALYSIS: THE BROAD ENVIRONMENT
Social Trends and Influences

The media have a powerful influence on people's behavior. Television, newspaper, and Internet images of the September 11 terrorist attacks, along with new reports of terrorist events, have caused society to lose confidence and changed peoples' traveling habits. Following are some of the major affects that these global events have had on travel:

- Consumers have had a tendency to travel to closer destinations and domestic travel. Compared with the first half of 2001, U.S. in-region trips increased 8 percent in the first half of 2002.[44]

- Consumers have shown a tendency for "safer" transportation methods, and air travel has significantly decreased. Compared to the first half of 2001, air travel declined over 10 percent in 2002. Meanwhile, during the same period, auto travel increased more than 3 percent.[45]

- Consumers are staying away from home for shorter durations of time. In 2001, most of the travel in the United States was made up short trips. More than half (about 55 percent) of all travel was for two nights or less.[46]

Economic Trends and Influences

The U.S. economic recession that began in late 2000 has had a tremendous affect on the hospitality industry. The Travel Industry Association of America expected that after falling nearly 6 percent in 2001, domestic and international travel spending would continue to be soft in 2002. Further, it is not expected to recover to the record 2000 levels until sometime in 2004.[47] The following industry indicators further depict the influence that the recession has had on the industry:

- The industry occupancy rate was 63.3 percent in the second quarter of 2002, down from the 64.5 percent occupancy rate in the second quarter of 2002.
- The average daily rate was $83.80 in the second quarter of 2002, 3.1 percent less than the corresponding 2001 figure.
- Revenue per available room (RevPAR), which is a key indicator of industry productivity, was $53.06 in the second quarter of 2002, a 4.8 percent decrease from second quarter of 2001.
- Industry room supply increased 1.7 percent in the second quarter of 2002. However, this was significantly down from the 2.6 percent supply growth that took place in the second quarter of 2001.[48]

Political Trends and Influences

Politics has had both a positive and negative impact on the hospitality industry. The positive impact has resulted from various new policies and programs that the federal government has implemented to stimulate the hospitality industry. For example, the Travel Industry Association of America and the U.S. Department of Transportation's National Scenic Byways program have announced a joint marketing partnership called "See America's Byways." This program began in the fall of 2002. "This new partnership

is yet another example of how public and private industry can work together to leverage our resources and to use the SeeAmerica brand to promote the entire USA," remarked William S. Norman, president and CEO of TIA. He further stated, "Through See America's Byways, we will be promoting the all-American road trip on the most scenic, historically and culturally significant roads in our nation."[49]

At the same time, the uncertain relationship between the United States and the Middle East significantly influenced the domestic and international tourists' decisions. Further, the war with Iraq could was expected to have an even more detrimental impact on the industry.[50]

Technological Trends and Influences

Cutting-edge technology has greatly influenced traveler behavior and the industry's way of doing business. From the consumer's point of view, technology has created a heightened expectation. In addition, the increased use of all types of electronic devices means that the hospitality industry must be able to accommodate the needs of its traveling customers. Some of the specific effects of technology on the industry are:

- A higher demand for customized holidays. Consumers believe that vacations should be suited to their specific needs. Although this requires more effort for hospitality companies, advanced information technology does make greater customization possible.[51]
- An increase in online booking. Out of all consumers who used the Internet to make travel arrangements in 2002:
  - 77 percent bought airline tickets for a trip taken in the past year (30 million adults)
  - 57 percent booked overnight lodging accommodations (22 million adults)
  - 37 percent made rental car reservations
  - 25 percent purchased tickets to a cultural event

    A smaller proportion of online travel bookers purchased travel packages, sporting events tickets, amusement park tickets, and museum tickets for a trip taken within the past year.

- A need to stay "wired" while traveling. 2002 trends indicated that business travelers have a high propensity to staying wired through portable electronics. Specifically:
  - 69 percent took a cellular phone on at least one business trip;
  - 25 percent took a laptop computer;
  - 16 percent took a handheld personal digital assistant; and
  - 13 percent took a pager.

  Leisure travelers were less likely to stay connected when traveling, but the numbers show that a significant proportion does travel with portable communication devices:
  - 61 percent took a cellular phone;
  - 9 percent took a laptop computer;
  - 9 percent took a pager; and
  - 5 percent took a handheld personal digital assistant.

  In addition, a significant proportion of travelers used the Internet or e-mail when away from home. This includes 42 percent of business travelers and 22 percent of leisure travelers.[52]

In addition to consumers, the industry itself has been influenced by technological advances. New software for customer relations management and tracking Web customers can provide hotel companies with the opportunity to learn more about their customers and provide customized service at the individual level. In addition, the integration of computer systems within a property and between a property, the chain, and global distribution systems can reduce costs while improving communication, efficiency, and effectiveness. The hotel industry has made an effort to reap the benefits of technology, as the U.S. hotel industry alone spent close to $8 billion on information technology between 1995 and 1999. However, while technology can provide distinct advantages, these expenditures have not provided

the same kind of return that has been realized in other industries.[53]

ENVIRONMENTAL ANALYSIS: THE INDUSTRY

Industry Overview

The hospitality industry is composed of various levels of hotels that share an objective of providing the traveling public with adequate shelter when they are away from home. Beyond this basic definition, the industry has evolved to providing a consistent, unique, and pleasant experience for guests. Large chains play a significant role in the industry. These chains typically take the form of companies that own and operate large chains of hotels and franchising companies that sell the use of their brand names to buyers that uphold the standards of the chain.

In addition, because the industry seeks to appeal to such a wide consumer base, hotels within a particular chain tend to offer similar amenities, services, and prices in order to provide a consistent "face" to the consumer. Further, the chains, and therefore the hotels within them, are categorized into one of the following six segments, based on pricing in 2002.[54]

- *Luxury.* Luxury hotel chains offer the most in-room and on-property amenities of all hotel segments. They usually offer meeting services and on-site retailers, and they must have at least one restaurant. These hotels typically have the highest levels of customer satisfaction. Luxury hotels have an average daily rate of $199 per night and fall within the top 10 percent to 15 percent of their markets' price tier. Chains in this segment include InterContinental, Ritz-Carlton, and Four Seasons.

- *Upscale.* Upscale chains include full-service restaurants, meeting facilities, and a full range of hotel services. Upscale hotels have an average daily rate of $121 and fall within the top 25 percent to 30 percent of their markets' price tier, although they will not have the highest rates if the market also includes a luxury hotel. Chains in this segment include Crowne Plaza, Marriott, and Hilton.

- *Extended Stay*. Extended-stay chains are a relatively new concept. Rooms at these hotels include a sitting room, bedroom, and kitchen area. These hotels also have on-property laundry facilities and often provide a complimentary full breakfast. As the name implies, guests usually stay at these hotels for extended periods. Rates are usually quoted on a weekly or monthly basis; however, the average daily rate for this segment is $89 and hotels in this segment usually fall between the 40th and 70th percentiles of the local markets' price tier. Chains in this segment include Staybridge Suites, TownePlace Suites by Marriott, and Homewood Suites by Hilton.

- *Midscale with Full Food Service*. These chains include hotels with an on-property, full-service restaurant. Hotels in this segment may also offer meeting facilities, business amenities, and fitness services. Hotels in this segment have an average daily rate of $83 and are typically between the 40th and 70th percentiles of the local markets' price tier. Chains in this segment include Holiday Inn Select, Holiday Inn Hotels and Resorts, Courtyard by Marriott, and Wyndham Garden Hotels.

- *Midscale with Limited Food Service*. Chains in this segment do not have on-property restaurants and offer limited services. The segment has an average daily rate of $75 and includes hotels that typically fall within the 40th and 70th percentiles of the local markets' price tier. Chains in this segment include Holiday Inn Express, Comfort Inn, Hampton Inn, and Best Western.

- *Economy/Budget*. Economy/budget chains offer very limited services and do not have restaurants or food service (except for coffee and light breakfast). Hotels in this segment differ from midscale hotels because they are cheaper to build and therefore have lower

quality interior and exterior features. Economy/budget hotels have an average daily rate of $63 and are included in the bottom 30 percent of their markets' price tier. Chains in this segment include Super 8, Days Inn, Motel 6, and Econo Lodge.

Although each of these segments is affiliated with a number of chains, it is important to note that independent hotels are also classified into one of these segments. However, since the industry is dominated by chains, independent hotels are typically left out of any discussion regarding the industry's segments.

Distribution Channels

Hotel rooms are generally sold through four distribution channels. These four channels are via the chain or hotel, in person (walk-ins), through a travel agent, or via the Internet. It is estimated that breakdown of reservations by booking source is as follows:

- 65 percent to 70 percent are made through the chain or hotel;
- 5 percent to 10 percent are walk-ins;
- 10 percent to 15 percent are made though a travel agent; and
- 5 percent to 10 percent are made via the Internet.[55]

Internet bookings can be further broken down into those that are made directly with a hotel company's Web site and those that are made through an intermediary such as Orbitz.com, PriceLine.com, or Hotels.com. In 2002, it was estimated that 54 percent of booking would be made via the hotel company, while 46 percent would be made via an intermediary's site. This trend was expected to continue into 2003; however, the percentage of reservations made via the hotel company has been declining slightly since 1999. Intermediary sites are beneficial to consumers because they provide a means to compare hotels and offer lower prices. On the other hand, they are detrimental to hotel companies because they promote "brand erosion," which is the removal of any differentiation that may exist between competitors.[56] Although hotel companies may prefer not to sell their product through intermediary sites, the events of September 11, 2001, forced them to sell rooms through every possible channel.[57]

Customers

The customers of the hotel industry tend to travel for four main reasons: vacation, business, group meetings and conventions, and other reasons such as to visit family or to attend a special event. For 2001, the breakdown of the four categories showed that:

- 29.5 percent traveled for business;
- 27.0 percent traveled for a group meeting or convention;
- 23.7 percent traveled for vacation; and
- 19.8 percent traveled for other reasons.[58]

The 2001 averages indicate that the typical leisure guest rooms consisted of two adults who were between 35 and 54 years of age, had a household income of $69,147, traveled by car, and paid an average daily rate of $87. On the other hand, the typical business guest rooms consisted of one man who was between 35 and 54 years of age, is employed in a professional or manager level position, had an average household income of $76,394, and paid an average daily rate of $95.[59] This age group, which is typically referred to as the baby boomers, accounted for more stays in 2001 than any other age group. This age group registered more than 248 million trips, and excluding the cost of transportation to their destination, they spent an average of $489 per trip.[60]

Besides the breakdown mentioned above, it is also important to note the significance of international guests. 2001 was a record year, as 45.5 million international travelers visited the United States. Out of these guests, slightly over half were from Canada and Western Europe (22.9 million). September 11 had a significant effect on the international traveler (and the domestic traveler), as the increase in international travelers between 2000 and 2001 was 10.7 percent less than it was between 1999 and 2000.[61]

Industry Size and Growth

Figures for 2001 indicate that the U.S. hotel market was composed of 41,393 properties and 4.2 million rooms. Industry-wide sales were $103.6 billion, and occupancy percentage of the entire industry was 60.3 percent (2.53 million room nights sold). Pretax profits were $16.1 billion.[62]

Although the supply of rooms increased by 100,000 between 2000 and 2001, the number of properties actually decreased. Sales and occupancy also decreased from 2000 to 2001. Sales decreased by $4.9 billion and occupancy decreased by 3.4 percent (2.61 million rooms nights sold). Finally, pretax profits decreased by 33 percent.[63] Much of this downturn can be attributed to the affect that September 11 had on the latter half of 2001. However, the downturn of the economy has also had an impact that carried into 2003. A more positive outlook is in store for 2004.[64]

The hotel industry is certainly reactive to outside forces. At the same time, it is important to note that the industry is also resilient and has still sustained long-term growth. Industry revenue has steadily risen from $62.8 billion in 1990 to $103.5 billion in 2001. In addition, the average daily rate has risen every year between 1991, which had an average daily rate of $58.08, and 2001, which had an average daily rate of $88.27.[65]

Competition

While the hotel industry is divided into six segments, most of the major hotel companies operate chains in more than one of the segments. Therefore, it is beneficial to compare the size of various competitors within each segment and across the industry as a whole.

In terms of rooms, at the end of 2001 the five largest companies across all six segments were: (1) Cendant with 553,771 rooms and 6,624 hotels, (2) Six Continents with 511,072 rooms and 3,274 hotels, (3) Marriott International with 435,983 rooms and 2,398 hotels, (4) Accor with 415,774 rooms and 3,654 hotels, and (5) Choice Hotels International with 362,549 rooms and 4,545 hotels.[66] Descriptions of Six Continents' four main competitors are as follows:

- Cendant is a diversified company that is involved with financial services, real estate services, car rental agencies, travel services, and the hotel industry. Its hotel operations include franchising more than 6,400 hotels under the following brands: Amerihost Inn, Days Inn, Howard Johnson, Knights Inn, Ramada, Super 8, Travelodge, Villager, and Wingate Inn. The brands are primarily within the midscale and economy/budget segments of the industry. Cendant is based in Parsippany, New Jersey.[67]

■ Marriott International operates and franchises more than 2,200 hotels via the following brands: Marriott, Renaissance, Courtyard by Marriott, Residence Inn by Marriott, Fairfield Inn by Marriott, TownePlace Suites, SpringHill Suites, The Ritz-Carlton, Ramada, and Marriott Conference Centers. Marriott's brands fall within each of the six hospitality segments. The company is based in Washington, D.C.[68]

■ Accor is involved in the hotel industry, travel services, casinos, and other specialized services such as employee care and assistance. Its hotel operations include owning, franchising, and leasing more than 3,700 hotels under the Motel 6, Studio 6, Red Roof, Coralia, Thalassa, Sofitel, Novotel, Atria, Orbis, Parthenon, All Seasons, Mercure, Suitehotel, Ibis, Etap Hotel, and Formule 1 brands. Accor's presence is within each hotel segment except for the luxury segment. The company is based in Paris.[69]

■ Choice Hotels International franchises approximately 4,400 hotels under the Comfort, Comfort Inn, Comfort Suites, Quality Inn, Sleep Inn, Clarion, Econo Lodge, Rodeway Inn, and MainStay Suites brands. The brands are primarily in the midscale, economy/budget, and extended stay segments. The company is based in Silver Spring, Maryland.[70]

A further examination of competition by segment shows that the five largest brands within each of the six industry segments are as follows:

■ Luxury:
   1. InterContinental (Six Continents)—45,278 rooms
   2. Westin (Starwood)—44,965 rooms
   3. Renaissance (Marriott)—44,773 rooms
   4. Le Meridien—37,667 rooms
   5. Fairmont—19,222 rooms

■ Upscale:
   1. Marriott—158,112 rooms
   2. Sheraton—127,904 rooms
   3. Radisson—100,874 rooms
   4. Hilton Hotels—86,063 rooms
   5. Hilton International—66,246 rooms

■ Extended Stay:
   1. Studio Plus Deluxe Studios (Extended Stay America)—32,809 rooms
   2. Suburban Lodge (Suburban Lodges of America, Inc.)—16,885 rooms
   3. Homestead Studio Suites—14,899 rooms
   4. Hawthorne Suites (U.S. Franchise Systems, Inc.)—12,711 rooms
   5. Homestead Suites by Hilton—11,603 rooms

■ Midscale with Full Food Service:
   1. Holiday Inn (Six Continents)—294,493 rooms
   2. Quality Inn (Choice)—84,760 rooms
   3. Courtyard by Marriott—78,785 rooms
   4. Mercure (Accor)—72,536 rooms
   5. Four Points by Sheraton—27,631 rooms

■ Midscale with Limited Food Service:
   1. Best Western—306,851 rooms
   2. Comfort Inn (Choice)—131,647 rooms
   3. Hampton Inn (Hilton)—117,806 rooms
   4. Holiday Inn Express (Six Continents)—103,522 rooms
   5. Novotel (Accor)—57,917 rooms

■ Economy/Budget:
   1. Days Inn (Cendant)—164,092 rooms
   2. Super 8 (Cendant)—125,016 rooms
   3. Ramada (Cendant)—120,515 rooms
   4. Motel 6 (Accor)—90,276 rooms
   5. Ibis (Accor)—60,939 rooms[71]

Although the industry is divided and competition exists within and across each segment, hotel companies are having a tough time creating services that are unique to their operations. This brand erosion, as described above, is the result of companies following in the successes of their competition. In other words, different hotel companies are offering very similar products. Additionally, the proliferation of the Internet has also reduced any differences between the various hotel companies.

Nevertheless, several innovations have been successful. For example, Westin has introduced the concept of the Heavenly Bed, a comfortable bed distinct to its hotels that has proven to be a customer favorite. Technology has also been an enabler of differentiation, as Carlson has used it to implement "Look to Book," a patented program through which travel agents receive frequency points for booking stays at Carlson properties.[72] Finally, in an attempt to provide the guest with a different experience at each hotel property, companies such as Loews Hotels are moving away from a standard hotel type to a more diversified hotel that represents the uniqueness of its location.

Entry Barriers, Exit Barriers, and Fixed Costs

Entering the hotel industry has become quite a daunting task. The overbuilding that took place throughout the 1990s has saturated most of the key U.S. markets, making it extremely difficult to find a good site on which to build a hotel.[73] In addition, the prevalence of brand erosion, high capital costs, and high fixed costs (fixed costs typically account for 10 percent to 15 percent of a hotel's revenue) have recently acted as deterrents for entering the industry.[74] These deterrents, coupled with the fact that financial institutions are unwilling to provide capital for new projects, has made it extremely difficult to enter the industry.[75]

For companies already in the industry, it is just as difficult to leave as it is to enter. The hotel product is very specific, and this makes it difficult to apply the industry's tangible resources to other industries. Possible scenarios include the conversion of hotels to apartments, condominiums, or office buildings. However, these are costly scenarios and are therefore rarely a reality. The only plausible option would be to reuse the land, as it has become a scarce commodity. But because this option requires the demolition of existing capital, it could be justified only if the site were extremely valuable and unique.

Suppliers

A large variety of industries provide the products and services that are necessary to operate a hotel. Some of the major product categories of suppliers include cleaning and maintenance, food and beverage, soft goods, furniture, technology, and guest amenities. Service supplier categories include education and associations, professional services such as housekeeping assistance, and sales and marketing.[76] Most of the suppliers distribute their goods via a variety of outlets including the Internet, phone, and catalogs. Regardless of the category, almost all of suppliers offer generic goods that could be used in the hotels of almost any segment. On the other hand, there are exceptions that allow brands to incorporate unique elements into their hotels. For example, as mentioned above, the Westin hotels feature the Heavenly Bed. This bed, specially created for Westin by Simmons, is one of the few items that can be purchased from only one supplier.[77]

Along with the suppliers mentioned above, a new type of supplier is also emerging at the chain level. Many chains are now setting up intermediary Web sites that often offer lower prices than other outlets. This type of procurement has made it even easier for hotels because all of the products on the intermediary sites are from approved vendors. Therefore, hotels do not have to spend time determining whether a particular product is within the established standards of the chain. An example of this type of intermediary supplier is ChoiceBuys.com, which provides one location through which hotels in any of Choice Hotels International's eight chains can buy all the supplies they need.[78]

Substitutes

The hotel industry has several major substitutes that depend on the type of traveler. The major substitutes for the leisure traveler are friends and family, recreational vehicles, and cruise boats. For business travelers, corporate apartments and tele-conferencing have become the major substitutes to the hotel industry.

The most used substitute for the leisure traveler would be friends and family. Homes are larger than they use to be, and extra bedrooms have allowed friends and family to stay in their hosts' home rather than at a hotel. In response to this, some chains recently encouraged people to put up their friends and family at hotels as a simpler, less-hectic solution.

Another substitute for the leisure guest is the recreational vehicle (RV). A 2001 study conducted by the University of Michigan shows that U.S. own-ership of RVs has reached record levels. Nearly 1 in 12 of the nearly seven million vehicle-owning households in the United States now owns an RV. This is a 7.8 percent increase from the previous four years and a 42 percent gain over the previous twenty-one years.[79] Older generations as well as families with children are taking advantage of this option because it is generally a less stressful means of traveling. Traveling and sleeping in an RV equates to having all the comforts of home at all times, including full kitchens and even bathrooms with showers. RVs are no longer simple vehicles charac-terized by the pop-up camper and having to use a campground's communal bathrooms.

Lastly, cruise boats are acting as substitutes to leisure travelers vacationing at coastal destinations. Travelers who would normally travel these destinations by plane and stay in hotels or resorts are now able to visit tourist locations by day and sleep on the cruise boat by night, as it travels to the next destination. This option has given travelers the comfort of unpacking one time for trips spanning several locations. After September 11, cruise travel rebounded dramatically, increasing 3.8 percent in the first half of 2002. It is expected to meet its target of 7.4 million cruisers by the end of the year.[80]

For business travelers, a substitute is the corpo-rate apartment. Some companies are realizing that renting apartments for employees who are doing temporary projects away from home is cheaper than putting them up in hotels for weeks at times. It was estimated that more than 64,000 people would live in corporate apartments in 2002.[81] These apartments often come with weekly or even daily housekeeping. Corporate apartments are approximately $14 a day cheaper than extended stay hotels, and they provide the advantage of knowing that there will be a vacancy for the entire stay. Companies no longer have to worry about major events that may occupy all of the hotel rooms in a particular city. Lastly, while the quality of room supplied by certain hotel chains may be unknown, corporate apartments provide compa-nies with the certainty that their employees will receive high-quality accommodations.

Another option for business travelers is to sim-ply not travel at all. "Corporate America is scaling back company travel policies . . . and even canceling meetings in favor of teleconferences."[82] The events of September 11 have increased this trend. Technology has rapidly developed to accommodate both audio and videoconference calling as substitutes to travel. Businesses are now able to save on travel costs by conducting meetings from their own offices via telecommunication lines. In most cases, the equip-ment cost of these technologies can be paid off within a few canceled trips.

Basic Strategies of Competitors

Every hotel chain has the strategy to be the best at what it does. While some hotel chains are better than others, they are all striving to come up with some sort of a sustainable competitive advantage. Most hotel companies struggle to define their competitive advantage. In fact, most changes in the industry are the result of hotel companies "copying" innovations created by the competition. For example, at one point a hotel made the historical decision to include shampoo with the room. This would be its competi-tive advantage. But once an innovation such as this is introduced, every hotel adopts the same practice and the competitive advantage disappears. This "follow-the-leader" mentality has been occurring for decades. Other examples of this trend range from providing a free breakfast to including basic ameni-ties like irons and boards in all of the guest rooms.

In-room high-speed Internet access has been the latest industry attempt to differentiate from one hotel to the next. Mark Hamilton, director of the Technology Research and Education Center at the

Conrad N. Hilton School of Hotel and Restaurant Management, comments, "From an overall technology standpoint in the hospitality industry, hotels are in catch-up mode as related to other industries in the world. The hospitality industry is conservative in nature and hotel companies are reluctant to invest in new amenities without knowing whether they will recover their costs in the end. It would be a competitive disadvantage for hotels of the future not to have high-speed Internet access."[83]

Another strategy hotels use in trying to differentiate themselves is through sheer numbers. For example, larger chains have a greater ability to retain their customers by referring customers to other hotels within their chain. The customer recognizes that an expected level of quality comes with each hotel whether it operates in the United States or Brazil.

A newer strategy being adopted by hotel chains is customer relations management. Wyndham's ByRequest program is one of the innovative leaders in this area. By consistently customizing their guest's rooms and amenities across all hotels and for every stay, Wyndham may have found a competitive advantage over its competition.[84] Whether it will be sustainable is yet to be seen. The company presently feels that this service level might lead to a successful edge over the competition. However, if other chains copy the program, Wyndham would experience brand erosion.

Overall, it is difficult to develop a significant and successful strategy over other competing hotel chains. It has been proven that hotel chains retaliate to competitive moves by matching or exceeding any other chain that comes up with a new advantage in the industry. For customers, aggressive competition has led to hotels offering more amenities and customized services for equal or lower rates. However, such tactics have also proven to hurt hotels by requiring them to offer more value to keep up with the competition, and this correlates to a decrease in profits.

External Stakeholders

The key external stakeholders in the hotel industry are the financial institutions, local communities, distribution channels, labor unions, suppliers, and customers. Each of these stakeholders has a different level of importance that depends on location.

Financial institutions control the industry's ability to grow or remodel. When markets become saturated, these institutions tend to not lend as much money for new construction as they would in an area that is not as developed. Additionally, depending on the economy, financial institutions know when hotels are earning low revenue that could affect whether loans are paid on time. This could make loans for remodeling difficult to obtain.

Local communities also have a large impact on the hotel industry. In fact, community-supported hotels have much higher rates of survival. A local community provides a source of labor and supports the areas surrounding the hotel by developing restaurants and other entertainment facilities. Safety, friendliness, and respect for the environment around the hotel are key aspects of a community that attract customers to a hotel.[85]

Distribution channels, which include everything from travel agents to online booking agents such as Expedia, are major industry stakeholders. Without them, the hotel industry would not be as developed as it is today. Although many distribution channels promote brand erosion, the advancements in technology have caused Internet bookings to become an important factor for many hotel chains. Through this technology, customers have the ability to search hotel listings quickly and make decisions based on cost as well as quality. Rates along with pictures and descriptions aid in this process. Even though there are issues pertaining to electronic distribution, the Internet will continue to be a driving force in the industry.

In certain geographic areas, labor unions are very important to hotels. While it is difficult to thoroughly discuss labor unions in all areas, it is important to note that for some areas, labor unions can be the most important stakeholder. Without proper negotiations and careful detail to maintaining relationships, a labor union can lead to the demise of a successful hotel.

Although suppliers offer many similar products that hotels can choose from, they also can be important stakeholders because they give the industry new innovations that help develop competitive advantages.

This can range from Kohler's BodySpa shower[86] to OnCommand's pay-per-view systems.[87] By building partnerships with suppliers, hotel chains can offer amenities that were previously not available. As mentioned earlier, an example would be Westin's Heavenly Bed, which resulted from a partnership with Simmons Beautyrest. Through this innovation, Westin has had incredible success in increasing occupancy, overall guest satisfaction, guest loyalty, and even at-home sales of the mattress.[88]

Finally, Customers are the stakeholders that have most dramatically shaped the industry. Hotels must change as customer's needs and wants change. As mentioned earlier, the story of Charles Kemmons Wilson shows how the hotel industry can adapt to consumer needs. Wilson's 1951 trip with his wife and five children helped him realize that roadside motels were generally unclean, cramped, and overpriced. In addition, these hotels charged additional fees for each child. As a customer, he saw a need for better accommodations for traveling families, and in 1952, he opened the first Holiday Inn as a response to the need for a family-friendly hotel. Holiday Inn is an example of a company that entered the hotel industry in order to satisfy the needs of the customer.[89]

Global Industry

The hotel industry can be found in practically every country in the world. The World Travel Tourism Council (WTTC) states that global tourism, of which hotels are a major part, is the largest industry in the world with $4 trillion in annual sales and a workforce that exceeds 260 million people.[90] Wherever people live, there is a need for hotels to house others who come to visit. There are many advantages for a hotel chain to be represented in more than one nation. Brand recognition is one of the most important motivators in developing a multinational or global strategy. Having a global presence provides loyal guests with the ability to stay with a brand they trust, regardless of where they are traveling to. With more than 3,200 hotels in 100 countries, Six Continents is an example of a globally recognized brand.[91]

ORGANIZATIONAL ANALYSIS

Turning to the internal operation of the company, top managers have crafted a strategic direction for the company that includes both corporate and business level strategies.

Corporate Strategy

Six Continents aims to create long-term sustainable growth in shareholder value through developing and strengthening the leading brands within its core businesses of high-growth international hotels and high-return restaurants and pubs. Six Continents is deploying its strong management, global infrastructure and substantial financial resources to drive superior returns from the expansion of its proven brands.[92]

Corporate Vision Statement

How we do business is an integral part of why we do business. We want to inspire our customers to return to our brands again and again and the way we behave is key to delivering this vision.[93]

Corporate Value Statement

Our values outline how we aim to conduct business and motivate people to succeed within Six Continents. These values are:

- Delighting our customers again and again
- Winning by a mile
- Generating innovation and change
- Behaving with integrity
- Valuing and trusting our people
- Respecting our communities

Every one of Six Continents' hotels, restaurants and pubs and bars is part of a wider community. All carry the responsibility to act in a way that respects the social, economic and environmental well-being of the wider world. As a company, we recognize that we will win in the long term and deliver shareholder value only if we behave properly at all times. Responsible corporate citizenship has a direct impact on our shareholder value.[94]

Hotel Business Strategy

Six Continents Hotels' goal is to extend the worldwide distribution of its range of high-quality hotel brands through a diverse portfolio of owned and leased hotels, managed contracts, and franchises. The strategy for achieving this is to make its brands the preferred choice for the guest, thus enhancing revenues and returns for the hotels in its system, which, in most cases, are owned by third-party investors.

Retail (Restaurant) Business Strategy

Six Continents Retail's strategy is to concentrate on expanding the distribution of distinctive retail brands and format in the attractive segments of the pub, bar, and restaurant markets.

Management Action and Influential Stakeholders

As previously mentioned, management at Six Continents was divided on the strategic direction of the company. A report in the August 2002 edition of *Caterer & Hotelkeeper* magazine states that "chief executive Tim Clarke reportedly favors a de-merger, while Chairman Ian Prosser is reportedly against a split."[95] One of the more outspoken and harsh critics of Six Continents' corporate strategy and of Prosser was fund manager Hermes.

On October 1, 2002, Six Continents finally made the decision to demerge its hotel and retail businesses and return the cash to shareholders from the sale of Bass to Interbrew. Upon that announcement, David Pitt Watson, managing director of Hermes UK

Focus Fund, which owned 3 percent of Six Continents, stated, "We are very pleased at the demerger and return of cash to shareholders. This will form two strong focused companies, which will deliver good returns to shareholders."[96]

Prior to the demerger announcement, it was decided that Ian Prosser would step down as chairman at the end of 2002. That was a supposedly tricky negotiation, since it was reported that Prosser had planned to stay on as chairman for another two to three years. This report had supposedly "prompted fury among shareholders, led by Hermes, Axa Investment Managers, and M&G Group. "There would have been war if Ian had not agreed to go next year," said one company insider.[97]

Change is occurring throughout the entire Six Continents organization and franchisees are glad to see it. In June 2002, Stevan Porter was named the new president of North American operations, replacing John Sweetwood, who stepped down in June to pursue other opportunities. Also stepping down was Ravi Saligman, brand president of the Americas. Six weeks after Porter took over the position, a new executive team was named. According to Porter, the strategy behind the change was "building its mid-scale and upscale brands, upgrading its technology infrastructure and finding additional ways to increase revenue through operations and major hotel investments around the world."[98] (See Appendices A and B for more detailed information on the senior management team and the board of directors.)

Influential franchisees applauded the move for several reasons. First, they were glad to see someone from inside the organization take the helm of North American Operations (Porter's previous position was chief operating officer of the Americas). Second, the franchisees were excited that Porter came into the position with an hotelier background and experience in franchising.

The support of the franchisees is important to Six Continents, especially in the United States. The Americas region—encompassing the United States, Canada, Mexico, Central and South America, and the Caribbean—is the largest operating region of Six

Continents. It includes 2,700 properties and nearly 300,000 guestrooms.[99]

Operating Characteristics

Six Continents is a hospitality conglomerate that employs approximately 80,000 employees worldwide, 57 percent of whom work full time and 43 percent part time.[100] The organization is divided into three distinct businesses: Retail (Restaurant and Pub), Hotels, and Soft Drinks. In 2001, total sales for Six Continents PLC surpassed $5.9 billion.

The Retail (Restaurant and Pubs) unit was operating only in the United Kingdom but recently entered the German market. The operation includes two groups. The first is the Restaurant Group, with more than 500 branded suburban restaurants and food-led outlets. The second is the Pubs & Bars Group, with more than 350 branded outlets.[101] In 2001, the Six Continents retail business reached $2.3 billion.

The hotel business is made up of owned and leased, franchised and management contract hotels in approximately one hundred countries. Six Continents offers a wide spectrum of global hotel brand accommodations that suit a variety of markets from the upscale to the budget conscience. Hotels in the Six Continents portfolio include: Inter-Continental, Crowne Plaza, Holiday Inn, Holiday Inn Select, Holiday Inn SunSpree, Holiday Inn Express, and Staybridge Suites.

Hotel assets grew in 2002 and continued growth looks promising. According to the company's 2002 Interim Financial Statement, "An indicator of future growth, the pipeline of hotels waiting to enter the Six Continents Hotel system remains healthy despite the difficulties surrounding the hotel industry; as of March 31, 2002 the pipeline stood at 490 hotels with 66,800 rooms, of which 28% of the rooms were in the upscale brands."[102] The number of hotels in the Six Continents system grew over the twelve-month period. At the end of March 2002, there were 3,279 hotels compared with 3,267 the year before. In 2001, sales for the Six Continents hotel and soft drink businesses reached $3.6 billion.

- *InterContinental:* An international upper-upscale brand with 135 locations in more than seventy-five countries. Generally located in the heart of the world's major cities and in exclusive resort locations.

- *Crowne Plaza:* An upscale, international brand that operates 160 hotels in forty countries, Crowne Plaza is renowned for its expertise in managing meetings and in servicing the needs of business travelers. Meeting facilities are flexible, with professionally trained staff to handle any request. Crowne Plaza is positioned in key urban, suburban, and airport locations.

- *Holiday Inn:* The full-service Holiday Inn Hotels and resorts offer guests the dependable service and amenities for both business and leisure travelers.

- *Holiday Inn Select:* Located throughout North and South America near business centers and airports. Holiday Inn Select provides business travelers with special services and amenities to make their stay as comfortable and productive as possible.

- *Holiday Inn SunSpree Resorts:* Found in more than twenty-five locations in the United States, Canada, the Caribbean, and Mexico. The casual atmosphere and modern facilities make it easy for families to relax and have fun together.

- *Holiday Inn Express:* The modern limited-service hotel for value-oriented travelers who expect clean rooms and convenience, all delivered in an atmosphere of informal hospitality. Holiday Inn Express hotels are the smart choice for travelers who want dependable quality, comfort, and convenience without all of the extras.

- *Staybridge by Holiday Inn:* The newest member of the Six Continents Hotels corporate family and is the latest evolution of the all-suite extended stay concept.

Unique Physical Resources

The global network of hotels provides Six Continents with tremendous economies of scale. In addition, the portfolio of brands owned by Six Continents, has a high level of brand identity. Holiday Inn alone is one of the most recognizable hotel brands in the world with locations in nearly one hundred countries.

The large amount of capital ($3 billion) from the sale of the Bass Brewing business has allowed Six Continents to purchase highly recognizable properties that bring immediate attention to their hotel brands. An example is the recent flag change of the Regent in Hong Kong to an Inter-Continental. This 514-room, five-star hotel was purchased in December 2001 for $346 million. The strategy behind the purchase was to relaunch the Inter-Continental brand. Kevin Croley, Six Continents Hotel's vice president of sales, Asia Pacific, and marketing, southern Asia, points out, "The Regent Hong Kong maintained a landmark identity. It offered a high degree of elegance and sophistication. In this regard, as the Hotel InterContinental Hong Kong, it is a defining property for the new InterContinental style."[103] The acquisition allowed Six Continents an immediate opportunity to showcase the Inter-Continental hotel brand.

In addition to the financial assets that allow Six Continents to purchase a hotel such as the Hong Kong Regent, the company has also developed value through strong brand identity. In June 2001, the company completed a deal in Sao Paulo to flag an enormous 780-room convention center and hotel with the Holiday Inn brand. Once completed, in 2003, the $50 million hotel will be the largest Holiday Inn in the world, connected to the largest convention center in Latin America.[104] A strong brand also translates into a loyal network of franchisees. As one hotelier, George Glover, stated, "Holiday Inn Franchisees are a little different—they bleed green," referring to the brand's long association with the color green in its logo.[105]

Six Continents was the first hotel company to offer Web bookings. And today, Information Technology software and hardware is another unique resource that drives Six Continents' business. According to Eric Pearson, vice president of e-commerce, "Earlier this year (2002), we passed another major milestone—$2 million booked in a single day direct to our Web sites."[106]

Six Continents was in the process of centralizing all of the hotels within its portfolio. Complete migration of all Six Continents' hotels to the new central reservation system (CRS)—HOLIDEXPlus—was expected to be completed by mid-2003. This new system means hotels can now provide more detailed descriptions of their properties, rates, and promotions to the various global distribution systems (GDS) and travel Web sites.[107]

Using Day Communique technology, Six Continents has recently reengineered its global Internet reservation system. Guests reserving through any Six Continents Hotels Web site can choose from any one of the 3,300 properties throughout the world and check availability and rates and then book online.[108]

In October 2002, Six Continents agreed to a deal with ATG, a leading developer of online customer relations management (CRM) applications. ATG will develop software that will provide Six Continents with more precision in marketing campaigns, and personalization for the company's network of Web sites. According to Eric Pearson, vice president of e-commerce, "ATG Commerce allows Six Continents Hotels to standardize on a platform that incorporates our existing back-end systems into our long term Internet strategy."[109]

A last component to the Six Continents technology strategy is the implementation of the webValidator by iPerceptions Inc. The purpose of the software is to "provide fast and economical market research on a user's behavior throughout their Web site experience."[110]

Overarching Marketing Strategy

In the wake of the demerger news, Six Continent's marketing strategy received a lot of attention. Six Continents is now a multibranded, global lodging company that is no longer part of a publicly held, Britain-based conglomerate. Six Continents presented this simplified and refocused business model to 1,600 franchisees in November 2002.[111]

An article from Hotelbusiness.com noted that the strategy for Six Continents is to clearly define each of its brands with consistent service and product. The following outlines the brand marketing strategy for each of the hotels:

- Staybridge Suites is putting an emphasis on its long-staying customers, rather than trying to fill units with transient guests who may be cutting into opportunities to host extended-stay visitors.

- Holiday Inn Express has a new breakfast concept in the form of Express Start, a sharply defined breakfast experience that is being mandated for all 1,200 North American properties beginning next year.

- Holiday Inn has its new balanced, full-service prototype, aimed at being more appealing to developers with its lower cost per key. The carefully planned model may be used to replace aging Holiday Inns throughout the system, said executives.

- In the upscale arena, Crowne Plaza is now being called the "Place to Meet," having staked its future on small to midscale meetings. A new logo will also be introduced. These initiatives are an attempt to create a niche for a brand name that doesn't "own a space in the public's mind."

- InterContinental has a $20 million advertising campaign to pull in the international business traveler, whose many needs will now be consistently met at every property carrying the upper upscale's moniker throughout the globe.

Marketing Tactics

Six Continents uses a variety of marketing efforts to draw customers to its hotels. Major initiatives have included Priority Club Rewards, Six Continents Club, Internet-based marketing, direct mail, advertising, and promotion.

Priority Rewards, Six Continents' loyalty program, includes 13 million members and includes all of Six Continents' brands. In April 2002, Six Continents relaunched its rewards program to make it easier and faster for guests to use and redeem points. The reason for the relaunch and the renewed focus on ease and speed was addressed by Susan Mulder, director of consumer marketing: "It used to be all about getting people in your program. Once they were in, you were done. Now everybody carries two or three frequent guest cards in their wallet, so the challenge now is much greater."[112]

The Six Continents Club is another marketing tool that is specific to the chain of InterContinental hotels. With a membership base of roughly 130,000, the Six Continents Club offers guests value-added benefits and rewards for each stay at an InterContinental. The importance of this program is highlighted in Six Continents' marketing collateral material: "Six Continents Club members account for approximately two percent of InterContinental guests, yet yield more than 10 percent of total room revenue.[113]

One of the newer marketing tactics that has been extremely successful for Six Continents is its Web-based "best rate" initiative called "Lowest Internet Rate Guaranteed." According to an article in *Travel Weekly*, the initiative is a promise to beat by 10 percent the cheapest rate that a customer can obtain through any online travel site."[114] According to a six-month review of the program, it was working:[115]

- Internet bookings shot up 80 percent over the previous year—compared to Internet bookings in general, which averaged 40 percent.

- Hotels are regaining control of their inventory and capturing the margins that would have otherwise gone to wholesalers.

- Challenges to the guarantee average about one out of every thousand bookings, or less than one-tenth of 1 percent of people who book on the Internet, confirming that Six Continents pricing is the best available.

Much of the refocusing change that is now occurring within the Six Continents organization may have been foreshadowed in a June 2001 interview that Tom Oliver, chairman and CEO of Hotels, did with Hotelbusiness.com. In the interview, Oliver stated that "trying to drive brand development in a market with so many moving parts" is probably the company's top problem at this time, though trepidations about human resources, return on investment, and quality assurance similarly take priority on a regular basis.[116]

Employee Benefits and Training

At the end of fiscal 2001, Six Continents offered various incentive programs to its employees. For example, employees could participate in the Employee Savings

Share Scheme, which provided the option to buy ordinary shares at a nominal price. This opportunity is provided to employees who have been with the company for at least one year and is open to all employees, including executive directors.

Six Continents also offers a variety of training programs to ensure that its employees have all the skills required to perform and enhance their daily duties. "At Six Continents Hotels we are committed to 'growing our own'—providing employees with training and development opportunities throughout their career with the organization."[117]

Employees of the group are provided training skills based upon individual needs and assessments. They receive managerial training to enhance their leadership and communication skills as well as technological training in computer applications. Training opportunities are available irrespective of their position in the company. The specific training programs include:

- *Your Career with Six Continents Hotels.* The goal of this program is to ensure that all employees in the Six Continents Hotels network have the opportunity for ongoing professional and personal development. The program is composed of four distinct phases: entry-level training, supervisory training, operational management, and management education. Within each phase, employees work at their own pace, and their learning is supported by workshops that strengthen skills and emphasize matters important to the company and the individuals.[118]

- *In the Customers' Shoes.* The objective of the program is to enhance customer satisfaction by developing excellent service skills among employees.

- *Corporate Management Traineeships.* This twelve- to eighteen-month training program focuses on hotel operations and people management.

- *Hospitality Operations Traineeships.* This program focuses on practical training in key areas of the hospitality industry such as Front Office, Food and Beverage (F&B), Housekeeping, and Kitchen Attending.

- *Apprenticeships.* The company provides apprenticeships to chefs in their first four years at the hotels. After completing the program, chefs can transfer to different properties within the group.

- *Milestones.* This program allows employees with potential to become general managers by learning from current general managers and other senior management. It provides development in leadership and management capability, technical competences, use of initiative, and strategic thinking.

Labor Unions

As stated in the industry analysis, hotels were significantly affected by the September 11 attacks. In spite of this fact, labor unions have continued to pressure hotel employers and have scored some victories in key cities. Specific to Six Continents, Holiday Inn has had some serious problems with labor unions. Recently, employees have used guerrilla tactics to boycott non-union hotels. For example, during a realtors conference at St. Paul, Minnesota, the employee demonstrators gave hotel guests unexpected wake-up calls at 7 A.M. Consequently, the hotel owner agreed to the "labor peace agreement."[119]

Relationships with Customers, Suppliers, and the Community

Six Continents attempts to develop customer relationships by providing unique services that are not provided by other hotel companies. Six Continents was the first hotel chain to provide customers with the service of booking rooms with mobile devices and credit cards. They used Air2Web technology to provide access to loyalty accounts, itineraries, hotel directories, and other customer services.

Six Continents Hotels also helped create an online supply system called Avendra. Through Avendra, Six Continents Hotels allows its owners and operators to cut costs significantly through procurement and purchasing power capabilities. Avendra is a founding member of, is a "Web enabled strategic supplier of business-to-business procurement solutions for the hospitality and related industries."

According to Six Continents, Avendra adds worth to owners and operators through "hospitality expertise, largest purchasing power, supply chain management expertise, and flexible access to programs."[120]

In regards to community relations, the chairman and CEO of Six Continents Hotels, Tom Oliver, states that "Six Continents Hotels strongly believes in supporting communities in which our hotel brands have a presence. Through our charitable giving programs we are able to positively impact the well-being of our consumers all over the world."[121] Six Continents donates to a number of charities and social organizations. Specifically, the company gives to educational institutions, raises funds for children organizations, and contributes to environmental conservation programs through the Conserving Our Planet program.[122] Additionally, employees are encouraged to participate in the community and share in the sense of responsibility to the social, economic, and environmental well-being of society.

Organizational Culture

Six Continents' high performing culture supports the organization's overall strategy. As stated earlier, Six Continents' corporate value statement notes the importance of "delighting our customers again and again." Therefore, Six Continents prides itself in providing guests with the best service possible. This is supported by the multitude of training programs available to employees. Furthermore, the company bases its success on its employees' behavior with customers and the company's relationship with shareholders. Hence, the culture works in line with the interests of the customers, shareholders, suppliers, and others.[123]

Competitive Advantage

Six Continents Hotels competes with a wide range of facilities offering various types of lodging options and related services to the public. The competition includes several large and moderate-sized hotel chains offering luxury, upscale, extended stay, and midscale accommodations.

As noted earlier, the Six Continents loyalty program, Priority Rewards, is one of the largest of its kind. The program has ties with more than forty airlines, which offer frequent-flier miles for stays at any Six Continents property. The program also has similar tie-ins with credit card and car rental companies. Enhancing Six Continents' marketing competency is its cutting-edge technological advancements that manage both existing and new customer relations.[124] These advancements include e-commerce, reservation technology (Holidex and HIRO), and guest-tracking systems.

Performance of individual hotels is highly seasonal; however, with 3,200 hotels in almost one hundred countries, Six Continents is able to use diversity as a means to combat this seasonality. Additionally, Six Continents Hotels includes a strong portfolio of five recognizable hotel brands across each price point. A clear indicator of its brand cachet is evidenced through the nearly 70 percent of Holiday Inn customers who are walk-ins.

Financial Summary

Despite recessionary market conditions, Six Continents posted favorable results in 2001. This favorable performance is attributed to continued development within its retail and hotel businesses. Sales were up 2.1 percent and operating profits were up as follows:

- Six Continents Hotels increased by 13.6 percent.
- Six Continents Retail increased by 1.1 percent.
- Britvic Soft Drinks increased by 23.9 percent.[125]

Please refer to Appendices C through G for more financial information regarding sales and assets figures, income statements, balance sheets, profit and loss statements, and RevPAR statistics.

UPDATE: DEMERGER COMPLETE

On April 15, 2003, six months after announcing it would be demerging, Six Continents split its hotel and soft drink business from its retail division, creating two separate companies. The retail business is now Mitchells & Butlers. The hotel group named Six Continents since 2001 has taken the name of its luxury line, InterContinental Hotels Group PLC.

In preparation for the split, Six Continents assembled a new senior team, although Steve Porter continues as President of the Americas. Talk of a hostile takeover by Capital Management and Investment (CMI) in the months preceding the demerger subsided when the Owners' Association of Six Continents Hotels (IAHI) voiced severe opposition. Many of these franchisees considered terminating their license agreements and leaving the system if the takeover and/or breakup of the company would have occurred according to Jay Fishman, Chairman of the IAHI Board of Directors.[126]

Acquisition of Kansas-based Candlewood Suites brand in late 2003 increased InterContinental's portfolio to six brands and their management portfolio by more than 30 percent in the Americas. Candlewood Suites, a midscale brand was acquired for $15 million in cash and permits InterContinental to be licensor on all current and future franchise agreements. This acquisition is viewed by Steve Porter, President for the Americas, as a way to expand hotel supply share in a segment in which the firm has experience.[127] As the new demerged firm enters 2004, it is focused on management and franchise growth. According to Richard North, the Chief Executive of InterContinental Hotels Group:

> "The most global hotel company now has a clear and robust strategy, a truly global brand portfolio, significant global scale, a wealth of talent at all levels of the company, and tremendous opportunity to grow in a number of markets."[128]

Notes

1. Hospitality Net, www.hospitalitynet.org/news/All_Latest_News/4013424.html, 15 November 2002.
2. J. P. Pederson, ed., *International Directory of Company Histories*, Vol. 38 (Detroit: St. James Press, 2001).
3. Ibid.
4. Ibid.
5. Ibid.
6. Ibid.
7. Ibid.
8. D. Atkinson, "Bass to Sell Crest Group to Concentrate on Holiday Inns," *The Guardian* (London), 1 March 1990.
9. S. Butler, "Bass Pays 55 M [Pds] for Four Holiday Inn Hotels," *Financial Times* (London), 22 May 1987.
10. D. Churchill, "Bass Buys a Holiday Inn Hotel Chain for 475 M," *Financial Times* (London), 16 September 1987.
11. Six Continents, History Page, http://www.sixcontinents.com/aboutus/history.htm, 15 November 2002.
12. G. Strauss, "Holiday Inns Sold; Britain's Bass to Buy Chain for $2.23 B," *USA Today*, 25 August 1989.
13. J. P. Pederson, ed., *International Directory of Company Histories*, Vol. 38 (Detroit: St. James Press, 2001).
14. G. Strauss, "Holiday Inns Sold; Britain's Bass to Buy Chain for $2.23 B," *USA Today*, 25 August 1989.
15. K. Wilson and R. Kerr, *Half Luck, Half Brains: The Kemmons Wilson Holiday Inn Story.* (Hambleton-Hill, 1996).
16. J. P. Pederson, ed., *International Directory of Company Histories*, Vol. 38 (Detroit: St. James Press, 2001).
17. Hoovers Online, Company Profiles, http://www.hoovers.com/premium/profile/8/0,2147,41788,00, 15 November 2002.
18. Bass Brewery, History Page, http://www.bassbrewers.com/about/history.html, 15 November 2002.
19. J. P. Pederson, ed., *International Directory of Company Histories*, Vol. 38 (Detroit: St. James Press, 2001).
20. N. Cope, "Reckitt & Colman Sell Foods Arm to Unilever," *The Independent* (London), 2 May 1995.
21. Six Continents, History Page, http://www.sixcontinents.com/aboutus/history.htm, 15 November 2002.
22. J. P. Pederson, ed., *International Directory of Company Histories*, Vol. 38 (Detroit: St. James Press, 2001).
23. A. Yates, "Bass to Snap Up Inter-Continental with Pounds 1.7 bn Offer," *The Independent* (London), 21 February 1998.
24. C. Seward, "Holiday Inn Parent Buying Luxury Chain," *The Atlanta Journal and Constitution*, 25 February 1998.
25. H. Ezell, "Holiday Hospitality to Enter Extended-stay Hotel Business," *The Atlanta Journal and Constitution*, 15 October 1997.
26. J. P. Pederson, ed., *International Directory of Company Histories*, Vol. 38 (Detroit: St. James Press, 2001).
27. A. Clark, "Bass Falls to Interbrew," *The Guardian* (London), 15 June 2000.
28. L. Baker, "Bass Calls Time as Interbrew Buys Beer Unit for Pounds 2.3 bn," *The Independent* (London), 15 June 2000.
29. G. Strauss, "Holiday Inns Sold; Britain's Bass to Buy Chain for $2.23 B," *USA Today*, 25 August 1989.
30. A. Osbourne, "End of an Era as Bass Name Makes Way for Six Continents," *The Daily Telegraph* (London), 28 June 2001.
31. Six Continents, Strategy Page, http://www.sixcontinents.com/aboutus/strategy.htm, 15 November 2002.
32. Yahoo Finance, Company Information, http://yahoo.marketguide.com/MGI/busidesc.asp?target=/stocks/companyinformation/busidesc&Ticker=SXC, 15 November 2002.
33. Hospitality Net, www.hospitalitynet.org/news/All_Latest_News/4013424.html, 15 November 2002.
34. Ibid.
35. Yahoo Finance, Company Information, http://yahoo.marketguide.com/MGI/busidesc.asp?target=/stocks/companyinformation/busidesc&Ticker=SXC, 15 November 2002.

36. Hotel Business, http://www.hotelbusiness.com/links/archive/archive, 15 November 2002.

37. Hoovers Online, Company Profiles, http://www.hoovers.com/premium/profile/8/0,2147,41788,00, 15 November 2002.

38. Yahoo Finance, Company Information, http://yahoo.market-guide.com/MGI/signdevt.asp?target=/stocks/companyinformation/signdevt&nss=yahoo&rn=A0313&pos=11#2001-08-27T00:33:00, 15 November 2002.

39. A. Yates, "Bass to Snap Up Inter-Continental with Pounds 1.7 bn Offer," *The Independent* (London), 21 February 1998.

40. Hoovers Online, Company Profiles, http://www.hoovers.com/premium/profile/8/0,2147,41788,00, 15 November 2002.

41. Hotel Business, http://www.hotelbusiness.com/links/archive/archive, 15 November 2002.

42. Hospitality Net, www.hospitalitynet.org/news/All_Latest_News/4013424.html, 15 November 2002.

43. Ibid.

44. Hospitality Net, "TIA Forecast Shows Slow Road to Recovery for Travel and Tourism Industry," http://www.hospitalitynet.org/news/9-11_Aftermath/4013560.html, 15 November 2002.

45. Hospitality Net, "Leisure Travel Up, Business Travel Down for First Six Months of Year—TIA Reports," http://www.hospitalitynet.org/news/9-11_Aftermath/4013245.html, 15 November 2002.

46. Travel Industry Association of America, "Length of Trip," http://www.tia.org/Travel/tripChar.asp, 28 November 2002.

47. Travel Industry Association of America, "Travel Market Segments," http://www.tia.org/Travel/TravelTrends.asp, 28 November 2002.

48. Hospitality Net, "Smith Travel Research Announces Second Quarter and First Half 2002 U.S. Lodging Industry Results," http://www.hospitalitynet.org/news/Market_Reports/STR_-_Market_Reports/4012814.html, 28 November 2002.

49. Hospitality Net, "Travel Industry Partners with U.S. Department of Transportation for Joint Promotion to See America's Byways," http://www.hospitalitynet.org/news/4012126.html, 19 November 2002.

50. Hospitality Net, "War Dampens Hotel Turnaround in 2003—Research Companies Estimate How War Effects the Recovery for Branded Hotels," http://www.hospitalitynet.org/news/Market_Reports/PKF_Consulting_(USA)/4013464.html, 19 November 2002.

51. Hospitality Net, "A Year after 9-11: Climbing Towards Recovery—WTO Reports," http://www.hospitalitynet.org/news/4013195.html, 28 November 2002.

52. Travel Industry Association of America, "Travel Market Segments."

53. P. Brown, "Investment in Information Technology: The Multi-Billion Dollar Game of Chance," *Hospitality Business Review* 4, no. 1 (2002): 28–38.

54. M. Grewitt, J. D. Power and Associates, "J. D. Power and Associates Reports: Top U.S. Hotel Chains Ranked on Guest Satisfaction," http://www.jdpa.com/presspass/pr/pressrelease.asp?ID=149, 18 November 2002; Environmental Protection Agency, "Hotel/Motel Amenity and Category Definitions," http://yosemite.epa.gov/estar/business.nsf/content/pm_eligibility_hotel_def.htm, 18 November 2002.

55. M. Starkov, Hospitality Net, "The Internet: Hotelier's Best Ally or Worst Enemy?—What Went Wrong with Direct Web Distribution in Hospitality?" http://www.hospitalitynet.org/news/4013469.html, 19 November 2002.

56. G. Piccoli, "Wyndham International: Fostering High-Touch with High-Tech," Teaching note created 10 October 2002, 3.

57. M. Starkov, Hospitality Net, "The Internet: Hotelier's Best Ally or Worst Enemy?—What Went Wrong with Direct Web Distribution in Hospitality?" http://www.hospitalitynet.org/news/4013469.html, 19 November 2002.

58. American Hotel and Lodging Association, 2002 Lodging Industry Profile, http://www.ahla.com/infocenter/lip.asp, 18 November 2002.

59. Ibid.

60. Travel Industry Association of America, "Travel Market Segments."

61. American Hotel and Lodging Association, 2002 Lodging Industry Profile, http://www.ahla.com/infocenter/lip.asp, 18 November 2002.

62. Ibid.

63. Ibid; American Hotel and Lodging Association, 2001 Lodging Industry Profile, http://www.ahla.com/infocenter/2001.pdf, 18 November 2002.

64. W. Amstutz, Hospitality Net, "Economic Events to Restrain Lodging Demand Growth Through Remainder of 2002 PwC Reports," http://www.hospitalitynet.org/news/4013058.html, 18 November 2002.

65. American Hotel and Lodging Association, 2002 Lodging Industry Profile, http://www.ahla.com/infocenter/lip.asp, 18 November 2002.

66. S. Walchuk, Hotels Magazine Online, "Hotels' Corporate 300 Rankings," http://www.hotelsmag.com/0702/images/300_corporate_ranking.pdf, 19 November 2002.

67. Cendant Corporation, Lodging Franchises Page, http://www.cendant.com/about-cendant/lodging_franchises.html, 19 November 2002.

68. Marriott International, Corporate Information Page, http://www.marriott.com/corporateinfo/glance.asp, 19 November 2002.

69. Accor Hotels, Hotels Page, http://www.accor.com/sa/groupe/act.htm?adresse=act1_idx, 19 November 2002.

70. Choice Hotels International, Corporate Information Page, http://www4.choicehotels.com/ires/en-US/html/CorporateProfile?sid=OvhHM.29$4_KXTV.4, 19 November 2002.

71. S. Walchuck, Hotels Magazine Online, "Hotels' Corporate 300 Rankings: The Largest Brands," http://www.hotelsmag.com/0702/images/300_largest_hotel_brands.pdf, 19 November 2002.

72. S. B. Heintzeman, Information Technology for Hospitality Managers (HA772) guest lecture at Cornell University on 6 November 2002.

73. S. Marx, Hotel Source, "Opportunities Still Abound in 'Hot Hotel Markets,'" http://www.hotelsource.com/topicsrelissues.html, 18 November 2002.

74. Equitymaster.com, http://www.equitymaster.com/research-it/sector-info/hotels/#kp, 18 November 2002; J. MacMillan, Hotel Online. "Cost Structures and the New 'Break Even,'" http://www.hotel-online.com/News/PR2002_3rd/Sept02_CostStructure.html, 19 November 2002.

75. E. Sahlins, HVS International, "HVS International Hotel Development Cost Survey 2002," http://www.hvsinternational.com/emails/journals/nyu2002/esahlins.htm, 18 November 2002.

76. Hotel and Motel Management, Suppliers Directory, http://www.mediabrains.com/client/HMM/BG1/search.asp, 19 November 2002.

77. Westin Hotels and Resorts, Heavenly Bed Page, http://www.starwood.com/westin/service/reservations_service.html, 19 November 2002.

78. Choicebuys.com, http://www.choicebuys.com/Comergent/en/US/direct/choice, 18 November 2002.

79. Recreation Vehicle Industry Association Online, RV Quick Facts Page, http://www.rvia.org/Media/fastfacts.htm, 15 November 2002.

80. Hospitality Net, "TIA Forecast Shows Slow Road to Recovery for Travel and Tourism Industry," http://www.hospitalitynet.org/news/9_11_Aftermath/4013560.html, 15 November 2002.

81. S. Gregory, "Corporate Apartments: A Real Home on the Road," *The New York Times*, 6 August 2002, C7.

82. "Air Leaders Struggle for a Way Back," *Advertising Age* Midwest region edition, 24 June 2002, S24.

83. K. Iacarella, "Hotel Technology That Meets Guest Expectations Gaining an Edge With Tech-Savvy Road Warriors," Cyberoom News Release, http://www.cyberoom.com/news_roadwarrior.htm, 15 November 2002.

84. G. Piccoli, "Wyndham International: Fostering High-Touch with High-Tech," teaching note created 10 October 2002, 3.

85. C. R. Goeldner and J. R. B. Ritchie, *Tourism* (Hoboken, N.J.: John Wiley & Sons, 2003), 300–304.

86. Kohler Company, "Kohler BodySpa Systems," http://www.us.kohler.com/tech/products/why_spas.jsp, 19 November 2002.

87. OnCommand Corporation, Information Pamphlet, "Turn On Something Good," 2002.

88. C. F. Leas, "The Bed Revolution," *Best Places Los Angeles*, 1st ed., ed. Stephanie Avnet Yates (Seattle: Sasquatch Books, 2001), 144–145.

89. S. A. McConnell, *Dun and Bradstreet/Gale Industry Reference Handbooks: Hospitality* (Farmington Hills: The Gale Group, 1999), xviii, 7.

90. Ibid.

91. Six Continents, What We Do Page, http://www.sixcontinents.com/aboutus/whatwedo.htm, 2 December 2002.

92. Six Continents, Strategy Page, http://www.sixcontinents.com/aboutus/strategy.htm, 20 November 2002.

93. Six Continents, Environment and Community Page, http://www.sixcontinents.com/environment/index.htm, 20 November 2002.

94. Ibid.

95. Hotel Business, "6C Downplays Demerger Talk," www.hotelbusiness.com/links/archive/archive_view.asp?ID=16626&search_variable, 19 November 2002.

96. D. Jones, "Six Continents to Spin Off Pubs, Return Cash," Reuters News, http://global.factiva.com/en/arch/display.asp, 19 November 2002.

97. Ibid.

98. Hotel Business, "6C Confirms New Lineup under Porter," http:www.hotelbusiness.com/links/archive/archive_view.asp?ID=16612&search_variable, 19 November 2002.

99. B. Adams, Hotel & Motel Management, "Franchisees Approve of Porter," http://global.factiva.com/en/arch/display.asp, 20 November 2002.

100. Six Continents, Form 20F, http://www.sixcontinents.com/pdf/20F02.pdf, 19 November 2002.

101. Six Continents, About Us Page, http://www.sixcontinents.com/aboutus/whatwedo_leisure.htm, 19 November 2002.

102. Six Continents, Presentations Page, Six Continents Interim Financial Statement for 2002, http://www.sixcontinents.com, 20 November 2002.

103. K. Crowley, "Price of Fame," *Hotels*, December 2001, http://web16.epnet.com/delivery.asp, 20 November 2002.

104. Hotel Business, "Bass to Flag Hotel in Sao Paulo Convention Center Complex," http://www.hotelbusiness.com/links/archive/archive_view.asp?ID=11012&search_variable, 20 November 2002.

105. Adams, "Franchisees Approve of Porter."

106. Yahoo Finance, "Six Continents Hotels Highlights Success of Online Initiatives and Outlines 2003 E-Commerce Goals," http://biz.yahoo.com/prnews/021119/attu010_1.html, 20 November 2002.

107. Hotel Business, "Six Continents Rolls Out Holidex Plus," http://www.hotelbusiness.com/links/archive/archive_view.asp?ID=16731, 19 November 2002.

108. "Six Continents Hotels Uses Day Applications to Deliver Personalized, Robust, Online Experience," http://ptg.djnr.com/ccroot/asp/publib/story_clean_cpy.asp?articles=BWR0230900775DJF, 19 November 2002.

109. Hoovers Online, "Six Continents Hotels Selects ATG For Next Generation Internet Business Platform," http://hoovnews.hoovers.com/fp.asp?layout=printnews&doc_id=NR20021028290.2, 20 November 2002.

110. "Online Customers Are a Priority for Six Continents Hotels," http://hoovnews.hoovers.com/fp.asp?layout=printnews&doc_id=NR200210281680.2, 20 November 2002.

111. Hotel Business, "6C Lays Out Brand Strategies at Global Investors Conference," http://www.hotelbusiness.com/links/archive/archive_view.asp?ID=17507&search_variable=6C, 20 November 2002.

112. "Six Continents Reinvents Priority Club," http://web16.epnet.com/delivery.asp?tb=1&_ug=dbs, 20 November 2002.

113. Six Continents Hotels, 2002 Marketing Collateral.

114. "Two Hotel Giants Play Beat the Web," http://web16. epnet.com/delivery.asp?tb=1&_ug=dbs, 20 November 2002.

115. Yahoo Finance, "Six Continents Hotels Highlights Success of Online Initiatives and Outlines 2003 E-Commerce Goals," http://biz.yahoo.com/prnews/021119/attu010_1.html, 20 November 2002.

116. Hotel Business, http://hotelbusiness.com/links/archive/archive /_view.aspID=15416&search_variable, 20 November 2002.

117. Employee Training and Development, http://www.sphc.com.au /aboutus/EmpTraining.htm, 20 November 2002.

118. Ibid.

119. M. Hughlett, *HERE News*, "Hotel Union Ends Boycott of Holiday Inn River Center," http://www.hereunion.org /herenews/HN020101RiverCentre.html, 4 December 2002; This was extracted from an article published in *The Union Advocate*, 10 October 2001. Used by permission. *The Union Advocate* is the official publication of the St. Paul Trades and Labor Assembly.

120. Six Continents Hotels, 2002 Marketing Collateral.

121. Six Continents, History Page, http://www.sixcontinents.com /aboutus/history.htm, 15 November 2002.

122. Six Continents, Environment Page, http://www. sixcontinentshotels.com/h/d/6c/c/2/dec/6c/1/en/sr /ep.html, 19 November 2002.

123. Six Continents, Business Conduct Page, http://6conti- nents.com/ourpeople/policies.htm, 20 November 2002.

124. Six Continents, Form 20F, http://www.sixcontinents.com /pdf/20F02.pdf, 19 November 2002.

125. Six Continents, Investor Relations Page, http://www. sixcontinents.com/investors/prelims01/results/highlights, 4 December 2002.

126. K. Amarante, "Swirling 6C Hostile Takeover Rumors Adopt Thunderous Tone," www.hotelinteractive.com/news/mailarticle, 24 February 2003.

127. K. Amarante, "InterContinental Acquires Candlewood Brand," http://www.hotelinteractive.com/news/articleview.asp?articleI D=2862, 28 October 2003.

128. K. Amarante, "6C Officially Changes Its Name To InterContinental," www.hotelinteractive.com/news/mailarticle, 15 April 2003.

APPENDIX A: SENIOR MANAGEMENT BIOGRAPHIES[1]

Sir Ian Prosser

Joined the group in 1969 and was appointed to the board in 1978. He became group managing director in 1984 and chairman and chief executive in 1987, relinquishing the role of chief executive on October 1, 2000. He is a nonexecutive deputy chairman of BP PLC and a nonexecutive director of Glaxo SmithKline PLC. He is a member of the CBI President's Committee and chairman of the Executive Committee of the World Travel & Tourism Council.

Tim Clarke

Joined the group in 1990, was appointed to the board in 1996 and became chief executive on October 1, 2000, having previously been chief executive of Six Continents Retail. He is a nonexecutive director of Debenhams PLC.

Richard North

Joined the group in 1994 as group finance director. He is responsible for finance, pensions, tax, and treasury. He is chairman of Britvic Soft Drinks and is a nonexecutive director of Leeds United PLC and FelCor Lodging Trust Inc.

Tom Oliver

Joined the group in 1997 and was appointed to the board in 1998. A U.S. citizen, he is chairman and CEO of Six Continents Hotels and a nonexecutive director of Interface Inc. Prior to working at Six Continents, Oliver was CEO of FedEx.

Richard Winter

Joined the group in 1994. He is the company secretary, responsible for legal, secretarial, assurance and internal audit services, and risk management.

Karrim Naffah

Joined the group in 1991. He is strategy director, responsible for group strategy, with additional responsibility for group information technology and property development.

APPENDIX B: BOARD OF DIRECTORS

Six Continents is a publicly held company traded on various stock exchanges. The managing body of the organization is a board of directors, composed of eleven members. Of the eleven, six are corporate agents and five are executives from outside the firm. Having already discussed the biographies of the executive team, the following is a list of board members and their backgrounds.[2]

Richard Carr

Appointed a director in 1996, he is the company's senior independent director. He is chairman of Chubb PLC, a nonexecutive director of Centrica PLC and Cadbury Schweppes PLC and a member of the CBI Council.

Robert Larson

Appointed a director in 1996. A U.S. citizen, he is a managing director of Lazard and chairman of Lazard Freres Real Estate Investors, LLC.

Sir Geoffrey Mulcahy

Appointed a director in 1989. He is group chief executive of Kingfisher PLC.

Bryan Sanderson

Appointed a director in August 2001. A former managing director of BP PLC, he is chairman of BUPA, Sunderland PLC, and the Learning and Skills Council.

Sir Howard Stringer

Appointed a director in May 2002. Formerly CEO of Tele-TV, he is chairman and CEO of Sony Corporation of America, is chairman of Sony Canada, chairman of Sony Electronics Inc., and a member of the board of Sony Europe.

1. Six Continents, About Us, http://www.sixcontinents.com /aboutus/management.htm, 20 November 2002.
2. Ibid.

APPENDIX C:
SALES AND ASSETS FIGURES

2001 Sales

	$ in millions	% of total
UK	$ 3,602	61%
US	$ 1,337	23%
Other regions in Europe, Middle East and Africa	$ 649	11%
Other Americas	$ 202	3%
Asia/Pacific	$ 149	2%
TOTAL	$ 5,939	100%

2001 Sales by Division

	$ in millions	% of total
Hotels	$ 2,792	47%
Restaurants	$ 2,293	39%
Soft Drinks & Other	$ 864	14%
(Adjustments)	$ (10)	N/A
TOTAL	$ 5,939	100%

APPENDIX D: INCOME STATEMENTS

Consolidated Income Statement Data

	Year ended September 30 (1)					
	2001 (2)	**2001**	**2000**	**1999**	**1998**	**1997**
	$	£	£	£	£	£
	(in millions, except per ordinary share and ADS amounts)					
Amounts in accordance with UK GAAP						
Turnover:						
Continuing operations	5,929	4,033	3,775	3,110	2,731	2,465
Discontinued operations	—	—	1,383	1,576	1,878	2,789
	5,929	4,033	5,158	4,686	4,609	5,254
Total operating profit before operating exceptional items:						
Continuing operations	1,164	792	776	664	572	498
Discontinued operations	—	—	129	160	186	303
	1,164	792	905	824	758	801
Operating exceptional items:						
Continuing operations	(63)	(43)	—	—	—	—
Discontinued operations	—	—	—	—	—	—
	(63)	(43)	—	—	—	—
Total operating profit:						
Continuing operations	1,101	749	776	664	572	498
Discontinued operations	—	—	129	160	186	303
	1,101	749	905	824	758	801

APPENDIX E: BALANCE SHEETS

Consolidated Balance Sheet Data		September 30 (1)				
	2001 (2)	**2001**	**2000**	**1999**	**1998**	**1997**
(in millions)	**$**	**£**	**£**	**£**	**£**	**£**
Amounts in accordance with UK GAAP						
Intangible assets	256	174	189	13	—	—
Tangible assets	11,110	7,558	6,683	5,794	4,870	4,431
Investments	391	266	249	528	706	596
Current assets	1,617	1,100	1,684	1,405	1,396	1,631
Total assets	13,374	9,098	8,805	7,740	6,972	6,658
Current liabilities	2,953	2,009	1,604	1,803	1,989	1,470
Long-term debt	1,498	1,019	1,213	2,101	1,886	1,097
Share capital	356	242	246	241	271	222
Shareholders' funds	8,010	5,449	5,379	3,313	2,577	3,769
Amounts in accordance with US GAAP						
Intangible assets	4,063	2,764	2,818	2,594	2,572	1,512
Tangible assets	9,379	6,380	5,130	4,211	3,956	3,153
Investments	301	205	254	505	603	578
Current assets	1,767	1,202	1,796	1,438	1,437	1,679
Total assets	15,510	10,551	9,998	8,748	8,568	6,922
Current liabilities	2,989	2,033	1,461	2,595	2,834	1,533
Long-term debt	1,166	779	1,152	1,111	822	846
Redeemable preference share capital	—	—	—	18	48	—
Share capital	356	242	246	223	223	222
Shareholders' equity	9,217	6,270	5,975	3,725	3,565	3,700

(1) The results for fiscal 1999 include 53 weeks' trading (Six Continents Hotels 12 months); all other fiscal years include 52 weeks' trading (Six Continents Hotels 12 months).

(2) US dollar amounts have been translated at the Noon Buying Rate on September 30, 2001 of $1.47 solely for convenience.

(3) For the purposes of UK GAAP, discontinued operations comprise Bass Brewers, Gala, Coral, Barcrest, BLMS and the leased pub business. Under US GAAP, discontinued operations comprise Bass Brewers, Gala, Coral, Barcrest and BLMS, but exclude the leased pub business which is not classified as a discontinued operation for the purposes of US GAAP.

(4) Each American Depositary Share represents one ordinary share.

(5) Long-term debt under UK GAAP includes amounts supported by long-term facilities, which are classified as current liabilities under US GAAP.

(6) Adjusted earnings per share are disclosed in order to show performance undistorted by abnormal items or, in respect of Financial Reporting Standard 15, the impact of adopting this standard.

Dividends

The Company has paid dividends on its ordinary shares each year since its formation in 1967. An interim dividend is normally declared by the board of directors in May of each year and paid in the following July. A final dividend is normally recommended by the board of directors in December following the end of the fiscal year to which it relates and is paid in the following February after approval by shareholders at the Annual General Meeting.

SIX CONTINENTS PLC CONSOLIDATED PROFIT AND LOSS ACCOUNT
Year ended September 30
(£ million, except per ordinary share amounts)

	2001			2000			1999		
	Before major exceptional items	Major exceptional items	Total	Before major exceptional items	Major exceptional items	Total	Before major exceptional items	Major exceptional items	Total
Turnover—	4,033	—	4,033	5,158	—	5,158	4,686	—	4,686
Analyzed as:									
Ongoing operations	3,889	—	3,889	3,775	—	3,775	3,110	—	3,110
Acquisitions	144	—	144	—	—	—	—	—	—
Continuing operations	4,033	—	4,033	3,775	—	3,775	3,110	—	3,110
Discontinued operations	—	—	—	1,383	—	1,383	1,576	—	1,576
Costs and overheads, less other income—	(3,241)	(43)	(3,284)	(4,264)	—	(4,264)	(3,878)	—	(3,878)
Group operating profit	792	(43)	749	894	—	894	808	—	808
Share of associates' operating profit	—	—	—	11	—	11	16	—	16
Total operating profit—	792	(43)	749	905	—	905	824	—	824
Analyzed as:									
Ongoing operations	755	(25)	730	776	—	776	664	—	664
Acquisitions	37	(18)	19	—	—	—	—	—	—
Continuing operations	792	(43)	749	776	—	776	664	—	664
Discontinued operations	—	—	—	129	—	129	160	—	160
Non-operating exceptional items—	(2)	2	—	3	1,231	1,234	(2)	(110)	(112)
Analyzed as:									
Continuing operations									
(Loss)/profit on disposal of fixed assets	(2)	—	(2)	2	—	2	(2)	—	(2)
Loss on disposal of operations	—	(36)	(36)	—	—	—	—	—	—
Provision against fixed asset investment	—	(36)	(36)	—	—	—	—	(110)	(110)
	(2)	(36)	(38)	2	—	2	(2)	(110)	(112)

APPENDIX F: PROFIT AND LOSS STATEMENT   C   E

Discontinued operations									
Profit on disposal of fixed assets	—	—	—	—	1	1	—	—	—
Profit on disposal of operations	—	38	38	—	1,231	1,231	—	(110)	(110)
	—	38	38	1	1,231	1,232	—	(110)	(110)
Profit on ordinary activities before interest—	790	(41)	749	908	1,231	2,139	822	(110)	712
Interest receivable	165	—	165	57	—	57	48	—	48
Interest payable and similar charges—	(224)	—	(224)	(209)	—	(209)	(188)	—	(188)
Profit on ordinary activities before taxation	731	(41)	690	756	1,231	1,987	682	(110)	572
Tax on profit on ordinary activities—	(190)	(19)	(209)	(197)	(90)	(287)	(177)	—	(177)
Profit on ordinary activities after taxation	541	(60)	481	559	1,141	1,700	505	(110)	395
Minority equity interests	(22)	—	(22)	(16)	—	(16)	(8)	—	(8)
Earnings available for shareholders (i)	519	(60)	459	543	1,141	1,684	497	(110)	387
Dividends on equity and non-equity shares—	(293)	—	(293)	(292)	—	(292)	(277)	—	(277)
Retained for reinvestment in the business	226	(60)	166	251	1,141	1,392	220	(110)	110
Earnings per ordinary share—									
Basic	—	—	53.2p	62.2p	—	192.9p	—	—	48.5p
Diluted	—	—	52.8p	—	—	191.6p	—	—	47.9p
Adjusted	60.1p	—	—	58.1p	—	—	—	—	—

(i) A summary of the significant adjustments to earnings available for shareholders (net income) that would be required had United States generally accepted accounting principles been applied instead of those generally accepted in the United Kingdom is set out in Note 33 of Notes to the Financial Statements.

APPENDIX G: REVPAR STATISTICS

RevPAR by Region, Ownership & Brand (Quarter Ended June 2002)

Americas:	Occupancy %		ADR (US$)		RevPAR (US$)	
	Actual	Growth % Pts.	Actual	Growth % Pts.	Actual	Growth % Pts.
Owned & Leased						
Intercontinential	65.0%	0.4%	166.25%	−10.3%	107.99%	−9.7%
Crowne Plaza	71.0%	−4.4%	116.28%	−3.3%	82.59%	−8.9%
Holiday Inn	65.5%	−1.1%	76.03%	−6.1%	49.80%	−8.0%
Staybridge	70.1%	−4.3%	85.84%	−2.6%	60.18%	−8.2%
Managed						
Intercontinential	50.6%	−6.1%	130.65%	−6.1%	66.10%	−16.2%
Crowne Plaza	65.3%	−0.9%	110.00%	−11.0%	71.95%	−12.3%
Holiday Inn	66.5%	−4.9%	81.26%	−6.2%	54.04%	−12.6%
Holiday Inn Express	65.7%	3.9%	84.93%	15.0%	55.79%	−9.6%
Franchised						
Intercontinential	51.1%	2.9%	104.10%	−11.9%	53.18%	−6.6%
Crowne Plaza	55.9%	−8.4%	106.64%	7.4%	59.59%	−6.6%
Holiday Inn	64.2%	−1.7%	79.81%	−2.2%	51.16%	4.7%
Holiday Inn Express	66.7%	−0.2%	72.81%	−0.7%	48.59%	−0.9%
Staybridge	66.7%	9.6%	82.56%	−1.1%	55.09%	15.5%
Total						
Intercontinential	55.1%	−0.8%	134.38%	−9.1%	74.04%	−10.3%
Crowne Plaza	59.5%	−6.4%	108.54%	N/A	64.59%	−9.6%
Holiday Inn	64.5%	−1.9%	79.74%	−2.6%	51.39%	−5.4%
Holiday Inn Express	66.7%	−0.1%	72.92%	−0.8%	48.65%	−1.0%
Staybridge	68.3%	2.0%	84.15%	−2.4%	57.50%	−0.5%

RevPAR Variance to Last Year

Americas:	11 months to Aug 2002	H2 (to Aug 2002)	H2 v H1 (% pts.)
Intercontinential Owned & Leased	−16.5%	−4.2%	20.9%
Crowne Plaza Owned & Leased	−21.9%	−16.2%	10.7%
Holiday Inn – total system	−8.6%	−4.4%	8.4%
Holiday Inn Express – total system	−1.8%	0.0%	3.8%

Source: http://www.sixcontinents.com/pdf/011002t.pdf.

Starbucks' Entry into China

Starbucks Coffee International, a subsidiary of Starbucks Coffee Company, recently celebrated its first step into southern China by opening a new store in the country, the first one in Shenzhen. The store is owned by Coffee Concepts, a joint venture between Starbucks and Hong Kong's Maxim Group, who together opened thirty-two Starbucks stores in Hong Kong between 2000 and 2002.[1] At the opening, Pedro Man, president of Starbucks Coffee Asia Pacific Ltd., the Asian division of Starbucks Coffee International, said:

> As we celebrate the opening of our first store in Southern China today, we mark yet another key milestone in the history and tradition of more than thirty years at Starbucks. The heart of the Starbucks brand lies in two very important cornerstones—our coffee and our people. Our passion for coffee means applying our coffee expertise and the highest standards of excellence to every detail of the coffee, from selecting and roasting the beans, to brewing the perfect cup of coffee.… At the same time, our people are highly valued partners in creating the unique Starbucks Experience. It is their passion, knowledge, unsurpassed expertise and enthusiasm which helps to create a truly outstanding coffee experience for our customers.[2]

Written by Adam Baru, Yinian Hou, Vikas Patel, Bill Spinnenweber, Anjali Talera, and Kem Wilson under the direction of Jeffrey S. Harrison at the School of Hotel Administration, Cornell University.

This case study was written for the purposes of classroom discussion.

Starbucks' success in Asia has surprised many people. But the executives at Starbucks have been surprising critics for many years. How did a small coffee company from Seattle with eleven stores in 1987[3] grow into an international company with nearly 6,000 stores worldwide?[4]

THE STORY OF TWO COMPANIES AND ONE MAN'S VISION

Starbucks Coffee, Tea and Spice opened its first store in April 1971 in the Pike Place Market in Seattle. Its original owners, Jerry Baldwin and Gordon Bowker, had a passion for dark roasted coffee, which was popular in Europe but hard to come by in America in the 1960s. "They founded Starbucks for one reason: They loved coffee and tea and wanted Seattle to have access to the best."[5] Starbucks stood not only for good coffee, especially dark-roasted coffee, but also for educating its customers about its product.

Jerry, a lover of literature, named the company Starbucks, after the first mate in *Moby Dick,* because it "evoked the romance of the high seas and the seafaring tradition of early coffee traders." The original store did not brew and sell coffee by the cup, but instead offered up a selection of thirty varieties of whole-bean coffee.[6] Although Starbucks was bringing high-quality coffee to Seattle, coffee was generally regarded as a produce item. In Italy, coffee bars serving up espresso drinks offered more than great coffee: they offered up a great coffee experience.[7] It took the vision of one man to turn coffee from a commodity into an experience. His name was Howard Schultz.

Howard Schultz was born in 1953, growing up in a housing project in Brooklyn. His father was a factory worker and truck driver, and his mother worked as a receptionist. He received a football scholarship to Northern Michigan University, where he earned a BS in communications, and was the first member of his family to graduate from college. He started as a sales trainee at Xerox and then moved to Hammerplast, a Swedish housewares company, where he rose to vice president of U.S. sales.[8] It was while he was at Hammerplast that Howard discovered Starbucks, which was a customer of his. After visiting the company and meeting its owners, he knew that he wanted to be part of Starbucks and see it grow nationwide. Baldwin and Bowker hired Schultz as director of retail operations and marketing in 1982.[9]

While traveling through Italy to learn more about the coffee business, Schultz was amazed that the country supported about 200,000 espresso bars, with 1,500 in the city of Milan alone. Convinced that this was the way to get Starbucks to appeal to a greater number of people, he proposed the idea to his bosses. He finally convinced them to test the idea in a new downtown Seattle store in 1984. The test was a great success, but the owners decided not to expand the concept. This disagreement caused Schultz to leave the company in 1985 and start his own coffee-bar company, Il Giornale.[10]

Later that year, Schultz met up with Dave Olsen, who had run a successful coffeehouse in Seattle called Café Allegro. Café Allegro was a place where students and professors would hang out, studying philosophy or debating U.S. foreign policy while drinking cappuccinos. Café Allegro was more in the European café tradition than it was in the Italian stand-up espresso bars that Schultz had seen in Milan. Café Allegro was what Starbucks later became, a gathering place in the neighborhood.[11]

Schultz and Olsen shared a passion for coffee and shared views on how to run a business. Schultz's strengths were communicating the vision, inspiring investors, raising money, and planning for growth. Olsen had a deeper understanding about how to operate a retail café, hire and train baristas, and ensure the best quality of coffee. It never occurred to Howard and Dave to become competitors; instead they were inspired by the idea of joining forces.[12]

They opened up the first Il Giornale in April 1986, determined to have it feel like a genuine Italian-style coffee bar. They had to eventually adapt some of their concepts to fit their customers, such as varying the music from only opera and selling coffee in paper cups to boost carryout business. The business was a success, and the chain expanded to a second Seattle store and its first international store, in Vancouver, in April 1987.[13]

That same year, the owners of Starbucks, Schultz's previous bosses, wanted to sell off their business, which consisted of six retail stores and a roasting plant. Schultz and Olsen raised the $3.8 million and purchased Starbucks in August. They changed the name of all the stores to Starbucks because of the stronger brand name it had in Seattle and among mail-order customers. Schultz had great plans for expansion even then, promising investors that Starbucks would open 125 stores in five years.[14]

During the next five years, Starbucks remained a privately held company and expanded its number of stores at a faster pace than planned. With a base of eleven stores in 1987, Starbucks opened fifteen stores in 1988 and twenty in 1989. Seeing that their targets were being met easily, they stepped up their expansion efforts and had 165 stores by 1992. Their expansion was limited to the Pacific Northwest, Chicago, and parts of California. They practiced a strategy of market saturation and building up customer loyalty. This loyalty helped their mail-order business, which reached many people who have tried Starbucks coffee but did not live near a retail store.[15]

BECOMING A PUBLIC COMPANY

Starbucks' managers refused to franchise the stores because they did not want to jeopardize the quality of their product, and they needed additional capital to keep up their expected growth. In 1991, Schultz and company decided to seek out an initial public offering and raise capital by making Starbucks a public company. On June 26, 1992, Starbucks stock was listed on NASDAQ. The offering was priced at $17 per share, but it immediately jumped to $21. The IPO raised $29 million for Starbucks and by the closing bell the company's market capitalization stood at

$273 million. This was only five years after Schultz and company bought the company for $4 million.[16]

With more capital on hand, the company could boost its expansion efforts. In April 1993, Starbucks opened its first East Coast store in Washington, D.C. The company then moved its efforts to New York and Boston in 1994. This growing success throughout the country prompted Starbucks to think more globally.[17]

A SUCCESSFUL BRAND NEEDS SUCCESSFUL MANAGERS

Starbucks was able to expand so rapidly because of solid investments in larger facilities before it needed them and by hiring confident, experienced managers who knew how to expand the business. Howard Schultz's management philosophy is to invite creative conflict and debates. "If there is no tension, I don't think you get the best result."[18] Two key people on Starbucks' management team were Howard Behar and Orin Smith.

As Starbucks expanded in 1989, Howard Schultz hired Howard Behar because he was familiar with opening and running many stores at once. He had twenty-five years' experience within retailing in the furniture business and as an outside developer. In 1990, Howard Schultz and his team hired Orin Smith as chief financial officer. Smith had an MBA from Harvard and was accustomed to managing far larger and more complex organizations than Starbucks. Smith had worked as budget director for the state of Washington for five years and before that for Deloitte and Touche for thirteen years.[19]

Behar and Smith joined Starbucks because they had a deep understanding of the passion and the potential of the business. Many other people had a significant part in the growth of Starbucks, but Howard Schultz, Howard Behar, and Orin Smith (otherwise known as H_2O) were the core of the management team that would lead the company for many years to come.[20] The driving force of the management trio is that they stand for the vision, the soul, and the fiscal responsibility of Starbucks.[21]

In 1994, Starbucks International was formed and Behar was named president. Schultz remained chairman and CEO but stepped down as president.

He was replaced by Smith, who took over many of the day-to-day responsibilities.[22]

In July 2000, Howard Schultz showed his commitment to Starbucks' plan to expand globally by stepping down as CEO and assuming the role of chief global strategist. While the company has grown incredibly since he took over, Schultz said: "We're only in the infant stages of what Starbucks is going to be."[23] Orin Smith is now CEO, and Howard Behar returned from retirement in September 2001 to become the head of North American operations.[24] Dave Olsen is the senior vice president for culture and immersion. He is right at the heart of Starbucks, where the core purposes and values come together. Schultz says that Starbucks would not be what it is today if Olsen had not been part of his team.[25]

THE EMPLOYER OF CHOICE

In the late 1980s, Howard Schultz and his team recognized that building a company like Starbucks would be a difficult task. They envisioned a national retail company with company-owned stores that depended highly on part-time workers.[26] Schultz believed that in order to build respect and confidence with customers, the company first had to build respect and confidence with the employees.[27] Howard saw this benefit as a part of his core strategy: "Treat people like family, and they will be loyal and give their all. Stand by people, and they will stand by you."[28]

In one sense the company is not only about coffee, but also about the experience created in the stores and in the company. Howard and his team wanted to bring a passionate commitment to the quality of the coffee and the company that they were building. They wanted to be proud of the equity in their name. They wanted to employ people who would share a sense of pride that was bigger than the job they were doing. They would attract people who were well educated and were eager to communicate their passion for coffee.[29] That is why employees are highly trained in the subtleties of coffee tasting so that they can provide information to customers.[30]

Since the early days of Starbucks, employees have had a major impact on the direction of the company. Even today, Starbucks' management stands in front of the employees in open forums everywhere the company does business to discuss the previous quarter's result. They discuss openly the plans, decisions, strategies, and concerns, because it is a part of the Starbucks culture that people shall have the opportunity to say what they feel, and what they feel is recognized as important to management. Howard Schultz recognized the tremendous trust developed when people feel a sense of belonging through their participation in the decisions.[31]

Howard Schultz wanted Starbucks to be the employer of choice for many people. He saw his father struggle through life working at low-paying jobs where he was treated poorly, and he sought to treat his employees the best he could. He planned to do this by offering a higher wage than other restaurant and retail stores and by offering benefits that weren't available elsewhere. He felt that offering these benefits was a key competitive advantage that attracted more knowledgeable and eager people. In late 1988, the company began offering health benefits to all full-time and part-time employees, the only company at its time to do so. Then in August 1991, Starbucks started its Bean Stock program, which made all employees in the company eligible for stock options, making all the employees "partners" in the company.[32] The purpose of the program was to educate employees on the importance of creating value and profits by linking them to shareholder value.[33]

Management wanted to make sure that the foundation on which it was building the company was linked to everyone in the organization, which would give the company the ability to retain the staff and their values. Schultz believes that a skilled and motivated workforce is an essential element to service quality; in other words, "Satisfied partners create satisfied customers."[34] Starbucks is still one of the few publicly held companies in the country to offer stock options and full health and dental coverage to all its full-time and part-time employees. These policies have contributed to a turnover rate that is well below the industry average.[35] Howard Schultz recognized that the foundation of Starbucks' success was the company's passionate commitment to the quality of coffee that it bought and roasted and to its view of its employees as business partners and not simply a line item.[36]

MARKETING THE BRAND NAME

Howard Schultz always believed that high-quality coffee would speak for itself, but gradually he and his team realized that they needed to be more proactive in clarifying and elevating the Starbucks message as competition grew greater. In 1994, Schultz was looking for a senior marketing director to tell the Starbucks story to the world. By 1995, he found Scott Bedbury, who had worked as Nike's director of advertising from 1987 to 1994. When Bedbury began to work for Starbucks, he found himself challenged because Starbucks was not only a brand, but also an importer, a manufacturer, a retailer, a wholesaler, and a direct-mail business. He had never known a company that could survive by doing all five, but he found many similarities from his work with Nike, a shoe manufacturer.

Until Bedbury joined Starbucks, the company had spent little money on advertising. The same year, Schultz had just made a decision to find a new advertising agency that could express Starbucks' brand personality: a passionate, entrepreneurial company dedicated to providing great coffee that enriches everyday moments for millions of people.

Bedbury believed that Starbucks should be a "knowing" company with the latest jokes, the latest music, and the latest personalities within politics, literature, sports, and cultural trends. When Bedbury started working for Starbucks, Schultz made him decide about advertising partners. Bedbury chose Goodby, Silverstein and Partners, an award-winning San Francisco agency that had created "Got Milk?"

After the contract was signed with Goodby, Bedbury began to carry out marketing research for Starbucks together with Jerome Conlon, a market research expert from Nike. They developed the Big Dig, a three-stage, nine-month research project that began with focus groups of customers in three cities. They asked the customers: Why do people come to Starbucks? How do they envision an ideal coffeehouse? They watched and analyzed the customers' and potential customers' perceptions of the coffee and the Starbucks experience.

Bedbury and Conlon found that the customers in their thirties and forties were generally happy with the Starbucks experience. However, the people in their twenties wanted more from a coffeehouse. They wanted a unique and funky place where they could hang out at night, not a quick to-go place on the way to work. Starbucks faced a huge challenge, the need to maintain and yet strengthen the brand to attract such a diverse group of consumers. The research helped the management team members understand that they needed to rethink their marketing strategy.[37]

Starbucks brand image continues to increase in spite of a harsh economic environment. But what makes Starbucks conspicuous is not its rapid development but its low expenses on advertisement. Starbucks only spends $30 million per year, which accounts for 1 percent of its income. This money is usually spent on promoting new flavors and new services such as in-house wireless Internet service. The common cost to other similar businesses normally goes as high as $300 million a year. The core value of Starbuck is actually "relationship," including the relationship between customers, employees, suppliers, and business partners. It has been repeatedly proved by many successful companies that it is essential to motivate the whole company to build a trustful, mutual-benefit, and long-term relationship among the customers, the employees, the suppliers, and the business partners. Starbucks is the model of the relationship-centered company.[38]

EXPANDING INTO NEW MARKETS

Starbucks expanded its brand not only through its retail stores, but also through various new products and partnerships. Starbucks has tried out new concepts such as expanded food menus and drive-through service, but both options were not pursued because the management felt that it took away from the core business.[39] In 1994, Starbucks created a new drink called a Frappuccino, a cold drink made from ice, coffee, sugar, and low-fat milk. It was a hit, drawing many non–coffee drinkers into the store and increasing sales on hot days. A bottled version sold in grocery stores through the North American Coffee Partnership, a joint venture between Starbucks and Pepsi.[40]

The Starbucks traditional business model departed in the late 1990s from selling its coffee only from its own outlets. Starbucks' strategy acknowledged

that the only way to sustain the company's growth rate is to open more shops and to expand through supermarket and retail channels. Schultz and his team are now focused on the big picture, rather than on store-by-store execution, as was done a decade earlier.[41] (See Exhibit 1.[42])

To further build its customer base Starbucks also formed more strategic partnerships to get access to more of their target customers. Such partnerships have made it possible to drink Starbuck's coffee at Nordstrom, at Barnes & Noble, on Holland America cruise lines, and at Starwood Hotels.[43] In order to offer its products in airports and schools, Starbucks also made strategic alliances with Host Marriott and Aramark.[44]

In 1996, the first Starbucks cup of coffee was served in a United Airlines flight as a result of a strategic alliance with that airline. The deal was perceived as an "incredible growth opportunity" because the flights would expose the Starbucks brand to numerous potential customers each year.[45]

In 1998, Starbucks launched a partnership with Kraft, a unit of food and tobacco giant Philip Morris, to distribute whole beans and ground coffee to more than 20,000 grocery stores in the United States. The key to all these ventures is in creating a premium-priced brand where earlier there were only cheaper commodity-type products. Demand for premium beans is on the rise, Starbucks found, while sales of plain old coffee have decreased.[46]

In an effort to target smaller offices that don't require brewing equipment or full breakroom service, Starbucks now provides ground-coffee packets through office supply dealers, such as Staples, Office Max, and Office Depot.[47]

Starbucks has expanded its reach into many markets that it feels complement its core strategy. Starbucks also offers a line of teas produced by its wholly owned subsidiary, Tazo, an Oregon-based tea company.[48] Starbucks has a partnership with Dreyer's Grand Ice Cream to market gourmet ice cream and worked with Seattle's Redhook brewery to develop a coffee-flavored stout. Starbucks even expanded into the music industry, partnering with Capitol Records to sell specialized musical compilations in Starbucks stores.[49]

EXHIBIT I	STARBUCKS' VISION, MISSION, AND GOALS, 2001

Vision: To establish the company as the most recognized and respected brand in the world.

Starbucks mission and enterprise strategy:

Establish Starbucks as the premier purveyor of the finest coffee in the world while maintaining our uncompromising principles as we grow. The following six guidelines will help us measure the appropriateness of our decisions:

- Provide a great work environment and treat each other with respect and dignity
- Embrace diversity as an essential component in the way we do business
- Apply the highest standards of excellence to the purchasing, roasting, and fresh delivery of our coffee
- Develop enthusiastically satisfied customers of all the time
- Contribute positively to our communities and our environment
- Recognize that profitability is essential to our future success

Starbucks environmental mission statement:

Starbucks is committed to a role of environmental leadership in all facets of our business. We fulfill this mission by a commitment to:

- Understanding of environmental issues and sharing information with our partners
- Developing innovative and flexible solutions to bring about change
- Striving to buy, sell and use environmentally friendly products
- Recognizing that fiscal responsibility is essential to our environmental future
- Instilling environmental responsibility as a corporate value
- Measuring and monitoring our progress for each project
- Encouraging all partners to share in our mission

Company goals:

- Continue to rapidly expand its retail operations
- Grow its Specialty Operations
- Selective pursue other opportunities to leverage the Starbucks brand through the introduction of new products and the development of new distribution channels

Starbucks retail goals:

To become the leading retailer and brand of coffee in each of its target markets by selling the finest quality coffee and related products, and by providing superior customer service, that fosters a high degree of customer loyalty. Starbucks strategy for expanding its retail business is to increase its markets share in existing markets and to open stores in new markets where the opportunity exist to become the leading specialty coffee retailer.

SOCIAL RESPONSIBILITY

Starbucks and its shareholders have committed themselves to social responsibility. The company's responsibility begins with being accountable to its stakeholders—its partners, customers, suppliers, investors, community members, and others. The company so values communicating openly about its business practices and performance that it began publishing an annual corporate social responsibility report in fiscal year 2001.[50]

In order to pursue its values, Starbucks entered a partnership with The Center for Environmental Leadership in Business. Together, they developed guidelines that they believe not only protect their high standards, but also promote the high-quality coffee market. The guidelines are based on the following criteria:[51]

■ Quality baselines that are based on maintaining Starbucks quality standards.

■ Social conditions that are based on conforming to local laws and applicable international conventions related to employee wages and benefits.

■ Environmental issues based on growing and processing standards that contribute to conservation of soil and water and to biological diversity.

■ Economics issues that will benefit rural communities by boosting producer, income, expanding employment and educational opportunities, and enhancing local infrastructure and public services.

Even with the high standards that Starbucks holds itself to, the company faced demands from many social and environmental groups. Environmental activists such as the Organic Consumers Association (OCA) complain about Starbucks' use of milk from cows that have been treated with growth hormones. Starbucks responds to this complaint by offering organic milk for an extra charge.[52]

Social activists in Central America have accused Starbucks of abusing poor coffee farmers by paying them low prices for the coffee beans. In an attempt to protect its brand image, Starbucks developed guidelines to pay farmers a premium price if they meet certain standards. However, some human rights organizations say this doesn't address the underlying poverty that is "killing coffee farmers and their families." In general, activists suggest: "It's time for Starbucks to share the wealth."[53] In response to these demands, Starbucks encourages farm groups who sell coffee beans to Starbucks to pay acceptable wages, avoid child labor, and provide acceptable living conditions.[54]

In an effort to build its image, the company entered into licensing agreement with TransFair USA to market and sell Fair Trade–certified coffee. The fair trade coffee market has evolved as part of a worldwide movement to help coffee producers in developing countries by having certified cooperatives sell directly to imports/roasters at or above minimum price.[55]

Starbucks formed a partnership with Conservation International to promote environmentally sound methods of growing coffee.[56] Furthermore, Starbucks invested $200,000 to support environmentally friendly crops in Mexico, only to find out that these crops had better taste and had a greater economic potential.[57] Starbucks also donates old beans to charity, and at the same time it maintains the highest levels of quality by brewing only fresh beans.[58]

STARBUCKS' CURRENT FINANCIAL STATE

On Wall Street, Starbucks is viewed as the latest great growth story. It soared more than 2,200 percent over the decade from 1992 to 2001, surpassing Wal-Mart, General Electric, PepsiCo, Coca-Cola, Microsoft, and IBM in total return.[59] As shown in Exhibit 2,[60] earnings per share increased from $0.03 to $0.46 during 1992 to 2001. However, Starbucks has never given out dividends, instead reinvesting all profits into the business.

Starbucks' sales have increased with an average of 20 percent annually since the company went public in 1992, hitting $2.6 billion in 2001.[61] In 2001, Starbucks had a debt/equity ratio of 0.4 and a return on equity ratio of 14.4 percent. See Exhibit 3 for 2001 year-end financials.[62]

From 1997 to 2001, revenues grew at 31 percent, net income at 61 percent, and assets at 21 percent. See Exhibit 4[63] for Starbucks' annual income statement and Exhibit 5[64] for annual balance sheet. In the first three quarters of 2002, sales climbed 24 percent to $2.4 billion, while profits rose 25 percent to $159.5 million.[65]

With more than 5,700 retail locations worldwide, Starbucks serves nearly twenty million customers a week,[66] and in September 2001 Starbucks employed 54,000 people, as shown in Exhibit 6.[67]

In December 2001, Starbucks had 9,650 shareholders, which includes employees' shares. The board of directors consists of nine people, including Howard Schultz as the chairman of the board. See Exhibit 7 for the Board of Directors.[68]

EXHIBIT 2	STOCK HISTORY

Year	Stock Price ($)			P/E		Per Share ($)		
	FY High	FY Low	FY Close	High	Low	Earns.	Div.	Book Value
Sep-01	25.66	13.46	14.84	56	29	0.46	0	3.62
Sep-00	22.63	10.69	20.03	91	43	0.25	0	3.05
Sep-99	20.50	7.88	12.39	76	29	0.27	0	2.62
Sep-98	14.98	7.19	9.05	79	38	0.19	0	2.22
Sep-97	11.19	6.53	10.45	66	38	0.17	0	1.68
Sep-96	8.97	3.63	8.25	64	26	0.14	0	1.46
Sep-95	5.53	2.69	4.73	61	30	0.09	0	1.10
Sep-94	4.06	2.38	2.88	81	48	0.05	0	0.47
Sep-93	3.53	1.69	3.42	88	42	0.04	0	0.40
Sep-92	2.06	1.28	1.89	69	43	0.03	0	0.36

EXHIBIT 3	2001 YEAR-END FINANCIALS

Debt ratio	0.40%
Return on equity	14.40%
Cash ($ mil.)	113.2
Current ratio	1.33
Long-term debt ($ mil.)	5.8
Shares outstanding (mil.)	380
Dividend yield	0.00%
Dividend payout	0.00%
Market value ($ mil.)	5,639.90

EXHIBIT 4	INCOME STATEMENT*

	Sep 01	Sep 00	Sep 99	Sep 98	Sep 97
Revenue	2,649.00	2,169.20	1,680.10	1,308.70	975.389
Cost of goods sold	2,068.00	1,684.30	1,326.20	996.959	751.006
Gross profit	581	484.9	353.9	311.74	224.383
Gross profit margin	21.90%	22.40%	21.10%	23.8%	23.0%
SG&A expense	151.4	110.2	89.7	77.575	57.144
Depreciation & amortization	177.1	142.2	107.5	72.54	52.8
Operating income	252.5	232.5	156.7	109.21	86.2
Operating margin	9.50%	10.70%	9.30%	8.3%	8.8%
Total net income	181.2	94.6	101.7	68.372	55.211
Net profit margin	6.80%	4.40%	6.10%	5.2%	5.7%
Diluted EPS ($)	0.46	0.25	0.27	0.25	0.35

*All amounts in millions of U.S. dollars except per-share amounts.

EXHIBIT 5	BALANCE SHEET*				
	Sep 01	**Sep 00**	**Sep 99**	**Sep 98**	**Sep 97**
Cash	113.2	70.8	66.4	101.66	70.13
Net receivables	90.4	76.4	47.6	50.97	31.23
Inventories	221.3	201.7	180.9	143.12	119.77
Total current assets	593.9	459.8	386.5	337.28	317.55
Total assets	1,851.00	1,493.10	1,252.50	992.75	857.15
Short-term debt	62.7	57	64.2	33.63	28.58
Total current liabilities	445.3	313.3	251.6	179.47	145.47
Long-term debt	5.8	6.5	7	0	165.02
Total liabilities	475.1	344.8	291.5	198.45	323.44
Total equity	1,375.90	1,148.40	961	794.30	533.71
Shares outstanding (millions)	380	376.3	366.6	170.193	156.642

*All amounts are in millions of U.S. dollars except shares outstanding.

EXHIBIT 6	HISTORICAL FINANCIALS AND EMPLOYEES*			
Year	**Revenue ($ mil.)**	**Net Income ($ mil.)**	**Net Profit Margin**	**Employees**
Sep-01	2,649.0	181.2	6.80%	54,000
Sep-00	2,169.2	94.6	4.40%	47,000
Sep-99	1,680.1	101.7	6.10%	37,000
Sep-98	1,308.7	68.4	5.20%	26,000
Sep-97	966.9	57.4	5.90%	25,000
Sep-96	696.5	42.1	6.00%	16,600
Sep-95	465.2	26.1	5.60%	11,500
Sep-94	284.9	10.2	3.60%	6,128
Sep-93	163.5	8.5	5.20%	4,585
Sep-92	93.1	4.1	4.40%	2,853

*All amounts are in millions of U.S. dollars except employees.

INTERNATIONAL EXPANSION INTO ASIA

Schultz's team is hard pressed to create new profits in a home market that is quickly becoming saturated with 4,247 stores across the United States and Canada. However, there are still eight states with no Starbucks stores. In Seattle, there is a Starbucks outlet for every twenty-four square miles; in Manhattan, Starbucks has 124 cafes, which is one for every twelve thousand people. With such a concentration, analysts give Starbucks until late 2004 before it saturates the U.S. market, but Starbucks expects to increase the number of outlets worldwide to 10,000 in three years. The company is convinced that it can export its American-brewed concept around the world.[69]

Starbucks opened its first store outside of the United States and Canada in Tokyo in August 1996. Japan was chosen because it is the third largest coffee importer in the world. Schultz felt going to Japan was an essential part of Starbucks International's expansion plan. For all its international operations

EXHIBIT 7	BOARD OF DIRECTORS

Howard Schultz
Starbucks Corporation
Chairman of the board and chief global strategist

Orin C. Smith
Starbucks Corporation
President and chief executive officer

Howard Behar
Starbucks Corporation
President, North American Operations

Barbara Bass
Gerson Bakar Foundation
President

Graig J. Foley
Wickham Capital Corp.
President

Gregory B. Maffei
Kibble & Prentice
President and chief executive officer

Arlen I. Prentice
Kibble & Prentice
Co-chairman and chief executive officer

James G. Shennan, Jr.
Trinity Ventures
General partner

Graig E. Weatherup
The Pepsi Bottling Group, Inc.
Chairman and chief executive officer

Schultz decided it was best to form partnerships with local operators. The Tokyo store was opened as a joint venture with Japanese retailer and restaurant operator Sazabu Inc.[70] In six years, the number of Japanese stores has grown to 368, beating Starbucks' own projections.[71]

Starbucks now operates about 1,200 international outlets, with plans for continuing rapid expansion.[72] A large portion of Starbucks' international business is throughout Asia. There are 850 Starbucks locations in fourteen Asian and Pacific markets: Japan, Singapore, Philippines, Thailand, Malaysia, South Korea, Beijing, Shanghai, Hong Kong and Macau as well as Australia, New Zealand, Taiwan, and Indonesia.[73] Starbucks will continue expanding its presence throughout Asia, and Howard Schultz feels that one day the company may be operating more stores in Asia than it does in North America.[74]

CHINESE POLITICAL ENVIRONMENT

History

China is a communist country. The economic system operates within a political framework of Communist Party control. The government used to control the whole economy. After the People's Republic of China was created in 1949, the founder of the country, Mao Zedong, ruled the country in a highly centralized way.[75] Coupons were distributed by each level of the government to the civilians to exchange for daily necessities. This practice continued until after the Cultural Revolution, a ten-year struggle between Mao and the other communist leaders.

After 1978, with the help of Premier Zhou En Lai, Deng Xiaoping controlled the country. He gradually introduced market-oriented reforms and decentralized economic decision making.[76] Under his rein, China abandoned the old planning and distributing system. As a result, the national output quadrupled by 2000.

Jiang Ze Min, the successor of Deng Xiaoping, followed Deng's train of thought. The market was further opened to foreign trade and investment. More and more foreign investors trooped in to fight for market share. China became the second largest economy after the United States, measured by purchasing power parity, even though by 2001 its GDP per capita was only US $4,300.[77] Foreign investment in China continues to increase rapidly.[78]

Recent Issues

The Sixteenth Communist Conference In the 16th central committee conference of the Sixteenth Chinese Communist Party Conference held on November 8, 2002, President Jiang Ze Min stated that the country would manipulate the market only by distributing resources, creating an environment where all the economic players have equal opportunity to use the resources and enhance the movement of the merchandise and manufacture factors. The government will monitor the market, adjust the economy, and manage the public service.[79] This conference further ensured that the opening-up policy will continue.

This new policy action will reduce government intervention in privately owned business, attracting more foreign investment to the country. However, although privately owned businesses account for 60 percent of China's GDP, one-fifth of each privately owned business is owned by the government. The growth rate of nationally owned business is lower than 10 percent. China's economy hasn't got on the track of sustainable development. In terms of leadership changes, in September 2001 the Chinese Communist Party started making important changes. Provincial leaders, who normally held their positions until age seventy, were replaced earlier than usual.[80] Another of the changes that took place after the Sixteenth National People's Conference was the election of Hu Jintao as new president of China.

World Trade Organization In 2001, with China entering the World Trade Organization, the Chinese market started to share the same rules as the global market. The internal policy making will be more transparent and the government function will be strained by the law frame of the WTO.

The development of China supplied great opportunities for foreign investors. However, because of the special economic policies in China, investors may still meet unexpected difficulties. For example, foreign investors willing to invest in China will have to apply for a special government investment license. In some small cities, bribery is necessary to get the license.

When Starbucks entered the Chinese market in 1999, the company had to deal with more rigid business policies in China. At that time, Chinese government functions were not strained by the law frame of the WTO. Now, tariffs are lower to foreign investors as well. This actually supplies a low-cost and low-risk operational environment, so that the advanced technology, managerial experience, and marketing network will be better jointed with the low-cost labor Chinese market and other marketing potentials. This "WTO effect" may inspire Starbucks, as the majority

of the famous international corporations already in China, to consider further investments in China.[81]

CHINESE ECONOMIC ENVIRONMENT

Economic Development Process

The Chinese market is considered the fastest growing and the most powerful market in the world in terms of its gigantic population and the overall rising economic growth. China's invitation for foreign investment started in 1978. But from 1978 to 1992, although the amount of investment increased every year, the accumulated amount was only $23.4 billion.[82]

During the 1990s, more foreign businesses trooped in to compete in the market. From 1992 to 1995, foreign investment in China developed rapidly. This was followed by an adjustment period of two years and a low period of three years. Total foreign investment went down from $45.5 billion in 1998 to $40.7 billion in 2000, a drop of 10.5 percent. After the adjustment, the quality and quantity of the investment increased significantly, making the number of foreign companies investing in China increase tremendously.[83] Direct foreign investment in China recovered with a record increase of 14.7 percent during the first nine months of 2002.[84]

China's economy recovered quickly after the Asian financial crisis that took place in 1997. From January to September 2002, the amount of foreign investment in China reached $39.56 billion, increased by 22.6 percent compared with the same period of the previous year. During the first nine months of 2002, the accumulated direct investment approved by the government and the accrued contract investment were $2,477.1 billion and $68.38 billion respectively, which represented increases of 33.4 percent and 38.4 percent.

Based on the analysis of China's historical economic data and economic development, it is estimated that the GDP of China will be higher than France in 2005. In 2020, China could be the third biggest economic power. By 2050, China could surpass Japan and become the second largest economy after the United States.[85]

The fast-developing economy attracted investors from various industries such as high technology and manufacturing. On the one hand, those foreign companies have created high-income potential customers for Starbucks. On the other hand, they may become Starbucks' supplier network in China. For example, Starbucks in Beijing is using Epson terminals for cash management. The stable economic environment promises investors like Starbucks a bright future.

SOCIOCULTURAL INFLUENCE

Social Trends

As China adopted market economy policies, more and more Western companies have been entering the Chinese market. U.S. companies in the food industry, such as McDonald's, KFC, and Pizza Hut, have been able to capture the Chinese customers' taste. The young generation of Chinese customers have been the most susceptible to the Western trend.[86]

Because rigid governmental legislation, which allowed Chinese people to have just one child, young married couples have more available purchasing power. Young married couples could save more money and the economy was growing. They want to spend more money on recreational activities, such as American fast-food restaurants.

China used to be a closed country twenty years ago. In that time, no one in China was familiar with the name McDonald's. But today, the lives of the Chinese people are full of foreign names. A girl wants a Barbie for her birthday gift. Couples celebrate their wedding anniversary in a Korean restaurant. Busy office workers order pizza for lunch. The increasingly wealthy Chinese people are willing to pay more for new experiences and better products and services.

The change of culture influences many aspects of people's lives. For example, China has traditionally been a tea-drinking country. Most people started to recognize coffee in 1980s from Nestle's slogan "Tastes great!"[87] However, now Chinese new generations not only drink coffee but require high-quality coffee. The Chinese, especially the petty bourgeoisie, want gourmet coffee instead of instant coffee. To them, coffee means only Starbucks.

As a result of the social unbalance, a social class called "petty bourgeoisie" emerged. They are the typical consumers of expensive foreign brands.[88] *Petty bourgeoisie* refers to an expanding group of wealthy and educated young people who are enthusiastic about chasing "taste" and "fashion." Qualifying to be a petty bourgeois, a person only uses Gucci bags, Rolex watch, and Chanel perfume; visits bars three nights a week to enjoy 1972 red wine; and travels overseas once a year. Petty bourgeoisie are the group of people who are most willing to spend money on expensive things that can show their social positions. Their inclination to accept the Western products demonstrates a social trend to connecting to the outside world. The petty bourgeoisie is getting bigger, probably supplying a stable consumer source for foreign brands.[89]

SOCIAL UNBALANCE

Currently, China has a problem with unbalanced distribution of income. There have been three main observations. First, the imbalance between the income of people in the cities and in the villages is still increasing. In 1998, the average income of people in the cities was over twice that of people in the villages. The second imbalance is the big discrepancy of income within the cities themselves. Since the economy was decentralized, the difference in income of the people in cities expanded rapidly. The income of the richest 10 percent was seven to eight times that of the poorest 10 percent. Sixty percent of the civilian wealth in the cities is owned by less than 9 percent of the population. The third imbalance is in the villages. Since village businesses exist only in wealthy areas, the distribution of the company income has not been balanced and therefore the difference in income is growing larger. In 1995, the income of the richest individuals was 18.1 times that of the poorest individuals. The income of the rich provinces of Guangdong, Zhejiang, and Jiangxi is 256 percent, 129 percent, and 59 percent higher than that of Shanxi, respectively.[90]

TECHNOLOGY ENVIRONMENT

Technology through the Wall in China

In the era of technology development, China is not an exception. Computers, Internet, and cell phones are part of people's lives. Companies rely on technology to manage their purchasing, control their cash, and serve their clients. The modernization of China's technology enables foreign investors to communicate in real time with their branches in China. In this way, the head offices outside of China get updated information from their Chinese branches.

The technology development in China also makes it possible for foreign investors to apply the latest technology to efficiently and effectively operate their branches in China. For example, Starbucks in China in 2002 started a strategic partnership with Compaq Computers. In this five-year agreement, Compaq will serve as the chief technology supplier and technical supporter to Starbucks.[91]

Some conservative groups in China believe that it will be difficult to develop the coffee market for Starbucks. First, coffee is by no means a mainstream beverage in mainland China. Compared with tea, coffee is a newcomer. The average annual coffee consumption of the whole country is only one cup per person. The total Chinese coffee production per year is only one thousand tons; in Brazil, the annual production is 1,500,010 tons. Furthermore, the weather of China is not suitable for growing coffee.[92]

THE CHINESE BEVERAGE MARKET

Tea, the classic Chinese beverage, represents more than 40 percent of total market volume. With more than 2,500 tea processing companies active, production of loose tea in 1998 came to 665,000 metric tons, of which one-third was exported. It was estimated that per capita tea consumption in 1999 was 27.5 liters (7.25 gallons). Tea bags and diet and instant teas make up only about 1 percent of the market, but ready-to-drink tea is becoming more popular, with more than one hundred brands.[93]

China exports approximately 200,000 tons of tea. And 18 percent of the total volume of tea is distributed throughout the world. In recent years, the price and consumption of crops have remained stagnant. However, the growth rate in the domestic market has remained highly competitive against numerous other beverages, which makes tea the leading Chinese beverage market.[94]

Since coffee and tea can substitute for each other, the competition between them will be fierce. In China, there is one competitive local coffee producer—Li Shen. However, Starbucks does not have a

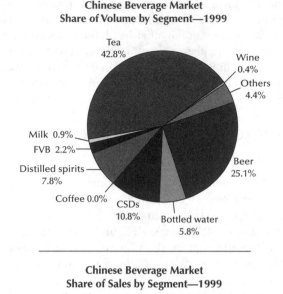

**Chinese Beverage Market
Share of Volume by Segment—1999**

- Tea 42.8%
- Wine 0.4%
- Others 4.4%
- Beer 25.1%
- Bottled water 5.8%
- CSDs 10.8%
- Coffee 0.0%
- Distilled spirits 7.8%
- FVB 2.2%
- Milk 0.9%

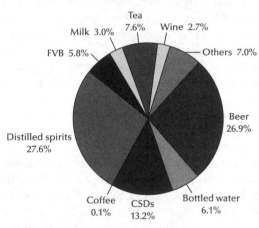

**Chinese Beverage Market
Share of Sales by Segment—1999**

- Tea 7.6%
- Wine 2.7%
- Others 7.0%
- Milk 3.0%
- FVB 5.8%
- Beer 26.9%
- Distilled spirits 27.6%
- Bottled water 6.1%
- CSDs 13.2%
- Coffee 0.1%

CSDs: Carbonated soft drinks; FVB: Fruit and Vegetable Beverages

Source: Beverage Marketing Corporation; Beijing Consultech; State Statistical Bureau (China)

problem supplying coffee beans to its Chinese stores. One of the sources of competitive advantage for Starbucks has been its ability to contact with coffee producers in the farthest places of the world. To sell a unique espresso coffee, Starbucks buys the best coffee beans from Africa, South America, and Indonesia, regardless of price.[95]

The statistics records in China show that, in 1990, the annual sales of coffee in the Chinese market was only 25,537 standard bags (60kg/bag). In 1995, this figure soared to 159,000 standard bags. By 2000, it was 318,000 standard bags. Compared to the annual U.S. coffee consumption per capita (4.02 kg), Chinese people don't drink a lot of coffee (0.01467 kg), but China is still deemed an enormous market for coffee.

Starbucks continues to try to expand its market in China, hoping that enough of that country's 1.3 billion people will put aside the country's old tradition of tea. So far Starbucks has opened over fifty locations in China, mostly in the more affluent cities of Shanghai and Beijing, where throngs of young workers are more open to Western products.

COFFEE COMPETITION

Zhen Guo Coffee, a Japanese chain, entered China in 1998. When Zhang Zhen De, the manager of Zhen Guo in China, realized that the car ownership rate of Yi Wu, a small city in the Zhen De province, was among the highest in China, he opened a Zhen Guo in Yi Wu. And after Zhen Guo opened its store, many local people became used to drinking coffee before they go to work.

After Zhen Guo captivated the Chinese people, coffee companies, such as Starbucks, Yi Shi, Xian Zong Lin of Taiwan and Jie Rong of Hong Kong, entered Shanghai. Even another American company, Seattle Coffee Company, is interested in investing in chain coffee stores.[96]

Once the coffee war started, choosing a right location became the strategic issue for each competitor. In choosing locations, Zhen Guo focused on less expensive venues, while Starbucks chose the most expensive locations. Zhang Jianhui, the general manager of Starbucks Shanghai, believes that a good location can maximize brand share. At the same time, Starbucks China applied the strategy used in the United States to the Chinese market: the coexistence of several Starbucks branches in the same area, which stimulates consumption. Within several hundred meters of the central business district of Nanjing, a city in central China, three Starbucks are already in place.

In May 2001, Taiwan Wang Wang Group and Taiwan Seattle Supreme Coffee aligned to invest in the Chinese mainland. The first Seattle Coffee Chain store under Wang Wang Group opened in Shanghai in October 2001. Another Taiwanese food chain called Ding Hao is said to be interested in chain coffee store as well. Even McDonald's is entering the coffee business and has opened its own coffee shop in Beijing.

STARBUCKS ORGANIZATION IN CHINA

Starbucks entered the Chinese market through a joint venture, as it has in other countries. In Beijing, Da Wei Sun is the manager of Starbucks' outlets. Da Wei Sun is fifty-five years old and was born in the northern city of Tian Jin, in eastern China close to Beijing. As a two-year-old, he moved to Hong Kong with his family. Sun spent his school years in Hong Kong in a middle-income family. He went to a university in Taiwan, where he obtained a bachelor's degree in business management. After graduation, he went to the United States, where he started working as a computer programmer in Texas. In the early 1980s, he traveled to a town near Chicago with a friend who was an employee at McDonald's. The trip changed his life. Through his friend he became interested in the functional model and managerial style of McDonald's. He researched it carefully and concluded that McDonald's had a lot of potential in China.

In 1984, Sun opened the first McDonald's in Taiwan, and it was a great success. Although Sun finally sold those restaurants and got involved in other industries, the whole industry acknowledged him as the person to introduce McDonald's to Taiwan. Sun not only made McDonald's in Taiwan prosperous, but he also trained managers. When the first McDonald's opened in Beijing, the first general manager was from Taiwan. From 1993 to 1994, Sun opened a Hard Rock Café in Taiwan. After two years of successful operation of Hard Rock, Sun sold it and started his career in the Chinese mainland.

On November 11, 1999, Sun opened the first Starbucks in Beijing's International Trade Center. In terms of Sun's believing in Starbucks' success in

China, he points out two major issues. "One is to integrate the western brand with local environment, and the other is to give your client a psychological space."[97] That is how Starbucks introduced its coffee to China. Besides, the pace of life is getting faster, and people in cities need a third space beyond home and office. Starbucks supplies such a "third space."[98]

In China, Starbucks chose to build its brand image first to its employees and then to consumers. Rather than mass advertising from the beginning to introduce its products as other food and beverage companies, Starbuck hires enthusiastic people who can build good interactive relationships with the customers.[99]

STARBUCKS' FUTURE IN CHINA

In May 2000, Howard Schultz went to Asia to open four stores in South Korea and China. In China, he went to Hong Kong to open the city's first Starbucks coffee store at Exchange Square, Central. Howard describes his experience:

> The store was packed with people,
> including many members of the press
> who had come to document the event.
> To celebrate the opening, I joined with
> our partners in Hong Kong to pour our
> heart shapes into a giant coffee press to
> symbolize pouring our hearts into this
> bustling store. We continued on to the
> opening of Hong Kong's second store at
> Hysan Avenue, Causeway Bay, where a
> traditional lion dance was performed to
> commemorate the event. The acrobatic
> dance was so remarkable that it stopped
> traffic. Afterwards, I joined our partners
> in dotting the eye of the lion to bring
> good luck. At the opening of each store,
> I witnessed the excitement and enthusi-
> asm of our partners and customers in
> these markets. As we prepared to move
> on, I couldn't help but reflect on this
> amazing journey.[100]

Starbucks entered Beijing in 1999. It now adds eight or nine stores per year each in the cities of Beijing, Hong Kong, and Shanghai.[101] With a population of over a billion people, China is a major opportunity for Starbucks. However, the Chinese market is drastically different than the U.S. market. Can Starbucks flourish there as it has done in the United States?

Notes

1. Business Wire. "Starbucks Celebrates First Store Opening in Shenzhen; Starbucks Brings Coffee Passion and Expertise to Southern China." Business Wire.com Archives. http://www.businesswire.com/cna-index.html. Visited 20 November 2002. Release dated October 18, 2002.
2. Business Wire. "Starbucks Celebrates First Store Opening in Shenzhen."
3. Bill McDowell. "The Bean Counters." *Restaurants & Institutions*, 15 December 1995, 44.
4. Jake Batsell, "Starbucks Closes Its Year Increasing Profit by 19 Percent." *Seattle Times* Web site. http://seattletimes.nwsource.com/html/home. Visited 20 November 2002. Release dated 15 November 2002.
5. Howard Schultz and Dori Jones Yang. *Pour Your Heart into It: How Starbucks Built a Company One Cup at a Time*. (New York: Hyperion Press, 1997), 29.
6. Schultz, 32–33.
7. Schultz, 52.
8. Stanley Holmes, Drake Bennett, Kate Carlisle, and Chester Dawson. "Planet Starbucks." *Business Week*, September 9, 2002, 100–106.
9. Alan Liddle, "Howard Schultz," *Nation's Restaurant News*, January 1995, 184.
10. Liddle.
11. Schultz, 81–86.
12. Schultz, 82–83.
13. Schultz, 84–89.
14. Schultz, 90–108.
15. Schultz, 110–115.
16. Schultz, 180–185.
17. Schultz, 190–204.
18. Holmes et al., "Planet Starbucks," 100–106.
19. Schultz, 154–156.
20. Schultz, 142–156.
21. Schultz, 154–156.
22. Schultz, 190–204.
23. Scott Hume. "Howard's Blend," *Restaurants and Institutions*, 1 July 2000, 45.
24. Holmes et al. "Planet Starbucks," 100–106.
25. Schultz, 83.
26. Schultz, 181.
27. Business Source Premier. "Interviews with Howard Schultz. Sharing Success," *Executive Excellence*, November 1999, 16.

28. Schultz, 127.
29. Schultz, 125.
30. "Starbucks' Stir up Brewing Coffee Culture," *Jakarta Post*. Business Source Premier, 23 June 2002.
31. Business Source Premier. "Interviews with Howard Schultz," 16.
32. Schultz, 123–135.
33. Schultz, 133–136.
34. Business Source Premier, "Interviews with Howard Schultz," 16.
35. McDowell, "The Bean Counters," 40–45.
36. Business Source Premier, "Interviews with Howard Schultz," 16.
37. Schultz, 260–265.
38. http://qiye.news.sohu.com/73/24/news203602473.shtml. Visited 17 November 2002.
39. McDowell, 52–55; Hume. "Howard's Blend," 54–56.
40. Schultz, 208–226.
41. Nelson D. Schwartz, "Still Perking after All These Years," *Fortune*, 24 May 1999, 203–207.
42. Schultz, 139; Starbucks, "Fiscal 2001 Annual Report," 19; Starbucks. http://www.starbucks.com. Visited 17 November 2002.
43. Schultz, 267–273.
44. Schultz, 173–174.
45. Scott Bedbury. "A New Brand World," *Brand Strategy*, April 2002, 30.
46. History of Starbucks, Press Release, http://www.starbucks.com. Visited 16 November 2002.
47. Reuters Limited, http://www.starbucks.com. Visited 4 November 2002.
48. History of Starbucks, Press Release, http://www.starbucks.com. Visited 16 November 2002.
49. Schultz, 208-226.
50. Starbucks, "Fiscal 2001 Annual Report," 51.
51. Starbucks, "Fiscal 2001 Annual Report," 17.
52. Phillip E. Barnes, "Business," *Business & Economic Review*, July–September 2002, 27.
53. Holmes et al. "For Coffee Growers, Not Even a Whiff of Profits," *Business Week*, 9 September 2002.
54. Milton R. Moskowitz, "Starbucks," *Business & Society Review*, Fall 1995, 73.
55. "History of Starbucks."
56. Organic Consumer's Association, http://www.organic-consumers.org, 21 May 2002. Visited 16 November 2002.
57. "Less Pollution, More Profits," *Bio Cycle World*, October 2001, 6.
58. Welsh et al., "Starbucks International Enters Kuwait," *Journal of Consumer Marketing* 15(2) (1998), 191–197.
59. Holmes et al., "Planet Starbucks."
60. http://www.hoovers.com/premium/fin_tables/5/0,2152,15745,00.html. Visited 29 October 2002.
61. Holmes et al., "Planet Starbucks," 100–106.
62. http://www.hoovers.com/premium/fin_tables/5/0,2152,15745,00.html. Visited 29 October 2002.
63. Starbucks 1998 and 2001 Annual Reports.
64. Starbucks 1998 and 2001 Annual Reports.
65. Holmes et al., "Planet Starbucks."
66. "Speed Meter, Starbucks Is Rolling," *Fast Company*, October 2002, 132.
67. http://www.hoovers.com/premium/fin_tables/5/0,2152,15745,00.html. Visited 29 October 2002.
68. Starbucks, 2001 Annual Report.
69. Holmes et al., "Planet Starbucks."
70. Richard L. Papiernik, "Starbucks' profitable Brew Turns Up Heat on Expansion," *Nation's Restaurant News*, 9 January 1996, 1, 4.
71. Holmes et al., "Planet Starbucks."
72. Ibid.
73. Business Wire. "Starbucks Celebrates First Store Opening in Shenzhen; Starbucks Brings Coffee Passion and Expertise to Southern China," *Business Wire.com Archives*. Visited 22 November 2002.
74. Schultz, 331.
75. Central Intelligence Agency, "The World Fact Book 2002," http://www.cia.gov/cia/publications/factbook/geos/ch.html# Govt. Visited 16 November 2002.
76. Central Intelligence Agency, "The World Fact Book 2002"
77. Ibid.
78. http://www.golden-age.com.cn/gold1/hjtxt/2002-5/0507.htm. Posted on 4 June 2002. Visited 22 November 2002.
79. http://cooltoy.yesky.com/20010515/1249148.shtml. Visited 14 October 2002.
80. Chen Yong Sheng, "The Macro-Economic Economic Situation 2001," 2.
81. http://www1.cei.gov.cn/hottopic/worldfrm.asp?class=17. Visited November 17, 2002.
82. http://www1.cei.gov.cn/hottopic/worldfrm.asp?class=17.
83. http://culture.9c9c.com.cn/food/coffee/topic_2653.html -. Visited 16 November 2002.
84. http://bbs.fudan.edu.cn/cgi-bin/bbs/bbsanc?path=/groups/rec.faq/Fashion/liu/xiaozi/M.1010233881.A -. Posted 15 March 2002. Visited November 22, 2002.
85. http://www1.cei.gov.cn/hottopic/worldfrm.asp?class=17. Visited 17 November 2002.
86. Mediachinanet, "Coffee Chain—War in Cups," http://market-info.mediachina.net/marketinfo_view.jsp?id=11160. Posted 23 August 2002. Visited 17 November 2002.
87. "Starbuck Dictionary," http://www.gemag.com.cn/gemedia/legend/0111021.asp. Visited 17 November 2002.
88. http://www1.cei.gov.cn/hottopic/worldfrm.asp?class=17. Visited 28 November 2002.
89. "competition," http://marketinfo.mediachina.net/marketinfo_view.jsp?id=11160. Posted 23 August 2002. Visited 28 November 2002.
90. Geng Shu. "The Annual Appraisal Report—The Current Social Situation: The Unbalanced Development."
91. "Starbuck Dictionary," http://www.gemag.com.cn/gemedia/legend/0111021.asp. Visited 17 November 2002.
92. Welsh et al., "Starbucks International Enters Kuwait."
93. Press Release, "Beverage Market in China," http://www.beveragemarketing.com/news2i.htm. Visited 28 November 2002.

94. Luo Shaojun (Director, Hangzhou Tea Research Institute, China), "The Present Condition and Future Prospect of Chinese Tea," 1999 World O-CHA (Tea) Forum in Shizuoka, http://www.o-cha.net/festa/o-chae/forum/99_s_1.html. Visited 2 December 2002.

95. Welsh et al., "Starbucks International Enters Kuwait."

96. "competition," http://marketinfo.mediachina.net/market-info_view.jsp?id=11160. Visited 2 December 2002.

97. http://www.dzdaily.com.cn/caijing/guanzhu/200209130753.htm. Visited 17 November 2002.

98. http://www.dzdaily.com.cn/caijing/guanzhu/200209130753.htm. Visited 17 November 2002.

99. http://qiye.news.sohu.com/73/24/news203602473.shtml. Visited 17 November 2002.

100. Starbucks, "Fiscal 2000 Annual Report," 14.

101. Ibid.

CASE 3

Fairmont Hotels & Resorts

With deep pockets, powerhouse partners, and a mandate to grow, Fairmont
is now a force to be reckoned with in
the luxury segment.

—Lodging News, August 2000[1]

Despite difficult times for the lodging industry,
Fairmont Hotels & Resorts, the largest luxury hotel
management company in North America—with
forty-one Fairmont hotels, located mostly in
Canada and the United States, plus thirty-nine
Canadian properties flying the Delta Hotels flag—
is in a singular position to grow. The company has
fused a longstanding history of luxury hotel management (under the Canadian Pacific and
Fairmont flags) with a fresh corporate structure
that emphasizes centrality, long-term planning,
and a conservative yet innovative approach to
brand expansion. The result? A reborn company
poised to compete against the biggest players in the
luxury hotel market.

With a strong brand foundation, an innovative
expansion plan driven by smart management, ready
cash, and a thumbs-up from industry analysts,
Fairmont Hotels & Resorts finds itself in a very

favorable position relative to its industry competitors. But will the Fairmont strategy prove worthwhile over the long term? Will the company be able
to "grow up," leaving its adolescence behind and
become a major contender with on the international
stage? Or is the company destined to remain a minor
player in the hospitality playing field?

HISTORY OF THE COMPANY

The Beginnings

The Fairmont brand was created in 1902 when the
daughters of James "Bonanza Jim" Graham Fair,
Tessie and Virginia Fair, began construction of the
Fairmont Hotel in San Francisco as a monument to
their father. The building was all but complete when
the Great 1906 Earthquake struck on April 18. Even
though most of San Francisco was destroyed during
the earthquake and subsequent fire, the Fairmont
remained standing with only some minor structural
damage. The Fairmont San Francisco officially
opened one year to the day after the Great
Earthquake, celebrating with a grand banquet.[2]

Even though the first Fairmont opened in
1907, the first hotel in the company now known as
Fairmont Hotels & Resorts (FHR) premiered two
decades earlier, when the Hamilton Princess
opened to Bermuda's balmy sea breeze in 1885.
Despite its pedigree, FHR can also be considered a
young company, as it became an independently
traded company on the New York and Toronto
stock exchanges in October 2001. FHR was created
from the merger of four hotel companies: Canadian
Pacific Hotels & Resorts, Delta Hotels, Princess

Authors Carol Ann Fisher (caf33@cornell.edu) and Cheryl Farr
Leas (cfl25@cornell.edu) are graduate students in the Masters in
Management of Hospitality program at the Cornell School of
Hotel Administration, class of 2004. This case was written under
the direction of Jeffrey S. Harrison. The authors wish to thank
Fairmont Hotels & Resorts for their kind support and gracious
co-operation in the preparation of this case study.

This case study is written for the purposes of classroom discussion.

Hotels International, and Fairmont Hotel Management. Canadian Pacific Hotels & Resorts, a division of Canadian Pacific Limited (CPL), was the driver behind this acquisition spree and forms the foundation of today's FHR, acquiring both Delta Hotels and Princess Hotels International, Inc. in 1998 and then a 67 percent interest in Fairmont Hotel Management in 1999.[3]

Canadian Pacific Railways— Brief History of a Conglomeration

CPL began as Canadian Pacific Railway (CPR), a company created in 1881 with the mandate to build a transcontinental Canadian railway within ten years. As described in CPR literature, "Canadian Pacific Railway was formed to physically unite Canada from coast to coast. Canada's confederation on July 1, 1867 united four eastern British North American provinces into a new country. Nova Scotia and New Brunswick were promised the Intercontinental Railway to link them with Central Canada—Quebec and Ontario. Manitoba, around the Prairies Red River settlement, joined the confederation in 1870. And British Columbia, on the west coast, was enticed into confederation in 1871—but only with the promise of transcontinental railway being built within 10 years to physically link it with eastern Canada."[4] Hence the creation of Canadian Pacific Railway in 1881.

In an effort to raise funding for its project, in 1883 the company issued 200,000 shares of common stock on the New York Stock Exchange (NYSE), becoming the first non-U.S. firm to be listed on the NYSE.[5] CPR's management team—known as "the syndicate"—used these funds, in addition to the government funds and land grants promised at the creation of CPR, to make rapid progress on the railway construction.[6] CPR completed the transcontinental railway six years ahead of schedule, on November 7, 1885, after only four years of construction.[7]

CPR entered the hotel industry early, building hotels and dining rooms along the railway as a service to passengers. William Cornelius Van Horne, who became general manager of CPR in 1882, envisioned a string of grand hotels along the railway. He is famously quoted as saying, "If we can't export the scenery, we'll import the tourists."[8] The first hotel, Mount Stephen House, opened in 1886, high in the Canadian Rockies. More hotels quickly followed, with the famed Banff Springs hotel opening in 1888, Château Lake Louise in 1890, and Le Château Frontenac in 1893.

Canadian Pacific also entered other industries. In 1886, CPR "chartered seven ships to carry tea and silk from Asia to the West Coast of Canada, thereby providing eastbound freight for the railway."[9] This was the start of what was to become CP Ships.

The land grants given to CPR to build the railway system led the company into mining and natural resources, as it had rights to all subsurface resources of the land. CPR was therefore involved in the coal, zinc, lead, gold, and silver businesses.[10] Also in 1886, while digging a well for water needed by its steam locomotives, CPR discovered natural gas deposits in Alderson, Alberta.[11] This was the beginnings of PanCanadian Petroleum.

Canadian Pacific Limited— from 1986 to 2001

By 1986, a century after the first natural gas discovery, CPL was Canada's second largest company with $15 billion (Canadian dollars, CAD) in revenue, nearly 100,000 employees, and total assets of CAD $17.7 billion.[12] This huge conglomerate faced difficult economic conditions in the 1980s with a reduction in demand for rail transportation as well as the collapse of oil prices in 1986.[13] The CEO, William Stinson, developed a plan to refocus CPL on four core businesses: freight transportation, natural resources, real estate (including hotels), and manufacturing.[14] The company began divesting its noncore divisions while streamlining the remaining businesses.

Though divesting had some positive impacts on CPL, the economic downturn of the early 1990s led to further losses for the conglomerate, given the weak prices for oil and gas. CPL responded by reorganizing and focusing on efficiencies. "CPL had slashed its workforce from more than 75,000 in the late 1980s to less than 40,000 by 1994, reflecting a significant liquidation of assets."[15]

In 1996, David O'Brien was appointed CEO of CPL. On the day he was appointed, O'Brien was quoted as saying: "In the 1960s and 1970s, the problem was to expand into new areas beyond our regulated railway and airline businesses. In the 1980s and early 1990s, it was to transform ourselves from a broadly based conglomerate, overseeing disparate businesses, into a more narrowly-based company focused on transportation, energy, real estate and hotels. Today, it is to maximize the potential of our core businesses while recognizing that we can excel only in a limited number of areas."[16] To do so, each of the five main companies—CP Rail (freight transportation), PanCanadian Petroleum (petroleum, oil, and natural gas), Fording (mining), CP Ships (regional ocean and inland transportation), and CP Hotels & Resorts—worked to increase their global competitiveness through strategic acquisitions and alliances.[17]

The focus on five key businesses culminated in the announcement on February 13, 2001 that Canadian Pacific would be divided into five separate companies, each to be publicly traded on both the New York and Toronto stock exchanges by the fall of 2001.[18] O'Brien stated, "We expect this distribution will not only unlock significant value now but also will provide sustainable value for Canadian Pacific's shareholders over the long term. As independent companies, each will be able to react decisively to the competitive forces in its own market, and pursue short and long-term strategies that are appropriate to its industry."[19]

As for Canadian Pacific Hotels & Resorts, this division was seen as a growth engine for the company. Through the late 1990s, they made several major acquisitions, enlarging its hotel management portfolio from twenty Canadian city center and resort hotels[20] to more than seventy hotels with 29,000 rooms in Canada, the United States, Mexico, Bermuda, and Barbados. Most of this growth was achieved through acquisition.[21] Also, when the company was split into the five businesses in 2001, CPL changed its name to Fairmont Hotels & Resorts, with this company retaining all assets not allocated to the other four divisions.[22]

Brief History of Hotel Companies Acquired by Canadian Pacific

Delta Hotels Delta Hotels began in 1962, with a single sixty-two-room motor inn in Richmond, British Columbia.[23] By 1998, the company managed or franchised thirty-four first-class properties and was owned by Realstart Group of Toronto and the Lai Sun Group of Hong Kong. Although twenty-seven of the thirty-four hotels were located in Canada, Delta Hotels had an international footprint with two hotels in the United States (in Orlando, Florida, and Phoenix, Arizona), two hotels in Cuba, two hotels in Thailand, one in the Philippines, one in Malaysia, one in Vietnam, and one in the Dominican Republic.[24] At the end of 2002, all international holdings had been divested in order to focus energies on the core Canadian portfolio.

Princess Hotels International Even earlier than Canadian Pacific Railway, Princess Hotels International opened its first hotel, Bermuda's Hamilton Princess, on January 1, 1885. The hotel was named in honor of Princess Louise, daughter of Queen Victoria, who visited the island in 1883. This hotel was built by Harley Trott, head of Trott & Cox, a steamship agent. Trott built the hotel to attract affluent Americans, who would summer in the Berkshires and winter in Bermuda. Over time, Princess Hotels grew to seven luxury resort properties with more than 3,000 rooms in Bermuda; Barbados; Acapulco, Mexico; and Scottsdale, Arizona.[25]

Fairmont Hotel Management L.P. Fairmont opened in San Francisco in 1907, and name "Fairmont" is synonymous with luxury hotels in San Francisco. However, the Fairmont brand did not grow to significant national and international prominence during the twentieth century. By 1999, only seven hotels were managed under the "Fairmont" name: the Fairmont San Francisco, the Fairmont San Jose, the Fairmont Boston Copley Plaza, the Fairmont Chicago, the Fairmont New Orleans, the Fairmont Dallas, and New York's Plaza[26] (which was managed as part of the group but has never worn the Fairmont name).

The San Francisco Fairmont changed hands several times. Tessie and Virginia Fair began construction in 1902 but sold it to brothers Herbert and Hartland Law in 1906. When Tessie Fair Oelrichs returned to San Francisco in 1908, she repurchased the hotel from the Law brothers, eventually selling it to D. M. Linnard in 1924. In 1945, Ben Swig, an East Coast businessman, purchased the hotel and created the Fairmont Hotel Company.[27] Richard Swig managed this hotel company until his death in 1997.[28] As chairman, Richard Swig spearheaded the expansion of Fairmont Hotels to seven U.S. cities.

After the death of Richard Swig, a new player took over management of Fairmont Hotels—Maritz, Wolff & Co., a private investment fund based in Los Angeles, which owns interests in many luxury hotels. In 1998, Maritz, Wolff acquired a 50 percent stake in the Fairmont Management Co. from Swig Company, with management contracts for the Plaza in New York City as well as Fairmont-branded properties in San Francisco, Dallas, Boston, Chicago, New Orleans, and San Jose. At the same time, Maritz, Wolff acquired a 50 percent stake in three of the Fairmont properties, in San Francisco, Dallas, and New Orleans.[29] The remaining 50 percent stake in both the management companies and the properties continued to be owned by Kingdom Hotels, a company associated with Saudi Prince Alwaleed bin Talal bin Abdul Aziz Saud.

In 1999, a decision was made to create Fairmont Hotels & Resorts in association with Canadian Pacific Hotels. In commenting on the decision, Lewis Wolff declared, "We have agreed, in principle, to a business combination with Canadian Pacific that not only expands our portfolio of luxury properties nearly fivefold, but also puts Fairmont into the resort category. And this is only the beginning of the Fairmont brand's expansion."[30]

Canadian Pacific Hotels— from 1986 to 1999

In the late 1980s and throughout the1990s, when the CPL conglomerate was facing difficulties, Canadian Pacific Hotels was performing strongly—it was seen as a growth lever within the group. In 1988, Canadian Pacific Hotels acquired Canadian National Hotels, the hospitality division of Canadian National Railway.[31] This added key properties to the Canadian Pacific Hotels group, including the Château Laurier in Ottawa and Jasper Park Lodge in Alberta.

On January 25, 1996, for the first time in its history, Canadian Pacific Hotels unveiled "a logo designed solely for its distinctive collection of hotels,"[32] with the launch of the logo coinciding with the 110th anniversary of the company. The logo portrays "CP" in a monograph style surrounded by twelve golden maple leaves, representing the ten provinces and two territories that then made up Canada, and topped with a royal crown, a visual cue to the château hotels in the collection, "considered by many to be the jewels in our crown."[33] The logo "combines the proud heritage of Canadian Pacific Hotels with the contemporary standards our guests enjoy at our world-class hotels. With the rebirth and revitalization of Canadian Pacific Hotels now complete, we are well positioned to begin our next century as Canada's leading hotel company."[34]

In 1997, Canadian Pacific Hotels created the Legacy Hotels Real Estate Investment Trust (REIT). As a REIT, Legacy's purpose is to provide unitholders with "regular stable and growing cash distributions."[35] Eleven of the city-center Canadian Pacific Hotels were sold to that REIT. Commenting on this sale and creation of the REIT, David O'Brien, then the president and CEO of Canadian Pacific Limited, stated that this act "allowed us to surface the real estate value in these properties while maintaining long term management contracts."[36] The funds generated by selling off certain properties to the Legacy REIT were used for an aggressive acquisition strategy in the coming years.

In May 1998, Canadian Pacific Hotels acquired Delta Hotels for CAD $93 million. Delta Hotels had been founded in 1962 in Richmond, British Columbia, and had grown to be Canada's largest first-class hotel management company.[37] At the time of the sale, Delta Hotels managed or franchised thirty-four properties with around 10,000 rooms and 6,500 employees.[38] With Delta Hotels, Canadian Pacific Hotels doubled its size in Canada, and one of the reasons for the acquisition was to capitalize on opportunities for synergies in support services.[39]

From the beginning, Canadian Pacific Hotels intended to manage Delta as a distinct brand from Canadian Pacific Hotels. William R. Fatt, chairman and CEO of Canadian Pacific Hotels, said at the announcement of the acquisition, "The Delta name is recognized by business and leisure travelers. We want to maintain the product, while encouraging the brand to grow under our leadership."[40]

In August 1998, Canadian Pacific Hotels acquired Princess Hotels International for CAD $865 million. Princess Hotels operated seven luxury resorts with more than 3,000 rooms, "which expanded our network beyond Canada to the U.S., Mexico, Bermuda, and the Caribbean."[41] As large, landmark luxury destination resorts, the Princess resorts were similarly positioned to CP hotels and an ideal match for the CP portfolio. With the Delta Hotels and Princess Hotels acquisition, Canadian Pacific Hotels became the fourth-largest resort hotel operator in North America and the Caribbean.

In one fell swoop, this Canadian player had taken the international stage, but with a regional brand name. As David O'Brien, CEO of Canadian Pacific, stated in April 1999, "While the Canadian Pacific Hotels name is strong in Canada, having a well-known U.S. retail brand and landmark hotels in key U.S. cities will significantly enhance our ability to grow in North America and beyond."[42] So Canadian Pacific cast its eye on Fairmont.

In April 1999, Canadian Pacific Hotels announced that it had agreed with Kingdom Hotels (USA) Ltd. and Maritz, Wolff & Co., to create a hotel management company to be called Fairmont Hotels & Resorts (FHR).[43] Canadian Pacific would hold a 67 percent interest in FHR while Kingdom and Maritz, Wolff would each hold 16.5 percent interest. At that time, there were seven Fairmont hotels, in Boston, Chicago, Dallas, New Orleans, New York, San Francisco, and San Jose.[44]

By April 1999, Canadian Pacific Hotels had divested Delta Hotels of all non-Canadian properties, except for the Delta Orlando in Florida.[45] It was decided from the beginning that the Fairmont name would be the brand used for expansion for the luxury hotels and resorts portion of its operations. Although Fairmont only had seven properties at the time, "the brand had a level of recognition that was well in excess of what would be expected" for its size, says Fairmont CEO William Fatt. "We were searching for a brand name that would be recognizable to the American marketplace, and Fairmont fit."[46] As a result, when the company opened its next new hotel in Vancouver in 1999, it bore the name the Fairmont Vancouver Airport.[47]

Fairmont Hotels & Resorts— 1999 and Beyond

In October 1999, Canadian Pacific formed Fairmont Hotels & Resorts, managing thirty-six luxury properties in resort and city center locations across North America and the Caribbean.[48] At that time, all seven Princess Hotels were rebranded as "Fairmont Princess" Hotels. In 2000, all of the Canadian Pacific hotels were rebranded "Fairmont," such as The Fairmont Banff Springs and The Fairmont Château Lake Louise.[49]

Despite the rebranding using the Fairmont name, the parent company remained Canadian Pacific Hotels & Resorts, with four divisions: Fairmont Hotels & Resorts, Delta Hotels, Canadian Pacific Hotels Real Estate, and Legacy Hotels REIT.[50]

After 1999, no new hotel companies were acquired, but new properties were added to the hotel portfolio. The Fairmont Miramar Santa Monica was added to the portfolio in late 1999, the Fairmont Kansas City at the Plaza in 2000 and the Fairmont Kea Lani in February 2001.[51]

After CPL split into five companies on October 1, 2001, Fairmont Hotels & Resorts began trading as an independent company on the Toronto and New York stock exchanges on October 3 under the FHR ticker symbol.[52] Canadian Pacific Hotels & Resorts was no more.

After FHR became an independent company, expansion continued outside of North America with the Fairmont Dubai opening in February 2002. FHR has a minority interest in this hotel, while His Highness Dr. Sheikh Sultan bin Khalifa Al Nahyan of Abu Dhabi owns the majority of the hotel.[53] In North America, Fairmont added three new properties in 2002: the Fairmont Sonoma Mission Inn & Spa; the Fairmont Orchid, Hawaii; and the Fairmont Washington, D.C.[54]

In mid-2003, the Fairmont Olympic Hotel, Seattle, which formerly flew the Four Seasons banner, joined the Fairmont family of hotels.[55] Further additions are planned with the Fairmont Coco Beach Resort in Puerto Rico and Fairmont Abu Dhabi Resort, both scheduled to open in 2005.[56]

On July 25, 2002, Kingdom Hotels announced its intention to exchange its 16.5 percent stake in Fairmont Hotels Inc., the hotel management company, for shares in Fairmont Hotels & Resorts, in a transaction in which Kingdom Hotels would acquire approximately 4 percent of the outstanding shares in FHR.[57] This transaction was completed on September 23, 2003, when FHR issued 2.875 million shares to Kingdom Hotels in exchange for the 16.5 percent stake in Fairmont Hotels Inc., equivalent to 3.7 percent of FHR outstanding shares. Commenting on this transaction, Prince Alwaleed stated, "We are pleased with this transaction as it provides us with a broader exposure to all of FHR's assets, not only the management business. Kingdom intends to be a long-term investor and we look forward to our continued relationship with FHR."[58]

ENVIRONMENTAL ANALYSIS

FHR competes in the strongly competitive hotel and lodging industry, focusing on the first-class and luxury segments of the market. In addition to the specifics of the lodging industry, FHR is affected by change in the overall travel, tourism and hospitality industries, as well as broader macroenvironmental trends.

Broad Environment

The World Travel & Tourism Council forecast that travel and tourism demand would achieve 2.9 percent real growth in 2003 and 4.6 percent real growth per annum between 2004 and 2013.[59] Travel is allocated between personal or leisure travel and business travel, with personal travel making up the largest share of the industry.

A major engine behind the growth in travel and tourism spending are baby boomers, who believe they possess an inalienable right to travel. Real median family income (after adjusting for inflation) has increased by 11.8 percent since 1982 alone.[60] And as post–World War II babies have matured into affluent boomers with a great deal more discretionary income than previous generations enjoyed, they are using those extra dollars to travel more.[61]

Younger generations have also been bitten by the travel bug; as travel has become more accessible and affordable, they consider a long-haul flight to Eastern Europe or Southeast Asia to be just as viable as a road trip to the Grand Canyon.[62] And, with increased globalization of business, international travel has also become extremely common for business travelers. According to a 1997–1998 Gallup poll, 81 percent of entire U.S. adult population had flown at least once, and two out of every five U.S. citizens flew during 1997–1998.[63]

The growing senior group, the population over fifty years of age, are also traveling more. Though they may have less total income than consumers age twenty-five to forty-nine, they tend to have more disposable income and more time available for travel. "From 1990–1998 the U.S. population grew by 9% and Americans traveled at fourfold that amount—an impressive 36%. But even more impressive is that during the 1990s travel among those 55+ grew by an astounding 50%, mainly in the leisure travel category."[64]

Despite these positive trends, travel and tourism has suffered recently, especially among North American travelers. The Travel Industry Association of America (TIA) tracks an overall traveler sentiment index, measuring consumers' interest in leisure travel and their perceived ability to travel. Consumer travel sentiment has been below par (100 percent) in recent years, dipping as low as 93.7 percent on first quarter 2002.[65]

Although consumer travel in the United States slowed after the terrorist attacks on September 11, 2001, this chart shows that consumer travel had actually begun to decline as the economy slowed down in late 2000. After rebounding briefly in early 2002, consumer sentiment dropped again in late 2002 as economic recovery was slow to appear and the possibility of a United States–led war with Iraq arose. Despite the favorable long-term global trends toward more travel, the North American travel industry has suffered.

The TIA commented that in early 2003, consumers feel that travel is very affordable right now; however, they continue to be concerned about having enough money to take a trip, most likely an indication of their uneasiness over the state of the economy. Consumers also are very concerned about having the time available to travel, which may explain the slight drop in interest in taking a pleasure trip. The uncertainty created by these factors is probably contributing to the current late booking patterns seen throughout the travel industry.[66]

Consumers have also changed their travel patterns. In forecasting travel for the summer of 2003, the TIA's senior vice president of research and technology, Dr. Suzanne Cook, commented that "the rather dramatic shifts that Americans have made in their travel preferences in the past twenty months, such as more driving trips, closer-to-home travel and more rural destinations, are still apparent. While we expect these trends to remain strong this summer, they may not be as exaggerated as we saw last year, reflecting Americans' gradual return to their more traditional travel patterns."[67]

Business travel has declined sharply since 2000, due to economic slowdown as well as due to the terrorist attacks in September 2001. Given the uncertain economic environment, most businesses are engaging in cost-cutting activities, trying to maintain a level of profitability while waiting for the recovery and growth period to start. A favorite target of cost cutting is corporate travel budgets. This results in decreased number of travelers as well as decreased spending per trip due to a lowering of authorized quality levels.[68]

Directly related to the uncertain economic trends is an increase in uncertainty for businesses. Corporations are often taking a "wait-and-see" approach to investments while at the same time they are actively looking for cost reduction opportunities.[69] Given the uncertainty around future investments and cost control efforts, companies are delaying decisions on any planned activities. More companies are waiting until the last minute before scheduling meetings and business trips to see customers and suppliers. This

affects the hotel business, as it results in a fundamental change in booking windows.[70]

The rapid expansion of technology has significantly affected hotel pricing. Technology has backed the creation of more flexible travel management systems, allowing corporations to implement and monitor travel policies for business travel. By accessing online hotel pricing—typically through the corporate travel agent's systems—corporations can price competitive hotels in the same market, making more and more decisions based on price alone.

The second impact, for both leisure and business travelers, are the Web search engines that can very quickly price shop for hotel rooms. Hotel companies have discovered a serious dark side to the new distribution frontier and transparency of pricing information. Now that anyone with a Web browser has access to the same global distribution systems as travel agents via such Web sites as Expedia, Travelocity, and Orbitz, hotel room-night pricing is approaching the economist's ideal of "perfect" information.[71] Thus, hotels must be willing to match their competitors' prices or lose market share.[72]

PricewaterhouseCoopers believes there has been a fundamental shift in lodging demand since 2001:

> Beginning in the Fall of 2001, ongoing security alerts, travel concerns involving safety and convenience, and lower consumer confidence and personal wealth due to stock market declines and volatility have caused lodging demand to trail the long-run trend line by approximately five percent, or 130,000 occupied room nights per night in 2002. PricewaterhouseCoopers believes that the combination of the many factors, some of which will continue well into the future, will result in a permanent structural resetting of demand that has not occurred since the Great Depression.[73]

Though Canada suffered from cancellations after the terrorist attacks on September 11, 2001, the Canadian hospitality industry was not as profoundly touched as the U.S. industry by the terrorist attacks and the impending U.S. war against Iraq in late 2002.

An estimated 780,000 room-nights were canceled in Canada's major urban and resort markets in September and October 2001, as a direct result of September 11.[74] Recovery occurred more quickly, however. "Canadian RevPAR showed solid increases, by some 5% in 2002, which is in sharp contrast to the decline of almost 3% forecast in the United States."[75] However, the Canadian hotel market was dealt its own severe blow in 2003 with the outbreak of SARS in Toronto. In first quarter 2003, national hotel occupancy averaged a mere 53 percent, and the nation lost an estimated $92.2 million (CDN) in hotel room revenue in the month of April alone.[76]

Travelers are increasingly preoccupied with security given the threat of terrorism. Though these threats are primarily against the United States and select Middle East countries, they do have a knock-on effect on all tourism in North America and abroad, as travelers hesitate to board airplanes. Many hotel guests are looking for increased security from hotel companies as part of their overall preoccupation with security.[77]

The Lodging Industry

As 2003 began, the lodging industry faced challenges from a soft economy. "Relatively weak business spending, cutbacks in the airline industry, price-sensitive consumer, and the threat of terrorism and war are all taking a toll on travel activity," noted Standard & Poor's in an industry survey.[78] How is the industry organized to take on these challenges?

Categorizing Hotel Guests There is no single "typical" lodging customer, per se. Among lodging customers as a whole, 23.7 percent are on vacation, 29.5 percent are transient business travelers, 27.0 percent are attending a conference or group meeting and 19.8 percent are traveling for other reasons such as family or a special event.[79] Hotels typically categorize their customers as business versus leisure. Within each category, there are other subsegments, such as whether the traveler is transient or associated with a group, or whether a business traveler is linked to a corporate business or an association. Typical abbreviations are "free independent traveler" (FIT) and "social, military, education, religious, or fraternal" (SMERF).

The hotel business is a cyclical business. Hotels that cater to the business traveler tend to be busier in midweek than at the weekend. Resort hotels tend to be busier in high season when the weather is better than in the off-season. Each property will track historical occupancies—by market segment when possible—to determine their cyclical pattern by day of the week, month, and season. Smith Travel Research, a hospitality consulting company that serves as the premier source of daily competitive market data in the accommodations industry, provides comparable data for a given city or a select competitive set that a property can use to complete its understanding of the cyclical nature of their business.

Like the broader travel and tourism industry, the hotel business is also subject to changes in travel patterns due to the underlying economic conditions or due to shocks to the hospitality industry such as war, terrorism, or health scares like SARS. Smith Travel Research estimates that hotel occupancy levels dropped 3.1 percent in early 2001 due to economic difficulties, and then full-year occupancy levels dropped 5.7 percent given the additional impact of the terrorist attacks on September 11, 2001.[80] In May 2003, Canada's national newspaper, *The Globe and Mail,* reported that "the anticipated 80-per-cent occupancy rate at some Toronto hotels has fallen below 40 per cent as a result of the [SARS] disease and in at least one hotel dipped into the single digits. Statistics Canada said yesterday that 12,000 of the city's hospitality workers lost their jobs last month."[81]

As an example of changes in travel patterns, Standard and Poor estimated that business travel was down in 2002 due to two primary reasons. First, travelers were trading down, staying in hotel rooms at lower price points than before the economy took a turn for the worse. Second, businesses seemed to be sending fewer staff to out-of-town meetings and conferences.[82]

With all of these changes in customer behavior, has FHR invested smartly—and enough—to better understand its customers?

Categorizing Hotel Properties The American Hotel & Lodging Association estimates that there are 41,393 hotel properties and 4.2 million rooms in the United States.[83] (See Exhibit 1.)

EXHIBIT 1	TOTAL U.S. HOTEL PROPERTIES BY CATEGORY[86]			
	Property		**Rooms**	
By Location				
Suburban	13,660	33.0%	1,231,682	29.4%
Highway	17,454	42.2%	1,327,518	31.7%
Urban	4,453	10.8%	666,820	15.9%
Airport	3,401	8.2%	469,247	11.2%
Resort	2,425	5.0%	490,496	11.7%
By Rate				
Under $30	1,695	4.1%	95,378	2.3%
$30–$44.99	7,101	17.2%	503,167	12.0%
$45–$59.99	13,722	33.2%	1,017,463	24.3%
$60–$85	11,563	27.9%	1,200,559	28.7%
Over $85	7,312	17.7%	1,369,058	32.7%
By Size				
Under 75 rooms	21,580	52.1%	954,057	22.8%
75–149 rooms	13,820	33.4%	1,479,206	35.3%
150–299 rooms	4,397	10.6%	878,724	21.0%
300–500 rooms	1,091	2.6%	404,967	9.7%
Over 500 rooms	505	1.2%	468,671	11.2%

many ways, including by price (budget hotels, midscale hotels, luxury hotels); by location (suburban, urban, highway, airport, or resort) or by property type (full-service hotels, limited service hotels, resorts, all-suite hotels, or convention hotels).[84] Goldman Sachs has a more restrictive definition:

> Hotels are typically divided into two types: either full-service hotels or limited-service hotels. Full-service hotels are generally mid-price to upscale hotels featuring restaurants, meeting and convention space, and include more labor-intensive services such as room and concierge service. In contrast, limited-service hotels typically do not include food and beverage service and have limited additional amenities.[85]

Hotel performance is tracked by occupancy (the number of rooms sold divided by the total number of rooms available) and the average daily rate (ADR) charged for the room, as shown in Exhibit 2.

The average daily rate charged by a hotel will, of course, depend on the local market and competition. It will also depend on the type of property and services offered by the hotel. Properties are rated by independent agencies against a variety of criteria. In North America, there are two major rating systems that travel agents and tourists use to judge a property: American Automobile Association's (AAA) Diamond Rating and Mobil's Star Rating.

The AAA Diamond Rating is designed to assess quality in each of the following six areas: management and staff; housekeeping and maintenance; exterior, grounds, and public areas; room décor, ambiance, and amenities; bathrooms; and guest services. The rating system extends from a One Diamond property to a Five Diamond property. The AAA Diamond Rating system is summarized as follows:[88]

- *One Diamond:* "These establishments typically appeal to the budget-minded traveler. They provide essential, no-frills accommodations. They meet the basic requirements pertaining to comfort, cleanliness, and hospitality."

- *Two Diamond:* "These establishments appeal to the traveler seeking more than the basic accommodations. There are modest enhancements to the overall physical attributes, design elements, and amenities of the facility typically at a moderate price."

- *Three Diamond:* "These establishments appeal to the traveler with comprehensive needs. Properties are multifaceted with a distinguished style, including marked upgrades in the quality of physical attributes, amenities, and level of comfort provided."

- *Four Diamond:* "These establishments are upscale in all areas. Accommodations are progressively more refined and stylish. The physical attributes reflect an obvious enhanced level of quality throughout. The fundamental hallmarks at this level include an extensive array of amenities combined with a high degree of hospitality, service, and attention to detail."

- *Five Diamond:* "These establishments reflect the characteristics of the ultimate in luxury and sophistication. Accommodations are

| EXHIBIT 2 | U.S. LODGING PERFORMANCE IN OCCUPANCY AND ROOM RATE BY CATEGORY, 2001–2002, ACCORDING TO SMITH TRAVEL RESEARCH[87] | | | | | | |

Segment	Occupancy (%)		Average Daily Room Rate (U.S. $)		Percent Change (2001–2002)		
	2001	2002	2001	2002	Room Revenue	Rooms Available	Rooms Sold
Industry, total	61.2%	60.5%	$ 85.05	$ 83.53	–1.2%	1.8%	0.6%
By Price							
Luxury	67.1%	67.2%	$ 114.32	$ 138.41	–2.1%	2.0%	2.1%
Upscale	63.2%	63.2%	$ 93.67	$ 91.26	–0.3%	2.3%	2.3%
Midprice	59.5%	58.4%	$ 69.96	$ 68.61	–1.5%	2.4%	0.5%
Economy	57.3%	55.9%	$ 54.55	$ 54.42	–1.4%	1.3%	–1.2%
Budget	59.1%	57.0%	$ 41.32	$ 42.72	–0.8%	–0.5%	–4.1%
By Location							
Urban	63.8%	63.8%	$ 125.71	$ 121.66	–0.7%	2.7%	2.7%
Suburban	62.0%	61.1%	$ 81.51	$ 79.99	–1.1%	2.2%	0.8%
Airport	64.8%	63.4%	$ 80.73	$ 77.31	–4.9%	1.6%	–0.6%
Highway	58.8%	58.1%	$ 65.67	$ 65.38	0.0%	1.6%	0.4%
Resort	62.8%	61.9%	$ 137.27	$ 135.57	–2.8%	–0.1%	–1.6%

first class. The physical attributes are extraordinary in every manner. The fundamental hallmarks at this level are to meticulously serve and exceed all guest expectations while maintaining an impeccable standard of excellence. Many personalized services and amenities enhance an unmatched level of comfort."[89]

In 2003, the coveted Five Diamond rating was given to only seventy-seven properties in North America. Of these properties, sixty-six were in the United States, three in Canada, five in Mexico, and three in the Caribbean.[90] For Fairmont Hotels & Resorts, only one property in its portfolio earned this distinction—the Fairmont Scottsdale Princess.

The Mobil Travel Guide uses a star rating, allocating between one and five stars to each property.

- *One-Star Hotel.* Provides a recommendation to a property that is limited in its amenities and services provided, however is focused on providing a value experience while meeting travelers' expectations. The property can be expected to be clean, comfortable, and convenient and has met Mobil Travel Guide standards and expectations at the One-Star level.

- *Two-Star Hotel.* Provide consumers with a clean and comfortable establishment but also with expanded amenities or distinctive environment. A Two-Star property is an excellent place to stay or dine.

- *Three-Star Hotel.* Recognizes an excellent property that provides full services and amenities. This category ranges from exceptional hotels with limited services to elegant restaurants with less-formal atmosphere.

- *Four-Star Hotel.* Honors properties for outstanding achievement in overall facility and for providing very strong service levels in all areas. These award winners provide a distinctive experience for the ever-demanding and sophisticated consumer.

- *Five-Star Hotel.* Indicates that a property is one of the very best in the country and consistently provides gracious and courteous service, superlative quality in its facility, and a unique ambiance that is all its own. The hotels and restaurants at the Five-Star level are consistently and proactively responding to consumer's needs, and they continue their commitment to excellence, doing so with grace and perseverance.[91]

Mobil grants the star rating based on an assessment of service detail, facilities detail, guest room detail, and specialized facility detail.[92]

The luxury segment of the hotel market includes four- and five-star (or diamond) rated hotels. These properties offer an exceptional level of personalized service and a complete range of amenities and facilities, such as dining options, meeting and convention spaces, and recreational activities. Hotel staff-to-guest ratios are highest in luxury hotels.

The "first-class segment" of the hotel market typically refers to three- and four-star (or diamond) properties. Though still offering high-quality services and amenities, they are somewhat below luxury quality standards.[93]

As of the end of 2002, only one FHR property bore the prestigious AAA Five Diamond award: the Fairmont Scottsdale Princess. In comparison, the Four Seasons and Ritz-Carlton brands had twenty and seventeen properties, respectively, on AAA's North American list.[94] With its hotel portfolio, is FHR a serious contender in the luxury arena? In 2003, the five-diamond Four Seasons Seattle became the Fairmont Olympic Hotel, Seattle, which may put the matter to test. Will Fairmont management be able to maintain this coveted designation?

Categorizing Hotel Companies While some hotel properties are run as independent businesses, most hotel properties belong to a hotel company involved with multiple properties. However, the owner of the hotel property does not necessarily have to be the manager of the hotel property. Many hotels have two masters: an owner *and* a management company.

Hotel companies select the business model they wish to operate from three main categories. The hotel company can own and operate its own property, thereby keeping all revenues and expenses related to the operation (for example, New York City's Waldorf-Astoria is owned and operated by Hilton). The company can be a management company only, operating a property that belongs to a third party in exchange for a management fee (i.e., Four Seasons)—usually a base fee of 4 to 5 percent of total hotel revenues plus a variable incentive fee of 5 to 30 percent based on profit performance. Lastly, the hotel company can possess a brand name that it franchises to other hotel operators in exchange for a royalty franchise fee of 5 percent of hotel revenues (such as Choice Hotels, which encompasses such brands as Days Inn, Comfort Inn, Comfort Suites, and Clarion). Many hospitality companies use a combination of these three models.[95]

Each business model has different finance structures and different benefits and drawbacks. In the whole-ownership model, an owning company is responsible for all development costs and has total control of operations. Owners benefit from a greater reward in growing markets, but they are generally highly leveraged and must bear the sole burden of the high-fixed-cost expense structure when top-line revenues slow in times of economic downturn. Owners can choose to share the rewards and burdens of ownership with partners via mezzanine financing, sliver equity sales, and other leverage models.[96]

The management structure allows hotel companies to grow aggressively with minimal capital risk. Management companies bear less operating leverage, since fees are deducted from total hotel revenues, but they benefit less dramatically than owners do from upturns in the economy (since they earn a minority fraction of profits). Furthermore, while a management company maintains total control over the day-to-day operation of the hotel, property maintenance and capital expenditure projects must be negotiated with and approved by the property owner; therefore, the management company maintains less control over the total quality of the product. Management companies sometimes own up to a 20 percent sliver-equity interest in their properties, which gives the management company more leverage at the negotiation table.[97]

In the franchise model, hotel companies can broaden their brand net with little capital risk. The franchising brand contributes no capital at the property level; rather, any corporate-level capital investment goes to national and international promotion of the brand. The hotel company also bears no operating leverage. However, the brand also has no control over property management or maintenance—which can put brand quality and customer perception of the brand at risk.[98]

The hotel industry is made up of a multitude of players. Most are publicly traded companies, such as Cendant, Marriott, and Fairmont, while some major players—such as Carlson Cos. (Radisson, Country Inns) and Hyatt Hotels—are privately held. (See Exhibit 3.)

The late 1990s saw a fast and furious wave of consolidation in the U.S. lodging market. For instance, Starwood acquired Sheraton and Westin, Hilton acquired Doubletree, Bass acquired InterContinental to form Six Continents (now InterContinental Hotels Group), and Marriott acquired Ritz-Carlton and Renaissance among a plethora of other merger activity. Despite the wave of consolidation between 1998 and 2001, "no single lodging company encompasses hotels (including franchises) that account for more than 15% of all hotel rooms in the United States."[100] Goldman Sachs believed in 2003 that domestic consolidation was just about over for the time being as United States-based hoteliers look internationally for expansion opportunities.[101]

Built on the acquisition of the Fairmont and Princess hotel groups by Canadian Pacific Hotels & Resorts in the late 1990s, FHR maintains a mixed business model as both an owner and a manager of hotel properties. Does this business model allow FHR to balance risk and reward and achieve the best of both worlds—or does it result in a splintered focus?

Operating Profit and Financing in the Hotel Business Beginning in 1925, the hospitality industry has continually developed and revised the Uniform System of Accounts for the Lodging Industry (USALI). This turnkey system provides detailed information about accounts, classifications, formats, and the uses of financial statements. It

EXHIBIT 3	SUMMARY OF LARGEST HOTEL COMPANIES, BASED ON NUMBER OF AFFILIATED ROOMS WORLDWIDE AS OF DECEMBER 2002[99]		
Company	**Major Brands**	**Number of Properties**	**Number of Rooms**
Cendant Corp.	Days Inn, Ramada (in U.S.), Super 8, Howard Johnson, Travelodge (in North America)	6,654	552,528
Six Continents Hotels (now InterContinental Hotels Group)	Holiday Inn, InterContinental, Crowne Plaza	3,300	515,000
Marriott International	Marriott, Renaissance, Courtyard, Residence Inn, Fairfield Inn, Ritz-Carlton	2,505	454,587
Accor S.A.	Motel 6, Mercure, Ibis, Novotel, Red Roof Inn, Hotel Sofitel, Formule One	3,800	425,000
Choice Hotels International	Comfort Inn, Comfort Suites, Sleep Inn, Clarion, EconoLodge, Quality Inn	4,426	360,000
Hilton Hotels	Hilton, Hampton Inn, Doubletree, Embassy Suites, Homewood Suites	2,058	334,704
Best Western International	Best Western	4,043	306,444
Starwood Hotels & Resorts	Sheraton, Westin, W, Luxury Collection, St. Regis, Four Points by Sheraton	745	225,382
Carlson Hospitality Group	Radisson, Country Inns & Suites, Regent International, Park Inn	814	136,507
Hyatt Corp.	Hyatt Regency, Park Hyatt, Grand Hyatt	122	59,000
Total		**28,467**	**3,369,152**

Source: Graves, Tom, "Standard & Poor's Industry Surveys: Lodging & Gaming," February 6, 2003; p. 7.

includes basic financial statements like a balance sheet and income statement, supplemented by "over 25 supplementary departmental operating statements and appendices covering budgeting and forecasting, a discussion of compiling revenues by market source, forms of statements, breakeven analysis and a uniform account numbering system."[102]

The USALI is a property-level system, not intended to be used at the corporate or consolidated level. It provides a framework to support comparisons of operational results between similar properties. It also organizes results around departments, such as the rooms division or the food and beverage division, rather than on a more simple income statement for a property as a whole.

As of 2001, the U.S. hotel industry derived 73 percent of its revenues from selling room nights. Other sources of revenue include food-and-beverage sales (9 percent) and telecommunications charges (2 percent).[103]

Under the USALI, expenses at a property level are tracked by department—rooms, food and beverage, and so on. From departmental profit, indirect costs—such as sales, general, and administrative costs—are deducted. These indirect costs are called Undistributed Operating Expenses (UOE) in the USALI. Hotel management fees, rent, property taxes, interest expenses, depreciation, and amortization are subtracted from income after undistributed operating expenses, resulting in the property's net income before taxes.

As of 2001, undifferentiated operating expenses accounted for 24 percent of U.S. lodging industry expenses, while departmental costs accounted for 38 percent, other fixed costs for 18 percent, management fees for 4 percent, and pretax income for 16 percent of expenses.[104, 105] PricewaterhouseCoopers believes that the breakeven point for the industry in terms of overall room occupancies has dropped to a record low of 47.4 percent in 2002, compared to a breakeven point of above 60 percent in 1995.[106] However, breakeven should rise slightly in 2003 as sales and marketing budgets will be increased to stimulate demand and market share, and because labor costs will also rise, mostly due to increasing medical benefit costs in 2003.

Facing an overall drop in occupancies since 2000, PricewaterhouseCoopers believes that the hospitality industry has reacted fairly swiftly to the changing economic situation. "The U.S. lodging industry will save $3.4 billion [in 2002] as a result of cost-cutting measures that were put in place in 2001. PricewaterhouseCoopers forecasts U.S. lodging industry aggregate profits will be $17.1 billion 2002, an increase of 1.8% over 2001. Without these actions, profits would have decreased by 18.5% to $13.7 billion in 2002."[107] Some typical cost-cutting actions undertaken by the hospitality industry include reductions in the number of employees and/or in the number of hours worked, cutbacks in advertising spending, and reduction in the opening hours of the food and beverage outlets offered at the hotel.

The hospitality industry is a "high overhead" business, characterized by significant capital investments in land, buildings, furnishings, and equipment for the hotel and surrounding installations. Typical capital expenditure needs are met by finding sources of outside funding. For existing building, mortgages, and bank loans may be negotiated on existing properties, typically up to 65 percent of the value. Mezzanine financing may be secured, funding another 20 percent of value of a building; but as this is unsecured financing without the collateral of the building, the debt costs are higher than with the mortgage.[108]

Rather than through debt financing, hotel development can be funded using equity vehicles. For instance, a real estate investment trust (REIT) can be established whereby unitholders buy trust units for cash, and this cash is invested by the REIT in hotel real estate. (In turn, unitholders are typically interested in the stable, constant dividend streams generated by investment in REITs.) The REIT purchases the property and contracts the management of the property to a third party. Another equity funding source would be issuing new shares in the hotel company itself; the company would then use this capital to invest in new hotel development.

Hotel companies dedicate significant efforts to maximize the investments made in their properties. As an industry standard, 5 percent of revenues is set aside as a reserve for replacement, taking care of the replacement of furniture, fixtures, and equipment due to normal wear and tear in the guestroom and throughout the hotel as items are used by both guests and staff. Most companies have a design and construction department that handles all aspects of new development and renovations, from centralized purchasing, ensuring that the best price is paid for furniture and equipment, to design teams, working with architects and general contractors to ensure that new developments are completed on time and within budget without sacrificing quality levels. Hotel companies typically find economies of scale in these types of operations when design, construction, and renovation teams work on a large number of properties, with more purchasing and negotiating power due to their larger size. This is typically a competitive advantage over smaller companies.

People at the Property Level   The largest portion of hotel operations expenses is salaries, benefits, and employee meals, an estimated 45.1 percent of all expenses at a property level.[109] As the hotel industry is a service industry, staff are needed to provide guests with the service levels that are expected. The range of staff working at a given property is wide: housekeeping attendants, kitchen attendants, chefs, front office staff, accounting, sales managers, and so on. As with any service industry, hotels find it difficult to maintain service quality standards, as even the most well-trained staffs and well-intentioned employees are subject to the daily variances of human behavior. (See Exhibit 4.)

Room to Grow?   There are three ways to grow in the hotel industry:

1. *Increase sales or profits at existing properties.* This can include refurbishing or expanding a property, reflagging the property as a different brand as a means to drive increased sales, improving cost efficiencies at the property, or taking advantage of wider distribution networks.

2. *Open new units.* New development involves selecting a location, completing the design and construction of the new facility, and launching the new hotel.

3. *Make acquisitions.* Acquisitions can target either a specific property or another hotel company in order to acquire several properties in one transaction.

The lodging industry has extremely high barriers to entry, since location is everything—especially its proximity to such demand drivers as shopping, entertainment, business centers, and transportation hubs. Just because you build it doesn't mean they'll come: New hotels rarely, in and of themselves, generate demand.

The huge capital investment required to build a new property, or to buy an existing one, also acts as a barrier to entry. Even for those who have the cash, real estate must be available in the right place at the right time. More often than not, existing hotels have already chosen the best locations. Even the most ardent hotel chain faces an uphill battle in adding a London property to its portfolio, for instance. A hotel company might try to draw customers to a new Docklands location, but there's no way to replicate the Dorchester's prime Hyde Park location for all the cash in the world.

Over the last decade, FHR has focused most of its growth efforts on making acquisitions and renovating existing properties in order to increase profits. Will the company be able to maintain these growth rates—and will it be enough to satisfy shareholders and the capital markets?

Branding   A given property can be managed as an independent hotel, such as the Greenbrier Resort in the scenic Allegheny Mountains of West Virginia, or it can be affiliated with a brand such as Hilton or Best Western. Standard & Poor's estimates that about 70 percent of U.S. hotel/motel properties are affiliated with a chain.[111] Some of the benefits of belonging to a brand are the shared name recognized by guests for a certain price and amenity level, as well as access to a central reservation system with established links to telephone, online, and travel-agent booking channels. In exchange for potential for increased sales and distribution, the hotel property will pay royalty fees to the brand owner for the use of the brand. The property then pays reservations fees for all bookings completed by the central reservation office.

As hotel companies seek to diversify and offer the appropriate product to the right customer segment, different brands are used to clearly position the product in the mind of the customer. These can either be brand extensions—extending an existing

EXHIBIT 4 MAJOR FUNCTIONAL AREAS FOUND IN FULL-SERVICE HOTELS[110]

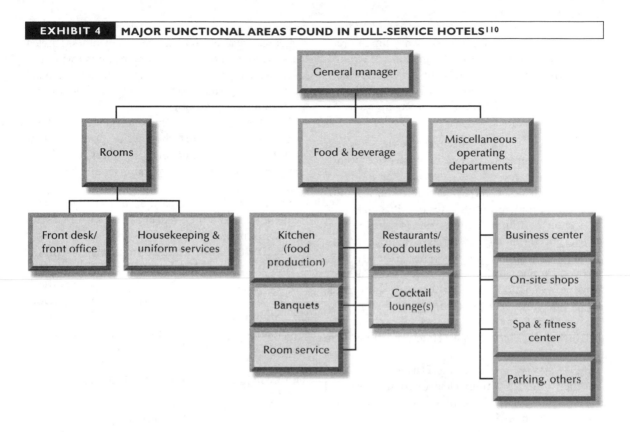

brand name to a new product—or a new brand.[112] Some examples:

- **Starwood's** brands include *St. Regis*, luxury full-service hotels and resorts; *The Luxury Collection*, luxury full-service hotels and resorts; *Sheraton*, global midscale to luxury full-service hotels; *Westin*, upper-upscale full-service hotels and resorts; *W*, boutique city-center hotel targeting the stylish and upscale business traveler; and *Four Points by Sheraton*, a midpriced full-service hotel for budget conscious travelers.[113]

- **Hyatt Corporation's** brands include *Hyatt Regency*, Hyatt's core brand, midsized upscale hotels targeting leisure and business travelers; *Grand Hyatt*, large business destination hotels servicing leisure and business travelers as well as conventions and meetings; and *Park Hyatt*, smaller luxury-class hotels targeting individual transient travelers.[114]

- **Marriott's** brands include *Marriott,* flagship quality first-class and upscale hotels targeting leisure and business travelers; *J. W. Marriott,* upper-upscale luxury hotels; *Ritz-Carlton Hotels,* upper-upscale luxury hotels targeting the individual traveler; *Bvlgari Hotels & Resorts*, a new cobranding partnership with Bvlgari for the luxury leisure market; *Renaissance,* quality full-service brand with the ambiance of a boutique hotel; *Courtyard by Marriott,* for the budget-conscious business traveler; *Marriott Residence Inn,* an extended stay product for the business traveler; *Fairfield Inn by Marriott,* quality lodging at an affordable price; *TownePlace Suites by Marriott,* a midpriced, extended-stay brand; *SpringHill Suites by Marriott,* moderately priced, all-suite properties; *Marriott ExecuStay,* fully furnished but temporary corporate housing; *Marriott Executive Apartments,* overseas corporate housing for longer term leases; *Marriott Grand Residence Club,* fractional property ownership in premium second-home destinations; *Marriott Vacation Club,* vacation ownership resorts; and *Horizons by Marriott Vacation Club,* value-oriented vacation ownership resort communities.[115]

Most successful hotel brands are the ones that clearly communicate to guests what price points, services, and amenities to expect. Starwood's W Hotels, for instance, have been successful in building a brand that communicates that it is an urban, city-center boutique hotel offering for the business traveler in terms of amenities and price points. Other hotel brands, on the other hand, such as Starwood's Sheraton brand, suffer from a wide range of variation between branded properties, from the nondescript cement block Sheraton Gateway San Francisco Airport Hotel to the luxurious Sheraton Maria Isabel Hotel and Towers in Mexico City.[116]

FHR has two main brands, Fairmont and Delta. Are their brand positions clear to guests, staff, and the industry at large? Are these enough brands for FHR—or too many?

Trends in Customer Relationship Management

Because the cost of acquiring new customers is very high[117]—and the benefit of retaining loyal customers is tremendous—hotel companies are working to better understand their customers. Capitalizing on the investments made in technology at the property level as well as at the centralized level with central reservation systems, most hotel companies are building customer relationship management data warehouses that can be used to improve target marketing.

One of the main benefits of understanding customers better through data warehousing is the ability to develop product offerings that fit the needs and price sensitivities of different guests. By segmenting the market, hotels can tailor services and amenities to the customer base being served, such as oversized desks and high-speed Internet access capabilities in rooms used by frequent business travelers. Prices can also be tailored to fit the budget and perceived value that different segments of guests have for different services and amenities. The Waldorf-Astoria, for instance, recognized the customer need for a more exclusive hotel product with higher service levels and guest room amenities. This led to the creation of the Waldorf Towers, a hotel-within-a-hotel, which provides guests with private elevators accessed through an elegant residential-scale lobby separate from the main lobby.[118]

Customer relationship management (CRM) databases also support the loyalty programs that almost every hospitality company offers to frequent guests. Marriott, for instance, claims more than fourteen million members in its Marriott Rewards program, which allows guests to accumulate points for frequent stays and then redeem them with free stays or other bonuses.[119]

FHR has two loyalty programs: Fairmont President's Club and Delta Privilege, both recognition programs rather than reward programs. Both brands also maintain guest data warehouses. Does this combination of resources give FHR the right information at the right time to service its guests appropriately and maximize customer loyalty?

The Boutiquing of the Hotel Industry

> Attracting trendsetters and celebrities, boutique hotels have ushered in the return of the hotel lobby as a downtown social-gathering spot, an important urban function on the wane since the grand hotels of the golden age when hotels were at a city's epicenter of fashion, politics, and high society. Grand hotels have long been associated with their stylish interiors. Although at a different scale, but in greater quantity, this new attention to innovative style in many ways is a return to the grandeur of nineteenth-century hotels—cosmopolitan, elegant, and distinctive—a culture of design.
>
> —*Hotel Design, Planning & Development,* 2001[120]

Hotels offer their guests a bed and bath for the night, but they also offer so much more. The *National Business Travel Monitor 2002* surveyed frequent business travelers and asked what they are looking for in a hotel or motel, as shown in Exhibit 5.

EXHIBIT 5	WHAT BUSINESS TRAVELERS ARE LOOKING FOR IN A HOTEL OR MOTEL EXPERIENCE[121]		
Criteria		**2001**	**2002**
Clean/well-maintained rooms		99%	98%
Friendly and efficient service		97%	95%
Diversity of restaurants on premises		67%	65%
A casual atmosphere, three-meal restaurant		75%	69%
24-hour room service		62%	54%
Free local phone calls		85%	80%
Offer express check-in and checkout		88%	85%
Computer data ports in room		57%	56%
High-speed Internet access in room		53%	54%
VCR in room		42%	37%
Printer in room		41%	37%
Multi-line telephone in room		29%	32%
Exercise facilities		53%	54%
Spa services		42%	43%
Specially equipped rooms for female travelers (e.g., separate vanities, makeup mirrors, hair dryers, increased security)		58%	47%
Concierge or executive floor		41%	36%

Source: Yankelovich Partners, *National Business Travel MONITOR 2002*, May 10, 2002; pp. 75–76.

Most important to the traveler is the comfort of the bed provided in the guestroom. Westin Hotels & Resorts conducted a study called "Sleeping on the Road," which concludes:

- Travelers say they get less sleep on the road as compared with home (49%); sleep fewer hours (51%); and are more likely to wake up in the middle of the night in a hotel bed (31%).

- The quality of sleep travelers receive on the road is worse (50%) and 31% claim their performance on the road has suffered because of a bad night's sleep in a hotel room.

- Most business travelers (82%) dislike something about hotel beds compared with their beds at home. These criticisms center around the mattress being too soft (27%) or too hard (21%) as well as there not being enough pillows (16%).

- By far, travelers said that a comfortable bed is the most important item in a hotel room

(49%). All other hotel room items, including a fax, a good shower, the TV, a large desk and a minibar, were mentioned by less than 10% of the travelers.[122]

As travelers become more sophisticated in their tastes, they select hotels based on the quality of stay they provide and the status they bestow. As new properties are built, hotels are designing larger guestrooms with more amenities, when the market will bear the price differential involved in offering these services. It is difficult for existing hotels to keep up with changing trends in terms of property design. After all, properties designed in the early 1900s were built to respond to a market where a twin bed, a dresser, and a small writing desk were the standards. It wasn't until Ellsworth Statler opened the Buffalo Statler hotel in 1908 that private baths, full-length mirrors, telephones, and built-in radiators became standard for each guestroom.[123] With capital reserves for renovation peaking at around 5 percent of revenue at a property level, are there enough funds for older properties to renovate and meet changes in guest expectations?

In the 1980s, a new fad hit the hotel industry: the boutique hotel, building on the increasing sophistication of hotel guests' tastes. Ian Schrager and Steve Rubell (with their legendary nightclub, Studio 54) are thought of as the main pioneers behind this new concept because of their "dramatic design makeover of Morgans, a small, dilapidated midtown [New York City] building"[124] in 1984. Boutique hotels tend to be small, urban hotels, many times with fewer than 100 rooms (although Schrager's own Hudson hotel, one of New York's newest boutiques, blooms at 1,000 rooms). Though there is no industrywide accepted definition of a boutique hotel, they tend to be thought of as small, fashionable and independent, associated with adjectives such as *fashion, intimate, glamour, style, chic, outré, hip, flair, elegant,* and *cool.*[125]

In many ways, boutique hotels are outperforming the rest of the hospitality industry, but the picture is not all rosy. *The Wall Street Journal* indicates that "while boutique occupancy rates are still above the industry average, bookings fell almost twice as fast as those at similar-priced properties from 2000 to 2002, according to Smith Travel. Furthermore, these days the boutiques' very chicness may be costing them some guests, because many aren't on company 'approved' travel lists and lack work-friendly amenities like business centers or high-speed Internet access."[126] In addition, the *Journal* indicates that the maintenance budgets at many boutique hotels have been sharply cut given the difficult economic situation for hotels today. Owners insist that this hasn't affected service or caused a sharp decline in business.

More traditional hotel companies are adapting to changing market needs and responding to the boutique hotels by designing new and innovative hotel experiences for their guests. Starwood, with W Hotels, is the only major hotel company to have launched a boutique brand. But other hotel companies have undertaken renovation projects that add more design elements to their hotels, giving the properties a "boutique" look and feel, as the industry realizes that unique and provocative design appeals to the model traveler looking for an experience. Marriott, for instance, positions its Renaissance brand as one that offers the "ambiance of a boutique."[127] Other hotel companies and individual properties have undertaken renovation projects to make their hotels more fashionable and similar to boutique concepts.

Can Fairmont maintain and refresh its portfolio of iconic and destination hotels to take advantage of the individual nature of its portfolio of heritage properties and showcase them in the light of new trends toward individualistic style and design? Or are the renovation costs too dear?

ORGANIZATIONAL ANALYSIS
Corporate Structure

FHR is both a hotel management company as well as a property owner. The parent company has five main divisions, which are either in the hotel management or the hotel ownership segment.[128] (See Exhibit 6.)

- **Fairmont Hotels Inc.** ("Fairmont"),[130] 83.5 percent owned by FHR: Fairmont manages forty-three luxury city center and destination resort properties in six countries: the United States, Canada, Mexico, Bermuda, Barbados, and the United Arab Emirates. With more than 20,000 rooms managed under the Fairmont flag, the company is North America's largest luxury hotel management company (only Ritz-Carlton comes close in number of rooms managed). The remaining 16.5 percent ownership share is held by Maritz, Wolff & Co., the private investment fund.

- **Delta Hotels Limited** ("Delta"), 100 percent owned by FHR: As of December 2001, Delta was the largest first-class hotel management company in Canada, with thirty-nine managed or franchised full-service, midmarket city-center, airport, and resort hotels located throughout Canada, with more than 11,000 rooms under management.

- **FHR Real Estate Corporation** ("FHRREC"), 100 percent owned by FHR: FHR has ownership interests ranging from 20 percent to 100 percent in twenty Fairmont-managed properties and three Delta-managed properties.

| EXHIBIT 6 | FHR CORPORATE STRUCTURE AS OF DECEMBER 31, 2002[129] |

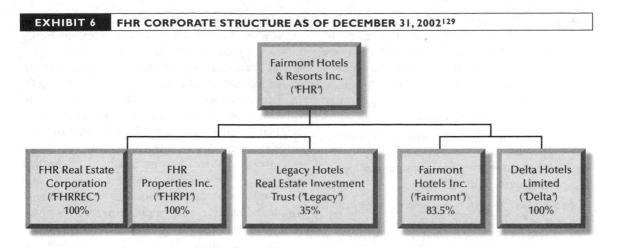

FHR Properties Inc. ("FHRPI"), 100 percent owned by FHR: A real estate company that holds the real estate assets, primarily a large undeveloped land block in Toronto. A second large undeveloped parcel on Vancouver's Coal Harbour was sold in March 2003 to the province of British Columbia for the expansion of Vancouver's Convention & Exhibition Centre.[131]

Legacy Hotels Real Estate Investment Trust ("Legacy"), 35 percent owned by FHR: A Canadian REIT with twenty-two luxury and first-class hotels and resorts in Canada and one in the United States. All properties are branded either "Fairmont" or "Delta" except for one Sheraton-branded property in Calgary (under Fairmont management).

Fairmont Hotels & Resorts became an independently traded company on October 3, 2001, when it was listed on the Toronto and New York stock exchanges. As of December 31, 2002, there were 78.8 million shares of common stock outstanding for FHR, and the per-share-price in December 2001 ranged between USD $23 and $24.[132] Market capitalization at the end of December 2002 was between USD $1.8 and $1.9 billion.

One of the major shareholders of FHR is Prince Alwaleed bin Talal bin Abdul Aziz Al Saud of Saudi Arabia, co-owner of a handful of Fairmont-flagged properties, including the Plaza in New York City and the Fairmont San Francisco. As of February 10, 2003, he owned approximately 4.9 percent of FHR's issued and outstanding shares.[133]

Legacy Hotels Real Estate Investment Trust

Legacy Hotels Real Estate Investment Trust is an unincorporated closed-end real estate investment trust created in 1997 by the declaration of Trust in Alberta.[134] Initially, the Trust purchased eleven Canadian city-center hotels and grew to hold twenty-two properties in Canada and one in the United States by the end of 2002.[135]

Legacy provides this definition of a REIT: "A REIT is an entity for the ownership and management of a portfolio of income-producing properties. Interests in the Trust are held by its unitholders. Each unit represents an equal beneficial interest of the holder thereof in the Trust. A substantial portion of the Trust's cash is distributed regularly to unitholders."[136]

Trusts are meant to provide stable income to investors and have many structural constraints to ensure that stability. The Canadian Institute of Public and Private Real Estate Companies, CIPREC, highlights five key components of Canadian REITs that provide this stability:

- *Conservative leverage:* the Declaration of Trust sets out a maximum debt capacity for the REIT.

■ *Professional management:* investors benefit from professional management of the portfolio and the underlying properties—often a hybrid of asset management acumen and industry-specific operational expertise.

■ *Regulatory requirement:* similar to any public company, REITs are required to comply with securities legislations and the rules of the applicable stock exchanges including those of continuous disclosure, insider trading and the sale of units.

■ *Board of Trustees:* in keeping with the principles of good corporate governance, the Board of Trustees (including independent or unrelated Trustees), governs the operations of the REIT, approving key decisions such as change in management, acquisitions and dispositions, the assumption or granting of mortgages and the granting of options under an option plan.

■ *Steady distributions:* REITs are required to distribute virtually all distributable income to unitholders. Monthly or quarterly distributions are intended to be steady and increasing over time as the RIT and its profitability grows. Yields are typically more attractive than on debt investments.[137]

As a REIT, Legacy's initial and continuing objectives are to "provide unitholders with regular, stable and growing cash distributions and to maximize future distributions and unit values through the superior management of the portfolio and through the acquisition of additional hotel properties, primarily in Canada."[138]

When Legacy was created in 1997, the senior management team was composed of Canadian Pacific Hotels & Resorts' senior management team: William R. Fatt, Legacy president and chief executive officer; Chris J. Cahill, Legacy executive vice president; and M. Jerry Patava, executive vice president, chief financial officer and treasurer.[139] Major changes to Legacy's management structure were made in March 2003, when Neil J. Labatte was named president and chief operating officer. At the same time, an executive search was begun for a full-time chief financial officer.[140]

Financial analysts praised this move. Goldman Sachs wrote, "On Friday afternoon Fairmont Hotels took a major step in the right direction, in our opinion, as it announced its intentions to eliminate top shared management between itself and Legacy REIT. ... This move will not only allow both Fatt and Patava to concentrate more solely on FHR, but it eliminates a major stumbling block for investors who perceived a conflict of interest between the shared executive structure. Investors had been fearful that any asset sale purchases between Legacy and Fairmont was 'conflicted' by the shared management. This fear disappears and should allow for freer transactions between the two companies."[141]

As of December 31, 2002, Legacy Hotels had 89.36 million units outstanding, of which 35 percent are held by FHR.[142] Units are traded on the Toronto Stock Exchange. In December 2002, units were trading between CAD $7.00 and $7.50, giving Legacy a market capitalization of between CAD $625 million and $670 million at that time.[143]

Mission, Vision, and Values

The stated mission of Fairmont Hotels & Resorts is as follows:

> We will earn the loyalty of our guests by exceeding their expectations and providing warm and personal service in distinctive surroundings.[144]

In order to deliver on this mission, Fairmont describes its vision as the following:

> We will be the **luxury hotel Brand** of choice recognized worldwide for distinctive style.
>
> We will inspire an open innovative learning organization that is energetic and exciting for **our Colleagues.**
>
> We will demonstrate a relentless commitment to understand, anticipate, and fulfill the needs of **our Guests.**
>
> We will deliver superior operating performance and financial returns for **our Owners and Investors** to ensure growth for the company and reinvestment in our hotels.[145]

Fairmont recognizes four key values as central to all of its relations with its internal and external stakeholders: respect, integrity, teamwork, and empowerment. The companywide emphasis is on giving each employee—both at the corporate and the property level—the tools, training, authority, and support he or she needs to make informed decisions and take appropriate actions to deliver the highest level of service excellence to Fairmont guests. The goal is to empower employees to create customized experiences that make lifetime memories for guests—what Fairmont calls "wow" experiences.[146]

But, for all of its aged assets and historic brand equity, Fairmont is an infant company. Creating an empowered culture and making precise and elegant service that says "Fairmont" a standard throughout the brand—a brand filled with decades-old hotels with legacy employees, property-unique processes, and entrenched inefficiencies—may be some years away.

Strategic Direction

[W]e are committed to the foundation of our strategic plan: to solidify our preeminent position in the luxury segment by expanding the Fairmont portfolio into critical North American markets and by aggressively expanding our brand presence to increase awareness and loyalty.

—William R. Fatt, Chairman and CEO[147]

A three-pronged overarching strategy—the GEM strategy—drives the growing company by emphasizing three key concepts:

- *Globalize:* Expanding Fairmont's unrivalled portfolio of forty-one city-center hotels and world-class resorts; grow brand awareness on a global scale; expand the customer base, especially loyalty program members; and increase distribution depth and breadth.

- *Energize:* Investing in Fairmont's employees to drive a new level of service excellence, guest and employee satisfaction, and market perception; and reposition assets for luxury market leadership as appropriate.

- *Maximize:* Capitalizing on key products—including Fairmont's new branded spa product, Willow Stream; Fairmont Gold, the company's "hotel within a hotel" product; and Fairmont President's Club, the guest recognition program—to increase revenue per available room (RevPAR), improve return on investment, and grow brand awareness.

This core strategy is focused on increasing revenues and net income by growing the brand through "selective acquisitions" and securing new management agreements in key North American gateway cities, resort destinations, and prime international markets.[148] In its first full year as a public company, 2002, Fairmont entered four new markets (reflecting a portfolio growth of 10 percent), improved its competitive yield in most properties, grew overall brand awareness, and led the industry with EBITDA growth of 22 percent—all despite a challenging economy.

Fairmont also took its first steps beyond North America in 2002, opening the Fairmont Dubai in partnership with His Royal Highness Dr. Sheikh Sultan bin Khalifa Al Nahyan, crown prince of Abu Dhabi. New U.S. markets adding Fairmont properties in 2002 were such prime destinations as Washington, D.C. (the Fairmont Washington, D.C., formerly the Monarch); the Big Island of Hawaii (The Fairmont Orchid, Hawaii); and California's Sonoma Valley wine country (the Fairmont Sonoma Mission Inn & Spa). The company expects to add two to four hotels annually. Among the future additions are a Puerto Rico destination resort and an Abu Dhabi resort—Fairmont's second Middle East property—both on the drawing board for 2005.[149]

Still, Fairmont sees the greatest opportunities for growth—both through purchase acquisitions and the acquiring of new management contracts—in the U.S. market, where the company can build on its established infrastructure and increasing brand awareness. Fairmont also sees growing its presence beyond the eleven of the top twenty-five U.S. markets it currently occupies as central to growing its brand awareness. Cities targeted for growth include Seattle, Miami, Orlando, Denver, San Diego, Las Vegas, and Philadelphia.[150] "Expansion outside of North America will be opportunistic, with equity partners who have an influence in their respective region and a willingness to invest in hotel real estate."[151]

President and COO Chris Cahill forecasts single-asset acquisition as the most likely avenue for continued growth.[152] Cahill also emphasizes the desire not for unchecked growth, but a product-matched portfolio. "We're not interested in just adding hotels. Instead, we want to do what we do well."[153]

Maximizing operating performance of existing assets—including both managed and owned hotels—is also seen as key to future success. A number of Fairmont-owned and -managed hotels have recently undertaken renovation programs in order to increase EBITDA and RevPAR. FHR recently invested $200 million in six of its owned hotels. Both Bermuda properties, the Fairmont Hamilton Princess and the Fairmont Southampton, the Fairmont San Francisco (which completed an $85 million redo in 2000), the Fairmont San Jose (which recently got a $67 million expansion—only to debut just as the bottom dropped out of the high-tech market), as well as the landmark Fairmont Banff Springs (which received a whopping $80 million treatment), are among those who have undergone a major facelift in recent years. Profit-enhancing capital improvements continued through 2003—when the focus was be on such properties as the Fairmont Château Lake Louise; the Fairmont Orchid, Hawaii; and the two Acapulco properties—and into 2004.[154]

Additional efforts to push revenue growth include more focused marketing programs and sales efforts. Incremental investments in Fairmont's own branded spa product, Willow Stream—The Spas at Fairmont, golf courses, retail, and the new Fairmont Heritage Place "private residence club" vacation ownership product (under development in Acapulco and Bermuda) are seen as valuable for the company because they broaden the chain's revenue streams and support the Fairmont brand's luxury positioning.[155]

Fairmont also sees building brand loyalty through its guest recognition program, the Fairmont President's Club, as a route to building a luxury brand image and increasing revenues. "These members are increasing the amount they spend with Fairmont, as they stay at our new properties and are willing to pay higher rates for specialized products and services," chairman and CEO William Fatt wrote.[156]

Despite its emphasis on historic assets, Fairmont has also carved a niche for itself as the most technologically advanced hotel company in the industry. Fairmont is the only luxury hotel brand to offer wireless and high-speed Internet service at each of its hotels. The company sees riding the cutting-edge of technology as central to its success, since more than half of its guests are business travelers. Fairmont has formed a long-term partnership with Cisco and deployed a unified, self-supported, end-to-end Cisco broadband network to connect even its most remote hotels.[157] Risk sharing through such partnering is a keynote of Fairmont's strategic plan—be it with Legacy Hotels as its real estate investment partner, Cisco in network building, or His Highness Dr. Sheikh Sultan bin Khalifa Al Nahyan in expansion abroad.[158]

As a regional brand comprising only 4 percent of Fairmont's earnings, Delta Hotels is not considered to be a growth vehicle for FHR (to the chagrin of some Delta employees). Delta has established a bulkhead position for Fairmont in Canada and erected barriers to entry for other first-class chains. However, for the brand to grow, it would have to compete head-to-head against such midluxury powerhouses as Hilton and Westin in the United States, which would require more investment than the company is willing to put forth—at this time, anyway. However, Delta is a solid moneymaker and is seen by Fairmont's corporate leaders as a great place to attract and develop talent. Anywhere from forty to sixty managers a year—including hotel general managers—cross over between the brands.[159]

Despite its focus on aggressive growth, Fairmont does not see itself as a risk-taking company. Fairmont will never be a first-mover, says president and COO Chris Cahill, who prefers to do proper research, choose a direction, then implement plans swiftly and decisively. "We want to be around for another hundred years."[160]

Product Portfolio

The Fairmont Brand Despite its sophomore status as a young company, Fairmont Hotels & Resorts' identity is defined by an unrivaled portfolio of iconic hotels and resorts that share two key brand messages—"Unrivalled Prominence" and "Places in the

Heart," expressions of both the geographic centrality and landmark presence that define the largely historic collection—and four key features:

- Premier "best address" locations in city centers and resort areas with nearly insurmountable barriers to entry
- Irreplaceable architecture that reflects the drama of the surrounding landscape and captures the energy of its community
- Whether old or new, a timeless, classic style
- Service excellence that creates long-lasting "wow" experiences for guests[161]

Many Fairmont hotels and resorts—including the full portfolio of original Canadian Pacific hotels and the seven original Fairmont hotels—are grand historic structures that dominate their markets with a distinctive profile, a rich history, and a legendary reputation for quality. Many of the company's hotels were among the first buildings to be erected in the young cities and pristine wilderness areas across Canada and the United States, and the communities and outdoor resorts they occupy often grew up around them. As of December 2001, the average age of Fairmont's (then) forty-one hotels (now forty-three) was 56.5 years, with an average of 497 rooms and 30,200 square feet of meeting space (or 60.8 square feet per guest room).[162]

From the beaches of the Caribbean, Mexico, and Hawaii to the heart of fashion-forward cities like New York, Vancouver, and Dubai, the company prides itself at offering a luxury guest experience that is uniquely "Fairmont." Among the iconic collection are legendary urban dwellers like the New York's Plaza hotel, the Fairmont New Orleans, Quebec City's Fairmont Le Château Frontenac, and Toronto's Fairmont Royal York. Grand Canadian provincial resorts include the Fairmont Château Lake Louise, the Fairmont Jasper Park Lodge, the Fairmont Banff Springs, and the Fairmont Château Whistler, queen of Canadian ski country. Sunny resorts such as Bermuda's Fairmont Southampton, Maui's Fairmont Kea Lani, and the Fairmont Acapulco Princess dominate some of North America's best beach destinations. "Legends in the making" include the Fairmont Scottsdale Princess and the new-in-2002 Fairmont Dubai.

Market Positioning Fairmont Hotels & Resorts occupies a unique position in the lodging market. From a purely competitive perspective, the Fairmont brand competes in the upper-upscale segment, which includes both pure luxury brands such as Four Seasons and Ritz-Carlton as well as first-class brands like Hyatt, Marriott, Sheraton, Westin, and Hilton. There is a $60 average daily rate differential between these two segments. With a blended brandwide average daily rate of ADR $168, Fairmont is positioned squarely between them, clearly above the first-class brands (by about $20) but below the pure luxury brands.[164] President and COO Chris Cahill, who has called this territory "Fairmontland," considers Fairmont's unique midmarket position to be a source of strategic competitive advantage for the firm.[165] (See Exhibit 7.)

Roughly 45 percent of Fairmont's properties are located in resort markets, 55 percent in city centers. Fairmont's clientele is split almost evenly between group (46 percent) and transient (54 percent) business, and almost evenly between leisure (46 percent) and business (54 percent) travelers. Most hotels are "group houses," catering heavily to the meetings, conventions, and events markets. The typical Fairmont hotel has about 500 rooms and approximately 30,500 feet of meeting space; only Hyatt and Westin hotels carry more square footage of meeting space per guest room on average.[167] As such, Fairmont is seen as the brand of choice for luxury groups and meetings; this is a market that Fairmont openly embraces and actively solicits. Nevertheless, the company also has a keen interest in growing its leisure business.

Despite its achievements in becoming a significant player in the luxury hotel segment in just a few short years, the Fairmont brand is still relatively young and unknown, especially compared to key competitors such as Four Seasons and Ritz-Carlton. Fairmont Hotels & Resorts had unaided brand awareness of only 14 percent in 2002.[168] While this position represents a significant improvement of 250 percent over the past three years, Fairmont still has a long road to travel in building a brand that is widely recognized on a global scale. Increased brand awareness is a major goal for the organization, as it is seen as the most direct path to increased sales and growth.

EXHIBIT 7   BUSINESS MIX VS. THE COMPETITION[166]

Positioning within the Group Market

Fairmont Hotels & Resorts

Hyatt

Westin Hotels & Resorts

The Luxury Collection

The Ritz Carlton

Four Seasons Hotels & Resorts

Meridien

Leading Hotels of the World

Positioning within the Transient Market

The experts seem to think that Fairmont can do it. "Everyone in the 4- and 5-star market is looking over their shoulder at Fairmont," industry analyst Paul Keung of CIBC World markets told *Hotels* magazine, which named Fairmont as a growing brand to watch in May 2002.[169] Year after year, the brand continues to strengthen its position: twenty-seven Fairmont properties were named to *Condé Nast Traveler*'s "Gold List" in 2003, up from twenty-one in 2002.[170]

Delta Hotels   Delta's collection of thirty-nine first-class city-center, airport, and resort hotels are positioned to compete with such first-class brands as Sheraton and Marriott in Canada's hospitality landscape. The brand's blended RevPAR for 2002 was about $54, while its blended ADR was just over $85.[171]

While Delta's portfolio complements Fairmont's Canadian collection, and while economies of scale are maximized behind the scenes, no link connects the two brands publicly. Even most behind-the-scenes corporate functions are handled separately, including human resources and sales and marketing, although information technology and finance are shared.[172]

While Delta is not a viewed as a source of growth for Fairmont, it does not remain stagnant, either. Eighteen properties have been added to the brand (although a few that fell outside the brand definition were divested) and $50 million spent on capital improvements since 1998. The brand was honored by Canada's National Quality Institute in 2000 with the Canada Award for Excellence (the national equivalent of the United States' Malcolm Baldrige National Quality Award) for achievement in leadership, planning, performance, and customer service.[173] And its position as the largest first-class hotel management company in Canada guarantees it a high profile.[174] (See Exhibit 8.)

Management Structure and Operational Characteristics

Key Managers All senior officers have been in place since the rebranding of Canadian Pacific Hotels as Fairmont Hotels & Resorts on October 1, 2001. The senior management team is a young and dynamic group of personalities largely composed of executives who rose through the ranks of Canadian Pacific.

While President and COO Chris J. Cahill often serves as the public face of the company, the FHR management style is team driven, rather than being ego driven or dominated by a single personality. There is much solidarity and trust among this tightly knit group of key managers, who share a strong history, which is unique for a company as young as FHR. As a result, the management culture is one of empowerment, in which managers are able to make their own decisions and carry a range of opinions. Healthy debate rules, as long as corporate decisions are supported on a companywide basis at the end of the day.

William R. Fatt—chief executive officer: Appointed CEO of Fairmont Hotels & Resorts on October 1, 2001, Mr. Fatt originally was appointed chairman and chief executive officer of Canadian Pacific Hotels & Resorts in January 1998. While he also serves as vice chairman and a trustee of Legacy Hotels Real Estate Investment Trust,[176] Mr. Fatt no longer serves as CEO of Legacy Hotels Real Estate Investment Trust now that steps have been taken (as of March 2003) to distance the REIT from its parent company, Fairmont.[177] From January 1998 to October 2001, Fatt served as executive vice president of Canadian Pacific Limited; previously, from 1990 to 1998, he was chief financial officer of Canadian Pacific Limited. A Toronto native, Fatt came to Canadian Pacific from the Morgan Bank of Canada.[178]

As a relative newcomer to the hospitality industry, Mr. Fatt has set the tone for empowerment and healthy delegation of responsibilities within the company by relying on his team of seasoned hotel executives to build the portfolio and the brand. He described his job this way: "In part, I'm a cheerleader, trying to encourage change in direction or operating practice, and I have to be the person holding the purse strings. I try to recognize my own limitations, where others in the company can do something better, and I limit my projects to a few areas where I am more skilled."[179]

Chris J. Cahill—president and chief operating officer: Chris Cahill, the company's highest profile executive, was appointed president and COO of Canadian Pacific Hotels & Resorts in January 1998 and continues to shepherd the company through its transformation into Fairmont Hotels & Resorts. He is also executive vice president and a trustee of Legacy Hotels Real Estate Investment Trust,[180] as well as a member of the Board of Directors of Delta Hotels.[181] Mr. Cahill boasts a hands-on background in hospitality. He served as executive vice president and vice president of sales at Canadian Pacific Hotels, and he capped a fifteen-year tenure at Delta Hotels as vice president of operations. He holds an MBA from the University of Toronto.[182] Youthful, energetic, and easygoing, Cahill is most responsible for institutionalizing the culture of responsibility and empowered decision-making at Fairmont.

Insiders report that it was Mr. Cahill who first saw Canadian Pacific's collection of heritage hotels and the Fairmont group of hotels as a marriage made in hospitality heaven. The merger made sense to all stakeholders, he said in 2000. "For employees, there are tremendous career opportunities. ... For our customer base, CP loyalists now have many more properties at their disposal in the U.S. And hotel owners now find they have assets in a much larger brand."[183]

John M. Johnston—executive vice president, development: John Johnston serves as executive vice president of development as well as chairman of Delta Hotels Limited. Previously, he had served as president of Delta Hotels from October 1998. Unlike many Fairmont executives who came through the Canadian Pacific or Delta ranks, Mr. Johnston's thirty-five-year career in hospitality includes key positions at Loews Hotels and Four Seasons Hotels and Resorts (another Toronto-based company).[184]

EXHIBIT 8	DELTA BRANDED PROPERTIES AS OF DECEMBER 31, 2002[175]

Property	Location	Year Opened	Ownership	Total Rooms	Meeting Space (Sq. Footage)
Delta Sun Peaks Resorts	Sun Peaks, British Columbia	2002	FHRREC 26%	226	11,000
Delta Victoria Ocean Pointe Resort and Spa	Victoria, British Columbia	1992		245	14,100
Delta Vancouver Airport	Richmond, British Columbia	1973	Delta	412	15,400
Delta Vancouver Suites	Vancouver, British Columbia	1998	FHRREC 34.8%	225	2,700
Delta Pinnacle	Vancouver, British Columbia	2000		434	15,700
Delta Whistler Resort	Whistler, British Columbia	1982		288	10,250
Delta Whistler Village Suites	Whistler, British Columbia	1997		207	4,000
Tantalus Lodge	Whistler, British Columbia	1980		76	1,300
Delta St. Eugene Mission Resort	Cranbrook, British Columbia	2002		125	4,400
Delta Bow Valley	Calgary, Alberta	1981		398	10,000
Delta Calgary Airport	Calgary, Alberta	1979	Legacy	296	19,500
Delta Lodge at Kananaskis	Kananaskis Village, Alberta	1988		321	16,000
Delta Edmonton Centre Suite Hotel	Edmonton, Alberta	1987		169	12,000
Delta Edmonton South Hotel & Conference Centre	Edmonton, Alberta	1975		237	31,900
Delta Bessborough	Saskatoon, Saskatchewan	1935	Legacy	225	18,000
Delta Regina	Regina, Saskatchewan	1988		274	28,700
Delta Winnipeg	Winnipeg, Manitoba	1974	Legacy	392	18,100
Delta London Armouries	London, Ontario	1987		245	9,500
Delta Meadowvale Resort and Conference Centre	Mississauga, Ontario	1981		374	30,200
Delta Toronto Airport West	Mississauga, Ontario	1976	Legacy	296	14,100
Delta Chelsea	Toronto, Ontario	1975		1,590	21,500
Delta Toronto East	Toronto, Ontario	1982	Legacy	368	22,000
Delta Pinestone Resort	Haliburton, Ontario	1976		103	15,000
Delta Sherwood Inn	Port Carling, Ontario	1939		49	3,500
Delta Grandview Resort	Huntsville, Ontario	1911		128	8,800
Delta Rocky Crest Resort	MacTier, Ontario	1965		65	3,000
Delta Ottawa Hotel and Suites	Ottawa, Ontario	1975	Legacy	328	12,000
Delta Montreal	Montreal, Quebec	1986		456	16,000
Delta Centre-Ville	Montreal, Quebec	1977	Legacy	711	22,600
Delta Sherbrooke Hotel and Conference Centre	Sherbrooke, Quebec	1989		178	17,800
Delta Trois-Rivières Hotel and Conference Centre	Trois Rivières, Quebec	1991		159	18,300
Delta Brunswick	Saint John, New Brunswick	1981		254	12,800
Delta Beauséjour	Moncton, New Brunswick	1972	Legacy	311	24,000
Delta Halifax	Halifax, Nova Scotia	1974	Legacy	296	9,000
Delta Barrington	Halifax, Nova Scotia	1980	Legacy	200	6,700
Delta Sydney	Sydney, Nova Scotia	1987		152	5,500
Delta Prince Edward	Charlottetown, P.E.I.	1984	Legacy	211	25,000
Delta St. John's Hotel and Conference Centre	St. John's, Newfoundland	1987		276	18,000

He thus brings a valuable outside perspective to the executive roundtable.

M. Jerry Patava—executive vice president and chief financial officer: Jerry Patava serves as executive vice president and chief financial officer, positions he also held under the Canadian Pacific banner since January 1998.[185] As of March 2003, Mr. Patava is no longer chief financial officer of Legacy Hotels Real Estate Investment Trust—a move made not only to appease shareholders wary of the close relationship between Fairmont and Legacy,[186] but also to herald the maturing status of the relationship between management company and REIT. Mr. Patava is also a holding company veteran, having served as vice president and treasurer of Canadian Pacific Limited until joining Canadian Pacific Hotels & Resorts.

Unlike many CFOs, Mr. Patava climbed the ranks to CFO not from accounting and audits, which is the most common practice, but from capital markets and corporate treasury, which is more relevant to his current position. "As a CFO, more of my time is spent on capital market issues than it is on accounting and control-type issues . . . with a strong controller, I am able to devote more of my time to financial marker issues."[187] He also notes that his experience in investment banking has been extremely helpful in his role as CFO. "Whether it is going through public offerings, managing large complicated financings, understanding how the sellers of those products work—all that is very valuable to me. It really helps me in my negotiations as well. It makes it hard to fool me."[188]

Thomas W. Storey—executive vice president, business development and strategy: Tom Storey joined the company as executive vice president of business development and strategy in February 2001, just prior to the Canadian Pacific–Fairmont merger. Mr. Storey was with Promus Hotels, a hotel management and ownership company, from 1997 to 2000; before Promus, he was vice president of sales and marketing at Doubletree Hotels. Unlike all of Fairmont's other key executives, Mr. Storey is based in Scottsdale, Arizona,[189] although he keeps an active office in Fairmont's Toronto headquarters.

John S. Williams—executive vice president, operations: John Williams was the first executive to wear both the Canadian Pacific and Fairmont hats. He was appointed executive vice president of operations for Fairmont in August 2000. Prior to that date, he served as senior vice president, British Columbia for Canadian Pacific Hotels from May 1995, and he held the same position for Fairmont's U.S. and Mexican hotels from September 1998.

Terence P. Badour—executive vice president, law and administration and corporate strategy: Terry Badour served parent holding company Canadian Pacific Limited as corporate counsel and assistant secretary until joining Canadian Pacific Hotels & Resorts as vice president, general counsel and corporate secretary in 1998.

Timothy J. Aubrey—senior vice president, finance: Formerly vice president of technology, Tim Aubrey was appointed senior vice president of finance in January 2003.[190] Before that appointment, he was responsible for establishing Fairmont Hotels & Resorts as the technology leader in the hospitality industry by rolling out an innovative cobranded Cisco high-speed backbone network and a shared-services IT support system to all Fairmont properties. From 1995 until joining CP Hotels in 1998, Mr. Aubrey served as manager of information systems of Canadian Pacific Limited.[191]

Neil J. Labatte—senior vice president, real estate; president and chief executive officer, Legacy Hotels Real Estate Investment Trust: In March 2003, Neil Labatte was appointed president and chief executive of Legacy Hotels REIT, replacing Mr. Fatt as a more mature, arm's-length relationship was forged between Fairmont and Legacy.[192] He continues to hold the position as senior vice president, real estate, at Fairmont Hotels & Resorts.[193] A former National Hockey League draftee for the St. Louis Blues, Mr. Labatte built his career as founder, principal, and board member of A. E. W. Mexico Company, a real estate investment management company. He served as president and COO of Legacy from July 1999 until his recent promotion to chief executive.[194]

John L. Pye—president, Delta Hotels: Like many his Fairmont counterparts, John Pye is a career Delta Hotels and Canadian Pacific man; in fact, he began his career as a bellman at the very first Delta hotel in Vancouver. He served as the general manager of the

Fairmont Scottsdale Princess and as regional vice president overseeing all of Fairmont's southern U.S. properties before ascending to the top position at Delta Hotels.[195] Even though Mr. Pye is the top figure in the Delta Hotels pyramid, he is not part of the FHR executive team.

Corporate Operations FHR corporate functions are centralized in handsome offices on six floors of the Canadian Pacific Tower in the Toronto Dominion Centre in the heart of downtown Toronto, Ontario. Approximately 220 employees operate out of these offices.[196] A secondary U.S. corporate office is still maintained in San Francisco and staffs about fifteen employees, mainly "to give support" to the U.S.-based hotels and resorts.[197] In addition, Fairmont has four small regional offices located in cities across Canada, offering localized support to the Canadian properties.[198] One floor of the Toronto offices is dedicated to Delta Hotels operations, which runs most of its own corporate functions (the major exceptions are Technology Services and Finance, which support all of FHR).

All corporation-wide decision making and support functions are centralized in the Toronto offices, which feature the executive offices as well as departments devoted to all main functional areas:

- Operations
- Brand marketing and communication (including public relations)
- Business development and strategy
- Asset management
- Design and construction
- New development
- Finance and accounting
- Food and beverage
- Human resources
- Investor relations
- Law
- Office services
- Rooms
- Sales and distribution
- Spa

- Technology services
- Treasury

Traveling is a way of life for the majority of these corporate managers, who are responsible for disseminating brandwide information and brand messages throughout the worldwide network of properties and regional sales offices.

Supporting the Fairmont brand, about seventeen regional sales offices are located throughout North America and Europe, in such cities as Chicago, Dallas, Los Angeles, Ottawa, Vancouver, London, Frankfurt, and Mexico City. The Global Reservation Centre—the nerve center of any hotel company, including Fairmont—is located in Moncton, New Brunswick.[199]

Fairmont maintains its centralized top-down organization by dividing its property network into a dozen regions:

- *California Region:* Fairmont San Francisco, Fairmont San Jose, Fairmont Sonoma Mission Inn & Spa, Fairmont Santa Monica
- *Scottsdale:* Fairmont Scottsdale Princess
- *Central Region:* Fairmont Copley Plaza Boston, Fairmont Chicago, Fairmont Kansas City, Fairmont Dallas, Fairmont New Orleans, Fairmont Washington, D.C.
- *New York Region:* The Plaza
- *British Columbia Region:* Fairmont Hotel Vancouver, Fairmont Waterfront, Fairmont Empress, Fairmont Vancouver Airport, Fairmont Whistler
- *Alberta Region:* Fairmont Banff Springs, Fairmont Château Lake Louise, Fairmont Jasper Park Lodge, Fairmont Hotel Macdonald, Fairmont Palliser, Sheraton Suites Calgary (under Fairmont management)
- *Central Canada Region:* Fairmont Château Laurier, The Fairmont Royal York, The Fairmont Winnipeg, The Fairmont Algonquin, The Fairmont Newfoundland
- *Eastern Region:* Fairmont Le Château Frontenac, Fairmont Le Manoir Richelieu, Fairmont the Queen Elizabeth, Fairmont Tremblant, Fairmont Kenauk, Fairmont Le

Château Montebello, Fairmont Royal Pavilion, Fairmont Glitter Bay

- *Dubai:* Fairmont Dubai
- *Hawaii Region:* Fairmont Kea Lani, Maui; Fairmont Orchid, Hawaii
- *Bermuda:* Fairmont Southampton, Fairmont Hamilton Princess
- *Mexico Region:* Fairmont Acapulco Princess, Fairmont Pierre Marques

Each region is overseen by a designated general manager (often the GM of the most prominent hotel in the region) who also carries the title of regional vice president. For example, the general manager of the Fairmont San Francisco oversees the California region, while the GM of Toronto's Fairmont Royal York oversees the Central Canada Region.[200]

This property-level structure is likely to continue to shift as Fairmont grows. The organization chart expanded from eight to twelve regions in less than two years thanks to the addition of such properties as the Hawaii resorts and the Fairmont Dubai. What's more, regions shift as qualified general managers move throughout the company. For example, John Pye oversaw the South Central Region (including the Fairmont Scottsdale Princess, the Fairmont Dallas, the Fairmont New Orleans, the Fairmont Acapulco Princess, and the Fairmont Pierre Marques)[201]—a region that was reorganized into two after he was elevated to the position of president of Delta Hotels. Clearly, fluidity in this area is not seen as a problem, as long as the fundamental structure remains in place.

Owners vs. Management: Dueling Interests?

While Legacy Hotels and FHR Real Estate own, or own equity interest in, the majority of the properties wearing the Fairmont flag, outside entities own others, such as The Plaza in New York and the Fairmont San Francisco, which are co-owned by Maritz, Wolff & Co. and Saudi Prince Alwaleed's Kingdom Hotels. These outside entities have the final say on capital improvement projects ranging from renovations to the installation of high-speed Internet connections.

Owner/management contracts require certain brand-standard obligations from owners, such as the use of the Global Reservation Centre and a bevy of operational brand standards. While every contract includes a capital reserve for replacement of goods (usually between 4 percent to 5 percent of a hotel's annual revenues as per Legacy's policy),[202] even Legacy Hotels might veto a brand-enhancing capital improvement project in one of its own assets in the interest of paying dividends to its unitholders. Might Fairmont find it a challenge to implement brandwide standards across a portfolio of nonstandard hotels with owners who are less concerned about building a brand and more concerned about bottom-line EBITDA growth? For this young brand, the answer to this most important question remains to be seen.

Centralization vs. Outsourcing

Fairmont's centralized, hands-on management philosophy is strongly evidenced in its approach to information technology. The company has taken a "nontraditional approach" relative to its competitors by serving as its own application service provider (ASP) and Internet service provider (ISP), and even by staffing its own twenty-four-hour technology help desk serving both Fairmont guests and employees around the world out of its corporate office. Fairmont's guest-data collection and warehousing for customer relationship management (CRM) is also highly centralized at the corporate level.

Top-down centralization of information systems at the corporate level benefit both the corporate and property cost structure and facilitates growth, according to Fairmont: "[A]s we expand, it makes it a lot easier to offer [IT] as a service to new ownership groups."[203] Fairmont corporate "sells" these shared services to its owners for an agreed-upon fee designated in the management contract. Calling the Fairmont approach "highly unusual," Mark Hamilton of Evans & Chastain Consulting notes that "I don't know of [another] hotel company that owns its infrastructure to this extent."[204]

Fairmont's human assets in IT are also highly centralized. Fairmont corporate employees oversee all aspects of information management at each Canadian property. These property-based IT employees report directly into corporate headquarters rather than to their respective general managers.[205] U.S.

properties are functioning more independently, though—at least for now. They are not free agents, however. "We do communicate very regularly to make sure they are aware of our corporate initiatives."[206]

Fairmont's practice of serving as its own IT consultant rather than outsourcing such functions, as many hospitality companies do, is emblematic to the company's shoulder-to-the-grindstone, do-it-yourself approach that has turned such traditional cost centers as information technology and food and beverage into revenue generators. When questioned about Fairmont's penchant to operate its own restaurants over outsourcing, executive food and beverage director Serge Simard remarked, "We want to control our own destiny." The result has been food-and-beverage operations that are known for high quality and consistently outperform the competitive set in terms of profitability.[207] A similar approach has been to building the Willow Stream spa brand, versus the less risky—but less controllable—option of partnering with a well-known spa brand, as Wyndham Hotels & Resorts has with the Golden Door.[208]

Although this "do it yourself" approach has reaped benefits for Fairmont until now, does the company have enough internal resources to leverage as it continues to grow? Is this scrappy, independent approach evidence of hardheadedness in a company that simply wants to do things its own way—or not? Will commitment to this approach ultimately put a cap on Fairmont's growth potential, or drive it?

Procurement: Participation in Avendra Fairmont has shown a willingness to outsource when it makes fiscal sense—to an extent. Fairmont joined forces with Marriott, Hyatt, Six Continents, and Club Corp USA in January 2001 to establish Avendra, which operates the largest Web-enabled, business-to-business hospitality procurement network for North American hospitality and related industries as an independent contractor.[209] Avendra's customer base now exceeds 1,600 hotels, representing 300,000 rooms, and more than 250 golf courses and clubs. Avendra's programs are supported by nearly 500 suppliers, representing more than 700,000 items.[210]

The Avendra alliance provides such critical mass that cost savings in procurement are tremendous—especially for a small player like Fairmont, which has been able to realize savings in procurement through Avendra that it couldn't possibly imagine on its own. Simultaneous integration and outsourcing of existing procurement operations, as well as improved relationships with properties, have been additional benefits for the company.[211]

Property Integration When Canadian Pacific Hotels acquired Princess Hotels International in 1998, the executive committees from all of the Princess hotels spent a week in Toronto at Canadian Pacific's offices for an orientation session introducing them to brand standards, human resources programs and other corporate programs. The intention of this orientation was for the two organizations to learn from each other, adapting different practices from each as a way to develop "best practices" for the combined group.[212] According to Melanie Wendeler, at the time a revenue manager for Canadian Pacific Hotels—and now director of hotel integration for Fairmont Hotels & Resorts—a team of Canadian Pacific representatives from various property-level departments—accounting, technology, human resources, revenue management, and so on—was then sent to each property. There was no formal program, but each integration team member was to work with their counterpart to ensure the property understood any changes that needed to be made.[213]

At a property level, the integration strategy was—and continues to be—to retain as many of the existing management and staff at an acquired property while selectively placing existing staff in open positions to ensure that the corporate culture and values are understood and implemented throughout the brand.

When Canadian Pacific and Fairmont merged, extensive executive-level integration workshops were held so that a joint understanding of corporate goals, mission, and vision could be developed and agreed upon.[214] Focus groups were organized at each property, contributing to the definition of the corporate values of respect, integrity, teamwork, and empowerment. Carolyn Clark, vice president of human resources, "It was incredible to see the similarity of definitions" between the two organizations."[215] The mission statement that FHR uses today was drafted during these integration workshops.

After 1999, integration focused less on integrating a group of hotels into FHR and more on integrating single properties into the company. The Fairmont Miramar Santa Monica joined the group in 1999, the Fairmont Kansas City at the Plaza in 2000 and the Fairmont Kea Lani, Maui, in 2001. In 2002, the acquisition pace continued with the addition of the Fairmont Sonoma Mission Inn & Spa, the Fairmont Orchid, Hawaii, and the Fairmont Washington, D.C. But the most significant integration task since the creation of FHR was the opening of the Fairmont Dubai in the United Arab Emirates. FHR was contacted by the office of His Highness Dr. Sheikh Sultan bin Khalifa Al Nahyan of Abu Dhabi in February 2001, and an agreement was struck in May of that year for Fairmont to manage and operate the property. The hotel opened in February 2002, after FHR's integration team completed all pre-opening tasks including selecting and hiring the management and staff; selecting and procuring the furniture, fixtures and equipment for the hotel; finding lessees for the residual apartments and offices that coexist in the multifunctional property; and implementing a sales organization to distribute the room nights local and international guests—all on a fast-forward schedule.

As a result of the intensive acquisition calendar of 2002, property integration is now a somewhat institutionalized process. Integrating single properties is done by a small team whose size and participants vary depending on the situation at each property. The team can and does call upon experts from various areas of the hotel when creating the integration team. Representatives from the departments of human resources, technology services, sales and distribution, rooms, food and beverage, and finance and accounting are assembled on temporary assignment from various properties throughout the brand as needed.

When an existing property is acquired, the amount of time the integration team will spend at the property varies; integration at the Fairmont Orchid took place over five weeks, whereas integration at the Fairmont Washington, D.C., was only three weeks. For the Fairmont Dubai, given that it was a hotel opening—and in such a new environment, no less—the integration team was in place longer, up to eight months.[216] Various factors contribute to the length of the integration process, such as the type of property

(resort vs. city center) as well as the number of open positions to fill following the acquisition. FHR prefers to place a small number of FHR people at each newly acquired property as a way to ensure that the corporate culture is understood and accepted. Fairmont does not impose lengthy brand standards and requirements on newly acquired properties; instead the integration team works with the property's management and staff to understand what brand standards must be met in what priority order.[217] Another key component of the integration process is ensuring the technical integration of the property, establishing links between the property's systems and the central reservation system and guest data warehouse used by FHR.

Since 2001, all integration tasks are coordinated through the integration department at the corporate offices of FHR. This is a very small department, with only a vice president, rooms and hotel integration, and a director of hotel integration. The role of this department is changing, as the integration process is becoming somewhat more formalized. Since early 2003, this department developed and tracked all-encompassing acquisition budgets for the projects under by the department. The department is also developing a knowledge database called DevNet, hosted on the companywide intranet, myFairmont.com, as a repository of documents relating to new and potential projects. The department is also more fully involved in all phases of the acquisition, from the preliminary due diligence to developing initial pro formas to the first meetings with executives as well as integration after an acquisition agreement has been signed.

Once a property is handed over to its permanent management team, the integration department is no longer involved—primarily because all business travel done by the integration team is reallocated back to the property's budget. At present, no procedure is in place for corporate integration executives to return to properties after integration to ensure that the corporate culture has been accepted or that brand standards are being met. As Melanie Wendeler states, "We haven't had the luxury to go back [to a property] four months after integration to see what worked and what didn't work."[218] Is this the appropriate integration process for a company whose strategic direction is to add two to four new hotels a year through acquisition?[219]

Employees and Corporate Culture

Engaged, well-trained employees will create good experiences, bring people back, drive profitability. We take this seriously.

—Chris Cahill, president and COO[220]

Currently, Fairmont Hotels & Resorts employs roughly 23,000 people throughout its organization, with another approximately 8,000 people employed by Delta Hotels. With a total annual expenditure of about $491 million on wages, benefits, and recruitment and training programs, human resources adds up to a major investment for the hotel company. In fact, 37.1 percent of revenues are dedicated to wages and benefits. The average full-time employee costs the company $32,100, and generates $86,400 in annual revenue on average.[221] Approximately 15 percent of employees are in management positions, 85 percent are salaried and hourly.

The average length of service for a Fairmont employee is six years, which is considered lengthy in the hospitality industry. While a full 43 percent of the Fairmont workforce has been employed by Fairmont for less than two years, 22 percent has more than ten years' experience at the company; the average length of service is 9.05 percent.[222] Carolyn Clark, the vice president of human resources, reports the turnover rate to be well below the industry norm.[223]

Most managers are hired from within. In fact, 68 percent of all corporate and property-level managers who took new positions in 2002 were internal candidates.[224] Property-level managers are often moved throughout the company in order to communicate the corporate message, spread the talent pool, and keep top talent interested and engaged. The twenty-year-old company-wide Pathfinder job-posting program makes it easy for employees around the world to apply for transfers or promotions, especially now that all postings are fully accessible through the companywide intranet, myFairmont.com.

While an arm's length distance is often kept between the two brands, talent often moves between the Delta and Fairmont brands. There were forty-one interbrand transfers of managers in 2002, with twenty-four moving from Fairmont to Delta properties and seventeen moving from Delta to Fairmont properties. Furthermore, managers are often transferred from Canadian properties—those closest to the heart of the company—to properties in the United States and abroad in order to extend the corporate culture through the wide network of properties. In fact, thirty-six managers were moved from Canada abroad in 2002.[225] For example, when Fairmont needed a seasoned general manager to open its first property outside of North America, it called on Michael Kaile, who had spent the previous three years as GM of the Fairmont Hamilton Princess in Bermuda, had opened the Fairmont Waterfront in Vancouver, and also had experience opening hotels abroad—in Kuwait and Bangkok—for other hotel companies.[226]

HR Strategy: Service Plus The stated mission of Fairmont Hotels & Resorts—"We will earn the loyalty of our guests by exceeding their expectations and providing warm and personal service in distinctive surroundings"[227]—is built on the provision of "warm and personal service," which cannot be provided by physical structure, but only by human capital. Thus, at the very heart of the company lies its commitment to human resources (HR) and employee performance. Fairmont's "people vision"—its HR strategy—drills down into this goal:

We will be known for superior service excellence by attracting and retaining the industry's most talented and engaged colleagues, relentlessly committed to providing WOW experiences that will create "Places in the Heart."[228]

The stated corporate values—respect, integrity, teamwork, and empowerment—further support Fairmont's people strategy and link it to both brand equity and financial success, as do key planks in the corporate vision:

We will demonstrate a relentless commitment to understand, anticipate, and fulfill the needs of our guests;

We will inspire an open, innovative learning organization that is energetic and exciting for our colleagues;

We will deliver superior operating performance and financial returns for our owners and investors.[229]

This intersection of mission, vision, and values describe an ideal hospitality company as one that emphasizes proactive service and offers developing opportunities to its employees. Fairmont believes that respect, instruction, and empowerment lead to happy and productive employees—which, in turn, lead to satisfied customers.

In order to realize its full investment in human capital, Fairmont uses an integrated HR management system called Service Plus, a four-pronged system—actually a legacy program from Canadian Pacific Hotels—designed to attract and retain the best available employees through structured selection, strong leadership development, culture and skills training for service excellence, and employee reward and recognition. The result is a satisfying workplace peopled by motivated employees, who in turn serve happy and satisfied customers, which leads to sustainable and profitable growth.[230]

Key success factors include performance management (with a strong emphasis on empowerment in decision-making and guest empathy),[231] leadership training, succession planning, and incentive programs, such as systematic awards and distribution of stock options.[232] But the most critical success factor—in Fairmont's estimation, anyway—is the use of the Gallup structured interview for selection and advancement.[233]

Gallup Structured Interview: Key to Selection

Fairmont Hotels & Resorts uses a structured interview designed by the Gallup Organization as its primary selection tool for all new employees, at both corporate and property levels as well as for those making significant job changes within the organization. Fairmont has been using the Gallup structured interview since 1988, though only recently has the company used Gallup to measure employee performance relative to their initial scores.[234]

The structured interview is designed to determine how an applicant's talents fit with the requirements for success in a particular job category through their responses to sixty-five standardized questions. Currently, there are seven Gallup interviews in use. Profiles differ by position, talent profile, and job expectations.[235] Front-of-house employees, for example, are measured on their ability to relate to and empathize with guests and colleagues; their problem-solving

skills; such customer-impact skills as positivity and winning others over ("woo"); and achievement-oriented goals.[236] Different sets of questions apply to heart-of-house positions without direct guest contact (such as housekeepers and engineers), culinary staff, sales personnel, floor managers, executive staff, and so on. The resulting talent profile for each applicant is compared to the required talents for the job, which are constantly updated from the best practices of top performers from throughout the company.[237] Cultural fit is emphasized over technical skill, which can be acquired through training.[238]

Fairmont believes deeply in the validity of the Gallup structured interview. Indeed, all evidence seems to indicate that the system has helped Fairmont align its human resources strategy with its overarching business strategy by helping the company identify new hires with a desire to serve and promote the Fairmont brand.

Every potential Fairmont employee must go through at least one Gallup interview, and the talent profiles generated are kept on hand for future promotion and movement within the company. To track employee performance after the fact, Fairmont and Gallup have decided on metrics that focus on driving profitability, such as room-night revenue for salespeople and upsell revenue for front-desk staff. Other nonfinancial metrics, such as safety incidents, absentee rates, and guest comments, are collected. Fairmont has realized the need for even more performance measures to ensure the validity of the selection process across the entire company, and it has committed to developing these by 2004.[239]

The Direct Impact of Service Plus Service Plus as a whole, and the Gallup structured interview in particular, has been shown to directly affect Fairmont's bottom line. Statistics show that Gallup-"recommended" employees are two to three times more productive than employees who are not Gallup approved:[240]

- Gallup-approved front-desk employees produce nearly three times more annual upsell revenue vs. the team average (165 percent vs. 63 percent)

- Gallup-approved food-and-beverage managers generate more revenue per square foot

($213 vs. $180) and more covers per hour (26.3 vs. 22.8)

- Gallup-tested food and beverage (F&B) employees report roughly half the health and safety incidents that other F&B employees do
- Sales managers who have received Gallup's stamp of approval generate 8 percent more annual revenue ($4,147,456 vs. $3,825,680 in 2001)[241]

Fairmont also credits the expansion and refinement of Service Plus with improving both employee satisfaction and the company's rising customer satisfaction scores from J. D. Power & Associates, which describes itself as the largest and most widely recognized gatekeeper of historical customer satisfaction data for the hospitality industry.[242] Fairmont reports a 6 percent improvement in employee satisfaction with their work from 2000 to 2002, measurable improvements in other key employee feedback areas, and improvement on 88 percent of key customer satisfaction drivers over the same time period.[243] What's more, companywide guest satisfaction was reported in November 2002 to be nearly 4 percent improved over year-to-date performance.[244] Hotels that are entirely staffed with Gallup-screened employees, such as the Fairmont Vancouver Airport, carry some of the Fairmont brand's highest employee satisfaction and J. D. Power customer satisfaction scores.[245]

But, despite the success of the Gallup structured interview in the selection process, might Fairmont have too many "legacy" employees to put it to effective use in establishing a brand-consistent, service-oriented workforce?

Compensation Practices Pay scales at Fairmont Hotels & Resorts are competitive—in the top quartile but not the industry's highest. Approximately 50.7 percent of nonmanagerial property-level employees are unionized, and paid on union-negotiated wage scales. Unionized employees are paid on a single pay rate not based on performance, while nonunion employees generally have at least some incentive-based pay.[246]

FHR does have a Key Employee Stock Option Plan (KESOP) as well as a Directors' Stock Option Plan (DSOP). The KESOP plan allows options to be granted whereby an employee may purchase common shares at a price per share not less than the market value at the date when the option is granted. Options are vested over a four-year period, and options expire nine years after the grant date. The DSOP plan granted 8,000 options to each nonemployee director as of October 2001, with an additional 4,000 options granted annually. Like the KESOP plan, the options allow the directors to purchase common shares at market-value price when the option was granted. They can be exercised immediately and expire ten years after the grant date.[247]

Internal Marketing Achieving employee buy-in to corporate decisions is a key to success for a company like Fairmont, which relies heavily on its human capital as a major source of strength. "Internal marketing is critical," confirms Brian Richardson, vice president of brand marketing and communications, even to such undebatable issues as the switch from the Canadian Pacific to the Fairmont name.[248]

Every employee throughout the company—no matter where they are based—has access to company information via myFairmont.com,[249] the intranet system that serves as the company's primary internal communication tool. MyFairmont.com is used to communicate information ranging from employee promotion announcements and human resources policy changes to e-mail blasts about new property acquisitions and special "friends and family" rates at hotels throughout the brand.

Close connections between executive, management, and line-level employees are key. President and chief operating officer Chris Cahill hosts regular group lunches so he can talk to each corporate-level employee one to one at least once a year, and he conducts management reviews with Carolyn Clark, the vice president of human resources, so he always knows where the company's best talents lie. Inclusive "launch" parties hosted by corporate executives celebrate every new acquisition. What's more, a general "open door" policy and a culture of empowered time management and decision making reigns.

The emphasis on human resources has been a great success for Fairmont Hotels & Resorts, which was honored by *Maclean's Magazine* as one of Canada's "Top 100 Employers" in 2002 and was named among the best in the 2003 edition of *Canada's Top 100 Employers*.[250] Delta Hotels was recognized by *The Globe and Mail,* the national newspaper of Canada, as one of the "50 Best Companies to Work for in Canada" for the third consecutive year in 2003.[251]

Marketing

For Fairmont Hotels & Resorts, the emphasis is on honing its brandwide marketing programs, all in the name of boosting the company's brand recognition among the traveling public, strengthening its luxury positioning, and communicating the message that Fairmont is committed to providing "outstanding" service.[252] Doing so, however, is not about splashy, expensive, one-size-fits-all advertising. Rather, the focus is on identifying the most valuable customers for Fairmont and target-marketing directly to them through special initiatives—most notably the Fairmont President's Club guest-recognition loyalty program and technology-enabled customer relationship management.

Fairmont Gold "The size issue"—the typical Fairmont hotel has 500 rooms or more—can often create a gap between service management and service perception. "That's one reason for Fairmont Gold," reports Brian Richardson, vice president of brand marketing and communications, "Slowly, we're breaking down the bias" that Fairmont is just a group house.[253]

Fairmont Gold is the brand's own pure-luxury hotel within-a-hotel product, designed to offer the highest levels of luxury service to independent corporate or leisure guests[254] in exchange for an additional rate premium above the standard rate (for example, typically CAD $90 above the base rate at Toronto's Fairmont Royal York).[255] Fairmont Gold is an exclusive floor or floors boasting:

- Dedicated check-in and high-guest-ratio concierge service
- A private lounge with complimentary continental breakfast, all-day coffee and tea, evening hors d'oeuvres, and an honor bar
- Complimentary high-speed Internet access in the guestroom and the lounge
- Upgraded room amenities, including higher quality décor, terry bath robes, and the like

- Complimentary boardroom privileges and light secretarial services[256]

Fairmont Gold has certainly enhanced Fairmont's luxury positioning in the marketplace. Travel agents who have booked Fairmont Gold generally report it to be superior to club floors offered by other top hotel brands.[257]

Fairmont Gold is so important to Fairmont's brand identity, in the company's estimation, that the plan is to install Fairmont Gold floors in each Fairmont hotel; as of the end 2002, they were located in sixteen properties (including a brand-new Fairmont Gold floor at Bermuda's Fairmont Hamilton Princess).[258] Properties that were to receive the Fairmont Gold treatment in 2003 included the Fairmont Château Lake Louise and the Fairmont Orchid, Hawaii.[259]

Fairmont President's Club Fairmont's loyalty program, the Fairmont President's Club, is seen as a prime growth vehicle for Fairmont, because its members—the guests most familiar with and loyal to the Fairmont brand—"are increasing the amount they spend with Fairmont, as they stay at our new properties and are willing to pay higher rates for specialized services" like Fairmont Gold.[260] "Fairmont President's Club equals personalization," says Brian Richardson.[261]

Launched in 2000, the Fairmont President's Club boasted 131,000 active members (while the Delta Privilege Program has 66,000 active members) in early 2002, a number that had climbed to roughly 175,000 by late 2002.[262] Rather than being a points-gathering program for future stays, the Fairmont President's Club is a guest recognition program that rewards guests immediately with an enhanced level of service at every stay.

Membership is free. Guests register their preferences on the Fairmont.com Web site in a profile that Fairmont then uses to customize the guest room to the guests' needs (in theory, at least). Such preferences include type of room (smoking or nonsmoking), type of pillow (feather or hypo-allergenic), proximity to elevators, newspaper preference (local or national), and the like. Members also benefit from exclusive check-in, complimentary local and toll-free calls, and discounts at Fairmont retail stores.[263]

Frequent guests can achieve Gold or Platinum status and score extra benefits that keep them coming back for more, such as free suite upgrades, priority room access with free high-speed Internet access, personalized luggage tags, and more.[264]

Customer Relationship Management

"It's a cluttered world, so relevance"—of the messages you send to your clientele—"is key. You can only do this if you use the information you have."—Brian Richardson, vice president of brand marketing and communications[265]

How does Fairmont gather relevant information? Three words: customer relationship management (CRM). The company has invested extensive resources into a robust data warehousing effort with a marketing and a CRM engine in order to gather guest preferences and perform strategic data analysis to better understand what guests are interested in and develop guest profiles and targeted products suited to their needs (like, for instance, Fairmont Gold).

Customer relationship management data are collected via the Web portals and stored in a centralized data warehouse together with the data collected by both the property management systems (PMSs) and central reservation system (CRS), so that employees are able to provide customized service to the guests throughout the portfolio.[266] Employees are encouraged to enter into the database as many guest preferences—particularly for President's Club members, the company's most loyal clientele—as they can gather during a guest's stay. The goal is to personalize the member's experiences more finely with every stay. When front-desk and reservations agents are speaking to guests, "they can view their preferences, see what their stay history is, and provide enhanced service," explains Sean Taggart, Fairmont's director of strategic analysis. "They will know if the guest visited five of our properties, how much they spent with us, how many nights they stayed with us. ... If we do it right, it will enable us to capture information so we can wow the guest."[267]

Guests who stay on Fairmont Gold floors end up with even more comprehensive guest data profiles, thanks to the attentiveness of Fairmont Gold concierges. "On the Gold floor is where we get most of the information to make sure the next stay is personalized," says Chris Cahill, president and COO.[268]

Members of Fairmont's loyalty program, the President's Club, can score an extra level of service by registering their preferences in their personal profile in the Web site, as noted above. The guest-data warehouse can merge information gathered from guests' online behavior (via self-selected options on the Web site) and data observed and input by hotel employees via the Intranet portal. This allows Fairmont to gather more complete information to better personalize the guest's hotel experience, both on return visits to the Web site and once they arrive on property.[269]

What's more, Fairmont has recently stepped up its effort to gather and manipulate data on all guests, not merely President's Club members.[270] "We run both our loyalty program [the President's Club] out of [the guest data warehouse] as well as all enabled marketing communication, which enables e-mail and direct communication with all of our guests, both loyalty program and non-members," reports Sean Taggart.[271] The guest-data mining drives the engine behind just about every marketing campaign, both at the property- and brand-management level. "We support the properties and their marketing efforts to help them execute a program leveraging guest data warehouse, and we develop national programs at corporate office."

Fairmont also purchases external data to drive marketing campaigns, especially to target nonusers who do not yet know Fairmont but match the profile of "best user." "We are spending more dollars here because it is more relevant, targeted, useful," notes Brian Richardson.[272]

Distribution Fairmont sees travel agents that drive business to the brand as some of their best customers, and has focused on using technology to customize the way it communicates with agency partners based on their booking habits. "I see us focusing on specialist agencies that target specific destinations or types of travel," says Tom Storey, executive vice president of business development and strategy. "If you can see which agencies are driving business, you want to find ways to continue to educate and reward those agencies."[273]

The company launched a page on the Fairmont Web site specifically to meet the needs of travel agents. The company has also expanded its relationship with Virtuoso, a network of travel agencies devoted to luxury travel, in order to expand its distribution network and raise its luxury profile.[274]

Fairmont caters similarly to its luxury meeting planners, who also number among Fairmont's best customers. Meeting planners have a bevy of ways to file requests for proposals (RFPs) from the company, including through Fairmont.com and AskFairmontFirst, a toll-free hotline exclusively for group travel planners that guarantees to start moving on any request within one hour of initial contact—and generate a full-color Fairmont eProposal in PDF format, complete with photos.[275] The company has also built a brandwide pricing structure that protects group rate integrity by ensuring that meeting planners are consistently getting the most favorable rates. "We price for our best customers first to make sure they are protected, and work 'up' to transient business," says Ian Wilson, executive director of distribution management.[276]

Fairmont has also worked to put an end to what Mr. Wilson calls "e-steria," or price inequities across distribution channels that resulted from the intersection of a softening travel economy and a rise in Internet bookings from intermediaries that would guarantee room nights to worried hoteliers in exchange for deeply discounted rates.

Fairmont monitors Internet distribution channels—Expedia, Travelocity, Orbitz, and others—at the corporate level to be sure that there is never more than a $5 rate difference across channels. The company also negotiates with online merchants centrally—properties are no longer allowed to do so themselves. "It hurts our brand positioning if our hotels are underpriced," says Mr. Wilson. "Fairmont hotels don't deserve to be commoditized."[277]

Fairmont is investing in industrial-strength technology in order to better manage its sales and distribution efforts. In 2003, it deployed the Delphi Multi-Property Edition 9.1 sales system throughout the brand.[278] Delphi combines prospect and customer information with the room, meeting, and catering sales data that is so important to Fairmont's group focus. The rollout is scheduled to be complete by the end of 2004. Furthermore, in autumn 2003 the company launched a more attractive and interactive Fairmont.com, which generates more personalized information and allows for more dynamic package-building and booking. The company hopes to drive more transient business and leisure traffic away from third-party sites to Fairmont's own site.

Strategic Partnering

> Co-branding is defined as when two or more well-known brands are combined in an offer. Each brand sponsor expects that the other brand will strengthen preference or purchase intention.
>
> —Philip Kotler, *A Framework for Marketing Management*[279]

Fairmont enjoys the risk diversification and increased attention, garnered, at a low relative cost, from both traditional and nontraditional marketing partnerships. Fairmont's marketing budget is similar to most chains': 1.5 percent of revenues. However, at Fairmont, it adds up to fewer actual dollars for marketing, since the funds must be split between sales and marketing—and a brand with large group business requires a large sales organization. As a result, cooperative relationships are key to Fairmont's marketing success.[280]

In addition to setting up traditional partnerships with airlines such as Air Canada and American Airlines and with American Express,[281] the company has also formed nontraditional cobranding partnerships with such companies as Porsche, Moët & Chandon, Nieman Marcus, and A&E Networks, among others.[282] For example, Fairmont has yielded positive results—mainly a wealth of valuable public relations "buzz"—from the "Tour de Fairmont" package in partnership with Porsche. The package includes four nights' accommodations (two at the Fairmont San Francisco and two at the Fairmont Sonoma Mission Inn & Spa); use of a new Porsche Boxter, 911, or Cayenne for four days; a bottle of Moët & Chandon champagne; and a tank of gas—all for just $7,990.[283]

While such partnerships can be extremely valuable—especially in building Fairmont's brand positioning, there are certain challenges. First of all, each partner must have a constituency that interests the other.[284] Both brands must also be on relatively equal footing; one partner cannot be so strong that it dilutes the other partner's brand or to cause brand confusion. Also, each partner needs to have the resources to support the partnering program—and its inherent liabilities. And, for Fairmont, the partnership must support the company's ultimate objective: the selling of guestrooms.[285]

As with most new ventures, Fairmont generally takes a cautious approach to cobranding relationships. The relationship with Porsche Cars North America, for example, started out informally—first with one test promotion, then a second test promotion. "It has progressed," notes Thatcher Brown, director of business development and the driving force behind many of Fairmont's nontraditional partnering relationships.[286]

Financial Concerns

The main drivers behind the earning power of hotel companies are the ability to fill rooms and to collect a competitive rate for their services. The following table presents an overview of occupancy, average daily rate (ADR) and revenue per available room (RevPAR) for each of Fairmont's main business lines. (See Exhibit 9.)

Each of the four main divisions at FHR contributes differently to the overall earnings of the company, as each has a different claim on the revenues and expenses generated by operations. For instance, managed properties contribute only management fees to overall revenues, while all revenues generated by owned properties contribute to overall revenues once they are prorated for FHR's share in ownership. Because of this, Fairmont's real estate division contributes the bulk of the earnings to the company—78 percent of the earnings before income tax, depreciation, and amortization (EBITDA) of the group in 2002.[288]

For FHR, cash and cash equivalents on hand at December 31, 2002, totaled $49 million, a decrease of $4 million from 2001.[289] This cash is used for current operations, to make new investments, and to fund hotel capital improvement projects. Cash is typically generated from hotel operations in excess of cash needed to fund these operations. Additional cash is raised as needed from lines of credit, issuing

EXHIBIT 9	**OPERATING STATISTICS FOR FAIRMONT HOTELS & RESORTS BY BUSINESS LINE**[287]

	Year Ended December 31,	
	2002	**2001**
Owned Hotels		
Worldwide		
RevPAR	112.69	114.14
ADR	180.93	185.11
Occupancy	62.3%	61.7%
Canada		
RevPAR	95.14	94.15
ADR	145.16	145.77
Occupancy	65.5%	64.6%
U.S. and International		
RevPAR	138.02	143.07
ADR	239.69	249.17
Occupancy	57.6%	57.4%
Fairmont-Managed Hotels		
Worldwide		
RevPAR	105.37	107.48
ADR	162.04	167.55
Occupancy	65.0%	64.1%
Canada		
RevPAR	86.63	84.15
ADR	127.41	128.43
Occupancy	68.0%	65.5%
U.S. and International		
RevPAR	130.45	139.78
ADR	213.64	224.57
Occupancy	61.1%	62.2%
Delta-Managed Hotels		
RevPAR	53.84	54.49
ADR	85.23	84.08
Occupancy	63.2%	64.8%

RevPAR is defined as revenues per available room.

ADR is defined as average daily rate.

Comparable Hotels are considered to be properties that were fully open under FHR management for at least the entire current and prior period. Given the strategic importance of the acquisition of The Fairmont Kea Lani Maui, it has been included in FHR's operating statistics on a pro-forma basis as if owned since January 1, 2001. Comparable Hotels statistics exclude properties where renovations have had a significant adverse effect on the properties' primary operations. For the annual periods of 2002 vs. 2001. The Fairmont Hamilton Princess. The Fairmont Southampton, and The Fairmont Pierre Marques have been excluded.

also has the option of selling owned properties to Legacy to generate cash. Yet another source of cash is the significant operating and capital losses inherited from Canadian Pacific Limited. These losses allow FHR to significantly reduce taxes payable and therefore increase cash.[290]

Below, key financial facts for each division are highlighted.

Fairmont Hotels Inc. (Fairmont) As a hotel management company operating forty-one resorts and city-center hotels, Fairmont's main revenues are generated from hotel management fees and incentive fees. Because of the small revenue base, this division only contributes 15 percent of the overall EBITDA of the company.[291] (See Exhibit 10.)

Delta Hotels Limited (Delta) As with Fairmont, Delta only contributes its management fees to overall revenues of FHR. Revenues under Delta management are much smaller than for Fairmont, both because the number of guestrooms at Delta is just over half the number of Fairmont rooms, and because the average

daily rate for Delta is lower than for Fairmont. As a result, Delta contributes only 4 percent of FHR's overall EBITDA.[293] (See Exhibit 11.)

FHR Real Estate Corporation (FHRREC) FHRREC has ownership interests ranging from 20 percent to 100 percent in twenty-three properties (see Exhibit 12). All revenues and expenses are direct revenues and expenses of FHR, prorated for ownership participation. Because of this, this division contributes 78 percent of the group's overall EBITDA.[295] The assets contributing to this 78 percent include the Fairmont Château Lake Louise; the Fairmont Château Whistler; the Fairmont Banff Springs; the Fairmont Scottsdale Princess; the Fairmont Kea Lani, Maui; the two Acapulco properties; and the two Bermuda properties.[296]

In addition to the hotel properties, FHRREC also has significant holdings in undeveloped land, mainly two large undeveloped land blocks in Toronto and Vancouver.[298] According to SalomonSmithBarney, the value of these blocks is approximately $150 million, and FHR is "under contract to sell four of the

---

EXHIBIT 10   **FINANCIAL PERFORMANCE OF FAIRMONT HOTELS INC.[292]**

Highlights

(U.S.$ Millions)	2002	2001	2000
Revenues under management	$ 1,316.2	$ 1,252.9	$ 1,297.4
Revenues	$ 41.3	$ 39.9	$ 43.3
EBITDA	$ 28.9	$ 24.1	$ 31.9
Total properties	41	37	36
Total guestrooms	20,396	18,564	18,143

Contribution to EBITDA

15%

EXHIBIT 11   **FINANCIAL PERFORMANCE OF DELTA HOTELS LIMITED[294]**

Highlights

(U.S.$ Millions)	2002	2001	2000
Revenues under management	$ 312.5	$ 317.9	$ 328.0
Revenues	$ 11.4	$ 10.4	$ 11.9
EBITDA	$ 8.1	$ 7.6	$ 8.6
Total properties	38	38	35
Total guestrooms	11,200	11,211	11,810

Contribution to EBITDA

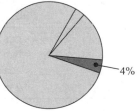

4%

EXHIBIT 12	FINANCIAL PERFORMANCE OF FHR REAL ESTATE CORPORATION[297]

Highlights

(U.S.$ Millions)	2002	2001	2000
Revenues	$ 516.6	$ 489.6	$ 464.7
EBITDA	$ 143.4	$ 126.1	$ 143.5
Total properties (100% owned)	16	15	14
Total guestrooms (100% owned)	7,408	6,871	7,507
Total properties (partially owned)	7	5	4
Total guestrooms (partially owned)	2,078	1,626	1,248

Contribution to EBITDA

78%

Vancouver plots and plans to sell all of the land within two to five years."[299] The large undeveloped parcel on Vancouver's Coal Harbour was sold in March 2003 to the province of British Columbia for the expansion of Vancouver's Convention and Exhibition Centre.[300] In addition to these key undeveloped lands, unused land surrounds the Fairmont Princess properties. This land is being used for a new brand, Fairmont Heritage Place, a private residence club already under development in Acapulco and Bermuda.

Legacy Hotels REIT Legacy Hotels REIT owns twenty-two properties in Canada and one in the United States. The goal of the REIT is to distribute the bulk of its net income to its unitholders. For instance, the REIT generated a net income of CAD $55.1 million in 2002 and a distributable income of CAD $50.9 million.[301] The main difference between net income and distributable income is the capital replacement reserve set aside for ongoing maintenance of the properties as well as for profit improvement projects in which the REIT can invest. (See Exhibit 13.)

Legacy grew in 2002, mostly due to two new acquisitions. First, Legacy acquired the Fairmont Washington, D.C. (formerly the Monarch) and contracted with FHR for the management of this property; second, it acquired the Sheraton Suites Calgary Eau Claire (currently under Fairmont management), acting as a funding source for FHR.[303]

Legacy's overall cash position as of December 31, 2002, was strong: CAD $46.2 billion in cash and cash equivalents, representing 2.4 percent of the total assets of the company. This strong cash position is targeted for funding future acquisitions, though some cash will be distributed to unitholders as distributable income. Legacy uses subscriptions from unitholders to fund most of its growth, but it has raised additional funds through mortgage and debenture debt. Total long-term debt as of December 31, 2002, equaled CAD $744.9 million, of which $157.3 million was considered the current portion.[304] Given this total debt level—the debt-to-equity ratio is 0.72—Legacy has the financial flexibility to pursue future investments.

EXHIBIT 13	FINANCIAL PERFORMANCE OF LEGACY HOTELS REIT[302]

Highlights

As reported by Legacy Hotels REIT (Cdn$ Millions)	2002	2001	2000
Revenues	$ 647.6	$ 606.8	$ 501.7
EBITDA	$ 146.0	$ 140.2	$ 121.7
Total properties	23	21	19
Total guestrooms	10,290	9,558	8,500

Contribution to EBITDA

3%

Overall Financial Position of Fairmont Hotels & Resorts (FHR) When FHR began trading publicly as an independent company, most analysts pegged it to outperform its peer group. For instance, Raymond James gave FHR an "outperform" rating due to many factors, including FHR's significant operating leverage allowing it to benefit from hotel recovery; heritage properties in markets with high barriers to entry; a low long-term-debt-to-market capitalization ratio; and its strategic relationship with Legacy.[305] When Raymond James made this evaluation, FHR's long-term-debt-to-market capitalization ratio was 13 percent, among the lowest of its peer group.

Despite a difficult year for the hospitality industry, analysts still look favorably on FHR. CIBC World Markets assessed FHR in February 2003 and concluded that "we believe FHR to be one of the strongest names in difficult times."[306] By the end of 2002, FHR's long-term debt had risen to just over $460 million from $245 million in 2001, primarily due to the acquisition of the Fairmont Orchid in Hawaii. Market capitalization in February was $1.7 billion, giving a new long-term-debt-to-market capitalization ratio of 0.27, in line with its peer group.

Financially, FHR seems well positioned for continued success. Will this financial position remain strong if recovery in the hospitality industry occurs later than expected?

CONCLUSION

Fairmont Hotels & Resorts has made significant achievements since 1999 in growing the company and growing the brand on an international scale. The short-term goal of Fairmont Hotels & Resorts is to have fifty-five properties in North America, boosted by a worldwide reputation for high-quality assets with "a sense of place" and luxury service "that is warm and genuine," President and COO Chris Cahill said in 2002.[307]

Fairmont Hotels & Resorts seems to be favorably positioned to accomplish these goals. But has the company taken on too much, too soon?

Can the current corporate resources continue to provide the infrastructure needed to integrate new hotels into the Fairmont brand—or have company resources been overextended in the name of rapid growth? Is the company focusing enough resources

on ensuring that their current guest service levels meet and exceed guest expectations in a manner that will build the Fairmont name into the luxury hotel brand of choice?

It may be time for FHR to take stock before pursuing further growth, in order to ensure that the appropriate corporate-level processes and infrastructure are in place and so that too-rapid growth doesn't spin the company out of management's control. Or is the FHR approach well grounded as it leverages FHR's current strengths and strategic partnerships with Legacy Hotels Real Estate Investment Trust; Maritz, Wolff & Co.; Kingdom Hotels; and His Royal Highness Dr. Sheikh Sultan bin Khalifa Al Nahyan, crown prince of Abu Dhabi?

Industry analysts are bullish on their expectations for Fairmont Hotels & Resorts' success. Are they making the right forecasts?

Notes

1. LodgingNews.com, "75 Profiles in Leadership: William R. Fatt, Chairman/CEO, Fairmont Hotels & Resorts," http://www.lodgingnews.com/lodgingmag/2000_08/2000_08_46.asp, 15 May 2003.

2. Fairmont San Francisco, "History of the Hotel," http://www.fairmont.com/FA/en/CDA/Home/Hotels/AboutHotel/CDHotelHistory/0,2992,nav%253D7%2526entity%25255Fvalue%253D100117%2526property%25255Fseq%253D100117%2526entity%25255Fkey%253Dproperty%25255Fseq,00.html, 6 February 2003.

3. "Fact Sheet: New Hotel Management Company Fairmont Hotels & Resorts Inc.," Hotel Online, 19 April 1999, http://hotel-online.com/News/PressReleases1999_2nd/Apr99_CPFactSheet.html, 2 May 2003.

4. Canadian Pacific Railway, "CPR Heritage: A Brief History," http://www.cprheritage.com/history/display1.htm, 17 May 2003.

5. J. P. Pederson, ed., "Canadian Pacific Railway," *International Directory of Company Histories*, vol. 45 (St. James Press, 2002), 78.

6. Ibid.

7. Canadian Pacific Railway, "CPR Heritage," http://www8.cpr.ca/cms/English/About+Us/CPR+Heritage/default.htm, 17 May 2003.

8. Fairmont.com, "Our History," http://www.fairmont.com/FA/en/CDA/Home/AboutFairmont/CDAboutFairmont/0,2949,code%25255Ftype%253DHIST%2526category%25255Ftype%253Dbrand%25255Fcopy,00.html, 2 May 2003.

9. Pederson, "Canadian Pacific Railway," 79.

10. Ibid.

11. Canadian Pacific Railway, "CPR Heritage: A Brief History."

12. Ibid.

13. Pederson, "Canadian Pacific Railway," 80.

14. Ibid.

15. Ibid., 81.

16. C. Osakwe, and P. Hedges, "The Diversification Discount: The Case of Canadian Pacific Limited. Working Paper Number 2002-17," November 2002, Haskayne School of Business, University of Calgary, 8.

17. Ibid., 9.

18. Canadian Pacific, Press Release. "Canadian Pacific to Enhance Shareholder Value by Spinning Off Its Businesses," 13 February 2001.

19. Ibid.

20. Canadian Pacific, *Canadian Pacific 1998 Annual Report,* 3.

21. Ibid., 2.

22. Osakwe and Hedges, "The Diversification Discount," 5.

23. DeltaHotels.com, "Delta Hotels: A Canadian Hotel Management Success Story," http://www.deltahotels.com/about, 17 May 2003.

24. Canadian Pacific Hotels, Press Release, "Canadian Pacific Hotels to Acquire Delta Hotels," 10 March 1998, 1.

25. Canadian Pacific, *Canadian Pacific 1998 Annual Report,* 4.

26. "Fact Sheet: New Hotel Management Company Fairmont Hotels & Resorts Inc.," Hotel Online.

27. Fairmont San Francisco, "History of the Hotel."

28. "Richard Swig, Chairman of Fairmont Hotel Management Company, Dead at Age 72," Hotel Online, 25 September 1997, http://hotel-online.com/News/PressReleases/SwigObituary_Sept97.html, 18 May 2003.

29. "Maritz, Wolff Co. Reaches Agreement to Acquire 50% Stake in Fairmont Hotels in San Francisco, Dallas and New Orleans," Hotel Online, 16 March 1998, http://www.hotel-online.com/News/PressReleases1998/FairmontAgreement_March98.html, 18 May 2003.

30. Wolff DiNapoli, Press Release, "Fairmont and Canadian Pacific Hotels Form New Company," 19 April 1999, http://www.wolffdinapoli.com, 18 May 2003.

31. Canadian National, "Our Story: The Drive to Compete 1980–1992," http://www.cn.ca/companyinfo/history/en_AboutOurStory.shtml, 17 May 2003.

32. Canadian Pacific Hotels, Press Release, "Revitalized Canadian Pacific Hotels Unveils New Logo," 25 January 1996, 1.

33. Canadian Pacific Hotels, "Symbols of Excellence," *Dialogue* internal magazine, January 1996, 1.

34. Canadian Pacific Hotels, "Revitalized Canadian Pacific Hotels Unveils New Logo," 2.

35. Legacy Hotels Real Estate Investment Trust, *1998 Annual Report,* 2.

36. Canadian Pacific, *Canadian Pacific 1998 Annual Report,* 12.

37. DeltaHotels.com, http://www.deltahotels.com/about, 2 May 2003.

38. Canadian Pacific Hotels, Press Release, "Canadian Pacific Hotels to Acquire Delta Hotels," 10 March 1998, 1.

39. Canadian Pacific, *Canadian Pacific 1998 Annual Report,* 54.

40. Canadian Pacific Hotels, "Canadian Pacific Hotels to Acquire Delta Hotels," 2.

41. Canadian Pacific, *Canadian Pacific 1998 Annual Report,* 3.

42. "Fact Sheet: New Hotel Management Company Fairmont Hotels & Resorts Inc."

43. Ibid.

44. Ibid.

45. Ibid.

46. S. P. Webber, "The Future of Fairmont," Travel Agent, 23 September 2002.

47. Canadian Pacific, *Canadian Pacific 1999 Annual Report,* 6.

48. Ibid.

49. Ibid., 1.

50. Ibid.

51. Ibid., 10.

52. New York Stock Exchange, "Listed Companies," http://www.nyse.com/listed/p1020656067970.html?displayPage=%2Flisted%2F1020656067970.html, 18 May 2003.

53. Fairmont Hotels & Resorts Inc., *Fairmont Hotels & Resorts 2001 Annual Report,* 4.

54. Fairmont Hotels & Resorts Inc., *Fairmont Hotels & Resorts 2002 Annual Report,* 6.

55. Legacy Hotels Real Estate Investment Trust, Press Release, "Legacy Hotels Real Estate Investment Trust to Acquire the Olympic Hotel in Seattle," July 3, 2003.

56. Fairmont Hotels & Resorts Inc., *Fairmont Hotels & Resorts 2002 Annual Report,* 19.

57. Fairmont Hotels & Resorts, Press Release, "Kingdom Hotels Subsidiary Exchanges Interest in Fairmont Management Company for a Stake in Fairmont Hotels & Resorts Inc.," 25 July 2002, http://ir.thomsonfn.com/InvestorRelations/PubNewsStory.aspx?partner=Mzg0TlRVd05BPT1QJFkEQUALSTO&product=MzgwU1ZJPVAkWQEQUALSTOEQUALSTO&storyId=84975, 19 May 2003.

58. Fairmont Hotels & Resorts, Press Release, "Fairmont Hotels & Resorts Inc. Announces Closing of Exchange Transaction," 23 September 2002, http://ir.thomsonfn.com/InvestorRelations/PubNewsStory.aspx?partner=Mzg0TlRVd05BPT1QJFkEQUALSTO&product=MzgwU1ZJPVAkWQEQUALSTOEQUALSTO&storyId=84982, 19 May 2003.

59. World Travel & Tourism Council, "Executive Summary: Travel & Tourism a World of Opportunity. The 2003 Travel & Tourism Economic Research," 3, 13.

60. C. R. Goeldner and J. R. B. Ritchie, *Tourism,* 9th ed. (New York: John Wiley & Sons), 307.

61. S. K. Neilsen, "Determinants of Air Travel Growth," *World Transport Policy & Practice* 7, no. 2 (2001): 28–37.

62. Goeldner and Ritchie, *Tourism,* 307.

63. Ibid., 127.

64. M. Snyder, "Senior Travelers: Active, Affluent, and On the Go," *HSMAI Marketing Review,* Winter 2000/2001, 39.

65. Travel Industry Association of America, Press Release, "TIA Traveler Sentiment Index Down Only Slightly in Second Quarter 2003," 2 May 2003, http://www.tia.org/Press/pressrec.asp?Item=272, 18 May 2003.

66. Ibid.

67. Travel Industry Association of America, Press Release, "Summer Travel Season Will Start Off Slow and Gain Momentum; 2.5% Increase Expected by End," 14 May 2003,

http://www.tia.org/Press/pressrec.asp?Item=274, 18 May 2003.

68. "Better Insight into the Business Traveler Critical for the Industry's Success," *Hotel Online,* 18 September 2002, http://www.hotel-online.com/News/PR2002_3rd/Sept02_BizTravel.html, 18 May 2002.

69. "The Fed Says Economic Activity Remains Subdued," *The New York Times,* http://www.nytimes.com/aponline/business/AP-Economy.html, 5 March 2003.

70. J. Higley, "The Incredible Shrinking Booking Window," *Hotel & Motel Management,* 17 February 2003, http://www.hotel-motel.com/hotelmotel/article/articleDetail.jsp?id=47632, 5 March 2003.

71. R. Britton, Managing Director of Advertising, American Airlines, lecture at Cornell University School of Hotel Administration, 22 November 2002.

72. Ibid.

73. PricewaterhouseCoopers, Press Release, "Lodging Industry Demand Is Reset at a Lower Base," 24 February 2003, 1.

74. Colliers International Hotels, "Canadian Hotel Investment Report 2002: Moving Forward," 2.

75. Colliers International Hotels, "INNvestment Canada," Fourth Quarter 2002, 1.

76. PKF Consulting, "Monitoring Canada's Accommodation Industry during a Challenging Year—2003—The Impact of the Iraq War & SARS Quarter 1 2003 Results—Executive Summary," May 2003, 1–2, http://ftp.canadatourism.com/ctxUploads/en_publications/MCA2003.pdf, 16 May 2003.

77. C. A. Enz, and M. S. Taylor, "The Safety and Security of U.S. Hotels: A Post–September 11 Report," *Cornell Hotel and Restaurant Administration Quarterly* 43 (2) 2002.

78. T. Graves, "Standard & Poor's Industry Surveys: Lodging & Gaming," 6 February 2003, 1.

79. American Hotel & Lodging Association, "2002 Lodging Industry Profile," http://www.ahma.com/products_info_center_lip.asp, 18 May 2003.

80. Graves, "Standard & Poor's Industry Surveys: Lodging & Gaming," 1.

81. G. Galloway and J. Gray, "Hotel Workers Want E1 Guidelines Relaxed," *The Globe and Mail* (Toronto), 10 May 2003.

82. Graves, "Standard & Poor's Industry Surveys: Lodging & Gaming," 2.

83. American Hotel & Lodging Association, "2002 Lodging Industry Profile."

84. T. Powers and C. W. Barrows, *Introduction to the Hospitality Industry,* 245–255.

85. Goldman Sachs, "The Essentials of Lodging Investing," May 2003, 10.

86. American Hotel & Lodging Association, "2002 Lodging Industry Profile."

87. Smith Travel Research data, in Graves, "Standard & Poor's Industry Surveys: Lodging & Gaming," 6 February 2003, 3.

88. American Automobile Association, "Lodging Requirements & Diamond Ratings Guidelines," http://www.aaanewsroom.net/Main.asp?CategoryID=9&SubCategoryID=22&ContentID=25&, 18 May 2003.

89. Ibid.

90. American Automobile Association, "2003 Five Diamond Winner List," http://www.aaanewsroom.net/Files/5Dwinners2003.doc, 18 May 2003.

91. Mobil Travel Guide, "Mobil Stars: Behind the Stars," http://www.mobiltravelguide.com/index.jsp?menu=rating_criteria, 18 May 2003.

92. Mobil Travel Guide, "Mobil Stars: Five Star Winners," http://mobiltravelguide.com/mtg_rating_criteria_fivestar.jsp, 18 May 2003.

93. Fairmont Hotels & Resorts Inc., *Annual Information Form,* 28 March 2002, 11.

94. American Automobile Association, "2003 Five Diamond Winner List."

95. Goldman Sachs, "The Essentials of Lodging Investing," May 2003, 12.

96. Ibid.

97. Ibid.

98. Ibid.

99. Graves, "Standard & Poor's Industry Surveys: Lodging & Gaming," 7.

100. Ibid.

101. Goldman Sachs, "The Essentials of Lodging Investing," 22.

102. R. S. Schmidgall, *Hospitality Industry Managerial Accounting,* 85.

103. Goldman Sachs, "The Essentials of Lodging Investing," 54.

104. Ibid., 56.

105. Smith Travel Research, in Goldman Sachs, "The Essentials of Lodging Investing," May 2003, 52.

106. PricewaterhouseCoopers, Press Release, "PricewaterhouseCoopers Forecasts Lodging Industry Expenses Will Rise in 2003," January 3, 2003, http://www.pwcglobal.com/extweb/ncpressrelease.nsf/docid/8C2AEB4032E1791385256CBC004952D4?OpenDocument, 19 May 2003.

107. PricewaterhouseCoopers, Press Release, "Lodging Industry Will Save $3.4 Billion in 2002 as a Result of Immediate Cost-Cutting Measures Taken in Late 2001," 14 January 2002, http://www.pwcglobal.com/extweb/ncpressrelease.nsf/DocID/659B7C814B4047B885256B730063B7E2, 19 May 2003.

108. Powers and Barrows, *Introduction to the Hospitality Industry,* 313–314.

109. The Hospitality Research Group, PKF Consulting, *Trends in the Hotel Industry USA Edition 2001,* 64.

110. Powers and Barrows, *Introduction to the Hospitality Industry,* 275.

111. Graves, "Standard & Poor's Industry Surveys: Lodging & Gaming," 17.

112. P. Kotler, *A Framework for Marketing Management,* 2nd ed. (Upper Saddle River, N.J.: Prentice Hall, 2003), 222.

113. Standard and Poor's, "Stock Reports: Starwood Hotels & Resorts," 21 September 2002, 2.

114. Hyatt Corporation, http://www.hyatt.com/corporate/hyatt/index.jhtml?ssnav=0, 19 May 2003.

115. Marriott, http://marriott.com/corporateinfo/glance.asp#mhrs, 19 May 2003.

116. Sheraton, http://www.webeventplanner.com/directory/sheratongatewaysfairport and http://www.starwood.com/sheraton, 19 May 2003.

117. The Wall Street Transcript, "CEO of Fairmont Hotels & Resorts Provides a Sense of the Health and the Outlook for Large Luxury Hotels," http://www.twst.com/notes/articles/pah209.html, 14 November 2002.

118. W. A. Rutes, R. H. Penner, and L. Adams, *Hotel Design Planning & Development* (New York: W. W. Norton & Company, 2001), 153.

119. Graves, "Standard & Poor's Industry Surveys: Lodging & Gaming," 9.

120. Rutes, Penner, and Adams, *Hotel Design,* 28.

121. Yankelovich Partners, *National Business Travel Monitor 2002,* 10 May 2002, 75–76.

122. Goldman Sachs, "The Essentials of Lodging Investing," 73.

123. B. McDonough et al., *Building Type Basics for Hospitality Facilities* (2001), 6.

124. Rutes, Penner, and Adams, *Hotel Design,* 26.

125. Ibid.; McDonough, *Building Type Basics for Hospitality Facilities,* 6, 52.

126. P. Bhatia, "Known for Their Good Looks, Hipster Hotels Trim Upkeep," *The Wall Street Journal,* 7 March 2003.

127. Marriott, http://marriott.com/corporateinfo/glance.asp#mhrs, 19 May 2003.

128. Fairmont Hotels & Resorts Inc., *Fairmont Hotels & Resorts 2002 Annual Report,* 2, 21.

129. Ibid., 19.

130. From a branded perspective, the company is publicly known as "Fairmont Hotels & Resorts"; from a legal perspective, the hotel management company is "Fairmont Hotels Inc." or "Fairmont."

131. Fairmont Hotels & Resorts, Press Release, "Fairmont Hotels & Resorts Inc. Completes Coal Harbour Land Sale," 4 March 2003, http://ir.thomsonfn.com/InvestorRelations/PubNewsStory.aspx?partner=Mzg0TlRVd05BPT1QJFkEQUALSTO&product=MzgwU1ZJPVAkWQEQUALSTOEQUALSTO&storyId=85018, 18 May 2003.

132. Fairmont.com, "Investor Relations," http://ir.thomsonfn.com/InvestorRelations/StockQuote.aspx?product=MzgwU1ZJPVAkWQEQUALSTOEQUALSTO&partner=Mzg0TlRVd05FRT1QJFkEQUALSTO, 18 May 2003.

133. Fairmont Hotels & Resorts, Press Release, "Fairmont Hotels & Resorts Inc. Completes Acquisition of the Fairmont Copley Plaza Boston," http://ir.thomsonfn.com/InvestorRelations/PubNewsStory.aspx?partner=Mzg0TlRVd05BPT1QJFkEQUALSTO&product=MzgwU1ZJPVAkWQEQUALSTOEQUALSTO&storyId=85012, 18 May 2003.

134. Legacy Hotels Real Estate Investment Trust, *Legacy Hotels Real Estate Investment Trust Annual Report 1997,* 1.

135. Ibid.

136. Ibid.

137. Canadian Institute of Public and Private Real Estate Companies, "Report on REITs: An Introduction to Real Estate Investment Trusts," 28 August 2002, B4.

138. Legacy Hotels Real Estate Investment Trust, *Legacy Hotels Real Estate Investment Trust Annual Report 1997,* 1.

139. Ibid., 24.

140. Legacy Hotels Real Estate Investment Trust, Press Release, "Legacy Hotels Real Estate Investment Trust Announces Changes to Management Structure," 7 March 2003 http://micro.newswire.ca/releases/March2003/07/c8285.html/54430-0, 18 May 2003.

141. Goldman Sachs, "FHR Takes Major Step in Right Direction—Eliminates Shared Mgmt with Legacy REIT," 9 March 2003, 1.

142. Legacy Hotels Real Estate Investment Trust, *Legacy Hotels Real Estate Investment Trust Annual Report 2002,* 34.

143. Toronto Stock Exchange, http://tse-cdnx.com/HttpController?GetPage=CustomQuoteForLGYPage&SelectedSymbol=LGY.UN, 18 May 2003.

144. The Fairmont Learning Organization, "My Fairmont/Service Plus," September 2001, 11.

145. Ibid.

146. Ibid., 1, 10.

147. Fairmont Hotels & Resorts Inc., *Fairmont Hotels & Resorts 2002 Annual Report,* 7.

148. Fairmont Hotels & Resorts Inc., *Annual Information Form,* 28 March 2002, 17.

149. Fairmont Hotels & Resorts Inc., *Fairmont Hotels & Resorts 2002 Annual Report,* 4–6, 18–19.

150. Interview with M. Jerry Patava, Chief Financial Officer, Fairmont Hotels & Resorts, 9 January 2003.

151. Fairmont Hotels & Resorts Inc., *Fairmont Hotels & Resorts 2002 Annual Report,* 6.

152. M. S. Lerner, "Chains to Watch," *Hotels,* May 2002, http://www.hotelsmag.com/0502/0502sr.html, 17 May 2003.

153. Interview with Chris J. Cahill, President and Chief Operating Officer, Fairmont Hotels & Resorts, 8 January 2003.

154. Fairmont Hotels & Resorts Inc., *Fairmont Hotels & Resorts 2002 Annual Report,* 6–7, 38; Webber, Sara Perez, "The Future of Fairmont," *Travel Agent,* 23 September 2002.

155. Ibid., 7.

156. Ibid., 5.

157. Cisco.com, "Cisco Systems and Fairmont Hotels & Resorts Offer Best-of-Breed High-Speed Connectivity to Guests," 12 November 2001, http://newsroom.cisco.com/dlls/corp_111201c.html, 17 May 2003.

158. Fairmont Hotels & Resorts Inc., *Fairmont Hotels & Resorts 2002 Annual Report,* 15.

159. Interview with Chris J. Cahill, President and Chief Operating Officer, Fairmont Hotels & Resorts, 7 January 2003.

160. Presentation by Chris J. Cahill, President and Chief Operating Officer, Fairmont Hotels & Resorts, to Cornell University School of Hotel Administration, 6 September 2002.

161. The Fairmont Learning Organization, "My Fairmont/Service Plus," September 2001, 9.

162. Fairmont Hotels & Resorts Inc., *Annual Information Form,* 28 March 2002, 20.

163. Fairmont Hotels & Resorts Inc., *Annual Information Form 2003,* 19; Fairmont.com, "Welcome to the Fairmont Olympic Hotel, Seattle," http://www.fairmont.com/FA/en/CDA/Home/Hotels/AboutHotel/CDHotelHomePage/0,2993,property%25255Fseq%253D100142,00.html, 16 October 2003.

164. Presentation by Jennifer L. Chase, Executive Director of Business Development, Fairmont Hotels & Resorts, at Cornell University School of Hotel Administration, 29 January 2003.

165. Interview with Chris J. Cahill, President & Chief Operating Officer, Fairmont Hotels & Resorts, 7 January 2003.

166. Presentation by Jennifer L. Chase.

167. Ibid. Fairmont averages 59.9 square feet of meeting space per guest room, while Hyatt averages 69.5 square feet and Westin averages 67.1; the next closest competitor is Ritz-Carlton, with 56.3.

168. Ibid.

169. Lerner, "Chains to Watch."

170. Fairmont Hotels & Resorts Inc., *Fairmont Hotels & Resorts 2002 Annual Report,* 13.

171. Ibid., 27.

172. Interview with Chris J. Cahill.

173. DeltaHotels.com, "Delta Hotels: A Canadian Hotel Management Success Story," http://www.deltahotels.com/about, 18 May 2003.

174. Fairmont Hotels & Resorts Inc., *Fairmont Hotels & Resorts 2002 Annual Report,* 23.

175. Fairmont Hotels & Resorts Inc., *Annual Information Form 2003,* 23.

176. Fairmont.com, "Fairmont Hotels & Resorts, Inc.; Directors & Senior Officers," http://www.fairmonthotels.com/fatt.asp, 16 May 2003.

177. Hospitality.net, "Strategic Partner of Fairmont Hotels & Resorts Inc. Announces Management Changes," 10 March 2003, http://www.hospitalitynet.org/news/All_Latest_News/4015089.print, 16 May 2003.

178. Fairmont.com, "Fairmont Hotels & Resorts, Inc.; Directors & Senior Officers," http://www.fairmonthotels.com/fatt.asp, 16 May 2003.

179. Hospitality.net, "Strategic Partner of Fairmont Hotels & Resorts Inc. Announces Management Changes."

180. Fairmont.com, "Fairmont Hotels & Resorts, Inc.; Directors & Senior Officers," http://www.fairmonthotels.com/cahill.asp, 16 May 2003.

181. *National Hotel Executive,* "Leadership Profile: Chris J. Cahill," http://www.hotelexecutive.com/profiles/Executives/50.asp, 16 May 2003.

182. Ibid.

183. C. Hendsill and M. Gostelow, "People Matters: Employee Recruitment and Retention Tactics," *Hotels,* March 2000, http://www.hotelsmag.com/0300/0300pti.html, 16 May 2003.

184. Fairmont.com, "Fairmont Hotels & Resorts, Inc.; Directors & Senior Officers," http://www.fairmonthotels.com/johnston.asp, 16 May 2003.

185. Fairmont.com, "Fairmont Hotels & Resorts, Inc.; Directors & Senior Officers," http://www.fairmonthotels.com/patava.asp, 16 May 2003.

186. Hospitality.net, "Strategic Partner of Fairmont Hotels & Resorts Inc. Announces Management Changes"; Goldman Sachs, "Fairmont Hotels & Resorts: Recent Weakness Provides Sound Entry Point for Long-Term Investors," 25 November 2002, 2.

187. CFO.com, "Former Investment Banker Says It's Best for Aspiring CFOs to Work Both Sides of the Capital Markets Street," 16 November 2001, http://www.cfo.com/printarticle/0,5317,5830|,00.html, 16 May 2003.

188. Ibid.

189. Fairmont.com, "Fairmont Hotels & Resorts, Inc.; Directors & Senior Officers," http://www.fairmonthotels.com/storey.asp, 16 May 2003.

190. Fairmont.com, "Fairmont Hotels & Resorts, Inc.; Directors & Senior Officers," http://www.fairmonthotels.com/aubrey.asp, 16 May 2003.

191. Ibid.

192. Hospitality.net, "Strategic Partner of Fairmont Hotels & Resorts Inc. Announces Management Changes."

193. Dow Jones Business News, "Legacy Hotels REIT Names Neil J. Labatte Pres, CEO," 7 March 2003, http://216.239.37.100/search?q=cache:H_l6btwifXsC:biz.yahoo.com/djus/030307/1749000696_1.html+neil+labatte+fairmont+dow+jones&hl=en&ie=UTF-8, 16 May 2003.

194. Fairmont.com, "Fairmont Hotels & Resorts, Inc.; Directors & Senior Officers," http://www.fairmonthotels.com/labatte.asp, 16 May 2003.

195. DeltaHotels.com, "Leadership Team," http://www.deltahotels.com/about/pye.html, 17 May 2003.

196. Fairmont Hotels & Resorts & Legacy Hotels, "Management Directory," January 2003.

197. LodgingNews.com, "75 Profiles in Leadership: William R. Fatt, Chairman/CEO, Fairmont Hotels & Resorts," http://www.lodgingnews.com/lodgingmag/2000_08/2000_08_46.asp, 16 May 2003; Fairmont Hotels & Resorts & Legacy Hotels, "Management Directory."

198. Fairmont Hotels & Resorts & Legacy Hotels, "Management Directory."

199. Ibid.

200. Ibid.

201. The Fairmont Learning Organization, Handbook, "My Fairmont/Service Plus," September 2001, 3.

202. Legacy Hotels Real Estate Investment Trust, *Legacy Hotels Real Estate Investment Trust Annual Report 2002,* 21.

203. Interview with Vineet Gupta, Executive Director of Technology (now Vice President of Technology), Fairmont Hotels & Resorts, 25 November 2002.

204. B. Brewin, "Hotel Chain Becomes Its Own Service Provider," *Computerworld,* 15 October 2001, http://www.computerworld.com/managementtopics/xsp/story/0,10801,64752,00.html, 18 May 2003.

205. Interview with Vineet Gupta.

206. Ibid.

207. Interview with Serge Simard, Executive Director of Food and Beverage, Fairmont Hotels & Resorts, 10 January 2003.

208. Wyndham Hotels & Resorts, http://www.wyndham.com/search/main.wnt, 19 May 2003.

209. Internet Travel News, "Fairmont Joins Avendra," 26 January 2001, http://www.internettravelnews.com/itn/news_display.asp?id=1353, 9 December 2002.

210. WiredHotelier.com. "Fairmont Hotels & Resorts Joins Hospitality Procurement Venture with Marriott, Hyatt, Bass, and ClubCorp," 24 January 2001, http://www.wiredhotelier.com/news/4006948.htm, 18 May 2003.

211. Interview with Vineet Gupta.

212. Interview with Carolyn Clark, Vice President of Human Resources, Fairmont Hotels & Resorts, 15 January 2003.

213. Interview with Melanie Wendeler, Director of Hotel Integration, Fairmont Hotels & Resorts, March 7, 2003.

214. Interview with Carolyn Clark.

215. Ibid.

216. Interview with Melanie Wendeler.

217. Ibid.

218. Ibid.

219. Fairmont Hotels & Resorts Inc., *Fairmont Hotels & Resorts 2002 Annual Report*, 18.

220. Interview with Chris J. Cahill.

221. Presentation by Bonnie Holbrook, Director of Corporate Human Resources, Fairmont Hotels & Resorts, 18 February 2003. Figures reported are in U.S. dollars unless otherwise noted.

222. Ibid.

223. Interview with Carolyn Clark.

224. Ibid.

225. Ibid.

226. Interview with Michael Kaile, Regional Vice President and General Manager, Fairmont Dubai, 8 March 2003; interview with Chris J. Cahill.

227. Presentation by Jennifer Chase.

228. Presentation by Bonnie Holbrook.

229. Ibid.

230. Interview with Carolyn Clark.

231. The Fairmont Learning Organization, Handbook, "My Fairmont/Service Plus."

232. Presentation by Bonnie Holbrook.

233. Interview with Carolyn Clark.

234. T. Tritch, Theresa, "Fairmont's Talent Strategy Delivers Results," *Gallup Management Journal*, 13 March 2003, http://gmj.gallup.com/op/article.asp?i=325, 27 March 2003.

235. Ibid.; interview with Carolyn Clark.

236. Presentation by Bonnie Holbrook; interview with Carolyn Clark.

237. Tritch, "Fairmont's Talent Strategy Delivers Results."

238. Interview with Carolyn Clark.

239. Tritch, "Fairmont's Talent Strategy Delivers Results."

240. Presentation by Jennifer Chase.

241. Presentation by Bonnie Holbrook; Tritch, "Fairmont's Talent Strategy Delivers Results."

242. J. D. Power & Associates, http://www.jdpower.com/travel/jdpa_ratings/jdpa_ratings.asp, 27 March 2003.

243. Presentation by Jennifer Chase.

244. Marcia Bogue, Memo, Director of Guest Satisfaction, Fairmont Hotels & Resorts, "October Guest Commentary," 25 November 2002.

245. Interview with Carolyn Clark.

246. Presentation by Bonnie Holbrook.

247. Fairmont Hotels & Resorts Inc., *Fairmont Hotels & Resorts 2002 Annual Report*, 64.

248. Interview with Brian Richardson, Vice President of Brand Marketing and Communications, Fairmont Hotels & Resorts, 17 February 2003.

249. Interview with Kyla McCrae, Human Resources Recruiter, Fairmont Hotels & Resorts, 26 November 2002.

250. Fairmont.com, "Employment," http://www.fairmont.com/FA/en/CDA/Home/AboutFairmont/CDEmployment/0,2951,code%25255Ftype%253DEMP%2526category%25255Ftype%253Dbrand%25255Fcopy%2526brand%25255Fseq%253D1000011,00.html, 18 May 2003; *Canada's Top 100 Employers*, online at http://www.canadastop100.com, 18 May 2003; Fairmont Hotels & Resorts Inc., *Fairmont Hotels & Resorts 2002 Annual Report*, 17.

251. DeltaHotels.com, "Delta Hotels: A Canadian Hotel Management Success Story," http://www.deltahotels.com/about, 18 May 2003; Fairmont Hotels & Resorts Inc., *Fairmont Hotels & Resorts 2002 Annual Report*, 17.

252. S. P. Webber, "The Future of Fairmont," Travel Agent, 23 September 2002; Fairmont Hotels & Resorts Inc., *Fairmont Hotels & Resorts 2002 Annual Report*, 5; interview with Brian Richardson.

253. Interview with Brian Richardson.

254. Fairmont Hotels & Resorts Inc., *Fairmont Hotels & Resorts 2002 Annual Report*, 5; Fairmont Hotels & Resorts, Press Release, "Fairmont Gold—A Hotel within a Hotel," 2003.

255. Fairmont Hotels & Resorts, http://www.fairmont.com/FA/en/CDA/Home/Secure/Reservations/CDRMRsvnSearchResults/0%2C3045%2C%2C00.html, 20 May 2003.

256. Ibid.

257. Webber, "The Future of Fairmont."

258. Ibid.

259. Fairmont Hotels & Resorts Inc., *Fairmont Hotels & Resorts 2002 Annual Report*, 8.

260. Ibid., 5.

261. Interview with Brian Richardson.

262. Fairmont Hotels & Resorts Inc., *Annual Information Form*, 28 March 2002, 29; interview with Sean Taggart, Director of Strategic Analysis, Fairmont Hotels & Resorts, 12 December 2002.

263. Fairmont Hotels & Resorts, Press Release, "Fairmont President's Club," 2003.

264. Ibid.

265. Interview with Brian Richardson.

266. Fairmont Hotels & Resorts Inc., *Fairmont Hotels & Resorts 2001 Annual Report*, 10.

267. Interview with Sean Taggart.

268. Webber, "The Future of Fairmont."

269. G. Haussman, "Fairmont Debuts Internet-Based E-Business Strategy," *Hotel Interactive*, http://www.hotelinteractive.com/news/articleView.asp?articleID=1294, 3 December 2002.

270. Interview with Brian Richardson.

271. Interview with Sean Taggart.

272. Interview with Brian Richardson.

273. Webber, "The Future of Fairmont."

274. Ibid.

275. Interview with Suanne Zankowski, Director of Global Sales Solutions, Fairmont Hotels & Resorts, 15 January 2003.

276. Interview with Ian Wilson, Executive Director of Distribution Management (now Hotel Manager, Fairmont Royal York), 15 January 2003.

277. Ibid.
278. Hotel Online, "Fairmont Hotels & Resorts Plans to Deploy Delphi Multi-Property Edition v9.1 to Connect and Cross-Sell 40+ Properties," 19 June 2003, http://hotel-online.com/News/PR2003_2nd/Jun03_NewmarketFairmont.html, 7 August 2003.
279. Kotler, *A Framework for Marketing Management*, 223.
280. Interview with Brian Richardson.
281. Fairmont.com, "Partners & Programs," http://www.fairmont.com/FA/en/CDA/Home/AboutFairmont/CDPartners/0,2952,code%25255Ftype%253DPRPGM%2526brand%25255Fcode%253DFA%2526loyalty%25255Fcode%253DPRES%2526brand%25255Fseq%253D1000011,00.html, 20 May 2003.
282. Presentation by Brian Richardson.
283. Fairmont.com, "Packages & Promotions." Package expired 31 December 2003.
284. Interview with Brian Richardson.
285. Interview with Thatcher Brown, Director of Business Development, 28 March 2003.
286. Ibid.
287. Fairmont Hotels & Resorts Inc., *Fairmont Hotels & Resorts 2002 Annual Report*, 27.
288. Ibid., 3.
289. Ibid., 35.
290. Ibid., 36.
291. Ibid., 3.
292. Ibid.
293. Ibid.
294. Ibid.
295. Ibid.
296. Ibid., 2.
297. Ibid.
298. Ibid., 3.
299. M. Rietbrock and D. Richter, "SalomonSmithBarney: Fairmont Hotels & Resorts: Initiation of Coverage," 24 June 2002, 12.
300. Fairmont Hotels & Resorts, Press Release, "Fairmont Hotels & Resorts Inc. Completes Coal Harbour Land Sale."
301. Legacy Hotels Real Estate Investment Trust, *Legacy Hotels Real Estate Investment Trust Annual Report 2002*, 1.
302. Fairmont Hotels & Resorts Inc., *Fairmont Hotels & Resorts 2002 Annual Report*, 3.
303. Legacy Hotels Real Estate Investment Trust, *Legacy Hotels Real Estate Investment Trust Annual Report 2002*, 3.
304. Ibid., 7, 25.
305. G. Mifsud, "Raymond James: Checking into the Lodging Sector," 15 October 2003, 23–24.
306. P. Keung, "CIBC: Fairmont Hotels & Resorts Inc. Reports Strong 4Q; Maintain Thesis As FHR Well Positioned in 2003," 3 February 2003, 1.
307. Webber, "The Future of Fairmont."

APPENDIX 1: FHR CONSOLIDATED BALANCE SHEET AT DECEMBER 31, 2002, AND DECEMBER 31, 2001

	As at December 31 (in millions of U.S. dollars)	
	2002	2001
Assets		
Current assets		
Cash and cash equivalents	$ 49.0	$ 52.7
Accounts receivable	47.0	48.2
Inventory	12.5	11.6
Prepaid expenses and other	10.9	8.8
	$ 119.4	$ 121.3
Investments in partnerships and corporations	68.9	58.8
Investment in Legacy Hotels REIT	96.4	56.4
Investments in land held for sale	88.8	92.1
Property and equipment	1,441.1	1,261.9
Goodwill	123.0	106.0
Intangible assets	201.7	149.8
Other assets and deferred charges	83.7	75.1
	$ 2,223.0	$ 1,921.4
Liabilities		
Current liabilities		
Accounts payable and accrued liabilities	$ 105.7	$ 109.1
Taxes payable	5.3	2.1
Dividends payable	2.4	1.6
Current portion of long-term debt	72.3	94.5
	$ 185.7	$ 207.3
Other liabilities	78.4	74.4
Long-term debt	463.2	245.2
Future income taxes	96.4	64.1
Non-controlling interest	—	25.0
	$ 823.7	$ 616.0
Shareholders' Equity		
Common shares	$ 1,191.5	$ 1,162.4
Contributed surplus	141.9	142.4
Foreign currency translation adjustments	27.4	20.2
Retained earnings (deficit)	38.5	(19.6)
	1,399.3	1,305.4
	$ 2,223.0	$ 1,921.4

Source: Fairmont Hotels & Resorts Inc., *Fairmont Hotels & Resorts 2002 Annual Report,* p. 48. Note that only two years history of Fairmont Hotels & Resorts balance sheets are provided here. The balance sheet for 2000, presented in the Fairmont Hotels & Resorts Annual Report 2001, includes assets and liabilities from Canadian Pacific Limited (CPL), as this was before the demerging of the company into five independent companies. As this balance sheet is not comparable, it is not included here.

APPENDIX 2: FHR CONSOLIDATED STATEMENT OF INCOME FOR YEARS ENDING DECEMBER 31, 2002, AND DECEMBER 31, 2001

	For the Years Ending December 31 (in millions of U.S. dollars)		
	2002	**2001**	**2000**
Revenues			
Hotel ownership operations	$ 516.6	$ 489.6	$ 464.7
Management operations	36.1	34.3	41.8
Real estate	37.9	13.4	10.2
Operating revenues	590.6	537.3	516.7
Other revenues from managed and franchised properties	27.7	29.4	25.2
	618.3	566.7	541.9
Expenses			
Hotel ownership operations	367.9	358.8	320.8
Management operations	15.7	18.6	14.6
Real estate	26.4	15.5	10.5
Operating expenses	410.0	392.9	345.9
Other expenses from managed and franchised properties	27.7	29.4	25.2
	437.7	422.3	371.1
Income from investments and other	17.7	18.7	24.3
Operating income before undernoted items	198.3	163.1	195.1
Amortization	52.4	50.7	40.6
Other (income) expenses, net	(4.9)	10.1	10.7
Reorganization and corporate expenses	2.2	156.9	65.7
Interest expense, net	19.1	69.6	44.5
Income (loss) before income tax expense (recovery), non-controlling interest, goodwill amortization and discontinued operations	129.5	(124.2)	33.6
Income tax expense (recovery)			
Current	12.0	21.1	42.5
Future	23.8	(120.7)	(67.4)
	35.8	(99.6)	(24.9)
Non-controlling interest	1.2	1.1	4.2
Income (loss) before goodwill amortization and discontinued operations	92.5	(25.7)	54.3
Goodwill amortization, net of taxes	—	2.5	1.9
Income (loss) from continuing operations	92.5	(28.2)	52.4
Discontinued operations	—	923.9	1,065.9
Net income of the year	92.5	895.7	1,118.3
Preferred share dividends	—	(5.4)	(8.2)
Net income available to common shareholders	$ 92.5	$ 890.3	$ 1,110.1
Weighted average number of common shares outstanding (in millions)			
Basic	78.4	78.9	79.5
Diluted	79.7	79.0	79.8
Basic earnings (loss) per share			
Income (loss) from continuing operations	1.18	(0.36)	0.66
Discontinued operations	—	11.71	13.41
Net income	1.18	11.28	13.96

Source: Fairmont Hotels & Resorts Inc., *Fairmont Hotels & Resorts 2002 Annual Report,* p. 50.

4

Living a Vision at Hillerman Hotels

Sitting in the fashionable Café Lupe, an upscale restaurant owned by the company Carl Gregg worked for, were the company's owners, investors, and top corporate personnel. Hillerman Hotels, a wholly owned subsidiary of the parent Hillerman Enterprises, was headquartered in Phoenix, Arizona, with a portfolio of over a dozen midscale and upscale hotels and three trendy upscale restaurants. The hotel group was gathered for one of its irregular, informal celebrations of success. As Gregg, the executive vice president of operations, raised his glass to join in the merriment, he wondered to himself whether his facial expression gave away the feelings he was suppressing. Gregg was torn—earlier in the day this same group discussed the possibility that the Westward Hilton and Towers, the only property in the Hillerman portfolio he had personally ever run as a general manager, might be sold. An inquiry from a REIT (real estate investment trust[1]) as to the property's availability had prompted the discussion.

The Hillerman Hotels subsidiary owned and managed all of its hotels, branding them with a variety of different midpriced and upper-priced hotel franchisers. The portfolio had grown over a twelve-year period to around a dozen properties at any given time. The number wasn't stable because the

Written by Cathy A. Enz of Cornell University and David L. Corsun of the University of Nevada–Las Vegas. This case is reprinted with permission of the *Case Research Journal*. This case was written as the basis for class discussion. The events described are not intended to illustrate either effective or ineffective management practices. The names of the organization and its members have been disguised at the request of the owners and investors. The affiliation with the Hilton Brand was not altered.

corporate strategy was to take advantage of opportunities to buy undervalued, underperforming properties and turn them around. Each hotel was operated as a fully self-sufficient operation. When the opportunity to sell a property at healthy profit presented itself, Hillerman's management team had, in the past, generally taken advantage of the market opportunity. With the exception of a second Phoenix property managed as an independent (unbranded) hotel and acquired in 1995 to be the group's flagship, no property was supposed to be untouchable. Perhaps coincidentally, since Gregg had moved into his corporate position back in 1992, only one Hillerman property had been sold. The portfolio had remained relatively stable, and its owners or investors had never broached selling the Westward. The investors were reaping healthy benefits from the portfolio.

Gregg knew that Kerry Glenn, whose money was behind Hillerman Hotels, felt as strongly about the Westward and the people who worked there as he did. Glenn owned the largest share of Hillerman Hotels as well as a major share of the parent company. Her visibility in the local community as a patron of the arts and civic leader was legendary. While Glenn was attached to the Westward, Gregg also understood that it was impossible for every decision to equally benefit owners, customers, and employees. He knew there were times when decisions would have an obvious ill effect on one group of stakeholders. Was the possible sale of the Westward Hotel one of those decisions? Was he too attached to this particular hotel because he had been its general manager when Hillerman bought it out of bankruptcy at the end of 1989? Gregg's thoughts drifted back nearly ten years to the year before he arrived in Phoenix.

PROJECT PERSPECTIVE

Carl Gregg grew up in the hospitality industry. He worked as a teen in his family's restaurant in Buffalo, New York. Through his twenties and thirties, Gregg used his restaurant experience to move into the hotel side of the industry, starting out in the food and beverage area. Over the course of about twenty years, he worked his way across the eastern half of the country, gaining the experience required to be a hotel general manager (GM). Prior to joining Hillerman, Gregg had over five years of experience as a GM. When Hillerman hired Gregg in 1988, he was brought on in a consulting role. Specifically, Gregg did project work for Hillerman in the Midwest, solving previously identified business problems.

Project work gave him an opportunity to view an operation from a very different vantage point from when he was a GM. Being removed from the day-to-day operation, Gregg was able to see aspects of the business that might be less clear to the manager occupied with running the entire operation. The short-term nature of his project assignments and their focus on specific problems with everything else removed from consideration allowed Gregg the liberty of a broader, big-picture perspective. He attributed two previous projects and experiences to radically shaping his feelings about the business when he entered the Westward.

The first project was a small Chicago hotel in which the employees were considering unionization. When Gregg arrived he found an all-white management staff and an almost all-black employee population and no interaction between the two. On his first visit he went to the cafeteria and listened to employees. Through informal conversations he learned which issues bothered the employees. The problems were mostly small things that could easily be remedied—things like the quality of employee meals. However, the senior management of the hotel was unaware of these employee issues because they had separated themselves from employees and formed a tightly knit group. The management never ate in the employee cafeteria and spent very little time in communication with the staff. Gregg did not make radical changes at this hotel, but he did listen carefully to the employees and spent time with them. In describing this experience, Gregg said it "taught me that managers devalue others when they overvalue themselves. I discovered the importance of creating a work environment that celebrates, nurtures, and values people. It is important to create a business environment in which every job and every employee is treated with dignity and respect. People want to care, but this work environment forced the workers to hide themselves."

The impact the work environment has on the individual came home to Gregg one evening when he drove past a schoolyard and spotted one of the hotel's employees playing basketball. As he watched the game he noticed that this worker, whom Gregg knew to be slow, uncooperative, and lacking initiative, was leading a group of his friends in a fast-paced and cooperative team effort. Gregg wondered how this person could be so different outside the workplace. Perhaps, he thought, it's because the work environment doesn't give the worker permission to be himself. This thought stuck with Gregg. Before he left this hotel several months later, new management had been brought in and the union drive was defeated by a vote of 72–2. Gregg elected to move on rather than serve as the new general manager, although the job was offered to him.

Gregg's second experience taught him to truly value the guests' perspective and experiences. Living for ninety days in a hotel plagued with quality problems, Gregg was a guest of sorts himself and he spoke with other guests daily. During this assignment he rediscovered what he knew from childhood about committing to the satisfaction of the guest. "I grew up in the restaurant business, and my parents taught me to be close to the customer. It seems that when you become a manager you start to focus on how to manage versus how to live a commitment to customers." Rather than viewing guest concerns as problems, he discovered through interaction with customers that one could trust their experiences and get something valuable and satisfying from responding to their concerns. He also noticed that most customers were present in the hotel at very specific times in the morning and evening and these were the times it was most important for the manager to be available to talk with guests. An everyday commitment to listening to guests was one powerful way of committing to their satisfaction.

These projects gave Gregg a new way of thinking and feeling about the hotel business. He began to feel his way toward a new management philosophy, but the quality of his personal life was suffering. After a year of living on the road and away from his family, Gregg wanted a stable position. However, to become a general manager again was not very appealing to him. As a GM, he had grown tired of the frustrations that came with the job. He was tired of the long hours, the constant people problems, and the cyclical nature of the business. In bad times, even when he worked very hard, the overleveraged and overbuilt industry had conspired to make him feel bad about his performance. The main people problems were high turnover and a lack of commitment from staff who were not into what they were doing. He had felt frustration at his inability to get employees excited or committed in the past. Gregg learned a great deal from the project work that occupied his time, and he also knew he needed to make a change. His children and his wife needed him to be more present in their lives too.

ARRIVING AT THE WESTWARD

The Westward Hilton was bought out of bankruptcy when the previous owner was forced to sell the property. For nearly five years the hotel had been operating at a loss, and the property and the people who worked in it were depressed. The physical plant was in bad shape and no capital had been devoted to renovation and upkeep. When Hillerman purchased the hotel, Gregg was given the opportunity to become the Westward's general manager. Mostly because of his desire to settle in one place for a while, he took the assignment. Gregg also thought he might take advantage of this opportunity to put his evolving management philosophy into practice.

During his first visit to the hotel—prior to becoming GM—none of the managers greeted him. Gregg was placed in a Towers level (one of the three floors of rooms with a private concierge and other special services) suite with "a lot of stuff." He got

chocolates, cheese, and a vast array of amenities, but not a note or phone call from the management. His first impression was that the management of the hotel was not sensitive to what the guest might want, but had automatically assumed that more amenities in the sleeping room would satisfy the customer. "They were thinking more and more stuff rather than sincere and genuine care." Gregg observed that the Westward's management had a traditional command and control style. In addition, their beliefs statement was borrowed from Ritz Carlton Hotels, a chain of highly regarded luxury hotels (see Exhibit 1). In Gregg's opinion the hotel was trying to be something it was not, and the beliefs were not genuine.

Gregg arrived at the Westward with a deep belief that all hotel companies and their managers have a moral obligation to make the work experience a positive one. Throughout his career, he had experienced the dark side of the hotel business in which generations of negative conditioning and abusive behaviors justified managers' willingness to undervalue the people who clean rooms and sweep floors for a living. The managers in Chicago reminded him by their bad example that he must break down these beliefs. Deep inside, after years of experience in the business he was convinced that caring about employees could be profitable.

> I didn't arrive at the Westward with a strategic plan, just a new feeling. My project work taught me to get close to the customer and value the employees. I was determined to start by making a real emotional commitment to the hotel.

THE WESTWARD HILTON AND TOWERS

The Westward Hilton was a nine-year-old, thirteen-story, full-service hotel built in 1980. The hotel tower and attached lobby sat on 8.5 acres on a city block at the southeast corner of Camelback Drive and Northern Avenue in Phoenix. The hotel contained approximately 151,000 square feet, occupied by three hundred guest rooms, board and conference rooms, executive offices, a fitness center, and the main lobby area. The exterior of the hotel was reflective glass

EXHIBIT 1 — THE RITZ CARLTON GOLD STANDARDS

The Credo	The Ritz-Carlton Hotel is a place where the genuine care and comfort of our guests is our highest mission.
	We pledge to provide the finest personal service and facilities for our guests who will always enjoy a warm, relaxed, yet refined ambiance.
	The Ritz-Carlton experience enlivens the senses, instills well-being, and fulfills even the unexpressed wishes and needs of our guests.
Motto	We are Ladies and Gentlemen serving Ladies and Gentlemen.

Source: Ritz Carlton information that is printed by corporate headquarters on a small, laminated card that can be folded and placed in a wallet.

main lobby area was situated in a single-story, attached building that included the main entrance to the hotel, reception desk, guest services area, a lobby lounge, and a gift shop.

After several years of Hillerman's ownership, and substantial renovations, the hotel had 13,000 square feet of flexible meeting space, including fourteen salons and three ballrooms. The gift shop was leased month-to-month to a third party. The hotel also included a free-standing 8,000-square-foot restaurant. The interior finish of the lobby area primarily consisted of inlaid terrazzo pavers, a combination of painted drywall and vinyl wall coverings, and recessed and track incandescent lighting. A landscaped courtyard led to the Hilton's outdoor pool, hot tub, and sun deck. Directly off the lobby was a bright and airy southwestern style atrium finished in rich earth tones.

Each guest room included a full bath, a king or two queen beds, a chaise longue and ottoman, a work desk, an armoire, one or two nightstands, and three or four lamps. The standard guest rooms featured twenty-four-hour in-room dining, free cable channels with HBO, coffee/tea maker, minibar, alarm clock radio, card key access, PC phone line, modem hookup, oversized desk, and complimentary newspaper. Executive business rooms also included fax/copier machine, desk jet printer, VCR, two private phone lines

with speakerphone, and a calculator. The top three Towers floors offered a complimentary continental breakfast buffet every morning, hors d'oeuvres every evening, exclusive registration and checkout, business services, a cocktail honor bar, and video phone. Morning and evening maid service and nightly turndown service were also provided on these floors.

THE VISION THING

"What does this hotel want to be?" was a critical question for Gregg. He felt the previous management tried to make the hotel something it was not. But what was this hotel to become? This was clearly a critical question. By imitating the Malcolm Baldrige Award–winning Ritz Carlton Hotels' beliefs, the previous management was not focused on how to position this hotel. For Gregg's first three or four months, during their meetings the managers talked unendingly about the successful large convention hotel across the street. This hotel had a lounge and a constant flow of leisure and convention customers. The conversations all seemed to be variations of a "Gee, if we were only like them" theme.

Finally, Gregg had enough. The turning point came in one staff meeting when he told his staff the following:

> Let's not focus on what we are not.
> Focus on what we are. We don't have to
> be that hotel. Let's stop wishing we were
> that and start being this. Look, we are a
> small hotel—we don't want lots of
> groups. We should be providing a different product and service to a different
> customer. Look at all the problems they
> have. It is a noisy hotel with long lines.
> Do we want that? No! We can become
> the number one corporate FIT (frequent individual traveler) hotel in
> Phoenix. We are a small hotel, we can
> be warm and friendly, let's use what we
> have and make it work. Stop focusing
> on them. Focus on what we are and
> what we can become. We are going to
> take the high-end guest, focus on the
> FIT through uncompromising superior
> quality and extraordinary service. We

are going to actively listen to guests and employees, anticipate market needs, liberate ourselves from old ways of doing things, and provide a wonderful employee experience.

The job of envisioning a new future for this hotel was made possible by years of capital investments and support from the new owners. Capital was needed to position the hotel above the competition. The repositioning would not have been possible if Hillerman's owners had not been willing to invest in fully renovating the hotel with a clean, modern, and comfortable look. Exhibit 2 provides a summary of the capital improvement costs.

The restaurant was redesigned and reconstructed in 1991, three years after the hotel's purchase. The renovation was done at a cost of $1,800,000 (including furniture, fixtures, and equipment). It was expanded from its original structure and leased to an independent restaurant group that raised the visibility and prestige of the food and beverage operation. Gregg believed the restaurant operation was a powerful tool in repositioning the hotel.

The equal value and appreciation of the interests and needs of owners, customers, and employees was the foundation for the vision creation process, according to Gregg. Uninterrupted owner support, continued affiliation with a well-regarded hotel brand like Hilton, and management with a commitment to guest, employee, and owner satisfaction were essential.

The vision emerged in discussion with the senior management staff, but was not written down initially. According to Gregg, it was a change in thinking, first and foremost.

> We were going to become the best corporate hotel positioned at the top end, but I approached this vision by doing

EXHIBIT 2	RENOVATION AND CAPITAL IMPROVEMENTS

Year	Capital Improvement Costs
1991	$ 4,300,000
1992	$ 2,800,000
1993	$ 1,000,000
1994	$ 200,000

three things: living my values, constantly talking about our vision, and modeling the vision every day. The plan was shockingly devoid of systems or procedures. I felt it and was deeply into it. The hotel needed an identity in the minds of the employees, and my job was to bring a deep belief in what this hotel could become to these people. Leadership in my opinion is about believing so deeply that people don't doubt. I was more a Civil War leader than a World War II general. My agenda? Focus and model, focus and model. I just did what seemed right at the time.

Gregg's vision of what the Westward aspired to become was the precursor to the formal corporate vision of Hillerman Hotels and the foundation for the guiding principles that would follow. It was not until 1995, almost six years later and well into Gregg's tenure as corporate executive vice president of operations, that he formally fashioned the set of guiding principles that explicitly conveyed the essence of Hillerman Hotels and the Westward Hilton. The principles were taught company-wide. Managers, upon completing their initial training and orientation, were given a daily planner with a twenty-two-page insert titled "Our Daily Compass: Hillerman Hotels, Inc. Guide to Leadership and Management." Among other things, including the corporate vision and mission, the insert included the guiding principles.

1. Dignity—We value everyone equally and highly.

2. Values—We insist that values like honesty, trust, integrity, respect, and fairness determine our decisions.

3. Focus—We establish priorities and concentrate on doing the most important things first.

4. Achievement—We all give our best effort to ensure team success.

5. Balance—We strive to maintain a balance among employees, customers, and owners.

Back in 1989, Gregg also arrived at the simple statement, *the friendliest place to visit*. This was a vision that remained with him and came to guide all the hotels in the portfolio. Gregg explained the meaning of the vision as follows:

> In the future, our customers and peers will say that we are the friendliest place to visit. The relationship between our employees and our guests should resemble that of the relationship between two friends; this is the hospitality experience we wish to provide. We will achieve this vision when the customer experiences a total commitment from all of us to the friendliest customer service anywhere.

The mission statement, which followed from the vision, was captured in the phrase "Making people's lives better through business." Gregg noted that:

> We will achieve our vision by making our employees', customers', and owners' lives better. Employees' lives are made better by treating them with dignity, rewarding and recognizing their contributions to our success, and providing a safe, secure, flexible, and fun working environment. Customers' lives are made better by providing a safe environment, excellent service, friendliness, and that extra thoughtfulness that makes visiting the Westward like visiting a friend. Finally, we make our owners' lives better by ensuring that the hotel is a leader in return on investment, [a] positive influence on the local community and successful on a long-term basis. We aspire to be a role model for other companies in the service industry: admired for the support we provide to our employees, the friendly experience we provide to our customers, and the exceptional rewards and satisfaction we provide to our owners.

Gregg was determined that his vision would become more than the GM's platitudes, neither acted on by subordinates nor lived by the executive in charge. He wanted to live his principles and pass them on to his management team to help guide their actions. It was his desire that all the employees of the Westward share the vision, mission, and principles. He wanted to make being a part of the Westward Hilton a different work experience. For Gregg, the mutual success of owners and employees depended on the acceptance and practice of the vision. But Gregg knew that good practice required more than inspiration, it required good strategic thinking.

STRATEGIC PLANNING

"What's possible?" is the question Gregg used to guide the strategic planning process. He insisted that the major issue for strategic thinking was to focus on what could be. "Identifying and removing the barriers between what is and what's possible" is how he proceeded to develop the plan.

> Our strategic plan allowed us to dream, ponder, and wonder what could be. Most planning is from today forward in a process of increases over a five-year period to get to a point. This is "present-forward" thinking. In this approach you rely on "the plan" and history to drive your thinking.

In contrast, Gregg introduced a future-backward thinking approach in which one creates an almost impossible future position and determines what needs to be done to achieve this target.

> Our strategic planning forced us to change our operation by setting objectives that seemed impossible. By thinking about the future and backing into implementation it was quite clear that we couldn't get to what is possible by doing what we already were. Future-backward thinking forced the staff to rethink what they do. This approach could easily backfire if failure to reach the target resulted in getting the crap kicked out of you. Trust was critical and made possible by having all targets and incentives at levels below the strategic plan.

Gregg did not confuse strategic planning with making budget. There was no penalty for failure.

Sure there was tension. We wanted to create that. It's okay if they felt like they failed. It's not okay if they felt I felt like they failed. The difference is important. We seduced them into a future, but not at their expense.

Gregg willingly admitted that he had no idea of how to get the hotel to the possible targets. "All I knew is that we could only achieve these targets if we became more skilled and did things differently."

Reports, forecasts, and analysis were the hallmarks of this strategic thinking system. In housekeeping, for example, daily labor costs were tracked and scheduling of labor was carefully synchronized with forecasts. To produce loyalty and retention, revenue information was assembled on customer segments and product/service offerings were bundled to provide a carefully targeted customer with the products she or he desired. Gregg did not believe in yield management, a system in which pricing is adjusted based on projected occupancy and proximity to the desired reservation date in order to fill the hotel. He believed in establishing relationships with guests and focusing on rates that were consistent and of high value.

After setting a vision and defining the target guest, the Westward's business mix changed with a decrease in group business and an increase in the business transient segment. Mini profit and loss statements were created for each department so they could keep track of expenses as each day passed. Gregg believed that daily accountability versus monthly accountability was a key to enabling the staff to carefully and intelligently manage the business.

CLOSE TO THE CUSTOMER

Even five years later, many employees remembered Gregg for his vigilance—standing in the lobby Monday through Friday from 7:00 to 9:00 A.M. when most customers entered or exited the hotel. During his ten-hour-a-week commitment to being close to the customer he saw and solved problems. Gregg talked with guests and got a feel for what was and what was not working.

If three or four guests mentioned they didn't get a wake up call we could locate and solve that problem quickly. If people needed their bags carried in or employees needed a hand in performing a job I was there to help. My job was to expedite, to help both employees and customers.

Gregg accomplished two things by hanging out in the lobby. He had the contact with the customer he so valued and believed in, and he modeled the commitment to guest satisfaction. He also showed employees that he would and could do their jobs and that he was there to help them.

I decided when I arrived at the Westward that I was willing to invest ten hours of my 50–60 hours per week to contact with the guests. The key job of a manager is to lead, to set an example and to focus on real problems and activities.

Gregg's actions were important, but getting others to live the vision required improving business practices too. He started by taking the customer comment card questions provided by the corporate staff of Hilton and using them somewhat differently. At the time, the typical approach in the industry was to have customer comment cards in the sleeping rooms, and few customers ever responded. When customers did respond, the hotel or guest mailed the cards directly to the brand's corporate headquarters, where the corporate staff provided a tracking service as part of the fees attached to brand affiliation. Problem issues were then identified, and monthly or quarterly reports were passed back to the GM, management company, or owners of an individual hotel. General managers then chose to send a letter or call the dissatisfied customer and apologize or offer some form of service recovery. Some hotel chains responded from the corporate headquarters and the individual hotels never received the comment card information.

At the Westward, Gregg made small but significant modifications in the existing system. First, customers were asked to complete the cards at checkout, substantially increasing the completed responses from 2–3 percent when he became GM to 75 percent of all guests. A core of forty questions was put into ten sets of four questions, with one set per comment card. The cards were randomly distributed so all forty questions were responded to by multiple guests. Because they included only four questions, scored on a seven-point scale where 1 = poor and 7 = excellent, the guests completed the cards in ten to fifteen seconds while waiting for their folios to print. The cards were then entered and tracked through the property management system, and reports were created daily. The customer tracking report was provided to management, but also posted in the employee gathering places for all employees to view. A sample of the Daily Guest Comment Report is shown in Exhibit 3. Daily huddles, or brief five- to ten-minute meetings at the beginning or end of a shift, were used to share the survey results with employees. As Gregg noted,

> We had been doing the survey for some time, but didn't realize the quantum improvement in the guest experience until we began sharing the guests' feedback with the people who were actually doing the work. Once we started showing people the results of the survey, they started making changes on their own. The improved scores were a direct reflection of team performance and they all wanted to succeed. The sharing of information tapped into the employees' basic desire to be whole and good. They wanted to fill the gap, and we did not need a program or process. It was magic. We gave people the information they needed to know and they did what needed to be done. There was no structure or guide. Just a belief that you give people information and they will set about fixing the problems. People love to close gaps. Evidence of our success lies in the data—96 percent of the guests indicated their intent to return and the repeat rate was 50 percent.

VALUING OTHERS

> Another strong, powerful part of our management philosophy was that you need to be willing to do what you ask of others. You can't expect the people to care anymore than you do. People

watch what you do. You lose ground if people can't trust you.

Gregg spent plenty of his time in the employee cafeteria and in the lobby with customers. These were lessons that his project days had brought home, and he put his learning to the test in his own hotel.

Gregg's human resource approach was deeply rooted in his belief in the dignity of all employees regardless of position or background. In describing his approach, he said:

> Human dignity was the most important principle for managing. My philosophy was that everyone must be treated with respect and given opportunities to learn and grow. A manager's highest priority is to treat her or his employees with dignity. Employees, customers, and owners are all linked together and excellent service and exceptional facilities are essential to compete, but something more is required to truly win. That something extra is the realization that keeping the customer is entirely in the hands of the employees. Each job and task and each person in the hotel is important and deserving of respect. I believe in nurturing the entrepreneurial spirit in everyone—whether the general manager, valet attendant, kitchen steward, or front desk. All people in the workplace perform better when treated with dignity.

Gregg realized that in the Phoenix market good service and quality facilities were a minimum expectation of customers. Excellent service was taken for granted, and the competition could deliver just as easily as the Westward could. Given this competitive environment, the question was, what could the Westward do to attract and retain customers over time? For Gregg, the answer was to build a strong system of rewards for the employees. "The opportunity for advancement and bettering oneself must be available to each employee. Satisfied employees create satisfied guests, and satisfied guests return and remain loyal."

The philosophy behind the design of the wage and benefit system fit with Gregg's notion that dignity was important. He said:

EXHIBIT 3	GUEST COMMENT DAILY REPORT

Today's Performance Metrics

TODAY'S % CARDS/W RM#S = 45.6%
TODAY'S CHECK OUT = 68
TODAY'S TOTAL CARDS = 35
TODAY'S % OF RETURN = 51.5%
TODAY'S RIO CHARGES = 1,384
TODAY'S RIO PER OCC ROOM = $4.86

**WESTWARD HILTON
GUEST COMMENT
DAILY REPORT
DATE: 1-26-97**

**Period to Date (PTD)
Performance**

PTD CHECK CUT = 1,401
PTD TOTAL CARDS = 549
PTD % OF RETURN = 39.2%
PTD RIO CHARGES = 23,249
PTD RIO PER OCC RM = $3.70

Return Again as %	Today Total Score	PTD Total Score 94.92%	Goal	Difference
Critical Services				
Overall responsiveness	6.36	6.48	6.50	(0.02)
Will return again	6.54	6.64	6.50	0.14
Rate this Hilton overall	6.48	6.26	6.50	(0.24)
Friendliness				
Reception staff friendliness	6.57	6.51	6.50	0.01
Departure desk friendliness	ERR	6.75	6.50	0.25
Lobby lounge friendliness	4.00	6.19	6.50	(0.31)
Operator friendliness	6.50	6.48	6.50	(0.03)
Room service friendliness	7.00	6.60	6.50	0.10
Banquet friendliness	ERR	6.52	6.50	0.02
Total	6.25	6.52	6.50	0.02
Cafe Tijera Restaurant				
Dining experience	6.00	5.96	6.50	(0.54)
Breakfast F&B quality	ERR	6.27	6.50	(0.23)
Breakfast staff service	5.50	5.78	6.50	(0.72)
Dinner staff service	6.00	6.10	6.50	(0.40)
Dinner F&B service	6.67	6.00	6.50	(0.50)
Total	6.14	6.03	6.50	(0.47)
Room Service				
Prompt service	7.00	6.09	6.50	(0.41)
Friendly service	7.00	6.60	6.50	0.10
Food-beverage quality	7.00	6.44	6.50	(0.06)
Overall experience	5.83	6.18	6.50	(0.33)
Total	6.30	6.33	6.50	(0.17)
Banquet Event				
Prompt service	6.80	6.55	6.50	0.05
Friendly service	ERR	6.52	6.50	0.02
Food-beverage quality	6.00	6.27	6.50	(0.23)
Total	6.50	6.43	6.50	(0.07)
Towers				
Will return again	ERR	ERR	6.50	ERR
Towers lounge overall	ERR	6.61	6.50	0.11
Total	ERR	6.61	6.50	0.11
Lobby Bar				
Prompt service	6.33	6.37	6.50	(0.13)
Comfort & decor	ERR	6.11	6.50	(0.39)
Lobby staff friendliness	4.00	6.19	6.50	(0.31)
Total	5.40	6.22	6.50	(0.28)

(Continues)

| EXHIBIT 3 | GUEST COMMENT DAILY REPORT *(CONTINUED)* |

Return Again as %	Today Total Score	PTD Total Score 94.92%	Goal	Difference
Reception				
Reception staff friendliness	6.57	6.51	6.50	0.01
Check-in efficiency	6.33	6.45	6.50	(0.05)
Door/bell staff assistance	ERR	6.45	6.50	(0.05)
Total	6.50	6.47	6.50	(0.03)
Departure				
Front desk friendliness	FRR	6.75	6.50	0.25
Check-out efficiency	7.00	6.77	6.50	0.27
Bell staff promptness	6.75	6.52	6.50	0.02
Total	6.80	6.68	6.50	0.18
Services				
Tele operator friendliness	6.50	6.48	6.50	(0.03)
Mail-message delivery	6.00	6.46	6.50	(0.04)
Laundry-dry cleaning	7.00	6.70	6.50	0.20
Fitness center	7.00	6.05	6.50	(0.45)
Total	6.50	6.41	6.50	(0.09)
Accommodations				
Room cleanliness	5.67	6.45	6.50	(0.05)
Room comfort & decor	6.00	6.61	6.50	0.11
Room TV-radio quality	6.33	6.09	6.50	(0.41)
Price/value of room	5.00	6.33	6.50	(0.17)
Total	5.75	6.39	6.50	(0.11)
Bathroom				
Bathroom cleanliness	6.25	6.51	6.50	0.01
Bathroom amenities	7.00	6.48	6.50	(0.02)
Public bathroom cleanliness	6.00	6.38	6.50	(0.12)
Total	6.29	6.47	6.50	(0.03)
Efficiency				
Check in efficiency	6.33	6.45	6.50	(0.05)
Check-out efficiency	7.00	6.77	6.50	0.27
Total	6.50	6.61	6.50	0.11
Total overall report w/o RIO	6.38	6.47	6.50	(0.03)
Total overall report	6.37	6.44	6.50	(0.06)

(Continues)

EXHIBIT 3 GUEST COMMENT DAILY REPORT (CONTINUED)

WESTWARD HILTON & TOWERS
GUEST COMMENT DAILY REPORT
'97

Today's Performance Metrics

TOTAL OCCUPIED ROOMS	=	285
CALCARDS WITH ROOM #'S	=	31
TODAY'S CHECK OUT	=	68
TODAY'S TOTAL CARDS	=	35
TODAY'S % OF RETURN	=	51.37%
TOTAL % CARDS W/RM #'S	=	45.59%
TOTAL CAFE TIJERA CHANGES	=	1,383.88

Period to Date (PTD) Performance

PTD OCCUPIED ROOMS	=	6,289
PTD TTL CARDS W/ROOM NUMBER	=	1,401
PTD CHECK OUT	=	549
PTD TOTAL CARDS	=	
PTD % OF RETURN	=	39.19%
PTD RIO CHARGES	=	23,249

	Today's Total Comment	1	2	3	4	5	6	7	Today's Total Points	Today's Score	PTD Total Points	PTD Total Score	PTD Total Comment
Efficient check-in	3					1		2	19	6.33	303.00	6.45	47
Guest room comfort & decor	3					1	1	1	18	6.00	304.00	6.61	46
Exp. of room for price paid	3				1	1	1		15	5.00	285.00	6.33	45
Overall dining exp. at Cafe Tijera	1						1		6	6.00	143.00	5.96	24
Overall responsiveness to needs	11				1		4	6	70	6.36	1,433.00	6.48	221
Efficient room service delivery	1							1	7	7.00	201.00	6.09	33
TV prog/reception quality	3						2	1	19	6.33	286.00	6.09	47
Banquet staff friendliness	0								0	ERR	137.00	6.52	21
Room service staff friendliness	1	1						1	7	7.00	264.00	6.60	40
Bathroom amenities & towels	1							1	7	7.00	311.00	6.48	48
Efficient check-out	1							1	7	7.00	318.00	6.77	47
Guest room cleanliness	3			1				2	17	5.67	613.00	6.45	95
Cafe Tijera dinner staff service	1						1		6	6.00	177.00	6.10	29
Lobby lounge staff friendliness	2						1		8	4.00	198.00	6.19	32
Guest room bath cleanliness	4						3	1	25	6.25	332.00	6.51	51
Room service F&B quality	2							2	14	7.00	218.00	6.44	34
Lobby lounge staff promptness	3						2	1	19	6.33	242.00	6.37	38
Rate this Hilton on overall basis	21					3	5	13	136	6.48	1,686.00	6.26	289
Arrival-front desk friendliness	7				1			6	46	6.57	384.00	6.51	59
Overall room service experience	6			1	1			4	35	5.83	247.00	6.18	40
Banquet staff responsiveness	5						1	4	34	6.60	144.00	6.55	22

(Continues)

EXHIBIT 3   GUEST COMMENT DAILY REPORT (CONTINUED)

	Today's Total Comment	1	2	3	4	5	6	7	Today's Total Points	Today's Score	PTD Total Points	PTD Total Score	PTD Total Comment
Fitness center	2							2	14	7.00	116.00	6.05	19
Telephone operator friendliness	6					1	1	4	39	6.50	259.00	6.48	40
Mail/message delivery	4					1	2	1	24	6.00	181.00	6.46	28
Cafe Tijera breakfast F&B quality	0								0	ERR	163.00	6.27	26
Departure-front desk friendliness	0								0	ERR	297.00	6.75	44
Public bathroom cleanliness	2					1		1	12	6.00	217.00	6.38	34
Banquet F&B quality	3					1	1	1	16	6.00	163.00	6.27	26
Cafe Tijera breakfast staff service	2					1	1		11	5.50	133.00	5.78	23
Laundry/dry cleaning services	2							2	14	7.00	67.00	6.70	10
Cafe Tijera dinner F&B quality	3						1	2	20	6.67	192.00	6.00	32
Departure-prompt bellman assist.	4						1	3	27	6.75	274.00	6.52	42
Arrival-prompt bellman assist.	0						3		0	ERR	213.00	6.45	33
Lobby comfort & decor	0								0	ERR	275.00	6.11	45
Towers lounge overall	0								0	ERR	238.00	6.61	36
Likelihood you will return	35		1	3	4	2	8	24	229	6.54	3,641.00	6.64	548
Totals without Cafe Tijera	138	0	1	3	4	12	33	85	880	6.38	13,846	6.47	2,140

451

Wages had to be competitive and fair, but based on the position held, not seniority. We surveyed the market to determine what fair and competitive wage rates should be. By doing job analysis we determined the worth of each position and then compensated on the worth of the job. I don't believe in individual performance–based pay because I can't figure out how to accurately measure individual performance. I'm better off not trying to reward performance when there is no good way to measure it. That's why all merit pay was based on the performance of the hotel.

Fifty percent of employee bonuses were tied to customer comment scores. In a simple and understandable bonus system, managers as well as hourly employees, both part time and full-time, received quarterly bonuses based on customer scores, house profit, and employee turnover.

The details of the bonus plan are shown in Exhibit 4. "Performance appraisal was separate from salary review," Gregg said. "Discussion of pay and performance together is confusing. Instead we used performance appraisals to discuss future development and acknowledge contributions."

Selection, Orientation, and Training

Gregg felt that getting the "right" people for the Westward culture was the key to implementing the hotel's vision, but an intuitive and values-based process.

We didn't do anything special. We looked for fit versus skill when we hired people. Did they share our values? After several years we began to use a management committee consensus-process approach. Mostly we tried to talk people out of coming to work for us. We were different, and if you couldn't buy into our values, or you didn't want to live with these principles, we didn't want you. Our values were not negotiable. We didn't have a formal orientation either. You picked up the values from everyone in the hotel. It wasn't necessary for top management to tell everyone—the people you worked with told you. We . . . saw training as a last resort. Training should be for helping people get over the hump once they've exhausted their own resources. If a person needed a skill then they were provided training to handle that need. We were committed to filling the gaps, but we don't have a formal training program. We supported cross-training to help build employee opportunities."

In the last couple of years, Hillerman invested in the Stephen Covey training on "The Seven Habits of Highly Effective People" to help managers and line employees live the company's vision and were pleased with the results. Carl Gregg, along with a manager from each property, was certified as a Covey trainer so they were able to do this training in-house.

Communication

Gregg expressed that "providing information to people is a form of respect. Information not only flows to employees, but from them as well." All employees met once per quarter at a property-wide meeting to discuss and review quarterly results of the hotel. The meeting included a question and answer period and the distribution of quarterly bonuses. Department meetings were held once a month, and at daily huddles managers and line employees reviewed customer service issues. Surveys were used to obtain feedback from employees as well as guests and owners. Cross-department task forces were assembled and disassembled quickly to respond to special problems. Plus, the company communicated in many one-on-one, personal ways. Key to all the information exchange was management's emphasis on listening and praise.

Culture

In discussing the culture he and his team created at the Westward and were attempting to inculcate throughout Hillerman, Gregg stated:

We had a family environment and were dedicated to one another and to high levels of customer service. I believed that managers should figure out what employees value and value that. We

EXHIBIT 4	BONUS PROGRAM

Hillerman Hotels, Inc.
1994 Quarterly Bonus Program
Westward Hilton

General Manager

A. All employees are eligible unless they have had written disciplinary action during the quarter. You must be employed at the end of the quarter to be eligible for a bonus. The base salary on the attached schedule will be used, for any vacant positions, in determining bonuses. Employees hired during the quarter will receive a pro-rated bonus based on the following:

Hired any time during the first month of the quarter	66%
Hired any time during the second month of the quarter	33%
Hired any time during the last month of the quarter	0%

"Bonus Quarters" are as follows:

1st Quarter	December, January, February
2nd Quarter	March, April, May
3rd Quarter	June, July, August
4th Quarter	September, October, November

This is an optional program designed to reward employees for performance above the average. This program may be altered or discontinued at any time at the sole discretion of Hillerman Hotels, Inc.

B. A prerequisite to payment of any bonuses will be the achievement of at least the minimum/maximum levels stated below for all three criteria as follows. Budgeted house profit may be adjusted from published numbers to compensate for unusual or unbudgeted events or material time differences.

	Min/Max
Employee turnover (annualized)	37.3%
Customer comment card score	6.25
House profit —1st quarter	$589,000
2nd quarter	$735,000
3rd quarter	$598,000
4th quarter	$697,000

C. Quarterly bonuses are based on the Hillerman triangle as follows:

Triangle Stakeholder	Measurement
Employee	Employee turnover during the quarter, annualized
Customer	Customer comment card quarterly weighted average score
Owner	House profit

(Continues)

started to do a back to school function for employees because we knew how important the family and education was for our workers. We invited the families to the party and distributed school supplies. It made everyone feel good. We did a Christmas party too—focused around the family with gifts to all the kids from Santa Claus. I think our culture is strong because we have a sense of community and a sense of purpose outside of the job.

I think we created a business environment where people could be themselves. They wanted to care. In the

| **EXHIBIT 4** | **BONUS PROGRAM (CONTINUED)** |

Year 6
Quarterly Bonus Program
Westward Hilton

General Manager

The criteria for receiving bonuses will be as follows:

	Level 1	Level 2	Level 3	Level 4
Employee turnover (annualized)	34.8%	32.3%	29.8%	27.3%
Customer comment card score	6.30	6.35	6.40	6.45
House profit —1st quarter	$639,000	$689,000	$739,000	$789,000
2nd quarter	$785,000	$835,000	$885,000	$935,000
3rd quarter	$648,000	$698,000	$748,000	$798,000
4th quarter	$747,000	$797,000	$847,000	$797,000

The basis for calculation of the bonus will be a percent of the employee's quarterly base salary as follows:

	Level 1	Level 2	Level 3	Level 4
Employee turnover (annualized)	2.66%	5.66%	8.66%	11.66%
Customer comment card score	2.66%	5.66%	8.66%	11.66%
House profit	2.66%+A	5.66%+A	8.66%+A	11.66%+A

A. 3.25% of the first $50,000 over minimum house profit for the level achieved.

typical work environment people must hide their true self. I think we gave people permission to be themselves, to be different. I think our low levels of turnover were critical to our culture. Lots of people like to argue that low turnover is essential because of the costs, but I think high turnover does more damage because it assaults the culture.

We had a high level of trust and also a level of tolerance and forgiving that I think are unique. We had an older woman in the laundry area who was with the hotel from the beginning who took two fifteen-minute naps each day. Can you imagine how most hotels would deal with an employee who sleeps on the job? I think we may have less talent, but we leverage it by being stronger as a whole. It's like a basketball team that doesn't have one superstar, but a whole group of average players who together do extraordinary things.

Success helps too. We started to see some dramatic positive results from our efforts at the Westward and that certainly lifted people's spirits. Good news feeds the emotional psyche. When we got into the Westward it had good people in it, but the culture was dominated by a traditional command and control management that didn't let the hard working and caring employees contribute the way they could. The culture flourished with our guiding principles and I don't think management can easily change it. But sure, it could go back to that. You bring in bad management, good people leave, turnover increases, and suddenly the work environment is different. Nothing lasts forever.

BUT DID IT MAKE MONEY?

Living a vision is in the details. "It is a slow and continuous process, and you must stick with it," reflected Gregg. But the ability to do so with the performance pressures of owners and the demands of customers is an ongoing battle. The results at Westward were dramatic support for the Carl Gregg vision. For six years, the Westward Hilton performed at or near the top of the Phoenix market, as indicated by the market penetration index show in Exhibit 5. According to the PKF Advisory, the Westward Hilton outperformed the Phoenix market by over ten occupancy points and $15 in average daily rate in 1996. Exhibit 6 shows the Hilton's position among its primary market competitors, the upscale chain market, the Phoenix market, and the Phoenix North markets. This performance was due in part to the redirection of the hotel's marketing efforts away from groups and more toward transient corporate travelers. According to recent investor reports, the above-average penetration was caused by the hotel's chain affiliation with Hilton Hotels and its highly visible location. Westward Hilton was in the top ten of all Hilton Hotels with an increase in profitability of 400 percent over the 1989–1996 period. House profit increased from the takeover (1989) figure of $798,895 to $4,025,254 (1996). Exhibit 5 shows the changes in house profit, guest comment scores, and employee turnover in addition to market penetration. The hotel's revenue per available room (REVPAR, calculated by dividing room revenue by the number of available rooms) rose from a rate of $30.30 in 1991 to a 1996 rate of $68.93. Exhibit 6 shows the Westward's market penetration based on market data from Smith Travel Research. Exhibit 7 provides summary Profit and Loss statements for the hotel for the five years 1992–1996.

NEW GENERAL MANAGERS ARRIVE

As one subordinate noted, Gregg had a clear employee emphasis, he was a caring person, and people felt good working for him. This employee indicated that Gregg was a master at showing interest in people's work. He noticed the small things and acknowledged everyone with a friendly greeting. He fostered a work environment that was informal, responsive, and trusting, not intimidating. The guide for behavior was "do the right thing." His focus was always on the questions "how does it impact our employees, customers, and owners?" and "are all three parties taken care of?" He would be a hard act to follow, and for some at the property the managers who followed Gregg were simply not up to the task.

Five general managers came and went from the Westward Hilton in the five years after Gregg moved into his corporate position. While the departures of the managers were for a variety of reasons, Gregg blamed himself for being too controlling as the executive vice president of operations of Hillerman Hotels. Even after his promotion to the position of supervising the general managers of several hotels, he was still deeply involved in the life of the Westward. His presence was everywhere in the hotel and remained strong. "I didn't trust it would continue to work. I was not confident in those that followed me and I was afraid that what we had built would not last." But last it did, and the results continued to be positive.

WHY SELL?

Bringing his thoughts up to the present, Gregg thought it might be the right time to sell—Hillerman had had a good seven-year run at the Westward. Plus, it truly was a sellers' market, as the high offering price for the hotel indicated. New products had come on board in the Phoenix market, and the hotel's performance might have peaked. Phoenix was experiencing explosive growth in new hotel room supply, with projections of around three thousand new rooms for 1997. Growth was particularly strong within the upper economy and midmarket segments. Much of the new hotel development was being undertaken by REITs and other public lodging companies, which were establishing or expanding their portfolio or brands, according to E & Y Kenneth Leventhal Real Estate Group's National Lodging Forecast. The overall supply growth in 1996 was 4 percent, while demand growth was 3.6 percent. All market segments experienced healthy ADR (average daily rate) growth. Twenty-eight hotels were under construction and an additional twenty-five were in permit

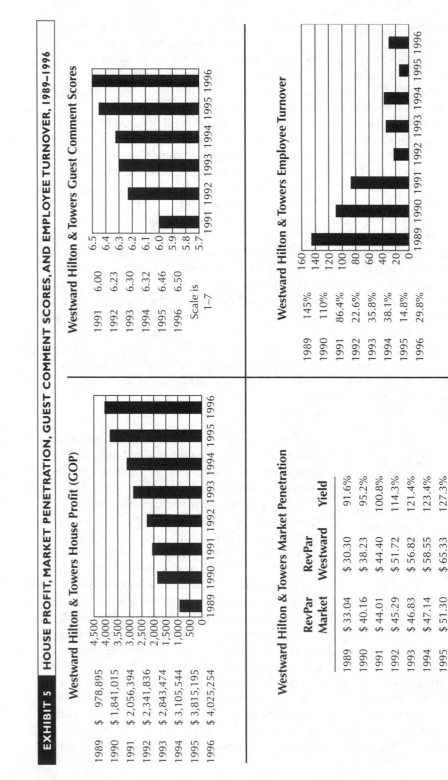

Westward Hilton & Towers House Profit (GOP)

Year	GOP
1989	$ 978,895
1990	$ 1,841,015
1991	$ 2,056,394
1992	$ 2,341,836
1993	$ 2,843,474
1994	$ 3,105,544
1995	$ 3,815,195
1996	$ 4,025,254

Westward Hilton & Towers Guest Comment Scores

Year	Score
1991	6.00
1992	6.23
1993	6.30
1994	6.32
1995	6.46
1996	6.50

Scale is 1–7

Westward Hilton & Towers Market Penetration

Year	RevPar Market	RevPar Westward	Yield
1989	$ 33.04	$ 30.30	91.6%
1990	$ 40.16	$ 38.23	95.2%
1991	$ 44.01	$ 44.40	100.8%
1992	$ 45.29	$ 51.72	114.3%
1993	$ 46.83	$ 56.82	121.4%
1994	$ 47.14	$ 58.55	123.4%
1995	$ 51.30	$ 65.33	127.3%
1996	$ 54.25	$ 68.93	127.0%

Market   Westward

Westward Hilton & Towers Employee Turnover

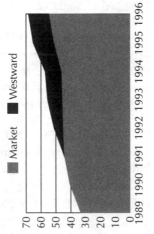

Year	Turnover
1989	145%
1990	110%
1991	86.4%
1992	22.6%
1993	35.8%
1994	38.1%
1995	14.8%
1996	29.8%

EXHIBIT 6	WESTWARD HILTON MARKET PENETRATION COMPARED TO PHOENIX MARKET, NORTH PHOENIX, COMPETITIVE SET, AND THE YAVAPAI CONVENTION CENTER & HOTEL, 1989–1996

Westward Hilton Market Penetration

Year	Westward Hilton RevPar	Westward Hilton Yield Index	Yavapai Convention	Phoenix Market	North Phoenix	Competitive Set
1989	30.30	103.50	33.09	29.27	39.40	33.04
1990	38.23	109.00	41.77	35.07	46.96	40.16
1991	44.40	121.60	46.15	36.50	49.57	44.01
1992	51.73	140.70	45.31	36.76	48.88	45.29
1993	56.82	154.70	43.95	36.79	49.73	46.83
1994	58.55	154.70	40.76	37.85	51.18	47.14
1995	65.33	168.20	50.85	38.83	52.73	51.30
1996	68.93	172.80	51.90	39.90	53.95	54.25

Market Share Report Room Sales Percentage

Westward Hilton % of...	1989	1990	1991	1992	1993	1994	1995
Phoenix Market	0.9	0.9	1.2	1.2	1.3	1.3	1.3
Luxury Market	1.7	1.9	2.4	3.6	5.3	4.1	3.9
Upscale Chain	5.5	6.2	4.9	5.2	5.6	6.1	5.8
Phoenix North Market	3.6	4	3.7	4.2	4.5	4.8	4.8
Competitors	11.6	12.5	13.9	13.7	13.9	15.2	15.5

Market Analysis

	Competitive Set		Westward Hilton	
	Occupancy	Room Rate	Occupancy	Room Rate
1989	58.9	56.14	53.1	57.06
1990	64.9	61.90	62.3	61.37
1991	66.2	66.53	63.7	69.66
1992	63.9	70.89	67.3	76.92
1993	64.2	72.94	71.5	79.48
1994	62.4	76.04	72.2	81.08
1995	66.0	77.70	77.4	84.36

Source: Smith Travel Research.

(*Continues*)

EXHIBIT 6	WESTWARD HILTON MARKET PENETRATION COMPARED TO PHOENIX MARKET, NORTH PHOENIX, COMPETITIVE SET, AND THE YAVAPAI CONVENTION CENTER & HOTEL, 1989–1996 (*CONTINUED*)

Major Competitors Figure

Competitive Set Includes	Rooms
Marriott Northside	500
Radisson Suite Hotel	175
Holiday Inn Select	335
Yavapai Convention Hotel	635
Embassy Suites	255
Hilton North	165
Hilton Southwest	295

Market Performance

Market Segment	Occupancy						
	1989	1990	1991	1992	1993	1994	1995
Westward Hilton	43.20%	49.20%	51.50%	56.20%	56.00%	72.20%	77.40%
Luxury	52.00%	54.20%	51.90%	52.30%	53.20%	66.70%	69.00%
Phoenix Market	48.40%	51.80%	47.20%	50.80%	49.20%	62.90%	62.10%
Phoenix North	51.40%	53.80%	49.60%	50.40%	52.00%	64.60%	65.10%
Chain upscale	55.30%	57.10%	57.30%	48.90%	48.60%	68.00%	69.50%
Competitors		50.60%	49.80%	51.20%	52.00%	62.40%	66.00%

Market Sample, 1989–1995

	Census Rooms	Sample Rooms	Sample Percentages
Phoenix	35,871–38,709	26,638–32,054	74.3%–82.8%
Luxury	12,483–7,632	9,688–7,565	77.6%–99.1%
Upper Tier	18,746–2,530	14,217–2,530	75.8%–100%

stages, for a total of 53 projects under development. The long-term outlook for Phoenix was strong with its 300 days of sunshine, good transportation support, natural wonders, and abundance of golf courses.

Hillerman Hotels, though, wasn't exactly desperate for the money. The rest of the portfolio was performing well—with the exception of one recently acquired property, all were profitable—and the parent company, which owned and operated a bank and several other businesses, was profitable. Further, all the Hillerman businesses were privately held, with Kerry Glenn being the majority shareholder in all. Thus, there was little of the short-term performance pressure to which publicly held companies are subject.

Gregg knew that at their next formal meeting, the seven people in the management/ownership group he was drinking and laughing with now would make a decision that, one way or another, would affect people's lives at the Westward. Perhaps selling would even affect the way Hillerman's employees at the other properties would feel about the company. On the other hand, because of his small equity stake in the hotel, Gregg stood to benefit handsomely from the sale.

EXHIBIT 7	PROFIT AND LOSS STATEMENTS FOR THE WESTWARD HILTON, YEARS 1992–1996				
	1992	**1993**	**1994**	**1995**	**1996**
Average room rate	76.87	79.47	81.08	84.45	89.87
Available rooms	111,300	107,380	107,380	107,380	107,380
Occupied rooms	74,324	78,221	79,790	84,703	84,105
Tot revenue/available rooms	74.01	82.40	83.37	92.24	97.96
Total hotel sales	8,237,533	8,956,357	8,951,885	9,904,653	10,518,539
Total room revenue	5,713,321	6,216,092	6,469,286	7,153,322	7,558,599
Salaries/benefits	928,398	1,031,178	989,548	1,041,332	1,070,538
Operating expenses	486,914	532,679	562,225	543,406	574,986
Rooms dept. profit	4,298,009	4,652,234	4,917,513	5,568,584	5,913,075
Total food revenue	1,755,529	1,755,340	1,530,531	1,831,253	1,967,293
Cost of sales	497,479	412,231	346	431,682	477,152
Salaries/benefits	733,792	667,220	584,787	633,299	698,491
Other expenses	157,970	143,462	101,962	128,100	102,552
Food dept. profit	366,289	532,427	467,665	638,172	689,097
Total beverage revenue	289,027	267,369	221,814	264,812	286,811
Cost of sales	70,469	61,430	55,724	61,698	65,652
Salaries/benefits	90,543	66,081	53,344	57,642	60,129
Other expenses	23,562	18,702	17,117	15,091	12,266
Bev. dept. profit	104,453	121,157	95,628	130,382	148,764
Tele. dept. profit	143,858	114,305	175,778	178,381	239,809
Misc. dept. profit	156,807	309,958	280,178	179,957	171,077
Minibar dept. profit	2,502–	23,574	20,352	27,696	29,262
Admin. & general exp.	830,125	734,436	750,262	770,521	858,796
Sales dept. expense	512,092	723,359	609,725	589,576	608,293
Franchise expense	360,274	417,790	430,171	493,294	596,234
Utilities expense	506,720	521,620	565,720	500,879	540,489
Maintenance & repair	515,866	538,472	525,691	553,707	562,017
House profit	2,341,836	2,817,977	3,105,544	3,815,195	4,025,254
Taxes, ins., & leases	560,922	545,531	502,153	420,155	432,599
Employee incentives	112,613	83,339	112,505	280,244	198,619
Corporate charges	323,012	322,022	316,127	314,506	316,100
Interest/financing	1,194,690	1,297,496	1,145,475	1,094,002	1,407,831
Other gains losses	1,369–	25,405	50,280	77,130	76,960
Income before non cash	149,229	594,994	1,079,563	1,783,418	1,747,064

(Continues)

Gregg thought to himself,
My one regret is that I didn't prepare people for this possibility. I don't believe we can protect people; we can only tell them it may not last forever. We should have prepared them. We should have made it clear that this is not forever—it's an investment and we should try to enjoy it for as long as we can. Everyone benefited from being involved with that property—from being part of a place that was so positive. I just worry that selling will

EXHIBIT 7	PROFIT AND LOSS STATEMENTS FOR THE WESTWARD HILTON, YEARS 1992–1996 (CONTINUED)				
	1992	**1993**	**1994**	**1995**	**1996**
Occupied rooms					
Individuals	47,283				54,800
Regular rack		1,630	2,014	2,465	
Corporate		14,519	12,352	7,599	
Spec. corp. & secr.		32,873			
Gov't, military		1,660	1,157		
Long term 5–29		947		473	
Long term 30+					
Via			30,476	38,071	
Good neighbor			4,253	6,292	
Subtotal individ.	47,283	51,629	50,252	54,900	54,800
Groups	10,253				19,292
Corporate		7,581	8,876	11,894	
Gov't, military		345			
Other		5,264	18	1	
Smerf			4,934	5,134	
Associates			2,207	2,721	
Subtotal groups	10,253	13,190	16,035	19,750	19,292
Contracts					
Corp., airline, RR					
Package/discount	16,788				10,013
Weekend		6,949	7,375	7,332	
Limited, club		6,453	6,128	2,721	
Subtotal pkg./disc.	16,788	13,402	13,503	10,053	10,013
Total rooms occupied	74,324	78,221	79,790	84,703	84,105

catch people flat-footed. We have created such a high trust level that people didn't even ask questions when we had investors visit the property. It embarrasses me that I didn't prepare them.

Gregg lifted his glass and smiled sadly as he thought of his friends and colleagues at the Westward. He took a long swig of his martini and muttered to himself, "I just don't know for sure what the right thing to do is." He was glad to have the weekend ahead to think about his vote and, if he decided to vote to hold, how he would try to convince the others, especially Glenn, to hold the property.

Notes

1. Real estate investment trusts are corporations that pay no income tax on their earnings (similar to a mutual fund) so long as they pay 95 percent or more of their profits to shareholders. REITS provide the advantages of corporate ownership to shareholders but also offer tax advantages. As a result, REITs have become very attractive to many investors.

CASE 5

Can Continental Airlines Continue to Work Hard, Fly Right, and Fund the Future?

We weren't just the worst big airline. We lapped the field.

—CEO Gordon Bethune[1]

When Gordon Bethune arrived in Continental Airlines' executive offices in February 1994, he almost turned around and left. Continental was the lowest-performing of the major U.S. airlines. It had the worst on-time record, filed the most mishandled-bag reports, and received customer complaints at a rate of nearly three times the industry average.[2]

Worst of all was employee morale. Sick time, turnover, on-the-job injuries, and worker's compensation claims stood at record highs, and a culture of mistrust reigned. Airport employees were so embarrassed by the company that they ripped the logo patches from their shirts to avoid having to answer for the company's behavior to customers and airport coworkers.[3]

Within two years, Continental Airlines was transformed from almost-certain doom as one of the worst performers in the airline industry into a standard-bearer in all respects: profitability, reliability, customer service, and employee satisfaction. And despite the turmoil in which the airline industry finds itself in the post–September 11 world, Continental continues to survive. The key is a well-

Written by Stephane Duchenne, Carol Ann Fisher, Cheryl Farr Leas, Yash Krishna, Michel Rugema and Yongqing Yang at the School of Hotel Administration, Cornell University.

This case study was written for the purposes of classroom discussion. It is not to be duplicated or cited in any form without the copyright holder's express permission.

focused brand and a clearly defined corporate culture in which everybody works together to win.

A SHORT HISTORY OF CONTINENTAL AIRLINES

Continental Airlines has such a fascinating history that it has been the subject of at least two books. *Maverick* tells the Continental Airlines tale from 1937 to 1980, the forty-three-year span when the airline's guiding influence was Robert Forman Six, CEO for forty of those years.[4] *From Worst to First* takes over the narrative in 1994, revealing how the current CEO, Gordon Bethune, turned a woefully unprofitable company—Continental Airlines declared bankruptcy twice between 1983 and 1990—into one of the most admired airline companies in the industry today.[5] Exhibit 1 contains some of the highlights of Continental Airlines' history.

The Maverick Years

Louis Mueller and Walter T. Varney created Varney Speed Lines in 1934. Varney transported mail and some passengers in the southwestern United States. In July 1936, Mueller sold 40 percent of the company to Robert Forman Six, who renamed the fledgling carrier Continental Airlines in 1937—and went on to become one of the greatest leaders of the industry. In *Maverick*, author Robert J. Serling states: "Without question, he is as complex a person who ever headed an airline. He is hard, quick-tempered, profane and dictatorial. He is also soft, warm-hearted, sentimental, deeply religious and generous."[6]

EXHIBIT 1	HIGHLIGHTS OF CONTINENTAL AIRLINES' HISTORY

1934	Louis Mueller and Walter T. Varney create Varney Speed Lines
1936	Mueller sells 40% of the company to Robert Forman Six who will manage the company for forty years
1937	Varney Speed Lines is renamed Continental Airlines
1945	Continental has 400 employees and serves twenty-six cities
1953	Continental merges with Pioneer Airlines and expands its route to forty-six cities
1959	The Boeing 707 is introduced to the fleet
1967	Air Micronesia is created to serve routes in Micronesia region
1978	The Airline Deregulation Act is enacted and will change the nature of flying forever
1979	Some oil producing countries create a cartel; the price of jet fuel skyrockets
1980	Robert Forman Six retires
1980	Frank Lorenzo buys Continental
1983	Continental Airlines files for Chapter 11 bankruptcy protection for the first time
1986	Lorenzo acquires Eastern Airlines, People Express and Frontier Airlines
1987	"Continental Express" is created to bring increased traffic to hub cities
1988	Continental negotiates an alliance with SAS, which buys 18.4% of Continental
1990	Frank Lorenzo is declared "unfit" by Congress and is forced out of the company
1990	Continental Airlines files for Chapter 11 bankruptcy protection a second time, citing rising fuel costs and reduced travel following the Gulf War
1994	Gordon Bethune is elected CEO of Continental Airlines
1995	The "Go Forward Plan" is adopted; it will lead Continental Airlines to success
1997	Continental achieves a record annual profit of $640 million
1998	Northwest and Delta issue competing bids for Continental; Continental chooses a complex code-share strategic relationship with Northwest, and Northwest agrees to have Continental run as an independent but complementary business
2001	Continental buys back all common shares held by Northwest Airlines; for the first time since 1983, the carrier no longer has an outside controlling shareholder
2001	Terrorists attack the United States using commercial aircraft as weapons, with strikes on New York, Washington, and Pennsylvania on September 11
2002	Continental announced a $139 million loss for the second quarter of 2002. The company promises a return to profitability, but will it be able to find profitability and avert the crisis of filing for Chapter 11 bankruptcy protection for a third time?

When Six took over as Continental's CEO, his long-term goal was to provide reliable and profitable flights, which would eventually fly beyond the borders of the United States.[7]

In the years preceding World War II, Continental flew to destinations that included El Paso, Texas; Albuquerque, New Mexico; Las Vegas, Nevada; and cities within Colorado. As the war approached its end, Continental expanded its regional route structure with service between Denver, Colorado, and Kansas City, Missouri, and between El Paso and San Antonio, Texas. By 1945,

the company had 400 employees and served twenty-six cities.[8]

Determined to expand its role as a regional airline, Six merged Continental with Pioneer Airlines in 1953 and expanded its routes to forty-six cities. The larger carrier provided service to every city in Texas with more than 100,000 inhabitants.[9]

In June 1959, Six determined to set Continental apart from its main competitors, who were then just joining the jet age. He introduced the Boeing 707 into the fleet. To maintain its small jet fleet, Continental developed an innovative "progressive maintenance" program that enabled the jet fleet to fly seven days a week, sixteen hours a day.[10]

In the 1960s, Continental doubled its route structure and achieved its goal of flying internationally. The airline began servicing routes to Southeast Asia, and it launched charter services to such European cities as Frankfurt, London, Paris, and Rome. In 1967, Continental won a five-year contract for routes to Micronesia. Out of the pact a new enterprise was born to fly the routes: Air Micronesia (informally known as "Air Mike").[11]

The Era of Deregulation

Federal regulation of domestic airline fares and markets ended with the Airline Deregulation Act of 1978.[12] What followed was a period of evolution that changed the nature of flying. The goal of the act was to promote competition within the industry. It essentially gave airlines unrestricted rights to enter new routes without Civil Aeronautics Board (CAB) approval. The companies could also exit any market as well as raise and lower fares at will.

At the same time, the oil-producing countries in the Middle East formed a cartel and raised the price of jet fuel 88 percent in 1979, capped by an additional 23 percent in 1980. Higher jet fuel costs—combined with tumbling fares and increased passenger loads due to increased competition after deregulation—caused Continental's profits to drop. Although deregulation allowed Continental to add eighteen routes in 1979, it also brought about an end to the airline's long stretch of sustained profitability.

By 1980, after forty years of service at Continental, Robert F. Six was no longer involved with the day-to-day operations at Continental; still, he remained chairman of the board of directors. Due to losses, Continental suffered its first decrease in workforce in forty-five years of operation. Employee morale was at an all-time low. Help came in the form of a merger with Texas International, led by Frank Lorenzo, in 1982. Lorenzo became chairman, president, and chief executive officer of the new Continental Airlines. The merger allowed Continental to provided flight service to four continents—and

Six's goals were at last achieved. It did not provide an instant solution to the pressures of deregulation and increasing oil prices, however. Lorenzo was unsuccessful in negotiating restructured salaries for unionized employees, and, in late 1983, Continental filed for Chapter 11 bankruptcy reorganization.

Lorenzo reacted strongly to the filing. He fired the entire staff, closed the doors to the airline for three days, and emerged with a company about one-third Continental's original size. By firing all employees, Lorenzo was able to reopen Continental with a nonunion staff.[13] The new company regained its competitive position by the end of the year, posting a small profit by the end of 1984. In 1986, Continental reported the largest profits in the airline's fifty-one-year history. In the same year, Lorenzo acquired Eastern Airlines, People Express, and Frontier Airlines, which gave Continental the largest route network in the United States.

Under Lorenzo's direction, Continental adopted the dual strategy of developing hubs and strategic alliances as a way to remain competitive in the era of deregulation. Continental needed a steady flow of passengers to and from its hub cities, so it created Continental Express in 1987 as a means to deliver passengers to hub airports for onward flights, and it formed a global alliance with Scandinavian Airlines (SAS) in 1988 in which SAS acquired 18.4 percent of Continental.

While the partnership with SAS has long since ended, Continental continues to follow this two-pronged strategy. The airline's hubs in Newark, Cleveland, Houston, and Guam are fundamental to Continental's route design. Its large family of partners are as important as its hubs, as they allow passengers traveling to overseas markets to connect to other destinations using the alliance's market routes.

Working under Frank Lorenzo was not an easy experience, however. The CEO position was in constant turmoil between 1980 and 1990, with six chief officers filling the position in ten years. In fact, all employees found conditions under Lorenzo difficult to endure. Labor relations under Lorenzo were amazingly bitter between 1980 and 1990. On October 26, 1989, remarks printed in the *Congressional Record* stated that "Frank Lorenzo has sabotaged a distinguished airline and disrupted the lives of its employees"—and Congress declared him "unfit" to run an airline. In 1990, Lorenzo was forced out of Continental, and Holland Harris took command. Harris was unable to work a rapid turnaround. Citing rising fuel costs and the impending Gulf War, Continental in 1990 filed for Chapter 11 bankruptcy protection for a second time.

Climbing the Ladder from Worst to First[14]

In 1993, Continental Airlines emerged from bankruptcy when leveraged buyout firm Air Partners, led by David Bonderman, invested $450 million in the company. In an attempt to compete with low-cost carriers, Continental launched a new company in 1993 called Continental Lite—which turned out to be not only unprofitable, but also detrimental to the already floundering image of Continental Airlines. Continental Lite was dismantled in 1995.

When Gordon Bethune left Boeing to become president of Continental in 1994, stakeholders despised the company—travelers, employees, and shareholders alike. However, under his leadership, Continental achieved twenty-one consecutive profitable quarters and has won more awards for customer satisfaction than any other airline.

The turnaround of Continental Airlines wasn't magic—far from it. Rather, it was the result of decisive leadership and a simple and clearly defined strategy that focused on understanding who the airline's target market is, improving products to compete in the marketplace, increasing revenues, and giving employees the power and enthusiasm to make success happen.[15]

Believing that there was nowhere to go but up, newly minted CEO Gordon Bethune and his chief operating officer, Greg Brenneman, defined the Go Forward Plan.[16] Its cornerstones are:

- *Fly to Win:* The marketing plan, which focused on identifying who Continental's customers are and how the company can best meet their needs.

- *Fund the Future:* The financial plan, which laid the foundation for profitable growth.

- *Make Reliability a Reality:* The product plan, geared to realizing tangible results for customers and employees alike.

- *Working Together:* The people plan, defining a workplace culture of trust, involvement, empowerment, performance-based incentives, civility, and respect.

Major aspects of the plan included bonuses to travel agents to book passengers to Continental, bonuses to employees if the flights landed on time, and a significant reduction in management/employee barriers. This four-point vision statement laid the foundation for Continental's reinvention—and it continues to drive both brand identity and corporate culture today.

But Is Continental Ready to Face Fundamental Shifts in the Airline Industry?

On January 17, 2001, Continental Airlines announced its financial results for the year 2000, proudly announcing six straight years of profitability. This continued profitability was even more remarkable when compared with Continental filing for Chapter 11 bankruptcy protection for the second time in seven years in 1990. The "Go Forward Plan" allowed Continental to improve operational performance and working environment for employees and achieve sustained profitability.[17] In early 2001, all indications pointed to a solid and enduring recovery for Continental Airlines.

But then the foundations of the airline industry were shaken to the core on September 11, 2001. The federal government grounded all flights in response to the terrorist attacks on New York City and Washington, D.C. The unprecedented suspension of airline operations continued until September 14, 2001, when Secretary of Transportation Norman Mineta allowed certain general aviation flights back into the U.S. airspace in late afternoon.[18]

In the last four months of 2001, Continental Airlines, the fifth largest airline company in the United States (as measured by 2001 revenue passenger miles), lost $189 million despite a $417 million grant from the federal government.[19] During the first nine months of 2002, Continental's net loss was $342 million,[20] with Continental losing $1.3 million each day of the year; by year's end, Continental's net losses totaled $451 million.[21] On August 11, 2002, U.S. Airways filed for Chapter 11 bankruptcy protection.[22] Given this turbulent environment, will Continental Airlines be able to survive and prosper?

THE ENVIRONMENT

Continental Airlines is battling for its survival in an extremely turbulent broad environment that has forced many carriers, including the mighty United Airlines, to the brink of bankruptcy.[23] In fact, the entire commercial air transport industry operates in a complex web of sociocultural, economic, technological, political, and competitive forces. Competition is fierce, and investments needed to succeed are high. At the end of 2002, air carriers were still trying to figure out how to navigate the shock waves resulting from the terrorist attacks of September 11 as well as a sea change in business travel patterns that may well be permanently undermining the legacy carriers' long-standing business models.

Industry Overview

The world's airlines carry 1.4 billion passengers per year,[24] and the airline industry is a significant part of the American economy. In 2000, the U.S. airline industry launched more than 24,600 flights a day, employed 680,000 people, and recorded $129.5 billion in revenues.[25]

Since 1978, when federal government regulation of domestic fares and markets ended with the Airline Deregulation Act,[26] passenger demand for air transportation has grown at an average rate of 4 percent per year. As the Air Transport Association reported in 1999, "Now there are more than twice as many people fly today as did two decades ago, and at prices that have dropped dramatically. These facts reflect that the airline industry is an economically vibrant, highly competitive and productive industry."[27]

During 2000, the U.S. airline industry provided services to 666.2 million passengers. However, in 2001, the number of passengers dropped to 622.1 million, a decrease of 6.6 percent.[28] The airline industry measures its capacity in terms of Available Seat Miles (ASMs), and its utilization of that capacity in terms of Revenue Passenger Miles. By comparing the two, the industry calculates its passenger load factor. Exhibit 2 describes recent trends in U.S. airline traffic and operations.[29]

The airline industry has a clear size-based classification structure, according to airline revenue base:[30]

- *Major Airlines:* Carriers that have annual revenues exceeding $1 billion. The leading nine U.S. airlines are, in order, United Airlines, American Airlines, Delta Air Lines, Northwest Airlines, Continental Airlines, Southwest Airlines, US Airways, America West Airlines, and Alaska Airlines.

- *National Airlines:* Carriers that have annual revenues that between $100 million and $1 billion. National airlines include JetBlue, Frontier, and Midway.

- *Regional Airlines:* Carriers that have annual revenues of less than $100 million. Regional airlines include AccessAir, Ameristar Jet Charter, Falcon Air Express, Laker Airways, and Sun Pacific.

Commercial airlines have two major types of customers: travel passengers, and clients who ship cargo. The U.S. airlines transport more than 665 million passengers and nearly 30 billion ton miles of cargo annually; in the United States more than 1.8 million passengers fly every day. On average, airlines generate 75 percent of their revenues from passengers, while 15 percent of revenues are from cargo transport fees; another 10 percent in revenue

EXHIBIT 2	U.S. AIRLINE TRAFFIC AND OPERATIONS				
(All figures in millions)	**1997**	**1998**	**1999**	**2000**	**2001**
Revenue passenger enplaned	594.7	612.9	636.0	666.2	622.1
Revenue passenger miles	603,419	618,087	652,047	692,757	651,663
Available seat miles	857,232	874,089	918,419	956,950	930,486
Passenger load factor (%)	70.4%	70.7%	71.0%	72.4%	70.0%

is generated from additional fees, such as the sale of in-flight alcoholic beverages and entertainment.[31] Airlines compete for travel passengers by offering products differentiated by destination, class of service, frequent-flier programs, change restrictions, in-flight amenities—and, of course, price.

The industry is characterized by high fixed costs. Roughly 80 percent of airline costs are fixed in that they do not vary depending on customer demand.[32] Equipment costs are very high, especially for aircraft, which require large maintenance expenditures. Airlines also make significant investments in facilities infrastructure, such as airports and maintenance facilities. In 2001, "the total value of these investments, net of depreciation, reached $89.6 billion of assets totaling $158.4 billion," reports the Air Transport Association of America.[33] Labor costs, including both fixed and variable components, absorb about 40 percent of total industry revenues and represent the largest portion of expenses for an airline. While labor costs continue to rise sharply, industry watchers report no sign of labor productivity improvements since 1996.[34] After salaries and wages, the second-largest operating cost for airlines is jet fuel.

The Airline Industry Changes: Deregulation (1978) Before 1978, the Civil Aeronautics Board (CAB) regulated airline activity in the United States, controlling routes that airlines could fly and the fares they could charge. The federal Airline Deregulation Act of 1978 phased out the government's control over airfares and services in the domestic market. Since 1978, market forces have determined the price, quantity and quality of domestic air services. The act sparked a fundamental shift in the history of the airline industry, leading to improved service, lower airfares, and increased air travel—all benefits derived from free-market competition.[35]

Deregulation opened the airline industry market for existing airlines as well as newcomers, since airlines no longer needed to apply to the CAB for authorization to fly the routes they wanted to operate. As a result, the airline industry has witnessed the entry (and exit) of many low-fare carriers, as well as several established airlines that could no longer compete in the new environment, such as Pan Am and Eastern Airlines.[36]

Increased competition brought more scheduled U.S. passenger carriers and more convenient travel options than what was available twenty years ago. In 1978, there were thirty scheduled passenger airlines classified by the Civil Aeronautics Board; after deregulation, the number of scheduled U.S. carriers peaked at forty-nine in 1985. At the end of 1998, there were forty-two large scheduled certificated air carriers.[37]

However, significant operational limits hamper the development of new airlines. At an increasing number of major airports, the lack of gate access stands in the way of new entrants and becomes the new-entry barrier.[38] Existing leases for gate access give leaseholding airlines exclusive rights to an airport's gates over a long period, commonly twenty years, which prevents entrants to a market access to these gates. In some cases, major airlines that have the exclusive-use gate leases will sublease to other airlines, including startup airlines, at nonpreferred times and at high premiums.[39]

Since deregulation, consumers in most communities have experienced some dramatic changes in the level of air service. The General Accounting Office defines service levels for a given community as a combination of several factors: number of departures, number of available seats, number of destinations served nonstop from the community, and number of jet departures (compared to the number of turboprop departures). "In general, airports serving larger communities have benefited from a greater increase in overall quality of air service . . . than those serving smaller communities."[40] Thanks to the hub-and-spoke operating structure favored by the major airlines—particularly such legacy carriers as American, Delta, Continental, and United—domestic destination availability has increased by 35 percent to 40 percent over the past twenty years.[41]

During the period 1978 through 1998, domestic Revenue Passenger Miles (RPM) grew at almost double the rate of the growth of the economy, while regional RPMs grew at over five times the rate. (From 1978 to 1998, average GDP increased 2.6 percent per year, while air carrier RPMs increased 4.8 percent and regional RPMs increased 14.3 percent.) International travel has grown at an even faster pace than domestic travel: In the past twenty years, international RPMs have grown at 1.5 times the rate of growth of domestic RPMs, reaching 7.0 percent per year.[42]

Increased competition following deregulation also resulted in lower airfares. The U.S. General Accounting Office reports that, overall, average airfares declined by about 21 percent in constant dollars between 1990 and second quarter 1998.[43] Price competition was unleashed by deregulation, according to the Air Transport Association. By the end of the 1990s, roughly 90 percent of all passenger miles traveled were traveled on discounted-fare tickets, at an average discount of 65 percent off the posted coach fare.[44]

Another Sea Change: The Terrorist Attacks of September 11, 2001 The terrorist attacks on New York City's World Trade Center and the Pentagon on September 11, 2001 changed the airline industry. In an unprecedented move by order of the federal government, the U.S. airline system was suspended for several days after the attacks. According to the Air Transport Association (ATA), the industry suffered losses of $1.4 billion as a result of the shutdown. Furthermore, the global airline business lost $11 billion in 2001, with losses in the U.S. market along reaching $9 billion. The ATA's forecast that the U.S. airline industry would lose another $6 billion in 2002 as the turbulence from the attacks persisted[45] proved to be a conservative estimate; ultimately, the net losses incurred by the top ten U.S. carriers alone totaled $11.3 billion in 2003.[46]

Influential Forces in the Industry Environment

Customers Airline passengers include business travelers and leisure travelers. Business travelers accounted for about 34 percent of domestic airline revenue in 2000 and 36.3 percent in 1999, but for only about 15 percent of domestic RPMs and 10 percent of capacity.[47] Business travelers have historically paid a premium for travel. Despite leisure travelers' accounting for around 85 percent of RPMs, their fares generated only 66 percent of the revenues.

Leisure travelers are traditionally price-sensitive, so airlines have discounted fares for leisure travelers—typically requiring advance purchase and including restrictions on changes and refunds. Airlines will also offer deeply discounted last-minute fares to leisure travelers to fill capacity on undersold flights.

Travel-agent intermediaries are the primary distribution channels of air travel to customers, generating roughly 70 percent to 80 percent of all airline bookings. Some 135,000 travel agents and 29,000 travel agencies operate throughout the United States.[48] However, the rate of bookings conducted through travel agents is declining as travelers have easier access to direct travel bookings through online services.[49]

Suppliers In the large commercial aircraft market, there are two main worldwide manufacturers: Boeing and Airbus. For smaller regional jets, the main suppliers are Embraer, Bombardier, and Saab. Even though these aircraft manufacturers' business success is significantly intertwined with the success of the commercial airline industry, they also make significant sales to governments and military establishments. For example, 60 percent revenue of Boeing comes from commercial airplanes, 39 percent from integrated defense systems funded by governments, and 1 percent from other sources.[50]

When acquiring the aircraft, airlines also deal with multiple other vendors, selecting options in categories such as engines—essentially from Pratt & Whitney, General Electric, or Rolls Royce—interiors, and entertainment systems. Most airlines also work with specialty finance companies that structure financing in loans or leases. GE Capital, Boeing Capital, International Lease Finance, GATX, and CIT are the leading financiers of aircraft in the world.

Fuel supply enables airlines' daily operation, and it is a significant expense for the industry. In 2001, fuel costs accounted for 14.9 percent of total airline expense. For each airline, fuel expenditures can vary significantly, depending on the age and fuel efficiency of the fleet and the length of flights conducted by the airline. Variations also come from the fluctuation in oil prices on the world's commodity markets. Fuel cost in 2001 was lower than in 2000, only 14.9 percent of total expenses in 2001 compared to 15.4 percent in 2000. Standard & Poor's reported in early 2002 that "jet fuel price changes are less important today than they were in 1980, when fuel accounted for 30 percent of industry cost."[51]

Most airline carriers have to hedge their fuel costs by striking deals with suppliers or by buying and selling futures on the commodities market. In this way, by setting up financial options, they can limit the fluctuations in fuel prices and have more predictable operating costs.

Another key supplier in the airline industry is the labor unions. Wages and salaries are the single highest-operating expense of any airline. The industry is highly unionized, leading to inflexible wage costs and labor structures. There are three large unions in this industry: the Airline Pilots Association, the International Association of Machinists and Aerospace Workers, and the Association of Flight Attendants. Over the last business cycle, from 1992 to 2001, labor costs in the airline industry increased dramatically and gave airlines a heavy financial load. For example, "pilot costs increased by 127% at Continental, 79% at America West, and 59% at American."[52] Labor negotiations between the airlines and unions consume significant time and effort by management and union representatives, as "at any given time, a half-dozen or more contracts may be in negotiation."[53] Negotiations and concessions at one airline typically causes unions at the other airlines to demand reopening of negotiations to match industry standards—and these tactics and negotiations often cause strife and contention in the industry. Some newer entrants to the industry, such as JetBlue, are not yet unionized, giving them a significant competitive advantage.

Competitors The airline industry is highly competitive, with numerous airlines operating in all sectors. In the United States alone, according to the Air Transport Association, at the end of 2001 there were fifteen major airlines (with annual revenues exceeding $1 billion), thirty-nine national airlines (revenues from $100 million to $1 billion), and forty-seven regional airlines (revenues under $100 million).[54] In addition, U.S. airlines compete with non-U.S. airlines for international routes and for alliances that allow customers to find continuing services in routes not covered by U.S. airlines.

In general, there are two basic business models for major U.S. airlines: a full-service model based on hub-and-spoke route maps, and a limited-service, low-cost point-to-point model. In general, airlines that existed before the 1978 Deregulation Act operate in the hub-and-spoke model. This is often called the "legacy" model.[55] Other airlines, notably Southwest Airlines, developed the low-cost point-to-point model after deregulation.

Legacy carriers may have profound structural disadvantages thanks to the high cost of unionized labor, overly complex route networks, and decades of intensive economic regulation in both the United States and Europe[56]—which is why newly created airlines like JetBlue Airways are avoiding the limited flexibility imposed by the hub-and-spoke structure by basing their business models on the Southwest model. This new breed of low-cost carriers boasts a less expensive, less unionized workforce as well as the more flexible point-to-point route structure. In addition to JetBlue, this alternative business model is serving a growing list of profitable carriers like the United Kingdom's easyJet, Canada's WestJet, and Ireland's Ryanair,[57] which are able to compete toe-to-toe with legacy carriers in many major markets. Their presence, simply by exerting downward pressure on prices, benefits even consumers who don't choose to fly them.

Despite the inherent competitiveness of this industry, airlines do work together when part of alliance and strategic partnerships. Partnering with one or more competing or complementary carriers allows airlines to offer more services—a broader route network serving more destinations, increased flight frequency, better frequent-flier programs—at the same time they expand their access to customers and lower their own costs by sharing airport infrastructure, engaging in joint procurement, developing cooperative advertising budgets, and much more.[58] Benefits depend on the nature of the alliance—whether it's a marketing or code-share agreement, or even a franchise or equity-transfer relationship. In order to provide international service, for instance, having a global partner means a U.S. airline can feed traffic through to this partner through an international hub, generating cost savings and smooth connection for all parties. For example, Northwest and China Air have developed a code-sharing strategy to exploit the promising China/U.S. line. In the domestic market, airline companies may share cargo and passenger terminals to save cost and consolidate sales. Continental Airlines has an extensive marketing alliance with Northwest Airlines that includes code-sharing and shared frequent-flier programs.

But airlines also continue to compete fiercely for client bases on particular routes, many times in spectacular price wars. When JetBlue announced a deeply discounted ticket on the route between Oakland, California and Washington, D.C. in August 2002, it triggered a price war on the East Coast–West Coast line. United Airlines responded immediately by matching its fares at the same price level as JetBlue, in the hopes that United will be able to maintain higher fares on other noncompeting flights. These price wars have put pressure on airfare yields since deregulation occurred in 1978.

One way to avoid price wars is to develop frequent-flier loyalty programs. In many cases, the privileges that come with membership in these reward programs—upgrades, priority on standby, access to business lounges, and so on—-are enough to convince members to fly with an airline at a somewhat higher fare than one offered by the competition on the same route.

Flying in Turbulence: The Broad Environment

> It's scarcely news that 2001 was the worst year ever for U.S. airlines.
>
> —Unisys R2A Transportation Management Consultants[59]

External factors have a tremendous impact on any industry—and possibly more on airlines than most industries, due to their high fixed costs and limited flexibility in adapting to changes.

Sociocultural Forces Baby boomers believe they possess an inalienable right to travel. Real median family income (after adjusting for inflation) has increased by 11.8 percent since 1982 alone.[60] And as post–World War II babies have matured into affluent boomers with a great deal more discretionary income than previous generations enjoyed, they are using

those extra dollars to travel more.[61] Younger generations have also been bitten by the travel bug; as travel has become more accessible and affordable, they consider a long-haul flight to Eastern Europe or Southeast Asia to be just as viable as a road trip to the Grand Canyon.[62] With increased globalization of business, international travel has also become extremely common for business travelers. According to a 1997–1998 Gallup poll, 81 percent of the entire U.S. adult population had flown at least once, and two out of every five U.S. citizens flew during 1997–1998.[63]

However, seasonality in travel demand is a constant issue for airlines. Temporal changes in patterns of travel demand result in overdemand for air travel in some periods and low load factors in others.[64] The airlines' product—seat miles—are highly perishable, and excess capacity is a chronic problem. In fact, American Airlines reports that 30 percent of its seat capacity went unused in 2001.[65]

Demand for flights in all seasons turned downward after the terrorist attacks of September 11, 2001. North Americans felt a new vulnerability to terrorism, which they had largely been able to dismiss as somebody else's problem. Airlines—the vehicle of choice for the most devastating terrorist attack on U.S. soil ever—have borne the brunt of travelers' resulting security fears. The tangible results have been devastating. The airline industry experienced a record loss of $7.7 billion in 2001, with air traffic down in all domestic and international markets a total of 5.9 percent—the largest drop in air traffic in U.S. history.[66] All of the major domestic carriers—with the exception of Southwest Airlines—experienced substantial financial losses in 2001.[67] Similar (albeit less devastating) declines also occurred after the TWA and other hijackings in 1985–86; the Pan Am Lockerbie disaster of 1988; and the Gulf War in 1990–91.

As a result, carriers have responded with cuts in service; available seat miles were down 2.8 percent in 2001 over the previous year, with the number of scheduled flights are down by about 600 per day. Furthermore, carriers shrunk their fleet size by decommissioning aircraft that are less fuel-efficient and more maintenance intensive and by postponing deliveries on roughly one-third of the new aircraft that they had planned to take delivery on in 2002 and 2003.[68]

Based on the recovery pattern that followed each of these blows, the airline industry is facing a slow turnaround; it is likely to take some time to build air travel back to what are considered "normal" levels of demand.[69] The outbreak of war in Iraq in early 2003 made the possibility of quick recovery little more than a pipe dream for the suffering air carriers.

Further complicating matters post–September 11 has been the increased security measures at airports, which can substantially lengthen flight-departure lead time—sometimes by as much as an hour or more—and add to an increased distaste for unnecessary air travel as travelers find themselves subjected to multiple body and bag searches. Furthermore, extra security taxes have been passed on to passengers,[70] resulting in increased ticket prices without any revenue benefit for the already strained carriers. Many short-haul travelers are resorting to other forms of travel in order to avoid such delays and hassles, such as the train;[71] Amtrak's Acela trains, for example, can deliver travelers point-to-point along Northeast Corridor routes such as New York to Boston or to Washington, D.C., in roughly the same amount of time it takes to fly.

Technological Forces The Internet, which has revolutionized the way airline passages are bought and sold, has opened up a whole new world of direct distribution for carriers. Airlines can sell directly to consumers via their own Web sites at a fraction of the cost of employing customer service agents to take call-center reservations. Furthermore, easy-to-navigate Web sites with up-to-the-minute availability, pricing, schedule, and fleet information, have diminished the need for intermediaries; as a result, carriers have been able to cut back on base commissions to travel agents.[72] According to Standard & Poor's, most major airlines had cut their commission rates to 5 percent of fares, with a $20 cap on domestic round-trip fares, by late 2001 (down from 8 percent of fares with a $50 cap); total commissions paid in 2001 accounted for approximately 4 percent of airline industry costs, down from 6.2 percent in 2000 and 10.9 percent in 1993.[73]

However, airlines have discovered a dark side to the new distribution frontier and transparency of pricing information. Now that anyone with a Web browser has access to the same global distribution systems as travel agents via such Web sites as Expedia, Travelocity, and Orbitz, airfare pricing is now approaching the economist's ideal of "perfect" information.[74] Thus, the legacy carriers must be willing to match their competitors' prices—including the prices offered by their more flexible low-cost competitors, such as Southwest, JetBlue, easyJet, and a variety of regional carriers—or lose market share.[75] As a result, leisure airfares were running at approximately 20 percent below their five-year average by mid-2002.[76]

Technology has dramatically changed all aspects of airline operations, from reservations through engineering; the result has been reduced labor costs, greater efficiency, and improved customer service.[77] Reservation systems have evolved from telephone operators to airline Web sites, while airlines now have the ability to trace luggage in a matter of minutes rather than days. "Ticketless travel"—e-ticketing—has been embraced by customers and airlines alike for its ease of use and cost-effectiveness. United Airlines reports that electronic ticketing costs fifty cents per ticket, while issuing a paper ticket costs $8, since fourteen additional accounting and processing procedures are required; the other major carriers are experiencing similar cost benefits from e-ticketing.[78]

Self-service electronic check-in, automatic upgrades for loyalty-program members, and other innovations have also become a norm for travelers. Such innovations have helped to allay travelers' frustrations with increased security measures and other post–September 11 bureaucracies associated with flying.

Global Economic Forces

> Had terrorists not attacked, the major hub-and-spoke carriers would still be facing the competitive Waterloo today.
>
> —Holman Jenkins,
> *The Wall Street Journal*[79]

While it's easy for the airline industry to place the blame for its economic troubles on the trauma of September 11, the reality is that corporate belt tightening and the prevailing economic recession had been putting enormous financial pressure on the airlines since early 2001. As a result, major carrier revenues were already in steep decline in the first six months of that year.[80] However, financial pressure on airlines was exacerbated by September 11, when air traffic was completely stalled for days, followed by an unprecedented decline in ticket sales. The downturn in business travel had already begun in early 2001, when corporate earnings fell. "Based on information from a sampling of ATA member airlines, domestic business traffic fell 5.5% during the first eight months of the year [2001], while personal and pleasure traffic increased 5.1%. Over the last four months of [2001], the decline in business traffic quadrupled to 24.2% and personal pleasure traffic reversed its course, falling 18.0%."[81]

Furthermore, cost-conscious corporations have become newly price sensitive. Businesses are no longer willing to pay the exorbitant full fares that they used to consider a fact of life in the days before the economic downturn took hold and scandal rocked the corporate world. Companies have also realized a new willingness to rely on "virtually there" technologies such as e-mail, video conferencing, and instant messaging in lieu of actually sending their employees on the road for face-to-face meetings around the globe. As a result, business travel—the most lucrative business in the industry—only generated about 30 percent of airline revenues in 2001, down from roughly 52 percent of total airline revenues in 1982, and about 15 percent of total Revenue Passenger Miles (RPMs) in 2001 according to Standard & Poor's estimates.[82] While the horizon got a little brighter in 2002—with business travel accounting for 37 percent of aggregate industry revenues and 21 percent of RPMs, according to Standard & Poor's[83]—a return to historic levels is unlikely.

All signs seem to indicate that the recession-era decline in business travel, combined with the new transparency in pricing available online and the decline in air travel due to fears of terrorism, likely signal a permanent sea change in both business and leisure travel purchasing patterns. These fundamental shifts have lead to the commodization of airlines, with price—rather than competitive advantages in service—being the primary driver behind consumer behavior.[84] Carriers haven't given up on creating competitive advantage for themselves, however; most airlines currently see frequent-flier loyalty programs targeted to keep regular customers coming back to be their best long-term hedge against commodization.

Further aggravating the industry's financial problems are high fixed costs, which allow airlines little elasticity, or freedom, to shrink and grow as demand dictates.[85] As a result, enormous losses resulting from the convergence of the recession pattern, increasing price competition, and the downturn of demand resulting from September 11 have driven cash flows deeply into negative territory, and the overall health of the industry is threatened.[86] U.S. carriers have laid off 80,300 employees since September 11; the largest layoffs occurred at American Airlines and United Airlines, which furloughed 20,000 employees each, followed by US Airways (11,000 employees), Northwest Airlines (10,000), and Continental (8,500). Only Southwest Airlines and Alaska Airlines did not lay off staff.[87]

Uncertainty in the price of oil is a major destabilizing factor. While jet fuel prices actually declined from $0.83 to $0.73 per gallon from 2001 to 2002, Goldman Sachs' Energy Research Group reported that a decline in available inventories would make oil prices increasingly volatile in the future.[88]

Political and Legal Forces Few other industries are as dependent on world governments as the airlines industry.[89] Despite the end of deregulation in 1978, U.S.-based airlines continue to answer to governmental agencies. The Federal Aviation Administration (FAA), an offshoot of the Department of Transportation, is the industry's primary regulatory body, policing the safety, labor, and operating procedures as well as aircraft fitness and emissions levels.[90] The most recent trend from the FAA has been the opening of new gate slots and expanded landing rights at congested airports.[91]

The Air Transport Association (ATA) of America is the cooperative trade association maintained by the domestic airlines that, in effect, serves as the industry's own self-policing agency, focusing largely on issues of safety, security, technological innovations, and cooperative industrywide service improvements. A similarly structured agency, the International Air Transport Association (IATA), serves as the global self-regulating body for the worldwide air transport network.[92]

U.S. airlines are subject to whatever local regulations are in place whenever they fly international skies. The degree of regulation varies from country to country; formal bilateral accords govern reciprocal landing rights, the number of international carriers that can operate within the country, and other matters[93]—and the reins on the international operation of U.S. carriers can be tight.

But the U.S. had signed "open skies" agreements with nearly one hundred countries as of 2002, reducing economic regulations, lowering entry barriers, and opening the playing field for code-sharing and other strategic partnering alliances between U.S. and international carriers. Still, some legislators have tried to regulate competition by curbing the formation of global alliances, especially those between U.S. and European Union carriers,[94] and by restricting the foreign ownership of U.S. airlines.[95] Still, Standard & Poor's reported in 2002 that "international deregulation seems unstoppable and it will follow the pattern seen in the U.S. industry."[96]

THE INTERNAL ORGANIZATION

During this past year of unimaginable challenges, Continental relied even more heavily on the fundamentals that have made us successful. Although no one could have anticipated the events of last year, our culture of Working Together developed over the last years, including relationships with employees, customers, vendors, and distribution partners, proved to be our most valuable resource for weathering the storm precipitated by the terrorist attacks of Sept. 11.

—Gordon Bethune, CEO, and Larry Kellner, president[97]

Continental Airlines is a major U.S. air carrier engaged in the business of transporting passengers, cargo, and mail. As of January 31, 2002, Continental flew to 123 domestic and 93 international destinations and offered additional connecting services through domestic and foreign alliances. These destinations are serviced by Continental; by Continental's wholly owned subsidiary, Continental Micronesia,

Inc. (CMI); and by ExpressJet Airlines, Inc., doing business as Continental Express. Continental does have a controlling interest in ExpressJet, holding 53.1 percent of its shares, following an initial public offering for ExpressJet in April 2002.

Continental is the second largest U.S. carrier to Latin America and serves more destinations in Mexico than any other U.S. airline. Continental is the largest carrier in the New York City metropolitan area and operates the only hub in the region (across the Hudson River from Manhattan in Newark, New Jersey).

Strategic Direction

Our goals are simple—they are our customers' goals. We continue to deliver a high-quality product each and every day, getting our customers where they want to go, on-time and with their bags, while providing pre-flight and in-flight service that is globally recognized for consistency and excellence.[98]

Continental Airlines has clearly defined set of goals that portray their strategic direction. Theirs is a simple, straightforward, and flexible mantra. The Go Forward Plan plainly explains what the company's goals are, what the challenges are it faces, and how the company will measure success.

The Go Forward Plan is a four-pronged approach:

- *Fly to Win:* The Market Plan
- *Fund Our Future:* The Financial Plan
- *Make Reliability a Reality:* The Product Plan
- *Working Together:* The People Plan

In practice since 1995, the Go Forward Plan has enabled Continental to achieve one of the most impressive turnarounds in American corporate history.

Fly to Win (The Market Plan)

Achieve above-average profits in a changed industry environment. Grow the airline where it can make money and keep improving the business/leisure mix. Maximize distribution channels while reducing distribution costs and eliminating non-value-added costs.[99]

Continental's marketing plan focuses on meeting the needs of the changing market to maximize profits for stakeholders. Continental concentrates on flying to cities where people want to go, and doing so in a clean, safe, and reliable manner. Continental leverages hubs with significant market strength that generate large amounts of revenue—namely New York City, Houston, Cleveland, and Guam in the Pacific.

Continental wants to provide the products and services that customers value, such as new airplanes with large overhead baggage bins, an award-winning frequent-flier program, and good food. The airline uses technology to eliminate non-value-added costs. It has updated its Continental.com Web site so customers can book flights, review their frequent-flier accounts, and check flight status all from a personalized home page.[100]

Funding Our Future (The Financial Plan)

Manage our assets to maximize stockholder value and build for the future. Reduce costs with technology. Generate strong cash flow and improve financial flexibility by increasing our cash balance.[101]

"Funding Our Future" lays the foundation for Continental's profitable growth by focusing on strengthening their balance sheet, reducing fleet age, and building and financing new hubs.

The events of September 11, 2001 had a staggering effect on Continental's financial health. The subsequent Stabilization Act provided Continental with $400 million in direct federal grants, out of a total of $5 billion granted to the industry, to cover the losses caused by the government-imposed shutdown and the terrorist attacks. The act also authorized up to $10 billion in loan guarantees, an offer Continental has yet to apply for. But the airline did undertake a series of cost-saving initiatives that include the continued grounding of aircraft and a roughly 20 percent reduction in flight schedules.

Making Reliability a Reality (The Product Plan)

Deliver an industry-leading product we are proud to sell. Rank among the top of the industry in the key DOT measurements: On-time arrivals, baggage handling, complaints and involuntary denied boarding. Keep improving our product.[102]

Continental has focused its efforts over the past six years on running a great airline that takes customers where they want to go safely, on time, and with their bags meeting them when they get off the plane. The airline has a trophy case full of awards to prove their success with customer satisfaction. In 2001, Continental was once again ranked number one in on-time performance among major U.S. hub carriers. In 2001, Continental had an 82.2 percent on-time arrivals rate. It was also named *Air Transport World*'s airline of the year in 2001 for the second time in five years.[103]

Continental has worked closely with the federal government to increase security at airports and in airplanes. The number of security screening lanes at hubs has been increased to reduce waiting time. Cockpit doors have been replaced with stronger, more impenetrable ones. Continental plans to keep the standards high even with the loss in demand.

Continental also looks to technology to make air travel quicker, more reliable, more convenient, and more user-friendly for their customers. Almost 90 percent of their tickets sold are e-tickets, and the airline has been aggressive about introducing eService check-in kiosks, which allow customers to check in, change seats, request upgrades, or purchase tickets at airports.[104]

Working Together (The People Plan)

Help well-trained employees build careers they enjoy every day. Treat each other with dignity and respect. Focus on safety; make employee programs easy to use and keep improving communication. Pay compensation that is fair to employees and fair to the company.[105]

Continental strives to be a company whose employees enjoy coming to work every day and are valued for their contributions. By becoming more involved in company decisions, working in an environment of civility and respect and receiving performance-based incentives, Continental's employees are motivated to keep the airline on top. In 2001, Continental was once again placed in *Fortune*'s list of the top "100 Best Companies to Work For."[106]

Ownership Structure

Continental's stocks are traded under the symbol CAL at the New York Stock Exchange. Continental offers preferred securities of trust, preferred stock, common stock, and Treasury stock.

Preferred Securities of Trust Trust preferred securities are issued in certain structured finance transactions, generally to raise capital. Trust preferred securities pay regular dividends, are immensely flexible, and may be converted into shares of common stock.

In November 2000, Continental Airlines Finance Trust II, which is wholly owned by Continental, completed a private placement of five million 6 percent convertible preferred securities. These term income deferrable equity securities have a liquidation value of $50 per preferred security and are readily convertible into shares of Class B common stock at a conversion rate of $60 per share of Class B common stock. Distributions on the preferred securities are payable by the trust at an annual rate of 6 percent of the liquidation value of $50 per preferred security.[107]

Preferred Stock The year 2001 began with the completion of a transaction with Northwest Airlines that resulted in a single class of common stock and equal rights for all holders of common stock, while strengthening and extending the broad commercial alliance between Continental and Northwest to make sure their customers have the long-term benefits of an expanded network. Judge Dennis Page Hood called the arrangement "a victory for consumers, who will benefit from lower fares and better airline service. This is the result we have sought all along. It will ensure that Northwest and Continental remain independent competitors."[108]

Northwest acquired stock representing more than 50 percent of the voting interest in Continental

in 1998 and entered into a separate marketing alliance at the same time. As of December 31, 2001, one share of Series B preferred stock was outstanding, which is owned by Northwest Airlines. On September 30, 2002 (end of the third quarter), Continental had $248,000,000 as redeemable preferred stock.

On August 23, 2002, Delta, Continental, and Northwest confirmed that they were seeking approval for a ten-year marketing pact, which would begin next spring. The agreement requires Northwest to exchange its class A Continental shares that carry ten votes per share for $450 million in cash and a lesser number of Continental B shares that carry one vote per share. In addition, Northwest would receive preferred stock in Continental that would give it the right to veto a proposed combination between Continental and other carriers under certain conditions. After the new deal is completed, Northwest will retain 7 percent of the voting interest in Continental and an equity stake of less than 5 percent.[109]

Common Stock Continental has one class of common stock issued and outstanding, Class B common stock. Each share of Class B common stock is entitled to one vote per share.

Treasury Stock A stock repurchase program was started in 1998 under which Continental repurchased a total of 28.2 million shares of Class B common stock for a total of $1.2 billion through September 30, 2002. The program was suspended during 2001.

Employee Stock Purchase Program All Continental employees are eligible to participate in an employee stock purchase program under which they may purchase shares of Class B common stock at 85 percent of the lower of the fair market value on the first day of the option period or the last day of the option period. During 2001, Continental issued 710,394 shares of Class B common stock.

Stock Price The stock price for the fifty-two-week period ending November 17, 2002, ranged from $3.59 and $35.25.[110] The shares showed a slight growth, in the intervening weeks due to the steps taken by Continental toward financial recovery. With threats of war with Iraq and the constantly changing broad environment, however, the market found it difficult to predict how Continental will be affected next. The airline fluctuated throughout most of 2003, but it started a persistent climb toward the $20 mark in the third quarter.[111]

Operating Characteristics

Continental's primary business is focused on transporting passengers to various destinations in the United States and throughout the world. Although Continental does provide some cargo and mail service, this business generates only 6 percent of the revenue of the whole group while passenger services generate the remaining 94 percent of revenue.

Prior to the September 11 terrorist attacks, Continental flew more 2,500 flights a day. For the year ending December 31, 2000, Continental had 86,100 million available seat miles. On September 15, 2001, Continental announced a 20 percent systemwide reduction in its flight schedule.[112] Two days later, Continental discontinued service on ten routes (see Exhibit 3).[113] By the end of December 2001, Continental had reduced its operations to 84,845 million available seat miles.

In the United States, Continental has designed its route network based on a hub-and-spoke system. This system allows airlines to bring passengers from lightly traveled areas, typically in smaller planes, to a single point where passengers can take a second flight, typically on larger planes. The goal is to generate higher load factors on the longer flights. This system is the opposite of a point-to-point system, where direct flights connect each airport to the others. The major airlines also use the hub-and-spoke design to achieve significant market penetration in the hub cities. Continental has four principal hubs: Newark, Cleveland, Houston, and Guam. By building hubs in strategic cities, airlines can build significant market share in their hub locations. For instance, Continental had a 73.7 percent market share in Houston and a 56.0 percent market share in Newark for the twelve months ending June 2001.[114]

The hub-and-spoke model does create some inflexibilities for an airline. It becomes almost impossible to develop direct point-to-point route between non-hub cities even if there is demand for it. Some sources of inflexibility include the difficulty obtaining gate space in the point-to-point cities, and not having local crews available to service the routes.

Equipment Fleet As of December 31, 2002, Continental had 554 aircraft in its fleet, of which one-fourth are owned and three-fourths are leased.[115] Continental has purchase commitments (orders) for an additional eighty-six aircraft and options to acquire one hundred more aircraft. Exhibit 4 details the types of aircrafts and the manufacturers.[116] It does not include the fifty-six jet aircraft and nineteen turboprop aircraft that Continental has put out of service after September 11.

Despite putting scores of aircraft out of service, Continental took delivery of twenty Boeing jet aircraft during the first nine months of 2002. Continental has been progressively updating its fleet of aircraft and reducing the number of models used. "Since the beginning of 1996, Continental has reduced the number of fleet types from eight to five (777, 767, 757, 737 and eventually outgoing MD80s) and cut its average mainline fleet age to 6.5 years from 13.6 years."[117]

Service Continental has made great strides to improve service performance during the ticketing and check-in process, both to make the process more

EXHIBIT 3	ROUTES DISCONTINUED AFTER SEPTEMBER 11, 2001

Cleveland–Atlantic City, NJ	Newark–Daytona Beach, FL
Houston–Abilene, TX	Newark–Düsseldorf, Germany
Houston–San Angelo, TX	Newark–Houston/Hobby
Houston–Tyler, TX	Newark–London Stansted
Houston–Waco, TX	Newark–Melbourne, FL

EXHIBIT 4	**COMPOSITION OF CONTINENTAL'S FLEET**

Aircraft Type	Total Aircraft	Firm Orders	Options	Seats in Standard Configuration	Average Age (in Years)
777-200ER	18	—	3	283	3.3
767-400ER	16	—	—	235	1.3
767-200ER	10	—	2	174	1.8
757-300	4	11	11	210	1.0
757-200	41	—	—	183	5.9
737-900	12	3	12	167	1.3
737-800	77	38	35	155	2.8
737-700	36	15	24	124	4.0
737-500	65	—	—	104	6.7
737-300	58	—	—	124	16.1
MD-80	29	—	—	141	16.7
Total Mainline Jets	**366**	**67**	**87**		**7.0**
ERJ-145XR	18	86	100	50	0.1
ERJ-145	140	—	—	50	2.6
ERJ-135	30	—	—	37	2.3
Regional Jets	**188**	**86**	**100**		**2.3**
Grand Total	**554**				

Source: Continental Airlines, Inc., *2002 Annual Report,* for period ended December 31, 2002, 21.

efficient for customers as well as to reduce its own operating costs.[118] One of the key measures of service in the airline industry is on-time arrivals. Continental offers superb performance for on-time arrivals. For all of 2002, over 84 percent of Continental's flights arrived within fourteen minutes of the planned arrival time, compared to an industry average of around 82 percent.[119]

Continental Airlines decided, in the wake of September 11, that it would not decrease the services it provides during flights, unlike most other major airlines. Continental continued to offer meals, including hot meals, during its flights. It continues to offer free magazines to fliers. This continued service may make up for some of the increased frustration that travelers have with air transportation after September 11. The increased security measures have meant longer lines at the airport, waiting to check in and screen bags, waiting to pass through security checkpoints, and waiting to board the aircraft while random screening is being conducted.

Financial Concerns

Before September 11, 2001, the financial perspective for the U.S. airline industry was beset with problems—but these problems were masked by a boom in travel. As a result, most major airlines posted significant profits during the 1990s.

The financial problems stem from the high fixed costs the industry has, primarily from equipment costs and expensive union labor contracts. As an example of equipment costs, JetBlue Airways purchased ten Airbus A320s in January 2002, a deal valued in excess of $500 million.[120] In another example of the high industry costs, the pilots at United Airlines staged a strike in 2000 that cost the airline around $700 million. As a result of the strike, the pilots received "the most expensive contract in history: An immediate pay raise of 22% to 28% and a 4.5% annual raise through 2004."[121] Although this is an extreme case, all airlines must work with a number of unions—pilots, flight attendants, and mechanists unions especially—which creates high labor cost for the industry as a whole.

As each airline has pursued different equipment acquisition tactics and different labor relations strategies, the cost structure between different airlines varied widely; however, most of them were fairly profitable during the 1990s.[122] The combined effect of the economic downturn and the reduced travel after September 11 caused the airline industry's finances to veer significantly off course in 2001. *Air Transport World* estimates that the global airline industry losses in 2001 were the worst in history, an estimated $11.0 billion, and expected industry losses of $7.5 billion in 2002. For the U.S. airline industry specifically, *Air Transport World* estimated losses of $9.0 billion in 2001 and $6.0 billion in 2002.[123] In reality, the top ten U.S. carriers alone shouldered a loss of $11.3 billion in 2002, with Standard & Poor's forecasting a narrower $6.4 billion loss for 2003.[124] Continental was operating at about a 75 percent passenger load factor through 2002, with a breakeven passenger load factor of nearly 78 percent.[125]

Continental generates its revenues through a combination of traffic volumes and pricing. Continental reduced its flight schedule after September 11, which resulted in reduced revenue per seat miles and available seat miles. In addition, Continental practiced fare discounting in an attempt to generate more demand for its services and to persuade those who might wish to cancel or delay their travel to instead fly with Continental. In one example, Continental offered double miles to frequent fliers, which led to increased free trips and thereby, discounted flights overall.[126]

As a result, Continental announced a 3.0 percent decrease in passenger revenue in the three months ending September 2002, compared to the same period in 2001. The airline attributed this to "continued traffic and capacity declines and fare discounting following the 2001 terrorist attacks and the continuing weak economy. Yield was 3.4% lower."[127]

Congress passed the Air Transportation Safety and System Stabilization Act (H.R. 2926) on September 22, 2001, in response to the crisis. Continental accepted slightly over $400 million in a federal grant as part of the Stabilization Act. This grant was considered revenue, to make up for the immediate lost business due to the temporary suspension of all flights on September 11. The government was also granting debt guarantees, based on an application review process. Continental did not apply for any of these guarantees, but it reserved the right to do so in the future depending on liquidity needs.[128]

Security costs have increased overall since September 11. For instance, all cockpit doors needed to be reinforced, an operation that Continental completed on October 22, 2001. Continental feels that most of these additional costs cannot be passed on to the consumer.[129] Given the low customer demand for air travel and the substantial discounts that most air carriers are marketing to customers, airlines will have to absorb the additional security costs.

In addition to the costs to increase security, the airline is also responsible for its share in the costs of installing baggage-screening equipment in each airport. These machines, some of which cost $1 million each, are purchased by the airlines and operated by the Transportation Security Agency.[130]

Continental's wages and salaries represented 35 percent of total operating revenues in 2001. Wages have always been the largest expense item for all airlines, as a services industry requires significant labor investment. Immediately after September 11, Continental announced that it would furlough 12,000 employees. Continental has reduced this number to about 8,000, but it has in any case significantly reduced its workforce. The costs of this reduction were significant, around $29 million in severance and continued benefits for furloughed employees.[131]

Continental has firm purchase commitments for 171 jets, including sixty-seven Boeing jets and 104 Embraer regional jets.[132] The estimated aggregate cost of Continental's commitment to Boeing is $2.5 billion. Aircraft were to be delivered starting in the fourth quarter of 2003 and continuing through 2008. No financing is currently in place for these acquisitions. As for the Embraer regional jets, the estimated total cost is $2.1 billion.[133]

Continental has been successful in managing its fuel costs, which account for 14 percent of its revenues. There was a significant decrease in fuel costs in 2002 compared to 2001.[134] In addition, Continental's younger fleet is more fuel-efficient, further enhancing fuel cost savings. Another benefit of the younger fleet of aircraft will be lower maintenance costs, especially when compared to other major U.S. air carriers.

In its *2001 Annual Report,* Continental indicated that its goal is to have $1.5 million in cash on hand, a significant increase from its previous target of $1 million, as a buffer against operating at a loss for the next few periods and against additional unknown changes to the economy and the airline industry. In its search for the additional cash balance, Continental decided to sell off part of one of its subsidiaries. As of December 31, 2001, Continental was the parent company of two wholly owned subsidiaries:

- ExpressJet Airlines, Inc. (formerly Continental Express, Inc.)
- Continental Micronesia, Inc.

In April 2002, Continental conducted an initial public offering (IPO) for 30 million of the common shares in ExpressJet as a way of increasing the company's cash balance. After the IPO, Continental retained a 53.1 percent controlling interest in ExpressJet. In addition, this IPO raised a significant amount of cash for Continental, as net proceeds totaled $300 million.[135] Continental retained the right to liquidate its remaining interest in ExpressJet once the 180-day lock-up period expired.[136] Continental does not plan to sell its remaining stake in ExpressJet, but the stake could be used to raise cash in the future.

See Exhibit 5 for five years of financial statements (1998 through 2002) for Continental Airlines.

Marketing

It's one thing for a company to know itself—and another thing altogether to be able to tell its story to everyone else. Continental Airlines has enjoyed great success by formulating a smart, no-nonsense public image that goes hand-in-hand with its strategic mission.

Brand Definition: "Work Hard. Fly Right."

The public knows Continental's Go Forward program as "Work Hard. Fly Right." The simple, snappy ad campaign—which features little more than the airline's signature blue-and-white globe and a series of short, to-the-point messages[137]—was launched in 1998 under the creative guidance of advertising firm NW Ayer & Partners. The campaign continues to be a strong public face for the airline. In fact, while other airlines worked to redefine their public images after the September 11 attacks, Continental recommitted itself to its "Work Hard. Fly Right." branding.[138]

The Kaplan Thayer Group (KTG) took over Ayer in April 2002[139] without causing a hiccup in Continental's public image. In fact, KTG—one of Madison Avenue's most brazen and successful ad agencies—seems to taking "Work Hard. Fly Right" in fresh directions: The agency allied with digital innovator Semaphore Partners in July 2002 to unify the ad campaign and Continental's Web site,[140] and it later partnered with cutting-edge cartoonists FlickerLab to create animated TV spots for the airline.[141] Continental's willingness to invest in its public image—it was the lone major carrier to increase its media budget at the end of 2001[142]—has helped the airline maintain one of the sleekest images among an increasingly ragtag band of competitors.

Commitment to Customer Service

> Guess which two airlines constantly top industry studies for customer satisfaction?
>
> You got it, Continental and Southwest.
>
> —*Investor's Business Daily*[143]

When Gordon Bethune took over Continental as CEO, he understood the value of branding, so much so that he cut the advertising budget in half until the company could build a product worth promoting.[144] To be reborn, the airline need more than a Madison Avenue image—it needed results.

Key to Continental's turnaround has been an emphasis on empowering employees at every level to offer the best service possible, and gauging success with tangible performance measures, both internally and against competitors. Doing so "got every employee

EXHIBIT 5	FINANCIAL STATEMENTS

Consolidated Balance Sheet
($ Millions, Except per Share Data)

Year Ended December 31,

Fiscal Year End	2002[1]	2001[2]	2000[3]	1999[4]	1998[5]
Assets					
Current assets:					
Cash & equivalents	$1,225	$1,132	$1,371	$1,198	$1,399
Short-term investments	117	—	24	392	—
Accounts receivables, net	377	404	495	506	449
Spare parts and supplies, net	248	272	280	236	166
Deferred income taxes, prepayments & other current assets	310	336	289	274	340
Total current assets	2,277	2,144	2,459	2,606	2,606
Property & equipment, net	6,968	6,153	5,163	4,173	3,065
Other non-current assets (including routes, airport operating rights & other intangibles, net)	1,495	1,494	1,579	1,444	1,667
Total assets	$10,740	$9,791	$9,201	$8,223	$7,086
Liabilities & stockholders' equity					
Current liabilities:					
Accounts payable	$930	$1,008	$1,016	$856	$843
Current maturities of long-term debt & capital leases	493	355	304	321	231
Air traffic liability	802	1,014	1,125	962	854
Accrued payroll & other current liabilities	621	569[6]	535	636	514
Total current liabilities	2,296	2,946	2,980	2,775	2,442
Long-term debt & capital leases	5,222	4,198	3,374	3,055	2,480
Other long-term liabilities	1,572	1,243[7]	995	800	860
Commitments & contingencies					
Mandatorily redeemable preferred securities of subsidiary trust holding solely convertible subordinated debentures	241	243	242	—	111
Minority interest & redeemable preferred stock of subsidiary	12		—	—	—
Redeemable common stock	—	—	450	—	—
Stockholders' equity:					
Preferred stock	—	—	—	—	—
Class B common stock	1	1	1	1	1
Additional paid-in capital	1,391	1,069[8]	379	871	634
Retained earnings	910	1,361	1,456	1,114	659
Accumulated other comprehensive income (loss)	(395)	(130)[9]	13	(1)	(88)
Treasury stock, at cost	(1,140)	(1,140)	(689)	(392)	(13)
Total stockholders' equity	767	1,161	1,160	1,593	1,193
Total liabilities & stockholders' equity	$10,740	$9,791	$9,201	$8,223	$7,086

1. Continental Airlines, *2002 Annual Report*, 23.
2. Ibid.
3. Continental Airlines, *2001 Annual Report*, 24.
4. Continental Airlines, *1999 Annual Report*, 38-39.
5. Ibid.
6. $523 in accrued payroll and pensions and $291 in accrued other liabilities, resulting in $3,191 in total current liabilities reported in *2001 Annual Report*, 24.
7. $998 in other long-term liabilities reported in *2001 Annual Report*, 24.
8. $1,071 in additional paid-in capital reported in *2001 Annual Report*, 24.
9. ($132) in accumulative other comprehensive loss reported in *2001 Annual Report*, 24.

(Continues)

EXHIBIT 5	FINANCIAL STATEMENTS (*CONTINUED*)

Income Statement ($ Millions)

Year Ended December 31,

Fiscal Year End	2002[10]	2001[11]	2000[12]	1999[13]	1998[14]
Operating revenue:					
Passenger-related revenues	$ 7,862	$ 8,457	$ 9,308	$ 8,116	$7,456
Cargo, mail and other	540	512	591	523	471
	8,402	8,969	9,899	8,639	7,927
Operating expenses:					
Wages, salaries and related costs	2,959	3,021	2,875	2,510	2,218
Aircraft fuel	1,023	1,229	1,393	756	727
Aircraft rentals, landing fees and other rentals	1,535	1,484	1,376	1,268	659
Maintenance, materials and repairs	476	568	646	603	582
Depreciation & amortization	444	467	402	360	583
Reservation and sales, commissions	592	809	981	990	414
Passenger services	296	347	362	352	294
Fleet impairment losses, severance and other special charges	242	124	—	81	122
Other	1,135	1,193	1,135	1,104	1,627
Stabilization Act grant	12	(417)	—	—	—
	8,714	8,825	9,170	8,024[15]	7,226
Operating income	(312)	144	729	615[16]	701
Nonoperating income (expense):					
Interest expense	(356)	(295)	(251)	(233)	(178)
Interest capitalized	36	57	57	55	59
Interest income	24	45	87	71	—
Gain on sale of Amadeus	—	—	—	297	55
Other, net	(7)	(65)	(60)[17]	(7)[18]	11
	(303)	(258)	(167)[19]	183[20]	(53)
Income (loss) before income taxes and extraordinary charge	(615)	(114)	562[21]	798	648
Income tax (expense) benefit	202	29	(219)[22]	(310)	(248)
Distributions on preferred securities of trust	(10)	(10)	(1)	—	(13)
Minority interest	(28)	—	—	—	—
Income (loss) before income taxes and extraordinary charge	—	$ (95)	348	488	387
Cumulative effect of accounting changes, net of taxes	—	—	—	(33)	—
Extraordinary charge, net of income taxes	—	—	(6)	—	(4)
Net income (loss)	$ (451)	$ (95)	$ 342	$ 455	$383
Basic earnings (loss) per share	$ (7.02)	$ (1.72)	$ 5.62	$ 6.54	$6.34
Diluted earnings (loss) per share	$ (7.02)	$ (1.72)	$ 5.45	$ 6.20	$5.02

10. Continental Airlines, *2002 Annual Report*, 22.
11. Ibid.
12. Ibid.
13. Continental Airlines, *2001 Annual Report*, 23.
14. Continental Airlines, *1999 Annual Report*, 37.
15. $8,039 in total operating expenses reported in *1999 Annual Report*, 37.
16. $600 in total operating income reported in *1999 Annual Report*, 37.
17. ($51) in other nonoperating income (expenses) reported in *2001 Annual Report*, 23.

18. $8 in other nonoperating income reported in *1999 Annual Report*, 37.
19. ($158) in total nonoperating income (expense) reported in *2001 Annual Report*, 23.
20. $198 in total nonoperating income reported in *1999 Annual Report*, 37.
21. $571 in income (loss) before income taxes and extraordinary charges reported in *2001 Annual Report*, 23.
22. ($222) in income tax benefit (expense) reported in *2001 Annual Report*, 23.

(*Continues*)

EXHIBIT 5	FINANCIAL STATEMENTS (*CONTINUED*)

Consolidated Statement of Cash Flows ($ Millions)	Year Ended December 31,				
Fiscal Year End	**2002**[23]	**2001**[24]	**2000**[25]	**1999**[26]	**1998**[27]
Cash flows from operating activities:					
Net income (loss)	$ (451)	$ (95)	$ 342	$ 455	$ 383
Adjustments to reconcile net income (loss) to net cash:					
Depreciation & amoritization	444	467	402	360	294
Fleet disposition/impairment losses	242	61	—	81	122
Deferred income taxes	(179)	(40)	224	293	224
Gain on sale of Amadeus	—	—	—	(297)	—
Gain on sale of other investments	—	—	—	(29)	(6)
Changes in operating assets & liabilities:	(138)	101	(4)	(37)	(137)
Cumulative effect of change in accounting principles	—	—	—	33	—
Other	4	51	(58)	(83)	(4)
Net cash provided by operating activities	(78)	545	906	776	876
Cash flows from investing activities:					
Purchase deposits refunded (paid) in connection with aircraft deliveries	146	(95)	(63)	(1,174)	(818)
Capital expenditures	(539)	(568)	(511)	(706)	(610)
Sale (purchase) of short-term investments	(117)	24	368	(392)	—
Proceeds from sale of Amadeus, net	—	—	—	391	—
Other	(34)	(15)	138	(6)	(30)
Net cash used in investing activities	(544)	(654)	(68)	(659)	(698)
Cash flows from financing activities:					
Proceeds from issuance of long-term debt, net	596	436	157	453	737
Issuance capital stock		241	334	38	56
Payments on long-term debt & capital lease obligations	(383)	(367)	(707)	(295)	(423)
Proceeds from sale of ExpressJet, net	447	—	—	—	—
Proceeds from issuance of preferred securities of trust, net	—	—	242	—	—
Purchase of common stock	—	(451)	(450)	(528)	(223)
Proceeds from issuance of common stock	23	241	92	38	56
Other	—	(11)	3	—	—
Net cash used in financing activities	683	(152)	(663)	(318)	196
Net change in cash & cash equivalents	61	(261)	175	(201)	374
Cash & cash equivalents—beginning of period	1,102	1,363	1,188	1,399	1,025
Cash & cash equivalents—end of period	$ 1,163	$ 1,102	$ 1,363	$ 1,198	$ 1,198
Supplemental cash flows information:					
Interest paid	$ 345	$ 314	$ 276	$221	$ 157
Income taxes paid (refunded)	(31)	(4)	7	18	25
Investing & financing activities not affecting cash:					
Property & equipment acquired through issuance of debt	908	707	808	774	425
Capital lease obligations incurred	36	95	53	50	124
Conversion of 6-3/4% convertible subordinated notes	—	—	—	230	—
Conversion of trust originated preferred securities	—	—	—	111	134
Sale-leaseback of Beech 1900-D Aircraft	—	—	—	81	—

23. Continental Airlines, *2002 Annual Report,* 24.
24. Ibid.
25. Ibid.
26. Continental Airlines, *1999 Annual Report,* 40-41.
27. Ibid.

heading in the same direction," reflected president and COO Greg Brenneman in 1998.[145]

Keeping the eye on the prize has resulted in unprecedented success for a major U.S. carrier. Continental Airlines enjoyed the industry's strongest consistency in service metrics over the four years ending in 2002.[146] Operational performance included an 82.2 percent on-time arrivals rate for 2001—making Continental number one among U.S. hub carriers for on-time performance—and a 99.2 percent flight completion rate in 2001.[147] Its on-time record and mishandled-bags record were the best in the industry for the first half of 2002.[148] What's more, the carrier cancels half as many flights than the industry as a whole, and canceled only 0.2 percent of its scheduled flights in the first half of 2002. The result has been a slate of industry and customer-service awards unrivaled by any other U.S. carrier in recent years.[149]

The airline is an innovator behind the scenes, too: Its call-center quality assurance program is an industry leader.[150] In fact, Continental is so widely acknowledged for its success in the customer-service arena that it sells consulting services to outside firms—both within and outside the airline industry—in call-center management, customer service, and sales training.[151]

Target One: Business Travelers   By placing greater emphasis on product differentiation over pricing relative to its competitors, Continental emphasized its commitment to business travelers,[152] despite the fact that the business world is cutting back on travel budgets, redirecting its traveling executives to the coach seats, replacing face-to-face meetings with video and teleconferencing, and generally cutting back on corporate travel across the board.[153]

Establishing the goal to earn and retain business travelers as part of the Go Forward Plan, a postturnaround Continental has proven its willingness to do almost anything to keep them on board: Bethune has even thrown a party at home for the 100 top fliers in the innovative and award-winning OnePass program,[154] an *Inside Flyer* Freddie Awards "Best Elite-Level Program" winner in 2000 and 2001[155] as well as a key factor in Continental's five consecutive J. D. Power and Associates consumer satisfaction awards.[156] These key travelers played a key factor in the airline's return to profitability.[157]

Today, the emphasis is on providing a competitive advantage via cutting-edge technology and convenience. The airline caused a stir by introducing the world's widest business-class seats—offering 170-degree recline, 6.5 feet of sleeping space, and privacy hoods with personal reading lights—to its award-winning Business First class at cost of $15 million in March 2002—exactly the time that all of its competitors were looking for ways to cut costs.[158] Other perks added after September 11 to keep business travelers have included adding security checkpoints, automated check-in kiosks, and free in-flight movies. As a result of Continental's heightened appeal to business travelers, the airline has realized the smallest relative decline in traffic of the six largest carriers.[159]

Strategic Alliances

Continental has realized incredible successes with strategic partnerships that expand its reach both domestically and around the globe. The carrier's long-term alliance with Northwest Airlines, in place through 2025,[160] is unprecedented in scope. The two carriers have built one of the industry's largest international route maps through extensive code-sharing and route system design. They also offer frequent-flier and executive club reciprocity, regularly engage in cooperative marketing efforts, and have negotiated joint contracts with major corporate clients and travel agents.[161]

Continental Airlines president Larry Kellner calls the alliance with Northwest, which generated $140 million in incremental revenue in 2001, "an absolute home run." It is considered to be the only domestic alliance offering enough scope and utility to attract corporate buyers.[162] The domestic network was expanded in August 2002, when a marketing agreement with Delta[163] formed a Continental-Northwest-Delta alliance controlling a remarkable 36 percent of the domestic market share.

Other domestic code-sharing partners include Gulfstream International Airlines (in which Continental owns 28 percent),[164] Hawaiian Airlines, Alaska Airlines, Horizon Air, Mesaba Aviation (Northwest's commuter airline), CommutAir, and American Eagle Airlines. The airline's international code-share alliance partners include KLM Royal Dutch Airlines; Virgin Atlantic Airways; Air China;

Air Europa, Spain's largest carrier; Panama-based Copa Airlines (in which Continental owns a 49 percent equity stake); Emirates, the official airline of the United Arab Emirates; and Taiwan-based EVA Air.[165] A new code-share alliance with regional carrier British European Flybe was awaiting final approval in November 2002.[166] Continental believes that forming such strategic alliances was the best way to expand the airline's foreign product line.

Continental's partnering emphasis is on quality rather than quantity, however: The airline dropped an eight year old code-share agreement with America West in March 2002[167] and declined an alliance with troubled carrier US Airways in June 2002.[168]

Continental Airlines expanded its code-share options further in March 2002 by launching a creative air/rail alliance with Amtrak. Passengers are now able to travel between Newark Airport and one of the seventeen Amtrak connection cities on the Northeast Corridor line under one reservation.[169]

Another example of Continental's "outside the box" thinking was the November 2002 announcement that Dallas-based Travelweb had forged an agreement with Continental to become a private-label net-rate hotel distribution affiliate for the airline's consumer Web site. Under the agreement, Continental provides its customers with one-stop shopping—and itself with a level of vertical integration—by marketing Travelweb's net-rate hotel room inventory to customers through Continental.com.[170]

Corporate Culture

We knew we had to balance those three elements:
The customers, the employees, and the shareholders.

—Larry Kellner[171]

We treat our people well, and in turn, they treat our customers well.
Happy employees equal customer satisfaction.

—Chief executive officer
Gordon Bethune[172]

Continental's Go Forward Plan has defined a corporate culture that emphasizes superior customer service; employee involvement, open bilateral communication, and tangible goal-reward systems at every level; strong, transparent leadership that employees could see in action; and pro-active decision making, for better and worse.

Vocal, Action-Oriented Leadership In 1994, one of Gordon Bethune's first acts as CEO was to bridge the gulf between executives and employees.[173] He promoted a culture of openness, rewarding good work with tangible rewards. "We wanted to let our people feel involved, that they belonged, that they were important—no matter what their role or position in the company," says Bethune.[174]

The emphasis continues to be on keeping employees informed at every level. Company goals, plans, initiatives are regularly communicated to all employees, from senior managers to baggage handlers.[175] Employees receive daily on-time arrival updates via e-mail, as well as weekly voice mail messages from their CEO.[176] "When management wakes up in the morning, it's 'What do we need to tell people today?'" states David Messing, Continental's managing director of public relations.[177]

Post–September 11 layoffs were announced to employees throughout the company hours before the press was informed.[178] "Consistent—even persistent—communications is our mantra," reports Bonnie Reitz, the airline's senior vice president of sales and marketing.[179]

Outspoken leadership is also key to Continental's spearheading industry position. The airline was the first to respond to the attacks of September 11 with fiscal and job cuts. Bethune was the first industry leader to raise the need for government financial assistance[180] and the first top airline executive to make the talk-show rounds to assure U.S. fliers that it was safe to board domestic carriers again. He has also leads the call for a "common sense" approach to airline security.[181]

The media has responded in kind to Continental's openness. Journalists report that Continental's executive and public relations staffs are responsive and available in both good times and bad.[182]

Employees Continental Airlines employed 42,900 employees as of December 31, 2001.[183] Although layoffs of 12,000 were announced on September 15,

2001, the company ultimately limited furloughs to 8,000, or about 21 percent of the total workforce.[184] Approximately 55 percent of furloughed employees voluntarily accepted retirement or leaves of absence. Not only has the company avoided further large-scale layoffs as of November 2002, but also several hundred employees were recalled to assist with enhanced airport security requirements around the country.[185]

The Value of High Morale When *Fortune* magazine named Continental number fifty-five of its "100 Best Companies to Work For" in January 2002—it was the company's fourth year in a row on the list—the magazine reported that 90 percent of employees reported that they intended to work at Continental until they retire.[186] What's more, the company is recognized for its diversity; *Hispanic* magazine named Continental to its "Most Opportunities for Hispanics" list of employers for the third year in a row in 2001.[187]

The value of Continental's workforce and the high morale that the executive team has generated among its employees should not be underestimated. In fact, in its mid-2002 "buy" report, Goldman Sachs named Continental's employees as the company's most distinctive competitive advantage: "High employee morale helps produce a more consistently reliable service product, sustaining Continental's revenue edge."[188]

The "Pay-for-Performance" Innovation

> When the customers won, the employees did, too.
>
> —President and COO
> Greg Brenneman[189]

An innovative monthly cash-reward incentive program has been a key driver in transforming Continental's on-time performance "from worst to first." In 1995, as a key component of their turnaround plan, Bethune and Brenneman introduced a pay-for-performance plan in which each of its (then) 35,000 nonmanagerial employees would receive a $65 cash bonus in any month that Continental ranked among the top five airlines for on-time departures.[190]

Everyone in the company won when the airline hit its on-time goals: "Booking agents, public relations folks, even that guy who waved the orange flashlights."[191] The incentive plan turned out to be a direct driver of performance: The carrier was first in on-time performance within two months of instituting the program.[192] The program was such a success that, in 1996, the $65 payout occurred only if Continental ranked among the top three on-time airlines; if it ranked first, the reward was $100.

The power of teamwork instituted a sea change in employee morale: It also played a central role in reducing employee turnover, sick days, and on-the-job injuries, as well as setting new standards for employee empowerment.[193]

The airline renewed its commitment to the plan in 2002, despite its annual cost of approximately $44 million, coupled with the devastating financial losses that followed September 11;[194] in fact, the company paid out the cash rewards in eleven out of twelve months in 2001.[195] While some might view cutting the pay-for-performance program as a way for the company to save cash in the short term, Continental sees it as essential to the airline's continued success in the long term.

Other Rewards Continental has also won over employees with its Perfect Attendance Recognition Program, which awards quarterly bonuses to employees with a spotless attendance record. In addition to the monetary reward, the company awarded eighteen Ford Explorers to employees in 2001 as part of the program.[196]

Continental's profit-sharing plan ties employee compensation to company objectives, "to ensure that our coworkers would win when our investors did," notes Greg Brenneman.[197] Virtually all Continental employees (except those whose collective bargaining agreements require other compensation) receive about 15 percent of the company's annual pretax earnings.[198] Continental also supports a scholarship program that funded educations for ninety-six Continental employees in 2002.[199]

The company's high employee satisfaction rate is still surprising, considering its reputation for low pay relative to the rest of the industry.[200] Goldman Sachs analysts report that mechanics' wage rates are 20 percent below other large-hub carriers (a gap that has closed somewhat with a new contract signed in October 2002; see the next section); Continental pilots receive 40 percent less pay than their peers at other airlines; and pensions and benefits packages are smaller across the workforce, relative to the rest of the industry.[201]

Union Relations While corporate-union relations are traditionally fraught with tension across any industry, Continental has established generally better-than-cordial relations with most of its heavily unionized employee ranks: roughly 45 percent of employees belong to unions.[202] This has been no small feat, thanks to the bitter union relations history formed under former owner Frank Lorenzo, who alienated his workforce in the 1980s by breaking union contracts as a cost-cutting measure, not to mention the pay gulf between Continental employees and their industry peers.[203]

The airline quelled some labor unrest by striking a four-year deal with the International Brotherhood of Teamsters, which represents the airline's 3,400 unionized mechanics and related workers, in October 2002. The airline agreed to attractive wage and retirement-benefit increases as well as strengthened job protections, at the same time that rival United Airlines was trying to squeeze wage cuts out of its labor groups.[204] The airline's 6,750 flight attendants, represented by the AFL-CIO's Association of Flight Attendants, have contracts through September 2004.[205]

Most vocal about compensation, job protection, and other issues is the Air Line Pilots Association, the United States' largest pilots union. The union's Continental Master Executive Council (CAL ALPA) represents the 6,500 pilots employed by Continental Airlines and Continental Express.[206] The union does not hesitate to speak out: When Gordon Bethune and his senior staff accepted 62.5 percent bonuses for first-quarter 2002 because the airline had bettered its loss targets—even though hundreds of pilots remained on furlough—union spokesman John Prater called the move "galling."[207] In mid-November 2002, the pilots union gave the green light to Continental's code-share plan with Northwest Airlines and Delta Airlines.[208]

CONCLUSION

At the end of 2001, Continental Airlines was the fifth largest airline company in the world,[209] employing 50,000 people and flying to 216 destinations. Continental serves more destinations in Mexico and Central America than any other U.S.

airline. It also serves more Japanese cities than all other U.S. carriers.[210] In 2002, Continental recorded the highest on-time performance among the large hub carriers. It received its eighth consecutive Freddie award, the Oscar of frequent-flier programs, for the best elite program.[211]

However, the events of September 2001 and the poor industry situation since has led Continental to make huge cuts in capacity and introduce a series of cost-cutting measures to meet what the airline considers to be dramatic changes in the marketplace. "These are challenging times in our industry and we need to do something now," said Gordon Bethune. "US Airways declared bankruptcy and United is likely to soon follow. While we remain committed to running a clean, safe, and reliable operation, we need to do some aggressive belt tightening so we don't end up like them."[212] Continental posted a $139 million loss in its second quarter 2002 and total capacity was expected to be down by roughly 17 percent for 2002 compared to the previous year.[213]

The economic slowdown of the economy forced some changes upon the company, but it has stuck to its four-part mission. Its Go Forward Plan has helped it make the remarkable turnaround, and the airline hopes this will see it through present and future.

Still, Continental faces significant challenges on all fronts. The emphasis has been on increasing customer fees, belt-tightening and attrition over layoffs, and cost efficiency through e-ticket distribution innovations. But with the airline bleeding cash and its stock price showing a decline and high variability, how long can it hold its shareholders at bay? Given the current turmoil in which the industry finds itself, can the airline maintain the programs that have been key to its turnaround success?

In the bigger picture, can this "legacy" carrier, designed around a hub-and-spoke system with rigid labor-union commitments and significant fixed costs in equipment and facilities, modify its business fundamentals enough to compete effectively with the new breed of low-cost point-to-point carriers and ultimately return to profitability?

With the airline's glorious past and unsure future, only time will tell if Continental will come out of one of the worst tourism slowdowns as a winner or a loser.

Notes

1. G. Bethune and S. Huler, *From Worst to First: Behind the Scenes of Continental's Remarkable Comeback* (New York: John Wiley & Sons, 1998), 4.

2. Ibid.

3. Ibid, 5–6; also G. Brenneman, "Right Away and All at Once: How We Saved Continental," *Harvard Business Review* (September–October 1998), HBR OnPoint product no. 4193, 12.

4. R. J. Serling, *Maverick* (Garden City, NY: Doubleday, 1974).

5. Bethune and Huler, *From Worst to First.*

6. Serling, *Maverick,* 321.

7. Ibid., 37.

8. Serling, *Maverick.* Also online at http://www.boeing.com /commercial/aeromagazine/aero, 8 November 2002.

9. Ibid.

10. Ibid.

11. Continental Airlines, "History 1959 to 1977," http://www.continental.com/company/history/1959-1977.asp, 10 November 2002. The contract became a permanent operation that became Continental Micronesia and celebrated thirty years of success in 1998.

12. The Department of Transport and its affiliated agency, the Federal Aviation Administration (FAA), continue to regulate the industry with regard to safety, labor, operating procedures, aircraft fitness, and emission levels. J. Corridore, *Standard & Poor's Industry Surveys: Airlines,* 21.

13. Public Broadcasting System, "Innovators: Frank Lorenzo," http://www.pbs.org/kcet/chasingthesun/innovators/florenzo.html, 2 December 2002.

14. Bethune and Huler, *From Worst to First.*

15. Ibid.; introduction, "The Idea in Brief."

16. Ibid., 4–5.

17. Continental Airlines, "History 1991 to Now," http:// www.continental.com/company/history/1991-now.asp, 18 November 2002.

18. Federal Aviation Agency Press Release, "Secretary Mineta Re-Opens Skies to General Aviation," 14 November 2001, reference DOT 97-01, http://www2.faa.gov/index.cfm/apa /1062?id=1408, 13 November 2002.

19. Continental Airlines, *Continental Airlines 2001 Annual Report,* 6, 18.

20. Continental Airlines, *Securities & Exchange Committee Quarterly Report for Continental Airlines, Inc.* for period ending 30 September 2002, 3.

21. Continental Airlines, *2002 Annual Report,* 22.

22. S. Carey, "UAL Posts $889 Million Loss for Third Quarter," *The Wall Street Journal,* 21 October 2002, A3; S. Power and S. Carey, "Panel Rejects United's Call for Federal Loan Guarantee," *The Wall Street Journal Online,* 5 December 2002, http://online.wsj.com/article/0,,SB1039043151540787993,00. html, 5 December 2002.

23. Associated Press, "United Airlines, Mechanics Hoping to Prevent Bankruptcy," 1 December 2002, http://www.cnn.com /2002/TRAVEL/12/01/united.airlines.ap/index.html, 3 December 2002.

24. C. R. Goeldner and J. R. B. Ritchie, *Tourism: Principles, Practices, Philosophies,* 9th ed., (Hoboken, N.J.: John Wiley & Sons) 124.

25. Ibid., 125.

26. Corridore, *Standard & Poor's Industry Surveys: Airlines,* 21.

27. Air Transport Association of America, *Facts & Figures of the U.S. Scheduled Airlines 1999,* http://www.air-transport.org.

28. Air Transport Association of America, *2002 Annual Report,* 6.

29. Ibid., 7.

30. Corridore, *Standard & Poor's Industry Surveys: Airlines,* 28 March 2002, 16.

31. Air Transport Association of America, "Keeping Customers First," http://www.customers-first.org, 17 November 2002.

32. R. Britton, Managing Director of Advertising, American Airlines, lecture at Cornell University School of Hotel Administration, 22 November 2002.

33. Air Transport Association of America, *2002 Annual Report,* 13.

34. Ibid., 2, 12.

35. A. E. Kahn, "Airline Deregulation," *The Concise Encyclopedia of Economics,* http://www.econlib.org/library/Enc/Airline Deregulation.html, 4 December 2002.

36. Corridore, *Standard & Poor's Industry Surveys: Airlines,* 8.

37. U.S. General Accounting Office, "Barriers to Entry Continue to Limit Benefits of Airline Deregulation," 13 March 1997.

38. Ibid.

39. Ibid.

40. U.S. General Accounting Office, "Airline Deregulation: Changes in Airfares, Service Quality and Barriers to Entry," March 1999, 11.

41. Kahn, "Airline Deregulation."

42. U.S. General Accounting Office, *20 Years of Deregulation, 1978 to 1998,* 1998.

43. U.S. General Accounting Office, *Airline Deregulation: Changes in Airfares, Service Quality and Barriers to Entry,* March 1999, 2.

44. Kahn, "Airline Deregulation."

45. Corridore, *Standard & Poor's Industry Surveys: Airlines,* 28 March 2002, 1.

46. Corridore, *Standard & Poor's Industry Surveys: Airlines,* 25 September 2003, 1.

47. Corridore, *Standard & Poor's Industry Surveys: Airlines,* 28 March 2002, 3.

48. Ibid., 20.

49. Ibid.

50. The Boeing Company, http://www.boeing.com, 13 November 2002.

51. Corridore, *Standard & Poor's Industry Surveys: Airlines,* 28 March 2002, 3.

52. Unisys, *Unisys R2A Scorecard: Airline Industry Cost Measurement,* October 2002, 14.

53. Corridore, *Standard & Poor's Industry Surveys: Airlines,* 28 March 2002, 19.

54. Air Transport Association of America, *2002 Annual Report,* 19.

55. For instance, see comments about "legacy carriers" on p. 3 of Unisys, *Unisys R2A Scorecard.*

56. Britton lecture.

57. Unisys, *Unisys R2A Scorecard.*

58. Corridore, *Standard & Poor's Industry Surveys: Airlines,* 28 March 2002, 14.

59. Unisys, *Unisys R2A Scorecard,* 1.

60. Goeldner and Ritchie, *Tourism,* 307.

61. S. K. Neilsen, "Determinants of Air Travel Growth," *World Transport Policy & Practice* 7, no. 2 (2001), 28–37.

62. Ibid.

63. Goeldner and Ritchie, *Tourism,* 127.

64. Ibid., 124.

65. Britton lecture.

66. Air Transport Association of America, *2002 Annual Report,* 9.

67. Unisys, *Unisys R2A Scorecard,* 1.

68. Air Transport Association of America, *2002 Annual Report,* 10.

69. Goeldner and Ritchie, *Tourism,* 125.

70. *The Bulletin,* "The Price of Airport Security," http://bulletin.ninemsn.com.au/bulletin/eddesk.nsf/All/4DD4F67689A6B1B3CA256C47001FB3DC (viewed 12/2/02); ABC KGO-TV, "The Price of Security," 18 October 2002, http://abclocal.go.com/kgo/news/101801_nw_airport_baggage.html, 2 December 2002.

71. About.com, "Airport Estimated Wait Times," http://businesstravel.about.com/library/weekly/aa010102a.htm, 3 December 2002.

72. Corridore, *Standard & Poor's Industry Surveys: Airlines,* 28 March 2002, 11–12; Goldman Sachs Global Equity Research, *Airlines: United States,* 23 April 2002, 12.

73. Corridore, *Standard & Poor's Industry Surveys: Airlines,* 28 March 2002, 20.

74. Britton lecture.

75. Ibid.

76. Goldman Sachs Global Equity Research, *Airlines,* 9.

77. Ibid.

78. Corridore, Jim. *Standard & Poor's Industry Surveys: Airlines,* 28 March 2002, 12.

79. Unisys, *Unisys R2A Scorecard,* 2.

80. Ibid.

81. Air Transport Association of America, *2002 Annual Report,* 9.

82. J. Corridore, *Standard & Poor's Industry Surveys: Airlines,* 28 March 2002, 15.

83. J. Corridore, *Standard & Poor's Industry Surveys: Airlines,* 25 September 2002, 18.

84. Britton lecture.

85. Ibid.

86. Air Transport Association of America, *State of the U.S. Airline Industry: A Report on Recent Trends for U.S. Air Carriers, 2002-2003,* http://www.airlines.org/public/industry/bin/state.pdf, 1, 11.

87. Air Transport Association of America, *2002 Annual Report,* 2.

88. Goldman Sachs Global Equity Research, *Airlines,* 21.

89. Britton lecture.

90. Corridore, *Standard & Poor's Industry Surveys: Airlines,* 28 March 2002, 21.

91. Federal Reserve Bank of San Francisco, "FRBSF Economic Letter: Competition and Regulation in the Airline Industry," 18 January 2002, www.frbsf.org/publications/economics/letter/2002/el2002-01.html, 4 December 2002.

92. Goeldner and Ritchie, *Tourism,* 129–130, 589, 591.

93. Corridore, Jim. *Standard & Poor's Industry Surveys: Airlines,* 28 March 2002, 21.

94. Goldman Sachs Global Equity Research, *Airlines,* 23 April 2002.

95. Federal Reserve Bank of San Francisco, "FRBSF Economic Letter."

96. Corridore, *Standard & Poor's Industry Surveys: Airlines,* 28 March 2002, 14.

97. Continental Airlines, *Continental Airlines 2001 Annual Report,* 3.

98. Ibid., 4.

99. Ibid., 5.

100. Yahoo Finance, "Continental Redesigns Web Site to Offer More Functionality for Customers," 16 September 2002, http://biz.yahoo.com/prnews/020916/dam021_1.html, 14 November 2002.

101. Continental Airlines, *Continental Airlines 2001 Annual Report,* 10.

102. Ibid., 13.

103. Ibid. See Appendix 1 for an expanded list of Continental's most recent awards.

104. ProQuest, "Continental Introduces 'New Functionality' to Its Self-Service Check-in System Airports," 15 October 2002.

105. Continental Airlines, *Continental Airlines 2001 Annual Report,* 16.

106. Continental Airlines, Press Release, "Continental Airlines Makes the Fortune 100 Best Companies to Work For List for Fourth Year in a Row," 22 January 2002, http://online at www.continental.com, 19 November 2002.

107. Continental Airlines, *2001 Annual Report,* 27.

108. U.S. Department of Justice, Press Release, "Department Announces Tentative Settlement in Northwest-Continental Lawsuit," 6 November 2000, http://www.usdoj.gov/atr/public/press_releases/2000/6905.htm, 2 December 2002.

109. Airwise News, "Three U.S. Airlines Seek Marketing Deal," 23 August 2002, http://news.airwise.com/stories/2002/08/1030123190.html, 5 December 2002.

110. As quoted at Yahoo! Finance, 17 November 2002.

111. Range was $4.16 to $21.70 for the 52-week period ending 29 October 2003, as quoted at Yahoo! Finance, 30 October 2003. See Exhibit 5 for annual diluted earnings/loss per share.

112. Continental Airlines, Press Release, "Continental Airlines Announces Long-Term Schedule Reduction and Furlough of 12,000 Employees," 15 September 2001, http://online at www.continental.com, 19 November 2002.

113. Continental Airlines, Press Release, "Continental Airlines Capacity Reduction Ends Service to 10 Cities," 17 September 2001, http://www.continental.com, 19 November 2002.

114. Corridore, *Standard & Poor's Industry Surveys: Airlines,* 28 March 2002, 9.

115. Continental Airlines, *Continental Airlines 2002 Annual Report,* 21. Also Continental Airlines. *Securities & Exchange Committee Quarterly Report for Continental Airlines, Inc.,* own/lease proportions for period ended 30 September 2002, 14.

116. Continental Airlines, *2002 Annual Report,* 21.

117. G. Engel and M. Gruetzmacher, *Goldman Sachs Global Equity Research: Continental Airlines,* 17 June 2002, 11.

118. Continental Airlines Presentation to Salomon Smith Barney Transportation Conference, 14 November 2002.

119. Ibid.

120. JetBlue Airways, Press Release, "JetBlue Orders 10 Airbus A320 Aircraft Valued in Excess of $500 Million," 14 January 2002.

121. "United They Fall," *The Wall Street Journal,* 21 October 2002, A14.

122. S. McCartney, "Southwest Sets Standard on Costs," *The Wall Street Journal,* 9 October 2002, A2.

123. Corridore, *Standard & Poor's Industry Surveys: Airlines,* 28 March 2002, 1.

124. Corridore, *Standard & Poor's Industry Surveys: Airlines,* 25 September 2003, *1.*

125. Corridore, *Standard & Poor's Industry Surveys: Airlines,* 28 March 2002, 33.

126. Continental Airlines, Press Release, "Continental Airlines Offers Double Miles for Its Frequent Flyers," 5 November 2001.

127. Continental Airlines, *Securities & Exchange Committee Quarterly Report for Continental Airlines, Inc.,* 19.

128. Ibid., 32.

129. Continental Airlines, *Securities & Exchange Committee Quarterly Report for Continental Airlines, Inc.,* 28.

130. Corridore, *Standard & Poor's Industry Surveys: Airlines,* 28 March 2002, 2.

131. Continental Airlines, *Securities & Exchange Committee Quarterly Report for Continental Airlines, Inc.,* 15.

132. Embraer regional jet orders were cut to eighty-six by December 31, 2002, although Boeing mainline jet orders held firm. Continental Airlines, Inc., *2002 Annual Report,* 21.

133. Ibid., 14–15.

134. Ibid., 22.

135. Continental Airlines, *Securities & Exchange Committee Quarterly Report for Continental Airlines, Inc.,* 8.

136. Continental Airlines, Press Release, "Continental Airlines Announces Pricing of Initial Public Offering of Regional Airline Subsidiary," 17 April 2002, http://www.continental.com, 19 November 2002.

137. See appendix of this case study for examples from the October 2002 issue of *Continental,* Continental Airlines' inflight magazine.

138. L. Petrecca, "Air Leaders Struggle for a Way Back," *Advertising Age,* Midwest region edition, 24 June 2002, S24.

139. A. Fass, "Ayer, One of Madison Avenue's Oldest Names, Is Fading Away," *The New York Times,* 8 April 2002, http://query.nytimes.com/search/restricted/article?res=F709 1FF93E590C7B8CDDAD0894DA404482, 14 November 2002.

140. Semaphore Partners, Press Release, "Kaplan Thaler and Semaphore Partners Forge Alliance," 23 July 2002, http://www.semaphorepartners.com/site/WhoWeAre /PressRelease.aspx?cid=1284, 16 November 2002.

141. FlickerLab, Press Release, "FlickerLab Completes Another National TV Spot for Continental Airlines," August 2002, http://www.flickerlab.com, 16 November 2002.

142. Petrecca, "Air Leaders Struggle for a Way Back."

143. Keri, "Satisfaction, Profits Fly Hand in Hand," *Investors Business Daily,* 30 January 2001, http://www.investors.com /ibdArchives/ArtShow.asp?atn=657041934134188, 14 November 2002.

144. G. Brenneman, "Right Away and All at Once: How We Saved Continental," *Harvard Business Review* (September–October 1998), HBR OnPoint product no. 4193, 9.

145. Brenneman, "Right Away and All at Once."

146. Engel and Gruetzmacher, *Goldman Sachs Global Equity Research,* 6.

147. Continental Airlines, *Continental Airlines 2001 Annual Report,* "2001 Accomplishments" ii, 11–12; completion factor excludes flights canceled due to the events of September 11, 2001.

148. Engel and Gruetzmacher, *Goldman Sachs Global Equity Research,* 6; also "Airline Performance Hot; 88% of Flights on Time in September," *USA Today,* 8 November 2002, B5.

149. See appendix for partial list.

150. L. Hollman, "A Not-So-Quixotic Quest for Quality," *Call Center Magazine,* July 2002, 18–32.

151. Continental.com, "Business Training Solutions," www.conti-nental.com/programs/solutions/default.asp?SID=191C87255 FE14B0EA62F1DF96F4D55B9, 14 November 2002.

152. D. Jonas, "CO Puts Premium on Biz Travel," *Business Travel News,* 25 March 2002, 3.

153. Petrecca, "Air Leaders Struggle for a Way Back."

154. K. H. Hammonds, "Business Fights Back: Continental's Turnaround Pilot," *Fast Company,* December 2001, 96.

155. The Freddie Awards, http://www.freddieawards.com /live@event/fred14th, 19 November 2002.

156. J.D. Power Consumer Center, http://www.jdpower.com/travel /search.asp?CatID=4, 14 November 2002.

157. Hammonds, "Business Fights Back."

158. Jonas, "CO Puts Premium on Biz Travel"; D. Jonas, "Continental Broadening BusinessFirst Seats," *Business Travel News,* 25 March 2002, 3, 14.

159. S. McCartney, "Flights of Fancy: Continental Airlines Keeps Little Things, and It Pays Off Big," *The Wall Street Journal,* 4 February 2002, A1.

160. Continental Airlines, *Continental Airlines 2001 Annual Report,* 18–19.

161. Ibid., 19.

162. Jonas, "CO Puts Premium on Biz Travel"; Also D. Jonas, "CO-NW Deals with KLM Further Transatlantic Alliance," *Business Travel News,* 13 May 2002, 3.

163. Delta Air Lines, Press Release, "Delta Air Lines Signs Marketing Agreement with Continental Airlines and Northwest Airlines," 23 August 2002, http://www.delta.com, 14 November 2002.

164. Continental Airlines, *Continental Airlines 2001 Annual Report,* 19.

165. Ibid.; also http://www.continental.com/company/alliance /default.asp?SID=AE733239090942C3916E1BDDF2D9F3A0, 19 November 2002.

166. http://www.continental.com/company/alliance
/flybe.asp?SID=AE733239090942C3916E1BDDF2D9F3A0,
19 November 2002.

167. *Consumer Reports Travel Letter,* June 2002, 4.

168. Airwise News, "Continental Shelves US Airways Alliance
Talks," 3 June 2002, http://news.airwise.com/sto-
ries/202/07/1025721393.html, 15 November 2002.

169. "Continental Airlines and Amtrak Will Launch an Air/Rail
Codeshare Agreement," *Airports,* 12 March 2002, 4.

170. Yahoo! Finance, "Travelweb Selected by Continental Airlines
as Online Net-Rate Hotel Distribution Affiliate," 18
November 2002, http://biz.yahoo.com/bw/021118/180118_1.
html, 2 December 2002.

171. Keri, "Satisfaction, Profits Fly Hand in Hand."

172. "Top Talent and Passionate Employees," *HRM Guide USA,* 10
April 2002, http://www.hrmguide.net/usa/commitment/pas-
sionate_employees.htm, 15 November 2002.

173. Keri, "Satisfaction, Profits Fly Hand in Hand."

174. "Top Talent and Passionate Employees," *HRM Guide USA.*

175. Ibid.

176. T. Raphael, "Continental Stays on Course," *Workforce,* June
2002, 16.

177. S. D. Green, "Internal PR Keeps Continental Flying Toward
Profit," *PRWeek USA,* 18 February 2002, http://www.sherri-
green.com/Internal%20pr%20keeps%20continental%20fly-
ing.htm, 15 November 2002.

178. Ibid.

179. R. A. Grant, "Making the Connection," *Lodging,* March 2002,
http://www.lodgingnews.com/lodgingmag/2002_03
/2002_03_19.asp, 16 November 2002.

180. Green, "Internal PR Keeps Continental Flying Toward Profit."

181. F. Fiorino, "Bethune Urges Common Sense Approach to Airline
Security," *Aviation Week & Space Technology,* 24 June 2002, 65.

182. Green, "Internal PR Keeps Continental Flying Toward Profit."

183. Continental Airlines, *2001 Annual Report,* 7.

184. Ibid., 20.

185. Ibid.

186. As quoted in Continental Airlines, *Continental Airlines 2001
Annual Report,* 14.

187. Continental Airlines, *Continental Airlines 2001 Annual
Report,* "2001 Accomplishments," ii.

188. Engel and Gruetzmacher, *Goldman Sachs Global Equity
Research: Continental Airlines,* 1.

189. Brenneman, "Right Away and All at Once: How We Saved
Continental," 10.

190. M. Knez and D. Simester, "Making Across-the-Board
Incentives Work," *Harvard Business Review* 80, no. 2
(February 2002): 16–17.

191. Keri, "Satisfaction, Profits Fly Hand in Hand."

192. Ibid.

193. Knez and Simester, "Making Across-the-Board Incentives Work."

194. Raphael, "Continental Stays on Course."

195. Continental Airlines, *Continental Airlines 2001 Annual
Report,*" introduction, "2001 Accomplishments."

196. Ibid.; also Green, "Internal PR Keeps Continental Flying
Toward Profit."

197. Brenneman. "Right Away and All at Once: How We Saved
Continental," 11.

198. Ibid.; also Continental Airlines, *Continental Airlines 2001
Annual Report,* 28–29.

199. Continental Airlines, *Continental Airlines 2001 Annual
Report,* 14.

200. Vault.com, "Continental Airlines," http://www.vault.com
/companies/company_main.jsp?co_page=1&product_id=72
0&ch_id=283, 14 November 2002.

201. Engel and Gruetzmacher, *Goldman Sachs Global Equity
Research,* 10.

202. Ibid.

203. Green, "Internal PR Keeps Continental Flying Toward Profit."

204. Reuters, "Continental, Mechanics in Tentative Deal," 18 October
2002, Yahoo! Finance, http://biz.yahoo.com/rb/021018
/airlines_continental_union_1.html; "Continental and
Teamsters Settle," *The New York Times,* 19 October 2002, C4;
Engel and Gruetzmacher, *Goldman Sachs Global Equity
Research,* 10.

205. Association of Flight Attendants, AFL CIO Web site,
http://www.flightattendant-afa.org/negotiations_status.asp,
19 November 2002; Engel and Gruetzmacher, *Goldman Sachs
Global Equity Research,* 10.

206. Continental Airlines Master Executive Council, Press Release,
"Pilots Wait to See What Continental Airlines' New Code-
Sharing Contracts Mean for Them," 26 August 2002,
http://www.calalpa.org/cgi/newsystem/one_press.asp?IDNe
ws=398, 19 November 2002.

207. D. Reed, "Continental Execs Qualify for Bonuses," *USA Today,*
15 October 2002.

208. M. Brannigan and N. Harris, "Delta Pact with Pilots Bolsters
Code-Share Plan," *The Wall Street Journal,* 18 November
2002, A2.

209. As measured by 2001 revenue passenger miles.

210. Engel and Gruetzmacher, *Goldman Sachs Global Equity
Research: Continental Airlines,* 2.

211. The Freddie Awards, http://www.freddieawards.com/win-
ners.htm, 4 December 2002. For a list of Continental's most
recent awards, see Appendix 1.

212. Continental Airlines, Press Release, "Continental Airlines,
Responding to Market Changes, Implements Measures to
Increase Revenue, Reduce Costs," 20 August 2002,
http://www.continental.com, 3 December 2002.

213. Airwise News, "Continental Tightens Its Belt," 20 August
2002, http://news.airwise.com, 3 December 2002.

We continue to build on a foundation that is rock solid, the result of more than 40 years of consistent thought and action. From this solid base, we expect a strong rebound in earnings when geopolitical issues stabilize and the economy improves. Over the next decade, we intend to continue to build on these foundations, and believe the best is yet to come.

—Isadore Sharp, Four Seasons' founder, chairman and CEO[1]

The luxury hotel management company known as Four Seasons Hotels & Resorts has been successful in the face of such challenges as a rough capital market and the affects of September 11. The company set a benchmark by ending 2001 with the strongest balance sheet in Four Seasons history. And, while the post–September 11 world continues to challenge the organization and the industry, Four Seasons has shown that it can maintain profitability while opening new properties across the globe.

Four Seasons continues to maintain strong liquidity and the high cash reserves that can facilitate

growth. The goal? To continue to expand, spreading Four Seasons' distinctive brand of hospitality throughout the world while retaining its commitment to its employees and its guests' experiences.

THE CREATION OF FOUR SEASONS

Four Seasons Hotels & Resorts was founded by Isadore "Issy" Sharp. Isadore's father, Max Sharp, emigrated from Poland to Palestine in 1920 and to Toronto, Canada in 1925. There, Max Sharp purchased and refurbished houses, then sold them at a profit. Isadore Sharp joined his father after graduating from Toronto's Ryerson Polytechnical Institute with high grades in architecture. However, his dream was to build his own hotels. For five years, he tried to find banks and venture capitalists to invest in his hotel project. Finally, he convinced Cecil Forsyth, who managed the mortgage department at Great Western Life Insurance Company, to provide $700,000 in capital. Isadore's brother in-law, Eddie Creed, and his best friend, Murray Koffler, also contributed $150,000 each to Sharp's project.[2]

Sharp's 126-room Inn on the Park opened in the spring of 1961. The final cost of the project totaled nearly $1.5 million. Despite the hotel's location in a poor downtown Toronto neighborhood known as a red-light district, the hotel's innovative design attracted wealthy customers. In a short period the Four Seasons became known as an upscale casual hotel.[3]

Written by James A. Fantaci, Serpil Halici, Michalis Stathokostopoulos, Vincent Trapenard, Phoebe Ullberg, and Elizabeth Willars under the direction of Jeffrey S. Harrison at the School of Hotel Administration, Cornell University.

Sharp built his second venture, Toronto's Inn, in a desolate area in the north section of the city where, in 1963, the only nearby business was a large garbage dump. Great Western Life Insurance Company lent him $1 million for the project, based on his success with the Four Seasons Motor Hotel. Soon after Toronto's Inn opened, the area that Sharp had chosen for the 569-room resort hotel became a corporate suburbia. Other hotels soon followed Sharp to this location. Sharp went public with Four Seasons in 1969.[4]

GROWTH AND EXPANSION

Isadore Sharp's first hotel outside of Canada was in London's historic Hyde Park. The 277-room hotel was opened in 1970 and featured amenities modern to the time such as air conditioning. The hotel enjoyed a 95 percent occupancy rate despite its higher-than-average room rates. During the early 1970s, Sharp concentrated on developing hotels in less urban areas. The hotels were characterized by their small size, luxury amenities, and excellent service. During the early 1970s he opened hotels in several destination locations such as Nassau and Israel.[5] In 1972, a partnership with the Sheraton division of ITT Corporation resulted in a 1,450-room hotel in Toronto. However, this partnership did not last and Sharp sold his shares in 1976 in order to return to the development and operation of smaller hotels. That year, Sharp purchased his first American property in San Francisco and opened a Four Seasons Hotel in Vancouver. The following year, 1977, Four Seasons assumed the management of the Ritz-Carlton Chicago.[6] During the early to mid-1970s, Four Seasons shares had climbed as high as $22 and dropped as low as $4. In 1977, Sharp and his partners accumulated all the shares of stock and turned Four Seasons from a public company into a private company.

In the 1980s, Four Seasons returned to its core luxury hotel business and took advantage of the booming economy by opening new properties in many countries.[7] Like many hoteliers, Sharp applied a strategy of managing properties instead of owning them. By doing this, the hotels opened under the Four Seasons name between 1980 and 1985 had a combined value of over $500 million, yet cost the company only $15 million. In addition to adding properties to the management portfolio during this time, Four Seasons was also buying many properties.[8] Since 1977, Four Seasons had been a privately held company, but in 1985 Four Seasons was taken public for the second time in its history. Sharp personally held 29 percent of Four Seasons equity and 83 percent of the votes in order to eliminate takeover threats.

Four Seasons' acquisition of Regent International Hotels in 1992 created the largest network of luxury hotels in Asia and Australia. The acquisition also expanded Four Seasons into the Far East, making it a global competitor in the luxury market. In 1992 and 1993, hotels were opened in Bali, Milan, and London, and new construction and acquisition was under way in Singapore, New York, Mexico City, Paris, Berlin, Jakarta, and Prague. In addition, resort properties were under development in Hawaii and California. In 1994, Saudi Prince Alwaleed bin Talal bin Abdufaziz al Saud bought 25 percent of the company stock for $167 million, which provided Four Seasons with financial leverage to build and buy properties worldwide.[9] In the mid-1990s, Four Seasons signed an agreement with Carlson Hospitality Worldwide to develop the Regent brand of its hotels around the world through establishing franchise agreements and management contracts. Under the agreement, Four Seasons continued to manage nine of the Regent hotels and had the option to manage any new Regent hotels. It also received a percentage of the revenues generated by Carlson.[10] The company launched its first vacation timeshare property in California in 1997. That year, properties opened in Las Vegas; London; Paris; Punta Mita, Mexico; and Scottsdale, Arizona.[11] In 2000, the Four Seasons Hotel Cairo, Four Seasons' first hotel in the Middle East, was opened. The company also opened hotels in Dublin, London, Paris, and Prague. For a complete list of properties and their operating characteristics by region, see Exhibits 1 and 2.

The terrorist attacks on the United States on September 11, 2001, affected the hospitality industry worldwide. The response of Four Seasons to these events can be illustrated by Sharp's response to his

EXHIBIT I	**SUMMARY HOTEL OPERATING DATA AS OF DECEMBER 31, 2002**				
	2002	**2001**	**2000**	**1999**	**1998**
All managed hotels[1]					
Worldwide					
No. of properties	57	53	48	47	42
No. of rooms	15,433	14,598	14,081	13,779	12,782
United States					
No. of properties	23	23	22	22	20
No. of rooms	7,248	7,248	6,971	6,982	6,374
Canada/Mexico/Caribbean/South America					
No. of properties	8	8	5	5	4
No. of rooms	1,762	1,762	1,341	1,340	1,200
Asia/Pacific					
No. of properties	14	12	13	13	13
No. of rooms	4,119	3,619	4,221	4,202	4,344
Europe/Middle East					
No. of properties	12	10	8	7	5
No. of rooms	2,304	1,969	1,548	1,255	864
Stabilized hotels[2]					
Worldwide					
No. of properties	46	45	42	39	38
No. of rooms	12,834	12,744	12,478	11,355	12,155
Occupancy	64.6%	65.0%	72.6%	69.8%	70.4%
Average daily rate (ADR)	$ 289	$ 287	$ 281	$ 272	$ 253
Revenue per available room (RevPAR)	$ 187	$ 187	$ 204	$ 190	$ 178
Gross operating margin	30.0%	32.1%	36.3%	35.5%	34.5%
United States					
No. of properties	22	22	21	20	20
No. of rooms	6,971	6,971	6,761	6,348	6,368
Occupancy	66.7%	67,1%	76.8%	74.9%	74.6%
Average daily rate (ADR)	$ 321	$ 331	$ 334	$ 317	$300
Revenue per available room (RevPAR)	$ 214	$ 222	$ 256	$ 237	$ 224
Gross operating margin	28.0%	30.8%	36.4%	36.2%	35.0%

Source: Four Seasons Hotels & Resorts, *2002 Annual Report,* 31–32.

[1] The table does not include the 249-room Four Seasons Hotel Riyadh. Four Seasons commenced management of this property after December 31, 2002.

[2] "Stabilized" hotels were fully open under Four Seasons management throughout the given year and during the last quarter of the prior year.

(Continues)

EXHIBIT I	SUMMARY HOTEL OPERATING DATA AS OF DECEMBER 31, 2002 *(CONTINUED)*				
	2002	**2001**	**2000**	**1999**	**1998**
Canada/Mexico/Caribbean/South America					
No. of properties	5	4	4	3	4
No. of rooms	1,341	1,145	1,145	1,004	1,200
Occupancy	63.8%	64.3%	67.6%	68.4%	70.3%
Average daily rate (ADR)	$ 261	$ 220	$ 212	$ 181	$ 213
Revenue per available room (RevPAR)	$ 167	$ 141	$ 143	$ 124	$ 149
Gross operating margin	30.9%	30.5%	29.8%	33.0%	34.5%
Asia/Pacific					
No. of properties	10	11	12	11	11
No. of rooms	2,715	3,080	3,682	3,132	4,197
Occupancy	63.9%	61.3%	66.2%	59.9%	63.3%
Average daily rate (ADR)	$ 164	$ 163	$ 179	$ 174	$ 157
Revenue per available room (RevPAR)	$ 105	$ 100	$ 119	$ 104	$ 99
Gross operating margin	33.7%	35.5%	36.7%	33.1%	31.2%
Europe/Middle East					
No. of properties	9	8	5	5	3
No. of rooms	1,007	1,540	890	871	390
Occupancy	58.4%	62.9%	73.3%	68.7%	78.5%
Average daily rate (ADR)	$ 380	$ 368	$ 314	$ 321	$ 465
Revenue per available room (RevPAR)	$ 222	$ 231	$ 230	$ 221	$ 365
Gross operating margin	34.6%	36.2%	39.8%	37.0%	42.4%

shareholders: "Basic ethical values, culture, trust, leadership and employee commitment—these are the underlying determinants of corporate success on which we based our decisions this past September." Addressing the near future of the company, he said: "Looking ahead, plans remain on track for further openings through 2002 and 2003. . . . We are well positioned for the economic recovery and subsequent increase in business travel expected later in 2002."[12]

THE ENVIRONMENT

There are two important features to consider when addressing the social component of the environment in which the Four Seasons exists: demographics and social values. Changes in these features of the social environment affect the travel and hospitality industry and can be observed in three trends including the ease of travel, the demographics of travelers, and the demographics of the workforce. Travel has become easier and cheaper, making business and leisure travel more accessible to the general population. Another trend affecting the industry is the age structure of the population.[13] Members of the baby-boom generation are becoming more affluent as they age. They represent an increasingly important seniors market, a market that will have the time, money, and good health to travel. In addition, the demographics of the workforce are changing; the educated, white-collar segment of the population is increasing. This segment of the population has the money to travel for leisure and jobs requiring travel for business.

Technology is an important tool hotels use to communicate with their customers. The technological environment in which the Four Seasons exists is focused on two major influences: the Internet and internal hotel computer systems. The increased use of the Internet by consumers as well as businesses

EXHIBIT 2   **PROPERTIES MANAGED BY FOUR SEASONS HOTELS AND RESORTS**

Hotel/Resort/Residence Club & Location	Approximate Number of Rooms/Units	Approximate Equity Interest[1]
United States		
Four Seasons Hotel Atlanta, *Georgia*	244	—
Four Seasons Hotel Austin, *Texas*	291	—
Four Seasons Resort Aviara, *California*	329	7.3%
Four Seasons Residence Club Aviara, *California*	120	7.3%
The Regent Beverly Wilshire (Beverly Hills), *California*	395	—
Four Seasons Biltmore Resort (Santa Barbara), *California*	217	—
Four Seasons Hotel Boston, *Massachusetts*	274	—
Four Seasons Hotel Chicago, *Illinois*	343	—
The Ritz-Carlton Hotel Chicago, *Illinois*	435	—
Four Seasons Hotel Houston, *Texas*	404	—
Four Seasons Resort Hualalai at Historic Ka'upulehu,	243	—
Big Island of Hawaii	357	
Four Seasons Resort & Club Dallas at Las Colinas, *Texas*	424	
Four Seasons Hotel Las Vegas, *Nevada*	285	
Four Seasons Hotel Los Angeles, *California*	380	
Four Seasons Resort Maui at Wailea, *Maui, Hawaii*	285	
Four Seasons Hotel Newport Beach, *California*	370	
Four Seasons Hotel New York, *New York*	210	
Four Seasons Resort Palm Beach, *Florida*	364	
Four Seasons Hotel Philadelphia, *Pennsylvania*	202	100%
The Pierre (New York), *New York*	277	—
Four Seasons Hotel San Francisco, *California*	210	3.9%
Four Seasons Resort Scottsdale at Troon North, *Arizona*	44	71%
Four Seasons Residence Club Scottsdale at Troon North, *Arizona*	450	3.4%
Four Seasons Olympic Hotel (Seattle), *Washington*[2]	259	—
Four Seasons Hotel Washington, *District of Columbia*		
Canada/Mexico/Caribbean/South America		
Four Seasons Hotel Buenos Aires, *Argentina*	165	—
Four Seasons Hotel Caracas, *Venezuela*	212	—
Four Seasons Resort Carmelo, *Uruguay*	44	—
Four Seasons Hotel Mexico City, *Mexico*	240	—
Four Seasons Resort Nevis, *West Indies*	196	—
Four Seasons Resort Punta Mita, *Mexico*	140	—
Four Seasons Hotel Toronto, *Ontario, Canada*	380	—
Four Seasons Hotel Vancouver, *British Columbia, Canada*	385	100%

Source: Four Seasons Hotels & Resorts, *2002 Annual Report,* 28–29.

[1] While Four Seasons often initially makes investments or advances in order to obtain new management agreements (or enhance existing management agreements), the corporation openly seeks to limit its total long-term capital exposure to no more than 20 percent of a property's total equity.

[2] The Four Seasons Olympic Hotel (Seattle) transferred management contracts to Fairmont Hotels & Resorts in mid-2003.

(Continues)

| EXHIBIT 2 | PROPERTIES MANAGED BY FOUR SEASONS HOTELS AND RESORTS *(CONTINUED)* |

Hotel/Resort/Residence Club & Location	Approximate Number of Rooms/Units	Approximate Equity Interest[1]
Asia/Pacific		
Four Seasons Resort Bali at Jimbaran Bay, *Indonesia*	147	—
Four Seasons Resort Bali at Sayan, *Indonesia*	54	—
The Regent Bangkok, *Thailand*	356	—
The Regent Chiang Mai, *Thailand*	75	—
The Regent Jakarta, *Indonesia*	365	—
The Regent Kuala Lumpur, *Malaysia*	468	—
Four Seasons Resort Maldives at Kuda Huraa, *Maldives*	106	—
Four Seasons Hotel Shanghai, *China*	443	21.2%
Four Seasons Hotel Singapore, *Singapore*	254	—
The Regent Singapore, *Singapore*	441	—
Four Seasons Hotel Sydney, *Australia*	531	15.2%
Grand Formosa Regent Taipei, *Taiwan*	539	—
Four Seasons Hotel Tokyo at Chinzan-so, *Japan*	283	—
Four Seasons Hotel Tokyo at Marunouchi, *Japan*	58	—
Europe/Middle East		
Four Seasons Hotel Amman, *Jordan*	195	8%
Four Seasons Hotel Berlin, *Germany*	204	100%
Four Seasons Hotel Cairo at The First Residence, *Egypt*	271	—
Four Seasons Hotel Dublin, *Ireland*	259	—
Four Seasons Hotel Istanbul, *Turkey*	65	—
Four Seasons Hotel The Ritz Lisbon, *Portugal*	283	—
Four Seasons Hotel Canary Wharf, *England*	142	—
Four Seasons Hotel London, *England*	220	12.5%
Four Seasons Hotel Milan, *Italy*	118	—
Four Seasons Hotel George V Paris, *France*	245	—
Four Seasons Hotel Prague, *Czech Republic*	162	—
Four Seasons Hotel Riyadh, *Saudi Arabia*	249	—
Four Seasons Resort Sharm el Sheikh, *Egypt*	140	—

around the world profoundly affects the production, marketing, and distribution practices of the hospitality industry. The Internet is increasingly being used by consumers to research, book, and pay for hospitality services. In response, hoteliers have adopted the Internet as a tool to market their products. The second major technological trend concerns hotels' internal computerized systems. Industry researcher Alberto Landero addresses the constant evolution of new systems, machinery, and software to aid the hospitality operator: "Major developments include new PMS systems, new reservations systems, new safety and security systems and some new facility designs that enhance customer appeal and ease of operation."[14] He says information technology enables companies to more easily test new processes and establish new strategies.

The industry is in the process of major consolidation. The formation of strategic alliances, which was used as a growth vehicle during the second half of the 1990s, is becoming increasingly important. Strategic alliances or mergers/acquisitions are becoming the primary vehicle for hotel industry international expansion, instead of new development, franchising, or management contracts.[15]

There is increasing awareness of the fact that the hospitality industry can generate a lot of economic growth.[16] A decline in a number of traditional industries has resulted in a need for jobs in the tourism and hospitality sectors.[17] However, hospitality is a very cyclical, so it does not counteract general economic influences.[18] Investments in hospitality-related real estate have grown significantly, reflecting an increase in the development of tourism facilities internationally. Researches have observed that, in today's global economy, international boundaries have been reduced. The rise of e-commerce together with globalization will continue to increase the presence of the hospitality industry in the international market.[19]

When considering the globalization of the hospitality industry, the influence of politics must also be considered. Emerging business markets resulting from the changing global political environment represent an important source of investment for multinational corporations. Taxes, regulations, and legislation related to the hotel industry differ from one international market to another.[20] In the United States, political lobbying and resulting changes in legislation are of concern to the hospitality industry. Further political influences in the industry regard the hotel industry's impact on the environment. Governmental regulations and social activism may restrict expansions and operations. The current political situation between the Middle East and the United States could greatly affect the whole industry. Four Seasons' expansion into the Middle East has been progressing in the past several years, with several new properties scheduled to open. The success of new and existing properties in this region could be jeopardized by political unrest.

THE LUXURY SEGMENT

For its customers, a luxury hotel provides opulence, truly superior customer service, and striking physical surroundings. Individuality of brand is a key competitive advantage in this segment. Each brand offers superior service, and amenities between brands are comparable. What distinguishes one brand from one another is the unique style of service offered. At the Four Seasons, this philosophy is declared as the Golden Rule: "treating others as you would like to be treated."[21] At Ritz-Carlton, it is translated as "ladies and gentlemen serving ladies and gentlemen."[22] Customer loyalty is gained and nurtured through the consistent application of customer-centric philosophies such as these throughout each brand.

Historically, changes in the economy have not impacted the luxury hotel segment as drastically as other segments of the industry. The president of St. Regis Hotels, Atef Mankatios, illustrated this: "When the economy stalls a little bit, the people most affected are in the middle segment of the market. The top end movers and shakers continue to travel and utilize the high-end hotels."[23] This was reinforced by Wolf Hengst, president of Worldwide Hotel Operations for Four Seasons, when he commented on continued customer loyalty in times of economic recession: "Our customers tend to be more loyal because they have to continue doing their business. They're there to function at the highest level at all times."[24] In the late 1990s and early 2000s, the industry saw a change in the mix of its customers. While luxury hotels have traditionally focused heavily on the business traveler, between 1996 and 2001 the industry saw the volume of business guests decrease by 3.5 percent and the percentage of leisure guests grow by 14.2 percent.[25] The downturn in the economy in combination with business travel slowing as a whole[26] has pulled value conscious business guests from the luxury segment into lower segments.[27] The lower segments of the market have additionally cannibalized the luxury segment's business clientele by offering new services tailored for their needs[28] such as Wyndham ByRequest, a customer relationship management model.

The leisure customer has different requirements than those of the business traveler and differing definitions of luxury. When asked in a *Travel and Leisure* survey how they identify luxury, 22 percent of leisure customers surveyed identified luxury with perfect service; 19 percent with divine décor; 18 percent with a category that encompasses amenities, food, view, and spa; 14 percent with spacious rooms; 13 percent with high-quality linens; 8 percent with swank bathrooms; and 6 percent with privacy.[29] The business traveler has different needs such as access to technology, good room service, business facilities, and amenities and service targeted at making the guest feel at home. The increase in leisure customers dictates a re-evaluation of services for the luxury segment. Regardless of the market segment from which they come, all customers of the luxury hotel demand spit-and-polish customer service with a personal touch in the highest-quality surroundings.

Traditionally, hotels have distributed their product by way of travel agents working through the Global Distribution Network and through customer reservations systems that link the properties together at a reservations center. Within the past ten years, the Internet has become a strong force in reservations distribution, and it is predicted to continue to grow in its influence. Jason Ader, an analyst with Bear Stearns, predicts that visits to Web sites offering hotel reservations continue to increase at rapid rates.[30] In online distribution, price is a focus, whereas price is not a strong source of differentiation among brands in the luxury hotel market. So while the luxury segment may not see high returns from Web sites offering hotel reservations, the increased Internet traffic gives the luxury segment an opportunity to express its particular brand through its own Web site. Indeed, analysts have stated that with branding, the hotel "box" or brand is becoming part of the distribution system.[31] Members of the luxury segment have realized this and have developed Web sites popular with Bear Stearns' Jason Ader, who rates Hyatt's, Starwood's, and the Four Seasons' sites as among the best.[32]

The Ritz-Carlton, Fairmont Hotels & Resorts, Starwood Hotels & Resorts, and Four Seasons are consistently ranked as top competitors in the luxury segment. However, the distinction between luxury and upscale hotels is often blurred. In terms of relative size, Starwood is the largest brand.

- Ritz-Carlton manages forty-five luxury hotels and resorts scattered across several continents. It also manages three Ritz-Carlton Clubs time-share properties.[33]

- Fairmont manages forty-three properties in Canada, the Caribbean, Mexico, the United Arab Emirates, and the United States. Its Delta Hotels division manages another thirty-nine hotels and resorts in Canada. Through Fairmont Hotels and Resorts Real Estate and a 35 percent stake in Legacy Hotels, FHR holds an ownership interest in forty-two properties.[34]

- Starwood Hotels & Resorts Worldwide maintains 750 properties in eight countries. Its portfolio includes such brands as Four Points, Sheraton, St. Regis, Westin, and W Hotels. Starwood owns or leases about 170 of its hotels and manages or franchises the rest. It also operates fifteen timeshare resort properties through Starwood Vacation Ownership (formerly Vistana), and it owns the deluxe hotel chain European Ciga Group, which it was planning to sell.[35]

- Four Seasons manages fifty hotels and resorts under its own brand, plus several Regent Hotels, The Ritz-Carlton in Chicago, and the Pierre in New York. It has ownership interests in about dozen properties.[36] See Exhibit 3 for a complete list of Four Seasons–managed properties.

Additional brands that compete in the luxury market are Park Hyatt, St. Regis, Le Meridien, Mandarin Oriental, The Peninsula, and Loews.[37] Consolidation is increasingly used in the hotel industry as a growth tactic. Currently, eight hotel companies account for two-thirds of the branded hotel properties in the United States.[38] In times of prosperity, mergers and acquisitions create an appealing investment option, and in times of economic downturn, the company may increase efficiency by functioning like a "factory," with consolidated technology and advantages of scale in relationships with their suppliers.[39]

Luxury hotels differentiate themselves from upscale hotels and from other hotels in the segment through their brand-name recognition, quality of service, and quality of accommodations, location, and room rates.[40] Of these, brand is a key differentiator in this segment. Brand can account for 80 percent of marketing efforts in the hotel industry.[41] Brand encompasses the philosophy of service, the quality of the physical properties, the prestige associated with staying at a brand's property and the consistency of service of the organization.

In the luxury segment, individuality of these key elements is what differentiates each brand from the others. Additional differentiation may come with the uniqueness of property or the size of the property. Loews is one brand that chooses to customize its properties for the individual community and culture in which each property resides. Park Hyatt keeps its properties small in order to best serve its guests. Ritz-Carlton's formal service and traditional property style distinguishes that chain. Starwood and Four Seasons approach service with progressive style tailored to each market and consistent application of superior service.

The luxury segment has been slow to differentiate itself through technology offerings to its guests or by technological systems that enable information gathering on their customers, opting for more human-based information gathering.[42] However, in 2002, Four Seasons signed with MICROS systems to have a property management system installed to link all of its properties.[43]

Price is not as important as a source of competition as it is in other segments of the lodging industry. The focus of competition is on increasing and improving guest services, which already stand at the highest in the industry. These services take time and capital to implement. When one leader in the segment makes improvements in guest services, the other members of the segment respond, but not rapidly, with their own service improvements. Strategies for the competitors in this segment focus more on growth of property numbers than on change in product. Consistency is a hallmark of the brands in this segment.

Luxury hotels make up 17.6 percent of the total hotel market share.[44] In the current economic market, while the hotel industry as a whole can expect lower returns, luxury hotels may feel the sting of this trend less, as analysts predict. The high-end segment of the market was the fastest growing segment in the late 1990s, and the trend is expected to continue.[45] According to the Urban Land Institute, the upscale/luxury segment of the industry should continue to outperform the midpriced/economy segment for at least the next few years[46]

Development of brand-new properties is likely to slow in times of economic uncertainty. The cost of building and equipping luxury facilities is estimated at $375,500 per room, while development of budget and economy properties is estimated at $48,900 per room.[47] The cost of property development represents a very high barrier to nonestablished brands trying to enter this segment of the market, and it also represents a barrier to expansion for established brands in tough economic times. Industry analysts predict that this is part of the reason that the luxury hotel sector remains robust: "Luxury hotels remain very strong, but developing them is difficult. We don't do a lot of it, and that's why they remain strong," noted Chase Burritt, national director of hospitality services for E&Y Kenneth Leventhal in Miami.[48]

Companies in the luxury segment of the hotel industry have been increasingly moving into hotel management, which has lower perceived risk and often lower costs than ownership. Currently, Four Seasons shows 54 percent of its sales are related to management activities and 46 percent to hotel ownership.[49] Four Seasons shares the list of largest management companies with competitor Fairmont Hotels & Resorts.[50] The fixed costs in this sector of the industry are high, and hotels typically have a hard time producing returns that are comparable to its downscale counterparts.[51] Part of the high fixed costs in the luxury segment can be attributed to the great number of supplies necessary for operations. Furnishings, housekeeping products, linens, sundries, high-quality foods, and uniforms are but a few of the products that a luxury property needs. The list of suppliers is extensive, each hotel often having different sources. In addition, Four Seasons customizes many of its products and sundries, making each high-quality product associated with their brand.

A number of key stakeholders influence this segment of the market. The costs of building and maintaining properties of the quality demanded of the segment require a large amount of debt financing, typically provided by financial institutions. Without that support, the capital for growth would be unattainable. Minor renovations may happen as often as every ninety days, as in Ritz-Carlton's "care" program.[52]

Continued customer loyalty is essential in raising capital. Though the price of luxury accommodations are high, the cost of development and maintenance are even higher, hence luxury hotels are often not able to charge their guests the amount needed to fully cover the true expenses of the operation.[53] Repeat, frequent business is an important element in the segment's success. Union activity is of concern with regard to luxury hotel construction and staffing. Unions are dealt with on a local basis.

Hotels in this segment strive to be present in any thriving business and financial center in the world. They open in emerging markets and ones showing important presence in the world market over time. The Four Seasons is currently present in twetny-five countries and plans to expand into another nine. Four Seasons competitor Starwood Hotels, designated the "World's Best Global Hotel Company" by *Global Finance* magazine in 2000,[54] was specifically cited for its accelerated global expansion. Another competitor in the luxury segment, Le Meridien Hotels and Resorts, has earmarked $550 million for global expansion by 2004, with Hong Kong and China its major targets.[55]

Though it would seem in this time of economic downturn that expansion would not be wise, industry leaders think that now is precisely the time to be expanding. Michael Saglid, managing director Asia Pacific for Le Meridian, expressed that it was best to enter during a down market.[56] This is echoed by Four Seasons' director of Worldwide Operations, Wolf Hengst, who said, "Down cycles actually provide us with opportunities for accelerated growth, to strengthen our product and grow into new markets."[57]

With Asia Pacific emerging as a financial center, luxury hotels are focusing on expansions there as well as in South America and Europe. The customer-centric models that luxury hotels employ require a great deal more understanding of local culture than do large chains, which provide a more homogenous product. The strong philosophies of customer service that permeate the culture of the organizations in this sector aid in providing a consistent product to each market.

BRAND AND CULTURE

Four Seasons' strategic direction is based on the strength of its brand name. George Stalk Jr., senior vice president of Boston Consulting Group's Toronto office, wrote in the 1999 publication *The CEO as Brand Manager* that "Total Brand Management is the essence of the Four Seasons hotel chain's success."[59] Four Seasons' focus on brand management is not only a feature of how it became successful, but is also an integral part of Four Seasons' global expansion strategy. Four Seasons articulated the importance of its brand recognition as a means of achieving a competitive advantage:

> The core business strategy of Four Seasons continues to be to enhance its industry position and overall profitability through a focused, international expansion program that capitalizes on the strengths of its core management operations and the value of its brand name.... The Corporation believes that the strength of its brand name, its global marketing presence and its operational expertise result in RevPAR premiums and strong operating profitability for luxury hotels under its management and provide Four Seasons with a competitive advantage in obtaining new management contracts worldwide.[60]

Four Seasons has become a dominant luxury brand that is defined by high levels of personal service and the creation of quality experiences for their guests. Their brand is used as a source of competitive advantage. They have established a strategy that uses the Four Seasons name to not only extend their core strength of hotel management globally, but also to enter new business areas, like residential properties and fractional ownership.[61]

One of Four Seasons' additional strengths is in their values, which is an important component of their operational expertise. In its statement of values (Exhibit 3), expressed in the company's *2002 Annual Report,* Four Seasons refers to their staff as their "greatest asset," and stresses the importance of treating people well.[62] Four Seasons has been noted as taking the extra step to improve the work environment of its staff. CEO Isadore Sharp believes a "successful brand experience" depends on those who create that experience and how those people are treated by top managers.[63] The entire corporate philosophy at Four Seasons hinges on the Golden Rule: "treating others as you would like to be treated."[64]

Four Seasons believes that each of its employees needs a sense of dignity, pride and satisfaction in what they do. Satisfying customer needs depends upon a united effort of all the employees of the company. Teamwork makes the employees more effective,

respecting each employee's contribution and importance. A main component of teamwork is integrity. The company considers integrity as a vital factor that must influence the ethical behavior of management and employees. Four Seasons' reputation is based upon this integrity, and the executive team sees integrity as critical to the success of the company.

Four Seasons made the decision early on to focus solely on the high-end customer and concentrate on hotel management rather than real estate. Moreover, they made the decision to pursue a global strategy. They leveraged their brand and strategic relationships to gain position in key destinations across the world. They continue to grow their portfolio, expanding into new areas and "prime locations."[65] Four Seasons has formed strategic relationships with investors, which has helped them expand management operations and development opportunities. Additionally, they have built relationships with several different small private

---

| EXHIBIT 3 | FOUR SEASONS HOTELS & RESORTS: OUR VALUES—OUR GOALS, OUR BELIEFS, OUR PRINCIPLES |

Who We Are

We have chosen to specialize within the hospitality industry, by offering only experiences of exceptional quality. Our objective is to be recognized as the company that manages the finest hotels, resorts, residence clubs and other residential properties wherever we operate. Our goal is to create properties of enduring value using superior design and finishes, and support them with a deeply instilled ethic of personal service. Doing so allows Four Seasons to satisfy the needs and tastes of our discriminating customers, and to maintain our position as the world's premier luxury hospitality company.

What We Believe

Our greatest asset, and the key to our success, is our people. We believe that each of us needs a sense of dignity, pride and satisfaction in what we do. Because satisfying our guests depends on the united efforts of many, we are most effective when we work together cooperatively, respecting each other's contribution and importance.

How We Behave

We demonstrate our beliefs most meaningfully in the way we treat each other and by the example we set for one another. In all our interactions with our guests, customers, business associates and colleagues, we seek to deal with others as we would have them deal with us.

How We Succeed

We succeed when every decision is based on a clear understanding of and belief in what we do and when we couple this conviction with sound financial planning. We expect to achieve a fair and reasonable profit to ensure the prosperity of the company, and to offer long-term benefits to our hotel owners, our shareholders, our customers and our employees.

Source: Four Seasons Hotels & Resorts, *2002 Annual Report,* inside cover.

equity and institutional investors, many of which have interests in more than one property. Three investors own interest in five or six properties, and Prince Alwaleed bin Talal bin Abdulaziz al Saud holds a significant minority interest of 25 percent in Four Seasons Limited.[66]

Prince Alwaleed bin Talal has made significant investments in Four Seasons properties, and is expected to continue to invest in several Four Seasons projects in the Middle East, including Amman, Cairo, Riyadh, Alexandria, Sharm el Sheikh, and Beirut. The Sharm el Sheikh resort was recently finished while other properties are in differing stages of development. Prince Alwaleed bin Talal finds local investors in the Middle East to help finance ownership of the properties and arranges management contracts with the Four Seasons. This has helped Four Seasons expand in a new market and is beneficial for two additional reasons: first, because hotel groups are heavily taxed on property ownership in the Middle East, and second, because Four Seasons wants to remain primarily a management company.[67]

As of the close of 2003, Four Seasons had twenty-one branded properties under construction or development around the world, from Jackson Hole to Qatar, with thirteen boasting a residence club or other residential component.[68] Although the Four Seasons' current strategy focuses on property management, it does have a 100 percent lease ownership on three properties: the Pierre in New York, the Four Seasons Vancouver, and the Four Seasons Berlin. These investments were established early on in Four Seasons' corporate development. Now, because of the nature of the lease, if Four Seasons wanted to sell the hotels, it would be hard to do so and retain the management contract. However, Four Seasons continues to have small equity positions in other properties within its global portfolio.

MANAGEMENT AND ORGANIZATION

Four Seasons prefers to develop its senior management team from within the company to retain consistency, work ethic, and the culture that has made it successful. The senior management of Four Seasons is made up of the CEO and founder, Isadore Sharp; the president of Worldwide Hotel Operations, Wolf H. Hengst; and the president of Worldwide Business Operations, Kathleen Taylor. The experienced corporate executive management team consists of eight people and has an average of twenty-two years' experience at Four Seasons. They collectively determine the global strategic direction for the company. They are supported by twenty-six vice presidents, who are responsible for numerous aspects of daily operations, and sixty general managers and regional vice presidents. The company employs 350 people in its various corporate offices, including the central reservation office and sales offices. In addition, there are over 25,000 people employed by Four Seasons worldwide.

Four Seasons is a publicly traded company listed on both the Toronto Stock Exchange and the New York Stock Exchange, under FSH and FS, respectively. The corporation reported total assets of $970,624,000 and consolidated revenues of $284,674,000 in 2002.[69] The Board of Directors is made up of thirteen people, including Isadore Sharp; see Exhibit 4 for a complete list of directors; Exhibit 5 for a list of the company's executive officers; and Exhibit 6 for complete consolidated financial statements.

Sharp's entrepreneurial spirit and vision of combining friendliness and efficiency with the finest traditions of international hotel keeping have transformed the Four Seasons from a modest motor hotel in Toronto to a leading global operator of hotels and resorts.[70] Sharp's vision for Four Seasons has been adopted by the rest of the company. His objectives were the same then as they are now: to position service as one of the company's core competencies, to develop medium-sized hotels of extraordinary quality, to follow the Golden Rule, and to concentrate investment in management expertise rather than real estate in order to distinguish the hotel brand by reputation. Sharp believes that employee loyalty and treating employees well at all levels of the company translates into a stronger culture, and, thus better service for Four Seasons' guests.[71]

Taylor and Hengst are both possible candidates to eventually lead the Four Seasons brand. Sharp, at

EXHIBIT 4	BOARD OF DIRECTORS
Isadore Sharp	Chairman and CEO, Four Seasons, Inc.
Brent Belzberg	Managing Partner, Torquest Partners, Inc.
Edmond M. Creed	Retired Executive
Frederick Eisen	President and CEO, The Eisen Corp.
H. Roger Garland	Corporate Director
Nan-b de Gaspe Beaubien	Co-Chair, Business Families Foundation, and Co-Chair, Philbeau Company
Charles S. Henry	President, Hotel Capital Advisers, Inc.
Murray B. Koffler	Partner, The Koffler Group
Heather Munroe-Blum	Principal and Vice Chancellor, McGill University
J. Robert S. Prichard	President and CEO, Torstar Corp.
Lionel H. Schipper	President, Schipper Enterprises, Inc.
Anthony Sharp	President, AD Sharp Development, Inc.
Simon M. Turner	Principal, Hotel Capital Advisers, Inc.
Benjamin Swirsky	Chairman and CEO, Beswir Properties, Inc.
Shuichiro Tamaki	Executive Vice President, Japan-Mexico Hotel Investment Co., Ltd.

Source: Four Seasons Hotels & Resorts, *2002 Annual Report,* 67.

EXHIBIT 5	EXECUTIVE OFFICERS
Isadore Sharp	Chairman and Chief Executive Officer
Sarah Cohen	Vice President, Corporate Counsel & Assistant Secretary
Wolf H. Hengst	President, Worldwide Hotel Operations
Douglas L. Ludwig	Executive Vice President, Chief Financial Officer & Treasurer
Craig O. Reith	Vice President Finance and Assistant Treasurer
Kathleen Taylor	President, Worldwide Business Operations
Randolph Weisz	Executive Vice President, General Counsel and Secretary

Source: Four Seasons Hotels & Resorts, *2002 Annual Report,* 67.

70 years old, has mentioned retiring but continues to hold his position. Hengst describes his job as "I get the heads on the beds and hot soup in the bowls."[72] Hengst has been with Four Seasons for over twenty-two years and had a hands-on role in many of Four Seasons' international expansion efforts. He characterizes himself as a bit compulsive and obsessive, and he stresses the importance of skills, honesty, and integrity in a leader.[73]

Taylor has become the primary dealmaker for Sharp. Sharp admits that when Taylor joined the company he thought that she had the potential to make top management. Taylor joined the company in 1989 as corporate counsel and rose to the presidency of Worldwide Operations in only ten years.[74] She became involved in all of the acquisition and deal structuring of the company by the late 1990s. Taylor was in charge of the international development function, and after numerous accolades she assumed the position of president of Worldwide Operations in 1999. Both Hengst and Sharp have stated that her down-to-earth approach to business is one of her strong suits.[75] She multitasks between being a mother and a senior manager, and is thought by many people, including Hengst, to be the future of Four Seasons.

SELLING "FOUR SEASONS"

Four Seasons' corporate office, located in Toronto, is responsible for the development and coordination of

EXHIBIT 6	CONSOLIDATED FINANCIAL STATEMENTS

Consolidated Balance Sheet ($ Thousands)

	2002[1]	**2001**[2]	**2000**[3]	**1999**[4]	**1998**[5]
			Year Ending December 31,		
Assets					
Current assets:					
Cash & cash equivalents	$ 165,036	$ 210,421	$ 218,100	$ 222,245	$ 17,591
Receivables	85,594	78,450	94,265	60,931	58,610
Inventory	2,609	3,074	2,806	2,869	1,681
Prepaid expenses	4,718	2,492	1,499	1,754	1,952
	257,957	294,437	316,670	287,799	79,834
Long-term receivables	207,106	201,453	167,214	129,174	150,866
Investments in hotel partnerships & corporations	146,362	141,005	172,579	116,010	76,761
Fixed assets	74,593	50,715	46,342	39,748	31,464
Investment in management contracts	222,835	201,460	189,171	186,025	131,705
Investment in trademarks & trade names	6,329	33,784	34,829	35,306	39,268
Future income tax assets	17,460	17,745	21,771	6,864	7,152
Other assets	37,982	39,782	35,821	31,213	228,006
Total Assets	**$ 970,624**	**$ 980,381**	**$ 984,397**	**$ 832,139**	**$ 545,056**
Liabilities & Shareholders' Equity					
Current liabilities:					
Accounts payable & accrued liabilities	$ 40,362	$ 50,813	$ 71,345	$ 57,311	$ 49,666
Long-term obligations due within 1 year	2,668	1,188	1,152	1,005	1,062
	43,030	52,001	72,497	58,316	50,728
Long-term obligations	126,386	118,244	203,736	186,126	163,925
Shareholders' Equity:					
Capital stock	321,601	319,460	316,640	308,993	300,805
Convertible notes	178,543	178,543	178,543	178,424	4,784
Contributed surplus	4,636	4,784	4,784	4,784	11,236
Retained earnings	264,016	285,619	202,760	94,150	13,578
Equity adjustment from foreign currency translation	32,412	21,730	5,437	1,346	13,578
Commitments & contingencies	801,208	810,136	708,164	587,697	330,473
Total Liabilities & Shareholders' Equity	**$ 970,624**	**$980,381**	**$ 984,397**	**$ 832,139**	**$ 545,056**

[1] Four Seasons Hotels & Resorts, *2002 Annual Report, 73.*

[2] Ibid.

[3] Four Seasons Hotels & Resorts, *2000 Annual Report, 56.*

[4] Ibid.

[5] Four Seasons Hotels & Resorts, *1998 Annual Report, 62.*

(Continues)

the overall marketing strategies for the portfolio of Four Seasons–managed hotels. The marketing strategy addresses both building international awareness for the Four Seasons brand and developing local market potential for specific hotels. Four Seasons' marketing is targeted at the luxury segment of the global marketplace. Four Seasons estimates that it derives 69 percent of its business from business travelers and groups and 31 percent from the leisure sector.[76]

The corporate marketing staff oversees the planning and implementation of the hotel marketing program. This includes organizing the training and development program for the global sales force as well as the local sales and marketing staff. Four

| **EXHIBIT 6** | **CONSOLIDATED FINANCIAL STATEMENTS (CONTINUED)** |

Consolidated Statement of Retained Earnings
($ Thousands)

	Year Ending December 31,				
	2002[6]	**2001**[7]	**2000**[8]	**1999**[9]	**1998**[10]
Retained earnings—beginning of year	$ 285,619	$202,760	$ 94,150	$ 11,236	$ (54,961)
Effect of adoption of new accounting standards for intangible assets	(26,366)	—	—	—	—
	259,253	202,760	94,150	11,236	(54,961)
Net earnings	21,231	86,486	103,074	86,479	69,702
Declared dividends	(3,633)	(3,627)	(3,605)	(3,565)	(3,505)
Repurchase of shares	(12,835)	—	—	—	—
Effect of adoption of new accounting standards for pension benefits	—	—	(7,476)	—	—
Effect of adoption of new accounting standards for income taxes	—	—	16,637	—	—
Loss of redemption of convertible notes	—	—	(20)	—	—
Retained earnings—end of year	$ 264,016	$ 285,619	$202,760	$ 94,150	$ 11,236

[6] Four Seasons Hotels & Resorts, *2002 Annual Report,* 74.

[7] Ibid.

[8] Four Seasons Hotels & Resorts, *2000 Annual Report,* 58.

[9] Ibid.

[10] Four Seasons Hotels & Resorts, *1998 Annual Report,* 64.

(Continues)

Seasons has a global sales force of more than one hundred people in thirteen integrated sales offices around the world. The key objectives of the sales force are to attract group and corporate business travelers for the hotels and resorts and to establish contacts with travel agencies.[77]

The local marketing strategy concentrates on developing luxury rooms and food and beverage sectors for hotels locally and regionally. In addition to promoting the hotel as a center of community activity, the staff has a goal of developing local revenues, particularly from catering.[78] The Four Seasons management company also provides an international corporate advertising program that develops and places advertising for Four Seasons hotels and oversees individual hotels' programs. Corporate advertising and marketing programs are designed to enhance consumer awareness of Four Seasons' luxury service and the value that such services provide to the business and leisure traveler.[79]

One of Four Seasons' marketing tools takes advantage of a superior reservation system and pro-

prietary technology. Four Seasons staffs one reservation center for all Four Seasons–branded hotels and resorts, providing reservation services in the local language in major North American, Asian, and European cities in twenty-five markets. Customers are also reached by electronic reservations through the global distribution network, as Four Seasons' reservation systems are fully integrated with international airline booking systems.[80] Another growing distribution channel is the Internet. Four Seasons' Web site—www.fourseasons.com—was recently redeveloped to improve its content. The navigation of the site, its links to search engines, reservation capabilities, and referral to other reservation channels were made more efficient.[81] Four Seasons receives corporate sales and marketing fees, centralized reservation service fees, and corporate advertising fees from all managed hotels, enabling it to recover a substantial portion of the costs of providing these services.[82]

Although Four Seasons uses standard approaches to reach its customers, the excellent support provided

EXHIBIT 6	**CONSOLIDATED FINANCIAL STATEMENTS** *(CONTINUED)*

Consolidated Statement of Operations
(Income Statement) ($ Thousands)

	Year Ending December 31,				
	2002[11]	**2001**[12]	**2000**[13]	**1999**[14]	**1998**[15]
Consolidated revenues	$ 284,674	$ 303,106	$ 347,507	$ 277,548	$ 248,778
Management operations:					
Revenues	$ 147,894	$ 160,672	$ 185,294	$ 143,984	$ 126,947
General & administrative expenses	(65,9033)	(65,416)	(59,532)	(54,858)	(47,064)
	81,991	95,256	125,762	89,126	79,883
Ownership operations:					
Revenues	$ 141,290	$ 147,500	$ 161,061	$ 132,371	$ 126,055
Distributions from hotel investments	1,321	1,510	9,047	8,310	2,732
Expenses:					
Cost of sales & expenses	(156,374)	(152,663)	(148,590)	(125,214)	(112,485)
Fees to management operations	(5,831)	(6,576)	(7,895)	(7,117)	(6,956)
	(19,594)	(10,229)	13,623	8,350	9,346
Earnings before other operating items	62,397	85,027	139,385	97,476	89,229
Depreciation & amortization	(14,837)	(16,242)	(14,028)	(12,492)	(15,164)
Other income (expense), net	(22,860)	30,698	8,669	3,587	865
Earnings from operations	24,700	99,483	134,026	88,571	74,930
Interest income, net	3,235	6,740	4,190	409	(3,802)
Earnings before income taxes	27,935	106,223	138,216	88,980	71,128
Income tax expense					
Current	(5,743)	(15,711)	(33,412)	(1,665)	(1,136)
Future	(1,118)	(3,087)	1,796	(836)	(290)
Increase (decrease) in future income tax assets	157	(939)	(3,526)	—	—
	(6,704)	(19,737)	(35,142)	(2,501)	(1,426)
Net earnings	$ 21,231	$ 86,486	$ 103,074	$ 86,479	$ 69,702
Earnings per share	$ 0.61	$ 2.48	$ 2.98	$ 2.52	$ 2.06
Diluted earnings per share	$ 0.59	$ 2.27		—	—

[11] Ibid.

[12] Four Seasons Hotels & Resorts, *2000 Annual Report*, 55.

[13] Ibid.

[14] Ibid.

[15] Four Seasons Hotels & Resorts, *1998 Annual Report*, 61.

(Continues)

to its distribution channels and networks and the exclusive focus on high-end travelers has made it a success.[83] Staying focused on the luxury market and the Four Seasons name has been a successful marketing tool. The significant premium in revenue per available room (RevPAR) that Four Seasons generated over and above its competition is evidence of its effective corporate marketing strategies. The Four Seasons Hotel London is an example of the success of Four Seasons' marketing strategies. Even though it is located in an extremely competitive market, over the past thirty years the hotel has been the best performing luxury property in London. Much of this success can be attributed to Four Seasons' reputation as a hotel company that expects excellence from employees at all levels.[84]

| **EXHIBIT 6** | **CONSOLIDATED FINANCIAL STATEMENTS (CONTINUED)** |

Consolidated Statement of Cash Flows
($ Thousands)

	Year Ending December 31,				
	2002[16]	**2001**[17]	**2000**[18]	**1999**[19]	**1998**[20]
Cash provided by (used in):					
Operations	$ 41,763	$ 75,510	$ 102,633	$ 106,787	$ 74,961
Financing					
Long-term obligations, including current portion:					
Issued	2,342	469	645	—	45,562
Repaid	(1,203)	(103,427)	(1,071)	(46,458)	(10,461)
Issuance of shares	5,653	2,820	7,647	8,188	2,423
Repurchase of shares	(16,495)	—	—	244,721	—
Dividends paid	(3,639)	(3,625)	(3,579)	(3,539)	—
Other			(71)	(423)	(678)
Cash used in financing	(13,342)	(103,663)	3,571	202,489	36,846
Capital investments					
Increase in long-term receivables	(32,316)	(52,428)	(69,984)	(80,976)	(68,476)
Decrease in long-term receivables	3,423	29,080	24,861	3,997	2,178
Hotel investments	(9,451)	(22,088)	(43,262)	(40,535)	(21,921)
Disposal of hotel investments	4,566	88,629	-	34,025	12,781
Purchase of fixed assets	(31,085)	(9,639)	(11,137)	(13,016)	(13,885)
Investment in trademarks, trade names & management contracts	(1,598)	(8,212)	(6,938)	(1,182)	(19,819)
Other assets	(7,809)	(6,319)	(6,537)	(5,171)	(7,179)
Cash provided by (used in) capital investments	(74,270)	19,023	(111,997)	(102,858)	(116,321)
Increase (decrease) in cash & cash equivalents	(45,849)	(9,130)	(5,793)	206,418	(8,016)
Increase (decrease) in cash & cash equivalents due to unrealized foreign exchange gain (loss)	464	1,451	1,648	(1,764)	272
Cash & cash equivalents—beginning of year	210,421	218,100	222,245	17,591	25,335
Cash & cash equivalents—end of year	$ 165,036	$ 210,421	$ 218,100	$ 222,245	$ 17,591

[16] Four Seasons Hotels & Resorts, *2002 Annual Report,* 75.

[17] Ibid.

[18] Four Seasons Hotels & Resorts, *2000 Annual Report,* 58.

[19] Ibid.

[20] Four Seasons Hotels & Resorts, *1998 Annual Report,* 64.

Four Seasons' training program reflects the entire philosophy and culture of Four Seasons Hotels & Resorts. General orientation, core standards training, and job shadowing are regular training protocol for all employees. Four Seasons trains all its employees with the same type of manual and standard courses so that all the hotels work on the same premise.[85]

Superior and consistent service are attributes synonymous with the Four Seasons brand. These attributes are instilled in its employees through a developmental training program.[86] New hires are immediately oriented to this value system. Each new employee is interviewed by top management and then participates in a seven-part orientation program spread over twelve weeks, culminating in an overnight stay in the hotel to experience all aspects of service, just as a guest would. Mentor relationships are developed both formally and informally.[87]

Besides formal training, employees learn by example from managers and by observing managers' behavior. Managers build an environment based on respect and leadership that allows the employee, with confidence, to take care of the guest. It should be no surprise, then, that a *Fortune* magazine named Four Seasons as one of the hundred best companies to work for in North America.[88] Four Seasons believes that it must maintain its service-oriented culture, which is facilitated by an unusually high ratio of thoroughly trained employees to guests.[89] Furthermore, Four Seasons spends a good portion of its training budget developing employees it already has.[90] In addition, Four Seasons indirectly maintains good relationships with their employees by maintaining good communications with unions.

In the changing workplace and economic environment, the role of mediators is evolving. Unions have shifted from resolving contract disputes to facilitation and training of both sides, leading to more effective bargaining and communications, joint problem solving, and innovative conflict resolution methods. Two unions, the Hotel Employees & Restaurant Employees Union and the Service Employees International Union, which represent the majority of hotel employees, have become models for improved labor-management relations.[91]

Most hoteliers worry that opposition to a union could lead to extensive delays in getting permits and approvals from local governments, which have long had the reputation of being friendly to labor unions. Developers and operators generally don't want to risk fighting the union during the construction or opening of a property, so most hotels try to maintain good relations with unions.[92]

Four Seasons takes a collaborative approach with unions. Where union representation is strong, Four Seasons has recognized that if it works with unions it can actually gain competitive advantage. Although there are times of conflict, Four Seasons is more open than ever to finding common ground with unions.[93]

Four Seasons recognizes that relationships with external stakeholders can help its bottom line.

Because of the complexity of the Four Seasons product, travel agents can be quite helpful in helping sell the product. Four Seasons hotels recognize the value of travel agents in directing business their way. Travel agents are consulted to determine how Four Seasons should market its products. Travel agencies that would like to feature a Four Seasons property on their own Web sites can create a customized minitour of the hotel.[94] These sales tools help agents further strengthen Four Seasons' brand and what it represents. Agencies that give Four Seasons a major share of their luxury business are invited to become a preferred partner with the company, entitling them to receive such support as joint marketing, staff education, and special access to key executives.[95]

Strategic relationships are an important source of future development opportunities to expand Four Seasons' management operations. Four Seasons has established relationships with numerous institutional and private equity sources that invest in and develop luxury hotels.[96] Other competitive relationships include hotel owners, such as Prince Alwaleed bin Talal bin Abdulaziz. Any failure by Four Seasons to maintain satisfactory relationships with the owner of a significant number of properties could reduce the corporation's return on operations. Additionally, since Four Seasons manages a portfolio in twenty-five countries, the maintenance of solid business relationships with both governments and local communities is crucial to Four Seasons' reputation and future.[97]

THE FINANCIALS

Four Seasons generally enjoys a healthy position in the market, but there have been some downturns. In 1982, bearing a significant amount of long-term debt, the corporation began selling properties, negotiating long-term contracts that allowed Four Seasons to continue the administration of the properties. About $31.2 million worth of assets were sold, and the company raised additional money through the sale of stock. These actions enabled Four Seasons to return to a strong financial position.

Another tactic the company used to maintain its financial health was seen in its reaction to a decline in profits during the 1970s. In that instance, Sharp and the Board of Directors turned the company private in order to regain control.[98]

In 1992, Four Seasons acquired Regent International Hotels. In the same year, the company experienced one of its major downturns, almost losing the management contracts of its hotels. The sale of 25 percent of the corporation to Saudi Prince Alwaleed bin Talal ensured that the company was able to maintain its management of these properties. In the mid-1990s, the company formed a joint venture with Carlson Hospitality Worldwide, giving Four Seasons a great competitive advantage in reaching customers in the luxury segment.[99]

The company expected its average daily room rates for 2002 to be roughly equivalent to 2000 ($281) and 2001 ($287), and it met that estimation with a $289 average daily rate for 2002.[100] However, a significant drop in across-the-board occupancy (from 72.6 percent in 2000 to 64.6 percent in 2002) and a commensurate drop in RevPAR, or revenue per available room (from $204 in 2000 to $187 in 2002), increases in cost of sales, and losses in foreign exchange and investments led to a serious, but expected, decline in net earnings (from $103.1 million in 2000 to $86.5 million in 2001 to $21.2 million in 2002).[100]

Four Seasons has adopted aggressive but practical measures to control costs. These actions have enabled them to maintain a significant RevPAR premium compared to their competitors. It has also maintained a good, albeit declining, corporate profit margin (59.3 percent in 2001, 55.4 percent in 2002) on its management business, and a better-than-fair market share of approximately 122 percent.[101] The company believes that its ability to control costs without compromising service has positioned it well for the anticipated recovery of the economy and lodging demand.[102]

Four Seasons' major financial objectives are summarized in these points:[103]

- To accomplish compounded earnings per share growth of 20 percent per year over the long term

- To accomplish an average return on capital of 10 percent over the corporation's long-term cost of capital

- Maintain an investment grade credit rating and a low cost of capital

- Focus on ongoing improvements in operating profit margins (both at property and corporate level)

- Maintain a policy of tax efficiency

- Maintain a prudent risk profile

- Invest in technology

As part of its business strategy, Four Seasons invests a portion of its available cash on new management agreements or on enhancing existing management arrangements. New loans or investments will take place only when the overall economic return improves.

CONCLUSION

Four Seasons' culture, brand, and global strategy are an integral part of its success. While there are opportunities, such as expansion in the Middle East, these opportunities are also risky because of the unstable nature of the economy and the political environment of the area.

Nevertheless, Four Seasons Hotels & Resorts has spent more than forty years nurturing a culture and reputation based on respect, fairness, financial prudence, and the strength of the Four Seasons brand as synonymous with luxury. The future of global politics and the economy may be uncertain, but for Four Seasons "culture and reputation" are sure to remain an important tool the company will use to navigate through challenging markets and prosperous times alike.

Notes

1. Four Seasons Hotels & Resorts, *2002 Annual Report,* p. 2.
2. Tina Grant, "International Directory of Company Histories" (St. James Press), V. 29, 198–200.
3. Ibid.

4. Ibid.
5. Ibid.
6. Ibid.
7. "Hoover Company Profile," www.hoovers.online. Visited 15 November 2002.
8. Ibid.
9. Grant, "International Directory of Company Histories."
10. "Group Therapy—The History of Four Seasons," *Catering and Hotel Keeper,* 22 March 2001.
11. "Hoover Company Profile," www.hoovers.online. Visited 15 November 2002.
12. Four Seasons Hotels & Resorts, *2001 Annual Report.*
13. Tourism Victoria, "Strategic Plan: Trends Analysis," http://www.tourismvictoria.com.au/strategicplan/plan2002_2006/1_introduction/trends_analysis.htm.
14. Alberto E. Landero, "Analysis of Current Trends in the Hospitality Industry through Content Analysis of Hotel-Online Internet News Service," *Hotel Online,* http://www.hotel-online.com/News/PressReleases/AnalysisHotelOnline_Sept1997.html. Visited November 2002.
15. Hospitality.net, "The TBR/WTTC Index of Leading Economic Indicators Declined 0.3 Percent in August—August Decline Was the Third in the Past Four Months," http://www.hospitalitynet.org/news/Association_Update/4013653.html. Visited December 2002.
16. Hotel News Resource, http://www.hotelnewsresource.com/studies/hvs052702.htm. Visited November 2002.
17. Landero, "Analysis of Current Trends in the Hospitality Industry through Content Analysis of Hotel-Online Internet News Service."
18. Keith C. Su, "Economic Trends & Influence on Hospitality Industry: The Case of U.S. Lodging Industry," *Hotel Online,* http://www.hotel-online.com/Trends/AdvancesInHospitalityResearch/CaseofUSLodgingIndustry1998.html.
19. Tourism Victoria, "Strategic Plan: Trends Analysis."
20. Landero, "Analysis of Current Trends in the Hospitality Industry through Content Analysis of Hotel-Online Internet News Service."
21. Four Seasons Hotels & Resorts, *2001 Annual Report,* 3.
22. Robert Green, "Baldrige Award Winner Profile: An Interview with Horst Schulze, President and COO of The Ritz-Carlton Hotel Co. LLC," *Quality Digest,* http://www.qualitydigest.com/aug00/html/baldrige.html.
23. Christina Brinkley, "Empty Rooms: U.S. Hotels Struggle to Cope with Drop in Guests since Attack," *The Wall Street Journal,* 28 September 2001. Online. Factiva. http://global.factiva.com/en/arch/print_results.asp. Visited November 2002.
24. Business Travel News, "Four Seasons Weathering Storm (One-on-One)," http://ga.primark.com/ga/Articles/GetRDS.asp. Visited November 2002.
25. Stephen Rushmore, Dana Michael Ciraldo, and John Tarras, *Hotel and Lodging Market Research Handbook* (Richard K. Miller & Associates, 2001).
26. Brinkley, "Empty Rooms: U.S. Hotels Struggle to Cope with Drop in Guests since Attack," 28 September 2001. Online. Factiva. http://global.factiva.com/en/arch/print_results.asp. Visited November 2002.
27. Rushmore et al., *Hotel and Lodging Market Research Handbook.*
28. Ibid.
29. Ibid.
30. Vito Racanelli, "Weekday Trader: Net Is Win/Win for Travel Industry, Public," *Barron's Online,* 17 June 1999. Online. Factiva. http://global.factiva.com/en/arch/display.asp. Visited November 2002.
31. Roger Cline for Arthur Andersen, "Brand Marketing in the Hospitality Industry—Art or Science," Summer 1996. http://wotel-online.com/Trends/Andersen/Brand_Marketing.html. Visited November 2002.
32. Ibid.
33. Ritz-Carlton Profile, Hoover's Online, http://www.hoovers.com/co/capsule/5/0,2163,41695,00.html. Visited November 2002.
34. Fairmont Profile, Hoover's Online, http://www.hoovers.com/co/capsule/7/0,2163,40897,00.html. Visited November 2002.
35. Starwood Profile, Hoover's Online, http://www.hoovers.com/premium/profile/7/0,2147,10747,00.html. Visited November 2002.
36. Four Seasons Hotels & Resorts, *2002 Annual Report,* 28-29.
37. Maurice Robinson, "And Then There Was One . . . Consolidation in the Hospitality Industry," *Hotel Online,* Summer 1997. http://www.hotel-online.com/Trends/KPMG/Articles/ThenThereWasOne.html. Visited November 2002.
38. Rushmore et al. *Hotel and Lodging Market Research Handbook.*
39. Robinson, "And Then There Was One."
40. Four Seasons Hotels & Resorts, *2001 Annual Report.*
41. Rushmore et al., *Hotel and Lodging Market Research Handbook.*
42. Daniel Connolly, "Shifting Paradigms: Using Information Technology to Enhance Service Dyads in Luxury Hotels," *Journal of Hospitality & Leisure Marketing,* Vol 7/2 2000. Online, Hospitality Database. Visited November 2002.
43. "MICROS Completes Global Deployment of Four Seasons Hotels and Resorts Central Reservations and Customer Information Systems; Begins Global deployment of OPERA Property Management System," PR News Wire, 14 May 2002. Online. Factiva. http://global.factiva.com/en/arch/display.asp. Visited November 2002.
44. Rushmore et al., *Hotel and Lodging Market Research Handbook.*
45. Ibid.
46. "Healthy Market Should Prevail Despite Construction Slowdown," *Hotel and Motel Management,* 2 June 2001. Online. Proquest. http://proquest.umi.com/pdqweb. Visited November 2002.
47. Stephen Rushmore, "Development Cost Can Determine Feasibility," *Hotels,* March 2002.

48. Joe Gose, "The Ground Floor: Hotel Industry Puts On Brakes as Overbuilding Threatens, Especially of Luxury Properties Downtown," *Barron's Online,* 19 July 1999. Online. Proquest. http://proquest.umi.com/pdqweb. Visited November 2002.

49. Four Seasons Hotels Inc. Profile, Hoover's Online. http://www.hoovers.com/premium/profile/2/0,2147,43682,00.html. Visited November 2002.

50. Rushmore et al., *Hotel and Lodging Market Research Handbook.*

51. Stephen Rushmore, "How to Manage the Lower Returns of Luxury, 5-Star Hotels," *Hotels,* February 2001.

52. Maria Vallejo, "Four Seasons Solidifies Its Hold as Asians Stumble," *Business Travel News,* 22 February 1999.

53. Connolly, "Shifting Paradigms: Using Information Technology to Enhance Service Dyads in Luxury Hotels."

54. PR Newswire, "Starwood Honored as 'World's Best Global Hotel Company' by *Global Finance Magazine,*" 2 October 2000. Online. Factiva. http://global.factiva.com/en/arch/display.asp. Visited November 2002.

55. Sandy Li, "Le Meridian Resumes Presence in SAR while Looking Further North," *South China Morning Post.* Online. Factiva. http://global.factiva.com/en/arch/display.asp. Visited November 2002.

56. "Healthy Market Should Prevail Despite Construction Slowdown," *Hotel and Motel Management.*

57. "Four Seasons Weathering Storm," *Business Travel News.*

58. Marriot Inc., *2001 Annual Report.*

59. George Stalk Jr., "CEO as Total Brand Manager." Boston Consulting Group Consumer & Retail Publication. 1999, 2.

60. Four Seasons Hotels & Resorts, *2001 Annual Report,* 23.

61. Nancy Schwartz and Shauna Emerson O'Neill, "Leveraging Brand Strategy in the Travel Industry," *Mercer on Transport & Travel,* Spring/Summer 2001, 18.

62. Four Seasons Hotels & Resorts, *2002 Annual Report,* inside cover.

63. Stalk, "CEO as Total Brand Manager."

64. Four Seasons Hotels & Resorts, *2001 Annual Report,* 3.

65. Roger Martin, "How Four Seasons Weathered Global Competition," *National Post,* 13 May 2002.

66. "Mubarak, Abdullah Open New Four Seasons Sharm El Sheikh Resort," *Travel & Tourism News Middle East,* Volume 19, Number 11. http://www.ttnworldwide.com/News.asp?Article=1344. Visited 19 November 2002.

67. John Rossant, "Apples Arabian Knight?" *Business Week,* 21 April 1997, http://www.businessweek.com/1997/16/b352385.htm. Visited 12 November 2002.

68. Four Seasons Hotels & Resorts, *2002 Annual Report,* 30.

69. Four Seasons Hotels & Resorts, *2002 Annual Report,* 72–73.

70. Four Seasons Profile, Fourseasons.com. http://www.fourseasons.com/about_us/company_information/about_us_10.html. Visited 16 November 2002.

71. *Lodging Magazine,* http://www.lodgingnews.com/lodgingmag/2000_08/2000_08_93.asp . Visited 12 November 2002.

72. Siobhan Roberts, "In All Seasons as Dealmaker for Fast-Growing Four Seasons Hotels, Kathleen Taylor Must Make Luxury Pay—Even in Fearful Weather," *The Globe and Mail,* Metro section, 28 December 2001.

73. Wolf H. Hengst, *Lodging Magazine,* http://www.lodgingnews.com/lodgingmag/2001_08/2001_08_30.asp. Visited 16 November 2002.

74. Four Seasons Hotels & Resorts, *2001 Annual Report.*

75. Jeff Higley, "Head of the Class: Down-to-Earth Approach Helps Multitasking Lawyer Scale Four Seasons' Ladder. (Kathleen Taylor, Co-president of Four Seasons Ltd.)," *Hotel & Motel Management,* 5 November 2001.

76. Four Seasons Hotels & Resorts, *2001 Annual Report.*

77. Ibid.

78. Robert C. Lewis, *Cases in Hospitality Strategy and Policy,* 282–303.

79. Four Seasons Hotels & Resorts, *2001 Annual Report.*

80. Ibid.

81. Lewis, *Cases in Hospitality Strategy and Policy.*

82. Four Seasons Hotels & Resorts, *2001 Annual Report.*

83. Martin, "How Four Seasons Weathered Global Competition."

84. Business Source Premier Database, "A Plan for Four Seasons." Visited 16 November 2002.

85. Proquest database, "Training the Top Tool in Battle to Keep Workers." Visited 5 November 2002.

86. Ibid.

87. Alicia Johnson, "An Incentive System for All Seasons," *Management Review* (August 1986).

88. Proquest database, "Strategic Approaches to Lodging Excellence." Visited 5 November 2002.

89. Grant, "International Directory of Company Histories."

90. Four Seasons Hotels & Resorts, *2001 Annual Report.*

91. Federal Mediation & Conciliation Service, http://www.fmcs.gov/annuals/94-95rpt/pm.htm. Visited 5 November 2002.

92. "For Hoteliers, the Word for Today Is Cooperation," *The Wall Street Journal,* 8 April 1998.

93. Ibid.

94. Tourism Victoria, "Strategic Plan: Trends Analysis."

95. Ibid.

96. Grant, *International Directory of Company Histories.*

97. Four Seasons Hotels & Resorts, *2001 Annual Report.*

98. "A Plan for Four Seasons," Business Source Premier database. Visited 16 November 2002.

99. Ibid.

100. Ibid.

101. Ibid.

102. Four Seasons Hotels & Resorts, *2001 Annual Report.*

103. Ibid.

Multibranding at Yum! Brands Inc.: Thinking Outside the Bun

Intense competition, slow same-store sales, and a sluggish economy have plagued quick-service restaurant (QSR) chains for several years. By June 2003, McDonald's same-store sales had fallen for each of the previous twelve months, with the first quarter of 2003 producing McDonald's first quarterly loss since becoming a public company in 1965.[1] Based on fifteen years of market and demographic trends, McKinsey and Company consultants projected that the fast-food segment of the industry would grow revenues by just 1 percent a year over the next eight years, less than half the 2003 rate.[2] Among the largest restaurant chains, aggressive efforts to retain their market shares led to excessive discounting. To regain profitability, they have moved away from price discounting and are scrutinizing potential site locations, upgrading menus and décor, investing in training programs for crew members, and developing customer-loyalty marketing programs.[3]

Yum! Brands Inc., with three top-ten chains, is one of the major players in the highly competitive fast-food segment of the industry and is the world's largest restaurant company with 33,000 stores in more than 100 counties.[4] The other large holding companies with multiple brands include McDonald's Corporation, Diageo PLC, Brinker International, CKE Restaurants, Wendy's International, Darden Restaurants, Allied Domecq Quick Service Restaurants, Outback Steakhouse, and AFC Enterprises. Together these large

---

Written by Professor Cathy A. Enz of Cornell University. This case was written as the basis for class discussion. The events described are not intended to illustrate either effective or ineffective management practices.

companies account for $107.5 billion in sales, or 51.8 percent of total restaurant industry sales.[5]

The top 400 largest chains reported a total sales gain of 5.6 percent in 2002 for a total of $207.6 billion. McDonald's was at the top of the list with around $40.5 billion in sales, followed by Burger King with $11.3 billion. The third and fourth largest chain restaurants were Kentucky Fried Chicken (KFC) ($10.3 billion sales) and Pizza Hut ($7.8 billion sales), both owned by Yum! Brands.[6] While the burger segment is the largest, accounting for 33.7 percent of the top 400 chains' sales, the fastest growing segment is coffee/snacks, which includes concepts like Starbucks and Krispy Kreme Doughnuts.

The maturing of the fast-food industry has forced the key players to rethink their strategies and reinvent their operations. Management reorganization, new product development, aggressive marketing, and strategic redirection helped the industry leaders rebound in late 2003. McDonald's same-store sales were flat in 2001 and dropped 1.5 percent in 2002. However, in October 2003 the corporation posted its strongest monthly U.S. sales gain in five years, with a 15 percent increase after an extensive global reorganization of senior management.[7] Wendy's International Inc. attributed customer response to the chain's new Homestyle Chicken Strips as one explanation for its reported same-store sales jump of 7.6 percent during the same period.[8]

In spite of recent sales turnarounds, some observers wonder if fast food will continue to prosper given changing consumer tastes and recent obesity lawsuits.[9] Burger King, the second largest fast food chain in the United States, has struggled in recent years. Diageo PLC, an international brewing and spirits conglomerate, sold the chain in the fall of 2002 for a low price of $1.6 billion.[10] In fact, an estimated 18 to 20 percent of Burger King franchisees were behind on royalty payments, although the chain was "encouraged" in 2003 by sales of the new low-fat chicken baguette line.[11] Nevertheless, one of Burger King's largest franchisees, AmeriKing, with 320 units, was in Chapter 11 bankruptcy in 2003 and intended to sell its entire portfolio of restaurants.[12]

The first Americans to grow up with fast food, the baby-boom generation (individuals born between 1946 and 1964), have matured and are seeking alternative dining options. The emergence and rapid growth of the "quick casual" segment is evidence of this trend. Quick-casual restaurants provide limited or self-service concepts, usually featuring "upscale" menu items such as gourmet soups, salads, and sandwiches.[13] As the baby boomers search for fresher and more nutritious food, fast casual chains such as Panera Bread Co., Atlanta Bread Co., Cosi Inc., Café Express LLC, Corner Bakery Co. and Pei Wei Asian Diner are capturing lunchtime. Most fast-food chains have responded by altering their menu items, adding salads, and changing ingredients. Market Fresh sandwiches, introduced by Arby's, and artisanal breads at Subway, Quiznos Sub, and Togo's Eateries are just a few examples of product innovations. In July 2003, Taco Bell introduced its "Outside the Bun" Caesar salad and a chicken Caesar grilled stuffed burrito. The burrito contains grilled all-white-meat chicken, romaine lettuce, crunchy red tortilla strips, and a Caesar dressing, wrapped in a tortilla.[14] Analysts attribute McDonald's line of premium salads as a major factor in its mid-2003 rebound.

As part of its strategy, McDonald's has made a variety of investments in fast-casual concepts, including the acquisition of Boston Market, Chipotle Mexican Grill, and Donatos Pizza. Boston Market, a quick-casual concept, was purchased in 2000, and McDonald's immediately began a turnaround effort that including remodeling stores and the menu. Russ Smyth, a senior manager responsible for the fast-casual activities at McDonald's, notes that these partnerships enable the firm to reach a different type of consumer.

In reference to the healthy-dining consumer, "No matter what we do," he says, "we won't be able to attract those people to the Golden Arches."[15] McDonald's also owns a 33 percent share in Pret A Manger, a fresh-sandwich concept, with an option to buy the chain outright in 2005.[16] With a recent revitalization plan, McDonald's hopes to attract new customers, encourage existing customers to visit more often, and create brand loyalty. The plan includes upgrading service, improving training, and enhancing the taste and relevance of its food.[17] The chain will focus its brand loyalty on young adults, kids, and moms. Jim Cantalupo, McDonald's chairman and chief executive officer, explained the plan as follows:

> When we embarked upon our revitalization plan earlier this year, we announced that in 2003 we would sharpen our focus and take the actions necessary to optimize the business. We've made progress toward this goal with October marking the first full month that our unprecedented "i'm lovin' it" campaign reached customers around the globe. This new brand positioning is bringing a new attitude and energy to life for our customers and crew. The management changes we announced earlier this week are another example of how we are making the best use of our talent and resources. During the fourth quarter, we will take additional actions to revitalize the business. These will include making decisions related to our Partner Brands and implementing the recently announced plans for revitalizing our business in Japan. These actions, along with the completion of annual impairment testing, will result in charges in the fourth quarter 2003.[18]

Multiple branding is likely to be a part of the future for all of the major players as they rethink their strategies. While McDonald's strategy has been to develop its brands separately, the company could capitalize on cobranding in the future. In contrast, Yum! Brands Inc. is betting on a multibranding strategy, in which the firm puts more than one of its brands into the same store in the hope of raising sales and leveraging operating efficiency. This *Fortune* 300 company, based in Louisville, Kentucky, is able to execute a multi-branding strategy easily because it operates five well-known brands: A&W All-American Food, Kentucky Fried Chicken (KFC), Long John Silver's, Pizza Hut, and Taco Bell. Sales for the global system totaled $24.2 billion in 2002, up from $22.3 billion in 2001.[19]

Before May 2002, Yum! Brands Inc. was called Tricon Global Restaurants to represent its three major brands, Kentucky Fried Chicken, Pizza Hut, and Taco Bell. Tricon was established as an independent, publicly owned company when it was spun off from PepsiCo, which owned and franchised the three quick-service restaurant brands worldwide.[20] The name change to Yum! Brands Inc. came in March 2002 after the acquisition of Yorkshire Global Restaurants. With this acquisition, the company added two additional QSR brands: Long John Silver's and A&W All-American Food. With five brands in hand, the name change better reflects the entire portfolio of restaurants as well as the company's New York Stock Exchange ticker: YUM. Exhibit 1 provides a brief overview of the company's earnings per share (EPS).

FIVE LEADING RESTAURANT BRANDS

In 2002, Yum! Brands opened a record 1,051 new international system restaurants. Key to the company's continued growth, the international business represents 35 percent of system sales, 31 percent of revenue, and one-third of operating profits with about 12,000 restaurants, compared to McDonald's more than 16,000 units internationally.[21] McDonald's is considered the primary competitor internationally with earnings of over $1 billion in international profit, compared to Yum! Brand's $400 million and Burger King's $50 million.[22]

The brands that drive international growth are primarily KFC with 6,800 restaurants and Pizza Hut with 4,400. With a goal of doubling the number of international restaurants by 2013, Yum! Brands is focused on China, Mexico, the United Kingdom, and South Korea. These four countries receive the majority of the firm's capital investments because of high returns.[23] Brand operations in China include approximately 800 KFCs and 100 Pizza Huts. The company has carefully positioned itself in China with the largest real estate team of any company in any industry and a distribution system that gives it coverage in every major province and hence access to most of China's 1.3 billion residents. Other parts of the world offer challenges, as the firm tries to get up to scale in Continental Europe, particularly in Germany with KFC, and in India with Pizza Hut. A recent joint venture in Brazil will help expand the KFC brand in South America.

Since 1999, the corporation has been strategically reducing its share of total system units by selling company-owned restaurants to existing and new

EXHIBIT 1	YUM! BRANDS INC. EARNINGS PER SHARE FOR 2002 AND 2001					
	2002	**2002**	**2002**	**2002**	**2002**	**2001**
	Q1	**Q2**	**Q3**	**Q4**	**FY**	**FY**
Ongoing operating EPS	$ 0.40	$ 0.45	$ 0.49	$ 0.56	**$ 1.91**	**$ 1.61**
Impact of NFAs	(0.02)	(0.02)	(0.03)	(0.01)	**(0.09)**	0.01
	0.38	**0.43**	**0.46**	**0.55**	**1.82**	**1.62**
Impact of unusuals	0.02	0.02	0.01	0.01	**0.06**	—
Reported EPS	**$ 0.40**	**$ 0.45**	**$ 0.47**	**$ 0.56**	**$ 1.88**	**$ 1.62**

Source: Yum! Brands, "Investor Relations," http://www.yum.com/investors/sss.htm (December 2, 2003).

franchisees. A total of 174 units were refranchised (sold) in 2002, although the bulk of refranchising was conducted in 2000, with sales of 757 restaurants, and in 2001 with sales of 233 units.[24] In addition, 224 restaurants were closed in 2002 because of poor performance or relocation. For several years Yum! Brands has worked to help franchisees struggling under high levels of debt. In 2001, it waived past-due royalties owed by overleveraged Taco Bell operators.[25] In addition, it sold or closed approximately 5,200 company-operated restaurants. The closing and selling of stores helped the company reduce the $4.5 billion in long-term debt that it carried after being spun-off by PepsiCo in 1997.[26] In 2002, the company charged expenses of $8 million to operating profit to allow for

doubtful franchise and license fee receivables in the Taco Bell system. Compared to 2001, franchise and license expenses decreased by $10 million or 18 percent in 2002, as a result of financial restructuring of certain Taco Bell franchisees in 2001. Overall, system sales increased by 9 percent to $1,243 million in 2002, with same-store sales up 2 percent. Exhibit 2 provides a summary of operating performance.

The corporation is divided into five divisions—A&W All-American Food combined with Long John Silver's, KFC, Pizza Hut, Taco Bell, and Yum! Restaurants International. Each division is led by a president, a president and chief operating officer, a president and chief concept officer, or, in the case of the international division, a chairman. The board of

---

EXHIBIT 2   **WORLDWIDE OPERATING RESULTS (IN MILLIONS, EXCEPT PER SHARE AMOUNTS)**

	2002					2003		
	Q1	Q2	Q3	Q4	FY	Q1	Q2	Q3
Company sales	$1,426	$1,571	$1,705	$2,189	$6,891	$1,597	$1,723	$1,765
Franchise and license fees	188	196	210	272	866	205	213	224
Revenues	1,614	1,767	1,915	2,461	7,757	1,802	1,936	1,989
Food and paper	439	482	517	671	2,109	492	532	544
Payroll and employee benefits	395	422	457	601	1,875	450	473	473
Occupancy and other operating expenses	369	405	450	582	1,806	430	462	481
Company restaurant expenses	1,203	1,309	1,424	1,854	5,790	1,372	1,467	1,498
General and administrative expenses	182	215	219	297	913	203	208	212
Franchise and license expenses (b)	10	9	12	18	49	7	6	7
Other (income) expenses (c)	7	5	9	—	21	(4)	(2)	(7)
Refranchising net loss (gain) (c)	(3)	(3)	(3)	(10)	(19)	7	—	6
	1,399	1,535	1,661	2,159	6,754	1,585	1,679	1,716
Operating profit before special items (d)	215	232	254	302	1,003	217	257	273
Interest expense, net	34	33	45	60	172	42	42	39
Income tax provision	64	65	65	71	265	57	70	67
Earnings before special items (d)	$117	$134	$144	$171	$566	$118	$145	$167
Tax rate before special items (d)	35.3%	32.5%	31.0%	29.8%	32.0%	32.6%	32.3%	29.0%
Company sales	100%	100%	100%	100%	100%	100%	100%	100%
Food and paper	30.8	30.7	30.3	30.6	30.6	30.8	30.9	30.8
Payroll and employee benefits	27.7	26.9	36.8	27.5	27.2	28.2	27.4	26.8
Occupancy and other operating expenses	25.9	25.7	26.4	26.5	26.2	26.9	26.9	27.3
Restaurant margin	15.6%	16.7%	16.4%	15.4%	16.0%	14.1%	14.8%	15.1%

Source: Yum! Brands, "Investor Relations," http://www.yum.com/investors/sss..htm (December 2, 2003).

directors is composed of thirteen individuals, with two from Yum! Brands, five from retail companies like Target Corporation and Kohl's Supermarkets, and another five from banks or investment firms.[27] The other member is the chairman of the board of Harman Management Corporation, one of KFC's largest franchisees. David C. Novak, the chairman of the board and chief executive officer of Yum! Brands, served as president of the company and was a brand group president for KFC and Pizza Hut when they were owned by Pepsi-Cola.

Four of the Yum! brands are global leaders in their categories of chicken, seafood, pizza, and Mexican food. As a percentage of QSR category sales, Yum! Brands holds 65 percent in the Mexican-style category with Taco Bell, 46 percent in chicken with KFC, 33 percent in seafood with Long John Silver's, and, 15 percent in pizza with Pizza Hut.[28] Although a smaller player in the large hamburger segment, A&W is the longest-running quick-service restaurant in America. The top twenty-five quick-service chains' sales and unit volumes are shown in Exhibit 3. As the table indicates, four of the brands are in the top twenty-five in the quick service sector.

| EXHIBIT 3 | TOP 25 QUICK-SERVICE/LIMITED-SERVICE CHAINS |

Chain	2002 Sales (in millions)	Number of Units (as of 1/1/03)
1. McDonald's	$40,457.6	30,025
2. Burger King	11,300.0	11,400
3. KFC	**10,300.0**	**12,362**
4. Pizza Hut	**7,800.0**	**12,030**
5. Wendy's	7,500.0	6,253
6. Subway	5,773.0	17,558
7. Taco Bell	**5,400.0**	**6,432**
8. Domino's Pizza	3,961.7	7,230
9. Starbucks	3,382.0*	5,886
10. Dunkin' Donuts	3,000.0	5,500
11. Dairy Queen	2,730.0*	5,710
12. Arby's	2,695.0	3,403
13. Sonic Drive-In	2,243.0	2,576
14. Jack in the Box	2,239.6	1,871
15. 7-Eleven	2,118.5	5,823
16. Papa John's	1,857.6	2,792
17. Hardee's	1,813.6	2,229
18. Tim Hortons	1,700.0	2,348
19. Popeyes	1,432.0*	1,672
20. Chick-fil-a	1,372.8	1,074
21. Little Caesars	1,200.0	2,700
22. Carl's Jr.	1074.6	987
23. Baskin-Robbins	913.0	4,700
24. Church's Chicken	900.0*	1,481
25. Long John Silver's	**828.0***	**1,249**

Source: "400 Rankings," *Restaurants & Institutions*, 15 July 2003 pg. 25.

* *Restaurants & Institutions* estimate.

Kentucky Fried Chicken

Kentucky Fried Chicken (KFC) was founded in 1939 by Colonel Harland D. Sanders, who pioneered what he called "Sunday Dinner, Seven Days a Week" and what is now frequently referred to as "home meal replacement"—selling complete meals to carry out.[29] KFC specializes in chicken dinners that include Original Recipe, Extra Crispy, Twister, and Colonel's Crispy Strips chicken with a variety of "home-style" sides. More than 300 other products, such as Chunky Chicken Pot Pie in the United States and a salmon sandwich in Japan, are offered in various locations worldwide.

Franchising began in 1952, and the unit count had risen to 6,600 units by the time KFC was acquired by PepsiCo in 1986.[30] Now almost eight million customers are served daily in the more than 11,000 restaurants. This long-established brand is located in more than eight countries and territories. Trying to differentiate the brand from other QSR products, in 2002 the company introduced the "There's fast food. Then there's KFC" advertising campaign with Jason Alexander, a well-known actor from the *Seinfeld* show. In spite of these efforts, sales remained flat. Entering 2003, the entire QSR segment came under harsh criticism by activists who claimed the rise of obesity in children is attributed to meals that are high in fat and calories. In an effort to present its chicken products as "healthy," KFC developed an advertising campaign that has many crying foul. KFC began in late 2003 airing a national advertising campaign that identifies the fried chicken products as low fat. In the advertisements KFC Original Recipe Chicken Breasts are compared to Burger King Whoppers. A company press release stated:

> "We want to set the record straight. Consumers should no longer feel guilty about eating fried chicken," said Scott Bergren, KFC's Executive Vice President, Marketing and Food Innovation. "Consumers will be surprised to learn they can enjoy fried chicken as part of a healthy, balanced diet. Of course, they should eat all food in moderation, and

balance that with an appropriate amount of exercise—it's all about energy in, energy out."[31]

Many have criticized KFC for jumping on the healthful-alternatives bandwagon without having a healthful product. An editorial in *Advertising Age* characterized the ad campaign as "laughable, and damaging." The editorial called for the ads to be pulled off the air immediately. As the editorial suggested, "In the long history of absurd, misleading and ludicrous ad claims, the campaign's positioning of KFC's breaded, fried chicken as a part of a healthy diet merits special derision. It damages the credibility not just of KFC but of the entire marketing industry."[32] A 6 percent decline in same-store sales was reported by KFC for September 2003 compared to the previous year.[33] The troubles may not stop there; the U.S. Federal Trade Commission (FTC) is investigating the television commercial's claims, asking the company to explain and justify with evidence the claim that its products can help consumers eat more healthfully and lose weight.[34]

Pizza Hut

Pizza Hut, the recognized leader in the $33 billion pizza category, is the largest pizza restaurant chain in the world, with 10,600 units in more than 100 countries; more than 6,600 units are in the United States. The company was named Best Pizza Chain in America in a national consumer survey published by *Restaurants & Institutions* magazine. Like many restaurants started by entrepreneurs, the company began when two college-age brothers borrowed $600 from their mother to purchase second-hand equipment and rent a small building on a busy intersection in Wichita, Kansas.[35] The year was 1958, and the concept of a pizza parlor was new but promising. A year later the first franchise unit was opened, and the first international restaurant opened in 1968 in Canada. Units in Mexico, South America, Australia, Europe, the Far East, and Africa were quick to follow. Nearly 3,200 units were in operation by 1977, when PepsiCo acquired the company.

Pizza Hut is known for six core pizzas: Pan Pizza, Thin 'N Crispy, Hand-Tossed Style, Stuffed Crust, The Chicago Dish, and The Big New Yorker. The company continues to refine and develop products, including the Fit 'N Delicious Pizzas. These pizzas have half the cheese of the regular Thin 'N Crispy recipes, generous portions of tomato sauce, and toppings that include lean meats and fresh vegetables. Fitting in with the trend for lower-fat foods, a slice contains only 3.5 to 5 grams of fat, depending on the selection of available toppings— according to the company, that is 25 percent less fat than a regular recipe, Thin 'N Crispy pizza.

Taco Bell

Taco Bell was started in 1962 by Glen Bell in Downey, California. Until the company went public in 1966, the banks would not lend the company money and financing was often secured by private borrowing.[36] A former Los Angeles policeman, Kermit Becky, bought the first Taco Bell franchise in 1964. This store did tremendous volumes from the beginning, inspiring other franchisees, as Becky himself frequently cleared $10,000 in one month. In 1975, Glen resigned as chairman of the board, and three years later, he sold Taco Bell's 868 units to PepsiCo, Inc.[37] The deal made Glen Bell a major PepsiCo shareholder and an enormously wealthy man.

A variety of innovations followed in the 1980s, including the installation of drive-through windows, value pricing, and free drink refills. Taco Bell's compact carts, kiosks, and in-line units begin appearing in airports, gas stations, retail stores, cinemas, stadiums, and schools in the early 1990s. These Express businesses provided Taco Bell food in a variety of locations that would not merit a full-store operation.

With 6,000 restaurants in the United States and more than 35 million consumers served each week, Taco Bell generated $5.4 billion in systemwide sales in 2002. Like the other brands in the company, Taco Bell has introduced a variety of advertising campaigns, including the popular talking Chihuahua campaign. This effort received the advertising industry's highest honor, the EFFIE, in 1998.

Long John Silver's

The recently acquired Long John Silver's brand is the largest quick-service seafood chain, with more than 1,200 units and 14,000 employees worldwide. This seafood concept, begun in 1968, was inspired by Robert Louis Stevenson's classic book *Treasure Island*. The restaurants offer seafood prepared in a secret batter of wheat, corn, and other natural ingredients.[38] As the concept grew, the menu expanded beyond the familiar hush puppies and batter-dipped fish, chicken, and shrimp to include sandwiches, salads, and desserts. One new promotional item in stores during the fall of 2003 was lobster-stuffed crab cakes. While one of the smaller brands in the Yum! corporation, Long John Silver's serves 3.8 million customers per week and sells 45 million pounds of fish per year.[39]

For years Long John Silver's was a publicly traded company called Jerrico Inc. A leveraged buyout in 1989 led by the company's senior management and a New York investment firm resulted in the company's becoming private.[40] The next year the company's other restaurant concepts were divested and the firm devoted all of its resources to the operation of Long John Silver's. A decade later, Long John Silver's merged with A&W Restaurants, resulting in the creation of Yorkshire Global Restaurants.

A&W All-American Food

It was 1919 when, using a formula he had purchased from a pharmacist in Arizona, Californian Roy Allen made a batch of creamy root beer, selling the first glass for a nickel.[41] Allen took on a partner, Frank Wright, and together they started America's first fast-food chain, A&W, in 1923 in Lodi, California. By 1933, there were more than 170 franchised outlets operating in the Midwest and West. Allen retired and sold the business in the early 1950s to a Nebraskan named Gene Hurtz who formed the A&W Root Beer Company with more than 450 A&W restaurants nationwide. The company was sold in 1963 to the J. Hungerford Smith Company, which had manufactured A&W Root Beer concentrate since 1921. A few years later the company was purchased by the United

Fruit Company of Boston. In 1970, United Fruit was acquired by the AMK Corporation, which formed a new corporation, United Brands Company. A&W was sold again in 1982 to A. Alfred Taubman, a developer of shopping centers and real estate. In 1994, Sagittarius Acquisitions, Inc., headed by Sidney Feltenstein purchased the company from Taubman. Yorkshire Global Restaurants was created in 1999, following the merger of Long John Silver's and A&W All American Food Restaurants. Yorkshire, becoming the parent company for both brands in 2000.

A STRATEGY FOR GROWTH

The vision of Yum! Brands Inc. is to offer customers food they crave so that they will return again and again, while using customer-focused teams. With 750,000 associates worldwide, customer service training is a key priority. The company developed a program called CHAMPS to guide operations training. CHAMPS stands for Cleanliness, Hospitality, Accuracy, Maintenance, Product Quality, and Speed. The company has developed a "Customer Mania" training program that its proponents argue puts process and discipline around all aspects of operations related to customer satisfaction.[42] The skills managers are teaching the front-line team members include how to listen to the customer, how to be empathetic to customer needs, how to exceed expectations

within reason, and how to recover from mistakes.[43] To guide employees, Yum! has developed a list of founding truths (see Exhibit 4) and a statement of how employees work together (see Exhibit 5).[44]

Customer Mania includes a CHAMPS Excellence review, in which 150 of the company's best managers are sent out to the restaurants to inspect the stores and ensure that the CHAMPS standards are being met. The company has made an $18 million investment in this training program in the hopes that it will give the firm a competitive advantage. Aylin Lewis, chief operating officer of Yum!, notes, "Typically you see a company roll something out, and that's the end of it. We will be training four times a year. This is a permanent commitment to quality training. Once is not going to be enough."[45]

The entire fast-food industry struggles with poor customer service. For example, in a company memo sent to a McDonald's franchisee, the following message was bluntly summarized:

> We are meeting our speed of service standard only 46% of the time, and 3 out of 10 customers are waiting more than four minutes to complete their order. Our 800 number has confirmed that . . . the number of complaints . . . for rude service, unprofessional employees and inaccurate service has risen steadily.[46]

EXHIBIT 4	**FOUNDING TRUTHS**

Our Founding Truths

People Capability First . . . satisfied customers and profitability follow

Respond to the Voice of the Customer . . . not just listen

The RGM is Our #1 Leader . . . not senior management

Run Each Restaurant Like It's Our Only One . . . avoid the trap of the averages

Recognition Shows You CARE . . . people leave when you don't

Great Operations and Marketing Innovation Drive Sales . . . no finger pointing

Operation Discipline Through Process and Standards . . . consistency—not "program of the month"

Franchisees are Vital Assets . . . operate as one system, not two

Quality in Everything We Do . . . especially the food

Source: Yum! Brands, "Yum! Values," http://www.yumcareers.com/yumvalue_framesetup.html (December 2, 2003).

EXHIBIT 5	HOW WE WORK TOGETHER

How We Work Together

Customer Mania

We not only listen and respond to the voice of the customer, we are obsessed to go the extra mile to make our customers happy.

Belief in People

We believe in people, trust in positive intentions, encourage ideas from everyone and actively develop a workforce that is diverse in style and background.

Recognition

We find reasons to celebrate the achievements of others and have fun doing it.

Coaching and Support

We coach and support each other.

Accountability

We do what we say, we are accountable; we act like owners.

Executional Excellence

We beat year ago results by continuously improving and innovating. We follow through with daily intensity.

Positive Energy

We execute with positive energy and intensity — we hate bureaucracy and all the nonsense that comes with it.

Teamwork

We practice team together, team apart after productive conflict.

Source: Yum! Brands, "Careers at Yum!," http://www.yumcareers.com/yumvalue_framesetup.html (December 2, 2003).

The Hardee's chain also has a new program that focuses on employee training. Andrew Puzder, the president and CEO of CKE, has made a commitment to customer service in the poorly performing Hardee's chain. He notes, "Our program focuses on taking care of the customer. It's our only solution. The fact is that if the customer comes in and the restaurants aren't ready, the customer isn't coming back. We want people to have an opportunity to find out how good our food is. So our emphasis now is on training, changing the culture, and paying more attention to cleanliness and service."[47] According to industry watchers, it's about time, while Hardee's franchisees are mixed on CKE's efforts. In contrast, Yum! is getting results. One Taco Bell restaurant manager from Florida described the Customer Mania program as follows:

> Customer Mania has provided us with a super edge in hiring great Team Members and in keeping the great ones

we've put so much effort into training. We're building a reward and recognition culture, one that gets our team pumped up and excited about satisfying each and every customer. It's a great culture we're creating and it makes a big difference in the store day to day and makes people want to stay.[48]

Yum! hopes to become the best restaurant operator in the world through the execution of the Customer Mania program. This program is viewed as an important strategy implementation activity, while five long-term growth drivers help shape corporate strategy. Below are the five dimensions believed to be essential to corporate progress and growth.

1. *International Expansion:* Yum! Brands' number-one goal is to drive global expansion with its category-leading brands. In 2002, the company opened a record 1,051

international restaurants and increased international system sales 9 percent prior to foreign currency conversion.

2. *Multibrand Expansion:* Yum! Brands is the worldwide leader in multibranding, offering consumers more choice and convenience at one restaurant location from a combination of two of the company's brands. The company and its franchisees operate more than 1,975 multibrand restaurants, generating $2 billion in annual system sales. Approximately 350 systemwide multibrand restaurants were opened in 2002.

3. *Portfolio of Leading Brands:* U.S. systemwide same-store sales increased approximately 4 percent in 2002 while U.S. same-store sales at company restaurants increased approximately 2 percent.

4. *Global Franchise Fees:* Global franchise fees, a significant factor in annual profits and cash flow, grew 6 percent to $866 million in 2002. Global franchise net restaurant growth was 2 percent.

5. *Strong Cash Generations and Returns:* Yum! Brands generated $1.3 billion in cash from all sources in 2002, more than fully funding capital expenditure needs, allowing free cash flow for share repurchase and some repayment of debt. Return on invested capital is 18 percent, in the restaurant industry's top tier.[49]

Accomplishing the growth that Yum! envisions will require careful measurement and attention to performance results. To benchmark its performance, the company has identified five key measurement areas, shown in Exhibit 6. Adding more multibrand units is one of the key performance targets.

TRANSFORMING THE INDUSTRY THROUGH MULTIBRANDING

Higher unit volumes are at the heart of the corporate multibranding strategy. For years, McDonald's has been the envy of the industry with twice the volume of the typical KFC or Taco Bell. McDonald's has seven types of food (burgers, chicken, fish, salads, eggs, waffles, and pancakes), but KFC and Taco Bell are each focused on one food category. No one looks for a KFC or Pizza Hut burger. According to Dave Deno, chief financial officer at Yum!, "The biggest thing that multi-branding offers is the chance to

---

| EXHIBIT 6 | FIVE KEY MEASURES OF PERFORMANCE |

Important Measures

1	International system-sales growth (local currency) Number of new international restaurant openings Net international unit growth Net U.S. unit growth	**3** Number of multibrand restaurant locations Number of multibrand units added
2	U.S. system-sales growth U.S. blended same-store sales	**4** Growth in franchise fees New restaurant openings by franchisees
		5 Cash generated by the business Cash generated after capital spending Operating margin Return on invested capital

Source: Yum! Brands, "Our Vision," http://www.yum.com/investors/vision.htm (December 2, 2003).

leverage our existing assets that have lower volumes than say a McDonald's for instance."[50] Early efforts at cobranding were combinations of KFC–Taco Bell and Taco Bell–Pizza Hut. The net result of these efforts was the addition of between $100,000 and $400,000 per unit in average sales increases. One franchisee, Larry Durrett, president of Southern Multifoods, Inc., opened the first cobranded Taco Bell–Long John Silver's and explains why multibranding is such a powerful idea for franchisees.

> Multibranding has a dramatic impact on the customer. It's a barrier-breaker for families, meaning that sometimes kids like to eat different things than adults. If you've got an A&W/Long John Silver's, like we do in South Texas, you can see how it offers something for everyone. More globally, though, if you have a KFC/Taco Bell, you might get someone who wants a taco one day and who will come back the next day for chicken. When we add volume to these restaurants through multibranding, we add incremental profits that we could not have gotten any other way. For example, if you take a good restaurant—like a $900,000 Taco Bell—and add a $400,000 Long John Silver's, you have added incremental profits that would be impossible to get any other way.[51]

Soon the company began to try combinations of KFC and Taco Bell with Long John Silver's and A&W. Before the acquisition of Yorkshire Global Restaurants, the two parent companies engaged in four years of partnering with multibranding. Testing the concept with eighty-three KFC–A&W units, six KFC–Long John Silver's operations, and three Taco Bell–Long John Silver's gave Yum! an opportunity to experiment with the concept. It was not until the concept had yielded positive results that Yum! Brands acquired Yorkshire Global. Yum! CEO David Novak plans to aggressively drive Yum!'s growth with multibranding, arguing, "Multibranding is going to transform the industry. Consumers do want more choice."[52] Now with the addition of the two new brands, the company gained the advantage of attracting franchisees with even more brands under the same corporate entity.

While Yum! Brands is the most aggressive company to use this strategy, Allied Domecq PLC has combined its Baskin-Robbins, Dunkin' Donuts, and Togo's Eateries into a single location to boost lunch business. Carl's Jr., a regional brand operated by CKE Restaurants, has cobranded with Santa Barbara Restaurant Group's Green Burrito chain to enhance its dinner business. Both of the parent companies of these brands share the same chairman, William Foley.[53] For McDonald's, "It is certainly a matter of when, not if," it experiments with multibranding, according to a spokesperson for the company back in 2001.[54] The time appears to be now, as McDonald's began in 2003 to experiment with new concepts in existing stores. Eleven units in Indiana have added a diner, and one unit in Nebraska has a three-in-one concept with a McDonald's traditional menu, an upscale sandwich shop, and a separate treat area with baked goods and desserts.[55] Indeed, the chairman of Yum! Brands may be correct that multibranding will be the biggest sales and profit driver for the fast-food segment since the advent of the drive-through window.

The benefits of multibranding include increasing sales volumes and unit profitability. Yum! reports that each time it combines brands in a unit, sales have jumped 30 percent.[56] In addition, putting two or more concepts under the same roof can spread business out during several parts of the day. For Allied Domecq, the addition of the Togo's chain allowed them to move beyond impulse snack or breakfast items into lunch and dinner periods. By offering two or more brands these companies can also enter into smaller trade areas with expensive real estate. "Now we can go into trade areas that we couldn't go into with an individual brand," notes Chuck Rawley, chief development officer for Yum![57] Sharing crew, storage, and production space permits a more efficient use of the asset.

The dramatic improvements in unit sales and the need to modernize and remodel outdated stores have motivated Yum! Brands to remodel much of its existing asset base. Unit design in the past had been decentralized to the brand level, but in 2002 it was centralized with the creation of a new corporate position, senior vice president for concept design and multibranding.[58] Design is now connected to brand marketing and consumer preferences rather than a development function.

Multibranding is not without challenges. Potential problems may include encroaching on existing units' sales, and the ability to operate substantially more complex store level operations. While encroachment does not appear to be a serious issue, execution of these new concepts is. To handle the needed operational capability to operate more complex restaurants

the company has developed simplified operating and training systems.[59]

The goals, as stated by CEO David C. Novak, are to take both KFC and Taco Bell to the distribution levels of Burger King, which has 8,000 units in the United States and to have volumes of at least $1.1 million per restaurant.[60] The company operates more than 1,975 multibrand restaurants worldwide, which generate sales of $1.2 billion each year. It hopes to more than triple its cobranded units by 2007.[61] Exhibit 7 shows the number of multibranded restaurants by concept combination.

EXHIBIT 7	NUMBER OF MULTIBRANDED UNITS

	Worldwide							
	2001	2002				2003		
	Q4	Q1	Q2	Q3	Q4	Q1	Q2	Q3
KFC								
Taco Bell	665	665	673	690	703	708	714	719
Pizza Hut	183	186	191	208	229	239	240	244
A&W	71	81	94	118	161	182	199	230
Taco Bell/Pizza Hut 3'n'1	45	48	49	50	51	50	51	52
Long John Silver's	5	6	7	7	12	16	19	35
Chock Full o' Nuts	3	2	—	—	—	—	—	—
Wing Works	1	1	13	16	24	24	26	26
Total	973	989	1,027	1,089	1,180	1,219	1,249	1,306
Taco Bell								
Pizza Hut	554	574	587	608	608	610	614	625
Long John Silver's	2	3	3	5	7	21	21	26
Backyard Burgers	—	—	1	2	3	3	8	8
A&W	—	—	—	—	—	1	2	2
Total	556	577	591	615	618	635	645	661
Pizza Hut								
KFC	—	—	1	1	1	1	1	1
Taco Bell	—	—	5	5	5	5	6	6
Wing Works	—	—	—	—	1	3	3	3
Pasta Bravo	—	—	—	—	1	1	3	3
Wing Streets	—	—	—	—	—	—	2	29
Backyard Burgers	—	—	—	2	2	2	2	—
Total		—	6	8	10	12	17	42
Long John Silver's								
A&W (a)	—	—	133	149	167	171	174	196
Total	1,529	1,566	1,757	1,861	1,975	2,037	2,085	2,205

Source: Yum! Brands, "Investor Relations," http://www.yum.com/investors/sss..htm (December 2, 2003).

The latest experiments include the partnering of Pizza Hut with the fifteen-unit fast-casual Pasta Bravo chain, headquartered in Aliso Viejo, California.[62] Pasta Bravo serves a variety of freshly prepared pasta dishes family style. Menus include a $12.95 bucket of spaghetti and meat sauce serving four to six people. The partnership is in the form of a licensing agreement, in which limited tests in primarily franchisee-operated dine-in units will determine whether this pairing is viable for expansion.

THE FUTURE

Should Yum! Brands partner or acquire another quick-service or a fast-casual chain? What would be a good menu category to add to the current portfolio? "If you pair a hot emerging brand with a proven one, in a real estate context that already has strong drawing power, you can take advantage of complementary natures for frequency, reach and freshness," according to Sarah Palisi-Chapin, CEO of the restaurant research and development firm Enersyst.[63] While the fast-food industry struggles to reinvent itself and hold on to the affluent, quality-driven baby boomers, new concepts may need to be developed for the emerging Generation X and Y palates. If so, how should Yum! Brands experiment with its multiple branding?

Notes

1. "Who Moved McDonald's Cheese?" *Display & Design Ideas*, June 2003, 3.
2. M. B. Horn, E. A. Ledet, and S. Rauch, "Fast Food Hits the Brakes," *McKinsey Quarterly* 2 (2002): 9.
3. S. Hume, "Back to the Future," *Restaurants & Institutions*, 15 July 2003, 20.
4. Yum! Brands Inc., "Investors," http://www.yum.com/investors/default.htm, 21 November 2003.
5. Ibid.
6. S. Hume, "400 Rankings," *Restaurants & Institutions*, 15 July 2003, 25.
7. A. Garber, "Supersized: McD Sales Jump 15% in October," *Nation's Restaurant News*, 17 November 2003, 1.
8. "Wendy's U.S. Same-store Sales Jump 7.6.% in October," *Nation's Restaurant News*, 17 November 2003, 12.
9. M. Boltz Chapman, "Future of Fast Food," *Chain Leader*, July 2003, 8.
10. D. Milton, *Standard & Poor's Industry Surveys: Restaurants* (New York: McGraw Hill, 2003).
11. A. Garber, "Turnaround Plans Bring Changes to McD, BK franchisees," *Nation's Restaurant News*, 10 November 2003, 125.
12. Ibid., 125
13. D. Milton, *Standard & Poor's Industry Surveys: Restaurants*.
14. "Taco Bell Launches Portable Ceasar Salad," Press Release, June 27, 2003, http://www.tacobell.com, 25 November 2003.
15. K. Macarthur, "Boston Market Ads Make Dinner a Focus," *Advertising Age*, 20 January 2003, 34.
16. D. Philadelphia, "Tastier, Plusher—and Fast," *Time South Pacific*, 30 September 2002, 51.
17. McDonald's, "2002 Summary Annual Report," http://www.mcdonalds.com/corporate/investor/financial-info/annual/report/letter/page2/index.html, 25 November 2003.
18. "McDonald's Reports Record October Sales Up 18% and Further Steps in Revitalization Plan," Press Release, http://www.mcdonalds.com/corporate/press/financial/2003/11072003/index.html, 25 November 2003.
19. Yum! Brands Inc., *Annual Report for 2002*; Tricon Global Restaurants, *Annual Report for 2001*.
20. Yum! Brands Inc., "Investing in Yum! Brands Inc.," http://www.yum.com/Investors/default.htm, 21 November 2003.
21. Yum! Brands Inc., *Annual Report for 2002*, 29.
22. Yum! Brands Inc., *Annual Report for 2002*. pg. 10.
23. Ibid., 4.
24. Yum! Brands Inc., *Annual Report for 2002*, 31.
25. A. Spector, "Tricon Mounts Taco Bell Bailout," *Nation's Restaurant News*, 26 February 2001, 1.
26. Ibid.
27. Yum! Brands Inc., "About Yum! Brands, Board of Directors," http://www.yum.com/about/boardofdir.htm, 29 November 2003.
28. Ibid.
29. Kentucky Fried Chicken, "About KFC," http://www.kfc.com/about, 24 November 2003.
30. Yum! Brands Inc., "Our Five Brands," http://www.yum.com/about/divisions.htm, 21 November 2003.
31. Kentucky Fried Chicken, Press Release, "KFC Sets the Record Straight," 28 October 2003, http://www.kfc.com/about/pr/102803.htm, 24 November 2003.
32. "KFC Blunders in 'Health' Ads," Advertising Age, 3 November 2003, 22.
33. "Chain Update: Latest from Yum, Red Robin, Others," *Foodservice Equipment & Supplies*, October 2003, 20.
34. M. Wilde, A. Steinberg, and B. Wilke, "FTC Examines Health Claims In KFC's Ads," *The Wall Street Journal, Eastern Edition*, 19 November 2003, B1.
35. Pizza Hut, "About Pizza Hut: Our Story," http://www.pizza-hut.com/about/default.asp, 24 November 2003.
36. Taco Bell, "History," http://www.tacobell.com, 24 November 2003.
37. Ibid.

38. Long John Silver's, "Home," http://www.ljsilvers.com, 1 December 2003.

39. Long John Silver's, "FAQ's," http://www.ljsilvers.com/about/faq.htm, 1 December 2003.

40. Long John Silver's, "Ownership," http://www.ljsilvers.com/about/ownership.htm, 1 December 2003.

41. A&W All-American Food, "The First Frosty Mug," http://www.awrestaurants.com/about/mug.htm, 24 November 2003.

42. Tricon Global Restaurants, *Annual Report 2001*, 3.

43. Ibid.

44. Yum! Brands Inc., "Founding Truths," http://www.yum.com/investors/vision.htm, 21 November 2003.

45. D. Berta, "YUM!'s 'Customer Mania' Program Seeks to Add Passion to Service," *Nation's Restaurant News*, 10 June 2002, 8.

46. D. Eisenberg, "Can McDonald's Shape Up?" *Time*, 30 September 2002, 52.

47. P. Siudzinski, "Catch a Falling Star," *Restaurant Business*, 1 February 2001, 16.

48. Yum! Brands Inc., *Annual Report for 2002*, 7.

49. Yum! Brands Inc., "Overview," http://www.yum.com/investors/overview.htm, 2 December 2003.

50. A. Zuber, "Accelerated Multibrand Growth Plan Puts Tricon in Driver's Seat," *Nation's Restaurant News*, 25 February 2002, 64.

51. Yum! Brands Inc., *Annual Report for 2002*, 15.

52. B. Sperber, "Tricon's Menu Redefines Multi-Branding Concepts, "*Brandweek*, 18 March 2002, 7.

53. A. Zuber, "To Market, to Market: Chains Find Strength in Numbers, Use Co-branding as Growth Vehicle," *Nation's Restaurant News*, 5 February 2001, 45–48.

54. Ibid.

55. A. Garber, "Thinking Outside the Box," *Nation's Restaurant News*, 20 October 2003, 71–74.

56. Sperber, "Tricon's Menu Redefines Multi-Branding Concepts."

57. Zuber, "To Market, to Market."

58. Garber, "Thinking Outside the Box."

59. Yum! Brands Inc., *Annual Report for 2002*, 7.

60. Ibid., 6.

61. L. Lohmeyer, "New Pizza Hut Prototype Pushes YUM Multibrand Growth Strategy," *Nation's Restaurant News*, 10 February 2003, 1.

62. J. Peters, "Yum! Brands Steps Up Co-branding with Pizza Hut–Pasta Bravo Pairing," *Nation's Restaurant News*, 5 August 2002, 1; "Yum! Slates New Format Test, Airs Service Details," *Restaurant Business*, 15 August 2002, 13; "Pizza Hut's New Pasta," *Chain Leader*, September 2002, 4.

63. Sperber, "Tricon's Menu Redefines Multi-Branding Concepts."

Glossary

accounting controls   Ensure that the financial information provided to internal and external stakeholders is accurate and follows generally accepted accounting practices (GAAP)

acquisition   An organization buys a controlling interest in the stock of another organization or buys it outright from its owners

acquisition premium   The percentage amount paid for shares of stock above their market value prior to the acquisition announcement

activist groups   Organizations formed with the purpose of advancing a specific cause or causes; public-interest groups represent the position of a broad cross-section of society, while special-interest groups focus on the needs of smaller subgroups

administration   Support activities of the value chain consisting of general management activities, such as planning and accounting

agency problem   Exists when top managers attempt to maximize their own self-interests at the expense of shareholders

aggressive strategy   These firms use every available resource in an effort to overwhelm rivals, thus reducing the chance that any countermove will be effective

alliance   An arrangement between two or more firms that establishes an exchange relationship but that has no joint ownership involved

analyzer strategy   Occupies a position in between a prospector strategy and a defender strategy; firms attempt to maintain positions in existing markets while locating growth opportunities on the fringes

antitrust laws   Established by governments to keep organizations from getting large and powerful enough in one industry to engage in monopoly pricing and other forms of noncompetitive or illegal behavior

average daily rate (ADR)   A commonly used measure of hotel performance; ADR is the average daily rate per rented room, or the mean price charged for all hotel rooms sold in a given period

avoidance strategy   Competitive strategy in which a firm avoids confrontation completely by focusing on a particular niche in the market in which other firms have little interest

bank centered economies   Banks and other financial institutions play the most significant role in the external capital markets

bargaining power   Economic power that allows a firm or group of firms to influence the nature of business arrangements for factors such as pricing, availability of products or services, purchase terms, or length of contract

barriers to imitation   Barriers intended to prevent existing competitors from imitating sources of cost savings or differentiation

basic research   Activity associated with pushing back the boundaries of science as we know it

behavioral controls   A special set of controls used to motivate employees to do things that the organization would like them to do, even in the absence of direct supervision; they include bureaucratic controls, clan control, and human resources systems

benchmarking   A tool for assessing the best practices of direct competitors and firms in similar industries, then using the resulting "stretch" objectives as design criteria for attempting to change organizational performance

best value strategy   A firm pursues elements associated with cost leadership and differentiation simultaneously

board of directors   In publicly owned companies, a group of individuals who are elected by the voting shareholders to monitor the behavior of top managers, therefore protecting their rights as shareholders

broad environment   Forms the context in which the firm and its operating environment exist, including sociocultural influences, global economic influences, political/legal influences, and technological influences

buffering   Techniques designed to stabilize and predict environmental influences and therefore soften the jolts that might otherwise be felt as the organization interacts with members of its external environment

builder-type culture   Growth is the primary goal in the organization

bureaucratic control   Rules, procedures, and policies that guide the behavior of organizational members

business angels   Wealthy individuals who provide startup capital to entrepreneurs

business definition   A description of the business activities of a firm, based on its products and services, markets, functions served, and resource conversion processes

business-format franchising   A popular form of franchising in hospitality firms; this approach to franchising involves a franchisor selling a way of doing business to its franchisees

business intelligence   The collection and analysis of information on markets, new technologies, customers, competitors, and broad social trends, as well as information gained from internal sources

business-level strategy   Defines an organization's approach to competing in its chosen markets

business-level strategy formulation   Pertains to domain direction and navigation, or how businesses should compete in the business areas they have selected; sometimes these strategies are referred to as competitive strategies

business plan   A plan that contains the details of how a new venture will be carried out

capital intensity   The extent to which the assets of an organization are primarily associated with plants, equipment, and other fixed assets

capital requirements   Costs associated with starting a business

CEO duality   Occurs when the CEO also chairs the board of directors

change-style leadership   The CEO formulates strategy and then plans the changes in structure, personnel, information systems, and administration required to implement it

Chapter 11   A legal filing under the Federal Bankruptcy Code of the United States; allows an organization to work out a plan or arrangement for solving its financial problems under the supervision of a federal court

chief executive officer (CEO)   Common title for the highest-ranking manager in a firm

chief information officer (CIO)   A high-level manager who oversees the collection, analysis, and dissemination of information

clan control   Socialization processes through which an individual comes to appreciate the values, abilities, and expected behaviors of an organization; closely linked to the concepts of culture and organizational ethics

code of ethics   Communicates the values of the corporation to employees and other stakeholders

codified knowledge   Knowledge that can be communicated completely via written means

collaboration strategy   Firms combine resources in an effort to gain a stronger resource position; various forms of interorganizational relationships can lead to collaboration

collaborative-style leadership   The CEO works with other managers to create a strategy; participants are then responsible for implementing the strategy in their own areas

collusion   Formal price-setting cooperation among firms

commander-style leadership   The CEO formulates strategy and then directs top managers to implement it

competitive dynamics   The moves and counter-moves of firms and their competitors

competitive tactics   Techniques firms use—such as advertising, new product launches, cost reduction efforts, and quality improvements—to win market share, increase revenues, and increase profits at the expense of rivals

concentration   A corporate-level strategy in which the firm has virtually all of its resource investments in one business area

conglomerate   A large, highly diversified firm

consortia   Specialized joint ventures encompassing many different arrangements; consortia are often a group of firms oriented toward problem solving and technology development, such as R&D consortia

control systems   Systems used to measure and monitor firm activities and processes, as well as motivate or encourage behaviors that are conducive to desired organizational outcomes; the tools of strategy implementation

core knowledge   Scientific or technological knowledge that is associated with the actual creation of a product or service

core values   The underlying philosophies that guide decisions and behavior in a firm; also called organizational values

corporate entrepreneurship   Involves the creation of new business ventures within existing corporations

corporate-level distinctive competencies   Derived from the ability to achieve shared competitive advantage across the business units of a multi-business firm

corporate-level strategy formulation   Refers primarily to the selection of business areas in which the organization will compete and the emphasis each area is given; also includes strategies for carrying out the corporate-level strategy

corporate matrix structure   The corporate-level counterpart to the project matrix structure described earlier; organizes businesses along two dimensions, such as product and function

corporate raiders   Organizations and individuals who engage in acquisitions, typically against the wishes of the managers of the target companies

craftsman-type culture   Quality is the primary driver of the corporate culture

creative destruction   The inevitable decline of leading firms because competitors will pursue creative opportunities to eliminate the competitive advantages they hold

crescive-style leadership   The CEO encourages lower-level managers to formulate and implement their own strategic plans, while still filtering out inappropriate programs

crisis management   Processes associated with preventing, detecting, or recovering from crises

cultural-style leadership   The CEO formulates a vision and strategy for the company and then works with other managers to create a culture that will foster fulfillment of the vision

defender strategy   A conservative strategy intended to preserve market share

deliberate strategy   Implies that managers plan to pursue an intended strategic course

differentiation   Requires the firm to distinguish its products or services on the basis of an attribute such as higher quality, more innovative features, greater selection, better service after sale, or more advertising

diversification   Occurs when a firm expands its business operations into new products, functions served, markets, or technologies

divestiture   A reverse acquisition; business assets are sold off or spun off as a whole business

domestic stage of international development   Organizations focus their efforts on domestic operations, but begin to export their products and services, sometimes through an export department or a foreign joint venture

dot-coms   Internet-based businesses; the name comes from the fact that many of these businesses have an Internet address that ends in .com, as in Amazon.com

downscoping   Involves reducing diversification (refocusing) through selling off nonessential businesses that are not related to the organization's core competencies and capabilities

due diligence   Involves a complete examination of a merger or acquisition, including such areas as management, equity, debt, sale of assets, transfer of shares, environmental issues, financial performance, tax issues, human resources, customers, and markets

e-commerce   Describes business dealings that are electronically based, such as e-tailing (retailing through the Internet), exchanging data, business-to-business buying and selling, and e-mail communications

economic dependence   Occurs when stakeholders rely on an organization to provide economic resources such as a salary, interest payments, tax revenues, or payment for goods and services supplied to the firm

economic environment   Influences and trends associated with domestic or global economies, such as economic growth rates, interest rates, the availability of credit, inflation rates, foreign exchange rates, and foreign trade balances

economic perspective   Defines the purpose of a business organization as profit maximization

economic power   Derived from the ability to withhold services, products, capital, revenues, or business transactions that the organization values

economies of scale   Cost savings that occur when it is more efficient to produce a product in a larger facility at higher volume

emergent strategy   Implies that the existing strategy is not necessarily planned or intended, but rather a result of learning through a process of trial and error

emerging economies   Economies that have historically been dominated by government influence, with poorly developed financial capital markets; some of these economies are now pursuing privatization programs that put economic assets in the hands of private citizens

employee stock ownership plan (ESOP)   Reward system in which employees are provided with an attractive method for acquiring stock in the companies where they work

enactment   The perspective that firms do not have to submit to existing environmental forces because they can influence their environments

enterprise strategy   Joins ethical and strategic thinking about the organization; it is the organization's best possible reason for the actions it takes

entrenchment   Occurs when managers gain so much power that they are able to use the firm to further their own interests rather than the interests of shareholders

entrepreneurial discovery   Entails channeling resources toward the fulfillment of a market need; the intersection of a need and a solution

entrepreneurial tasks   Recognition or creation of an opportunity, creation of a business plan, securing startup capital, and actual management of the startup through its early stages

entrepreneurship   The creation of new business

entry barriers   Forces that keep new competitors out, providing a level of protection for existing competitors

environmental determinism   The perspective that the most successful organization will be the one that best adapts to existing forces—in other words, the environment "determines" the best strategy

environmental discontinuities   Major, unexpected changes in the social, economic, technological, political, or internal environments that necessitate change within organizations

environmental uncertainty   A result of not being able to predict precisely what will happen with regard to the actions of external stakeholders and other external influences; results in organizational uncertainty

exit barriers   Costs associated with leaving a business or industry

exporting   Transferring goods to other countries for sale through wholesalers or a foreign company

external environment   Stakeholders and forces outside the traditional boundaries of the firm; they can be divided into the broad and operating environments

family-centered economies   Families hold a lot of the stock in large corporations, allowing them a lot of control

feedback control   Provides managers with information concerning outcomes from organizational activities

financial controls   Based purely on financial measures such as ROI

financial intermediaries   A wide variety of institutions—including banks, stock exchanges, brokerage houses, investment advisers, mutual fund companies, pension fund companies, and other organizations or individuals—that may have an interest in investing in the firm

financial risk   The risk that a firm will not be able to meet its financial obligations and may eventually declare bankruptcy

financial strategy   Primary purpose is to provide the organization with the capital structure and funds that are appropriate for implementing growth and competitive strategies

first-movers   Firms that stay at the forefront of technological advances in their industries

five forces of industry competition   Forces that largely determine the type and level of competition in an industry and, ultimately, the industry's profit potential; they include customers, suppliers, entry barriers, substitute products or services, and rivalry among existing competitors

fixed costs   Costs associated with plants, machinery, or other fixed assets

focus strategy   A firm targets a narrow segment of the market through low-cost leadership, differentiation, or a combination of low cost and differentiation

food contractors   Provide restaurant services to commercial, industrial, university, school, airline, hospital, nursing home, recreation and sports center institutions; the institution may provide the facilities and personnel for these operations; examples of contractors include Aramark Corporation, Compass Group, and Sodexho Alliance

Foreign Corrupt Practices Act (FCPA)   A response to social concern about bribes paid by U.S. companies to foreign government officials; it defines the "rules-of-the-game" for U.S. companies when they operate in foreign countries

foreign exchange rates   The rates at which currencies are exchanged across countries; this is a major source of uncertainty for firms operating in foreign countries

foreign trade balance   A measure of the relative value of imports to exports from one country to another

formal power   Occurs when stakeholders have a legal or contractual right to make decisions for some part of an organization

formal structure   Specifies the number and types of departments or groups and provides the formal reporting relationships and lines of communication among internal stakeholders

franchising   A licensing strategy in which two independent companies form a contractual agreement giving one (the franchisee) the right to operate a business in a given location for a specified period under the other firm's (franchisor) brand; franchisees agree to pay fees and royalties, and they may also agree to make advertising contributions as a percentage of unit revenues

full-service restaurants   Restaurants that offer eat in service, expansive menus, and prices that range from low to high; these restaurants are divided into three segments: family, grill-buffet, and dinner houses

functional-level strategy   The collective pattern of day-to-day decisions made and actions taken by managers and employees who are responsible for value-creating activities within a particular functional area

functional-level strategy formulation   The details of how functional resource areas—such as marketing, operations, and finance—should be used to implement business-level strategies and achieve competitive advantage

functional strategy audit   Through evaluation of functional-level strategies on the basis of internal consistency, consistency across functional areas, and the extent to which each functional strategy supports the overall strategies of the firm

functional structure   A business-level structure organized around the inputs or activities that are required for producing products and services, such as marketing, operations, finance, and R&D

generic business strategies   A classification system for business-level strategies based on common strategic characteristics

geographic and customer-based structures   A business-level structure organized around geographic locations or customer types serviced

global integration   The process through which a multinational organization integrates its worldwide activities into a single world strategy through its network of affiliates and alliances

global product/market approach   Companies use one product design and market it in the same fashion throughout the world

global resource advantage   A source of competitive advantage resulting from the ability of a global organization to draw from a much broader and more diversified pool of resources

global stage of international development   The organization has become so global that it is no longer associated primarily with any one country

gross operating profit (GOP)   The difference between operating revenue and expenses, or income after undistributed operating expenses; GOP is calculated by subtracting total undistributed operating expenses from total operated departments income

group-centered economies   Groups of companies manage the use of internal capital as a replacement for external capital markets

horizontal integration   Involves acquisition of an organization in the same line of business

hospitality   Defined in the *Oxford English Dictionary* as the reception and entertainment of guests, visitors, or strangers with liberality and goodwill

hospitality industry   A group of businesses that welcome travelers and guests by providing accommodation, food, and/or beverages

hostile acquisition   An acquisition that is not desirable from the perspective of the managers of a target company; unexpected acquisition announcements typically are considered hostile

human resource management   Support activities of the value chain associated with human-based activities such as recruiting, hiring, training, and compensation

human resources strategy   The pattern of decisions about selection, training, rewards, and benefits

hypercompetition   A condition of rapidly escalating competition

hypothesis development and testing   Organizations should test their decisions to see if they are appropriate or likely to be successful; hypothesis development is a creative process, whereas hypothesis testing is an analytical process

inbound logistics   Primary activities of the value chain that include activities associated with acquiring inputs that are used in the product

industry consolidation   Occurs as competitors merge

industry life cycle   Portrays how sales volume for a product category changes over its lifetime, from the introduction stage through the commodity or decline stage

industry revolutionaries   Firms that invent business concepts

industry supply chain   The sequence of activities in an industry from raw materials extraction through final consumption

information systems strategy   Plan for using information systems to enhance organizational processes and strategy

inimitable resources   Resources that are possessed by industry participants but are hard or impossible to completely duplicate

initial public offering (IPO)   Entails sale of stock to the public and investors

innovation   A new idea, a recombination of old ideas, or a unique approach that is perceived as new by the individuals involved; innovation is the combination of both invention and commercialization

intangible relatedness   Occurs any time capabilities developed in one area can be applied to another area

intangible resources   Organizational assets that are hard to quantify, such as knowledge, skills, abilities, stakeholder relationships, and reputations

integrative knowledge   Knowledge that helps integrate various activities, capabilities, and products

intelligent opportunism   The ability of managers at various levels of the organization to take advantage of unanticipated opportunities to further intended strategy or even redirect a strategy

interlocking directorate Occurs when a director or executive of one firm sits on the board of a second firm or when two firms have directors who also serve on the board of a third firm

internal controls A set of controls that firms use to guide internal processes and behaviors; specifically, behavioral, process, and accounting controls

international expansion The process of building an expanding operational presence; this can lead to global resource advantages

international stage of international development Exports become an important part of organizational strategy; operations and marketing are tailored to the needs of each country

interorganizational relationships A term that includes many types of organizational cooperation or partnerships

intrapreneurship Corporate entrepreneurship, or the creation of new business ventures within existing corporations

joint venture An entity that is created when two or more firms pool a portion of their resources to create a separate jointly owned entity

knowledge economy Refers to the importance of intangible people skills and intellectual assets to developed economies

lateral (horizontal) organization Refers to the horizontal communication and coordination mechanisms that occur across departments or divisions, such as direct contact, teams, task forces, a community of practice, and integrator positions

learning curve Demonstrates that the time required to complete a task will decrease as a predictable function of the number of times the task is repeated

legal perspective Ethical behavior is defined as legal behavior

leverage A measure of a firm's long-term or total debt relative to its assets or equity; a common measure of financial risk

leveraged buyouts (LBOs) Private purchase of a business unit by managers, employees, unions, or private investors

licensing Selling the right to produce and/or sell a brand name product, often in a foreign market

limited partnership A business form in which the partners' management responsibility and legal liability are limited

liquidity A measure of a firm's ability to pay short-term obligations

low-cost leadership strategy A firm pursues competitive advantage through efficient cost production; also called cost leadership

management company In the hotel industry, management companies run the operation of a hotel; they may also be a franchisor and/or owner; examples include Interstate Hotels and Resorts, Tharaldson Enterprises, and Westmont Hospitality

management contract A contract between an owner and a management company in which the owner agrees to make a payment from the operation's gross revenues to the management company in exchange for running the business with full management responsibility

market-centered economies Economies with well-developed infrastructures, business environments, and external capital markets

market development Involves repositioning a product or service to appeal to a new market

market penetration Competing with a single product or service in a single market

marketing and sales Primary activities of the value chain associated with processes through which customers can purchase the product and through which they are induced to do so

marketing strategy Plan for collecting information about customers or potential customers and using this information to project future demand, predict competitor actions, identify new business opportunities, create products and services, and sell products and services

mental model A view of how the world works; mental models should include an understanding of both the internal and external organizations and the interaction between the two

merger Occurs when two organizations combine into one; acquisitions are the most common type of merger

mission statement Defines what the organization is and its reason for existing; often contains all of the elements of strategic direction—including vision, business definition, and organizational values

monopoly An industry in which one firm is the only significant provider of a good or service

multidivisional corporate-level structure A corporate-level structure in which each business exists as a separate unit reporting to top management

multidomestic product/market approach Entails handling product design, assembly, and marketing on a country-by-country basis by custom tailoring products and services around individual markets' needs

multimarket competition Firms compete in multiple markets simultaneously

multinational stage of international development The organization has marketing and production facilities throughout the world

network A hub-and-wheel configuration with a local firm at the hub organizing the interdependencies of a complex array of firms

network structure A business-level structure in which operating units or branches are organized around customer groups or geographical regions

newly industrialized economies (NIEs) Countries that have recently experienced high levels of growth in real gross domestic product

occupancy A commonly used measure of hotel performance; occupancy is calculated by dividing the number of rooms sold by the number of rooms available and multiplying by 100

oligopoly An industry characterized by the existence of a few very large firms

operating environment Consists of stakeholders with whom organizations interact on a fairly regular basis—including customers, suppliers, competitors, government agencies and administrators, local communities, activist groups, unions, the media, and financial intermediaries

operating goals Established in an effort to bring the concepts found in the vision statement to a level that managers and employees can influence and control

operations Primary activities of the value chain that refer to transforming inputs into the final product

operations strategy Emerges from the pattern of decisions made within the firm about production or service operations

organizational crises Critical situations that threaten high-priority organizational goals, impose a severe restriction on the amount of time in which key members of the organization can respond, and contain elements of surprise

organizational culture The system of shared values of an organization's members

organizational ethics A value system that has been widely adopted by members of an organization; often used interchangeably with the term "organizational values"

organizational fit Occurs when two organizations or business units have similar management processes, cultures, systems, and structures

organizational governance How the behavior of high-ranking managers is supervised and controlled; for example, the board of directors is responsible for ensuring that managerial behavior is consistent with shareholder interests

organizational scope The breadth of an organization's activities across businesses and industries

organizational structure Reporting relationships and the division of people into groups, teams, task forces, and departments within an organization

organizational values The underlying philosophies that guide decisions and behavior in a firm; also called core values or organizational ethics

outbound logistics Primary activities of the value chain related to storing and physically distributing a final product to customers

outsourcing Contracting with another firm to provide goods or services that were previously supplied from within the company; similar to subcontracting

owner/manager structure In this form, the owner is the top manager and the business is run as a sole proprietorship

Pacific Century Refers to a forecast that the world's growth center for the twenty-first century will shift across the Pacific Ocean to Asia

partnership   A business form in which the partners each contribute resources and share in the rewards of the venture

patent   Legal protection that prevents other companies from using a firm's innovation

performance-based compensation plan   Reward system in which compensation varies depending on the success of the organization

pioneer-type culture   The emphasis is on new product and new technology development

political environment   Influences and trends associated with governments and other political or legal entities; political forces, both at home and abroad, are among the most significant determinants of organizational success

political power   Comes from the ability to persuade lawmakers, society, or regulatory agencies to influence firm behavior

political strategies   All organizational activities that have as one of their objectives the creation of a friendlier political climate for the organization

premise control   Use of information collected by the organization to examine assumptions that underlie organizational vision, goals, and strategies

process controls   Use immediate feedback to control organizational processes

product/market structure   A business-level structure that organizes activities around the outputs of the organizational system, such as products, customers, or geographical regions

product- or service-based structure   A business-level structure organized around the outputs of the organization system

product/service development   Introduction of new products or services related to an existing competence of the firm or development of truly new-to-the-world products not related to the core business of the firm

product/service differentiation   Attributes associated with a product or service that cause customers to prefer it over competing products or services

pro-forma financial statements   Forward-looking income statements, balance sheets, and cash flow statements that are based on predictions of what will happen

project matrix structure   A hybrid business-level structure that combines some elements of both functional and product/market structures

prospector strategy   An offensive strategy in which firms aggressively seek new market opportunities and are willing to take risks

quick-service restaurants   Eat-in or take-out operations with limited menus, low prices, and fast service; these restaurants are commonly called fast-food or fast-service restaurants; examples include McDonald's, Burger King, KFC, and Taco Bell

R&D/technology strategy   Plan for developing new products and new technologies

radical innovations   Major innovations that influence more than one business or industry

radical restructuring   Major changes to a firm's direction, strategies, structures, and plans

reactor strategy   Describes firms that don't have a distinct strategy; they simply react to environmental situations

real estate investment trusts (REITs)   A corporation or trust that has at least 75 percent of its investments in real estate; REITs do not pay income tax so long as they pay back to shareholders 95 percent or more of their profits

reengineering   A restructuring approach that involves the radical redesign of core business processes to achieve dramatic improvements in productivity cycle times and quality

related acquisitions   Occur when the acquiring company shares common or complementary resources with its acquisition target

related diversification   Diversification that stems from common markets, functions served, technologies, or products and services

religious perspective   Religious teachings define appropriate behavior

reputation   An economic asset that signals observers about the attractiveness of a company's offerings based on past performance

resource-based approach to strategic management   Considers the firm as a bundle of resources; firms can gain competitive advantage through possessing superior resources

resource complementarity Occurs when two businesses have strengths in different areas

resource procurement Support activities of the value chain related to the purchase of inputs for all of the primary processes and support activities of the firm

restructuring Involves major changes to an organization's strategies, structure, and/or processes

retaliation strategy A firm threatens severe retaliation in an effort to discourage competitors from taking actions

retrenchment A turnaround strategy that involves tactics such as reducing the workforce, closing unprofitable plants, outsourcing unprofitable activities, implementing tighter cost or quality controls, or implementing new policies that emphasize quality or efficiency

revenue per available room (RevPAR) A commonly used measure of hotel performance; RevPAR is calculated by dividing total revenue by the number of hotel rooms available for sale

S corporation Formerly called the Subchapter S corporation, this corporate form allows tax advantages in the United States that are similar to those associated with a partnership

salesman-type culture These firms are excellent marketers who create successful brand names and distribution channels and pursue aggressive advertising and innovative packaging

service Primary activities of the value chain associated with providing service to enhance or maintain product value—such as repairing, supplying parts, or installation

situation analysis Analysis of stakeholders inside and outside the organization, as well as other external forces; this analysis should be conducted at both the domestic and international levels, if applicable

Six Sigma A philosophy based on minimizing the number of defects found in a manufacturing operation or service function

social responsibility The duty of an organization, defined in terms of its economic, legal, and moral obligations, as well as discretionary actions that might be considered attractive from a societal perspective

social stake Occurs when a stakeholder group not directly linked to the organization is interested in ensuring that the organization behaves in a manner that it believes is socially responsible

sociocultural environment Influences and trends that come from groups of individuals who make up a particular geographic region

spin-off A type of divestiture in which current shareholders are issued a proportional number of shares in the spun-off business

stakeholders Groups or individuals who can significantly affect or are significantly affected by an organization's activities

stakeholder approach to strategic management Envisions the firm at the center of a network of constituencies called stakeholders; firms can gain competitive advantage through superior stakeholder management

start-up capital The financing required to begin a new venture

steward A leader who cares deeply about the firm, its stakeholders, and the society in which it operates

strategic business unit (SBU) structure A multidivisional structure in which divisions are combined into SBUs based on common elements they each possess

strategic control Refers to a combination of control systems that allows managers excellent control over their firms

strategic direction Pertains to the longer-term goals and objectives of the organization; this direction is often contained in mission and vision statements

strategic fit Refers to the effective matching of strategic organizational capabilities

strategic flexibility A firm can move its resources out of declining markets and into more prosperous ones in a minimum amount of time

strategic-group map Categorizes existing industry competitors into groups that follow similar strategies

strategic intent A vision of where an organization is or should be going; similar to the strategic concept of "vision" defined previously

strategic leadership   Generally refers to leadership behaviors associated with creating organizational vision, establishing core values, developing strategies and a management structure, fostering organizational learning, and serving as a steward for the firm

strategic management   A process through which organizations analyze and learn from their internal and external environments, establish strategic direction, create strategies that are intended to move the organization in that direction, and implement those strategies, all in an effort to satisfy key stakeholders

strategic planning process   The formal planning elements of strategic management that result in a strategic plan; this process tends to be rather rigid and unimaginative

strategic reorientation   A significant realignment of organization strategies, structure, and processes with the new environmental realities

strategic surveillance   The process of collecting information from the broad, operating, and internal environments

strategic thinking   A somewhat creative and intuitive process that leads to creative solutions and new ideas

strategy formulation   The process of planning strategies, often divided into the corporate, business, and functional levels

strategy implementation   Managing stakeholder relationships and organizational resources in a manner that moves the organization toward the successful execution of its strategies, consistent with its strategic direction

structural inertia   Forces at work to maintain the status quo; they may include systems, structures, processes, culture, sunk costs, internal politics, and barriers to entry and exit

subcontracting   Acquiring goods and services that used to be produced in-house from external companies

substitute products/services   Products or services provided by another industry that can be readily substituted for an industry's own products/services

sustainable competitive advantage   Exists when a firm enjoys a long-lasting business advantage compared to rival firms

synergy   Occurs when the whole is greater than the sum of its parts

tacit knowledge   Knowledge that is difficult to articulate in a way that is meaningful and complete

tangible relatedness   Means that the organization has the opportunity to use the same physical resources for multiple purposes

tangible resources   Organizational assets that can be seen, touched, and/or quantified, such as plants, money, or products

technological environment   Influences and trends related to the development of technologies both domestically and internationally

technology   Human knowledge about products and services and the way they are made and delivered

technology development   Support activities of the value chain associated with learning processes that result in improvements in the way organizational functions are performed

thinking in time   Recognition that the past, present, and future are all relevant to making good strategic decisions

top management team (TMT)   Typically a heterogeneous group of three to ten top executives selected by the CEO; each member brings a unique set of skills and a unique perspective

tourism clusters   Geographic concentrations of competing, complementary, and interdependent firms that work together to provide the tourism experience

trade association   Organizations (typically nonprofit) that are formed by firms in the same industry to collect and disseminate trade information, offer legal and technical advice, furnish industry-related training, and provide a platform for collective lobbying

trade barriers   Factors that discourage international trade, such as tariffs and import quotas

trademark   Legal protection that prevents other companies from making use of a firm's symbol or brand name

traditional approach to strategic management
Analysis of the internal and external environments of the organization to arrive at organizational strengths, weaknesses, opportunities, and threats (SWOT), which form the basis for developing effective missions, goals, and strategies

transaction cost economics   The study of economic transactions and their costs

transaction costs   The resources used to create and enforce a contract

transnational structure   A corporate-level structure that organizes businesses along three dimensions: nation or region, product, and function

travel and tourism industry   A variety of interrelated businesses that provide services to travelers; the tourism industry includes a broad range of businesses like airlines, bars, cruise lines, car rental firms, casinos, entertainment firms, hotels, restaurants, travel agents, timeshares, tour operators, and recreational enterprises

triad regions   Three dominant economic regions in the world; namely, North America, Europe, and the Pacific Rim

Uniform System of Accounts   These standardized industry accounting systems provide many supplementary operating statements covering budgeting and forecasting; the *Uniform System of Accounts for the Lodging Industry* (USALI) and the *Uniform System of Accounts for Restaurants* (USAR) are designed with the special needs of the industry in mind and permits comparisons with industry standards

U.S. Sentencing Guidelines (USSG)   Compulsory guidelines courts must use to determine fines and penalties when corporate illegalities are proven

universalist perspective   Appropriate behavior is defined by the question: "Would I be willing for everyone else in the world to make the same decision?"

unrelated acquisitions   Occur between companies that don't share any common or complementary resources

unrelated diversification   Diversification that is not based on commonality among the activities of a corporation

utilitarian perspective   The most appropriate actions generate the greatest benefits for the largest number of people

value chain   A representation of organizational processes, divided into primary and support activities that create value for the customer

venture capitalists   Individuals or groups of investors that seek out and provide capital to entrepreneurs

vertical integration   Exists when a firm is involved in more than one stage of the industry supply chain; a firm that vertically integrates moves forward to become its own customer or backward to become its own supplier

vision   Expresses what the organization wants to be in the future

visionary leadership   Pertains to envisioning what the organization should be like in the future, communicating the vision, and empowering followers to enact it

wholly owned foreign subsidiary   A business venture that is started from scratch; sometimes called a greenfield investment

Index

SURVEY OF LONDON
VOLUME XXXIX

PREVIOUS VOLUMES
OF THE SURVEY OF LONDON

*Original edition out of print. Photographic facsimile available from the Greater London Council Bookshop, County Hall, London, SE1 7PB, or from A.M.S. Press Inc., 56 East 13th Street, New York.

† Out of print.

No. 66 Brook Street, now the Grosvenor Office: chimneypiece in first-floor front room in 1976. Edward Shepherd lessee, 1725

SURVEY OF LONDON

GENERAL EDITOR: F. H. W. SHEPPARD

VOLUME XXXIX

The Grosvenor Estate
in Mayfair

PART I
General History

THE ATHLONE PRESS
UNIVERSITY OF LONDON
Published for the Greater London Council
1977

Published by
THE ATHLONE PRESS
UNIVERSITY OF LONDON
at 4 Gower Street, London WC I

Distributed by
Tiptree Book Services Ltd, Tiptree, Essex

U.S.A. and Canada
Humanities Press Inc, New Jersey

ISBN 0 485 48239 8

Printed in Great Britain
at the University Press, Oxford
by Vivian Ridler
Printer to the University

Preface

The publication of this volume of the *Survey of London* coincides with the tercentenary of the establishment of the Grosvenor Estate in London. In advancing the printing of this volume by a year, the Greater London Council is giving special prominence to one of the most extraordinary and successful developments in our city. The increasingly tight control exercised by the Estate in modern times not only over the architecture but also over the use of newly erected buildings, has contributed to making Mayfair a harmonious and to a large extent visually united whole. Georgian, Victorian and Edwardian elements blend into a cohesive and dignified entity. Only occasionally, some later buildings may be felt to be unwelcome intruders.

Situated in the very heart of London, alongside Oxford Street, the capital's largest shopping thoroughfare, the area described in this volume has Grosvenor Square as its focal point, famous for its connection with the United States of America. Their mighty new embassy building dominates the western end of the large square, while the statue of Franklin Delano Roosevelt constitutes the main feature of its open space. Other embassies, including those of Italy and Japan, are sited close by. It is no accident that so many foreign missions have sought out this part of London where they exist side by side with a prosperous business community, fine residences, and some of the capital's most prestigious hotels and restaurants. The very name of Mayfair has become a byword for quality, not least because of the prevalence of strong and characteristic architecture and the total absence of mean or derelict streets.

This is the first part of the *Survey of London*'s study of the Grosvenor Estate in Mayfair. It contains a general account of the history and architecture of the estate, and will be followed by a detailed description of individual buildings which is now in course of preparation.

The Grosvenor family's estates in what are now Mayfair and Belgravia were acquired by Sir Thomas Grosvenor through his marriage on 10 October 1677 with Mary Davies, the daughter and heiress of a scrivener in the City of London. In Mayfair, development for building began in the 1720's, and within a few years Daniel Defoe was describing the 'amazing Scene of new Foundations, not of Houses only, but as I might say of new Cities' which were then springing up on the western outskirts of London. Many of the leading architects and builders of the day, notably Colen Campbell, Roger Morris and Edward Shepherd, worked on the Grosvenor Estate. Despite widespread rebuilding during the last hundred years, several splendid examples of the original Georgian work still survive, and many of the Victorian and Edwardian buildings are equally notable.

Hitherto only a few of these buildings have been studied in any detail, and the history of the estate itself—of its first development and of its subsequent management down to the present day—has remained largely unknown. The production of this volume has been made possible by the decision of the Grosvenor Estate Trustees to allow the Council's *Survey of London* staff access to their historical records kept at the Grosvenor Office in Mayfair and at Eaton Hall in Cheshire. The Council is most grateful to them and their staff at the Grosvenor Office, and in particular to Mr. Guy Acloque, for this essential assistance in the study of London's historic fabric.

On behalf of the Council I should also like to thank all those people who have given help in the preparation of this study. Many of their names are recorded in the List of Acknowledgments in this volume, and much of the research for it could not have been done without their generous assistance. I am particularly grateful to my colleagues, the advisory members of the Historic Buildings Board— Sir John Betjeman, Sir Hugh Casson, Sir Osbert Lancaster, Mr. Ian Phillips, Sir Paul Reilly and Sir John Summerson—who have given their valuable time and profound knowledge at numerous meetings of the Board. I would also like to express my great appreciation to the elected members of the Board for their devotion to the task of preserving the architectural heritage of our great city.

This volume has been prepared under the General Editorship of Mr. F. H. W. Sheppard. On the basis of research started in 1973, he and the Assistant Editors, Mr. J. Greenacombe and Mr. V. R. Belcher (all of the Director-General's Department) wrote the historical portions of the text and edited all the material. Latterly they were assisted in research and editing by the Deputy Editor, Mr. P. A. Bezodis. The typing was done by Mrs. K. Hill, who prior to her retirement in 1976 had typed the whole of the texts of seven volumes of the *Survey*, and by Mrs. B. Crawford, who also assisted with proof reading. All the contributions made by the staff of the Historic Buildings Division of the Department of Architecture and Civic Design were produced under the aegis of Mr. Ashley Barker, Surveyor of Historic Buildings. These contributions comprise portions of the text written by Mr. Andrew Saint, the Architectural Editor, who in 1974 took over from Dr. Malcolm Airs the organisation of the photographic and drawing programmes. The principal photographers were Mr. Alan Turner, Mr. Graham Slough and Mr. Stephen Tozer of the Council's Photographic Unit. The drawings were made in the Historic Buildings Division under the general guidance of Mr. F. A. Evans, M.B.E., and after his retirement in 1975, of Mr. John Sambrook. The authorship of each individual drawing is acknowledged in the List of Figures. I should like here to add a word of special appreciation for the outstanding contribution made by Mr. Evans, whose drawings appear in all eighteen of the volumes of the *Survey* published since 1949.

LOUIS BONDY
Chairman, Historic Buildings Board
Greater London Council
County Hall
March 1977

Acknowledgments

The principal acknowledgment of assistance received by the Council in preparing this volume must be to the Trustees of the Grosvenor Estate for their great courtesy in making available the records of the Mayfair estate, without which this study would have been impossible. It is a pleasure to acknowledge at the same time the ready assistance given to the Council's officers in their work by the members of the staff of the Grosvenor Office, and of the Trustees' solicitors, Boodle, Hatfield and Company.

For the work of Fernand Billerey on the estate his widow, Madame V. H. Billerey, and his son Mr. L. V. A. Billerey gave both encouragement and much valuable information. Mr. Jonathan Blow hospitably provided an opportunity to discuss the work of his father, Detmar Blow, and to examine the numerous architectural drawings in his possession. Mr. Geoffrey Singer, formerly Chief Surveyor to the Grosvenor Estates, very kindly read parts of the text at successive stages of their production.

Particular acknowledgment should also be made to Mr. Edward Hubbard and to Dr. J. M. Robinson for their generosity in allowing use to be made of their post-graduate theses on John Douglas and Samuel Wyatt respectively.

The Council tenders its grateful thanks to the following individuals, institutions and corporate bodies who have helped to make the work on this volume possible by providing or giving access to information or by allowing the inspection of buildings in their ownership or occupation:

Mr. Guy Acloque; Mr. Bengt Åkerrén; Mrs. Jill Allibone; H.E. the American Ambassador; Margaret, Duchess of Argyll; Miss Catherine Armet; Miss Rosemary Ashbee; Viscountess Astor; Mr. E. H. Aucott; Miss A. S. Bagshawe; Mr. Eustace Balfour; Mr. Nicolas Barker; the Duke of Beaufort; Mrs. Denis Berry; Mrs. E. K. Berry; Mr. G. C. Berry; Mr. T. S. Blakeney; H.E. the Brazilian Ambassador; Mrs. W. Broekema; Mr. O. Bateman Brown; Mr. S. Bywater; Mrs. Ann Campbell; Lady Iris Capell; the Earl of Carnarvon; Mr. Wayne Carter; Mrs. Carvalho; Mrs. Bridget Cherry; Miss Sarah D. Coffin; Mr. S. R. Coggan; Mr. H. M. Colvin; Mr. John Cornforth; Dr. Maurice Craig; Mr. Alan Crawford; the Earl of Crawford and Balcarres; Mr. Stephen Croad; the late Miss Jacqueline Cromic; Miss Helen Cundy; Mrs. Joan Cundy; Mr. J. Cutileiro; Mrs. Monica Dance; the Countess of Denbigh; Lady D'Erlanger; Mr. E. V. Dommett; Mr. Ian Doolittle; Mrs. M. P. G. Draper; Mr. William Drummond; Mr. Peter Dunne; Mrs. C. Dutnall; Rev. Fr. F. Edwards, S.J.; H.E. the Egyptian Ambassador; Frances, Lady Fergusson; Mr. R. B. Fisher; Rev. John Gaskell; Mr. A. Stuart Gray; Mr. B. Lund Hansen; Mr. John Hardy; Mrs. T. H. Harker; the Earl of Harrowby; Mr. M. D. Heber-Percy; Mr. J. B. Henderson; Mr. Nicholas Hill; Bishop A. Hornyk; Lady Hulse; H.E. the Indonesian Ambassador; Mr. R. Irving; H.E. the Italian Ambassador; H.E. the Japanese Ambassador; Mr. Edward Joy; Miss A. M. Kennett; Mrs. Geraldine Kunstadter; Mrs. Nancy Lancaster; Mr. Michael Levey; Mrs. Christine Loeb; the Hon. Christopher McLaren; Mr. Byron Maile; Mr. C. E. Mansfield; Miss Betty R. Masters; Mr. R. Mellin; Lord Methuen; Mr. E. Croft Murray; Mrs. Virginia Murray; Mr. R. G. Must; Mr. David Nickerson; Mrs. Y. Nothman; Prof. D. P. O'Brien; Miss Susan Orde; Sgr. L. Orsi; Count Guy de Pelet; Sir Nikolaus Pevsner; H.E. the Portuguese Ambassador; the Earl of Radnor; Mr. A. Ramsey; Mr. P. M. Rayner; Mrs. Margaret Richardson; Mr. Michael Robbins; Miss Mary L. Robertson; Mr. Michael Ross-Wills; the Marquess of Salisbury; Mr. A. W. Saxton; Mr. I. B. Scott; Mr. T. Shearing; Mrs. Smallpeice; Mr. F. T. Smallwood; Mr. R. A. H. Smith; the Duke of Somerset; Mr. H. D. Steiner; Miss Dorothy Stroud; Miss E. A. Stuart; Sir John Summerson; Miss M. Swarbrick; H.E. the Swedish Ambassador; Dr. Eric Till; Mrs. M. Travis; Mrs. P. A. Tritton; Miss Elmira Wade; Mr. Clive Wainwright; Mr. B. Weinreb; Mrs. H. J. Whetton; Mr. J. W. Wilcox; Mr. R. H. Harcourt Williams; Mrs. Dorothy Wimperis; Dr. E. J. Wimperis; Mr. R. McD. Winder; Sir Hugh Wontner; Mr. A. C. Wood.

Alpine Club; American Church in London; Ashmolean Museum; Messrs. Barrington Laurance; Barrow Hepburn Group; Bedfordshire Record Office; Bell Faultless Partnership; Berkshire Record Office; Biddle Holdings; Bodleian Library; John Bolding and Sons; British Library; British Optical Association; British Standards Institute; Buckinghamshire Record Office; Carmarthenshire Record Office; Casanova Club; Cheshire Record Office; Chester City Record Office; Church Commissioners; Claridge's Hotel; Sibyl Colefax and John Fowler; Brian Colquhoun and Partners; Commonwealth Secretariat; Connaught Hotel; Conservatoire National Des Arts et Métiers; Cornwall Record Office; Corporation of London, Guildhall

Library, and Record Office; *Country Life*; County and District Properties; Cumbria Record Office; Derbyshire Record Office; Devon Record Office, Exeter; Drummond's Branch, Royal Bank of Scotland; Duchy of Cornwall Office; Dudley Public Library; Durham Record Office; East Sussex Record Office; Essex Record Office; John Garlick Ltd.; Glamorgan Record Office; Gloucestershire Record Office; Thos. Goode and Co.; Green and Abbott Ltd.; Guildford Muniment Room; Gwent County Record Office; Gwynedd Archives Service, Caernarvon; Hammerson Group of Companies; Hampshire Record Office; Harkness House; Harrowby MSS Trust; Haslemere Estates; C. E. Heath and Co.; Hereford Record Office; Hertfordshire Record Office; Hoare's Bank; House of Lords Record Office; Huntingdon (Cambridgeshire) Record Office; Henry E. Huntington Library; The Honourable Society of the Inner Temple; Kent Archives Office; King's College, Cambridge; Lambeth Palace Library; Lancashire Record Office; Leeds Archives Dept.; Leicestershire Record Office; Lenygon and Morant Ltd.; Lincolnshire Archives Office; London Library; Lucas Industries Ltd.; Mallett at Bourdon House; Merchant Taylors' Company; Metropolitan Museum of Art; Messrs. Millar and Harris; Museum of London; National Library of Ireland; National Library of Wales; National Monuments Record; National Register of Archives; National Register of Archives (Scotland); National Trust (Hughenden Manor); W. H. Newson and Sons; Niedersächsische Staats- und Universitätsbibliothek, Göttingen; North Humberside Record Office; North Yorkshire Record Office; Northamptonshire Record Office; Nottinghamshire Record Office; Oxfordshire Record Office; Peabody Trust; Public Record Office; Public Record Office of Northern Ireland; Rank Organization; Royal Institute of British Architects; Royal Photographic Society; The John Rylands University Library of Manchester; Savile Club; Scottish Record Office; Sesame Club; Sheffield City Libraries; Shropshire Record Office; Sir John Soane's Museum; Somerset Record Office; Sotheby's Belgravia; Staffordshire Record Office; Robert Stigwood Organization; Suffolk Record Office; Surrey Record Office; Thames Water Authority; Trollope and Colls (City) Ltd.; Tupperware Company; Ukrainian Catholic Cathedral; University College of North Wales, Library; University of Hull, Brynmor Jones Library; University of Nottingham, Library; Victoria and Albert Museum; Voice and Vision Ltd.; Warwickshire Record Office; West Sussex Record Office; Westmoreland Properties; Williams and Glyn's Bank; Wiltshire Record Office; Worcestershire Record Office; Yorkshire Archaeological Society; Zinc and Lead Development Associations.

Contents

Plates *at end*

End Pocket

List of Plates

List of Figures

Note. Many of the following drawings show the buildings conjecturally restored to their presumed original state, and should in no case be taken as a precise record of present appearance.

TABLES

END POCKET

CHAPTER I

The Acquisition of the Estate

For three hundred years the Grosvenor family has owned large estates in what are now some of the most valuable parts of Westminster. These estates were acquired in 1677 through the marriage of Sir Thomas Grosvenor with Mary Davies, the infant daughter and heiress of a scrivener in the City of London. In the process of time Mary Davies's inheritance was developed for building, and the Grosvenors became the richest urban landlords in the country, the lustre of their name—for long synonymous with wealth and fashion—being gilded by successive advancements in the peerage, culminating in the dukedom of Westminster in 1874. Today the bulk of that inheritance is still, despite the sale of some of the less select parts, enjoyed by her descendants, and is now administered by the Grosvenor Estate Trustees.

The marriage portion which the guardians of the twelve-year-old Mary Davies were able to offer the young Cheshire baronet Sir Thomas Grosvenor in 1677 consisted of some five hundred acres of land, mostly meadow and pasture, a short distance from the western fringes of built-up London. Not all of this was to be available in immediate possession and the income from the land was at that time relatively small, but its potential for future wealth was realized even then. The area with which this volume is particularly concerned was only a part of that vast holding, approximately one hundred acres in extent and sometimes called in early deeds The Hundred Acres,[1] lying south of Oxford Street and east of Park Lane. With only minor exceptions this part of Mary Davies's heritage has remained virtually intact to the present day and forms the Grosvenor estate in Mayfair. The history of the ownership of this land before it came into the possession of the Grosvenor family is, however, best told as part of the history of the larger holding which the third baronet acquired on his marriage. To a considerable extent this story, and that of the personalities involved in it, have been recounted in the two volumes by Charles Gatty entitled *Mary Davies and the Manor of Ebury* and only a brief outline will be attempted here.

The Manor of Ebury

Most of the London estates which now belong or have belonged to the Grosvenor family—and all of that with which this volume is concerned—once formed part of the manor called Eia in the Domesday survey but later known as Eye, from which Eybury or Ebury derives. Although the manor's original bounds have not been determined

with certainty it probably occupied the territory between the Roman road along the present course of Bayswater Road and Oxford Street on the north, the Thames on the south, the Westbourne river on the west, and the Tyburn, which was also known as Eye or Ay(e) Brook, on the east.[2] Even these relatively straightforward bounds are difficult to define because these tributaries tended both to change course and to have more than one outlet to the Thames. In the case of the Tyburn the westernmost of several channels, perhaps originally little more than a drainage ditch, seems to have formed the eastern boundary of the manor in its southern part.

After the Norman Conquest Geoffrey de Mandeville obtained possession of the manor, one of many which he took in reward for his services in the Conqueror's cause. Before the end of William's reign de Mandeville had given the manor to the Abbey of Westminster and it remained in the Abbey's ownership until 1536 when it was acquired by Henry VIII.[3] During this long period two areas came to be distinguished from the main manor, but although sometimes termed manors it is doubtful whether they had entirely separate jurisdictions.[4] The areas were Hyde in the north-west corner, now incorporated into Hyde Park, and Neyte or Neat(e) in the heart of the district later known as Pimlico. The so-called manor or bailiwick of Neat presents particular problems. In seventeenth- and eighteenth-century title deeds the estate belonging to the Grosvenors is described as the site of the manor of Ebury and parcel of the bailiwick of Neat,[5] but the use of these terms appears merely to have followed that in early leases in which they were probably employed loosely to describe farms. In fact the Neyte was formerly a manor house or grange of the Abbots of Westminster situated between the modern Warwick Way and Sutherland Row,[6] and its site, together with some thirty-six acres to the south and east, were not included in Mary Davies's inheritance, having been granted away separately by the Crown after 1536, and thus did not pass into the ownership of the Grosvenor family.

Surrounded by other lands belonging to Westminster Abbey the manor had lost its identity as a unit of landholding before the end of the Middle Ages, and the process of disintegration continued after its acquisition by the Crown. The many documents and maps which survive show that the subsequent history of its descent is extremely complex, but as few of these complexities affect the history of The Hundred Acres in Mayfair no attempt will be made here to unravel all of them. The 'Manor of Hyde' was enclosed into Hyde Park by

Henry VIII, and he or his successors also added some land on the east to his new park, for fifteen acres called Tyburn Close and forty acres near Stonehill (apparently the north-eastern and south-eastern extremities of the park) were specifically excluded from subsequent leases and grants of Ebury manor. Other stated exceptions in such transactions were the lands around the 'Manor of Neate'.[7]

Although not specified other lands which appear originally to have been within the manor became detached when it was in the hands of the Crown, including a substantial part of Mayfair south of The Hundred Acres. Among these was a large close or series of fields called Brick Close which was later to form part of the Berkeley estate,[8] and other fields which were incorporated into the manor or bailiwick of St. James. Some six or seven acres to the north of the modern Brick Street were, however, retained; they were included in a schedule of property to be sold to pay the debts of Alexander Davies, Mary Davies's father, by Act of Parliament in 1675,[9] and therefore did not pass to the Grosvenors.

Of the areas in Mayfair which apparently became separated from the manor, that which presents the most puzzling aspects is a plot with a frontage to Park Lane, about three acres in extent, immediately to the south of the Grosvenor estate, now occupied by the Dorchester Hotel and parts of Deanery and Tilney Streets. When first leased for building in the 1730's this was described as waste ground belonging to the manor of Knightsbridge in the ownership of the Dean and Chapter of Westminster.[10] The Dean and Chapter had acquired the manor (the full title of which was the manor of Knightsbridge with Westbourne Green) from Henry VIII in 1542[11] although it had belonged to Westminster Abbey in the Middle Ages. How that manor came to include a parcel of waste ground in the middle of the manor of Ebury is unclear. In Grosvenor estate documents of the eighteenth century the area is defined as 'a common or waste… called Ossulton Common'.[12] The name Osolstone is also used to describe this spot in a deed of 1614 and in the same document Park Lane is described as 'the highwaye from Osolstone to Tiburne'.[13] The name is also marked on an early manuscript map among the Grosvenor archives which relates to this deed. In the records of Westminster Abbey there are references to a farm 'at Osolueston' which belonged to the manor of Eye, and other references to Ossulston, always as part of this same manor.[14] The evaluation of this evidence in determining the location of the assemblies or courts of the Hundred of Ossulston, the ancient area of jurisdiction which included London, is not within the scope of this volume, and the apparent conflict of evidence about the manorial history of this small area remains unresolved.

Most of the remainder of Ebury manor was let by the Crown in two leasehold entities, the fields of one intermingling with those of the other. Reversionary leases were also granted, apparently as a way of rewarding faithful service, well before the current leases expired, and to complicate matters further each reversionary lease came to be held by more than one person so that partitions of the land had to take place when the previous leases fell in early in the seventeenth century.[15]

In 1618 a moiety of one lease was bought for £4,760 by trustees acting for Sir Lionel Cranfield, the ambitious merchant who held several offices of state under James I and was later impeached for corruption.[16] By this purchase Cranfield became the direct leaseholder of a large part of the manor including The Hundred Acres. He also contemplated purchasing the other moiety, which he estimated would cost about £5,000 or £6,000, but was evidently unable to complete the transaction before his fall, for this leasehold interest remained outstanding until its expiry in 1675.[17] In 1623, however, James I sold the freehold reversion* of the manor to two 'gentlemen' of London, John Traylman and Thomas Pearson, for £1,151 15s. By a conveyance dated the day following they in turn disposed of it for the same amount to two representatives of Cranfield, by then Earl of Middlesex and Lord High Treasurer of England.[19] The price was equivalent to thirty years' purchase of the nominal Crown rents obtained under leases granted by the Tudors, and by buying the manor in fee farm Cranfield could no doubt claim that he was preserving the King's rent, low as it was. Not only did the grant convey all of the manor with the exception of those parts already detached from it and a royal mulberry garden (now part of the site of Buckingham Palace and its grounds), but additionally some land elsewhere was included. Particularly important for the later history of the Grosvenor estate were some twenty acres at Millbank on the south side of Horseferry Road, for it was here that the first speculative building on the estate took place.

In 1626, when his personal and financial fortunes were at a low point, Cranfield sold his interests in the manor and the additional lands for £9,400 to Hugh Audley (also spelt Awdley or Awdeley), a clerk of the Court of Wards and Liveries who amassed a considerable fortune by lending money.[20] Although Cranfield had thus made a handsome profit on the two sums he had laid out, he felt that Audley had driven a hard bargain.[21] Audley held the property until his death at an advanced age in 1662. During this long period he sold some small parcels of land and bought others which had probably once belonged to the manor,[22] but when he died the estate he had purchased in 1626 was still virtually intact. By a settlement made shortly before his death he left the bulk of the land

---

* In strict terms the manor was sold in fee farm, for a perpetual annual rent of £38 7s. 10d. (equal to the total rent due under the existing leases) was payable to the Crown. In 1663 this rent was granted by Charles II to the Earl of Sandwich[18] and was thereafter paid to the Earl and his descendants.

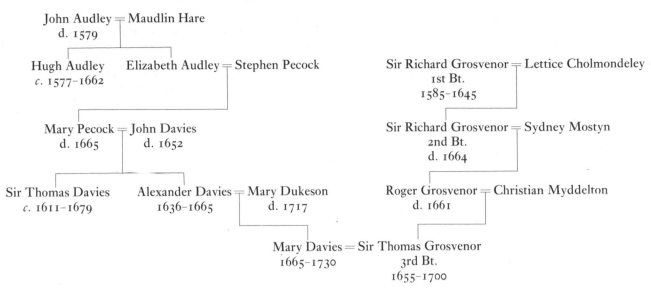

Abridged pedigree of Audley, Davies and Grosvenor families

to his great-nephew Alexander Davies and the detached part at Millbank (known as Market Meadows) to the latter's brother Thomas Davies, later Sir Thomas Davies, who was Lord Mayor of London in 1676-7.[23] After Audley's death Thomas Davies sold his holding for £2,000 to his brother[24] so that Alexander Davies possessed all of Audley's former estate in the area.

Alexander Davies was a scrivener by profession and had worked for Audley.[25] Although scriveners were technically the draftsmen of deeds they also undertook many of the functions later associated with lawyers, particularly the management of investments for clients, and Davies probably had access to ready supplies of capital. He decided to embark on speculative building on his new property and as the site chose Market Meadows at Millbank, which he had purchased from his brother. He let the land along the river front for building, reserving a large plot at the southern end as the site of a mansion for his own occupation. This was later called Peterborough House and then Grosvenor House when it became the principal London residence of the Grosvenor family in the first half of the eighteenth century. In 1665, however, 'in the time of the...great Sicknesse' Alexander Davies died at the age of twenty-nine, leaving the speculation unfinished, his mansion half built, and an infant daughter less than six months old as his heir.[26] This was the Mary Davies who was to marry Sir Thomas Grosvenor in 1677.

Alexander Davies had settled the estate on trustees for the benefit of his heirs with provision for an annuity of £100 to be paid to his widow.[27] The settlement did not extinguish her right of dower, however, and so his widow, also named Mary, could claim a life interest in a third of the property. She quickly remarried, her second husband being John Tregonwell, a Dorset squire, and was here-after, of course, known as Mrs. Tregonwell. Despite the potential wealth of the estate the immediate problem facing the Tregonwells was the settlement of Alexander Davies's debts. He had not paid the £2,000 purchase money for the land at Millbank and had borrowed heavily to finance his building programme. Nearly £2,000 more had to be spent on the unfinished mansion to make it habitable and there were annuities and interest charges on the estate. A substantial part of the land yielded no income as it was still subject to the leasehold interest granted by the Crown (previously referred to) which was not due to fall in until 1675. John Tregonwell later claimed to have advanced a considerable amount of his own money in settling Alexander Davies's affairs,[28] and in 1675 an Act of Parliament was passed enabling some property to be sold to pay the debts.[9] Specified in the Act were Goring House (on the site of Buckingham Palace) and some twenty acres adjoining, five acres which now lie in the north-western corner of Green Park, the seven acres in Mayfair to the north of the line of Brick Street referred to above, and twenty-two acres in Knightsbridge. The land in Knightsbridge was repurchased by the Grosvenor family in 1763.[29] The Act also provided that several fields in the Mayfair portion of the estate should be held in dower by Mrs. Tregonwell. About fifty-six acres were involved, constituting the western part of The Hundred Acres. This had some effect on the building history of the area as the dower lands were exempted from subsequent settlements and were held under a different tenure when building leases came to be granted.

Despite these temporary difficulties, however, there was no doubt about the eligibility of the infant Mary Davies as a future wife for some aspiring young nobleman. In 1672 an agreement was drawn up whereby she was to be married to the Hon. Charles Berkeley, the eldest son of John, first Baron Berkeley of Stratton, as soon as she reached her twelfth birthday, when she would be of age to consent to the match. As part of the contract Lord Berkeley paid £5,000 immediately to John Tregonwell, partly in recompense for money spent in finishing Alexander Davies's mansion and in the upbringing of Mary; he also agreed to settle land of a considerable annual value either on, or in trust for, the couple by the time of the ceremony.[30] The marriage, however, never took place. According to an account preserved in the Grosvenor archives and probably drawn up by Mrs. Tregonwell[31] the reason was that Lord Berkeley was unable to provide the land. Although he was a rich man he had recently built an expensive mansion, Berkeley House in Piccadilly, and at about this time he purchased Brick Close in Mayfair, immediately to the south of the fields belonging to Mary Davies.[32] The breakdown of these plans mattered little for within a few months of her twelfth birthday a husband had been found for her in the twenty-one-year-old baronet, Sir Thomas Grosvenor.

The Grosvenor Marriage

The marriage between Mary Davies and Sir Thomas Grosvenor took place on 10 October 1677 in the church of St. Clement Danes, where the bride's grandfather, Dr. Richard Dukeson, was rector.[33] The Grosvenors were an ancient Cheshire family claiming a somewhat tenuous descent from Hugh Lupus, first Earl of Chester, one of William the Conqueror's foremost knights and possibly his nephew. By the seventeenth century they owned land in Chester, Cheshire, Denbighshire and Flintshire and also valuable lead mines in the last two counties. In 1622 Sir Richard Grosvenor was created a baronet by James I, and Sir Thomas, his great-grandson, was the third baronet. The family seat was at Eaton Hall, near Chester.

All Sir Thomas Grosvenor's prospects from the marriage were in the future. In deference to her tender years his bride remained for at least two years in the care of a guardian aunt, and as part of the marriage bargain he had to expend a considerable sum of money. Lord Berkeley's £5,000 had to be repaid with interest, and among other sums required to be disbursed John Tregonwell received £1,000 for a reversionary interest in the estate which would arise in the event of the death of Mary Davies before reaching the age of twenty-one, and which he had prudently acquired by assignment.[34] While a settlement of the estates in Cheshire and North Wales for the benefit of any male heirs of the marriage in order of primogeniture was made shortly after the ceremony,[35] a similar settlement of that part of Mary Davies's lands which was free from dower had to await her twenty-first birthday and was finally made in 1694.[36] The total annual rental value of the London estates in 1677 was £2,170, but one third of this was payable to Mrs. Tregonwell in

dower, and after annuities and other payments the clear income from the rest amounted to £824.[37] Besides this income, some £3,400 were obtained in 1681 when thirty-five acres were sold, apparently by royal wish, to the Earl of Arlington.[38] The land involved now constitutes parts of the grounds of Buckingham Palace, Green Park and Hyde Park Corner. A further two and a half acres in Chelsea, now or formerly part of the grounds of the Royal Hospital, were also sold.[39]

Sir Thomas Grosvenor died in 1700 leaving three sons under the age of twelve; a daughter also was born a month after his death. All three sons eventually succeeded to the baronetcy. Sir Richard, the eldest, died in 1732. His brother, Thomas, succeeded him for only seven months before his death in Naples early in 1733. The youngest son, Robert, then became the sixth baronet until his death in 1755; he was the only one of the three brothers to leave any issue.

The effect of the settlement of 1694 was that on her husband's death Dame Mary Grosvenor, as Mary Davies was now styled, was left a life interest in the London estate, with the exception of those parts held in dower by her mother. She had already shown signs of mental instability during her husband's lifetime and her illness was no doubt accelerated by his death. In 1701 while in Paris she married, or was inveigled into a bogus marriage by, Edward Fenwick, the brother of a Roman Catholic chaplain she had taken into her household. Four years of legal disputes ensued until the supposed marriage was annulled by the Court of Delegates in 1705.[40] In the same year a commission of lunacy was appointed to enquire into her mental state. She was adjudged insane and committed to the care of Francis Cholmondeley of Vale Royal in Cheshire, who had been appointed one of the guardians of her children by Sir Thomas Grosvenor's will.[41] As a result the revenues from her estate were paid into the Court of Chancery to be invested for her benefit, and any change in the use or disposition of the land could only be made by leave of the Court. Dame Mary lived on without regaining her faculties until 1730.

In 1708 Sir Richard Grosvenor married Jane Wyndham, daughter of Sir Edward Wyndham of Orchard Wyndham in Somerset. In return for a marriage portion of £12,000 he agreed to make a new settlement of the estates in his possession and of those in which his mother had a life interest, in part to secure a jointure for his wife.[42] In view of his mother's lunacy, however, it was only possible to do this with the authority of an Act of Parliament which was duly obtained in 1711 when he had reached the age of twenty-one.[43] The effect of the settlement was to preserve the descent of the estates in the male line, firstly to his male heirs if any and then to his brothers and their male heirs. Jane Grosvenor died in 1719 without issue and Sir Richard married again. His second wife was Diana Warburton, daughter of Sir George Warburton of Arley in Cheshire. This time a dowry of £8,000 was provided and a new settlement was drawn up, but its effect was to preserve the same contingent remainders as earlier ones.[44] Diana Grosvenor died in 1730, also without issue.

A clause was inserted in the Act of 1711 to enable Sir Richard Grosvenor to grant building leases for any term up to sixty years of the land in London in which his mother held a life interest (but excluding the land held in dower by Mrs. Tregonwell). The Act referred to some old and ruinous buildings which might be rebuilt, but otherwise there is no indication that any specific development was then planned.

In 1717 Mrs. Tregonwell died[45] and the third of the estate which she had held in dower passed in fee simple to Dame Mary Grosvenor. The income from this land was also henceforth administered on her behalf by the officials of the Court of Chancery.

CHAPTER II

The Development of the Estate 1720-1785

'I passed an amazing Scene of new Foundations, not of Houses only, but as I might say of new Cities. New Towns, new Squares, and fine Buildings, the like of which no City, no Town, nay, no Place in the World can shew; nor is it possible to judge where or when, they will make an end or stop of Building.... All the Way through this new Scene I saw the World full of Bricklayers and Labourers; who seem to have little else to do, but like Gardeners, to dig a Hole, put in a few Bricks, and presently there goes up a House.' So wrote Daniel Defoe in *Applebee's Weekly Journal* in 1725.[1] He was describing the amount of building work then going on in west London. Periodic bursts of activity in house building had been common in the western suburbs of London since the Restoration, but Defoe described the latest phase which followed the Hanoverian succession as 'a kind of Prodigy'.[2] Within a dozen years builders had moved from Hanover Square through the City of London's Conduit Mead estate well into the Grosvenor estate and even north of Oxford Street, in the vicinity of Cavendish Square. More deeds were registered in the Middlesex Land Register in 1725 than in any other year until 1765—an indication of the feverish level reached by building speculation at that time. On the Grosvenor estate, where development began in 1720, only a handful of houses were occupied before 1725, but in that year the parish ratebooks show many more houses filling up and the new streets on the estate were formally named, an occasion marked by a 'very splendid Entertainment' given by Sir Richard Grosvenor.[3]

The relative stability which followed the Peace of Utrecht and the crushing of the Jacobite rebellion provided a favourable climate in which building developments could be undertaken, and there seems to have been plenty of capital available for mortgages even during the years of the South Sea Bubble, but it is difficult to find adequate demographic reasons why there should have been so many houses built in the decade after 1715. As far as we know the population of London was not rising substantially at this time,[4] but the inexorable movement of fashion westwards, partly out of the fear of disease in the more crowded parts of the capital, may have provided much of the impetus. Defoe remarked on the contrast between the depopulation of the older parts of the metropolis and the creation of new *faubourgs* in the west. 'The City does not increase, but only the Situation of it is a going to be removed, and the Inhabitants are quitting the old Noble Streets and Squares where they used to live, and are removing into the Fields for fear of Infection;

so that, as the People are run away into the Country, the Houses seem to be running away too.'[5]

Against this background the decision of the Grosvenor family in 1720 to lay out The Hundred Acres in Mayfair for building is not a particularly remarkable one. The extent of the building scheme—stretching as far west as Park Lane—may have been a bold gesture, but the timing of the enterprise must have been largely dictated by the fact that builders had already reached the eastern boundary of the estate in their development of the adjoining Conduit Mead property in the vicinity of New Bond Street, and the men who initially carried through the operation on the Grosvenor lands were almost without exception those who were still working on the neighbouring estate.[6]

The Ground Landlord and his Role

A certain circumspection on the part of the ground landlord was to be expected on the Grosvenor estate during the first half of the eighteenth century, for Sir Richard Grosvenor and his brothers were country gentlemen rather than metropolitan entrepreneurs. Worthy, honest and perhaps a trifle dull, they appear to have made little mark on the national scene. They represented Chester at Westminster on the family interest as Tories, and in 1722 Sir Richard's name was included in a secret list drawn up by the Jacobites of those members of the nobility and gentry who, they thought, 'may be inclinable to join' a rebellion.[7] The Grosvenors were, however, Protestants, and there is no overt evidence that they were disloyal to the Hanoverian dynasty. The decision to erect a statue of George I as the centrepiece of the grand square which was to dominate the estate layout was probably prompted not merely by considerations of expediency, and architects and speculators more generally associated with Whig patrons apparently found little difficulty in co-operating with them. Of the three brothers who succeeded in turn to the baronetcy, Richard, the eldest, and Robert, the youngest, appear to have been most concerned with events in Mayfair. Indeed a dispute which occurred when Thomas Grosvenor became fifth baronet in 1732 suggests some degree of estrangement from his younger brother. He replaced the agents who managed the Middlesex estates, Richard and Robert Andrews, by a man of his own choice, but was apparently unable to persuade them to hand over the documents in their custody, and eventually brought a case against them in the Court of Exchequer.[8] They were supported in their resistance by Robert Grosvenor, ostensibly on the grounds that they were also acting for him as one of the executors of Sir Richard Grosvenor's will. A consideration in the minds of Sir Thomas Grosvenor's opponents was that he was a sick man (he died in Naples in February 1733) and that it might in turn prove difficult for them to obtain the papers necessary for running the estate from his executors on his death.[9] Robert Grosvenor was actively involved in the development of Mayfair even before he became sixth baronet in 1733. He often looked after the family's interest in London while Sir Richard Grosvenor was at Eaton and lived in a new house on the site of the present No. 10 Upper Grosvenor Street from 1730 to 1733,[10] probably while Grosvenor House, Millbank, was being reconstructed. He was also a lessee (from his brother) of parts of the estate, particularly on the south side of Grosvenor Square,[11] and this property, which was largely developed by speculative builders under sub-leases in the normal manner, was referred to as his trust estate.

Robert Grosvenor's son Richard, who succeeded his father as seventh baronet in 1755 and was created Baron Grosvenor in 1761 and Viscount Belgrave and Earl Grosvenor in 1784, appears to have been a different type of person from his father and uncles. With a disastrous marital life which led to a notorious scandal when he brought an action for adultery against George III's brother, the Duke of Cumberland,[12] and with a fondness for the turf which brought him to near ruin, he represents a transition between the country gentry and the sophisticated aristocracy of the Grosvenor family in the nineteenth and twentieth centuries. A series of sycophantic letters written to him by William Pitt the elder[13] suggests that he was also fully aware of the advantages to be gained by bestowing his political favours shrewdly and it was through Pitt's influence that he was raised to the peerage. He once described Pitt as 'the shining light or rather the blazing star of this country'.[14] The hectoring tone of some of the letters written to him by his London agent, however, suggests an exasperation at delays in obtaining crucial decisions affecting his affairs, and indicates that he was less than decisive in matters of estate policy.[15]

Until 1730 the position of the Grosvenor family as landlords was complicated by the mental derangement of Dame Mary Grosvenor and the different tenures under which the land in Mayfair was held. By the Act of 1711 Sir Richard Grosvenor had power to grant leases for up to sixty years of those parts of the estate in which his mother held a life interest, but not of the land which was then held in dower by his grandmother, Mrs. Tregonwell, and which his mother was to inherit in fee simple in 1717. The lands in which Dame Mary Grosvenor had only a life interest were in the eastern part of The Hundred Acres, and as this was the quarter from which development would naturally proceed, the problem of the fee-simple land was not an immediate one. The first difficulty was that the Grosvenors thought a term of sixty years

would not be a sufficient inducement to builders, even though sixty-one- and sixty-two-year leases were accepted during the contemporary development of the Burlington estate, and even shorter terms were granted in Conduit Mead. From the beginning a longer term was evidently intended for parts of the Grosvenor estate for in the very first building agreement, concluded with the estate surveyor, Thomas Barlow, in August 1720, it was specified that leases were to be granted for sixty years and 'a further term of years...as shall be agreed to be granted for building the new intended Square'.[16] Other agreements made in 1720 were either for sixty years (although the leases granted under them were for longer periods), or for ninety-nine years even though no power existed as yet to grant such a term.[17] The first lease (dated 15 July 1721) was for sixty years from Midsummer 1721, but this term was extended by a subsequent deed.[18]

This unsatisfactory situation was resolved in 1721 by a deed dated 2 June in which forty-three acres were conveyed in trust for the use of Sir Richard Grosvenor and his heirs with a proviso that leases could be granted for any term not exceeding ninety-nine years.[19] This deed explains the peculiar terminology of the early estate leases which were granted for sixty years under the Act of 1711 and a further term under the deed of 2 June 1721. This further period was generally thirty-nine years making ninety-nine in all, but for the area to the east of Davies Street an eighty-year term overall was more usual, the ninety-nine-year lease to Thomas Barlow of a large plot on the south side of Grosvenor Street to which he was entitled under the building agreement referred to above being the one notable exception.[20] Barlow, himself, granted only one sub-lease for a longer term than eighty years and several, chiefly of plots for stables, were for sixty or less,[21] the reversionary term under his direct Grosvenor lease eventually considerably enhancing the value of his estate (see page 19).

Although no leases of the western part of The Hundred Acres, which was held by Dame Mary Grosvenor in fee simple, were granted until 1727, builders were interested in staking a claim in this territory as soon as the development of the estate got under way.[22] Accordingly a petition was presented to Chancery in 1721 asking that Robert Myddelton of Chirk Castle in Denbighshire, who was then the legal guardian of Dame Mary Grosvenor, should be empowered to grant leases of this land for up to ninety-nine years. The necessity for such a term was explained by 'the intended buildings being very large'. The request was granted, subject, however, to the approval of each lease by the Master in Chancery who administered the revenues from Dame Mary's estates—a costly and time-consuming procedure.[23] The laying out of Grosvenor Square, the site of which included part of Dame Mary's lands, made the matter urgent, and after more abortive approaches to Chancery another Act of Parliament was obtained in 1726 by which Myddelton (or any subsequent guardian) acquired power to grant ninety-nine-year leases, the consent only of Dame Mary's heir apparent being required.[24]

Myddelton was a party to all the agreements and leases concluded while Dame Mary Grosvenor was still alive. In leases of the land in which she held only a life interest Sir Richard Grosvenor was the grantor or first party and Myddelton the second, the latter nominally consenting to the transaction on behalf of Dame Mary; but in leases of the fee-simple land, Myddelton was the first party with Sir Richard Grosvenor as consenting party. The precise niceties of the correct order were not always followed in agreements, which did not have the same long-term legal force as leases.

Dame Mary Grosvenor died in January 1730 and within a few months Sir Richard Grosvenor had taken steps to simplify the whole tenure of the estate by means of the legal device of a common recovery which abolished the entail imposed in the settlement of 1694.[25] He now held all the London estates in fee simple, but in his will he established a new entail by bequeathing his property to his next brother Thomas and his male heirs in order of birth, and failing issue in that line, to his youngest brother Robert and his male heirs likewise.[26] It was not until 1755 that Sir Richard (later first Earl) Grosvenor, who had recently succeeded to the estate, abolished this entail by similar legal means.[27] For the rest of the eighteenth century encumbrances on the title to the estate did not arise through complexities of tenure but were monetary, eventually leading to the establishment of a trust whereby the control of the estate was taken out of Lord Grosvenor's sole charge (see page 37).

The peculiar circumstances that over several years the revenues from Dame Mary Grosvenor's estates, after expenses and allowances, had been 'frozen' in the Court of Chancery enabled the Grosvenors to aid the development of their Mayfair lands in a practical manner. By 1721 £8,490 was held in Chancery besides any interest which might have accrued on this sum.[28] Although they had some difficulty in freeing this money, as several Chancery petitions testify, the Grosvenors were eventually able to use it (and a good deal more) in a series of measures designed to assist the builders who took land on their estate.

Until Sir Richard Grosvenor's death the sewers which were laid under most of the new streets were built at his initial cost, the money being recovered from lessees on the granting of their leases, usually at the rate of six shillings per foot frontage for those plots which fronted on to the streets under which the sewers lay.[29] The sewers drained into 'the Great Sewer called Aybrooke' and were at first constructed without the leave of the Westminster Commission of Sewers. It was not until 1726 that the Commissioners discovered this, but they then gave permission for the work to be continued on payment of a lump sum of £204 (computed at £2 per acre on 102 acres) to the Commission.[30] Cash books among the Grosvenor records contain a day by day account of income and expenditure on the London estates beginning in 1729; these include several payments 'for sewering' to building tradesmen who also worked on the houses being erected. George Barlow, John Barnes and Thomas Hipsley, bricklayers, Lawrence Neale, carpenter, and Stephen Whitaker, brickmaker, 'on account of digging work', were paid some £300 between them for such work in 1729.[31] In the later years of the development, however, the building agreements suggest that the construction of sewers was often undertaken by the developers rather than the ground landlord.[32]

Although under the terms of agreements and leases road-making was the responsibility of undertakers and their lessees, some stable yards which formed the boundary between blocks of land taken under building agreements were laid out at the Grosvenors' expense, the money being recovered, as in the case of sewers, from lessees according to the footage of their plots abutting on the yard.[33] John Mist, paviour, was paid for 'paving the stable yard between Grosvenor Street and Brook Street with the horsepond and way leading thereto'.[31] The majority of mews, however, lay completely within large areas developed under one agreement and were not, therefore, made at the Grosvenors' cost.

Apart from the expense of the sewers, the principal capital cost met by the Grosvenor family and retrieved later, where possible, from builders, was in the laying out of Grosvenor Square. By an agreement of June 1725[34] between Sir Richard Grosvenor and the various building tradesmen and others who were already in possession of the land fronting on to the square under building agreements, Sir Richard undertook to lay out the square garden* and surround it with a brick wall topped by a wooden fence, access being provided through four iron gates. In the centre of the enclosure was to be a gilded equestrian statue of George I (by John Nost). The cost of the garden (£350) and the statue (£262 10s.) was specified and rates for the other work set out. The signatories agreed to repay Sir Richard's costs within one month of the work being completed, the sum due from each being determined by the extent of his frontage to the square. An initial rate of 20s. per foot frontage was assessed, but later Sir Richard also met the cost of paving the square around the oval enclosure and a final payment of 40s. 9d. per foot frontage was eventually sought, not always successfully, from the building lessees of the houses in the square.[36]

The sums laid out by the Grosvenors in these ways were in effect interest-free loans (not always repaid) which were designed to advance the progress of development. Another and more important method of achieving

---

* The work was to be done by one of his own tenants, John Alston, a gardener from Pimlico, who also provided the design for the garden layout.[35]

this object was by the granting of mortgages. An Order in Chancery of October 1722 required the Master to whom the administration of Dame Mary Grosvenor's finances had been entrusted, John Borrett, to provide mortgages at 5 per cent interest to builders approved by Sir Richard Grosvenor, his brothers and sister and Robert Myddelton. The first such loans were made in December 1722 for various amounts, generally between £400 and £600.[37] Borrett died shortly afterwards and some difficulties being encountered in securing the co-operation of his successor as Master in Chancery, permission was granted for Richard Andrews, the Grosvenors' London agent, to execute mortgages in his own name.[38] Between 1726 and 1729 Andrews lent £11,800, mostly to builders working in and around Grosvenor Square, in a series of transactions which have been preserved among the estate records.[39] Although he appears also to have been lending money on his own account, the survival of these records suggests that he was here acting as trustee for the Grosvenors. When Dame Mary Grosvenor died in 1730 an account was drawn up of her personal estate in which were itemized the various sums owing to her on mortgages to builders. Several correspond with the amounts advanced in Andrews' name and they totalled in all £9,450 (some of the principal no doubt having been repaid).[40]

The Grosvenors took a particularly direct concern in the building of Grosvenor Square, no doubt regarding its successful prosecution as the key to the progress of the whole enterprise. As already indicated, Robert Grosvenor was the head lessee for most of the south side and several of the mortgages referred to above were granted to builders who had sub-leases from him. He also apparently had one house built directly (No. 42), which he sold to the master builder Benjamin Timbrell in 1731.[41] He also assisted in the building of the important east side, which was developed uniformly by another master builder, John Simmons, by purchasing improved ground rents from Simmons while the building operations were still in progress. Between 1731 and 1733 he provided over £2,000 in this manner towards the completion of four houses, including the large centre house with a seventy-foot frontage.[42] Robert Grosvenor was also prepared to intervene elsewhere to bail out builders who found themselves in difficulties,[43] and after he succeeded to the baronetcy in 1733 he continued the policy of providing mortgages; at his death in 1755 he was owed £7,700 by builders (including £1,700 by Elizabeth Simmons, the widow of John Simmons).[44]

A less direct but probably equally valuable way of assisting builders was by allowing arrears of ground rent to accumulate. Sometimes quite substantial sums were involved. At Christmas 1731 £3,600 was owing, but Lady Day appears to have been the quarter day on which most accounts were settled, and the arrears at the end of that quarter are therefore probably more significant, the highest such total—£2,595—being at Lady Day 1732. At Sir Richard Grosvenor's death shortly afterwards the debt amounted to £2,988 and some attempt was made to clear this, but £1,239 remained outstanding and was probably never recovered.[45] In 1733 (on the succession of Sir Robert Grosvenor) a new account was begun, but arrears continued to mount up and by Lady Day 1744 totalled £2,060.[46] This was reduced in succeeding years, and on the succession of Sir Richard (later first Earl) Grosvenor in 1755 the practice of allowing rent to stand uncollected for long periods was discontinued.[47] Although evidence about the administration of the estate in these years is scanty, there is no indication that builders were hounded for back rent, and a willingness on the part of the Grosvenors to condone such casualness in the payment of rent must have helped builders to maintain an essential cash flow, particularly in the early years.

A measure of the extent to which the development of its estate was fostered by the Grosvenor family is shown in the previously cited account of Dame Mary Grosvenor's personal estate drawn up after her death in January 1730. Besides the £9,450 due on mortgages granted to builders, £12,000 was owed on a mortgage by Sir Richard Grosvenor (not necessarily, of course, used to promote the development) and £2,000 similarly by Robert Grosvenor. A further item was a debt of £4,747 due from Sir Richard Grosvenor 'to make good to the Personal Estate all such Sums of Money as have been disburst thereout to Carry on the new buildings, more than has been received from those buildings'.[40]

The Estate Agent

Little is known about the background of Richard Andrews, who was variously described as the agent, steward or 'receiver of the rents' for the Grosvenors' London estates when building began in Mayfair in 1720. He was then living 'next door to the blew Boar' in Great Russell Street, St. Giles-in-the-Fields,[48] and had first been employed as steward by Dame Mary Grosvenor in 1700, when he was some thirty-five years old.[49] In 1706 he was dismissed for alleged malpractice but was reinstated again in 1716 largely as the result of entreaties by Anne Grosvenor, Sir Richard's sister.[50] By 1730 his salary was £80 per annum and he also had an assistant, his second son Robert, at £50 per annum.[51] Robert Andrews was a member of the Inner Temple, being admitted in January 1725 when he was about twenty years old,[52] and he practised as a solicitor. He not only acted as London agent for the Grosvenors but also conducted the family's legal business in the capital.[53] No doubt partly because of his professional position Robert Andrews took a more considerable role in the management of the estate than his father, even before the latter's death in 1734 or 1735. He lived in a house in Grosvenor Street (No. 10, now demolished) from 1730,[54] and was also involved in parish affairs. He acted as attorney for the Vestry of St. George's, Hanover Square, between 1736 and 1744 and was a Vestryman from 1741.[55] In 1763, the year of his death, he was still acting as London agent for the first Baron (later first Earl) Grosvenor.

A brief hiatus occurred, however, in the long steward-ship of the Andrews family on the death of Sir Richard Grosvenor, the fourth baronet, in July 1732, when, as indicated earlier, his successor Sir Thomas Grosvenor wished to put his own man in charge. His agent was Robert Barbor, a contemporary of Robert Andrews at the Inner Temple, but the Andrewses refused to give Barbor the books and papers necessary to run the estate. Sir Thomas brought an action in the Court of Exchequer to force them to hand over the documents, but he died in Naples in February 1733, probably before the case had come to a decision. The Andrewses always had the confidence of Robert Grosvenor, now sixth baronet, and Barbor dropped out of the picture. He submitted a bill for services rendered to the late Sir Thomas, but he was probably little involved in the affairs of the estate.[56]

Both Richard and Robert Andrews were more directly involved in the development of the estate than their positions as agent would seem to warrant. Both took areas of the estate under building agreements and leases and proceeded to develop them as independent speculators by granting sub-leases to builders.[57] Robert Andrews, in particular, secured some handsome profits in improved ground rents:* for instance he obtained over £130 per annum from one large plot which he held under a direct Grosvenor lease, and £120 from another.[58] He was also concerned with others in the building of the Grosvenor Chapel in South Audley Street, eventually becoming its sole proprietor.[59] Both he and his father lent money to builders on mortgage,[60] but it is not always possible to distinguish those occasions in which they were advancing their own capital from those in which they were acting for the Grosvenors. The possible conflict between the Andrewses' role as agents (and trustees) negotiating with other developers and builders, especially after 1730 when there was no estate surveyor, and their activities as speculators profiting from the development them-selves, did not seem to concern either themselves or the Grosvenors (with the possible exception of Sir Thomas Grosvenor, who, among other charges in the case brought against them in the Exchequer, alleged that they owed money in ground rents).[8]

Certainly Robert Andrews was a successful, and, by whatever means, a relatively wealthy man at the time of his death in 1763. His salary from the Grosvenor family was then £150 per annum,[61] but, besides his solicitor's business, he also held a post in the Excise Office and was the lessee of some revenues of the Duchy of Cornwall called the Post Groats, worth £400 per annum. Besides his residence in Grosvenor Street he also had a house

in Acton, and his estate and effects were valued at £18,000.[62]

One of Robert Andrews' executors was his son-in-law and successor as the Grosvenors' London agent, Thomas Walley Partington, also a solicitor. Andrews' will estab-lished very complicated trusts, and the difficulty in carry-ing these out led to a case in Chancery in 1789, Andrews v. Partington,[63] in which certain legal principles were laid down on how long the number of persons eligible to claim a share in a settlement (in this case the number of Robert Andrews' grandchildren) could remain uncertain. The problem arose because Andrews' son, the Reverend Robert Andrews, had twelve surviving children at that time and claimed that he might have still more. The decision in Andrews v. Partington that a numerically open class of beneficiaries normally closes when the first member becomes entitled to claim his share (in this instance when the first grandchild reached the age of twenty-one) constituted an important legal precedent.[64]

Thomas Walley Partington, who was born in 1730, came from a prominent Chester family.[65] His father, Edward Partington, was an attorney who acted for the Grosvenors in that city.[66] Thomas Walley was admitted as a student to the Inner Temple in 1746[67] and in 1750 he was working as a clerk to Elisha Biscoe, a solicitor whose clients included a number of builders on the Grosvenor estate.[68] By 1753 he was associated with Andrews[69] and in the following year he married the latter's daughter, Elizabeth.[70] From 1757 he occupied a house in Brook Street and shortly afterwards also took over an adjoining house (the joint plot, later numbered 55, being on the site of Claridge's Hotel).[71] At the time of his death in 1791 he also had houses in Shepherd Street (probably the modern Dering Street near Hanover Square) and at Offham in Sussex. He does not appear to have been as directly involved in the development of the estate as his predecessors, but like Robert Andrews he had achieved relative prosperity when he died. According to the terms of his will his personal estate alone was worth at least £20,000.[72]

By 1779 Partington had formed a partnership with Edward Boodle,[73] who had at one time probably been his assistant (an Edward Boodle witnessed a Grosvenor estate deed in 1767).[74] After Partington's death Boodle became the London solicitor for the Grosvenors and occupied the premises in Brook Street which had been Partington's (they are entered in the ratebooks in 1789–91 as Partington and Boodle's).[71] The firm of Partington and Boodle, which became Boodle Hatfield and Company at the end of the nineteenth century, continued to occupy premises on the estate, in Brook Street until 1836 and then at No. 53 Davies Street, where its present offices are situated.[75] Thus a remarkable degree of continuity can be traced from Richard Andrews, who was appointed

---

* I.e., the difference between the total rent which he obtained by his sub-leases to builders and the rent which he had to pay to the ground landlord under his head lease.

receiver of the rents for Dame Mary Grosvenor's estates in Middlesex in 1700, to Messrs. Boodle Hatfield and Company, who are solicitors to the Grosvenor Estate at the present day.

The Estate Surveyor

Thomas Barlow, who was the estate surveyor when building commenced, was a carpenter by trade. Little has heretofore been known about Barlow but he emerges as one of the most important master builders working in west London in the early eighteenth century. The earliest known reference to his building work is in a deed of 1701 concerning a house, probably built by him, in Albemarle Street,[76] and he was also the builder of other houses in that vicinity.[77] His address at that time was in Maiden Lane, in Covent Garden,[78] where he was the building lessee of houses in Southampton Street in 1708 and undertook repairs to St. Paul's Church in 1714-15.[79] In 1715, however, he appears in a more significant role as 'agent' for Lord Scarbrough in negotiations with the 'Fifty Churches' Commissioners over the siting of a church near Hanover Square.[80] In view of Barlow's later position on the Grosvenor estate and the fact that Lord Scarbrough was the promoter of the development of the Hanover Square area[81] there must at least be a possibility that Barlow was responsible for the layout of that development. He was certainly deeply involved in the building operations there and appears to have been the builder of several of the houses with a distinctively Baroque appearance in St. George Street.[82] He was at one time owner of the freehold of the site of St. George's Church, but conveyed the ground to General William Steuart who in turn gave it gratis to the Commissioners.[83] Barlow was also active in the development of the Conduit Mead estate and built himself a house in New Bond Street where he lived until his death.[84] Barlow Place (formerly Mews) off Bruton Street is named after him.[85]

In a petition addressed to the Lord Chancellor Sir Richard Grosvenor stated that he had appointed Barlow on 10 August 1720 'to Lett Severall Feilds or Closes... to build upon' and that 'a Scheme or Plann of the Said Intended Building has been Drawn by the said Barlow'.[86] The purpose of this petition was to enable money to be freed from Dame Mary Grosvenor's account in Chancery in order to build sewers and to pay Barlow's expenses and salary. He was to receive £50 for the initial work he had undertaken and then £50 per annum 'besides his Reasonable Expences' (which generally amounted to £10 per annum).[87] He continued to act as estate surveyor until his death in January 1730,[88] but to what extent he exercised control over the operations of builders is difficult to determine. In one building agreement for a plot on the south side of Grosvenor Street and the south-east corner of Grosvenor Square it was stated that 'all and every of the houses which shall be built on ye said piece of Ground fronting Grosvenor Street aforesaid shall be built so as to range in their fronts in such manner as Mr Thos. Barlow the present Surveyor of the said Lunatick's Estate, or other the Surveyor or Surveyors... for the time being shall hereafter direct and appoint',[89] but this was an unusually explicit reference to Barlow, perhaps because the south side of Grosvenor Square was to be set back from the line of Grosvenor Street. As the author of the layout he appears to have been responsible for staking out plots on the ground and making some adjustments when building was under way, even correcting a 'grand mistake' in one instance.[90] The fact that several early leases were witnessed by the master of the Mount Coffee House (on the site of the present No. 80 Grosvenor Street), which was built by Barlow and was one of the earliest buildings on the estate to be completed (by November 1721), suggests that negotiations with builders may well have been conducted in that establishment.[91] One of Barlow's functions was the assessment of the value of houses in order that money held in Chancery could be made available to their builders on mortgage.[37] In general, however, neither the wording of agreements and leases, nor the surviving visual evidence suggest that Barlow exercised a very firm control over building operations, and when he died in 1730 it was not considered necessary to appoint a successor. Robert Andrews took over some of his functions and the post of estate surveyor remained vacant until the 1780's, when the assessment of fines on the renewal of leases posed new problems which led to the employment of William Porden.

Like Richard and Robert Andrews, Barlow was also directly concerned in the development. He was the recipient of the first building agreement (dated 8 August 1720, two days before his official appointment) covering the area bounded on the north by Grosvenor Street, on the west by Davies Street, and on the south and east by the boundaries of the estate (no. 1 on plan A in the end pocket), and he subsequently held all this land under one lease granted in July 1721. For this he paid the very low ground rent of £67 per annum, or 2s. per foot frontage calculated on the frontage to Grosvenor Street only.[92] Within this area he built the Mount Coffee House and No. 75 Grosvenor Street (both now rebuilt) and some coach-houses and stables in Grosvenor Mews, developing the rest of his land by sub-leases to other builders or occupiers. In improved ground rents alone he obtained a profit of £280 per annum on this sub-development, which was substantially complete by the time of his death.[93]* He also took other parts of the estate under building agreements, including (jointly with Robert Andrews) the area bounded by Upper Brook Street on the south, Park Street on the west, North Row on the north and North Audley Street on the east (no. 55 on

---

* For the subsequent rise in value of this large leasehold plot see page 19.

plan A), the largest plot to be covered by a single agreement.[94] Building here had, however, hardly begun before his death.

Barlow was one of the founder-directors of the Westminster Fire Office in 1717[95] and was also one of the initial Vestrymen of the parish of St. George, Hanover Square, chosen by the 'Fifty Churches' Commissioners in 1725.[96] On his death in January 1730 he was described as 'a very noted Master-Builder'.[88] In a complaint brought in Chancery by his descendants against one of his executors it was stated that he left a leasehold estate which brought in about £600 per annum in ground rents and £400 in rack rents, several freehold houses and a personal estate of upwards of £1,000.[97] While there may have been some exaggeration in these figures there is little doubt that Barlow's career as a builder had been eminently successful. He left the bulk of his estate to his son, Richard, who died in 1740 'haveing greatly wasted and outrun his fortune'.[98]

The Layout

There was nothing remarkable about the terrain of The Hundred Acres either to pose difficulties or create opportunities for Barlow in devising his layout. The ground sloped gently from a high point in the north-west corner to the valley of the Tyburn in the east, the lowest level being in the south-east corner. The only topographical feature of any note was the remnant of one of the fortifications erected during the Civil War and known by the eighteenth century as Oliver's Mount.[99] Probably by then little more than a raised earthwork, it was, however, sufficiently recognisable to give its name to Mount Field and subsequently to Mount Street, Mount Row and the Mount Coffee House, and the development which began in 1720 was often referred to initially as 'the new buildings about Oliver's Mount'. So completely was it obliterated in the course of building that its exact location is difficult to pinpoint, but the evidence of a map of 1717 and some vague references in documents suggest that it stood near the junction of Mount Row and Carpenter Street, where a public house called Oliver's Mount was established.[100]

Barlow's layout of the Mayfair estate is an exercise in disciplined, straightforward town planning—a grid of wide, straight streets with a grand *place* in the centre—which makes no concession at all to the irregular boundaries of the land. The positioning of the main east-west streets, and consequently of the square which lies between them, links up with the layout of the Hanover Square area. Brook Street and Upper Brook Street are direct continuations of that part of Brook Street which joins the south side of Hanover Square, while Grosvenor Street and Upper Grosvenor Street are aligned with the axis of St. George's Church (which had, however, not been built although its site had been determined upon when the Grosvenor estate layout scheme was made). In Brook

Street Sir Richard Grosvenor had to take leases of land in Conduit Mead, which lay between his estate and the Hanover Square estate, and enter into agreements with builders there—in one instance allowing a builder to have land on his estate on especially favourable terms—in order to prevent them building across the proposed line of Brook Street and thus blocking up this important line of communication with older established parts of the West End.[101] The reason for the positioning of Grosvenor Street is less obvious. Barlow knew that the street could not be extended as far as St. George's Church in order to provide a monumental 'vista-stopper', for the course of the narrow Maddox Street, which was to skirt the north side of the church, had been decided by 1718, and frontages to the street west of its intersection with St. George Street were being developed by the following year.[102] It is possible, though highly unlikely, that Barlow foresaw that the steeple of the church (the design of which had not even been decided) would provide an effective terminal point to the view down Grosvenor Street from the west, but, more prosaically, it may be that he simply chose a convenient position for the street parallel with Brook Street. From the wording of his own building agreement of August 1720 Barlow originally anticipated that Grosvenor Street would be extended as a sixty-foot-wide road as far as New Bond Street,[16] but in the event the street narrows at the eastern boundary of the estate. This awkward transition is effected by bringing forward the frontage of No. 80 Grosvenor Street where Barlow originally built the Mount Coffee House.

There are several references in documents to a grand plan in which the layout was expressed,[103] but this does not appear to have survived. A small sketch plan is folded loosely in a notebook in which Robert Andrews kept a brief record of agreements and leases:[104] several comments are written on it and it may have been a working copy of the grand plan. It is somewhat misleading, however, as a record of the intended layout, for it seems that some streets were added to the sketch plan at a date later than the original drawing. The best record of the layout as originally planned is the map of the whole of the Grosvenors' London property drawn in 1723 by John Mackay,[105] which shows Mayfair as set out for building (Plate 1). This part of the map has the measurement of foot frontages inscribed, suggesting that it may have been taken from Barlow's grand plan, and at the foot of the map the area is described as 'Grosvenor Buildings or the Fields Commonly called Oliver's Mount Fields; being Partly built and a Square And Eleven Principal Streets designed As per Plan...'. Few mews are shown, except in the area developed by Barlow himself, and the sites of these were probably worked out in the course of development. The evidence of this map suggests that alterations in the layout were made as building proceeded, particularly in the western part of the area. More streets were formed than originally intended, including Green Street, and the site of the projected chapel was altered. That some of these changes were variations from the initial scheme is confirmed by documentary evidence.[106]

The extent of The Hundred Acres enabled Barlow to plan on a lavish scale. Grosvenor Square itself measures 680 feet × 530 feet between the building lines and covers over eight acres, its spaciousness increased by setting the houses in the square thirty feet back from the frontages of the streets leading into it (a device also used in Hanover Square, but not in Cavendish Square). The main east–west streets—Grosvenor Street and Upper Grosvenor Street, Brook Street and Upper Brook Street—were intended to be sixty feet wide and most of the remaining streets fifty feet. Even the mews were spacious, an impression now enhanced by the relatively recent widening of their entrances, which were originally left deliberately narrow to make the stable yards less obtrusive. Long, straight, unbroken lines of terrace frontage, so favoured by the early Georgians, abound, and would have been even more extensive if the original layout scheme had been scrupulously followed.

The Course of Development

The translation of Barlow's plan into the realities of bricks and mortar took over half a century to complete. The last leases, for sites in the north-west corner of the estate, were not granted until 1777,[107] by which time it was necessary to consider renewals of the earliest leases. The progression of the development was generally, and logically, from east to west, but the pace was by no means even. On the rudimentary evidence of the dating of estate leases (some leases being of large plots which were sub-let in smaller sites) there was considerable building activity throughout the 1720's, with 1725 and 1728 as the peak years, a slow-down from 1733 to 1735, a new surge to another peak in 1740, a considerable decline throughout the 1740's and early 1750's (only six leases were granted between 1741 and 1755), and a gradual development of the remaining unbuilt land over the next twenty or so years. The marked reluctance of builders to take sites near the north end of Park Lane and the western end of Oxford Street was probably due to the proximity of Tyburn gallows, situated at the present junction of Edgware Road and Bayswater Road, where public executions attended by vast and tumultuous crowds continued until 1783.

In general the frontages to Oxford Street and Park Lane were not regarded with any favour by either the officers of the estate or by builders. The whole development was at first noticeably turned inwards towards Grosvenor Square and away from the extremities of the estate, with the exception of the eastern boundary where it was clearly desirable to link up with existing streets. Although areas on the north side of Brook Street and

Grosvenor Square extending as far as Oxford Street were taken under building agreements as early as 1723–5, the completion of buildings along the frontage to Oxford Street was in some cases delayed for over thirty years.[108]

In 1766 John Gwynn remarked disparagingly on 'that heap of buildings lately erected from Oxford-Road to Hyde Park Corner, whose back-fronts are seen from the Park'.[109] The wording of early building agreements for ground at the western edge of the estate suggests that this orientation was a matter of deliberate policy (although the layout shown on Mackay's map envisages buildings along the Park Lane frontage). Under these agreements ground rents were to be calculated by the extent of frontage along Park Street, and while it was usual to include provisions against the siting of coach-houses and stables along that street or in any of the main east–west streets, no such restriction applied to Park Lane.[110] In fact stabling was built there on a site now occupied by part of Grosvenor House.[111] One short terrace of houses facing the park called King's Row was built in the 1730's (on the site of the present Nos. 93–99)[112] but it was set back from Park Lane and quickly shielded from the road by a screen of trees (Plate 13a, b). Even in the 1750's when Norfolk (now Dunraven) Street was laid out the houses were built with their back elevations overlooking the park and their garden walls forming the Park Lane frontage (Plate 19b, c). In 1791 William Porden, the estate surveyor, remarked on the opportunity lost 'in originally laying out the ground of making a handsome front towards Hyde Park',[113] and it is not clear why Park Lane was so ostracized. Certainly in the nineteenth century it was a very busy road and was originally quite narrow: some stretches were widened in the course of building on adjacent land.[114] The park was concealed by a brick wall which was not entirely replaced by iron railings until 1828,[115] and, although a gate was provided at the cost of Sir Richard Grosvenor for the benefit of his tenants (Grosvenor Gate),[116] the prospect from ground level at least could not have been very attractive.

Building Agreements

Over the long period which was required to cover The Hundred Acres with buildings some ninety-three or more pre-lease building agreements were concluded with prospective undertakers,* the vast majority of whom were building tradesmen. The originals or counterparts of ninety of these agreements have survived among the Grosvenor Estate records, and the existence of three others is recorded although the documents themselves are lost.[117] There are a few plots for which no agreements have been found, but in at least two instances it is likely that no agreements were made before leases were granted —a frontage to Oxford Street taken by a brickmaker in

---

* The term undertaker is here used to mean someone who undertakes the development of a parcel of land under a building agreement.

exchange for an existing lease of a brickfield there, and 185 feet on the south side of Grosvenor Square leased to Robert Grosvenor.[118] The areas taken under building agreements are shown on plan A in the end pocket. They varied from single house sites to large plots covering several acres, the biggest being that taken by Thomas Barlow and Robert Andrews in 1725 (no. 55 on plan A). In most cases the agreements were made some considerable time before leases were granted of the land covered by them, and as soon as they had been signed they became negotiable documents. In 1728, for instance, Robert Grosvenor bought an existing agreement for a plot on the west side of Park Street (no. 61 on plan A) for thirty guineas 'and divers other good Causes and valuable Considerations',[119] and the houses subsequently built there became part of his trust estate. In a few instances agreements were surrendered and replaced later by others, but in most cases where the original undertaker was unable to fulfil his contract the benefit of his agreement was assigned to someone else.

Although the agreements do not follow a standard form they are generally similar in wording and indicate, at least on paper, a marked degree of laxity in the control of building operations. Under them Sir Richard Grosvenor or his successors (or in some cases Robert Myddelton, for the reasons indicated earlier) agreed to grant a lease or leases of the ground when building had reached a certain stage. This was usually expressed as within forty days of the first and second floors of the house or houses being laid, or within forty days of tiling-in. Sometimes it was specified that the street before the front of the house(s) should be levelled and paved to the middle before leases were granted, but more specific paving clauses were contained later in the documents.

When the ground taken included a frontage to a stable yard a stipulation was usually made that future lessees were to be granted the right of use of the stable yard and the horse pond, watering place, pump, water and dung place to be made available there on paying to the ground landlord a share of the costs of making the yard and its appurtenances proportionate to the amount of foot frontage to the yard. This requirement was invariably repeated later in the document, perhaps to emphasise the responsibility of the undertaker to ensure that such costs were met, and lessees were also required to pay their share of keeping the mews in repair on the same basis of assessment. Most stable yards were, however, situated entirely within the limits of the areas taken and in the majority of these cases no reference was made to them in agreements, the provision of mews presumably being at the cost (and possibly also the discretion) of the undertaker. Clauses relating to the use of such yards were, however, often inserted in leases, specifying that the lessee was to pay his share of the cost of making the mews, but not to whom the cost was to be paid.[120]

Clauses specified the term of years for which leases were to be granted and the ground rent payable for the whole ground taken under each agreement. These ground rents are discussed in detail on pages 17–19. As stated earlier, the leasehold terms not only varied from one agreement to another but were sometimes exceeded when leases were granted; and little attempt was made to provide a common starting or ending date for such terms, even at the beginning of the development. Under the first agreement of all the terms were calculated from Lady Day 1721, but the second and several subsequent contracts merely stipulated that they were to begin on the last quarter day before the date of each lease. From time to time, notably in the 1730's and in the 1750's, attempts were made to achieve some degree of uniformity in the dates on which leases would fall in, but the long delay before the development was completed nullified such efforts, and the last leases granted did not expire until 1864,[121] over sixty years later than the earliest ones.

Besides his ground rent each lessee was, in almost every instance, required to pay an extra rent if he allowed his premises to be used for certain noxious trades. This extra rent was usually fixed at £30 in the main streets, but was sometimes only £10 in the lesser ones, such as Mount Street. The list of such trades varied, being generally longer for plots fronting on to the principal streets, but some of the variations appear to have been arbitrary, and some leases contained longer or shorter lists than their parent agreements.[122] The most commonly restricted trades were:—butcher (both shop and slaughter-house), tallow chandler, soapmaker, tobacco-pipe maker, brewer, victualler, coffee-house proprietor, distiller, farrier, pewterer, working brazier and blacksmith. Occasionally in later agreements sugar baker and glassmaker were added, and in the leases of No. 88 Brook Street, No. 9 Grosvenor Square and a plot in Duke Street the occupations of roasting cook, boiling cook, silk dyer, hatmaker and 'scowerer of cloths' were also discouraged in this way.[123] More usually trades were omitted from the list, either in agreements or individual leases, particularly those of butcher (although slaughter-houses were generally still included), victualler, coffee-house keeper, farrier, pewterer, brazier and blacksmith. In some of the extensive back land of large plots only a common brewer or a melter of tallow was required to pay the increased rent.[124] However, in the whole area fronting north on Grosvenor Street and west on Davies Street, which was taken by the estate surveyor, Thomas Barlow, at the beginning of the development, no trades at all were restricted.[92]

The assumption implicit in this general policy was, evidently, that the extra rent would be a sufficient deterrent to the establishment of undesirable trades. The Grosvenors could hardly have been satisfied with the relatively insignificant additions to their income as compensation for the damaging effects of some of these trades if they had been conducted near to expensive houses. A tallow chandler was unlikely to prove a satisfactory neighbour for an earl or a marquis. A similar device had been used when building leases of Alexander

Davies's land at Millbank were granted in 1663 but there the penalty for noxious trades had been assessed at £200 per annum,[125] a sum more likely to discourage would-be practitioners of undesirable arts. In the eighteenth century, however, in this as in so many other matters on the estate, much seems to have been left to the good sense of builders and future tenants.

The agreements also stipulated that all leases were to contain 'Common usuall and necessary Covenants', a remarkably vague phrase to cover a crucial area of estate management, embellished in the first agreement to read, 'such common and reasonable Covenants and Agreements as are usually contained in Leases of Houses in London'. No doubt builders knew what to expect and the leases were somewhat more explicit (see below).

Although the clauses relating to the actual building operations varied in detail from document to document they followed in essentials a formula worked out in several early agreements. By this the undertaker was at his own costs within eighteen months to build, tile in and enclose on the ground floors (i.e., put in the doors, windows and internal shutters), or cause to be built, on the front of his plot, a good and substantial brick dwelling house or houses to range uniform in the fronts (i.e., follow a common building line with adjoining houses). Within twenty-four months he was to finish the house or houses and back buildings, put up good iron rails before the front and posts in the street, and do the rough and smooth paving work in the street. The work was to be completed 'as fully and amply in every Respect as if all the Particulars for Building had been herein expressly mencioned and Sett Down'. He was also to make the stables and back buildings as low as they conveniently could be and cover them with slate. The time allowed for completion was often varied, Barlow for instance being simply enjoined to proceed 'with all convenient speed', and was, in any case, rarely adhered to.[126] In some instances where agreements covered ground with more than one street frontage the undertaker was only required to build houses on the principal frontages, while other brick buildings, or brick walls where there were no buildings, sufficed for the other fronts (including Park Lane, as stated earlier).[127] In later agreements the type of paving to be used was more clearly indicated: footways up to the posts separating them from the roadways were to be laid with Purbeck stone, and the roadways before each plot with good rag or other paving stones to the middle.

What is perhaps most remarkable about these building requirements is their lack of precision, even by the relatively lax standards of the day.* In the absence of any further contracts (and the only others that have been found are between the principal undertakers and other builders taking plots from them or between builders and prospective purchasers) these agreements seemingly provided the only form of control in writing which the landlord and his officers had over the buildings to be erected on the estate. All that could be ensured under them was that a house would be of brick, would adhere to a uniform building line with its terrace neighbours, and being 'good and substantial' would presumably not fall down. Of course, it was also supposed to conform to the London Building Acts of 1707 and 1709 which required certain standards of construction, chiefly in order to prevent the spread of fires.† In only two instances was the amount of money to be spent on building specified—both, surprisingly, in Mount Street, where one undertaker was required to expend £300 within two years and another £200 within twelve months in erecting buildings 'for dwelling in'.[129] Under some agreements for Brook Street the houses to be built were required to be 'large'[130] while in Grosvenor Square (where the agreements tended to be slightly more comprehensive and will be discussed more fully below) it was sometimes stipulated that houses were to be not less than thirty feet wide by thirty feet deep. In general, however, throughout the long course of the whole development it was not considered necessary to modify substantially the terminology first employed, and the last agreement made in 1765 was hardly more explicit than those of 1720.

The undertaker had to guarantee that the leases offered by the ground landlord would be accepted, and on the execution of his lease, the lessee was to pay for the use of any sewer built in front of his plot, usually at the rate of six shillings per foot. At first this sum was paid to Sir Richard Grosvenor, but after his death in 1732 it was more usual to specify that the money was to be paid to whomsoever was entitled to receive it, and the phrase 'if he [the undertaker] doesn't build same' was occasionally inserted.[131] It was also usually stated in early agreements that a separate lease was to be granted of each house built, but this was often ignored and it became common practice to let large areas of ground under one lease after the total ground rent to be obtained from any particular plot had been secured by leases already granted, and in some cases even before.

The final clause in all but a handful of agreements required all disputes between the parties concerned, or between one builder and another, to be submitted to three named referees, or any two of them. Any decision made by them was to be accepted and obeyed within forty days. Exactly how this proviso worked out in practice is not known, but it may have made up for some of the deficiencies in the earlier clauses. In theory, at least, if the Grosvenors or their estate officers were not satisfied

---

* A model agreement of 1724 for developing the Cavendish-Harley estate in St. Marylebone, although also couched in general terms, contains more detailed provisions relating to the building work including the types of materials to be used; and an agreement of 1711 for building on the Bedford estate in Covent Garden also specified the storey heights and timber scantlings to be employed.[128]

† But the Acts were not always scrupulously observed, e.g. No. 72 Park Street where in the first three storeys the window frames are not set back the requisite four inches from the front of the reveals.

with the way building operations were being conducted they could submit a complaint to this panel of arbitrators. Unfortunately no record has survived of the way in which this procedure operated in practice—if it did at all—but it may be significant that provision for it was still being made in the last agreements concluded. One agreement stipulated that the parties concerned should act upon any decisions made in this manner 'without having recourse to Law or Equity',[132] and behind the employment of this device there may have been a desire to prevent the protracted lawsuits which so often arose in the course of building operations.

The referees who were chosen to adjudicate on disputes included some of the best-known architects and building tradesmen of the time. For agreements made between 1720 and April 1724 they were almost invariably Nicholas Dubois, James Gibbs and Thomas Barlow, although there is no indication that Dubois or Gibbs were in any other way connected with the development of the estate. Until his death in 1730 Barlow was always a member of the panel. Others who served as referees were Edward Bussey junior, surveyor; Benjamin Timbrell, carpenter; Joseph Stallwood, bricklayer; Edward Shepherd; Colen Campbell (for the last four agreements dated before his death in 1729); John James; — Barton, surveyor; Thomas Phillips, carpenter; Roger Morris; Robert Andrews; James Horne; Robert Scott, carpenter; John Phillips, carpenter; Thomas Walley Partington; William Timbrell, carpenter; and George Shakespear, carpenter.

Some agreements contained additional stipulations relating to the specific circumstances of a particular plot. In an agreement of 1723 with Edward Shepherd for an area on the north side of Brook Street with long frontages to Davies Street and Gilbert Street it was laid down that no stables or coach-houses were to be built in these 'cross streets' within two hundred feet of Brook Street.[133] Restrictions on the siting of stabling can be found in other agreements but were more frequently inserted in leases. Later agreements for the south-western area of the estate contained clauses reserving to the ground landlord the right to grant free passage to and from neighbouring estates along South Street or South Audley Street, with power to stop up the roads leaving only a footway.[134] Edward Shepherd, who contracted for part of the west side of South Audley Street as far as the southern boundary of the estate, received a concession granting him right of way into the adjoining property of the Dean and Chapter of Westminster which he held on lease, but this privilege did not extend to other nearby estate owners (such as Lord Berkeley and Sir William Pulteney) or their tenants without permission.[127] It is doubtful whether these conditions had any practical effect, but they were no doubt inserted in case undesirable developments on adjoining properties should require the restriction of communication with them. An agreement of 1720 for the eastern end of Brook Street made reference to the construction of arches and shores over the Tyburn brook

to carry the roadway. One of the joint undertakers of this agreement also held adjoining land in Conduit Mead on lease and covenanted to continue Brook Street into that estate at its full width as far as his holding permitted.[135] When Augustin Woollaston, who may have been a brickmaker by trade, took land at the western edge of the estate in 1725 he had to contract to use any bricks which he might make from brick earth dug out of the ground there for his building operations on the estate, particularly the north side of Grosvenor Square, where he also held land under agreement.[136]

Even for Grosvenor Square itself, however, there were remarkably few extra provisions. The first agreements for the east and west sides in November 1724 and February 1725 were, indeed, hardly more explicit than those for other streets, but by March and April 1725 more clauses were being written into agreements for the other sides, and these were also inserted in leases of houses on the east and west sides. A share of the costs of making the enclosure in the centre of the square and maintaining the garden was to be paid, but the only additional requirements affecting the building operations were that an area eight feet wide from house front to pavement was to be made in front of each house, a ten-foot-wide pavement was to be laid with Purbeck stone, and the roadway from thence 'quite home to the said intended Square' was to be laid with 'common paving'. In fact the paving work around the enclosure was done at Sir Richard Grosvenor's initial expense and was subsequently added to the charge of laying out the garden, as stated earlier. A surprisingly late addition to such agreements (although contained in all leases or sub-leases of individual house sites in the square) was a clause granting to tenants the 'Liberty and Privilege in Common with other Tenants fronting on the said new intended Square of walking within the Garden designed to be made in the said new intended Square and of having and keeping a Key or Keys to the Gate or Gates thereof'.[137] Endorsements were added to some of the agreements for ground fronting on to the square stipulating that the houses erected should be at least thirty feet wide and thirty feet deep.[138] This condition was included in the last agreement (for the south side), but was still ignored in the case of No. 35, which, according to the dimensions given in the building lease, had only a twenty-five-foot frontage to the square.[137] Several other houses on corner sites in the square were also less than thirty feet in width.

Building Leases

In some cases, as has been indicated, some of the more notable deficiencies in agreements were corrected in the leases granted under them.[139] There were 460 such leases of plots ranging in size from individual house sites (and in one case part of a yard[140]) to extensive areas which were then sub-let in smaller building plots by their lessees.

Although by no means uniform, the leases generally followed a standard pattern. They were usually granted in consideration of buildings erected, in course of erection, or to be erected; the payment of rent; and the performance of covenants. Each was of a plot of ground and the building or buildings standing on it or to be erected there. Even in leases of individual house plots the phrase 'and all other buildings built or which may be built' on the same was often added, no doubt to cover stabling, offices or other out-buildings; but this phrase, if interpreted literally, gave the lessee complete freedom to cover the ground with whatever buildings he wished.

The term of years granted by such leases and the extra rent payable if undesirable trades were practised have been discussed above; the ground rents will be examined separately in the next section.

The 'common usual and necessary covenants' referred to in the agreements are set out fully in the leases themselves. The lessee undertook to pay the ground rent and the extra rent payable if he practised a noxious trade; to pay his share of the cost of making and keeping in repair the stable yard, if applicable; to finish the building within a specified time in a workmanlike manner; to put up rails and posts, and do the necessary paving work to the middle of the street; to build his stables or other buildings at the back of his plot to as low a height as possible; to maintain the premises in good repair; to surrender the buildings at the end of the leasehold term with their fittings intact; to allow to the landlord or his agents the right of inspection at least twice each year, and to put right any defects thereby discovered within three months. A further clause gave to the landlord the right of repossession in case of non-payment of rent in the usual manner of such leases.

The time limit laid down for completing buildings was usually six months but this was often varied. In leases of large areas containing a number of house plots a longer time was frequently allowed, and in one instance the lessee was merely required to finish his buildings 'with all Convenient Speed and as soon as may be'.[141] For houses in Grosvenor Square twelve or eighteen months were generally allowed. Many instances could be cited of houses which were not completed within the allotted span and there is no evidence of any attempt on the part of the Grosvenors or their officers to enforce such provisions rigidly. In one case, when a builder died after being in financial difficulties, partially built houses were standing in a deteriorating condition ten years after a lease of them had been granted to him, but Robert Andrews, acting for Sir Robert Grosvenor, agreed not only to remit the arrears of ground rent due but also to pay a small sum to the builder's principal creditor in return for an assignment of the lease in trust for Sir Robert.[43]

Additional covenants were included in leases whenever particular circumstances demanded. Often these were concerned with the siting of coach-houses and stables. In leases of plots which had their principal frontages on major streets such as Brook Street or Grosvenor Square and long return frontages to other streets such as Davies Street or Duke Street, a condition was often inserted that the building of stabling in the latter streets was either prohibited or only allowed if no entrance directly into the street from the stable was constructed, access being obtained from the mews at the rear.[142] Among the more unusual stipulations about the location of stabling was that contained in leases of sites on the south side of South Street in which it was stated that if lessees built stables on their plots they were not to keep dung in the street but were to 'sink a place...in the said Street...for the holding and keeping of such Dung and...cover the same over in a Safe manner even with the Surface of the said Street'.[143] In leases of plots with frontages on to stable yards, the use of the yard and its facilities was granted in common with other lessees of plots abutting on the yard.

The building leases for Grosvenor Square contained provisions about the square garden. In return for the privilege of 'walking in' the enclosure the lessee had to pay an additional annual rent (calculated at 9d. per foot frontage), the proceeds of which were to be used for maintaining the garden, watering the roadway in the square, and paying a gardener to look after the enclosure.

Ground Rent

Although the amounts of ground rent payable under individual leases differed widely, a general consistency can be discerned in the sums required under the various building agreements. The rent demanded for each piece of ground was either expressed as a rate per foot frontage on the principal front of the land (and occasionally on more than one front when the plot lay between two streets) or as a lump sum, which can sometimes be reduced to an equivalent rate per foot frontage.

In early agreements covering sites in Grosvenor Street and Brook Street the ground rents were usually 6s. per foot on the Grosvenor Street frontages and 5s. on Brook Street, the plots being generally 150 or 200 feet in depth.[144] For substantially larger pieces of ground on the north side of Brook Street, with back land extending as far as Oxford Street, however, the rate was increased. In an agreement for the area bounded by Brook Street on the south, Davies Street on the east, Gilbert Street on the west and Oxford Street on the north the ground rent charged was 9s. per foot, assessed on the Brook Street frontage, but the agreement was not carried out and when a new one was made with another developer this rate was reduced to 8s. per foot.[145] The latter rate was also paid for the remaining frontage of Brook Street as far west as Duke Street, with an equally extensive 'hinterland'.[146]

On the south side of the eastern part of Mount Street, where the southern boundary of the estate or the location of the parish burial ground prevented any great depth of site, sixty to seventy feet being the average, rents of only 2s. to 2s. 6d. per foot frontage were asked.[147] Even on the north side, however, the figure was at most 3s., although the building plots (if not the house sites as eventually built) extended back for some 150 feet.[148] Mount Street was probably never originally intended to be more than a minor street, and the building of the parish workhouse on the south side in 1725-6 was in keeping with its lowly status.[149]

The ground rents for Grosvenor Square were not significantly different from those for Brook Street or Grosvenor Street. The first builder to take an extensive frontage to the square (the whole of the east side) was John Simmons, carpenter, in November 1724, and for 350 feet with a depth of 260 feet he agreed to pay £112 per annum, equivalent to slightly over 6s. per foot frontage.[150] For the same number of feet on the west side the undertaker's rent was £150, but his plot had greater depth and abutted at the rear on Park Street.[151] On the north side the rents ranged from approximately 8s. to 10s. per foot, but, as at the western end of Brook Street, the plots extended northwards for about 600 feet.[152] Most of the south side was let by Sir Richard Grosvenor to his brother Robert at only 2s. per foot frontage, but in the agreements which he made with builders Robert Grosvenor charged the equivalent of 10s. per foot frontage for sites which reached as far as the north side of Mount Street.[153]

To the west of Grosvenor Square the ground rents were more variable and, in view of the large areas often involved, were generally more favourable to builders than in the eastern part of the estate. For the extensive rectangle of ground between Upper Brook Street, North Row, Park Street and North Audley Street, for instance, Thomas Barlow and Robert Andrews were jointly charged only £150 per annum (apparently calculated as 5s. per foot frontage on either the Park Street or North Audley Street fronts, or 2s. 6d. on both).[94] Apart from the section of South Audley Street lying to the south of South Street, where the rents were equivalent to between 6s. and 9s. per foot frontage (and where houses of a high quality were built),[154] 5s. per foot for one frontage alone appears to have been the maximum amount charged here until the 1750's. It was not until June 1765 that a ground rent of a substantially different order was required when John Phillips, carpenter, had to pay £320 per annum for the last undeveloped piece of ground, the area bounded by Oxford Street, Park Lane, North Row and Park Street. This sum is equivalent to between 13s. and 14s. per foot if assessed on the long east-west frontage to Oxford Street, or to exactly £2 per foot on Park Street.[155]

The precise ground rent charged was no doubt often arrived at after negotiation with the builder or developer interested in a piece of ground. As early as 1721 Major Joseph Watts, who was one of the promoters and first directors of the Chelsea Waterworks Company,[156] had entered into an agreement to build on the whole site now occupied by Grosvenor House, and the rent charged had been 4s. per foot on the Park Street frontage (400 feet).[157] No building was then taking place so far westward and some five years later Watts appears to have wanted to reduce his commitment. Robert Andrews explained the situation to Sir Richard Grosvenor in 1726: 'Major Watts was this morning with Mr. Barlow and Me', wrote Andrews, 'about taking as much of the Ground He formerly held as would be sufficient for the building three houses upon. Mr. Barlow offered it for 10s. per ft. by Gros. Street front the whole depth into Mount Street but the Major woud have it for 6 and intends to write to You, to shew how reasonable it is for a person that has been so serviceable to the Family as he has been by projecting the Waterworks to have such a favour allowed him, of which I thought it proper to give You this informacion not doubting but You will easily make him sensible his Merrit is not so great in regard to his Services done the Family as he imagines.'[158] The rent now demanded by Barlow was in fact higher than the rate which he had been charging to the east of Grosvenor Square, and apparently no accommodation was possible for Watts did not develop any of the site. Andrews' letter also suggests that a somewhat more optimistic view of the ground rents obtainable in the western part of the estate was taken at this date than proved realistic in the event.

In 1734 Edward Shepherd, the architect and builder, who had already built several houses on the estate, made an offer of only 18d. per foot frontage for a very large plot between Park Lane and Park Street with a depth of about 600 feet from Oxford Street, the rent to be calculated on the north front alone. Andrews assessed the plot as worth 2s. per foot frontage on both the Park Lane and Park Street fronts: the difference was between £33 2s. 6d. as offered by Shepherd and £125 as computed by Andrews, who noted that 'there is no foundation to agree'.[159] Sir Robert Grosvenor duly turned down Shepherd's offer, but it was not until 1765 that the last part of this ground was eventually taken, the total ground rent received from it then amounting, however, to over £500.

Some parts of the estate were let to undertakers on particularly favourable terms in return for services rendered. The agreement with Major Watts in 1721 referred to above was no doubt the result of his role in promoting the Chelsea Waterworks Company which supplied the new houses with water. Another plot at the western edge of the estate was taken by Francis Bailley, carpenter, who was then building in Conduit Mead, in return for the assignment of some of his land there to Sir Richard Grosvenor to enable Brook Street to be carried through from Hanover Square to the Grosvenor estate. Bailley's rent was 5s. per foot frontage, 'being a cheaper price than the other ground thereabouts was…designed to be let for',[160] but he, like Watts, did not eventually build there. For similar reasons the triangular area now bounded by Brook Street, Davies Street and South Molton Lane was also made available at a very low rent to two developers who had interests in Conduit Mead: parts of this site to the north of Davies Mews were not built over for many years.[135] We have already seen that in the very first agreement, made with the estate surveyor Thomas Barlow, for the extensive area to the south of Grosvenor Street and east of Davies Street, a ground rent of only 2s. per foot frontage on the Grosvenor Street front alone was required. No doubt this was partly in return for Barlow's services in laying out the estate and seeking builders to work there, but he was, of course, paid a fee for these activities, and another consideration in Sir Richard Grosvenor's mind may have been a desire to let Barlow have a piece of land on terms that would enable him to raise sufficient capital to develop it quickly and profitably, and thereby attract other builders to the estate. In 1730 the promoters of the Grosvenor Chapel were granted land adjacent to its site, on both sides of South Audley Street, at a rent of only 1s. per foot frontage in consideration of their 'hazard and expense' in building the chapel.[161] They were also allowed a five-year peppercorn term instead of the usual period of between two and three years.

The scale of ground rents on the Grosvenor estate was a good deal lower than that in nearby developments for which comparable evidence is available. In Albemarle Ground (the area of Albemarle Street, Stafford Street, Dover Street and Grafton Street) in the late seventeenth century rents ranged from approximately 5s. to 13s. 9d. per foot frontage for building plots varying from sixty-five to one hundred feet in depth, and the leases ran for only some fifty or fifty-one years.[162] On the Burlington estate (Cork Street, Clifford Street and Savile Row area), where building took place contemporaneously with the Grosvenor estate, the ground rents appear to have been calculated initially on the basis of 1s. per foot frontage for every ten feet of depth and varied between 7s. and 16s. per foot frontage for sixty-one- or sixty-two-year terms.[163] The calculation of the ground rent obtained from the development of Conduit Mead is complicated by the fact that some ground there was assigned to builders rather than leased to them. The total rent received for the twenty-seven or so acres was £1,076, or about £40 per acre. A report of 1742 estimated, however, that only two-thirds of the acreage had been let for rent, and if assessed on this proportion alone the figure was £60 per acre.[164] This compares with the final sum of £31 per acre secured in ground rents on the Grosvenor estate in Mayfair by its initial development,* and in Conduit Mead the leases were for less than fifty years.

All of these areas were much smaller than the Grosvenor estate, and in The Hundred Acres, where house building was being pushed some way beyond the existing urban limits, it was probably necessary to keep the ground rents at a low level in order to attract builders, particularly to the land near Hyde Park, where the rents were at first lower, in fact, than was desired or originally anticipated. In the event, however, several undertakers were able to obtain a handsome surplus in improved ground rents over the rent which they paid to the Grosvenors.

A remarkable example of the rise in value of such leasehold property occurred in the large area to the south of Grosvenor Street and east of Davies Street let to Thomas Barlow, the estate surveyor, in 1721 on a ninety-nine-year lease at £67 per annum. This was the largest piece of the Grosvenors' Mayfair lands to be let under a single lease and covered about six acres, now embracing, in terms of present streets and buildings, Nos. 55–81 (consec.) Grosvenor Street, Nos. 2–26 (even) Davies Street, Grosvenor Hill, Bourdon Street and Place, Broadbent Street, Jones Street and Nos. 25–31 (consec.) Berkeley Square. In this estate within an estate Barlow sub-let the land in building plots for at most eighty years (with one exception) and often for sixty or less, and from it he obtained some £280 per annum in improved ground rents over the £67 he had to pay, and £160 in rack rents. When Barlow's property was sold at auction in 1745 for the benefit of his descendants this very large plot fetched some £7,000. In 1792, however, when the whole area was again put up for auction, several of the sub-leases had already expired and others were shortly due to do so, giving purchasers the prospect of a considerable return in rack rents for the remaining twenty-eight years of the original Grosvenor lease, besides the possibility of renewals on favourable terms, and the sum realised amounted to over £58,000.[165]

Within the general framework of the ground rents laid down in agreements, the rents at which individual building plots were let varied widely and often bore no relation to the size or importance of the site. Sometimes the total ground rent required under an agreement was secured by leases of only a small part of the ground, and the remainder would be let (often in one lease) at a token rent, usually 3s. 4d. per annum.[166] Some huge pieces of land embracing two or three acres were let for such nominal sums, particularly between Oxford Street and the backs of house plots in Grosvenor Square and Brook Street. Even the rents of adjoining house sites could vary widely. To take one instance, No. 5 Grosvenor Square, with a forty-five-foot frontage, was leased to John Simmons, its builder, in May 1728 for £22 10s. per annum while No. 4, with a seventy-foot frontage, was leased to him in September of the same year for 4s. per annum, both for ninety-nine-year terms.[167] No doubt such variations were often made for the builder's convenience, to enable him to make a quick sale, possibly at an enhanced price, of a house at a low ground rent, or, as in Simmons's case, to enable him to create an improved ground rent which he could sell to raise money for his building operations.

---

* If the improved ground rents received from Sir Robert Grosvenor's trust estate are added the Grosvenors' total rental from their Mayfair lands amounted to £34 per acre.

Architects and Builders

The names of some 290 individuals who were connected with the building trade, either as practitioners of its arts and crafts or as suppliers of materials, are recorded in the documentary evidence relating to the development of the estate. These were the men who entered into building agreements, were direct lessees of the Grosvenors, or were sub-lessees of developers, and it can reasonably be assumed that there were also many more sub-lessees whose names have not been traced. While by no means all of them can have aspired to the description of 'master builders' they were nevertheless in business in a substantial enough way to be parties to various legal instruments, and must have been supported by countless journeymen, labourers and apprentices. Their activities on the estate were, of course, spread over the whole sixty-year period of its first development but the names of a substantial number of them occur in documents dating from the first decade, and it is not difficult to envisage Defoe's 'World full of Bricklayers and Labourers'.

A handful of these 290 can justifiably be called architects, although only two were actually so described. One of these was Colen or Colin Campbell, who described himself as Architect to the Prince of Wales when he was granted a building lease in 1726,[168] and the second was John Crunden, who was the building lessee of a terrace of houses in Hereford Street in 1777.[169] The others usually styled themselves 'esquire' or 'gentleman'. They included William Benson, whose architectural career had already been cut short before he appeared on the estate; Edward Shepherd; Thomas Ripley; Roger Morris; and Thomas Archer, who had a house built in Grosvenor Square but apparently not of his own designing. In the case of Shepherd and Morris, however, the line dividing them from an outstanding master builder like Benjamin Timbrell is indeed fine.

Any discussion of the role played by architects in the development of the estate must begin with the enigmatic presence of Colen Campbell. Sir Richard Grosvenor was a subscriber to all three volumes of *Vitruvius Britannicus* published in Campbell's lifetime and Eaton Hall is featured in the second volume of 1717, but no account of any dealings with Campbell has survived in the family archives, and if Sir Richard Grosvenor and his brothers had any views on architecture they remain obscure. Campbell was the lessee of two adjoining house plots in Brook Street in 1726 and on one of these he built the still-surviving house (No. 76) in which he lived until his death there in 1729 (Plate 33c; fig. 2e on page 107).[170] The ground on which these houses were built, however, was originally taken under a building agreement by Edward Shepherd, and it was as Shepherd's nominee that Campbell received his lease. In fact Shepherd had agreed to make the site available to Israel Russell, painter-stainer,

and Campbell had subsequently obtained an assignment of Russell's agreement with Shepherd in 1725. Russell witnessed the lease.[168]

Although No. 76 and the now demolished No. 78 Brook Street are the only buildings which can with some certainty be attributed to Campbell, his involvement in the development of the estate was undoubtedly more extensive. We have already seen that in four agreements concluded shortly before his death he was named as one of the referees for settling disputes.[171] More directly, an engraving in the Gibbs Collection at the Ashmolean Museum shows the elevation and plan of 'Seven New intended Houses on the East Side of Grosvenor Sq^r as Designed by Colen Campbell Esqr 1725' (Plate 4b). The engraving was probably intended for publication, but the circumstances in which the design was made are a mystery. An agreement to undertake the development of the east side of the square had been signed by the builder John Simmons in November 1724.[150] Whether Simmons commissioned Campbell to provide a design, whether Sir Richard Grosvenor procured a design which he hoped Simmons would follow, this being the first side of the square to be taken by a builder (although no stipulation that any overall design had to be adhered to was made in the agreement), or whether Campbell's contribution was unsolicited is not known. Perhaps significantly there is some similarity between the east side as built by Simmons and Campbell's scheme. Simmons's façade was much plainer but it was nevertheless treated as a symmetrical composition with the ends and centre given additional emphasis (Plate 5). 'By this means', to quote Sir John Summerson, 'the block assumed the character of a single palatial building, and an important step had been taken towards a new conception of street architecture'.[172] Campbell's design was for seven houses, and Simmons's range, as viewed from the square, also appeared to consist of seven houses, but, in fact, contained an extra house on the south side with its entrance in Grosvenor Street. As in Campbell's design, the centre house as built was wider than the rest, but it had a frontage of seventy feet rather than sixty as shown by Campbell, and there were corresponding differences in the dimensions of the other houses. A reference in a letter by Robert Andrews in 1726 to a dispute with Simmons over sewers may be pertinent although it hardly clarifies matters. Andrews wrote, 'It was an unlucky misunderstanding at first but such a Genr! design as that is seldom ever carried on without oversights of that kind which makes it the more pardonable'.[158] Part of Simmons's composition survived in a little-altered state at No. 1 Grosvenor Square until *c.* 1936 and can be seen on Plate 8a.

There is another design by Campbell for Grosvenor Square, architecturally very similar, dating from 1725 in the Royal Institute of British Architects. This consists of an elevation and plans for three houses with a combined frontage of approximately 185 feet.[173] Again nothing is known about the history of the design. It is, however, interesting to note that in April 1725 Robert Grosvenor was granted a lease by his brother of 185 feet of frontage on the south side of the square, but by August he was contracting with builders to sub-let the ground to them in building plots of such dimensions that the execution of Campbell's design would have been impossible.[174] Edward Shepherd took 180 feet on the north side of the square in 1725,[175] but he eventually built four houses there, three of them to his own rather grand design, which, although Palladian, cannot be related to Campbell's.

Two other designs attributed to Campbell in the R.I.B.A. have been associated with Grosvenor Square,[176] but they show astylar blocks in the manner of his Old Burlington Street houses or of his own house in Brook Street, and the dimensions do not fit any of the sides of the square.

One of the associates of Campbell who lived on the estate was John Aislabie, a former Chancellor of the Exchequer who had been discredited by the South Sea Bubble. In 1729 Aislabie concluded the purchase of No. 12 Grosvenor Square, on the north side, from its building lessee, John Kitchingman, a timber merchant, moving in during that year.[177] The house, which was demolished in 1961, had a Palladian façade (fig. 2a on page 106) and interior decorative features in the manner of Campbell.

Another member of Campbell's circle who had a house on the estate was William Benson, the architect of Wilbury House in Wiltshire, which was an early example of the Palladian revival. He had been made Surveyor-General of the King's Works in 1718, having manoeuvred Wren out of the office, only to be dismissed himself for incompetence in the following year.[178] Campbell was his Deputy Surveyor and Chief Clerk but also lost his position on Benson's disgrace. Benson was, however, well compensated financially and among other perquisites received the reversion of the office of Auditor of the Imprests.[178] In 1725 he and his brother Benjamin (who had replaced Hawksmoor as Clerk of the Works at Whitehall in 1718) jointly took an assignment of a building agreement for thirty-six feet of frontage on the south side of Grosvenor Street, where they had two narrow houses built (Nos. 45 and 46, now demolished).[179] William Benson lived in No. 45 from 1726 until 1752 and was succeeded as occupant by John Aislabie Benson, his son.[71] Whether Benson designed these houses, or what, indeed, they looked like is not known, and he is chiefly of interest in the history of the estate as a mortgagee of Sir Richard Grosvenor, to whom he lent £10,000 in 1732,[180] probably in connection with the extensive work then being undertaken at Grosvenor House, Millbank.

Of the architect-builders who worked on the estate, Edward Shepherd must rank as the most important, both in terms of the original extent of his work and of the amount surviving. He is first recorded on the estate in 1721 as the assignee of an agreement for a plot on the south side of Brook Street now occupied by part of Claridge's Hotel. In 1723 he was granted a lease of the house which he had erected (No. 47), and is there described as a plasterer, which accords with Vertue's account of his career.[181] In November of the same year he entered into an agreement to build on the north side of Brook Street between Davies Street and Gilbert Street,[133] and in the course of this development (and others on the estate) he progressed from calling himself a plasterer to firstly a 'gentleman' and finally an 'esquire'. It was for part of this ground in Brook Street that Colen Campbell was granted a building lease in 1726 in the circumstances described above, and, in view of instances where Shepherd obtained leases for building tradesmen who did work for him, it is possible that the two men were professionally associated in some way. Between 1726 and 1729 they lived within two doors of each other, Shepherd at No. 72 Brook Street and Campbell at No. 76.[71] Certainly by the end of the 1720's Shepherd had graduated from being a plasterer to being an assured if not outstandingly distinguished architect, and Campbell may have been his mentor.

In the absence of any evidence to the contrary it can be conjectured that Shepherd was responsible for the design of the elaborate interior of No. 66 Brook Street (now part of the Grosvenor Office), of which he was the building lessee in 1725 (Frontispiece, Plates 6c, 9a).[182] Four years later he assigned the house to its first occupant, Sir Nathaniel Curzon, and Curzon's account at Hoare's Bank records payments to Shepherd and his mortgagee but none to any other architect.[183]

His most remarkable design during these years, however, was for three houses on the north side of Grosvenor Square (Nos. 18, 19 and 20 in the modern sequence) which he united behind a Palladian façade of red brick above a rusticated, stuccoed ground storey with an attached hexastyle Corinthian portico as its centrepiece (Plate 5). The design was presumably in existence by April 1728, when an agreement with a bricklayer who was to work on the houses made reference to 'the modell plann or forme and elevation...which hath been made or drawn by the said Edward Shepherd'.[184] Originally the composition was symmetrical but within a few years it was made to seem unbalanced when the adjoining corner house (No. 21) was refaced to match its neighbour. Robert Morris wrote in 1734 that 'the same Architect did compose a regular Range for that whole Side, in which he has shown a Nobleness of Invention, and the Spirit and Keeping of the Design is not unworthy of the greatest British Architect; but the unpolite Taste of several Proprietors of that Ground prevented so beautiful a Performance from being the Ornament of that Side of the Square'.[185] That he had Shepherd in mind is suggested by his reference elsewhere to 'that Grandeur of Esqr; Shepherd's [range] on the North'.[186] The only other undertaker on the north side was Augustin Woollaston, a brickmaker, who received his frontage at the same time as Shepherd (March 1725),[187] but the first building leases of his ground were granted in 1726,[188] some two years before those of Shepherd's houses.

No. 12 North Audley Street, which has an interior as fine as that of No. 66 Brook Street, was built on part of the 'hinterland' of Shepherd's ground on the north side of Grosvenor Square (no. 54 on plan A), presumably for its first occupant, Colonel (later Field-Marshal and Earl) Ligonier, who paid a rack rent to Shepherd for some five years before purchasing the house outright in 1735.[189] Although Shepherd was almost certainly the builder, there is a possibility that he was here working to another's designs, for on stylistic grounds there is a strong case for attributing the design of the interior, and in particular the splendid long gallery at the back (Plate 11), to Sir Edward Lovett Pearce, the Irish Palladian architect who provided a design (probably unexecuted) for a house for Ligonier near Dublin.[190]

Other large and apparently well-appointed houses by Shepherd in North Audley Street have been demolished but in South Audley Street more has survived of the range from No. 71 to No. 75 where he was the undertaker.[127]

Thomas Ripley's known work on the estate is confined to one house, No. 16 Grosvenor Street, for which he was the building lessee in 1724. He too had graduated in rank, from 'carpenter' in 1720 when he entered into an agreement to build on this plot to 'esquire' on receipt of the lease.[191] The first occupant of the house was Lord Walpole,[71] the eldest son of Sir Robert Walpole, and it was to the latter's influence rather than his own skill that Ripley owed his advance in the world. Ripley was also one of the first builders to take ground in Grosvenor Square, signing an agreement to develop the whole of the west side in 1725.[151] He was one of the parties to the arrangement with Sir Richard Grosvenor for the laying out of the square garden, but by the time building leases of his plot were granted in 1728 he appears to have relinquished all his interest under the building agreement to Robert Scott, carpenter, and Robert Andrews,[192] and there is no indication that he had anything whatsoever to do with the heterogeneous mixture of houses which made up that side of the square.

Roger Morris is first encountered on the estate in 1727 when (as a bricklayer from St. Marylebone) he was given possession of some ground in Green Street by Thomas Barlow and Robert Andrews, who were the undertakers for a larger area of which Morris's plot formed part. He built a house for himself at No. 61 Green Street, living there from 1730 until his death in 1749, and the building lessee of the neighbouring house on the west (formerly No. 60, but now joined to No. 61) was James Richards, who was the master carver of the King's Works and an associate of Morris.[193] In 1738 Morris, who had become master carpenter of His Majesty's Ordnance, built a large block of stables for the Second Troop of Horse Guards on the site now largely occupied by Green Street Garden.[194] To the east of the Guards' stables, on the west side of Park Street, he was also responsible in his capacity as developer for the erection of a terrace of narrow-fronted and apparently unremarkable houses between Wood's Mews and Green Street, all since demolished. The lessee of one of these houses was his kinsman, Robert Morris, the author of the favourable comment about Edward Shepherd's houses in Grosvenor Square quoted above, who lived in Park Street from 1739 until his death in 1754.[195]

The evidence relating to the part played by other notable architects is more fragmentary and in some cases entirely speculative. Nicholas Dubois, James Gibbs and, briefly in 1730, John James were named in several building agreements as parties to whose judgment disputes were to be submitted, and Isaac Ware witnessed the agreement with Thomas Ripley for the west side of Grosvenor Square, but none of these architects is known to have been involved in any building work on the estate. Henry Flitcroft is known to have undertaken alterations to No. 4 Grosvenor Square (the great centre house on the east side) for its second occupant, Lord Malton,[178] but his name also occurs in other circumstances in which his role is less clear. In 1728 he provided a mortgage of £400 on No. 12 Upper Grosvenor Street, which the master builder Benjamin Timbrell was then building for his own occupation,[196] and seven years later he witnessed an assignment of No. 6 Upper Brook Street (now demolished) from Edward Shepherd, who had built and briefly occupied the house, to Lord Gower.[197] Flitcroft was also associated with Timbrell in other enterprises, and, perhaps coincidentally, the widow of the Duke of Kent's son, whom Lord Gower was to marry in the year following his move to Upper Brook Street, had previously lived in a house built by Timbrell at No. 9 Clifford Street on the Burlington estate.[198] Later architects such as Sir Robert Taylor, James and Samuel Wyatt, or the Adam brothers, who certainly worked in the area, fall into a somewhat different category, for they were adapting or embellishing existing houses for clients rather than concerning themselves with the first development of the estate.

It is impossible to give details of the work of all of the building tradesmen whose names are known, and information about those who worked in the principal streets is contained in the tables on pages 172–95. Nevertheless the contribution of a few may be singled out. Prominent among the builders, if only by the continual recurrence of the name, was the family of Barlow. At least three generations of the family, which came from Forebridge, Stafford, worked as bricklayers on the estate, but lack of biographical information and the practice of giving the same Christian names to successive generations have made it impossible to determine exact relationships, or, in some cases, to be sure which member of the family was responsible for a particular building. There were four Williams, and probably two Johns and two Georges who were all involved in building work. The eldest William Barlow, sometimes described as William Barlow senior, was the son of Hugh Barlow of Stafford, husbandman, and was apprenticed to a member of the Tylers' and Bricklayers' Company in 1705.[199] He himself took as apprentice in 1715 another William Barlow, son of George Barlow of Stafford, mason, and therefore perhaps his cousin,[200] and this may be the William Barlow, sometimes described as William Barlow junior, who built the two adjoining houses, No. 88 Brook Street and No. 9 Grosvenor Square.[201] William Barlow senior was extensively involved in the earliest building activity at the eastern edge of the estate and continued to be active until his death in 1743. He was appointed bricklayer to the parish of St. George, Hanover Square, in 1725, and in this capacity helped to build the workhouse on the south side of Mount Street.[202] He was also one of the four proprietors of the Grosvenor Chapel.[203] None of the houses of which he was the building lessee have, however, escaped rebuilding. His grandson, Sir George Hilaro Barlow, was created a baronet in 1803.[204] No relationship has been discovered between the Barlow family of bricklayers and Thomas Barlow, carpenter, who was the estate surveyor.

The position of Benjamin Timbrell as one of the foremost master builders working in the West End of London in the first half of the eighteenth century is well known,[178] but his work on the Grosvenor estate has not so far been recorded. He was the building lessee of some ten substantial houses there (including at least two in Grosvenor Square), of which No. 52 Grosvenor Street (Plate 8c; fig. 16 on page 136), No. 69 Grosvenor Street and No. 12 Upper Grosvenor Street survive in part. The latter was his own residence, where he lived from 1729 until 1751.[71] He was almost certainly involved in the building of other houses where he was not the direct lessee, and of the four proprietor-builders of the Grosvenor Chapel he is the most likely to have provided the design (fig. 7 on page 119). As one of the original vestrymen of the parish of St. George, Hanover Square, he often supplied plans for parish buildings, including the workhouse.[205] His son, William, also worked as a carpenter on the estate[206] and his daughter, Martha, married John Barlow,[207] the son of William Barlow senior.

With Thomas Barlow and Benjamin Timbrell, Thomas Phillips, carpenter, was one of the relatively few non-aristocratic vestrymen appointed by the 'Fifty Churches' Commissioners in 1725 to govern the new parish of St. George, and he also assisted in the design and execution of parish buildings including the workhouse (with Timbrell).[208] He had been employed, with Timbrell, as carpenter for the building of the church of St. Martin in the Fields and enjoyed a high standing in his trade.[178] On the Grosvenor estate he built houses in Brook Street and Grosvenor Square. From 1723 until his death in 1736 he lived in one of these houses, No. 39 Brook Street[209] (later partly rebuilt by Jeffry Wyatville), and his nephew, John Phillips, also a well-known master builder, lived there from 1741 until his death in 1775 or 1776.[210] John Phillips was the undertaker for the last area of the estate to be developed—in the north-west corner—

and he was probably the builder of the two large, detached houses erected there, Camelford House and the house later called Somerset House, the latter apparently to his own design.[211]

John Simmons, carpenter, the builder of the east side of Grosvenor Square, was the son of John Simmons, citizen and cooper of London, and was himself a freeman of the Merchant Taylors' Company.[212] He was probably the John Simmons, joiner, who worked for Gibbs at the church of St. Mary-le-Strand.[213] Besides his considerable undertaking in Grosvenor Square he also built several houses in Brook Street, Grosvenor Street and Upper Brook Street. He had a house and workshop on the Grosvenor estate at Millbank,[214] and he was thus one of the few builders working on the Mayfair estate who did not live either there or in adjacent parts of the parish of St. George, Hanover Square. After his death in 1738 his widow, Elizabeth, continued his business until her own death in 1755. When their grand-daughter married in 1778 she was able to provide a dowry consisting of some property at Millbank and eight houses in Mayfair (including two in Grosvenor Square) which had been leased to John or Elizabeth Simmons and were then still owned by their descendants, having in the meantime been let on short-term leases at rack rents.[215]

Other builders who had a substantial impact on the development of the estate included Robert Scott, carpenter, who was also one of the proprietors of the Grosvenor Chapel (with Timbrell, William Barlow senior and Robert Andrews);[203] he was the builder of some ten houses in Grosvenor Street, Grosvenor Square and Upper Grosvenor Street, and of numerous other houses in the lesser streets where he was often joint lessee. Lawrence Neale, carpenter, who lived at No. 24 Upper Grosvenor Street (on part of the site now occupied by No. 93 Park Lane) from 1730 to 1745,[71] was responsible for over a dozen substantial houses, including three in Grosvenor Square. Richard Lissiman, mason, who was the son of a gunsmith from Colwall in Herefordshire and who died in 1733, was the building lessee of several houses in Grosvenor Street, including the important trio of Nos. 33-35 (consec.), and Upper Grosvenor Street.[216] Another builder who died at an early stage in the development was John Green, from whom Green Street almost certainly takes its name. He was drowned in 1737 when he fell into a well he was inspecting for the Marquess of Carnarvon at No. 43 Upper Grosvenor Street, a house which he had himself built some six years previously. He was then living in Green Street and was described as 'a very wealthy Builder'.[217] In the middle years of the eighteenth century the names of John Spencer, carpenter, and Edmund Rush, mason, appear regularly in the estate records, both as builders and developers of substantial areas in the vicinity of South Street, Portugal Street (now Balfour Place), Green Street, Norfolk (now Dunraven) Street, and the west end of Upper Brook Street where house-building was still in progress in the 1750's. Spencer lived on the estate for several years, latterly at No. 60 Green Street (now joined to No. 61), but in 1771 he was declared bankrupt and quit his house, his subsequent movements being unknown.[218]

Building Methods and Finance

Sufficient evidence has come to light about the methods used by builders in the development of the estate to provide several specific examples of modes of building practice which were undoubtedly widespread in the eighteenth century. There are examples of co-operation between builders trained in different crafts, both directly in the few cases where specific contracts have survived, and indirectly in the granting of leases. The contracts are instances of what Sir John Summerson has called 'a remarkably efficient system of barter'[219] whereby the need for cash was reduced by offsetting one man's carefully costed work against that of another. In 1724 Edward Shepherd, who held under agreement the ground on which Nos. 66–78 (even) Brook Street were built, contracted with Thomas Fayram, mason, that he would procure a lease or assignment to Fayram of No. 68 Brook Street, then 'lately built but not finished', and in return Fayram was to pay him £606, half of which was to be in cash and half in mason's work, presumably at No. 66 and other houses in that range (see Plates 6c, 33c). The rate at which Fayram's work was to be measured was carefully set down, viz.—2s. per foot for Portland block, 1s. per foot for superficial plain work, 1s. 3d. per foot for the same moulded, 5s. per foot for white and veined marble chimneypieces and slabs, 2s. 6d. per foot for white and black marble squares, 1s. 6d. per foot for Portland paving, 1s. per foot for plain firestone hearths, 7d. per foot for Purbeck paving and 1s. 10d. per foot for Purbeck steps.[220]

An agreement drawn up four years later between Shepherd and Francis Drewitt, bricklayer, is even more informative. Shepherd, who was then in possession of a piece of ground on the north side of Grosvenor Square under an agreement of 1725, undertook to obtain for Drewitt a lease of No. 20, which was to be built according to Shepherd's plan and elevation, this being one of the houses forming his Palladian composition discussed above. Shepherd was to supply sufficient place and grey stock bricks at the rate of £3 5s. per rod,* and Drewitt was to do the bricklayer's work on two houses to be built by Shepherd in the square, presumably No. 19 and No. 21 (the latter being leased to Shepherd's brother, John, a plasterer).[221] For this Drewitt was to be allowed £1 6s. per rod including ornaments. He was to carry out the work according to Shepherd's plans and elevation and under Shepherd's direction. In return Shepherd was to

do the 'Plaistering worke' on the front of Drewitt's house (namely the entablature, 'Rustick Story', cellar storey and the ornaments to the windows) at the lowest price customarily charged for such work. As soon as the respective work of each was finished the account was to be settled between them and Drewitt was to pay Shepherd the balance before he received the lease.[184] Drewitt, who signed documents with a mark, obtained £400 by mortgaging this agreement before the lease was granted.[222] The lessee of No. 18, the easternmost house in Shepherd's Palladian group, was Thomas Fayram,[223] with whom presumably a similar contract was made.

An unusually explicit reference to the barter system is contained in an agreement of 1755 between Edmund Rush, mason, who was principally responsible for the development of Norfolk (now Dunraven) Street, and Jacob Hancock, painter, who contracted to take a building lease of a plot on the east side of the street. The document states that 'Edmund Rush shall do and Perform or cause to be done and Performed all the Masons Bricklayers and Carpenters Works wanting and Necessary to be done in and about the building and Finishing the Carcass of the said Messuage or Tenement or other buildings to be Erected and built upon the said Peice of Ground...and whatever Sum of Money the same shall amount to... the said Edmund Rush doth hereby agree to Accept and Take out in Work and Business to be done by the said Jacob Hancock for the said Edmund Rush in his Trade or Business as a Painter'.[224] Other lessees of houses in the same range as Hancock's included a carpenter, a bricklayer, a mason, a carver, a plumber and another painter,[225] and similar arrangements were probably made with them, for Rush granted the lease in each case.

The mutual co-operation of several building lessees responsible for a long terrace range can often be assumed but surviving contracts between them are rare. One such is an agreement of 1742 between Elizabeth Simmons, the widow of John Simmons, on the one part, and Joshua Fletcher, mason, John Barlow, bricklayer, Lawrence Neale, carpenter, John Smith, timber merchant, and Robert Andrews, on the other. Elizabeth Simmons was in possession of 189 feet of frontage along the north side of Upper Brook Street to the west of No. 21, presumably as the result of an agreement made between her late husband and Robert Andrews, who was the head lessee of the ground, and she and the others mutually agreed to build seven houses there (Lawrence Neale being responsible for two). She covenanted to build her house 'with the same Expedition' as the others 'to the Intent that the whole of the said peice of Ground may be built upon and such Buildings carried up at one and the same time', and, moreover, she undertook to employ Fletcher, Barlow and Neale on the house in their respective trades, it also being stipulated that Neale was to obtain his timber from

* A clause was added at the end of the agreement substituting red bricks for grey, and for this change Drewitt was to make 'a reasonable allowance', presumably meaning that he was to pay for these at a higher rate. The houses were somewhat unusually faced with red bricks.

Smith's firm. For this work she was to pay them 'in ready Money', as she herself had no building skill to offer in return.[226] The seven houses, Nos. 22-28 (consec.) Upper Brook Street, were built, nearly though not quite as arranged (see table on pages 186-7).

Although the barter system could lessen the dependence of a builder on a supply of ready money, it could not eliminate the need for cash altogether. Some of the accounts of John Jenner, bricklayer, have survived among the records of a Chancery case which followed his death in 1728. These include bills from various tradesmen who had supplied materials or worked for him, with statements of what proportion of the account had already been settled. In only one is there a direct indication that part of the payment had been made in kind, Henry Huddle, carpenter, having done work amounting to £404, of which he had received £306 in cash and lime. One or two other instances of reciprocal arrangements can, however, be assumed from the system of accounting, for an account book kept by Jenner's executor contains entries of money received from Francis Commins, mason, partly in payment for bricklayer's work (presumably done by Jenner) on the same day as he, Commins, was ostensibly paid money for mason's work. Nevertheless for the most part Jenner and later his executor appear to have had to meet their commitments in cash.

The bills also provide evidence about the cost of materials and workmanship. For carpentry Huddle charged £7 per square (100 square feet on plan) for a house in Grosvenor Square, £3 per square for a house in Brook Street which Jenner built for 'Mr. Hogg' (presumably Thomas Hogg, lime merchant), and 45s. per square for coach-houses and stables. For 'Act of Parliament' bricks James Whitaker, brickmaker, received £1 per thousand. Daniel Wheatley, carver, submitted a bill in which his prices ranged between 3s. 6d. per foot for a frieze, 1s. 2d. per foot for bed moulding, 8d. per foot for door and window architraves and 3d. per foot for 'cornish'. He also charged £6 for thirteen fronts of Ionic caps (presumably to pilasters).[227]

Enrolments of many of the mortgages whereby builders raised money on the security of their leases, or in some cases of their pre-lease agreements, are in the Middlesex Land Register. The sum borrowed is not always stated, but there is sufficient evidence, nevertheless, to indicate the general pattern of long-term borrowing. The majority of mortgages were for amounts ranging between £100 and £500, chiefly at 5 per cent interest (the maximum allowable by law), although additional sums were often provided by mortgagees as building progressed. In 122 mortgages of building leases for streets other than Grosvenor Square between 1722 and 1760 the average amount borrowed initially from each mortgagee was £470. This rather high average figure is explained by a few instances in which substantial sums were involved. Richard Lissiman mortgaged No. 34 Grosvenor Street during the course of building for firstly £1,300 and then

a further £1,125 from the same mortgagee.[228] Benjamin Timbrell borrowed at least £2,000 in two instalments on the security of a house on the site of the present Nos. 71-72 Grosvenor Street,[229] and No. 40 Upper Grosvenor Street was also mortgaged by its building lessee for a similar sum.[230] In Grosvenor Square, where the scale of operations was bigger, the loans were often of £1,000 and upwards. No. 38 was mortgaged for £3,500 by its building lessee, Israel Russell, painter-stainer, to a citizen and clothworker of London.[231] Nos. 12 and 25 were each mortgaged for £3,000,[232] and it can be assumed that similar or greater sums were borrowed for the building of other houses in the square where detailed record of the transactions has not survived.

The mortgagees came from a variety of stations in life, one of the largest sources of capital on the Grosvenor estate being, as we have already seen, the ground landlord. Among the many gentlemen and esquires were doubtless a number of solicitors and barristers, some of them identifiable by addresses in the Inns of Court. Widows and spinsters were prominent in providing the small sums necessary to maintain the essential flow of cash to builders, but a high proportion of mortgagees were tradesmen living or working in the several Westminster parishes. Among them were two apothecaries, a cordwainer, three fishmongers, a gingerbread baker, a linen-draper, two oilmen, a pattern-maker, a peruke-maker, a poulterer and a woollen-draper.[233] From slightly further afield were a brewer of St. Giles and a gardener of Chelsea,[234] while there were also merchants or tradesmen with City connexions, some of them members of various livery companies including the Clothworkers', Ironmongers', Goldsmiths', Cooks', and Farriers'.[235] There were also several instances in which builders obtained mortgages from timber merchants, brickmakers or even fellow craftsmen, but these were no doubt sometimes *post hoc* securities for materials supplied or work done. Few of the mortgagees were from outside London and most of these had addresses in the Home Counties. One of the most important was Philip Stone, a maltster from Shepperton, who lent money to several builders.[236] Richard Lissiman's mortgagee for No. 34 Grosvenor Street, mentioned previously, did hail from the provinces, however, being a gentleman from Hambledon in Hampshire. The clergymen mortgagees included Dr. John Pelling, the rector of St. Anne's, Soho, who advanced £2,000 to Edward Shepherd towards the building of No. 19 Grosvenor Square.[237] Among noble lenders were the Earl of Uxbridge, Baron Carpenter and the Dowager Lady Gowran; and Lady Mary Forester of Hampton Court lent £2,000 to Benjamin Timbrell.[238] At the other end of the social scale Richard Wood, a coachman, lent £100 on a mortgage of a house in South Street.[239] Institutional lenders are more difficult to identify, because the deeds relating to their loans were often executed in the names of individuals and do not mention the name of the firm or company concerned, but there is no evidence that they played a major role in the supply of money to builders on the Grosvenor estate. A notable exception was the series of mortgages, amounting to £7,000 by 1743, obtained by Edward Shepherd from Christopher Arnold and Richard Hoare, goldsmiths, which were, in fact, loans from Hoare's Bank.[240]

Little is known about the majority of mortgagees apart from their names and sometimes their occupations, but John Aldred, a former seaman, is an exception. He had been captain of the 'Rochester', a man of war, and in 1710 was 'Commander of the Forces in Newfoundland'.[241] In 1731, when he was living in St. Marylebone, he began lending money to builders on the estate, and between then and 1734 he executed at least six mortgages for a total of £2,500.[242] In 1733 he took up residence in a new house at No. 15 Upper Brook Street (Plate 44b, far right, now demolished) of which he was already the mortgagee and lived there until his death in 1740 (see table on page 187).[243] He also had a country house in Buckinghamshire, and at the time of his death he was able to leave legacies of over £6,000, including £2,000 each to St. Bartholomew's and St. Thomas's Hospitals.[244]

Although much of the loan capital needed for the development of the estate was no doubt channelled through attorneys, scriveners were also very important in providing similar services. They not only acted as witnesses to transactions but were also sometimes parties themselves. James Swift of St. Martin-in-the-Fields, for instance, made several loans to builders, including £2,750 to Benjamin Timbrell and £2,000 to Thomas Knight, joiner, on mortgages of Nos. 28 and 47 Grosvenor Square respectively.[245] Whether he was using his own money or funds entrusted to him by his clients for investment is not known, but he also witnessed other mortgages,[246] as did several of his fellow scriveners.[247] The foremost member of this profession connected with the estate, particularly during the early years of its development, was John Hodson of St. Paul's, Covent Garden. He was probably an associate of Thomas Barlow, the estate surveyor, who had also lived in Covent Garden, and he witnessed both Barlow's agreement with Sir Richard Grosvenor for the large plot on the south side of Grosvenor Street and the resultant building lease.[92] He was also an executor of both Thomas Barlow's and his son Richard's wills.[248] No doubt profiting from this connexion he was able to extend his practice on the estate and witnessed a considerable number of building agreements and leases relating to it. He also provided a number of mortgages to undertakers and builders,[249] but in 1743 he suffered a fate more usually associated with his builder-clients when he was declared bankrupt.[250]

Evidence about other sources of funds apart from mortgages is less readily available. The accounts of John Jenner show that builders operated on an extensive system of short-term credit for materials and sometimes workmanship.[227] William Packer, carpenter, who was the building lessee of a house in Grosvenor Square, must

have encountered financial difficulties for his lease was assigned in trust to creditors, and the deed of sale of the house contains a list of his creditors and their occupations. They included three timber merchants, a brickmaker, an ironmonger, a sawyer, two carvers, a turner, a joiner, a blacksmith, a painter, a lighterman, a butcher, a baker, a coal merchant, a carman and two victuallers including the proprietor of the Mount Coffee House.[251] Borrowing on the security of bonds and promissory notes was no doubt also a widespread practice, but little evidence of this has survived. There is, however, a reference to Robert Andrews lending £400 on a bond to Thomas Knight, the builder of No. 47 Grosvenor Square, before any mortgage of the property had been made,[252] and in 1743 Job Beasley, a servant to a resident of Putney, complained that he had purchased two promissory notes drawn on a builder who became bankrupt, but 'coming but Seldom to London', he had missed the declaration of the dividend.[253] Several mortgages must in fact have been executed to cover money already advanced and in many cases doubtless already spent.

One way to raise capital without borrowing was to sell annuities. This method would only be available to the large-scale undertaker with a considerable annual income, but there are examples of its use by builders on the Grosvenor estate. Thomas Barlow raised £1,500 by selling an annuity of £100 out of the rents and profits of his ground on the south side of Grosvenor Street,[254] representing a return for the purchaser of just over $6\frac{1}{2}$ per cent.

When building was well under way it was possible for the larger operator to obtain cash by selling the improved ground rents which he had created in the course of development. There are several instances of this practice on the Grosvenor estate, where the level of rents required by the ground landlord was so favourable to undertakers. Unfortunately, as in the case of mortgages, much of the evidence occurs in the Middlesex Land Register, where the sums of money involved are only rarely stated, but from the available information the rate at which improved ground rents were bought varied widely. John Baker, esquire, was the purchaser in several such transactions, usually paying between sixteen and nineteen years' purchase, representing an annual return of about $5\frac{1}{2}$ to 6 per cent on his investments. In April 1725 he paid £320 for ground rents of £20 per annum arising out of subleases of houses in Brook Street (sixteen years' purchase),[255] but in December of the same year he paid £142 10s. for rents amounting to £7 10s. (nineteen years' purchase).[256] In the following year he paid £635 for several houses on the east side of Duke Street let on subleases at rents totalling £35,[257] and two years later he paid Edward Shepherd £1,100 for a rent of £59 9s. from thirteen houses in James (now Gilbert) Street (both between eighteen and nineteen years' purchase).[258] In 1728 Henry Huddle, carpenter, paid a sum equivalent to twenty years' purchase to buy the rent for which he was liable under a sub-lease of a plot in Mount Street.[259]

In some cases, however, the rate was twenty-one years or longer, giving a return of under 5 per cent. A document among the papers relating to John Jenner, referred to earlier, values the improved rents arising from his building activities at twenty-two years' purchase. This may well have been an optimistic assessment, for in 1729 Francis Commins, mason, paid £210 for £10 worth of rents from Jenner's executor.[260] In 1739 Abraham Crop, a merchant, bought a plot of ground on which a rent of £69 10s. had been secured for £1,459 10s.[261] Both these sums were equivalent to twenty-one years' purchase, and this was also the basis on which Robert Grosvenor paid John Simmons for the improved ground rents of houses on the east side of Grosvenor Square in 1731-2. In 1733, however, he bought the increased rent of the large centre house there at twenty-three-and-a-half years' purchase,[42] his willingness to pay this exceptionally high price being probably due to his wish to provide a stimulus to the whole development by the completion of such an important house.

The builder who was fortunate would find a purchaser for a house either before work had begun or when the building was only in carcase. In a few instances leases were granted to the first occupants of houses on the estate rather than to building tradesmen, but in only one of these cases has the contract which was presumably made as a matter of course between the respective parties come to light. This is an agreement of 1769 concerning the large house at the north end of Park Lane (later known as Somerset House, Plate 14b) which was leased to Viscount Bateman in 1773.[262] By this contract John Phillips, who held the land under a building agreement of 1765 (no. 92 on plan A), undertook to build a house and stables for Bateman at a cost of £6,500 plus an extra £500 for an abatement in ground rent. The document contains several detailed provisions relating to the building work including the dimensions of the timbers to be used.[263] At No. 48 Upper Grosvenor Street (fig. 2c on page 107), where the lessee, Colonel William Hanmer, was the first occupant, the builder of the house, Robert Phillips, bricklayer, was a party to the lease,[264] and it is known that a contract for building the house was made between Phillips and Hanmer. It apparently contained detailed specifications and was endorsed with accounts of the partial payments made by Hanmer as the work progressed.[265]

Two examples of large and imposing houses which were purchased before completion are Nos. 34 and 52 Grosvenor Street, both of which survive, albeit in altered states (Plates 8c, 9b; figs. 16-17 on pages 136-7). A building lease of No. 52 was granted to Benjamin Timbrell in November 1724,[266] and in March 1725 Sir Thomas Hanmer, the former Speaker of the House of Commons, agreed to pay Timbrell £4,250 for the house which was 'now erected or in building' and was 'to be finished in the best manner now used'.[267] Hanmer's accounts show that

the payments were spread over eighteen months as building work progressed, and he moved in at Michaelmas 1726. As well as the purchase money Hanmer paid sums to other craftsmen for work in fitting up the house, and Timbrell allowed him a reduction of £60 from the stated price 'for the Staircase', presumably because Hanmer had employed Giovanni Bagutti, the eminent Italian plasterer, on the embellishment of the staircase compartment rather than entrust the work to Timbrell.[268]

A similar arrangement was made at No. 34 Grosvenor Street, for which Sir Paul Methuen paid £4,500 to its building lessee, Richard Lissiman, in 1728, some three years after Lissiman had been granted the lease.[269] Methuen held back £500 of the purchase money until certain works were completed and a memorandum was drawn up setting these out in detail. Among the specifications was the instruction that Lissiman should 'wainscoat the Staircase with Oak, in the same manner as the Staircase is wainscoated, in the house where Sir Thomas Hanmer now lives. And...cover all that part of the Staircase and Sealing above it, that is plaisterd, with Ornaments of Stucco, to the Satisfaction of Sir Paul; But with this Express condition, that Mr. Lissiman is not to be at any greater Expence for the same then [sic] forty pounds. So that if Sir Paul should be desirous to have it done very finely Mr. Lissiman shall be obliged to contribute forty pounds towards ye Charge of it, and no more'.[270] Surviving bills indicate that Methuen, too, made extra payments to craftsmen for work at the house, although there is no bill for plasterwork.[271]

A shortened version of one contract shows that shortly after receiving his building lease of the house on the west corner of Duke Street and Grosvenor Square William Barlow junior agreed to complete the house according to the requirements of Thomas Archer of Whitehall, esquire (the architect), after which Archer was to have the option of purchasing it for £1,600. Although all the provisions are not known Archer's general instruction seems to have been that the house should be finished in the same manner as No. 9 in the square, at the opposite corner of Duke Street, which Barlow had built previously.[272] Barlow borrowed £650 from Archer to complete the house, but in January 1727 he was declared bankrupt, and by November of the same year Archer was complaining that the house was still unfinished and was 'now in a ruinous and destructive manner, open and exposed to the wind and rain'.[273] In February 1728 Barlow's assignees in bankruptcy conveyed the house to Archer for an unknown amount.[274]

Undoubtedly the most unusual method of selling a house was the raffle held for No. 4 Grosvenor Square, the centre house on the east side with a seventy-foot frontage (the largest in the square). This imposing mansion was built by John Simmons and was valued at £10,000, but it was described by his widow as 'not being every Body's Money'. She devised a scheme to sell 39,999 tickets at 5s. 3d. each, with a free ticket for anyone who bought twenty-four. The raffle, which was held on 8 June 1739, was won jointly by the wife of a grocer in Piccadilly and her lodger, who sold the house to the Duke of Norfolk. According to *The Gentleman's Magazine* the Duke paid £7,000, but the deeds seem to indicate that the price was only £4,725, a remarkably low sum for such a large house.[275]

The highest price known to have been paid for a new house on the estate was £7,500 in 1730 for No. 19 Grosvenor Square, which was described as 'the fine House...built by Mr. Shepherd the famous Architect'.[276] With a sixty-foot frontage and a handsome Palladian façade it was perhaps originally the grandest house in the square. In 1731 No. 7 Grosvenor Square was let to Lord Weymouth for seven years at a peppercorn rent for the first year and £396 per annum thereafter with an option to purchase the house within three years for £6,400, the price to include four coach-houses in the mews behind.[277] Other known prices paid to their builders for houses in the square were £5,250 for No. 18, £4,800 for No. 17, £4,200 for No. 12 and £3,400 each for Nos. 44 and 46.[278] No. 34, however, which was a smaller house on a corner site, sold for £1,750.[279]

Substantial sums were also paid for houses in other streets. The £4,500 paid by Sir Paul Methuen for No. 34 Grosvenor Street, a house with a forty-three-foot frontage, and the £4,250 paid by Sir Thomas Hanmer for No. 52 in the same street, with a fifty-foot frontage, have already been cited. No. 51 Grosvenor Street (fig. 2b on page 106), another imposing five-bay house next door to Hanmer's, was purchased in 1726 by Sir John Werden for £3,900.[280] According to a contemporary newspaper report the Hon. John St. John paid £4,000 in 1738 for a house with over forty feet of frontage which now forms part of No. 75 South Audley Street, and from the evidence of his account at Hoare's Bank Sir Nathaniel Curzon paid £3,000 in 1729 for No. 66 Brook Street (Frontispiece; Plates 6c, 9a), both of these houses being built by Edward Shepherd.[281] Another large house with a thirty-five-foot frontage on the site of the present No. 32 Grosvenor Street was sold in 1726 for £2,800 to Charles Edwin, a Welsh landowner who was later M.P. for Westminster.[282]

The £5,000 paid in 1740 by the second Baron Conway (later created Earl and finally Marquess of Hertford) for No. 16 Grosvenor Street, a house with a fifty-five-foot frontage, comes into a slightly different category. Although Lord Conway paid the money to Thomas Ripley, the builder of the house, he was not the first occupant, No. 16 having already been inhabited for some fifteen years by Lord Walpole, the son of Sir Robert Walpole, who was Ripley's principal patron, and other instances have been found where houses acquired an enhanced value after having been lived in for some years.[283]

Prices in the region of £1,000 appear to have been usual for smaller houses in the principal streets. The 'Fifty Churches' Commissioners paid £1,300 to its builder for No. 15 Grosvenor Street,[284] and No. 35 Grosvenor Street

was sold for only £1,250[285] even though it stood next door to Sir Paul Methuen's grand house which cost him nearly four times that sum, and moreover was built at the same time by the same builder. Another house in Grosvenor Street, on the site of No. 65, was purchased by a widow in 1726 for £1,240.[286] On the north side of Brook Street to the east of Davies Street prices were significantly lower, two houses on the site of the present Nos. 52 and 54 with twenty-foot frontages selling for £500 and £550 in 1725.[287] In the lesser streets, with one or two notable exceptions, they tended to be lower still. In 1737 Captain Robert Booth paid only £180 to Edward Shepherd for No. 11 North Audley Street,[288] a house which still survives behind a later façade and which was even smaller than its twenty-two-foot frontage suggests. A house in James (now Gilbert) Street sold for £250 in 1726 and one in South Audley Street in 1730 for £275.[289]

Rack-rental values also varied widely. In auction particulars dating from about 1745 of the estate which had belonged to Thomas Barlow, the annual value of twenty-five houses on the south side of Grosvenor Street is given.[21] The average was £88, the highest being £220 for a house with a forty-two-foot frontage built by Benjamin Timbrell. Francis Salvadore, a merchant in the City, paid Edward Shepherd £250 per annum on behalf of the Portuguese ambassador for No. 74 South Audley Street,[290] and the Earl of Chesterfield paid £240 yearly for No. 45 Grosvenor Square (with an option to purchase the house for £4,200 which he did not take up).[291] There is, however, a remarkable contrast between the £396 per annum paid by Lord Weymouth for No. 7 Grosvenor Square and the annual rent of £24 which Richard Barlow, Thomas Barlow's son, paid Edward Shepherd for a house in North Audley Street.[292] Some houses built by John Jenner in Mount Row were valued at an even lower figure, for his widow stated that five of them were worth annually only £60 altogether.[293]

Perhaps understandably there is more clear evidence about the failures of builders than their successes, but some at least left their descendants in a comfortable if not vastly wealthy state. The example of Thomas Barlow, who was also the estate surveyor, is given on page 12. Thomas Richmond, a carpenter from Soho who built three houses in Grosvenor Square, left an estate consisting chiefly of leasehold houses worth over £8,000 at his death in 1739.[294] Edward Shepherd, although indebted to Hoare's Bank, was also in a basically sound financial position at the time of his death in 1747. His widow sold some of his property to clear his debts, and after a long series of disputes the bulk of his estate was sold at the end of the eighteenth century for over £13,000.[295] When Benjamin Timbrell died in 1754 his daughter claimed that he owned freehold land and houses to the annual value of £1,000 and leasehold ground on which he had built 'several large and magnificent Dwelling Houses', which, together with his money, stocks and other securities, gave him a personal estate of £20,000, but that his executors were defrauding her of her share of the inheritance by claiming that he died in mean and low circumstances.[296] One is more inclined to believe her side of the story, but even a successful builder such as Timbrell could find his affairs severely compromised at times. John Green was described as 'a very wealthy Builder' at the time of his unfortunate demise in 1737[297] and when his son died two years later he was said to be 'possessed of a plentiful Estate',[298] but nevertheless the Grosvenors do not appear to have been able to recover the money owed by Green towards the cost of making the garden in Grosvenor Square.[36] It may be noted that, with the possible exception of Green, all of these builders had extensive interests outside the Grosvenor estate.

The bankruptcy records for the years 1720–75 show that commissions of bankruptcy were awarded against 38 of the 290 known builders or allied tradesmen working on the estate.[299] There is, however, evidence that many builders became insolvent without actually being declared bankrupt and that in several cases the assets of a builder at his death were insufficient to meet his liabilities. A document among the estate records dating from about 1738, with revisions made some years later, lists the amounts still owing from builders for the laying-out of the garden of Grosvenor Square.[36] This indicates that of the thirty-one builders or firms to take plots around the square, eight became bankrupt and at least another eight died either insolvent or with insufficient funds to complete the payments.* Of the eight bankruptcies, seven can be confirmed from other sources and there is little reason to doubt the basic accuracy of this record, which was intended to aid in the recovery of money owed to the estate. Typical of several marginal comments on the document is that beside the name of Francis Bailley which reads 'A prisoner many years and not worth a shilling', with the single word 'dead' added later, evidently to conclude the matter.

Some indication of the narrow margin under which builders operated is given in a letter from the builder Roger Blagrave's solicitor to Robert Andrews in 1744 or 1745. Blagrave, who built several substantial houses in South Audley Street, South Street and Park Street, had apparently made an addition to one of his houses which extended beyond the limits of his building plot and was consequently having difficulty in obtaining a building lease. His solicitor claimed that as a result Blagrave was unable to borrow money to complete the house and concluded, with no doubt pardonable overstatement on behalf of his client, that 'The Man has laid out all his Substance and many Years Constant Labour in these Houses and if he Cannot Obtain a Term in this peice must be inevitably Ruined and cannot get Money to pay his Journeymen another Weeks Wages and is really very Deserving'.[300]

Other Features of the Development

Of the two features often considered essential for the success of a large scheme of development—a church and a market—the Grosvenor estate initially provided only the former. In some ways this might have been considered the less needed, for the large new church of St. George, Hanover Square, was consecrated in 1725 and the Grosvenors assisted firstly the 'Fifty Churches' Commissioners and then the authorities of the new parish after its formation in 1725 in a series of ways. In 1723 they sold the freehold of one and a half acres near the southern boundary of their estate to provide a burial ground for the church.[301] The price of £315, or £210 per acre, if calculated on the normal basis of thirty years' purchase of an assumed ground rent of £7 per acre, was little more than the agricultural value of the land and was well below the potential value realized in the course of development. They later also sold the freehold of No. 15 Grosvenor Street at thirty years' purchase of the ground rent of £4 10s. to the Commissioners as a residence for the rector of St. George's,[302] and allowed a workhouse for the parish to be built in Mount Street on a ninety-nine-year lease.[303]

The provision of a chapel near the western boundary of the estate was, however, planned from the first,[105] and when the land for it was made available in 1730 to the three building tradesmen and Robert Andrews who were jointly to build it, the words of the agreement made it plain that spiritual considerations were subordinated to practical aims. The preamble stated that, 'As well for the Conveniency and Accomodation of the severall Tenants or Inhabitants of new Houses lately built… lyeing in and about Grosvenor Square…As also for the Encouraging and promoting of building in Generall upon such parts of the said Estate as yet remain unbuilt It hath been adjudged and thought proper to erect a Chappell'.[203] Sir Richard Grosvenor assisted the chapel's proprietors by granting contiguous building land in South Audley Street to them at very low ground rents, but apart from reserving pews for his family and servants he did not directly involve himself in its erection and management, even though it eventually became known as the Grosvenor Chapel (Plate 12b; fig. 7 on page 119). In 1732 he sold the fee simple of its site to the rector and churchwardens of St. George's as a means of resolving the problem that the vaults under the chapel could not be consecrated for burials unless the ground were held freehold by the parish.[304]

The burial ground and the sites of the rectory and chapel were the only parts of the estate sold freehold during the eighteenth century. Another Anglican proprietary chapel, St. Mary's, was, however, built in 1762 on leasehold ground at the south-east corner of Park Street and Green Street.[305]

---

* It should be noted that these failures did not necessarily arise from the engagements in Grosvenor Square alone, for the builders concerned also had commitments elsewhere.

The Grosvenors did not promote the development of a market on their estate until the 1780's when Grosvenor Market, occupying an inconveniently situated site at the north-east corner of the estate in the northern part of the triangle bounded by South Molton Lane, Davies Street and Davies Mews, was erected partly by speculative building and partly under contract.[306] It was not a success, for a rival market called St. George's Market had just been established to the east of James (now Gilbert) Street. This was on part of a large plot on the north side of Brook Street which had been leased in 1726 to Edward Shepherd for ninety-nine years, and in this lease the only trades listed as noxious had been those of brewer and melter of tallow.[307] The ground landlord therefore had virtually no control here, and in many other areas of the estate few trades were restricted and shops had been established from an early date. A petition by the builders of Grosvenor Market complained of such shops, particularly those of butchers, who, the petitioners thought, were defying their lease covenants, in Oxford Street, Chapel Street, North and South Audley Streets, North Row, Park Street, Davies Street, Mount Street and Duke Street.[308] Both the Westminster poll books of 1749 and a list of householders in the parish of St. George, Hanover Square, dating from c. 1790, show that a substantial proportion of the occupants of these and other streets were indeed tradesmen (see Chapter V).[309] Grosvenor Market nevertheless struggled on for some decades, but it gradually ceased to be a centre for retail trade, and the whole site was re-developed in 1890.

Taverns and coffee houses were also, originally, extremely numerous, and the very first building to be completed on the estate was probably the Mount Coffee House at the eastern end of Grosvenor Street.[310] Although some attempt was made in early building agreements to restrict them to the mews or minor streets they were soon to be found in all parts of the estate except Grosvenor Square. In the main streets they were generally confined to corner sites where the entrance and sign could be sited less obtrusively in a side street or alley.[311] The death in 1739 of Mr. Fellows, master of the Three Tuns tavern in Grosvenor Street, was reported in *The London Daily Post*, where he was described as 'well known among the Builders; and is said to have died rich'.[312] Building workers no doubt provided a large part of the clientele of such places in the early years.

A supply of water was obtained from the Chelsea Water Works Company, which was incorporated under an Act of 1722 and which obtained a royal warrant in 1725 to build a reservoir at the eastern edge of Hyde Park to supply *inter alia* the new buildings about Oliver's Mount (Plate 2). Water for the reservoir came from a system of basins and canals connected with the Thames on the Grosvenors' Pimlico property, and at first had to be raised to the higher levels of Mayfair by horse power until pumping machinery was installed in 1742. The reservoir was converted into an ornamental basin with a fountain in the middle in 1835 and its (much diminished) site is now occupied by the fountain to the south of Grosvenor Gate.[313]

The Chelsea Company's supply was, however, by no means adequate at all times and for all purposes. In 1742 a man who was employed by the inhabitants of Grosvenor Street to water the roadway during the summer complained to the Westminster Commissioners of Sewers of irregularities in supply, 'the said Water not coming in sometimes for a fortnight together'. He sought permission to obtain the water which he needed from the common sewer flowing under Avery Row, and this request was granted.[314] Some houses had private wells, as is evidenced by the fate of John Green, the builder, who drowned when he fell into one at No. 43 Upper Grosvenor Street.

An ancient conduit pipe, which originally carried water from springs at Paddington to the City of London, ran under the north-west corner of the estate a short distance to the south of Oxford Street. Clauses were written into agreements and leases of plots in the area protecting the rights of the proprietors of the London Bridge Water Works Company (who had been granted a lease of the conduit system by the City Corporation) to have access to the pipes and any conduit heads. When the present No. 449 Oxford Street was being rebuilt in 1875 a conduit head was discovered underneath the former house on the site in a good state of preservation, and drawings were made of it. Another was situated further west, on the east side of Park Street near the corner with Oxford Street, and was housed in a building which belonged to the City Corporation, presumably by right of the medieval charters granting to the City the ownership of the pipes and other features of the system. In 1866, when this corner of Park Street and Oxford Street was first being redeveloped, the Grosvenor Estate paid £2,470 to the Corporation to buy the freehold of the ground on which the 'conduit house' stood.[315]

Conclusion

The development of the Grosvenor estate in Mayfair proceeded with great pace until 1740, and then in a more desultory fashion as the momentum of building slowed throughout the metropolis. In 1741 the builder Roger Blagrave was complaining about paying rates on several of his houses in South Street which were standing empty,[316] and of the thirty-eight builders on the estate who are known to have become bankrupt, nine suffered this fate during the years 1740 to 1742. In 1754 the parish Vestry drew attention to the unsatisfactory state of the western end of Upper Brook Street, where land on the south side had stood vacant for some time,[317] and the twenty-year gap between the dates when sub-leases were granted to the builders of No. 35 (1737) and No. 34 (1756)[318] suggests a considerable slackening in demand over this period. Nevertheless, despite the lapse of over fifty years before building work on the estate was completed, the basic layout scheme was adhered to with little alteration, and on the whole the development can be accounted a success. Horwood's map of 1792–9 shows that some 1,375 houses were built on the estate, besides many other buildings such as coach-houses, stables, workshops, riding houses, chapels and a workhouse. The evidence of ratebooks suggests that there were few very long delays in filling houses once built and the presence among the early occupants of many people of rank and wealth indicates that fashionable society was well represented from the very start (see Chapter V).

Sir John Summerson has remarked that in the eighteenth century 'Ground landlords rarely found it practicable to dictate the architectural character of the buildings on their land. They might set out the lines of the streets and squares, but once the building agreements were signed the control of elevations was virtually out of their hands'.[319] This was certainly true on the Grosvenor estate. The Grosvenors commissioned the severely rectilinear layout and provided a good deal of practical assistance to builders but they appear to have eschewed any overall aesthetic control. The only notable case in which architectural uniformity was achieved was on the east side of Grosvenor Square, where a composite elevation with centre and wings was created by the undertaker John Simmons. Edward Shepherd did the same in a slightly grander style with three houses on the north side, but they were not even in the centre of the long range of thirteen houses there. In the description of the square in the 1754 edition of Stow's *Survey* the author remarks that the lack of uniformity in the houses had been criticized but concludes that 'they are so far uniform, as to be all sashed and of pretty near an equal Height'.[320] Much the same could be said of the other streets. The kind of overall architectural composition which John Crunden achieved in the 1770's with a small group of three houses in Park Street between North Row and Hereford Street (Plate 13c) was very much the exception, and, of course, in this case dated from the end of the development. Elsewhere the generality of plain brick façades no doubt provided a measure of homogeneity, and most houses appear to have been of three storeys with basements and garrets (an effect now largely obscured by the addition of one or more extra storeys to many houses), but the storey heights were by no means uniform and the width of frontages differed widely.*

An example of the suspicion with which building tradesmen regarded attempts to produce uniformity occurs in the agreement of 1742 to build a group of seven houses in Upper Brook Street, previously mentioned on page 24. Here the words 'that the said Houses shall have a continued Brick Facie through the same and the several Windows thereof shall respectively rainge with each other so as to make a regular Line of Building as to the said Facie and Windows' have all been struck through, the alteration being insisted upon by the several building tradesmen who were parties to the agreement before they would execute the deed.[226]

The most important houses were generally built in Grosvenor Square and the principal east–west streets, viz.: Brook Street and Upper Brook Street, Grosvenor Street and Upper Grosvenor Street. There were exceptions, notably Bourdon House in Davies Street, Roger Morris's own house at No. 61 Green Street, Ligonier's house at No. 12 North Audley Street, the range for which Edward Shepherd was undertaker at Nos. 71–75 (consec.) South Audley Street and the group of houses opposite at Nos. 9–16 (consec.), all of which survive in some form. Some of the larger houses built in Park Lane and the north-western corner of the estate at a late date also deviated from the general pattern, and, from the evidence of the social status of their occupants, the houses at the south end of Park Street with gardens extending to Park Lane were of some quality. Even some of the smaller houses in streets like North Audley Street, Duke Street or South Street—selling at about £200 to £300 or renting at approximately £25 per annum—were, however, by no means insubstantial. The house on the east side of North Audley Street which Richard Barlow rented from Edward Shepherd in 1733 for £24 had a yard or garden and a stable behind, and consisted of three storeys and a basement. The rooms above ground were 'wainscotted all round from bottom to top' and had Portland stone or marble chimneypieces.[321] Houses built by John Jenner on the south side of Mount Row, which was essentially a mews, were of low annual value, but an insurance policy on one of them for £200 shows that it had three storeys and a garret with four rooms wainscotted and four Portland stone chimneypieces.[322]

Some of the houses in Mount Row were sub-divided from the time of first letting, and, despite the reputation of Mayfair as a preserve of the rich, there was originally a good deal of accommodation for the less well-to-do, not least on the Grosvenor estate. There were a number of courts and passages, some of them opening out of the principal streets, and several of the mews had dwelling houses as well as stables and coach-houses built in them, particularly Adams Mews (now Row), Grosvenor Mews (now Grosvenor Hill, Bourdon Street and Bourdon Place), Lees Mews (now Place), Mount Row and Reeves Mews. In the northern part of the estate, where large blocks of land had been let under single leases with few restrictive covenants, streets like James (now Gilbert) Street and Bird (now Binney) Street were laid out in rows of narrow-fronted houses which had very little open space at the rear. These houses in the vicinity of Gilbert Street were rebuilt during the years 1822 to 1833 in the

---

* For instance, the plots on the south side of Grosvenor Street between Davies Street and the Mount Coffee House sub-leased by Thomas Barlow, the estate surveyor, had the following frontages (in feet): 17½, 19, 25, 36, 36, 24, 18, 20, 17, 19, 21½, 35, 28, 20, 35, 35, 42, 34, 34, 22, 26, 37, 19½.

first major redevelopment scheme to take place on the estate, but there is no evidence that any desire to raise the social *cachet* of the area lay behind the decision of the Grosvenor Estate to sanction this speculative venture by the builder Seth Smith.

Brown's Court, which lay between North Row and Green Street, and was one of several such alleys on the south side of North Row, is an example of the lower level of housing provided on the estate. The ground on which it was laid out was part of the large area bounded by North Row, North Audley Street, Green Street and Park Street which was leased *en bloc* in 1728 at a ground rent of four shillings per annum.[323] The lease stipulated merely that 'good and substantial' houses should be built on the

NORTH   ROW

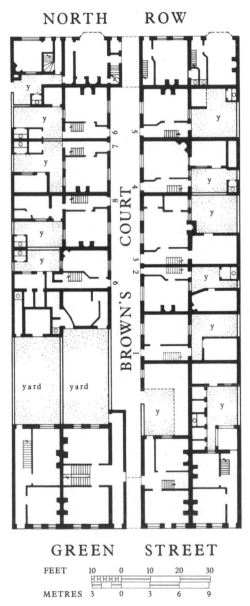

GREEN   STREET

FEET	10	0	10	20	30
METRES	3	0	3	6	9

Fig. 1. Brown's Court with adjoining houses in Green Street and North Row. Ground-floor plan in *c.* 1800

main street frontages and the only restricted trade was that of a brewer. In 1730 John Brown, bricklayer, was granted a sub-lease of part of this ground[324] and by 1739[71] he had built nine tiny two-storey houses along a ten-foot-wide court entered from Green Street and North Row through even narrower arched passageways. Some of the houses had garrets and cellars but several had neither. Each house was virtually one room deep with a yard behind, and the small closet wings belonging to some of the houses shown in the ground plan of the court at the end of the eighteenth century (fig. 1) may have been additions. Brown's Court was largely, or perhaps completely, rebuilt in 1824[325] and was swept away during the redevelopment of the north side of Green Street at the end of the nineteenth century.

Some idea of the unsatisfactory condition of that area of the estate which lay immediately to the south of Oxford Street at the beginning of the nineteenth century can be gleaned from a letter written in 1816 to Lord Grosvenor by Edward Boodle, his lawyer. He had been induced, he wrote, 'to be of a Committee of Inhabitants to go round a part of the Parish between the North side of Grosvenor Square and Green Street, and the South side of Oxford Street', and he had 'never experienced in one day more scenes of distress and misery than presented themselves to us in the course of that day's investigation'.[326] The first Duke of Westminster was later to make the improvement of this area one of his major philanthropic concerns, and in the late nineteenth century several blocks of working-class dwellings were erected to the north of Grosvenor Square and Brook Street. They replaced the run-down houses which were the legacy of the treatment of this part of the estate as a relative backwater from the start of development.

The extensive stabling required by the occupants of the larger houses—many had more than one coach-house—spilled out from the mews into the lesser streets. Some attempt was made to limit this by provisions in building agreements, but stabling with access directly into the roadway was built in South Street, Park Lane and Oxford Street among others, and parts of the frontages of the 'cross streets' (as the north-south streets were called) were taken up with either garden walls or the flank walls of coach-houses and stables. Several large blocks of stables and 'riding houses' were also built, usually for army regiments, the largest being that provided in the 1730's by Roger Morris for the Second Troop of Horse Guards between Green Street and Wood's Mews. The presence of such buildings does not seem to have been considered detrimental to the amenities of the estate; no specific restrictions appear to have been placed on their use, and care was taken in the leasing of adjoining plots to preserve their light:[327] for the stables built by Morris a plot on the south side of Green Street was even left vacant to be used as a 'dung place'.[328]

For the ground landlords the principal benefit of the development lay, of course, in the distant future when the terms of the first building leases would come to an end, and renewals could be granted at greatly enhanced rents with premiums or fines payable on renewal. In the meantime, however, some years elapsed before their income from the new buildings even matched their expenditure. The agricultural rent received from the fields in Mayfair in the early eighteenth century was between £3 and £4 an acre,[329] or probably somewhat less than £400 for the whole estate there. Once the land had been turned over to the builders the income from ground rents did not begin to exceed this figure until 1725,[45] and it was during these early years that the Grosvenors were spending heavily in the promotion of their new development. If the account of Dame Mary Grosvenor's personal estate at her death in 1730 is taken at its face value, the money spent for this purpose up to that time exceeded the total income received from the speculation by over £4,500.[40] In 1732, however, Sir Richard Grosvenor was able to reap an early advantage from the whole project by borrowing £10,000 at 4 per cent interest from one of his tenants, the loan being made on the security of the newly created ground rents of houses in Brook Street, Grosvenor Street and Grosvenor Square.[180] As more and more houses were built the income gradually increased, and in 1743 this loan was repaid.[330] Eventually the ground rents received from the whole of The Hundred Acres amounted in 1768 (before any leases had been renewed) to £3,133 per annum, or £31 per acre,[331] plus £312 per annum received in improved rents from Sir Robert Grosvenor's trust estate.[332]

Because of the great extent of their landholdings in various parts of England and Wales, it is difficult to determine the effect of the development of Mayfair upon the Grosvenor family's finances, but there is little doubt that the reversionary value of the houses there as building leases began to fall in was a crucial factor in helping to preserve solvency at a difficult period. By the 1770's the affairs of Lord Grosvenor had reached a parlous state: besides his establishment at Eaton he maintained a racing stable at Newmarket costing over £7,000 a year and paid out another £9,400 annually in jointures, annuities and interest charges on mortgages (including £1,200 to his estranged wife). He had apparently been living beyond his means for some time and in 1779 his debts amounted to over £150,000.[73] On the advice in particular of his London agent, Thomas Walley Partington, he contemplated selling all of his estates in Middlesex with the exception of The Hundred Acres in Mayfair and Grosvenor Place in Belgravia. He prevaricated, however, much to the annoyance of Partington, who concluded one letter with remarkable frankness, 'Do my Lord recollect what I laid before you…and for Gods sake as you value your own peace of mind, resolve upon something before Lady Day'.[333] Eventually in 1785 his estates were conveyed to five trustees, viz.: his brother Thomas Grosvenor, the Right Honourable Thomas Harley, the bankers Robert and Henry Drummond, and Thomas Walley Partington, to sell some lands and use the money, together with the remaining rents, to discharge the debts.[334] Over the next twenty years the increasing income from fines and higher rents as leases were renewed in Mayfair helped to retrieve the situation (see page 38), and in the event none of the London estates had to be sold. With the management of the estate passing to trustees and the appointment of an estate surveyor to advise on policy with regard to lease renewals in the 1780's, however, a new stage in the history of the estate had effectively begun.

CHAPTER III

The Administration of the Estate 1785-1899

Between the completion of the first building development in *c.* 1780 and the accession of the second Duke of Westminster in 1899, which may be regarded as the start of the modern phase of the history of the estate, four members of the Grosvenor family held the property. During this period Baron Grosvenor was created Earl Grosvenor in 1784, and his son and great-grandson were respectively advanced to the Marquessate of Westminster (1831) and to a dukedom (1874), the latter being the only wholly new dukedom in the peerage of the United Kingdom (apart from those connected with the Royal House) to be created in the whole of the reign of Queen Victoria.[1] Two younger brothers of the second Marquess of Westminster also held distinct peerages, one as Earl of Wilton and the other as Baron Ebury, and in 1886 the Marquess's youngest son was created Baron Stalbridge.[2] Thus in the closing years of the nineteenth century four members of the Grosvenor family sat in the House of Lords, all of them being, moreover, closely related by the marriages of both the second Marquess and the first Duke to the almost equally resplendent dynasty of Leveson-Gower, possessors since 1833 of the Dukedom of Sutherland, plus (in 1846) the Earldom of Ellesmere. And in the House of Commons other members of the Grosvenor family sat in one of the two seats for the City of Chester from 1715 to 1874 without a break. For forty-two years of this period they held both the Chester seats, while other members of the family often represented other constituencies.[3]

This rapid social or dynastic advancement was matched by a corresponding growth in the wealth of the family, which was increasingly based upon the London estates. At a dinner party in 1819 the Chancellor of the Exchequer (Nicholas Vansittart) informed the American minister in London that the property-tax returns showed that Earl Grosvenor was one of the four richest men in England, with an annual income of 'beyond one hundred thousand pounds, clear of everything'.[4] At that time the enhancement of revenue from the Mayfair portion of the estate by the renewal of the original building leases was still at an early stage, and the development of Belgravia and Pimlico had hardly even begun. In the succeeding decades these two sources produced a torrent, and in 1865 the Grosvenors were described as 'the wealthiest family in Europe —perhaps...the wealthiest uncrowned house on earth'.[5]

Professional Advisers and Estate Staff

During the period covered by this chapter each of the four successive owners of the Grosvenor estate took an active part in the administration of their London properties, and this is described later. Their professional advisers were nevertheless influential. The most important of these were the successive partners in the legal firm of Partington and Boodle. After the death of Thomas Walley Partington in 1791 these were Edward Boodle (d. 1828),[6] and his nephew John Boodle,[7] who from 1806 had a house in Davies Street before removing first, in 1829, to his uncle's house at No. 55 Brook Street until 1836, and then to No. 53 Davies Street (now the Grosvenor Office).[8] The latter appears to have been used principally, or solely, as an office, John Boodle's residence from this time being in Connaught Square; and he also had a property called Heath Farm, near Watford. After his death in 1859 his effects were valued at 'under £14,000'.[9] Since at least 1838 he had been in partnership with his younger son, William Chilver Boodle, his son-in-law, Edward Partington, and his first cousin (Edward Boodle's son), Henry Mitford Boodle.[10] In 1858 they were joined by Henry Mitford's son, Henry Trelawny Boodle, both then living in Leinster Gardens, Bayswater.[11] Henry Mitford died at his house in Tunbridge Wells in 1878, leaving a personal estate of 'under £8,000';[12] Edward Partington, who lived at Gloucester Place, Hyde Park, died in 1883 leaving a personal estate of 'under £24,206',[13] and William Chilver Boodle, who had lived first in Connaught Square but latterly in Dover, died in 1887, leaving personal estate of 'under £11,694'.[14] The surviving partner, Henry Trelawny Boodle, was joined in 1897 by his two sons, Trelawny Frederick and Walter Trelawny Boodle,[11] and died at his house on Wimbledon Common in 1900 leaving effects valued at £48,892.[15] With the admission of G. F. Hatfield to a partnership in 1899 the name of the firm became Boodle Hatfield and Company.[11] Trelawny Frederick died in 1930 and his brother Walter Trelawny —the last of the Boodles to be connected with the firm— in 1931.[16]

Until the death of Edward Partington in 1883 the firm entered itself in the directories as 'Boodle and Partington, conveyancers'. Thereafter only the names of the individual partners appear, but in 1898 the entry becomes 'Boodle and Co., solicitors' and in 1899 'Boodle Hatfield and Co., solicitors'. It was in fact a firm of lawyers with many other clients besides the Grosvenors, and with one exception its members were paid by the Grosvenors by fee, not by regular salary. The one exception was Edward Boodle, whose financial difficulties led in 1807 to his borrowing several thousand pounds from the second Earl Grosvenor,[17] and in return the latter agreed to pay him partly by fee and partly by a regular salary of some £250 per annum.[18] It follows, therefore, that none of the partners—not even Edward Boodle, who in 1808 was 'in high spirits' upon being offered the receivership of the estates of the late Lady Bath[19]—ever devoted the whole of his attention to the affairs of the Grosvenor estate. Henry Trelawny Boodle, for instance, as solicitor to the Marquess of Northampton, had at least one other client with property problems even more complex and probably time-consuming than those of the Grosvenors in Mayfair and Belgravia.[20]

The Grosvenors' advisers also included in the latter part of the eighteenth and throughout most of the nineteenth centuries a succession of 'agents'. The first recorded of these was John Boydell, a nephew of Alderman John Boydell, the engraver and print publisher who became Lord Mayor of London in 1790, and a brother of the Alderman's partner, Josiah Boydell. The Boydell family came from Shropshire and Flintshire, and another of John Boydell's uncles, Thomas Boydell, was in Earl Grosvenor's service at Eaton, evidently as steward. John Boydell is known to have been the Earl's London agent from at least 1787 until 1791, when he became insolvent. He lived at a house in Stratton Street,[21] and his functions included the management of the Earl's London household, the payment of tradesmen's bills, servants' wages and sometimes of expenses at Newmarket. At that time the Earl's financial affairs were in an extremely disordered state, and John Boydell seems to have got into the habit of accepting bills of exchange in his own name, partly, at any rate, in order to pay the Earl's more pressing creditors. In 1791 John Boydell fell ill and the Earl, feeling 'much uneasiness from the apparent irregular management of his Household affairs', discovered that many tradesmen's accounts had not been paid for five or six years. In the ensuing investigation John Boydell was declared insolvent, and the Earl paid his assignees in bankruptcy some £2,500. Both Edward Boodle and Josiah Boydell were active in these inquiries, and the former said of John Boydell that his 'errors appear to be of the head and not the heart'.[22]

The next agent was Abraham Moore, a London barrister who was appointed in 1796 after the manager of the family lead mines in North Wales had proved 'a most decided Knave', having 'gone off to America, loaded with more spoils than those of' Earl Grosvenor himself, whose income from this source in 1800 amounted to over £18,000.[23] At that time Earl Grosvenor was so deeply in debt that he had 'no regular disposable income at all but what is derived from Cheshire and North Wales',[24] and Moore's main function seems to have been (in addition to the management of the mines) the imposition of some sort of order on the Earl's embarrassingly disordered financial affairs. In 1809-12 he was paid a salary of £500 per annum, but he also received fees for the management of an election at Chester,[25] and like the Boodles he had extensive other commitments, regularly

absenting himself from his chambers in the Temple for weeks at a time to practise on the Western Circuit, as well as to attend to such other matters as 'holding the Eton College courts'. His correspondence gives an impression of great efficiency, his constant orders to Edward Boodle, and more particularly to the steward at Eaton Hall and to the local manager of the Welsh mines, being followed up in the latter case by annual personal visits to Eaton during the Long Vacation.[26] But in the long run a part-time agent did not prove a success, for in 1821 it was discovered that Moore had been supporting his numerous financial transactions 'by a most ingenious fraud', thereby cheating the second Earl Grosvenor, who now described him as 'one of the greatest Scoundrels in existence', of very large sums of money.[27] Like his predecessor at the lead mines he too departed to America, where he died at Jersey City in the following year.[28]

After these débâcles the next agent was a man of altogether lesser status than Moore. This was Edmund Empy,[29] who seems to have been employed by Earl Grosvenor as a clerk at a salary of £50 per annum as early as 1802.[30] In 1808, when Moore and a mentor of the second Earl Grosvenor, John Hailstone, were chivvying Edward Boodle to re-organise his office, Hailstone reported to the Earl that 'you will see how we are driving on with Boodle. We have got a separate room in his house for *our* clerk, a measure which I was determined to carry at the point of the bayonet, for if this plan is effective it will depend on keeping our authority paramount and distinct.'[31] This clerk, employed by Earl Grosvenor but working in Boodle's office, was probably Empy, and from his installation 'at the point of the bayonet' in Boodle's premises evidently originates the arrangement whereby the salaried staff of the Grosvenor Office and the quite separate staff of the Grosvenors' lawyers were housed under the same roof—an arrangement which continued at No. 53 Davies Street until 1923, and is even now perpetuated by their occupation of adjacent premises which still share a common entrance at No. 53.

Empy did not have overall control of the administration of the Earl's affairs as had Moore. He seems indeed to have been only concerned with the London properties, where he was occupied with the collection of rents, the renewal of leases and the general maintenance of the estate.[32] The tone of letters addressed to him by the second Earl from Eaton suggests that even in London his position was a relatively subordinate one.[33]

Empy lived at No. 100 Park Street from 1823 to 1841,[34] when he seems to have retired; he died at Tunbridge Wells in 1845 or 1846.[35] He was succeeded by Abraham Howard, who is described as 'agent to the Marquess of Westminster' at the Grosvenor Office, No. 9 (now 53) Davies Street, and sometimes as a conveyancer. He lived at No. 2 Eccleston Square[36] where he died in 1864, leaving effects 'under £5,000'.[37] His successor, Frank Burge, from 1864 to 1870, was initially paid £300 per annum, later raised to £400. His duties were to keep the accounts and letterbooks, enter up rentals and leases, and fill in in colour all lease plots on maps of the London estate. His office hours were from 10 a.m. to 4 p.m., and he was to attend the weekly Board meetings on Wednesday evenings; he was not to take any other employment.[38] In 1865 an auditor of the Marquess's London estates was also appointed, at a salary of £100, later raised to £300.[39]

Neither Burge nor the next agent, William R. Glennie (1871–92), were lawyers,[11] but Glennie had previously been in the employment of the second Marquess of Westminster since at least 1855, possibly as steward at Grosvenor House.[40] In 1885 he was receiving a salary of £600 per annum, and after his retirement in 1892, a pension of £400.[41] He lived at Berkeley Lodge, Wimbledon,[11] and at his death in 1902 he left effects valued at £8,860.[42] His successor, Charles Robert French, had also previously been in the family's service, again probably as steward at Grosvenor House, and in 1895 his salary was £480 per annum.[43] He remained agent until 1918, living at Evelyn Gardens, South Kensington; he died in 1922, leaving effects valued at £3,877.[44]

In addition to their lawyers and their salaried 'agents', the Grosvenors also employed a series of 'surveyors', all of whom were architects of some distinction with their own independent private practices, and whose works are discussed elsewhere. The first (after the death of Thomas Barlow in 1730) was William Porden (c. 1755–1822), who was appointed by the first Earl Grosvenor in or soon after 1784,[45]* when valuations of properties on the Mayfair estate for the renewal of the original building leases were beginning to require professional advice. He was paid a retaining fee or salary of £200 per annum, but he also charged a fee for other work for Earl Grosvenor, notably at Eaton Hall and Grosvenor House.[50] His successors from 1821 were Thomas Cundy I, II and III, who held the position of surveyor successively to 1890. Cundy II and III both received salaries varying from £300 to £500 per annum,[51] but their principal remuneration was by fee for the extensive works which they superintended for the Grosvenors;[52] and probably Thomas Cundy I was paid in the same way.† From 1890 to 1910 the estate surveyor was Eustace Balfour, whose partner in private practice was Thackeray Turner.

Thus throughout the whole of the nineteenth century (and indeed even later) the only full-time salaried staff employed by the Grosvenors for the administration of their Mayfair estate, not to mention the development of those in Belgravia and Pimlico, were the 'agents' and

their clerical assistants. After Moore's defalcation in 1821 the importance of the post of agent was greatly and no doubt intentionally reduced, and its subordinate position is clearly seen in the fact that it was H. T. Boodle and not W. R. Glennie who gave evidence relating to the Grosvenor estate to the Select Committee of the House of Commons on Town Holdings in 1887.

In the management of their almost equally great wealth the Dukes of Bedford contrived a different system. Like the Grosvenors, they had very valuable London properties and large country estates, but they 'were advised firstly by a peripatetic chief agent, and secondly, by the local stewards of each estate'. All of them were full-time salaried employees, often they seem to have been lawyers, and at least one of the agents, Rowland Prothero, later Lord Ernle and President of the Board of Agriculture from 1916 to 1919, was a man of great distinction. From 1815 onwards they compiled annual reports on the condition of the estates, thereby providing successive Dukes of Bedford (and later, their grateful historians) with a bird's-eye view of the general situation.[54] In 1887 it was the steward of the London estates in Covent Garden and Bloomsbury who gave evidence—very ably—to the Select Committee on Town Holdings; and it is hard to resist the conclusion that the administrative system on the Bedford estate was in the nineteenth century better organised than on the Grosvenor.

The Estate in Trust, 1785–1808

Towards the end of the eighteenth century tenants on the Mayfair estate began to apply to Lord Grosvenor for the renewal of their leases. The first such applicant, in 1774, was Lord Grosvenor's own lawyer, Thomas Walley Partington, for the two houses which he occupied on the south side of Brook Street. Although the original leases did not expire until 1801 and 1804 they were nevertheless renewed to 1826 at the same low ground rent as hitherto, with no additional restrictive covenants and without a fine.

In the north-eastern portion of the estate virtually all of the original building leases had been granted for only eighty years instead of the more usual ninety-nine years, and in 1778–81 Lord Grosvenor evidently intended to renew the leases here for terms the expiry dates of which would correspond roughly with those in nearby areas of the estate. In 1778–9 he therefore employed (Sir)

---

* The exact year of his appointment is uncertain. In 1785, when he may have been working in James Wyatt's office,[46] he was appointed surveyor to the Vestry of St. George's, Hanover Square,[47] and by 1786 he was certainly in Earl Grosvenor's employment. But in a letter written by him in 1814 to the second Earl Grosvenor he stated that 'I have now been 30 years in the service of your Lordship and your Lordship's Father', which, if correct, means that he was appointed in 1784.[48]

In 1783–6 John Jenkins was also acting as surveyor for Lord Grosvenor in the erection of Grosvenor Market, and for works at Lord Grosvenor's houses at No. 45 Grosvenor Square, Millbank and Salt Hill. In 1787 the payment of his fees for the latter three items, amounting to some £100, was witnessed by Porden.[49] There is no evidence that Jenkins was concerned in the general management of the Grosvenor estate.

† One of Thomas Cundy III's daughters married a son of Henry Mitford Boodle.[53]

Robert Taylor and George Shakespear to make a detailed plan of the north-eastern portion, to estimate the repairs needed at each house, and to assess the value of the fines to be paid by the tenants in order 'to make up their present Terms 41 years from Michaelmas 1778'.[55]* In 1780 two leases, one in Grosvenor Street and the other in Davies Street, were renewed in conformity with this intention, and 'fines' or premiums were exacted for the first time; but the policy was abandoned soon afterwards. In Davies Street the extra rent payable if certain listed undesirable trades were practised was £60 per annum, whereas in Grosvenor Street it remained at the original figure of £30.[56]

With many more similar applications certain to be received during the next few years, the renewal terms to be offered would clearly require careful consideration, and this was probably the principal reason for Lord Grosvenor's appointment of a surveyor to advise him.

The extra revenue to be derived from the fines payable on the renewal of the Mayfair leases was indeed already being regarded as the salvation of the estate from the enormous debts which, as we have already seen in the previous chapter, had been incurred by the first Lord Grosvenor. As early as 1772, when he was wanting to borrow another £5,000, Partington was 'presuming to remind your Lordship that when you borrowed the last money you determin'd it should be *the last* you would borrow'.[57] By April 1779, however, the situation was worse, and with debts of over £150,000 Lord Grosvenor was compelled to mortgage all his estates to the Right Honourable Thomas Harley, the bankers Robert and Henry Drummond (with whom Lord Grosvenor had banked since 1765), and Partington, who, as trustees for all the creditors, agreed to 'advance to his Lordship a Sum sufficient to pay all his Lordship's Debts in London, at Newmarket and elsewhere'. In return Lord Grosvenor undertook 'to give up his racing System by Selling and disposing of his Horses as soon as the then next meeting should be over', and to order all his rents (except £1,000 per annum for the support of Eaton Hall, Chester, and Halkyn Hall, Flintshire) to be remitted to the trustees for the payment of family jointures and of the interest on his debts. Lord Grosvenor was to be allowed £4,000 per annum, and the residue was to provide a sinking fund for the discharge of the principal sums—'which Fund was to be assisted by Fines to be now received for renewing Leases in Middlesex'.[58]

But this arrangement was not strict enough to salvage Lord Grosvenor (who did not in fact sell his horses until 1796),[59] and in 1781 Partington was exhorting him to 'turn your thoughts to what passed in April 1779, when your Friends stepped forward to save your Lordship from impending disgrace—pardon the word, but I call it so, because you had numerous creditors who would

have brought disgrace upon you, had you not satisfyed them by the Assistance of such Friends as I believe no Nobleman in such a situation ever met with; by their means every Debt was paid, and a Plan laid down to retrieve your affairs—Think my Lord how these Friends must feel at the present situation of your Affairs, and how hurt they must be to find their most friendly efforts ineffectual, and that instead of securing your Lordship they are likely to suffer great inconvenience themselves.'[60]

Even this and other 'fruitless representations' from Partington proved ineffective, however,[61] and in 1785 Lord Grosvenor was finally compelled to convey virtually all his estates to the same trustees as in 1779 plus his brother Thomas Grosvenor, upon trust to sell several properties, but excluding those in Mayfair.[62] The revenue shortly to arise from the renewal of the Mayfair leases was again thought of as an important factor in 'reducing the enormous Debt', and when these new dispositions were still in course of discussion, Partington urged Lord Grosvenor that 'in my humble opinion the sooner your Lordship appoints your Surveyor the better'.[61]

It was therefore in these extremely inauspicious circumstances that the renewal of many of the original building leases in Mayfair was commenced. In the history of any great estate this is the time when the initiative in determining the future character of the property returns to the ground landlord, and the decisions made are therefore of crucial importance. In the 1780's there were few, if any, precedents to follow, for many of the London estates originally developed under the leasehold system in the late seventeenth or early eighteenth centuries had since been broken up, and almost the only survivors of any size were those of the Crown and the Dukes of Bedford. On the former there seems, at any rate until 1794, to have been no settled policy respecting renewals or rebuildings.[63] Although on the Bedford estate in Covent Garden it had been the practice since the middle of the seventeenth century to require payment of a fine for renewal of leases, some of which prohibited certain trades without licence from the ground landlord, the impact of estate policy there was not great.[64] And the same seems to have been true further west on the numerous small estates in the northern part of the parish of St. James, where the falling-in of original leases was not responsible for any identifiable turn of the fabric towards neglect or renewal.[65]

So the Grosvenor estate authorities had to formulate their own policies with little guidance from elsewhere, and as the sole object of the trustees established in 1785 was to pay off the debts they naturally adopted a course which would bring in money quickly. This was by granting renewals at a low ground rent but subject to a large fine for such a term as would, with the remaining years of the existing original lease, make up a total term of sixty-three years.

---

* The very detailed plan made by Taylor and Shakespear forms the basis of fig. 4 on pages 110-11.

The first such lease granted by the trustees was in 1786,[66] and with some modifications in the ratio between the ground rent and the fine, this remained one of the basic features of estate policy in Mayfair for about a hundred years, and even then was not permanently abandoned. For the discharge of Lord Grosvenor's debts it proved eventually successful. Between 1789 and 1808 fines for the renewal of leases in Mayfair totalling over £180,000 were received,[67] and in the latter year the trust of 1785 was dissolved, the debts (with a few trifling exceptions) having been paid off. Some estates in Cheshire and Wales had had to be sold, but all those in London had been preserved intact.[68]

The authors of this policy were presumably Lord Grosvenor's surveyor and his trustees, two of whom, Robert and Henry Drummond, were bankers and therefore expert in money matters. The surveyor was William Porden, who held the post for some thirty-seven years before being finally superseded in 1821. Throughout this period he maintained his own private architectural practice, and (as previously mentioned) was paid a retaining fee or salary of £200 per annum by Lord Grosvenor. For valuations made for the renewal of leases he also received a fee of two guineas from the applicant, which was subsequently deducted from the fine payable to the trustees;[69] and for architectural work for Lord Grosvenor he also charged a commission of five per cent.[70] From 1796 until his death in 1822 he lived in Berners Street.

At first, as Partington had correctly foreseen in 1784, 'the money to be raised by renewing Leases' went 'but a little way' towards paying off the debts.[61] But in 1789 twelve leases were renewed, yielding fines totalling £6,581,[67] and this increase of business led at about this time to the establishment of a Board, the first known meeting of which was on 9 January 1789.

The records of the Grosvenor Board are contained in forty-six volumes of minute books extending from 1789 to about 1920. Throughout this period the Board dealt primarily with the renewal of leases, and also with any other matter affecting the estate. When the development of Belgravia, and later of Pimlico, began, the records became more voluminous, and later in the nineteenth century the amount of information recorded in each entry—which had at first been extremely sparse—became considerably more detailed. But throughout the whole period the method of entry remained basically the same: each item of business was entered, with the date, under the name of the applicant (or, in later years, of the address of the premises under consideration), generally on a new page, but sometimes, when space permitted, half way down beneath a short item of other completed business. Often in later years the entry for one item may extend over many pages and several volumes, and sometimes the chronological sequence of entries is confused by references back to a previous page or even volume where a blank space was deemed a suitable place to continue the record.

The names of those present at meetings were never recorded, but the members of the Board were, evidently, one or more of the partners from Boodle and Partington, the estate surveyor, the agent, and of course, whenever he desired to come, the reigning member of the Grosvenor family. The other trustees do not seem to have attended. The meetings were held weekly, until about 1838 at Boodle's office in Brook Street[71] and subsequently in 'the Board Room' at the Grosvenor Office at No. 53 Davies Street. In 1808 some fifty items of business were being considered at a single meeting, and the drafting of the minutes was evidently done by Lord Grosvenor's clerk and future agent, Edmund Empy.

The part played by the successive owners of the estate in the deliberations of the Board naturally varied according to the personal disposition of each holder of the Grosvenor family title. Often they were absent, 'out of town' or otherwise committed, but in general they seem to have attended assiduously when possible, and of course their wishes (sometimes conveyed in their absence in writing) overruled those of the other members of the Board. The first Earl Grosvenor made at least two decisions of some long-term importance, insisting in 1794 that in the renewal of leases the first claimant should be the owner of the existing lease,[72] and in 1791 (at Porden's instance) refusing to renew the leases of the houses on the site of the modern Nos. 93-99 (consec.) Park Lane in order to facilitate rebuilding at a later date.[73] He also provided the name for a 'Row of new buildings in the Road leading to Chelsea', and even concerned himself in such a trivial matter as the repair of a parish watch-house; but he wisely refused to interfere with the valuations which Porden made for the renewal of leases.[74]

Until 1808 the main object of the Board was to pay off the debts on the estate, and 'Lord Grosvenor's general terms' for renewal were therefore (as Edward Boodle informed an applicant in 1796) to extend 'the subsisting term to 63 years from the time of granting the renewal upon payment of a fine proportionate to the number of years to be added and calculated upon the rent or annual value after deducting the ground rents and land tax'.[75] The fine was payable immediately, but the new rent did not commence until the expiry of the original term. Whenever an application was received Porden would inspect the house and assess the annual value or rack rent, and also the appropriate ground rent which, until the debts were paid off, was kept very low in order to maximise the fine. The amount of the fine was then calculated, evidently by Boodle or Empy, and the terms sent to the applicant.

These calculations were based, at least as early as 1795, upon the published 'Tables of calculation', sometimes referred to as 'Smart's Tables'.[76] Commencing in 1707 John Smart, described as 'at the Town-Clerk's Office, London', had published several editions of Tables of Simple and Compound Interest, which were evidently used at first by the Grosvenor Board. In 1802, however, Francis Baily, the astronomer, published greatly improved

Tables for the purchasing and renewing of Leases,...with rules for determining the value of the reversion of estates after any such leases, which quickly ran through several editions and in 1811 were pirated (much to Baily's annoyance) by the architect William Inwood, whose compilation had by 1880 achieved twenty-one editions.[77]

The theory behind the tables was carefully explained by Baily. 'The sum paid down for the grant of a lease may be considered as so much money paid in advance for the annual rents, as they become due; or...it is such a sum given to the lessor as will enable him, by putting the money out to interest at the given rate, to repay himself the rack rent of the estate, or the yearly value of his interest therein, during the given term: all we have to do, therefore, in this inquiry, is to find out such a sum as, put out to interest at the rate required, will enable him to do this.'[78] This was done in his tables,[79] which gave the number by which the annual value was to be multiplied (referred to as the number of years' purchase) in order to obtain a lease for a given number of years, separate tables being provided for various rates of interest ranging from two to ten per cent.

On the Grosvenor estate, however, the leases being granted did not come into force immediately, but in reversion on the expiry of the subsisting term. In such cases the sum to be paid by the lessee for the addition of any number of years to the unexpired part of an old lease was equal to the difference between the value of the lease for the *whole term* (on the Grosvenor estate, sixty-three years) and the value of the unexpired part of this term already in the lessee's possession.[80] When this difference, expressed in years' purchase, had been calculated from the relevant table—that for five per cent was used on the Grosvenor estate at this time—the answer was multiplied by the annual value of the property after deduction of the ground rent and land tax, and provided the amount of the fine to be paid.*

During the course of negotiations for renewals countless calculations of this kind were made on the Grosvenor estate throughout the nineteenth century. The renewals were made for many years to the owner of 'the original lease from Lord Grosvenor's ancestor',[82] as the first Earl had decided in 1794.[72] This was often not the occupant, and the practice produced unsatisfactory results when the occupant had recently made improvements at his own expense. Thus in 1819 the Board minutes record that in the case of a public house in Grosvenor Mews (now Bourdon Street) the absentee head lessee had 'been in no respect a beneficial tenant to Lord Grosvenor, and should he treat for the renewal, it will only be to make a profit of the man who has been responsible for [the property]...; this system of giving an option to Lessees

under such circumstances has been attended with considerable inconvenience to Lord Grosvenor, and is contrary to the practice of other large estates in London, who treat only with the occupier unless the original improver be living. On the Duke of Northumberland's estate the occupiers only are treated with.'[83]

In this particular case the head lessee refused to treat, and ultimately the renewal was granted to the occupant, but when the two parties were competing against each other, preference was given to the head lessee, even though the Board were fully aware that he would thus be able to continue to make a profit by charging the occupant a higher rent than that stipulated in the ground lease.[84] It was not until 1873 that a particularly extortionate example of this sort of practice, at No. 9 Upper Grosvenor Street, led the third Marquess of Westminster, on the strong recommendation of Thomas Cundy III, to renew to the occupant,[85] and two or three years later this was stated to be the usual practice.[86]

At first the rigidity of the system adopted by the Board for the assessment of fines met with hostility from some applicants. The Bishop of Gloucester, for instance, on being informed in 1795 that the fine for the renewal of the lease of his house at the corner of Davies Street and Grosvenor Street would be £3,010, 'expressed his surprize at the magnitude of the fine, and said he supposed it amounted to a prohibition to renew'.[87] But the fact that the calculation of the fines was made upon scientifically based published tables and could therefore be checked by the applicant meant that unless he was able to dispute Porden's valuation, he had no valid objection. And haggling over the amount of the fine was also generally useless, as the Marquess of Hertford, living in Grosvenor Street, found when he was politely informed in 1795 that 'however desirous Lord Grosvenor may be to meet his Lordship's wishes on all occasions, it is utterly out of his power to comply with them in this instance as the gentlemen who act as trustees of his Lordship's estates cannot without a flagrant breach of their trust submit to take £1,174 18s. 6d. less than the Tables of calculation warrant them in asking for the renewal'.[88]

The successful levy of fines did, however, depend upon the capacity of applicants to pay them, and when this capacity was much reduced by the financial crises of the later 1790's some modification of the Board's policy had to be made. Whereas the total yield from fines for renewals in Mayfair averaged £7,268 per annum between 1789 and 1792, it fell between 1793 and 1800 to an annual average of £3,183, and in 1794 nothing at all was paid.[67] In 1799 Samuel Stephens, a picture-frame maker and head lessee of a house in Brook Street, stated that 'from the difficulties of the times he is not able to raise money to pay the Fine

---

* *Example.* At No. 17 Grosvenor Street in 1800, John Morris, the applicant for a renewal, had one year unexpired in the subsisting term, and sixty-two years were therefore to be added. Baily's five per cent table shows that the value of a sixty-three-year lease was 19.075 years' purchase, and of the subsisting one-year term was 0.952. The value for adding sixty-two years was therefore 19.075— 0.952 = 18.123 years' purchase. Porden valued the house at £240 per annum, which after deduction of his recommended ground rent of £18 and the land tax of £11 12s. was reduced to £210 8s. This latter sum, multiplied by 18.123, gives a fine payable of £3,813.[81]

for the renewal of the lease of his House' and therefore asked for a shorter-term repairing lease at a rack rent.[89] He was told that, 'as Lord Grosvenor's object must be to renew upon Fines', he could not have a lease at a rack rent so long as there was any possibility of renewing on a fine to any applicant who might present himself. Several such candidates did apply, but they all withdrew, and ultimately Stephens was granted a repairing lease at a rack rent, without a fine, for twenty-one or thirty-one years.[90] At about this time there were several other such cases,[91] and, again in 1799, one applicant to whom a thirty-one-year lease was granted was informed that Lord Grosvenor had now 'generally assented to the measures of granting repairing leases of such of the houses now nearly expiring as cannot be renewed upon a fine',[92] this being clearly preferable to allowing houses to stand empty.

Lord Grosvenor himself had not much helped his trustees in their efforts to pay off his debts. In 1791 he was borrowing yet more money,[93] and we have already seen that although he had agreed in 1779 to sell his race-horses he did not in fact do so until 1796, and three years later he was still active at Newmarket.[94] In 1798 his financial situation was critical once again, even his allowances to his son and his estranged wife being in arrears, and numerous creditors were hounding him for payment.[95] To one such the new agent, Abraham Moore, wrote, 'We literally have not the means of paying…at present. Lord Grosvenor's income is curtailed above one third during [the] continuance of the war and his London property rendered till the return of Peace incapable of improvement.'[96] In November 1798 Moore was 'almost destitute of means to support the ordinary expenses of Lord Grosvenor's reduced establishment',[97] and although his successful exploitation of the lead mines in North Wales yielded over £18,000 in 1800,[98] he had to tell Countess Grosvenor, whose allowance was again in arrears, that she would have to wait 'until I can turn some lead into money'.[99] In July 1801 he even had to borrow 'to prevent an execution going into his Lordship's house'.[100]

The full extent of Lord Grosvenor's debts at the time of his death on 5 August 1802 is not known, but in December 1804 the trust debt still amounted to over £108,000.[101] His son and heir, Robert, second Earl Grosvenor and later first Marquess of Westminster, was a very different man from his spendthrift father, and was evidently determined to discharge all the debts as fast as possible. This (as previously mentioned) he managed to do, with a few small exceptions, by 1808, when the trust of 1785 was dissolved, and completely by 1809.[102] Some lands in Cheshire and North Wales had been sold, but this astonishing recovery seems to have been largely due to the upturn of the national economy, which coincided roughly with the first Earl's death. This improved financial climate encouraged tenants to apply for the renewal of their leases, many of which had only a few more years to run, and was reflected in the receipt

between 1801 and 1807 of fines from Mayfair totalling £114,553 (annual average £16,364) and from the North Wales lead mines between 1800 and 1804 of £139,460 (annual average £27,892).[103] It was also a remarkable testimony to the virtually limitless resilience of the Grosvenor family's vast resources.

The liquidation of the first Earl's debts in 1808–9 provides a convenient standpoint from which to examine the progress of the Mayfair estate during the previous twenty years. In general, this was the period when, mainly through the renewal of the original leases, the ground landlord began to exert his authority more strongly than hitherto. In those easy-going days, however, the extent of this control was still not very great, and only two major innovations seem to have been made.

The first of these, made in 1795, was to insert a clause in new leases requiring the tenant to insure his premises against fire.[104] After the burning of the Pantheon in Oxford Street in 1792 there was much public interest in the dangers of fire, and in 1793 the Duke of Bedford had started, in his repairing and building leases, to specify constructional preventive measures[105]—a policy not adopted on the Grosvenor estate until many years later. For some years after 1805 the second Earl Grosvenor's tenants were required to insure with the Globe Insurance Office, from which he had recently borrowed £30,000,[106] or by 1815 with 'some responsible Insurance Office'.[107]

The second innovation was, whenever reasonably possible, to insert in new leases of premises in certain of the 'best' streets an undertaking on the part of the lessee not to use the property for a 'Tavern, Coffee House or Public House or any Open or Public Shop nor for any Art, Trade or Manufactory whatsoever'.[108] This ban applied in Grosvenor Square, Upper Grosvenor Street, Upper Brook Street and Park Lane, and with some exceptions, in Grosvenor Street and Brook Street. It also applied to certain houses which backed on to Park Lane, notably the west side of New Norfolk (now Dunraven) Street and, at its southern extremity only, the west side of Park Street.[67]

The implementation within the best streets of the ban on 'any art, trade or manufactory whatsoever' was not always possible (except in Grosvenor Square, where commerce had never intruded), for by 1790 a substantial proportion of the houses in even some of these streets was already occupied by tradesmen, some practising the very trades listed in the original leases as having to pay the £30 surcharge on the ground rent. Thus in Grosvenor Street at least twelve out of some seventy-four occupied houses on the estate there, and in Brook Street some twelve out of forty on the estate, were in 1790 occupied by tradesmen, largely concentrated in both streets at the eastern ends.[109] So when Francis Grosse, a perfumer, applied to renew the lease of one of these houses in Grosvenor Street, no objection was raised, he agreeing in 1795 to accept the ban on a 'tavern, coffee house or public house or any open or public shop' in exchange for the omission of 'nor for any art, trade or manufactory whatsoever'.[110] Similarly, there was no objection in 1799 to Samuel Stephens, the picture-frame maker of Brook Street previously referred to, and the Board minutes record that 'the clause prohibiting any open or publick Shop must be qualified so as not to restrain him from carrying on his own business'.[111] Even the lease of the Lion and Goat public house at No. 5 Grosvenor Street was renewed in 1800 without difficulty,[112] but some trades were regarded as obnoxious, Porden in 1818, for instance, advising the Board not to renew the lease of a tallow chandler in or very near Upper Brook Street.[113]

Sometimes it was evidently for financial reasons that leases were renewed to tradesmen in these best streets. Thus in 1802 No. 43 Brook Street, having stood empty for a year after the expiry of the original lease and the refusal of the head lessee to renew on fine, was leased by Lord Grosvenor's authority to Pellot Kirkham as a hotel, despite this use being 'contrary to the restrictions contained in the leases of the other houses that have been renewed in Brook Street'.[114] Three years later, in precisely similar circumstances, William Wake of Wake's Hotel, Covent Garden, was allowed to open a hotel nearby at No. 49 Brook Street (now part of the site of Claridge's Hotel), and in both cases Lord Grosvenor actually helped them by using 'his influence' to obtain magistrates' licences for the sale of alcohol.[115] Extensions of trade in the principal streets were evidently not undertaken lightly, however, for in 1805 a bookseller's application to take No. 51 Brook Street (also now part of the site of Claridge's Hotel), which had been empty for over a year, was refused, and the house remained empty for another two years before being ultimately let on fine to a private resident. But pressure for permission to use houses in this part of Brook Street as hotels was evidently very strong, and although an application made by the lessee in 1812 on behalf of a hotel keeper, James Mivart, to use this house as a hotel was personally refused by Lord Grosvenor, Mivart was nevertheless using it as 'a private lodging house' in the following year.[116] It is to these establishments of Wake's and Mivart's that Claridge's Hotel traces its origin.

By about 1835, when all the leases in these best streets had been renewed, the effect of this policy seems to have been to rid Upper Grosvenor Street and Upper Brook Street of any such trade as had insinuated itself there in the eighteenth century. In Grosvenor Street and Brook Street it largely prevented any further commercial incursions until many years later. Those parts of these two streets which lay outside the eastern boundary of the Grosvenor estate had evidently become largely commercialised during the eighteenth century, and (as mentioned above) trade had even gained a footing here within the estate, particularly on the north side of Brook Street east of Davies Street. Commercial pressure, expressed principally through difficulty in finding private residents willing to take houses adjoining or opposite to

tradesmen, must therefore have been very strong here. The census of 1841 shows, however, that in Grosvenor Street there had been virtually no change since 1790 in the ratio of commercial and domestic occupation, while in Brook Street the slight increase of trade was due to the establishment of hotels.[117]

In all except these best streets the restrictive covenants which lessees were required to accept in their new leases on other parts of the estate were at first surprisingly lax. These were merely to pay the rent, maintain the premises, permit the landlord to inspect them and give notice to repair them within three months, and to surrender them peaceably at the end of the new term; and if the rent were in arrears, the landlord could resume possession. Undesirable trades were at first controlled in the same way as hitherto, by the payment of an additional annual ground rent (generally still £30) if the premises were used by a butcher, slaughterman, tallow chandler or melter, soap maker, tobacco-pipe maker, brewer, victualler, coffee house keeper, distiller, farrier, pewterer, working brazier or blacksmith—this list being virtually identical with that contained (wholly or in part) in the original building leases. In 1799, however, a complete ban was placed on all these listed trades, plus that of hotel keeper, and this ban was also extended, by an important new proviso, to include any 'other noisome or offensive Trade or Manufactory whatsoever',[118] thus applying to the whole of the estate a restriction only a little less severe than that in the best streets already referred to.

Hitherto, throughout the greater part of the estate the ground landlord's control had rested primarily—at least until individual leases were renewed—upon the clause in the original lease requiring the £30 surcharge on the ground rent for the practice of some or all of the trades listed above. Numerous trades were left unrestricted, and in 1806, for example, Lord Grosvenor was unable to prevent the conversion to an upholsterer's shop of No. 76 Grosvenor Street (where in any event the original lease of the whole large block in which it stood had omitted all restriction on specified trades).[119] Even tallow-melting had not everywhere been restricted, which perhaps explains why in 1819 the estate authorities allowed it to continue at a site in Chandler (now Weighhouse) Street in the mistaken belief that the original lease did not prohibit it there.[120] But generally, where the appropriate restriction existed in the original lease, a threat to enforce payment of the surcharge seems to have secured the suppression of such nuisances as those caused by butchers, slaughtermen, blacksmiths and tallow chandlers.[121] Sometimes this took a long time. In the case, for instance, of John Holland, a tallow-melter in South Audley Street, who had renewed his lease in 1795,[122] Edward Boodle had in 1800 'perceived a most offensive smell proceeding from the house', but threats to enforce the £30 surcharge, followed by demands for its payment (with six years of arrears) and refusal to renew his lease when it should next expire seem to have produced little lasting improvement until 1817, when the Board was informed that 'since Mr Holland has been spoken to, the work has been carried on…in such a manner as not to be offensive'.[123]

No example of the £30 surcharge being actually paid has been found, and both this and the ban imposed in 1799 upon any 'noisome or offensive Trade or Manufactory whatsoever' seem to have been used primarily as reserve powers to secure reasonable neighbourly conduct rather than interpreted literally. Thus Robert Mansbridge, a 'spruce beer brewer' had the lease of his house in Brook Street renewed in 1800 without difficulty, but when two years later he asked 'that the prohibitory clause respecting a brewhouse might be struck out of his lease, being fearful that it would affect him', he was told by the Board that 'as he had exercised his profession on the premises for many years unmolested, he had no occasion to be under apprehension for the future while he conducted it as he had hitherto done, but that the clause could not be dispensed with because it would leave him or his successors the liberty of making a brewery of a very different kind, to the essential inconvenience of his neighbours'.[124] And another reserve power—that of threatening to refuse to renew the lease when it should come up for negotiation—was sometimes used to abate nuisances which did not actually contravene the existing covenants—e.g. the beating of 'beds and feathers' on the roof of a house adjoining Grosvenor Square,[125] a steam engine off Oxford Street[126] or a house of ill-fame in New Norfolk (now Dunraven) Street,[127] or in Brook Street 'the constant disturbance…suffered particularly in the night from the violent kicking and plunging of Lord Penrhyn's horses'.[128]

The treatment of public houses reflected the different policies pursued by the first and second Earls, and also the changing social conditions on the estate. In 1793 there were some seventy-five pubs on the estate (excluding those in Oxford Street),[129] and the first Earl seems not to have objected to the renewal of their leases, even in the case of those in the best streets.[130] At first the second Earl reluctantly continued this policy, an applicant in Upper Grosvenor Street being informed in 1809 that 'Lord Grosvenor would not be sorry to see the public house discontinued as such, though his Lordship would not insist upon it'.[131] Starting around 1815, however, he refused to renew the leases of any public houses in the best streets,[132] and elsewhere he also sometimes refused to do so.[133] But pubs were a valuable source of revenue, and between 1815 and 1824 several large London brewers, including Meux, Reid and Company, Combe, Delafield and Company (both now part of the Watney's chain) and Whitbread's, were competing against each other for renewals. Meux, Reid had already acquired the sub-leases of several houses on the estate, but Lord Grosvenor refused to treat with them until and unless the head lessee had declined to do so.[134] Combe, Delafield and Meux, Reid both rejected Lord Grosvenor's first terms out of hand,[135] but ultimately, after receiving some encouragement from the Estate,[136] Meux, Reid negotiated nine new leases on payment of a fine of upwards of £7,000,[137] one of the advantages of treating with a brewer being his greater capacity to repair and even occasionally to rebuild his premises. By 1828, on the eve of the Beer Act of 1830, the total number of licensed premises on the estate had declined at most very slightly (if at all),[138] the suppression of some pubs being partly counterbalanced by the establishment of new hotels, particularly at the eastern ends of Brook Street and Grosvenor Street.

During Porden's reign as surveyor (c. 1784-1821) rebuilding was hardly ever made a condition for the renewal of a lease, and very little took place. Such little as tenants did undertake was evidently regarded by the Board as either an 'improvement' or as normal maintenance work.[139] Sometimes such 'improvements' were considerable, but in general the Board did not interfere, provided that they did not contravene the lease in question and were not injurious to the estate or the neighbours.[140] At the western ends of Upper Brook Street and Upper Grosvenor Street the building of projecting awnings and balconies which interfered with the neighbours' view of Hyde Park was gradually controlled by the insertion of special restrictive covenants in new leases,[141] and when Lady Cunliffe, living in New Norfolk (now Dunraven) Street wanted to block up five or six windows she was told that she would 'be liable to the expence of opening and restoring them at the expiration of her lease'.[142] Outgoing tenants' liabilities for dilapidations were carefully enforced, sometimes by a Court order.[143]

But although there was little actual rebuilding, Porden did initiate three long-term improvement schemes, all of which ultimately had a happy outcome. In 1791 he persuaded Lord Grosvenor not to renew the leases in King's Row (now the sites of Nos. 93-99 consec. Park Lane) so that in due course 'a handsome front towards Hyde Park' might be built in place of the original tumbledown agglomeration here.[144] This policy was maintained on a number of occasions,[145] and after Porden's death his aim was achieved—for the most part in 1823-8 (Plate 19a). Similarly, improved lines of frontage for the north side of Berkeley Square and the west end of Bourdon Street, projected by Porden in 1800-3, were implemented shortly after his death.[146]

His third scheme achieved a quite different object from that intended. In 1789 he had suggested that Green Street might be extended eastward from North Audley Street to Duke Street. But unfortunately he made this suggestion immediately after the lease of a substantial part of the ground needed had been renewed for sixty-three years, and so when the property was put up for sale in 1792 Lord Grosvenor's trustees had to buy up their own lease at a price of 1,500 guineas—despite the enormous debts then encumbering the estate.[147] In 1795 the land was leased on a short-term basis to the St. George's Volunteer Corps, but the arrangement did not prove a happy one, for in 1798 several of the officers—including 'Major Harrison the coal merchant and Captain Gunter the confectioner'—refused to pay Lord Grosvenor his rent 'until their demands on his Lordship are paid'.[148] After the return of peace in 1802 the ground was leased (determinable on six months' notice) for upholsterers' workshops, but in 1818 Porden recommended that the cost of buying up the rest of the ground needed would be too great, and that therefore 'the proposed opening should be given up, and the neighbourhood continued to be occupied (as it now is) by workshops etc, which although not the most respectable in appearance, Mr. Porden states to be of great value'.[149] Shortly afterwards, however, the site was sold (with other adjacent ground) to the Church Building Commissioners,[150] and St. Mark's Church was built upon it in 1825-8.

Generally, during the years between 1785 and 1808 the first and second Earls Grosvenor, their Board and their trustees began to make some impact upon the evolution of the estate. Primarily this was done through their policy of, whenever possible, renewing leases on fine to provide terms of sixty-three years to come. The fact that leases could nearly always be renewed on these terms whenever the lessee chose to apply meant that the expiry dates of these renewed leases varied greatly from one house to another.* In 1794 Lord Grosvenor did decide that no lease should be renewed if the existing one had more than fifty years to run,[151] but even this rule could be subject to exceptions.[152] The Estate was therefore committing itself far ahead, but without any long-term policy, for the making of the leases of adjacent sites co-extensive with each other seems only to have been done at the lessee's request, and even then evidently as a favour.[153] The result of this practice was to make simultaneous rebuilding on adjacent sites much more difficult, and hardly any such reconstruction in fact proved possible until the 1880's and 1890's, when the effects of a less haphazard and more flexible policy in the granting of the third generation of leases began to produce approximately simultaneous expiry dates, notably in Mount Street and parts of South Audley Street. In many other parts of the estate, however, the original individual plots have never been merged, and in some cases the original houses still stand on them.

The Free Estate, 1808-45

Robert, second Earl Grosvenor, and from 1831 first Marquess of Westminster, held the family estates from 1802 until his death in 1845. He had inherited them from his father unentailed, but still subject to the trust created in 1785 for the payment of massive debts. These he had, as we have already seen, virtually discharged by 1808, when the trust was dissolved; thereafter he was the absolute master of all his numerous properties.

At the time of his succession in 1802 the second Earl was aged thirty-five. In his marriage, the Grosvenors' 'old luck with heiresses had not deserted them', his wife being Eleanor, only surviving daughter and heiress of Thomas Egerton, first Earl of Wilton. He had sat in the House of Commons since 1788 as a supporter of Pitt, but after the latter's death in 1806 he joined the Whigs. In later years he supported the Reform Bill, and in 1831 was raised to the rank of Marquess of Westminster. A near-contemporary, writing in 1865, described him as 'An admirable man of business, an honest politician, his character was deformed only by a thrift, always more or less apparent in the family, which in him rose to a mania ...the thrift which gives rise to stories such as those told of the Marquess is unusual, and has done much to lower the great popularity of the house'.[154]

Within a year or two of his succession he began to use his vast wealth to the full—or if not quite to the full, with more purpose than his father in recent years. While still paying off the old debts he bought more lands in Cheshire 'very desirable to him' for some £30,000,[155] and in 1804 he began the rebuilding of Eaton Hall on a huge scale to Gothic designs by Porden.[156] In 1806 he bought the Agar Ellis collection of pictures for 30,000 guineas, having previously spent £20,000 on a suitably impressive house in which to house it and his own family. This was Gloucester House in Upper Grosvenor Street, hitherto occupied by George III's brother, the Duke of Gloucester, until his death in 1805.[157] Renamed Grosvenor House, this now became the family's principal London residence. Old Grosvenor House at Millbank was pulled down in 1809,[158] and No. 45 Grosvenor Square, where Earl Grosvenor's father had lived in preference to Millbank, was sold. After spending large sums on alterations and redecorations Earl Grosvenor moved into the new Grosvenor House in 1808.[159]

After this tremendous initial burst of expenditure the pace slackened somewhat, but in later years he continued to buy pictures, enlarge Grosvenor House, and above all, buy more land—notably the Pulford estate in Cheshire (1813, £80,000), the Shaftesbury estate in Dorset (1820, £70,000, much enlarged in later years), the Stockbridge estate in Hampshire (1825, £81,000) and Moor Park, Hertfordshire (1827, £120,000). He also kept up his father's racing stud.[160]

The growth of the Earl's income was, however, well able to support these outlays. Between 1768 and 1782 the rental of the Mayfair estate only had been about £3,450

---

* Thus the building leases of two adjacent houses granted in 1730 for 99 years would both expire in 1829. One lessee might apply for a renewal in 1790, when he still had 39 years unexpired. He would be granted a reversionary term of 24 years to give him a total of 63 years to come, and his new lease would expire in 1853. But his neighbour might not choose to apply for a renewal until 1820, when he had only 9 years of the original term unexpired. He would be granted a reversionary term of 54 years, and his new lease would not expire until 1874.

per annum, but by the time of the second Earl's succession in 1802 it had risen to £5,550. This modest increase was largely due to the expiry around 1801 of a number of the original leases granted only for eighty years, and to the grant of a few short-term leases on rack rents. But by far the greater part of the yield from the estate at this period took the form of fines, which (as previously mentioned) amounted between 1789 and 1808 to over £180,000. After 1808 there is a gap in the records of fines received, but the yield no doubt continued high, for many leases were being renewed.

By 1820 the rental had risen to over £8,000, but in the following year it bounded up to nearly £20,000.[161] The reason for this was that the increased reversionary ground rents due on leases renewed on fine in previous years now became payable for the first time, the original ninety-nine-year leases granted in 1721 having now expired. This was, of course, a continuing process, reflecting the rate of building and the grant of leases a century earlier; and there were also a great many original leases still to be renewed at greatly enhanced rents. So by 1825 the Mayfair rental rose to over £41,000,[161] and by 1835 to some £60,000.[162] Nor was this and the unrecorded fines anything like all, for it was in these years that the large-scale development of the great estate in Belgravia and Pimlico began to yield a much increased crop of ground rents. The Earl's expenditure, colossal as it was, was not therefore excessive in relation to his resources, and although he had between 1826 and 1829 to mortgage his estates for £130,000, he was still able to repay the whole amount in 1835-6.[163] When he died in 1845 he left his estate with no encumbrances other than those providing for his family.

As well as being thrifty he was, indeed, 'an admirable man of business' (at least until his latter years), and being dissatisfied with the existing administration of his properties he began in 1807 to attempt to reform the workings of Edward Boodle's office. In this uphill struggle—started evidently in anticipation of the forthcoming dissolution of the trust of 1785—he was assisted by his friend John Hailstone, the geologist, whom he had first met at Trinity College, Cambridge, in the 1780's. Boodle, it appears, was in financial difficulties of his own, and he was also dilatory beyond belief, some of his clients not having received any bills for his services since 1780. This must have adversely affected Lord Grosvenor's affairs, relying so heavily as he (even with the active Abraham Moore as his agent) and his forbears did, almost of necessity, upon the firm of Boodle and Partington. So for some years, and particularly during the Earl's frequent absences from London, Hailstone concerned himself with introducing a semblance of efficiency into the management of the Grosvenor business in Boodle's office in Brook Street.

In February 1807 Boodle was complaining of 'great fatigue and headache owing to his exertions', possibly caused by an 'experiment' made by Hailstone, which a few days later was said to have 'failed intirely. At the rate he is capable of travelling the business would not be finished in the next generation.' A year later Hailstone was reporting that 'Our operations have certainly wrought an evident change for the better in Mr. B. who now seems to exert himself in good ernest'[164]—a reference, probably, to the installation of Lord Grosvenor's own clerk, Edmund Empy, in Boodle's office (see page 35). This seems, indeed, to have been the only enduring success of the whole campaign, for Hailstone continued to refer sarcastically to Boodle as 'the energetick', and in February 1808 he concluded that 'It is equally impossible to drive him beyond his easy amble as the bold P out of his curvets'.[165]

'The bold P' was, of course, a facetious reference—habitual in this correspondence—to the Earl's surveyor, William Porden, who was also a victim of this early attempt at the introduction of 'business efficiency' methods. From his house in Berners Street Porden himself had at first joined in the game of making fun of Boodle, describing him (in a letter of 1803 to the Earl) in his rather incongruous capacity of an officer in the volunteers as 'armed cap-a-pie, in Sash and Gorget, and Kavan-Hullar Beaver, going, to be comfortably inspected in a heavy Rain'.[166] But pleasantries of this kind soon ceased, for Porden too was incurably dilatory. In 1807 Hailstone wrote that 'I seldom miss a day but I walk to the House [Grosvenor House] and sometimes spur the bold P. till he is ready to lash out at me'.[167] In 1808 Lord Grosvenor, at Eaton, was exasperated with Porden because there was no mason working there, the last having departed after 'a tiff' with Porden—'this, you know, must be the effect of P. rages'. Two years later he was 'out of all Patience at Porden's delays about things here', and soon afterwards Hailstone was told that 'if you can give any elastic Vigour in Brook or Berners Street, you will do great things'.[168] Indeed, of all the professional men employed by the Earl, only the agent, Abraham Moore, escaped criticism—at least until his massive embezzlements were discovered in 1821.

It is, however, easier to get rid of an architect than of the family solicitor, and so Edward Boodle survived until his death in 1828, while Porden was eventually superseded in September 1821.[169] By then he was aged about sixty-six, and in addition to his exasperating dilatoriness there had in the past been disagreements with the Earl about his fees[170] and possibly also about matters of estate policy. Porden was certainly not the man to have day-to-day charge of the impending development of Belgravia, and he died a year later at his house in Berners Street, in September 1822.[171] His successor, Thomas Cundy I, an architect and builder of Ranelagh Street (now Beeston Place and the eastern end of Ebury Street), where he owned several leasehold houses,[172] at once initiated a rebuilding policy in Mayfair—possibly at the Earl's behest—but he died in 1825 without having had enough time to make any great impact there. He was succeeded by his son, Thomas Cundy II, who held the post for over forty years and whose influence upon the fabric of the Grosvenor properties in Mayfair—greater, perhaps, than that of any single other architect except Edmund Wimperis—may still be seen, in one way or another, in many of the main streets on the estate.

Porden's departure coincided with the discovery of Abraham Moore's defalcations, and although Porden was in no way involved in Moore's crimes, this simultaneous change of architect and agent does seem to have inaugurated a new and more autocratic régime. Having to rely upon a new surveyor, a new agent (Empy) of substantially lower status than his predecessor, and the irremovable Edward Boodle, Lord Grosvenor was evidently very much in personal command of his estates in the remaining years of his life. And there is no doubt that he liked to have his own way, for his daughter-in-law said of him that 'When Lord Grosvenor is possessed of an idea one might just as well talk to the winds'.[173]

But if the day-to-day administration of the Grosvenor estates in London in the first two decades of the nineteenth century does not seem to have been very efficient, the basic principle of management adopted in *c.* 1786—renewal for long terms on fine—was sound; and its long-term as well as its financially immediate effects were beginning to become apparent, as the hard-pressed Edward Boodle pointed out in 1814 in a letter to Lord Grosvenor. In 1809 the fourth Viscount Grimston (later first Earl of Verulam) had in the normal way been granted on fine a reversionary term of sixty-three years to come on his house, No. 47 Grosvenor Square, only to find, four years later, that 'a radical defect in the original building of the house' required its complete rebuilding, which he duly undertook at a cost of £12,900.[174] This prompted Boodle to make one of the rare general comments to be found in the records of the Grosvenor Office: 'it is, I confess, highly gratifying to me to witness the good effects of that system of renewal which was peculiar to your Lordship's Estate, altho' it has been since adopted by other considerable Proprietors of Ground and houses in this Metropolis. Lord Grimston has furnished a striking instance in favor of it, by having followed his renewal with completely rebuilding his House, and upon a very improved Plan. While this system shall be pursued the Estate will be kept not merely in good heart and condition, but will keep pace in modern improvements with all the Neighbouring property, and having from its situation so much the advantage of all the adjacent Estates, will preserve its consequence as long as Hyde Park remains unbuilt upon.'[175]

Under the second Earl the detailed application of the 'sixty-three year reversionary renewal on fine' policy was frequently altered. This was particularly evident in his decisions about the ratio between the rent and the fine. During the course of the nineteenth century this ratio was reversed, the low rent and high fine of the early years being gradually replaced by a high rent and a low fine. The change was not a smooth one, however, and its ups and downs evidently reflected disagreements between the current possessors of the estate on the one hand and their legal and professional advisers on the other.

The latter always advocated high fines and low rents, by means of which (to quote Messrs. Boodle in 1845) the tenant 'has a larger Interest in the House and is more likely to improve the Property':[176] or (to quote Porden in 1821) 'the making the Rents on renewal too high, causes the Property to be neglected near the expiration of the lease'.[177] The attitude of the current possessors varied, however. Generally, they favoured higher rents and lower fines, but although they could and did overrule their professional advisers, there were other factors—notably their own expectation of life—to be taken into account.

Connected with the ratio between rent and fine was the question of how long before the expiry of a lease the current possessor of the estate was prepared to treat for its renewal. As we have already seen, the first Earl had at first renewed to any of his tenants willing to pay a fine, but the effect of this had been to commit the estate far ahead without any long-term policy and to create wide divergences in the expiry dates of such renewed leases. In 1794 he had therefore decided not to renew when the existing lease had more than fifty years still to run,[178] and the second Earl reduced the period still further, by 1815 to thirty years,[179] and by 1823 to ten years.[180] Subsequently, however, he reversed this policy, by 1834 his rule being not to renew when the unexpired term had more than twenty years to run,[181] and at this level it remained until his death in 1845.[182]

In the years prior to 1808, when the first Earl's debts were being paid off, the reversionary rent fixed at each renewal was kept extremely low in order to maximise the fine; generally it amounted to only about one tenth of the annual value of the property. After 1808 it was fixed at 'one fifth (or at most one fourth) of the improved annual value of the house',[183] and in 1816 the ground rent was sometimes as much as one third of the annual value.[184] In 1821 Porden was resisting an applicant who wanted the rent to be well over half the total value—'he should be absolutely required to pay half in Fine and half in Rent, which will bring our practice back to nearly what it was, till lately'—and he asked Lord Grosvenor to make this a standing order. But 'His Lordship thinks otherwise at present'.[185] Shortly afterwards this upward movement of the rent went even further, an applicant for stables in North Row having to be told that 'he must pay a fine of at least $\frac{1}{5}$ part' of the annual value.[186]

In order to understand why in the early 1820's the second Earl favoured high rents and lower fines it is necessary to bear in mind that by greatly reducing the length of time before the expiry of a current lease in which he was prepared to treat for its renewal, he had postponed a great many such renewals. At that time he knew that about one third of all the original leases on the Mayfair estate were still unrenewed, and that most of

them would expire during the next decade or so. As in
1820 he was aged fifty-three, he seems to have thought
that it was in his own best interests to charge a high rent
and a low fine on such renewals in order to maximise his
future income when the old leases expired—hence his
disagreement with Porden, concerned with the long-term
standards of upkeep of the estate.

Later on, however, his interests changed. By 1835
almost all the original leases had been renewed at greatly
increased rents,[162] and his own expectation of life had,
of course, diminished. Relatively few more renewals were
to be expected before his death, and in any case he might
not live to enjoy the benefit of the enhanced reversionary
rents arising from them. So in the last decade of his life
it was better for him to have higher fines and lower
reversionary rents, for thereby he had the immediate
use of the fines, either as capital or, invested, as income.
By 1834, therefore, he was encouraging applications to
renew by extending the period in which he was prepared
to treat from ten to twenty years before the expiry of the
existing lease, and at some unknown date he reverted to
his earlier ratio of one quarter rent and three quarters
fine—much to the satisfaction, no doubt, of Cundy and
Messrs. Boodle.[187]

His son, the second Marquess of Westminster, reversed
this policy immediately after his succession in 1845. In
order to facilitate rebuilding he inaugurated a more
flexible leasing policy (though still normally based on
the sixty-three-year term) and he therefore reduced the
period for renewal negotiations in anticipation of the
expiry of existing leases from twenty to ten years, where
it remained for the rest of the century and beyond.
Contrary to Messrs. Boodle's advice, however, he raised
the proportion of the rent from one quarter to one half.[188]
In 1845 he was aged fifty, and just as his father had done
at the same age, he favoured higher reversionary rents,
payable within not more than ten years. By this means
he evidently hoped to enjoy both the fine and at least some
years of the enhanced rents. By the time of his death in
1869 the rental of the Mayfair estate had risen from some
£60,000 in 1835 to £80,000 in 1870.[189]

In 1866, however, the 'half rent, half fine' formula was
changed to two-thirds rent and one-third fine[190]—a change
possibly caused by tenants' inability to raise capital in
that year of financial crisis. This policy was continued by
his son, the third Marquess (later first Duke), who succeeded to the title in 1869 at the age of forty-four.[191]

But whatever variations were from time to time made,
it was always an essential object of successive owners to
keep the estate, as Edward Boodle phrased it, 'in good
heart and condition'. In the early years of the nineteenth
century this had been comparatively easy, for the value
of all individual properties on the estate were rising. Thus,
to take one of many examples, Porden valued Colonel
(later Field-Marshal) Thomas Grosvenor's house at the
corner of Grosvenor Street and Grosvenor Square at £300
per annum in 1797, £360 in 1803, and £500 in 1808, and

his reports in these years constantly refer to 'the general
increase in the value of property'.[192] But after reaching
a peak in about 1812 a decline began, and from 1814 to
at least his retirement in 1821 he was often reporting that
'the value of property is falling'.[193] Tenants often had
such difficulty in paying their fines that they were allowed
to pay them in two six-monthly instalments (with interest),
and B. F. Hardenburg, the sculptor, was even permitted
to pay his over a five-year period without interest.[194] This
fall in values corresponded in date with the slump of
1811–16 in London building, but its continuance after
building had picked up again may perhaps have been due
to competition from the great new residential districts
then being built in Tyburnia and on the Portman and
Crown estates in St. Marylebone.

The existence of these new rivals for aristocratic
patronage may have prompted a more positive attitude
to rebuilding on the Grosvenor estate in Mayfair. This
new policy was started very shortly after the appointment
of Thomas Cundy I as the new surveyor in the autumn
of 1821, and he was instrumental in enforcing it: but it
may equally well have originated with the Earl himself,
who, with the vast increase of the 1820's in rents from the
Mayfair estate, could now well afford to forgo a little of
this extra revenue by encouraging rebuilding.

From 1822 onwards applicants for the renewal of
dilapidated properties were encouraged, or occasionally
required, to rebuild, and in such cases they were also
required to do so in accordance with 'a plan approved by
Lord Grosvenor's surveyor' (i.e. Cundy).[195] Usually the
term granted did not exceed sixty-three years, and despite
the lessee's rebuilding expenses, he still often had to pay
a fine as well as a ground rent, even in such streets as
Upper Grosvenor Street and Park Lane, where rebuilding
would no doubt be costly.[196] In South Street and on the
north side of Berkeley Square, however, where a number
of 'first rate' houses were built in the 1820's, terms ranging
between ninety-six and ninety-nine years were granted,
those in South Street being also subject to a fine.[197] Some
of these houses still survive (Plate 24c).

Thus the foundations of the Grosvenor rebuilding
policy, by which large parts of the estate were in later
years to be transformed, were laid in the early 1820's by
the second Earl and Thomas Cundy I. In the next two
decades some rebuilding took place, notably in Green
Street, Bourdon Street and around South Street, while
in the Weighhouse Street area substantial redevelopment
was undertaken by the builder Seth Smith, some sixty-
three small houses being built there between 1822 and
1833. But when the original houses were still in good
condition, the second Earl and first Marquess was
generally content, until almost the end of his life, to
pursue in renewal negotiations the old policy of adding
to the existing term to give sixty-three years to come,
without requiring rebuilding or even alterations to the
front.[198] And he would probably have agreed with Messrs.
Boodle's verdict of 1845 upon the satisfactory results of

this policy: 'very few renewals which have been negociated have gone off [i.e. proved abortive] and for many years not a single House has been on hand [i.e. untenanted], and the Marquess of Westminster's name as a Landlord has obtained that Opinion with the Public that nearly every person would give more for a Lease on His Lordship's Estate than on any other'.[199]

But Thomas Cundy II was evidently not so satisfied, and in May 1844 he had an interview with the Marquess, who agreed 'to Mr Cundy's suggestion for improving the appearance of the houses in Grosvenor Square by the addition of stucco work to the fronts with porticos, window dressings, cornices and balustrades to such of the houses as may be thought to require it'. In future, in terms for the renewal of leases of houses in the square, stipulations to this effect were to be included, and a design was to be submitted by the applicant.[200]

Before anything could be done, however, the first Marquess died, on 17 February 1845; and it was to be under the aegis of his son, the second Marquess, that the transformation of the outward appearance of the estate was to be commenced.

The Estate Entailed, 1845-99

Richard Grosvenor, second Marquess of Westminster (1795-1869), had married the youngest daughter of the first Duke of Sutherland. He had represented Chester or one of the Cheshire constituencies as a Whig from 1818 to 1835,[2] but after his father had presented him in 1831 with Motcombe House, near Shaftesbury, on the Dorset estate, he had spent most of his time there in simple domesticity, surrounded by his wife and their numerous children. Daily family prayers, the instruction of his elder children in Latin verse and the works of Shakespeare, and other such preoccupations had formed the routine of this 'deeply serious...high-principled, reserved' man,[201] who after his death was said by *The Times* never to have risen 'to the height of his opportunities'. He was, however, considered to have administered 'his vast estates with a combination of intelligence and generosity not often witnessed...His gift of a fine Park to the city of Chester' being regarded as 'an instance of almost princely munificence.'[202]

But within his family, and even in a wider circle, he had an evidently well-deserved reputation for parsimony, an attribute which, although originating in his youth,[203] was perhaps aggravated by the terms on which he had inherited much of the family wealth. His father—equally renowned for his thrift—had left a will of such complexity that it took the family solicitor, John Boodle, two hours to read.[204] By it the London estates were entailed to trustees for the use, firstly, of his eldest son, the second Marquess, for life, and then for life to his grandson, Hugh Lupus, the future third Marquess and first Duke; and the trust so established had, moreover, been extremely

strictly drawn.[205] Finding himself thus restricted, the second Marquess's frequent lectures to young Hugh Lupus, about his 'idleness, listlessness and weak moral character' had evidently been intensified, and when in 1856 the latter had asked his father for financial help in addition to the income of £8,000 per annum already settled on him, the second Marquess had refused. 'With only a life interest in this strictly curtailed property I am sorry I cannot aid you.'[206] Nevertheless he did contrive to buy yet more lands, paying for them out of his own income from the settled estates, at a total cost of £195,000.[207]

At about the time of his death in 1869, his rents from the Mayfair estate alone amounted to *c.* £80,000 per annum.[189] Between 1845 and 1864 receipts from fines or premiums payable to the trustees on the renewal of leases amounted to £108,538. About half of this appears to have been used to discharge family encumbrances created by the first Marquess, but in 1864 there remained £55,584, the income from which (invested at three per cent) was payable to the second Marquess.[208]

Hugh Lupus, third Marquess and first Duke of Westminster (1825-99) was in some respects similar to his father. He, too, served his political apprenticeship in the House of Commons (as Liberal M.P. for Chester, 1847 69), married firstly a Leveson-Gower—his first cousin, a younger daughter of the second Duke of Sutherland, who bore him a large family—was deeply religious, and was regarded with some awe by his sons. But he was not known for thrift or parsimony. Although he never gambled he revived the Grosvenor racing stud (winning the Derby four times) and between 1870 and 1880 he rebuilt Eaton Hall, which once more became the family's out-of-town headquarters, at a cost of some £600,000.[209] He was a vigorous supporter of a variety of philanthropic causes, and unlike his father, he remained to the time of his death active in politics, where his admiration for his friend and neighbour, Gladstone, did not prevent his opposing both Gladstone's abortive Reform Bill of 1866 and the Irish Home Rule Bill of 1886. But despite the first of these disagreements it was Gladstone who recommended the Marquess for a dukedom in 1874—apparently for little other reason than the deep respect in which he was almost universally held; and although the second rift lasted longer, the old friendship was ultimately renewed.[210] The Duke, in fact, managed somehow to personify the generally prevalent idea of how a great rich nobleman should conduct himself, and after his death it was admiringly said of him that 'He could pass from a racecourse to take the chair at a missionary meeting without incurring the censure of the strictest'—a remarkable tribute at any time, but particularly so in the Victorian era.[211]

The Duke's biographer, Mr. Gervas Huxley, states that the settled properties of which he had become in 1869 the new life-owner 'were valued at close on £4,000,000, after deducting the capital value of all encumbrances, and consisted of the whole of the London estates and part of the Cheshire, Chester, and Halkyn estates. He also inherited the absolute ownership of Eaton Hall, Halkyn Castle, and the bulk of the Cheshire, Chester, and Flintshire properties', with a capital value of some £750,000. 'The Dorset and Wiltshire properties owned by the second Marquess were unsettled and had been left to his widow for her lifetime', with remainder respectively to her younger son and her son-in-law.[212]

Only two important additions to his own personal estates were made by the third Marquess and first Duke— Reay Forest in Sutherlandshire, which he leased from his relatives the Dukes of Sutherland, and where he used Lochmore Lodge for his summer holidays; and Cliveden, Buckinghamshire, which he inherited in 1868 from his mother-in-law, the Dowager Duchess of Sutherland.[213] In 1893, however, he sold Cliveden to William Waldorf Astor for £250,000 to enable him to make provision for his children—fifteen in all, eleven by his first wife, who died in 1880, and four by his second—of whom eleven were still living in 1893.[214]

On the settled estates (which included the London properties) the entail created by the first Marquess could be broken when the first Duke's son, Victor Alexander, Earl Grosvenor, came of age. This was done in 1874, the estates being resettled[215] upon the first Duke and his son successively for each of their lives, and then upon Earl Grosvenor's eldest son as tenant in tail male.[216] Earl Grosvenor died in 1884, and soon after the succession of his son to the dukedom in 1899 the estates were once again disentailed and resettled (see pages 67, 79).[217]

During the time of the third Marquess and first Duke the rental from the Mayfair estate alone rose from c. £80,000 per annum in 1870 to c. £116,000 in 1882, and to c. £135,000 in 1891.[218] Between the resettlement of 1874 and the Duke's death in 1899 receipts from the fines or premiums payable to the trustees on the renewal of leases in Mayfair amounted to some £650,000. From this at least £200,000 was spent on improvements to the Duke's settled estates in both Cheshire and London, some of the very large mortgages incurred by the Duke were paid off, and provision was made for various members of the Duke's family. The running balance was placed on deposit and in the 1890's the interest therefrom was paid to the Duke as income.[219]

With the accession of the second Marquess in 1845 it is clear that the administration of the Mayfair estate became much stricter than hitherto. Ever since the precipitate flight of Abraham Moore, the agent, and the supersession of Porden, the surveyor, in 1821, the first Marquess had kept matters very much in his own hands; but by 1845 he was aged seventy-eight, and chiefly in Belgravia he had sometimes allowed building to proceed without formal leases or contracts, transferred ground rents from one contract to another, and through a casual system of record keeping generally got into a muddle, principally in his dealings with Thomas Cubitt. Within six months of his father's death, therefore, the second Marquess obtained a private Act of Parliament to set these matters right; and power was also obtained for the trustees established by the first Marquess's will to enter into contracts for the granting of leases—a power not adequately provided for in the will.[220]

The main object of the second Marquess's stricter management was to preserve and enhance the overall value of the estate, and—in the days before the statutory protection of buildings of historic or architectural interest —this of necessity involved the periodic rebuilding of outworn portions of the fabric. Rebuilding therefore became for the first time an integral part of estate policy. But rebuilding could generally only be undertaken when individual leases expired, for the purchase of subsisting leases was expensive and only rarely undertaken at this date; and as hitherto virtually no attempt had been made to make the leases of adjoining sites expire simultaneously, it followed that at first rebuilding could only be done on individual sites. Co-ordinated rebuilding over several adjacent sites would only become possible later, when the effect of renewing leases of adjacent sites for comparatively short terms all expiring contemporaneously had had time to make itself felt.

The second Marquess took an active interest in the architecture of his estates, and such evidence as exists suggests that he favoured co-ordinated schemes of rebuilding.[221] The old policy of renewing to applicants for such a term as would, with their subsisting leases, give them sixty-three years to come, was therefore no longer followed as a matter of course. Instead, both he and his successor considered each site in relation to its neighbours, and although they sometimes continued the old policy, they more frequently refused to renew beyond the date of expiry of the longest subsisting lease in any particular range of houses. At that date, when all the leases would expire at about the same time, the rebuilding of the whole range could at last be considered. Thus, for instance, at Nos. 1–8 (consec.) Upper Brook Street, the subsisting leases granted between 1810 and 1824 under the old haphazard policy expired at various dates between 1873 and 1887, but by short renewals of varying lengths granted between 1859 and 1876 they were all made to expire in 1886 or 1887.[189]

The increased flexibility of this policy made it possible in due course to phase the rebuilding of large parts of the estate over a number of years. Rebuilding entailed sacrificing the immediate in favour of the long-term interest of the estate, since the ground rents were lower than the receipts which would have been obtained on rack rents, and usually there were no fines. It also entailed much administrative work for the estate officers, and some social disturbance for the adjacent residents. It was therefore important that not too much rebuilding should take place at any one time, and these factors were clearly in the second Marquess's mind when he stated in 1867 that 'I do not wish any new work to be taken in hand beyond what is now marked out but shall renew the Leases as they occur at short periods as we have done before, in order to give future opportunity for blocks being formed for local improvements'.[221] Thus to revert to the example of Upper Brook Street, Nos. 1–8 were not in fact rebuilt in 1887, for in 1881 the lease of No. 5 had been extended by the first Duke to 1906. In the early 1880's a considerable amount of rebuilding was already in progress or in prospect, notably in Mount Street, Oxford Street and the artisans' dwellings around Brown Hart Gardens, and between 1881 and 1886 the leases of the other seven houses in Nos. 1–8 Upper Brook Street were all also renewed to 1906, thereby merely postponing the opportunity to rebuild.[218]

The reign of the second Marquess was therefore more one of preparation for than of actual rebuilding, and what did take place was mostly on individual sites—notably three separate blocks of artisans' dwellings in Bourdon Street, and one in Grosvenor Market, ten mansions in Grosvenor Square, and a number of houses at the east ends of Brook Street and Grosvenor Street. But in the mid 1860's he was at last able to carry out two large schemes, one in Belgravia and one in the north-west corner of Mayfair, where the original building leases granted in the latter part of the eighteenth century were now expiring. In Belgravia he rebuilt part of Grosvenor Place and extended it southward (as Grosvenor Gardens) to Victoria Station (opened in 1860), both the layout, which included the formation of two triangular gardens, and the very large new houses being designed by Thomas Cundy III. In Mayfair the rebuilding of Hereford Street, parallel with and set back from Oxford Street, also to designs by Cundy III, began in 1866. By that time it was already well known that the Marquess was 'determined to pull down and rebuild on his estates whenever he has an opportunity'.[222]

But although his opportunities for such wholesale clearances had been very limited, and even rebuilding on individual sites had been restricted in scope, the second Marquess did nevertheless make very considerable alterations in the outward aspect of his Mayfair property, and the stamp of his taste, as executed chiefly by Thomas Cundy II, is still very apparent in many surviving buildings there. This imprint was made by requiring tenants, as a condition for the renewal of their leases, to execute precisely specified modifications to the then still Georgian elevations of their houses.

As we have already seen, the idea of 'improving the appearance of the houses in Grosvenor Square by the addition of stucco-work to the fronts with porticos, window dressings, cornices and balustrades to such of the houses as may be thought to require it' had already been suggested by Cundy II to the first Marquess in 1844;[200] but the latter had died a few months later. This suggestion was evidently at once approved by his suc-

cessor, for in May 1845 Cundy's clerk was measuring the fronts of the houses on the south side of Grosvenor Square, the occupants being informed that the new Marquess was 'anxious to obtain a correct design for some proposed improvements'.[223] He was, however, intending to go much further than Cundy had suggested, for in November 1845 he sent John Boodle two very important 'instructions for future renewals' of leases. Firstly, in all future leases there was to be a covenant requiring 'no alteration of the frontage without permission from the Grosvenor Estate Office'; and secondly, all houses of four or more windows' width were 'to have a Doric Portico with fluted or plain Pillars carried out to the end of the area railing'.[224]

The elevational alterations which, in negotiations for the renewal of leases of houses in the principal streets, tenants were now usually required to execute, were generally designed by Cundy II. The applicant had to sign a bond, often of over £1,000, to ensure the due performance of the works, which generally included the addition of a Doric open porch and sometimes a balustrade in front of the first-floor windows (both in Portland stone), cement dressings to the windows, and a blocking course, balustrade or moulded stone coping at the top. Sometimes an additional storey was to be built, plate glass might be required for all the windows, and occasionally also works of improvement in the domestic offices in the basement. Attached to the bond there was usually a detailed specification of the works and a copy of Cundy's design.[225]

The effect of this policy, which was vigorously pursued throughout the whole of the second Marquess's reign from 1845 to 1869, was to make the principal streets on the estate, hitherto purely Georgian in appearance, look increasingly like those of South Kensington (see page 133). Over twenty examples of fronts entirely designed or altered by Cundy II (latterly assisted by his son Thomas Cundy III) still survive. These are chiefly in Brook Street, Upper Brook Street and Grosvenor Street, and originally, before later rebuildings, there were many more, notably some dozen in Grosvenor Square alone, for the south range of which he produced in 1849 a complete scheme of 'suggested alterations'.[226]

Tenants or builders engaged in the complete rebuilding of individual houses also found it convenient to have Cundy as their architect, or at least for him to provide the elevation, for they knew that his work would be acceptable to the Marquess; and sometimes it was made a condition of rebuilding that Cundy should design the new front.[227] Thus in Grosvenor Square (Plate 25) he and/or his son did ten houses. Four of these were for tenants (Nos. 18, 20, 21 and 30, all demolished), another four for the builder C. J. Freake (No. 4, which still survives, and Nos. 10, 26 and 40, all demolished), and one each for the builders Wright Ingle (No. 42, demolished) and Sir John Kelk (No. 2, demolished). Ingle also employed him at the still-surviving Nos. 11 Upper Brook Street and 20 Grosvenor Street, as did Kelk at No. 128 Park Lane.

For the prolific local builders John Newson and his son George John Newson he did Nos. 14, 23 and 24 Grosvenor Street and Nos. 48–50 (even) Brook Street, all of which still survive, as well as others now demolished.

The Cundys did not always have a free hand, however, for the Marquess sometimes rejected even their designs. At No. 21 Grosvenor Square, for instance, he refused to allow Venetian windows, despite the evident wishes of both Cundy III and the tenant (who was of course paying for the new house there);[228] and when in 1848 Cundy II produced 'for the Marquess's consideration' two drawings showing the existing elevation and 'his proposed elevation' for all the houses on the north side of Brook Street east of Davies Street, it was recorded that 'the Marquess does not approve the proposed plan, and Mr Cundy takes it away'.[229] Subsequently, however, four houses in this range (Nos. 48, 50, 56 and 58, all still surviving) were rebuilt to elevational designs by Cundy, but presumably in a different manner to that originally proposed.

The elevational alterations required by the second Marquess involved the tenants in considerable expense, but there is little evidence that they objected on this ground. When the works were very extensive, as in the case of Miss Mary-Anne Talbot at No. 24 Grosvenor Square, which had a long flank elevation to Upper Brook Street, the fine was reduced or remitted to suit the financial convenience of the tenant; but the full annual value of the house was nevertheless expressed in the ground rent, which was raised from £13 (on a lease granted in 1792) to £460, in exchange for a renewal of only thirteen and a quarter years to come (1855–68).[230] She and her sister were, however, very wealthy women, for in 1862 they were able to sell their Portobello estates in North Kensington for building for over £100,000.[231] At the still surviving No. 15 Upper Grosvenor Street Arthur Ward was required in 1862 to provide a porch, balcony and window dressings (designed by Cundy) in exchange for a reversionary extension of only ten years, from 1871 to 1881; but he had to pay a fine of £1,125 and (from 1871) a rent of £215 instead of £50.[232] For tenants as rich as those in the best streets of the Grosvenor estate, the cost of the Marquess's 'improvement' requirements were almost trivial. Porches were fashionable and popular, and the records of the Metropolitan Board of Works show that quite a number of them were erected voluntarily by tenants, sometimes without the approval of the Grosvenor Board. Many of these have been lost through later rebuildings, but at least one, badly designed in 1867 by Henry McCalla, architect, still survives at No. 68 Grosvenor Street.[233]

In one case, however, the Marquess's requirement to erect a stone balcony at first-floor level was resisted on stylistic grounds, though unsuccessfully. This was at No. 41 Upper Brook Street (now demolished), where Sir Henry Meux, the brewer, had in 1851 commissioned Samuel Beazley to make extensive alterations. The Marquess's intention was to make the house correspond outwardly with its neighbour, No. 42, which had an elegant iron balcony erected in previous years. Beazley had therefore designed a similar iron balcony for No. 41, but nevertheless the Marquess (down at Motcombe House in Dorset) rather perversely instructed Cundy to insist on a stone balcony, and this was duly put up, not without much mutual acrimony. Beazley died shortly afterwards,[234] and when the lease of No. 42 came up for renewal a few years later Cundy and his master were able to have the offending iron balcony there replaced by one of Portland stone corresponding to Meux's at No. 41.[235]

Obedience to the Marquess's architectural commands was, indeed, almost unavoidable, and the only known example of successful defiance was provided by a woman. This was Mrs. Gwynne Holford of No. 36 Grosvenor Square, who, having signed a bond for £1,000 to comply with his behests and paid a fine for renewal, then refused to do the work (for what reason is not recorded). Ultimately in 1869 she was excused, on forfeiture of £300 of her bond. But this reprieve was granted not by the implacable second Marquess but during his last fatal illness by his son and heir; and it may be doubted whether the father would have been so lenient.[236] In later years, when this formidable lady applied for another renewal, the first Duke and Thomas Cundy III wisely required her only to insert plate glass in the windows, but she died in 1881 before the completion of negotiations.[237]

The extensive up-dating of the plain old Georgian fronts and the complete rebuilding of some houses were only the most apparent and most immediately effective manifestations of the altogether stricter régime inaugurated by the second Marquess. His control was, of course, mainly exercised through the covenants contained in his leases, which were much more carefully drawn than hitherto. But whilst he could make the immediate execution of elevational alterations a condition for the grant of a reversionary lease, the new covenants which he inserted into such leases did not become operative until the expiry of the subsisting term. Many of the existing leases on the estate still had long terms to run, moreover, and often there was therefore no opportunity to renew them on stricter terms during his years in charge. Thus as late as 1876 the tenant of a house in Norfolk (now Dunraven) Street held under a sixty-year lease granted in 1820 did not have to obtain the first Duke's consent to make alterations because 'at present the old lease is in force'.[238] And although immediately after his succession in 1845 the second Marquess began to refuse to renew when the existing lease had more than ten years to come,[239] there was nevertheless a time lag of varying length but seldom less than of about a decade before many of his leasing innovations could take effect.

The single most important of these innovations was the covenant requiring 'no alteration of the frontage without permission from the Grosvenor Estate Office'.[239]

Commencing in 1845 this clause has been inserted in all subsequent Grosvenor leases, the phrase 'no alteration of the frontage' being soon extended to any part of the exterior of a building, any additional or substituted building, or any change in the 'architectural appearance', this last including even the enclosure of the sides or front of projecting porches.[240]

As the existing leases which did not contain this clause gradually expired this new covenant gave the second Marquess and his successors a vice-like control over the outward appearance of the buildings on their properties which has never been relaxed, and which has in some considerable measure been responsible for the high visual quality of many parts of the Grosvenor estates in London. With the passage of time this instrument of control was, moreover, refined still further. In 1851 the Marquess approved a design by Cundy II for area railings 'for general adoption', and a specimen of it was made 'for the inspection of the lessees'.[241] Beginning in 1854 all leases contained a covenant requiring stucco-work to be painted once every seven years and all wood and ironwork twice.[242] A few years later the stucco was required to be painted 'of a stone colour', and the work was to be done in every leap year, thus ensuring 'that houses were kept clean simultaneously and the general appearance was good'.[243] In 1866 'Words [were] to be added to the forms of lease to prohibit alterations to chimney pots',[244] and soon afterwards tenants were required to clean and repoint the brickwork every seven years.[245]

But the outward appearance of the buildings was not the only field in which the Grosvenors' control was greatly extended in the middle years of the nineteenth century. In his later years the first Marquess had begun to require his tenants to contribute a fair share to the repair of party walls—hitherto sometimes a troublesome cause of dispute—and to notify the Estate Office of any assignments of head leases.[246] His successor at once began to stipulate a right for his officers to make a schedule of fixtures in all leased premises,[247] in order to prevent the removal of such fixtures at the end of a lease, some of them, particularly chimneypieces, being of considerable value.

More important than these purely administrative changes, however, were those innovations concerned with the uses to which any particular property might be put. We have already seen that in the 'best' streets in the latter part of the eighteenth century a ban had been placed, wherever reasonably possible in the then existing circumstances, upon 'any art, trade or manufactory whatsoever'.

In Grosvenor Square always, and in the other 'best' streets sometimes, the second Marquess extended this ban to professional use as well, doctors and surgeons being the main target for exclusion; and he also prohibited his tenants in these 'best' streets from doing or permitting anything which 'may be or become a nuisance or annoyance' to either himself as ground landlord or to the adjoining tenants.[248]

Elsewhere on the estate leases had since 1799 contained a list of prohibited trades followed by 'or other noisome or offensive Trade of Manufactory whatsoever'. In the second Marquess's time this list of prohibited trades—now considerably longer*—was at first concluded with the greatly strengthened formula 'or any other trade or business that shall be a nuisance or annoyance to the neighbourhood'.[250] By the 1860's, however, this phrase had become even more stringent as 'any other trade, business or occupation which in the judgement of the Marquess of Westminster shall be deemed objectionable or a nuisance to the neighbours'.[251]

With control of this nature there was in practice hardly any difference between the phraseology of the lease of a mansion in Grosvenor Square and that of a coach-house in a mews: the Marquess, and later the first Duke, could and did specify precisely for what purpose any building might be used. Thus some leases for premises in Brook's Mews granted in 1887 forbad the practice there of 'any art, trade, business' or even profession, and required the tenant to use them 'as a private dwelling house only and the said demised coach house and stable as a private gentleman's coach house and stable for horses only, and the rooms over the same...for the lodging of servants or others to be employed in or about the said demised premises and for no other purpose'. When, as sometimes happened, mews premises were to be used for purposes other than 'a private gentleman's coach house and stable', a manuscript addition was inserted into the standard printed lease which came into general use in the 1880's. Thus a lease of 1891 of other premises in Brook's Mews banned all trades, businesses or professions except that of jobmaster and horse-dealer; and a few years later a similar lease contained the usual ban, followed by an exception in favour of the business of the Stohwasser and Winter Puttee Legging and Military Equipment Corporation Limited.[252]

The granting of exceptions such as these had of course to be made judiciously. It was all very well to ban hog-skinners, catgut-spinners, horse-boilers and such like

---

* In 1887, when the list reached its maximum extent, a tenant in Brook's Mews undertook not to use the premises as a forge, place of public entertainment or museum, and not to carry on any of the following trades: butcher, pork butcher, fishmonger, slaughterer, knacker, horse boiler, hogskinner, cat gut spinner, cart-grease or varnish maker, melter of tallow, soap boiler, melter of fat, tripe boiler, tripe seller, sausage maker, sugar baker, fellmonger, dyer, scourer, alehouse keeper, beerhouse keeper, tavern keeper, licensed victualler, gambling or betting house keeper, brass or iron founder, blacksmith, whitesmith, coppersmith, working brazier, pewterer, tin or iron plate worker, packing-case maker, undertaker, coffin maker, glass maker, farrier, goldbeater, beater of flax, hemp or feathers, beater of carpets, bone boiler, cork burner, chimney sweeper, dealer in soot, dealer in second-hand clothes, boots or shoes, dealer in old iron or marine stores or any other trade, business or employment 'which shall be dangerous or a nuisance or annoyance' to the adjoining tenants and occupiers.[249]

from the estate, but not even its most august residents could do without butchers or fishmongers, nor their servants without licensed victuallers, all of which trades were in general also prohibited, but of which there had always, of necessity, been quite a number of practitioners. So exceptions in their favour had to be made, although, as we shall see later, this did not prevent the first Duke from making a great reduction in the number of licensed victuallers. But subject only to the limitation of having to allow for the basic human requirements of all the residents, the ground landlord's control of the use of all premises had, well before the end of the nineteenth century, become complete and total. And later additions to the lease covenants, such as the prohibition of the display of goods for sale on the pavements, the exhibition of bills or placards, or the keeping of 'living fowls' were all relatively minor.[253]

The new restrictive covenants contained in mid nineteenth-century Grosvenor leases were not, however, the only means of control. No regular inspections of the properties on the estate were made at that time (except immediately prior to the grant of a new lease), because it had been found that the system of usually exacting a fine on renewal gave the tenant 'the greater interest during the term' and thus provided 'a guarantee against breaches of the covenants of his lease'.[254] But despite the lack of inspection, the Grosvenor Board (meeting weekly at 3 p.m. on Tuesdays or Thursdays 'except when Marquess in town')[255] seems to have known what was going on, and frequently required tenants to conform. In 1858-61, for instance, Lord Chesham made unauthorised alterations to the rear of his new house, No. 20 Grosvenor Square, and after being told to remove them a compromise was reached;[256] and in 1864 George (later Viscount) Goschen was made to stop building an unauthorised conservatory at his house at the corner of Park Lane and Mount Street.[257]

The Board was, in fact, well informed—sufficiently so to know in 1853 that 'in all the modern stables there are water closets', but that in those held under old leases privies were still prevalent, and that therefore new leases of stables should require the formation of properly drained water closets.[258] In 1869 it knew of the existence of nineteen slaughter-houses in Mayfair, Belgravia and Pimlico, all prohibited under the terms of the respective leases. All of them were, however, 'in commercial neighbourhoods', and after enquiries had been made among the neighbours it was found that only four were a nuisance. The owners of these were told to stop, but, in the days before the freezing of meat, slaughtering had to be done near the point of consumption and at least one slaughterman was subsequently reprieved provided that he 'uses every precaution to prevent nuisance'.[259] In the more delicate purlieus of Grosvenor Street, however, Colonel Augustus Meyrick was in 1865 prohibited from keeping a cow, despite his lawyer's opinion that 'some gentlemen like to keep a cow in London'.[260] But prostitutes presented a more difficult problem, here on the Grosvenor estate as elsewhere, and although the existence of brothels in Gilbert Street and Chapel (now Aldford) Street was known to the Board, no effective action seems to have been taken against them.[261]

Commencing in 1864, when extensive rebuilding in Grosvenor Place and Gardens in Belgravia was in progress, a clerk of works was employed 'to inspect the building works generally over the Estate'. His salary, and also the considerable fees due to Thomas Cundy III (although the latter did not succeed his father as surveyor until 1867) were paid out of a new Improvement Account, opened at the same time. The receipts paid into this account came mainly from the proceeds of the auction sales of the old materials and fixtures of houses about to be demolished, of which there were quite a number at that time. In 1864, for instance, the proceeds of the sale at two adjoining houses in Grosvenor Square (about to be rebuilt by C. J. Freake as a single house) amounted to £843. Payments out were mostly to the St. George's Vestry for road, pavement and sewer works executed on behalf of the Estate, principally no doubt at Grosvenor Place and Gardens. From time to time, when expenditure exceeded the income from the sales, the Marquess transferred additional funds from his private account.[262]

The rebuildings in Grosvenor Place and Gardens and in Hereford Street, Mayfair, in the mid 1860's were the forerunners of the very extensive rebuildings which took place in Mayfair in the 1870's, 80's and 90's. These operations, and the antecedent demolitions, caused much disturbance to adjoining occupants. In 1861 the second Marquess therefore began to prohibit the dusty noisy work of demolition during the London social 'Season', when all important personages were sure to be in residence in their town houses. In that year C. J. Freake, about to rebuild No. 26 Grosvenor Square, was required to demolish the old house in August and September after the Season was over,[263] and in 1865 Sir John Johnstone had to demolish No. 30 in February and March before it had begun.[264] Soon afterwards the cleaning and pointing of brickwork was interdicted in the months of May, June and July,[265] and in 1875 Sir John Kelk was forbidden to commence work on No. 3 Grosvenor Square until 1 August as 'it is the rule of the estate that no works of this nature should be commenced during the London season owing to the annoyance which would be caused to the neighbours'.[266] It was not, indeed, for nothing that the second Marquess, who had inaugurated this policy, now continued by his son, was known (to quote *The Building News* in 1865) to be 'determined to have none but tip-top people on his estates'.[222]

Rules of this kind were required in order to minimise the upheavals caused by the colossal rebuilding programme executed under the auspices of the third Marquess and first Duke during his thirty years' reign (1869-99). This rebuilding was probably larger in scope than any carried out on any other London estate (except, perhaps, that of the Crown) in the whole of the nineteenth century, and at the time of writing (1976) large parts of the existing fabric of the Grosvenor estate in Mayfair date from these years. It included the whole of Mount Street, Duke Street, Aldford Street and Balfour Place; almost all of South Audley Street north of South Street; all of the north side of Green Street and a quarter of the south side; almost all of the south side of Oxford Street from Davies Street to Park Lane; most of the west side of North Audley Street and the south side of Bourdon Street; substantial parts of Park Street and several mews (Adams Row, Balfour Mews, Mount Row and North Row); part of the north side of South Street; the Carlos Place quadrant on an improved frontage, and the realignment of the north end of Davies Street; three new churches, two schools, new Vestry offices, a library and a dozen blocks of artisans' dwellings.

Notably absent from this list are the houses in the principal streets. Half a dozen of the mansions in Grosvenor Square were in fact rebuilt in these years (Nos. 3, 27, 33, 34, 41 and 39 'practically') and the great block of Claridge's Hotel reared itself in Brook Street; but in Grosvenor Street and Upper Grosvenor Street there was hardly any rebuilding and none at all in Upper Brook Street. It was in these streets, principally, that the second Marquess's policy of elevational improvements to designs, usually by Thomas Cundy II, had been most rigorously applied. Because the houses here were generally in the hands of wealthy tenants they were already in good order, and although the first Duke's procedure in renewing leases in the principal streets, as elsewhere, was to make the terms of all the houses in any single range expire at approximately the same time, rebuilding was nevertheless often postponed when that time arrived, as at Nos. 1–8 Upper Brook Street, previously mentioned— presumably because the Duke wished to limit the amount of rebuilding going on at any one time and felt that the claims of other lesser streets were more urgent.

The first Duke inherited the long-term results of the second Marquess's leasing policy and was able to rebuild whole ranges to a single design. Almost all his rebuilding was done in this way, rather than on individual sites, and it is because so little rebuilding took place in his time in Brook Street, Grosvenor Street, Upper Brook Street and Upper Grosvenor Street that so many of the original houses there, though often greatly altered, have survived. When in his early years (1899–c. 1914) the second Duke turned his attention to these four 'best' streets, there had been a partial reaction away from renewal in whole ranges, and he often favoured individual refronting or rebuilding. So by the chance of this change of fashion they, or at any rate their individual sites, survived again, and although in later years a number of blocks of flats or offices have been built, these four streets still retain in some measure—and certainly more than anywhere else on the estate—the domestic flavour of the original development.

The first Duke's preference for rebuilding in ranges rather than on individual sites provided architects on the estate with new problems and opportunities, and this is at any rate one reason why the buildings erected in his time are so strikingly different from those built under his father. But their own architectural tastes also differed, and these differences reflected current changes in Victorian fashion. Whereas the second Marquess had liked and required the Italianate stucco widely prevalent in London in the 1850's and 60's, his son was a supporter of the Queen Anne Revival and a fervent admirer of the new 'South Kensington' red-brick and terracotta manner. Throughout the whole of his reign he championed the new modes and materials, and only two months before his death in 1899 he commented on a proposal in Duke Street 'the more red brick the better'.[267]

This difference in taste extended to the architectural embellishment of existing buildings. In 1856, for example, the second Marquess had required the applicant for a reversionary lease of No. 14 Grosvenor Square to erect an open Doric porch, remove the iron balcony at first-floor level and substitute three stone balconettes and add a square attic storey. This had not been done because the tenant later decided not to renew, but in 1878 the first Duke required a dormer attic instead of a square one, and the retention of 'the present character of the brick front'.[268] Stone or stucco porches, balconies, balustrades and window dressings were, in fact, now becoming things of the past, and it is hardly an exaggeration to say that all important surviving Georgian brick fronts without these embellishments are so because they did not have their leases renewed during the second Marquess's time—Nos. 76 Brook Street and 36 Upper Brook Street are cases in point. The tastes of the second and third Marquesses were indeed so different that in dealing in 1899 with an application to renew the lease of No. 55 South Audley Street, now the sole survivor of three houses built in white brick in 1859 to designs by Cundy II (fig. 14b on page 134), the Duke commented that he 'objected to the appearance' of this trio 'and would not consent to any arrangement for perpetuating it'.[269]

It was also presumably for reasons associated with the Duke's personal taste in architecture that, despite the enormous volume of rebuilding, Thomas Cundy III was hardly employed at all in Mayfair. He had succeeded his father as estate surveyor in 1867 and held the post until his resignation in 1890, aged seventy. Although he worked extensively on the Belgravia and Pimlico estates, where he designed churches and schools and (as previously mentioned) the new houses in Grosvenor Gardens and Place,[270] his work on the Mayfair estate consisted chiefly of planning for future rebuilding, routine administration, repairs and embellishments. The only row of houses designed by him there was that in Hereford Gardens, the rebuilding of which had started in the days of his father, Thomas Cundy II, and of the second Marquess, and he also did a number of commercial buildings in

Oxford Street. The records of the Grosvenor Estate Board contain hints of several disagreements between the Duke and Cundy,[271] and the stuccoed domestic buildings of Cundy's private practice in South Kensington are unlikely to have been to the Duke's taste.[272] This, doubtless, was the reason for Cundy's virtual exclusion from design work in the predominantly brick purlieus of Mayfair.

Cundy's successor as estate surveyor, Eustace Balfour,* was appointed by the Duke in 1890.[274] He was a brother of the future Prime Minister, a grandson of the second Marquess of Salisbury, and his wife, besides being a daughter of the eighth Duke of Argyll, was also a niece of the Duke of Westminster.[275] In architectural matters his well-mannered brick and stone fronts were entirely acceptable to both the first Duke and to his grandson and successor the second Duke, and he (and/or his partner, Thackeray Turner) worked extensively on the Mayfair estate, particularly in the south-west corner around Aldford Street and Balfour Place. He seems to have resigned in 1910 owing to bad health, and died in 1911, aged fifty-seven.[276]

Numerous other architects were of course employed in the Mayfair rebuildings during the first Duke's time, but before discussing the various ways in which they obtained their commissions it is necessary to examine the mechanics of the whole process. The general leasing policy continued to be to renew for comparatively short periods coterminous for all the houses in any particular range. In 1889 fear of the possibility of leasehold enfranchisement, then much in public debate, made the Duke and his Board decide not to renew (except in the case of rebuilding) for more than twenty years,[277] and in the 1890's this was generally reduced to ten years.[278] Under the deed of resettlement of 1874 the Duke's trustees now had power to accept surrenders of existing leases,[279] and this was sometimes done with the co-operation of an intending building lessee, who bought up the existing leases and then surrendered them to the estate as part of his rebuilding contract. In 1882 the Settled Land Act enabled trustees to spend capital money on improvements,[280] and at about this time the Grosvenor trustees occasionally bought outstanding leases themselves to expedite rebuilding. Thus in 1880 they bought a number of leases for the site of St. Mary's Church, Bourdon Street, and in the 1890's those of several in Mount Street, Park Street and Green Street,[281] the capital being repaid to the trustees by the building lessee or his nominee on the completion of rebuilding, and allowed to him by a reduced ground rent.[282]

From about 1876 onwards the Duke also began, in blocks where he intended to rebuild, to refuse applications for renewals. Many such applicants held leases with up to ten years still to run, and thus, at any rate in theory,

they had some warning of their impending forced disturbance. Generally they were told that at the end of their term their property would be rebuilt, 'required for estate purposes', or 'probably wanted for improvements'. Between 1876 and 1899 nearly one hundred and fifty such applications were refused.

By all these means the Duke was able to obtain an increasingly tight yet flexible grip on his estate, and the final years prior to rebuilding provided an opportunity to decide the future character of a range or block about to be redeveloped—a process in which Cundy III was much involved. In 1877, for example, he was already planning the new frontage line for Charles Street (now Carlos Place), while in the block bounded by Green Street, Park Street, Wood's Mews and Norfolk (now Dunraven) Street he was required in 1880 to plan the future rearrangement of the plots.[283] In 1884 the Duke approved his preliminary plan for the adjoining block to the east and decided that 'there shall be no shops in Park Street but small private houses, and that a model lodging house shall be built in the mews at the rear of Green Street, with an open space to Green Street westward of Hampden House. Rebuilding to be carried out gradually as opportunity arises'—most of which was in due course effected.[284] Shops at the west end of Mount Street and in Green Street were to be eliminated in favour of 'small private houses' when rebuilding took place, and they were also intended to go at the eastern end of Brook Street,[285] but elsewhere they were encouraged—'The Duke wants shops in South Audley Street'.[286]

Rebuilding leases granted by the second Marquess in the 1850's and 60's for private houses had generally been for seventy-seven years, but under the first Duke the normal term was increased to eighty years for commercial properties as in Oxford Street, and to ninety years for private houses in and around Grosvenor Square.[287] In the mid 1880's ninety years became the normal term throughout the whole of Mount Street, and in some premises where terracotta was required to be used an extra six months at a peppercorn rent was granted in addition to the normal allowance of one year.[288] Negotiations for a building lease culminated in the signature of a building contract containing detailed specifications, to which in 1888 Cundy III suggested adding a clause requiring fireproof construction. In 1890 the specifications were tightened up by Eustace Balfour.[289]

From the mid 1870's onwards it was the practice, whenever possible, to treat first of all with the occupant for both the renewal of leases and the grant of rebuilding leases. In the case of private houses to be rebuilt individually there was seldom any difficulty. Thus Dr. Joseph Walker, in occupation of part of No. 22 Grosvenor Street and in possession of the whole of the adjoining No. 21, a lodging house, accepted terms for the rebuilding

---

* As commander of the London Scottish Royal Volunteer Corps (a position to which he had risen from the ranks) from 1894 to 1902 he was often referred to as Colonel Balfour.[273]

of both houses in 1898-9, the lodging-house keeper evidently having no wish to treat; or Sir John Kelk, wanting a house in Grosvenor Square, bought the lease of No. 3 and after being granted a renewal, proceeded to rebuild it completely (now demolished). The Duke's policy in such cases was to 'let to a gentleman for his own occupation' rather than to a speculator,[290] and if the occupant under an expiring lease did not wish to rebuild, a rebuilding lease was generally offered to some other gentleman known to be looking for a site in the locality. No. 41 Grosvenor Square was rebuilt by C. H. Wilson, M.P., in this way in 1883-6, and No. 27 by the Earl of Aberdeen in 1886-8 (fig. 22 on page 150). There was seldom if ever any shortage of takers.

When—as more usually happened in the first Duke's time—a whole range of private houses was to be erected simultaneously, building was invariably done by a speculator of known substance, generally a builder. Thus, for example, Matthews, Rogers and Company built Nos. 2-11 (consec.) Green Street (1891-5), Daw and Son Nos. 14-22 (even) Park Street and 68 Mount Street (1896-7) and Higgs and Hill Nos. 2-12 (even) Park Street (1897-c. 1900, now partly demolished). Usually each rebuilding site was offered by the Board to a reputable speculating builder, but occasionally a speculator applied for a site and got it, as in the case of J. T. Smith at Nos. 106-116 (even) Park Street and 19 Green Street (1887-8), or of Holloways at Nos. 40-46 (even) Brook Street (1898-9). Similarly in November 1890 Trollopes applied for and obtained the very important site of Nos. 6-9 (consec.) Mount Street, 1-8 (consec.) Carlos Place and 1-15 (odd) Mount Row, and in the following year they obtained the site of Nos. 45-52 (consec.) Mount Street by competitive public tender— apparently the only occasion when this method of selection was used in those years.*

But when shops, and particularly a whole range of them, were to be rebuilt, there were very considerable problems, which were closely examined in 1887 by the Select Committee of the House of Commons on Town Holdings. The shopkeepers naturally feared the loss of their goodwill through enforced removal, and (to quote from H. T. Boodle's evidence to the Committee) the Estate Board therefore generally recommended 'that the occupier, if he is capable of rebuilding, shall be the person to rebuild, so that the question of disturbing him does not arise'. In certain cases, moreover, the Duke had 'found it practicable to allow old tenants to rebuild, even when the new elevations form part of one general design …two or three of them adjoining combine and employ the same architect and builder'.[291]

This had indeed happened during the time of the second Marquess at Nos. 489-497 (odd) Oxford Street, which were rebuilt in 1865-6 with elevations in the French style by Thomas Cundy III (Plate 27b). Here the individual shopkeepers who were the rebuilding lessees combined together to employ a single builder, Mark Patrick and Son, and even agreed among themselves to reduce the number of original plots in order to obtain wider frontages for their shops. This block has been demolished, but another with similar elevations by Cundy survives at Nos. 407-413. Here in 1870-1 Peter Squire, manufacturing chemist and chemist in ordinary to the Queen, was the rebuilding lessee for four old shops and houses, one of which had hitherto been in his own occupation, and which he rebuilt as two—now Nos. 411 and 413 Oxford Street. Shortly afterwards his neighbour, a fruiterer, was the rebuilding lessee for the adjoining two shops and houses (Nos. 407 and 409). This completed the short range between Binney Street and Duke Street, and at about the same time the adjoining range (also short) to the west was rebuilt, the building lessee for No. 415 being T. B. Linscott, a confectioner, for the centre portion J. M. Macey, a builder, and for the western portion the trustees of the Association in Aid of the Deaf and Dumb, who built a church there (all now demolished). Macey built all three portions, No. 415 and the church (Plate 29c) under contract with the respective lessees, and the centre evidently as a speculation on his own account.

Linscott had at first been 'rather reluctant to rebuild', but the Duke and his advisers had insisted that it was 'absolutely necessary that his house should be pulled down'. Some years later, however, H. T. Boodle said that 'whenever he [Linscott] sees me, he thanks me for having been firm, and having advised him to rebuild. He says, his profits are a great deal more than they had been for years; it has immensely improved his business, and he sees how short-sighted he was in wishing to retain the old house.'[292] With this encouraging example several other Oxford Street tradesmen became building lessees in later years, notably a linen draper in 1875-6 at Nos. 431 and 433, who had previously occupied the adjoining shops, and Thrupp and Maberly, the coach-builders, who in 1884-7 rebuilt their own premises (now demolished) between Lumley and Balderton Streets.

This procedure, in which each tradesman/rebuilding lessee acted on his own individual account, negotiating terms with the Grosvenor Board and then employing a builder to put up the new house and shop, was at first employed elsewhere on the estate. In 1875, for instance, W. J. Goode began the rebuilding of his own shop at

---

* Other examples of ranges of private houses built by speculators include: Charles Fish, 51-54 (consec.) Green Street, 1882-3; Robert Edis, 105-115 (odd) Park Street and 25-31 (consec.) Green Street, 1891-4; Trollopes, 34-42 (even) Park Street, 1895-9; Colonel Bird, Balfour Place, east side, 1891-4; W. H. Warner, the block bounded by Mount Street, Balfour Place, Aldford Street and Rex Place, 1891-7; William Willett, 39-47 (odd) South Street, 1896-8; William Cubitt and Company, 94-104A (even) Park Street, 1896-8, and 55-59 (consec.) Green Street, 1897-8; Bywaters, 16-19 (consec.) Dunraven Street, 1897-8.

Nos. 18-19 South Audley Street, and in 1882 Henry Lofts, an estate agent with offices in Mount Street due to be rebuilt soon, was the rebuilding lessee for Nos. 34 Berkeley Square and 130 Mount Street, which adjoined each other. But in the mid 1880's a substantial frontage of over ninety feet on the south side of Mount Street was leased in two blocks to two local businessmen for rebuilding to designs prepared by the same architect, Ernest George (Plate 34b). This site had hitherto been occupied by part of the St. George's Workhouse, which was now removed to Pimlico, and simultaneous rebuilding by more than one lessee was therefore relatively easy to arrange, there being no occupants with claims to be considered. The two lessees were W. H. Warner, Lofts's partner in the firm of Lofts and Warner, and Jonathan Andrews, a builder with premises on the north side of Mount Street soon due for demolition.

This precedent was followed, in more elaborate form, in the rebuilding of most of the rest of Mount Street east of South Audley Street during the ensuing decade. On the south side of Mount Street the Grosvenor Board arranged for the rebuilding of Nos. 125-129 (consec.) by four local shopkeeper-lessees in 1886-7 (Plate 34c); Nos. 116-121 (consec.) by four shopkeepers and a surgeon, all local (1886-7); Nos. 94-102 (consec.) in 1889-91, and Nos. 87-93 (consec.) Mount Street (Plate 34a) and 26-33 (consec.) South Audley Street (1893-5), each by five local shopkeepers or businessmen.

On the north side of Mount Street similar consortia were formed at Nos. 1-5 consec. (1888-9, Nos. 1-3 now demolished), and at Nos. 27-28 Mount Street and 34-42 (consec.) South Audley Street (1888-9). And the same procedure was followed in parts of other predominantly commercial streets, notably in South Audley Street, at Nos. 61-63 consec. (1889-91) and Nos. 64-68 consec. (1891-3); in Duke Street at Nos. 55-73 odd (1890-2); and in Oxford Street at Nos. 385-397 odd (1887-9). Generally each group of lessees employed a single building contractor—Perry Brothers, for instance, at Nos. 87-93 (consec.) Mount Street and 26-33 (consec.) South Audley Street, or Kirk and Randall at Nos. 55-73 (odd) Duke Street; but when one of the lessees was himself in the building trade, he was sometimes allowed to do the building on his own site. Thus at Nos. 94-102 (consec.) Mount Street Bywaters were the contractors for four of the lessees, but the fifth, Andrews, being a builder, was permitted to do his own construction work provided that 'the bricks and terra cotta are obtained from the same source as the other houses so that the colour may be alike';[293] and similarly at Nos. 116-121 (consec.) Mount Street W. W. Weir, an upholsterer, was allowed 'to build his own house', he being 'experienced in building works'.[294]

The administrative labour required to establish and supervise these tradesmen's consortia and their architects (who will be discussed later) was very considerable and could only have been attempted on such a large rich estate as that of the Grosvenor family. Even there it evidently placed considerable strain on the Duke's advisers, for when a private resident whose lease had only four more years to come applied in 1884 for a renewal he was brusquely told that 'the matter could not be pressing and must await more pressing renewals'.[295] This, perhaps, was one reason why, despite the Duke's evident wish to treat so far as possible with commercial occupants, commercial sites were nevertheless quite often offered to speculators, just as sites for residential ranges always were. This practice, which entailed much less work for the estate staff, was first adopted in the 1870's when Thomas Patrick, of Mark Patrick and Son, builders, became the rebuilding lessee of Nos. 443-451 (odd) Oxford Street (1876-8), his architect being J. T. Wimperis. It was continued at Nos. 57-60 (consec.) South Audley Street, where James Purdey, the gunmaker, who had not hitherto had any premises on the estate, began in 1879 to buy up the subsisting short-term leases with a view to rebuilding. This was done in 1881-2, Purdey taking the prominent corner with Mount Street for his shop while the rest of the building was used as residential chambers —a successful speculation evidently, for in 1892 he rebuilt the adjoining No. 84 Mount Street and signed a contract to rebuild No. 31 Green Street (both private houses).

In South Audley Street Purdey had clearly been allowed to rebuild because the previous occupants preferred to sell their old leases to him and remove rather than undertake to rebuild for themselves; and lack of applications to rebuild from occupants may sometimes have been the reason why commercial sites were offered to speculators. But this was at any rate not altogether the case on the west side of Duke Street, where in August 1886 Boodle invited J. T. Wimperis, the architect, to treat for the site now occupied by Nos. 54-76 even (Duke Street Mansions).[296] As previously mentioned, Wimperis had already acted as Patrick's architect at Nos. 443-451 (odd) Oxford Street, and in 1884-6 he had at his own suggestion acted as both architect and lessee for the building of chambers and one shop at the corner site of Nos. 56 South Audley Street and 44 Mount Street (Plate 33d). In August 1886 Boodle undoubtedly knew that one of the occupants of the Duke Street site, E. L. Armbrecht, a chemist, wanted to rebuild,[297] but the building contract and subsequently the new lease for the whole range were nevertheless granted to Wimperis. The Board's allegedly unfair treatment of Armbrecht was subsequently investigated at great length by the Select Committee of the House of Commons on Town Holdings. Boodle's defence of his conduct was no doubt legalistically sound, but his assertion that, if Armbrecht had been allowed to rebuild, the erection of a block of artisans' dwellings at the rear of the site would have been 'obstructed' was not very convincing, and the suspicion remains that Wimperis got the contract in preference to an occupant because he was known from previous experience to be efficient and because he could, as both lessee and architect, undertake the whole range single-handed.[298]*

But despite the criticism implied in the Select Committee's enquiries, the Grosvenor Board continued to offer commercial sites to speculative builders. In 1891 the site of Nos. 25–29 (consec.) North Audley Street, after being refused by several other firms, was taken by Matthews, Rogers and Company, the first of a number of speculations undertaken by them on the Grosvenor estate. Four of the five shops which they built here were sold on completion to Mount Street tradesmen disturbed by rebuilding there. Trollopes in 1893–5 built Nos. 75–83 (odd) Duke Street (Plate 35b), half as a speculation and half under contract with a dressmaker whose previous premises on the opposite side of the street were to be demolished; and the same firm also built Nos. 10–12 (consec.) Mount Street in 1894–6 under a similar arrangement for No. 10 with a firm of auctioneers previously occupying other premises in the street about to be rebuilt. Holloways were the lessees for the adjoining Nos. 14–26 (consec.) Mount Street in 1897–8 (Plate 34a; fig. 20c)—evidently at Boodle's suggestion[300]—and in 1898 Bywaters accepted an offer of the site of Nos. 31–38 (consec.) North Audley Street, they having previously built the adjoining No. 30 under contract with a firm of saddlers who had negotiated a rebuilding lease.

When the amount of contemporaneous rebuilding of ranges of residential property is also taken into account, it is clear that a very considerable volume of speculative building was proceeding on the estate, particularly in the mid 1890's. The Board was therefore concerned that this work should be of good quality, and in 1896 it drew up 'a list of builders whose names may be put down as reliable in case any building sites offer'. These were Stanley Bird, Colls and Company, William Cubitt and Company, Higgs and Hill, Holloway, Lucas Brothers, Matthews, Rogers and Company, Mowlem and Company, Sprake and Foreman, George Trollope and Sons, and William Willett.[301] In the distribution of its favours among these firms the Board attempted to be fair, and so when Trollopes applied for a vacant site in Balfour Mews the Board decided that 'Messrs. Trollope have already had far more sites [on the estate] than any other builders in London and their application cannot be acceded to'. The allocation of important work was not, however, necessarily confined to these firms—Daw, for instance, who was not on the list, was granted the site in Balfour Mews.[302] But the Board was nevertheless very careful about what firms should be allowed to build on the estate, and whenever a lessee who was not himself a builder invited tenders for the rebuilding of his premises, he was required to consult the Board about the names of the firms to be invited to tender. Failure to do so produced an admonishment—'The names ought to have been sent

in the first instance before any of the builders were asked to tender'.[303]

These administrative mechanics of the Duke's rebuilding were one of the chief subjects which interested the members of the Select Committee of the House of Commons on Town Holdings in their prolonged examination of H. T. Boodle in 1887. But they were not in the least interested in the architects who designed the new buildings. Who these architects were, and how they were chosen, is however a matter of importance in the history of the estate.

The architects known to have worked on the estate during the first Duke's time included several of the foremost practitioners of the day—for instance, W. D. Caröe, Ernest George, J. J. Stevenson and Alfred Waterhouse—and many of the others were drawn from the middle ranks of the profession. The hacks, who proliferated in the late nineteenth century, did not in general get much work here. The relatively high standard of design which therefore resulted may be largely attributed to the discriminating influence of the Duke himself and of his advisers.

This influence varied with each building or range of buildings, and there was never any set procedure in the selection of architects. Sometimes there is no evidence about how the choice was made, but the Duke's influence and authority must generally have been strong, even when not directly exerted. All designs had to be submitted to the Board, and in most cases they were closely examined by the Duke himself, who often only approved them after considerable modification. After about 1875 all prospective rebuilding lessees knew that the Duke would insist on red brick in the Domestic Revival manner, and even when they were allowed to choose their own architect, their choice must have been greatly affected by this knowledge.

In 1887 their choice was still further circumscribed. The Board minutes record that 'With regard to the architects for rebuilding plots, the Duke wishes the following names to be selected from by the rebuilding tenants: one architect to be employed for each block of buildings. Mr. Norman Shaw, Mr. [J. T.] Wimperis, Mr. [R. W.] Edis, Mr. [T.] Chatfeild Clarke, Mr. [J. T.] Smith, Mr. [Thomas] Verity, and Mr. Ernest George'.[304]

In practice this list was not exclusive,[305] and was changed from time to time (see page 147). In 1894 it consisted of J. MacVicar Anderson, Ingress Bell and Aston Webb, A. J. Bolton, H. C. Boyes, W. D. Caröe, T. Chatfeild Clarke, T. E. Collcutt, R. W. Edis, Ernest George and Peto, Isaacs and Florence, C. E. Sayer, J. J. Stevenson and J. T. Wimperis.[306]

The way in which this list of 'approved' architects was used varied greatly. In cases—comparatively rare—when a private gentleman wanted to rebuild a single house for his own occupation, he was generally allowed to choose

---

* On the expiry of his lease at Lady Day 1887 Armbrecht took temporary premises on the east side of Duke Street on a yearly tenancy, but in 1890 he was accepted by the Board as one of the rebuilding lessees for Nos. 55–73 (odd) Duke Street.[299]

for himself, subject to the Duke's approval. Sir John Kelk, for instance, seems to have done so in the appointment of John Johnson at No. 3 Grosvenor Square (1875–7, demolished), and it was evidently the lessee, C. H. Wilson, who chose George Devey for No. 41 Grosvenor Square (1883–6, demolished). Both these appointments were made before the existence of the 'approved' list, but its existence did not prevent Lord Windsor from selecting Fairfax B. Wade, who was not on it, for his large house at No. 54 Mount Street (1896–9, Plates 36a, 37), overlooking the garden of Grosvenor House—a choice which evidently pleased the Duke, who firmly overruled his Board's objections to Wade's elevational designs.[307] Similarly, when Lord Ribblesdale proposed Sidney R. J. Smith—likewise not on the list—for No. 32 Green Street (1897–9) the Duke consented and appointed Smith as architect for the adjacent sites in Norfolk (now Dunraven) Street and North Row as well (Plate 36b).[308] But when the Earl of Aberdeen announced that he did not intend to have an architect at all for the rebuilding of No. 27 Grosvenor Square (1886–8, demolished), the Duke insisted that there should be one, and the appointment was evidently made by him or by Boodle, the choice being J. T. Wimperis, who, it may be noted, had recently had several other commissions on the estate.[309] Even for private gentlemen the safest course was perhaps that adopted by Dr. Joseph Walker at Nos. 21 and 22 Grosvenor Street (1898–9), who attended the Board 'and, of course, leaves the question of architect to the Duke. After he has left the Board, it is suggested to ask the Duke if he would allow Mr. Balfour [the estate surveyor, probably present at this meeting] to be the architect.'[310]

But most of the private houses built in the first Duke's time were, as we have already seen, built in ranges by speculating builders, and in these cases the architect was almost always appointed by the Duke himself or by the Board with his approval. When, for instance, the builders Higgs and Hill were in 1896 offered terms for the site of Nos. 2–12 (even) Park Street, they were told that A. H. Kersey (not on the list) was to be the architect.[311] In the same year Boodle, at a Board meeting at which the Duke was evidently not present, successfully suggested H. O. Cresswell as architect for Nos. 94–104A (even) Park Street, Boodle being under the impression that Cresswell was on the approved list, although no record of this has been found.[312]

Boodle seems, indeed, to have had his own share of influence in the choice of architects. In 1886 he approached J. T. Wimperis about the site of Nos. 54–76 (even) Duke Street, and it was he who proposed in 1891 that the Board should 'communicate with Col. Edis as to any clients of his who might be desirous of rebuilding' on the large

L-shaped site at the north-west corner of Park Street and Green Street. R. W. Edis had already rebuilt Nos. 59 and 61 Brook Street in 1883–6 (one being intended for his own occupation)[313] and he was also one of three architects on the 'approved' list of 1887 who sometimes acted as speculator as well as architect for large sites on the estate.* At Boodle's corner plots Edis ultimately took on the whole site himself, and between 1891 and 1894 he designed and built Nos. 105–115 (odd) Park Street and 25–31 (consec.) Green Street. This was evidently successful from his point of view, for in 1894–6 he was clamouring for more building sites. But the Board would not oblige him. He had 'seriously departed' from the estate specification, and it was therefore decided that 'he should not be offered further sites'. Furthermore, 'The Board do not think it expedient that an architect should speculate on the estate, as architects are wanted to design and supervise the buildings of others'.[314]

A not very different practice adopted by two large firms of builders, who liked to use their own 'tame' architect, was not, however, objected to. At four sites where rebuilding was undertaken by George Trollope and Sons in the 1890's, his brother, John E. Trollope, of the firm of Giles, Gough and Trollope, was the architect (Nos. 6–9 consec. Mount Street, 1–8 consec. Carlos Place (Plate 34d) and 1–15 odd Mount Row, 1891–3; Nos. 45–52 consec. Mount Street, 1891–3; the Barley Mow, Duke Street, 1895–6; and Nos. 34–42 even Park Street and 53 Mount Street, 1895–9); but at another site the Duke required him to use someone else (Nos. 75–83 odd Duke Street, W. D. Caröe, 1893–5). Similarly Matthews, Rogers and Company agreed in 1891 to rebuild Nos. 25–29 (consec.) North Audley Street to designs by the Duke's nominee, Thomas Verity, who was probably insisted upon because there was a public house (the Marlborough Head) to be rebuilt at the adjoining No. 24 and Verity had already done another public house on the estate, the Audley Hotel (1888–9), to the Duke's hard-won satisfaction. But in all their subsequent work on the estate Matthews, Rogers and Company were always allowed to use 'an architect in their own firm', M. C. Hulbert.[315]

By far the most prolific architect of private houses was, however, the new estate surveyor appointed in 1890, Eustace Balfour, who seems to have been able to get whatever work he wanted and then, sometimes, delegate it to his partner in private practice, Thackeray Turner. As early as 1891 he is recorded as declining to act as architect at Nos. 2–8 (consec.) Green Street because 'he would like to transfer his services to the Portugal Street site'.[315] In this south-western part of the estate he (and/or Turner) did so much work during the 1890's that Balfour Place (formerly Portugal Street) and Balfour Mews were named after him. It included Nos. 1–6 (consec.) Balfour Place

---

* The other two were J. T. Smith, lessee and architect for Nos. 106–116 (even) Park Street and 19 Green Street (1887–8), and J. T. Wimperis, lessee and architect for Nos. 56 South Audley Street and 44 Mount Street (Audley Mansions, 1884–6) and for Nos. 54–76 (even) Duke Street (Duke Street Mansions, 1887–8).

(1891-4); the whole block bounded by Mount Street, Balfour Place, Aldford Street and Rex Place (1891-7, see Plate 35a); Alfred Beit's mansion at No. 26 Park Lane (1894-7, demolished), where Balfour's employment by Beit as architect was made one of the conditions of the contract for the rebuilding lease (Plate 38a); Nos. 14-22 (even) Park Street, 68 Mount Street and stables on the west side of Rex Place (1896-7); and the east side of Balfour Mews (1898-9). Elsewhere on the estate the firm of Balfour and Turner did No. 10 Green Street (1893-5) and St. Anselm's Church, Davies Street, of 1894-6 (Plate 38b), and in 1897-8 Balfour was diplomatically— and successfully—asking for Nos. 21-22 Grosvenor Street and 40-46 (even) Brook Street (1898-9).[316]

In the choice of architects for the rebuilding of shops and commercial premises there was very wide variety of practice. In the 1860's and early 1870's, as we have already seen, both the second Marquess and the third Marquess and future first Duke required their tenants in Oxford Street (which was the first commercial street to be extensively rebuilt) to use elevational designs supplied by the estate surveyor, Thomas Cundy III; and some-times the tenants employed obscure architects of their own to design the internal disposition of their buildings. Nos. 407-413 (odd) Oxford Street are cases in point. But the Duke's success in 1875 in persuading W. J. Goode to start the rebuilding of a large shop in South Audley Street to designs by Ernest George in the red-brick manner of the Queen Anne Revival (Plate 32) seems to have aroused his architectural ambitions. So when the next phase of commercial rebuilding began in the later 1880's he often nominated architects whose work reflected his own tastes.

The first such nominee was J. T. Wimperis, who had already done two jobs on the estate—Nos. 443-451 (odd) Oxford Street (1876-8) and Nos. 34 Berkeley Square and 130 Mount Street (1880-2)—his selection as architect in both these cases having been made by the building lessee. Subsequently he had applied successfully to be both lessee and architect for Nos. 56 South Audley Street and 44 Mount Street of 1884-6 (Plate 33d), and in 1886 he was invited by the Board to act in the same dual capacity at Nos. 54-76 (even) Duke Street (1887-8).[317] Thomas Chatfeild Clarke, who had also been responsible for the design of various buildings erected in Oxford Street since 1883, was invited to design Nos. 385-397 (odd) Oxford Street (1887-9), despite the objections of one of the rebuilding lessees, who wanted to have someone else: in 1890 it was decided that he should be the architect for Nos. 64-68 (consec.) South Audley Street (1891-3), which were about to be rebuilt by local tradesmen, this commission being subsequently extended to the adjoining Nos. 69 and 70, designed by his son Howard Chatfeild Clarke in 1898-1900.[318] In 1889 'Mr. Boodle suggests and the Duke approves of Mr. Caröe being the architect' for a group of tradesmen in the rebuilding of Nos. 55-73 (odd) Duke Street (1890-2), and in 1892 the Duke nominated Caröe for the nearby Nos. 75-83 (odd) Duke

Street, to be rebuilt by Trollopes and one shopkeeper (Plate 35b).[319] Thomas Verity and (after his death in 1891) his son Frank were the Duke's selections for Nos. 24-29 (consec.) North Audley Street (1891-3), probably (as we have already seen) because this range included a public house, Thomas Verity having already done the Audley Hotel satisfactorily. But for his death Thomas Verity would probably also have been appointed for the Barley Mow at No. 82 Duke Street (1895-6), which went instead, on Boodle's suggestion, to John Trollope with Trollopes as builders, despite the objection of the publican-lessee, who wanted 'a Mr. Frampton, a friend of his, to be the architect'.[320] And although Auguste Scorrier, hotel keeper and prospective lessee for the re-building of the very important Coburg (now Connaught) Hotel at the corner of Mount Street and Carlos Place, ultimately got the man he wanted, he was made to under-stand that the choice was not his to make. After he had been imperiously informed in November 1893 that 'the architect had not been decided upon by the Duke' his solicitors, displaying a finesse which was on this occasion conspicuously absent in Boodle's office, politely suggested that the Duke might make his selection from one of three architects, namely Lewis H. Isaacs of Isaacs and Florence, William J. Green and E. T. Hall. As neither Green nor Hall seems ever to have designed a hotel, whereas Isaacs had done the Victoria in Northumberland Avenue and the Imperial at Holborn Viaduct, the Board took the hint and in January 1894 'the Duke appoints Mr. Isaacs the architect'.[321]

Sometimes the Duke's influence in the choice of an architect is apparent, even though he did not act directly. At Nos. 104-111 (consec.) Mount Street (1885-7) W. H. Warner, the estate agent and one of the rebuilding lessees, took the lead in submitting designs by Ernest George. He may well have done so because he knew from W. J. Goode's experience in South Audley Street in 1875 that George's work would be acceptable; and so it proved, after the Duke had required the height of the proposed buildings on this north-facing site to be reduced to admit more light to the houses opposite (Plate 34b).[322] After 1887 groups of shopkeepers who were negotiating for the rebuilding of a range to one design were sometimes sent the Duke's list of 'approved' architects, from which they were to choose.[323] Ernest George and Peto were probably selected in this way for Nos. 1-5 (consec.) Mount Street (1888-9, Nos. 1-3 demolished), and Thomas Verity almost certainly so at Nos. 27-28 Mount Street and 34-42 (consec.) South Audley Street (1888-9).

At what turned out to be the largest range of buildings by a single architect on the whole of the Mayfair estate the Duke's influence was rather more uncertain. This range, by A. J. Bolton, consisted of the new Vestry Hall on the south side of Mount Street (1886-7, now demolished, site occupied by No. 103), Nos. 94-102 (consec.) Mount Street (1889-91), Nos. 87-93 (consec.) Mount Street and 26-33 (consec.) South Audley Street and the new public library (1893–5). In 1883 the Vestry of St. George's arranged with the Duke to buy the freehold of part of the old workhouse for the site of the new Vestry Hall, and then 'invited the competition of four architects' for the new building. Bolton was chosen by the Vestry,[324] but the Duke, who was himself a vestryman, evidently did not much like the design, and Bolton was required to call at Grosvenor House, where the Duke 'told him of his wishes and requested to have an altered elevation'.[325] By 1887, however, when he opened the new Vestry Hall on 23 April,[326] the Duke's opinion of Bolton's work had perhaps changed somewhat, for when both the Vestry clerk and Bolton himself asked in 1888 that 'the latter, who acted for the Vestry building, may be the architect for the proposed new houses' at the adjoining Nos. 94–102 (consec.) Mount Street, the Duke agreed. He did, however, stipulate—rather in vain, as it turned out—that 'he would like a repetition of the houses' (not in fact themselves identical) by Ernest George at Nos. 104–111 (consec.); and in 1892 he appointed Bolton architect for the rebuilding lessees at Nos. 87–93 (consec.) Mount Street and 26–33 (consec.) South Audley Street, stipulating in this case—with more effect—that Nos. 94–102 Mount Street 'are to be copied'.[327] By this time Bolton had won a competition for the design of the public library in Buckingham Palace Road, Victoria, also on the Grosvenor estate, where the Duke had presented a freehold site gratis,[328] and in April 1891 the St. George's Library Commissioners asked the Duke for a site for a library in Mayfair. Here he agreed to grant them a ninety-year lease, but before the building contract was exchanged 'the question who is to be the Architect selected by the Duke' was discussed at a Board meeting in his absence, when it was 'felt that, as Mr. Bolton is building all the adjoining houses, his Grace may possibly select him, although he is understood not to have altogether approved of his [Bolton's] design for the Free Library in Buckingham Palace Road'. Despite his evidently still only qualified approval of Bolton he did ultimately agree, 'if the Vestry so desired'.[329]

Bolton's original appointment in 1884 for the first stage of this range—the Vestry Hall—was undoubtedly due to the Vestry, and the Duke's displeasure at the choice (mentioned above) was manifested again in 1887 when Bolton's name was not included on the first list of 'approved' architects. Perhaps in this case it would have been difficult, though certainly not impossible, for him to have resisted the Vestry's decision, but other cases show that even shopkeepers were sometimes allowed their own free choice. In 1880 William Lambert, surveyor, was the choice of James Purdey, the gunmaker, for Nos. 57–60 (consec.) South Audley Street (1881–2), and in 1889–91 he acted for the completion of this range (Nos. 61–63 consec.) by other commercial lessees. Edwin Hollis, a pork butcher, was allowed to have J. S. Moye

for Nos. 399–405 (odd) Oxford Street (1880–2, demolished), and Thrupp and Maberly had Henry S. Legg at Nos. 421–429 (odd) Oxford Street (1884–7, demolished) despite Thomas Cundy's objection that he did 'not consider that Mr. Legge [*sic*] will be very suitable as he knows nothing of him'.[330] At Nos. 125–129 (consec.) Mount Street (1886–7) it seems likely that the four shopkeeper/rebuilding lessees chose W. H. Powell themselves, for in August 1885 the Board received letters 'from and on behalf of Mr. Powell…giving testimonials as to his fitness to be the architect for some of the rebuilding tenants in Mount Street'.[331] At that time there was as yet no list of 'approved' architects, but Powell's name did not appear on it in 1887 or in later years.* Similarly the four shopkeepers and a surgeon who were the rebuilding lessees at Nos. 116–121 (consec.) Mount Street (1886–7) seem to have chosen J. T. Smith themselves. When Smith submitted an elevation on their behalf in 1885 'his Grace did not approve of it as he thought the buildings very high and too elaborate in decoration'. But he later agreed to a revised version, 'though it appears to me to be overdone and wanting in simplicity',[333] a view which many others may still share, but which the Duke does not seem to have held very strongly, since in the following year he allowed Smith to be the lessee and architect for private houses at Nos. 106–116 (even) Park Street and 19 Green Street, and in 1887 included him in the 'approved' list.

When E. McM. Burden, a Duke Street chemist about to rebuild Nos. 78 and 80 there (1887–8), submitted designs by his brother, R. H. Burden, in 1886, he was 'told that the Board do not think the drawing good enough for the site, but the Duke will decide'. R. H. Burden 'had not had experience in street architecture', and ultimately on Boodle's suggestion J. T. Wimperis, who was then in course of rebuilding the nearby Nos. 54–76 (even) Duke Street, was called in to revise Burden's designs.[334] Such ducal dislike of commercial lessees' architectural tastes was probably the reason for the compilation of the 'approved' list in 1887, but even in later years complete freedom of choice was sometimes still allowed. Thus Walton and Lee, auctioneers, were allowed in 1893 to nominate H. C. Boyes for No. 10 Mount Street, although he was not on the list of 1887. This choice was evidently considered to be satisfactory, for in 1894 Boyes became the architect (for Trollopes) for the adjoining Nos. 11 and 12 as well, and his name was put on the revised list of that year.[335] In 1896 Holloways, the builders, negotiating for the rebuilding of Nos. 14–26 (consec.) Mount Street (Plate 34a; fig. 20c), successfully asked that Read and Macdonald (never on the list) 'whom they can highly recommend, may be the architects'.[336] And a firm of saddlers was allowed to have Henry S. Legg (likewise never on the list) at No. 30 North Audley Street (1896–7), despite Eustace Balfour's recommendation of Ernest

---

* Perhaps because he subsequently migrated to Natal, where he died in 1900.[332]

George; and when the adjoining Nos. 31–38 (consec.) were rebuilt a year later by the contractors Bywaters, Legg was again the architect, this time at the instigation of the Board.[337]

In addition to the rebuilding of private houses and shops there were two other categories of buildings in which the Duke's philanthropic temperament prompted him to take an active personal interest. These were artisans' dwellings and public houses.

During the second Marquess's time (1845–69) several small blocks of artisans' dwellings had been built on the Mayfair estate—St. George's Buildings and Grosvenor Buildings, Bourdon Street (1853 and 1869), by the St. George's Parochial Association (Plate 30a, b), and Bloomfield Flats, Bourdon Street (1856) and Oxford House, Grosvenor Market (1860, demolished), by a local builder, John Newson.[338] The Grosvenor Estate did not initiate any of these schemes, but between 1866 and 1875 the second Marquess and his successor, the first Duke, were both intimately involved in much larger projects in Pimlico, first in conjunction with the Metropolitan Association for Improving the Dwellings of the Industrious Classes, and later with the Improved Industrial Dwellings Company. In Mayfair the latter also built Clarendon Flats (formerly Buildings), Balderton (formerly George) Street in 1871–2 (Plate 30c), and in 1880 the Duke was already considering with the Company a very large scheme for improved dwellings between Grosvenor Square and Brook Street on the south and Oxford Street on the north, to be implemented when the existing leases expired in 1886.[339] Thus this project was in existence well before the tremendous public outcry of 1883 about the prevailing conditions of working-class housing, and between 1886 and 1892 nine blocks of dwellings were built in that area (Plate 31). They and Clarendon Flats provided accommodation for some two thousand people, this being seven hundred more than the scheme displaced, and the Company was bound in its contract with the Duke 'to offer to the persons who are now residing...upon that portion of his estate, the opportunity of occupying the dwellings as they are from time to time erected'.[340] The Duke himself paid the cost of laying out a large garden in what is now Brown Hart Gardens—later converted into a roof 'garden' above the Duke Street Electricity Sub-station (Plate 31b). His annual rental for the whole area redeveloped fell from £2,193 under the old leases to £502 under the new ones granted to the Company.[341]

The Duke's policy towards public houses reflected a more severe side of Victorian philanthropy; and it also exhibits more clearly than in any other aspect of the estate's administration the vast powers which he possessed as ground landlord. We have already seen that the second Earl and first Marquess (1802–45) had begun to try to reduce the number of pubs, and that in 1828, on the eve of the Beer Act of 1830, there were around seventy-five on his Mayfair estate. At about the time of the accession of the third Marquess (later first Duke) in 1869 there were still about forty-seven pubs and beer shops there,[342] and encouraged no doubt by the changes of 1869–72 in the licensing laws he decided to make a further drastic reduction in their numbers. In the ensuing years the great majority of applications to renew pub leases, whether from publicans or from great brewers like Watney's or Meux, were rejected outright. In 1874, for instance, Hanbury's were peremptorily informed that they could not have a renewal of the Swan in Oxford Street because 'on public grounds it is essential to reduce the number of public houses on the estate',[343] while Watney's in 1879 were told that the site of their Coach and Horses in Grosvenor Mews (now Bourdon Street) was 'already promised for the Parochial Institution'.[344] By 1891 no less than thirty-nine pubs and beer houses had been abolished on the Mayfair portion of the estate alone, and only eight still survived.[345] Today there are only five.

The motive for this massacre was, of course, the promotion of temperance,[346] and in c. 1884 a branch of the Church of England Temperance Society was established in the parish with the Duke's blessing.[347] In the newly rebuilt artisan quarter around Brown Hart Gardens he provided a drinking fountain, and he would have liked to establish a 'cocoa house' there too, had not the proposed lessee replied that he did not 'see much chance of making cocoa rooms in the place spoken of pay'.[348] Pubs did, however, pay, and their wholesale diminution was only achieved 'at a great pecuniary loss' to the Duke.[346] The Board could indeed state, in answer to a question about the Duke's policy towards pubs, that 'the question of loss does not influence the Duke in deciding upon this or any other matters affecting the good of the tenants or the improvement of London'.[349]

The mere abolition of pubs was, however, only one of the formidable prongs with which the Duke assailed the drink interest, for the surviving few were subjected to a regimen of controlling discipline of almost Spartan intensity. In the rebuilding of pubs the lessees had their architects chosen for them, of course, and at the Hertford Arms, 94 Park Street (now demolished) the tenant had to build his pub (to H. O. Cresswell's design) in a wholly domestic manner outwardly indistinguishable from the adjoining range of private houses.[350] At the corner of Mount Street and South Audley Street Watney's were only allowed to rebuild the Bricklayers' Arms (now the Audley Hotel) in 1888–9 on condition that they surrendered the lease of another nearby pub, and in the new building there was to be no entrance from South Audley Street. Even such a favoured architect as Thomas Verity had his first designs returned with the comment that 'His Grace thinks that the elevation...is too gin-palace-y in Mount Street'.[351]

Beginning in 1871 the Marquess (later Duke) also sought to reduce the hours of opening. These were certainly long—on weekdays, 4 a.m. to 1 a.m. (except Saturdays, midnight), and on Sundays 1 p.m. to 3 p.m. and 5 p.m. to 11 p.m. Sunday opening was, however, what particularly offended the Duke, and at first he admitted 'that there would be difficulties in London in reducing the hours, however desirable'.[352] But in 1880 he decided that he would, in renewing leases, 'prohibit the houses being opened on Sundays except for drinking off the premises from 1 to 3 o'clock'.[353] This draconian decree was sometimes relaxed to facilitate the exchange of leases, and by 1895 Sunday drinking on the premises between 1 and 3 o'clock seems to have been generally allowed. But in that year he refused to allow F. W. Bevan, the licensee and rebuilding lessee of the Barley Mow in Duke Street (who was risking his own capital of over £4,000 in rebuilding by an architect and contractor both chosen by the Duke), to open on Sunday evenings; and although he subsequently did allow off-the-premises trade on Sunday evenings[354] he still had all the publicans completely at his mercy, thanks to the ingenious drafting of his pub leases.

These, in the list of prohibited trades, *included* that of licensed victualler, but a 'conditional licence' was attached, by which the Duke granted consent, personal to the lessee, to practise the trade of licensed victualler, provided that 'the said trade or business be respectably conducted to my satisfaction', that the peculiar Grosvenor restrictions on Sunday opening be observed, and that 'I or other the landlord for the time being may revoke this licence at any time if in my or his absolute discretion there shall have been a breach of any or either of the above conditions'.[355] With this power to revoke his own licences whenever he, at his sole discretion, might think fit, the Duke had much more power over the pubs on his estate than the licensing authorities themselves.

The control of pubs shows in its most extreme form the full extent of the Duke's authority over his estate. But there were other fields in which it was at any rate in theory not much smaller, although practical difficulties sometimes prevented its full use. It should, however, be noted that the Duke usually exerted his power to achieve objects generally congenial to at least the wealthy residents for whom the estate primarily catered. His control, through his leases, over the use to which individual buildings might be put is a case in point and has already been discussed. The results of this can still be clearly seen in Mount Street, where prior to its complete rebuilding in the 1880's and 90's, shops, private houses and apartments let 'to people coming up to town' were all mixed together. The Duke's policy, which could only be implemented at the time of rebuilding, was to have all the shops east of South Audley Street and only private houses to the west. 'Our experience', Boodle stated in 1887, 'is that tradesmen like what they call "a market". They like all the shops to be together, and private gentlemen naturally like their houses to be together without shops.'[356] Similarly the grandees residing in Upper Grosvenor Street (of whom the Duke himself was one) probably liked his decision in 1873 that 'professions as well as trades and businesses should be excluded from Upper Grosvenor

Street,...without, however, interfering with professional men under existing leases.'[357]

Policies of this kind could, however, only be implemented gradually, and elsewhere trade was now so long established that its removal, however desirable it might be thought to be, was sometimes abandoned. In 1880, for instance, a tailor at No. 62 Grosvenor Street was refused a renewal because 'businesses are being excluded from Grosvenor Street as the leases expire',[358] but Collard's, the piano makers at No. 16 were granted an extension without difficulty in 1888;[359] while in Brook Street some attempt seems to have been made to eliminate shops,[360] but Claridge's Hotel was allowed to be rebuilt there in the 1890's. The eastern end of Brook Street was, indeed, becoming steadily less residential in character, while in Grosvenor Street the Alexandra Ladies' Club was admitted to No. 12 in 1887;[361] and discreet new businesses, notably that of 'Court dressmaker', were even allowed, provided that there was 'no show of business except a small brass plate, and the door to be kept shut except for ingress and egress'.[362]

Sometimes the Duke's requirements must have been irksome even to residents in the best streets. His liking for plate glass in the windows of private houses was not always popular, and his idiosyncratic fondness for stucco-work to be painted orange, as he himself had the Grosvenor Office at No. 53 Davies Street done in 1883 ('like that at the bottom of Waterloo Place') must have been vexatious to some tastes.[363] For railings he seems to have changed in the mid 1870's from stone colour to 'chocolate or red', but in later years the new red brick 'Queen Anne style' houses had to have their railings and window frames painted white.[364]

More usually, however, his actions did probably enjoy considerable support among his tenants. His objection to building work during the London Season, his preference for wood blocks—quieter but more expensive than granite—for the repaving of Oxford Street, and his strict control of advertising on his portion of the same street, are obvious instances.[365] In the 1870's and early 1880's the disfigurement of the estate by the erection of telegraph and telephone posts and wires was vigorously opposed, the proprietors being required to sign an acknowledgment that their installations were held on sufferance only, subject to three months' notice to quit.[366] When the new electric lighting companies obtained power in 1883 to put up posts and wires, subject to the control of the local authorities, the Board thought that 'a combination should be effected with other landlords to require all the electric wires to be put underground'.[367] And well-founded complaints from tenants were often taken up—against 'the uproarious conduct' of the children at the Ragged School in Davies Mews, or the constant standing of carriages outside the Grosvenor Gallery, or, from the Duchess of Marlborough against a dentist in Grosvenor Street whose activities were visible from her house opposite, and whom the Board politely requested 'to put up a muslin curtain to prevent his dentistry patients being seen'.[368]

Nor was such concern confined to outward and visible (or audible) matters. From the 1870's onwards it became common for the Board, in the renewal of leases, to insist that water closets should be externally lit and ventilated instead of (as was sometimes hitherto the case) from the staircase.* The installation of lifts—first recorded in 1884[370]—produced a new type of problem through the frequent complaints of neighbours about the noise of their operation. In the mews behind the great houses extensive works of modernization were often required, particularly when Eustace Balfour was the estate surveyor (1890–1910), the following being a typical requirement —'Modernise the stabling as regards accommodation for a married coachman and one helper, providing at least four rooms (every room to have a fireplace) and a separate w.c. for the use of the helpers. The helper's room to be approached directly from the staircase, and to be kept quite distinct from the coachman's quarters…'[371] In many mews the old narrow entrances were widened by the demolition of corner houses, and in conjunction with the Vestry urinals à la mode française were provided for the army of outdoor servants who worked there 'the Duke was most anxious for a great many more urinals being erected in the Parish and in London generally'. And when Lord Manners's coachman complained that the urinal in Reeves Mews 'could be seen into from his upper windows', the Board acted with as much promptness as it had in the case of the Duchess of Marlborough and the dentist in Grosvenor Street.[372]

In addition to the extensive rebuildings and the general maintenance of the estate, a number of important other improvements were made during the first Duke's time. Communication between Berkeley Square and Grosvenor Square was greatly improved by the demolition of some projecting property of the Duke's at the east end of Mount Street (c. 1880), and by the widening and realignment of Charles Street (now Carlos Place, c. 1891). Several other streets were widened during the course of rebuilding, notably Duke Street, North Audley Street, South Audley Street north of South Street, and Mount Street, the land given up by the Duke for this last alone being worth £50,000.[373] Several short new streets were formed or realigned and widened—Red Place, Carpenter Street, Rex Place and Balfour Mews—and in 1898 the important realignment of the north end of Davies Street, first mooted in the 1830's,[374] was at last achieved, thereby providing greatly improved communication between Berkeley Square and Oxford Street.[375] When the Metropolitan Board of Works made improvements at Hyde Park Corner—some distance from the Grosvenor estate—at the public expense, the Duke of Westminster was the only landowner to make a voluntary contribution (of £3,000) to the cost, 'in consideration of the additional value that was given to his property'.[376] And when in 1890 the disused burial ground to the east of the Grosvenor Chapel was converted by the Vestry into a public garden the Duke, who had envisaged this improvement as long ago as 1874, began, and continued for the rest of his life, to pay £100 per annum towards the cost of its upkeep.[377] It was not indeed for nothing that the chairman of the Royal Commission of 1884–5 on the Housing of the Working Classes said publicly that he did 'not think that anybody on the Commission would be disposed to doubt the excellent management of the Westminster Estate'.[378]

In 1899, the last year of the Duke's life, there was a marked decline in the volume of rebuilding on the Mayfair portion of the estate. A phase of reduced activity was beginning, and his own tremendous impact upon the area had probably exhausted itself. In 1887, when this impact had not yet made itself fully felt, Boodle had stated before the Select Committee of the House of Commons on Town Holdings that the Duke's aim was 'to have wide thoroughfares instead of narrow, to set back the houses in rebuilding so as to obtain broad areas and a good basement for the servants…He also wishes to have effective architecture, to insist upon good sanitary arrangements in houses, to promote churches, chapels, and schools, and open spaces for recreation'. All this he had done chiefly 'because he desires better houses, and he is a great lover of architecture and likes a handsome town, and he would sacrifice enormously to carry that out on his estate'.[379]

By insisting so often upon rebuilding he undoubtedly had sacrificed the very considerable extra income which he could have obtained by leasing at rack rents. Boodle stated that 'rebuilding involves a loss of about two-thirds of the income'.[380] In Mount Street the total new ground rents amounted in 1898 to £8,343 per annum,[381] but if no rebuilding had taken place the rack rental from this one street would have been worth about £20,000 a year.[382] In 1897 the rental of the estate was actually said to have 'diminished, owing to the pulling down'.[383] The Duke's decision to go ahead with rebuilding on a large scale cannot therefore have been an easy one.

Yet despite the rebuildings the rental of the Mayfair estate nevertheless rose (as we have already seen) from c. £80,000 per annum in 1870 to c. £135,000 in 1891. About two thirds of this increase took place before the most intense phase of rebuilding began around 1886; and it should, of course, be remembered that although in rebuilding the Duke forfeited about two thirds of what he could have obtained by rack renting, his income still rose, because the new ground rents were substantially higher than the old ones.†[380]

---

* Even in Mayfair it does not appear that a constant supply of water was provided until 1893–4.[369]

† Some examples of the new ground rents, measured in square feet: stables, 7d.–9d.: Duke Street, 9½d.: houses in Aldford Street and Balfour Place area, 1s.: Mount Street east of South Audley Street, 1s. 3d.–1s. 6d.: Green Street, 1s.–1s. 8d.: public houses, 1s. 4d.–1s. 6d.

The extent of his sacrifice was therefore a matter of degree. But it was certainly one which no other London landlord made on the same scale, and the fact that he did make it gave substance to Boodle's claim that 'the Duke certainly takes the lead in the improvement of London'.[384] Nor should his success in the re-creation of 'a handsome town' on his estate be decried. It was an age when the quality of municipal street improvement was at its lowest ebb, and Mount Street was a vastly different kettle of fish from Shaftesbury Avenue or Charing Cross Road.

If the Duke had reason to be satisfied, so too did his rebuilding lessees, for according to Boodle they 'almost invariably' got their money back, and 'with a very large profit'. There was never any shortage of applications for sites, and the case (previously mentioned) of T. B. Linscott, the Oxford Street confectioner who had at first been 'rather reluctant to rebuild' but whose business had subsequently grown very rapidly, was 'usual in good thoroughfares'.[385] According to the estate agent W. H. Warner, who had no axe to grind in the matter, probably not a single one of the Mount Street lessees was 'dissatisfied with his bargain'.[386]

Throughout the 1880's and 90's the Board received numerous requests from architects and builders for sites, most of which were refused, occupants being (as we have seen) generally preferred. Those favoured few whose applications were successful, such as Edis or Trollopes, were almost always anxious to have more sites—a sure testimony to the financial success of their operations on the estate. Except in Balfour Place and Balfour Mews, where the market was sluggish for S. G. Bird in 1894 and for W. A. Daw in 1900,[387] speculators never seem to have had any difficulty in finding tenants or purchasers for their new buildings, and the high prices which they demanded were sometimes noted with interest by the Board, £16,000 for No. 68 Mount Street (W. A. Daw, ground rent £150) and for No. 78 Mount Street (W. H. Warner, ground rent £116), being cases in point.[388] The new houses in Green Street, although less expensive than those at the west end of Mount Street, were also evidently much sought after. In 1892 the Hon. Alfred Lyttelton bought one of them from the builders, Matthews, Rogers and Company, for £7,000, but sold it soon afterwards for £8,600 to F. Leverton Harris, who in turn re-sold it in 1896 for £12,600—an appreciation of eighty per cent in the course of four years.[389]

The market in Grosvenor Square was buoyant too. In reference to 'houses which have been rebuilt on a ground-rent, and afterwards sold for sums far exceeding the cost of building them', Boodle cited one house which 'cost 12,000l., and was sold for 18,000l.', and another which 'cost 18,000l. and was sold for 23,000l., and was afterwards sold again for 35,000l.'. No. 42, rebuilt as a speculation by the builder Wright Ingle in 1853–5 at a cost of less than

£20,000, was sold in 1886 (without any addition to the original seventy-seven-year lease) for £30,000.[390] In 1878 Holland and Hannen were thought to have made a profit of about £8,000 in selling No. 39 to the Marquess of Lothian for £23,500 after having 'practically had to rebuild the house';[391] and in the 1890's Matthews, Rogers and Company's speculations in refurbishing Nos. 11 and 13 were probably correspondingly successful.

But although the Duke himself, his rebuilding lessees and the speculative builders were all probably pleased with the changes made on the estate, there were other people who were not. There were some who merely did not like the Duke's taste in architecture. When the renumbering of the houses in Grosvenor Square was in contemplation, the Earl of Harrowby took the opportunity to complain to the Vestry 'that the character of the Square has much deteriorated of late and its Appearance has been destroyed by the recent erection of houses like public institutions'. The Earl's own architectural tastes were probably rather old-fashioned, but this did not, however, prevent his expressing a deeper and more general source of grievance when he continued that 'Anyhow, ordinary courtesy should have led the Grosvenor Estate Board to have consulted the old and existing tenants of the other houses, though recent experience has unfortunately shown that their interests are no longer consulted by the Estate Board in the arrangements with the new builders'.[392]

It was during the very years that the renewal of the Mayfair estate was being so vigorously carried through that the leasehold system, of which the Grosvenor estate formed such a conspicuous example, was first seriously criticised. During the 1880's several abortive 'leasehold enfranchisement' bills were discussed in Parliament,[393] both the Royal Commission of 1884–5 on the Housing of the Working Classes and the Select Committee of the House of Commons of 1887 on Town Holdings examined the workings of the system in some detail, and the Duke himself was from time to time attacked in the press and in a number of pamphlets.[394] Great urban landlords, and dukes in particular, were being challenged for the first time, and the death duty clauses in Sir William Harcourt's Finance Act of 1894 only added to their tribulations.[395] Public attitudes towards them, hitherto ignored, suddenly became important to them in the new political climate emanating from the Reform Act of 1884. Boodle did battle on the Duke's behalf in the correspondence columns of *The Times*, and the Marquess of Salisbury (the sometime Prime Minister) helpfully suggested to his nephew Eustace Balfour, the Grosvenor estate surveyor, 'that the number of the Duke's houses might be ascertained to disabuse the public mind as to the Dukes of Bedford and Westminster owning practically the whole of the area within the County of London'.*[396]

---

* The Grosvenor Board had 'no objection' to having such a count made, but considered (the science of public relations having not yet been invented) that 'it may be doubtful in which way it should be utilized'.[396]

The most pungent critic of the leasehold system in general and of the Duke in particular was Frank Banfield, whose series of articles in *The Sunday Times* was published in book form in *c.* 1888 under the title *The Great Landlords of London*. In his chapter on the Grosvenor estate he attacked the Duke for sometimes giving preference to speculative builders before occupants, and for compelling prospective lessees in businesses with valuable goodwill to rebuild at their expense but to his architectural taste. 'I like fine streets as much as any one, but I object to see numbers of Englishmen forced to tax their capital so heavily and perilously merely to suit the dictatorial architectural caprices of a millionaire Duke.' He also asserted that 'tenants do not receive that consideration which is their due', being often left in ignorance 'right up to the end of their lease, whether they can renew or not', and criticised the estate (in the person of H. T. Boodle) for its 'take it or leave it' attitude when offering rebuilding terms, and for the unreasonable stringency of some of the lease covenants.[397]

In reference to this last he cited the case of a butcher in Mount Street, Edgar Green of No. 117, who was one of the lessees for the rebuilding of Nos. 116-121 (consec.) and who in his lease had had to 'sign away the right to hang carcases' in front of his shop window. When he had nevertheless displayed meat outside, Boodle had asked him to desist, but had also invited him 'to make an application to the Duke for leave to hang a moderate quantity of meat in the window in front if he wished to do so instead'. Green had then attended a meeting of the Board to put his case, and the Duke had said he would 'call and see the shop on his way home' to Grosvenor House. Subsequently he wrote to Boodle that 'I think Butcher Green's exhibition of prominent carcases of sheep may be permitted as an ornament to the street, as I have told him'.[398]

This case shows that, on occasion, the autocratic powers possessed by the Estate were used with discretion; but generally the criticisms made by Banfield and others were criticisms of basic features of the leasehold system itself. It was (at any rate on the Grosvenor estate) the function of the head lessee to improve, by building or rebuilding, the ground let to him on a long lease at a low rent. But whereas at the time of first development the prospective lessee was free to accept or reject the terms offered by the ground landlord, at the time of rebuilding he already often had a considerable amount of capital vested in the site in the form of goodwill, and in negotiation for terms the scales were therefore weighted against him. Boodle might claim with justice that no advantage was 'taken of a tradesman's good will, created by his own industry, so as to exact high terms from him', but he did also admit that 'in many cases of rebuilding it is impossible to let the old tenants rebuild. The tenants would not be equal to it . . . Great care has to be taken as to who rebuilds.' In the eyes of the Estate the tenant had a moral right to be 'fairly considered' at the expiry of his lease, and every

effort was made to minimise the disturbance of rebuilding 'by endeavouring to find accommodation for the tenants displaced in the neighbourhood, as far as possible'; but 'if the necessities of the estate for public improvement require that he should go, he must go'.[399]

The Duke's rebuilding programme did undoubtedly cause a great deal of disturbance and some resentment. E. L. Armbrecht, the Duke Street chemist previously referred to, for instance, wrote to the Duke inviting him 'to imagine our positions reversed. Were your Grace a dispensing chemist, and I the Duke of Westminster, what would you then think of your landlord if, in the full knowledge that you had given the best of your life to the development of a business, I did not scruple to confiscate interests acquired at such a cost.'[400] And Thrupp and Maberly, coachbuilders in George (now Balderton) Street, complaining of the way in which they had been treated by Boodle in the matter of loss of light through the building of Clarendon Buildings opposite, asked the Duke to 'infuse into the managers of the Estate more urbanity and consideration of the feelings of others. We suppose it tends to save time to refuse to discuss matters, to say, "This is my plan, that is our form of lease, not a word shall be altered, you have only to accept or reject". But such a course is not a pleasant one to tenants.'[401]

Compulsory displacement, loss of business and a sense of grievance were all part of the price that had to be paid under the leasehold system for the Duke's improvements; but Boodle was able to make a good case for his contention that these improvements would not have been made at all if the estate had been divided into a multitude of small ownerships. In support of this he cited the case of Bond Street, where most of the tenants 'have leases perpetually renewable by right, and these leases in point of duration are practically equivalent to separate freeholds. No grand improvement, such as widening the street, is, therefore, made on a comprehensive scale, and Bond-street is, and will remain, unless the Metropolitan Board of Works steps in at an enormous cost to the ratepayers, one of the most inconveniently narrow thoroughfares in London.'[402]

Yet despite this disadvantage Bond Street nearly a century later still keeps its standing among the commercial streets of the West End; and this shows that it was not only due to the Duke's rebuilding policies and the general efficiency of his property management that the Grosvenor estate in Mayfair retained and has continued to retain its pre-eminence among the great estates of London. From the time of its first development in the eighteenth century it has always enjoyed immense advantages of topographical position. At first it was a natural refuge for the *beau monde* in westward retreat from the once fashionable but soon crowded and declining streets of Covent Garden and Soho. Then the proximity of Hyde Park came to be regarded as an added attraction— as was not the case in the early eighteenth century. Still more important, the existence of the park on the western boundary of the estate dammed up further migration directly westward. Thus Mayfair is one of the few areas of London to benefit from the outward movement of the well-to-do without later suffering from it. No surface railway or railway constructed on the cut-and-cover principle has ever been built either on or even near the Grosvenor estate there, nor has it ever had undesirable neighbours of lesser social distinction, whose mere existence in adjacent streets might have detracted in course of time from its own *bon ton*. It has, in fact, had good fortune as well as natural advantages. With strict management and a determined programme of renewal as well, it is hardly surprising that in the first Duke's time it was generally regarded as the first among the big estates in London.[403]

CHAPTER IV

The Estate in the Twentieth Century

The death of the first Duke of Westminster on 22 December 1899 was, in retrospect, as great a landmark in the history of the Grosvenor estate as the death of Queen Victoria thirteen months later was to be in the history of the nation. In the palmy days of the late nineteenth century dukes had still been able to do pretty much as they pleased with their own, just as Imperial Britain had with her Empire; and if ominous rumblings could sometimes be heard, little attention was as yet paid to them.

But in the early years of the twentieth century dukes and all landed aristocrats found themselves on the defensive for the first time, and after Lloyd George's budget proposals of 1909, the Parliament Act of 1911 and the war of 1914–18 they were in full retreat. As early as 1873 it had been said of the great estate owners of London that 'Their position of affluence is independent of virtue or vice, prudence or folly. They exist; that is their service. It was the sole service of most of their ancestors.'[1] Views of this kind were not widely held in the 1870's, but fifty years later they seemed almost commonplace; and after the lapse of another fifty years the mere survival of so many great urban estates, even in attenuated form, provides in itself a notable tribute to the tenacity and adaptability of their owners and managers in the conduct of the great retreat.

The reign of the second Duke of Westminster, Hugh Richard Arthur, extended from 1899 to 1953. He was the grandson of the first Duke, his father having died in 1884, and at the time of his succession he was still a minor, about to go out to the South African War, where he served until 1901.[2] In their general mode of living there could hardly be a greater contrast between the peripatetic second Duke and his staid Victorian predecessor; and since his death he has in general attracted a bad press. *The Times* obituaries virtually restricted themselves to praising 'his business acumen', the efficiency of the administration of the Grosvenor estates, and his breadth of vision in extending his domains to Southern Africa and British Columbia.[3] But the politician and diarist Henry Channon described him more frankly as 'magnificent, courteous, a mixture of Henry VIII and Lorenzo Il Magnifico, he lived for pleasure—and women—for 74 years. His wealth was incalculable; his charm overwhelming; but he was restless, spoilt, irritable, and rather splendid in a very English way. He was fair, handsome, lavish; yet his life was an empty failure...'[4] Other comments of this kind could be cited, and it is therefore worth noting that immediately after the Duke's death Sir Winston Churchill, who was then Prime Minister,

issued a statement publicly acknowledging their long friendship. 'As a companion in danger or sport he was fearless, gay, and delightful...Although not good at explaining things or making speeches, he thought deeply on many subjects and had unusual qualities of wisdom and judgment. I always valued his opinion. His numerous friends, young and old, will mourn and miss him, and I look back affectionately and thankfully over half a century of unbroken friendship.'[5]

Soon after his return from South Africa the new Duke married for the first time, and the estates were resettled.[6] After the first Duke's death estate duty assessed at over £600,000 had become payable (more than 90 per cent of it arising from the London properties), and for the first time in the history of the estate sales were resorted to to meet taxation. In 1902 Watney's, the brewers, bought the freehold of property in Victoria Street in the vicinity of the Stag brewery. In 1906 Westminster City Council purchased land adjoining the railway near Victoria Station, and St. George's Hospital bought that part of its site at Hyde Park Corner which stood on the Grosvenor estate. The last instalment of duty on the London estates was paid in that year.[7]

Immediately after the first Duke's death all rebuilding and improvement schemes not already commenced had been stopped, 'having regard to the money required for estate duties',[8] and very little rebuilding took place until 1906. By that time property values on the estate were falling for the first time within living memory—a matter of some surprise, perhaps, for modern readers apt to associate Edwardian Mayfair with limitless opulence—and although there was a recovery in rebuilding in the years 1906–14, the volume of work in progress at any one time has never approached that of c. 1886–96.

Hitherto, values on the estate had risen steadily by about ten per cent per decade,[9] but they had begun to fall in about 1901.[10] Three years later the Estate Board admitted that the market was 'bad',[11] and in 1905 the Duke was informed that for some time past the number of applications for the renewal of leases had declined. Some houses in the hands of lessees were unoccupied,[12] and in 1906 Sir Christopher (later Lord) Furness, in tentatively applying for the renewal of No. 23 Upper Brook Street, stated that he was 'undecided as to whether to take a fresh house in some other part of London, as the neighbourhood was becoming so depressing by reason of so many notice boards and empty houses'.[13]

This depreciation lasted until at least 1909 and particularly affected the larger houses. In that year the value of houses in Grosvenor Square was said by an experienced estate agent to have fallen by 50 per cent since about 1901, and there were no less than ten houses—a fifth of the whole square—to let, 'whereas seven or eight years ago it was very difficult to purchase a house' there.[14] And for the renewal of the lease of Hampden House, Green Street, the Board was forced in negotiations with the Duke of Abercorn to reduce its terms from a rent of £1,000 and a premium of £25,000 in 1904 to a rent of £850 and a premium of £10,000 (plus works estimated at £2,400) in 1909.[15]

The fall in values certainly extended throughout the whole of the West End.[16]* Fears aroused by Lloyd George's budget programme of 1909 also had their effect, the Duke of Abercorn's agents forecasting in that year that the depression 'seems likely to become more acute, especially in view of prospective legislation'.[17] But the Estate's own leasing policy, practised by the first Duke and at first continued by his successor, of generally renewing for very short terms, often of only ten years or even less, was also a contributory cause. Although renewals of up to sixty-three years were still occasionally granted,[18] they were now very much the exception, and by 1904 both occupants and the speculative builders who often took houses for modernisation followed by a quick sale, were all complaining of the difficulties caused by short leases. Occupants pointed out that family trust money could not be invested in short leases, that it was becoming increasingly difficult to sub-let houses for the Season,[11] and that if they only occupied their houses for six months of the year they could 'get a flat at Claridge's for £3 10s a day', which was not more than the cost of running a house.[19] Speculators, such as William and Haden Tebb, clamoured for extensions of their terms, laying all the blame for their inability to sell upon the fact that 'people will not purchase a short leasehold, no matter how attractive and up to date the house may be'. The Tebbs had bought eight houses in the best streets 'at the top of the market' in 1900–2 for a total of over £61,000, all except one of them on leases of less than ten years. By 1906 they were glad to sell one of them (No. 41 Upper Brook Street) at a loss of over £7,000, while at No. 6 Upper Grosvenor Street, on which they had spent £8,500, the caretaker reported that 'Mr. Tebb would sell for £3,000 or almost give the house away.'[20]

At first the Board had ignored such complaints, and although (as previously mentioned) it admitted in 1904 that the market was 'bad', the estate surveyor, Eustace Balfour, still thought that values would continue to rise, as hitherto, at about ten per cent per decade.[9] In the following year, however, the Board was uncertain whether values would in future rise or fall, and there were also fears that 'the attractions offered on the Portman Estate and the Portland Estate on the north side of Oxford Street

may depreciate the value of houses on the Grosvenor Estate'. In the spring of 1905 the Duke was therefore advised to grant longer renewals[21] and in May he agreed.[22] Less than two years later this decision was reinforced by political forebodings occasioned, evidently, by the accession of the Liberal government, the view of G. F. Hatfield, the Duke's solicitor, in January 1907 being that 'having regard to future legislation it would be well to get houses occupied for long terms.'[23]

Renewals for sixty-three years to come were now, once more, often granted, particularly in the principal streets, and in 1910 the Board stated explicitly that 'generally, 63 years leases should be granted wherever possible as the lessee will be more likely to look after and improve the property'.[24] This reversal of policy had very important results, for some houses now listed as of historic or architectural interest might well not have survived into the era of statutory protection but for the long renewals granted after 1905. Cases in point include No. 34 Grosvenor Street (renewed in 1905), No. 59 Grosvenor Street (1910) and No. 76 Brook Street (1911).

These long renewals were granted subject, usually, to the payment of a fine or premium, and almost always subject to extensive works of modernisation. Sometimes such works were accepted in lieu of a premium (as at No. 59 Grosvenor Street, for instance), and were evidently on occasion much needed. In 1905, for instance, a prospective lessee of No. 22 Norfolk (now Dunraven) Street, stated that 'the house is uninhabitable. The drainage is rotten: there is no lavatory that could be passed [by the local authority], being in the middle of the house; there is no hot and cold water and no bathroom.'[25] And in 1910 No. 21 Grosvenor Square (built to designs by Thomas Cundy II and his son in 1855–8) was said to have 'no gas or electric light and no bathrooms...There are no W.C.'s in the house except on the back staircase, and they are small and inconvenient. There is no serving room and no lift from the kitchen.'[26]

Externally, no alterations were generally demanded, except in the case of a number of important houses, which were refronted in stone. This was first done by the builder John Garlick, who in 1901–2 took No. 18 Grosvenor Street as a speculation and included a new stone front in his improvements.[27] At almost the same time, in 1902, No. 45 Grosvenor Square was refronted in Portland stone for the tenant by Edmund Wimperis and Hubert East (Plate 44a). From 1905 the process gathered pace: Garlick, for example, in that year provided No. 47 Upper Grosvenor Street, which, again, he had taken as a speculation, with a new brick and stone front designed by R. G. Hammond. The Board thought the new elevation to be 'a great improvement',[28] and in 1906, in the course of negotiations for a long renewal of the lease of No. 75 South Audley Street, the Duke's solicitor, G. F. Hatfield, suggested

* See, for instance, *Survey of London*, vol. XXIX, 1960, page 13 n. for difficulty in disposing of private houses in Cleveland Row, St. James's, in 1905.

that the lessee, the banker H. L. Bischoffsheim, might be required to refront in stone. Ultimately he agreed to do so,[29] and the same stipulation was subsequently made in the renewal of the leases of the adjoining Nos. 73 and 74 South Audley Street (Plate 44c). Several other houses, chiefly in Upper Grosvenor Street (Plate 44d), were similarly treated (or completely rebuilt with stone fronts) between 1905 and 1916, but after the war of 1914–18 the practice was generally discontinued, probably on grounds of excessive cost.

The change of leasing policy made in 1905 to renewals for long terms had important repercussions on rebuilding policy, which were carefully considered by the Board. In the words of the Duke's solicitor, the estate at that time had been for some decades 'divided into blocks, and it is the custom to renew the leases of all the premises in the various blocks for periods which make them coterminous, so that the whole of any particular block may be pulled down and rebuilt at the same time'.* This procedure was not in practice followed as effectively as this statement suggests, but in so far as it was pursued, it provided a number of advantages. These were that large sites 'for public and other purposes' could be provided, inconvenient boundaries could be rectified and rights of light and air settled, streets could be widened and new thoroughfares formed, and blocks could 'be treated architecturally as a whole, thus giving scope for a more effective design'. But there were also disadvantages. Sometimes there was 'a good house in a block which does not require rebuilding, and its removal with the block is a loss to the estate', leasing problems often arose, and 'Many people do not care to live in a house forming part of a block of houses all built on the same plan, but would prefer a house built to suit their own requirements, and according to their own design.' Ultimately it was therefore decided that 'no hard and fast rules applicable to the whole [estate] can be carried out with advantage'. Many 'houses might be rebuilt separately without detriment...', and 'each district and each house or existing separate leasehold in each district should be considered and dealt with individually. In this way, it is believed that the estate can be further developed, the present rentals maintained, and the general welfare of the estate improved.'[12]

Thus when rebuilding recommenced in 1906 a more pragmatic approach than hitherto was adopted. On the one hand, there were to be no more great schemes such as those executed by the first Duke in Mount Street, Carlos Place, Balfour Place and Mews, or in the 'artisan quarter' to the north of Grosvenor Square; and on the other hand, individual rebuildings were not to be encouraged, at any rate if the estate surveyor, Eustace Balfour, had his way, 'The experience that we have had as to individual rebuilding' being, so he informed the Board in 1907, 'so disastrous from the point of view of general improvement that it is only in cases of special necessity that I now advocate it.'[31] Instead, Edmund Wimperis (who after Balfour's retirement due to ill health in 1910 held the post of estate surveyor until his resignation in 1928) prepared in 1911 a ten-year rebuilding programme. This marked out fifteen blocks, or more accurately groups of generally up to about a dozen adjacent properties due for successive redevelopment year by year.[32]

Under these new dispositions a substantial amount of rebuilding took place between 1906 and 1914, and, after the interruption caused by the war of 1914–18, more of Wimperis's programme was completed in the 1920's. Commercial buildings were almost always built in ranges, and generally consisted of shops with flats or offices above, H. T. Boodle having noted as long ago as 1880 that 'flats should be encouraged for the upper classes as well as the working classes as they are found of great use'.[33] Examples of this type of development include Nos. 375–381 (demolished) and 439–441 (odd) Oxford Street (both 1906–8), Nos. 16–20 (consec.) North Audley Street (1908–9, originally shops with a hotel above), Nos. 39–42 (consec.) North Audley Street (1908–9), and Nos. 4–26 (even) Davies Street and 55–57 (consec.) Grosvenor Street (1910–12, Plate 47a). Houses were sometimes built in ranges, sometimes in pairs, and sometimes individually. Ranges include Nos. 37–43 (odd) Park Street (1908–10, Plate 46b), Nos. 80–84 (even) Brook Street and 22–26 (consec.) Gilbert Street (1910–13, Plate 45d), and Nos. 44–50 (even) Park Street and 37–38 Upper Grosvenor Street (1911–12, Plate 46a). Pairs were built at Nos. 2 and 3 Norfolk (now Dunraven) Street and Nos. 49 and 50 Upper Brook Street (both in 1907–8) and there were also about twenty-five individual rebuildings in Grosvenor Square and the principal residential streets. All the ranges, for both commercial and residential use, were undertaken as speculations by reliable builders such as Higgs and Hill, Matthews, Rogers and Company, or William Willett, but whereas individual houses had hitherto been usually rebuilt by an intending resident for his own occupation, many of them were now taken by builders as speculations, there being, evidently, fewer private gentlemen willing to build for themselves. Nos. 19 Upper Grosvenor Street (1909–10) and 75 Grosvenor Street (1912–14), for instance, were rebuilt as speculations, and so too were all four of the houses in Grosvenor Square rebuilt between 1906 and 1914.

In two different places on the estate advantage was taken of the upheavals caused by rebuilding to form a private communal garden in the centre of a block. In 1910, in one of his last reports to the Board, Balfour had advocated the gradual rebuilding of the rectangle bounded by Green Street, Park Street, Wood's Mews and Norfolk (now Dunraven) Street, the clearance of the stables and garages in the centre and the formation of 'a large common

---

* It may be noted that a similar policy had been followed on the Crown Estate with similar results.[30]

garden'.[34] This idea was subsequently executed by Edmund Wimperis, and although rebuilding in the block was not completed until *c.* 1924, it was sufficiently far advanced by 1914 for the garden for the use of all the residents to be laid out to Wimperis's designs (Plate 47b). The cost was paid by the trustees of the estate, the garden being viewed as an improvement, and its upkeep was provided for from a small private rate levied on the residents. The proposal to form this garden 'resulted in largely increased ground rents being obtained' for the houses shortly to be built around it,[35] and Wimperis therefore had no difficulty in persuading the Board to approve the formation of a similar, though smaller, garden in the centre of the block bounded by South Street, Waverton Street, Hill Street and South Audley Street. The almost complete rebuilding of three sides of this block was about to begin in 1914, and a garden, again designed by Wimperis, was formed here in 1915–16.[36]

During the years 1906 to 1914 the choice of architects for new buildings was nearly always tacitly surrendered by the Duke and the Board to the lessees. Plenty of work nevertheless still came to the estate surveyor. The silversmith John Wells, for instance, probably chose Balfour and Turner for the rebuilding of Nos. 439 and 441 Oxford Street (1906–8) in order to minimise the possibility of disagreements with the Board during his absence in New York, where he had other business interests.[37] Wimperis and/or his partners in private practice designed many of the new houses around the Green Street and South Street gardens, the large range comprising Nos. 4–26 (even) Davies Street, 55–57 (consec.) Grosvenor Street and the adjoining flats between Davies Street and Grosvenor Hill known as The Manor (1910–12), and he also had a number of other important commissions. On one occasion—at the prominent corner site of Park Lane and Oxford Street—the Board clearly favoured an architect of whom it approved (Frank Verity) and when in 1907 Higgs and Hill presented unacceptable plans for Nos. 37–43 (odd) Park Street the Board asserted that it 'should have been consulted first before an architect was employed'. Higgs and Hill were told that 'it is customary to submit to the Board a few names of architects for approval',[38] but some years previously they had had much trouble at Nos. 2–12 (even) Park Street with an architect— A. H. Kersey—nominated by the first Duke,[39] and this time they were determined that the architect should not 'be their master'. Mr. Higgs therefore produced a list of ten architects acceptable to him, from which the Board struck out five names, and Higgs and Hill then chose one of the survivors—W. D. Caröe.[38] This was a sensible compromise, but the case of Ralph Knott—the architect chosen by the lessee for the refronting of No. 21 Upper Grosvenor Street—whose designs were ultimately accepted by the Board despite strong dislike of them,[40] shows that there was now marked reluctance to use the Estate's authority in the choice of architects. In 1909 the Board informed an inquirer that 'more liberty is now given to the lessees to select their own architects',[41] and the sole occasion where the old authority was unequivocally asserted was in the building of the present Nos. 44–50 (even) Park Street and 37–38 Upper Grosvenor Street (Plate 46a). This site overlooked the garden of Grosvenor House, and the Duke required the lessee, the builder Willett, to employ Detmar Blow as architect.[42]

In general, however, the second Duke was not so assiduous in attention to the management of his estate as his grandfather had been. His restless mode of living and his dislike of London[43] precluded his regular involvement in administrative matters, and he appears to have only seldom attended the meetings of the Board. He seems to have accepted Hatfield's statement, made in 1905, that 'legislation is constantly curtailing the rights of the landowner and extending the power of the Public Authorities over all new buildings, thus reducing the necessity for street widening and such like improvement at private expense';[44] and even when the chance of making such an improvement did arise, as in the redevelopment of the block bounded by Green Street, Park Street, Wood's Mews and Norfolk (now Dunraven) Street, he 'left the question of dealing with this block to the Board'.[45] He did, however, make statements of broad intent from time to time, as, for instance, in 1907, when he 'in a general way expressed a wish for the erection of small houses on his estate';[46] and he was frequently consulted on matters which concerned himself, on controversial matters of taste, and on matters of policy.

In the building of Nos. 44–50 (even) Park Street and 37–38 Upper Grosvenor Street, mentioned above, the Duke was consulted in the choice of architect because of the proximity of the site to the garden of Grosvenor House. His appointment of Detmar Blow may perhaps have been due to his liking for the pleasing appearance of Blow's earlier No. 28 South Street (Plate 45a),[47] and it was possibly this liking which had led in turn to the Duke's commissioning Blow in about 1911 to design a hunting lodge for him at Mimizan in the Landes country between Bordeaux and Bayonne.[48] The Duke's own architectural tastes always, indeed, inclined towards 'the traditional', and in her *Memoirs*, Loelia, Duchess of Westminster, stated that he was 'most decidedly…a lover of old buildings'.[49] As we shall see later, these deeply rooted preferences led him to preserve several fine houses on the estate, but it is nevertheless doubtful whether he was as actively interested in current architectural matters as his grandfather had been. He did not, for instance, distinguish between the character of Blow's work and that of C. S. Peach, architect—with much assistance from Eustace Balfour—of the Duke Street Electricity Sub-station, whom he also explicitly desired to be given work on the estate, but whom Balfour considered to have 'no artistic perceptions'.[47] And it was perhaps from this lack of knowledge that sprang the Duke's modest reluctance to impose his own tastes on others.

This reluctance sometimes led to difficulties with the members of his own Board, particularly in such matters as the rival merits of large or small window panes. Balfour's view was that it was 'impossible to get good architecture with large panes',[50] but small panes were unpopular with many lessees, and when Knott's client at No. 21 Upper Grosvenor Street threatened to abandon her contract 'if the small panes are insisted upon' the matter was referred to the Duke, who 'saw no objection' to large panes.[51] Similarly at No. 20 Upper Grosvenor Street the Countess of Wilton (who was said by her builder, G. H. Trollope, to be 'very difficult') 'talked about throwing up the terms if she could not have large panes', and appealed from the Board to the Duke, who decided that 'a subdivision of the panes is not to be insisted upon'. Balfour could only lament that 'if permission is given there is no knowing where such windows will stop',[52] and thereafter all serious attempt to impose small panes on reluctant lessees seems to have been abandoned.[53] In the renovation and enlargement of Bourdon House, Davies Street, where he was himself in 1910 the architect for the Duke, he was, however, very careful to provide panes of the correct 'period' size.[54]

At No. 6 Upper Brook Street the uncertainty and unreliability of the Duke's decisions in architectural matters had a very unfortunate outcome. In the latter part of the eighteenth century this house had been virtually rebuilt, with extensive interior embellishments, to designs evidently by Samuel Wyatt (fig. 8a on page 121). Balfour thought it 'interesting architecturally, being probably an "Adams house"'[55] and in 1912 Wimperis said that it had 'the most distinctive front of any in the neighbourhood, and that it certainly ought to be preserved'.[56] In that year Lord Elphinstone was granted a sixty-three-year lease and was about to start renovating when he discovered that the stone front was structurally unsound and must be rebuilt.[57] The Board then required him to rebuild the front in Portland stone 'to the same design as at present', and in consideration of his extra cost agreed to grant him a ninety-year lease.[56] But the members of the Board refused to allow him to erect a projecting porch, it being their unanimous opinion that the character of the front would be destroyed by such an addition. Lord Elphinstone then wrote personally to the Duke, who informed the Board that Elphinstone 'would not have the porch'.[58] Four months later, however, the Duke happened to meet Lord Elphinstone in Paris, 'which reminded him of the porch. His Grace was rather inclined to let him have it, but did not wish to go against the opinion of the Board.'[59] At about the same time Wimperis noticed that the new front was not being rusticated in accordance with the previously existing work, and as this was 'an essential characteristic of the design...its repetition should be insisted upon', at an extra cost of only about £25. But Lord Elphinstone regarded rustication as 'a continual eyesore' and asked that the whole matter should be placed before the Duke once more.[60] When this

was done the Duke decided that the rustication should not be insisted upon, and in the light of this the Board resolved that it was not worth while to attempt to prevent the erection of a porch, the justly exasperated Wimperis considering 'that as the previous design is not to be followed, the addition of a porch is not important'.[61] Thus the original far-sighted intention to reproduce Wyatt's design was largely frustrated: and in 1936 the Duke seems to have raised no objection to the total demolition of the house by a speculator.

The loss, largely unrecorded, of this fine house was far from being the only such case on the estate during the second Duke's long reign, the similar fate of Grosvenor House and a number of the mansions in Grosvenor Square providing other obvious examples. It must be said, however, that during the early decades of the twentieth century there is little evidence to suggest that the surviving Georgian buildings or their often fine interior embellishments were greatly admired by the Grosvenor Estate's lessees or tenants. It was not until 1944 that public opinion on this subject was sufficiently strong for buildings of architectural or historic interest to be listed to ensure their statutory protection under the Town and Country Planning Act of that year. The losses of such buildings on the Grosvenor estate were matched all over London and throughout the country and should therefore be considered in the context of the times.

The Duke himself was, indeed, personally responsible for the preservation of several of the finest houses on his estate, despite the loss of income which sometimes resulted therefrom. In 1907 he finally refused (after first consenting) to allow the rebuilding of Nos. 9–16 (consec.) South Audley Street, contrary to Balfour's advice that this range should be demolished, and that the Duke would 'get a larger income if the premises are pulled down'.[62] In 1908 he refused—again ignoring Balfour's recommendation—to allow the demolition of No. 44 Grosvenor Square because of its historical associations, this being the house to which the news of the Battle of Waterloo was brought to the Prime Minister, Lord Liverpool, on 21 June 1815, and where in 1820 members of the Cabinet were to have been assassinated at dinner by the Cato Street Conspirators;[63] and when, a few months later, a large Georgian mural painting was discovered, concealed behind canvas, on a former staircase wall in the same house, he granted the lessee a remission of rent in consideration of the expense and inconvenience of preserving it.[64]

After the Duke's death No. 44 Grosvenor Square was demolished in 1968, the mural being, however, removed to the Victoria and Albert Museum.[65]

At Camelford House, which with Somerset House and other adjoining property formed part of a large and very valuable site at the corner of Park Lane and Oxford Street, the Duke's attempt to preserve was similarly frustrated, though much more quickly. Here the Duke had in November 1909 approved negotiations with J. Lyons and Company for the demolition and rebuilding of both Camelford

House and Somerset House, but immediately afterwards he revoked this decision and authorised an offer of terms for Camelford House to Mrs. Beatty, wife of Captain (later Admiral of the Fleet, Earl) Beatty. When his solicitor, G. F. Hatfield, went to see the Duke 'his Grace stated that it would be a pity to pull the house down, particularly having regard to No. 40 [Somerset House] having historical associations.* His Grace was told that... if the rebuilding did not take place, there would be a loss of about £6000 a year. His Grace stated that on a big estate like the Grosvenor something had to be sacrificed for sentiment and association...'[67] Unfortunately, however, Mrs. Beatty declined the terms, and as no other prospective occupant appeared, Camelford House was demolished in 1912.

At No. 11 North Audley Street the Duke's intention to preserve has, however, been maintained to the present time. The house itself is not of outstanding quality but the adjoining No. 12 is one of the very finest examples of Georgian domestic architecture on the whole estate, and the two houses share a unified façade and have from time to time been occupied as one. In 1883 the first Duke had decided to renew the leases of both Nos. 11 and 12, despite his intention to rebuild most of the rest of North Audley Street, the Duke's view, in the case of No. 12, being that 'it will be a pity to pull down the house owing to the beautiful room etc.'.[68] In 1913, however, the Board thought that an adjoining site in Balderton Street would be greatly improved if that of No. 11 were added to it, and with the second Duke's approval the lease of the house was therefore purchased by the Estate for this purpose. This had no sooner been done than the Duke began to have doubts about allowing its demolition. 'He was told that the object of purchasing the lease was that the house might be pulled down', but he nevertheless insisted that 'this ought not to be done and gave instructions accordingly'. Six months later the Board, still anxious about the site in Balderton Street, decided that 'the Duke be asked again about this house', but in the ensuing interview with Hatfield he reiterated that 'the house should be neither let or pulled down', and in 1914 he brusquely dismissed a suggestion for a skating rink here.[69] After standing empty for some years No. 11 was subsequently occupied by the Duke's daughter, Lady Ursula Filmer-Sankey,[70] before being reunited with No. 12 in 1948–9.

Thus Nos. 9–16 (consec.) South Audley Street and No. 11 North Audley Street all owe their survival directly to the second Duke, and it was through no lack of effort on his part that No. 44 Grosvenor Square and Camelford House have been demolished. Other decisions of his also show his concern for old buildings. During the pre-war years he affixed plaques on a number of houses commemorating the former residence of such distinguished occupants as Warren Hastings and Benjamin Disraeli,[71] and at the latter's house, No. 93 Park Lane, permission

was refused for the addition of a bow window on the Park front, the house being regarded as 'somewhat historical'.[72] When asked for his views on the matter in 1912, he refused to countenance a proposal to demolish the church of St. George's, Hanover Square, and to build a new parish church on the site of the Grosvenor Chapel in South Audley Street.[73] And for various different purposes he was also responsible for the thorough renovation, at the Estate's own expense, of several important houses— Bourdon House, Davies Street (1909–11), Nos. 53 Davies Street (1922) and 66 Brook Street (1925–6), and No. 9 South Audley Street (1930–2).

Immediately after the outbreak of the war of 1914–18 the Duke joined the armed forces, serving at first as a temporary Commander, R.N.V.R., with armoured cars in France, and subsequently in North Africa, where he was awarded the D.S.O. in 1916. In the following year he was appointed personal assistant to the Controller, Mechanical Warfare Department, at the Ministry of Munitions.[2] At about this time Grosvenor House was taken over by the Government at the Duke's invitation, and after the return of peace he made his London home at Bourdon House, Davies Street.

Until the war the Grosvenor estates had survived largely intact. Small pieces of the Belgravia and Pimlico properties had been sold to pay estate duty after the first Duke's death; but after 1906 hardly any more land had been sold for some years, the Thames Bank Distillery site (1909) and several small pieces required by the London County Council, all in Pimlico, being relatively minor exceptions.[7] The second Duke had, however, bought a large estate in Rhodesia,[74] and very large mortgages and family charges dating from the first Duke's time were still outstanding.[75] It was probably in order to meet some of these liabilities that the second Duke had sold one of his outlying properties, Halkyn Castle, Flintshire, and the surrounding estate, in 1911–12.[76] But he had steadfastly refused to sell his London properties, despite half a dozen offers made for them in 1914[77] and despite the example of the Duke of Bedford's sale of his Covent Garden estate in that year.

Between 1917 and 1923, however, the Duke made massive sales, and for the first time these included substantial portions of the London properties. During this period many other landed proprietors were also selling their estates, and of the years 1918–21 it has been said that 'Such an enormous and rapid transfer of land had not been seen since the confiscations and sequestrations of the Civil War, such a permanent transfer not since the dissolution of the monasteries in the sixteenth century'.[78] The Duke of Westminster's contribution to this process was, firstly, the sale of the western portion of the Eaton estate in Cheshire for some £330,000 between 1917 and 1920, followed, between 1920 and 1923, by portions of the Pimlico properties, mainly in the vicinity of Victoria,

---

* Warren Hastings had lived there from 1789 to 1797.[66]

which raised some £1,100,000.[79] In 1921 two of the most famous pictures in the Grosvenor collection (Gainsborough's *Blue Boy* and Reynolds's *Mrs. Siddons as the Tragic Muse*) were also sold for £200,000.[80] By that year mortgages and family charges of over £900,000 had been paid, and the remaining encumbrances amounted to some £400,000.[81] After 1923 no more sales were made for several years, the only notable exception being that of No. 75 South Audley Street in 1925, on very favourable terms for the Duke, to the Egyptian Government for its London Legation (now Embassy).[82]

Throughout the whole of the war the routine management of the estate had been largely left in the hands of the Board, but in addition to his decision to sell part of the Eaton lands the Duke had made one other disposition of far-reaching importance. This was the appointment of the architect Detmar Blow to his personal staff in 1916.

Blow was then aged about forty-nine, and prior to the outbreak of war in 1914 he and his partner, Fernand Billerey, had had a flourishing private practice. As a young man and a very accomplished draughtsman, Blow, while drawing the church in Abbeville, had been befriended by the aged Ruskin, who had taken him on a tour of France and Italy and subsequently introduced him to Morris and Burne-Jones. In England he had learnt the technique of building at first hand by apprenticing himself to a working mason, and in 1892 he had won the R.I.B.A. Pugin Studentship.[83] Later in the 1890's he had been associated with Philip Webb in several commissions,[84] and he was a close friend of Lutyens,[85] who was two years his junior. Much, indeed, of Blow's work at this time had close affinities with that of Lutyens, particularly in his use of local materials, his gift for graceful scholarly design in the 'traditional' manner, and his insistence on the highest standards of building craftsmanship—all to be seen in his country house work, on which his early fame chiefly rested.

In 1905 Blow entered into partnership with the French architect Fernand Billerey (1878–1951). Billerey was the son of the official architect of the Department of Eure in Normandy, through whose life-long friendship with an English industrialist he had obtained a fluent command of English. He had studied in Paris, immersing himself in the Beaux-Arts tradition and learning drawing from Rodin before winning a scholarship for travel in Italy and Greece. According to family tradition, he worked at some point as an assistant at the Church of the Sacré Coeur in Paris, and had first met Detmar Blow in Italy.[86] But by September 1902 Billerey was in London in Blow's office, where he was evidently working for him as an assistant.[87] At that time Blow had chambers at No. 9 King's Bench Walk, and it was from this address that the partnership of Blow and Billerey began to function from 1905.[88]*

Hitherto Blow's practice had been almost exclusively in the country, No. 28 South Street, on the Grosvenor estate, 1902–3, being the only notable exception. Between 1906 and 1914, however, most of the partnership's chief commissions were in the West End of London, either for the design of large new houses such as No. 9 Halkin Street or No. 10 Smith Square, or for extensive interior embellishments, as at No. 10 Carlton House Terrace or the Playhouse, Northumberland Avenue. The style of some of this work was markedly different from Blow's earlier 'English Renaissance' manner, and years later the comment was made that 'his more formal style may be said to have dated from the association' with Billerey.[89] Just as Lutyens and so many contemporaries were becoming increasingly enthusiastic about the English classical tradition, so the new partnership of Blow and Billerey turned for inspiration, at any rate in London, to the corresponding French tradition, which was also enjoying growing popularity. This is particularly apparent in two commissions executed on the Grosvenor estate, Nos. 44–50 (even) Park Street and 37–38 Upper Grosvenor Street of 1911–12 (Plate 46a), and the façade of No. 46 Grosvenor Street of 1910–11 (fig. 25 on page 156), both very different in manner from Blow's earlier No. 28 South Street (Plate 45a), and in both of which Billerey's hand is unmistakably evident. Billerey was, in fact, 'a very, very good architect' in the opinion of such a discriminating critic as Professor Goodhart-Rendel,[90] who described the work of the partnership in these years as 'French architecture in London, architecture of the highest order, and of the kind which leads an Englishman to despair. It must take not a lifetime, but generations of inherited experience to produce the easy certainty with which Mr. Billerey has grouped the houses in Park Street, has modelled the galleries in "The Playhouse", has turned the vault over the staircase of No. 10 Carlton House Terrace.'[91]

Between 1905 and 1914 the partnership of Blow and Billerey was one of the most distinguished architectural practices in London. In 1914 it was, at all events, prosperous enough for Blow to buy a farm near Painswick in Gloucestershire, where he designed and built himself a very beautiful house (never fully completed) in the traditional 'Cotswold' manner, and into which he moved in January 1917. In the ensuing years he acquired by successive purchases an estate of over a thousand acres there.[92]

After the outbreak of war, however, the practice diminished greatly. Billerey went off at once to become an officer in the French army, in which he served as an interpreter for the duration,[86] and one of the few remaining commissions left for Blow was the restoration and embellishment of Broome Park, near Canterbury, for Earl Kitchener, who spent many 'happy hours' there 'with

---

* But according to the obituary notice of Blow published in *The Times* in 1939 'It was the late Mr. John Tweed, the sculptor, who introduced Blow to Mr. Billerey when he was looking for a partner.'[89]

his architect and friend, Mr. Blow...'.[93] In June 1916, however, Kitchener was drowned when H.M.S. *Hampshire* disappeared while *en route* for Russia, and it was at this unpropitious moment in his fortunes that, a few months later, Blow was invited by the Duke of Westminster to become, in effect, his private secretary.

At that time the Duke had known Blow for some years. His liking for Blow's No. 28 South Street (1902–3) had evidently led, as we have already seen, to his commissioning Blow to design and build the lovely single-storey hunting lodge at Mimizan. In 1908 he had appointed Blow as architect for Nos. 44–50 (even) Park Street and 37–38 Upper Grosvenor Street, which overlooked the garden of Grosvenor House; and in 1911 Blow and Billerey had worked for the Duke in the layout of formal gardens at Eaton Hall.[94] Thus at the time of this strange appointment—the immediate occasion for which was the departure to the war of the Duke's previous private secretary, Colonel Wilfred Lloyd—Blow and the Duke were already well known to each other, and their sixteen years of close association now about to begin, was evidently tinged with an element of personal friendship which was often acknowledged by the Duke with great generosity. But for Blow his employment with the Duke nevertheless meant, virtually, the end of his career as a creative artist whilst still at the height of his powers.

At the time of Detmar Blow's appointment in 1916 Edmund Wimperis had been the estate surveyor for six years. This was still a part-time appointment, and in association with a succession of partners he also conducted a flourishing private practice, the offices of which were conveniently situated in South Molton Street, some two minutes' walk from the Grosvenor Office in Davies Street. By 1916 his ten-year rebuilding programme of 1911 was already in process of execution, and his provision of private communal gardens for some of the residents of new houses in Green Street and South Street had proved very successful.

When war broke out in August 1914 another stage in Wimperis's rebuilding programme was about to be implemented, Matthews, Rogers and Company having contracted to rebuild almost the whole of the block surrounded by Upper Brook Street, Blackburne's Mews, Culross Street and Park Street. In October 1914, however, the contract had been placed in abeyance for the duration.[95] Wimperis had been quick to realise that, as the Board admitted, 'the conditions which the War had imposed had revolutionised the circumstances dealing with property...',[96] and in 1915 he drew the attention of the Board to the success of a tenant who had 'converted stabling in Aldford Street into a little house making it the best bijou house in London'. Wimperis was 'convinced that was the type of thing for which there was a great demand',[97] and in the 1920's he was able to prove his conviction in Culross Street, where several decrepit small houses and stables were rebuilt or refurbished (Plate 50a, b) and provided with a small communal garden on the lines of those in

Green Street and South Street. The age of the mews house in a fashionable district had arrived.

It was also Wimperis who persuaded the Board itself to undertake, on occasion, the cost and risk of refurbishing obsolescent houses after their leases had expired. Hitherto this work had always been left to building speculators, who had taken a short lease, made improvements and relied on a quick sale for their profit. In 1918 the Board discussed 'the advisability of spending money on houses to be let as a general policy', and Wimperis urged, in relation to No. 10 Upper Grosvenor Street, that 'he would prefer that the Duke should spend money and take the risk of finding another tenant rather than a speculator should make a profit'.[98] This particular case does not seem to have been successful, but at No. 58 Park Street in 1919 the Estate, at Wimperis's instigation, spent some £570 on improvements, chiefly to the basement, and at once found a tenant willing to accept terms based on an annual value enhanced by £100. Subsequently Wimperis commented that 'I have in the past so often advocated a policy by the Grosvenor Estate of spending sums of money on improving premises that are in hand in order that His Grace the Duke of Westminster may himself reap the benefit of the improvement, that I wish to draw attention to the success of this policy in the case of No. 58 Park Street.'[99] In the 1920's this practice was adopted on numerous occasions elsewhere on the estate.

Thus when Detmar Blow entered the Duke's service Wimperis had already proved, and was to continue to prove, his worth as the estate surveyor. But with the benefit of hindsight it is easy to see that the involvement of two successful architects, both in their prime, in the management of the estate might lead to trouble, and this was not long in coming. Some mutual dislike perhaps already existed, for at No. 46 Grosvenor Street in 1910 Blow, having obtained the Board's approval for the proposed new façade there, had built it to a different design, and Wimperis, as estate surveyor, had stopped the work for a while until matters could be sorted out; similarly at Nos. 44–50 (even) Park Street and 37–38 Upper Grosvenor Street friction had arisen in 1910–12 through Blow's changes of intention. In 1920, however, Wimperis was protesting at Blow's frequent interferences and 'personal assumption of my responsibilities', and eventually he offered his resignation.[100]

By this time it was Blow who had the Duke's confidence, and although Wimperis's resignation was not accepted, he was clearly the loser in this trial of strength. He remained as estate surveyor for some years, and although his duties were not re-defined (as Blow had in the spring of 1920 promised that they should be) they seem in fact to have been largely restricted to routine matters such as dilapidation claims, the drawing of lease plans and the approval of plans of works to be done by lessees.[101] He was not, for instance, consulted when the future development of Park Lane was under discussion.[102] Some architectural work for the Estate still came his way, however, for instance in Culross Street, the renovation of the Grosvenor Office at No. 53 Davies Street and of Nos. 55 and 57 (1922), and of the adjacent No. 66 Brook Street (1925-6), to which his own office as estate surveyor was then removed. But a growing proportion of his time was spent (in partnership with W. B. Simpson, and later also L. Rome Guthrie) on his own private practice. During these years this included several important new buildings on the estate—e.g. No. 38 South Street (1919-21, Plate 45c), Mayfair House in Carlos Place (c. 1920-2), the flats in Park Street known as Upper Feilde at No. 71 and Upper Brook Feilde at No. 47 (1922-4 and 1926-7, Plate 49a, b), Nos. 49-50 Grosvenor Square (1925-7) and No. 64 Park Street (1926-7). He resigned as estate surveyor in 1928,[103] but still practised privately in the 1930's. He died in 1946.[104]

After his victory over Wimperis, Blow was left in a position comparable with that of trusted minister in the court of an autocratic, pleasure-loving monarch: a not too fanciful analogy with Cardinal Wolsey and Henry VIII has, indeed, been suggested. It was Blow's wish 'to try and interest the Duke of Westminster in his Estate',[100] but the 1920's were the days when the Duke had two large yachts (the *Flying Cloud* and the steam yacht *Cutty Sark*) and a second hunting lodge in France (at St. Saens in Normandy) and his restlessness was such that during the whole course of his married life with his third wife he only once spent three consecutive weeks in the same place. Thus, while he 'enjoyed dictating the grand strategy and taking tremendous decisions' about his estates, regular personal involvement in their management was impossible;[105] and as, shortly before Wimperis's subjection, the Duke had decided that Boodle Hatfield's duties should be confined to purely legal matters,[106] Blow was left pretty much the master of all he surveyed.

He lived on the estate—at first at No. 31 and then at No. 9 Upper Grosvenor Street, and latterly at No. 3 Carlos Place. He was named as an executor of the Duke's will. He was one of the witnesses at the Duke's third marriage in 1930. When the Duke was in London he had frequent access to him; when the Duke was abroad he sometimes had power of attorney to act for him in certain matters, and when one of the Duke's trustees was out of the country he was granted similar power. He introduced his own personal methods of business procedure, entries in the series of Board Minutes, commenced in 1789, being, for instance, virtually discontinued. He advised the Duke in financial matters as well as in architectural matters, and after Wimperis's resignation he also acted as estate surveyor.[107] So it was not without reason that a builder anxiously trying to get a document signed by the Duke (who was then 'travelling about') informed the London County Council, 'I have sent the paper on to Mr. Blow, who acts for the Duke in all matters.'[108]

The period of Detmar Blow's ascendancy lasted from about 1920 until 1933. By chance, these were the final years in which great urban landlords could still treat their estates much as their forebears who had laid them out had been accustomed to do, as their own private property, broadly subject only to the landlord's covenants contained in their own leases, to the limitations of their own family settlements and to the statutory building regulations administered by the local authority and the district surveyors. Public overlordship by planning had barely started—town planning control in this part of London did not begin until 27 May 1935.[109] The zoning of land use, the redevelopment of outworn buildings, the style and aesthetics of architectural design, and the preservation or destruction of the historic fabric—all these were still, as they had always hitherto been, private matters for decision by the ground landlord and/or his advisers. On the Grosvenor estate Detmar Blow's years of eminence provided, both in their achievements and in their limitations, a fitting swansong for these traditional modes of private administration by which the estate had been hitherto managed.

These were years of much uncertainty for great urban landlords, who peered anxiously into the future to foresee what it might hold for them in the new social situation brought about by the war. On the Grosvenor estate it had not been clear, even before the war, whether the maintenance of an aristocratic residential enclave in Mayfair was still feasible, and in trying to move with the times the Board had sometimes been opposed by the tenants. In 1914, for instance, numerous objections from adjoining residents had compelled the Board to refuse to allow W. E. Hill and Son, the violin makers, to lease No. 75 Grosvenor Street (at the less fashionable east end of the street) and a private resident was not found for the house until 1917;[110] and even in socially less exclusive Park Street in 1912 the Board, after receiving similar protests, had to break its promise to allow a house agent at No. 88, one of the chief objectors being a dentist at No. 82, who stated that his patients 'would feel that he was losing caste if he had a business next door to him and they would drop off'.[111]

The Duke's own intentions were, moreover, still often unpredictable. We have already seen that he had attempted, at considerable financial sacrifice for himself, to keep Camelford House near the corner of Park Lane and Oxford Street, but that after Mrs. Beatty had declined his terms, the house had been demolished. A public outcry ensued when it became known that the new building was intended to have shops on the Park Lane frontage, but the Duke's reaction was that he did 'not see why from any sentimental feeling or moral obligation he should be prevented from carrying through a scheme which he believes would be of advantage to the estate'.[112] Nor did 'his inability to adapt himself to any change whatever', to which Loelia, Duchess of Westminster, refers,[113] prevent his abandoning Grosvenor House itself to the demolition contractors shortly after the war. Indeed, whatever may be thought of Grosvenor Estate policy towards the buildings on the Mayfair estate in the years between the wars, bedrock conservatism or absolute resistance to change had little part in it. And in matters of social policy the Duke was similarly pragmatic, as in 1917, when he overruled his Board's advice and gave permission for negotiations for the establishment of offices for the Japanese embassy in Upper Grosvenor Street, hitherto an exclusively residential preserve.[114]*

After the war of 1914–18 both the social and architectural problems confronting the Grosvenor Estate were, indeed, more perplexing than at any previous time, for the imponderable questions of the social future were matched by equally baffling questions about the future of 'modern architecture'. Writing in 1931 Sir Edwin Lutyens pointed out that 'Forty years ago steel construction was in its infancy. Reinforced concrete was untried. Motor cars, aeroplanes, and most of the mechanical contrivances that play so large a part in life to-day were unheard of.' 'It is inevitable and right', he continued, 'that these things should influence architecture, the machines no less than the materials',[116] but the practical question for the administrator of a great urban estate was the form which this influence should take. This was particularly difficult in the case of the Grosvenor estate, for, to quote Mr. Christopher Hussey writing in 1928, 'No residential area of the West End has preserved so nearly or so long its original character' as it had; and he, at all events, had no doubt that the success of the Estate in meeting this challenge was largely attributable to the influence of Detmar Blow.[117]

After the war only two large new private houses for single-family occupation were built—No. 38 South Street and No. 15 Aldford Street, both in 1919–21; but the impending demise of the great town mansions was not as clearly apparent then as it is now, for even as late as 1936 an extra storey containing servants' bedrooms was built at No. 25 Grosvenor Square, which was to be occupied 'as a single family dwelling house'.[118] Despite the obscurity of the future, flats (and the conversion of large houses into flats) became the main residential building form of the 1920's, the design of the new blocks—notably those by Wimperis and/or his partners in Park Street, and at the south-east corner of Grosvenor Square and in Carlos Place—generally comparing favourably with that of others being erected elsewhere in London. But relatively small new private houses were also provided, obsolescent stables and coach-houses in, for instance, Mount Row, Shepherd's Place, Lees Place, Blackburne's Mews and Culross Street, being replaced by modest dwellings, each intended for single-family occupation (Plate 50c, d)—a policy which often involved for the Duke the sacrifice, in the general interest of the estate, of the highest price obtainable for a particular site.[119]

Unlike the reign of the first Duke, that of the second was not marked by the provision of artisans' dwellings on the Mayfair estate. This did not, however, betoken any lessened awareness of the problem of working-class housing, for which the Duke made very generous provision elsewhere, evidently in part at the instigation of Detmar Blow.[120] In Pimlico he leased land at a peppercorn rent to the Westminster City Council—indeed he offered more land than the Council required;[121] and on his Millbank estate in 1928 he not only granted a similar lease to the Council of land worth £200,000, but through his trustees he also provided over £113,000 towards the cost of the flats to be built on the site.[122]†

Such changes as did take place in Mayfair reflected the Estate advisers' slow and careful reactions to social forces emanating from outside the estate's own boundaries. One of these advisers, writing in 1934 in defence of their recent policies, pointed out that 'Trade and business has, for many years, tended to move westwards'. With the advent of motor traffic, streets such as Grosvenor Street and Brook Street had become 'noisy and somewhat congested, and it was found that the houses nearest to Bond Street gradually became unsuitable for private occupation. When the advisers to the Estate had quite satisfied themselves that this change was in no way temporary but permanent, and that houses ceased to be occupied by private families, and that it was more than unlikely that they would be so occupied again, then they had to consider what should be allowed to be done with such premises, at the same time bearing in mind that some of the houses would in all likelihood remain in private occupation for a considerable time. Great care was, therefore, taken as to these changes of user. The first changes would be from purely private to professional occupation. That is, a house might be used by a doctor or a surgeon or a dental surgeon, but not by a veterinary surgeon. As time went on it was found advisable to allow quiet businesses such as dressmaker or milliner, and after a further lapse of time and experience, shop fronts were permitted in certain cases...The point is that the inevitable changes of user were throughout most carefully watched and controlled by the Estate's advisers in the interests of the Estate's tenants and the public generally.'[124]

The success of flexible attitudes of this kind in achieving a smooth transition into the hurly-burly of the 1920's and 30's was matched by corresponding flexibility in leasing policy, a notable innovation here being the Estate's willingness to buy out existing leases in order to expedite rebuilding or other change. In Detmar Blow's time some £361,000 was spent on the purchase of over fifty buildings, the money being provided by the Estate trustees out of capital.[125] That the management of the estate during these years was a success is attested by the facts that, in the mid 1920's, only half of one per cent of the buildings on it were unoccupied, and that the income from it was rising.[126]

---

* The negotiations ultimately proved abortive and the house, No. 10, was never in fact taken by the embassy.[115]
† Between 1929 and 1934 he sold the rest of the Millbank estate to a property company for over £900,000.[123]

But Blow's principal and most lasting impact on the estate was, of course, in the field of architecture. Here two of the most distinguished architects of the day—Lutyens and Billerey—were commissioned to act as consultants. It was altogether characteristic of the traditionally personal methods of estate management of which the second Duke and Blow were among the final exponents that these two artists should, evidently, have owed their employment to their personal connexions with Blow— long-standing friendship in the case of Lutyens, professional partnership in the case of Billerey; and the results of their work still adorn the estate, although that of Billerey was very substantially modified in the course of building.

After Edmund Wimperis's status as estate surveyor had been greatly diminished in 1920, the valuations and routine reports were often done by specially commissioned independent firms of surveyors such as Hillier, Parker, May and Rowden.[127] Relatively little rebuilding took place for some years after the war, however, and so it was not until 1923, when the Duke finally decided to permit the redevelopment of the Grosvenor House site, that any important problem of architectural design arose. After a number of false starts the redevelopment of the site was taken over by an experienced speculator, and the Estate called in Lutyens to act with Blow in looking after the Duke's interests.

Although Lutyens's functions were supposed to be restricted to considering and ultimately approving the design to be submitted to him by the lessee, he did nevertheless, in close conjunction with Blow, prepare revised elevations of his own, no doubt to the annoyance of the lessee's architects, the ubiquitous Messrs. Wimperis, Simpson and Guthrie, who provided the plans and structural workings. What were in appearance virtually Lutyens's designs for the new Grosvenor House were duly executed in 1926–30 (Plate 48c).

Although doubtless inevitable, such great changes as this in the face of London aroused protest and dismay. But the Duke, at all events, was satisfied with the new Grosvenor House, and it was doubtless due to his and/or Blow's influence that Lutyens was commissioned by Westminster City Council in 1928 to act as architect for the very large housing scheme (previously referred to) then impending on the Duke's Millbank estate. On the Belgravia properties Lutyens was responsible for the elevations of Terminal House, Grosvenor Gardens (1927).[128] In Mayfair he was again employed in 1928 by the Estate for a site almost as important as Grosvenor House, that of the proposed new Hereford House, a massive building in Oxford Street to contain a department store and flats above. Here the lessees, Gamages (West End) Limited, had their own architects, C. S. and E. M. Joseph, but the building had to be erected 'to the satisfaction of Sir Edwin Lutyens and Mr. Blow as… Estate Architects' and, rather as at Grosvenor House, this resulted in Lutyens being in effect the author of the

executed elevations.[129] At about the same time he acted in a similar capacity for shops and flats at Nos. 8–10 (consec.) North Audley Street, where the elevation is substantially his.[130] At the Estate's expense he also improved elevations for No. 8 Upper Grosvenor Street and provided a shop front at No. 138 Park Lane.[131] He was consulted over Aldford House (1930–2, architects G. Val Myer and F. J. Watson-Hart) and Brook House (1933–5, architects Wimperis, Simpson and Guthrie), and may have contributed to the elevations of the former (Plate 49d).[132] For all his work on the Mayfair portion of the estate executed between 1926 and 1933 his fees, paid by the Duke's trustees, amounted to over £12,000, some three-quarters of which were in respect of Grosvenor House.[133]

In view of the success of his work for the Duke it is perhaps surprising that it was not Lutyens, but Billerey, who was awarded what must have seemed at the time to be the greatest prize of all—the preparation of elevational designs for the coherent rebuilding of Grosvenor Square. The first conception of this bold idea almost certainly originated with Detmar Blow, as did the appointment of Billerey as architect; and it was through no fault of either of them that the scheme ultimately miscarried.

At the end of the war Billerey had returned to London to resume private practice, until about 1924 nominally at least still in partnership with Blow, and thereafter independently. In 1923 he had been employed by the Estate for preliminary work at Grosvenor House, and subsequently he had received several other very small routine commissions. In these post-war years Grosvenor Square presented perhaps the most intractable of all the problems confronting the Estate. The market for the rebuilding of its enormous houses had gone for ever, and those on the four corners suffered increasingly from the noise of motor traffic. When rebuilding was resumed, therefore, the first blocks of flats in the square were erected in the mid 1920's at the south-east corner, at Nos. 48 and 49–50 on either side of Carlos Place, to designs by, respectively, Wills and Kaula, and Edmund Wimperis and Simpson.

There was evidently some vague intention in the Duke's mind that the style of these two blocks should be repeated elsewhere in the square as opportunity arose,[134] but Wimperis resigned as estate surveyor in 1928, being succeeded by Blow, and in May 1929 Billerey was already concerning himself with the future of the square.[135] By this time the question of the general elevational design was becoming pressing, for the leases of Nos. 19, 20 and 21 at the western end of the north range were due to expire shortly. During the ensuing years Billerey produced a succession of elevational designs for the rebuilding of the north and south sides of the square,[136] and by September 1932 Blow had (in addition to overcoming numerous other difficulties) evidently persuaded the Duke to accept Billerey's proposals for the north range.[137] In January 1933 he finally approved on the Duke's behalf the now urgently needed elevations for Nos. 19–21.[138] But two months later he relinquished all his duties with the Grosvenor Estate.

If Billerey's designs for the north range, and his less fully developed proposals for the south side, had been executed unaltered, the new Grosvenor Square would have provided a fine example of the Beaux-Arts manner adapted to twentieth-century requirements. But this was not to be. The lease of No. 38 on the south side had already been renewed for a long term in 1928, thereby effectively precluding the complete rebuilding of this range within the foreseeable future. Immediately after Blow's sudden departure the Estate destroyed the simple elegance of Billerey's proposed treatment of the roof of the north range by permitting the insertion of a second range of attic windows at Nos. 19–21,[139] and this (plus a further increase in the height of the roof and other modifications) was continued in the subsequent rebuilding of the rest of this range, finally completed in 1964 (Plate 54b). On the south side the Estate authorities in 1934 failed to impose Billerey's designs in the rebuilding of Nos. 35–37; and although Billerey, acting for other clients at Nos. 45–47, was still attempting in 1938–9 to provide a coherent design,[140] his chances of success were much reduced by Blow's departure from the Estate Office. On the east side complete rebuilding had been blocked by the renewal of the lease of No. 4 in 1931 for a long term, and Billerey is not known to have produced any designs for this or the western range. The rebuilding of neither the south nor the east side has ever been completed, the nineteenth-century fronts still surviving at Nos. 38 and 4 respectively. Those portions which have been rebuilt, in imitation of Billerey's elevations for the north range, merely exemplify by comparison the rare quality and accomplishment of his work. Blow's original conception, and Billerey's designs for its realisation, have both been forgotten, and amongst the architectural critics the new Grosvenor Square has become the object of such epithets as 'grandiose', 'uninspiring' and 'unimaginative'.

Detmar Blow left the Duke's service in March 1933. He died at his home in Gloucestershire in 1939, aged seventy-one.[89] His departure was a considerable loss for good architecture on the estate, for thereafter neither Lutyens nor Billerey received any commission of any importance from the Grosvenor Office. Blow's successor as estate surveyor was George Codd, hitherto an assistant surveyor in the office, who held the post until shortly after the war of 1939–45.

Frederick Etchells was one of the few architects still consulted from time to time by the Estate after Blow's resignation. As early as 1923 he had been employed to prepare models for the Grosvenor House schemes;[141] at the Estate's expense he directed extensive alterations at No. 14 Culross Street in 1927 (Plate 50b), and in 1933 he prepared plans for the rebuilding of No. 4 Mount Row (now demolished).[142] The Estate authorities continued to consult him on a number of small matters until 1935,

but his fees for any one item seldom exceeded ten guineas. After Blow's resignation he did his best, though unsuccessfully, to prevent Codd from making further alterations in 1936 to Billerey's design for the centre portion of the north range of Grosvenor Square.[143]

By 1930 the Duke was over fifty years of age, and had no son of his own. Very large liabilities for estate duty were certain to occur after the Duke's death, and these, it was then thought, could only be met by sales of land. But if such sales were to be made quickly and on a large scale after the Duke's death, the market would inevitably be depreciated. The need to mitigate such an unfavourable situation and also to mitigate the impact of any future tax on ground rents provided some of the reasons why at about this time the Duke's advisers began to recommend the gradual sale of a few particularly valuable sites, the proceeds being of course available for investment.[144]

The implementation of this policy began in 1929 with the sale of part of the Millbank estate,[145] but the Duke was extremely reluctant to sell any part of Mayfair or Belgravia,[146] and it was not until 1930 that he agreed to do so. In 1930–2 the freeholds of the Connaught Hotel, Mayfair House (both in Carlos Place), Claridge's (Brook Street), Fountain House (Park Lane), Nos. 139–140 Park Lane, No. 32 Green Street and Nos. 415, 417 and 419 Oxford Street were all sold. There were also other sales in Pimlico (notably of the Victoria Coach Station site) and in Millbank.

There was, however, a new alternative to outright sales. Under the Settled Land Act of 1925 life tenants of settled land (such as the Duke) had been empowered to grant 999-year leases.[147] From the Grosvenor Estate's point of view, it was felt that this procedure would be advantageous because it would continue the mutually beneficial relationship between lessor and lessee, while by means of the covenants to be inserted in the leases, the maintenance and use of buildings on the estate could still be controlled.[148] Accordingly it had for the first time been employed in 1928 on the site of the present Fountain House, Park Lane, mentioned above. Here the lessees, the Gas Light and Coke Company (who ultimately bought the freehold outright), agreed, in exchange for a 999-year lease, to pay a large capital sum and a substantial rent, and to rebuild to designs to be approved by the Duke's architect.[149]

A number of similar leases were subsequently granted elsewhere on the estate.

During the war of 1939–45 the estate suffered severe damage by enemy action, and after the return of peace the problems with which it was faced were more difficult than ever before. A number of buildings had been totally destroyed, very many others severely injured, and even those which had survived with little or no damage were in urgent need of maintenance, which had perforce been largely suspended during the war. For several years after

1945 building licences had to be obtained before any substantial work could be started, and it was not until 1955, for instance, that the partially completed rebuilding of Grosvenor Square could be recommenced. In order to encourage the costly processes of restoration and/or improvement, the Estate's policy was to grant long leases, subject to the requirement that repairs, improvements, conversions or reconstructions should be carried out to the satisfaction of the Duke's staff. The expiry dates of these leases were arranged by blocks, to fit in with a comprehensive plan for the whole of both the Mayfair and Belgravia properties.[150]

Just when the estate was beginning to recover from the effects of the war the incidence of massive estate-duty payments, consequent on the death of the second Duke in 1953, postponed all plans for the future. During the latter part of his long reign he had instructed his chief agent, Mr. George Ridley, to 'go out into the world and seek investments in the Empire', and by a series of purchases he had extended the Grosvenor estates as far afield as Southern Africa and Australia. Shortly before his death he had bought Annacis Island in British Columbia, where he planned a great industrial estate, while at home he had initiated large schemes of afforestation in Cheshire, the Lake District, County Durham and in Scotland. On his estates in Scotland, too, the very substantial improvements which he had made there, and his support for the west coast fishing industry, had provided much local employment in the inter-war years. In a leading article The Times said of him that for more than half a century he had been 'the biggest private landlord in this country and probably in the world', and that 'It was in the management of his vast estates that his life found its best expression and achievement.'[151]

After his death it was reported in The Times that for years the Treasury had been taking ninety-five per cent or so of his income in taxes. Immediately after his death his estates in Britain were nominally valued at over £10 million, but the final figure upon which estate duty was assessed was very much larger,[152] and in 1971 The Daily Telegraph reported that some £17 million had been paid.[153]

Because he left no son, the resettlement made by the Duke in 1901 came to an end on his death in 1953, and subject to various family charges which he had created, he had been free to bequeath the settled estates as he wished. In order, if possible, to obviate for his descendants the recurrence of the enormous duty to which the estate would be liable on his own death, the Duke by his will divided the benefit of the bulk of the income from the Grosvenor properties among several members of the family. The heir to the title as third Duke was an elderly reclusive bachelor invalid, for whom financial provision had already been made. The income was therefore divided, in different proportions, between, firstly, the third Duke's heir-presumptive, his cousin, Colonel Gerald Hugh Grosvenor, who succeeded as the fourth Duke in 1963;

secondly, the latter's brother, Lieutenant-Colonel Robert George Grosvenor, who became the fifth and present Duke in 1967, the fourth Duke having had no son; and thirdly, their respective eldest sons, if any. Each of these beneficiaries was to receive part of his share of the income absolutely, but whilst the benefit of the income was thus divided, the bulk of the estates was to be held 'in fee simple' by trustees. The days when the reigning Duke, as tenant for life, was pretty much the director of the whole of the family fortunes, were, in fact, ended, and in order to preserve the totality of the estate, which had always been one of its strengths, the management of the whole vast concern was now handed over to very able professional trustees acting for all the beneficiaries.[154]

The sales made to pay the duties arising from the second Duke's death included a number of estates in the provinces and some of the family pictures.[155] In London the whole of the Pimlico properties to the south of Buckingham Palace Road were also sold, but in Mayfair virtually no more sales have been made since as long ago as 1933, apart from that of the new Grosvenor House, which was sold in 1935 under an option to purchase granted to the building lessee in 1925. In 1934 the second Duke had, indeed, categorically refused to sell the freehold of Aldford House, Park Lane,[156] and he would no doubt have been pleased by the successful resistance made after his death by his trustees to extreme pressure to sell the freehold of the site of the proposed new United States Embassy on the west side of Grosvenor Square. Here they finally agreed to give the site subject to one proviso—the return of 'the Grosvenor Family's 12,000 acres in East Florida confiscated by the American nation at the time of the War of Independence', a property which probably included Cape Canaveral (sometime Cape Kennedy). The American Embassy in London therefore remained, it is said, the only one in the world of which the United States Government did not own the freehold.[157] The Duke's desire to preserve the Mayfair estate intact was, indeed, evidently so strong that it had even extended to the repurchase of four sites previously sold or donated—those of the Vestry Hall in Mount Street, sold to the St. George's Vestry in 1883–5 and repurchased in 1930; of St. Anselm's Church, Davies Street, given by the first Duke to the Ecclesiastical Commissioners in 1893 and repurchased in 1939 after the demolition of the church; of the Connaught Hotel, Carlos Place, sold in 1930, and of No. 32 Green Street, sold in 1931, both repurchased after the war of 1939–45.

After the vast estate duties arising from the second Duke's death had been paid off, the trustees initiated a great expansion of the Grosvenor estates, which by 1967 had achieved a 'remarkable growth of assets'.[158] No duties were payable in 1963 on the death of the third Duke, who had no interest in the estate, and after the death of the fourth Duke in 1967 the senior trustee was still able to say that 'The management of the estates will go on as before and nothing is likely to cause any disintegration or fragmentation of the estates.'[155]

The new system of management inaugurated after the second Duke's death represented a fundamental departure from the previous administrative arrangements, which for more than two centuries had hitherto been, in the last resort, directed by the successive heads of the Grosvenor family. But the post-war years have, of course, also witnessed another equally fundamental innovation in the history of the estate—the assumption by the local authorities and the state, under successive Town and Country Planning Acts, of many of the functions hitherto discharged by the ground landlord. Town planning control, as we have already seen, had begun in Mayfair and in much of the rest of London in 1935, but its full impact did not make itself felt until after the war. For the Grosvenor authorities, with their long tradition of successful private management, this was a very difficult transition to make, and in 1934 the second Duke's advisers had even attempted, unsuccessfully, to have the estate excluded from planning control on the ground that the Estate Office already provided adequate supervisory machinery.[159] Accustomed as they were to making their own decisions in the best interests of the estate, the new planning legislation and its implementation by the local planning authority in the early post-war years often seemed, indeed, when viewed from the Grosvenor Office, to generate more heat (in the form of frustration and delay) than light.

After the war the Estate had wished the Mayfair portion of its properties to be used primarily for business purposes, while the Belgravia portion should be preserved as a primarily residential counterpart. This concept for the future character of Mayfair gave rise to considerable disagreement with the London County Council as the planning authority. After the devastation of the City of London by bombing, many of the large houses in Mayfair, hitherto in single residential occupation but at that time vacant, had been subdivided and converted wholly or partly to office uses, and numerous temporary planning consents of widely varying duration were granted for this purpose. In the altered social conditions of the post-war period the large tall ground- and first-floor rooms of many Mayfair houses were, in the Grosvenor authorities' view, no longer well suited for domestic occupation, but could readily find a new use as 'prestige offices'. By 1960 offices and private residential property each occupied about one third of the total floor space in the area, but the County of London Development Plan of 1951 had intended that ultimately most of Mayfair should be restored to residential use. This policy evoked a protest from the Grosvenor Office, which regarded the discouragement of offices as 'contrary to good estate management',[160] but it was nevertheless upheld and even strengthened by the Minister. When the Development Plan was reviewed in 1960 'it was decided that some houses should have their temporary office consents extended to December 31,

1990, others should be extended for shorter periods, and the remainder should have their temporary office consents extended until December 31, 1973, in order to give Westminster City Council time to formulate a policy for their future use.'[161]

Soon after the accession of the fifth and present Duke in 1967 the Grosvenor trustees (of whom the Duke himself was one) commissioned their own study of the future of their London estates, which was prepared by Chapman Taylor Partners and their fellow consultants and published in 1971 under the title *The Grosvenor Estate Strategy for Mayfair and Belgravia*. In his foreword to this work the chairman of the trustees acknowledged that during the previous twenty-five years or so 'The responsibility and the initiative for urban planning has shifted from the owner of a house or a street or an estate to the community—to its elected representatives and to their officers.'

In deciding to commission this study the trustees had felt that the post-war rebuilding phase being over, future developments or redevelopments should only be made in the context of a comprehensive planning framework. They were also much concerned at the deterioration of the environment, primarily caused by the intrusion of an ever-growing volume of motor traffic. The moment of publication of the *Strategy* proved extremely timely, for the shift of responsibility for urban planning from private to public hands, which had hitherto seemed (in the words of the chairman of the Estate trustees) 'both absolute and permanent', was then being modified by more conciliatory attitudes on the part of the public authorities. 'More recently a better balance has emerged: although the power of ultimate decision rests, as it should, with the community, the process by which that decision is reached welcomes the participation of everyone who is affected by it. This new attitude towards planning revives the estate owner's responsibility to look beyond the problems of the moment to the medium and longer term influences on his property—to the shape of the square, the pattern of the streets, the scale of the buildings.'[162]

The *Strategy* was also timely in that its preparation coincided with the designation in 1969 of most of the Grosvenor estate in Mayfair as a Conservation Area. This new planning concept had been created by the Civic Amenities Act of 1967, the object of designation being 'to preserve the character or appearance of areas of special architectural or historic interest, as distinct from individual buildings, to control development in such areas and to stimulate and encourage measures to improve the environment'.[163] In an area such as Mayfair (or Belgravia) conservation was clearly to have an important bearing upon future planning policies, and the *Strategy* took full account of it.

The planning objectives of the *Strategy* were 'to preserve what is of architectural value, to enhance the inherent character of the Estate, to relate street formation to environmental qualities and to establish a balanced mix of uses, including a full range of residential accommodation, confining redevelopment of high intensity to appropriate districts close to public transport facilities'.[164] The basic idea for the realisation of these aims was that 'A structure of high intensity development on the peripheries' should shield 'the conserved inner areas or hinterland' of the estates in both Mayfair and Belgravia.[165] Numerous detailed proposals for this purpose were put forward, the most important for Mayfair being the comprehensive redevelopment of the whole of the Oxford Street frontage from Davies Street to Marble Arch, and 'an active improvement policy' for most of the rest of the estate.[166] Through traffic was to be diverted from the internal roads on to the boundary roads of Oxford Street and Park Lane, the eight-lane carriageway of the latter, it was hoped, being eventually sunk below ground level; and the number of vehicular entry and exit points to and from the estate was to be reduced.[167] As the amount of redevelopment envisaged was 'likely to be relatively small' (except in the vicinity of Oxford Street), considerable emphasis was placed upon the maintenance and improvement of 'the existing character and the ambience of the environment'.[168] The mixture of office and residential uses, often uneasily combined within a single building, was to be sorted out, increased residential use in the mews or in Aldford Street being counterbalanced by more offices in streets bearing a greater volume of traffic, such as Park Street or Davies Street.[169] The first Duke's *chef d'œuvre*, late Victorian Mount Street, was to be 'preserved and maintained as long as economically possible', and the range of erstwhile stables and coachhouses on the south side of Bourdon Street was to be converted into a shopping arcade.[170] The conservation policy was, in general, to be 'largely one of infill in scale and in character with existing buildings'; and whenever redevelopment did become necessary, the *Strategy*'s authors 'strongly advise against imitations of former styles whether Georgian or Victorian'.*[171]

The *Grosvenor Estate Strategy* of 1971 is one of the most important privately commissioned planning studies yet to appear, and its reception in the press was generally favourable. *The Guardian*, for instance, commented that 'what shines through the Strategy is its real concern for the environment and an understanding of it'; and *The Observer* thought that 'almost everything that is said seems to be more or less right and aimed at making a happier, better place to live and work in. Above all, perhaps, the conclusions appeared to have been generated primarily by human considerations rather than financial ones.'[172]

An opposite view was, however, taken in *Official Architecture and Planning*, where it was stated that 'It is depressing, but probably inevitable, that the primary objective of the effort should be the realisation of the full development potential of some of the most distinctive parts of central London'.[173] This verdict must have been discouraging for the authors of the *Strategy*, who had intended it to provide 'a link of unity' between the public authorities and the Estate.[174] A link it is nevertheless proving to be, despite the strains to which all links are sometimes subject. Since its publication in 1971 detailed discussions have taken place between Westminster City Council, the Greater London Council and the Estate, and in 1973 the City Council decided that, subject to certain modifications, the *Strategy* 'would be one of the material considerations to which the Council will have regard in determining planning applications for the Mayfair and Belgravia areas...'[175]

These modifications, which were also sought by the Greater London Council, have been agreed to by the Estate, and include a smaller increase of offices and a greater increase of residential accommodation than had been envisaged in 1971; and the resolution of the vexed question of the 'temporary office permits' problem, it being agreed that some premises would revert to residential use and others would continue as offices during the life of each particular building. The Estate also undertook to increase its stock of low-income housing and for this purpose leased an important site in Pimlico to the Peabody Trust.[176] Recently the size of the hinterland of the Oxford Street area proposed in 1971 for comprehensive redevelopment has been greatly reduced by the exclusion of Green Street, Binney Street, Gilbert Street and the east side of Duke Street (parts of which had at first been intended for redevelopment) and the blocks of 'artisans' dwellings' built in this neighbourhood in 1886–92. These blocks are now to be retained, some of them are to be modernised, and the loss of residential accommodation caused by the conversion of some of the lower floors into shops will be balanced by new residential accommodation to be provided in Weighhouse Street. Nearby, the reconstruction of Bond Street Tube Station to serve both the existing Central Line and the new Fleet Line is already in progress. Here the London Transport Executive, the Grosvenor Estate and the developers, Metropolitan Estate and Property Corporation Limited, are co-operating in the building of a larger and more efficient station than that originally envisaged. Above the station there will be several shopping levels and floors of offices, and the completion of the scheme in about 1980 will mark the achievement of the first phase of the

---

* It may here be noted that the architectural assessments contained in the *Strategy* should be treated with caution. The classification on page 22 of buildings 'by four historical periods and three grades of architectural quality' (a classification in no way connected with that in the Secretary of State for the Environment's list of buildings of special architectural or historic interest) contains a number of errors, of which the identification of Nos. 91–103A (odd) Park Street, by Wimperis and Simpson 1913–c. 1922, as '1700–1800 Georgian' provides one example. Nor will the authors' sweepingly unfavourable judgments upon most of the twentieth-century buildings on the estate be universally accepted.

comprehensive redevelopment of the south side of Oxford Street which the Estate had first proposed in 1971.[177]

During the preparation of the *Strategy* (which was started in 1968) and during the ensuing years of prolonged discussions with the public authorities about the acceptance and/or modification of its proposals, the Estate had submitted itself to a 'self-imposed stand-still on major commercial and residential redevelopment in the interest of strategic planning', its view being that 'individual schemes cannot be properly assessed in isolation and must relate to an overall strategy to ensure that the correct overall land use balance is achieved'.[178] Adaptation to the exacting demands of post-war planning was not, however, the only new problem confronting the Estate in these years, for under the Leasehold Reform Act of 1967 some tenants acquired the right in certain circumstances to buy the freehold of their houses. The exercise of this right would have frustrated many of the policies pursued by the Grosvenor Estate over very many years, but for the Estate's success in obtaining the insertion of a safeguarding clause in the Act. This provided that when the Minister of Housing was satisfied that 'in order to maintain adequate standards of appearance and amenity and regulate redevelopment' in any area owned by a single landlord, it was 'likely to be in the general interest that the landlord should retain powers of management', he was to grant a certificate to that effect. This certificate had to be approved by the High Court,[179] and in 1973 the Grosvenor Estate became the only landlord with a significant holding in central London to obtain final approval for such a management scheme. The approved scheme related only to Belgravia,[180] but application has recently been made for another for Mayfair. The whole episode provides striking public recognition of the 'general benefit'[179] which, even in the age of public planning, can still arise from the Grosvenor Estate's administration of its London property.

CHAPTER V

The Social Character of the Estate

At Michaelmas 1726 Sir Thomas Hanmer, baronet, Member of Parliament for the County of Suffolk and ex-Speaker of the House of Commons, vacated his town residence at No. 12 Old Burlington Street, and his household moved into a new house at No. 52 Grosvenor Street for which the price was £4,250 (Plate 8c; fig. 16 on page 136). Sir Thomas himself was then still at his country seat at Mildenhall in Suffolk and his housekeeper supervised the move in good time for the master's return to town in November for the new London Season. Sir Thomas had only lived in Old Burlington Street, where he was also one of the first occupants, since about 1723, but his new house in Grosvenor Street was much larger and no doubt better fitted to accommodate his retinue of some fourteen servants.[1] In being so soon prepared to move to another newly developing district further to the west, where he would inevitably be once more surrounded by the noise and clutter of building operations, he was following the lead of his compeers, for several of his new neighbours belonged to the titled ranks of society. The Earl of Arran lived on one side of him and on the other was Sir John Werden, baronet, father-in-law of the second Duke of St. Albans who was also living here at about this time, while two doors away at No. 50 the first Earl of Uxbridge was a new arrival.[2]

An indication of the attraction of the new suburb around Grosvenor Square for the social élite can be gathered from the standing of the first occupants, i.e. householders, of the houses in the principal streets, viz. Brook Street and Upper Brook Street, Grosvenor Street and Upper Grosvenor Street, and the square itself. A full list of these occupants is given in the tables on pages 172–95, but it should be noted that they were not all resident at the same time, as the houses were erected over several years. Of the 277 houses built in these streets, 41 were first inhabited by peers and seven more by persons who were created peers or succeeded to peerages while living on the estate, making 48 (17.3 per cent) in all. A further 69 houses were first occupied by other persons of title, i.e. the wives, widows, sons or daughters of peers; baronets and knights (or their widows); and foreign nobility. Thus, in all, the initial householders of 117 of the 277 houses (42.2 per cent) belonged to the titled classes of society. The proportion was naturally highest in Grosvenor Square itself, where of the 51 houses 16 were taken by peers (31.4 per cent) and 19 more by other persons of title, making 35 (or 68.6 per cent) in all. In these principal streets 54 of the first occupants (19.5 per cent) sat in the House of Commons at some time during

their residence on the estate, 19 of them living in Grosvenor Square. Several of these M.P.'s also come into the category of persons of title and a few were Irish peers, who did not sit in the House of Lords and were thus eligible for election to the lower House.

The gathering momentum of the migration of fashionable society to the new estate can be seen from the number of members of both Houses of Parliament who had their town addresses there. In 1733 30 members of the Commons (5.4 per cent of the whole House) and 16 peers who could attend the Lords (8.3 per cent of the upper House) lived on the estate. By 1741 the numbers had increased to 45 (8 per cent) and 31 (16.3 per cent) respectively, and by 1751 to 49 (8.8 per cent) and 39 (23.3 per cent).[3]

On the whole the aristocracy and the gentry lived in the broad belt across the centre of the estate formed by the principal streets referred to above, but a few lived elsewhere, notably at the south ends of Park Street and South Audley Street, and later in Norfolk (now Dunraven) Street and Hereford Street, and, much later, in Park Lane. It was generally in these streets that the large households were concentrated, such as that of Sir Thomas Hanmer, already mentioned, or of Baron Conway (later Marquess of Hertford), who in 1746 had twenty-two servants at No. 16 Grosvenor Street. His steward kept a 'Grosvenor Street House Account' which shows that his annual expenses there amounted to little short of £3,000, of which £345 or only about 12 per cent was accounted for by his servants' wages, most of the remainder being spent on the payment of tradesmen's bills.[4]

The house account also itemised some of the travelling costs, including the carriage of trunks to London from other places, chiefly the Conways' seat at Ragley Hall in Warwickshire, and in these streets the comings and goings of the London Season must have been particularly marked. The influx of carriages into town at the beginning of the parliamentary session (in the eighteenth century usually in November, December or January) was quite noticeable. *The World* in January 1790 reported that 'London is now almost at the fullest:— every avenue yesterday was crowded with carriages coming into town.'[5] In the first half of the eighteenth century the parliamentary sessions generally lasted into the early summer, but in the latter half they usually extended into June, July or occasionally even August. Whenever it occurred, the commencement of the summer recess was soon followed by the departure of many of those residents who also had country houses. In September 1734 Mrs. Delany, who was then living at

No. 48 Upper Brook Street, remarked with characteristic independence to Dean Swift, 'The town is now empty, and by most people called dull; to me it is just agreeable, for I have most of my particular friends in town.'[6] It was during these uncomfortable, dusty months that the builders and upholsterers were called into the grand houses to prepare them for the next social round.

Even within those streets where the momentum of life must often have been regulated by the social calendar there were, however, a number of incursions from the world of trade. Victuallers established themselves, generally on corner sites, at the Mount Coffee House, the Three Tuns and the Red Lion in Grosvenor Street; the Barley Mow, the Cock and Bottle and John Dickins's coffee house in Upper Brook Street; and the Oval and the Wheatsheaf in Upper Grosvenor Street. Other first occupants known to have been tradesmen included an apothecary and a shoemaker on the north side of Brook Street, a grocer at the corner of Brook Street and Davies Street, and a cheesemonger and a tailor in Upper Brook Street; while William Campbell, upholsterer, had established himself in Grosvenor Street by 1727.[7] In a somewhat different category were the building tradesmen who occupied the houses they built in the main streets, sometimes for lengthy periods.

If trade made inroads into the principal streets, however, it dominated the lesser ones. The Westminster poll books of 1749[8] give a useful though imperfect guide to the occupations of many of the inhabitants of the estate at a time when such evidence is generally unavailable. In Westminster there was a particularly wide franchise, for the right to vote was vested in male householders paying 'scot and lot', i.e. the parish rates; of course the large class of women householders and the much smaller one of peers were excluded, and not all of those eligible to vote actually did so. The Westminster by-election of 1749–50 was, however, 'one of the most fiercely contested elections in the first half of the eighteenth century' and there was a very high poll. Charges of malpractice were brought, and the high bailiff was accused of 'allowing many votes by people who did not pay scot and lot and refusing those of others who did, and of having declined to produce the parish books showing who the legal voters were.'[9] Whatever the substance of these allegations the record has to be treated with caution. It consists of a meticulously written account of the names and occupations of the voters and the streets in which they lived. Some of the names in the poll books do not appear in the ratebooks but a close comparison is not always possible because of the loss of some ratebooks for the period of the poll. Nevertheless by correlating the two sources for certain streets and using only those names which can with reasonable certainty be confirmed as the occupants of the houses, a generalized picture can be built up.

In Mount Street, for instance, there were 116 houses entered in the ratebooks; 91 householders were seemingly qualified to vote and 66 of them did so. Of these 66 only nine described themselves as gentlemen or esquires, and one other (a schoolmaster) can be considered to belong to the professional classes. Excluding two coachmen and a turncock, 53 of the remainder (or 80 per cent of those who voted) were tradesmen. Thus almost one half of the ratepaying inhabitants of Mount Street were certainly tradesmen and the actual proportion was undoubtedly higher. Not only would many of the non-voting male householders have been engaged in trade, but so also would some of the female ratepayers, including the landlady of the Wheatsheaf tavern, and, quite possibly, a number of milliners; while at the poll the landlord of the Swan described himself as a gentleman. Of the 53 tradesmen who voted, 20 (37.7 per cent) belonged to the building and decorating trades; 14 (26.4 per cent) were purveyors of food and drink, including three victuallers and three chandlers; and 13 (24.5 per cent) were concerned with clothing or other wearing apparel.*

North Audley Street is a much shorter street with direct access from Grosvenor Square, but there the predominance of the trading element was just as pronounced. Of 36 householders paying rates 27 were eligible to vote and 25 did so. Of these 25 only five were gentlemen, esquires, or, in the case of Sir John Ligonier, a knight; one other was a schoolmaster but the remaining 19 (76 per cent of those who voted) were tradesmen. Five of them were builders or decorators, including a cabinet-maker; eight supplied food and drink, including three victuallers; and six worked in the world of clothing and fashion, including a staymaker and two peruke-makers.

In Davies Street, where most of the houses had been standing for twenty years or more, the pattern only varied slightly. Of 55 householders, 51 were entitled to vote and 44 of them did so. Three were gentlemen or esquires, and there were also a surgeon, a cook and a beadle, but 38, well over half of all the ratepayers in the street, were tradesmen. Of these 38, some five (13.2 per cent) were connected with building or decorating; 21 (55.3 per cent) were in the food and drink trades, including the resident victuallers of six taverns in the street and three chandlers; and six (15.8 per cent) supplied clothes, materials or wigs.

South Audley Street had its fashionable element, particularly at the south end, but over the whole street the tradesmen were still apparently dominant. Of 66 householders, 49 were eligible to vote and 38 exercised their franchise; 13 of these 38 were gentlemen or esquires and there was also one chairman, but the remaining 24 (63.2

* The occupations of the 53 tradesmen who voted in Mount Street were: (building and decorating trades) bricklayer, carpenter (6), carver, glassman, glazier, mason (3), painter (2), plasterer, plumber, smith, turner, upholsterer; (food and drink trades) baker, brewer, butcher (2), chandler (3), corn chandler, distiller, greengrocer, poulterer, victualler (3); (dress trades) breeches-maker, cutter, dyer, framework-knitter, laceman, linen-draper, peruke-maker (4), shoemaker, tailor (2); (other trades) apothecary, coachmaker, dealer in horses, lampman, saddler and snuffman.

per cent of the voters) were all tradesmen. Five of the 24 (20·8 per cent) pursued building or allied occupations; 14 (58.3 per cent) worked in the food and drink trades; only one, a peruke-maker, was concerned with clothing and fashion, but it is possible that some of the many single female householders were milliners. One at least was in trade, for Elizabeth Jones was the licensed victualler of the Albemarle Arms.

Some of the less salubrious areas of the estate lay immediately to the south of Oxford Street where land had been parcelled out in large blocks at low rents with few restrictive covenants in the original building leases. Two of these enclaves where building had progressed sufficiently by the mid eighteenth century for a coherent pattern of occupation to be established were the hinterlands behind the north side of Grosvenor Square between North Audley Street and Duke Street, and behind the north side of Brook Street between Duke Street and Davies Street. Here developers had laid out several narrow streets, viz. George (now Balderton), Queen (now Lumley), Brown and Hart Streets (now combined into Brown Hart Gardens) north of Grosvenor Square; and Bird (now Binney), James (now Gilbert) and Chandler (now Weighhouse) Streets north of Brook Street. The ratebooks show that by 1749 some 150 houses had been built in these streets and along the south side of Oxford Street. Several of them were let to tenants who did not pay rates and were thus ineligible to vote; against one such entry in the ratebooks where the ratepayer's name was left blank the collector had noted 'takes in vagabonds for Lodgers'. Nevertheless 92 ratepaying occupants of these streets did vote in the election of that year. Eleven were gentlemen, some of these being landlords like John Taylor who lived in one house in James Street himself and let half a dozen others to tenants; six fall into the general category of servants, including two coachmen and two chairmen; and 71 (77.2 per cent of the voters) were tradesmen. The remainder included a schoolmaster, a surgeon, a yeoman and a gardener. Of the tradesmen 26 (36.6 per cent) worked in the building trades, 22 (31 per cent) supplied food and drink including no fewer than eight victuallers, and 11 (15.5 per cent) were concerned with dress.

The impression created by the occupations of the voters in these streets could also be found in other parts of the estate. There were, however, some differences in the distribution of trades. Building workers were understandably most numerous in those parts of the estate where development was still in progress, in the streets to the north of Brook Street and Grosvenor Square, in the south-west corner around South Street and Chapel (now Aldford) Street, in Park Street and Green Street, and, more surprisingly, in Mount Street. Those involved in some capacity with horses or carriages, the wheelwrights, farriers, stable-keepers and coachmen, tended to live in the mews where there was clearly a good deal of residential accommodation. But, at this period, by no means all mews dwellers belonged to these or allied trades; in Grosvenor Mews, for instance, there were also victuallers, chandlers, builders, servants and a chimney-sweep among others. There was, however, no obvious concentration of food retailers and the numerous victuallers who presided over some 75 taverns or licensed coffee houses[10] were scattered throughout the estate. The chandler, that eighteenth-century Jack-of-all-trades, could also be found almost everywhere outside the five main streets.

The poll provides less evidence about the inhabitants of the principal streets, both because the presence of numerous peers and female householders (the latter accounting for over a third of the ratepaying occupants of Upper Brook Street alone) meant that fewer of them were eligible to vote, and because, of those who could have voted, a lower proportion exercised their right. Westminster tradesmen appear to have been more assiduous in using their political rights than the titled classes or country gentlemen. Many of these may indeed have been out of town, although the poll was taken during a parliamentary session. For comparative purposes the examples of Brook Street (that part on the Grosvenor estate only) and Upper Brook Street may be cited. There were then 94 houses already erected in the two streets and the householders of 54 of them were eligible to vote, but only 33 did so. Of these 33, gentlemen, esquires, 'honourables', knights, baronets, a general, a physician and a clerk account for 20, and the remaining 13 (39·4 per cent of the voters) were tradesmen, a surprisingly high number (considering that there may have been others who did not vote) for these august thoroughfares. They included two victuallers and a 'coffee man', all in Upper Brook Street at corner sites, two apothecaries, a linen-draper, a tailor, a wine merchant, a cheesemonger, a saddler, a smith, a glassman, and the master carpenter John Phillips at No. 39 Brook Street.

Thus by the mid eighteenth century, when the estate was still by no means completely built over, a coherent picture of its social composition had begun to emerge. It was that of a fashionable core of streets and a grand square occupied by the *beau monde*, encroached upon to a limited degree by residents engaged in trade, who in turn were to be found in overwhelming preponderance in the surrounding streets. Just as some tradesmen lived in the preserves of the socially distinguished, so also there were small coteries of the fashionable gathered in the outlying streets, and except in Grosvenor Square there was no strict segregation. The houses of the upper classes dominated physically by their size and by their large plots with long gardens extending to mews stabling at the rear, but they account for only about a quarter of the building fabric of the estate. The tradesmen, who formed such a substantial element of the population, evidently varied greatly in wealth and status, there being no doubt a considerable difference between, for instance, John Edmonson, saddler, of Upper Brook Street, who was listed in Mortimer's *Universal Director* of 1763, and the chandlers of Grosvenor Mews; and the gulf between the tradesmen of North Audley Street and the nearby inhabitants of Brown's Court or Parr's Buildings off North Row must have been almost as great as that between a well-established tradesman and his fashionable clientèle. Many of these tradesmen would have relied greatly on the patronage of the rich and titled inhabitants, as Lord Conway's household accounts testify; and in the case of the peruke-makers, of whom there were at least sixteen on the estate in 1749 (four of them in Mount Street), their dependence must have been almost complete.

Over fifty years ago Mrs. Dorothy George commented that 'Eighteenth-century London inevitably suggests the brilliant society which made up the world of politics and fashion. This small world of statesmen and politicians and placemen, of wits and rakes and fops, was so self-sufficient, so conscious that it was the only world that counted, that it imposes its point of view on us...We know little of the artisans and labourers, the shopkeepers and clerks and street-sellers, who made up the mass of the population.'[11] The nature of the evidence is such that it could hardly be otherwise, but at least sufficient can be gleaned from very fragmentary information to suggest that the impression generally prevalent that this part of Mayfair was the almost exclusive province of the well-to-do and the well-connected is in some respects highly misleading. Fortunately the somewhat crude outline of the social composition of the area that can be drawn from such evidence as that provided by the poll books of 1749 can be filled in by more detailed and reliable evidence in later years.

A Survey of Householders in *c.* 1790

The end of the eighteenth century was a quiet period in the history of the Mayfair estate. The building operations begun in 1720 had finally come to an end in the 1780's, and rebuilding on any significant scale did not start until the 1820's. A stable pattern of occupation therefore established itself in these years, and this is well illustrated by a detailed survey of the 'inhabitants' which was compiled in 1789-90 by the authorities responsible for collecting the assessed taxes in Middlesex.[12]

Though its provenance must connect it with taxation the real purpose of this survey remains unknown. It covers the whole of the parish of St. George's Hanover Square, street by street, listing the 'inhabitants' with their status or occupation and a wealth of other detail besides.* The term 'inhabitants' here seems to have been synonymous with the resident householders, but it also included non-residents who had businesses on the estate or let houses there to tenants. All householders were included (which was not the case with the poll books, previously discussed), but no information was given about the size of households or of the population as a whole.

The total number of these 'inhabitants'—excluding as far as possible non-residents and double entries—was 1526. These can be divided according to rank or occupation as shown in the accompanying Table.

The figures in this Table confirm the impression, already hinted at by the 1749 poll books, of a very heterogeneous population in which trade and commerce predominated. The residents of rank and fashion, who

Householders in *c.* 1790

Status or occupation of 'inhabitants'		Number of 'inhabitants'	% of total
Persons of title		129	8.5
M.P.'s (both with and without titles)		35	2.3
Professional		112	7.3
Trade		890	58.3
Food and drink	288		18.9
Dress and fashion	173		11.3
Building	164		10.7
Transport (including stable servants)	142		9.3
Other trades	123		8.1
Domestic servants		48	3.1
No occupation		343	22.5
less 'inhabitants' with dual status or occupations		−31	−2.0
		1526	100.0

* The headings under which the information sought by the survey was listed are as follows: 'House Number'; 'Inhabitants'; 'When Inhabited'; 'Furnished Houses'; 'Empty Houses'; 'Inmates Ground Floor'; 'Pays No Taxes'; 'Roman Catholics'; 'Widows and Spinsters'; 'Peers and Members of Parliament'; 'Army, Navy and Placemen'; 'Occupations'; 'Observations and Remarks'. The remarks usually include the sign of licensed premises, the nationality of aliens and sometimes the names of employers.

in this area might be expected to be numerically pre-eminent, are, however, not very easily identifiable in the survey, their presence being partly concealed in the 'no occupation' category, which includes 63 esquires and 24 gentlemen, and nearly 200 women. A better guide to the proportion of residents of rank and fashion is probably provided by *Boyle's Court Guide*, first published in 1792. Its 410 entries for the Grosvenor estate suggest that about a quarter of all householders on the estate belonged to this class.

The location of the various classes showed hardly any changes since the mid century. For those who could afford it Grosvenor Square was still the 'best address'—indeed one of the best in London. Of its 47 householders in 1790 thirty-one were titled, and these included three dukes, six earls (of whom one was Lord Grosvenor) and a viscount. Only slightly less fashionable were Upper Brook Street and Upper Grosvenor Street, which Mrs. Anne Damer, house-hunting in Mayfair in 1795, coupled with Grosvenor and Berkeley Squares as the 'ne plus ultra'.[13] In Upper Brook Street (where Mrs. Damer settled in 1799) 49 householders out of a possible 55 are listed in the court guide for 1792 and in Upper Grosvenor Street, 42 out of a possible 48. Brook Street and Grosvenor Street, always more vulnerable to commercial pressure than their extensions west of the square, were rather less exclusive, particularly towards their eastern ends. In Brook Street just under a quarter of all the householders were tradesmen and by 1805 the estate surveyor, William Porden, thought that the eastern half of the street was 'of such a mixed character of Houses as not to be thought an eligible situation for Persons of Rank'.[14] The newer developments in Hereford Street, Norfolk Street, Portugal Street and the south-west end of South Street were, however, all popular with fashionable residents. In South Audley Street the two facing groups of houses at the south end (Nos. 9–16 and 71–75 consec.) retained their fashionable *cachet* against commercial encroachments, as did the large houses overlooking the park at the south end of Park Street, and some of the houses on the south side of Green Street.

Titled people of all types accounted for 8.5 per cent of the 'inhabitants' listed in the survey. They included 37 peers (including Irish and Scottish peers), 18 baronets, 15 'honourables', and 39 'ladies'. Heading the list of peers was the Duke of Gloucester, one of George III's brothers, whose large detached house in Upper Grosvenor Street was later to become the London home of the Grosvenors. In addition to the Duke of Gloucester there were five non-royal dukes living on the estate. Foreign nobility was represented by the Hanoverian minister, Baron Alvensleben, at No. 37 Grosvenor Square, and the Duke of Orleans (Philippe Egalité) at No. 2 South Street, a house at the corner with Park Lane.

Several of the householders whose names appeared in the court guide were professional men. They included 'placemen' who were not also tradesmen; members of the armed forces; attorneys and lawyers; medical men (but not apothecaries) and architects. The 'placemen', of whom there were 32, were mostly either civil servants like Timothy Caswall of Davies Street, one of the Commissioners of the Salt Tax, or court officials, like Thomas Dupuis of Park Lane, the King's organist. Among the armed forces the Army was represented by fifteen officers and a surgeon, the officers ranging in rank from captain to general; the Navy's complement was two admirals, three captains and a surgeon. Three civilian surgeons were among the twelve householders who were medical men, the others being physicians, a dentist, a 'man mid-wife' and a chiropodist described as 'Operator to their Majesties for the Hands and Feet'. Another eight householders were attorneys, two of them being Earl Grosvenor's own lawyers, Edward Boodle and Thomas Walley Partington of Brook Street. Only two householders were described as architects, one being John Crunden, who occupied a house of his own designing in fashionable Hereford Street, and the other the little-known George Stoddart of South Street. Rather surprisingly the financial world had only one representative, George Brooks of Green Street, a founding partner in the banking firm of Dixon Brooks and Company, established in 1787 in Chancery Lane.[15]

More than half the householders on the estate in 1790 earned their living by trading in goods and services. Some 120 different trades were represented, ranging from muffin-makers to 'herald painters', but the main areas of activity were those concerned with food and drink, building, dress and fashion, and transport. The standing and scale of business of individual tradesmen evidently varied greatly. Twelve of them claimed to have the patronage of Royalty, the names of several appeared in the court guide, and the wealthy and fashionable inhabitants of Grosvenor Square naturally dealt with high-class purveyors, some of whom enjoyed metropolitan reputations. But at the other extremity were those who must have relied for their trade on the unfashionable but more numerous inhabitants of the lesser streets and mews.

The main shopping streets in 1790 were Davies Street, Duke Street, Mount Street, North and South Audley Streets, Oxford Street and Park Street—Mount Street being probably the most fashionable. The survey does not identify individual shops (except for a few occupied separately from the rest of the house), but as most tradesmen seem to have used their homes as their place of business, a good many ground-floor front rooms must have been turned over to trade. Some of them were fitted up with shop windows, as is shown on a plan of the east end of Brook Street in 1778–9 (fig. 4). Tradesmen had not at first needed the permission of the ground landlord to install shop windows, but from the 1760's estate leases contained a clause prohibiting the erection of bow windows[16]—evidently an attempt by Lord Grosvenor and his advisers to limit the proliferation of shop fronts.

The largest of the four main commercial groups were the food and drink trades, in which 288 tradesmen (some 19 per cent of all householders) were employed. Within this group the most numerous in a single occupation were the 74 licensed victuallers, of whom 73 occupied named licensed premises on the estate. Thus the number of public houses had hardly altered since 1750. Some losses in the older streets had been made up in the newer developments like Norfolk Street, but their distribution was as widespread as before, and among the principal streets only Grosvenor Square, Hereford Street and Portugal Street had none at all.

After the victuallers came the butchers, with 55 traders including poulterers and a tripeman. They were heavily concentrated in the north-east corner of the estate, particularly in St. George's and Grosvenor Markets (both exclusively food markets), where 35 butchers had their stalls. Their concentration in these two markets may have been the result of an attempt by Earl Grosvenor to take what was often an offensive trade out of the main streets. But even in the markets the butchers were not immune from complaints. In 1801, for example, a resident of Brook Street complained that on market days the stable yard behind her house was so crowded with cattle belonging to the butchers in St. George's Market that her carriage could not be 'aired' without running the risk of being 'gored by the bullocks'; and her neighbour objected to being disturbed in the morning by the bleating of sheep and calves.[17]

Less numerous than the butchers, but far more widely distributed, were the 43 chandlers whose main customers were the poorer inhabitants. Other householders in the food and drink trades included 28 greengrocers and fruiterers, 20 grocers, 18 bakers, 10 cheesemongers, 7 dairymen (including a cowkeeper in Green Street), and 6 fishmongers, one of whom was said to hawk his wares about the streets.

Slightly over 10 per cent of the householders were employed in what may broadly be termed the building industry. Apart from the regular building tradesmen— carpenters, bricklayers and the like—this group includes craftsmen and tradesmen associated with the decoration and furnishing of houses, principally upholsterers and cabinet-makers. Also included are four surveyors (none of them well known), but not the two architects previously mentioned. The carpenters, numbering 56, were by far the most numerous of any of the individual categories in this group. Many of them had their premises in the streets to the north of Grosvenor Square: in George Street, for example, where 14 of the 33 householders were employed in the building trades, there were seven carpenters. The most prominent member of the trade living on the estate was William Clarke of Little Grosvenor Street, described as carpenter to the 'Board of Works'. In addition to the carpenters there were 21 bricklayers, 12 masons, 11 plasterers, 9 glaziers, 6 plumbers and 2 slaters, but only one 'builder', William Rutledge of Mount Street.

Upholstery and cabinet-making was the best represented of the various furnishing trades, with 12 practitioners, some of them very well known. In Berkeley Square there was John Linnell, who had extensive workshops on the site of the present No. 25. Nearby at No. 70 Grosvenor Street lived Charles Smith, 'Upholsterer to their Majesties', while in Mount Street, which was soon to become a popular address with high-class furniture-makers, were to be found the cabinet-maker Edward Rawlings and the upholstery firm of Elward and Marsh, the latter much patronised by the Prince of Wales. (It is perhaps an indication of the standing of this firm that one of the partners, William Marsh, lived in a house in the fashionable part of South Street.) Altogether 29 building tradesmen had premises in Mount Street (20 per cent of all the householders there), numerically more than in any other street on the estate.

The dress and fashion trades employed a further 173 'inhabitants', many of whom lived in Mount Street, Oxford Street and Park Street. Twenty different types of tradesmen are represented in this group, including tailors, breeches-makers, mantua-makers, glove-makers, milliners, haberdashers, linen-drapers, perfumers, hairdressers and peruke-makers. Tailoring and shoemaking, which together engaged 77 householders, were the most widespread of these activities. On the other hand dressmaking and millinery, trades chiefly practised by women (who were, of course, often not householders), are certainly under-represented.

The 142 householders who derived their livelihood from the trades grouped under the heading 'transport' included 30 stable-keepers, 27 coachmen and 23 coachmakers as well as smiths, farriers, wheelwrights, saddlers, horse-dealers and coach-brokers. The large number of stable-keepers suggests that there was a substantial demand for commercial stabling in the area in addition to the private requirements of residents who kept their own horses and carriages. A few of the coachmen were in the employment of particular individuals, but the majority seem to have worked on their own account. The coachmakers included John Barnard of Park Street, coachmaker to the King, and Murdoch Mackenzie of the 'Rhedarium for the sale of coaches' which occupied the former Guards' stables built by Roger Morris between Green Street and Wood's Mews. Advertisements for the Rhedarium offered coaches and horses for sale by commission, 'neat Carriages of every kind to let for any space of time', 'Stallions to cover', and stables 'for gentlemen's horses to stand at livery'.[18] For new or inexperienced horsemen who might wish to improve their technique there was a riding academy in Queen Street, and a riding master in Park Street. Supplementing the horse-drawn transport were eight chairmen, one in the service of the Duchess of Devonshire, but the rest evidently self employed.

The remaining 123 tradesmen were employed in trades unconnected with any of the four main categories. These included fifteen coal dealers and twelve apothecaries, as well as stationers, chinamen, chimney-sweeps, tobacconists and watchmakers. Another twenty-one were the sole representatives of their trade on the estate, among whom were a piano-maker in Duke Street, a gunsmith in Mount Street, and a printer in Queen Street.

Apart from a few coachmen and other stable-servants, who traditionally lived over the mews stable, there were 48 householders engaged in some form of domestic service 'living out', evidently in their own houses. At first sight this may seem a surprisingly large number; but, as we have already seen, some families employed small armies of servants, more than could possibly be accommodated under one roof. (Lack of adequate servants' quarters in the original Georgian houses was one of the reasons why extra storeys were often added in the nineteenth century.) Married servants with families were no doubt obliged, and may have preferred, to provide their own accommodation. Many of the servants 'living out' were in the employment of the nobility resident both on the estate, like Lord Petre and Lord Abercorn, and elsewhere, like Lord Clive and Lord Powis. Lord Clive's porter had a house in Little Grosvenor Street which was only a few minutes' walk away from his lordship's own house in Berkeley Square, but a rather longer journey faced the Earl of Powis's cook on setting out from Green Street for the Earl's house in Portland Place. Domestic servants whose duties were specified in the survey included four porters, four valets and three cooks. Four of the Duke of Gloucester's pages had their own houses as did his cook, all within easy walking distance of Gloucester House. Lord Petre's butler, who shared his employer's Roman Catholic faith, lived in Green Street, not far from his master's mansion in Park Lane. Also included in the total number of domestic servants are three stewards, one combining the duties of steward to the Earl of Tankerville (who had extensive estates in Northumberland) with the business of a coal agent.

The survey of 1790 also provides information about the number of furnished houses and the number of sub-divided houses. Although there were probably more furnished houses than the 29 listed in the survey, they nevertheless represented only a small proportion of the 1400 or so houses on the estate. As the customers for these furnished lettings were most likely to come from the upper classes such houses were to be found almost exclusively in the fashionable streets. One upper-class occupant of a furnished house was the third Earl of Rosebery at No. 73 South Audley Street. The provision of furnished houses at this time was often in the hands of upholsterers and cabinet-makers, several of whom appear in the survey in the role of furnished-house proprietors. In Grosvenor Street the cabinet-makers Mayhew and Ince and the upholsterer Richard Taitt had a furnished house apiece, both however awaiting tenants in 1790, while at No. 65 Brook Street, a furnished house occupied by an 'esquire', the proprietor was the New Bond Street upholsterer Charles Elliott. But the ownership of furnished lettings was not confined to the professionals, for private owners would often let their town houses for brief periods while they themselves were away. Thus in Park Lane the second Earl of Warwick was enjoying possession of Camelford House during the absence abroad of Lord Camelford. Lord North, the former Prime Minister, used regularly to let his house at No. 50 Grosvenor Square while he occupied Downing Street: but 'conscious on how frail a basis his administration reposed, [he] would never let it for a longer period than one year. In consequence of this principle it annually changed possessors, and being frequently taken by newly-married couples, it obtained the name of Honeymoon Hall.'[19] Lord North's presence in his own house in 1790 did not deter the compilers of the survey from including No. 50 amongst the furnished houses. The demand for furnished houses, particularly by 'Families who spend but a short time in London', was soon to outstrip the supply and led naturally enough to the opening of several private hotels on the estate, one of the first of these being Kirkham's in Brook Street, which opened in about 1802.[20]

The sub-divided houses identified in the survey are those where one of the householders was said to inhabit only the ground floor; and almost all of these householders were tradesmen. Only 33 houses sub-divided in this way are listed, all of them in streets where commercial occupation predominated. There were also a few other houses apparently in joint occupation, and the occasional comment that an 'inhabitant' occupied one or more rooms provides further evidence of divided occupancy, which was doubtless far more widespread than the survey shows.

The London Season in 1841

We have already seen that as early as the 1730's and 40's many of the residents in the principal streets of the Grosvenor estate, and of course many more in other correspondingly fashionable parts of London, only spent part of each year in town, their seasonal movements being prescribed by those of the Court and by the dates of the parliamentary sessions. In the eighteenth century the number of people participating in this fashionable minuet between town and country cannot be even approximately calculated, but in the nineteenth century detailed information about the London Season was published for many years in *The Morning Post*, and this has been analysed for the year 1841.*

---

* This year was chosen in order to obtain supplementary material from the census of 1841. This census was preferred to those of 1851, 1861 and 1871 because the information contained in *The Morning Post* gradually becomes less detailed.

The Table opposite shows week by week the movements into and out of London of what *The Morning Post* called the 'Fashionable World'. Over four thousand movements are plotted, of which at least 15 per cent relate to residents on the Grosvenor estate in Mayfair; but the total size of the seasonal migration into and out of the capital must in reality have been substantially larger than that shown in the Table, because it may confidently be conjectured that many movements of both the 'Fashionable World' and its imitators were not publicly reported.

The year 1841 was not altogether a typical one because the general election by which the Tories displaced the Whigs was held in the latter part of the summer, but this serves to emphasize the extent to which the seasonal migration of the *beau monde* was influenced by the dates of parliamentary sittings. At the beginning of the year most people of fashion were out of town, either at home, visiting, or at Brighton. At the end of January there was the biggest influx of the year, for the opening of Parliament, and there then ensued a brief pre-Easter season,[21] marked by numerous dinners and soirées, the opening of the opera season, and the first royal levée. On 31 March, for instance, it was reported that Lady Compton Domville had held 'a very brilliant assembly' at No. 5 Grosvenor Square. 'The five spacious saloons in that superb mansion were most brilliantly illuminated.' Dancing 'to Weippert's band' had commenced at 11.30 p.m. and at 1.30 a.m. 'a most sumptuous supper' was served. And a day or two later Lady Anne Wilbraham had held 'a soirée dansante' at 'the family mansion in Lower Brook Street' (No. 68), at which 'Above 200 of the leading fashionables in town honoured her Ladyship with their company, as also the chief members of the corps diplomatique'.[22]

Early in April the adjournment of Parliament for the Easter recess and the removal of the Court to Windsor were accompanied by a substantial exodus, and Brighton filled up. With the reassembly of Parliament on 20 April, the Queen's return from Windsor, the first royal drawing-room, the reopening of the opera after Easter, and the first ball at Almack's there was a very large influx which marked the commencement of the main Season. Numerous arrivals at addresses principally in Belgravia, Marylebone, St. James's, Pall Mall and streets off Piccadilly, as well of course as Mayfair, were reported. The house agents did a brisk business in the letting of furnished houses 'for the Season', and the private hotels filled up, Mivart's and the adjacent Coulson's (formerly Wake's) in Brook Street being the most notable on the Grosvenor estate. Every Monday *The Morning Post* carried a column entitled 'Fashionable Arrangements for the Week', and on a single evening there were three separate receptions at various houses in Grosvenor Square alone. Other chronicled events included the Royal Academy exhibition, the Queen's levées, drawing-rooms and state balls, the Derby at Epsom, and Ascot races, the latter attended then as now, by the Queen from Windsor.

The prorogation of Parliament on 22 June and the imminence of a general election set off a gradual drift away from London. On 6 July Lady Compton Domville 'gave her farewell fête' in Grosvenor Square, the last ball at Almack's was held on the following night, and there were no more 'Fashionable Arrangements' in *The Morning Post*. Some emigrants went off on foreign tours, and it was reported that 'The fashionable departures for the German spas this season have been unusually numerous'.[23] There was also much visiting about from one country house to another, and Harrogate, Brighton, Goodwood races, yachting at Cowes, and shooting in Scotland all attracted their wealthy patrons.

But even at this 'dead' time of year fashionable London was never entirely empty. There were always some arrivals to report, and although the pattern of seasonal migration in the summer of 1841 was greatly distorted by the general election and the parliamentary session of 19 August to 7 October, which occasioned a considerable but short-lived influx, it is clear that even the most socially distinguished members of the 'Fashionable World' were often in London out of season. Such visits were, however, frequently of short duration, and the autumnal attractions of Buxton, Brighton, Leamington and Worthing, of racing at Newmarket, and above all of the hunting field, ensured that (after a brief influx in early December for the Smithfield Club's cattle show and annual dinner) London's social year had a quiet end, the twelve days of Christmas being generally celebrated out of town.

In addition to listing the arrivals in and departures from London *The Morning Post* also published 'changes' from one out-of-town address to another. Taken together all this information reveals the peculiarly peripatetic existence of the 'Fashionable World', while other records indicate the resources needed to sustain such a mode of life. The case of two earls and their families, both resident in Grosvenor Square, may be taken as examples.

The first Earl of Verulam had a town house at No. 47 Grosvenor Square and a country seat at Gorhambury Park, near St. Albans. The family estates in Hertfordshire and Essex were estimated in 1882 to contain some 10,000 acres yielding £14,000 per annum.[24] In 1841 the Earl was aged sixty-five; his wife was some nine years younger, and the youngest of their nine children was aged sixteen. On the night of the census (6–7 June) the Earl and Countess, two of their sons and one daughter were all resident in Grosvenor Square, where they were attended by seven male and eight female servants.[25] At Gorhambury House there were on the same night another seven female servants and one male servant, plus half-a-dozen other male servants in the adjoining stables.[26]

Towards the end of January the Earl had come up to Grosvenor Square from Gorhambury, where he was joined by the Countess, who had been visiting one of their married daughters, the Countess of Craven, at Combe Abbey near Coventry. Their eldest son, Viscount Grimston, M.P., still a bachelor, also joined them at

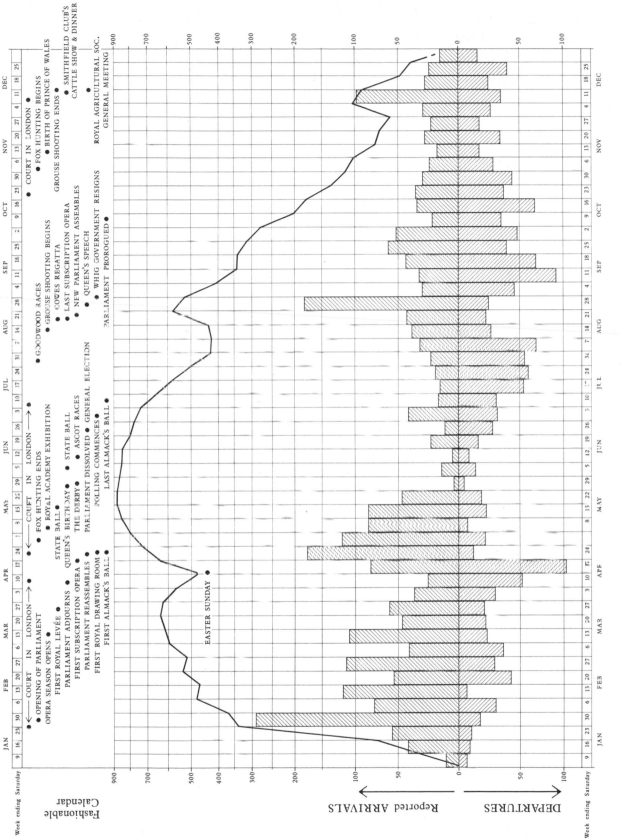

SEASONAL MIGRATIONS OF THE 'FASHIONABLE WORLD' IN 1841

This figure plots over 4,000 movements into and out of London of members of the 'Fashionable World', as reported in *The Morning Post* in 1841. Movements of single individuals or of married couples or of whole families are all expressed as one movement. Thus the total number of persons arriving and departing was in reality substantially larger than that given here.

The hatched columns show the total number of arrivals and departures reported in each week. Sometimes there was a time lag of up to ten days between the date of a movement and its publication.

The heavy black line shows the cumulative total of arrivals after subtraction of departures. The departures were not so fully reported as the arrivals, and to correct this shortfall the departures have been multiplied by a factor of 1.6.

Grosvenor Square from Ireland, all these arrivals coinciding with the opening of Parliament. In March the Earl and Countess went to the Duke of Rutland at Belvoir Castle, back to Grosvenor Square, and thence (with Lord Grimston and their youngest daughter) to Earl and Countess Amherst at Knole, Kent. Their return to Grosvenor Square in early April was soon followed by a visit by the Countess and her unmarried children to Longford Castle, Wiltshire, to stay with another of their married daughters, Viscountess Folkestone. By mid April the Earl of Verulam was at Newmarket, and a week later his family was back in Grosvenor Square. In mid May he and the Countess, with Lord Grimston and their unmarried daughter, were at Gorhambury for the races, but were back in town by 6 June. In the latter part of July the Earl and Viscount Grimston were visiting Mrs. Warde at the Squerryes, Westerham, before going to Buckhurst Park, Sussex, and ultimately to the Duke of Richmond at Goodwood. Meanwhile the Countess was entertaining her son-in-law and daughter, the Earl and Countess of Craven, at Gorhambury. At the end of August both the Earl and Countess of Verulam were in Grosvenor Square, but early in September the Earl and his son Viscount Grimston went off to the Marquess of Abercorn's shooting lodge in Inverness-shire, while the Countess and her youngest daughter went to Gorhambury. A few days later, however, the Countess and one of her sons were in Grosvenor Square on their way to Longford Castle again. By 24 September the Earl and Viscount Grimston were back at Gorhambury from their Caledonian foray, and a week later they too went on to Longford Castle. In mid October the Earl was said to be 'still at Newmarket', while the Countess, Viscount Grimston and her unmarried daughter left Grosvenor Square for visits to Mrs. Warde at the Squerryes and Earl Amherst at Knole. By the end of the month the Earl was back at Gorhambury before joining his wife at the Squerryes. In mid November they were at Gorhambury entertaining the Earl and Countess of Clarendon and 'a large circle of nobility and gentry around'. In December Viscount Grimston went to visit the Marquess of Abercorn at Baron's Court in Ireland, and on his way back to Gorhambury shortly before Christmas he stayed for a few days with his sister the Countess of Craven.

The second Earl of Wilton was a younger and considerably richer man than the Earl of Verulam. He was a younger son of the first Marquess of Westminster, having inherited his title from his maternal grandfather by special remainder. In addition to his town house at No. 7 Grosvenor Square he had a country seat at Heaton House, near Manchester, and a hunting lodge at Melton Mowbray. His estates, chiefly in Lancashire, Yorkshire and Staffordshire, were variously estimated in 1882 to be worth £31,000 or £65,000 per annum.[27] In 1841 he was aged forty-one, and by his wife (a daughter of the twelfth Earl of Derby) he then had four young children, the eldest of whom was aged eight. On the night of the census he, the Countess and two of their children were resident in Grosvenor Square, where they were attended by seven male and nine female servants.[28] At Heaton House on the same night there were a clerk, a housekeeper, three female servants and two grooms, while the residents in the cottages of the surrounding park included a gamekeeper and eight gardeners.[29] Egerton Lodge at Melton Mowbray was shut up for the summer, the only residents being an elderly couple evidently acting as caretakers.[30] The Earl's two younger children were at Walmer Castle, the official residence of the Lord Warden of the Cinque Ports, the Duke of Wellington, who was a friend and frequent correspondent of the Countess of Wilton. The Duke himself was not at Walmer, where the staff looking after the two children consisted of a housekeeper, one male and five female servants.[31]

Towards the end of January the Earl of Wilton had come up to Grosvenor Square from Eaton Hall, Chester (the home of his father the Marquess of Westminster), and left for Melton Mowbray for the hunting immediately after the opening of Parliament. A week or two later he was back in Grosvenor Square, but in mid February both he and the Countess were at Melton. In the first half of April they were successively at Belvoir Castle with the Duke of Rutland, Grosvenor Square, probably with the Duke of Wellington at Stratfield Saye, Melton Mowbray and Grosvenor Square again, before going with their children to Tunbridge Wells, perhaps staying in a rented house. In the latter part of April the Earl and Countess were both back in Grosvenor Square, but the Countess soon returned to Tunbridge Wells. Most of May seems to have been spent in Grosvenor Square, though the Earl was at the Derby at Epsom at the end of the month. Early in June the Countess took two of her children to Walmer Castle, but she was back within a few days to give 'a splendid entertainment' in Grosvenor Square, followed by a dinner party early in July. Soon afterwards she was for a few days at Heaton House—her only visit of the year—and then went (probably with her children) to a house near Ryde in the Isle of Wight. In due course she was joined there by the Earl, who was Commodore of the Royal Yacht Squadron, but by the end of August they were both at Grosvenor Square, where they gave a dinner for the Duke of Wellington. Mid September saw them once more at Ryde, and on 24 September *The Morning Post* reported that 'The Noble Earl purposes a cruise of a few weeks in his yacht, and will then go to Melton Mowbray for the hunting season'. This cruise seems to have taken in a visit to Walmer Castle, whence in early November he and the Countess returned by yacht to Ryde, and thence back to Grosvenor Square. On 9 November the Earl, 'unattended', arrived at Heaton House for his only and very brief visit of the year, and during the rest of the month there were visits with the Countess to Ryde, to the Duke of Beaufort at Badminton, and in early December to the Duke of Wellington at Stratfield Saye. By mid December they were at Grosvenor Square *en route* for Melton Mowbray, but on 22 December they were back in town *en route* for Stratfield Saye for Christmas. By 28 December the Earl was again in Grosvenor Square.

Most of the journeyings of both the Earl of Verulam and the Earl of Wilton were probably made by road, few railways having yet been built by 1841. Verulam's real home was evidently at Gorhambury, and as this was little more than twenty miles from London he seems to have spent less time at his house in Grosvenor Square (around seventeen weeks) than did the Earl of Wilton. Wilton's country seat was much further away, and its proximity to Manchester was perhaps already reducing its residential attraction.* To cater for his two principal sporting interests of hunting and yachting he therefore had two subsidiary houses out of town, at Melton Mowbray and Ryde, plus a third, perhaps mainly for his wife and family, at Tunbridge Wells. But it may be conjectured that none of these gave him a social position out of town comparable with that of Gorhambury for the Earl of Verulam, who was Lord Lieutenant of Hertfordshire for over twenty years. Despite his more numerous residences Wilton therefore seems to have spent rather more time in Grosvenor Square—around twenty-one weeks than Verulam.

Such influences of family heritage and of individual personal preference no doubt greatly affected the way of life of many other families moving about in the 'Fashionable World'. But it may be noted, firstly, that although neither of them was prominent in politics, the movements of both Verulam and Wilton conformed broadly with the general pattern of seasonal migration based on the parliamentary sessions; and, secondly, that even in out-of-season times of the year they (and particularly Wilton) were often in at least brief residence in Grosvenor Square.

The Censuses of 1841 and 1871

The vast amount of information about the demographic structure of the Grosvenor estate which is contained in the enumerators' books of the decennial censuses from 1841 onwards falls largely outside the scope of this volume, and only a brief analysis of those of 1841 and 1871 (the latter being the most recent for which the schedules are at present open to public inspection) can be attempted here.[32]

The results of this analysis are presented in the Table on page 94. At the outset it must be emphasised that the inter-censual comparisons made there should be treated with caution because the criteria upon which the censuses of 1841 and 1871 were taken differed in several important respects. But despite these differences, which are discussed below, some tentative evaluations can be made.

Firstly, the figures show that between 1841 and 1871 the total number of residents on the estate fell by 13 per cent. Almost all of this decline evidently occurred between 1841 and 1851, when the population of Mayfair as a whole, and of that other fashionable area, St. James's Square, also fell by a similar amount.[33] As will appear later, it seems that this decline was principally amongst the residents of independent means and their servants, rather than amongst those engaged in trade or non-domestic service; and it may be conjectured that some, at any rate, of this decline was due to the rival attractions of Belgravia, Kensington and Tyburnia.

Secondly, the figures show that only a very small proportion of the residents on the estate (some 5 to 10 per cent) belonged to the titled or leisured classes. The social *cachet* of a good address there might still, in Victorian times, be as highly prized as ever; but even in this citadel of the *beau monde* such residents were far outnumbered by the rest of the population.

The number of residents of title and leisure recorded in the census of 1841 is, however, more than double that recorded in the count of 1871, and this disparity requires examination. Some decline in their numbers evidently did take place, but it was probably not as great as the figures suggest, and the discrepancy can be largely explained by differences inherent in the two counts.

The first of these differences arose from the precise dates in 1841 and 1871 when the censuses were taken. That of 1841 was taken on 6–7 June, when Parliament was in session and the London Season was near its height, whereas that of 1871 was taken on 2–3 April, when both Houses had risen for the Easter recess, and many residents of wealth and fashion were therefore absent from their London homes: less than half the peers who are listed in *Boyle's Court Guide* as having addresses within the Grosvenor estate in Mayfair were actually resident there on the night of the census of 1871. In 1841 some eighty inhabited houses were not in substantially normal occupation (i.e. were occupied only by servants or caretakers), about forty of them in the principal streets, whereas in 1871 the number of such houses was 175, about one hundred of them being in streets where the titled and leisured classes generally lived. Furthermore, in 1841 the number of such occupants who may have been absent from their homes on the night of the census was in part counterbalanced by others who had taken houses for the Season, such as the Duke of Rutland, who was living at General Thomas Grosvenor's house, No. 50 Grosvenor Square, with two members of his family (and eleven servants).

A second important difference arises from the differing treatment of residents of independent means, which has resulted in a far larger number of such persons appearing in 1841 (906) than in 1871 (300). This divergence may be partly explained by the very catholic interpretation placed

---

* The house and park at Heaton were sold to Manchester Corporation in 1901.[27]

The Censuses of 1841 and 1871

	Census of 6–7 June 1841			Census of 2–3 April 1871		
		% of workers	% of total popn		% of workers	% of total popn
Inhabited houses and mews dwellings	1,753			1,645 (containing 2,711 households)		
Blocks of model lodgings				3 (containing 75 households)		
Uninhabited houses and mews dwellings	85			125		
Total population	17,064			14,829		
Residents of the titled and leisured classes	1,780		10.4	840		5.7
Peers	48			25		
Baronets	25			14		
Other persons of title	238			109		
Untitled independents	906			300		
Untitled landowners	not available			81		
Dependants of above	563			311		
Residents working for financial reward	9,213		54.0	8,422		56.8
Professional						
Army officers	83			50		
Naval officers	18			11		
Law	29			54		
Medicine	70			88		
Church	21			17		
Architects and engineers	11			6		
Total	232	2.5	1.3	226	2.7	1.5
Trade or service						
Servants	5,935	64.4	34.8	4,583	54.4	30.9
Transport	408	4.4	2.4	489	5.8	3.2
Dress and fashion	1,060	11.5	6.2	1,348	16.0	9.1
Food and drink	481	5.2	2.8	521	6.2	3.5
Building	270	2.9	1.6	202	2.4	1.4
Other trades	829	9.0	4.9	1,053	12.5	7.1

A 'household' (both as used in the above table under 1871 and in the text) comprises any distinct family group in which the head of the group is so described, or where an absent head is presumed by the designation of the first person within the group as wife, son, etc. Lodgers and boarders have not been counted as separate households. It has not been possible to determine the number of households in 1841 from the enumerators' books.

'Other persons of title' comprise peeresses; peers' widows, sons, daughters or daughters-in-law; wives or widows of baronets; knights and their wives or widows; and foreign nobles. In the 1841 census persons of independent means were generally classed simply as 'independent' and it has not been possible to determine the number of untitled landowners. In the figures derived from the 1871 census, in which more categories were used, 'Untitled independents' include fundholders, annuitants, gentlemen, and persons with 'income from dividends' or entered as of 'no occupation'. In both censuses M.P.'s who are described as such without any accompanying rank or profession are counted as independents. 'Dependants' include untitled relatives of the head of the household, and visitors, but governesses, servants, coachmen and grooms are excluded.

Soldiers' rank was not given in the 1841 census, and the 83 'Army officers' include eight residents whose addresses suggest that they may not have been commissioned.

In the 1841 census coachmen and grooms were generally entered as servants, but in 1871 they were classified separately. They then numbered 637, and for purposes of comparison have been included in the number of servants. Governesses, of whom there were 35 in 1841 and 48 in 1871, have also been classed as servants.

The parish workhouse on the south side of Mount Street was enumerated separately at each census and has not been included in the above table.

on the term 'independent' by the enumerators in 1841. They were instructed that 'Men, or widows, or single women having no profession or calling, but living on their means, may be inserted as *independent*',[34] but sometimes they extended this definition to embrace almost anyone with no occupation, including the wives and children of tradesmen. As far as possible the latter have been excluded in counting the number of 'independents' for the purposes of the Table, but some exaggeration in the total number of such persons is, nevertheless, probably inevitable. On the other hand there are numerous instances in both the 1841 and 1871 counts in which a householder's profession or occupation is not given, and, particularly in the latter year, many of the persons concerned are likely to have been untitled householders of leisure.

These differences in the time of year and in the methods of classification of the two counts point to the conclusion that in 1841 the number of titled and leisured residents was slightly overstated and in 1871 certainly understated. But despite these qualifications there is little doubt that there was indeed an overall decline between 1841 and 1871 in the number of such persons living on the estate. In Park Street, where many 'independents' lived in 1841, the number of residents occupying exactly the same number of inhabited houses dropped from 932 to 786 between the two censuses, and this pattern was repeated in other streets of 'middling' character. It is in such streets that persons living off moderate incomes, many of them women, would have lodged, and it may be that one of the factors in the general decrease in the population of the estate after 1841 was the migration of such people to the newly developing suburbs of Paddington and Kensington.

A similar decline in the number of M.P.'s listed in *Boyle's Court Guide* with addresses on the estate from 68 in 1840 to 49 in 1872 can no doubt be attributed to the same cause, but there was no corresponding diminution in the number of peers, who were perhaps more reluctant to leave such a long-established centre of fashion.

The residents who worked for financial reward comprised slightly over half the total population in both 1841 (53·99 per cent) and 1871 (56·8 per cent).* Very few of them were professional men, but the number of lawyers, physicians and surgeons had increased by 1871, while the number of army officers had fallen. 'City' men of business and commerce—bankers, stockbrokers and merchants—who at the turn of the century were to settle in the area in some numbers, were still very few.

In an area such as Mayfair most of the working population were engaged in supplying the wants of the relatively small number of wealthy residents, and by far the largest of these wants was, of course, for service, both domestic and out-door. In the census of 1841 grooms and coachmen (who were very numerous in this carriage-owning area) were generally classified as servants, and altogether servants amounted to over a third of the entire population (34 per cent) and to 64 per cent of all the working residents. Some 44 per cent of them were male.

By 1871 the total number of domestic servants, coachmen and grooms had fallen by nearly a quarter, but they still amounted to 30 per cent of the entire population and to 54 per cent of the working residents. Some 36 per cent of them were male. The domestic servants were now classified separately from the coachmen and grooms, and they alone numbered 3,898, equivalent to 26.3 per cent of the whole population and to 46.3 per cent of the working residents. Some 26 per cent of them were male.

Between 1841 and 1871 there was thus a substantial fall in the total number of servants, and in the proportion of male servants.

The census of 1871 demonstrates the extent to which the demand for domestic service was concentrated in a comparatively few very wealthy households. Some 63 per cent of all the households on the estate had no domestic servant, and thirteen per cent had one each, a further thirteen per cent had two or three servants, and only eleven per cent (303 households) had four or more. Expressed in a different way, some three hundred households with four or more servants employed almost 70 per cent of all the domestics on the estate in 1871.†

Comparable figures for 1841 cannot be calculated because of the difficulty of identifying separate households.

About three quarters of the three hundred houses with large domestic staffs in 1871 were in Grosvenor Square, Park Lane, Brook Street, Grosvenor Street, Upper Brook Street and Upper Grosvenor Street, and a similar concentration had no doubt existed in 1841. In Grosvenor Square in 1841 over 76 per cent of the residents listed in the census were domestic servants,‡ while in 1871 (when a greater proportion of householders and their families were absent on the night of the census) servants accounted for over 80 per cent of the inhabitants of the square. In those 43 houses which were in normal occupation at the time of the count in 1841, the average size of each household was 16.7, of whom 12.9 were servants. Twenty-six

---

* Excluding residents of the titled and leisured classes, the balance of the population consisted of the wives and children of the residents working in the professions, trade or service, students and all other untitled persons who left the 'occupation' column of the census schedule blank.

† These figures for servants may be compared with those for the Queen's Gate area of South Kensington in *Survey of London*, volume XXXVIII, 1975, p. 322.

‡ As has already been mentioned, the census of 1841 does not differentiate between domestic servants and coachmen and grooms, but the census of 1871, which does make this differentiation, contains hardly any coachmen or grooms resident in Grosvenor Square or other principal streets. It has therefore been assumed that in the census of 1841 the servants recorded at such addresses were indoor domestics and not stable staff, who were, of course, listed, also as 'servants', in large numbers in the nearby mews.

of these 43 houses had 12 or more servants, the largest number being at No. 44, where a staff of 23 attended to the Earl of Harrowby and four members of his family.

In 1871 the average size of household in the 29 houses in Grosvenor Square which were in normal occupation had declined to 13.8, of whom 10.8 were servants. The largest domestic establishment was at No. 41, the house of Sir Henry Meux, baronet, of the brewing family, where there were 21 servants. The largest complement of all, in either census, was at Dudley House, Park Lane, in 1871, where the Earl and Countess of Dudley, their infant son, a nephew and two nieces, were attended by 28 domestic servants, two coachmen and seven stable 'helpers'.

In 1841 domestic servants accounted for between 67 and 72 per cent of all the residents in Upper Brook Street, the western part of Grosvenor Street, and Upper Grosvenor Street. In the houses where normal occupancy existed on the night of the census the average size of each household was 10.9 in Upper Brook Street and 10.7 in Upper Grosvenor Street, and the average number of servants was 7.3. Households in the western part of Grosvenor Street averaged 12.8, of whom 9 were servants. In 1871 these figures had fallen only slightly, 66 per cent of the residents in these streets still being servants, and the average number of servants in each house being about seven. In the western half of Brook Street some 62 per cent of the residents were servants in both 1841 and 1871, but their numbers in the houses in normal occupation fell from an average of 7·0 to slightly below 5·7.

In addition to the domestic servants there were also the coachmen and grooms, of whom there were over six hundred living on the estate in 1871. Many of the great houses in Grosvenor Square and the streets leading off it had their own coach-houses and stables in the mews on to which they backed, but in the censuses the residents in the mews were almost always classified separately from their employers, and the precise number of stable staff belonging to any particular house cannot easily be found, even in the census of 1871, and in that of 1841 never: the previously mentioned case of Dudley House provides a rare exception, and the Marquess of Westminster's stables are known to have been near Grosvenor House in Reeves Mews, where in 1871 lived the head coachman and his family, an assistant coachman, a groom and two servants. The census of 1871 shows that in the yards and mews behind the principal streets, in such places as Adams Mews (now Row), Blackburne's Mews, Three Kings Yard and Wood's Mews, almost all the male working residents by then in fact worked with horses, the public-house keepers, of whom there were often one in each mews, being the most notable exceptions. A few farriers, jobmasters, ostlers, carmen, coachsmiths and such like could be found there, but by far the most numerous occupations were those of coachman and groom. In Three Kings Yard, for instance, ten of the twelve householders were coachmen or grooms, the other two being a female domestic servant and the keeper

of the public house at the corner of Davies Street. The latter and one footman were the only men not working in the stables. The entire population of this busy little working community lurking inconspicuously behind the fashionable mansions of Brook Street, Grosvenor Street and Grosvenor Square upon which it was so totally dependent and yet from which it was socially so totally divided, amounted to sixty-five persons.

Apart from demand for personal service, both indoors and outdoors, wealthy residents' other great want, sufficiently extensive to reflect itself in the general pattern of employment on the estate, was in the field of dress and fashion. But while demand for domestic service declined between 1841 and 1871, demand for services providing for personal adornment was increasing. The Table above shows that whereas in 1841 1,060 residents had work dependent on dress and fashion, a figure equivalent to 11.5 per cent of the working population of the estate, by 1871 the corresponding figures were 1,348 residents, amounting to 16 per cent of the working population. During this period the number of dressmakers rose from 310 to 507, and of tailors from 205 to 269, but laundresses remained constant at 116 and 113. The remainder included such trades as milliner, draper, hosier, hatter, haberdasher, bootmaker, dyer, waistcoat-maker, hairdresser, lace merchant and lace cleaner. Apart from domestic service these trades provided *in toto* by far the largest source of local employment for women.

Unlike many of the servants, coachmen and grooms, the residents engaged in these trades were scattered over many parts of the estate, with particular concentrations in the poorer areas immediately to the south of Oxford Street and in what are now Grosvenor Hill and Bourdon Street. Many of the women were the wives or daughters of householders engaged in quite different trades, and the needlewomen and laundresses in particular probably often worked at home, the sooty grime of London and the absence as yet of a constant water supply providing the latter with continuous and arduous work. There were, however, half a dozen employers of large, generally resident, staffs of needlewomen or shop assistants. In 1871 three of these—a dressmaker (whose staff of eleven lived elsewhere), a lace merchant and a linen-draper—were in South Audley Street, and there was one each in Mount Street (court dressmaker) and the eastern parts of Brook Street (milliner) and Grosvenor Street (silk mercer). The biggest of these establishments was that of Smith, Durrant, Mayhew and Loder, at Nos. 58-60 (consec.) South Audley Street, where Francis Loder, living in 1871 with his wife and two infant sons, employed a male staff of six assistants, four porters, two clerks and two apprentices, and a female staff of sixteen assistants, plus a female domestic staff of seven—all living in.

The demands of wealthy residents on the estate may also have been at least partly responsible for the number of local workers engaged in the coachbuilding trades. This demand was of course very small in comparison with those for personal service and the dress trades, the total number of workers in the trades of coachbuilder, painter, trimmer, smith, plater and springmaker being only 74 in 1841 and 81 in 1871. A large proportion of them lived in the area immediately south of Oxford Street, where they had been established for many years. This concentration may well, indeed, have originated in the low rents charged here at the time of the original development of the estate, for coachbuilding always required a considerable amount of space; but the close proximity of numerous wealthy customers was no doubt also an advantage, just as it is to-day for the motor-car dealers of Berkeley Square and Berkeley Street.

Few of the numerous other trades practised on the estate appear to have been notably directed towards the requirements of the rich residents upon which the occupations so far discussed did chiefly depend. Some of the firms (mainly shops) in which the 521 residents engaged in 1871 in the food and drink trades worked no doubt catered for expensive local tastes, and the poulterer John Baily, who employed sixteen men at his shop in Mount Street, was in later years known to the Duke of Westminster himself. But the relatively even distribution of the food and drink trade workers throughout all but the most exclusive residential parts of the estate suggests that most business was of a very local nature. In the High Victorian world of 1871 the 56 publicans living on the estate, at all events, are not likely to have been greatly dependent upon the custom of upper-class residents. Some of the 73 lodging-house keepers may, on the other hand, to judge from their numbers in such partly fashionable streets as Green Street, Park Street and Mount Street, have found much of their custom amongst persons of rank who had no town house of their own. It is a testimony to the accuracy of Anthony Trollope's observation that when, in *Framley Parsonage*, Archdeacon Grantly and his wife had occasion to come up to London they took lodgings in Mount Street, which in fact contained in 1871 the highest number of lodging houses of any street on the Grosvenor estate.

Although over half of all the residents on the estate worked in trade or service, there can have been little outward reflection of this in the streets, which were, of course, overwhelmingly residential in character except in such 'shopping' streets as Mount Street and Oxford Street. Dress and fashion, and domestic service, the two principal sources of employment in the area, were unobtrusive trades, and the noise made by the 'machinists' who are occasionally recorded in the census cannot have been so generally heard as in the industrialised quarters of London. Conditions in the two primarily labouring-class areas, immediately south of Oxford Street and in the south-eastern corner of the estate, must certainly have provided a striking contrast with those of the neighbouring Brook Street and Grosvenor Street, but even there the smell of horses must have been far more notable than the clatter of machinery.

The census of 1871 presents a detailed picture of the social composition of the estate as it existed about a decade before the commencement of widespread rebuilding in the early 1880's under the first Duke of Westminster's superintendence. This picture was made about a century after the completion of the original building development, and it shows very clearly how relatively little change had taken place during that period.

Aristocrats and gentlemen still lived mainly in Grosvenor Square and the four streets extending east and west from it. Norfolk (now Dunraven) Street, and the south ends of Park Street and South Audley Street were still fashionable, and Park Lane had come into its own in the early nineteenth century. Nor does the basic pattern of the seasonal movements of the fashionable world seem to have changed greatly since the mid eighteenth century, although November and December had probably become quieter because Parliament now seldom sat in those months.

The public houses in Upper Grosvenor Street and Upper Brook Street no longer existed, but such fashionable streets had become popular with physicians, of whom in 1871 there were three in the former and six in the latter. Rich businessmen were also beginning to appear in small numbers in the best streets—Joseph Baxendale, for instance, the senior partner in the firm of Pickford and Company, the carriers, which had some two thousand employees, lived at No. 78 Brook Street; and in addition to Sir Henry Meux in Grosvenor Square itself there were at least four brewers, those three of them (Sir Thomas Buxton, Sir Dudley Marjoribanks and Octavius Coope) who lived in Upper Brook Street each having a retinue of servants ranging between twelve and nineteen in number.

In both Grosvenor Street and Brook Street the number of tradesmen had declined since 1790, and members of the medical profession had settled there in large numbers. In Grosvenor Street in 1871 18 houses were occupied by physicians and surgeons and another five by four dentists and an oculist—equivalent to 31 per cent of all the houses in the street within the estate; and in Brook Street there were also 18 houses similarly occupied, plus another two by dentists, making 44 per cent of all the houses there within the estate. Another five houses in Brook Street were now occupied by two private hotels, Lillyman's at No. 43 and Claridge's at Nos. 49–55 (odd). Both these establishments had originated in the early nineteenth century, the former as Kirkham's, the latter as Wake's and Mivart's, and both belonged to that select class of hotel where 'no guests were received who were not known to the landlord either personally or through fit credentials …An unknown and unaccredited stranger could, by the mere chance latch-key of wealth, no more obtain access to such hotels as these than he could make himself to-day [1920] a member of some exclusive club by placing the amount of the entrance fee in the hands of the hall porter.'[35] At Claridge's, on the night of the census in

1871, the thirty-nine visitors were attended by sixty-six living-in servants—a number that probably included both personal domestics and the hotel staff.

In Mount Street, despite the presence of one peer, two M.P.'s and two foreign nobles, the commercial element of the population may have increased slightly since the mid eighteenth century, some 75 per cent of the householders being engaged in trade or domestic service. In North Audley Street, too, there seems to have been a small increase, for here all but four of the householders in 1871 were in trade, the exceptions being two widows, a surgeon and a schoolmistress; but in South Audley Street no perceptible change had taken place, some 65 per cent of the householders being tradesmen, and most of the 'independents' being still at the south end. Most of the tradesmen in these streets kept few domestic servants, the average number in the commercial households of North Audley Street, for instance, being only slightly over one each. In Mount Street, it may be noted, the residence of several butlers (described as head of household) with their families shows that at any rate senior domestics did not always live at their place of employment; but elsewhere on the estate (in Davies Street and Binney Street) there are instances of households consisting of butlers' wives and children without a husband or father, who was presumably 'living in' at his employer's house.

The parts of the estate on which substantial social change first took place were in the poorer areas occupied by the labouring classes. The two main such areas were immediately south of Oxford Street chiefly east of North Audley Street, and in the south-eastern extremity of the estate in the mews now known as Grosvenor Hill, Bourdon Street and Place, Broadbent Street and Jones Street. Both these areas had been relatively poorly occupied since the time of the original building development, and both were greatly altered in the second half of the nineteenth century by the building of blocks of model lodging houses. But whereas in the area immediately south of Oxford Street the first such block (Clarendon Buildings in Balderton Street) was still in course of erection at the time of the census of 1871 and had not yet been occupied, in the south-eastern corner of the estate several blocks had already been completed; and the effect of this innovation can therefore be compared, at any rate for the years between 1841 and 1871.

The two censuses show that in the twenty-nine four-storey houses with basements in Robert Street (now Weighhouse Street), parallel with Oxford Street, there was no significant change in the total numbers of residents. In 1841 there were 526 and in 1871, 512, the latter figure being about ten per cent more than the population of the whole of Grosvenor Square. The average number of residents per house was thus 18.1 and 17.65 respectively. Many of the inhabitants were coachmen, tailors, porters, labourers, building tradesmen, needlewomen and char-women. In 1871 each of the twenty-nine houses in this street contained an average of 4.9 separate households;

and the average number of residents in each household was 3.6 (compared with 13.8 for the houses in Grosvenor Square in normal occupation on the night of the census). Comparable figures for households in 1841 are not available.

But in the south-eastern mews area the building of several blocks of model lodging houses in the 1850's and 1860's greatly increased the overall population of this little working-class territory. In 1841 there were 805 residents in the 76 dwellings there, and in 1871 857 in 81 dwellings, the average number per dwelling remaining constant at 10.6. But by 1871 the new model lodging houses contained 287 extra residents; the total population of this densely packed little enclave, only some two and a half acres in extent, was thus 1,144, equivalent to nearly eight per cent of the population of the entire hundred-acre estate.

Despite such wide variety of social circumstances, Grosvenor Square and the principal streets had to a notable extent retained for over a century the original social *cachet* of their first development. This was not always the case in originally fashionable areas. Covent Garden Piazza, built in the 1630's to attract 'Persons of the greatest Distinction' had lost much of its social prestige within two generations, the growth of the adjacent market being partly responsible.[36] Its later seventeenth-century successors, Golden Square, containing 'such houses as might accommodate Gentry', Soho Square, said in 1720 to be 'well inhabited by Nobility and Gentry', and Leicester Square, had all suffered a considerable social decline within two or at most three generations.[37] On the Earl of Burlington's estate (Cork Street and Savile Row area), where building had begun at about the same time as on the Grosvenor estate, the process took a little longer, but substantial change had nevertheless taken place by 1850.[38] On the other hand, Berkeley Square, Cavendish Square, Portman Square and above all St. James's Square (built as long ago as the 1660's and 70's) had retained their original social character largely unchanged. These varying fortunes suggest that favourable topographical situation and the absence of adverse social influences from surrounding areas were of more importance in preserving the original social quality of an estate than either the terms of land tenure at the time of first building or the watchful management of a ground landlord intent on maintaining the value of his property.

The Last Hundred Years

The census of 1871 was taken about a decade before the commencement of the period of greatest change in the whole history of the Grosvenor estate in Mayfair since its first development for building. The widespread rebuildings initiated by the first Duke in the 1880's and 1890's have already been described from the historical viewpoint. Socially, they seem to have had two main effects—they increased the segregation both between class and class and between the private residents and the men of commerce; and they increased the proportion of private residents in a number of important streets on the estate, at least in part at the expense of the tradesmen.

These, at all events, are the impressions gained from such evidence—mainly the *Post Office Directories*—as is at present available. Sometimes they were the results of deliberate policies laid down by the Duke, and always they reflected the immiscibility of the numerous social gradations prevalent in the late Victorian and Edwardian world.

The provision of churches, schools, artisans' dwellings, a library and two public gardens, the removal of the work-house and the drastic reduction in the number of public houses, were all as much a part of the first Duke's achieve-ment as the replacement of hundreds of old and often dingy houses by solid expensive new ranges of shops and chambers and private dwellings. In many parts of the estate this tremendous tidying-up operation stamped Victorian social discipline and formality upon the more easy-going attitudes of earlier times, and even when it was not intentional, physical changes of this order of magnitude could not fail to produce correspondingly great social change as well.

The elimination of trade from certain streets or parts of them, and its concentration in others, were certainly intentional. This was done in Park Street, Green Street, Charles Street (now Carlos Place) and the western part of Mount Street which became exclusively residential, while shops were encouraged in South Audley Street.[39] Between 1871 and 1914 the number of both commercially and professionally occupied houses in the eastern part of Grosvenor Street was reduced, with a corresponding increase in private residence, and in Upper Grosvenor Street even the successful physicians and surgeons who had gained a foothold in the 1870's were eliminated. Only in the eastern part of Brook Street, where the proportion of commercial occupation increased between 1871 and 1914, did the Duke's separatist policies not prevail.[40]

Policies of this kind undoubtedly enjoyed the support of well-to-do residents, and after the first Duke's death in 1899 they were continued by his successor and his advisers. Some residents, indeed, notably those of Grosvenor Street and Park Street, were even successful in insisting that they should be adhered to in circum-stances in which the Estate Board would have preferred to relax them.[41]

The new buildings erected in the 1880's and subsequent years also had a marked effect on the social composition of the residents. The houses built in Green Street, the western part of Mount Street and in South Street (Nos. 39–47 odd) always found ready buyers,[42] but their high price restricted the market to purchasers with substantial means. And so too, in somewhat lesser degree, did the price of the new flats built over shops in such streets as South Audley Street and the eastern part of Mount Street. Wealth was what counted in the recruitment of residents, and even though the first and second Dukes both wanted to have what they regarded as 'small private houses' such as those in South Street, no concession was made to slender pockets, as Miss Walpole was crushingly informed when she inquired in 1895 'if it is the intention of the Duke to build middle class dwellings in South Street. She wishes to live near Farm Street Roman Catholic Church and the flats in Mount Street are too expensive.'[43]

As early as 1880 H. T. Boodle had foreseen that 'flats should be encouraged for the upper classes as well as the working classes as they are found of great use'.[44] At first these had been built over shops in the commercial streets, one of the earliest examples being Audley Mansions in South Audley Street of 1884–6 (Plate 33d). This type of building was evidently extremely successful, for it pro-vided a good address for both shopkeepers and private residents while keeping them quite apart from each other, the flats being approached by separate entrances. At corner sites, such as Audley Mansions, the private entrances could even be placed in a residential street (in this case the western part of Mount Street) while the commercial entrance could be at or round the corner in a shopping street.

By means of these large, carefully designed dual-purpose buildings the proportion of floor space in private use even in avowedly commercial streets could be sub-stantially increased. Although there is no firm evidence on this point, the internal disposition of the buildings themselves suggests that the shopkeepers now generally lived elsewhere instead of generally upstairs, as the census of 1871 (made before rebuilding) shows to have been hitherto the usual practice. Taking the number of entries in the *Post Office Directories* as a rough guide (the only one available) the proportion of tradesmen fell sub-stantially, and that of private residents rose correspond-ingly, between 1871 and 1914, in Mount Street, North and South Audley Streets and Duke Street. In Brook Street and Grosvenor Street (the whole of these streets on the estate being here considered) there were similar changes, though of lesser degree, and as we have already seen, trade was wholly excluded from Park Street, Green Street and the new Carlos Place. In about 1914, it may be hazarded, the private residents formed a larger proportion of the total population of the estate than ever before or since.

This increase finds indirect expression in the new social and financial origins of many rich residents willing and anxious to pay for a good address on the Grosvenor estate in late Victorian and Edwardian times—origins very different from those of the traditional landed aristocracy and gentry. Following the earlier example of the old-established brewers, it was now the turn of the new industrialists and capitalists, both native and foreign, to edge their way into even the innermost social sanctuary of Grosvenor Square itself, where at various times lived, for instance, Sir John Kelk the building contractor, Baron Furness the Hartlepool shipping magnate, Sir Edward Mackay Edgar the Canadian company director, Samuel Lewis the moneylender, and the financiers John Pierpont Morgan junior and Sir Ernest Cassel. In Park Lane lived two Duveens, in Park Street (in houses looking out across the garden of Grosvenor House to Hyde Park), two Rothschilds; and so on.[40]

It was in the houses of such people as these, and in those of such old families as were still able to afford to compete at the highest level in the fashionable world, that in the years before the war of 1914–18 the traditional social round of the London Season reached its last opulent and glitteringly artificial climax. Entry to and status within even the innermost circles could now generally be bought, for the cost in itself provided the necessary degree of exclusiveness. In 1905 Sir Ernest Cassel paid a premium of £10,000 for the renewal of the leases of Brook House, Park Lane, and the adjoining house, and spent £20,000 on adapting them to provide an appropriately magnificent setting for his receptions there, the proposed approach to the dining-room being specially designed 'level with the ground floor...(for the convenience of the King)'.[45] A few years later Mrs. Keppel, before starting to spend some £15,000 on the renovation of No. 16 Grosvenor Street, submitted her plans to the King, 'who had approved of them', but who probably only visited the house on a single occasion before his death in May 1910.[46] And from such central points as these a succession of ever-widening ripples spread out all over both the fashionable and the would-be fashionable worlds, powerful enough to confer a rent 'for the season' of up to £1,000 on even a house in noisy dusty Hereford Gardens.[47]

Matching the increased private residential use of parts of the estate after the great rebuilding was the apparent decline in the proportion of commercial use. If there were fewer businesses after the first Duke's reconstructions, it was, evidently, because the weakest had gone to the wall. In his evidence before the Select Committee of the House of Commons on Town Holdings, H. T. Boodle had said that 'in many cases of rebuilding it is impossible to let the old tenants rebuild. The tenants would not be equal to it', and he had admitted that compulsory displacements had been made.[48] These casualties had been amongst the little men (and women) with a shop or business at home or round the corner, and whose numbers (attested in the census of 1871) must have made much shopping and petty commerce so local in character before the rebuildings. The survivors, on the other hand, were the strongest and fittest—men like W. J. Goode, the South Audley Street china-dealer, whose business expanded from a single house (where he lived with his family)[49] to take in the whole frontage between South Street and the Grosvenor Chapel; or James Purdey the gunsmith, who after building his own premises in South Audley Street, was only too anxious to speculate elsewhere on the estate; or T. B. Linscott, the confectioner, whose shop in Oxford Street flourished greatly after he had reluctantly rebuilt it.[50] These were the men able to stimulate and then cater for the demands of a wealthy clientèle, primarily in the luxury and semi-luxury trades in which many of the shops of the area were now engaged. And in its hotels—now the other commercial speciality of the estate—the change from the old-fashioned comforts provided by William Claridge and Auguste Scorrier in adapted private dwellings to the discreetly spacious splendours newly built by Claridge's Hotel Company Limited and the Coburg Hotel Company Limited must have been just as great.

For the working-class residents on the estate the principal result of the first Duke's rebuildings was a great improvement in the standard of their housing. The blocks of artisans' dwellings built immediately south of Oxford Street, mainly between 1886 and 1892, provided new accommodation for nearly two thousand people—equivalent almost to fourteen per cent of the total population of the estate in 1871—and in the early years of the twentieth century the flats there were in very great demand, often from locally employed servants (butlers and valets in particular) and policemen.[51] In addition an unknown but very substantial number of residents in the mews were rehoused by the widespread rebuilding of coach-houses and stables in such places as Adams Row, Balfour Mews, Bourdon Street, Mount Row and Three Kings Yard. Some of these premises were of considerable size, space for six or seven stalls and three or four carriages being sometimes provided,[52] and even when complete rebuilding did not take place, tenants were often required, as a condition for the renewal of their leases, to execute extensive works of modernisation.[53]

Much of this great surge of improvement in the mews took place in the years immediately preceding the gradual eclipse of the horse by the motor car. By 1910 tenants on the estate were said to have a 'general desire to get rid of horses',[54] and the second Duke and his Board were granting increasing numbers of licences for the use of coach-houses and stables as garages. At about this time this process was taken a stage further by the occasional conversion of stables into dwelling houses, the first known example being at No. 2 Aldford Street in 1908;[55] and in later years the size and quality of these equine palaces was such that many of them proved well suited for adaptation to domestic use for residents no longer able or willing to live in a great house in one of the fashionable streets.

The outbreak of war in 1914 marked the commencement of fundamental changes in the social character of the estate. Throughout Mayfair as a whole the population had been falling slowly since as early as 1851, and although the first Duke's rebuilding may have temporarily reversed this process on the Grosvenor estate, numbers in Mayfair as a whole were again falling in the early twentieth century. For the estate by itself no reliable figures can be calculated for some sixty years after 1871, but during that period the resident population fell from 14,829 in 1871 to some 8,775 in 1931.* By 1961 it had declined still further to an estimated 4,354.[56]

It has already been conjectured that in the years before 1914 the private residents formed a larger proportion of the total population of the estate than ever before or since. Whether this conjecture is correct or not, the steep decline in the aggregate resident population reflects the great increase in the number of non-resident business users which has transformed the social make-up of the estate since 1914.

At the very top of the social scale the evidence of the *Post Office Directories* suggests that in the 1920's and 1930's there was little change in the number of peers, baronets, knights and other persons of title resident on the estate, despite the numerous new creations made in those years. The ritual of the social Season still continued, and in the unfashionable months cruises to the Mediterranean or the West Indies, or forays to shoot big game in Africa replaced the visits of earlier days to the German spas. But cocktail parties ('by far the cheapest way of entertaining') and 'Cheap cabarets and *intime* night clubs' were replacing the lavish private receptions of Edwardian times; and the prevalence of jokes about income tax collectors showed that it was now becoming 'almost a social stigma to be rich. It is fashionable to pretend to be poorer, not richer, than you are.'[57]

The lack of change in the number of residents of title obscures important internal changes, however. Old families were giving place to new, and by 1947 the titles of approximately half the peers resident on the estate had been created since 1900. Between 1921 and 1939 the Dukes of Portland and Somerset and Earl Fitzwilliam and the Earl of Durham all left Grosvenor Square, whilst the newcomers included two new barons (Illingworth and Selsdon). By 1939 four of the eight peers resident in the square lived in the new flats there, and the fifteenth Earl of Pembroke, one of whose eighteenth-century ancestors had had a house in the square, now lived in Three Kings Yard. In 1933 the first Viscount Furness left Grosvenor Square for Lees Place, and by 1947 even such a traditional grandee as the Duke of Sutherland had moved from Hampden House in Green Street to a flat in Park Lane.[40]

In addition to the continuing decline in their absolute numbers, many residents were thus occupying less space individually. By 1939 only about a quarter of all the houses in Brook Street, for instance, were still in private occupation, and a diagram prepared for *The Grosvenor Estate Strategy for Mayfair and Belgravia*, published in 1971, shows not a single building in the whole of either Brook Street or Grosvenor Street still in solely residential use.[58] By that time a substantial proportion of the surviving residents lived either in modern blocks of flats or in the mews and the lesser streets—Adams Row, Reeves Mews, Balfour Mews and Culross Street are cases in point—and Grosvenor Square itself could only be considered to be still predominantly residential by virtue of the two large hotels recently built there. The fall in the number of residents had, indeed, gone so far that throughout the whole estate only about one third of all the floor space was still, in 1960, in residential occupation[59]—a remarkable reversal of the traditional character of the area.

Some of the buildings hitherto in private use are now occupied by foreign diplomatic missions, for which imposing mansions provide an appropriate setting. In the eighteenth and nineteenth centuries embassies and legations had from time to time alighted for a while on different parts of the estate, but in 1910 there was only one—the Italian Embassy, then at No. 20 Grosvenor Square—and the permanent presence of a foreign diplomatic community here dates only from the 1920's. In 1921 there were seven embassies and legations (four of them in Grosvenor Square), but to-day there are nine, plus five high commissions and two consulates; and some of them are very large—notably the embassies of Egypt and the United States and the Canadian High Commission—and with their ancillary premises occupy more than one building.

A much greater proportion of the accommodation previously in private residential use had, however, been converted into offices, which in 1960 occupied about one third of all the floor space on the estate.[59] As early as 1929 *The Evening News* reported that 'Ancient families are leaving Mayfair and modern dressmakers or beauty or health specialists are arriving'; and 'a West End property expert' declared that Mayfair 'is going over to business as fast as it can...Not so long ago a large house... remained to let for a year without a single inquiry. At last a condition against the use of any part of it for business was withdrawn. It was snapped up then within the next 48 hours.'[60]

In the 1920's and 30's the Grosvenor Estate itself was 'strongly opposed'[61] to the spread of offices, but in 1934 the second Duke's advisers acknowledged that trade and business had for many years been moving westward, and in streets such as Brook Street and Grosvenor Street they had conducted a slow rearguard action, here and there permitting first a professional occupation (usually by a doctor or dentist), then an inconspicuous business (usually dressmaking) and finally, perhaps, a shop window. By 1939, however, this process had advanced a little further, for some of the doctors and dentists in their turn were beginning to move out of Brook Street and Grosvenor Street. Those that remained, instead of living there in individual houses as at first had been the practice, were congregating together in houses evidently

*The figure for 1931 is obtained by counting the number of resident voters contained in the electoral register and multiplying this figure by the factor of 1.505, provided by the Population Studies Section of the Greater London Council's Policy Studies and Intelligence Branch. The electoral registers cannot be satisfactorily used for this purpose prior to 1928, when women under thirty years of age were given the vote.

used only as non-resident consulting rooms, of which No. 86 Brook Street, for instance, contained some twenty sets. Even in Upper Grosvenor Street, where a few physicians and surgeons had again settled in the 1870's (only to be subsequently eased out again in favour of private residents), clubs, couturiers and other businesses began to appear in the late 1920's, soon after the building of the new Grosvenor House on the south side.

It was at this time of delicate transition that the impact of the war of 1939–45 tilted the balance heavily towards office use. During the war a number of buildings were requisitioned for this purpose, and after the destruction of large parts of the City of London by bombing, many businesses moved into the mansions of Mayfair, then often vacant through the departure of the residents to the country, and in rapidly changing social conditions no longer suitable for private occupation.[62] The Grosvenor Estate itself reversed its previous opposition to the growth of offices on its Mayfair properties, leaving Belgravia unchallenged as London's principal fashionable residential quarter. On the Mayfair estate the professions—no longer dominated by the doctors and dentists, who did not return in large numbers after the war of 1939–45—and the diplomats were joined by businessmen with either relatively small staffs or small headquarters staffs, all of whom required a prestigious address and often a sumptuous 'Board Room' office suite in an adapted Georgian or Victorian town house. Advertising and public relations firms (of which there were some thirty in 1965) found a natural milieu here; expensive restaurants did well, and many of the shops dealt in the fields of fashion or luxury. Despite this new emphasis on business and commerce the estate has thus maintained its traditional prestige; but in 1970 the *Post Office Directory* listed only one solitary duke as still resident there; and even the Duke of Westminster himself now lived in Belgravia.

The Architecture of the Estate

The Early Buildings

A glance at the map or a short walk through the district will show that the Grosvenors' Mayfair estate, with its regular grid of broad streets and narrow mews, conforms in layout and structure to the characteristic development patterns of early-Georgian London. But though some few surviving buildings still remain from that period, an equally casual inspection will reveal how much of the original basic stratum has been concealed, overlaid or obliterated. Nineteenth- and twentieth-century flats, shops, office blocks and hotels have taken over upon the peripheries of the estate, while its very centre of Grosvenor Square has been so thoroughly rebuilt that only the merest traces survive from the initial development there. The four main sides of the square, to follow this example further, are now nearly all given over to modern flats, hotels, and diplomatic buildings, with the exception of two embassies that occupy the only surviving 'houses', and even these houses (Nos. 4 and 38) are rebuildings or recastings of differing date, hardly related except in plot to the predecessors on their sites. Only along the four chief residential thoroughfares, Grosvenor, Upper Grosvenor, Brook and Upper Brook Streets and towards the bottom of South Audley Street, an outlying but always fashionable district of the estate, can the original Georgian fabric and character of the whole area be readily appreciated today.

Even here, as with the surviving houses of the square, qualifications have immediately to be made. Anywhere in these streets, what looks like a Georgian house may be only a Georgian façade; and, *vice versa*, what appears to be a Victorian or Edwardian rebuilding may just be a Victorian or Edwardian refronting. For throughout the smarter parts of the estate, one rich inhabitant has continually replaced another over the years; succeeding estate managers have, since the early nineteenth century, enforced a strict but variable set of demands for improvements (especially to fronts); and, latterly, there has occurred a near-universal change from single-family occupation to offices or flats. As a result, each and every house has been incessantly liable to refacing, internal alterations small and large, or complete rebuilding.

All this is a common pattern on London's older and larger leasehold estates, but it is particularly marked on the Grosvenor estate in Mayfair, for two perhaps connected reasons. One is that the district has never lost its high property values, nor since its construction fallen out of fashion; the other, that its acme of repute as an upper-class residential district was reached only quite recently, at the end of the last century and the beginning of this one. Viewed in this light, the older areas of the estate are a palimpsest, of no vast antiquity perhaps, yet subject to continual rewritings. What is remarkable is not so much that parts of the original are still decipherable, but that these should have so vividly affected, shaped and often fixed the labours of those that came after.

The method, organisation and chronology of the initial development on 'The Hundred Acres' have already been discussed in Chapter II. Something, too, has been said of the rationale of its plain and grid-like layout (Plate 1), evidently the work of the estate's first surveyor, Thomas Barlow. Ambitious in scale but aesthetically unadventurous, its chief debts were to its immediate predecessors and neighbours, Lord Scarbrough's Hanover Square development and the Cavendish-Harley estate north of Oxford Street, both of which schemes were initiated a little before development on the Grosvenor estate began in 1720.[1] The one obvious dramatic feature of Barlow's layout was, of course, Grosvenor Square— at 680 by 530 feet larger than any previous square laid out in London. In plan it had resemblances to Cavendish Square (c. 1719–24), the first London square to incorporate two roads at precise right-angles to each other running into the corners, thus making each side of the square in some degree a continuation of the grid of streets around it.[2] But in Cavendish Square this occurred in only the north-west and north-east corners, for on the south side the only road running out of the square did so from the middle, crossing Oxford Street and debouching into the north side of Hanover Square. Grosvenor Square takes the Cavendish Square principle to its logical conclusion, with two streets running into each corner, making eight altogether. But though the long north and south sides might naturally have been bisected by further streets running into the centre of the square, this was not done. The line of George Street (present-day Balderton Street) together with the passage known to have been projected from Providence Court into the middle of the north side of the square gives a hint that such a street may have been considered but abandoned.[3] If it had been cut through, the shorter frontages thus created would have lent themselves to expansive sites for individual noblemen's houses such as were encouraged in Cavendish Square. That some such scheme may seriously have been mooted is hinted at by the survival in the Grosvenor Office of a drawing (Plate 4a) showing neat plans and elevations for a large house on a corner site, bigger than anything ever built in

Grosvenor Square, with a 'front to ye square' of some seventy-five feet. Though there is nothing but its provenance to connect it with Grosvenor Square and it fails to fit any of the sites as actually developed, it may well be an early scheme for the west end of the north side, made at a time when palatial houses were possibly being contemplated. In style, this drawing with its distinctive pilasters and its aprons under the windows is much more consciously attuned to the English Baroque than anything actually built in the square, and has a flavour of the work of Thomas Archer (who did indeed have an interest on the north side of the square, though at the east end, on a site with which the drawing can have no connexion).

However, if this kind of scheme was ever seriously considered, it came to nothing. It may have been the difficulties encountered with individual noble lessees in Cavendish Square that helped to persuade Barlow and the Grosvenors to stick on all four frontages to the kind of terrace housing familiar from St. James's Square and Hanover Square, and now rising along Grosvenor and Brook Streets. This decision, together with the arrangement of streets at the corners, meant that Grosvenor Square was more integrated into the surrounding estate layout than any previous square in London. But to dispel just a little the insistent rectilinearity of the scheme, the building line on all four sides of the square was set back thirty feet from that of each of the incoming streets, as on the short sides of Hanover Square. This led to extra spaciousness in the square itself, and to the creation of four distinctive L-shaped corner sites; on one of these (Nos. 9 Grosvenor Square and 88 Brook Street in the north-east corner) something of the original fabric survives. Though the square was doubtless less easy to take in as a whole than is suggested by early engravings (Plate 5a), these corner sites must have helped to give to its peripheries some much-needed solidity, and thus contributed to its 'squareness'. In the centre, the oval garden probably had some slight softening effect upon the contours of the square, though the paths were strictly formal, the planting was minimal, and the whole scheme centred upon John Nost's gilded equestrian statue of George I in the middle. The garden layout (1725) was the work of the little-known John Alston; the traditional attribution to William Kent appears to have no basis.

One other obvious feature in the planning of the estate, also shared by the Hanover Square and Cavendish-Harley schemes, was the exclusion of its main public place of worship from the square. In any comparable French or Italian town-planning project of this date, a church or other public institution would have been the natural point of focus, but in England this was not the custom, despite the early precedent of St. Paul's, Covent Garden. St. George's, Hanover Square (1720–5), the parish church for the Grosvenor estate and a building with which Thomas Barlow was involved, had despite its importance been sited outside Hanover Square itself, rather as St. James's, Piccadilly, had been related to St.

James's Square some fifty years before. On the Cavendish-Harley estate, James Gibbs's Oxford Chapel (the modern St. Peter's, Vere Street) was situated well away from Cavendish Square and in no way emphasized. So too the Grosvenor Chapel was allotted an equally inconspicuous position in South Audley Street, though it did at least have the advantage of a vista along Chapel (now Aldford) Street. Nor can it have been deemed essential to the early success of development, for though it was projected from the start it was not built until 1730–2. At one stage indeed, Edward Shepherd thought of erecting a chapel in North Audley Street, again on a relatively modest site, but this came to nothing;[4] the Grosvenor Chapel, when built, became the estate's only place of established worship. Likewise, other special buildings, whether public or private, were equally slow to develop and tended to occupy peripheral sites. The layout, in fact, was designed with terrace housing alone specifically in mind, and it is the nature of this that must now be examined.

In the 1720's and 1730's it was not as yet feasible for a landlord to impose absolutely regular frontages upon the London speculative building lessees of the day. But if only because the Grosvenor estate was by far the biggest single area of high-class domestic building at the time, attempts were made here and there, notably in the square, to combine individual house fronts into the kind of disciplined architectural composition beloved of the Palladians. This has to be seen in perspective. Palladian ideals being as yet new in the 1720's, Barlow and the master builders who dominated the estate development still practised an architecture in the tradition of speculative building going back to the era of Nicholas Barbon fifty years before, but tempered by modest innovations from the school of Wren. Further, in conjunction with the short-lived period of the English Baroque, there appears to have been a reaction against uniformity of town-house fronts, especially for houses of the larger sort, and this was still reflected in the estate development. In Grosvenor Square, the only part of the area for which there is good evidence as to the original appearance of the houses, the variations were considerable. Some of them were due to the leasing history of the various plots, some to stylistic uncertainty following the onslaught of Palladianism, but some may have been the outcome of a conscious desire for variety. Almost certainly, the surrounding streets looked more uniform and more disciplined, but this would have been in the interests of economy rather than classicism. Nevertheless, the Palladian movement did have much influence on the estate. Colen Campbell, Roger Morris, William Benson, Thomas Ripley and Edward Shepherd, five important figures in the implementation of Palladian ideals, all had a hand in the development. Their precise involvement is specified elsewhere (see pages 20–2), but here something must be said of its nature and results.

It was upon Grosvenor Square that the new movement naturally concentrated its powers. Here Colen Campbell contributed in 1725 an intriguing but unexecuted design for the east side, known only from an engraving showing a front elevation and ground-floor plan of the whole composition (Plate 4b). The elevation presents a striking antithesis to speculative building traditions of the time: an absolutely even and symmetrical range dressed in the whole Palladian finery, with stone arches to the ground floor, first-floor balconies, an engaged order to the upper storeys, elaborate window dressings and balustrading with crowning statues masking the roof. The backs of the houses are shown on the plan as very curtailed but absolutely regular, while no allowance is made for the corner sites, so this was probably something of an ideal solution. Nevertheless John Simmons, the developer of the square's east side (Plates 5, 8a), did manage within the limits of a plain brick architecture to maintain the symmetry and regularity suggested by Campbell; he raised a central pediment and emphasized the ends, thus distinguishing the range from the rest of the square and other parts of the estate, and setting an important precedent for London street architecture.

Campbell was very likely involved in the two long sides of Grosvenor Square as well. A similar design of his for a block of three houses, perhaps for the south side, was again not followed, but on the north side the story is more intriguing. Though lavish in the scale of its houses, this side as built ended up as an irregular and frankly clumsy range because of the inclusion among its façades of two Palladian compositions with attached orders and pediments and, between them, a third less 'correct' interloper adorned with pilasters (Plate 5). Had these buildings balanced each other, all would have been well, but this they failed to do, thereby exciting the derision of acerbic critics such as James Ralph.[5] Close to the west end of the side Edward Shepherd's massive composition occupied three houses (Nos. 18–20, to follow modern numbering); near the middle, the pilastered part extended over two (Nos. 15 and 16), while to the right of centre there was just John Aislabie's elegantly pedimented house at No. 12 (fig. 2a), conspicuous amidst a run of otherwise orthodox fronts. Individually, Shepherd's development and the Aislabie house were of high merit, and since Colen Campbell had been patronised by Aislabie at Waverley Abbey and Studley Royal and was an associate of Shepherd's, he could have had some hand in either of these ambitious buildings. That a 'regular range' had at first been designed by Shepherd for the whole of the north side is claimed by Robert Morris,[6] and it would have been natural for Shepherd, though clearly the architect for his development, at least to consult Campbell. It may be no coincidence that the window surrounds on Campbell's surviving own house, the modest No. 76 Brook Street (fig. 2e), on a plot made available to him by Shepherd, appear to be similar in shape, character and material to the 'plaister' ones specified for Shepherd's Grosvenor Square houses.

So despite the participation of two experienced undertakers, Simmons and Shepherd, and the enthusiasm of Campbell, the pioneering Palladian, the attempt to build uniform classical frontages in the square met with very limited success. It was even harder where plots were parcelled out among different builders in smaller divisions. Outside the square, one such effort to impose a uniform frontage on a number of builders in Upper Brook Street as late as 1742 soon met with opposition and failed (see page 31). Normally, the different lessees and sub-lessees were building on plots of limited frontage with little or no restriction as to proportion and style, and so there was naturally opportunity for plenty of variation from house to house. Width of plot, height and number of storeys, proportions of windows, quality and type of brickwork on the front: all these features varied according to the position and status of the house in question (Plate 8b, c, e). The simple overall layout meant that these small tendencies to indiscipline were enlivening rather than disruptive, whereas an elaborate composition in town planning might have been wrecked by them.

Along the estate's chief streets and in most of the square, the effect was quite different from the monotonous regularity of later Georgian thoroughfares like Baker Street or Gower Street. Instead, the finished appearance must have consisted of variations upon the well-tried but ever fertile theme of flat, stock-brick fronts, of unpredictable width and slightly irregular height (fig. 2). Where two or more houses were undertaken together, there was sometimes no architectural break between them; more frequently, it was the practice to draw attention to the division by means of projecting brick piers or 'pilaster strips', a favourite device along the estate's main streets and one probably borrowed from the Hanover Square development. These curious strips, which can still be seen in places in Grosvenor Street, gave definition to the individual houses. Where adjacent plots were developed by a single builder, the strips would usually span the party wall. Elsewhere they were less formally organized, belonging sometimes to one house, sometimes to another (Plate 8c), and a few of the widest plots included two strips, to the deprivation of their narrower neighbours. Sometimes these strips were plain, sometimes rusticated like quoins. In the square itself, proper stone quoins were common (Plate 8a), but this seems to have been infrequent elsewhere, though there are surviving examples at No. 16 Grosvenor Street and Nos. 35–36 Upper Brook Street (Plate 6b; fig. 2f). At the ends of these unevenly divided but otherwise flat-fronted ranges, it became a charming habit to give the return frontages to some of the corner houses delightful bay windows or other features to the upper storeys, carried out on piers or pillars and sometimes projecting right over the pavement. Though the only examples that survive are those at Nos. 9 and 71 South Audley Street (Plate 6d), these upper-storey projections (which may frequently have been early additions) were not uncommon, and were also to sprout here and there along the main frontages.

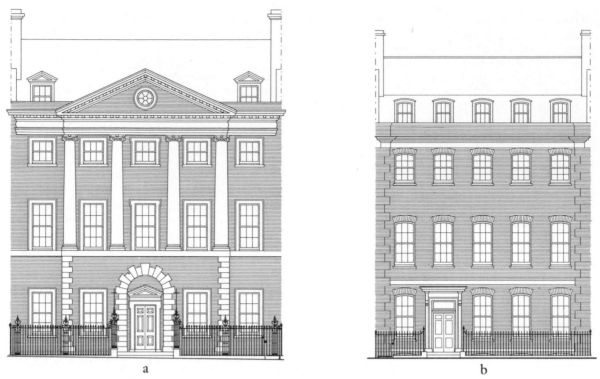

a   b

a. No. 12 Grosvenor Square. *Lessee*, John Kitchingman (timber merchant), 1727; *architect*, possibly Colen Campbell for John Aislabie, the first occupant. *Demolished*

b. No. 51 Grosvenor Street. *Lessee*, Israel Russell (painter), by direction of Benjamin Timbrell (carpenter), 1724

Fig. 2. EARLY-GEORGIAN ELEVATIONS

As for the fronts themselves, these were of anything between two and five windows' width. The windows generally were still segment-headed, with their wooden frames set well back in accordance with the Building Act of 1709, and their surrounds dressed liberally with red cutters and rubbers to set off the grey-brown of the stock bricks. Indeed many of the original fronts were probably quite colourful, to make up for the lack of stonework. Stone dressings were common only in the square and other special places; elsewhere, bold plaster cornices and wooden doorcases ruled the day. In height, there was rough uniformity along the main streets, but little attempt to make storey levels coincide. Three storeys above ground sufficed for Georgian wants, with a further one in the attic, usually with dormers perching over the cornice and set within a roof of double pitch, or more rarely treated as a fourth full storey flush with the front. The whole house would be raised upon a basement storey, its front area protected by stout iron railings (a feature often specified in the building agreements) and frequently containing an ornamental lead cistern.

Though none of these terrace fronts along the main streets remains absolutely unscathed, two sets of houses designed as pairs, Nos. 44 and 45 Upper Grosvenor

Street and Nos. 35 and 36 Upper Brook Street, are good but rather different types of survivors (Plate 6a, b; fig. 2f). Both pairs were built in two tones of brickwork; but in Upper Grosvenor Street the houses (*c*. 1727–31) have the segmental window heads and wooden doorcases typical of early development, whereas the later Upper Brook Street houses (*c*. 1737–42) adopt the embellishments by then familiar from the square, of string courses between the storeys, stone quoins, keystones, and rusticated door surrounds. All four of these houses have had balconies added and windows lengthened at first-floor level, and the Upper Grosvenor Street houses have been heightened. Similar changes have been made at Nos. 70 and 76 Brook Street, 51 Grosvenor Street, 10 and 13 South Audley Street, and 48 Upper Grosvenor Street, all terrace houses whose fronts still have much of their old character, without more than the most superficial admixture of stucco (fig. 2b–f).

Photographs of the lost Grosvenor Square houses confirm the slightly different picture there already suggested. The houses whose fronts survived best until the square's recent rebuilding were No. 1 on the east, Nos. 12, 14 and 17 on the north, No. 25 on the west, and Nos. 37, 44 and 46 on the south. But of this group, if those on the north

c. No. 48 Upper Grosvenor Street. *Lessee*, William Hanmer (esquire), 1727; *builder*, Robert Phillips (bricklayer)

d. No. 13 South Audley Street. *Lessee*, William Singleton (plasterer), 1736

e. No. 76 Brook Street. *Lessee*, Colen Campbell (architect), 1726

f. No. 35 Upper Brook Street. *Sub-lessee*, Anthony Cross (mason), 1737

and east side bear out the greater formality intimated in early engravings, the south side ones show the extent to which a pre-Palladian brick architecture continued even in the square. No. 44, one of a row of similar houses here, was particularly attractively organised, with the red dressings flanking the windows carried up without break between the floors to cornice level; this emphasized the pilaster strips at either end and gave the whole building a strong vertical accent, augmented by treating the attic as a full storey flush with the front (Plate 7).

The smaller residential houses of the estate have nearly all been demolished (Plate 8e). But the survivors show that they differed in scale and plan rather than in front from their superiors. A well-preserved group at Nos. 70–78 (even) Park Street, originally quite a respectable row of small houses and including an almost untouched façade at No. 72, gives an idea of the appearance of some of the secondary streets, a sequence of modest fronts in two tones of brick (Plate 8b). Further down the social scale, the disappearance has been total. Simplicity must have been the rule, since in many districts tenements with only a single room per floor were crammed into a riddle of back alleys, as in Brown's Court, Green Street, one of

the few places of this kind for which we have a reliable plan (see fig. 1 on page 32).

In general, most of the lesser houses on the estate followed the common London terrace plan. It is well known that in the late seventeenth century there evolved a standard arrangement for the smaller London terrace house, consisting of two rooms per floor, a dog-leg staircase rising alongside the back room and, often enough, an additional small rear parlour or closet facing the yard. This plan appears, for instance, throughout Nos. 70–78 (even) Park Street and in many places along the main streets where frontages were narrow (fig. 3a), but it could also be used outside a strictly residential context. At this period there were no special plans for shops, taverns or even small manufactories, and this established arrangement quickly proved itself both adaptable and economic. As a result the standard plan became the norm in streets of mixed character like Mount Street and Duke Street, where for over a century it steadily continued to perform the varied functions laid upon it.

But though this plan suited small houses, it would not do for the smarter parts of the estate, which abounded in generous frontages and deep plots leading right through to stables some 150 feet or more away. A separate servants' staircase was hard to include in the standard arrangement, and the areas of circulation and main stairs themselves tended to be cramped. Alternatives of several kinds were evolving for larger houses at the time the estate was being developed; consequently the individuality of the first-class Grosvenor estate house was more strikingly expressed in its plan than in its elevation (fig. 3).

Where a secondary staircase was felt to be *de rigueur*, the most fashionable plan, much employed on the recently built Burlington estate,[7] was to have a 'great stair' starting from the front compartment of the house inside the entrance hall and turning back towards the street, from which it was lit (fig. 3f). This staircase rose only to the first-floor reception rooms; the upper storeys were served by separate stairs (usually with a toplight high above) which was situated behind the great stair in the central or back compartment of the house and climbed most or all of the way from basement to attic. Houses of this kind were built throughout the square and surrounding streets where the plots were of thirty-foot frontage or over, allowing at least four windows towards the street, sometimes five, and therefore giving enough space for ample front rooms on ground and first floors beside the great stair. Examples with parts or more of the main stairs surviving can still be seen at Nos. 67 Brook Street, 34 and 59 Grosvenor Street (Plate 9b, d), and 14 and 74 South Audley Street, and plans remain of many other lost ones, e.g. at No. 43 Grosvenor Street (fig. 3f). It must have been a particularly common type in the square, but there documentation of the original plans is sadly scant.

Although this was the most distinctive and fully evolved type of plan for the larger terrace house, there were plenty of other options available. One was the central toplit staircase arrangement, whereby the entrance hall was left clear and the great stair, lit by a skylight high above, rose immediately behind to first-floor level, with the secondary staircase again behind that and sometimes relegated right to the very back of the house beyond a large reception room. The advantage of this disposition, which survives at No. 33 Grosvenor Street and can be clearly seen on plans of various demolished houses, for instance Nos. 43 and 45 Brook Street (fig. 3g, h), was to allow a large room facing the front at first-floor level, which compensated for loss of living space on the ground floor below. This plan was relatively novel when it first appeared on the Grosvenor estate, but was to grow in popularity throughout the eighteenth century; the lengthy rear wings often incorporated in such arrangements were commonly used as private suites, for the master of the house on the ground floor, for the mistress on the floor above. In its full form, the central toplit plan was again at its best for houses of four or five windows' width, but it could also be used in a curtailed version for those of three windows' width; in houses of this kind the need for a separate servants' staircase was beginning to be increasingly felt. A remarkable variant survives at No. 44 and originally existed also

at No. 45 Upper Grosvenor Street (fig. 3d), both three-bay houses, where the back stairs are in parallel to the main staircase, which is toplit from a low dome in the centre; this creates a fine effect but necessarily curtails the size of the rooms at front and back. In other houses of three windows' width, for instance No. 16 Upper Grosvenor Street (fig. 3b), the presence of a conventional dog-leg staircase did not inhibit the inclusion of a secondary one, placed behind the rear wing closet and accessible only through the back room on each floor. For houses on the estate without back stairs, a central staircase was also a common variant from the conventional type of plan, as it long had been. In various houses of lesser width of frontage like Nos. 10 and 73 South Audley Street and No. 38 Upper Brook Street (before alteration) the toplit stairs were thrust between front and back rooms with small closets or passages behind (fig. 3c). This was basically an old-fashioned arrangement, especially when the staircase was of the dog-leg variety, but it survived well into the 1730's and beyond.

Happily, there is good proof to show how heterogeneous the plans of the houses along the main streets really were. There survives at the Grosvenor Office a large body of ground-floor plans of individual houses, showing their state round about the beginning of the nineteenth century; these were made by William Porden and his assistants for the purposes of leasing, at the time that the estate management was being put upon a more professional footing. By this date many of the houses had already been altered, and as the drawings were done at different times they vary in detail and accuracy. But when used judiciously together with a survey made by Robert Taylor and George Shakespear in 1778-9 showing in detail the triangle within Davies Street, Grosvenor Street, and South Molton Lane/Avery Row (fig. 4), they demonstrate the variety of possible arrangement. For instance, the relative frequency of the three main plan types is given by the crude statistic that of some 120 fully enclosed terrace houses along Brook, Upper Brook, Grosvenor and Upper Grosvenor Streets for which the arrangement is known, 51 were of the conventional staircase type, 35 had their chief staircase in the front compartment, and 33 had some form of main central stairs. More sense can be made of these figures in terms of plot widths and the presence of secondary stairs. In Grosvenor Square, where frontages habitually exceeded thirty-five feet in breadth and had more than three windows, few if any houses had the conventional staircase arrangement, and none is known to have been without back stairs. In the surrounding streets, the houses of three windows' width and approximately twenty-five feet in frontage are the unpredictable ones. If they had back stairs, usually they adopted some form of main central staircase, but if they omitted back stairs, either the conventional type or a central staircase was possible. To sum up, a central staircase could be found in all kinds of houses, while a front compartment staircase tended to be reserved for those of

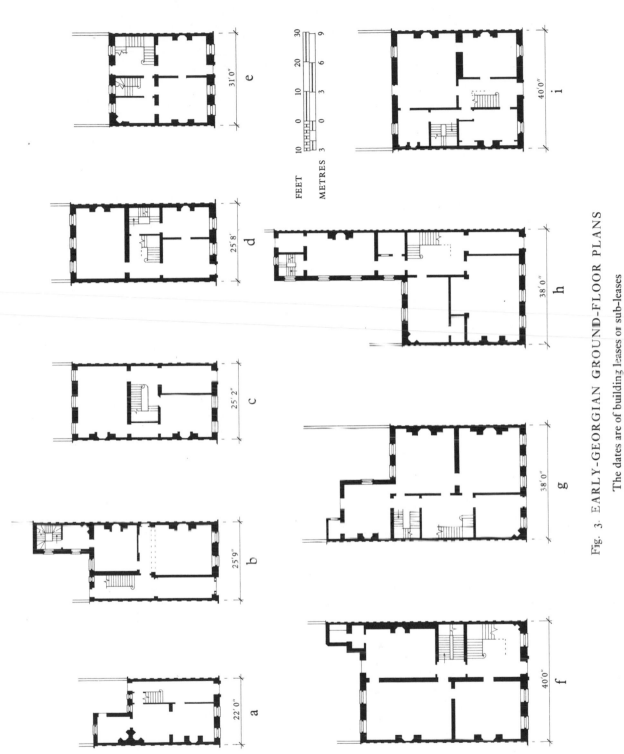
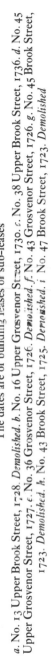

Fig. 3. EARLY-GEORGIAN GROUND-FLOOR PLANS

The dates are of building leases or sub-leases

a. No. 13 Upper Brook Street, 1728. *Demolished. b.* No. 16 Upper Grosvenor Street, 1730. *c.* No. 38 Upper Brook Street, 1736. *d.* No. 45 Upper Grosvenor Street, 1727. *e.* No. 36 Grosvenor Street, 1726. *Demolished. f.* No. 43 Grosvenor Street, 1726. *g.* No. 45 Brook Street, 1723. *Demolished. h.* No. 43 Brook Street, 1725. *Demolished. i* No. 47 Brook Street, 1723. *Demolished*

wide frontage and a conventional dog-leg staircase for narrow ones of three bays or less.

In houses of the largest size, the characteristics of the terrace house plan might be virtually lost and much of the spaciousness of the nobleman's free-standing town house could be obtained, despite enclosure. In examples like No. 47 Brook Street (with a frontage of forty feet but, curiously, only three windows towards the street) or No. 19 Grosvenor Square (five windows wide with a sixty-foot frontage), the entrance was in the centre of the façade, and the plan resolved itself into a series of separate but equal compartments *en suite*, with toplit stairs where required (fig. 3i). Despite the efforts of Simmons and Shepherd to create symmetrical compositions, this grandest of all the house types was the distinct exception, even in Grosvenor Square. Thus Isaac Ware, propagandizing in his *Complete Body of Architecture* on behalf of a Palladian programme for symmetrically planned town houses, found cause to complain of 'one very striking instance of placing the door out of the centre. This errs both in proportion and situation, and must be named as a caution to the young builder. The house is in Grosvenor Square; the edifice is large and conspicuous, but one is puzzled to find which is the way into it. It appears a house without a door, and when the eye is cast upon the little entrance at one side, one scarce knows how to suppose it is the door to that house; it seems to belong to the next.'[8]

An analysis of the plan types and plot widths offers no logical answer to the question of why small and large houses were so closely intermingled along the four main streets. In Grosvenor Street there was some tendency for the grander houses to be sited nearer the square, and there were few plots in Upper Brook Street and Upper Grosvenor Street with the width of frontage sometimes found in Brook and Grosvenor Streets, but to both these rules there are exceptions. The size of houses erected in any one area depended upon the inclinations, capacities and ambitions of the developers, especially when they were taking large plots, and not upon any clear conception on the part of Thomas Barlow or any other officer of the estate. To take one instance visible on the 1778-9 survey plan mentioned above (fig. 4), the north side of Brook Street between Davies Street and South Molton Lane was taken in 1720 by Henry Avery and Robert Pollard as one lot. Fifteen small houses, nearly all of conventional plan and probably of quite uniform appearance, were built here, though scarcely anything of them survives today. Yet immediately opposite on a strip of similar length along the south side of Brook Street, the land was divided between several undertakers; here only eleven houses were built, but these were of greater size and varying plan. The rich and the not-so-rich were therefore staring each other in the face, a situation which had polarized by the 1780's, when the majority of the houses on the north side

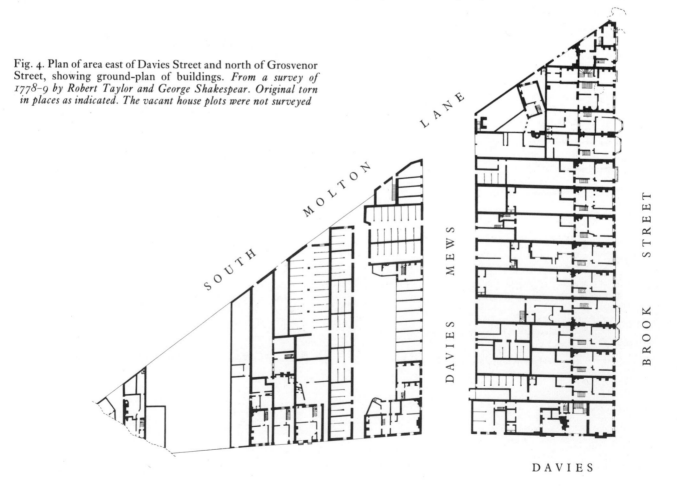

Fig. 4. Plan of area east of Davies Street and north of Grosvenor Street, showing ground-plan of buildings. *From a survey of 1778-9 by Robert Taylor and George Shakespear. Original torn in places as indicated. The vacant house plots were not surveyed*

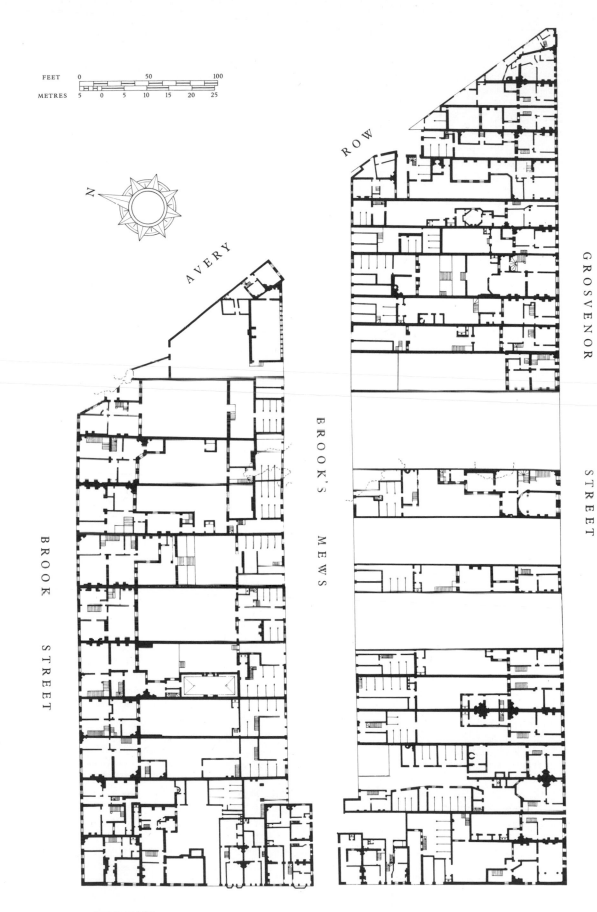

FEET 0 50 100

METRES 5 0 5 10 15 20 25

N

AVERY ROW

GROSVENOR STREET

BROOK'S MEWS

BROOK STREET

STREET

were occupied by tradesmen. In 1805, when William Porden was asked to consider the conversion of one of the south side houses into a hotel, he reported that the good houses here were neither so fashionable nor so profitable as they ought to have been, because of the proximity of lesser ones.[9] There was a similar contrast (though less sharp) in Grosvenor Street east of Davies Street, where most of the houses on the north side were smaller than those on the south. Why the better class of house in the eastern parts of both these streets occupied the south sides we do not know. In Upper Brook and Upper Grosvenor Streets, nearly all the houses had frontages of between twenty and thirty-five feet and there was much less unevenness between the sides.

Despite the remains of much original work here and there, a clear idea of how the interiors of these houses first appeared or how they functioned is hard to come by. In view of later attempts, often successful, to convey a 'period' authenticity in their redecoration, the nature of the original schemes cannot easily be seen objectively. The evidence of memoirs and correspondence is scanty, building accounts rarely survive and are even less frequently helpful; early inventories, however, are not so uncommon, and have been much depended upon for what follows.

From our review of its planning, it is plain that the early Georgian first-class terrace house on the Grosvenor estate was rarely a composition of great formality. One reflection of this is the nomenclature of rooms, which were most often designated not by their function but by their position or sometimes by their embellishment. On the ground floor were the parlours, usually 'fore parlour' and 'back parlour', the normal focus of private family activity. At first-floor level the front room, especially if it was at the head of a 'great stair', might be the grandest room of the house in which guests were received and entertained. More remarkably, the 'eating room' was often also at this level. It was certainly so at Handel's house, just off the estate at No. 25 Brook Street;[10] inventories of 1757 and 1772 show dining-rooms at first-floor level at Nos. 9 and 6 Grosvenor Square respectively;[11] and in 1756 Isaac Ware takes it for granted that the dining-room of an ordinary house would naturally come over the hall.[12] Still, by the mid century, dining-rooms were sometimes at ground level, more often at the front. Thus at No. 29 Grosvenor Square, a schedule of 1746 mentions one on the first floor, but by 1757 it has descended to ground level.[13] In the best houses, this change meant the re-organization of the ground-floor parlour so as to make a capacious room with a recess or sometimes a screen of pillars marking off the serving area, thus often curtailing the back room behind (figs. 3h, 4). By 1800 many of the houses on the estate had been altered in this way, but it is a moot point whether in some the change did not take place shortly after completion; at No. 50 Grosvenor Square, a surviving set of what appear to be very early plans already shows this arrangement.[14]

A dining-room on the first floor must have meant a long trek from the kitchen; this was most frequently in the basement along with the other 'offices' and normally faced the front area. But in at least one of the larger Grosvenor Street houses (on the site of the present Nos. 71–72), it had already been relegated from the start to a position 'away from the house',[15] and a similar arrangement, found at No. 16 Grosvenor Street in about 1763, was probably also original.[16] Such a long separation of kitchen and dining-room was inconvenient to gentry as well as to servants, who must have had to cross some of the important public spaces with hot dishes and dirty plates. But it seems not to have troubled the Georgian builders, or the inhabitants of their houses, still content to live at close quarters and without complete privacy.

The houses were certainly very fully occupied at certain seasons. In 1763 Lady Molesworth's reputedly 'small' house at No. 49 Upper Brook Street burnt down one night (a peril to which early Georgian town houses, with their stud partition walls, their wooden stairs, and their stretches of panelling, were prone). Horace Walpole says that seven inhabitants perished, another account claims ten, but certainly several escaped. This means that there were probably some fifteen people in the main house, though admittedly at a time when there were visitors, since Lady Molesworth 'to make room had taken her eldest daughter, of 17, to lie with her' in the front room on the second floor (a casual, crowded arrangement which would have been avoided at a later period).[17] Again, when in 1726 Sir Thomas Hanmer moved into his new house at No. 52 Grosvenor Street, one of the district's largest, it appears that he had at least fourteen servants (mostly male) in and around the house, besides his wife and family. But if these houses were intensively used, that was not the case all the year round. Hanmer's accounts show him, with fair regularity, living in Grosvenor Street between November and May and moving to the countryside for the rest of the year.[18] From the architectural point of view this seasonal migration meant that for some five months of the year the houses were merely looked after by servants, and therefore there was ample time and scope for the decorative improvements that were so frequently demanded, right from the early days of the estate's history.

There must always have been a wide variety in the degree and elaboration of internal finishing in these early houses. One useful hint for interpreting their original quality is the mix of panelling and plaster. The basic material was of course panelling, and on moving into her new house in Grosvenor Street (on the site of Nos. 71–72) in the early 1720's Lady Hertford was pleased to report 'that (except the garrets) there is not a corner unwainscotted'.[15] But though panelled interiors were practical, they were not in any way special. Many quite modest houses, for instance Nos. 7 and 8 Upper Brook Street or Nos. 70 and 74 Park Street, retain much panelling, while some of the more luxuriously appointed ones such as Nos. 71, 73 and 74 South Audley Street have, and probably always had, little (Plate 10a): prosaically enough, an early inventory of No. 45 Grosvenor Square records in the garden a wainscotted 'Boghouse'.[19] In fact deal panelling without any mouldings ('square work') could be cheaply run up and was regularly used in attics and up to dado level in basements. It could be framed directly on to internal brickwork, or be attached to studs to make thin partition walls not bearing any load. On the main floors, it would be more or less elaborated, with at the simplest a 'quarter-round' or 'ovolo' moulding (often carved with egg and dart) framing the panels, which were set back from the stiles and characteristically rose high in proportion to their breadth. One better than this was the raised and fielded panelling that formed the wainscotting of the parlours in the best houses. These were the two basic types of good panelling, which though subject to variation are nevertheless distinguishable from later imitations. The cornices in panelled rooms of high quality would include a run of egg and dart or of modillions; on bedroom floors, wooden box cornices seem to have been the norm.

However this wainscotting was originally treated, it is clear that at least in the best houses it was primarily regarded as a background to other things. Most of it was made from imported deal, which was very nearly always painted, and sometimes grained to look like oak. The tone of the painting remains a difficulty but light colours seem to have been the commoner. Ware must have been thinking of white or cream when he spoke in 1756 of panelling 'painted in the usual way' as lighter than stucco,[20] and in 1769 the building agreement for Lord Bateman's house in Park Lane (later Somerset House) specified that the main rooms should be left a dead white but the bedroom floor and attics a stone colour, presumably as a basis before the upholsterer moved in.[21] Later in the century, shades of green were popular for panelling and by 1800 stronger tones were frequent. But whatever its tone, the panelling served chiefly as a background for broad, brightly coloured areas of fabric, with mirrors ('pier glasses') frequently interspersed in between. Thus Sarah, Duchess of Marlborough, in 1732 tells her grand-daughter, then about to move into No. 51 Grosvenor Street: 'Though several people have larger rooms, what you have is as much as is of any real use to anybody, and the white painting with so much red damask looks mighty handsome. All the hangings are up in the four rooms above stairs except some pieces that are to be where the glass don't cover all the wainscott, and I think that will look very well.'[22] Thus too in an inventory of 1767 for No. 18 Grosvenor Square the bedrooms, which were probably panelled from head to foot, were called after their hangings and soft furnishings in general: 'green silk damask bedchamber', 'printed cotton bedchamber', 'green harrateen bedchamber' and 'blue mohair bedchamber'.[23] Such names reveal the crucial, sometimes tyrannical, part played by the upholsterer in finishing these houses. Little is known of the men who originally furnished the great Grosvenor estate houses, but of their successors there will be much to say.

Panelling apart, the joiner was of course responsible for doors, which on the main floors might have pediments and friezes, and occasionally for chimneypieces. But fireplaces were basically part of the mason's job, a point on which the early inventories are surprisingly unanimous. The good houses usually had marble fireplaces, often of no great pretension, right through to bedroom level, with Portland stone equivalents in the basement and the 'garrets'; the lesser houses were content with ordinary stone chimneypieces throughout. Perhaps because of their simplicity, few of these remain in either marble or stone; later accounts for Grosvenor Square mention the replacement of fireplaces with particular frequency. The characteristic early Georgian high chimneypieces have also rarely survived in their entirety, though there are wooden examples at No. 71 South Audley Street (Plate 10a) and a more elaborate one of marble below and plaster above on the first floor at No. 66 Brook Street (Frontispiece). This type of fireplace must have meant calling in a skilled carver or statuary specially for this task; thus Hanmer employed Rysbrack for a lost fireplace at No. 52 Grosvenor Street.[18]

Some elaborate survivals suggest that the plasterers were particularly active on the Grosvenor estate. To a degree their trade overlapped with that of the carpenters, since cornices could be of wood and walls could be panelled but either feature could be plastered instead. They may even in places have encroached upon the traditional spheres of other tradesmen. Because the houses were built by a mutual system of sharing jobs and bartering in labour, there had to be co-operation between the trades, but the actual lessee presumably had the final say as to the permanent finishings of his house and would naturally bias them in favour of his own craft. Certainly stucco was already gaining ground on the fronts of houses, especially where plasterers like Edward Shepherd were involved. For his group of houses at Nos. 18–20 Grosvenor Square (Plate 5), Shepherd agreed in 1728 to execute all the 'Plaistering worke of the front...(Vizt) The Intableture Rustick Story Cellar Story and ornaments to Windows',[24] and though exterior stuccowork remained unreliable in quality for fifty years and more after this, it is likely that several other houses on the estate took advantage of the material. Similarly, quite a few surviving interiors of quality can with fair certainty be ascribed to Shepherd, one of the most prolific and individual of the original developers, or to craftsmen close to him. These are Nos. 66 Brook Street, 72 Brook Street (for a time Shepherd's own house), 12 North Audley Street, and 71, 73 and 74 South Audley Street, all in a block taken by Shepherd and let to him and his associates. On the other side of South Audley Street five further houses, Nos. 9, 10, 12, 13 and 14, retain interesting ornamental plasterwork; here the plasterer William Singleton, of whom little is known, was one of the lessees.

What all these houses have in common is a series of entertaining decorative ceilings (fig. 5). More unusually,

◄ c

Fig. 5. EARLY-GEORGIAN PLASTER CEILINGS

a. No. 12 South Audley Street, ground-floor front room. *Lessee*, William Singleton (plasterer), 1737. *b*. No. 73 South Audley Street, ground-floor back room. *Lessee*, John Shepherd (plasterer), 1736. *c*. No. 74 South Audley Street, ground floor, main back room. *Lessee*, Edward Shepherd (esquire, formerly plasterer), 1736. *d*. No. 34 Grosvenor Street, over main staircase. *Lessee*, Richard Lissiman (mason), 1725

many of them also have interesting plasterwork to the walls as well. Nos. 12, 71 and 73 South Audley Street share in many of the principal rooms the characteristic of eccentric sunk plaster wall panels with shouldered heads (Plate 10a). These, clearly the plasterer's equivalent to wainscotting, were meant to receive pictures and hangings. Sunk plaster panels occur again at No. 66 Brook Street on the walls and ceilings of the ground-floor front room, as part of a more elaborate composition including pilasters, flowerpieces, and ornamental cartouches destined for 'pier glasses'. This house undoubtedly contains the finest of all Shepherd's surviving interiors on the estate, for besides this room there is a plaster-vaulted staircase (Plate 9a) leading on the first floor to a splendid and festive apartment, long recognized as one of the best Baroque interiors in London. It boasts elaborate doorcases, engaged Corinthian columns on all sides and, as a climax, an exuberant double-storey chimneypiece, marble below and plaster above, with a standing *putto* set in relief in the upper part (Frontispiece).

The surviving ceilings and staircase decorations of Shepherd and his circle show that, left to their own devices, they expressed themselves with an almost rustic floridity. This was not uncommon at the time, even with quite Palladian houses. William Kent was a fertile and frequently unclassical designer of ornament, and even true Italian *stuccadori* like Bagutti (who is known to have worked on the lost staircase at No. 52 Grosvenor Street[18]) could produce ceilings bordering on the quaint. This rampant style of plasterwork is well shown in four fine surviving ceilings at No. 73 South Audley Street, where Shepherd's brother John, also a plasterer, was the lessee (fig. 5b). They are highly compartmentalized compositions, relatively flat in relief; but within its borders each compartment breaks out into a rash of arabesques and strapwork patterns, with the occasional naturalistic flowerpiece or portrait medallion reserved for the sides or corners. The manner is too stiff to be connected with the real Rococo that was shortly afterwards to triumph in the great London *palazzi* of Chesterfield House or Norfolk House, and it may in part reflect surviving plasterers' traditions from an earlier period. This is not to say that Edward Shepherd could not turn out disciplined, dignified plasterwork when required to. The vaulting over the stairs at No. 66 Brook Street (Plate 9a), perhaps done specially for Sir Nathaniel Curzon, and the ceilings at No. 74 South Audley Street, originally the Portuguese ambassador's house (fig. 5c), are at once deeper in relief, severer in conception, and more gracious than his average production. Still more 'correct' is the plasterwork in the long gallery at No. 12 North Audley Street, the house that Shepherd probably built for Lord Ligonier and one of the outstanding survivals on the estate (Plate 11). Here Ligonier had a tripartite single-storey gallery built for himself at the back, very possibly designed by the Irish architect Edward Pearce; but though its proportions, plaster vaulting and engaged

columns show a restraining hand at work, there are still traces of Shepherd's florid manner. At No. 72 Brook Street, his own house, some hint of his idiosyncrasies also survives, despite much alteration. It should be added that Shepherd can have had no monopoly of high-class plasterwork. The two houses leased to William Singleton at Nos. 12 and 13 South Audley Street included accomplished plaster decorations (Plate 9c; fig. 5a), while much elaborate work of which we now know nothing must originally have been executed for houses in Grosvenor Square.

The last feature of these early Mayfair interiors that remains to be singled out is the treatment of the 'great stair'. As the most formal part of the house, the staircase had to be handled with fitting pomp. Up to this time, main staircases in enclosed town houses had usually been of wood, but the Grosvenor estate shows the joiner beginning to give ground to the mason and the smith. Here they were often built of stone, the steps cantilevered out from the wall and cut away on their undersides, with hand-wrought iron balustrades in simple, attractive patterns (fig. 6). There are good surviving examples in each of the three traditional staircase positions at Nos. 33 and 34 Grosvenor Street (Plate 9b; fig. 6c, f) and No. 16 Upper Grosvenor Street (fig. 6d). With a front compartment staircase, this might make part of a considerable architectural composition. Over the stairs would come an ornamental plaster ceiling (Nos. 14 and 74 South Audley Street, 34 and 59 Grosvenor Street, 20 Upper Brook Street), or even a plaster vault (No. 66 Brook Street). Sometimes this plasterwork was extended to the walls, as at No. 13 South Audley Street, where the decoration has been comparatively recently destroyed (Plate 9c). An inventory records similar treatment at No. 6 Grosvenor Square, and at No. 34 Grosvenor Street the lessee Richard Lissiman agreed in 1728 with Sir Paul Methuen, the intending occupant, 'to wainscoat the Staircase with Oak, in the same manner as the Staircase is wainscoated, in the house where Sir Thomas Hanmer now lives [No. 52 Grosvenor Street]. And...to cover all that part of the Staircase and Sealing above it, that is plaisterd, with Ornaments of Stucco, to the Satisfaction of Sir Paul.'[25] However this was evidently not done in exact accord with the agreement, for the surviving staircase at No. 34 Grosvenor Street, a fine and authentic example, is wainscotted from head to toe in elegantly elongated panels, with the plasterwork confined to the ceiling (fig. 5d).

Another and more dramatic alternative was to fresco the stairs. How common this was we do not know, but it was probably fairly regular in the 1720's and 1730's, having been done often enough in country houses since 1660, and having acquired a new impetus in London after William Kent painted the great stair at Kensington Palace. It certainly required craftsmen of ability, but they are usually anonymous. Israel Russell, a 'painter-stainer' who was one of the original lessees of some of the houses, may have specialized in this direction; another

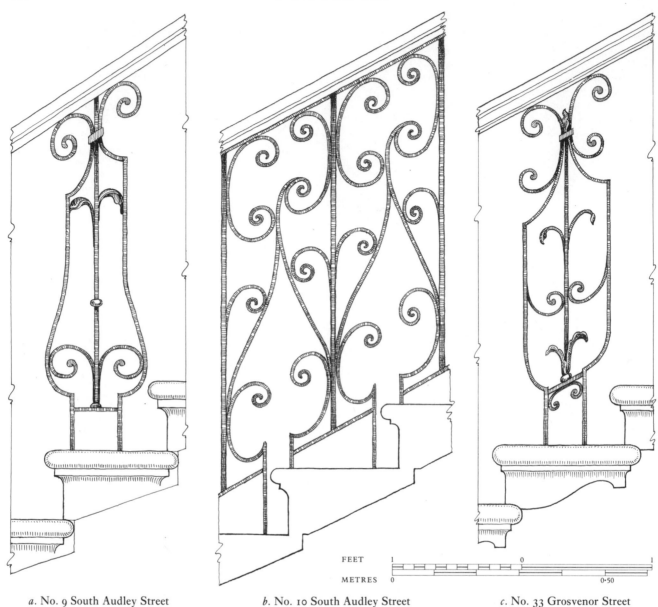

FEET

METRES

a. No. 9 South Audley Street　　　　*b*. No. 10 South Audley Street　　　　*c*. No. 33 Grosvenor Street

Fig. 6. WROUGHT-IRON BALUSTRADES FROM EARLY-GEORGIAN STAIRCASES

possibility is Mark Antony Hauduroy, who had worked with Shepherd at Chandos House and lived in one of his houses at No. 11 North Audley Street. A charming figurative staircase mural, found at No. 44 Grosvenor Square, was removed to the Victoria and Albert Museum before the destruction of that house. An attribution of this fresco has been made to John Laguerre, son of Louis Laguerre, and seems the more convincing in so far as an inventory of 1750 for No. 48 Grosvenor Street informs us that the 'Great Stair Case' was 'Wainscotted Rail'd high with Oak and the rest painted in a Composed Order with figures and Trophies done by John Legare'. Several of the other houses, especially in the square, must have

had painted staircases, though none survives; besides those mentioned, inventories allude to long-lost examples at Nos. 45 Grosvenor Square and 29 Grosvenor Square, the latter 'painted in Architecture and History'.[26]

To round off this discussion of the interiors of the great Grosvenor estate houses, the reader is referred to Appendix II, where he will find the full text of one of the several inventories mentioned above, that of 1733 for No. 45 Grosvenor Square. This will provide some idea of the typical positions, names and uses of the smaller rooms, as well as of the basic fixtures and fittings of such a house.

A few general comments can be added about the gardens

d. No. 16 Upper Grosvenor Street *e.* Dudley House, Park Lane (basement stairs, *f.* No. 34 Grosvenor Street
 from older house)

of these large houses. Sutton Nicholls's engraving of Grosvenor Square (Plate 5a) gives an idealized representation, showing in each back garden numerous straight gravel walks enclosing small grass plots or flower beds, with espaliered fruit trees against the walls, a few minor shrubs here and there, and the occasional architectural feature at the back to disguise a stable block. Though this picture of seventeenth-century formality may be misleading in many respects, it demonstrates that these town-house gardens were no mere plain and functional backyards. Even where a basement extended behind the main house, a proper garden could from early on be had, as an inventory of 1799 for No. 16 Grosvenor Street

shows; here the yard is described as 'covered with Lead Clayed and Gravelled for Garden'.[27] Yet another inventory, this time of 1742 for a house on the south side of Grosvenor Street, shows that the 'features' too were no mere figment of the imagination, for here there could be found 'an Alcove at the end of Garden after the dorick order covered with lead, the alcove back and sides wainscotted quarter round and raised pannells with a seat, Portland pavement before ditto'.[28]

Flowers in abundance were certainly common and, as time went on, so were fair-sized trees. Sir Thomas Hanmer's accounts of 1726–9 for No. 52 Grosvenor Street itemize several payments for tending flowers to gardeners (one of whom was French), and include a note to pay one man more 'when the flowers appear to be right in number and kinds'.[18] So too in 1734 Mrs. Delany, keeping her provincial sister up to date with details about her modest (but surviving) house at No. 48 Upper Brook Street, could write: 'You think, madam, that I have no garden, perhaps? but that's a mistake; I *have one* as big as your parlour in Gloucester, and in it groweth *damask-roses*, *stocks* variegated and plain, some purple, some red, *pinks*, *Philaria*, some dead some alive; and *honeysuckles* that never blow'.[29] And in 1748 Fanny Boscawen of No. 14 South Audley Street was boasting that 'my garden is in the best order imaginable, and planted with 100 shrubs and flowers'. Half a century later, still living in the same house, Mrs. Boscawen could in the more picturesque spirit of the age go further: ''tis well I have some trees, whose leaves wave close by me, and that about me I behold purple lilacs, white lilacs, and yellow laburnums in my own or my neighbours' gardens, and no bricks or tiles'.[30] How mature Mrs. Boscawen's trees were is hard to say, but they were probably bigger than the trees which in 1763 William Chambers was advising his client at No. 25 Grosvenor Square to trim and nail up against the wind, in a garden which contained wooden 'lattice work', that is presumably trellises for espaliers against the walls.[31] So from quite early days, there was a fair amount of variety, colour and greenery in all these gardens and by the end of the eighteenth century precious little austerity, if the Boscawen case is at all typical.

Finally, something must be said of the few larger buildings that interrupted the estate's original pattern of regular terrace housing. Here and there, especially west of Grosvenor Square, a few individual houses of size did spring up. Among these, pride of place must go to the freestanding house built in about 1730 for Lord Chetwynd in Upper Grosvenor Street near its west end. Though it was to become the future Grosvenor House little is known of its original appearance, except that Porden characterized the interiors as being in 'a heavy, antiquated, but respectable stile'.[32] This was written in 1805, just before the Grosvenors began their transformation of the house; at that time it was a sizeable, symmetrical villa in plan, set back some ninety feet from the south side of the street at the rear of a court with a narrow street entrance. In this respect it was like some of the large noblemen's houses that still in part survive on the north side of Piccadilly, but instead of having office wings flanking the court, the side plots were let off, so that the house must have been inconspicuous from the street. In the later eighteenth century other big houses were to be built close to the park in this western sector, but for nearly thirty years Lord Chetwynd's house stood alone.

For the largest surviving individual house of early date on the estate one must look further north, to No. 61 Green Street, later known as Hampden House. This was the home of the Palladian architect Roger Morris. Of the Palladians who were involved in the estate development,

Colen Campbell has already been discussed; Thomas Ripley built a very large house that survives in altered form at No. 16 Grosvenor Street but does not seem to have varied greatly in elevation from the estate norm; and William Benson may have been responsible for two small lost houses in Grosvenor Street of which, however, little is known. But Morris was evidently more ambitious on his own behalf. The result was the big brick house and spacious garden, dating from 1730, that survive at the east end of Green Street. This was then a relatively open position, with a few sizeable houses nearby in North Audley Street, some smaller but seemingly detached houses mainly belonging to other builders on either side of Morris's plot, and empty land close by on the north and west. It is now a gaunt and much altered building on both elevation and plan, but the slightly recessed wings and high central rooms of this seven-bay house still bear witness to Morris's ambition and wealth. By contrast, at the south end of Davies Street stands a much quainter survival, Bourdon House (Plate 12a). Built in about 1721–3 and therefore one of the earliest of houses on the estate, it still despite alterations and an added top storey keeps its modest brick character, with a south-facing pediment looking down on what must once have been the main approach, through a rather deeper front garden than now exists. Within, the interior has retained an early Georgian flavour almost better than any other house on the estate, and there is some excellent original woodwork in the 'ante-dining room' (Plate 10b).

These are the main early houses independent of any terrace arrangement of which something is known. There is little to add about the estate's few public buildings. Since there was originally no market, these really comprise only two, the parish workhouse that stood until 1886 on the south side of Mount Street, and the Grosvenor Chapel in South Audley Street. The workhouse, erected by Benjamin Timbrell and Thomas Phillips in 1725–6, was a functional and capacious building which could accommodate 160 persons and ran to no elaboration except a central cupola. The chapel (Plate 12b; fig. 7), erected in 1730–1, also involved Timbrell (with Robert Scott as fellow carpenter and William Barlow senior as bricklayer), and this is the more interesting since it bears distinct resemblances to James Gibbs's Oxford Chapel (St. Peter's, Vere Street) on which Timbrell had worked a few years before. Both are simple auditoria of similar length having galleries on three sides, with groined plaster vaults over the aisles and a curved ceiling to the nave, and on the outside two tiers of windows along the sides, and pedimented and turretted western features. A comparison is instructive, as it shows the difference in fluency between the work of the specialist architect and that of the master builder; but though the Grosvenor Chapel is second best in most respects and has been more altered than St. Peter's, its quaint steeple at the termination of Aldford Street provides one of the few minor features of town planning in the estate layout. Of original interior

FEET 10   0   10   20   30

METRES 3   0   3   6   9

Fig. 7. Grosvenor Chapel, west front as originally built in 1730-1

fittings it still retains its old stairs to the gallery, some pleasant panelling and plasterwork, an organ and a pulpit, but much else has been changed in subsequent restorations.

First Changes

Since the plots at the western end of the Mayfair estate were slow to let, a date at which the original development was finished is hard to pinpoint. Beyond Park Street building proceeded very spasmodically, especially in the north-west. Though little of the old fabric in this sector survives in recognizable form, one or two characteristics can be determined. Where rows of houses were built, they deviated little from the norm. Park Lane, then an unimpressive thoroughfare with a high wall on the park side, was reached at one point by the early 1730's, when King's Row, an ordinary set of small houses, was built at the end of Upper Grosvenor Street on the site of the present Nos. 93–99 (consec.) Park Lane. The lane in fact

presented a considerable problem to would-be developers, since the original estate grid had taken no account of its irregular course; plots west of Park Street, therefore, were of very variable size. Towards the south end of the estate, between Mount Street and South Street, the houses on the west side of Park Street occupied deep plots running right through to Park Lane, so the inhabitants certainly, and the houses probably, were of quality, but none of the fabric here remains.

Further north in Green Street, there is equally scant record of the appearance of the terrace houses; surviving lease plans show the usual variety of plan-type here, which suggests irregularities too in the elevations. A chapel was built at the south-east corner of Green Street and Park Street (1762), but it also was of small architectural significance. In Norfolk Street (now Dunraven Street), developed in the late 1750's with a good class of house, especially on the west side, there was again little or no uniformity. The survivors here, though much altered, do provide some idea of the original scale and quality. The houses on the west side are not deep, since Park Lane is close behind, but they are reasonably wide, often with a frontage of thirty feet or more; Nos. 21 and 22 Dunraven Street, the only ones for which old plans are known but probably reasonable guides for several others, had front compartment staircases and canted bays at the back. It must be emphasized that because Park Lane was at this date so inconsiderable, these rear bays facing towards the park were quite simple and cannot have been thought of as alternative fronts. King's Row, the only terrace actually entered from the lane itself, had completely flat fronts at this date, sheltered behind a screen of trees (Plate 13a, b). In the 1750's and '60's very little new development occurred on the estate, except in Norfolk Street, already mentioned, and Portugal Street, a short thoroughfare between Mount Street and Chapel (now Aldford) Street, on the line of what is now Balfour Place, where a few modest but well-inhabited houses were erected. Then in 1773 began the construction of Hereford Street, marking the completion of the ordinary estate development. This street, running west from close to the northern end of Park Street beyond North Row, has been entirely obliterated; it occupied a large part of the site of the present Hereford House, but was quite distinct from development along the south side of the Oxford Road. Even at this late date, the old pattern of individuality was scarcely disrupted, with a number of houses on the north side of different extent and, presumably, appearance. But for the south side of Hereford Street the architect and speculator was John Crunden (1740–1835), a capable designer in the Adam manner, and responsible for Boodle's Club in St. James's Street at just about this date. Along the main frontage Crunden erected a series of high-class houses with what were probably quite conventional façades except at No. 13, which boasted a pediment, perhaps because it was the only house visible from Oxford Street. But on the return frontage to Park Street, illustrated in one of Soane's lecture diagrams (Plate 13c), he attempted something more ambitious, a group of three houses with fronts of stucco or stone, the central one having touches of attenuated classical detail and a pediment. Crunden lived in the corner house with Hereford Street, and the centre house was Mrs. Fitzherbert's.

It was on this western part of the estate that there also arose a number of big houses distinct from any terrace arrangement, which were to be the precursors of the later Park Lane palaces. The first of these, Lord Chetwynd's house in Upper Grosvenor Street, has already been mentioned (page 118). Close by were the Park Lane mansions of Lord Petre (later Breadalbane House) and of Lord Dudley, the latter on the northern half of the site occupied by the present Dudley House. Both were five-bay houses, with high but plain brick façades, as befitted what was still a modest right of way of little pretension. Breadalbane House, designed in 1769 by James Paine with a complicated plan because of its restricted site, had the advantage over Dudley House of a pair of brief recessed wings (Plate 13b). Abutting Dudley House to the south, at the corner with modern Culross Street, stood another substantial house in an up-to-date Palladian style, shown on an aquatint of 1801 (Plate 13a). This engraving well conveys the ragged but not unattractive medley of backs and fronts which made up this part of Park Lane at that date.

Higher up and closer to Oxford Street, there was space for more large houses, but they took longer to get under way: Sir Thomas Robinson advised Lord Bute in 1762 against building a house here or on the Portland estate north of Oxford Street on the grounds that it was 'too farr either from publick business or publick pleasure'.[33] John Phillips the master carpenter eventually took a large area here, and was responsible for Lord Bateman's house, later Somerset House, erected in 1769-70 on a site now covered by part of Nos. 139-140 Park Lane, and probably for the building of Thomas Pitt's Camelford House (1773-4) on a site squeezed in between this and the Hereford Street development. Despite their proximity, they were dissimilar houses. Somerset House (Plate 14b) was very much a builder's house, always asymmetrical and probably never distinguished in elevation, without a particularly grand front even towards the park. But the owner of Camelford House, Thomas Pitt, was an amateur architect of accomplishment and an intimate of the young John Soane; so his house was of some moment, though inconspicuous from Oxford Street or Park Lane. A self-conscious late-Palladian villa (Plate 14a), it boasted a courtyard before it like that at Lord Chetwynd's house, canted bays at front and back, a strictly symmetrical plan, and able neo-classical interiors.

With these houses of the western sector, the names of well-known architects begin at last to crop up. But before Paine, Crunden or others had been active here, the houses in and around Grosvenor Square were already undergoing alteration. Hardly a noble family would change its London abode in the eighteenth century without manifold rearrangements and re-upholsterings, and these often involved architects. As early as 1743 Henry Flitcroft was undertaking works at No. 4 Grosvenor Square for the Earl of Malton, who had just moved in; this was to be followed by a series of improvements up to 1764, when the ageing architect superintended the stuccoing of the back of the house. This was the kind of job that one might expect to have been undertaken by an architect of the younger generation, William Chambers or his great rival Robert Adam. In fact in 1763 Chambers, just then building his fine early villa for the Earl of Abercorn at Duddingston, did also renovate the Earl's town house at No. 25 Grosvenor Square. This was often how high-class architects came to be involved in houses on the Grosvenor estate, altering them in sometimes quite trifling respects following more important country house work for the same client. Adam was in the field straight after Chambers in 1764-5 with a larger job, the internal updating for the Earl of Thanet of the stately No. 19 Grosvenor Square, the pedimented house by Edward Shepherd on the north side (Plates 15b, 17a, b). Each architect went on to cap the other's work with further commissions in the square, Chambers by redecorating No. 20 in 1767 for the Duke of Buccleuch, Adam with what amounted to a rebuilding of No. 26 for Lord Stanley (later the Earl of Derby) in 1773-4: this was the famous Derby House. Chambers also worked at No. 28 Grosvenor Street, while the Adam brothers were involved in one capacity or another at Nos. 5, 12 and 28 Grosvenor Square, at No. 16 Grosvenor Street (Plate 16b), at Claudius Amyand's house on the corner of Berkeley Square and Mount Street (Plate 15c), and perhaps too at No. 75 South Audley Street, the town house of Robert's great Scottish patron Lord Bute. The Adams' list is the longer not just because of their popularity or their better documentation but also because they were well placed to cultivate their contacts; from 1758 to 1771 they lived at No. 76 Grosvenor Street, a house which they appear to have altered but which is now long demolished.

By the turn of the century, plenty of well-known architects had acted in alterations of one kind or another. Thus John Vardy spent lavishly at No. 37 Grosvenor Square for the Duke of Bolton (1761); Robert Taylor appears to have rebuilt No. 33 Upper Brook Street (fig. 8b) in about 1768; the shadowy Kenton Couse made alterations at two houses in Grosvenor Square, in 1774-5 at No. 2 and in both 1764-5 and 1774-5 at No. 29; Henry Holland worked with his early partner Capability Brown at No. 75 South Audley Street (c. 1775) and, it seems, alone at Bourdon House (c. 1783); the less-known George Shakespear made changes at No. 41 Upper Brook Street in 1776-7; James Playfair added a gallery at No. 34 Grosvenor Square for Sir George Beaumont (1790); John Nash was supervising work at No. 34 Grosvenor Street (1798); and John Soane was in almost constant employment on major or minor estate works, the chief of them being the gradual internal reconstruction of No. 49 Grosvenor Square (1797

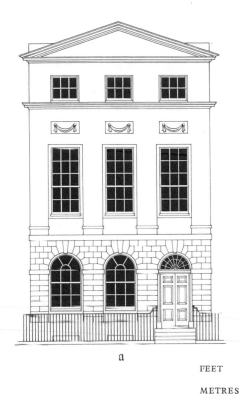

FEET 10 5 0 5 10
METRES 3 2 1 0 1 2 3

Fig. 8. MID-GEORGIAN ELEVATIONS

a. No. 6 Upper Brook Street. *Architect*, Samuel Wyatt, 1787–9. *Demolished*
b. No. 33 Upper Brook Street. *Architect*, probably Robert Taylor, *c*. 1768. *Now without pediment*

onwards). Soane, the best documented of these architects, had dealings with at least seventeen different houses on the estate in the course of his long career, and a similar intensity of practice hereabouts may be presumed for others. Frequently they were working simply as surveyors, valuing properties, bargaining on behalf of their clients, or acting as estate agents. A document of the 1740's at the Drawings Collection of the Royal Institute of British Architects in the hand of the architect John Sanderson describes and gives rough plans of a number of town houses, several of them on the Grosvenor estate, which he had evidently looked over on behalf of an intending purchaser;[34] rather later, Robert Mylne's illuminating diary is full of little entries mentioning visits to houses in a similar capacity,[35] while some letters of P. F. Robinson show that as late as the 1800's it was still common for eminent architects to find town houses for their customers.[36] Holland, Soane, S. P. Cockerell and Wyatville are all also recorded as 'acting' for clients in negotiations with the Grosvenor Office, no doubt usually in hope of rather than in connexion with more remunerative work.

One architect whose work on the estate is worth more than passing attention is Samuel Wyatt, who until recently has lived in the shadow of his brother James's greater reputation. In the earlier and more thorough period of his career James Wyatt did indeed work on two major houses in Grosvenor Square, No. 16 for William Drake of Shardeloes (1773–4) and the larger No. 41 for the dissolute Peter Delmé (1778), and made minor alterations at a third, the Grosvenors' own No. 45 (1783–4). Both No. 16 and No. 41 had ornamental ceilings of the new Adam type, and No. 41 was one of the first houses to have its front stuccoed in Higgins's patent cement. Having been his brother's reliable assistant and principal contractor in these two houses and in several other jobs, Samuel Wyatt struck out on his own in the late 1770's, with great success. Thus on the Grosvenor estate he is found in 1778 stuccoing the basement of No. 66 Brook Street with Higgins's cement for Assheton Curzon, the brother of Wyatt's first patron under Adam at Kedleston Hall.[37] In the ensuing period he acted in at least three lease renewals, altered one house (the western of the two on the site of No. 10 Grosvenor Square, in 1801–3), and virtually reconstructed two others (No. 6 Upper Brook Street for William Weddell in 1787–9 and No. 45 Grosvenor Square for Lord Petre in 1803–6). Weddell's house was of the greatest interest; having employed Adam to remodel his country seat at Newby Hall, for his town house he opted for the versatility and practicality of Samuel Wyatt. Wyatt seems to have excelled himself, achieving some ingenious interiors behind a stone pedimented front of only three bays (fig. 8a). He even earned himself the hyperbolic title of the 'wonder-working Chip' from a friend of Weddell's, whose surviving letters enthuse, as work proceeds, over 'the fine curve of the Trunk Cieling in the sky light', 'the light and airy look of the Eating room with the new circular end behind the columns', and finally, 'the Chip's new invented design for lighting the staircase, a fanciful *Machine*, that pours forth such a blaze of glory, that the Sun in it's meridian splendor will shew to it but as a *rush light*'.[38] Of all this interior work there is now no record except a few photographs of detail (Plate 17d), but they are enough to show that No. 6 Upper Brook Street was exceptional, even within Wyatt's *oeuvre*.

Like that house, nearly all the results of this first epoch of alterations have been swept away today. There is nothing recognizably by the Adams left on the estate, nothing by Chambers, just one room with characteristics of Holland's touch at Bourdon House, a few presumed fragments of the work of Brown and Holland at No. 75 South Audley Street, and little by the assiduous Soane except for a balcony and parts of a porch at No. 22 Dunraven Street (Plate 19c). However there are two major mid-Georgian survivals, No. 33 Upper Brook Street, a rebuilding of *c*. 1768 almost certainly by Robert Taylor for John Boyd of Danson Park, and No. 38 Grosvenor Square, a reconstruction of *c*. 1780 done so much in Samuel Wyatt's manner that an attribution to him is hard to resist. These houses are very different but equally important. No. 33 Upper Brook Street shows what could occur when updated Palladianism was applied to a modest three-bay house of little depth. Taylor reorganized the façade (fig. 8b) by putting the door in the centre, setting it and its flanking windows between small engaged columns carrying semi-circular heads, emphasizing the first floor with a sparing use of ornamental dressings, and topping the house with a neat pediment (now obliterated). Inside, the ground floor had to be limited to just two units, a spacious plaster-vaulted entrance hall and stairs, and a large octagonal room behind. Because this kind of arrangement left little compass for manoeuvre, mid-Georgian architects more frequently adhered to the basic lopsidedness of the townhouse plans that they inherited. That is what occurred at No. 38 Grosvenor Square, where a front compartment staircase may have been removed, and a deep back wing with windows to the side was certainly added, stretching right through to the stable block and ending with a private stair between the suites of the master and mistress of the house (fig. 9c). This wing was plastered over, and so also in all probability was the front to the square, since rebuilt. At the same time the interior was gutted throughout and refashioned with features of greater delicacy and lightness: a stone staircase with a lively iron balustrade and

oval toplight, drawing-rooms with voluptuous marble chimneypieces (Plate 17c), and plasterwork ceilings incorporating inset allegories painted in the fashionable manner of the Carracci (Plate 16c).

Such also, to judge from plans, was the character of Samuel Wyatt's No. 45 Grosvenor Square, and also of Derby House, Robert Adam's great masterpiece at No. 26 Grosvenor Square. Here again in both houses was a main central staircase generously toplit, and a long rear wing with a bow culminating in a private stair (fig. 9a, b). All three of these houses, in fact, betray the new preference for central stairs; the days of the front compartment staircase were over by 1770 and would not return. But at Derby House, with that extra conviction and fertility that separate him from his followers, Adam transformed the resulting sequence of straightforward rooms, each in itself symmetrical, into an eventful suite, by introducing circular and oval apartments and by blurring the contours of the other rooms with bowed ends, niches, vaults and pillared screens, so producing the effects of light and shade dramatized in Pastorini's famous perspective of the third drawing-room (Plate 15a). The intention to create such a suite even within the confines of a terrace house of fifty-foot frontage, despite attendant difficulties, is confirmed by the commentary on Adam's published plans, which refers to Derby House as 'an attempt to arrange the apartments in the French style, which... is best calculated for the convenience and elegance of life...The smallness of the scites upon which most London houses are built, obliges the artists of this country to arrange the apartments of the ladies and gentlemen upon two floors. Accordingly Lord Derby's are placed on the parlour story: the French, in their great *hôtels*, with their usual attention to what is agreeable and commodious, would introduce both these apartments upon the principal floor; but this we can only do in our country-houses, where our space is unconfined.'[39] So by 1773 French influence was already beginning to invade the London terrace house.

Adam's published plans of Derby House (fig. 9a) show also that the function of rooms was becoming more specified. As in some earlier houses, the kitchen was to be found here in the basement of the stable block facing inwards towards the paved court; because of smells, noise, and the danger of fire, such a position or one actually under the garden was to become standard in all subsequent rearrangements. In the main block of Derby House the reception rooms consisted of a 'great eating room' and library downstairs, and three drawing-rooms above, with appropriate antechambers on each floor. The private suites in the rear part of the wing referred to above, were a survival from the days of the 'great apartment', a concept ably explained in Fowler and Cornforth's *English Decoration in the 18th Century* (1974); they are a reminder that intimate friends would be received as a matter of course in these more sequestered parts of the house. One further point about Derby House,

Groom's room

Hay Loft

Laundry

Closet

Bed Chamber

Lady Derby's Dressing Room

Third Drawing Room

Second Drawing Room

First Drawing Room

Ante-room

▲ GROUND & ◀ 1st FLOOR

Upper part of Kitchen

Cabinet

Lord Derby's Dressing Room

Library

Great Eating Room

Parlour

Ante-room

Hall

a. No. 26 Grosvenor Square. *Architect for reconstruction,* Robert Adam, 1773–4. *Demolished*

▼ GROUND & ◀ 1st FLOOR

b. No. 45 Grosvenor Square. *Architect for reconstruction,* Samuel Wyatt, 1803–6. *Demolished*

▼ GROUND & ◀ 1st FLOOR

c. No. 38 Grosvenor Square. *Architect for reconstruction unknown, c.* 1780

Fig. 9. MID- AND LATE-GEORGIAN GROUND- AND FIRST-FLOOR PLANS

originally made by Soane in his Royal Academy lectures, is worth repeating; the front elevation was scarcely altered by Adam and retained its modest brick early-Georgian character, in token of the proud 'disregard to external appearance' of which English noblemen liked to boast.[40]

The 'Adam' style of interior decoration, exemplified by Derby House, looks radically new when compared with the efforts of Shepherd and his contemporaries. But there had certainly been a transition. Paine's ceiling design for the drawing-room of Lord Petre's Park Lane house (Plate 16a), published in the second volume of his *Plans, Elevations and Sections of Noblemen and Gentlemen's Houses*, combines the old deep compartments with a single painted roundel of the new type in the centre, and there is still a certain floridity to Adam's early ceiling designs such as that for Lord Hertford's drawing-room at No. 16 Grosvenor Street (Plate 16b). Nevertheless, the new style embodied archaeological sophistication of a kind that had been rare in earlier town houses. Not all designers could pick up its every resonance, but they were at least aware that a novel self-consciousness and unity were expected of their decorative schemes. This entailed the ousting of the heavy panelling that had been the hallmark of the original houses and a new supremacy for the more delicate skills of plasterer, painter, gilder, paperhanger, and last but not least, upholsterer.

Apart from a few master builders like Benjamin Timbrell and Edward Shepherd, the craftsmen responsible for the estate's original development remain shadowy figures. For the later Georgian period we are rather better informed. High-class architects like the Adams or the Wyatts brought with them experienced men whose practice was by no means exclusively metropolitan and who were no mere tradesmen. A few of them indeed appear to have enjoyed something of a monopoly within their trade. Thus the name of John Deval, mason (both father and son), appears in connexion with alterations at no less than five houses in Grosvenor Square (Nos. 2, 4, 16, 18 and 29) between 1736 and 1775, that is to say for almost all the houses in the square for which we have full records of work during the period. Sometimes this family firm was acting as mason-contractors, sometimes as specialized sculptors.

Another equally well-known name that constantly crops up is that of the great plastering concern of the two Joseph Roses. In 1764 Flitcroft was enthusing over the care taken by the elder Joseph Rose in stuccoing the back of No. 4 Grosvenor Square, which he thought would be 'an Example worthy of Imitation Mr Rose having taken great care in Chusing and mixing the materialls for it'.[41] Rose and his nephew went on to work in the 1760's and '70's at Nos. 16, 26, and 29 Grosvenor Square under James Wyatt, Robert Adam and Kenton Couse respectively, and doubtless did jobs at other houses of which we know nothing. By the turn of the century, plasterwork

was in general becoming less elaborate, and the Roses had been superseded by men like the William Rothwells, Soane's favourite plasterers, and Francis Bernasconi, who executed large contracts for Samuel Wyatt at No. 45 Grosvenor Square (1803-6) and for William Porden at Grosvenor House (1806-8).

One or two other special craftsmen are worth particular mention. Sefferin Alken was the carver in three of the mid-century jobs in Grosvenor Square already mentioned; Thomas Carter the younger worked as sculptor at No. 16 Grosvenor Square under James Wyatt and also elsewhere; Richard Westmacott the elder sculpted a chimneypiece at No. 41 Upper Brook Street; and John Mackell occurs constantly as a smith in contracts towards the end of the century. The early nineteenth-century bills for No. 45 Grosvenor Square and Grosvenor House include two names which were to become increasingly familiar in the years to come, those of Bramah for water closets and other ironwork at both houses, and of Skidmore for cast iron at Grosvenor House. Men like these were laying the foundation of firms of industrialized craftsmen in the modern sense at about this time. At the opposite end of the scale were the decorative artists, who held a particularly high status and operated more or less on their own; such were Antonio Zucchi who painted door panels at Derby House, and Biagio Rebecca, James Wyatt's choice for ceilings at No. 16 Grosvenor Square.

As elusive as any of these craftsmen but far more important for the history of the estate were the cabinet-makers and upholsterers, ancestors of the modern interior decorator. For obvious reasons, their work hardly survives in town houses at all. Yet because of their concern with the finishings of houses, they dealt directly with clients and frequently wielded much authority. Furnishings in the latest taste might be destined to last perhaps only a very few years before they were supplanted by something more up-to-date. But the lure of a spick-and-span interior was compelling, and certainly more powerful in London, where the proximity of neighbours encouraged rivalries, than in the country. Thus in 1748 we find Mrs. Boscawen rattling on to her absent admiral husband about their new house at No. 14 South Audley Street. 'This afternoon I saw company in my dressing-room for the first time since its being furnished...and everyone admired my apartment, which is indeed a very pretty one and wants nothing but the approbation of its Lord.' Then a little later: 'My house is an hourly expense to me, as you may imagine...My furniture, which is now pretty complete, costs many a penny. So elegant am I, that my fender is a Chinese rail. *Je connais des gens qui portent tellement envie à ma maison et à mes meubles qu'ils en sont presque malades*, and worry their husbands night and day to go out of that odious, beastly house.'[42]

Though Mrs. Boscawen's letters mention papers, hangings, chintzes, muslins, carpets and mattings galore, she includes only one craftsman's name, that of the famous early paperhanger Thomas Bromwich. In its later forms, firstly Bromwich, Isherwood and Bradley, later Isher-wood and Company, this firm also made papers for No. 29 Grosvenor Square (1777), No. 45 Grosvenor Square (1784) and for Grosvenor House (1807-8). In the later eighteenth century, wallpaper, as a cheaper and daintier background material, was increasing in popularity against hangings, and was available for quite humble houses. Surviving records of Joseph Trollope of West-minster reveal his firm at about the turn of the century papering houses of varying status, from Nos. 49 and 34 Grosvenor Street (the latter under Nash's guidance) to an evidently small house in South Audley Street, where Trollope was asked to 'take coals in return'.[43]

While very little is known of the earliest upholsterers who worked on the estate, the bills for alterations in houses in Grosvenor Square are soon full of the names of the most eminent concerns of the day: Vile and Cobb at No. 4 Grosvenor Square (1775 and later); William France, at No. 29 Grosvenor Square (1764); John Brad-burn, paid £2576 for work at the Marquis of Carmarthen's house, No. 2 Grosvenor Square, in 1774-5; and Chippen-dale, for whom posthumous works by his firm are recorded at No. 29 Grosvenor Square (1781-2) and No. 16 Grosvenor Square (1789).

For the display of their wares, cabinet-makers and upholsterers such as these required a proper shop, which tended to be strategically sited, close to fashionable society: Soho, Oxford Street, Bond Street, or increasingly the Grosvenor estate itself. A modicum of high-class trade has always flourished at the east end of Grosvenor Street, and here the firm of William Campbell (later George Campbell), advertised as 'upholders', had premises between 1727 and 1785, the first of several such enter-prises in the street. Not far away, on the north side of Berkeley Square (the only side on the Grosvenor estate), John Linnell, in succession to his father William Linnell, ran his famous workshops from 1763 until 1796. From here he was excellently placed to supply furniture to the local houses of the great, for example No. 16 Grosvenor Square in 1773-4, and No. 4 Grosvenor Square in 1776 and 1782-3. As a subcontracting carver to the building concern of John Phillips and George Shakespear, Linnell is likely to have done much other work on the estate. Then in Mount Street nearby was the establishment of William Marsh (Elward and Marsh), another celebrated up-holsterer who from about 1795 was in partnership with Thomas Tatham, a close associate and legatee of Linnell. Marsh and Tatham may possibly have inherited the goodwill of Linnell's business. In the firm's later incarna-tions as Tatham and Bailey, later Tatham, Bailey and Saunders, it became one of the dominating forces in the world of decoration, and included in its orbit two architects, C. H. Tatham, Thomas's brother, who lived for several years on the estate but is not known to have done substantial work hereabouts, and John Linnell Bond, who altered the Tatham and Bailey shop in Mount Street.[44]

By the early nineteenth century, to digress further into the obscure but influential world of these upholsterers, the commercial parts of the Grosvenor estate together with Bond Street had become virtually their most important centre of activity. From c. 1795 to 1814 Gillows, the well-known cabinet-makers who decorated the interiors of Grosvenor House and Eaton Hall under William Porden, held a lease of the grand house at Nos. 11-12 North Audley Street, and they retained the yards and workshops behind; these were premises additional to their main Oxford Street shops not far away, on part of the present site of Selfridges. In the next generation Thomas Dowbiggin had by 1816 started his very suc-cessful and high-ranking business in Mount Street, not far from Tatham and Bailey. For the following thirty-five years Dowbiggin was to work widely on the estate, sometimes as a speculator, before being absorbed into Holland and Sons, a firm which has only recently dis-appeared. Lastly, Thomas and George Seddon of Alders-gate Street took and probably greatly altered the large No. 16 Grosvenor Street in 1824 as their West End branch. Houses like this and Nos. 11-12 North Audley Street must have been fitted up not as mere places of work, but as elaborate showrooms. Into such centres these firms could entice the local gentry and nobility and tempt them to extravagance in their own homes.

The extent of upholsterers' work at this time is rarely known except when short-term speculation was involved. The seasonal occupation of fashionable Mayfair houses encouraged firms to buy up leases, refurnish the premises and let them at exorbitant rents for short periods, especially near the end of leasehold terms, a practice which could lead to serious problems (see Appendix III). In 1792 when the parish vestry of St. George's, Hanover Square, debated a rating question, they noted that 'when Gentlemen go into the Country leaving Furniture and a Person in their House (which generally wants more or less Repair every Year) such Gentlemen pay Rates for the whole Year; also that Upholsterers and others who left Houses ready furnished pay Rates for the whole Year though the Houses may be unlett for a great part of the Time'.[45] One example of such a house was No. 74 Grosvenor Street, for which the reputable cabinet-making concern of Mayhew and Ince are entered in the ratebooks 'for tenants' during the whole of the period 1778-1801; another may be No. 65 Grosvenor Street, where Taprell and Holland, ancestors of the firm of Holland and Sons, are entered between 1833 and 1847. It was a short step from this kind of practice, a perfectly normal one for upholsterers and house agents, to that of early hotels like Mivart's (later Claridge's) in Brook Street, by which an entrepreneur took on contiguous houses and let them to different clients for short periods, not just fully furnished but fully staffed as well.

After the Regency period, the advent of the professional builder began to scale down the broader activities of upholsterers, but in their heyday they are found acting on the Grosvenor estate as house agents and speculators far more often than architects, and quite frequently also as surveyors. In 1819 when the lease of No. 16 Grosvenor Street (the house eventually taken by the Seddons) came up for renewal, it was reported that 'three upholsterers have applied for the terms, viz Mr Key, Mr Rainy and Mr Johnston'.[46] No more is known of Rainy, but George Key was associated with a good cabinet-maker, Charles Smith, who had a house on the opposite side of Grosvenor Street, while John Johnstone of New Bond Street acted both as a major speculator (he took four houses in Grosvenor Street and one in Upper Brook Street between 1819 and 1824[47]) and also as agent and surveyor for the Duke of Newcastle in 1811, when the Duke was thinking of purchasing No. 75 South Audley Street.[48] Possibly the most ambitious speculator of this type was Charles Elliott, yet another well-known Bond Street upholsterer of high quality. Of the several large houses that Elliott took on, at least three radically altered or rebuilt by him between 1790 and 1810 survive: No. 66 Grosvenor Street, No. 18 Upper Grosvenor Street, and No. 65 Brook Street. One of them, No. 18 Upper Grosvenor Street, still has the appearance of a high-class speculative house of the 1790's, with its stucco façade (Plate 44d), neat central stone staircase, and Adam-style marble fireplaces; to these the original finishings would doubtless have added a spick-and-span flavour.

Of course upholsterers were not alone in such speculations. Since the start of estate development, builders or other tradesmen had often been the holders of head leases, merely subletting to gentry. Now others bought up the ends of leases, especially of houses that were dilapidated. In the period 1797–1819, for instance, a speculator called Bartholomew bought up at least six houses at the Bond Street end of Grosvenor Street in this way, radically improved and relet them.[49] The system frequently provoked dissatisfaction among their clients, who were not too happy to be so dependent upon 'tradesmen'. Thus in 1811 the economist David Ricardo bought No. 56 Upper Brook Street, a small new house built as 'infill' behind Nos. 24 and 25 Grosvenor Square, from the builder Charles Mayor, the original lessee of Nash's Park Crescent and very soon a spectacular bankrupt.[50] Ricardo, ironically disregarding the laws of the market at the whim of his wife and children, paid Mayor what he considered an 'enormous' price and was soon lamenting his decision: 'that Mayor of whom I bought the house was a complete knave, and from the holes in the chimnies, and the communication between them and the beams, he perhaps intended that it should be destroyed by fire, so that no one might ever find out the total insufficiency of the materials to support the house.'[51]

One might think that these were the kinds of difficulty that led to Lord Grosvenor's appointment of an estate surveyor in about 1784. But the evidence is clear that the main brief was financial, to compile an accurate record of property values and to make satisfactory terms when leases were renewed. When in 1778–9 Robert Taylor and George Shakespear were employed by the Estate to survey the area north of Grosvenor Street and east of Davies Street in detail, the purpose cannot have been to see where estate improvements could be effected but to get adequate information about this part of the estate in case of lease-renewals. William Porden, Lord Grosvenor's eventual choice as surveyor, was a relatively unknown architect at the time of his appointment. His selection is possibly a little surprising, since John Jenkins, a local surveyor, had recently been employed in some small family jobs for the Grosvenors; Jenkins had also designed the Grosvenor Market (1784–5), a modest group of houses and shops with a covered way behind, on the triangular stretch of ground at the top of Davies Street and South Molton Lane (the present Boldings site). Porden may have been chosen because he had been a pupil of James Wyatt, who had also been working for Earl Grosvenor, if only in a minor capacity, at his main town house, No. 45 Grosvenor Square. In any case Porden soon proved his worth and his individuality and was to handle estate matters with a stout and hearty independence for thirty-five years and more. A number of large architectural jobs away from the estate showed that he could design too, and that with talent and idiosyncratic taste. From 1804 he was working for the Prince of Wales at Brighton, and had started reconstructing Eaton Hall for Lord Grosvenor on the most lavish scale, in the Gothic style that he made no bones about favouring. Then in 1806–8 he became equally busy with his one major work on the Mayfair estate, Grosvenor House. This was the reconditioning of Lord Chetwynd's old house in Upper Grosvenor Street, which had passed to the Duke of Gloucester and was acquired by Lord Grosvenor in 1806 for use as the family's London seat.

There is no reliable record of the appearance of Grosvenor House when Porden had finished with it in 1808. Though well over £16,000 was spent, the only major change to the outside of the house was the addition of a bow towards the garden (Plate 18a). Most of the work, in fact, was interior and decorative, since the house was intended to show off Lord Grosvenor's collection of pictures to best advantage, and Porden prided himself on his particular taste and care in such matters. There was inevitable (and instructive) friction with the upholsterer, Gillow, who was often consulted by Lord Grosvenor, doubtless because he was less independent-minded than Porden. Disagreeing with Gillow about the colour of a dado, which he wanted 'sattin wood' in tone and Gillow a more dashing pink and white, Porden could damningly say of his opponent, 'in his own province, he is only governed by fashion'.[52] In the end, all turned out for the best; when Grosvenor House was thrown open in 1808, the results earned for Porden society's accolade. *The Times* was at its most orotund: 'Never do we recollect to have seen a more judicious and pleasing application of classical enrichments to domiciliary character and accommodation.'[53] There was, however, an argument about Porden's fee. Still, in 1817 Porden was again chosen as architect to add a gallery to accommodate Lord Grosvenor's growing picture collection.

The places where Porden significantly influenced the appearance of the rest of the Mayfair estate were few. Unlike later surveyors, he does not seem to have required plans for new houses or alterations to old ones to be submitted to him, nor did he solicit employment on the estate as a private architect. In the early years of his tenure relatively few leases were falling in, so his opportunities to assert himself architecturally or to promote a coherent policy for improvements were small. But one example of a notion of Porden's eventually bearing fruit was the reconstruction of King's Row (Nos. 93-99 consec. Park Lane), by the Grosvenor Gate into Hyde Park. As early as 1791 he saw that the jumbled appearance of Park Lane could be improved in places. He therefore persuaded Lord Grosvenor not to renew leases in King's Row so that in due course better houses could be built there. In 1808 Porden once more counselled against premature renewals, but it was not until 1823-8, after his death, that most of the range was rebuilt. Though the designs adopted were not uniform, Nos. 93-99 Park Lane remain one of the estate's most charming and individual ranges (Plate 19a). The only architect known to have been involved, John Goldicutt at Nos. 98 and 99, certainly did not have overall control. Yet somehow, since the plots were very shallow, the promoters all took up the idea suggested by the backs of houses fronting Norfolk (now Dunraven) Street higher up and Park Street lower down the lane, and canted out the new façades with a delightful set of bays, bows, iron balconies and verandas (Plate 19; fig. 10). This conception of backs turning into fronts was the vital factor in transforming Park Lane into a thoroughly fashionable address. Up and down the park frontage, bigger and better bays started to sprout on existing houses, while beyond the estate the reverberations reached Tyburnia.

In his last years as surveyor, Porden was sometimes represented at the Grosvenor Board by his son-in-law, Joseph Kay.[54] He retired in 1821, shortly before his death. By then the emphasis of Grosvenor estate development had shifted to Belgravia, the main sphere of activity of his successors, the Cundys. From their tenure of the surveyorship, a new phase in the character of the Mayfair estate may be dated.

The Reign of the Cundys

In September 1821 Thomas Cundy of Pimlico, architect and builder, succeeded Porden as the second Earl Grosvenor's surveyor. Cundy may have been recommended by his predecessor, as like Porden and Kay he had been a protégé of S. P. Cockerell, the district surveyor of St. George's, Hanover Square. He was certainly conversant with the Mayfair estate already, having altered two houses in Grosvenor Square, No. 7 (1808) and No. 30 (1815-16), acted in lease-renewals for two others (Nos. 11 and 29), and applied for the lease of at least one property close to Grosvenor House. His brother, the engineer Nicholas Wilcox Cundy, had also lived briefly first in Brook Street just off the estate, then in Norfolk (now Dunraven) Street.[55] But the decisive factor must have been Thomas Cundy's connexion with the 'Five Fields' area of Pimlico, towards which all eyes were now turning as the next logical place for expansion on the Grosvenor estates. By 1811 serious plans had already been laid for the development of Belgravia;[56] there were at least two false starts, but by the time that Cundy became estate surveyor development was about to take off, and since he operated from Ranelagh Street (now Beeston Place and the eastern end of Ebury Street) he was well placed to superintend affairs. For the next forty years Mayfair was to take a back seat, as a style both of development and of architecture was evolved for Belgravia and Pimlico, and then reflected back upon the older estate. The principal early figures in this evolution were the speculative builders, the great Thomas Cubitt, Seth Smith, and to a lesser degree Joseph, James and Thomas Cundy II, the sons of the estate surveyor.[57] But though Thomas Cundy I must have matured the layout of Belgravia, and certainly had a hand at the start of his sons' speculations there, he died in 1825 before matters were at all advanced. Thomas Cundy II, his eldest son, now took over the surveyorship to Lord Grosvenor, an appointment he was to hold for over forty years and then pass on in turn to his third son Thomas Cundy III, who retained the post until 1890. Day-to-day architectural control of the London estates was thus in the hands of the same family for nearly seventy years.

Officially the briefs of Thomas Cundy I and II seem to have exceeded Porden's in one important respect only. This was that the Cundys began to consider and approve plans for any new buildings or rebuildings undertaken by tenants. This duty, obviously evolved with Belgravia in mind, was to become vital on the Mayfair estate as well. Here a new era of general rebuilding, small perhaps compared to the volume of development further south, but still significant, was ushered in with the retirement of Porden. If the falling-in of Mayfair leases was partly the cause, the Cundys must also have encouraged this distinctly new policy, as it offered them greater opportunities as well as more responsibilities. The family certainly took their early chances in Belgravia while Thomas Cundy I still lived, and though Thomas Cundy II relinquished his interest in his brother Joseph's 'take' of land round Chester Square on becoming surveyor,[58] he probably continued designing for the family speculations, as his father had done.

How much Thomas Cundy II designed on the estates during the first twenty years of his surveyorship, before the accession of the second Marquess in 1845, is hard to

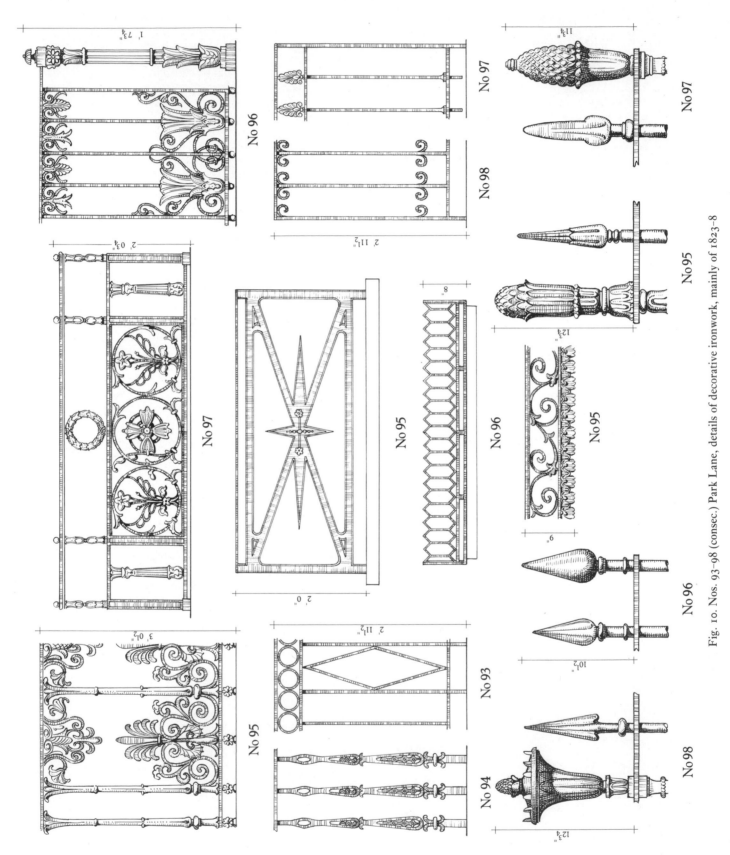

Fig. 10. Nos. 93–98 (consec.) Park Lane, details of decorative ironwork, mainly of 1823–8

say. Well before his father's death he had been engaged in the architectural side of the practice, and for works of the mid 1820's their hands are indistinguishable. What is undoubtedly true is that their most lucrative Mayfair commissions of this period were undertaken for the Grosvenors themselves. The first one, the reconstruction of Nos. 15 and 16 Grosvenor Square as Belgrave House, has hitherto escaped notice, but was a large business. In 1819 the second Earl Grosvenor's heir, Viscount Belgrave, had married Lady Elizabeth Leveson-Gower; the wealthy couple soon had children and wanted for a substantial London house. The answer was the pair of houses in the middle of the north side of the square, which between 1822 and 1824 were transformed by the Cundys into a regular palace, at a cost of over £12,000. They acquired a new stucco front some seventy-five feet in length, with four giant engaged columns running through first- and second-storey levels (Plate 20a). This illustrious mid-terrace composition must have been an influence on the façades of Belgrave Square, which were being evolved shortly after this date. The interior of Belgrave House, though modest on plan, can scarcely have been less magnificent, as John Davis, a Brook Street cabinet-maker, presented a bill for £3829 for work done here.

Immediately afterwards, in 1824, Earl Grosvenor initiated an even more massive rebuilding scheme for Grosvenor House itself. Porden had reconditioned the house but had scarcely enlarged it, and this was what the Cundys now prepared to do. Thomas Cundy I must have been a party to the scheme's inception, but all extant drawings date from after his death. The only major addition actually erected, the great picture gallery of 1826–7, was certainly in the hands of Thomas Cundy II, assisted in the execution of the work by his brothers, the short-lived mason James and the soon-bankrupted carpenter Joseph. As architects, the first two Cundys had neither the sophistication nor the individuality of a Porden: their Grosvenor House scheme, therefore, though lavish and imposing, was essentially pedestrian, relying much upon engaged columns for exterior effect (Plate 18a, b). In contrast to this heavy Roman effort, a chaster scheme submitted (without invitation) by Smirke makes one sigh for more imaginative patronage on the part of the second Earl Grosvenor (Plate 18c). Later, in 1842–3, Thomas Cundy II added a noble screen equipped with florid iron gates to front the courtyard towards Upper Grosvenor Street. Though modelled on Holland's Carlton House screen, it has been translated into the same sober Roman idiom (Plate 20c).

Still, the second Cundy does appear to have had a lighter side at times, if the façade of the Grosvenor Office at No. 53 Davies Street, a fresh and cheerful essay of the 1830's in the stucco of Belgravia, can be taken as his (Plate 20b). There is no evidence for the authorship of this engaging composition, enlivened by touches of Greek detail, but Cundy is the obvious candidate, and stylistic parallels

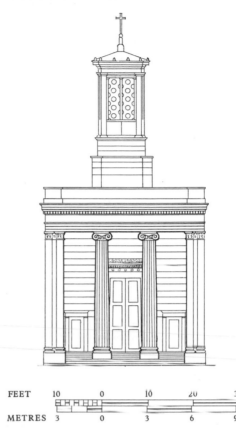

Fig. 11. St. Mark's Church, North Audley Street, west front. *Architect*, J. P. Gandy-Deering, 1825–8

with the demolished Belgrave House, also fronted in stucco, seem to suggest his hand. Meanwhile, he was also well supplied with out-of-town work for the Grosvenors, for instance at Moor Park in Hertfordshire, where over £15,000 was spent by Earl Grosvenor between 1828 and 1831.[59]

With the Cundys at the helm, the Greek Revival scarcely got an airing on the Mayfair estate. The chief exception is the work of that rare architect, J. P. Gandy-Deering. He was the winner in 1824 of a competition for the new church of St. Mark's, North Audley Street. The surviving portico and pronaos of his church (fig. 11) display able scholarship and exceptional purity of detail, and go some way to explain why the extant designs of another competitor, John Goldicutt, were not chosen. Goldicutt also participated in the redevelopment at Nos. 93–99 (consec.) Park Lane, but there was nothing very Greek in the outline of this range (Plate 19a). Here and elsewhere, lessees were mostly content to display the new fashion, as far as exteriors were concerned, in pretty cast-iron balconies and verandas on the fronts and backs of their houses (figs. 10, 12b). Again, Gandy-Deering was the exception. A unique and highly fashionable terrace of houses designed by him in *c.* 1825–35 at Nos. 14–24 (even) South Street (Lord Melbourne lived in one of them) manifested the same careful discipline and sense for proportions as his St. Mark's designs (Plate 24c; fig. 12c). So it is lamentable that only two forlorn houses in this row remain, while of other work by Gandy-Deering in the South Street area virtually nothing survives.

Another architect employed on the western half of the estate was William Atkinson. His rebuilt Dudley House (1827–8) is the most important house of this period to remain. Its stucco façade follows the lead of some of the simpler Regent's Park terraces, whilst some handsome passages of its interior decoration mark the point of transition from a chaste Greek style to the more fulsome manner associated with the Italianate of Charles Barry (Plate 21).

In the 1820's one or two interesting architects had their homes upon the estate, a circumstance which easily led to their employment here and there. One such was George Stanley Repton, son of the landscape gardener, who in 1821 was encouraged by his banking friends the Loyds to come and live close to them in Norfolk (now Dunraven) Street. His house, overlooking the park, has been demolished, but in the early 1820's he designed stabling in Wood's Mews for Samuel Jones Loyd, the future Lord Overstone (Plate 22c), and is likely to have done more work, either for Loyd or for himself. P. F. Robinson, an affable and ingenious ex-assistant of Porden's who is best known for his books of picturesque cottage designs, lived and worked for many years at a house on the site of the present No. 80 Brook Street; he altered Somerset House, Park Lane, in 1819 and on various occasions acted for his regular clients, the Osbaldestons, in their search for a Mayfair house;[36] an instructive account of one such episode, in connexion with No. 51 Brook Street, will be found in Appendix III. Though the houses of Repton and Robinson have disappeared, the more original residence of Jeffry Wyatt (Sir Jeffry Wyatville) still survives at No. 39 Brook Street (Plate 22a). Wyatt moved into this pleasant and unusually planned early Georgian house in about 1802, at which time he was partner in a building business with premises behind in Avery Row and Brook's Mews. As his architectural practice expanded he seems to have relinquished the building side, and shortly after 1821 he smartened up the old house substantially by remodelling several rooms, constructing a small circular entrance hall, and adding a large and long toplit gallery at first-floor level behind on the Avery Row side. The character of this work is classic in the manner of Soane, but far more subdued. Wyatt also acted in lease-renewals and altered several houses in Grosvenor Square, principally No. 6 in 1809 for the Marquess of Bath, his patron at Longleat, and he may also, like Robinson, have made a small addition at Somerset House, Park Lane (1811).

Other leading architects of the period are less well represented on the estate. Smirke's scheme for Grosvenor House was never seriously considered and his only other known design, a small addition at Camelford House, does not seem to have been built. The substantial works done by C. R. Cockerell at No. 88 Brook Street in 1824 have been swept away, and the house he altered for his brother at No. 1 Upper Grosvenor Street has been demolished. In Grosvenor Street there are few traces of the internal alterations made by Decimus Burton at No. 18 (1835–6), but rather more of those by Lewis Vulliamy at No. 51 (1836). Anthony Salvin is said to have worked at Grosvenor House in 1835, but the nature and extent of his employment remain a mystery. As for Charles Barry, he appears to have been employed on the estate only in his later career, and again his two known works, both refrontings, have disappeared. That at No. 41 Brook Street (1852–3) was not particularly significant, but his recasing of No. 2 South Street in 1852 was a lavish affair. This house, which had been enlarged by the Duke of Orleans, the famous Philippe Egalité, during his English exile (1789–90), had a return front to Park Lane, by then a highly fashionable address. Barry therefore dressed the building in a noble outfit of Italianate stucco façades with a festive and ornamental frieze, rather in the manner of some of the houses in Kensington Palace Gardens (Plate 22b).

In general, the reign of the second Earl Grosvenor and first Marquess of Westminster (1802–45) brought few drastic changes to the fabric in the smartest parts of the Mayfair estate. Since leases were often renewed without particular conditions, rebuilding occurred only as and when the lessees desired and was rarely prompted by the estate. Apart from the recasting of Belgrave House, only one house along the main sides of Grosvenor Square is known to have been completely rebuilt between 1804 and 1854, and that was No. 47, reconstructed in 1814–15 because of its poor state to the designs and under the superintendence of a little-known builder, Thomas Martin.

Yet elsewhere there was no shortage of building activity, a fact which is partly obscured by the spate of subsequent reconstruction in the first Duke's day. To take the clearest instance, a good deal of Davies Street and of the small streets south of Grosvenor Street and north of Brook Street was transformed in the 1820's and 1830's. The main operators were Seth Smith and, to a lesser extent, Thomas Cubitt, famed as developers in Belgravia. But both had built on the Mayfair estate before turning to Belgravia, Smith on the west side of Davies Street between Brook Street and Three Kings Yard (1818–20), Cubitt at the north end of Berkeley Square, next to the corner with Davies Street (1821–2). Cubitt was of course to outstrip Smith in Belgravia, but in Mayfair Smith was the bigger speculator. Yet of the sixty-three small but decent houses he put up between 1822 and 1833 in the Gilbert Street, Binney Street and Weighhouse Street area, possibly to the designs of William Maberley (Plate 23a), only a single one, No. 27 Gilbert Street, survives (fig. 12a); even his dissenters' chapel has disappeared. Cubitt's slightly later developments have fared no better. In 1837–40 he rebuilt

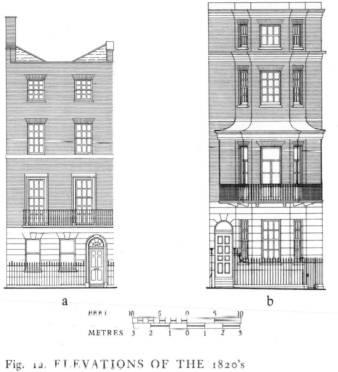

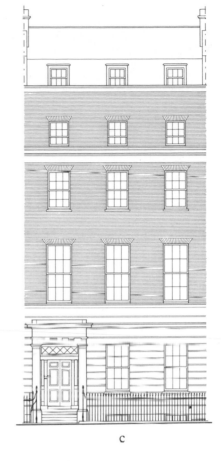

Fig. 12. ELEVATIONS OF THE 1820's

a. No. 27 Gilbert Street. *Builder*, Seth Smith, 1828-9. *Now extended*

b. No. 98 Park Lane. *Architect*, John Goldicutt, 1823-5

c. No. 16 South Street. *Architect*, J. P. Gandy-Deering, *c.* 1825-30. *Demolished*

much in the Grosvenor Hill–Bourdon Street area, a group of houses on the west side of Davies Street, and three substantial houses in Grosvenor Street. None of these remains. In Cubitt's case these enterprises may have been intended to take up the slack from his undertakings elsewhere, but Seth Smith's smaller workforce was more probably stretched by his Mayfair developments.

A third, much smaller improvement in this area that happily survives is the Running Horse public house together with Nos. 52–54 (even) Davies Street of 1839-40 (Plate 24b). This originally comprised the pub, a pair of houses, and building workshops behind, erected by the small contracting firm of Joshua Higgs and Company as their headquarters. Though the business here never seems to have grown to great proportions, a nephew of Joshua Higgs apprenticed here was to become co-founder of the much bigger Higgs and Hill.[60] Also, in the year of the firm's establishment at this address, 1839, a son, Joshua Higgs junior, submitted to the Select Committee on Metropolis Improvements an elaborate scheme for improving the north end of Davies Street with shops and a chapel in the Grecian style of Regent Street (Plate 24a). But the scheme came to nothing, and the top of Davies Street had to wait another fifty years for its improvement.

Two other districts underwent major change at this time. One was the Green Street area, where the presence of several minor architects and surveyors such as Samuel Erlam, Edward Lapidge and Daniel Robertson was a stimulus to rebuilding activity in the 1820's. A principal builder-speculator here was John Elger (Plate 23c), a native of Bedford who from about 1825 had a yard on the estate in South Street, east of South Audley Street. Over the following twenty years he took a substantial number of good sites in different parts of the West End, and he was also the builder of Thomas Cundy II's screen at Grosvenor House (1842-3). Elger's niece was to marry Thomas Cundy III, and in the 1840's his South Street premises were passed on to John Kelk, who in his turn relinquished them in about 1862 to George Smith and Company.[61] All these are highly reputable names in the London building world of the time, and all are frequently met with on the Mayfair estate. The connexions between these figures, though often unclear to us, were evidently crucial to their operations. Yet despite Elger's importance, the only estate work of his to survive in any recognizable form is No. 138 Park Lane (Plate 19c), a house at the corner with North Row, originally two premises but united by him in 1831-2.

The last district to be substantially redeveloped at this time, South Street, Chapel Street (now Aldford Street)

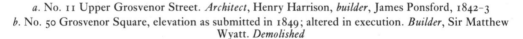

Fig. 13. EARLY-VICTORIAN ELEVATIONS

a. No. 11 Upper Grosvenor Street. *Architect*, Henry Harrison, *builder*, James Ponsford, 1842–3
b. No. 50 Grosvenor Square, elevation as submitted in 1849; altered in execution. *Builder*, Sir Matthew Wyatt. *Demolished*

and Portugal Street (now Balfour Place), also brings up its individuals, but by and large they are more obscure. The Gandy-Deering developments in the western part of South Street have already been mentioned. One of his associates here was James Gallier, who soon became bankrupt and departed to America, where he won some fame and fortune as an architect in New Orleans.[62] Gallier's chief backer was John Robson, who had a large coach manufactory behind the north side of South Street and the west side of South Audley Street and built houses hereabouts. In the late 1820's Robson, a Mr. Arber and Thomas Oliver divided a good deal of the ground round here for redevelopment, but there were other figures too such as William Skeat on the south side of Mount Street close to Park Lane (Plate 23b). Oliver and his successor John Feetham appear to have been the largest operators; they did much work in Portugal Street and Chapel Street and among the larger houses which Feetham took was No. 74 South Audley Street, where he altered the main house, pulled down the old Portuguese Embassy chapel behind, and erected stables on the site, which survive as the present No. 26 South Street (1833). It was probably also at this time that the Grosvenor Chapel acquired its present external dressings of stucco; major works were

undertaken by William Skeat in 1829–30, after the chapel had become the property of the parish.

The developments in this district also mark the first appearance of Wright Ingle, for nearly forty years a speculator upon the Mayfair estate. In the 1820's his activities were modest in scope, but they gradually enlarged. Between 1841 and 1851 he was absent from the estate scene, but in the following eleven years he was constantly at work altering or reconstructing one house or another, his largest single task being the rebuilding of No. 42 Grosvenor Square (1853–5). He eventually died in 1865, full of years and riches, and was buried in his native town of St. Ives, Huntingdonshire.[63] The two survivors from Ingle's speculations are Nos. 11 Upper Brook Street and 20 Grosvenor Street, a pair of similar small houses both of 1852–3. It is significant that though Ingle is sometimes described as a builder, he was not one in the ordinary sense of the word at least in his later years, nor so far as is known was he an architect. His enterprises of the 1850's were invariably erected by other building firms and usually, it appears, designed by Henry Harrison, an architect who lived for some years in Park Street and had experience of designing for speculative builders. In about 1843 James Ponsford, a major speculator in

Tyburnia, now developing apace on the other side of Hyde Park, called in Harrison to design a pair of large houses at Nos. 10 and 11 Upper Grosvenor Street (fig. 13a) and a smaller one behind at No. 62 Park Street. Those in Upper Grosvenor Street are among the few remaining examples on the Mayfair estate to adopt the full Belgravia manner: completely stuccoed with Italian porches, pedimented first-floor windows and iron balconies, and spaciously planned so as to include ample public space and internal light-wells. Harrison may also have designed a set of houses erected by Ponsford in North Audley Street (all now demolished), and he certainly altered Hampden House, No. 61 Green Street, and Derby House, No. 26 Grosvenor Square. Under Ingle's aegis he was responsible for Nos. 11 Upper Brook Street, 20 Grosvenor Street, and 42 Grosvenor Square, except for the façades. These, in accordance with a policy that must now be discussed, were the work of Thomas Cundy II (figs. 14, 15, 17).

The death of the first Marquess of Westminster in 1845 marked the start of a twenty-two year heyday for Thomas Cundy II. Just like his father before him and his son after him, the second Marquess celebrated his accession with an outburst of building. In the country, his principal architects were William Burn, who altered Eaton once again and designed a new house on the family's Fonthill estate in Wiltshire, and T. H. Wyatt, who scattered a handful of Grosvenor-financed churches across the Salisbury diocese, churches being the enthusiasm of the age.

But in London the Cundys still ruled supreme. Thomas Cundy II had already been laying his plans, for in 1844 he obtained the consent of the first Marquess to a proposition for adding stuccowork, porticos, window dressings, cornices and balustrades in Grosvenor Square to 'such of the houses as may be thought to require it. The terms for renewal in all houses to contain stipulations to this effect and a drawing to be submitted by the parties applying.'[64] This was more than a vague idea, it was a proposal for refronting on a vast scale. In May 1845 measurements were being taken from the façades of the south-side houses, the new Marquess telling inhabitants 'I am anxious to obtain a correct design for some proposed improvements';[65] four years later, Cundy produced to the Grosvenor Board 'a drawing showing his suggested alterations' for all the houses along this side.[66] There is also more than a suspicion that Cundy prepared a uniform elevation for the north side of the square. In 1855, at the time that substantial reconstruction on this side first became a practical proposition, an elevation of the whole frontage as existing was drawn; moreover, the houses eventually rebuilt here, No. 10 at the east end (fig. 15) and Nos. 20 and 21 at the west (Plate 25b), were allotted unusual and matching pilastered fronts, as though they were to form flanking wings to Nos. 15–16, formerly Belgrave House. (Soon after the Marquess had moved into Grosvenor House in 1845 this house became free.

It had then been taken by a speculative businessman, Kensington Lewis, and divided back into two in 1848–9, with some alterations to the front.) It appears therefore as if the Marquess and Cundy now conceived their old Belgrave House as the centre of a splendid composition embracing the whole north side of the square.

Whether, as all this implies, there was serious thought of refronting the whole square over a long period so as to make the houses 'range uniform' in the Belgravia manner is not clear. But it soon became apparent that the new policy had no prospects of quick advancement. The first practical opportunity to refront a house in the square did not come until 1851. By chance it was the famous Derby House, No. 26; Henry Harrison was the lessee's architect, and not unnaturally wanted a slightly different front from the type prescribed by Cundy. In the event Cundy designed the new façade, but probably with some concessions. A similar compromise with the new estate rule must have been reached at the next house to be refronted, the surviving No. 38 Grosvenor Square (1854–5); unlike most of the square it already had a completely stuccoed front, and therefore Cundy had to provide different detailing (Plate 25a).

Soon, Cundy and the second Marquess, knowing there was no chance of a quick, clean sweep in the square, were also soberly applying themselves by means of compulsory clauses in terms for new leases to refronting almost every house in the main streets as it came up for renewal. The first house that appears to have fallen under this fiat was No. 18 Grosvenor Street (since refronted again), for which Cundy provided an elevation in February 1846. At first the policy was slow to get off the mark, but by the mid 1850's it was well under way, and between 1850 and Thomas Cundy II's death in 1867 almost fifty separate refrontings can be traced as having been carried out in the major streets, nearly all in conjunction with lease renewals.

Although these refrontings had to be proceeded with piecemeal, it is not improbable that a coherent design existed for the frontages in each major street, to which Cundy turned when an individual house was being renewed. In 1848 he produced a general design for the north side of Brook Street east of Davies Street, and the wording of the original terms of renewal for Nos. 41 and 43 on the south side suggests that he may have proposed another one for this side. There is indirect evidence too for such a design on the north side of Grosvenor Street, where a large number of houses between Avery Row and Davies Street, some of them contiguous, were rebuilt or refronted with similar façades of a uniform height and with a distinctive frieze (fig. 14c). In Grosvenor Square nearly all the fronts rebuilt on the south and west sides had common characteristics, with stone dressings instead of the cement used in the side streets, harder and lighter bricks for the walling, and stone balustrades to the areas rather than iron railings (Plate 25). Even in South Audley Street, where little refronting took place in the Cundy era, the one block to be rebuilt, Nos. 53–55 (consec.) of

a   b   c

Fig. 14. ELEVATIONS BY THOMAS CUNDY II

a. No. 11 Upper Brook Street. *Builder*, Wright Ingle, 1852–3
b. No. 55 South Audley Street. *Builders*, Reading and William Watts, 1858–9
c. No. 17 Grosvenor Street. *Builder*, John Newson, 1855–6

1858–60, had its special, markedly ornamental design, though only No. 55 (fig. 14b) has survived to tell the tale.

Inevitably there were exceptions to the policy, especially early on, as the cases of Nos. 26 and 38 Grosvenor Square have already shown. Some few lessees escaped the condition of refronting or successfully rejected Cundy's elevations. At No. 2 South Street his design was supplanted by that of the lessee's own architect, Charles Barry, no doubt because of the latter's superior prestige; at No. 41 Brook Street Barry again had his own way. At No. 50 Grosvenor Square, the home of the aged General Grosvenor, Lord Robert Grosvenor (the brother of the Marquess) took charge of the rebuilding deemed urgently necessary in 1847. He brought in (Sir) Matthew Wyatt, the developer of Victoria Square and of much of Tyburnia, who was allowed to build the whole house, and the Marquess was reduced to twice requesting Wyatt to simplify and tone down his elevation, presumably because the originals (fig. 13b) were too brash for the estate norm. Generally, however, the Marquess supported Cundy to the hilt. At No. 41 Upper Brook Street, Sir Henry Meux and his architect Samuel Beazley had to submit to the

stone balcony insisted upon; and even so eminent a domestic architect as Burn, who had twice worked for the Marquess, had to employ an elevation by Cundy when he rebuilt No. 18 Grosvenor Square for Earl Fortescue in 1864–7 (Plate 54a).

The refronting policy raises several issues. What were the precedents? Were the Estate's motives primarily commercial or aesthetic? And was it the fruit of Thomas Cundy II's ambitions, or did it in the main reflect the desires of the tenants? Though the answers must in part be guessed, it is plain that Belgravia and its newer outliers westward, beyond Grosvenor land, lay at the root of Estate thinking. There, uniformity and the stucco style had proved an asset, not a liability, and there must have been some anxiety that Mayfair might go into decline unless something of the kind were tried there. Rebuilding, though frequently undertaken in the main streets and square during the period of the second Marquess, was often unrealistic, wasteful and unnecessary, and could deprive the estate of valued tenants; as there was no way of influencing internal alterations, refronting was the only other option. Nevertheless, the whole operation was to

FEET   10   5   0   5   10

METRES   3   2   1   0   1   2   3

Fig. 15. No. 10 Grosvenor Square, elevation to the square. *Architect*,
Thomas Cundy II, *builder*, C. J. Freake, 1864-6. *Demolished*

a degree eccentric. There was no obvious precedent, and the few successors, like the Bedford Estate's refronting of Russell Square at the turn of the century, were not strictly parallel. It was also a destructive policy. Thomas Cundy II and the second Marquess were not sensitive souls when it came to the architecture of the past, and in their anxiety to promote a revitalized Mayfair estate in good repair, not only did much of the Georgian appearance of the streets and square vanish, but many fine houses, including Derby House, were entirely destroyed. If the epochs of the second Marquess and the first Duke are compared, it cannot seriously be questioned that the first Duke built more that was of permanent merit and destroyed less of real value than his father had done.

Still, many of Cundy's fronts (Plate 25; figs. 14, 15, 17) were able compositions in their own right, especially where plots were broad enough to allow him adequate space. One fine surviving example, at No. 52 Grosvenor Street, involved Lord Radnor in large expenditure in 1854-5. This front (fig. 17) is still in the strict Italian style, with a deep cornice upon consoles, individual balconettes to the first-floor windows, and the cement rustication running evenly up the sides of the building. Later on, these elements begin to change. Another big surviving elevation is that to No. 4 Grosvenor Square, in fact a complete rebuilding of 1865-8 (Plate 25d). Here the basic material is the hard, unyielding white Suffolk brick so fashionable during this period; upon this have been fitted the conventional appendages of refronting policy, i.e. deep cornice and roof balustrade, window dressings, rusticated quoins, pediments to the first-floor windows (here supported on columns), first-floor balconies, stuccoed ground storey, and projecting open portico. But by this time the various details have something of a French flavour, consistent with the appearance of Thomas Cundy III as an important power under his father. Thomas Cundy III, who was, as will be seen, a designer of distinctive Francophile tendencies, was in fact paid for drawings for No. 4 Grosvenor Square. His first recorded appearance on the Grosvenor estate was in 1854-6, when the very large job of rebuilding Nos. 20 and 21 Grosvenor Square, ascribed in *The Builder* to 'the firm of T. and T. Cundy', was in fact almost entirely the work of the younger man.[67] From then on he played an increasing part

Fig. 16. No. 52 Grosvenor Street, elevation as originally built. *Lessee*, Benjamin Timbrell (carpenter), 1724

FEET 5 0 5 10
METRES 0 1 2 3 4

Fig. 17. No. 52 Grosvenor Street, elevation after refronting. *Architect*, Thomas Cundy II, 1854–5

in matters of design on the estate, and from 1864 until he replaced his father as estate surveyor in 1867 it is likely that a good proportion of 'Cundy' designs were his.

In the large majority of cases involving the Cundys, their role was confined to refronting, even where there was a complete rebuilding. Lessees and speculators acquiesced in this arrangement because they knew that Cundy designs would generally pass the increasingly stiff hurdle of acceptability for façades at the Grosvenor Office, while behind the fronts they could proceed much as they did elsewhere. As usual, we are best informed for Grosvenor Square (Plate 25). Here, out of ten reconstructions with Cundy fronts between 1853 and 1867, two actually were planned by the Cundys. These were Nos. 20 and 21, where they were employed directly by the tenants, no doubt through the mediation of the Grosvenor Office, and the successful builder, John Kelk, got the contract as the result of tendering for their already formulated plans. Only one other of these ten houses is known to have been planned by an independent architect acting directly for a client. This was No. 18, the house rebuilt by William Burn for Earl Fortescue. The remaining seven were probably all planned by large builders with experience in speculation, or more correctly by architects working under them according to an arrangement already common: No. 42 by Henry Harrison for Ingle, Nos. 10, 26 (the 1861-2 rebuilding), and possibly also Nos. 4 and 40 by William Tasker for Freake, and the other two by unknown designers, No. 2 under Kelk, No. 30 under George Trollope and Sons. Varying degrees of speculation were involved in these houses. Sometimes there was technically no speculation at all on the builders' part, as at No. 30 where it was the tenant who stood to gain, bringing in Trollopes and then selling on his own behalf the house that they built for him. In some other cases a client was found at an early stage, and not only was the lease granted to him but the finishings of the house and on occasions even the planning were determined by his requirements. Thus at No. 10 Grosvenor Square, Freake built a single house instead of the two he had originally contemplated for the site to meet the wishes of his client Lord Lindsay, who paid £35,000 for the privilege. At this house no less than four architects were involved in one way or another: Lewis Vulliamy, the Lindsay family's old architect, who was consulted over the planning at an early stage; Freake's architect Tasker, who actually provided the plans and was probably responsible for most of the interior; Cundy, who designed the fronts (fig. 15) on behalf of the Estate; and lastly a Mr. Young, a surveyor who was called in at the insistence of Lord Lindsay's solicitor to look over the specifications and proposed one major alteration.[68]

Nevertheless the critical role in most of these Grosvenor Square houses was that of the independent speculative builders, whose repute and reliability were vital to the successful carrying out of the refronting policy. Of Wright Ingle something has already been said. C. J. Freake was principally a Kensington figure, not widely active in Mayfair, but whose high status and respectability were affirmed by houses like those in Grosvenor Square: with Lord Lindsay, for instance, Freake could conduct his correspondence on a level almost of social equality. John Kelk too had broken through from the level of mere tradesman or entrepreneur to that of public benefactor and (eventually) baronet; his commitments on the estate were wider than Freake's. Trollopes on the other hand were an up-and-coming if somewhat faceless firm: they were to be incomparably the most important builders on the Grosvenor estate at the turn of the century.

But for the period of the second Marquess, the most significant and typical estate builder was none of these, but John Newson of Grosvenor Mews. According to tradition, Newson came to London in the 1830's from Woodbridge in Suffolk, took a contract for roadsweeping in Berkeley Square, and graduated via the making of trunks for maidservants into the building industry. Whatever the truth, he was big enough by 1835 to make a sizeable speculation in the Ebury Street district of Pimlico, where he built the delightful houses of Bloomfield Terrace in one of which he made his home.[69] He also had a Mayfair base and began here with a series of rebuildings near his workshops, in those parts of modern Grosvenor Hill and Bourdon Street that Cubitt had not touched. He then proceeded to larger works in the main streets, especially Grosvenor Street, where he rebuilt or worked on nine of the minor houses (Nos. 13, 14, 17, 23, 24, 25, 65, 79 and 80) between 1851 and 1857. Newson was small enough to employ outside architects. In the 1840's he had an association with the Mount Street cabinet-maker Thomas Dowbiggin,[70] while for the surviving No. 25 Grosvenor Street the recorded architect is F. W. Bushill, and for Nos. 79-80 Sydney Smirke (who had his office here). But Newson appears to have had a good understanding with Thomas Cundy II, and participated whole-heartedly in the refronting policy. Yet frequently, many of the surviving Newson houses with Cundy fronts turn out to be less than complete rebuildings and retain a few older features.

Though by no means an operator on the scale of Thomas Cubitt, and perfectly content to do contract as well as speculative work, Newson did well enough to build himself a country house, Haskerton Manor near Woodbridge, and buy other Suffolk property. On his retirement, one son took over his Mayfair interests, another his property and yards in Pimlico, and the latter side survives as W. H. Newson and Sons, timber merchants of Pimlico Road.[71] But what separates John Newson from the speculative builders of the previous generation is his interest in working-class housing. In the 1850's he built in Grosvenor Hill and Bourdon Street the first two blocks of an important series of 'model lodging houses' erected on the Mayfair estate: St. George's Buildings (1852-3) and Bloomfield Flats (1854-6), as well as the smaller Oxford House, Grosvenor Market (1860), now demolished. St. George's Buildings was for the newly formed St. George's Parochial Association, but Bloomfield Flats was Newson's own enterprise, and in both the initiative appears to have been his, at least according to Henry Roberts, who reports similar ventures by Newson elsewhere in London.[72] Roberts, the best-known of the early architects to specialize in working-class housing, was brought in to plan St. George's Buildings, an austere, galleried block of workman-like appearance (Plate 30a).

For the time the estate did not manifest much interest, but the second Marquess must have been impressed by the success of the experiment. In the 1860's he began to encourage much larger developments of working-class flats on his estates, at first with the Metropolitan Association for Improving the Dwellings of the Industrious Classes, later with the Improved Industrial Dwellings Company. Before the Marquess died in 1869 this campaign was mainly confined to Pimlico, so there are no I.I.D.C. blocks in northern Mayfair prior to Clarendon Flats in Balderton Street (1871–2). But in 1868–9 the St. George's Parochial Association did add to their previous ventures with a further block in Bourdon Street, Grosvenor Buildings, this time designed by R. H. Burden and built in two tones of brick to cheer up its essentially sober elevations (Plate 30b).

The last years of the second Marquess were ones of stylistic restlessness. Gothic had scarcely yet been seen on the estate, nor was it ever to secure more than a toehold. However when it did appear its teeth could be sharp, as was manifested in a chemist's shop at No. 26 South Audley Street, an eccentric and controversial creation of 1858 by Thomas ('Victorian') Harris demolished in the first Duke's rebuildings. Some of this kind of assertiveness percolated through to other styles deemed more suitable to town houses. In this context a number of significant schemes on the northern part of the estate, now almost entirely lost, must be mentioned. One was a single house. In 1866–9 Sir Dudley Marjoribanks rebuilt his residence at the corner of Upper Brook Street and Park Lane. The new Brook House was on the grand scale (Plate 27a); its architect was T. H. Wyatt, a choice possibly prompted by the Grosvenors (who had long patronized him in the country), and the style was rebarbatively French. It proclaimed for all Park Lane to see that the fustian classic of Thomas Cundy II had had its day upon the estate. But a little further north, larger developments were in the mid-1860's already springing up in confirmation of this message. These were the reconstructions of the whole of Hereford Street (soon to be called Hereford Gardens) and of a range nearby at Nos. 489–497 (odd) Oxford Street (Plate 27b), while further east at Nos. 411–413 (odd) rebuilding of a similar kind was contemplated but could not yet be undertaken.

Hereford Gardens and the Oxford Street ranges are inseparable from the Grosvenor Place improvements, that is to say the rebuilding of properties along Grosvenor Place and the laying out of Grosvenor Gardens on the eastern edge of the Belgravia estate. All of these works as built betray the hand of Thomas Cundy III working untrammelled by the restrictions of previous estate policy. Grosvenor Place itself had a complicated history and was the last of these improvements to be undertaken, but for Grosvenor Gardens, initiated in 1863, Thomas Cundy III provided designs for the street fronts; behind these, high-class builders were allowed to proceed much as they pleased. Cundy's elevations here were of a French-style Second Empire character and of an elaboration and colourfulness hitherto unknown in London terrace architecture, with tall mansards and pavilion roofs, lavish stone dressings, and plenty of red brick, terracotta and polychrome slatework. Though his inspiration was no doubt the New Louvre, mediated through such recent buildings as Burn's Montagu House and Knowles's Grosvenor Hotel, Cundy showed that he had learned something too from the proponents of Advanced Gothic.

The Mayfair schemes matured at the same time as Grosvenor Gardens and by the same methods, with Thomas Cundy III as architect for the elevations once again, but because the developments were smaller and the neighbourhood of Oxford Street was less fashionable, the façades were somewhat more sober, but with a similarly animated roof-line (Plate 14b). Hereford Gardens, the only strictly residential development of the three, was originally to comprise nine houses, which were to be set back from Oxford Street with an open space in front. The terms for its development were taken by Trollopes, but at a high price just before a big building slump, and they were soon in trouble with the venture. To make them easier to sell, twelve houses instead of nine were built and the elevations of six of these were simplified, so that the final result as built between 1866 and 1876 had little of the *brio* of Grosvenor Gardens. By contrast Nos. 489–497 (odd) Oxford Street, a block of shops with accommodation over, proceeded without a hitch in 1865–6, Mark Patrick and Son being the builders for all the lessees. The appearance of this handsome range (Plate 27b), with an unanswered pavilion at the Park Street corner, suggests that it may have been the Estate's hope to rebuild the remainder of the block up to North Audley Street when leases fell in. Further east, Cundy also in 1864–5 provided modest French-style elevations (with proposed terracotta dressings) destined for a rebuilding at Nos. 411–413 (odd) Oxford Street; these were eventually extended to Nos. 407–409, and the block was carried out in 1870–4. This rather forlorn range is now the only survivor of French-style elevations in Mayfair, but it testifies to what may have been the start of a systematic attempt by the second Marquess to smarten up the bedraggled appearance of Oxford Street, a policy frustrated by difficulties with leases and by his own death.

If the French-style developments of the Oxford Street area and of Grosvenor Place marked the end of the long sway of Thomas Cundy II, they were also in their way a turning point for his son. For though Thomas Cundy III succeeded as surveyor to the second Marquess on his father's death in 1867 and held this post under the first Duke right up until 1890, he was never again so largely employed as an architect on the Mayfair estate. He certainly did some smaller designing jobs under the first Duke, but his role was mainly confined to that of a surveyor. In fact the Duke seems firmly to have shut Cundy out from the architectural aspects of the great rebuilding undertakings he was to initiate from the 1880's. With his accession in 1869 (at first as third Marquess) the whole refronting policy finally collapsed, and yet another distinctive epoch in the estate's architecture was ushered in.

Ducal Heyday

The first Duke of Westminster was one of English architecture's great private patrons. Bodley, Clutton, Devey, Douglas, Edis, Lutyens, Robson, Wade and Waterhouse were among the different distinguished Victorian architects whom he employed in a personal capacity. But the range of talents engaged through him on estate work was far wider. On his estates, the notable architectural achievements of the Duke and his servants were twofold. Round Eaton Hall, the Cheshire countryside was studded with a series of internationally acclaimed cottages and model farms from the picturesque pencil of John Douglas, while in London, many of the more down-at-heel streets of the Mayfair estate were taken by the scruff of the neck, and then scrubbed, polished and outfitted anew. From this latter transformation there emerged a remarkable batch of buildings, almost invariably in the fresh red brick personally insisted upon by the Duke, and usually approximating in style to the 'Queen Anne', that undogmatic town-house manner initiated in the 1870's. Individually, these buildings are a mixed bag, some brilliant, some worthy, and some poor; together, they then offered and still offer a sharp, invigorating contrast with the character of the rest of the estate, and please in accordance with the old canon of variety within uniformity. Duke Street and Green Street both have a share in these virtues, but the great success of the first Duke's rebuildings was undoubtedly Mount Street, a thoroughfare whose *élan* and cheerful homogeneity are unique not just on the estate but in the whole of the West End (Plate 34a, b).

In contrast to his father, the first Duke felt a special affinity with and concern for questions of architecture, as the detailed comments and suggestions he made on Douglas's drawings for estate buildings round Eaton show.[73] For his London estates the second Marquess had continued to prefer the Italianate fashionable in his youth, though we have seen a more lavish French manner beginning to creep in under architects like T. H. Wyatt and Thomas Cundy III. But his son was keen to explore new possibilities; his tastes were in fact broad and eclectic. In 1863, several years before his father's death,

he had sauntered down from his home in Princes Gate to see the new brickwork of what is now the west side of the quadrangle of the Victoria and Albert Museum.[74] This visit may have fuelled his enthusiasm for red brick and terracotta. In 1875 the Duke was to ask for the use of these materials in connexion with the rebuilding of W. J. Goode's shop in South Audley Street, and to recommend Goode to view a certain house in South Kensington, no doubt one of the very recently erected ones by J. J. Stevenson or Norman Shaw. This suggests a partisanship for the idioms of 'South Kensington' and the Queen Anne revival, and certainly Mount Street and other developments testify to the sway that these styles were to enjoy upon the Duke's estates.

But he was no architectural dogmatist, except in this matter of brickwork being red. In the countryside, for instance, he was an avid enthusiast for half-timbering, a feature which he was sensible enough not to try and force upon his London estates. There is a suspicion, too, that it was he as Earl Grosvenor rather than his father who in 1864, as part of the improvements of the time in Belgravia and Pimlico, promoted an abortive limited competition for two blocks in Grosvenor Place, where it was his definite intention to live in a specially designed house.[75] The participants for the blocks were G. E. Street (Gothic), H. B. Garling (Gothic), Robert Kerr (French Renaissance with significant terracotta detailing) and Thomas Cundy III (designs lost, but presumably also French Renaissance), while E. M. Barry contributed an ornate villa design for a corner site, again in a French Renaissance style with terracotta details and presumably destined for the son and heir to the estates himself. Gothic designers like Street and Garling were not the sort of architects whom the second Marquess normally patronized, nor was competition his natural method of selection. Although the designs were set aside, the records show that Earl Grosvenor was involved before his succession in decision-making for all the big blocks actually erected by Cundy during this period, in Grosvenor Gardens (1864-9), Hereford Gardens (1866-76) and Grosvenor Place (1867-71).[76] No. 5 Grosvenor Place (now demolished), at the corner with Halkin Street, was indeed specially built in 1867-9 to Cundy's designs for the Earl,[77] though because of his father's death he appears never to have lived there. The French style of all these buildings, therefore, though not normally associated with his preferences, was probably one of the several facets of his catholic architectural taste, at a period when town-house styles were in a state of uncertainty and flux. At the least, the Earl was well versed in all questions of design upon the Grosvenor estates before his succession in 1869. His later patronage was to show that he was always more concerned to get the right architect for the right job, and to experiment accordingly, than to adhere to any one single man or style.

However, it is vital not to attribute too much to the personality of the first Duke. For a start, his important rebuildings in Mayfair belong only to the second half of his reign, from about 1885 to 1899, and were of course dependent upon the falling-in of leases, not upon personal initiative. Except in Oxford Street the years 1869 to 1885 were a reasonably quiet period on the Mayfair estate, during which the Duke had merely to maintain the smooth-running management machine perfected by the second Marquess, the Cundys and the Boodles. The only drastic change he made was to drop the refronting of houses, a policy which had already become something of a dead letter since the demise of Thomas Cundy II in 1867. He did indeed involve himself specially in the charitable projects inherited from his father, principally the campaign for better working-class housing in both Pimlico and Mayfair. But otherwise he was at first content to let the estate jog on much as before under the professionals.

Indeed as a dynast, a Liberal and a Balliol man, the first Duke was as much bound up with fulfilling the duties of family, politics, social life and conscience as with the artistic aspects of architecture. His patronage reflected these concerns and prejudices; Alfred Waterhouse, who rebuilt Eaton, was most likely the choice of the Liberal politician in him, while the very different Henry Clutton, architect for the Grosvenor House alterations, was probably the notion of the family man, as Clutton had worked for the Duke's father in-law at Cliveden. Eaton and Grosvenor House were in fact set in train shortly after he had succeeded as third Marquess in 1869, the latter perhaps in compensation for the unoccupied mansion in Grosvenor Place. The Grosvenor House job, though modest in comparison with Eaton and hardly affecting the exterior at first, was certainly lavish. The whole of the Cundy wing and most of the reception rooms in the old house were being redecorated from top to toe in 1870-2, and were certainly finished before the third Marquess was created first Duke in 1874. Clutton's outstanding features were the ceilings, magnificently painted, gilded, and in part designed by J. G. Crace. They varied between dainty neo-classicism in the saloon, dining- and drawing-rooms, and exceptional muscularity and depth in the Rubens room and the gallery (Plate 28b). The awesome 'chain-link' ribs of the gallery ceiling were of *cinquecento* inspiration, but the handsome painted frieze beneath was by a Frenchman, F. J. Barrias, and the Rubens room and many of the fittings throughout were in a candidly Empire style.

It is instructive thus to see Clutton, a Goth by instinct though certainly a Francophile one, and the Duke, an Englishman to his marrow and client for the most confident Gothic Revival house of its day at Eaton, turning automatically to French classicism, in however imaginative a rendering, as the natural answer for the grand town-house interior. The gallery ceiling was constructed under a special fireproof iron framework and could if it became necessary be hoisted to a higher position, proof not so much of the Duke's delight in prudent ingenuity as of his plans for the future extension of Grosvenor House. But as with his grandfather this was not to be.

In 1880-1 Clutton did add on a semicircular open loggia with Ionic columns at the newly conspicuous Park Lane end of the gallery wing, matching Cundy's exterior in general style and materials but once again using markedly French details (Plate 28a). Yet the fuller reconstruction of Grosvenor House forecast in 1871 never materialized, so that the interior, right up to demolition in 1927, remained much as Clutton had left it fifty years before.

Though the Duke's first thoughts were of rehousing himself, the claims of conscience and religion were being settled simultaneously. His uncle Lord Ebury had been instrumental in securing a favourable hearing for the Association in Aid of the Deaf and Dumb, when they brought their request for a chapel site before the Grosvenor Board in 1868. Earl Grosvenor, as the Duke then was, promised virtually for nothing a site in Oxford Street, upon which St. Saviour's Church was erected in 1870-3. The architect was Arthur Blomfield, brother-in-law to one of the Association's trustees. It was a valuable commission to him, for he went on to design the reconstructions of St. Peter's, Eaton Square, St. Mark's, North Audley Street and the new church of St. Mary's, Bourdon Street, all on the Grosvenor estates. St. Peter's, in Belgravia, does not concern us here, but Blomfield's three Mayfair churches (Plate 29) all showed the resourcefulness that this frequently humdrum architect could muster when faced with a special brief. St. Saviour's, Oxford Street, though conventionally 'second-pointed' in style, was given a centralized plan to ensure maximum visibility for the deaf and dumb, and a wooden octagonal vault above. On the other hand St. Mark's (1878), where since 1851 the Reverend J. W. Ayre had pursued an industrious ministry directed particularly towards the poor of his parish, was a prestigious reconstruction job. Here, Blomfield kept Gandy-Deering's portico and pronaos, but rebuilt the body of the church in the Romanesque style that was one of his occasional specialities. The result is a fine high-roofed vessel of considerable dignity, with internal walling of coloured brickwork and some fittings and glass of merit, though there have been several alterations since Blomfield's time. The third church, St. Mary's, Bourdon Street, was a less ambitious venture, built for the poor of the Grosvenor Mews district and entirely paid for by the Duke. It was a simple church in a Gothic rather old-fashioned for its date (1880-1), but it had two distinctive features, passage aisles and concrete piers, concrete being an expedient Blomfield sometimes used for cheapness. Some of the same craftsmen worked at the three churches. Maceys were the builders of St. Saviour's and St. Mary's, in both of which there were windows by Blomfield's favourite firm of Heaton, Butler and Bayne; while Thomas Earp did carving and Burke and Company mosaic work at St. Mark's and St. Mary's. Blomfield also provided clergy houses for St. Saviour's (1876-8) and St. Mark's (1887-8), next to the respective churches. The St. Mark's vicarage survives at No. 13 North Audley Street, an unexceptional brick house unusual only as a rare essay by Blomfield in the full Queen Anne manner and because of its fine position at the head of Green Street. Later again in the Duke's reign, the estate was to become even better 'churched'. In Duke Street, the King's Weigh House Chapel replaced Seth Smith's Robert Street Congregational Chapel, while in Davies Street there rose the unusual church of St. Anselm's; both of these important designs will be discussed later.

Behind St. Mark's, two further buildings still to be seen in Balderton Street (Plate 30c) highlight the concern of both vicar and landlord for the lot of the local working classes. One is St. Mark's Mansions (1872–3), an unusual institution for the Church of England at that date, combining a club, kitchen, mission room, classrooms and apartments in the same functional brick building by R. J. Withers. Adjacent is Clarendon Flats, originally Clarendon Buildings (1871–2), the first of the Improved Industrial Dwellings Company's blocks upon the Mayfair estate, complementing several others erected in Pimlico in this period in accordance with a policy worked out in the late years of the second Marquess.

But though his son approved and carried out this block, as he did with the others in Pimlico, he was when Clarendon Flats were finished to express 'his dissatisfaction at the elevation as built'.[78] Consequently, when fifteen years later the I.I.D.C. came to construct the large series of tenement blocks round the present Brown Hart Gardens and east of Duke Street (1886–92), their habitual type of elevation was dropped in favour of something more cheerful in the red-brick idiom of which the Duke was so fond, with a modicum of gables and decoration (Plates 30d, 31a, b). However, with working-class housing the plans were what mattered. The later I.I.D.C. blocks (fig. 18) adhere to the complete self-containment for each

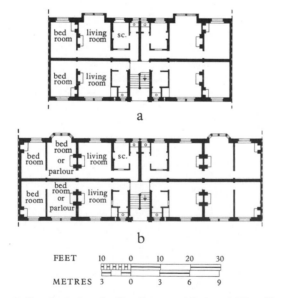

a

b

FEET   10   0   10   20   30

METRES   3   0   3   6   9

Fig. 18. Standard plans for flats, Improved Industrial Dwellings Company's estate, 1885. *a.* Three- and two-room flats. *b.* Four- and three-room flats (sc = scullery)

flat that was a hallmark of this company, but drop the awkward contours of Clarendon Buildings and their similar early ventures elsewhere and go instead for greater linearity of plan, more even ventilation, and better light. Who designed these flats we do not know, but the principal throughout their construction was the I.I.D.C. secretary, James Moore. Though the 'coffee tavern' that was to accompany them never materialized, they did enjoy the unusual amenity of communal gardens. The 'Italian Garden' in the centre of what is now Brown Hart Gardens was soon replaced by the Duke Street Electricity Sub-station, but the quiet little garden dividing the two parts of Moore Flats survives as a pleasant urban oasis between Binney Street and Gilbert Street.

Meanwhile, there was further expansion of working-class housing by other bodies. In 1883–4 a small parish institute was erected in Bourdon Street in combination with model dwellings, designed by Joseph Peacock and now demolished; between 1887 and 1890 the Artizans Labourers and General Dwellings Company tucked in two small blocks by F. T. Pilkington, one at Nos. 20 and 22 Lees Place, still surviving, the other in Mount Row, now gone; and for the St. George's Parochial Association, a body distinct from the vestry itself, their secretary and architect R. H. Burden designed a substantial block in North Row (1887–9) and extended Grosvenor Buildings in Bourdon Street (1891–2). As Thomas Cundy III and the Estate were behind the Association's initiative, Burden's North Row Buildings, though peppered with a few more Queen Anne touches, keep to a basic idiom compatible with the I.I.D.C.'s Brown Hart Gardens blocks.

Returning now to the early period of the Duke's reign, only a few houses along the four major streets were rebuilt in his first years. One such was No. 78 Brook Street, destroyed by fire in December 1872. Its replacement by C. F. Hayward, a tall, gaunt affair (1873–5), shows the Estate's predilections of the time: minimally Gothic elevations of the 'prescribed' red brick and stone, with 'numerous projections' for light and air (Plate 33c).[79] The biggest single block along these streets to undergo major change in the 1870's was Nos. 37–40 (consec.) Upper Grosvenor Street (now demolished), the leases of which had been planned to fall in so that the Duke's stables in Reeves Mews could be improved. Yet significantly in the event only Nos. 39 and 40 were completely rebuilt (1875–7). Though both houses have gone, they were a landmark in the return of individualism for terrace houses. Both had porticos, but their elevations were by no means uniform; No. 39, by Clutton, had a stone front, while No. 40, the home of John Walter, proprietor of *The Times*, was in brick. When Walter had dabbled in architecture before, at his country house, Bear Wood, he had employed the 'gentleman's architect' Robert Kerr and had had his fingers burnt for his pains, so for Upper Grosvenor Street he relied upon his surveyor, one S. Deacon, perhaps supplemented by his own efforts.

The only other big house to be rebuilt in these years was No. 3 Grosvenor Square (1875-7) by John Johnson for Sir John Kelk, with a rather restless front elevation again of stone, which the Duke was plainly prepared to allow if a tenant would run to it. Clearly it was drab stucco which he could not stomach, as he showed when he had the exterior of the Grosvenor Office painted orange in 1883.

If complete rebuildings of individual first-class houses were for the time rarer, the pace of internal reconstruction and redecoration never slackened. This was an age of large households and specialized servants, and Georgian town-house accommodation could not hope to meet Victorian requirements. Many tenants had long since begun adding extra storeys to answer this problem, and in 1874, when one of several attempts was being made to rationalize building regulations, a proposed height limit of sixty-five feet to the cornice was canvassed for London houses. E. M. Barry, giving evidence before the Select Committee on the eventually abortive Metropolitan Buildings and Management Bill, took as an example No. 66 Grosvenor Street, a house which he had just altered internally. This house then had a height to the cornice of 41 feet 6 inches, and Barry demonstrated how two good extra floors could be added and the main storeys raised behind a suitably embellished front, without exceeding the proposed limit. He also pointed out that the recently built Brook House, which actually exceeded the limits slightly, boasted merely two bedroom storeys below the cornice, whereas if pressed he could get in three at No. 66 within the limit, apart from the attics.[80]

If Brook House shows what spacious storey heights were then in vogue, the Grosvenor Street house is a typical instance of the predicament in which fashionable tenants found themselves. There was little they could do to alter the proportions of their reception rooms unless they undertook total reconstruction. Usually they had to content themselves with palliatives: building on at the back (though space here was at an increasing premium as more and more additions were made), putting on extra storeys, or rearranging the main rooms. Adding on servants' rooms was a rather anonymous sort of work, radically different from the great Grosvenor Square reconstructions of a hundred years before, in which leading architects had vied with each other. But occasionally distinguished men were still employed in additions or alterations; No. 49 Grosvenor Street was set about by Alfred Waterhouse in 1868-71, and in 1878-9 that rare architect Eden Nesfield is found engaged on one of his even rarer London works, the partial refurbishing of No. 26 Grosvenor Square. One development of these years was the more sensitive treatment, in some cases, of Georgian interiors, as at No. 19 Grosvenor Square, where Frederick Arthur presided in 1880 over a full restoration of the Adam work.

The coming of 'Queen Anne' in the mid 1870's gave a fillip to the staid progress of the Mayfair estate and

Fig. 19. Nos. 18 and 19 South Audley Street (Goode's), elevation. *Architects*, Ernest George and Peto, 1875-6

heralded the estate revolution of the 1880's and 1890's. Its indubitable harbinger was W. J. Goode's china and glass shop at Nos. 17-21 (consec.) South Audley Street (Plates 32, 33a, b). Goode's is a powerful and picturesque if slightly ungainly building by Ernest George and Peto, in the reddest of red brickwork and tricked out with the complete panoply of the new domestic revival: carved and moulded brick dressings and panels of great elaboration, mighty chimneys, touches of half-concealed tile-hanging, blue and white pots in the Oriental taste to enhance the façade, and within, dapper aesthetic interiors mingling stained glass, ceramic tiles and leather paper. Two points need to be emphasized about Goode's. Firstly, it is not a single composition; Goode began rebuilding on the enclosed sites of Nos. 18 and 19 in 1875, added No. 17 on the corner shortly after, and only extended his premises to Nos. 20 and 21 together with the houses in Chapel Place in 1889-91. The original design, therefore, though short-lived as an independent composition, seems to have

a. Nos. 104–108. *Architects*, Ernest George and Peto, 1885–7   *b*. Nos. 97–99. *Architect*, Albert J. Bolton, 1889–91

Fig. 20. MOUNT STREET REBUILDING: ELEVATIONS

involved only a pair of terrace houses, and in this context one can make sense of the Duke's advice that Goode's architect should look at a particular house in South Kensington (probably No. 8 Palace Gate by J. J. Stevenson, less likely No. 196 Queen's Gate or Lowther Lodge by Norman Shaw), and of the designs then produced by George (fig. 19), slightly asymmetrical but kept in order by two regular gables. Secondly, if the Duke's advice was helpful, it fell on receptive ears, for Goode himself was an enlightened 'artistic' tradesman, eager to reflect the latest taste. To him must be credited the employment of Ernest George and the consequent architectural panache of the building. Goode's in fact was a double precedent; besides being the Grosvenor estate's first Queen Anne building, it was apparently George's own first full essay in a style that was to be the medium of many of his happiest inventions. From two more of these Mount Street was to profit, while in the 1890's George went on to rebuild Motcombe in Dorset for the Duke's brother, Lord Stalbridge.

The street where the new manner was most quickly taken up was Oxford Street, where a systematic policy of rebuilding when the time was ripe appears to have been decided in the mid 1860's. The first rebuildings here had been in the French style favoured in the late days of the second Marquess, and Thomas Cundy III's Nos. 407–413 (odd) Oxford Street (1870–4) still survives as a reminder of the type. Under the first Duke, Queen Anne

was soon to prevail, but if Goode's shows how well the new style could be applied to commerce, in Oxford Street it was often watered down and degenerated into banality. The most prolific architect here was T. Chatfield Clarke, who designed a number of shops of variable style and merit, the best being the extant Nos. 385–397 (odd) of 1887–9 and the demolished Nos. 475–477 (odd) of 1887–8. But the first Queen Anne range appears to have been Nos. 443–451 (odd) of 1876–8, a perfunctory design by J. T. Wimperis notable only as an attempt at stylistic compromise between the French elevations provided for Oxford Street by Thomas Cundy III and the new preferences of the Duke. Wimperis, a prolific West End architect, was known to Cundy, and his later partner, W. H. Arber, came from a family of local surveyors equally established with the Grosvenor Board. Wimperis built quite widely on the estate, and a cousin of his was later to become its surveyor. He is a representative Queen Anne designer of varying accomplishment. His other surviving buildings include Nos. 130 Mount Street and 34 Berkeley Square (1880–2); Nos. 51–54 (consec.) Green Street (1882–3); Audley Mansions at the north-west corner of South Audley Street and Mount Street (1884–6); Duke Street Mansions, a block of shops and flats that straggles along the west side of that thoroughfare (1887–8); and the premises of John Bolding and Sons, the plumbers and sanitary engineers, in Davies Street (1890–1). The Berkeley Square house has a stylish interior; Audley

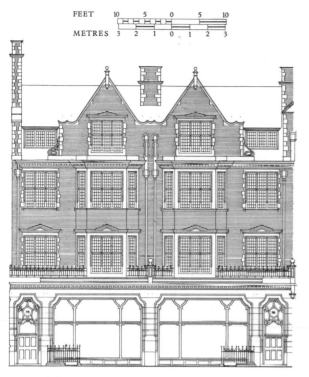

FEET 10 5 0 5 10
METRES 3 2 1 0 1 2 3

c Nos 23-26 *Architects,* Read and Macdonald, *builders,* Holloways, 1896-8

Mansions (Plate 33d) is one of the earliest and not the least satisfying set of high-class flats on the estate; and at Boldings, Wimperis's chunky pink blocks of terracotta make up a dignified elevation for yet another corner site, and skilfully conceal the nature of the only major surviving factory building on the whole estate. Though J. T. Wimperis was often a speculating architect he could ascend the social scale too, making alterations at No. 23 Grosvenor Square in 1876 and 1879, and completely rebuilding No. 27 Grosvenor Square in 1886-8. In several of these works, lowly as well as high class, he found room for a little stained glass, as if to validate his claims to just a touch of aestheticism.

The work of J. T. Wimperis offers a preview of the building types and styles soon to dominate in the great reconstructions of 1885-99. At much the same time rebuilding began in three separate areas, centred upon Mount Street, Duke Street and Green Street. By the turn of the century the first two districts were substantially complete, but in Green Street west of Park Street building activity was to recommence just before the war of 1914-18. The methods by which these rebuildings were organized and architects chosen are explained on pages 54-60; here it remains to consider the results, beginning with Mount Street.

To understand the genesis of present-day Mount Street (Plate 34), the most representative and best sector to take is the range on the south side between South Audley Street and the cul-de-sac opposite Carlos Place. Ignoring J. T. Wimperis's two corner blocks mentioned above, one may say that the reconstruction of the street began when Albert J. Bolton won a limited competition of 1884-5 for a Vestry Hall on the site of No. 103 (in the centre of this block), the freehold of which had been recently bought by St. George's Vestry. Of the Vestry Hall, one of only two losses in Mount Street, we know little except that the Duke preferred a rival design. Nevertheless in 1889-95 Bolton was allowed to build the adjacent Nos. 87-102 (consec.) to the west, together with the deep return plot to South Audley Street and the library in Chapel Place North. For the first part of this long frontage, the Duke had hoped but failed to get Bolton to follow the lines of Ernest George and Peto's designs at Nos. 104-111 (consec.) Mount Street (1885-7), the Vestry Hall's neighbour on the other side and the first block to be reconstructed in the body of the street at the Estate's initiative. These two ranges (Plate 34a, b) are archetypal for Mount Street. Both consist of shops with chambers over; both, so far as overall uniformity of design permits, are divided into distinguishable units, to suit the wants of different parties among the consortia that built them; and both boast street fronts spectacularly decked out in bluff pink terracotta. The differences are almost more illuminating. Bolton contents himself with a straightforward elevational division between shops and upper floors, arranges his flats in an orthodox manner, and where necessary leaves out a little of his normally riotous façade ornament (fig. 20b). But Ernest George boldly chooses two different styles for his lessees, a simple late French or Flemish Gothic for W. H. Warner (fig. 20a), a gentle Jacobean for Jonathan Andrews. He then binds his block together with a continuous roof, corresponding storey heights, and a line of firm arches over the shops. He also experiments with the planning of the chambers, providing conventional bachelor apartments for Warner's tenants over Nos. 104-108, but a brilliant split-level arrangement of larger flats over Andrews's portion, Nos. 109-111. Then, when Andrews decides to take the corner site with the cul-de-sac in 1891-2, George is able to extend his design two bays eastwards to cover Nos. 112-113 without a visible break, and to vary his plan again, this time with another arrangement of bachelors' flats.

The problems raised by this collective method of architecture were formidable. On the whole the Mount Street designers solved them most creditably. Of the two big blocks that followed in 1886-7 hard upon Ernest George's brilliant lead, J. T. Smith's Nos. 116-121 (consec.) appears overloaded in comparison with W. H. Powell's Nos. 125-129 (consec.), a disciplined range in orthodox Queen Anne taste (Plate 34c), with good touches in the planning of the flats. A capable architect, Powell designed a pair of corner houses which the Duke admired at Nos. 33-34 Grosvenor Square (now demolished) at the same time, but disappeared from the metropolitan scene shortly afterwards. The other building to be noted on this part of the south side of Mount Street is No. 114 by the Catholic architect A. E. Purdie (1885–8), which includes, behind its somewhat lumpy terracotta façade, presbytery accommodation, a hall and a chapel, all for the Church of the Immaculate Conception in Farm Street.

In 1888–9 work began on the north side of the street, with George and Peto again in the forefront of affairs. There was to be less terracotta along this side, so the high façades that George devised here (to the plans of others) between Davies Street and Carpenter Street at Nos. 1–5 (consec.) were of brick, with neat cut and moulded brick dressings in his whimsical early Flemish or French Renaissance manner. The western half only of this range survives. Progressing further west, the opening out of Carlos Place, formerly Charles Street, was one of the major Estate undertakings of the early 1890's. The pleasant houses around the eastern curve here (Plate 34d) are to the designs of John Evelyn Trollope, working for his brother George Haward Trollope's building firm (1891–3); the same combination was busy simultaneously on houses at Nos. 45–52 (consec.) Mount Street, in the sector west of South Audley Street where the Duke had decided that trade should be barred, and a little later at the adjacent No. 53 Mount Street and Nos. 34–42 (even) Park Street. On the western side of Carlos Place rose in 1894–6 the rebuilt Coburg (now Connaught) Hotel. It was designed by Isaacs and Florence, and much of its rich, original interior survives behind a somewhat banal façade. Further along the north side of Mount Street, at the east corner with South Audley Street, Thomas Verity's Audley Hotel (1888–9) was a very different animal from the Coburg; a 'public house bar' was at first prohibited in the Coburg, but the Audley, as one of the few pubs that escaped the scythe of ducal temperance, was frankly a drinking establishment. This truth is reflected in the block's popularly beefy two-tone appearance, albeit moderated from Verity's first elevations, which the Duke had rejected as too 'gin-palace-y'.[81] Between these two havens is the latest and possibly the most charming of the Mount Street ranges, Nos. 14–26 (consec.) by Read and Macdonald (1896–8), in a Tudor style handled with a convincing flair for overall composition and with effective Arts and Crafts touches in the stone dressings, ironwork and shop fronts (Plate 34a; fig. 20c).

Both Verity and Read and Macdonald were to work again on the west side of North Audley Street, another thoroughfare much rebuilt in the first Duke's time. Verity's Nos. 24–29 (consec.) North Audley Street (1891–3) is a big block of flats much like the Audley Hotel and again incorporating a pub; while Read and Macdonald designed another pretty block in their Mount Street idiom, unfortunately now demolished, at the corner with Oxford Street (Nos. 453–459 odd Oxford Street and 22–23 North Audley Street, 1900–2), and the stone mansion at No. 22 Grosvenor Square stretching up North Audley Street as far as Lees Mews, a not altogether happy speculation of 1906–7 by Holloways the builders.

Duke Street is more easily dealt with. On the west side the dominant feature, J. T. Wimperis's Duke Street Mansions (1887–8), evidently sited so as to enclose the Improved Industrial Dwellings Company's new blocks built round Brown Hart Gardens, looks like a coarser and bigger version of one of the Mount Street ranges. Then, before the present Electricity Sub-station was built, came the Duke's 'Italian Garden', a welcome open space, and to the south of this, a pair of undistinguished rebuildings at Nos. 78–82 (even) flanking Chesham Flats, the biggest of the I.I.D.C. blocks.

Opposite, however, are three notable buildings. At the north end Nos. 55–73 (odd), a long range of shops stretching through to Binney Street, has a large central Dutch gable, refined brick detailing, and very picturesque roof treatment. Reminiscent of Ernest George at his most flamboyant, it is in fact an early work by W. D. Caröe (1890–2), who went on to design the more remarkable Nos. 75–83 (odd) Duke Street, south of Weighhouse Street (1893–5). This is one of the estate's most original buildings, a compact, asymmetrical composition whose square profile and chimneys, clipped roof line, well-organized windows and graceful shop arches are all features eloquent of the Arts and Crafts spirit (Plate 35b). The handling of materials on both blocks is delicate and careful. Caröe had doubtless been given these jobs by the Duke on the strength of another design of his a little further east, the Hanover Schools in Gilbert Street (1888–9). This now-demolished building was a more orthodox composition in the School Board manner, but with an idiosyncratic outline and touches of adventurous detailing.

Between Caröe's two Duke Street ranges rises one of Mayfair's chief landmarks, Alfred Waterhouse's King's Weigh House Chapel (now the Ukrainian Catholic Cathedral), built in 1889–91 and serving as a replacement for both Seth Smith's Robert Street Chapel and the old Weigh House Chapel, which had been displaced from the City. The Weigh House congregation was independent and, on the whole, wealthy; originality, therefore, was to be anticipated. Waterhouse, in one of his few ecclesiastical ventures, complied, with an elliptical galleried auditorium candidly expressed outside as well as in, and a Romanesque street front of brick and terracotta designed with his customary rigour and culminating in a tall, cleverly balanced tower at the street corner (Plate 35b; fig. 21). Round into Binney Street the composition continues with a presbytery and associated buildings, of which not the least interesting feature is a meeting room in the attics with a fine open-timber roof. Though a late work, the King's Weigh House Chapel conveys in both conception and detail the energy and compulsiveness so characteristic of Waterhouse throughout his career.

Where ranges of houses were built, rather than the shops with flats over that make up the bulk of Mount and

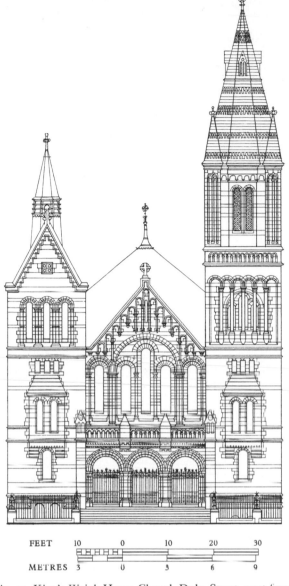

FEET 10 0 10 20 30

METRES 3 0 3 6 9

Fig. 21. King's Weigh House Chapel, Duke Street, west front. *Architect*, Alfred Waterhouse, 1889–91

Duke Streets, the results were by and large inferior, because the Grosvenor Board let direct to speculative builders and exercised less control over their designs. In any case, Queen Anne was a style evolved for individual houses, and rarely looked as well when strung out unrelieved along a domestic terrace. These are the reasons why Green Street is a duller and less distinguished thoroughfare than its commercial counterparts. As before, J. T. Wimperis was the Queen Anne standard-bearer here, with Nos. 51–54 (consec.) for Charles Fish the builder on the site of the Park Street chapel (1882–3). Most of the succeeding development of 1887–94 was opposite, on the north side, and neither the promoters nor the designers need to be individually mentioned here; the blocks uniformly consist of houses rather than 'chambers' or 'mansions', and are scarcely distinguishable from similar work elsewhere in London. The only prominent name is that of R. W. Edis, architect and specu-

lator for Nos. 25–31 (consec.) Green Street and 105–115 (odd) Park Street (1891–4). Edis had been in high favour earlier on, having been employed by the Duke himself both at Eaton and at Cliveden and having rebuilt the prominent Nos. 59–61 (odd) Brook Street, opposite the Grosvenor Office, together with the long return to Davies Street in 1883–6. But as a result of his activities in Green Street he fell from grace, for by the 1890's the Grosvenor Board had decided against allowing independent architects to speculate on their own behalf.[82]

The fate of Edis raises anew the question of the choice of architects who worked on the estate at this period. With Thomas Cundy III firmly in his place as surveyor and no more, the Duke and his estate managers could often select architects themselves. From 1887, shortly after large-scale rebuilding began, a list of 'approved architects' was inaugurated, a practice which may have been shared by other contemporary estates. This list was made up in the main of architects who had already built on the estate and conducted themselves without signal incompetence. The original seven of 1887 comprised the two doyens of contemporary domestic architecture, Norman Shaw and Ernest George, four middle-ranking names, T. Chatfeild Clarke, R. W. Edis, Thomas Verity and J. T Wimperis, and the rather dim figure of James Trant Smith, altogether an odd assortment.[83] Shaw's name was doubtless included out of pious hope; he never built anything on the Grosvenor estates, though he did at one stage sketch out a scheme for houses on the future Aldford House site.

Obviously the list was an amalgam of the Duke's suggestions, mainly aesthetic, and his advisers' business-oriented ideas. It was never exclusive, always haphazard and inconsistent, with names being inserted or dropped in an *ad hoc* manner. In 1891 Aston Webb and Ingress Bell were added, evidently at their own request and on the strength of their Victoria Law Courts at Birmingham, which the Duke 'highly approved of',[84] but they never worked on the estate. Basil Champneys, on the other hand, a leading Queen Anne architect, was never added to the list, although he applied for work on the estate and was championed by his friend and ex-pupil Eustace Balfour, the Duke's new estate surveyor.[85] At one stage Champneys prepared plans for reconstructing the Grosvenor Chapel, but these came to nothing, as did the suggestion that he should undertake part of Carlos Place.

In 1894 the revised list looked like this: J. Macvicar Anderson, Ingress Bell and Aston Webb, A. J. Bolton, H. C. Boyes, W. D. Caröe, T. Chatfeild Clarke, T. E. Collcutt, R. W. Edis, Ernest George and Peto, Isaacs and Florence, C. E. Sayer, J. J. Stevenson, and J. T. Wimperis.[86] Apart from Sayer, Webb and Bell, all these men had already worked on the Mayfair estate or were to do so in the future. Of those not already mentioned, Anderson and Collcutt seem only to have been involved in minor private house-alterations in Mayfair, but may have had work in Belgravia or Pimlico; Boyes designed a small and respectable block at Nos. 10–12 (consec.) Mount Street; and Chatfeild Clarke was active in Oxford Street, designing, besides his creditable Nos. 385–397 (odd), a long run of shops, all now demolished, between North Audley Street and Park Street: Nos. 461–463 (1886), 465 (1885), 467–473 (1885–6), 475–477 (1887–8), 479–483 (1883–4), and 485–487 (1883–4). He and (later) his son Howard also designed the large and ornate block at Nos. 64–70 (consec.) South Audley Street (1891–1900). J. J. Stevenson was responsible in 1896–8, by which time he had largely abandoned his early austere Queen Anne manner, for a small, select and ornamental little block of speculative houses for William Willett the builder, tucked away at Nos. 39–47 (odd) South Street.

Four men (H. Huntly-Gordon, E. W. Mountford, E. P. Warren and Howard Ince) were subsequently added to the list of 1894, most of them at their own request, but none of them is known to have worked on the Mayfair estate.[87] In fact the list was always something of a fiction. The real estate 'discoveries' such as the young W. D. Caröe owed their opportunities to the Duke's seeing something good by them and giving them a run for their money. Indeed the estate's appearance benefited more from the Duke's obsession with architecture and from his almost capricious desire to put a new architect or two through his paces every so often, than from the sound but staid advice of H. T. Boodle and the luminaries of the Grosvenor Office. Sometimes, of course, it was a lessee who came up with a good and previously unknown designer, as at Nos. 52–54 (even) Brook Street, where the young Percy Morley Horder displaced an incompetent architect and produced what must have been virtually his first work (1896–7), a neat brick design with mullioned windows in the manner of Voysey.

But a crucial contributor to the changing tone of the estate in the last years of the century was the new estate surveyor, Eustace James Anthony Balfour, who took over when the Cundy era finally came to a close with the retirement of Thomas Cundy III in 1890. Though a short list appears to have been made of candidates for the job, it was characteristic of the Duke that social and dynastic considerations in the end swayed his choice and led to his appointment of a man not on the final list. Eustace Balfour (1854–1911) was impeccably connected; his mother was a Cecil, his brother was A. J. Balfour the politician and future Prime Minister, his father-in-law was the eighth Duke of Argyll, and most critically of all his uncle by marriage was the Duke of Westminster himself. Balfour in fact was on terms almost of social equality with the Duke, and rather as in the case of Cecil Parker, the Duke's agent at Eaton and another of his nephews, this entitled him to a position of special eminence, since the estate, to quote Balfour's wife writing much later, 'was run, not as today on commercial lines, but more as a Principality'.[88] Balfour however was not an autocrat in the Parker mould, but a fastidious and to some extent withdrawn individual, with a strong feeling of class loyalty, an interest in shoot-

ing, and, at least in later life, a sense of commitment about his work with the army volunteer corps, in which he served as a colonel. Yet as a pupil of Basil Champneys he was also a conscientious and well-trained architect, he knew Burne-Jones, De Morgan, and others in early Arts and Crafts circles, and, having a horror of modern Gothic, he had been involved in some of the early work of the Society for the Protection of Ancient Buildings, a body with which his friend and partner since 1885, Hugh Thackeray Turner, had a lifelong association.

Thackeray Turner (1853–1937), a man of a reticence and modesty equal to Balfour's, had been brought up in Sir Gilbert Scott's office and then became his son George Gilbert Scott junior's trusted assistant. Deeply versed in English mediaeval churches, Turner ardently admired the principles of William Morris and the work of Philip Webb, and was a close companion of W. R. Lethaby, loyalties all discernible in his architecture, and most notably in the beautiful house he built himself at Westbrook outside Godalming in his beloved Surrey. Turner appears as the more active and abler architect of the two, and while Balfour was clearly in ultimate control of all the work they did on the Grosvenor estates, Turner seems to have been the busier at the drawing board.

Of designing the partnership had much to do, since the first Duke was disposed to give them the chances he had denied to Thomas Cundy III. The main area of their Mayfair activity was between Mount Street and Aldford Street. Here, and especially round the eponymous Balfour Place, they showed that Green Street was not an inevitability, in fact that one could combine with the speculative builder to get lively but disciplined street fronts in the brick style of the day. The first range by Balfour and Turner, Nos. 1–6 (consec.) Balfour Place (1891–4), is still tentative and unsatisfactory despite some imaginative planning. But the block bounded by Mount Street, Rex Place, Aldford Street and Balfour Place (1891–7), together with the stables on the east side of Balfour Mews (1898–1900), shows late Queen Anne elevations at their best, with delightfully shaped gables and individual touches of Arts and Crafts detailing and carving upon each house (Plate 35a). Further west, the firm designed another good range of houses fronting Park Street at Nos. 14–22 (even), which with A. H. Kersey's Nos. 2–12 (even) Park Street and Balfour and Turner's demolished Aldford House in Park Lane virtually completed the Duke's transformation of this sector. Elsewhere, they built Nos. 21–22 Grosvenor Street (1898–9) in brick with gay stone banding and a prominent pair of gables, the long range at Nos. 40–46 (even) Brook Street of 1898–9 (fig. 26a), the beautiful Webb-influenced stabling on the south side of Duke's Yard of 1900–2 (Plate 35c), and one odd house in the Green Street development, No. 10 of 1893–5, with delightful carving round the door probably by Thackeray Turner's sculptor brother, Laurence Turner, who worked on other of the firm's buildings on the estate. There were further works by Balfour and Turner under the second

Duke, but none so characteristic as these. All convey an originality passing at times into self-conscious eccentricity, a mood particularly marked in their two major demolished buildings on the estate, St. Anselm's Church in Davies Street (1894–6) and Aldford House (1894–7).

St. Anselm's, a building which by repute was largely or wholly the work of Thackeray Turner, was a typical Arts and Crafts attempt at style-blending (or style-bending). The interior (Plate 38b) was basilican, with more than a hint of *quattrocento* Florence in the texture of grey stone coupled pillars against white-plastered walls, and a few bald and massive fittings; but the tracery was Gothic and the exterior uncompromisingly plain except for some big buttresses and a vicarage building squeezed on to the site at the corner between St. Anselm's Place and Davies Street. In fact for all its originality it was a little-loved church, and when its demolition was being canvassed in 1938 even H. S. Goodhart-Rendel had to admit that 'St. Anselm's has always seemed to me a purely personal record of Thackeray Turner's particular tastes'.[89] And so it disappeared, to be replaced by the far less worthy British Council building.

Aldford House, the diamond magnate Alfred Beit's grand free-standing stone mansion in Park Lane, was also far from an unqualified success, partly because of difficulties over the site, partly because Balfour and Turner insisted on deploying the elements of classicism borrowed from nearby Dorchester House so casually and eccentrically. The result (Plate 38a), an ornate but stunted affair, earned a muted reception, soon dated like St. Anselm's, and therefore was the more easily demolished. There is no doubt that brick domestic buildings were the firm's *forte* on the Grosvenor estate, and these have happily nearly all survived.

Aldford House was one of the last-built of the Park Lane palaces, those ebullient mansions of the super-rich that adorned the park frontage from Marble Arch to Hyde Park Corner, interspersed among the more modest stucco houses. Though many were old, their halcyon days date from after the improvement of Park Lane as a thoroughfare about 1870. At the turn of the century those on the Grosvenor estate were as follows, from north to south: Somerset House, with Camelford House behind in its shadow (Plate 14); Brook House, which was to be transformed internally for the financier Sir Ernest Cassel in 1905–7; Dudley House, with its façade appearing by 1900 much as it does today (Plate 21a); Grosvenor House, whose westward aspect towards the park was opened out shortly before Clutton added his loggia in 1880–1; and finally Beit's Aldford House, below which Dorchester and Londonderry Houses raised their massive bulks.

Though Dudley House is the sole survivor from this galaxy, two grand houses of the 1890's still remain in 'also-ran' positions close behind the park frontage, to testify to its lure at that date. One is No. 32 Green Street, a corner house close to Park Lane, built for Lord Ribblesdale in 1897–9 to the designs of Sidney R. J. Smith.

Though a large, conventional edifice (Plate 36b), it is a valuable precursor of the subdued brick neo-Georgian soon to be so fashionable, and contrasts distinctly with the neighbouring Nos. 16–19 (consec.) Dunraven Street, where Smith allowed himself rein with some beefily detailed terrace housing. Much more spectacular is No. 54 Mount Street, on a similar corner site, but originally with an open view towards the park over the garden of Grosvenor House. This was the town house, built in 1896–9, of Lord Windsor, an affluent but discriminating client, whose profuse patronage fell on this occasion upon Fairfax B. Wade, never a prolific but, in his later practice, always an interesting architect. Wade's design (Plates 36a, 37) makes both Aldford House and No. 32 Green Street appear lacking in assurance. It has a festive pair of pedimented brick and stone elevations mixing French and English late seventeenth-century motifs, and a unique and forceful plan combining upper and lower vaulted halls, ample reception rooms, and unusually spacious office and sleeping quarters, all marked by many little originalities of conception and detail. Happily these palatial interiors still remain and must be counted one of the estate's surviving glories. They are possibly the only place on the Grosvenor estate where the true flavour of the late Victorian aristocracy at home still lingers on in Mayfair.

The other great survivor from this palmy period is Claridge's. This splendid and always exclusive hotel had long been operating in a handful of spacious houses stretching along Brook Street from the south-east corner with Davies Street when rebuilding was first contemplated in 1889. The Estate willingly fell in with the idea, for though commerce was at best tolerated along the main streets, this had to be an exception. The classes for whom Claridge's catered were precisely those whose good opinion mattered to the Estate; and, in a period of already shrinking rented accommodation, the hotel fulfilled the specific needs of the many gentlemen, noblemen, magnates and potentates, British and foreign, who wished to stay in town for a limited season and would in former years have hired a house on the estate for the purpose. Caröe was appointed architect and devised a comprehensive scheme with a courtyard, but after the promoters had got into financial difficulties and were bought out by the Savoy Hotel Company in 1893, he was replaced by C. W. Stephens. The main part of the hotel as rebuilt in 1894–8 is the work of Stephens, whose tall and ruddy brick elevations (Plate 39a) call for no great notice. But the lavish decorations of the main reception areas (Plate 39b) were given to Ernest George and Yeates, and although these were drastically altered in the 1930's, in these august apartments, something of the gracious, unhurried life-style of that late Victorian golden age also still obtains.

If such sumptuous edifices are symptomatic of the imperial spirit of the 1890's, that epoch's luxurious but formal way of life can be traced, too, in the vast extent and

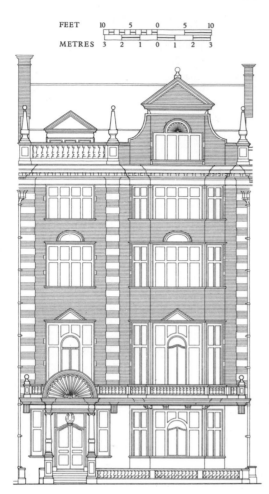

a. No. 41 Grosvenor Square. *Architect*, George
Devey, 1883–6. *Demolished*

b. No. 27 Grosvenor Square. *Architect*, J. T.
Wimperis, 1886–8. *Demolished*

Fig. 22. ELEVATIONS OF THE 1880's

expense of works privately undertaken between 1890 and 1914 in Grosvenor Square and the surrounding streets. This era saw the undoubted climax of the great houses of the estate, after which they were soon to decline and, nearly every one, fall victim to demolition or conversion. While the first Duke lived, there were indeed few entirely new terrace houses rebuilt along the main streets, but in the latter half of his reign, yet another tide of replanning and redecoration had begun to carry his smarter tenants along, until from the second Duke's accession in 1899 up to the war of 1914–18, the Mayfair estate was immersed in wave after frenetic wave of internal reconstructions and redecorations, sometimes engulfing the same house twice. For this period, records of many of these (to modern eyes) almost incredibly lavish conversions remain in photographs taken by the firm of Bedford Lemere after the work was done. From these a coherent picture of this part of Mayfair at the apogee of its fashion emerges.

The lead-up to this great splash was tentative. Possibly because of the prevalent tone of existing houses, 'Queen Anne' never somehow caught on on the estate as a style for the houses of rich individuals, as it did in Kensington and Chelsea. There are really only three candidates, all rebuildings in Grosvenor Square between 1883 and 1888. George Devey's No. 41 for C. H. Wilson, later Lord Nunburnholme, (1883–6) and J. T. Wimperis's No. 27 for the Earl and Countess of Aberdeen (1886–8) were both political gathering points for prominent Liberals. Neither was as typical a Queen Anne composition as Nos. 33 and 34, a busy pair of houses by W. H. Powell in the south-west corner (1886–8), which sported ample terracotta dressings, and bay windows and gables. In contrast to this, Devey, nearing the end of his career as a progressive country-house architect, still believed, even in town, in an irregular Jacobean front with a prominent multi-storey bay and casement lights, while Wimperis invested in equal protuberance coupled with a more cautious symmetry and some distinctly French detail (fig. 22). Both houses had newly specialized plans, Devey in particular showing ingenuity in getting natural light to the stairs and securing a storey-and-a-half ballroom (though Cundy, noticing his poor arrangement of the offices, could surprisingly inform the Grosvenor Board that 'he does not think that Mr Devey can have had any experience in planning a large house').[90] Wimperis, on the other hand, who had been brought in when the Duke insisted that the Aberdeens must have an architect, was well under the thumb of his employers, for whom an exotic 'Indian room' decorated by the firm of Liberty was devised at first-floor level next to the mews and accessible by a separate entrance, since it was destined mainly for meetings (fig. 24a). This is a token of how stable blocks were beginning to be squeezed out by expanding families at this period. By another late-Victorian innovation, dinner guests in the Aberdeens' 'Indian room' were accommodated at separate small tables, a change in fashion which opened up the possibility of new types of reception-room planning.[91] Yet by 1912 Wimperis's arrangements were sufficiently old-fashioned for No. 27 Grosvenor Square to require radical updating in both plan and décor.

Bedford Lemere's surviving photographs of No. 41 Grosvenor Square show this house at two dates, 1909 and 1926 (Plate 41). The opulence of interior finishing that they reveal is matched only by its transitoriness, and in this they may be taken as paradigms of the kind of continual renewal that so many of the houses in the square underwent in this era. Devey had indicated the lines that the decoration would have to follow, having designed the staircase details, fireplaces and panelling for at least some of the main rooms, and probably also the ceilings. But by a division of labour typical of the time, the main onus of the finishings must have been left to the professional 'interior decorator', as the old upholsterer was now beginning to call himself. His work, even more than that of the architect, was naturally subject to dramatic shifts in fashion. Thus by 1909 the Nunburnholmes' ballroom was given over to a riotous Viennese Rococo quite out of character with anything known about Devey; yet this in 1926 had in turn been ousted and the room redecorated in the cooler eclectic classicism of the years immediately after the war of 1914–18. By contrast the dining-room, an apartment still treated much in Devey's manner in 1909, with light-painted panelling up to dado level and framed tapestries above, had been enlivened seventeen years later by marbling parts of the panelling and fireplace, and by covering the whole of the upper walls with an old pictorial wallpaper.

Decorators' schemes such as these, characterized by their almost reckless extravagance and panache, were amazingly common on the estate during this era. Before 1914, however, they were invariably derivative in style, the common stylistic factor nearly always being France.

The French taste lurks behind so many stages of the history of interior decoration in Britain since the seventeenth century, cropping up even in English architecture's most chauvinist periods, and its importance in Mayfair is so great that it calls for a short excursus.

French-derived interiors were always far commoner in London than in the country. Chesterfield House and Norfolk House were decorated in a French Rococo taste at the height of English Palladianism; Carlton House revealed the Prince Regent as a regular Francophile; and York (now Lancaster) House and Apsley House show the conquerors of Bonaparte transformed into enthusiasts for 'Empire'. For all these jobs the upholsterers and other decorators were of equal or greater importance compared with the architects, and the numerous French immigrants among them naturally passed on their skills to Englishmen. So by the 1820's at the latest all the big Mayfair cabinet-making firms such as Tatham and Bailey, Dowbiggin (the decorator of Apsley House) and Seddon, had a good grasp of the French style of interior. But at this time it connoted an exclusive style reserved for the court or the nobility, which the ordinary Mayfair resident either did not want or could not afford. Earl Grosvenor, for instance, might well have chosen such a manner for Cundy's picture gallery at Grosvenor House, or his heir for the refashioned Belgrave House (Nos. 15 16 Grosvenor Square), though what evidence we have suggests that they did not do so. In fact the first French scheme of decoration on the Grosvenor estate of which there is reliable record was at Samuel Daukes's ballroom for the first Earl of Dudley at Dudley House, finished off in a dazzling Empire splendour of glass and gilding in 1858, by the Paris firms of Laurent and Haber (Plate 40a). Though the ballroom has gone, many passages of French craftsmanship survive in the fabric of Dudley House and presumably date from this time.

From this epoch on, the French manner was to grow in popularity and make more of a specifically architectural impact. Many mid-Victorian country houses espoused one French style or another, but in London, under the influence of Haussmann's Paris and especially after the building of a number of grand mansarded hotels, the impulse to go French was particularly strong. Under Thomas Cundy III at Grosvenor Gardens, Grosvenor Place and Hereford Gardens, and in great mansions like T. H. Wyatt's Brook House (Plate 27a), there emerged briefly in the 1860's a fully fledged French architectural style for the high-class London town house. Though the Queen Anne revival succeeded in putting a stop to this kind of street architecture, it did not establish itself widely as an aristocratic style for interiors, and here the French manner was never seriously challenged, instead gradually and imperceptibly broadening its own appeal, particularly for the mercantile bourgeoisie. As an international style, equally idiomatic in Paris, New York, Vienna or London, it became particularly popular with the foreigners who in increasing numbers made their homes in Mayfair. Not

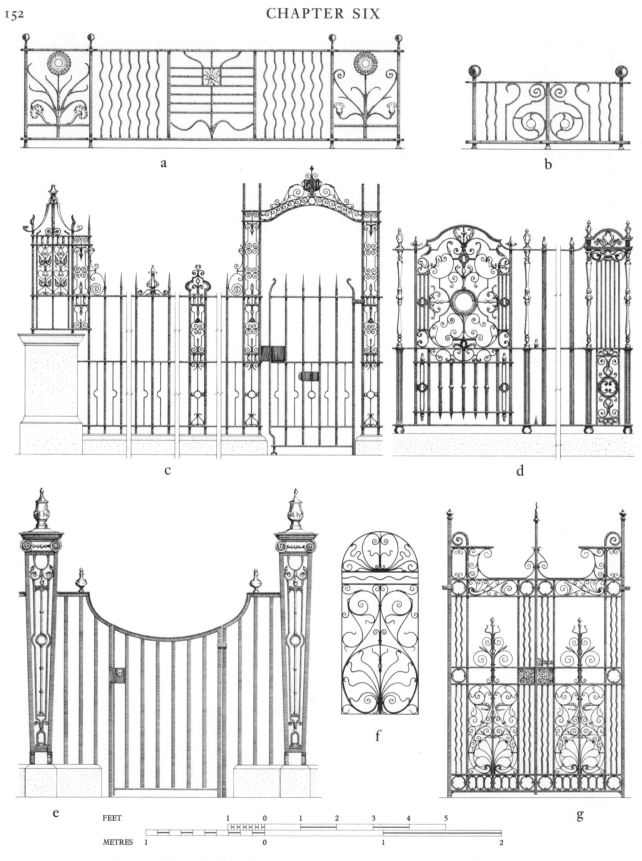

Fig. 23. VICTORIAN AND EDWARDIAN EXTERIOR IRONWORK

a, b. Goode's, South Audley Street. *c*. No. 10 Park Street. *d*. No. 54 Mount Street.
e. No. 28 South Street. *f, g*. No. 13 North Audley Street

just the peerage, but financiers, diplomats, industrialists and entrepreneurs of every variety were now crowding on to the estate, and lavishing more money than ever before on their town houses, in the attempt to make their mark on society. No longer was it merely tiresome tradesmen who were predictably uncivil to Boodle and the rest of the Duke's minions; magnates when making their whimsical alterations might also fret at estate restrictions, and more reverence had to be shown to them. Thus F. W. Isaacson, millionaire colliery owner, who in 1886 spent some £7,000 on improvements and decorations at No. 18 Upper Grosvenor Street, coupled a cheque for the renewal of his lease eleven years later 'with some expressions of a very offensive nature'.[92] What such persons in increasing numbers wanted and could now command was the French interior, which by 1890 was well on the way to becoming not just the natural idiom of the great Mayfair house, but a symptom of the conspicuous consumption of the day. Architects had either to learn how to manage the style or leave the job to the real professionals. Mostly they chose the latter course, and from this time dates the heyday of the interior decorator.

Two quite early but typical Grosvenor estate clients for the French interior were H. L. Bischoffsheim of Bute House, No. 75 South Audley Street, and Walter H. Burns of Nos. 69–71 (odd) Brook Street. Neither of them spared any expense. Bischoffsheim was a millionaire banker originally from Amsterdam, with close ties in Paris. Some time between 1873 and 1902, he transformed Bute House into a suite of immaculate *dixhuitième* rooms as a showcase for his famous collection of pictures and furniture (including the G. B. Tiepolo ceiling painting which found its way to the National Gallery in 1969). These interiors were to be supplanted in yet another French-style campaign of 1926–7; but Burns' palatial house in Brook Street survives behind a pair of unpromising exteriors as the Savile Club. Burns, an American who had married a sister of Pierpont Morgan and whose City job involved looking after the great financier's British interests, bought himself a country estate at North Mimms, Hertfordshire, where he employed Ernest George as his architect. Yet significantly for his town house Burns appears (in about 1890) to have put himself in the hands of a Parisian architect, the Dutch-born W. O. W. Bouwens van der Boijen,[93] who for the very extensive structural works relied heavily upon Trollopes the builders. The results (Plate 42b) were ornate, imposing, but haphazard, the climax being an enormous Louis XV ballroom now shorn of its once liberally frescoed ceiling.

There were various smart ways to procure a French interior. One was to buy original *boiseries* and other fittings—no problem for the big dealers like Duveen who now regularly dealt in 'period' rooms. Much panelling from decaying Parisian *hôtels* must have been shipped to England, cleaned, regilded, and neatly made up for the fashionable drawing-rooms of the period. One such

beneficiary was No. 66 Grosvenor Street, fitted out in 1913–14 for Robert Emmett (after alterations by W. H. Romaine-Walker) with Louis XV panelling from the Hôtel Cambacères in the boudoir, and Louis XVI panelling from the Hôtel Prunellé in the drawing-room.[94] This is just one case for which the evidence survives; in many other houses on the estate, imported originals cannot be reliably distinguished from modern copywork, such was the stylishness and craftsmanship of the crack interior decorating firms of the day.

The old upholstering concerns were now fading into the background or changing their complexion. Several of the new firms founded in this period still survive today. Among these, pride of place must go to Turner Lord and Company of Mount Street, who have been involved in works on the Mayfair estate, many major, ever since the early 1890's, when they were busy redecorating the Aberdeens' ballroom at No. 27 Grosvenor Square and enlarging the veranda on the front of Dudley House. A typical example of their high standards is No. 33 Grosvenor Street, thoroughly recast by Turner Lord in 1912 for Princess Hatzfeldt with a new stone front and delicate interiors, part French and part English. At this date and just after the war of 1914–18, this firm boasted full-time architects (W. Ernest Lord and Sidney Parvin) on their staff, and could design, build and decorate complete houses, for instance Nos. 41–43 (consec.) Upper Grosvenor Street (1912–14) and Nos. 42–44 Hill Street (1919), though in each case the Grosvenor Board insisted on the involvement of independent architects as well. Some other familiar firms like Maples, White Allom, Green and Abbott, and Lenygon and Morant came to prominence during this era. White Allom and Company in particular were as prolific in this period as Turner Lord. Their largest job, the recasting of the interior of Brook House, will be mentioned a little later, but work by them at No. 128 Park Lane (1905), No. 17 Upper Grosvenor Street (1906–7) and No. 59 Grosvenor Street (1910) should also be recorded here. Another firm of comparable status which does not survive today was the cabinet-making concern of Charles Mellier and Company, by whom several big schemes of decoration, apparently all in the French style, are known: Nos. 45 Grosvenor Square (1897, Plate 42d), 14 Grosvenor Square (1901–2), 19 Upper Brook Street (1903–4), 58 Grosvenor Street (1908–9) and 27 Grosvenor Square (1912).

No. 19 Upper Brook Street, one of the more extravagant of these works, was undertaken by Mellier under the supervision of W. H. Romaine-Walker, one of the few English-trained architects to take a real interest in French interior work and therefore a popular choice among plutocrats; besides this house and No. 66 Grosvenor Street, Romaine-Walker altered No. 128 Park Lane for Henry Duveen (brother and partner of the famous dealer Sir Joseph Joel Duveen), two houses in Park Street (Nos. 34 and 46) for members of the Rothschild clan, and No. 1 Upper Brook Street for C. F. Garland. After some

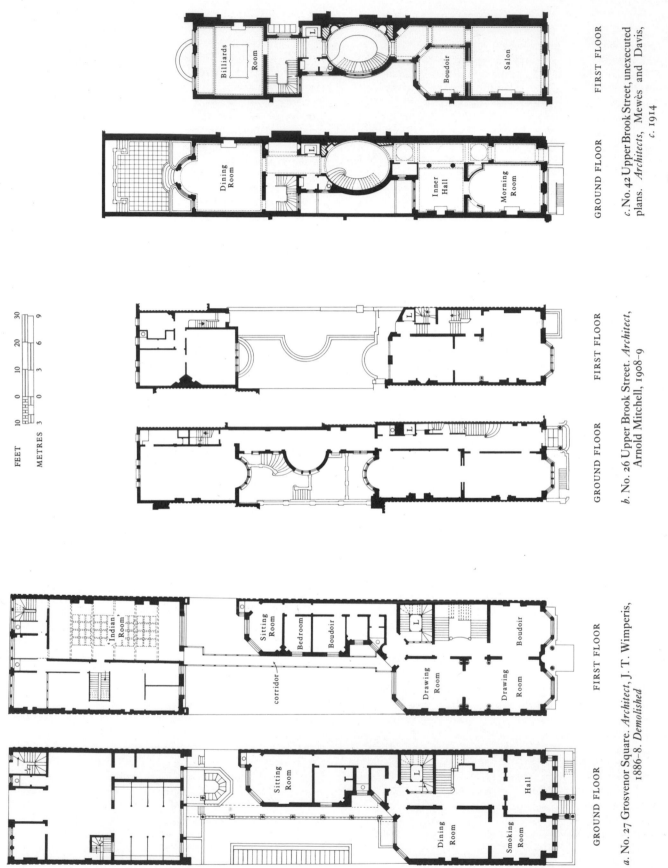

FIRST FLOOR

Billiards Room

Boudoir

Salon

GROUND FLOOR

Dining Room

Inner Hall

Morning Room

c. No. 42 Upper Brook Street, unexecuted plans. *Architects,* Mewès and Davis, *c.* 1914

FEET

METRES

FIRST FLOOR

GROUND FLOOR

b. No. 26 Upper Brook Street. *Architect,* Arnold Mitchell, 1908–9

FIRST FLOOR

'Indian' Room

Sitting Room

Bedroom

Boudoir

corridor

Drawing Room

Drawing Room

Boudoir

GROUND FLOOR

Sitting Room

Dining Room

Smoking Room

Hall

a. No. 27 Grosvenor Square. *Architect,* J. T. Wimperis, 1886–8. *Demolished*

Fig. 24. GROUND- AND FIRST-FLOOR PLANS, 1880–1914 (L = lift)

£20,000 had been lavished upon No. 19 Upper Brook Street, the Grosvenor Board felt obliged, not uniquely for this period, to warn the tenant that such reckless expenditure would not guarantee for him the renewal of his (very short) lease. The Board also noted that 'French workmen had decorated the house to fit and display his works of art', presumably under Mellier.[95] This was an old and by no means unusual tradition, dating back to Georgian times and beyond. On the estate, we have seen Parisian firms working at Dudley House, and by the Edwardian period this was a frequent occurrence. Thus Marcel Boulanger of Paris was commissioned in 1910 by Lady Essex (one of the many Americans who married into the English aristocracy at this period) for decorations at Bourdon House; he also carried out some decorations at Claridge's under the French architect René Sergent (1910), and worked at No. 27 Grosvenor Square (1912). The smartest thing, in fact, for a client to do if he could not command old French work was to command modern French craftsmen.

But a specifically late-Victorian and Edwardian development was the introduction of Beaux-Arts-trained architects as well as craftsmen. One such was Sergent at Claridge's, another Bouwens van der Boijen, mentioned earlier in connexion with Nos. 69–71 (odd) Brook Street. A third was Arthur J. Davis, English partner in the international firm controlled from Paris by Charles Mewès. Mewès and Davis, though best known for their great commercial successes like the Ritz Hotel, were also busy and capable domestic architects. From a number of estate jobs that fell to them, the remodelling of No. 27 Grosvenor Square in 1912 and an unbuilt speculative house design for Trollope and Colls at No. 42 Upper Brook Street (fig. 24c) excel in elegance and amplitude of plan.[96] But the outstanding survival is their complete rebuilding of No. 88 Brook Street, tactfully carried out behind the existing façade in 1909–10, and culminating in an architectural garden at the rear, small, sculptural, and tastefully *chic*. Such gardens, conservatories and verandas were now constantly being jammed into the few awkward remaining spaces between houses and mews, in an effort to instil yet more lushness into the tone of life in this palmiest of periods.

The most significant Beaux-Arts architect to appear on the Grosvenor estate scene was in fact a Frenchman, Fernand Billerey (1878–1951). Billerey came to England in about 1902 and joined up with Detmar Blow, an architect who, like his friend Lutyens, had struck out a line in very English small country houses and cottages, designed and constructed along fervent Arts and Crafts principles. Blow and Billerey were to feature largely in the twentieth-century history of the estate, and a fuller account of their careers will be found on pages 73–4. But at the time they went into partnership, Blow's only substantial independent job on the Mayfair estate was (and still remains) No. 28 South Street, the rebuilding of a stable as a private house, done in 1902–3 for a stockbroker, Sir

W. Cuthbert Quilter of No. 74 South Audley Street. The best feature of this house is its neat front elevation (Plate 45a), executed in a reticent neo-Georgian notable for its date but quite characteristic of Blow's beliefs and previous practice. A few years later Blow secured the job of designing the second Duke's French hunting lodge at Mimizan, and by 1911 the established team of Blow and Billerey was working on the gardens at Eaton, had started designing a big block of houses for the building firm of William Willett looking into the garden of Grosvenor House at the corner of Upper Grosvenor Street (Nos. 37 and 38) and Park Street (Nos. 44–50 even), and was engaged on a large new house on the site of two old ones at No. 46 Grosvenor Street, for the ostentatious financier Sir Edgar Speyer.

Stylistic and documentary evidence alike point to Billerey as the design partner for these and other of the firm's London works. The contrast between Blow's quaint and almost pugnaciously English manner in the country, and Billerey's sumptuous Beaux-Arts urban confections, reflects the schizoid state of Edwardian architecture and, indeed, society. In his elevations for both the Willett block and Speyer's house, Billerey insisted upon rigidly disciplined classical elevations in stone, with refined though sometimes overscaled French detailing (Plate 46a; fig. 25). As so often with this type of architecture, this could only be achieved in each case at the expense of true logic of plan; the elevations had constantly to be juggled to make them fit, often at the last moment, which failed to endear the architects to either the London County Council or the Grosvenor Board. To achieve the 'easy certainty of grouping' that impressed Professor Goodhart-Rendel at the Willett speculation (1911–12), one bay of the main façade covering Nos. 44–50 (even) Park Street fronts no more than a light-well.

But this is nothing compared with what occurs at No. 46 Grosvenor Street (1910–11). Here, since Speyer was obliged by the Board to arrange his house so that it could be converted back into two houses at some future date, Billerey's heroic three-bay elevation conceals many an oddity of plan. Not only do two asymmetrical staircases start from opposite ends of the entrance hall, but they are clothed in two styles, with a riot of flamboyant Gothic woodwork such as might be found in the Musée de Cluny clambering up one side (Plate 42a), and more modest Italian Renaissance detailing on the other. Indeed the whole of Speyer's house passes from exoticism to exoticism with dazzling rapidity, mixing features genuine and antique upon its path, until the comparative calm and familiarity of Louis XV are reached in the first-floor music room. The astonishing woodwork of No. 46 Grosvenor Street appears to have been put in by a Paris firm, L. Buscaylet, and though some of the craftsmen were British, such as W. Bainbridge Reynolds for metalwork (he designed a silver bath for Speyer) and George P. Bankart for plasterwork, the frescoes in the music room must have been painted by a Frenchman, most likely

Fig. 25. No. 46 Grosvenor Street, elevation. *Architects*, Blow and
Billerey, 1910–11

Billerey's close friend Henri Tastemain. Other members of Billerey's regular team of French craftsmen may have worked on the architect's most satisfying later job on the estate, the final and complete internal remodelling of Bute House, No. 75 South Audley Street, as the Egyptian Embassy, done in *c.* 1926–7 after Blow and he had parted company (Plate 43a). The decorous Louis XVI and Empire interiors on the first floor here were far removed from the flamboyance of No. 46 Grosvenor Street, and happily they remain to this day appositely furnished and kept up in the old style. As for Billerey's other post-war role on the estate, in connexion with the rebuilding of Grosvenor Square, this must be deferred till later.

If the interior embellishment of Speyer's house is the *ne plus ultra* of the exotic vulgarian, it is also a reminder that other styles besides French ones were common currency in the Edwardian years. Often, inhabitants stuck to something discreetly English for ground-floor rooms and went French only up at drawing-room level. Such a house is No. 26 Upper Brook Street, rebuilt in 1908–9 by Arnold Mitchell (fig. 24b); on the ground floor the front room is in the Adam style, the dining-room

behind and the room right at the back are panelled in Old English taste and allotted pretty plasterwork in the manner of the Bromsgrove Guild, but upstairs the inevitable French drawing-rooms appear. The decorators here may have been White Allom, who had in 1905–7 certainly done the lion's share of the work in transforming Brook House next door under Mitchell into yet another up-to-date magnate's palace, this time for Sir Ernest Cassel, financial confidante of Edward VII. Royal connexions with the estate were closer than ever at this time; indeed right at the end of the reign No. 16 Grosvenor Street became the home of Mrs. Keppel, after the typical fashionable renovation under F. W. Foster (1909–10). 'Adam' (often still termed 'Adams') such as Mrs. Keppel had here was the commonest rival to French, but there were plenty of other options. Beneath its French drawing-rooms, No. 24 Upper Brook Street boasted a series of rich ground-floor rooms (including a 'museum') hallowed by liberal helpings of polished and carved oak, half Jacobean and half Loire Valley in character, and no doubt the speciality of some interior decorator who held Ernest George in high regard (Plate 42c). Again, No. 33 Grosvenor

Street was briefly fitted up in 1910 for Auguste Lichtenstadt, a stockbroker, with drawing-rooms 'in the German medieval style',[97] but these were expeditiously removed only a year later when Princess Hatzfeldt took the house. Best of all, perhaps, Mr. J. Bland-Sutton, surgeon, of No. 47 Brook Street, doubtless hoping to outdo his many medical neighbours, in about 1904–5 introduced as his dining-room a reproduction ('of course to a smaller scale') of the Palace of Artaxerxes at Susa.[98]

Turning from these interiors to the development of street architecture during the early years of the second Duke's reign, it has first to be remembered that there was a marked downturn in the volume of total rebuildings promoted between 1899, the year of his accession, and 1906. This hiatus, together with the fact that Eustace Balfour was less closely attuned to the second Duke's taste and to his casual and sporadic way of dealing with architectural questions, led to some uncertainty as to design policy. One sure trend, however, was the decline of red brick along the main streets in favour of stone. The first instance of this seems to have been at No. 18 Grosvenor Street, where the builder John Garlick in 1901–2 provided a new stone front. In Grosvenor Square, No. 45 was refronted in Portland stone on the tenant's initiative by Edmund Wimperis and Hubert East in 1902 (Plate 44a); and when in 1906–7 Nos. 22 and 32 were both rebuilt speculatively, the fronts were again of this material. Sir Edgar Speyer and Princess Hatzfeldt both adopted stone at Nos. 46 and 33 Grosvenor Street respectively, and in Upper Brook Street practically all the many rebuildings of 1905–16 were stonefronted: Nos. 1, 2, 16–18 (Plate 44b), 25, 26, 37, 39, 41, 49–50 and 51. There was one exception, the now demolished No. 54 (1912–13). This was Ernest George's swansong on the estate (fig. 26b), a delightful brick house handled in the seventeenth-century manner to which he had always inclined, but with a gentleness and understatement far removed from the exuberance of his earlier work at Goode's in South Audley Street.

The new liking for stonework is of particular significance in two places. One is in the ranges facing Grosvenor House, where the Duke naturally took an interest and the estate managers therefore exercised special prudence. Hence the appearance of a now seemingly purposeless full order and pediment on the prestigious stone block at Nos. 37–38 Upper Grosvenor Street and 44–50 (even) Park Street by Blow and Billerey of 1911–12 (Plate 46a). Across the road from the Grosvenor House screen, too, reconstruction of individual houses with stone fronts was proceeding apace from 1906 onwards (Plate 44d). Balfour and Turner acquired the first job here, the rebuilding of No. 17 Upper Grosvenor Street, and a typically interesting and idiosyncratic job they made of it, with large expanses of small-paned windows and plenty of naturalistic carving. No. 19 by Maurice C. Hulbert has an able individual elevation (fig. 27a) and plan in the French manner, while for No. 21 another considerable talent, Ralph Knott

of County Hall fame (in partnership with E. Stone Collins), produced an attractively florid front with oval windows beneath the cornice (fig. 27b). Both Knott and the architects of the less interesting No. 20, probably Boehmer and Gibbs, came up against Balfour's opposition, for he plainly wanted small window panes throughout this range to match his own No. 17; but the pressures of the fashionable French style and of the social influences brought to bear upon his pliable master the Duke forced him to concede big plate-glass windows.

A little further east, at the north-west corner site between Park Street and Upper Grosvenor Street, comes an interesting illustration of the status by now attached to a stone front (Plate 46b). Here Caröe was chosen architect for a big speculative block at Nos. 37–43 (odd) Park Street, after the Estate had applied some pressure upon its undertakers, Higgs and Hill. Abandoning most of the stylistic mannerisms of his Nos. 75–83 (odd) Duke Street but retaining some similarities of outline, Caröe produced a design articulated in two separate parts. Both are in a wholehearted seventeenth-century French idiom, but with the ornate stone façades significantly confined to the corner site (No. 37 Park Street), while the northern portion, invisible from Grosvenor House, drops back quickly into a cheery red brick with stone dressings.

The other important set of stone fronts occurs in South Audley Street, near the southern boundary of the estate. Drastic reform in this area was contemplated in 1907, when a proposal to demolish the best houses on the east side, Nos. 9–16 (consec.), was after some indecision deflected by the Duke's innate conservatism. Opposite, on the west side, something like a Cundy refronting policy was followed, apparently for no more substantial reasons than fashion (Plate 44c). In 1906 H. L. Bischoffsheim, forced thus to set about the great No. 75, chose an obscure architect called Cyrille J. Corblet for the lushly classical façade which this house still presents (though the door has been moved); in 1908 Balfour and Turner refronted No. 74 in their idiosyncratic style; and in 1909 Paul Waterhouse followed with a new elevation to No. 73. But the policy went no further. Edwardian fronts of these years normally imply Edwardian houses behind. The rest of South Audley Street remained as it was, excepting for some major and controversial alterations to the interior of the Grosvenor Chapel by J. N. Comper in 1913.

By 1909 Balfour's constitution was breaking down, and a change in the surveyorship again became imminent. What Thackeray Turner and he had designed since the second Duke's accession, besides No. 17 Upper Grosvenor Street and the refronting of No. 74 South Audley Street, did not amount to much: an inconspicuous but pleasant building at Nos. 439–441 (odd) Oxford Street (1906–8) and a new wing at Bourdon House (1910), the latter on the personal initiative of the Duke. Balfour had, however, been instrumental in improving various designs which came before him in the course of estate work, notably

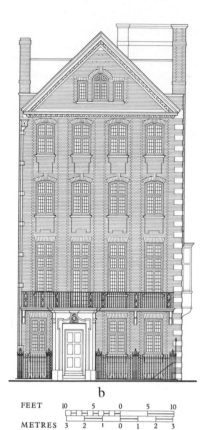

a   b   c

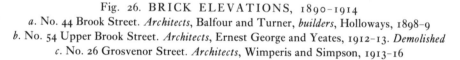

FEET   10   5   0   5   10
METRES 3 2 1 0 1 2 3

Fig. 26. BRICK ELEVATIONS, 1890–1914
a. No. 44 Brook Street. *Architects*, Balfour and Turner, *builders*, Holloways, 1898–9
b. No. 54 Upper Brook Street. *Architects*, Ernest George and Yeates, 1912–13. *Demolished*
c. No. 26 Grosvenor Street. *Architects*, Wimperis and Simpson, 1913–16

C. Stanley Peach's Duke Street Electricity Sub-station (1903–4). This heroic replacement for the Italian Garden is the Mayfair estate's fullest flight in Edwardian Baroque. Peach was a practical architect of much ingenuity and a pioneer in the planning and design of electricity stations; in 1890–2 he had already erected a generating station and some not uninteresting flats on the estate (now demolished) at the corner of Davies Street and Weighhouse Street. But his more ambitious elevations for the Duke Street Sub-station (possibly in part designed by C. H. Reilly, who worked briefly for Peach at this time) did not satisfy Balfour until he had expended much effort on them.

Balfour's successor as surveyor in 1910 was perhaps surprisingly not Detmar Blow, who had by now worked personally for the Duke, but Edmund Wimperis (1865–1946), son of E. M. Wimperis the painter, brother of Arthur Wimperis the playwright, and a cousin-once-removed and pupil of that J. T. Wimperis who had designed so much in Mayfair in the first Duke's day. At this date he was in partnership with J. R. Best at No. 61 South Molton Street and had already carried out a few substantial works on the estate: the refronting (with Hubert East) of No. 45 Grosvenor Square (1902, Plate 44a), a rebuilding at No. 1 Upper Brook Street (1907–8) and the first part of what was to be an attractive run of three stone elevations further west at Nos. 16–18 (consec.) Upper Brook Street (1907–16, Plate 44b). He it was who was to carry out the rebuildings now planned for the Green Street and Davies Street areas, and with his later partners W. Begg Simpson and L. Rome Guthrie to preside over the estate's gradual change of style to neo-Georgian.

No doubt because of their expense, the Edwardian liking for Portland stone façades was not shared by developers building on more than one plot. Therefore the only two ranges built on the estate in the period 1899–1906, Nos. 6–9 and 61–63 (consec.) Grosvenor Street (1900–1 and 1904–6), both adopt a rather dull late Queen-Anne brick style. Even in the square Joseph Sawyer's new No. 51 (1908–11), entered from Grosvenor Street, adhered to brick with stone dressings, out of loyalty to its neighbours. Edmund Wimperis's own first big undertaking is again in brick; it fronts Grosvenor Street at Nos. 55–57 (consec.), and Davies Street at Nos. 4–26

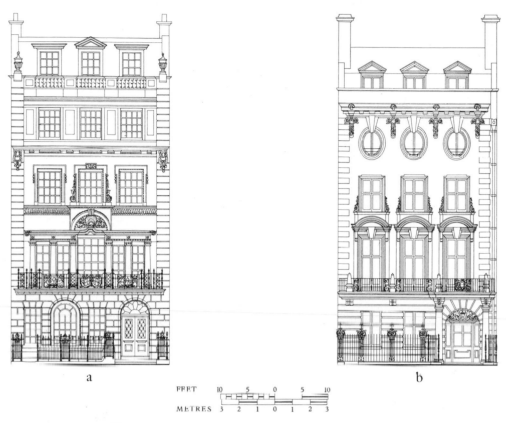

Fig. 27. EDWARDIAN STONE ELEVATIONS

a. No. 19 Upper Grosvenor Street. *Architect*, Maurice C. Hulbert, *builders*, Matthews, Rogers and
Company, 1909-10

b. No. 21 Upper Grosvenor Street. *Architects*, Ralph Knott and E. Stone Collins, 1908

(even), where it stretches all the way back to Bourdon House. Though already architect (with J. R. Best) for this development before becoming estate surveyor, Wimperis was at the helm by the time it was actually built (1910-12). It is not an elegant or entirely coherent building (Plate 47a), but, foreshadowing as it does the bulky blocks soon to multiply upon the estate, it is an important one. The incoherence is due only partially to the division of the range between three separate developers, for it exhibits a measure of stylistic uncertainty as well. Minimally French or neo-Grec still in some of the details at the Grosvenor Street corner, along Davies Street the building shows study of Lutyens and a hankering for the flatter, suaver possibilities of elevation offered by neo-Georgian. With the arrival of W. Begg Simpson in 1913 as a partner, the neo-Georgian contribution begins to outweigh the subdued half-French, half-Greek detailing that seems to have been the urban idiom natural to Edmund Wimperis, and the firm's work quickly improves. Nos. 75 Grosvenor Street of 1912-14 and 26 Grosvenor Street of 1913-16 (fig. 26c) are indications of the ample scope that neo-Georgian was to offer for individual

houses. Both façades are founded upon an entirely orthodox Georgian manner, but though they come closer than anything yet built on the estate to the original house-style of the area, their different proportions, subtle red-brick textures, and wooden window frames flush with the surrounds (a feature only legalized since 1894) make them distinctive. Yet if asked to design a front in stone, as at No. 39 Upper Brook Street (1913-15), elements of a more sober, less inventive classicism recurred in the work of Wimperis and Simpson.

To trace the evolution of neo-Georgian on the Mayfair estate a stage further one must look at Green Street. Here Edmund Wimperis was the agent of a policy agreed upon under Balfour to rebuild, on the south side between Park Street and Norfolk (now Dunraven) Street together with the deep return along those streets, 'small or moderate sized houses, of much the same frontage as those now standing, with a large common garden in the centre, and a motor house or motor houses towards Woods Mews'.[99] A similar decision was made for the short section of Waverton Street on the estate together with the return frontages to South Street and Hill Street. Though the houses here were to be fewer and bigger, the principle of completely rebuilding a range with some allowance for individualism of plan and elevation but with a communal garden behind was again followed. These policies, interrupted by the outbreak of war, remained pre-war in conception. Wimperis's firm was to design both the pleasant South Street and the Green Street gardens together with most of the houses, that is to say Nos. 38–39, 41–44, 46 and 48 (consec.) Green Street, 91–103A (odd) Park Street, 40A and 40B Hill Street and, after the war, the mighty No. 38 South Street. Despite some variety in elevation, most of these houses are generically similar (Plate 47b), with bow windows towards the gardens and decent neo-Georgian façades, most of them in two tones of carefully textured brick. Where the level of design, exterior or interior, rises higher, it is usually, like No. 46 Green Street, the largest house in this section of the street, a design to meet an individual's requirements by W. Begg Simpson (Plate 45b). But most of the houses were undertaken directly for big speculative builders, and are therefore merely decent and simple.

Well before this time, indeed shortly after the great rebuildings began in the 1880's, the procedure by which large and respectable firms of builders could speculate upon the estate had been formalized, and it remains to look at the character and achievements of some of the principal contractors. Compared to earlier developers, their power was more limited because the Grosvenor Board took a more stringent line towards design and would often prescribe architects for them. But on the other hand it was now easier for good builders to get hold of large rebuilding plots and work out, in co-operation with the Board, a unified design for a whole range, or even an area. This could secure them a better return. The frequency with which builders were offered 'takes' by the Estate naturally depended upon their efficiency, their quality of work, and, because of the social tone of the area, upon their speed and discretion.

For the period 1890 to 1914, there is no doubt that of the builders regularly working on the estate George Trollope and Sons were foremost in all these virtues. Trollopes had long been connected with the Grosvenor estates, having been house agents for Cubitt in Belgravia before they entered into block contracting.[100] In the 1860's they had taken plots in Grosvenor Gardens and were responsible for the whole of Hereford Gardens, but the latter undertaking was nearly disastrous for them and made them unpopular in the Grosvenor Office. However, by 1890, under George Haward Trollope, they had recovered their credit completely. In the Mount Street rebuildings they secured on their own account the whole of the block fronted by the eastern curve of Carlos Place and, further west, Nos. 45–52 (consec.) and 53 Mount Street and 34–42 (even) Park Street. These were all erected to the very respectable designs of their own architect, John Evelyn Trollope (of Giles, Gough and Trollope), brother to G. H. Trollope, but the firm was just

as ready to build to the designs of others. Fairfax Wade's No. 54 Mount Street, Balfour and Turner's Aldford House, W. D. Caröe's Nos. 75–83 (odd) Duke Street and C. W. Stephens's rebuilding of Claridge's were all works of the first importance carried out by them in the 1890's, while at Nos. 69–71 (odd) Brook Street Trollopes did the reconstruction for W. H. Burns under Bouwens of Paris. After the lull of 1899 to 1906 the firm took up their chances more selectively in the following new period of activity, here recasting a house direct for an aristocratic client (No. 20 Upper Grosvenor Street for the Countess of Wilton, or No. 44 Grosvenor Square for the Duchess of Devonshire), there going for designs to Edmund Wimperis (Nos. 2 Upper Brook Street, 75 Grosvenor Street) and even Mewès and Davis (No. 42 Upper Brook Street, unbuilt, fig. 24c), or, with greater orthodoxy, taking part of the block at Nos. 91–103A (odd) Park Street under Wimperis on lease from the estate. After the war of 1914–18 Trollope and Colls (as they had been since 1903) indulged little if at all in speculation but continued to do a lot of high-class private work. The reasons for their special reputation are not far to seek. They were a well-capitalized firm, relatively secure against fluctuations in building activity and therefore liable to be prompt in taking on, executing and completing contracts; they were diversified, including under their umbrella an estate agent's business which must have been the means of bringing them a proportion of their private work; they were staunch conservative builders with a tradition of opposition to the unions, which doubtless endeared them to much of their clientèle; and lastly, as specialists in high-class work, especially in superior joinery, they could always provide the elaborate materials and workmanship constantly specified in Mayfair but sometimes hard to obtain from lesser firms.

Other great concerns of comparable size to Trollopes did not on the whole work widely on the Mayfair estate at this time, though Higgs and Hill were the developers of A. H. Kersey's Nos. 2–12 (even) Park Street, W. D. Caröe's Nos. 37–43 (odd) Park Street and Joseph Sawyer's No. 51 Grosvenor Square, and William Willett of J. J. Stevenson's Nos. 39–47 (odd) South Street and the large Blow and Billerey block on the opposite corner to Caröe's in Park Street (Nos. 44–50 even) and Upper Grosvenor Street (Nos. 37 and 38), while Holloways promoted three separate major developments with Read and Macdonald as architects, Nos. 14–26 (consec.) Mount Street, 22 Grosvenor Square, and 453–459 (odd) Oxford Street together with 22 and 23 North Audley Street. Three smaller firms, however, deserve a special mention: Matthews, Rogers and Company, John Garlick and Sons, and F. Foxley and Company.

Matthews, Rogers had been building in Egerton Gardens, Kensington (under the name of Matthews Brothers), when in 1891 they took on their first Mayfair speculation at Nos. 25–29 (consec.) North Audley Street and 1–11 (consec.) Green Street. Thomas Verity was the architect appointed by the Estate for the North Audley Street elevation, but in Green Street the company was allowed to stick (except at No. 10) to its own architect, Maurice Charles Hulbert. Architecturally undistinguished, this range was very profitable and led Matthews, Rogers on to further developments fifteen years later, at Nos. 37 and 49-50 Upper Brook Street (1907-8), 19 Upper Grosvenor Street (1909-10) and 80-84 (even) Brook Street with 22-26 (consec.) Gilbert Street (1910-13). The surprise about these later houses is that they show the obscure Hulbert transformed from a dull builder's architect into a free and spirited interpreter of the Mayfair French Renaissance manner. Outstanding is the Brook Street range, which unites three large houses in a single composition built of judiciously picked orange-red bricks and creamy stone, with a row of smaller dwellings of equal quality running back into Gilbert Street (Plate 45d). Here and at No. 19 Upper Grosvenor Street the plans are as well and individually conceived as the elevations, while at Nos. 49-50 Upper Brook Street Hulbert showed what he could make of a pair of elaborate stone fronts in a more English style, Balfour having recommended that he 'take for a model the Adams house in St James Square formerly Sir Williams-Wynn's'.[101] Was Hulbert 'ghosted' for these excellent houses, as so many architects of the time reputedly were? The question, now virtually impossible to answer, should at least be raised.

John Garlick was a more prolific operator but visually his output is less striking. Garlick started out as a large-scale public-works contractor based on Birmingham, but according to an obituary in 1910, 'in later years he had given special attention to West-end mansions, in connexion with which his name was well known on the Portman, Grosvenor, and Cadogan estates'.[102] His first known appearance on the estate was in 1897 when, already over sixty years of age, he took a lease of No. 35 Grosvenor Square. Between then and 1910 his activity, usually but not invariably speculative, was incessant, and it unusually bridged the gap of 1899 to 1906 when few other speculative developments were proceeding. Sometimes Garlick went to outside architects, for example Edward I'Anson III for Nos. 6-9 Grosvenor Street (1900-1), R. Stephen Ayling and Lionel Littlewood at No. 32 Grosvenor Square (1906-7) or Edmund Wimperis at No. 1 Upper Brook Street (1907-8), but R. G. Hammond was his regular man. Several of the plainer surviving fronts of these years are due to Hammond, not a designer of particular talent: Nos. 61-63 (consec.) Grosvenor Street (1904-6), 51 Upper Brook Street (1905-6), and 47 Upper Grosvenor Street (1905), while No. 25 Upper Brook Street (1907-8) is his work in association with another builder. On the other hand the façade of No. 18 Grosvenor Street (1901-2), evidently the first case of an Edwardian stone 'refronting' on the estate, looks less like Hammond, more like Ayling and Littlewood. When Garlick died in 1910 (worth £88,863) he had headquarters

at No. 43 Sloane Street, Knightsbridge, a furniture shop at No. 40 North Audley Street, and substantial steam-joinery works in Manresa Road, Chelsea, for like other builders of this area he was a specialist in joinery. His son William J. Garlick continued the family's involvement in the area, building part of the big Wimperis block at Nos. 4-26 (even) Davies Street in 1910-12 and No. 26 Grosvenor Street in 1913-16, but after the war the firm faded from the Mayfair scene, though they still exist in Wandsworth today.

The third and last building firm of note begins to appear only late in the period. This is F. Foxley and Company, who from 1909 make frequent showings in the district surveyor's returns, mostly in the Green Street area and often in conjunction with F. W. Foster, architect and speculator. Foxleys built most of the Green Street houses designed by the Wimperis firm in the period 1913-16, together with much of the east side of Dunraven Street south of Green Street, but this apparently did not include the vast but not very accomplished Norwich House, No. 4 Dunraven Street (1913-16), a design by Foster based loosely upon Lutyens's No. 7 St. James's Square. The Foxleys-Foster relationship is unclear, but in 1914 Foster seems to have been using a firm of architects called H. H. Fraser and H. R. Peerless, suggesting that he himself was more of an entrepreneur than a designer. Foster was very busy in both Belgravia and Mayfair at this date and was responsible for No. 47 Grosvenor Square (1913-15), the last private house in the square to be completely rebuilt. He was badly hit by the housing slump when the war came, and disappears quickly from the scene. But the houses built by Foxleys are perfectly worthy, and Wimperis must have found the firm satisfactory, for they continued like Trollope and Colls to be trusted builders in the years after the war and to work often on the estate.

But along with much else, the war of 1914-18 spelt an end to the activities of the great self-capitalizing speculative builder. Soon the bottomless purse of the old Mayfair client began to close and as his servants slipped away one by one, the services of his town-house architect were in less and less demand. Though the interior decorator was to enjoy an Indian summer in the 1920's and '30's, the Mayfair house had started upon its inexorable decline.

Modern Times

Twentieth-century development upon the London estates of the Grosvenors, as previously, has kept in general respects of pattern and style to the ordinary progress of English architecture. Thus a conservative vein, gradually shorn of its classical attributes in response to the dictates of function and cost, has long persisted, giving way only very recently to the more forthright modes of the present day. But because of its homogeneity and its special blend of domestic and commercial occupation, the Mayfair estate is a good area in which to focus upon the conflicts and trials that have beset modern urban architecture. Here, more particularly, one may ponder upon the achievements and the failures of neo-Georgianism as a style not just for our houses but also for our city centres. The contrasts are struck most starkly in Grosvenor Square, scene of one of London's most ambitious and comprehensive rebuilding projects of modern times, yet with Eero Saarinen's American Embassy at flagrant stylistic odds with its three other sides. Elsewhere, in a less dramatic instance of the same seemingly contradictory tendencies, bulky blocks of flats and offices invaded the main streets, while 'bijou' Georgian-style houses sprang up in the refurbished mews behind. Complete uniformity in so large a compass could of course be neither expected nor applauded. Yet there can be no doubt that over the last fifty years the architectural personality of the estate has been continually in question.

After the war of 1914-18, it at first looked as though the Mayfair estate might quickly resume its old role as the doyen of high-class residential areas. Despite post-war shortages and high costs of building materials, the Green Street-Park Street and South Street-Waverton Street redevelopments were soon completed and two large individual houses erected, No. 38 South Street for Henry McLaren (later Lord Aberconway) by Wimperis and Simpson (1919-21), and No. 15 Aldford Street for Cuthbert Heath by George Crawley (1919-21). No. 38 South Street, 'the last private house of great size to be built in London' (as *The Times* was to call it),[103] was a sophisticated essay in the mature brick manner of Lutyens for a client who knew the great architect but did not choose to employ him, possibly fearing his expense. As if to compensate for the vast, pre-war scale of the rooms, its polished interiors, partly designed by Harold Peto, were in a restrained, up-to-date style (Plate 43b). Heath's house was more old-fashioned, a staid stone mansion with a garden frontage towards Park Lane and some elaborate ironwork; its architect, George Crawley, was an amateur of some standing, who seems equally to have enjoyed designing palatial edifices in the United States and stockbroker manors in Surrey.[104] Crawley also altered Aldford House close by, and at one stage produced a complex scheme of flats for the Grosvenor House site, so his connexions with this part of Park Lane were strong. But his epoch was over; no work of Crawley's survives on the estate, which began reaping the whirlwind of change soon after these two big houses were finished.

Park Lane is the most graphic illustration of the sudden change of tack. After five years of prevarication, Grosvenor House was torn down in 1927. Aldford House followed in *c.* 1930, Charles Barry's No. 2 South Street and its neighbours at much the same time, and in 1936, after only fifteen or so years of existence, No. 15 Aldford Street disappeared together with all its neighbours on the present Fountain House site. So by the war of 1939-45, the whole

of the Park Lane frontage of the estate south of Upper Grosvenor Street had been dramatically redeveloped and replaced by the high buildings familiar today. Further north, the rebuilding of Brook House and of Nos. 105-108 meant that only Nos. 93-99, No. 100 (Dudley House), and the two ranges between Nos. 117 and 138 including the backs of the houses in Norfolk (now Dunraven) Street (Plates 19, 21) survived as reminders of the old scale and dignity of this once charming thoroughfare. As brutally as the age of the great town house was over, the age of the high-rise block had begun.

In terms of mere extent, these big inter-war buildings were no novelty to Mayfair. Many of the ranges built during the first Duke's campaigns and, more recently, the block erected by Wimperis and Best at Nos. 55-57 (consec.) Grosvenor Street and Nos. 4-26 (even) Davies Street had been as ambitious. But (with the significant exception of Claridge's) they had been humanized by frequent subdivision, moderate height, and much plasticity, whereas now the revolution of steel-framing had unleashed a new scale of overall design. The first important example of steel-framing on the estate is the group of flats situated on the corner with Oxford Street at Nos. 139-140 Park Lane, and characterized by Goodhart-Rendel as 'much the best architecture that can be found in that thoroughfare'.[105] Erected in *c.* 1913-18 to the designs of Frank Verity, who had built a similar, smaller block of flats at No. 25 Berkeley Square some years earlier, the prominent Park Lane project attracted much attention and even made the favourably-inclined Grosvenor Board 'somewhat nervous as to the effect on the residents and public' (not least because the estate's only cinema was included behind).[106] Their apprehension cannot have diminished as building dragged on through the war years, but the various changes and delays did allow the capable and reliable Verity to mature an admirable set of neo-Grec elevations in stone to clothe his steel frame (Plate 48a).

For a few years it looked as though Verity's kind of idiom, with its capacity for easy translation into the smart Egyptian, Assyrian and Aztec modes of the 1920's, might have a future in Mayfair. But the only building overtly of this nature was the reinforced concrete garage in Balderton Street (1925-6, surprisingly by Wimperis and Simpson with strong support from structural engineers). Bolder and more conspicuous ventures of the Selfridges type do not seem to have been welcome on the estate. Nevertheless, one or two large stone-faced and steel-framed buildings did appear in the immediate post-war years. One, Brookfield House at Nos. 62-64 (even) Brook Street on the corner with Davies Street, was among the first purpose-built office buildings on the estate, with a bank on the ground floor. It had been projected in 1917, but when it was built in 1922-3 its architect Delissa Joseph was asked to make its elevation, at least towards Brook Street, 'as much as possible bear the appearance of a private residence'.[107]

Another and more meritorious example of steel-framing on the estate is the range of shops and offices at Nos. 415-419 (odd) Oxford Street, between Duke Street and Lumley Street (Plate 48b). This composite free-standing block, begun in 1923-4 with No. 419 designed by G. Thrale Jell (architect of the Piccadilly Arcade), was completed as one range in the same style by Wimperis, Simpson and Guthrie (No. 415 in 1926-7, No. 417 in 1935), but the overall design is probably Jell's. Because of its location on a candidly commercial street he was able to adopt the principles of Chicago, with plenty of window space for shops below and showrooms and offices above. America henceforward was to be an important factor in Grosvenor estate buildings. Just a little further east, another hint of changes to come occurred when in 1924 Charles Holden (of Adams, Holden and Pearson) did one of his earliest jobs for London's transport, the modest but prototypical remodelling of the exterior of Bond Street Tube Station with a neat stone frame, a canopy, and illuminated signs. It should be added that the station was no longer on the estate, as the site had been conveyed to the Central London Railway in 1897, so the Duke was in no way responsible for Holden's employment here.

For the core of the estate, still a distinctly domestic neighbourhood, those in architectural control had other ideas. Whatever frictions arose between Edmund Wimperis as estate surveyor and the second Duke's secretary Detmar Blow, they and their allies (Wimperis's partners W. Begg Simpson and L. Rome Guthrie, and Blow's old associate Fernand Billerey) were agreed in their adherence to a more or less classic style for future developments, and specifically to the type of reduced neo-Georgianism of 'Wrenaissance' embraced by Lutyens and his school for London buildings. These men, with the possible exception of Billerey, were broadly speaking architects of texture rather than structure. In the early 1920's their feeling was still primarily for domestic work, and they were firm believers in a refined neo-Georgian brick architecture as the right treatment for both private houses and flats. And by now, more flats were an inevitability. The too-great size of many of the old houses on the estate may have been just one of several factors contributing to a southward movement of the epicentre of fashionable Mayfair, to the more resilient areas of Hill Street and Charles Street. Something had to be done to keep the Grosvenor estate up to date, and flats and smaller dwellings were the most obvious answer. Thus for instance No. 7 Grosvenor Square was converted from one house into four in 1925, and in Upper Brook Street, where a grand house had been destined for the site of No. 42 before the war, what eventually went up in 1928-9 was a small luxury block of flats by T. P. Bennett. In a somewhat different vein of multi-occupation, No. 86 Brook Street was virtually rebuilt in 1922 to the discreet designs of C. H. Biddulph-Pinchard, becoming the headquarters of a team of consulting physicians and surgeons and gaining an elegant new front to Binney Street. There were still a few optimists, notably in the square, who were keen to expand their houses. One was Major Stephen Courtauld of No. 47 Grosvenor Square, for whom Vincent Harris added a music room (1926) and, further behind the house, a 'racquets court' (1924). Several such private courts appeared on the estate during these years, but this is the only one to survive conspicuously; its cheerful brick-and-pantiled façade can still be seen on the west side of Carlos Place, sandwiched between two large blocks. Again, as late as 1936 Collcutt and Hamp added bedrooms and radically altered the interior at No. 25 Grosvenor Square for Lady Cecilia Baillie. But subdivision and conversion were the commoner trends.

Still, conversion and infilling could by no means satisfy the demand. Therefore the firm of Wimperis, Simpson and Guthrie, who took the lion's share of major commissions on the estate in the mid 1920's, had like so many architects of the period to change the tenor of their work. A few words on the character of this firm are worth including. By this time Wimperis, Simpson and Guthrie were developing into one of the busiest and most respected practices in London, specializing in large commercial commissions throughout the West End, though the Grosvenor estate was their stronghold. The partners were Edmund Wimperis, still until 1928 the estate surveyor and ever the dignified and courteous Edwardian gentleman; W. Begg Simpson ('Simmy'), always dapper with a carnation in his buttonhole, and increasingly occupied by the business work of the firm; and L. Rome Guthrie, a Scot, son-in-law of William Flockhart, and established as a well-known architect before he joined the practice in 1925. At their office (just off the estate in South Molton Street) this trio presided benignly over an assiduous body of underlings. New jobs were normally assigned to one particular partner or another, though it is rarely possible to say which job went to whom. But it does appear that from the time of Guthrie's arrival he gradually took on more of the most important designing work, while Wimperis especially began to reduce his commitments.[108]

On the Grosvenor estate, the crucial buildings erected by the firm in the 1920's were not the occasional private houses like No. 38 South Street or the pert No. 64 Park Street, but their big new blocks of flats. These, like the houses, were designed with elevations of the elegantly textured red bricks (mainly from Daneshill) that were then fashionable, and for a time still sported ample classical details in stone. The first of these blocks was the justly admired Mayfair House, Carlos Place (1920-2). It was followed by three at the corner of Upper Brook Street and Park Street: Upper Feilde (1922-4), Upper Brook Feilde (1926-7), and No. 80 Park Street (1929-30). Also in the group is the important Nos. 49-50 Grosvenor Square (1925-7) in the south-east corner, precursor of much that was to follow in the square. Of these blocks of flats, Upper Feilde (at No. 71 Park Street) is worth singling out as an instructive early attempt to enliven an essentially plain six-storey elevation (Plate 49a); it embodies cleverly contrived bonding patterns, delicate diapers in the brickwork, and even a small gable or two. Close by, on Upper Brook Feilde (at No. 47 Park Street), the architects fought back against monotony by means of a giant order on the main front and, to get extra accommodation, crammed two storeys instead of one into the roof, above the line of the 'architecture' (Plate 49b). But here and in their big corner block at Nos. 49–50 Grosvenor Square, stretching back along the east side of Carlos Place, they came up against the problem then exercising half London's architects. How could a style that was domestic in scale be articulated to fit the height and density required in the new, large city buildings equipped for modern living? This was the real, practical crisis for neo-Georgianism: not the challenge of Corbusier, but its own ultimate lack of elasticity for urban buildings of scale. What so often occurred was that the style was gradually deprived of its most obvious appurtenances so as to minimize two quite distinct problems, those of cost and those of proportion. Divested of its stylistic features, it easily sank into monotony and fell prey to critics of new persuasions.

However, on the Grosvenor estates this steady tendency towards simplification was to be stoutly, if briefly, resisted at the behest of Detmar Blow, now in the ascendant at the Grosvenor Office. In an unusual step, two independent architects, Edwin Lutyens and Fernand Billerey, were called in to help on different Estate schemes of redevelopment, while a third, Frederick Etchells, was entrusted with a variety of minor employments. More than anything, it seems to have been the question of Grosvenor House, uninhabited by the Duke since the first World War and temporarily under Government occupation, that precipitated this move. As early as 1923, Billerey and Etchells had been involved by the Estate in proposals for the site, and several abortive schemes followed, notably one worked out by the New York architect Whitney Warren, and another by George Crawley and Gervase Bailey. But it was not until 1926, when proposals for a new building on the site of the old house were finally agreed upon, that Lutyens was called in.

From this time the short but vital era of architectural consultation begins. Its peak coincides in fact with Blow's heyday between 1928, when Wimperis relinquished the estate surveyorship, and his own abrupt retirement in 1933. In this period, loose but distinct spheres of interest speedily emerged. Lutyens took the big blocks ripe for redevelopment, principally Grosvenor House and Hereford House; Billerey was called in over the proposed rebuilding of Grosvenor Square; and Etchells quietly diverted himself with private commissions in the mews. At first sight the emergence of these particular individuals appears arbitrary: Lutyens, acclaimed first architect of the day and prince of English traditions of design; Billerey, reclusive and meticulous Beaux-Arts designer; and Etchells, young Vorticist painter, translator of Le Corbusier, Anglo-Catholic enthusiast, and clever amateur

in all the arts. Doubtless, the heterodoxy and informality of their characters appealed to Blow, weary of the steady efficiency of the Wimperis firm. Strong individualism was a particularly necessary quality for Lutyens and Billerey, since their job was to bestow grace and style upon the exteriors of a new set of buildings, most of which had a more mundane character and function than those of earlier epochs. What is remarkable is the extent to which their answers to the problems which Blow presented to them coincided uniformly in a reinforcement of that brick-classic tradition that was now gradually vanishing from so much of urban architecture.

The most graphic example of this is Grosvenor House. In 1926 A. O. Edwards, a speculator who had gained experience on part of the site of Devonshire House, came forward with a comprehensive scheme to include a hotel and flats, his architect being L. Rome Guthrie. It is said that Guthrie brought the job with him into the office of Wimperis and Simpson, whose ranks he joined as a partner at just this time. But by the time that Guthrie's drawings were complete, Blow had brought in Lutyens and made various suggestions to him. The deliberate plainness of Guthrie's submitted elevations evidently did not appeal to the Duke's advisers, and this gave Lutyens the chance to take over, alter and dramatize the façade-composition; and also to add some extra height. So Grosvenor House, as built in 1926–30, is in its plan basically Guthrie's and in its dress mainly Lutyens's: the hand of the latter is easily betrayed by the special brand of classicism employed on the ground storeys and on the high stone pavilions, so reminiscent of his work at Delhi (Plate 48c).

But there were other influences at work as well. Grosvenor House was intended by Edwards to cater 'specifically for the American market',[109] so in the layout good note was taken of American models and the complex was broken up into several separate blocks with deep set-backs from the street between them, instead of the internal light-wells traditional to Britain. Lutyens, who in 1925 had visited the United States for the first time, discovering much to admire in contemporary architecture there, had thought the skyscrapers 'growing from monstrosities to emotions of real beauty'.[110] Ever quick to adopt and perfect an idea, Grosvenor House shows him refining the American innovation of a crowning classical storey, as in his contemporary Midland Bank, Poultry, and Britannic House, Finsbury Circus.

At Grosvenor House, Lutyens was closely confined. His attic pavilions had to be limited to the ends of the four blocks, the linking bridges he had wanted between the two main portions were omitted, and the upward recession in mass for which he constantly strove in his later civic works could hardly be realized. The result was in fact a compromise and because of its great bulk inevitably controversial. It has never been thought wholly successful. Lutyens's official chronicler A. S. G. Butler believed that the criticism really stemmed from the fact that new Grosvenor House spelt the knell of one-time fashionable Park Lane as a residential street.[111] But a shrewd contemporary article in *The Times* sums up the real problem: 'what is the matter with Grosvenor House is precisely that it is not designed as a big building. It is an overgrown small building, stretching a familiar and endearing style of domestic architecture beyond its capacity to please. Every architectural style has its proper scale, and it is a fairly safe general rule that, if you greatly enlarge—or diminish—scale, you must change style.'[112]

Nevertheless Lutyens had furnished the estate with a spectacular building, and was to do so again, at Hereford House in Oxford Street. Here the whole of the Victorian development of Hereford Gardens together with the open space in front was destined to disappear in favour of a grand store for Gamages with flats above, to plans by C. S. and E. M. Joseph. Lutyens provided elevations in September 1928 and building took place in 1929–30. This time, though the site was more enclosed, the design problems were not so great and Lutyens could respond to the scale with the high recessed classical features that he loved on all four sides. Towards Oxford Street he also introduced a small engaged colonnade, thus restoring to the Grosvenor estate side of the street a little of the swagger stolen by Selfridges across the way. On the whole Hereford House, though a ruinous enterprise for Gamages, turned out more satisfactorily than Grosvenor House. It was beyond even Lutyens's power entirely to redeem the problems of scale. But in each case he had given a touch of distinction to what might otherwise have been just another pair of massive rebuildings.

The smaller rebuildings in which Lutyens was involved need briefer comment. One was Audley House, Nos. 8–10 North Audley Street, where he provided a sketch elevation for the block of shops and residential flats planned by J. Stanley Beard and erected in 1927–9. Like Grosvenor House and Hereford House, Audley House is of red brick with some distinguishing stone dressings. But at No. 8 Upper Grosvenor Street, also in 1927–8, Lutyens surprisingly was asked to improve a single stone house-elevation. For this and two other advisory jobs on further sizeable rebuildings along Park Lane, Aldford House (1930–2) and Brook House (1933–5), he was paid a standard fee of fifty guineas each time. It must have been an *ad hoc* consultative procedure, for he played no known part in either the decent Nos. 105–108 Park Lane of 1930–2 (Plate 49c), designed like the new Brook House by Wimperis, Simpson and Guthrie, or the inferior Nos. 56–62 Park Lane (1933–4), by Trehearne and Norman, Preston and Company. Billerey, too, was consulted on some of these sites, particularly Brook House, but there is good circumstantial evidence that neither he nor Lutyens had any substantial hand in the design of this interestingly planned block, where Guthrie once again was the principal architect. The best of all these buildings is the new Aldford House (Plate 49d), for which the archi-

tects were George Val Myer and F. J. Watson-Hart, designers of Broadcasting House. As usual, it is divided between banks and shops below and flats above, but the flats have continuous, canted balconies that form a horizontal banding to the block and contribute to a more lively and up-to-date treatment than any of its neighbours received. The receding top storeys, culminating in the surprise of end pediments and a gabled roof, suggest the possibility of a more extensive and specially constructive piece of intervention by Lutyens here, but this is not known for certain.

After Blow's eclipse, however, Lutyens was no longer used by the Grosvenor Estate as a consultant. He was briefly superseded by Sir Giles Gilbert Scott, who was well paid for advice on Fountain House, Park Lane (1935–8, also by Myer and Watson-Hart), but this appears to have been the single instance of his consultation. In a personal capacity, Lutyens also made a number of minor domestic alterations on the estate, from those at No. 12 Grosvenor Square, probably of 1895, to those at No. 5 Balfour Place in 1934, but none was of consequence.

It is surprising, possibly even disappointing, that the job of rebuilding Grosvenor Square did not fall to Lutyens, the only designer of the period who had the stature, temperament, and needful mixture of charm and aggression to force such a bold concept through to fulfilment. Fernand Billerey had no such natural advantages. Neither his French background nor his self-effacing modesty was calculated to work to his benefit in a situation where the support and co-operation of estate managers, speculators and fellow-architects had to be secured for the elevations that he was commissioned to impose upon them. Many of the difficulties Billerey did manage to overcome, but others turned out to be insuperable.

The chronology of the long-drawn-out Grosvenor Square rebuilding has already been given (see page 77), but it remains to consider the architectural character and assess the outcome of this great scheme. Today there is no longer any need to challenge on doctrinaire grounds Billerey's choice of style for Grosvenor Square as old fashioned, since the fashion which it represents has now passed into history. His neo-Georgian, in textured brick with ample stone dressings, tested, formalized and refined through contact with the Beaux-Arts disciplines that were his own particular strength, corresponded precisely with that partial view of eighteenth-century tradition that the guardians of the estate's image cherished most dearly. Nor can Billerey be blamed in any way for the failure to complete the square. Given the leasehold system of tenure, the rupture between his ally Blow and the Duke in 1933, and the depressed economic situation that persisted through the decade, a quick completion to unified designs was impossible. But one pertinent question, having little to do with style but much to do with history of Grosvenor Square, has to be asked. Was the conception of a unified, composed rebuilding of the square in itself a wise one?

In the eighteenth century, attempts to sustain a single composition along individual sectors of the square had succeeded on the east but failed on the north. Then in the Cundy era, though Blow and his associates probably did not know it, what appears to have been an attempt to secure uniformity by refrontings had also died the death. So a composed, classical Grosvenor Square was a recurrent theme, and because of modern leasing policies it stood real chances of success in the twentieth century. But the British, traditionally respectful of the rights of property, have been equally often rebels against formality in aesthetics and dictatorship in design, even when initiated by the very same landlords. So much the estate managers might have learned from the painful recent histories of Regent Street and Kingsway. In Grosvenor Square they were to get nearer to success, but a major factor in their frustration was to be the old conception of the London square in terms of individual, private plots. In this conception there was much aesthetic sense as well as practicality. The Grosvenor Square which the twentieth century demolished was not meant to be 'read' as one, but as a set of variations upon the domestic theme, to which the amenity of the garden gave relief. Though the old houses of that square could hardly all survive into the age of the apartment block, the case for judicious variety and gradual replacement was a strong one. Since modern developers press both for height and for breadth of frontage, the variations would certainly have been difficult to control; arguably indeed, uniform development has meant that Grosvenor Square has escaped the fate of, say, modern Golden Square or Hanover Square. But this has been at a cost. The long sides of today's square, however well composed, cannot comfortably be taken in at a glance. The thinning of trees and opening out of the central garden, though intended to pull the square together, actually draws attention to this problem. As a result, the modern visitor scurries through Grosvenor Square, absorbing little of the refined architecture that is about him, or at best fixing on the comparatively brash but finite bulk of the American Embassy upon its western side.

Billerey was in some measure alive to the dangers of an over-extended composition on the two long sides. Evidently the Place de la Concorde, most obvious of models for a large open square, was much before his Gallic consciousness. Indeed in a design of 1936 for the south side he actually divided the range into two, with a wide gateway in the centre. This was doubtless not feasible because of the sacrifice of space involved, but it was visually a good principle and makes the loss of his overall design for this side the sadder. It is only on the north, the one side completed recognizably to his design (except for the roof), that Billerey's grasp of an architecture of scale and texture, with its refinements of sculptural detail and brickwork and its small breaks

and recessions to avoid monotony, can be readily appreciated (Plate 54b).

Even on this side, and much more visibly on the others, variations of detail in parts of different date can naturally be found. These variations are more dramatically apparent on the return flanks and backs of the new Grosvenor Square, some of which have an interest of their own. The return flank along North Audley Street of No. 21, part of the first block to be rebuilt (1933–4), adopts the then fashionable light-well set back from the street, whereas at the other end of the north side, Lewis Solomon, Kaye and Partners' Europa Hotel (1961–4) has an expansive façade towards Duke Street incorporating a small drive-in. Brutally different again are the rear elevations of the square's other hotel, the Britannia by Richard Seifert and Partners (1967–9) at Nos. 39–44 in the middle of the south side; here, in compensation for the loss of a modern façade or entrance to the square, the design breaks with redoubled vigour towards Adams Row into the blocky pre-cast concrete idiom so characteristic of this firm. One of the minor entertainments of modern Grosvenor Square is to stroll around the neighbouring streets and mews and note how many disparate bedfellows in the way of embassies, hotels and flats can be found snuggling together under Billerey's all-enveloping classical counterpane.

Of the architects regularly employed to advise the Estate during this period, the third, Frederick Etchells, is something of an elusive figure, and his direct work for the Estate was much less far-reaching than that of Lutyens or Billerey. A dilettante of the best and most capable kind and an associate of Blow as far back as 1911,[113] Etchells liked small jobs with which to keep himself amused, and of these the Grosvenor estate had plenty. In 1923 he had a model prepared in connexion with one of the Grosvenor House proposals, a task he again undertook for Lutyens in 1929. By 1925 he was also being paid in connexion with a variety of small commissions, sometimes matters like lettering on signboards. But by the time that Wimperis retired in 1928, Etchells was privately establishing himself as monarch of the mews, with all that this now implied.

The 'bijou' mews house in Mayfair had, perhaps surprisingly, a short pre-war history. Possibly motors took up less space than horses, for as early as 1908 the Grosvenor Board agreed to the conversion of some of the stables in Balfour Mews and Streets Mews (now Rex Place) which were letting badly, and duly in that year No. 1 Streets Mews was turned into a private house (now No. 2 Aldford Street). Then after a gap of about five years, the architects Gilbert and Constanduros added a storey at No. 1 Balfour Mews (now No. 3 Aldford Street) for Monty Mendelssohn, a small speculator, and Stanley Barrett and Driver altered No. 17 Balfour Mews (now No. 23 South Street) for two maiden ladies, in both cases with the help of Thackeray Turner, joint architect of the original stabling here. By 1915, on the strength of the many applicants he had for his conversion, Matheson (as Mendelssohn now called himself) was able to report 'great demand' for what he was already speaking of as 'bijou' housing, and after the war this rapidly increased.[114] One of the first such post-war conversions, again undertaken by Matheson with Gilbert and Constanduros at No. 1 Mount Row in about 1919, was deemed worthy to be published in *Country Life* four years later.[115] Characteristically, as little as possible of the exterior was changed, but the whole of the inside was gutted and made elegantly French. As mews houses became the rage, especially among *chic* young people, many such private works of conversion were undertaken (Plate 50c, d) and many must remain unrecorded. But by 1925 the Estate was beginning to explore what might be done in three minor thoroughfares, Culross Street, Mount Row and Lees Mews (later Lees Place).

The main field of Estate endeavour was the sector of Culross Street east of Park Street, where there had always been a number of small independent houses. In 1926-9 Wimperis managed to shut up the short east-west section of Blackburne's Mews, behind the north side of Culross Street, and in its place his firm laid out a narrow little garden. Both sides of the street itself were thoroughly rebuilt, with Wimperis, Simpson and Guthrie undertaking No. 6 together with No. 64 Park Street, and Forsyth and Maule (with Mrs. Macindoe) Nos. 2 and 4, while much of the rest came under the sway of Etchells. He with his partner Gordon Pringle rebuilt or brushed up Nos. 1A and 5 and probably also Nos. 1, 3, 7 and 9 on the south side, and No. 14 on the north, all in a simple style enlivened with small fetching Regency details rather in the manner of Adshead and Ramsey's work on the Duchy of Cornwall Estate in Kennington (Plate 50a, b). Most of this took place between 1926 and 1928, and was so subtly done that it is hard to believe the transformation so complete or so modern. Further west in Culross Street there are one or two other nice mews houses (Plate 51a), for instance Ernest Cole's witty No. 25 (1929).

Having proved that an admirer of Corbusier could play a good hand in neo-Georgianism, Etchells produced another trick from his sleeve in Mount Row. Here the young T. P. Bennett in 1926-7 had designed the charming Nos. 12-14 (Wren House), with an intricate plan including a garage on the ground floor, reception rooms above, and round 'Hampton Court' windows to the bedroom storey (Plate 51c). Not to be outdone, Etchells in 1929-31 followed on with the neighbouring Nos. 6-10 (Tudor House), an irreverent group with a pair of half-hipped gables that look as though they had dropped in on Mayfair from some smart suburban estate (Plate 51d). Such slight interludes upon the staid Grosvenor scene were what Etchells loved; another, a restoration of a run of shops along Little Grosvenor (now Broadbent) Street, sadly failed to materialize, though drawings survive (Plate 51b). Further north and west in Lees Place (as Lees Mews became in 1930), his role was smaller but his

spirit of paradox as present as ever. With the pleasant neo-Georgian houses built in Shepherd's Place in the 1930's he was not involved, but in Lees Place itself he probably designed No. 14 (1930) and certainly the more formal Lees House, No. 4 (1930-1) for the Hon. Evelyn FitzGerald. Etchells was determined not to let the tall symmetrical neo-Georgian façade of Lees House be taken at its face value. In a tongue-in-cheek article for *The Architectural Review*, presumably written by himself, he pleaded that Lees House was a 'modern house, built for two modern people leading a highly modern life', and that its 'faint flavour of the eighteenth century . . . is as illusive and as unimportant as when Picasso, to compare small things with great, gives the world a bold experiment in the guise of an 1870 lithograph'; and in justification he pointed to the variations he had made on the 'typical London plan'.[116] The old traditional house plan was indeed at last beginning to fade away in metropolitan London, as domestic architects learned to deal with smaller sites and cope with conversions. Though Lees House and one or two other of the mews houses mentioned do still have two staircases, in most the demise of old Mayfair patterns of living was plain to behold.

In one respect the interwar period was still a golden age, and that was for interior decoration. Fashionable families who gave up their great houses and installed themselves in flats wanted and, on the whole, could still afford some compensation for their novel anonymity in the shape of good furniture and design. In this period there was probably more originality in decorating work than ever before. One little-remembered factor in the increasing separation of architecture from interior design was the apartment block, for in a flat there was no need to employ an architect but plenty of opportunity to display good taste. Decorating firms of the 1920's and '30's are recalled usually for their contributions to country houses, but blocks of flats like those in Grosvenor Square were their staple fare. Several such schemes were chattily written up in magazines like *Vogue* and *Harper's Bazaar*.

Most of the Mayfair decorators of the day still adhered to the traditional styles, but many hankered for modernity in one form or another. Despite the occasional go-ahead client, like the one who employed Serge Chermayeff to redecorate a flat at No. 42 Upper Brook Street shortly before 1935, or Mr. Saxon Mills, who got Denham MacLaren to 'scramble' the walls of his flat at No. 52 Grosvenor Street,[117] the traditional concerns naturally got the better of the market. But gone were the days when French stucco-work was reeled out by the yard; instead, firms like White Allom or Lenygon and Morant now offered quiet, relatively scholarly interiors, with panelling of waxed oak or subdued colouring, and the emphasis all upon the furniture, pictures and carpets. Much borrowing from old houses went on at this time, which Philip Tilden speaks of as 'a period when all Mayfair panelled its walls with pine stripped from old discarded Georgian houses, and which were limed to greyness, or waved to honey'.[118] Such was the character of Lenygon and Morant's transformation of No. 25 Upper Brook Street of 1933 (Plate 53a), of their work at No. 9 South Audley Street (1935) and of the surviving interiors at No. 45 Upper Grosvenor Street, where date and designer are unknown. Oliver Hill was, on the whole, equally reticent in his work of 1928 for Lord Forres at No. 70 Grosvenor Street (now demolished). A less individual but similar style of work could be had from the big department stores like Whiteleys, Harrods, Waring and Gillows and Maples, all of whom sported flourishing decorating sides between the wars.

For greater originality, still within a traditional framework, it was possible to go to one of a group of amateurs and ladies who did much for interior decoration in the 1920's and '30's. 'The conversion of stables and garages was an important part of Mrs. Beaver's business' in *A Handful of Dust*, and for Mrs. Beaver Evelyn Waugh could have had one or several personalities in mind. In Culross Street we have already seen a Mrs. Macindoe in operation at Nos. 2 and 4, but some more familiar names were active on and around the estate. Lady Sibyl Colefax, probably the best known of these women, began her decorating practice from rooms just out of our area in Bruton Street; her only known work on the Grosvenor estate in this period was the redecoration of No. 40A Hill Street in 1938. After the war, however, she joined forces with John Fowler in Wyatville's old house at No. 39 Brook Street, the gallery of which was separated off and redecorated as a private house for Mrs. Lancaster (doyenne of 1930's taste) in Fowler's inimitable manner, while the main house remains the headquarters of Colefax and Fowler. Another celebrated shop was that of Mrs. Guy Bethell and Mrs. Dryden, partners in an interior decorating firm called E. Elden at No. 84 Duke Street, just behind No. 10 Grosvenor Square;[119] they altered No. 9 Upper Grosvenor Street in 1928, and some surviving reliefs of this date by Gilbert Bayes in the back yard must relate to their work here.

Near Elden's shop, behind No. 9 Grosvenor Square, Somerset Maugham's wife Syrie had in the late 1920's and 1930's a 'wildly expensive corner block with "Syrie Ltd." in gold letters', where her estranged husband once uncharitably imagined her as 'on her knees to an American m-m-millionairess trying to sell her a chamber-p-p-pot'.[120] But Syrie Maugham did serious work. She is usually remembered for her obsession with white and her love of stripped furniture, though neither taste was greatly in evidence in her three known works on the Grosvenor estate—interiors at No. 48 Upper Grosvenor Street for the Whighams (1935), at Israel Sieff's flat in the new Brook House (1935), and at No. 47 Upper Brook Street (1936) for the Leveson-Gowers. Her work for the Whighams still survives, and not untypically the room with the most panache is the bathroom, that classic inner sanctum of the sybarite of the '30's, where good taste could surrender to luxury and ostentation, and modern materials come to the fore. 'Bathrooms nowadays look more expensive than any rooms in the house', commented *Vogue* in 1935.[121] There were other excellent bathrooms at nearby No. 44 Upper Grosvenor Street, as done up for Leo d'Erlanger and his very fashionable wife by Jansen of Paris, and at No. 12 North Audley Street where in 1932 the mysterious Marchesa Malacrida (with White Allom) put in for Samuel Courtauld a witty semi-circular bathroom of temple form (Plate 53d).

If wit was a prized commodity in interior decoration of the period, nobody was the readier with it than Rex Whistler, who painted a panel for Courtauld's bedroom in North Audley Street, and designed urns for the house's great gallery. More extensive were his murals of 1937 (now removed) for Lady Mountbatten's boudoir in the large double-storey penthouse at the top of the new Brook House; this had been designed specially for the Mountbattens by L. Rome Guthrie, penthouses as much as bijou mews houses being a feature of the age. At some point also Whistler sketched an interesting and in some ways prophetic suggestion for the replanting of Grosvenor Square, with formal paths converging on a central monument.

Classicism of Whistler's variety was sometimes combined with elements from the various *jazz-moderne* styles to convey freshness and humour in interiors of the 1930's. Such an instance was No. 25 South Street, a big private house built in 1932–3 by E. B. Musman for Sir Bernard Eckstein, and augmented and decorated in 1936–7 by Turner Lord and Company with flamboyant painted interiors and furniture (Plate 53c). In an appropriately lower but similar key were the various extensions to Claridge's Hotel. In 1926 Basil Ionides, a pioneer in several aspects of interior design between the wars, redecorated the restaurant and with the help of William Ranken put in some pretty engraved glass and some large modelled elephants. This scheme was not to survive for long in its entirety; in 1929 Oswald Milne constructed a new entrance foyer, remodelled the restaurant again (keeping the glass and the elephants), and followed these with large extensions east of the main hotel in 1930–1 and a penthouse on top in about 1936; in the same period many of the suites were refurnished. Milne's work (Plate 52) was carried out in a gay, up-to-the-minute manner, with copious help from subordinates like Marion Dorn for carpets and the Bath Artcraft Company, R. Burkle and Son, and Gordon Russell for the furniture. Even *Country Life* was compelled to admire 'the beauty of the freedom afforded by the revolution of the last ten years', at least in the shape that it took at Claridge's, duly denuded of too much French Cubism or German utilitarianism by the civilizing hand of 'a humanist such as Mr. Milne'.[122]

Though the façade of the Claridge's extension towards Brook Street, an essay in the stepped-back manner of the day, is less distinctive than Milne's interiors, it is more able than most of the comparable large inter-war blocks along the main streets. At first, a majority of these had been flats, but by 1939 encroachment by office blocks was under way, especially along Grosvenor Street. The residential character of the principal streets was now under serious threat. Following their appearance on the ground floors of new blocks, shop windows were beginning to be seen upon even the major old houses; in Grosvenor Street, one (since taken out) was installed when Keeble Limited, the decorators, converted No. 34 as their Mayfair showroom in 1936, and others appeared at about this time at Nos. 18 and 58. Probably the best of these was at No. 15 North Audley Street, where Albert Richardson put in a Regency Gothick shop front for the West End branch of B. T. Batsford in 1930. There was a natural tendency for commercial concerns to move into the old houses first, because new flats often had stringent rules about occupation, whereas these had to be relaxed for the houses because only firms could fill them economically. So the influx of commerce probably saved many of these houses from destruction, though office use naturally tended to detract from their interior character, sometimes very severely.

The war of 1939-45 of course speeded up the progress of commerce and left even fewer private householders in its wake. There were not many important architectural losses by bombing, the destruction of the picture gallery and ballroom at Dudley House being the worst, but the wear and tear of war confirmed the fate of the remnants of old Grosvenor Square. Here, a number of good houses were sacrificed to the rebuilding scheme, notably Nos 12 (1961) and 44 (1967), but outside the square few first-rate houses have disappeared since the war. Still, the onward march of commerce has led to further proliferation of office and apartment blocks. Before 1960 few of these buildings espoused an overtly modern style. Possibly the last block in the full neo-Georgian tradition was Nos. 76-78 Grosvenor Street (designed by P. Macpherson, of Hillier, Parker, May and Rowden, 1939-40), a building still in the brick manner of Wimperis, Simpson and Guthrie. A comparison with the estate's first big post-war block, the unambitious British Council headquarters on the site of St. Anselm's Church at No. 65 Davies Street, designed under austerity conditions by Howard, Souster and Partners (1948-50), shows the now pressing need for a new initiative. On the British Council *The Architectural Review* was predictably scathing, but still had to look abroad for support for the new aesthetic: 'the many foreign visitors the Council entertains will not be impressed by the heavy Georgian-style office block illustrated herewith'.[123] But the Grosvenor Estate was still a champion of neo-Georgian, as the stone-faced Drill Hall opposite the British Council at No. 56 Davies Street by Trenwith Wills (1950) testifies. Its architectural policies, if unadventurous, were at least more mannerly than in some other parts of London. As late as 1963-5 a development in Davies Street with a frontage at No. 53 Grosvenor Street was obliged to keep this façade in reasonably decorous adherence to the brick traditions of the street.

But the Modern Movement finally arrived on the Mayfair estate with a bang at the United States Embassy (1956-60), inevitably a foreign achievement. Old American associations with Grosvenor Square had been renewed when the embassy moved to the east side in 1938. Throughout the war the American presence strengthened, and was confirmed in 1947 by the replanting of the central garden as a memorial to President Franklin D. Roosevelt, which led to the felling of 'over sixty five mature trees'[124] and the setting up of a statue by Sir William Reid Dick in the centre. Then the west side, substantially complete still except for bomb damage at its north end, was after years of prevarication allotted to the new American Embassy, and a limited competition was held. Great care was taken not to outrage traditional Grosvenor sentiment, so much so that the American assessors outlined in the conditions of competition the need for an undogmatic building related in scale and materials to the rest of the square, while of the competitors it is recorded that 'some...were certainly chosen for their moderation'.[125]

The result was a win by an experienced competitor, Eero Saarinen, the runner-up being Edward D. Stone. A third participant, Minoru Yamasaki, produced a design with a strong Gothic flavour. But though Saarinen showed respect for the neo-Georgianism around him, there was nothing really Georgian about either his style or his materials. The building itself (Plate 55b) has brought a dramatic, internationalist change to the atmosphere of the very centre of the estate, still hard to assess fifteen years after completion. Many of Fello Atkinson's original criticisms in *The Architectural Review* remain as pertinent as ever. The Embassy's merits in his eyes were Saarinen's sensitivity to the square's scale and his determination to design a deeply relieved façade, which was met by slotting a complex grid of Portland stone window frames into the diagonal structural system developed after he had won the competition. On the other hand, because the huge building is set back from the street line on all three of its major sides (a condition which appears to have been part of the brief), it fails to enclose the square and therefore, paradoxically, is too small; set up on a podium as it is, it appears as an austere, free-standing temple rather than the palace or fortress that embassies traditionally have been and truly are. On a third point mentioned by Atkinson time has yet to tell: Saarinen looked forward to the day when the building would darken with dirt, and the gilded aluminium of the window frames would stand out against dark stonework.[126]

Since the American Embassy, it has never been quite so easy to be conservative on the estate again. Most big developments have taken the bull by the horns, some with reasonable success. Sir John Burnet, Tait and Partners have made a pair of lively contributions to the estate scene at Nos. 15-27 (odd) Davies Street (1963-5) and 399-405 (odd) Oxford Street (1967-70); another sizeable block is Grosvenor Hill Court between Bourdon Street and Grosvenor Hill, by Westwood, Piet and Partners (1962-6); while Fitzroy Robinson and Partners have blown the brazen trumpet of comprehensive redevelopment at Nos. 455-497 (odd) Oxford Street (1961-9). The wholesale rebuilding of this area was indeed a prominent feature of Chapman Taylor Partners' *Grosvenor Estate Strategy for Mayfair and Belgravia* (1971). Respect for 'conservation' (distinguished, however, from 'preservation') was there expressed, and also for many of the Victorian buildings. But in execution the visual transformation of the area would doubtless have been very great, not least because of the low architectural assessment in that report of the estate's numerous twentieth-century buildings of more-or-less 'period' character. In its assumptions about the successful juxtaposition of the indigenous styles of Georgian and modern times this careful and very interesting report already seems characteristic of its period. At present (1976) there has been a retreat from a number of these premises and objectives and the estate enters a period when more extensive conservation appears, for the moment, to have gained the upper hand.

APPENDICES

This table provides information about the initial development of Brook Street, Grosvenor Square, Grosvenor Street, Upper Brook Street, Upper Grosvenor Street and the part of South Audley Street between South Street and the estate boundary: the house plots and the areas covered by building agreements are shown on Plan A in the end pocket.

The house numbers are as at present or (where sites have been merged) are those of the original sites in the present sequence. Where the present site arrangement differs substantially from the original the numbers last in use when the original sites still existed are given (as at the corners with Park Street). Where sites were merged before the present sequence of numbers was adopted, as at No. 10 Grosvenor Square or No. 75 South Audley Street, the original houses have been distinguished as, for example, 10 (*east*) and 10 (*west*) or 75 (*north*) and 75 (*south*).

The building leases were granted by the head of the Grosvenor family, or by Robert Myddelton, the guardian of Dame Mary Grosvenor (see pages 7–8, 16–17, where general information about the leases can also be found).

House No.	Frontage in Feet	Date of Building Agreement	No. on Plan A	Undertaker	Date of Building Lease	Lessee
BROOK STREET, NORTH SIDE						
36	19				31 July 1724	Augustin Woollaston
38	16					
40	32				30 July 1724	Thomas Lansdell
42	16				do.	Thomas Couch
44	18				do.	do.
46	20				do.	Edward Buckingham
48	20				do.	Edward Austin
50	20	3 Dec. 1720	9	Robert Pollard, yeoman, and Henry Avery, bricklayer	do.	John Ellis
52	20				do.	John Howorth
54	20				do.	William Head
56	19					
58	19				31 July 1724	Ralph Harrison and Thomas Barlow
60	19					
62	19					
64	25				30 July 1724	Thomas Hogg
Here is Davies Street						
66	36				25 Jan. 1724/5	Edward Shepherd
68	36				do.	do.
70	32				1 April 1725	Lawrence Neale
72	22½	7 Nov. 1723	36	Edward Shepherd, plasterer	do.	Edward Shepherd
74	26				do.	Thomas Hogg
76	20					
78	30				1 April 1726	Colen Campbell
Here is Gilbert Street						

STREETS ON THE ESTATE

The rent is the sum specified in the building lease except where a separate sub-lease is indicated in the table, when the rent is the sum specified in that sub-lease.

Information about the first occupants is derived mainly from the ratebooks of the parish of St. George, Hanover Square, and because of the nature of the evidence there may be inaccuracies in the dates of residence given.

Principal sources: agreements and lease books in Grosvenor Office; Middlesex Land Register in Greater London Record Office; ratebooks in Westminster City Library; *Burke's Peerage*; *The Complete Peerage*; *Dictionary of National Biography*; *History of Parliament*.

Designation	Associated Builders and Architects	Rent £ s. d.	First Occupant	Period	House No.
esquire	William Barlow, bricklayer, party to lease	8	John Watts	1725–30	36
			Mr. Thickbroom	1726–8	38
joiner	do.; assigned to Daniel Marston, glazier	3 0 0	Slingsby Cressy, apothecary	1726–30	40
slater	William Barlow, bricklayer, party to lease	3 10 0	William Blackburne, shoemaker	1726–43	42
do.	do.	do.	Edward Thompson	1728–30	44
mason		4 0 0	William Winde, esq.	1728–32	46
bricklayer		do.	Mrs. Lewis	1728–30(d)	48
joiner		do.	General Joseph Sabine, M.P., Governor of Gibraltar	1728–39(d)	50
carpenter		do.	Humphrey Denby	1725–50	52
carpenter		do.	Joseph Crouchley	1725–52	54
	Sub-let 1724 to William Barlow, bricklayer, and by him to William Austin, carpenter	8 15 0	Elizabeth Allen	1728–30	56
gentleman		do.	Thomas Thickbroom	1728–30	58
carpenter	Sub-let 1724 to William Barlow, bricklayer, and by him to Thomas Lansdell, joiner	do.	Bennet Demages	1734–6	60
		do.	Ann Vincent	1728–31	62
lime merchant		5 0 0	Lady Drogheda, ?widow of 4th Earl (she d. 1735)	1731–5(?d)	64
plasterer		20 0 0	Sir Nathaniel Curzon, Bt., M.P.	1729–58(d)	66
do.	Assigned to Thomas Fayram, mason	15 0 0	Lawrence Shirley, esq.	1729–31	68
carpenter		8 0 0	Brigadier Robert Murray, M.P., s. of 1st Earl of Dunmore	1727–38(d)	70
gentleman		3 0 0	Edward Shepherd	1726–9	72
lime merchant	Assigned to Lawrence Neale, carpenter	10 8 0	William Cowper, esq.	1726–9	74
		19 12 0	Colen Campbell, architect	1726–9(d)	76
esquire, architect to H.R.H. the Prince of Wales	Israel Russell, painter-stainer, witness to lease		Hon. Henry Vane, M.P. (later 1st Earl of Darlington)	1727–34	78

House No.	Frontage in Feet	Date of Building Agreement	No. on Plan A	Undertaker	Date of Building Lease	Lessee
BROOK STREET, NORTH SIDE (continued)						
80	22				25 Aug. 1725	James Heathfield
82	25				do.	do.
84	32	27 April 1724	38	Augustin Woollaston, esquire	do.	Augustin Woollaston
Here is Binney Street						
86	32				do.	do.
88	50				26 April 1725	William Barlow jnr.
BROOK STREET, SOUTH SIDE						
39	26	12 Dec. 1720	11	Thomas Phillips, carpenter	9 March 1722/3	Thomas Phillips
41	32				22 July 1725	do.
43	35	21 Dec. 1720	20	David Audsley, plasterer	21 July 1725	David Audsley
45	38	17 Dec. 1720	13	George Pearce, plumber	10 May 1723	George Pearce
47	40	do.	14	Joseph Osborne, ironmonger (assigned to Edward Shepherd)	do.	Edward Shepherd
49	40				21 June 1725	George Pearce
51	29				22 June 1725	do.
53	30	25 May 1724	39	George Pearce, plumber	do.	George Barlow and William Head
55 (east)	18				do.	John Barnes
55 (west)	24	12 Dec. 1720	12	John Barnes, bricklayer	25 April 1724	do.
57	36				do.	do.
Here is Davies Street						
59	31				20 Aug. 1723	Edward Liney
61	18				25 Aug. 1725	William Jackling
63	30	24 Nov. 1720	7	Francis Bailley, carpenter	do.	do.
65	31				28 Feb. 1722/3	Henry Avery
67	31				do.	Francis Bailley
69	50	6 March 1724/5	50	do.	25 Aug. 1725	do.
71	31	24 Nov. 1724	44	John Simmons, carpenter	18 Feb. 1725/6	John Simmons
GROSVENOR SQUARE, EAST SIDE						
51	22				5 June 1731	John Simmons
1	30				4 June 1731	do.
2	44	24 Nov. 1724	44	John Simmons, carpenter	3 June 1731	do.
3	44				2 June 1731	do.
4	70				12 Sept. 1728	do.

Designation	Associated Builders and Architects	Rent £ s. d.	First Occupant	Period	House No.
carpenter	William Barlow jnr. party to lease	8 0 0	Captain (later Colonel) Mark Anthony Saurin	1727-31	80
do.	do.	do.	Eleanor Farmer	1728-41	82
esquire	Assigned to Lawrence Neale, carpenter	9 13 0	Margaret Graham	1728-36	84
do.	Assigned to Robert Umpleby, carpenter	do.	5th Earl of Northampton	1729-54(d)	86
bricklayer		22 0 0			88
carpenter		9 0 0	Thomas Phillips	1723-36(d)	39
do.		4 0 0	2nd Viscount Mountjoy	1725-8(d)	41
plasterer		9 0 0	16th Baron Abergavenny	1727-44(d)	43
plumber		do.	5th Earl of Coventry	1725-35 (moved to No. 3 Grosvenor Sq.)	45
plasterer		10 0 0	Sir John Buckworth, Bt., M.P.	1725-37 (moved to No. 13 S. Audley St.)	47
plumber		do.	Marquess of Hartington, M.P. (succ. as 3rd Duke of Devonshire in 1729)	1726-9	49
do.		4 0 0	'Sir August Humes'? Sir Gustavus Hume, Bt.	1727-9	51
bricklayer carpenter		7 10 0	Augustus Schutz, esq., Master of the Robes and Keeper of the Privy Purse to George II	1727-57(d)	53
bricklayer		4 10 0	Mr. Parker	1726-8	55 (east)
do.		4 0 0	? John Shepherd, plasterer	1725	55 (west)
do.		6 0 0	Edward Reculest, grocer	1726-46	57
paviour		7 10 0	Hugh Williams, esq., M.P.	1726-37	59
bricklayer		6 6 0	Abigail Jones	1729-31	61
do.		10 0 0	Robert Moore, esq.	1730-48	63
do.		9 6 0	Captain (later Colonel) Martin Madan	1727-31	65
carpenter		7 14 0	Nicholas Grice, esq.	1726-9	67
do.		6 3 0	Marquis de Montandré, Field-Marshal	1734-9(d)	69
do.		9 0 0	Hon. Capel Moore, s. of 3rd Earl of Drogheda	1729-37	71
carpenter		3 14 0	Mrs. Simmons or William Mabbott, esq., Director of E. India Co.	1741 1741-8	51
do.		do.	Lady Barker	1734-9	1
do.		4 0	Lady Mary Colley, d. of 6th Earl of Abercorn and widow of Henry Colley, M.P.	1735-6	2
do.		do.	5th Earl of Coventry	1735-51(d)	3
do.		do.	9th Duke of Norfolk	1739-41	4

House No.	Frontage in Feet	Date of Building Agreement	No. on Plan A	Undertaker	Date of Building Lease	Lessee
GROSVENOR SQUARE, EAST SIDE (continued)						
5	45				28 May 1728	John Simmons
6	45	24 Nov. 1724	44	John Simmons, carpenter	2 Aug. 1727	Chrysostom Wilkins
7	51				1 Aug. 1727	John Simmons
GROSVENOR SQUARE, NORTH SIDE						
[Former No. 8 now No. 88 Brook Street]						
9	30	27 April 1724	38	Augustin Woollaston, esquire	24 May 1725	William Barlow [jnr.]
Here is Duke Street						
10 (east)	30				5 May 1726	do.
10 (west)	36				4 May 1726	William Packer
11	34				6 May 1726	William Gray and John Brown
12	50	6 March 1724/5	51	do.	30 June 1727	John Kitchingman
13	32				14 Aug. 1727	Lawrence Neale
14	32				15 Aug. 1727	do.
15	44				21 Nov. 1727	Augustin Woollaston
16	32				22 Nov. 1727	Richard Davies
17	50	do.	52	do.	15 April 1729	Lawrence Neale
18	50				22 July 1728	Thomas Fayram
19	60	do.	54	Edward Shepherd, gentleman	23 July 1728	Edward Shepherd
20	50				24 July 1728	Francis Drewitt
21	20				25 July 1728	John Shepherd
Here is North Audley Street						
22	30	do.	55	Robert Andrews, gentleman, and Thomas Barlow, carpenter	28 Nov. 1728	John Kitchingman
23	21				26 Sept. 1727	Robert Andrews
GROSVENOR SQUARE, WEST SIDE						
24	33				22 June 1728	Francis Bailley
25	45				21 June 1728	John Green
26	50				20 June 1728	Charles Griffith
27	42	6 Feb. 1724/5	47	Thomas Ripley, esquire (assigned to Robert Andrews, gentleman, and Robert Scott, carpenter); Isaac Ware witness of agreement	19 June 1728	Robert Scott
28	44				18 June 1728	Benjamin Timbrell
29	44				17 June 1728	Thomas Richmond
30	36				15 June 1728	Joseph Stallwood
31	30				14 April 1729	John Sanger
32	26				15 April 1729	John Worrington

Designation	Associated Builders and Architects	Rent £ s. d.	First Occupant	Period	House No.
carpenter		22 10 0	Lady King, widow of 1st Baron King	1734–67(d)	5
plasterer		do.	Edward Chandler, Bishop of Durham	1730–50(d)	6
carpenter		25 0 0	2nd Viscount Weymouth	1731–9	7
bricklayer		18 0 0	Sir Thomas Samwell, Bt.	1727–30	9
do.	Finished according to agreement with, and assigned to, Thomas Archer, esquire [architect]	10 0 0	Thomas Bladen, esq., M.P.	1731–8	10 (east)
carpenter	William Barlow jnr. party to lease	14 8 0	John Campbell, esq., M.P., Lord of the Treasury	1729–67	10 (west)
bricklayers	William Barlow jnr. party to lease; Roger Morris supervised finishing of house	13 12 0	14th Baron (later Earl) Clinton	1729–51(d)	11
timber merchant		20 0 0	John Aislabie, esq., Chancellor of Exchequer 1718–21	1729–42(d)	12
carpenter		12 16 0	Dorothea Dashwood	1729–51	13
do.		do.	Sir William Strickland, Bt., M.P., P.C., Secretary at War	1729–35(d)	14
esquire	Assigned to Richard Davies, joiner	3 12 0	Thomas Duncombe, esq., M.P.	1729–46(d)	15
joiner		12 16 0	Lady Gowran, widow of 1st Baron Gowran	1729–44(d)	16
carpenter		20 0 0	2nd Earl of Albemarle	1730–54(d)	17
mason	John Deval, mason, did £300 worth of work in interior in 1736	25 0 0	2nd Earl of Rockingham	1737–45(d)	18
gentleman		26 0 0	7th Earl of Thanet	1730–53(d)	19
bricklayer		25 0 0	6th Earl of Mountrath, M.P.	1731–44(d)	20
plasterer		7 0 0	Sir Cecil Bishopp, 6th Bt., M.P.	1733–8	21
timber merchant		10 10 0	5th Baron (later Earl) Cornwallis	1730–9	22
gentleman	Assigned to John Worrington, paviour	6 6 0	John Evelyn, esq., M.P., Groom of the Bedchamber to Prince of Wales	1732–51	23
carpenter	Assigned to James Theobald, timber merchant	12 0 0	Lord Nassau Powlett, s. of 2nd Duke of Bolton	1735–8	24
joiner		19 2 6	Duchess of Rutland, widow of 2nd Duke	1733–51(d)	25
carpenter		21 15 0	Sir Robert Sutton, M.P., P.C., diplomat	1730–5	26
do.		17 17 0	4th Earl of Shaftesbury	1731–71(d)	27
do.		18 14 0	General Sir Charles Wills, M.P., P.C.	1730–41(d)	28
do.		do.	2nd Duke of Manchester	1732–9(d)	29
bricklayer	Thomas Richmond, carpenter, party to lease	15 6 0	Anne Jennings	1730–61	30
carpenter	do.	12 10 0	Sir Charles Gounter Nicoll, M.P.	1730–3(d)	31
paviour	do.	10 16 0	Lady Acklom or Charles Echlin, esq.	1729–30 1730–48	32

House No.	Frontage in Feet	Date of Building Agreement	No. on Plan A	Undertaker	Date of Building Lease	Lessee
GROSVENOR SQUARE, SOUTH SIDE						
33	35				22 Aug. 1727	William Moreton
		18 Nov. 1725	58	Richard Andrews, gentleman		
34	30				25 May 1728	Robert Scott and William Barlow snr.
Here is South Audley Street						
35	25					
36	35					
37	38					
38	39	29 April 1725	57	Robert Grosvenor, esquire	4 Feb. 1726/7	Robert Grosvenor
39	36					
40	45					
41	42					
42	38					
43	36					
44	36	(No building agreement found)			22 April 1725	do.
45	40					
46	35					
47	35	6 March 1724/5	48	Thomas Cook and Caleb Waterfield, carpenters	25 Oct. 1726	Caleb Miller
48	40				5 May 1726	Thomas Cook and Caleb Waterfield
Here is Carlos Place						
49	30	28 Jan. 1724/5	46	John Jenner, bricklayer	25 Jan. 1727/8	John Jenner
50	33				28 Jan. 1725/6	do.
GROSVENOR STREET, NORTH SIDE						
4 & 5	40				5 Feb. 1722/3	William Barlow and Robert Scott
6	18				do.	Robert Scott
7	18	2 Sept. 1720	3	William Barlow snr., bricklayer	do.	William Barlow
8	20				15 July 1721	William Mantle
9	31				8 Oct. 1722	Robert Scott
10	20				5 Feb. 1722/3	William Barlow
11	20				do.	John Cartwright

Designation	Associated Builders and Architects	Rent £ s. d.	First Occupant	Period	House No.
mason	Robert Scott, carpenter, and William Barlow snr., bricklayer, parties to lease	12 0 0	4th Earl of Inchiquin, M.P.	1731–6	33
carpenter bricklayer		5 15 0	Lady Bishopp, widow of Sir Cecil Bishopp, 5th Bt.	1729–50(?d)	34
	Sub-let 1728 to William Head, carpenter; George Barlow, bricklayer, party	8 10 0	Lady Mary Saunderson, d. of 1st Earl of Rockingham	1730–7(d)	35
	Sub-let 1727 to George Barlow, bricklayer; William Head, carpenter, party	14 0 0	Colonel (later General) Roger Handasyde, M.P.	1730–42	36
	Sub-let 1728 to Samuel Phillips, carpenter	15 0 0	2nd Earl of Scarbrough	1733–40(d)	37
esquire	Sub-let 1727 to Israel Russell, painter-stainer	14 0 0	4th Earl of Dysart	1733–9	38
	Sub-let 1728 to William East, esquire; Thomas Phillips, carpenter, party	14 8 0	William East, esq., M.P.	1727–31	39
	(Sub-let 1727 to Baron Carpenter)	13 10 0	1st Baron Carpenter, general, commander of forces in North Britain 1715	1727–32(d)	40
	Sub-let 1727 to Benjamin Timbrell, carpenter	14 14 0	Henry Bromley, esq., M.P. (later 1st Baron Montfort)	1728–34	41
	Built directly and sold in 1731 by Robert Grosvenor to Benjamin Timbrell, carpenter		Frederick Frankland, esq., M.P.	1731–7	42
do.	Sub-let 1727 to William Barlow [snr.], bricklayer	9 0 0	Duchess of Kendal	1728–43(d)	43
	Sub-let 1727 to Robert Scott, carpenter	do.	Oliver St. George, esq.	1728–31(d)	44
	Sub-let 1727 to Thomas Richmond, carpenter	1 0 0	Marquess of Blandford, M.P., g.s. of 1st Duke of Marlborough	1730–1(d)	45
	do.	13 10 0	Lord Glenorchy, M.P. (later 3rd Earl of Breadalbane)	1731–8	46
brickmaker	Assigned to Thomas Knight, joiner	17 10 0	5th Baron Baltimore, M.P.	1731–42	47
carpenters		20 0 0	Sir William Wyndham, Bt., M.P., Chancellor of Exchequer 1713–14	1738–40(d)	48
bricklayer		2 2 0	Henry Talbot, esq., b. of 1st Baron Talbot, Lord Chancellor	1728–61	49
do.		16 7 0	William Bumpsted, esq. or Hon. Anne Vane, mistress of Frederick, P. of Wales	1732 1733–6(d)	50
bricklayer carpenter		6 0 0	Richard Davies, victualler (Red Lion)	1723–32	4 & 5
do.		2 10 0	Frances Wyndham	1725–38	6
bricklayer		do.	Major James Haldane	1725–8	7
plasterer		6 0 0	Colonel Lloyd	1724–6	8
carpenter		6 10 0	Mrs. Rowe	1725–6	9
bricklayer		5 0 0	Mrs. Wallop	1724–5	10
blacksmith		6 0 0	Edward Cressett, esq.	1725–6(?d)	11

House No.	Frontage in Feet	Date of Building Agreement	No. on Plan A	Undertaker	Date of Building Lease	Lessee
				GROSVENOR STREET, NORTH SIDE (continued)		
12	30				15 Nov. 1723	Israel Russell
13	20	2 Sept. 1720	6	Mathew Tomlinson, carpenter (assigned to Benjamin Timbrell, carpenter)	30 Nov. 1723	Charles Griffith
14	20				do.	John Jenner
15	30	11 Jan. 1722/3	28	John Jenner, bricklayer	3 June 1723	do.
16	55	2 Sept. 1720	5	Thomas Ripley, carpenter	25 April 1724	Thomas Ripley
17	35	do.	6a	Robert Scott, carpenter	30 Nov. 1723	Robert Scott
18	35				do.	Thomas Richmond
19	20	22 June 1723	31	John Laforey, esquire	31 Oct. 1723	John Laforey
20	20	20 July 1723	32	Benjamin Whetton, bricklayer	30 Nov. 1723	Richard Lissiman
21	19½	9 Aug. 1723	35	Samuel Phillips, carpenter	do.	John Steemson
22	19½				do.	Samuel Phillips
23	23	4 Jan. 1720/1	21	George Chamberlen, carpenter, and George Wyatt, bricklayer	28 Jan. 1724/5	George Chamberlen
24	23				do.	George Wyatt
25	25				1 Aug. 1724	John Deane
26	25	2 Sept. 1720	2	John Deane, painter	do.	do.
27	20				26 Jan. 1724/5	Richard Davies
28	31½				10 Aug. 1725	do.
				Here is Davies Street		
29	18	19 July 1723	33	Francis Commins, mason	26 Nov. 1725	Francis Commins
30	19					
31	18				25 Aug. 1725	William Mantle
32	35	24 July 1724	41	Robert Scott, carpenter	20 April 1725	Robert Scott
33	35	10 July 1724	40	Richard Lissiman, mason	21 July 1725	Richard Lissiman
34	43				do.	do.
35	22				22 July 1725	do.
36	31				18 Feb. 1725/6	John Simmons
37	30				16 Feb. 1730/1	do.
38	30	24 Nov. 1724	44	John Simmons, carpenter	do.	do.
39	22				do.	do.
40	22				do.	do.
				GROSVENOR STREET, SOUTH SIDE		
43	40	17 Dec. 1720	17	John Pritchard, gentleman	12 April 1726	Benjamin Hoadly
44	20				12 May 1726	John Pritchard
45	18	20 Dec. 1720	18	Stephen Whitaker, brickmaker (assigned to William and Benjamin Benson)	31 Dec. 1725	William Benson
46	18				do	Benjamin Benson
47	24	22 Jan. 1724/5	45	John Jenner, bricklayer	29 July 1726	Colonel Charles Churchill
48	36	17 Dec. 1720	16	Henry Huddle, carpenter	22 June 1726	Henry Huddle

Designation	Associated Builders and Architects	Rent £ s. d.			First Occupant	Period	House No.
painter[-stainer]		9	0	0	Earl of Burford, M.P. (succ. as 2nd Duke of St. Albans in 1726)	1725-6	12
carpenter		6	0	0	Charles Miller, esq.	1726-32	13
bricklayer		do.			William Edwards, esq.	1725-30	14
do.		7	10	0	(Rectory of St. George, Hanover Square)	1725 onwards	15
esquire		15	15	0	Baron Walpole, s. of Sir Robert Walpole (later 2nd Earl of Orford)	1725-38	16
carpenter		10	0	0	James Vernon, esq., Clerk of the Privy Council	1725-55	17
do.		do.			Elizabeth Strangeways (later Duchess of Hamilton)	1725-9(d)	18
esquire		5	0	0	? Colonel Churchill	1725	19
mason		do.			John Herring, esq.	1725-43 (?d)	20
carpenter		4	17	0	— Smith, esq.	1725-6(d)	21
do.		do.			Major (later Colonel) William Duckett, M.P.	1726-49(d)	22
do.		6	15	0	Governor Morris, ? Bacon Morris, Gov. of Landguard Fort, Suffolk	1726-7	23
bricklayer		do.			Simon Smith, esq.	1726-30	24
painter		3	0	0	Mr. Davies	1725-6	25
do.		do.			John Harrison	1725-8	26
joiner		5	0	0	Elizabeth O'Court	1726-33	27
do.		8	10	0	Mary Butler	1727-48	28
					?		29
mason			3	4	Mr. Pitts	1727-8	30
plasterer		6	10	0	William Mantle	1726-7	31
carpenter		8	10	0	Lady Edwin (and her son, Charles Edwin, esq., M.P., who d. 1756)	1726(-56(d))	32
mason		10	10	0	Baron Sparre, Swedish Envoy	1727-36	33
do.		14	10	0	Sir Paul Methuen, M.P., P.C.	1728-57(d)	34
do.			3	4	William Turner, esq	1728-34	35
carpenter		9	0	0	Judith Ayliffe	1728-35	36
do.		5	0	0	Charles Evelyn, esq.	1733-5	37
do.		do.			Lady Gray, ? widow of Sir James Gray, Bt.	1733-44	38
do.		3	0	0	Marquess of Graham (succ. as 2nd Duke of Montrose in 1742)	1734-42	39
do.		do.			Thomas Colnit, esq.	1734-5	40
Bishop of Salisbury	John Jenner, bricklayer, party to lease; Robert Phillips, ? brick-layer, witness	15	0	0	Benjamin Hoadly, Bishop of Salisbury (later B. of Winchester)	1726-45	43
gentleman		6	0	0	John Pritchard	1726	44
esquire		5	8	0	William Benson, Surveyor-General of the King's Works 1718-19	1726-52	45
do.		do.			Benjamin Benson, brother of above	1727	46
		10	16	0	Colonel (later General) Charles Churchill, M.P.	1727-45(d)	47
carpenter		14	8	0	Lord Charles Cavendish, M.P., s. of 2nd Duke of Devonshire	1729-32	48

House No.	Frontage in Feet	Date of Building Agreement	No. on Plan A	Undertaker	Date of Building Lease	Lessee
GROSVENOR STREET, SOUTH SIDE (continued)						
49	36	9 Aug. 1723	34	Robert Herne, joiner (assigned to John Green)	21 Oct. 1725	John Green
50	36½				3 Nov. 1724	Charles Griffith
51	39½				do.	Israel Russell
		21 Dec. 1720	19	Benjamin Timbrell, carpenter		
52	50				do.	Benjamin Timbrell
53	40					
		17 Dec. 1720	15	William Waddell, plumber (assigned to Thomas Barlow, carpenter)	11 Jan. 1724/5	Thomas Barlow
54	31					
Here is Davies Street						
55	17½					
56	19					
57	25					
58	36					
59	36					
60	24					
61	18					
62	20					
63	17					
Here is Broadbent Street						
64	19					
65	21½	8 Aug. 1720	1	Thomas Barlow, carpenter	15 or 27 July 1721	Thomas Barlow
66	35					
67	28					
68	20					
69	35					
70	35					
71–72	42					
73	34					
74	34					
75	22					
76	26					

Designation	Associated Builders and Architects	Rent £ s. d.	First Occupant	Period	House No.
joiner		10 16 0	Earl Grandison	1727–35	49
carpenter		do.	1st Earl of Uxbridge	1726–43(d)	50
painter[-stainer]		11 14 0	Sir John Werden, Bt.: his son-in-law, 2nd Duke of St. Albans, also here 1726–7	1726–8	51
carpenter		15 0 0	Sir Thomas Hanmer, Bt., M.P., Speaker of House of Commons 1714–15	1726–46(d)	52
do.	John Prince, ? surveyor, witness to lease; sub-let 1725 to John Neale, carpenter	do.	Earl of Arran	1726–58(d)	53
	do.	12 0 0	Robert Knight, esq., M.P.	1729–36	54
	Sub-let 1724 to Samuel Phillips, carpenter	5 0 0	William Fellows, victualler (Three Tuns Tavern)	1725–39(d)	55
	do.	4 0 0	? Mrs. Robinson	1726	56
	Sub-let 1724 to Walter Lee, mason	8 0 0	Lady Stapleton, widow of Sir William Stapleton, Bt	1725–33	57
	Sub-let 1724 to John Green, joiner	12 12 0	Baron Ranelagh	1726–54(d)	58
	Sub-let 1725 to David Audsley, plasterer	10 0 0	Sir Robert Rich, Bt., M.P.	1726–42	59
	Sub-let 1723 to John Neale, carpenter	7 0 0	Anne Oldfield, actress	1725–30(d)	60
	Sub-let 1721 to George Worrall, plasterer	4 1 0	George Worrall or Lady Allen, ? widow of Sir William Allen, Bt.	1725 1725–36	61
	Sub-let 1721 to John Neale, carpenter	5 0 0	Mr. Munday	1725–8	62
	Sub-let 1723 to Thomas Sams, joiner	3 10 0	William Robertson	1726–30	63
	Sub-let 1724 to Edward Allen, carpenter	4 0 0	Mrs. Milton	1726–56	64
carpenter	Sub-let 1725 to do.	5 0 0	Lucy Killigrew	1726–9(d)	65
	Sub-let 1723 to Joshua Fletcher, mason	10 0 0	2nd Baron Barnard	1725–9	66
	Sub-let 1723 to Caleb Waterfield and Thomas Cook, carpenters	7 16 0	Lady Strafford, widow of William, Earl of Strafford	1725–31	67
	do.	6 0 0	Mary Fox	1725–32(d)	68
	Sub-let 1723 to Benjamin Timbrell, carpenter	10 0 0	Earl of Dalkeith (later 2nd Duke of Buccleuch)	1725–9	69
	Sub-let 1722 to Robert Hearne, joiner; Benjamin Timbrell party	do.	Godfrey Clarke, esq., M.P.	1724–34(d)	70
	Sub-let 1722 to Benjamin Timbrell, carpenter	do.	Earl of Hertford (succ. as 7th Duke of Somerset in 1748)	1724–48	71–72
	Sub-let 1722 to John James, bricklayer	do.	Sir Edward Ernle, Bt., M.P.	1724–9(d)	73
	Sub-let 1722 to Stephen Whitaker, brickmaker; John James party	do.	Lord Compton (later 5th Earl of Northampton)	1725–9 (moved to No. 88 Brook St.)	74
	Built by Thomas Barlow and let at rack rent		Mrs. Herne	1725–32	75
	Sub-let 1722 to William Waddell, plumber	7 0 0	John Dobson, esq.	1727–57	76

House No.	Frontage in Feet	Date of Building Agreement	No. on Plan A	Undertaker	Date of Building Lease	Lessee
GROSVENOR STREET, SOUTH SIDE (continued)						
77 } 78 }	37					
Here is the entrance to Grosvenor Hill						
79	19½	8 Aug. 1720	1	Thomas Barlow, carpenter	} 15 or 27 July 1721	Thomas Barlow
80						
81						
SOUTH AUDLEY STREET, EAST SIDE						
9	18				7 Dec. 1738	John Blagrave
10	18	24 May 1736	74	John Eds, carpenter	do.	Roger Blagrave
11	16				22 June 1737	George Thwaits
12	31	do.	73	William Singleton, plasterer	5 Aug. 1737	William Singleton
13	21				19 July 1736	do.
14	34				do.	Roger Blagrave
15	26	1 Feb. 1735/6	72	Roger Blagrave, carpenter	do.	do.
16	27				14 Feb. 1735/6	do.
SOUTH AUDLEY STREET, WEST SIDE						
71	20				19 July 1736	Thomas Skeat
72	19				do.	John Eds
73	20				do.	John Shepherd
74	56	24 May 1736	75	Edward Shepherd, esquire	do.	Edward Shepherd
75 (north)	26				do.	do.
75 (south)	{ 19½ { 22				do. do.	do. do.
UPPER BROOK STREET, NORTH SIDE						
1	23				27 May 1728	John Evans
2	30				16 June 1730	John Neale
3	20				do.	do.
4	31	6 March 1724/5	55	Thomas Barlow, carpenter, and Robert Andrews, gentleman	do.	David Audsley
5	31				do.	do.
6	30				19 Sept. 1732	Edward Shepherd
7	19				do.	Edward Cock
8	16				do.	do.
Here is Shepherd's Place						

Designation	Associated Builders and Architects	Rent £ s. d.	First Occupant	Period	House No.
	} Sub-let 1722 to William Waddell, plumber	12 19 0	William Robertson	1725-6	77
			George Bickford	1723-42(?d)	78
carpenter	Sub-let 1721 to John James, bricklayer, and David Audsley, plasterer	5 0 0	Thomas Hewson	1725-8	79
	Built by Thomas Barlow and let at rack rent		Francis Minetone (Mount Coffee House)	1721-3	80
	(? originally part of No. 80)		James Martin	?1736-48	81
carpenter	Roger Blagrave, carpenter, party	4 19 0	Susannah Jennings	1739-53	9
do.	Assigned to John Blagrave, carpenter, his son	do.	Catherine Sloper, estranged wife of William Sloper of West Woodhay, Berks., M.P.	1739-99	10
gentleman		4 10 0	George Thwaits	1738-44	11
plasterer		9 0 0	Hon. James Lumley, M.P., s. of 1st Earl of Scarbrough	1740-4	12
do.		6 6 0	Sir John Buckworth, Bt., M.P.	1737-41	13
carpenter	Assigned to John Blagrave, carpenter, his son	13 12 0	Jerome de Salis, esq.	1740-5	14
do.	do.	7 16 0	Barbara Cavendish, estranged wife of William Cavendish, g.s. of 1st Duke of Devonshire	1738-50	15
do.		4 1 0	John Tubb, chandler	1738-61	16
bricklayer		6 0 0	Samuel Greathead, esq., M.P.	1739-56	71
carpenter		8 0 0	Hon. Colonel Charles Ingram, M.P., s. of 3rd Viscount Irwin	1738-43	72
plasterer		10 8 0	George Ogle, esq., classicist and Chaucerian scholar	1738-46(d)	73
esquire		20 0 0	(Portuguese Embassy)	1747 onwards	74
do.		7 12 0	2nd Earl of Halifax	1739-46	75 (north)
do.		5 0 0 }	Hon. John St. John (later 2nd Viscount St. John of Battersea)	1738-48(d) }	75 (south)
do.		6 0 0 }			
joiner		6 4 0	Mary Fox	1732-4	1
carpenter		8 10 0	Archibald Hutcheson, esq., lawyer and economist	1732-40(d)	2
do.		6 6 0	Colonel Francis Byng, b. of Admiral Sir George Byng, 1st Viscount Torrington	1732-3	3
plasterer		10 10 0	Mrs. Trenchard	1733-8	4
do.		do.	Richard Powys, esq., M.P.	1734-7	5
esquire	John Shepherd, plasterer, party to lease	10 7 0	Edward Shepherd	1734-5	6
carpenter	do.	5 5 0	Lady Betty Lowther (and/or Sir Thomas Lowther, Bt., M.P.)	1735-7(d)	7
do.	do.	4 7 6	Thomas Burke	1733-6	8

House No.	Frontage in Feet	Date of Building Agreement	No. on Plan A	Undertaker	Date of Building Lease	Lessee
UPPER BROOK STREET, NORTH SIDE (continued)						
9	20				14 Oct. 1729	John Shepherd
9A	20				13 Oct. 1729	do.
10	34				25 May 1732	Edward Cock
11	15				26 May 1732	do.
12	38				1 March 1728/9	Elizabeth Alleyne
13	22	6 March 1724/5	55	Thomas Barlow, carpenter, and Robert Andrews, gentleman	28 Nov. 1728	William Davis
80 Park St.	20				22 Nov. 1728	Thomas and Samuel Gough and Richard Peacy
Here is Park Street						
14	22				23 July 1728	William Barlow jnr.
15A	18				1 April 1729	William Davis
15	20				2 April 1729	John Barlow
16	20				10 Oct. 1729	William Bennett
17	23				do.	John Panton
18	30					
19	30					
20	30					
21	30	6 March 1724/5	53	Augustin Woollaston, esquire (assigned to Robert Andrews, gentleman)		
22	31					
23	27				19 Sept. 1732	Robert Andrews
24	32					
25	30					
26	28					
27	18					
28	23					
29	46				16 May 1729	Francis Bailley

Designation	Associated Builders and Architects	Rent £ s. d.	First Occupant	Period	House No.
plasterer		5 5 0	John Dickins, coffee house keeper	1730–48	9
do.	Assigned to John Barnes, bricklayer	do.	Elizabeth Jenkins	1733–56	9A
carpenter		14 0 0	Sir Francis Head, Bt.	1732–41	10
do.		6 0 0	Catherine Hewsham	1734–8	11
widow		13 6 0	Elizabeth Alleyne	1730–7	12
carpenter	Daniel Marston, glazier, Thomas and Samuel Gough, bricklayers, and Richard Peacy, carpenter, parties to lease; assigned to Francis Jackman, timber merchant	4 0 0	Dr. Lovell	1736–7	13
bricklayers carpenter	Daniel Marston, glazier, party to lease; assigned to Francis Drewitt, bricklayer	3 0 0	Lady Vane, ? widow of 1st Viscount Vane	1739–41	80 Park St.
bricklayer	George Barlow, bricklayer, party to lease; William Allison, carpenter, witness	6 0 0	James Liverpoole, victualler (Barley Mow)	1736–46(?d)	14
carpenter	George Barlow and William Barlow jnr., bricklayers, parties to lease; assigned to William Jayne, carpenter	4 10 0	Thomas Marsh	1734 5	15A
bricklayer	George Barlow and William Barlow jnr., bricklayers, parties to lease; assigned to latter	5 0 0	Captain John Aldred, R.N.	1733–40(d)	15
carpenter	George Barlow, bricklayer, party to lease	8 0 0	'Lord Peters', ? 8th Baron Petre	1741–2	16
do.	do.	9 4 0	Major Weldon and/or Lady Charlotte Weldon	1734–8	17
	Sub-let 1737 to John Simmons, carpenter	12 0 0	1st Earl of Pomfret	1740–7	18
	do.	do.	3rd Viscount Doneraile, M.P.	1742–4	19
	Sub-let 1737 to William Atlee, painter; John Simmons, carpenter, mortgagee	do.	Mr. Fortnam, ? Richard Fortnam, bricklayer, son-in-law of John Simmons	1744–5	20
	Sub-let 1737 to John Simmons, carpenter	do.	Sir Edmund Thomas, Bt., M.P., Groom of the Bedchamber to Prince of Wales	1742–51	21
	Sub-let 1742 to Joshua Fletcher, mason	12 8 0	3rd Earl of Marchmont	1744–63	22
gentleman	Sub-let 1742 to Thomas Barratt, brickmaker, and John Barlow, bricklayer	10 16 0	Trafford Barnston, esq.	1747	23
	Sub-let 1742 to Lawrence Neale, carpenter	12 16 0	2nd Duke of Chandos	1746–54	24
	do.	12 0 0	Lady Frances Bland, widow of Sir John Bland, Bt.	1744–58(?d)	25
	Sub-let 1746 to Elizabeth Simmons, widow of John Simmons	11 4 0	Sir Francis Eyles(-Stiles), Bt.	1747–50	26
	Sub-let 1742 to do.	7 4 0	Samuel Spencer, esq.	1744–50	27
	Sub-let 1742 to Joshua Ransom, John Smith and Griffin Ransom, [timber] merchants; Richard Fortnam, bricklayer, a witness	9 4 0	Lady Sidney Beauclerk, widow of Lord Sidney Beauclerk and mother of Topham Beauclerk	1745–53	28
carpenter	Assigned to Thomas Phillips, carpenter, and eventually vested in his nephew, John Phillips, carpenter	4 0	14th Earl of Morton	1747–9	29

House No.	Frontage in Feet	Date of Building Agreement	No. on Plan A	Undertaker	Date of Building Lease	Lessee
UPPER BROOK STREET, SOUTH SIDE						
30	51					
31	23					
32	29					
33	31				25 Sept. 1736	William Barlow and Robert Scott (as execs. of Stephen Whitaker)
34	20					
35	28					
36	28					
37	28				do.	do.
38	25	11 May 1721	26	Stephen Whitaker, brickmaker	do.	Isaac Mansfield
39	20				do.	John Simmons
40	30				do.	do.
41	35				do.	William Barlow and Robert Scott (as execs. of Stephen Whitaker)
42	27				11 Dec. 1735	John Brown
43	23				do.	William Barlow and Robert Scott (as execs. of Stephen Whitaker)
44	21					
45	19					
46	17				14 Dec. 1734	William Arnott
Here is Park Street						
47	36					
48	19					
49	31½					
50	32½	6 Feb. 1724/5	47	Thomas Ripley, esquire (assigned to Robert Andrews, gentleman, and Robert Scott, carpenter); Isaac Ware witness to agreement	1 June 1728	Robert Andrews
51	31½					
52	20					
53	21					
Here is Blackburne's Mews						

Designation	Associated Builders and Architects	Rent £ s. d.	First Occupant	Period	House No.
	Sub-let 1756 to William Timbrell, esq., and John Spencer, carpenter, co-partners; Alexander Rouchead, mason, party	8 10 0	Mrs. Stanley	1757–64	30
	do.	do.	Thomas Ramsden, esq.	1759–91(d)	31
	Sub-let 1756 to John Barlow, bricklayer; Timbrell, Spencer and Rouchead (as above) parties	10 3 0	Sir Charles Hanbury Williams, M.P.	1758–9	32
bricklayer carpenter	Sub-let 1756 to Edmund Rush, mason; Timbrell, Spencer and Rouchead (as above) parties	12 8 0	Lady Anne Jekyll	1757–66(d)	33
	do.	5 9 0	Thomas Sanders, esq.	1757–75	34
	Sub-let 1737 to Anthony Cross, mason; Alexander Rouchead, mason, party	8 14 0	Duchess of Atholl	1746–8	35
	do.	7 5 0	6th Baron Ward (later 1st Viscount Dudley and Ward)	1742–57	36
do.	Sub-let 1736 to Stephen John Whitaker, brickmaker, and assigned by him to Lawrence Neale, carpenter	2 0	Lord Mark Kerr, general, s. of 1st Marquis of Lothian	1742–52(d)	37
plasterer	William Barlow, bricklayer, and Robert Scott, carpenter, parties to lease	8 15 0	Lady Delorain, widow of 3rd Earl of Delorain	1741–53 and 1773–94(d)	38
carpenter	do.; Isaac Mansfield, plasterer, witness	7 0 0	2nd Viscount Vane	1742–3	39
do.	do.	10 10 0	Hon. Nicholas Herbert, M.P., s. of 8th Earl of Pembroke	1742–75(d)	40
bricklayer carpenter	Sub-let 1736 to John Brown, bricklayer, and Anthony Cross, mason	12 5 0	Lady Georgiana Spencer, widow of Hon. John Spencer (later Countess Cowper)	1747–61	41
bricklayer	William Barlow, bricklayer, and Robert Scott, carpenter, parties to lease	8 2 0	Anthony Chute, esq., M.P.	1739–47	42
do. carpenter	Sub-let 1736 to William Arnott, carpenter	1 0	Lady Anne Cavendish	1739–80	43
	do.	6 16 0	Robert Bragg, esq.	1739–43	44
	Sub-let 1735 to do.	4 10 0	Robert Bogg	1738–47	45
do.		4 0 0	William Davis, cheesemonger	1737–69	46
	Sub-let 1730 to John Barnes, bricklayer	do	Thomas Mitchell	1732–4	47
	do.	do.	John Gill	1732–3	48
	do.	9 9 0	Duchess of Bolton	1731–49	49
	Sub-let 1730 to Israel Russell, painter[-stainer]; John Barnes, bricklayer, party	9 15 0	Countess of Shaftesbury, widow of 3rd Earl	1733–51(d)	50
gentleman	Sub-let 1730 to Edward Cock, carpenter; John Barnes, bricklayer, party	9 9 0	Arthur Stafford, esq., and/or Lady Stafford	1732–5	51
	do.	4 0 0	Robert Sheppard, tailor	1732–54	52
	Sub-let 1730 to John Barnes, bricklayer	3 0 0	Daniel Fitzpatrick, victualler (Cock and Bottle)	1730–40(?d)	53

House No.	Frontage in Feet	Date of Building Agreement	No. on Plan A	Undertaker	Date of Building Lease	Lessee

UPPER BROOK STREET, SOUTH SIDE (continued)

House No.	Frontage in Feet	Date of Building Agreement	No. on Plan A	Undertaker	Date of Building Lease	Lessee
54	38½			Thomas Ripley, esquire (assigned to Robert Andrews, gentleman, and Robert Scott, carpenter); Isaac Ware witness to agreement	19 Sept. 1729	John Green
55	20	6 Feb. 1724/5	47			
56	41½				8 Sept. 1729	do.

UPPER GROSVENOR STREET, NORTH SIDE

House No.	Frontage in Feet	Date of Building Agreement	No. on Plan A	Undertaker	Date of Building Lease	Lessee
1	28					
2	20					
3	18				16 April 1729	Thomas Richmond
4	17					
5	17	6 Feb. 1724/5	47	Thomas Ripley, esquire (assigned to Robert Andrews, gentleman, and Robert Scott, carpenter); Isaac Ware witness to agreement		

Here is Blackburne's Mews

House No.	Frontage in Feet	Date of Building Agreement	No. on Plan A	Undertaker	Date of Building Lease	Lessee
6	24					
7	20					
8	20					
9	30				1 June 1728	Robert Scott
10	33					
11	31					
12	36					

Here is Park Street

House No.	Frontage in Feet	Date of Building Agreement	No. on Plan A	Undertaker	Date of Building Lease	Lessee
37 Park St.	17					
13	20					
14	33					
15	32					
16	25	25 April 1724	37	Robert Andrews, gentleman	14 Feb. 1726/7	Robert Andrews
17	34					
18	34					
19	30					
20	30					

Designation	Associated Builders and Architects	Rent £ s. d.			First Occupant	Period	House No.
joiner		1	2	6	Jonathan Scull	1730-8	54
do.					? Joseph Reeve	1739	55
			17	6	(Originally added to curtilage of 25 Grosvenor Sq.; separate house not built here until 1810-13)		56
	Sub-let 1729 to Thomas Fry, carpenter	9	2	0	Lady Frances Erskine, widow of 22nd Earl of Mar	1736-42	1
	do.	6	10	0	George Ogle, esq., classicist and Chaucerian scholar	1737-8 (moved to No. 73 S. Audley St.)	2
carpenter	Sub-let 1729 to John Worrington, paviour; Thomas Fry, carpenter, party	5	17	0	John Gillard	1733-41	3
	do.	5	10	6	William Gillett	1731-55	4
	Sub-let 1729 to Thomas Fry, carpenter	5	0	0	Evan Brotherton	1731-4	5
	Sub-let 1728 to John Worrington, paviour	4	0	0	John Stokes, victualler (Oval)	1729-53	6
	Sub-let 1729 to William Waddell, plumber	6	0	0	John Lamp, esq.	1734 6	7
	do.				Captain Robert Hale	1732 50	8
do.	Mortgaged by Scott to Charles Serena, Italian plasterer	7	0	0	William Edwards, esq., Treasurer of New River Co.	1731-7(d)	9
	Sub-let 1728 to Benjamin Timbrell, carpenter	8	10	0	(Sir) Robert Grosvenor, M.P.	1730-3	10
	do.	8	0	0	Captain (later Major) Humphry Watson	1731-41(d)	11
	do.; Henry Flitcroft [architect], mortgagee		do.		Benjamin Timbrell	1729-51	12
	Sub-let 1732 to Richard Davies, joiner; John Mackreth, lime merchant, and Stephen Whitaker, brickmaker, parties	4	0	0	John Hughes	1737-46	37 Park St.
	do.	6	0	0	Thomas Miller	1734-6	13
	do.; assigned to Lawrence Neale, carpenter	13	0	0	6th Viscount Irwin	1736(d)	14
	do.		do.		Hon. Bussy Mansell, M.P. (later 4th Baron Mansell)	1736-50(d)	15
gentleman	Sub-let 1730 to Joshua Fletcher, mason; Mackreth, Whitaker (as above) and Thomas Hipsley, bricklayer, parties	10	12	6	Thomas Whichcot, esq., M.P.	1741-8	16
	Sub-let 1732 to Lawrence Neale, carpenter; Mackreth and Whitaker (as above) parties	13	12	0	Hon. Lawrence Shirley, s. of 1st Earl Ferrers	1734-8	17
	do.		do.		Thomas Boothby Skrymsher, esq.	1735-51(d)	18
	do.	12	0	0	Viscount Blundell	1734-56(d)	19
	do.		do.		John Nightingale, esq.	1735-6	20

House No.	Frontage in Feet	Date of Building Agreement	No. on Plan A	Undertaker	Date of Building Lease	Lessee
UPPER GROSVENOR STREET, NORTH SIDE (continued)						
21	29					
22	21	25 April 1724	37	Robert Andrews, gentleman	14 Feb. 1726/7	Robert Andrews
23	20					
24	19					
UPPER GROSVENOR STREET, SOUTH SIDE						
(Former 28 Park Lane)	28				8 April 1729	William Hale and Richard Lissiman
25	18				9 April 1729	do.
26	28	12 April 1728	65	Richard Lissiman, mason	16 Aug. 1729	Richard Lissiman
27	19				15 Aug. 1729	do.
28	20				14 Aug. 1729	do.
29	21				19 Sept. 1732	do.
30	34				do.	do.
31	19					
32	57					
33		(no building agreement found)			5 June 1731	1st Viscount Chetwynd
34	40					
35	26	5 June 1727	61	Thomas Goff, blacksmith (assigned to Robert Grosvenor)	11 Dec. 1735	Thomas Skeat
36	24				do.	John Eds
Here is Park Street						
56 Park St.	16					
37	21					
38	33				4 Oct. 1731	Richard Andrews
39	34					
40	36	18 Nov. 1725	58	Richard Andrews, gentleman		
41	36					
42	33				2 Oct. 1731	John Green
43	33				1 Oct. 1731	do.
44	25				3 Nov. 1727	William Draycott

Designation	Associated Builders and Architects	Rent £ s. d.	First Occupant	Period	House No.
	Sub-let 1732 to Lawrence Neale, carpenter; Mackreth and Whitaker (as above) parties; assigned to Benjamin Denne, mason	11 12 0	Leonard Smelt, esq., M.P.	1734–40(d)	21
gentleman	Sub-let 1732 to John Clarkson, carpenter; Lawrence Neale, carpenter, party	5 5 0	John Emmett	1737–51 (inter-mittently)	22
	Sub-let 1730 to John How, carver; Lawrence Neale, carpenter, party	4 15 0	? Mrs. Atheton or Lady Hubbard	1735 1736–44	23
	Sub-let 1730 to Lawrence Neale, carpenter; Richard Davies, joiner, a witness	3 10 0	Lawrence Neale	1730–45	24
masons		5 0 0	Richard Burket, victualler (Wheat-sheaf)	1730–7	(Former 28 Park Lane)
do.		4 10 0	Rev. Thomas Clark(e)	1730–45	25
mason		7 0 0	William Hale, mason, son-in-law of Lissiman	1730–6	26
do.		4 0 0	Captain Lawrence	1733–40	27
do.		5 0 0	Mrs. Burroughs	1734–8	28
do.		5 5 0	Charles Carter, esq.	1732–8	29
do.		9 7 0	Hon. Frances Bruce	1739–51	30
			Mary Hutchenson	1736–42	31
			George Wright, esq.	1736–42	32
	(Large mansion set back from road; later called Grosvenor House)	76 13 0	1st Viscount Chetwynd, M.P.	1732–6(d)	33
	Sub-let 1731 to Benjamin Timbrell, carpenter	8 0 0	Colonel Richard Pyott and/or Mrs. Pitts	1732–7	34
bricklayer	John Eds, carpenter, party to lease	9 10 0	2nd Viscount Chetwynd, M.P.	1738–41	35
carpenter		4 10 0	? John Powis	1737–9	36
	Sub-let 1731 to James Jenner, brick-layer; assigned to William Allison, carpenter	do.	John or Thomas Baswick	1731–4	56 Park St.
	Sub-let 1731 to Colonel Francis Williamson; James Jenner, brick-layer, party	5 10 0	Colonel Francis Williamson	1731–8	37
esquire	Sub-let 1731 to James Jenner, brick-layer	13 10 0	Richard Edgcumbe, esq., M.P. (later 1st Baron Edgcumbe)	1733–58(d)	38
	Sub-let 1731 to John Neale, carpenter; Charles Griffith, carpenter, party	13 12 0	3rd Earl of Jersey	1733–43	39
	Sub-let 1731 to Israel Russell, painter[-stainer]; John Eds, carpenter, party	13 4 0	Lord Lynne (later 3rd Viscount Townshend)	1735–41	40
	Sub-let 1731 to John Eds, carpenter	14 8 0	Hon. Henry Vane, M.P. (later 1st Earl of Darlington)	1734–9	41
joiner		13 4 0	7th Viscount Falkland	1734–6	42
do.		do.	Marquess of Carnarvon, M.P. (later 2nd Duke of Chandos)	1735–9	43
esquire	Charles Griffith, carpenter, party to lease	8 15 0	— Jolliffe, esq.	1731–2	44

House No.	Frontage in Feet	Date of Building Agreement	No. on Plan A	Undertaker	Date of Building Lease	Lessee
UPPER GROSVENOR STREET, SOUTH SIDE (continued)						
45	25				2 Nov. 1727	William Draycott
46	40	18 Nov. 1725	58	Richard Andrews, gentleman	12 Sept. 1728	Edward Cock
47	20				do.	Robert Phillips
48	20				28 Aug. 1727	William Hanmer

Designation	Associated Builders and Architects	Rent £ s. d.			First Occupant	Period	House No.
esquire	Charles Griffith, carpenter, party to lease	8	15	0	Sir George Oxenden, Bt., M.P., Lord of the Treasury	1732–7	45
carpenter		15	0	0	Lady Isabella Scott, d. of Anne, Duchess of Buccleuch	1733–48(d)	46
bricklayer		3	0	0	Francis Blake Delaval, esq., of Seaton Delaval	1732–8	47
esquire	Robert Phillips, bricklayer, party to lease and builder of house	10	0	0	Colonel William Hanmer	1729–41(d)	48

APPENDIX II

Schedule of Fixtures at No. 45 Grosvenor Square, 1733

This schedule is contained in a lease in the Grosvenor Office dated 3 December 1733 from Thomas Richmond, carpenter, to Philip Dormer, Earl of Chesterfield.

IN the Six Garretts—Eight Sash Windows compleatly glazed with inside Shutters thereto Three Portland Chimney pieces and Slabs and Hearths, Five Closetts with Doors to the same also Six Doors to the Garretts, A Skylight at the head of the great Stairs.

IN the two front Rooms on the two pair of Stairs Floor—Five Sash Windows compleatly glazed with inside Shutters and Iron fastnings thereto, The Rooms compleatly wainscotted, Two Marble Chimney pieces and Slabs with firestone Hearths and Covings, Three Closetts with Shelves and Doors to the same and two Doors to the Rooms.

IN the back Room next the Garden—Two Sash Windows compleatly glazed with inside Shutters and Iron fastnings thereto, The Room compleatly wainscotted, a Marble Chimney piece and Slab with firestone Hearth and Covings, Two Doors to the Room and two Closetts with Shelves and Doors to the same.

IN the two Rooms and dressing Room adjoining—Six Sash Windows compleatly glazed with inside Shutters and Iron fastnings thereto, Two Marble Chimney pieces and Slabs compleat A Portland one compleat, seven Cupboards with Doors and Shelves, The Rooms compleatly wainscotted, four Doors to the Rooms, Brass Knobs to all the Sashes and Shutters in this Floor.

IN the Room one pair of Stairs forward—Three Sash windows compleatly glazed with inside Shutters and Iron fastnings thereto, The Room compleatly wainscotted with Modillion Cornish & Dentill Bedmold around the same, Two Ionic Pillasters next the Chimney with the Entablature over them, A Marble Chimney piece with Slab Slips and Nosings with a Cornish over the Mantle, Firestone Hearth and Covings, Two Doors with Pediments over them.

IN the Room adjoining next the Garden—Two Sash windows compleatly glazed with inside Shutters and Iron fastnings thereto, The Room compleatly wainscotted, A Marble Chimney piece with Slab Slips and Nosings Firestone Hearth & Covings, A Door to the Room

IN the Middle Room—One Sash Window compleatly glazed with inside Shutters and Iron fastnings thereto The Room compleatly wainscotted, A Marble Chimney piece Slab Slips, firestone Hearth and Covings, a Door to the Room.

IN the Wing—Five Sash Windows compleatly glazed with inside Shutters and Iron fastnings thereto, the Rooms compleatly wainscotted with A Modillion Cornish around the same, Two Ionic Pillasters with the Entablature over them A Marble Chimney piece and Slab Slips and Nosings with a Cornish over the Mantle, Firestone Hearth and Covings Four Doors to the Rooms, A Water Closett adjoining to the Garden with a Marble Bason Bosses and Seat Compleat a Leaden Cistern on the Top of the same, Brass Knobs to all the Sashes and Shutters in this Floor.

IN the fore Parlour—Three Sash Windows compleatly glazed with inside Shutters and Iron fastnings thereto, The Room compleatly wainscotted, Two Doric Pillasters with the Entablature over them, A Marble Chimney piece and Slab Slips and Nosings, firestone Hearth and Covings, The Jaumbs continued above the Mantle with a Cornice over them.

IN the back Parlour—Two Sash Windows compleatly glazed with inside Shutters and Iron fastnings thereto the Room compleatly wainscotted, A marble Chimney piece with Slab Slips and Nosings, Firestone Hearth and Covings, two Doors to the Room.

IN the Middle Room—One Sash Window compleatly glazed with inside Shutters and Iron fastnings thereto the Room compleatly wainscotted A Marble Chimney piece with Slab and Slips, Firestone Hearth and Covings A Book press with Shelves and folding Doors to the same, A Door to the Room.

IN the Wing or great Room next the Garden—Five Sash Windows compleatly glazed with inside Shutters and Iron fastnings thereto, The Room compleatly wainscotted, Two Doric Pillasters with the Entablature over them A Marble Chimney piece with a Cornice over the Mantle Slab Slips and Nosings, Firestone Hearth and Covings one Door to the Room, and a Pair of Pedestall folding Doors.

IN the Hall and Staircase—Three Sash Windows compleatly glazed with inside Shutters and Iron fastnings thereto The Hall wainscotted compleat, Two Ionic Pillasters with the Entablature carved around the Hall (The Staircase Painted) A Wainscot Staircase with Twist Rails & Ballisters carved Bracketts, also the Caps of Columns and Pillasters a Portland Chimney piece Brass Knobs to all the Shutters and Sashes in this Floor.

IN the Housekeeper's Room below Stairs next the front Arey—Three Sash windows compleatly glazed with outside Shutters and plate Bolts, The Room compleatly wainscotted, a Closet with Door to the same, a Portland Chimney piece with Slab and Hearth, Three firestone Stoves with Grates and Boxes fixt to them, a Leaden Cistern with Pipes and Brass Cock to the same, a Door to the Room.

IN the Pantry next the fore Arey—One Sash Window compleat with outside Shutters and Plate Bolts thereto The Rooms wainscotted, A Portland Chimney piece and Slab, Two Closetts with Shelves, two Doors to the same, a Door to the Room, a Leaden Cistern with Pipes and a brass Cock to the same.

IN the Steward's Room—Two Sash windows compleatly glazed with inside Shutters thereto, The Room wainscotted about six foot high, a Portland Chimney piece and Slab, with firestone hearth, a Door to the Room.

Two Wine Vaults next the Passage with Binns, a Pantry with Shelves

IN the Servants Hall—Four Windows with inside Shutters Kirb and Iron Bars over Ditto in the Garden, The Hall wainscotted about six foot high, a Portland Chimney piece, Two Appartments divided off with Partions Story high, Leaden Pipes laid from the force Pump to the Marble Bason in the Middle Room Ground Floor, with a Brass Cock to one of them.

IN the Front Arey—Four Vaults with Doors.

IN the back Arey—A Vault with a Door, a Flatt covered with Lead leading to the Kitchen Passage in which is a Wine Vault with Binns, and a Door to the same.

IN the Kitchen Arey—a Cool Larder with a Bressimer Front wired, a Door to the same and two Dressers, a Deal Dresser in the Washhouse, a Pump compleat, and Elm Dresser and Sash Window in the Scullery, The flat over the Washhouse and Arey leaded, a Door to the same and Scullery, a Large Leaden Cistern with water pipes, Brass Cocks and Bosses with a Ball Cock to the same, a Pipe laid from the Cistern to the force pump in the Garden to convey the water into the Cistern at the Top of the water Closet

IN the Garden—A Boghouse wainscotted with a Door to the same, a leaden Bason with Bosses and wast pipes and Seat compleat.

IN the Kitchen—Three Sash Windows compleat, Two large Dressers and Shelves with Drawers under Ditto A Cool Larder adjoining with Dressers and Shelves, a Sash Window to the same, An Oven with an Iron Door, a Portland Chimney piece, four Stoves with Grates and Boxes set in Brick work with an Iron Rim around the same a Door to the Coal Vault and two Kitchen Doors, a Leaden Sink with a Pipe and brass Cock.

The Water laid from the Tree to serve the Cisterns in the front Arey, housekeeper's Room and Butler's Pantry, also the back Arey, the Kitchen Arey, washhouse and Sink in Kitchen.

IN the Rooms over the Scullery—A Sash Window with inside Shutters thereto, a Portland Chimney piece & Slab and Hearth, a Door to the Room.

IN the Room over the last mentioned Room—Two Sash Windows with inside Shutters thereto a Portland Chimney piece Slab and firestone hearth, a Door to the Room.

IN the Landry—Three Sash windows with inside Shutters and Iron fastnings thereto, a Portland Chimney piece and Slab, a Door to the Room

IN the Stables—Standings for twelve horses with turn'd Columns, Bailes, Rings, Chains, Staples, Racks and Mangers compleat, Two Corn Binns, outside Shutters to the Window, three Coach houses divided, a Hay loft over the Stables with a Window and Shutters to the same, three Windows with Shutters to the same belonging to Coachmen and Grooms Rooms over the Coachhouses, a Crane to the Hay loft Door, a Lead water trough to convey the wast water into the Stable Yard, The water laid into the Cistern in the Stables.

ABOUT the Outside of the House—Stone Steps and Iron Rails in the Front Arey, Iron Pallasades to Ditto and back Arey, Rain Lead Waterpipe, with proper Fastnings to all the outside Doors and Shutters.

Problems of short-term leasing: an episode

Short-term speculation and improvement played a vital part in the leasehold system, especially in the complex period at the end of one lease and the beginning of another one. But though they were essential for the needs of fashionable society in the eighteenth and nineteenth centuries, short-term occupiers could also by their nature, habits and interests dissuade other potential lessees from taking on the longer tenancies that were the life-blood of the system. Nowhere is this better highlighted than by the history of No. 51 Brook Street in 1802–6, as recorded chiefly in letters (now in the North Yorkshire County Record Office) from the architect P. F. Robinson to Mrs. Osbaldeston of Hutton Buscel, Yorkshire, a prospective lessee.

The head lease of No. 51 Brook Street, due to run out at Lady Day (25 March) 1804, was held by General Thomas Davies, who for some years had been sub-letting to tenants, the last of them a Frenchman, Mr. Grillion, who may have been running the house as a private hotel. Since the renewal terms offered by the Estate were high, both Davies and Grillion successively declined them. But Robinson, hearing of the house through an agent and having after inspecting it received 'very satisfactory answers' about the 'disagreeables to which Houses are liable', clinched the terms verbally on behalf of his client Mrs. Osbaldeston early in January 1803. Mrs. Osbaldeston was to have a sixty-two-year term from Lady Day 1804. Though the fine was higher than he had at first been led to believe, Robinson still thought the house a bargain, telling Mrs. Osbaldeston 'if I had money to lay out I do not know a speculation I would more willingly engage in than that of purchasing Houses in the neighbourhood of Grosvenor Square, improving and selling them. I think I could make a fortune. Houses in this quarter are so much sought after that the value encreases rather than otherwise.'

Nevertheless the fine was never paid and the deal was to fall through for two connected reasons. Firstly, Mrs. Osbaldeston was primarily interested in a town house which she could occupy for short periods, at most for the duration of the London Season, and not as the long-term investment which her architect was urging upon her. So much is clear from Robinson's letters of subsequent years about other London houses he looked into for her. Secondly, the subtenants were left in a confusing situation during the last year of General Davies's term.

Grillion's sub-lease expired in March 1803 and he was anxious to be relieved of his tenancy before that date if possible. But though Mrs. Osbaldeston herself took on a sub-lease of the following six months from April to September under General Davies, so as to be able to have a house for the Season of 1803 while postponing her final decision about a new lease, she declined to take over Grillion's last two months as well. This put Grillion 'in so great a rage', Robinson reported, 'that he swears neither I nor any person on your account shall enter the House while he has any power to prevent it. I calculate however upon his getting cool and seeing his interest a little better.' This duly occurred; Grillion performed some minor repairs and made over these two months to Mr. Polton, an upholsterer, who in his turn prepared to refurbish the house and looked for a short-term tenant. Polton naturally wanted the house for a longer period than two months; thinking of letting it for the Season, he applied to Robinson for the ensuing six months (April–September 1803). But Robinson advised against this unless Mrs. Osbaldeston were herself to live in the house as furnished by Polton during the period, 'as we otherwise shall get possession of the House at a Season when it will be impossible to put workmen in it [i.e. too late in the year] and you would have it on your hands during a winter in its present state.'

Mrs. Osbaldeston therefore kept these six months in reserve with a possible view to living in the house for the Season of 1803, while Polton found a two-month tenant in the shape of the Danish Ambassador. But in February 1803, Robinson was reporting gloomily that the house was 'dirty enough indeed, I believe it is in vain to look for cleanliness from a Frenchman and if Grillion or his agents are so unwise as to neglect their interest in not rendering it tolerable, we must search for another house pro tempora [*sic*]'. Whether Mrs. Osbaldeston actually did take the house for the Season is unclear, but the likelihood is that in the light of these reports she did not. Her enthusiasm for a long lease was also beginning to wane. In June 1803 Robinson sent sketches to her for proposed permanent alterations in stages and attempted to reconcile her to taking on the lease with the thought that the house could be easily sold at any time. 'The present time has the effect of encreasing the value of Houses' he argued; 'I have had some conversation with intelligent Builders, who agree in believing that Rents will universally be raised.' But by August Mrs. Osbaldeston had taken fright, and by Autumn 1803 she had definitely decided against taking the long lease. Though this led to difficulties with the Grosvenor Board and some talk in December 1803 of litigation, the subsequent immediate history of No. 51 Brook Street suggests that she was right and her architect wrong. After General Davies had surrendered the house empty in April 1804, it hung heavy on the Estate's hands for several years. Despite various proposals, one to convert it into a bookshop, no permanent tenant could be found until December 1806, when Sir Joseph Copley agreed to take a new long lease from Lady Day 1807. Even then the house remained private for only a few years, for in 1813 it was to become the first of a series of houses to be taken over as Mivart's Hotel, chief ancestor of the modern Claridge's.

References

ABBREVIATIONS

B.A.　　Building Act case, Greater London Council.

B.L.　　British Library, Reference Division.

Colvin　　H. M. Colvin, *A Biographical Dictionary of English Architects, 1660–1840*, 1954.

D.N.B.　　*Dictionary of National Biography.*

E.H.P.　　Eaton Hall Papers, archives of the Grosvenor family at Eaton Hall, Cheshire.

GBA　　Grosvenor Building Agreements in Grosvenor Office (numbered sequence, 1–92).

GBM　　Grosvenor Board Minutes, 46 volumes, 1789–*c.* 1920, in Grosvenor Office.

G.E.C.　　*The Complete Peerage*, ed. G.E.C., 1910–59.

GLB　　Grosvenor Lease Books, 45 volumes, 1721–1834, in Grosvenor Office.

G.L.R.O.(L)　　Greater London Record Office (London Records), County Hall.

G.L.R.O.(M)　　Greater London Record Office (Middlesex Records), Dartmouth Street.

G.O.　　Grosvenor Office, 53 Davies Street, W.1.

M.L.R.　　Middlesex Land Register in Greater London Record Office.

P.O.D.　　*Post Office Directories.*

P.P.　　*Parliamentary Papers.*

P.P.R.　　Principal Probate Registry, Somerset House.

P.R.O.　　Public Record Office.

R.B.　　Ratebooks of the parish of St. George, Hanover Square, in Westminster City Library, Buckingham Palace Road.

R.I.B.A.　　Royal Institute of British Architects.

W.C.L.　　Westminster City Library, Buckingham Palace Road.

CHAPTER I (pp. 1–5)

The Acquisition of the Estate

1. P.R.O., C66/880, m. 32.
2. William Loftie Rutton, 'The Manor of Eia, or Eye next Westminster', in *Archaeologia*, vol. LXII, 1910, pp. 31–58, from which most of the information about the early history of the manor is derived.
3. 28 Henry VIII, c. 49 in *Statutes of the Realm*, vol. III, 1817, pp. 709–12.
4. Rutton, *op. cit.*, p. 33.
5. E.g. G.O., early deeds and papers, no. 242.
6. Rutton, *op. cit.*, p. 34.
7. G.O., early deeds…, no. 11.
8. B. H. Johnson, *Berkeley Square to Bond Street*, 1952, pp. 10–21.
9. 27 Car. II, c. 2, private.
10. M.L.R. 1738/4/11.
11. *Calendar of Letters and Papers of Henry VIII*, vol. XVII, p. 392.
12. GBA 75.
13. G.O., early deeds, no. 15.
14. For Ossulston see Charles T. Gatty, *Mary Davies and the Manor of Ebury*, 1921, vol. I, pp. 51–60 and G.O., London Scrapbooks, vol. I, pp. 47–89.
15. G.O., early deeds, nos. 5–12, 15: B.L., Add. MS. 38104 (reproduced by London Topographical Society as *A Plan of the Manor of Ebury*, c. 1663–1670, 1915).
16. G.O., early deeds, nos. 26–7: Menna Prestwich, *Cranfield, Politics and Profits under the Early Stuarts*, 1966, pp. 258–9.
17. Prestwich, *op. cit.*, pp. 591, 601: B.L., Add. MS. 38104 (see ref. 15).
18. P.R.O., C66/3032, no. 8, m. 6.
19. G.O., early deeds, nos. 33–4.
20. *Ibid.*, no. 38: Gatty, *op. cit.*, vol. I, pp. 76–155 *passim*.
21. Prestwich, *op. cit.*, pp. 478–9.
22. B.L., Add. MS. 38104 (see ref. 15): Gatty, *op. cit.*, vol. I, pp. 97–8.
23. G.O., early deeds, nos. 101–2.
24. *Ibid.*, no. 107.
25. Gatty, *op. cit.*, vol. I, p. 119.
26. 27 Car. II, c. 2, private: Gatty, *op. cit.*, vol. I, p. 169.
27. G.O., early deeds, nos. 111–12.
28. *Ibid.*, no. 135.
29. G.O., chest B, bundle 9, 22 and 23 April 1763.
30. *Ibid.*, unnumbered early deeds, agreement of 12 Dec. 1672.
31. *Ibid.*, misc. box 3, 'An Acount at the Marage of my Daughter Grosvenor', quoted in Gatty, *op. cit.*, vol. II, pp. 186–92.
32. Johnson, *op. cit.*, pp. 51–9.
33. Gatty, *op. cit.*, vol. I, p. 222.
34. G.O., early deeds, nos. 170–1.
35. *Ibid.*, MS. vol. called 'Title Deeds', deed of 31 Oct. 1677.
36. *Ibid.*, early deeds, no. 242.
37. *Ibid.*, nos. 166, 181.
38. G.O., unnumbered early deeds, bundle of deeds of 1681; early deeds, nos. 242, 328.
39. *Ibid.*, early deeds, no. 242: *Survey of London*, vol. XI, 1927, p. 5.
40. Gatty, *op. cit.*, vol. II, pp. 54–182.
41. E.H.P., personal papers, 4th Bt., petition to Chancery, *c.* 1720; 3rd Bt., copy of will.
42. G.O., chest B, bundle 6, 12 June 1708.
43. 9 Anne, c. 22, private.
44. G.O., misc. box 21, abstract of title, [*c.* 1730].
45. *Ibid.*, London Scrapbooks, vol. II, p. 35.

CHAPTER II (pp. 6–33)

The Development of the Estate
1720–1785

1. Daniel Defoe, *A Tour Thro' London about the year 1725*, ed. Sir Mayson M. Beeton and E. Beresford Chancellor, 1929, pp. 97–8.
2. *Ibid.*, p. 21.
3. *Mist's Weekly Journal*, 17 July 1725.
4. M. Dorothy George, *London Life in the Eighteenth Century*, 1925, pp. 23–5: George Rudé, *Hanoverian London 1714–1808*, 1971, p. 4.
5. Defoe, *op. cit.*, p. 98.
6. Corporation of London Record Office, 'The City's Estate in Conduit Mead', [*c.* 1742–3].
7. Romney Sedgwick, *The House of Commons 1715–1754*, 1970, vol. I, pp. 64–5, 113, 203–4, vol. II, pp. 87–8.
8. P.R.O., E112/1181/954.
9. E.H.P., box 42/2, 23 Nov. 1732 and 9 Jan. 1732/3.
10. R.B.: M.L.R. 1731/2/382–3.
11. GLB II/66, IV/114.
12. G.E.C.: *D.N.B.*
13. E.H.P., personal papers, 1st Earl, letters from W. Pitt, 1759–60.
14. Sir Lewis Namier and John Brooke, *The House of Commons 1754–1790*, 1964, p. 557.
15. E.H.P., box 42/4, 14 Nov. 1772, 20 Feb. 1781, 17 May [? 1784].
16. GBA 1.
17. *Ibid.*, 2–7, 9–20.
18. GLB I/1, II/55.
19. G.O., chest B, bundle 6, 2 June 1721.
20. GLB I/2.
21. E.H.P., box 77/2, 'A Particular of Ground-Rents, and other Leasehold Premises, Late the Estate of Mr. Richard Barlow, deceased.'
22. G.O., chest B, bundle 6, 10 July 1723: E.H.P., item 1193, lease and plan book, p. 5.
23. G.O., misc. box 3, draft petition with accompanying letter of 27 Nov. 1725.
24. 12 Geo. I, c. 23, private.
25. G.O., chest B, bundle 7, 9–10 April and 11 May 1730.
26. P.R.O., PROB 11/655/284.
27. G.O., chest B, bundle 9, 14 Nov. 1755.
28. E.H.P., personal papers, 4th Bt., undated petition to Ld. Chancellor and letter from J. Sharp of 17 April 1722.
29. GBA *passim*.
30. G.L.R.O.(L), W.C.S. 51, pp. 229, 275, 378.
31. G.O., cash book no. 1.
32. GBA 87.
33. E.g. *Ibid.*, 13.
34. W.C.L., deed 143/1 (copy: original in possession of Williams and Glyn's Bank Ltd.).
35. G.O., agreement of 11 Nov. 1725, J. Alston and Sir Rd. Grosvenor; rent book, 'Old Estate', 1725–9.
36. *Ibid.*, 'The State of the Accot. for making up Grosvenor Sq.'.
37. *Ibid.*, chest B, bundle 6.
38. *Ibid.*, misc. box 3, draft petition with accompanying letter of 27 Nov. 1725: E.H.P., personal papers, 4th Bt., letter from Rbt. Grosvenor of 27 May 1725.
39. G.O., chest B, bundle 7.
40. E.H.P., personal papers, 3rd Bt., 'An Account of Lady Grosvenor's Personal Estate made up to 12 Jan. 1729'.
41. *Ibid.*, box 77/2, rough note of receipts and expenditure up to 1737: G.O., chest B, bundle 7, 19 May 1730: M.L.R. 1731/3/65.
42. G.O., Sir Rbt. Grosvenor's Trust Estate boxes, bundles of deeds relating to purchase of ground rents in Grosvenor Square.
43. *Ibid.*, bundle of deeds concerning leaseholds purchased from E. Bennett.
44. E.H.P., box 77/2, 'An account of the late Sir Robert Grosvenor's several Securities and Moneys due to him in Middlesex'.
45. G.O., rent books, Mayfair estate, 1724–9, 1730–2.
46. *Ibid.*, 1733–47.
47. *Ibid.*, 1755–63.
48. Lambeth Palace Library, MS. 2714, f. 12.
49. G.O., misc. box 3, deposition of Rd. Andrews [*c.* 1714].
50. E.H.P., personal papers, 4th Bt., letters of 10 June, 6 Nov. 1706 and 15 May 1716.
51. G.O., cash book no. 2.
52. Inner Temple Admissions Register, vol. II, p. 251, f. 1378: P.R.O., C24/1588/54, deposition of Rbt. Andrews.
53. G.O., misc. box 6, solicitor's bills.
54. R.B.: M.L.R. 1730/4/301.
55. W.C.L., C767, p. 34; C768, pp. 1, 106.
56. P.R.O., E112/1181/954: Inner Temple Admissions Register, vol. II, p. 252, f. 1379.
57. E.g. GBA 37, 58: GLB IV/115, IX/247–51: M.L.R. 1725–63 *sub* Andrews, Rd. and Rbt.
58. GLB IV/115, XI/278: M.L.R. 1726–47 *sub* Andrews, Rbt. (sub-leases).
59. GLB IX/236: W.C.L., C766a (at rear): M.L.R. 1751/1/567–8.
60. E.g. M.L.R. 1729/6/95; 1736/5/337.
61. E.H.P., item 1194, account book 1756–63.
62. P.R.O., PROB 11/891/415; C12/1086/1: *The Gentleman's Magazine*, vol. XXXIII, Sept. 1763, p. 465.
63. P.R.O., C12/1086/1; C12/1092/3.
64. R. E. Megarry and H. W. R. Wade, *The Law of Real Property*, 3rd ed., 1966, pp. 237, 508–9.
65. *Parish Register of the Holy and Undivided Trinity in the City of Chester 1532–1837*, ed. L. M. Farrell, 1914, p. 175.
66. G.O., misc. box 5, solicitor's bills.
67. Inner Temple Admissions Register, vol. II, p. 316, f. 1476.
68. M.L.R. 1750/3/117.
69. GLB XVI/412.
70. *Harleian Society Publications, Registers XI, St. George's, Hanover Square, Marriages*, vol. I, *1725–1787*, 1886, p. 53.
71. R.B.
72. P.R.O., PROB 11/1203/146.
73. G.O., chest C, bundle 10, 'State of Lord Grosvenor's Affairs', 1779.
74. GLB XVII/434.
75. R.B.: *P.O.D.*
76. P.R.O., C54/4883, no. 8.
77. B. H. Johnson, *Berkeley Square to Bond Street*, 1952, pp. 131, 147.
78. W.C.L., ratebooks of St. Paul's, Covent Garden.
79. *Survey of London*, vol. XXXVI, 1970, pp. 39n., 107, 107n., 312–13.
80. Lambeth Palace Library, MS. 2690, p. 206; MS. 2714, f. 7.

81. B. H. Johnson, 'Note on the early development of the sites of the buildings in Hanover Square and St. George Street, Westminster', typescript in possession of G.L.C. *Survey of London* section: Lambeth Palace Library, MS. 2714, f. 3.

82. Johnson, 'Note...', *ut supra*, pp. 13–14, 17.

83. *Ibid.*, p. 14: Lambeth Palace Library, MS. 2691, pp. 95, 97, 100–1, 118.

84. P.R.O., PROB 11/635/26.

85. Corporation of London Record Office, 'The City's Estate in Conduit Mead', [*c.* 1742–3], p. 2.

86. E.H.P., personal papers, 4th Bt., copy of undated petition to Ld. Chancellor with Order dated 11 Feb. 1720/1 entered on it.

87. *Ibid.*: G.O., cash books nos. 1 and 2.

88. *The Daily Post*, 22 Jan. 1730.

89. GBA 46.

90. E.H.P., item 1193, lease and plan book, pp. 2, 6–7.

91. M.L.R. 1721/6/196–7; 1722/3/337; 1723/5/294: GLB II/53.

92. GBA 1: GLB I/2.

93. G.O., misc. box 13, abstract of title to estate of Bird's trustees: E.H.P., box 77/2, 'A Particular of Ground-Rents ', *ut supra* (see ref. 21).

94. E.H.P., item 1193, lease and plan book, p. 32.

95. W.C.L., WBA 343/1.

96. *Ibid.*, C766, pp. 325–30.

97. P.R.O., C12/2201/2.

98. *Ibid.*, *loc. cit.*; PROB 11/635/26.

99. Norman G. Brett-James, *The Growth of Stuart London*, 1935, pp. 274–5, 281.

100. P.R.O., MPH 258; C11/2430/38: G.L.R.O.(M), L.V.(W) 68/33: G.O., plan of Oliver's Mount public house, *c.* 1816.

101. G.O., building agreements, bundle 5, 8 June 1722; chest B, bundle 6, 10 July, 26 Oct. 1723.

102. Johnson, 'Note...', *ut supra*, pp. 13, 15: M.L.R. 1719/5/267–8.

103. E.g. GBA 30: GLB I/9.

104. E.H.P., item 1193, lease and plan book.

105. G.O., John Mackay's map of the Grosvenor estate, 1723.

106. GBA 26: G.O., chest B, bundle 6, 10 July 1723.

107. GLB XVII/450–3, XVIII/454–60.

108. GBA 36: M.L.R. 1755/3/503; 1757/1/362.

109. John Gwynn, *London and Westminster Improved*, 1766, p. x, note.

110. GBA 26, 27, 37.

111. R. Horwood, *Plan of the Cities of London and Westminster ...*, 1792–9: G.O., estate surveyor's plans, vol. 1, p. 79.

112. M.L.R. 1726/2/407; 1727/5/394; 1730/4/340; 1732/3/322–4: R.B.

113. GBM 1/156.

114. E.H.P., item 1193, lease and plan book, p. 20.

115. Jacob Larwood, *The Story of the London Parks*, 1881 ed., p. 59.

116. G.O., misc. box 6, papers relating to Grosvenor Gate, 1724–5.

117. The information in this section is largely based on GBA *passim*.

118. GLB II/66, IV/120: M.L.R. 1719/6/36; 1727/1/62.

119. G.O., Sir Rbt. Grosvenor's Trust Estate boxes, agreement of 5 June 1727 with T. Goff and endorsement.

120. E.g. GLB V/132–3.

121. *Ibid.*, XVII/444–53, XVIII/454–60.

122. E.g. GBA 10 and GLB X/275, XI/276–7: GBA 16 and GLB VII/191: GBA 38 and GLB III/90.

123. GLB II/67, III/70, IV/109.

124. GBA 51: GLB V/142.

125. G.O., early deeds and papers, no. 149.

126. GBA 1, 23.

127. *Ibid.*, 75.

128. B.L., Add. MS. 18,238, ff. 30–2: *Survey of London*, vol. XXXVI, 1970, p. 38.

129. GBA 29, 30.

130. *Ibid.*, 36, 38.

131. *Ibid.*, 85, 87.

132. *Ibid.*, 30.

133. *Ibid.*, 36.

134. *Ibid.*, 72, 74, 81.

135. *Ibid.*, 9.

136. *Ibid.*, 53.

137. *Ibid.*, 57.

138. *Ibid.*, 48, 52.

139. The information in this section is largely based on GLB I–XVIII/1–460.

140. GLB XIII/348.

141. *Ibid.*, IV/115.

142. *Ibid.*, II/37, III/70.

143. *Ibid.*, XI/295, 297, 300, XIII/301.

144. GBA 2, 5–7, 12–13, 16–21.

145. *Ibid.*, 25, 36.

146. *Ibid.*, 38.

147. *Ibid.*, 10, 22, 24, 30, 42–3, 49, 56, 59, 62–4, 66.

148. *Ibid.*, 16–18, 23, 29.

149. W.C.L., C766, pp. 1–120 *passim*.

150. GBA 44.

151. *Ibid.*, 47.

152. *Ibid.*, 51–2, 54.

153. GLB II/66, IV/114: G.O., Sir Rbt. Grosvenor's Trust Estate boxes, building agreements of 3 Aug. 1725 and 6 April 1726.

154. GBA 72–5.

155. *Ibid.*, 92.

156. Information kindly provided by Mr. G. C. Berry, archivist to the Thames Water Authority.

157. GBA 27.

158. E.H.P., box 42/2, 31 June 1726.

159. *Ibid.*, box 77/2, letter of 19 Sept. 1734 from Rbt. Andrews.

160. G.O., chest B, bundle 6, 10 July 1723.

161. GBA 68–71.

162. Johnson, *Berkeley Square*, *ut supra*, pp. 103–7.

163. *Survey of London*, vol. XXXII, 1963, p. 452.

164. Corporation of London Record Office, 'The City's Estate in Conduit Mead', [*c.* 1742–3], inset report of sub-committee of 2 Nov. 1742, p. 16.

165. G.O., misc. box 13, abstract of title to estate of Bird's trustees; Bird v. Lefevre, sale particulars of 1792: Williams and Glyn's Bank Ltd., same sale particulars: E.H.P., box 77/2, 'A Particular of Ground-Rents...', *ut supra* (see ref. 21).

166. E.g. GLB III/90.

167. *Ibid.*, VI/156, VII/178.

168. *Ibid.*, IV/98.

169. *Ibid.*, XVII/450–3, XVIII/454–8.

170. *Ibid.*, IV/98: R.B.: *The St. James's Evening Post*, 9–11 Sept. 1729.

171. GBA 63-6.
172. John Summerson, *Architecture in Britain 1530 to 1830*, 1969 ed., p. 230.
173. *Catalogue of the Drawings Collection of the Royal Institute of British Architects. Colen Campbell*, 1973, [13], 1-2.
174. GLB II/66: G.O., Sir Rbt. Grosvenor's Trust Estate boxes, building agreements of 3 Aug. 1725.
175. GBA 54.
176. *R.I.B.A. Drawings Catalogue: Colen Campbell*, [13], 3-4.
177. GLB V/121: M.L.R. 1729/4/40; 1742/2/318: R.B.
178. Colvin.
179. GLB IV/94-5.
180. G.O., chest B, bundle 8, 26 March 1732.
181. GLB I/13: Colvin.
182. GLB II/50.
183. M.L.R. 1729/6/248: Hoare's Bank, Ledger K/98.
184. P.R.O., C105/32/1, agreement of 6 April 1728, E. Shepherd and F. Drewitt.
185. Robert Morris, *Lectures on Architecture*, [Part I], 1734, preface.
186. *Ibid.*, p. 85.
187. GBA 51-2.
188. GLB IV/102-3.
189. P.R.O., C105/32/1, manuscript plan of E. Shepherd's estate in N. Audley St.: M.L.R. 1735/1/285: R.B.
190. *Architectural Drawings in the Library of Elton Hall by Sir John Vanbrugh and Sir Edward Lovett Pearce*, ed. Howard Colvin and Maurice Craig, for Roxburghe Club, 1964, p. xliii and Catalogue, no. 6.
191. GBA 5: GLB I/28.
192. GLB VI/162.
193. M.L.R. 1730/4/178-9; 1731/5/13: R.B.
194. GBA 76: GLB XIII/342, XIV/360: M.L.R. 1738/5/29-30.
195. M.L.R. 1738/4/52: R.B.: P.R.O., PROB 11/812/334.
196. M.L.R. 1728/1/245; 1728/6/174: R.B.
197. M.L.R. 1735/5/10.
198. *Survey of London*, vol. XXXII, 1963, p. 477.
199. Guildhall Library, MS. 3045/2, entry of 1 Feb. 1704/5.
200. *Ibid.*, entry of 24 May 1715.
201. GLB II/67, III/70.
202. W.C.L., C766, pp. 5-6, 22.
203. GBA 67.
204. Rev. William Betham, *The Baronetage of England...*, vol. V, 1805, pp. 536-9.
205. W.C.L., C766, pp. 1, 16, 237, 325-30; C768, p. 172.
206. M.L.R. 1756/1/393-4, 505-8.
207. P.R.O., C12/356/33.
208. W.C.L., C766, pp. 1, 16, 120, 325-30.
209. GLB I/11: R.B.: Colvin.
210. P.R.O., PROB 6/151, Farrant, Nov. 1775; PROB 11/1016/87: M.L.R. 1776/3/353: Colvin.
211. GBA 92: GLB XVII/446: Northamptonshire Record Office, BH(K) 1185-6.
212. Information kindly provided by the Clerk of the Merchant Taylors' Company: P.R.O., PROB 11/689/103.
213. Colvin *sub* Gibbs.
214. G.O., rent book, 'Old Estate', 1730-2: W.C.L., ratebooks of St. Margaret's parish.
215. P.R.O., PROB 11/817/203; PROB 11/994/28: M.L.R. 1778/1/334: Badminton MSS., III·1·1, abstract of title to D. of Beaufort's stables.
216. Guildhall Library, MS. 5305/3, 12 Jan. 1691/2: P.R.O., PROB 6/109, f. 193v.: M.L.R. 1733/3/111.

217. GLB IX/245: *The Weekly Miscellany*, 15 July 1737.
218. M.L.R. 1762/3/10; 1772/3/237; 1773/2/453: R.B.: P.R.O., B4/21, S.22.
219. John Summerson, *Georgian London*, 1962 ed., p. 77.
220. P.R.O., C105/32/1, agreement of 11 March 1724/5, E. Shepherd and T. Fayram.
221. GLB VII/176.
222. M.L.R. 1728/4/47.
223. GLB VI/172.
224. G.O., building agreements, bundle 5, 20 Oct. 1755.
225. M.L.R. 1756/3/207, 230, 296, 482-3; 1756/4/133.
226. G.O., building agreements, bundle 5, 22 March 1741/2.
227. P.R.O., C105/21.
228. Corsham Court Archives, deed of 2 March 1727/8.
229. M.L.R. 1723/2/366; 1727/2/189.
230. *Ibid.*, 1733/2/162.
231. *Ibid.*, 1729/6/157.
232. *Ibid.*, 1727/4/212; 1728/2/67; 1728/4/132; 1728/5/449: G.O., chest B, bundle 7, 17 Oct. 1728.
233. M.L.R. 1721/4/94; 1725/3/233, 415; 1727/2/202; 1728/4/395; 1729/4/32; 1730/1/67; 1731/1/308; 1732/2/298; 1733/2/206; 1734/4/347; 1736/4/583; 1736/5/583; 1737/1/397; 1740/4/20.
234. *Ibid.*, 1724/4/227-8; 1728/2/336.
235. *Ibid.*, 1725/4/99; 1729/6/157; 1736/5/358; 1737/5/139; 1740/3/334.
236. *Ibid.*, 1723/3/129; 1723/6/414; 1725/1/442; 1725/2/74; 1726/4/111.
237. *Ibid.*, 1729/1/3; 1729/5/79.
238. *Ibid.*, 1723/2/366; 1727/2/189; 1728/1/257; 1728/2/67; 1737/5/324; 1738/5/30.
239. *Ibid.*, 1741/3/445.
240. *Ibid.*, 1736/4/47; 1738/4/258; 1738/5/206; 1751/2/676: Hoare's Bank, M/L 1743-73/13.
241. *The Gentleman's Magazine*, vol. X, Sept. 1740, p. 469.
242. M.L.R. 1731/3/278-81; 1732/5/414; 1734/2/24.
243. GLB VII/199 (variations vol.): R.B.
244. P.R.O., PROB 11/704/240.
245. M.L.R. 1728/5/299; 1728/6/398; 1729/3/174; 1729/4/325; 1730/6/4.
246. *Ibid.*, 1725/4/511; 1726/6/412; 1728/2/338; 1730/1/381.
247. *Ibid.*, 1728/1/420; 1728/2/336; 1737/1/279.
248. P.R.O., PROB 11/635/26; PROB 11/700/3.
249. M.L.R. 1725/2/181; 1726/3/70, 82; 1727/4/339; 1729/3/173.
250. P.R.O., B4/10, p. 280, no. 1791; C12/2200/59.
251. M.L.R. 1728/6/152.
252. *Ibid.*, 1728/1/181.
253. P.R.O., B1/17, p. 299.
254. M.L.R. 1728/6/159.
255. *Ibid.*, 1724/1/263-4, 266-9; 1725/1/48.
256. *Ibid.*, 1725/4/320.
257. *Ibid.*, 1726/6/168.
258. *Ibid.*, 1728/1/246.
259. P.R.O., C105/21, copy of deed of 12 Dec. 1728, J. Montigny to H. Huddle.
260. *Ibid.*, undated paper listing value of J. Jenner's property, and deed of 12 June 1729, J. Montigny to F. Commins.
261. M.L.R. 1739/2/252.
262. GLB XVII/444.
263. Northamptonshire Record Office, BH(K)1185.
264. GLB V/133.
265. *The Builder*, 23 Nov. 1867, p. 861.

266. GLB II/44.
267. Wiltshire Record Office, Radnor MSS., 490/630.
268. Suffolk Record Office, Bury St. Edmunds, Bunbury Papers, E 18/660.2.
269. GLB III/76: Corsham Court Archives, deed of 2 March 1727/8.
270. Corsham Court Archives, memo. of 2 March 1727/8.
271. *Ibid.*, bills, 1728.
272. M.L.R. 1726/3/301.
273. P.R.O., C11/1690/29.
274. M.L.R. 1727/1/410.
275. *The London Daily Post, and General Advertiser*, 19 June 1738; 7, 8, 9, 11 June 1739: *The Daily Post*, 16 Feb. 1739: *The Daily Gazetteer*, 11 June 1739: *The Gentleman's Magazine*, vol. IX, 1739, pp. 325, 437: Northamptonshire Record Office, Fitzwilliam (Milton) MSS., tin box 10, Mx, parcel 3.
276. Kent Archives Office, U455/T136: *The St. James's Evening Post*, 30 April–2 May 1730.
277. M.L.R. 1731/5/187.
278. Kent Archives Office, U791/T236: G.L.R.O.(L), O/179/4: M.L.R. 1729/4/40; 1730/4/37: *The London Daily Post*, 29 April 1738.
279. M.L.R. 1730/2/15.
280. Essex Record Office, D/DCc T55.
281. *The London Daily Post*, 23 Jan. 1737/8: Hoare's Bank, Ledger K/98.
282. M.L.R. 1726/1/134: Sedgwick, *op. cit.* (ref. 7 above), vol. II, p. 6.
283. Warwickshire Record Office, CR 114/Rag. iii/4: R.B.: Colvin.
284. Lambeth Palace Library, MS.2691, pp. 245, 254.
285. M.L.R. 1728/2/131.
286. W.C.L., deed 21/7.
287. M.L.R. 1725/3/443; 1725/5/400.
288. *Ibid.*, 1737/3/503.
289. *Ibid.*, 1726/5/198–9; 1730/1/91.
290. *Ibid.*, 1740/4/55.
291. G.O., chest B, bundle 8, 3 Dec. 1733.
292. M.L.R. 1731/5/187: lease of 15 Aug. 1733, E. Shepherd to R. Barlow, formerly in possession of Williams and Glyn's Bank Ltd.
293. P.R.O., C11/2430/38.
294. *Ibid.*, C11/2501/16.
295. *Ibid.*, C13/2851, Bevan v. Pearce.
296. *Ibid.*, C12/356/33.
297. *The Weekly Miscellany*, 15 July 1737.
298. *The Daily Post*, 10 Feb. 1739.
299. P.R.O., B4/3–21 *passim*.
300. G.O., misc. box 6, letter of 1 March 1744, E. Biscoe to Rbt. Andrews.
301. P.R.O., C54/5236, no. 7.
302. Lambeth Palace Library, MS. 2691, p. 254; MS. 2714, f. 59.
303. GLB VI/161.
304. W.C.L., C766, pp. 207, 210, 212–13, 229, 245; C766a, copies of deeds at back.
305. G.O., Park Street Chapel box, agreements of 13 July 1762.
306. GLB XXI/551–69: GBM 1/42–3, 211, 230, 262, 266, 290, 297: G.O., box Q, bundle 35; box S, bundle 157.
307. GLB IV/99.
308. G.O., box S, bundle 157, undated petition.
309. G.L.R.O.(M), TC/St.G/1–2.
310. M.L.R. 1721/6/196–7.
311. GLB VIII/219.
312. *The London Daily Post*, 13 June 1739.
313. Information kindly provided by Mr. G. C. Berry: Jacob Larwood, *The Story of the London Parks*, 1881 ed., p. 95.
314. G.L.R.O.(L), W.C.S. 53, p. 322.
315. A. Morley Davies, 'London's First Conduit System: A Topographical Study', in *Transactions of the London and Middlesex Archaeological Society*, n.s., vol. II, 1913, pp. 9–59: G.O., early deeds and papers, no. 44; misc. box 17, papers re conduit house, 1865–6: GBA 91–3: GLB IV/120; XVI/428–53; XVIII/454–60: GBM 14/8, 389–90, 400; 15/78–9, 182, 264: W.C.L., watercolour, C138 Oxford St. (6).
316. G.L.R.O.(L), W.C.S. 53, p. 308.
317. W.C.L., C 769, p. 82.
318. M.L.R. 1737/4/249; 1756/1/394.
319. John Summerson, *Architecture in Britain 1530 to 1830*, 1969 ed., pp. 229–30.
320. John Strype, *A Survey of the Cities of London and Westminster*, 1754–5 ed., vol. II, p. 688.
321. Lease of 15 Aug. 1733, E. Shepherd to R. Barlow, formerly in possession of Williams and Glyn's Bank Ltd.
322. P.R.O., C105/21; C11/2430/38.
323. GLB VII/183.
324. M.L.R. 1730/6/156.
325. GBM 9/420: G.O., lease particulars book A, No. 8 Green Street.
326. G.O., box P, bundle 133, 28 Dec. 1816.
327. GLB XIV/360.
328. *Ibid.*, XVI/413–14.
329. G.O., expired leases, 29 Oct. 1700 and 4 Dec. 1716.
330. *Ibid.*, box B, bundle 8, 28 Sept. 1743.
331. *Ibid.*, rent book, Mayfair estate, 1764–88.
332. *Ibid.*, rent books of Sir Rbt. Grosvenor's Trust Estate.
333. E.H.P., box 42/4, 20 Feb. 1781, 17 May [? 1784].
334. G.O., chest C, bundle 11, 5 April 1785.

CHAPTER III (pp. 34–66)

The Administration of the Estate 1785–1899

1. Gervas Huxley, *Victorian Duke. The Life of Hugh Lupus Grosvenor, First Duke of Westminster*, 1967, p. 101.
2. G.E.C.
3. Romney Sedgwick, *The House of Commons 1715–1754*, 1970, vol. I, p. 203; vol. II, pp. 87–8: Sir Lewis Namier and John Brooke, *The House of Commons 1754–1790*, 1964, vol. II, pp. 557–9: J. Vincent and M. Stenton, *McCalmont's Parliamentary Poll Book. British Election Results 1832–1918*, 1971, *passim*: G.E.C.
4. Richard Rush, *The Court of London from 1819 to 1825*, 3rd ed., 1873, pp. 8–10: see also Prince Pückler-Muskau, *Tour in England, Ireland and France in the Years 1826, 1827, 1828 and 1829*, 1940, pp. 40–1.
5. John Langton Sanford and Meredith Townsend, *The Great Governing Families of England*, 1865, vol. I, p. 112.

6. Hermione Hobhouse, *Thomas Cubitt, Master Builder*, 1971, p. 561.
7. G.O., box Q, bundle 143.
8. R.B.: *Boyle's Court Guide*.
9. P.P.R., will of John Boodle, 1859.
10. *Harleian Society Publications, Registers XXIV, St. George's, Hanover Square, Marriages*, vol. IV, *1824-1837*, 1897, p. 257: *Boyle's Court Guide*.
11. *P.O.D.*
12. P.P.R., will of H. M. Boodle, 1878.
13. *Ibid.*, will of Edward Partington, 1883.
14. *Ibid.*, will of W. C. Boodle, 1887.
15. *Ibid.*, will of H. T. Boodle, 1901.
16. *Ibid.*, index to wills: *P.O.D.*: *Boyle's Court Guide*.
17. G.O., memo. of 5 Jan. 1807.
18. *Ibid.*, Hailstone corresp., Grosvenor to H., 6 March 1809; Moore letter books, vol. 7, 2 March 1809.
19. *Ibid.*, Hailstone corresp., H. to Grosvenor, 27 Nov. 1808.
20. *P.P.*, 1887, XIII, *Report from the Select Committee on Town Holdings*, p. 319.
21. G.L.R.O.(M), TC/St.G/2.
22. G.O., box A, *passim*.
23. *Ibid.*, Hailstone corresp., Grosvenor to H., 27 Dec. 1795; Moore letter books, vol. 7, Aug. 1806.
24. *Ibid.*, Moore letter books, vol. 3, 5 April 1799.
25. *Ibid.*, Moore's accounts, 1809-17.
26. *Ibid.*, Moore letter books, *passim*, and especially vol. 8, Dec. 1811.
27. *Ibid.*, Hailstone corresp., Grosvenor to H., 2 Aug. 1821.
28. *Ibid.*, misc. box 21, abstract of title 1878, p. 39.
29. *Ibid.*, misc. box 15, 14 Aug. 1828.
30. E.H.P., box 76.
31. G.O., Hailstone corresp., H. to Grosvenor, 28 Jan. 1808.
32. Royal Bank of Scotland, Drummonds Branch, ledgers, Grosvenor accounts, 1815-45 *passim*.
33. G.O., misc. box 15, Grosvenor to Empy, 1822-8.
34. R.B.
35. P.R.O., PROB 11/2042/652.
36. *P.O.D.*: *Robson's Directory*, 1843.
37. P.P.R., index to wills, 1864.
38. G.O., misc. box 17, memo. re Mr. Burge, 16 Sept. 1864.
39. Royal Bank of Scotland, Drummonds Branch, ledgers, Grosvenor accounts, 1875.
40. *Ibid.*, Grosvenor accounts, 1855, 1865.
41. *Ibid.*, Grosvenor accounts, 1885, 1895.
42. P.P.R., index to wills, 1902.
43. Royal Bank of Scotland, Drummonds Branch, ledgers, Grosvenor accounts, 1875, 1895.
44. P.P.R., index to wills, 1922: *P.O.D.*
45. E.H.P., box 42/4, 17 May [? 1784]; 42/6, 2 Feb. 1814.
46. Information kindly supplied by Mr. H. M. Colvin.
47. W.C.L., C774, pp. 117-18.
48. G.O., misc. box 13, Porden valuations: E.H.P., box 42/6, 2 Feb. 1814.
49. G.O., box Q, bundle 35.
50. E.H.P., box 42/6, 24 Sept. 1809, 10 Nov. 1810; box 76, receipts *passim*.
51. G.O., account books of first Marquess, vol. 10, 1839-44 *passim*: Royal Bank of Scotland, Drummonds Branch, ledgers, Grosvenor accounts, 1875, 1885.
52. G.O., Cundy papers, 1864-6: GBM 15/3-4.
53. P.P.R., wills of H. M. Boodle, 1878, F. Boodle, 1891, and T. Cundy, 1895.

54. *Survey of London*, vol. XXXVI, 1970, pp. 41-2, 47, 49.
55. G.O., misc. box 12, Taylor and Shakespear's receipt, 1782.
56. GLB XXI/545-8.
57. E.H.P., box 42/4, 14 Nov. 1772.
58. G.O., chest C, bundle 10, 'State of Lord Grosvenor's Affairs', 1779, and mortgage, 1 April 1779.
59. *Ibid.*, Hailstone corresp., Grosvenor to H., 2 Sept. 1796.
60. E.H.P., box 42/4, 20 Feb. 1781.
61. *Ibid.*, box 42/4, 17 May [? 1784].
62. G.O., chest C, bundle 11, 5 April 1785.
63. *Survey of London*, vol. XXIX, 1960, p. 11.
64. *Ibid.*, vol. XXXVI, 1970, p. 36.
65. *Ibid.*, vol. XXXI, 1963, p. 13.
66. GLB XXI/549.
67. GLB *passim*.
68. G.O., chest D, 6 Feb. 1808.
69. *Ibid.*, box S, bundle 156, 15 Feb. 1817.
70. E.H.P., box 42/6, 10 Nov. 1810.
71. G.O., box R, bundle 147, 1 Feb. 1812.
72. GBM 1/45.
73. *Ibid.*, 1/156.
74. *Ibid.*, 1/141, 145; 2/218.
75. G.O., box Q, bundle 142, Jan. 1796.
76. GBM 2/95; 7/325.
77. Francis Baily, *Tables for the purchasing and renewing of Leases...*, 3rd ed., 1812, preface (B.L. pressmark 8506 f 13): Colvin *sub* William Inwood.
78. Baily, *op. cit.*, p. 4.
79. *Ibid.*, pp. 90-3.
80. *Ibid.*, p. 49.
81. GBM 1/116.
82. G.O., box Q, bundle 143, 14 Feb. 1814.
83. GBM 7/325.
84. *Ibid.*, 15/415, 492.
85. *Ibid.*, 17/470, 505; 18/90.
86. *Ibid.*, 18/275; 19/38.
87. *Ibid.*, 1/234.
88. *Ibid.*, 2/95.
89. *Ibid.*, 1/160: G.L.R.O.(M), TC/St.G/1.
90. GBM 2/204.
91. *Ibid.*, 1/161; 2/143; 3/172, 178.
92. *Ibid.*, 2/289.
93. G.O., chest C, bundle 12, 20 Aug., 3 Dec. 1791.
94. *Ibid.*, Moore letter books, vol. 3, 13 Feb. 1799.
95. *Ibid.*, vol. 2, 5, 12 Jan., 31 Aug., 5 Nov. 1798 and *passim*.
96. *Ibid.*, vol. 3, 1 May 1799.
97. *Ibid.*, vol. 2, 22 Nov. 1798.
98. *Ibid.*, vol. 7, Aug. 1806.
99. *Ibid.*, vol. 3, 3 Jan. 1800.
100. *Ibid.*, vol. 4, 18 July 1801.
101. *Ibid.*, box P, bundle 133, 11 Dec. 1804.
102. *Ibid.*, chest D, deed of 6 Feb. 1808 and endorsement of 12 April 1809.
103. *Ibid.*, Moore letter books, vol. 7, Aug. 1806: GLB *passim*.
104. GLB XXIV/678.
105. *Survey of London*, vol. XXXVI, 1970, p. 40.
106. G.O., chest D, bundle 14, 10 Oct. 1804: GLB *passim*.
107. GLB XXVIII/780.
108. *Ibid.*, XXI/575.
109. G.L.R.O.(M), TC/St.G/1.
110. GLB XXIV/678: GBM 1/188, 212.
111. GBM 2/204.
112. *Ibid.*, 2/309; 3/21: GLB XXV/701.

113. GBM 7/144.
114. *Ibid.*, 2/160-1; 3/160, 178: R.B.
115. GBM 4/83, 158: R.B.
116. GBM 3/288; 4/82; 5/273: G.O., box R, bundles 147-8, 27 Aug. 1812 and 11 May 1813.
117. P.R.O., HO 107/733/5, 6, 12.
118. GLB xxv/696-7.
119. GBM 4/85.
120. *Ibid.*, 6/215.
121. *Ibid.*, 1/13, 57; 2/76, 256; 3/34; 4/259.
122. GLB xxiv/683.
123. GBM 2/222; 5/275, 289, 308; 6/326: G.O., box P, bundle 133, 29 Aug. 1812.
124. GBM 3/22, 177.
125. *Ibid.*, 1/51.
126. *Ibid.*, 6/130.
127. *Ibid.*, 9/126.
128. *Ibid.*, 1/132.
129. G.L.R.O.(M), WR/LV, register 1793-1813.
130. GBM 2/309; 3/21, 65; GLB xxv/701.
131. GBM 5/25.
132. *Ibid.*, 6/87; 7/50, 319; 8/276; 9/35.
133. *Ibid.*, 8/464; 9/123.
134. *Ibid.*, 6/113, 139, 143-4.
135. *Ibid.*, 6/141-2, 163, 170.
136. *Ibid.*, 6/163-4; 8/263, 468.
137. *Ibid.*, 7/443; 8/210, 212, 249.
138. G.L.R.O.(M), WR/LV, St. Geo. Hall, 34, 1828.
139. GBM 4/315: G.O., box Q, bundle 143, 3 Sept. 1814.
140. GBM 5/322: G.O., misc. box 14, 8 April 1808.
141. GBM 4/148; 5/36, 303, 338.
142. *Ibid.*, 3/9.
143. *Ibid.*, 2/110, 5/101; 6/246; 7/25, 84, 453; 8/54.
144. *Ibid.*, 1/156.
145. *Ibid.*, 1/198, 212; 2/176; 4/232.
146. *Ibid.*, 3/74; 4/210.
147. *Ibid.*, 1/28, 235.
148. *Ibid.*, 2/37, 46, 163.
149. *Ibid.*, 3/204, 241; 7/178.
150. M.L.R. 1824/8/392.
151. GBM 1/288.
152. *Ibid.*, 1/187.
153. *Ibid.*, 5/281.
154. Sanford and Townsend, *op. cit.* (ref. 5 above), vol. I, pp. 122-3: G.E.C.
155. G.O., chest D, bundle 14, 10 Oct. 1804; box S, bundle 153, 11 Oct. 1804.
156. Colvin.
157. G.O., chest D, bundle 14, 2 Aug. 1806.
158. Gervas Huxley, *Lady Elizabeth and the Grosvenors, Life in a Whig Family, 1822-1839*, 1965, p. 58: GBM 4/299-300.
159. G.O., Hailstone corresp., Grosvenor to H., 11 Oct. 1802, and *passim* 1808-10.
160. Huxley, *Lady Elizabeth, ut supra*, pp. 6, 8, 59: G.O., misc. box 15, Jones to Grosvenor, 17 Aug. 1825.
161. W.C.L. and G.O., Grosvenor rent books.
162. G.O., lease particulars book A.
163. *Ibid.*, chest D, deeds 1829-36.
164. *Ibid.*, Hailstone corresp., H. to Grosvenor, 23, 27 Feb. 1807, 3 Feb. 1808.
165. *Ibid.*, 17 Feb. 1808, 10 March 1813.
166. E.H.P., box 42/6, 12 Nov. 1803.

167. G.O., Hailstone corresp., H. to Grosvenor, 23 Feb. 1807.
168. *Ibid., ut supra*, Grosvenor to H., 29 Aug. 1808, 15, 19 Nov. 1810.
169. GBM 8/491.
170. E.H.P., box 42/6 *passim*.
171. P.R.O., PROB 11/1665/35.
172. *Ibid.*, PROB 11/1708/72.
173. Huxley, *Lady Elizabeth, ut supra*, p. 17.
174. G.O., lease particulars book A: GBM 4/315: Hertfordshire Record Office, Grimston MSS., D/EV, F331.
175. G.O., box Q, bundle 143, 3 Sept. 1814.
176. *Ibid.*, misc. box 17, 'Remarks upon granting Leases...', 1845.
177. GBM 8/326.
178. *Ibid.*, 1/288.
179. G.O., box R, bundle 149, Sept. 1815.
180. GBM 9/295.
181. *Ibid.*, 8/3.
182. *Ibid.*, 12/33: 8 and 9 Vict., c. 33, private.
183. G.O., box Q, bundle 143, 14 Feb. 1814.
184. GBM 6/186.
185. *Ibid.*, 8/326.
186. *Ibid.*, 9/2.
187. *Ibid.*, 12/373, 375: G.O., misc. box 17, 'Remarks upon granting Leases...', 1845.
188. GBM 12/178; 13/541: G.O., misc. box 17, 'Remarks upon granting Leases...', 1845.
189. G.O., lease particulars book 1.
190. GBM 15/162.
191. *Ibid.*, 15/436; 18/88-9, 285, 352.
192. *Ibid.*, 2/122.
193. *Ibid.*, 5/245; 6/22, 124; 7/69, 247.
194. *Ibid.*, 7/479; 8/215.
195. *Ibid.*, 8/396.
196. *Ibid.*, 9/57, 215.
197. *Ibid.*, 9/75, 528: G.O., lease particulars book A.
198. GBM 12/73.
199. G.O., misc. box 17, 'Remarks upon granting Leases...', 1845.
200. GBM 12/117.
201. Huxley, *Lady Elizabeth, ut supra*, pp. 13, 14, 22, 52, 54, 56.
202. *The Times*, 2 Nov. 1869, p. 7.
203. Huxley, *Lady Elizabeth, ut supra*, p. 14: Huxley, *Victorian Duke* (see ref. 1 above), pp. 11, 13, 71-4.
204. Huxley, *Lady Elizabeth, ut supra*, p. 162.
205. Recited in 8 and 9 Vict., c. 33, private.
206. Huxley, *Victorian Duke, ut supra*, pp. 16, 73.
207. Huxley, *Lady Elizabeth, ut supra*, p. 167.
208. GBM 14/498.
209. Huxley, *Victorian Duke, ut supra*, pp. xi, xii, 67, 93, 95, 105, 114-18, 176-94: G.E.C.
210. Huxley, *Victorian Duke, ut supra*, pp. 76-80, 100, 150-1, 154, 160-5, 168-9.
211. *The Times*, 23 Dec. 1899, p. 6.
212. Huxley, *Victorian Duke, ut supra*, pp. 91-2.
213. *Ibid.*, pp. 34, 74, 92, 96, 130.
214. *Ibid.*, pp. 67, 120, 126: G.O., Trustees' accounts, 1893.
215. GBM 18/248.
216. G.O., misc. box 21, abstract of title, 1918: M.L.R. 1874/10/646.
217. G.O., misc. box 21, deed of resettlement, 1901.
218. *Ibid.*, lease particulars books 1 and 2.

219. *Ibid.*, Trustees' accounts; misc. box 21, deed of resettlement, 1901.
220. 8 and 9 Vict., c. 33, private.
221. GBM 15/438–9.
222. *The Building News*, 13 Oct. 1865, p. 712.
223. Papers of John Liddell, architect, in stock of B. Weinreb, Architectural Books Ltd., Lord Westminster to Lord Carnarvon, 22 May 1845.
224. GBM 12/178.
225. G.O., misc. box 17, bonds.
226. GBM 12/426–7.
227. *Ibid.*, 13/324.
228. *Ibid.*, 13/326, 348.
229. *Ibid.*, 12/353.
230. *Ibid.*, 13/312–13, 368: G.O., lease particulars books A and I.
231. *Survey of London*, vol. XXXVII, 1973, pp. 304–5.
232. GBM 14/305–6: G.O., lease particulars book I.
233. G.L.R.O.(L), M.B.W. Minutes, 10 May 1867, p. 565.
234. GBM 12/240, 480; 13/14–15, 62–3: G.O., misc. box 17, papers attached to elevation of No. 41 Upper Brook Street.
235. GBM 13/541; 14/9, 239, 261.
236. *Ibid.*, 15/282, 308, 352; 16/182.
237. *Ibid.*, 20/295.
238. *Ibid.*, 18/437.
239. *Ibid.*, 12/178.
240. W.C.L., WBA 429, see for instance bundle 98, lease of 65 Grosvenor Street, 20 Sept. 1854, and bundle 99, lease of 46 Grosvenor Street, 5 Aug. 1873.
241. GBM 13/76.
242. *Ibid.*, 13/291.
243. *Ibid.*, 13/516–20; 24/34–5: W.C.L., WBA 429, bundle 93, lease of 41 Grosvenor Square, 29 Sept. 1865.
244. GBM 15/178.
245. W.C.L., WBA 429, bundle 99, lease of 46 Grosvenor Street, 5 Aug. 1873.
246. *Ibid.*, bundle 93, lease of 13 Grosvenor Square, 1837.
247. *Ibid.*, bundle 93, lease of 15A Grosvenor Square, 7 Aug. 1848.
248. *Ibid.*, bundle 93, lease of 41 Grosvenor Square, 29 Sept. 1865; bundle 99, lease of 46 Grosvenor Street, 5 Aug. 1873.
249. *Ibid.*, bundle 189, lease of premises in Brook's Mews, 20 May 1887.
250. *Ibid.*, lease of No. 19 North Audley Street, 25 Feb. 1846.
251. *Ibid.*, bundle 189, lease of premises in Brook's Mews, 22 May 1862.
252. *Ibid.*, bundle 189, Brook's Mews leases, 1887, 1891, 1905.
253. *Ibid.*, bundle 189, Brook's Mews lease, 20 May 1887; bundle 93, lease of 45 Grosvenor Square, 1 July 1895.
254. GBM 12/373, 375.
255. *Ibid.*, 15/178.
256. *Ibid.*, 13/383–4, 389; 14/120, 122, 149.
257. *Ibid.*, 14/495.
258. *Ibid.*, 13/181.
259. *Ibid.*, 16/239–40, 253, 286.
260. *Ibid.*, 15/150.
261. *Ibid.*, 12/426; 15/402.
262. *Ibid.*, 15/200, 269, 441, 458–9, 513; 16/4: G.O., improvement account book, 1864–82.
263. GBM 14/195–7.
264. *Ibid.*, 14/290–1.

265. *Ibid.*, 17/220.
266. *Ibid.*, 18/423.
267. *Ibid.*, 27/498.
268. *Ibid.*, 13/446, 459–60; 19/280–1.
269. *Ibid.*, 27/487.
270. *The Builder*, 7 Dec. 1895, p. 426.
271. GBM 20/171–2; 21/383–4.
272. *Survey of London*, vol. XXXVIII, 1975, Plate 89b.
273. *The Builder*, 17 Feb. 1911, p. 222.
274. GBM 24/40.
275. *Who Was Who 1897–1915*.
276. GBM 35/470; 37/489–90: *The Builder*, 17 Feb. 1911, p. 222.
277. GBM 23/306; 24/20, 169.
278. G.O., Duke's instruction book, 1905–8, pp. 7–12.
279. GBM 18/248.
280. *P.P.*, 1884–5, XXX, *R.C. on the Housing of the Working Classes*, p. 52.
281. G.O., Trustees' accounts, 1874–1901.
282. GBM 24/322, 376; 25/312, 347, 455, 495–6.
283. *Ibid.*, 19/245; 20/379.
284. *Ibid.*, 21/518.
285. *Ibid.*, 20/371, 379; 21/19, 219; 25/2–3.
286. *Ibid.*, 22/467–8.
287. *P.P.*, 1887, XIII, *S.C. on Town Holdings*, p. 351.
288. GBM 22/402, 437–8, 539.
289. *Ibid.*, 23/385–6, 429; 24/40, 45: *P.P.*, 1887, XIII, *S.C. on Town Holdings*, p. 321.
290. GBM 25/82.
291. *P.P.*, 1887, XIII, *S.C. on Town Holdings*, pp. 325, 350.
292. *Ibid.*, p. 352.
293. GBM 24/127–8.
294. *Ibid.*, 22/397: *P.O.D.*
295. GBM 22/129.
296. *Ibid.*, 22/320.
297. *P.P.*, 1887, XIII, *S.C. on Town Holdings*, pp. 326, 354.
298. *Ibid.*, pp. 245–6, 326–8, 354, 361–2, 370–1.
299. *Ibid.*, p. 370: GBM 24/279–80.
300. GBM 26/407–8.
301. *Ibid.*, 26/451, 453.
302. *Ibid.*, 27/195–6.
303. *Ibid.*, 27/210.
304. *Ibid.*, 23/364.
305. *Ibid.*, 27/289.
306. *Ibid.*, 26/17.
307. *Ibid.*, 26/415–16.
308. *Ibid.*, 27/101–2.
309. *Ibid.*, 22/474, 486; 23/123.
310. *Ibid.*, 27/112.
311. *Ibid.*, 26/387–8.
312. *Ibid.*, 26/441.
313. *Ibid.*, 21/133–6; 22/320; 24/358.
314. *Ibid.*, 26/95, 376.
315. *Ibid.*, 24/480.
316. *Ibid.*, 27/112, 171.
317. *Ibid.*, 22/320.
318. *Ibid.*, 23/183–4; 24/463; 25/77; 27/209–10.
319. *Ibid.*, 24/171; 25/233.
320. *Ibid.*, 24/437, 477–8; 25/356; 26/263.
321. *Ibid.*, 25/509–10; 26/59–60.
322. *Ibid.*, 22/339–40.
323. Frank Banfield, *The Great Landlords of London*, [1888], p. 59.

324. *Annual Report of the Vestry of the Parish of Saint George Hanover Square*, 1883–4, p. 44; 1884–5, p. 34: GBM 21/463.
325. GBM 22/152–4.
326. *Annual Report, ut supra*, 1887, p. 38.
327. GBM 23/463–4; 25/199–200, 315–16.
328. *Ibid.*, 25/115–18, 225.
329. *Ibid.*, 25/127–8, 369–70.
330. *Ibid.*, 21/120, 122.
331. *Ibid.*, 22/402.
332. *R.I.B.A. Journal*, 3rd ser., vol. VII, 1900, p. 450.
333. GBM 22/398.
334. *Ibid.*, 23/99–100, 303–4.
335. *Ibid.*, 25/432, 511–12; 26/119–20.
336. *Ibid.*, 26/407–8.
337. *Ibid.*, 26/329–30; 27/67–8.
338. *P.P.*, 1887, XIII, *S.C. on Town Holdings*, p. 332.
339. GBM 20/212.
340. *P.P.*, 1887, XIII, *S.C. on Town Holdings*, pp. 333, 461–2.
341. GBM 23/107–8, 469: G.O., lease particulars book 2.
342. GBM 25/4.
343. *Ibid.*, 18/224.
344. *Ibid.*, 19/491.
345. *Ibid.*, 25/4.
346. *P.P.*, 1887, XIII, *S.C. on Town Holdings*, p. 335.
347. GBM 22/15.
348. *Ibid.*, 23/106, 428.
349. *Ibid.*, 24/17.
350. *The Architect*, 29 Aug. 1902, illustr. facing p. 136.
351. GBM 20/143; 23/213–14.
352. *Ibid.*, 17/61.
353. *Ibid.*, 20/38.
354. *Ibid.*, 26/301, 529: W.C.L., WBA 429, bundle 237, agreement of 16 Dec. 1895.
355. W.C.L., WBA 429, bundle 279, lease of 1 July 1881.
356. *P.P.*, 1887, XIII, *S.C. on Town Holdings*, pp. 329, 371.
357. GBM 18/11; 26/40.
358. *Ibid.*, 20/378.
359. *Ibid.*, 23/306.
360. *Ibid.*, 25/2–3.
361. *Ibid.*, 23/28.
362. *Ibid.*, 21/4; 26/15–16, 19–20.
363. *Ibid.*, 18/345; 19/331; 20/378; 21/222.
364. *Ibid.*, 18/246; 25/45, 333.
365. *Ibid.*, 16/458; 18/415–16, 477; 21/18; 24/12; 26/43–4.
366. *Ibid.*, 18/122, 124; 21/4, 6, 7.
367. *Ibid.*, 21/205–6, 249–50, 353, 358.
368. *Ibid.*, 16/365; 21/20, 217; 24/49, 401.
369. *Ibid.*, 26/1, 26.
370. G.L.R.O.(L), M.B.W. 1727/5, no. 152.
371. GBM 33/473.
372. *Ibid.*, 22/6; 26/18.
373. *P.P.*, 1899, XXXVI, *R.C. on Local Taxation*, pp. 277–82.
374. *Ibid.*, 1839, XIII, *First Report from S.C. on Metropolis Improvements*, plan 6.
375. *The Architect*, Supplement 2, 6 Jan. 1899, pp. 24–5.
376. *P.P.*, 1884–5, XXX, *R.C. on the Housing of the Working Classes*, pp. 468–9.
377. GBM 18/320: *Annual Report of the Vestry of Saint George's Hanover Square*, 1889, p. 41; 1890, p. 44.
378. *P.P.*, 1887, XIII, *S.C. on Town Holdings*, p. 332.
379. *Ibid.*, pp. 324–5.
380. *Ibid.*, p. 323.
381. GBM 27/270.
382. *P.P.*, 1899, XXXVI, *R.C. on Local Taxation*, p. 280.
383. *P.P.*, 1887, XIII, *S.C. on Town Holdings*, p. 336: GBM 22/77; 26/480.
384. *P.P.*, 1887, XIII, *S.C. on Town Holdings*, pp. 325, 347.
385. *Ibid.*, pp. 322, 352: GBM 23/332.
386. *P.P.*, 1899, XXXVI, *R.C. on Local Taxation*, p. 279.
387. GBM 26/149; 27/305.
388. *Ibid.*, 27/9.
389. *Ibid.*, 25/133; 26/337.
390. *P.P.*, 1887, XIII, *S.C. on Town Holdings*, p. 322.
391. GBM 19/170–1, 175, 262.
392. *Ibid.*, 23/487–8.
393. *Ibid.*, 20/388–9; 23/306; 24/169.
394. *Ibid.*, 24/20, 22; 25/34–5: *The Times*, 6, 9, 10, 12, 13, 15, 17 Feb. 1892: Frank Banfield's articles in *The Sunday Times*, published c. 1888 in book form as *The Great Landlords of London*.
395. GBM 26/23.
396. *Ibid.*, 25/382.
397. Banfield, *op. cit.*, pp. 60–1, 68, 71.
398. GBM 22/393.
399. *P.P.*, 1887, XIII, *S.C. on Town Holdings*, pp. 325, 326, 332, 362.
400. *Ibid.*, pp. 445–6.
401. GBM 17/143–4.
402. *P.P.*, 1887, XIII, *S.C. on Town Holdings*, p. 325.
403. *Ibid.*, p. 352.

CHAPTER IV (pp. 67–82)

The Estate in the Twentieth Century

1. John Macdonnell, *The Land Question*, 1873, p. 84.
2. G.E.C.
3. *The Times*, 21 July 1953, pp. 7, 8.
4. *Chips. The Diaries of Sir Henry Channon*, ed. Robert Rhodes James, 1967, p. 477.
5. *The Times*, 22 July 1953, p. 8.
6. G.O., misc. box 21, resettlement of 15 Feb. 1901.
7. *Ibid.*, Trustees' accounts, 1901–21.
8. GBM 28/33; 29/537.
9. *Ibid.*, 32/237–40.
10. *Ibid.*, 29/216.
11. *Ibid.*, 31/374.
12. G.O., Duke's instruction book, 1905–8, pp. 7–12.
13. GBM 34/333.
14. *Ibid.*, 34/384; 35/130, 139.
15. *Ibid.*, 31/398; 35/471.
16. *Ibid.*, 35/495; 36/355–6.
17. *Ibid.*, 35/470.
18. G.O., Duke's instruction book, 1900–4, p. 25.
19. GBM 33/345–6.
20. *Ibid.*, 32/172, 310; 34/345.
21. G.O., Duke's instruction book, 1905–8, pp. 7–12, 19.
22. GBM 32/161, 241.
23. *Ibid.*, 33/414.
24. *Ibid.*, 38/219.
25. *Ibid.*, 32/356.
26. *Ibid.*, 38/391.
27. *Ibid.*, 29/225–6.

28. *Ibid.*, 32/162.
29. *Ibid.*, 33/217–18.
30. *Survey of London*, vol. XXIX, 1960, pp. 12–13, 13n.
31. GBM 34/125, 264, 342.
32. *Ibid.*, 38/517.
33. *Ibid.*, 20/380.
34. *Ibid.*, 38/239–40.
35. *Ibid.*, 41/119–23, 223–4, 247–8.
36. *Ibid.*, 42/302–9.
37. *Ibid.*, 31/269–70.
38. *Ibid.*, 34/122, 124.
39. G.O., Duke's instruction book, 1900–4, p. 17.
40. GBM 35/418–19.
41. *Ibid.*, 35/227–8.
42. *Ibid.*, 35/429.
43. Loelia, Duchess of Westminster, *Grace and Favour*, 1961, p. 183.
44. G.O., Duke's instruction book, 1905–8, pp. 7–12.
45. GBM 38/240.
46. *Ibid.*, 34/124.
47. *Ibid.*, 35/429.
48. 'The Work of Mr. Detmar Blow and Mr. Fernand Billerey', in *Architectural Supplement to Country Life*, 26 Oct. 1912, pp. v–ix.
49. Loelia, Duchess of Westminster, *op. cit.*, p. 186.
50. GBM 31/411.
51. *Ibid.*, 35/419.
52. *Ibid.*, 36/193–5.
53. *Ibid.*, 35/539.
54. *Ibid.*, 37/221–2.
55. *Ibid.*, 31/264.
56. *Ibid.*, 39/344.
57. *Ibid.*, 37/536; 39/342–4.
58. *Ibid.*, 39/389–90.
59. *Ibid.*, 39/414.
60. *Ibid.*, 39/421–2.
61. *Ibid.*, 39/429.
62. *Ibid.*, 34/125, 263–4: G.O., Duke's instruction book, 1905–8, pp. 114–15, 133.
63. Reginald Colby, '44 Grosvenor Square, The Residence of Lady Illingworth', in *Country Life*, 27 July 1961, pp. 193–4.
64. GBM 35/152; 36/335–40, 372, 382, 384, 393.
65. Desmond Fitz-Gerald, 'The Mural from 44 Grosvenor Square', in *Victoria and Albert Museum Yearbook*, no. 1, 1969, p. 145.
66. R.B.
67. GBM 37/411–14.
68. *Ibid.*, 19/440.
69. *Ibid.*, 39/286, 328, 370: G.O., Duke's instruction book, 1912–14, p. 189.
70. GBM 42/209; 44/413.
71. G.O., Duke's instruction books, 1900–4, p. 146; 1905–8, p. 6; 1909–11, pp. 14–15; 1912–14, p. 85.
72. GBM 31/175.
73. G.O., Duke's instruction book, 1912–14, pp. 23–4.
74. *The Times*, 26 Jan. 1911, p. 6.
75. G.O., misc. box 21, printed abstract of title, 1918.
76. *The Times*, 24 Jan. 1911, p. 15; 15 Dec. 1911, p. 10; 20 June 1912, p. 20.
77. GBM 39/304–9; 42/218.
78. F. M. L. Thompson, *English Landed Society in the Nineteenth Century*, 1963, p. 332.

79. G.O., Trustees' accounts, 1901–21, 1921–7.
80. Loelia, Duchess of Westminster, *op. cit.*, p. 86.
81. G.O., Duke's instruction book, 1919–22, pp. 94–6, 142–4.
82. *Ibid.*, Duke's instruction book, 1923–5, p. 218.
83. Christopher Hussey, *The Life of Sir Edwin Lutyens*, 1950, p. 14: *Country Life*, 23 Sept. 1911, pp. 7*–10*: *R.I.B.A. Journal*, 3rd ser., vol. XLVI, 1939, p. 571.
84. *The Architectural Review*, vol. V, 1898–9, p. 173.
85. Hussey, *op. et loc. cit.*
86. Information kindly supplied by Madame V. H. Billerey and Mr. L. V. A. Billerey.
87. R.I.B.A. Drawings Collection, Blow drawings, No. 28 South St., sheet signed by Billerey Sept. 1902.
88. London County Council Minutes, 18 July 1905, p. 520: *P.O.D.*
89. *The Times*, 8 Feb. 1939, p. 16.
90. *The Architectural Review*, vol. 138, 1965, p. 263.
91. *Ibid.*, vol. LIII, 1923, p. 31.
92. Information kindly supplied by Mr. Jonathan Blow: Company House, file 249,996.
93. Sir George Arthur, *Life of Lord Kitchener*, 1920, vol. 1, p. 11.
94. 'The Work of Mr. Detmar Blow and Mr. Fernand Billerey', in *Architectural Supplement to Country Life*, 26 Oct. 1912, pp. xx–xxvii.
95. GBM 40/375–6, 381–4.
96. *Ibid.*, 43/213.
97. *Ibid.*, 42/225.
98. *Ibid.*, 44/496.
99. *Ibid.*, 45/483–4.
100. G.O., Wimperis correspondence, Jan. 1920.
101. *Ibid.*, Duke's instruction books, 1923–5, pp. 180–6; 1926–8, part II, pp. 563–5.
102. *Ibid.*, Duke's instruction book, 1926–8, part I, pp. 156–8.
103. *Ibid.*, Duke's instruction book, 1926–8, part II, pp. 419, 563–5.
104. P.P.R., index to wills, 1946.
105. Loelia, Duchess of Westminster, *op. cit.*, pp. 160, 163, 183, 198.
106. G.O., Blow letterbooks, 1918–19, Nov. 1919.
107. *Ibid.*, Duke's instruction books, 1923–5 to 1931–2, *passim*.
108. B.A. 41564.
109. London County Council Minutes, 4 June 1935, pp. 795–6.
110. GBM 39/23, 550: *P.O.D.*
111. *Ibid.*, 39/170, 455–7.
112. *Ibid.*, 40/165–6.
113. Loelia, Duchess of Westminster, *op. cit.*, p. 187.
114. GBM 44/406, 460, 463.
115. *Ibid.*, 44/463.
116. Sir Edwin Lutyens, 'What I think of Modern Architecture', in *Country Life*, 20 June 1931, p. 775.
117. Christopher Hussey, 'The Great Estates of London and their Development: The Grosvenor Estate', in *Country Life*, 21 April 1928, pp. 558–65.
118. B.A. 80871, in G.L.R.O.(L).
119. G.O., typescript of evidence given by A. C. H. Borrer to a public inquiry conducted for the Minister of Health, *c.* 1934, pp. 32–4.
120. GBM 45/67: *The Times*, 31 March 1926, p. 16.
121. *The Times*, 20 May 1924, p. 11; 31 March 1926, p. 16; 16 Feb. 1927, p. 7; 24 July 1929, p. 12.
122. *Ibid.*, 20 March 1928, p. 18; 31 Jan. 1929, p. 9.
123. G.O., Trustees' accounts, *passim*.

124. *Ibid.*, drafts of evidence given by A. C. H. Borrer to a public inquiry conducted for the Minister of Health, *c.* 1934, pp. 2–3, 29.
125. *Ibid.*, Trustees' accounts, 1922–33.
126. *Ibid.*, Duke's instruction books, 1923–5, pp. 108–9; 1926–8, part I, pp. 96–7.
127. *Ibid.*, Trustees' accounts, 1921–7.
128. Christopher Hussey, *The Life of Sir Edwin Lutyens*, 1950, p. 482.
129. G.O., Duke's instruction book, 1926–8, part II, p. 527.
130. *Ibid.*, Duke's instruction book, 1929–30, p. 184: B.A. 55136.
131. G.O., Trustees' accounts, 1928–33; Duke's instruction book, 1929–30, p. 409.
132. *Ibid.*, Estate Surveyor's unnumbered letterbooks, 21 July 1933: Hussey, *op. cit.*, 1950, p. 482.
133. G.O., Trustees' accounts, 1927–36.
134. *Ibid.*, solicitor's fee books, G37/455.
135. *Ibid.*, misc. letterbook, Codd to Billerey, 29 May 1929.
136. *Ibid.*, Estate Surveyor's letterbooks, 20/109, 143.
137. *Ibid.*, solicitor's fee books, G39/470.
138. *Ibid.*, solicitor's fee books, G41/433.
139. *Ibid.*, solicitor's fee books, G41/231, 277; Estate Surveyor's unnumbered letterbooks, 25 March 1936, p. 211.
140. Greater London Council, Building Regulation case 109691.
141. G.O., improvement accounts, Sept. 1923.
142. *Ibid.*, Duke's instruction book, 1933–4, p. 197.
143. *Ibid.*, Estate Surveyor's unnumbered letterbooks, Codd to Etchells, 25 March 1936.
144. *Ibid.*, Duke's instruction books, 1931–2, pp. 462–4; 1933–4, p. 358.
145. *Ibid.*, Trustees' accounts, Jan. 1929.
146. *Ibid.*, Duke's instruction book, 1926–8, part II, p. 373.
147. *The Times*, 26 Oct. 1932, p. 4.
148. G.O., Duke's instruction book, 1931–2, pp. 392–7.
149. *Ibid.*, Duke's instruction books, 1926–8, part II, pp. 506–7; 1931–2, p. 128.
150. Information kindly supplied by Mr. Geoffrey Singer.
151. *Ex. inf.* Mr. Singer: *The Times*, 21 July 1953, pp. 7, 8.
152. *The Times*, 21 July 1953, p. 7; 23 Oct. 1953, p. 5: P.P.R., will of Duke of Westminster, 1953.
153. *The Daily Telegraph*, 4 Nov. 1971.
154. P.P.R., will of Duke of Westminster, 1953: *The Times*, 23 Oct. 1953, p. 5.
155. *The Times*, 27 Feb. 1967, p. 3.
156. G.O., Duke's instruction book, 1933–4, p. 358.
157. *The Times*, 9 June 1966, p. 15: *The Director*, Aug. 1974.
158. *The Daily Telegraph*, 19 June 1967.
159. G.L.R.O.(L), L.C.C. file AR/TP/2/48.
160. *The Times*, 6 Oct. 1960, p. 9.
161. Michael Hanson, 'Private Houses Return to Mayfair', in *Country Life*, 15 Nov. 1973, p. 1601.
162. *The Grosvenor Estate Strategy for Mayfair and Belgravia*, 1971, Foreword.
163. *The London Gazette*, 8 May 1969, p. 4863.
164. *The Grosvenor Estate Strategy for Mayfair and Belgravia. Second Revision*, 1974, para. 4.
165. *Strategy*, 1971, p. 76.
166. *Ibid.*, pp. 88, 96.
167. *Ibid.*, pp. 148, 161.
168. *Ibid.*, pp. 78, 162.
169. *Ibid.*, pp. 99, 100, 103.
170. *Ibid.*, pp. 106, 108.
171. *Ibid.*, p. 78.
172. *The Guardian*, 4 Nov. 1971: *The Observer*, 31 Oct. 1971.
173. *Official Architecture and Planning*, Dec. 1971.
174. *Strategy*, 1971, p. 174.
175. Westminster City Council Minutes, 30 April 1973, adopting T.P. Committee Report of 15 March 1973: *Strategy…Second Revision*, 1974, para. 1.
176. *Strategy…Second Revision*, 1974, para. 12.
177. *The Grosvenor Estate Strategy Progress Oxford Street West One*, 1976.
178. *Strategy…Second Revision*, 1974, para. 11.
179. Leasehold Reform Act, 1967, c. 88, sec. 19.
180. *Strategy…Second Revision*, 1974, letter of 6 Sept. 1974.

CHAPTER V (pp. 83–102)

The Social Character of the Estate

1. Suffolk Record Office, Bury St. Edmunds, Bunbury Papers, E18/660.2: *Survey of London*, vol. XXXII, 1963, p. 557.
2. R.D.
3. *The Court Kalendar*, 1733, 1741: *The Court and City Register for 1751*.
4. Warwickshire Record Office, CR114A/253.
5. *The World*, 14 Jan. 1790.
6. *The Autobiography and Correspondence of Mary Granville, Mrs. Delany*, ed. Lady Llanover, part I, vol. I, 1861, p. 492.
7. R.B.: Ambrose Heal, *The London Furniture Makers from the Restoration to the Victorian Era 1660–1840*, 1953, p. 33.
8. G.L.R.O.(M), WR/PP, Reg. 5, 1749.
9. Romney Sedgwick, *The House of Commons 1715–1754*, 1970, vol. I, p. 287.
10. G.L.R.O.(M), L.V.(W) 68/449–56.
11. M. Dorothy George, *London Life in the Eighteenth Century*, 1925, p. 155.
12. G.L.R.O.(M), TC/St.G./1,2.
13. *Edward Jerningham and His Friends*, ed. Lewis Bettany, 1919, pp. 187–8.
14. E.H.P., box 42/6, Porden to Lord Grosvenor, 6 Nov. 1805.
15. F. G. Hilton Price, *A Handbook of London Bankers*, 1890–1, p. 53.
16. E.g. GLB XVII/435.
17. GBM 3/167.
18. *The World*, 15 May 1787, 23 Sept. 1789.
19. *Memoirs of Sir Nathaniel William Wroxall*, ed. H. B. Wheatley, vol. I, 1884, pp. 374–5.
20. GBM 3/160: R.B.
21. *The Morning Post*, 5 April 1841.
22. *Ibid.*, 3 April 1841.
23. *Ibid.*, 26 July 1841.
24. John Bateman, *The Great Landowners of Great Britain and Ireland*, 1971 ed., p. 457.
25. P.R.O., HO 107/733/12, f.38r, v.
26. *Ibid.*, HO 107/438/11, ff. 15–17.
27. G.E.C.
28. P.R.O., HO 107/733/12, f.26v.
29. *Ibid.*, HO 107/545/9, ff. 2–3.

30. *Ibid.*, HO 107/588/2, f. 43.

31. *Ibid.*, HO 107/470/17, f. 24.

32. The enumerators' books for 1841 are in P.R.O., HO 107/733/4-6, 8-16, and HO 107/734/5-6, 8-9. Those for 1871 are in P.R.O., RG 10/92-95, 97-99, 101-102.

33. R. Price-Williams, 'The Population of London 1801-81', in *Journal of the Statistical Society*, vol. 48, 1885, p. 389.

34. *P.P.*, 1843, XXII, *Abstract of the Answers and Returns: Enumeration Abstract*, p. 3n.

35. W. H. Mallock, *Memoirs of Life and Literature*, 1920, p. 71.

36. *Survey of London*, vol. XXXVI, 1970, p. 82.

37. *Ibid.*, vol. XXXI, 1963, p. 143; vol. XXXIII, 1966, p. 45; vol. XXXIV, 1966, pp. 424, 428-30.

38. *Ibid.*, vol. XXXII, 1963, pp. 442, 453, 454.

39. GBM 21/518; 20/371, 379; 21/19, 219; 25/2-3; 22/467-8.

40. *P.O.D.*

41. GBM 39/23, 550; 39/170, 455-7; *P.O.D.*

42. GBM 27/9; 25/133; 26/337.

43. *Ibid.*, 26/256.

44. *Ibid.*, 20/380.

45. *Ibid.*, 32/480.

46. *Ibid.*, 37/249, 254.

47. *Ibid.*, 42/116.

48. *P.P.*, 1887, XIII, *Report from the Select Committee on Town Holdings*, pp. 325-6.

49. P.R.O., RG 10/101, f.81v.

50. *P.P.*, 1887, XIII, *S.C. on Town Holdings*, p. 352.

51. GBM 42/223.

52. *Ibid.*, 27/195-6.

53. *Ibid.*, 33/473.

54. *Ibid.*, 38/219.

55. *Ibid.*, 35/50-1, 57, 70, 94; 36/45: G.L.R.O.(L), LCC/AR/BA/4/185/40/233.

56. *The Grosvenor Estate Strategy for Mayfair and Belgravia*, 1971, para. 83.

57. *Harper's Bazaar*, Jan. 1933, pp. 44-5; Feb. 1933, pp. 16-17; May 1933, p. 26.

58. *Strategy*, p. 37.

59. *The Times*, 6 Oct. 1960, p. 9.

60. *The Evening News*, 13 Sept. 1929.

61. *Strategy*, p. 201.

62. *Strategy*, pp. 201-2.

CHAPTER VI (pp. 103-70)

The Architecture of the Estate

1. John Summerson, *Georgian London*, 1962 ed., pp. 98-100, 105-111.

2. P. Lavedan, *Histoire de l'Urbanisme*, vol. II, 1959, fig. 193, p. 383.

3. GLB V/140-1: M.L.R. 1728/4/135.

4. P.R.O., C105/32/1, manuscript plan of E. Shepherd's estate in N. Audley St.

5. J. Ralph, *A Critical Review of the Publick Buildings...In, and about London and Westminster*, 1734, pp. 108-9.

6. Robert Morris, *Lectures on Architecture*, [Part I], 1734, preface.

7. *Survey of London*, vol. XXXII, 1963, fig. 92, p. 499.

8. Isaac Ware, *A Complete Body of Architecture*, 1777 ed., p. 320.

9. E.H.P., box 42/6, Porden to Lord Grosvenor, 6 Nov. 1805.

10. O. E. Deutsch, *Handel, A Documentary Biography*, 1955, p. 830.

11. Guildhall Library, MS. 8766: Wiltshire Record Office, Longleat MSS. 845/Schedule III/bundle 16.

12. Ware, *op. cit.*, p. 346.

13. Lincolnshire Archives Office, ANC 2B/19/2/6.

14. Bodleian Library, MS. North b. 24, f. 268.

15. Helen Sard Hughes, *The Gentle Hertford*, 1940, p. 63.

16. Warwickshire Record Office, CR114A/254.

17. *Horace Walpole's Correspondence with Sir Horace Mann*, vol. VI, 1960, ed. W. S. Lewis, Warren Hunting Smith and George L. Lam, pp. 138-41.

18. Suffolk Record Office, Bury St. Edmunds, Bunbury Papers, E18/660.2.

19. G.O., chest B, bundle 8, 3 Dec. 1733.

20. Ware, *op. cit.*, p. 469.

21. Northamptonshire Record Office, BH(K)1185.

22. *Letters of a Grandmother, 1732-1735*, ed. Gladys Scott Thomson, 1943, p. 78.

23. Bodleian Library, MS. North e.40.

24. P.R.O., C105/32/1, agreement of 6 April 1728, E. Shepherd and F. Drewitt.

25. Corsham Court Archives, memo. of 2 March 1727/8.

26. Desmond Fitz-Gerald, 'The Mural from 44 Grosvenor Square', in *Victoria and Albert Museum Yearbook*, no. 1, 1969, pp. 148-50: Staffordshire Record Office, D1161/1/2/2: Lincolnshire Archives Office, ANC 2B/19/2/6.

27. Nottinghamshire Record Office, DD4P 52/108.

28. Badminton MSS., 110.1.43.

29. *The Autobiography and Correspondence of Mary Granville, Mrs. Delany*, ed. Lady Llanover, vol. I, 1861, p. 476.

30. Cecil Aspinall-Oglander, *Admiral's Wife. Being the Life and Letters of The Hon. Mrs. Edward Boscawen from 1719 to 1761*, 1940, p. 80; and *Admiral's Widow. Being the Life and Letters of The Hon. Mrs. Edward Boscawen from 1761 to 1805*, 1942, p. 164.

31. John Harris, *Sir William Chambers*, 1970, p. 222.

32. E.H.P., box 42/6, Porden to Lord Grosvenor, [Nov. 1805].

33. Mount Stuart, Bute MSS., letter of Sir Thomas Robinson to Lord Bute, 15 Aug. 1762.

34. R.I.B.A. Drawings Collection, MS. G5/6.

35. A. E. Richardson, *Robert Mylne*, 1955, pp. 57-220 *passim*.

36. North Yorkshire Record Office, Dawnay Collection, ZDS.

37. J. M. Robinson, 'Samuel Wyatt', D.Phil. thesis, University of Oxford, 1973, pp. 426-7.

38. Leeds Archives Department, Ramsden Archives (Rockingham Letters), vol. 3b, nos. 128 and 142.

39. *The Works in Architecture of Robert and James Adam*, vol. II, 1779, Explanation of Plate I.

40. Sir John Soane's Museum, Soane Lectures, vol. X, no. 21.

41. Sheffield Central Library, Wentworth Woodhouse Muniments, R 185/3.

42. Cecil Aspinall-Oglander, *Admiral's Wife...*, 1940, pp. 68, 72.

43. G.L.R.O.(L), B/TRL/9, pp. 28, 31, 93, 206, 273, 307, 313, 381, 383.

44. Patricia Anne Kirkham, 'The Careers of William and John Linnell', in *Furniture History*, vol. 3, 1967, pp. 29-44: C. Proudfoot and D. Watkin, 'A Pioneer of English Neo-Classicism—C. H. Tatham', and 'The Furniture

of C. H. Tatham', in *Country Life*, 13/20 April 1972, pp. 918-21, and 8 June 1972, pp. 1481-6: R.B.

45. W.C.L., C775, pp. 20-1.
46. GBM 8/2.
47. *Ibid.*, 8/75, 135, 254; 9/125.
48. University of Nottingham, Newcastle MSS., Ne c 7009a.
49. GBM 2/279, 309; 3/20, 131, 234; 5/78.
50. Ann Saunders, *Regent's Park*, 1969, pp. 95-101, 178.
51. *The Works of David Ricardo*, ed. P. Sraffa, vol. 6, 1962, p. 52; vol. 7, 1962, pp. 16-17.
52. E.H.P., box 42/6, Porden to Lord Grosvenor, 9 Dec. 1807.
53. *The Times*, 2 June 1808, p. 3.
54. E.g. GBM 7/185, 205, 207, 208, 209.
55. R.B.: *Survey of London*, vol. XXXI, 1963, p. 279.
56. GBM 5/180 et seq.: Hermione Hobhouse, *Thomas Cubitt, Master Builder*, 1971, pp. 88-9.
57. Hobhouse, *op. cit.*, chapters V-VII: GBM 9/90; 10/1.
58. GBM 10/1.
59. G.O., Moor Park box, bills.
60. *Survey of London*, vol. XXVI, 1956, p. 12.
61. P.P.R., will of John Elger, 1888: M.L.R. 1826/1/571; 1844/8/969: R.B.: *P.O.D.*
62. *The Times*, 11 April 1832, p. 3: *Autobiography of James Gallier, Architect*, 1864: William R. Cullison and Roulhac Toledano, 'Our Architectural Heritage from the Brothers Gallier', in *New Orleans*, July 1970, pp. 30-5.
63. P.P.R., will of Wright Ingle, 1865.
64. GBM 12/426-7.
65. Papers of John Liddell, architect, in stock of B. Weinreb, Architectural Books Ltd., Lord Westminster to Lord Carnarvon, 22 May 1845.
66. GBM 12/426 7.
67. *The Builder*, 5 May 1855, p. 216: University College, London, Library, William Brougham MSS., letters from T. Cundy, 1854-9.
68. The John Rylands University Library of Manchester, Crawford MSS.
69. *Timber Trades Journal, Annual Special Issue*, Jan. 1965, p. 170: P.P.R., will of John Newson, 1873.
70. *Survey of London*, vol. XXXVIII, 1975, p. 17.
71. P.P.R., will of John Newson, 1873.
72. Henry Roberts, *The Progress and Present Aspect of the Movement for Improving the Dwellings of the Labouring Classes*, 1861, pp. 10-11.
73. Edward Hubbard, 'The Work of John Douglas (1830-1911)', M.A. thesis, University of Manchester, 1974.
74. Victoria and Albert Museum, Library, Diary of Henry Cole, 7 July 1863. Consulted by courtesy of Mrs. Cynthia Dutnall.
75. *The Builder*, 11 June 1864, p. 440. Drawings by Garling, Kerr and Street survive at the Grosvenor Office. For Barry's design see Sotheby's Belgravia Sale Catalogue, 11 March 1975, item 27.
76. GBM 14/523; 15/198; 16/39: *The Building News*, 6, 13 Oct. 1865, pp. 695, 712: *The Builder*, 23 Feb. 1867, pp. 121-3.
77. GBM 15/388-9.
78. *Ibid.*, 17/308.
79. *The Builder*, 25 Dec. 1875, p. 1153.
80. *P.P.*, 1874, vol. X, *Report and Minutes of Evidence of Select Committee of the House of Commons on the Metropolitan Buildings and Management Bill*, pp. 130-1, 180-1.
81. GBM 23/213-14.
82. *Ibid.*, 26/95, 376.
83. *Ibid.*, 23/364.
84. *Ibid.*, 25/27.
85. *Ibid.*, 24/411.
86. *Ibid.*, 26/17.
87. *Ibid.*, 26/297; 27/18-19, 285, 288-9.
88. Lady Frances Balfour, *Ne Obliviscaris*, 1930, vol. 2, p. 104. For Cecil Parker see Edward Hubbard, *op. cit.*
89. R.I.B.A. Library, Biographical File 774, H. S. Goodhart-Rendel to W. W. Begley, 8 Feb. 1938.
90. GBM 21/383-4.
91. Lord and Lady Aberdeen, '*We Twa*', vol. 1, 1925, pp. 280-2.
92. GBM 26/545.
93. Information supplied to Sir Nikolaus Pevsner by Mr. Clifford C. Makins, in April 1954.
94. Papers in the possession of Mr. H. D. Steiner of Steiner and Co.
95. GBM 32/328.
96. For No. 42 Upper Brook Street see *The Architect*, 4 April 1919, pp. 242 et seq.
97. GBM 38/203.
98. *The Building News*, 9 June 1905, p. 815.
99. GBM 38/239-40.
100. *The Builder*, 20 Dec. 1851, pp. 805-6.
101. GBM 34/291-2.
102. *The Builder*, 26 Feb. 1910, p. 240.
103. *The Times*, 10 Aug. 1974, p. 14.
104. Cuthbert Headlam, *George Abraham Crawley, A Short Memoir*, 1929.
105. *R.I.B.A. Journal*, 3rd ser., vol. XLIV, 1936-7, p. 1071.
106. GBM 39/200.
107. G.O., Duke's instruction book, 1919-22, pp. 133-5.
108. Information kindly supplied by Mrs. Loeb and Mrs. Carvalho, daughters of L. Rome Guthrie, and by J. R. Wilcox, Esq., assistant to Messrs. Wimperis, Simpson and Guthrie.
109. K. Jones and T. Hewitt, *A. H. Jones of Grosvenor House*, 1971, p. 24.
110. Christopher Hussey, *The Life of Sir Edwin Lutyens*, 1950, p. 460.
111. A. S. G. Butler, *The Architecture of Sir Edwin Lutyens*, vol. III, 1950, p. 35.
112. *The Times*, 6 Aug. 1930, p. 11.
113. B.A. 3440, note from Etchells on behalf of Blow and Billerey, 21 Sept. 1911.
114. GBM 42/225.
115. 'No. 1, Mount Row, W. and its conversion by Messrs. Gilbert and Constanduros', by R.R.P., in *Country Life*, 28 July 1923, pp. 131-2.
116. *The Architectural Review*, vol. LXXII, Sept. 1932, pp. 96-8.
117. Madge Garland, *The Indecisive Decade*, 1968, pp. 23-4.
118. Philip Tilden, *True Remembrances*, 1954, p. 162.
119. John Fowler and John Cornforth, *English Decoration in the 18th Century*, 1974, p. 17.
120. Beverley Nicholls, *A Case of Human Bondage*, 1966, pp. 51-2.
121. *Vogue*, 13 Nov. 1935, p. 69.
122. 'New Rooms at Claridge's Hotel', by C. H., in *Country Life*, 11 June 1932, pp. 663-5.
123. *The Architectural Review*, vol. CVIII, Oct. 1950, p. 274.
124. *Ibid.*, vol. 141, Feb. 1967, p. 133.
125. *Ibid.*, vol. 129, April 1961, p. 254.
126. *Ibid.*, pp. 252-65.

Index

NOTE

The symbols in the left-hand margin distinguish those persons who have worked, or are thought to have worked, on the fabric of the area, and the authors of unexecuted designs:

 a Architects, designers, engineers, and surveyors
 b Builders and allied tradesmen
 c Artists, craftsmen, and decorators

PLATES

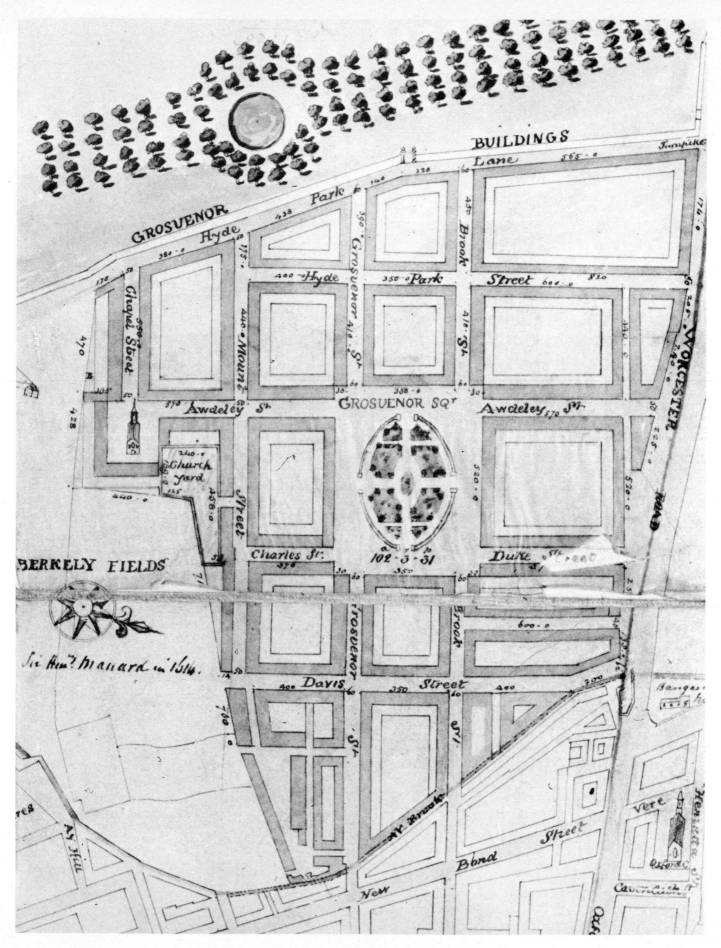

The intended layout of the estate as shown on John Mackay's map of 1723

2

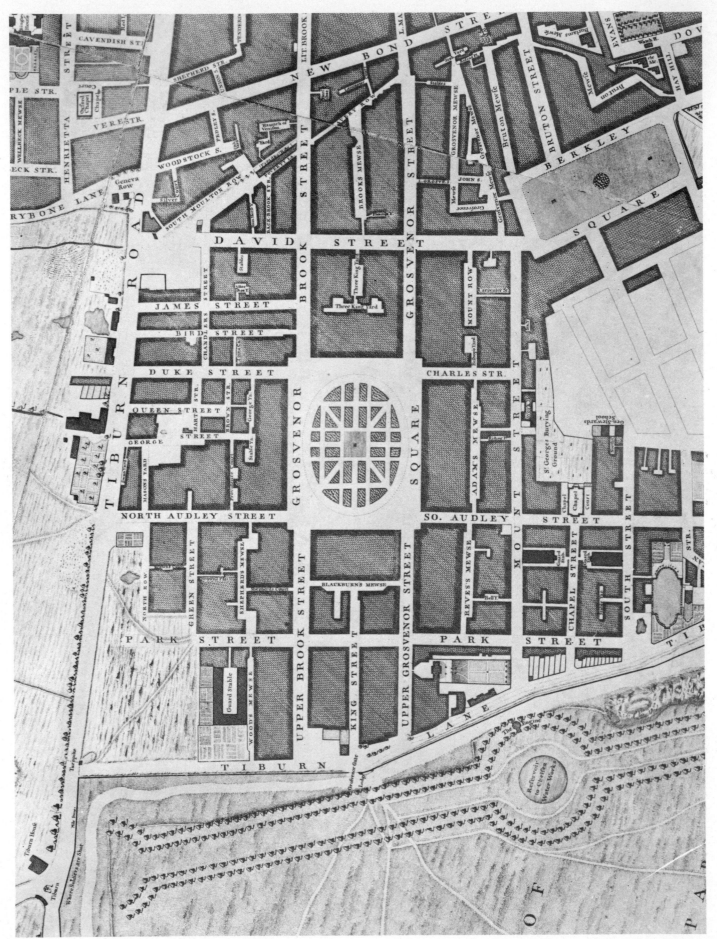

Extract from John Rocque's map of 1746

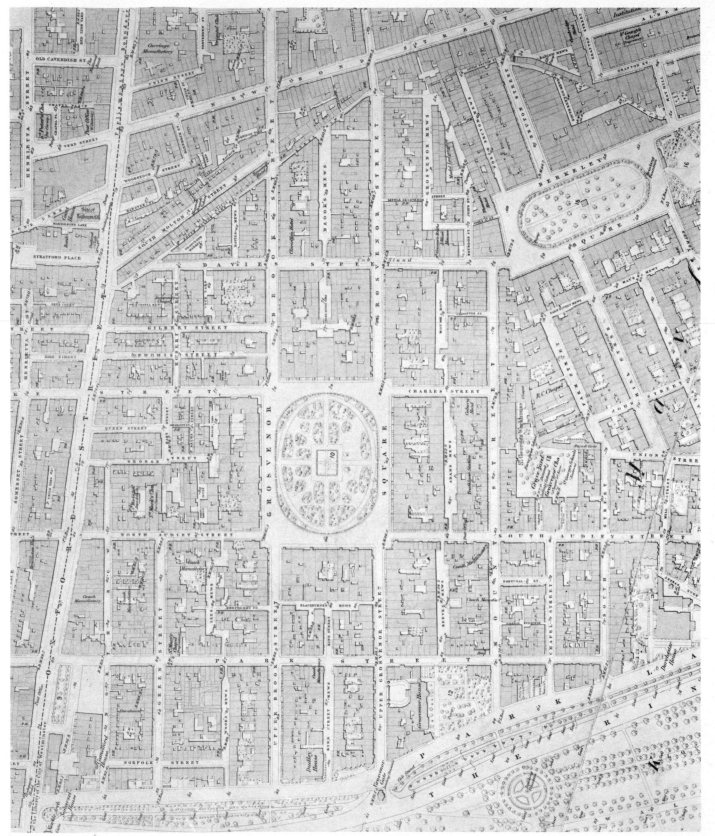

Extract from the Ordnance Survey map surveyed in 1869–70

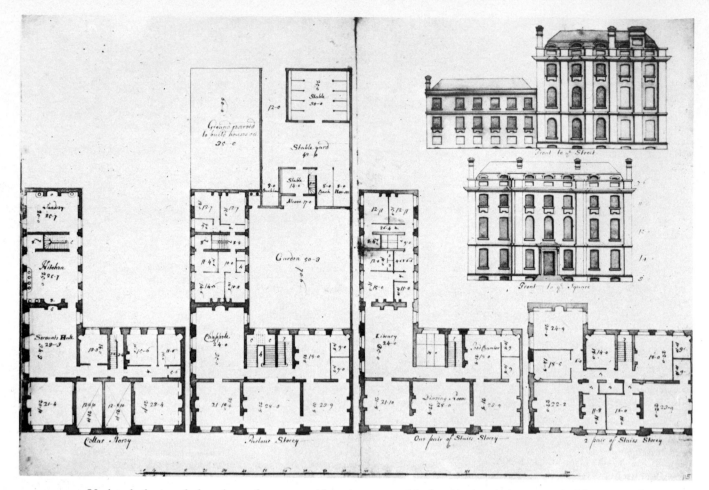

a. Undated plans and elevations of a proposed house, presumably for the square (pp. 103–4). *Not executed*

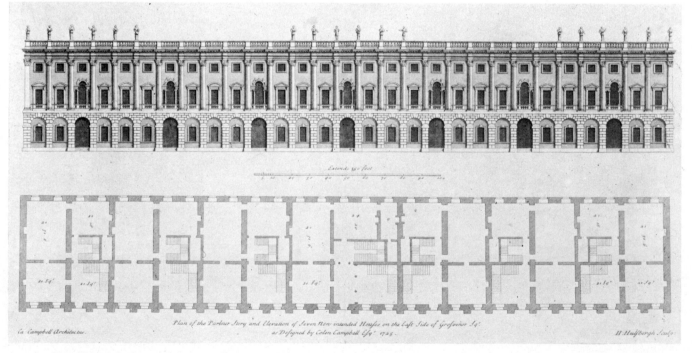

b. Ground-plan and front elevation for the east side of the square as proposed by Colen Campbell in 1725 (pp. 20, 104–5). *Not executed*

EARLY DESIGNS FOR GROSVENOR SQUARE

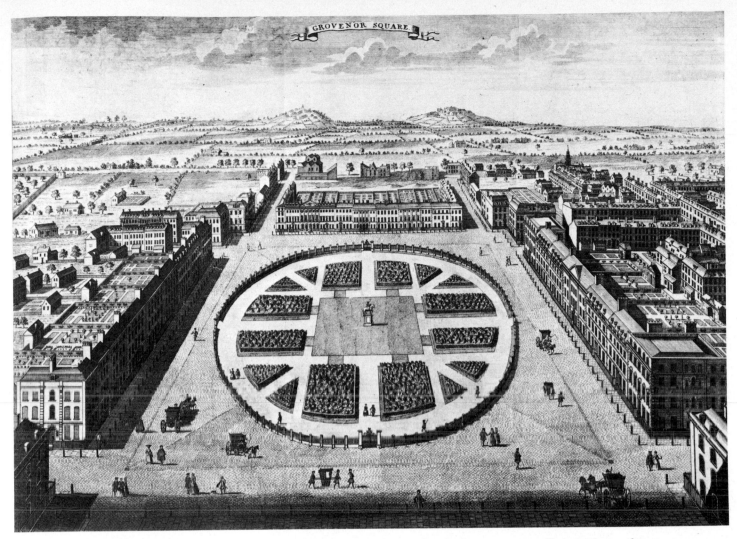

a. View looking north, *c.* 1730–5. The background appears to date from *c.* 1730 or earlier, the house fronts in the square from *c.* 1735

b. View looking east, *c.* 1741

EARLY VIEWS OF GROSVENOR SQUARE

6

a. Nos. 44–45 Upper Grosvenor Street in 1976. William Draycott (esquire) lessee, 1727. ?Charles Griffith (carpenter) builder

b. Nos. 35–36 Upper Brook Street in 1958. Anthony Cross (mason) sub-lessee, 1737

c. No. 66 Brook Street in 1973. Part of No. 68 on left. Edward Shepherd lessee of both houses, 1725. *Now the Grosvenor Office*

d. No. 71 South Audley Street in 1933. Thomas Skeat (bricklayer) lessee, 1736

EARLY-GEORGIAN EXTERIORS

No. 44 Grosvenor Square in *c*. 1874, with No. 43 (right) and No. 45 (left). Robert Scott (carpenter) sub-lessee of No. 44, 1727. *Demolished*

b. Nos. 70–78 (even) Park Street, *c.* 1730, in 1974 (No. 78 on left). Nos. 66 and 68 (on right) rebuilt in 1845–6

a (*above*).   No. 1 Grosvenor Square in 1932. John Simmons (carpenter) lessee, 1731. *Demolished*

c (*right*). No. 53 Grosvenor Street with No. 52 (right) in *c.* 1809. Benjamin Timbrell (carpenter) lessee of No. 52, 1724: John Neale (carpenter) sub-lessee of No. 53, 1725. *No. 53 demolished*

d. No. 50 Grosvenor Street in *c.* 1770–4. Charles Griffith (carpenter) lessee, 1724

e. Mount Street, west end of north side, in 1889. *Demolished*

EARLY-GEORGIAN EXTERIORS

a. No. 66 Brook Street, first-floor landing to main staircase in 1974. Edward Shepherd lessee, 1725. *Now the Grosvenor Office*

b. No. 34 Grosvenor Street, main staircase and landing in 1950. Richard Lissiman (mason) lessee, 1725

c. No. 13 South Audley Street, upper part of staircase in 1948. William Singleton (plasterer) lessee, 1736. *Plasterwork destroyed*

d. No. 59 Grosvenor Street, entrance hall and staircase in 1975. David Audsley (plasterer) sub-lessee, 1725. Woodwork of the staircase much restored

EARLY-GEORGIAN STAIRCASES

a. No. 71 South Audley Street, dining-room (ground-floor back room) in 1933. Thomas Skeat (bricklayer) lessee, 1736. Plasterwork of ceiling and walls probably by Edward Shepherd

b. Bourdon House, Davies Street, 'ante-dining-room' in 1909. William Bourdon (esquire) sub-lessee, 1723. Panelled throughout in wood. Fireplace of later date

EARLY-GEORGIAN INTERIORS: PLASTERING AND PANELLING

No. 12 North Audley Street, gallery in 1962, looking south. Columns and other ornamental details of plaster

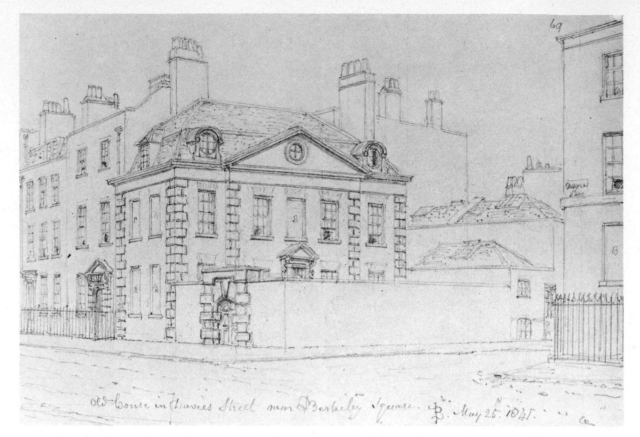

a. Bourdon House, Davies Street, in 1841, from south-west. William Bourdon (esquire) sub-lessee, 1723

b. Grosvenor Chapel, South Audley Street, in 1830, from south-west. *For the presumed original state of the chapel see fig. 7 on p. 119*

a. Park Lane, northern end from Hyde Park in 1799, showing King's Row (extreme right), the old Dudley House (right of centre with projecting porch), the end of Upper Brook Street (centre) and in the middle distance to left, the junction with Oxford Street. *Mostly demolished*

b. Park Lane, view looking south-east in *c.* 1807, showing houses in King's Row (left, behind trees), the south corner with Upper Grosvenor Street, and Breadalbane House (right). Grosvenor Gate lodge in foreground. *All demolished*

c. Park Street, elevational drawing of 1820 showing houses on west side between Hereford Street and North Row. John Crunden, architect, 1778. *Demolished*

a. Camelford House, Park Lane: north front in 1912. Hereford Gardens abuts to the left, Somerset House to the right. *Demolished*

b. Somerset House, Park Lane: house (right) and stables (centre) in 1912, from junction of Park Lane and Oxford Street. Outbuildings of Camelford House in left foreground with roofs of Hereford Gardens behind. *All demolished*

a. No. 26 Grosvenor Square (Derby House), perspective view of 'third drawing-room' in 1777. Robert Adam, architect, 1773–4. *Demolished*

b. No. 19 Grosvenor Square, the dome room in 1919. Robert and James Adam, architects, *c.* 1764–5. *Demolished*

c. Design for porch at Claudius Amyand's house, corner of Mount Street and Berkeley Square. Robert or James Adam, architect, probably *c.* 1761. *Either demolished or not executed*

THE ADAM BROTHERS ON THE ESTATE

c. No. 38 Grosvenor Square, ceiling of front drawing-room in 1953. Architect and painter unknown

b. No. 16 Grosvenor Street, design by Robert Adam for drawing-room ceiling, 1761. *Possibly not executed*

MID-GEORGIAN CEILINGS

a. Lord Petre's house, Park Lane (later Breadalbane House), engraving of drawing-room ceiling, 1783. James Paine, architect, 1766–70. *Demolished*

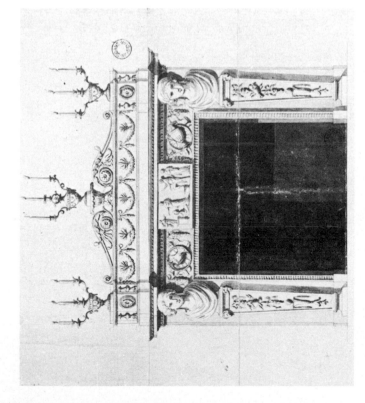

a. No. 19 Grosvenor Square, design by Robert Adam for chimneypiece in gallery, 1764

b. No. 19 Grosvenor Square, chimneypiece by Robert Adam in gallery in 1919. *Demolished*

c. No. 38 Grosvenor Square, chimneypiece in front drawing-room in 1953. Architect and carver unknown

d. No. 6 Upper Brook Street, chimneypiece in drawing-room in 1902. Samuel Wyatt, architect, 1787–9. *Demolished*

MID-GEORGIAN
CHIMNEYPIECES

a. South front in *c.* 1827–8, showing new gallery by Thomas Cundy I and II (1826–7), and (right) old house as altered by William Porden (1806–8). *Demolished*

b. Design of 1827 by Thomas Cundy II for enlargement, showing proposed new entrance front on south side masking gallery shown above. *Not executed*

c. Design of 1827 by Robert Smirke for enlargement, showing south front. *Not executed*

GROSVENOR HOUSE

a. Nos. 93–99 (consec.). The houses are numbered from right to left, and mostly date from the 1820's, with later additions

b. Nos. 26–31 (consec.) Dunraven Street, backs facing the park. Mid-Georgian houses with later additions, numbering from left to right. *All demolished*

c. No. 138 Park Lane (left) and Nos. 20–22 (consec.) Dunraven Street, backs facing the park. Mostly mid-Georgian houses with later additions. No. 138 Park Lane rebuilt by John Elger in 1831–2; No. 22 Dunraven Street (right) altered by (Sir) John Soane, 1801

PARK LANE, HOUSES FACING HYDE PARK IN 1927

a. Nos. 15 and 16 Grosvenor Square (Belgrave House), in *c*. 1932. Fronts by Thomas Cundy II, 1822–4. *Demolished*

b. No. 53 Davies Street (the Grosvenor Office), in 1973. Façade probably by Thomas Cundy II, *c*. 1836

c. Grosvenor House, screen to Upper Grosvenor Street in early 20th century. Thomas Cundy II, architect, and John Elger, builder, 1842–3. *Demolished*

EARLY WORKS BY THOMAS CUNDY II

a. Park Lane front in 1890. The veranda is Victorian

b. Ceiling in old dining-room, ground floor, in 1975

DUDLEY HOUSE, PARK LANE. William Atkinson, architect, 1827–8

a. No. 39 Brook Street in 1971, showing front as altered by Jeffry Wyatt, *c.* 1821. The shop front is of *c.* 1927

b. No. 2 South Street in 1927, from Park Lane. Façades designed by Sir Charles Barry, 1852. *Demolished*

c. Wood's Mews, design for stables for S. J. Loyd by George Stanley Repton, *c.* 1823

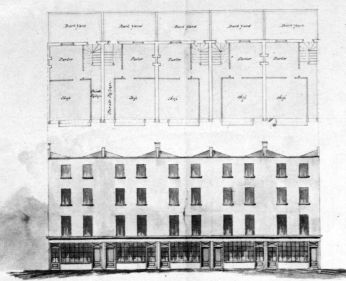

a. Ground-plan and elevation for houses and shops to be built by Seth Smith in the Gilbert Street and Weighhouse Street area. Drawing signed by [Seth] Smith and [?William] Maberley, 1821. *Demolished*

b. Elevation of houses to be built by William Skeat at the west end of Mount Street, *c.* 1830. *Demolished*

c. Elevation with section of houses to be built by John Elger in Green Street, *c.* 1825. *Demolished*

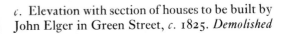

REBUILDING OF THE 1820'S AND 1830'S

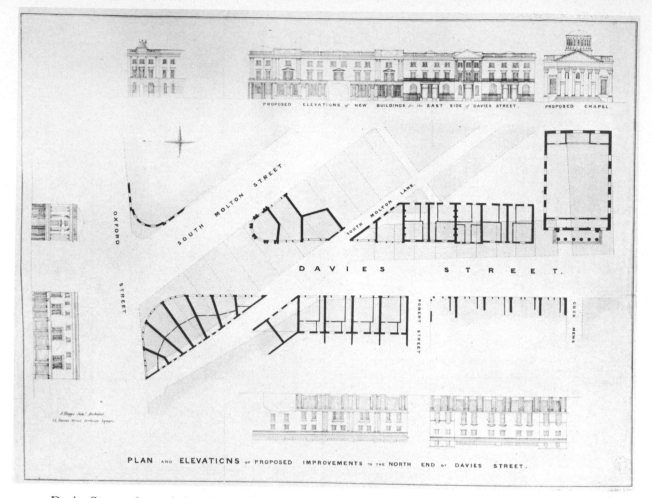

PLAN AND ELEVATIONS OF PROPOSED IMPROVEMENTS TO THE NORTH END OF DAVIES STREET.

a. Davies Street, plan and elevations to show improvements at north end suggested by Joshua Higgs junior, 1839. *Not executed*

b. Nos. 50 (Running Horse), 52 and 54 Davies Street in 1968. Joshua Higgs, builder, 1839-40

c. Nos. 14-24 (even) South Street (right to left) in *c.* 1931. J. P. Gandy-Deering, architect, *c.* 1825-35. *Mostly demolished*

a. No. 38 Grosvenor Square in *c*. 1931. Front altered in 1854–5

b. Nos. 20 and 21 Grosvenor Square in *c*. 1932–3. Complete rebuilding by John Kelk, 1855–8. *Demolished*

c. No. 26 Grosvenor Square in 1902. Complete rebuilding by C. J. Freake, 1861–2. *Demolished*

d. No. 4 Grosvenor Square in 1976. Complete rebuilding by C. J. Freake, 1865–8

FRONTS DESIGNED BY THOMAS CUNDY II AND III

a. Front drawing-room in 1975

b. Chimneypiece in 1975

No. 4 Grosvenor Square, Interiors. C. J. Freake, builder, 1865–8

a. Brook House, Park Lane, 1866–9. Perspective view by T. H. Wyatt, architect, showing fronts to Park Lane and Upper Brook Street (right). *Demolished*

b. Nos. 491–497 (odd) Oxford Street in *c.* 1931. Thomas Cundy III, architect, 1865–6. *Demolished*

THE FRENCH STYLE IN THE 1860's

28

a. The loggia at the west end, added in 1880–1, from Park Lane, shortly before demolition in 1927

b. The gallery, with the Rubens room beyond, in 1889. Frieze painted by F. J. Barrias, 1872. *Demolished*

GROSVENOR HOUSE, REMODELLING BY HENRY CLUTTON, 1870–2 AND 1880–1

c. St. Saviour's, Oxford Street, 1870–3, from north in *c.* 1922. *Demolished*

b. St. Mark's, North Audley Street, interior as remodelled by Blomfield in 1878: view looking east in 1971

a (left). St. Mary's, Bourdon Street, 1880–1, from south-west in 1956. *Demolished*

CHURCHES DESIGNED BY ARTHUR BLOMFIELD

a. St. George's Buildings, Bourdon Street, from west. Henry Roberts, architect for plan, and John Newson, builder, 1852–3

b. Grosvenor Buildings, Bourdon Street, from east, with Grosvenor Hill to right. R. H. Burden, architect, 1868–9

c. Clarendon Flats, Balderton Street (Improved Industrial Dwellings Company, 1871–2), from south, with St. Mark's Mansions (R. J. Withers, architect, 1872–3) on left

d. Balderton Flats, Balderton Street and Brown Hart Gardens (Improved Industrial Dwellings Company, 1887), from south-west

WORKING-CLASS HOUSING. Photographs of the early 1930's

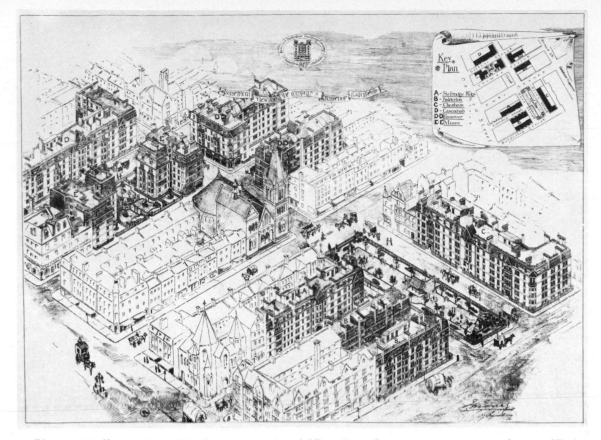

a. Plan and bird's-eye view of the Improved Industrial Dwellings Company's estate east and west of Duke Street, 1886–92

b. Improved Industrial Dwellings Company's estate, in *c.* 1930, showing blocks on north side of Brown Hart Gardens and (right) King's Weigh House Chapel, from garden of Duke Street Electricity Sub-station

WORKING-CLASS HOUSING

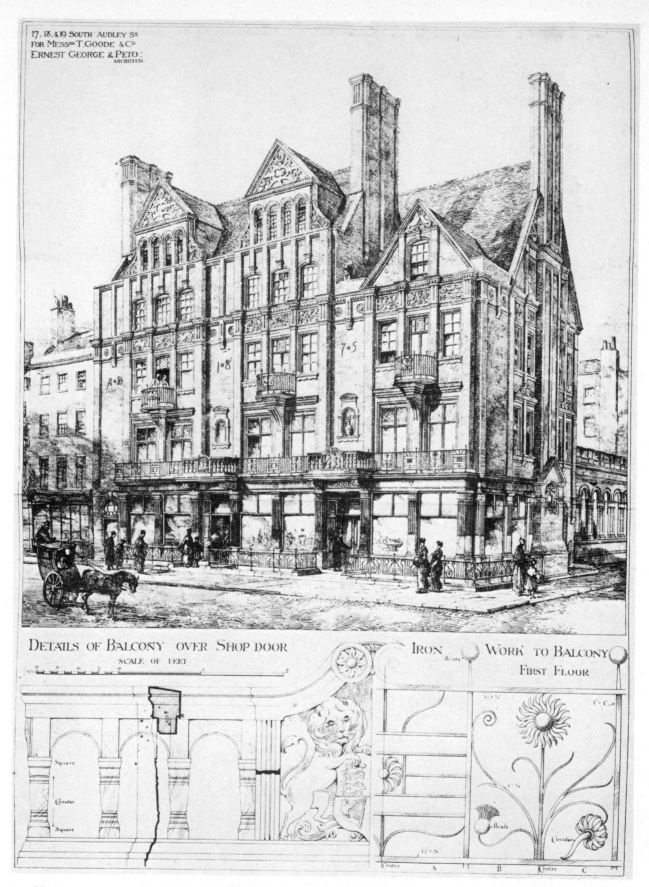

Nos. 17–19 (consec.) South Audley Street. Perspective and details, showing extent of rebuilding by Ernest George and Peto, architects, in 1875–6

GOODE'S, SOUTH AUDLEY STREET

a, *b*. Goode's, South Audley Street, details in 1975: *a* (*left*), detail of stained glass window, *b* (*right*), chimney facing South Street. Ernest George and Peto, architects, 1875–6

c. No. 78 Brook Street, with Nos. 76–68 (even) to right, in 1875. C. F. Hayward, architect of No. 78, 1873–5

d. Audley Mansions, Nos. 56 South Audley Street and 44 Mount Street, perspective view of 1885. J. T. Wimperis, architect, 1884–6

34

a. Looking west in 1976, showing in foreground parts of (left) Nos. 87–102 (A. J. Bolton, architect, 1889–95) and (right) Nos. 14–26 (Read and Macdonald, architects, 1896–8)

b. South side in 1976, showing (left) Nos. 104–113 (Ernest George and Peto, architects, 1885–92); (centre right) No. 103 (Wimperis, Simpson and Guthrie, architects, 1936–8); and (far right), Nos. 87–102 (A. J. Bolton, architect, 1889–95)

c (*left*). Nos. 125–129 in 1968, from Carpenter Street. W. H. Powell, architect, 1886–7

d (*right*). Nos. 4–7 Carlos Place, from south-west in *c*. 1897. Giles, Gough and Trollope, architects, George Trollope and Sons, builders, 1891–3

MOUNT STREET RECONSTRUCTION

35

b. Nos. 75–83 (odd) Duke Street in 1975 (W. D. Caröe, architect, 1893–5), with King's Weigh House Chapel to left

c. Duke's Yard: stable block on south side from Binney Street in 1968. Balfour and Turner, architects, 1900–2

a. Nos. 7 and 8 Balfour Place, from south-east in 1894, with part of return to Aldford Street. Balfour and Turner, architects, 1891–4

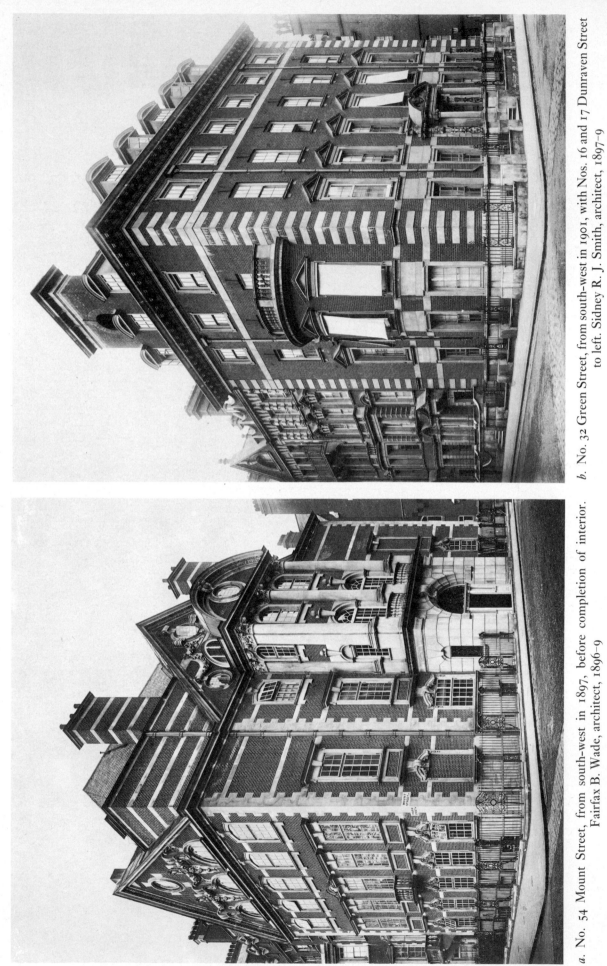

a. No. 54 Mount Street, from south-west in 1897, before completion of interior.
Fairfax B. Wade, architect, 1896–9

b. No. 32 Green Street, from south-west in 1901, with Nos. 16 and 17 Dunraven Street
to left. Sidney R. J. Smith, architect, 1897–9

TOWN HOUSES OF THE 1890's

No. 54 Mount Street, entrance hall in *c.* 1911. Fairfax B. Wade, architect, 1896–9

a (*above*). Aldford House, Park Lane (1894–7), fronts to Aldford Street (left) and Park Lane (centre) in 1897. *Demolished*

b (*left*). St. Anselm's Church, Davies Street (1894–6), interior looking east in *c*. 1938. *Demolished*

BUILDINGS DESIGNED BY BALFOUR AND TURNER

a. Perspective view showing entrance front in Brook Street and return front in Davies Street, by C. W. Stephens, architect, 1897

b. The billiard-room in 1898. Interior decorations by Ernest George and Yeates, architects, 1896–8.
Destroyed

CLARIDGE'S HOTEL, NEW BUILDING

a. Dudley House, Park Lane, ballroom in 1890. Samuel Daukes, architect, and Laurent and Haber, decorators, *c*. 1858. *Destroyed*

b. No. 26 Grosvenor Square, drawing-room in 1902. Howard and Sons, decorators. *Demolished*

INTERIORS IN THE FRENCH STYLE

a (above). In 1909.
Decorators unknown

b (right). In 1926.
Decorations perhaps
by Keeble Limited,
1919

No 41
Grosvenor
Square, the
Ballroom.
Demolished

a. No. 46 Grosvenor Street, Gothic staircase in 1970. Blow and Billerey, architects, and L. Buscaylet, decorator, 1910-11

b. Nos. 69-71 (odd) Brook Street, ballroom staircase in 1975. W. O. W. Bouwens van der Boijen and assistants, architects and decorators, *c.* 1890

c. No. 24 Upper Brook Street, entrance hall and staircase in 1917. Decorator unknown. *Now simplified*

d. No. 45 Grosvenor Square, conservatory in 1897. Charles Mellier and Company, decorators. *Demolished*

VICTORIAN AND EDWARDIAN INTERIORS

a. Bute House, No. 75 South Audley Street, hall and staircase in 1927. Fernand Billerey, architect, *c.* 1926–7

b. No. 38 South Street, hall and staircase in 1924. Wimperis and Simpson, architects, and Harold Peto, decorator, 1919–21

INTER-WAR ENTRANCE HALLS

44

a. No. 45 Grosvenor Square in 1910. Edmund Wimperis and Hubert East, architects of front, 1902. *Demolished*

b. Nos. 16 (centre) and 17 (left) Upper Brook Street in 1913. Edmund Wimperis and J. R. Best, architects, 1907–13

c. Nos. 73 (centre right), 74 (left centre) and 75 (far left) South Audley Street in 1943. Front of No. 73 by Paul Waterhouse (1909), of No. 74 by Balfour and Turner (1908), and of No. 75 by Cyrille J. Corblet (1906–7)

d. Nos. 17–21 (consec.) Upper Grosvenor Street (right to left) in 1927. No. 17 by Balfour and Turner (1906–7); No. 19 by Maurice C. Hulbert (1909–10); No. 20 probably by Boehmer and Gibbs (1909); and No. 21 by Ralph Knott and E. Stone Collins (1908)

ELEVATIONS IN STONE, 1900–1914

a. No. 28 South Street in 1903. Detmar Blow, architect, 1902–3

b. No. 46 Green Street in 1976. Wimperis and Simpson, architects, 1913–15

c. No. 38 South Street, rear elevation from South Street garden, in 1924. Wimperis and Simpson, architects, 1919–21

ELEVATIONS IN BRICK, 1900–1920

d. Nos. 25 and 26 Gilbert Street in 1974. Maurice C. Hulbert, architect, and Matthews, Rogers and Company, builders, 1910–12

45

a. Nos. 37 and 38 Upper Grosvenor Street and Nos. 44–50 (even) Park Street, from north-west in 1912. Blow and Billerey, architects, and William Willett, builder, 1911–12

b. Nos. 37–43 (odd) Park Street, from south-east in 1911. W. D. Caröe, architect, and Higgs and Hill, builders, 1908–10

STONE-FRONTED RANGES

a. Nos. 55–57 (consec.) Grosvenor Street (right to left) and Nos. 4–26 (even) Davies Street (right to left), from north-west in 1976. Wimperis and Best, architects, 1910–12

b. Nos. 38–45 (consec.) Green Street (left to right), backs from Green Street garden in 1916. Mostly by Wimperis and Simpson, 1913–16

BRICK-FRONTED RANGES

a. Nos. 139–140 Park Lane, from west in 1968. Frank Verity, architect, *c*. 1913–18

b (*above*). Nos. 415–419 (odd) Oxford Street, from north-east in 1976, showing return front to Duke Street. G. Thrale Jell and Wimperis, Simpson and Guthrie, architects, 1923–35

c (*right*). Grosvenor House, Park Lane, from north-west in 1931. Sir Edwin Lutyens and Wimperis, Simpson and Guthrie, architects, 1926–30

a. Upper Feilde, Upper Brook Street and Park Street, from south east in 1976. Wimperis and Simpson, architects, 1922–4

b. Upper Brook Feilde, Upper Brook Street and Park Street, from north-east in 1976. Wimperis, Simpson and Guthrie, architects, 1926–7

c. Nos. 105–108 (consec.) Park Lane, from west in *c.* 1932. Wimperis, Simpson and Guthrie, architects, 1930–2

d. Aldford House, Park Lane, from north-west in 1932. George Val Myer and F. J. Watson-Hart, architects, 1930–2

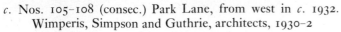

INTER-WAR FLATS

a (*left*), *b* (*right*). Nos. 10–14 (even) Culross Street (right to left), in 1926 and 1976, before and after alterations of 1926–7, mainly by Etchells and Pringle

c (*below left*). No. 3 Lees Place (stables to No. 23 Grosvenor Square) in 1890 before conversion. J. T. Wimperis and T. N. Arber, architects, 1889

d (*below right*). No. 3 Lees Place in 1976 after conversion. H. Douglas Kidd, architect, 1932

MEWS HOUSES AND CONVERSIONS

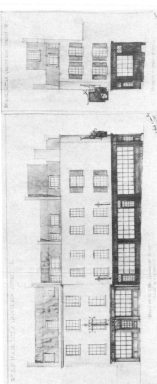

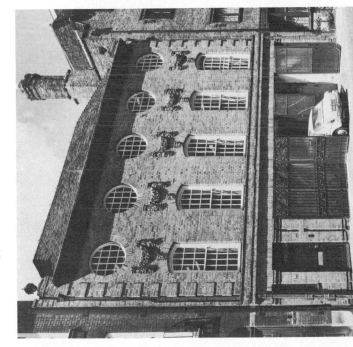

b. Broadbent Street (formerly Little Grosvenor Street), elevations by Etchells and Pringle for proposed conversion of shops, 1927. *Not executed*

d. Tudor House, Nos. 6–10 (even) Mount Row, in 1968. Frederick Etchells, architect, 1929–31

a. Nos. 21–25 (odd) Culross Street (left to right), fronts in 1976. No. 25 by Ernest Cole, 1929

c. Wren House, Nos. 12 and 14 Mount Row, in 1968. T. P. Bennett, architect, 1926–7

MEWS HOUSES AND CONVERSIONS

b. Vestibule and entrance hall of extension building in 1932. Oswald Milne, architect, 1930–1

a. Main entrance hall in 1930. Oswald Milne, architect, 1929

CLARIDGE'S HOTEL, INTERIORS OF 1929–31

a. No. 25 Upper Brook Street, drawing-room in *c.* 1933. Lenygon and Morant, decorators, 1933

b. No. 42 Upper Brook Street, bedroom of Mrs. F. J. Wolfe's flat in 1939. Decorators unknown

c. No. 25 South Street, sitting-room in 1937. W. Turner Lord and Company, decorators, 1936–7

d. No. 12 North Audley Street, bathroom in 1975. Marchesa Malacrida and White Allom and Company, decorators, 1932

INTERIORS OF THE 1930's

54

a. North side in *c.* 1910, showing fronts of Nos. 10–20 consec. (right to left). *Demolished*

b. North side in 1976, showing fronts of Nos. 10–21 consec. (right to left). Elevations by Fernand Billerey, architect, executed 1933–64

GROSVENOR SQUARE REBUILDING

a. West side in *c.* 1930 from North Audley Street, showing No. 21 (extreme left), No. 22 (extreme right), Nos. 24–32 consec. (centre right) and Nos. 33–34 (centre distance). *All demolished except No. 22*

b. West side in 1961 from south-east, showing entrance front and Upper Grosvenor Street front of United States Embassy. Eero Saarinen, architect, 1956–60

GROSVENOR SQUARE REBUILDING

Grosvenor Estate, Mayfair, aerial view from the south-east in 1973. Berkeley Square is in the right foreground, Grosvenor Square in the centre, and Hyde Park at the top left